AN INTRODUCTION TO LITERATURE

AN INTRODUCTION TO
LITERATURE

Fiction | Poetry | Drama

Ninth Edition

Edited by

Sylvan Barnet, *Tufts University*
Morton Berman, *Boston University*
William Burto, *University of Lowell*

SCOTT, FORESMAN AND COMPANY
Glenview, Illinois Boston London

Library of Congress Cataloging-in-Publication Data

An Introduction to literature: fiction, poetry, drama / edited by
  Sylvan Barnet, Morton Berman, William Burto. — 9th ed.
      p.   cm.
  Includes indexes.
  ISBN 0-673-39875-7
    1. Literature—Collections.   I. Barnet, Sylvan.   II. Berman,
  Morton. III. Burto, William.
  PN6014.I57 1989   88-10103
  808.8—dc19   CIP

1 2 3 4 5 6 7 8 9 10 — RRC — 94 93 92 91 90 89 88

Printed in the United States of America

Cover art

> John Opper, *Blue and Yellow Verticals*. Archer M. Huntington Art Gallery,
> The University of Texas at Austin, Michener Art Fund, 1970.

Acknowledgments

Edward Albee. *The Sandbox*. Reprinted by permission of William Morris
Agency, Inc. on behalf of the author. Copyright © 1960 by Edward Albee.

W. H. Auden. "The Unknown Citizen," "Musée des Beaux Arts," and
"Lay Your Sleeping Head, My Love." Copyright 1940 and renewed 1968 by W. H.
Auden. Reprinted from *W. H. Auden: Collected Poems,* edited by Edward Mendelson,
by permission of Random House, Inc. and Faber and Faber Ltd.

Toni Cade Bambara. "The Lesson" from *Gorilla, My Love* by Toni Cade
Bambara. Copyright © 1972 by Toni Cade Bambara. Reprinted by permission of
Random House, Inc.

Donald Barthelme. "The Balloon" from *Unspeakable Practices, Unnatural
Acts* by Donald Barthelme. Reprinted by permission of International Creative
Management, Inc. Copyright © 1967 by Donald Barthelme. First published in
The New Yorker.

Elizabeth Bishop. "The Fish," "Filling Station," and "Poem" from *The
Complete Poems 1927–1979* by Elizabeth Bishop. Copyright 1940, © 1976 by Elizabeth
Bishop. Copyright © 1979, 1983 by Alice Helen Methfessell. Reprinted by permission
of Farrar, Straus and Giroux, Inc.

Gwendolyn Brooks. "We Real Cool" from *The World of Gwendolyn Brooks.*
Copyright © 1959 by Gwendolyn Brooks. Reprinted by permission of the author.

Raymond Carver. "Cathedral" from *Cathedral* by Raymond Carver.
Copyright © 1981, 1982, 1983 by Raymond Carver. Reprinted by permission of
Alfred A. Knopf, Inc.

(Acknowledgments continue on p. 1227)

Preface

"A big book," said Callimachus, "is a big misfortune." He might have added that a big book is heavy. Aware that many instructors have found needlessly bulky most of the textbooks designed for introductory courses in literature, the editors and publisher of *An Introduction to Literature* have produced a book that is smaller than most books intended for such courses. They have kept in mind Dr. Johnson's maxim: "Books that you may . . . hold readily in your hand are the most useful after all."

The relative brevity of this volume has been achieved partly by assuming that much of what is included here will please the instructor and therefore need not be reinforced by numerous alternative selections, and partly by refusing to allow the editorial apparatus to usurp the province of the classroom. Both of these points deserve further comment.

We have offered much material that can be called "classical," both to keep the bulk down and because we believe that students ought for the most part to read first-rate material. There is something wrong with a book that includes a dozen stories of the last year or two and nothing by Hawthorne. We include some very recent work (of the thirty-three short stories, twelve are by living writers), and about half of the selections are from the twentieth century, but we have tried not to neglect such classic writers as Shakespeare, Dickinson, Hawthorne, and Whitman. Classic works, of course, are not the same things as chestnuts. "Classics," Maurice Beebe has explained, "are in a sense the freshest of stories simply because they obviously may be seen in many different lights and even yet have not given up all their secrets. The chestnuts are those stories that — like 'Haircut,' 'The Necklace,' and 'The Furnished Room' — give up all their secrets on an initial reading and hence require as little classroom discussion as they have evoked published criticism. I see no objection to a text made up primarily of classics."

The editorial material is brief and yet fairly complete. The paradox is easily explained: this book does not try to do what only the teacher can do. The proper place for a detailed discussion of responses to stories, poems, and plays is, we believe, the classroom. Textbook discussions that for pages drag the student through a short poem or story rarely accomplish much. The object of an anthology of literature is to allow students to read and to think and perhaps to write down their responses; it is doubtful if a long exegesis stimulates a student to experience literature. We have tried in our editorial apparatus and especially in our glossary to give succinct definitions of the terms commonly used in talking about literature and to *begin* (but by no means to finish) a lively encounter with literature. About half the selections in the book are briefly discussed or have questions appended in an effort to stimulate responses; the other half are unsullied. We have kept in mind Frost's remark: "You don't chew a poem — macerate a poem — for an evening's pleasure, for a Roman holiday. You touch it. You are aware that a good deal of it is missed."

USING THE BOOK

Probably most instructors teach fiction, then poetry, and then drama — the order followed here. But the three sections can be taught in any sequence, because each is relatively independent: for example, symbolism is discussed in each of the three sections, and although the three discussions have a cumulative effect, any of the three can be used first. This flexibility runs throughout the book; we hope that instructors will not feel that the first chapter must be taught first. Indeed, the first chapter — a survey of some theories of literature — can be used effectively midway or even at the end. There is a similar flexibility within the three chief sections of the book: one can teach everything straight through a section, or skip one's way through a section, or bring in wherever one wishes the stories and poems that conclude the sections. Perhaps the only chapter in the book that ought to be taught at a specific time, or not taught at all, is the second chapter, "Reading and Responding to Literature." If instructors think it is useful, they will want to assign it very early in the term, possibly even for the second meeting of the class.

An appendix, "Writing Essays about Literature," is partly drawn from Sylvan Barnet's *A Short Guide to Writing about Literature*, fifth edition (1985). It includes not only information about manuscript form and three sample essays by students (one explication and two analyses), but also detailed suggestions that may help students to choose a topic and get their responses down on paper.

Suggestions that will help generate responses are not, however, limited to this appendix. Each of the three genres includes a chapter entitled "Summing Up," which provides questions that students may put to themselves as they think about whatever works they read.

What else is new besides the three chapters called "Summing Up"? Chapter 2 ("Reading and Responding to Literature") is new, and so is the "Glossary of Literary Terms." But most important, this edition of *Introduction to Literature* includes twelve new stories, thirty-seven new poems, and four new plays; among the eleven plays there are now not only two Greek tragedies (*Oedipus the King* and *Antigone*), but also two tragedies by Shakespeare (*Hamlet* and *Macbeth*).

If this new edition has been strengthened and enhanced, it is primarily because of encouraging comments from users of the earlier editions. Among the new selections are stories by Chekhov, Kate Chopin, Kafka, Bobbie Anne Mason, and Louise Erdrich and poems by Drayton, Herrick, Christina Rossetti, Amy Clampitt, Adrienne Rich, Craig Raine, and Rita Dove. The drama section in particular has been enlarged and now includes three short plays (Chekhov's *The Brute*, Albee's *The Sandbox*, and Clare Boothe Luce's *Slam the Door Softly*) as well as eight full-length plays (*Oedipus the King, Antigone, Hamlet, Macbeth, A Doll's House, The Glass Menagerie, Death of a Salesman*, and Marsha Norman's recent Pulitzer Prize–winning play, *'night, Mother*). We would like to call special attention to Clare Boothe Luce's play, which is a late twentieth-century rewrite of *A Doll's House*. So far as we know, this play has never before been included in a book of this sort.

Finally, after this elaborate explanation of what has been done, we wish to thank people who helped us do it: Linda Bamber, David Cavitch, Charles Christensen, Robert Cyr, Joan Feinberg, Arthur Friedman, David Giele, Bradford Gray, Nancy Grayson, Martha Hicks-Courant, Billie Ingram, X. J. Kennedy, Martha Lappen, Judy Maas, Deirdre McDonald, Patricia Meier, Joseph Opiela, Ronald E. Pepin, Carolyn Potts, Virginia Pye, William Roberts, Clair Seng-Niemoeller, Virginia Shine, Marcia Stubbs, Helen Vendler, Charles L. Walker, and Ann Chalmers Watts.

Our thanks also to the many users of the earlier editions who gave us advice on how and where to make improvements. We are especially grateful for the comments and suggestions offered during preparation of the ninth edition. In particular we wish to thank the following scholars: Priscilla B. Bellair, Carroll Britch, Don Brunn, Malcolm B. Clark, Terence A. Dalrymple, Franz

Douskey, Gerald Duchovnay, Peter Dumanis, Estelle Easterly, Adam Fischer, Martha Flint, Robert H. Fossum, Gerald Hasham, Richard Henze, Catharine M. Hoff, Grace S. Kehrer, Nancy E. Kensicki, Linda Kraus, Juanita Laing, Martha McGowan, John H. Meagher III, Stuart Millner, Edward Anthony Nagel, Peter L. Neff, Robert F. Panara, Ronald E. Pepin, Jane Pierce, Robert M. Post, Kris Rapp, Mark Reynolds, John Richardson, Donald H. Sanborn, Marlene Sebeck, Frank E. Sexton, Peggy Skaggs, David Stuehler, James E. Tamer, Carol Teaff, C. Uejio, Hugh Whitmeyer, Manfred Wolf, Joseph Zaitchik.

S. B.
M. B.
W. B.

Contents

6. *Style*   83

A Note on Tone.

Eudora Welty, Livvie   85

7. *Summing Up: Reading Fiction Responsively*   99

8. *A Collection of Short Fiction*   102

Drama

1
Some Theories of Literature

WHAT IS LITERATURE?

Literature is sometimes defined as anything written, but this definition is both too broad and too narrow. Although it is true that anyone can ask the Department of Agriculture for "literature" about canning artichokes, surely we can distinguish between literature in the sense of any writing and literature in the sense of verbal works of art. On the other hand, to say that literature must be written or printed is too narrow, because it excludes such oral literature as ballads that are sung and stories that are recited.

We can begin by saying that literature is (to quote Robert Frost) a "performance in words." It has in it an element of entertaining display, and surely we expect literature to afford pleasure. That literature is an adult game, a sort of make-believe, is suggested in some of the words we apply to pieces of literature — "fiction," "story," "tale," "play."

Now, what makes literature pleasant? Without attempting a complete answer, perhaps we can say that a literary work seizes our interest and more or less — at least for a moment — makes the rest of the world fade or vanish. If the writer has done the job well, our attention is focused on the work, and we are at least partially detached from our usual surroundings. Consider, as an analogy, our reaction when we suddenly get a whiff of new-mown hay. We are walking along a road, either fretting about a dozen things or engaged in a pleasant vague reverie, when suddenly we smell the hay. At once we are caught up, keenly interested in this experience, intensely aware of this one thing, a thing that seems complete and satisfying in itself. For the moment we forget about the time of day, the dust of the road, the heat of the sun, and we find in this thing which is complete, whole, independent, something that catches us up and delights us. A work of art has this power to catch us up momentarily, and to delight us.

But it may well be objected that *Hamlet* is surely more than a load of hay. Art, it is commonly said, offers truth as well as pleasure. Such a view is at least superficially plausible, but when we begin to think about it, we encounter problems. What "truth" is there in *Hamlet*? The characters in the play are fictional, so we cannot say that Shakespeare is giving us a true picture of Danish history. There is a ghost in the play, but many people today have serious doubts about the existence of ghosts. Perhaps we will seize on certain lines, such as "Neither a borrower nor a lender be," but even this much-quoted line can hardly be defended as an unquestioned truth: there are surely times when it is good to borrow or to lend.

Let us leave *Hamlet* (though not with the implication that the concept of truth is irrelevant to it) and glance at an amusing short poem, "Tender-handed touch a nettle," written more than two hundred years ago by Aaron Hill. (A nettle is, in the words of a dictionary, a plant whose leaves are covered with "hairs that secrete a stinging fluid that affects the skin on contact.")

> Tender-handed touch a nettle,
>   And it stings you for your pains,
> Grasp it like a man of mettle,
>   And it soft as silk remains.
> So it is with human natures,
>   Treat them gently, they rebel,
> But be as rough as nutmeg graters,
>   And the rogues obey you well.

It is true that if "tender-handed" you touch a nettle it will sting, and that if you seize it firmly you will not feel the sting, but is it true that if you treat people roughly they will "obey you well"? Some people, perhaps. But isn't it apparent that whatever value Hill's poem has (and many children have enjoyed it during its two centuries) is not in its botany or in its psychology, but in its engaging impudence, in its *playful* assertion that all people are "rogues" who need to be knocked about. The meter, the rhyme, the pun on mettle/metal, and the comparison to a nutmeg grater hardly allow us to take the piece very seriously. We value it more for the pleasure that it offers than for the truth it claims to offer.

What literature is, and what sort of truth (if any) it offers, are big problems, and they have not yet been solved to general satisfaction. There is a diversity of theories, and nothing is gained by pretending that everyone knows or agrees what literature is or does. But most theories of literature can, without much distortion, be put into one of three pigeonholes — which can be called "imitative," "expressive," and "affective" — and these are what we want to talk about first. Good literature deserves to be talked about as well as read and enjoyed, and such discussion may help sharpen a reader's perceptions.

THE IMITATIVE THEORY

The imitative theory holds that art is an imitation of something. In his *Poetics*, Aristotle (384–322 B.C.) says that a tragedy is an imitation of an action that is serious and complete. Because imitation now has pejorative associations, it is well to think of Aristotle's *mimesis* as not only "imitation" but also "re-creation" or "representation." In an artistic imitation, Aristotle holds, a form is re-created or re-presented in a substance not natural to it. Thus, Michelangelo imitated Moses in stone; van Gogh imitated sunflowers in pigment on canvas; Shakespeare imitated Caesar in an actor's words and gestures. Music, too, Aristotle holds, is imitative; Tchaikovsky imitates Napoleon's defeat in Russia in the "1812 Overture." Aristotle would have approved of Thomas De Quincey's remark that although no one whistled at Waterloo, one might whistle Waterloo. The imitative instinct, of course, is not the artist's private possession. A child says to another, "You be the cop and I'll be the robber and you say 'Halt' and I'll run away." This natural tendency to imitate is combined, Aristotle says, with a tendency toward rhythm or pattern, and the result can be a work of art.

In its simplest form the imitative theory appeals to the naive: "How lifelike that wax apple is!" "How like a Frenchman that actor looks!" But more sophisticated people may ask: "What is so pleasing about a wax apple? There are plenty of real apples for us to look at." Aristotle's theory includes such a close copy of nature as a wax apple, but by coupling imitation with harmony, Aristotle goes further. He says that art is superior to history because although history must stick to the facts, art refines nature, showing, one might say, not what happened but what should have happened in a world free from accident. The artist is a sort of greenhouse keeper, producing not the rose that grows wild, cankered, and stunted, but the rose that has fulfilled all its potential, the rose that is more a rose than any wild rose. The artist, in short, does not imitate servilely; the artist re-creates reality and presents it to us in a fashion in which we see its essence more clearly.

It is only half-true, then, to say that Aristotle's imitator is a maker of an imitation. (This idea of the artist as a maker, by the way, survives dimly in the word "playwright" — "wright" being a maker, as in "shipwright," and having nothing to do with "write.") Because the artist's imitation is more than a copy of what is apparent to every eye, the imitation is in some measure a creation. It is imaginative and interpretive; it reflects a special view of reality.

The imitative theory often includes the notion that art gives us not only pleasure but also knowledge, insight into the nature of reality. If you say that we enjoy wax apples simply because we enjoy seeing exhibitions of skill at imitation, you are not introducing the criterion of knowledge. If, however, you say that by looking at the imitation we come to know something about reality, you are saying that art furnishes knowledge, and that its value depends partly on its truth. This problem of truth does not arise in all the arts: no one asks the Taj Mahal to be true. But many people want their literature to be true — to be an illuminating reflection of reality. The danger, of course, is that the reader may turn literature into a message: hunting for detachable tags ("There's a divinity that shapes our ends," "To thine own self be true"), the reader reduces the whole work to a neat moral and gives A's to those works whose messages seem right. But what does anyone really learn from a work of literature? Do we learn from *Julius Caesar* not to be a tyrant? Or not to assassinate a tyrant? Or the difficulty of assassinating a tyrant and getting away with it? Surely we knew all this before.

Perhaps the answer to the question "Does literature give knowledge?" is that we do not learn from literature how to act in a particular situation (we'll never get the chance to be Roman tyrants), but we do learn something about life in general. After seeing a play, we feel that we have achieved at least a momentary understanding of some of the facts of life. The happenings in the book or on the stage not only resemble things in real life, but also clarify real life, making us say: "Yes, people are like that, but I hadn't noticed it before." James Baldwin has said that in *Julius Caesar* he discovered the tension between idealism and blind passion, or, to put it another way, the guilt that is part of a hero's "desperate singlemindedness." When we read a piece of literature, we may have known intellectually that this or that is so, but what earlier had been a lifeless platitude now becomes a vital part of our being. James Joyce expressed the view that literature imitates life and influences behavior when he complained to a publisher who refused to issue his book of short stories, *Dubliners*:

> It is not my fault that the odor of ashpits and old weeds and offal hangs round my stories. I seriously believe that you will retard the course of civilization in Ireland by preventing the Irish people from having one good look at themselves in my nicely polished looking-glass.

2 THE EXPRESSIVE THEORY

The second theory, usually called the expressive theory, can be treated more briefly. It holds that the artist is not essentially an imitator but one who expresses his feelings. D. H. Lawrence said, "One sheds one's sicknesses in books, repeats and presents again one's emotions to be master of them." Here is a powerful expression of feeling, thinly disguised as a statement about the ancient Israelites:

> When Israel was in Egypt's land,
>   Let my people go!
> Oppressed so hard they could not stand,
>   Let my people go!
>
> *(Chorus)*
> Go down, Moses,
> 'Way down in Egypt's land;
> Tell old Pharaoh,
> Let my people go!

One understands easily enough what Frederick Douglass, a fugitive slave, meant when he said that songs can relieve an aching heart, and that he often sang to drown his sorrow. Two quotations from William Wordsworth may be useful. "Poetry," he said, "is the spontaneous overflow of powerful feelings"; the poet's job is "to treat of things not as they *are* . . . but as they *seem* to exist to the *senses,* and the *passions.*" (This is by no means a complete summary of Wordsworth's theories, but it is enough to illustrate the gist of expressive theories.)

The artist's vision, the theory holds, is more inward than outward; the work of art is not an imitation of the external world but an expression of the internal world, the embodiment of an emotion. This theory sometimes holds that "truth" has nothing to do with literature. Art expresses an artist's feelings, and his feelings cannot be true or false. They simply exist. Sometimes, however, an expressive theory insists that a work is true if it is sincere. We do not ordinarily say that laughter or tears are true or false, but if we discover that the laughter or tears are hypocritical rather than sincere, we call them false. Since, however, the reader of a piece of literature cannot know if the author was sincere, the criterion of sincerity is valueless. We cannot say that *Julius Caesar* is sincere; perhaps Shakespeare wrote it merely to make money. We cannot even say that his sonnets reflect his true feelings; though Wordsworth said that in them Shakespeare "unlocked his heart," how can we be sure? Furthermore, writing that is indubitably sincere is not necessarily good writing. Aldous Huxley is surely correct in his observation that "a bad book is as much labor to write as a good one; it comes as sincerely from the author's soul."

Moreover, what value does expressive writing have? One can reply it is valuable for the writer: "If I don't write to empty my mind," Byron said, "I go mad." Yeats, at the end of his career, put it less heroically: "I have sometimes wondered if I did not write poetry to find a cure for my own ailment, as constipated cats do when they eat valerian." But if this relief from pressure is its only value, the written piece might just as well be left lying on the writer's desk. Most expressions of emotions, after all, are valueless to everyone but the person expressing them. Our laughter, mumblings, and cries of despair are all very expressive and afford us a relief, but who would call them works of art that are of value to other people?

Advocates of the expressive theory argue that by showing us how he sees and feels something, the writer may pluck the blinders from our eyes and melt the ice around our heart. He may jolt us out of our usual rut and widen the area of our sensibilities. Wordsworth's view of daffodils may force upon us the awareness that our own views are narrow. An awareness of how other people feel is, after all, a way of expanding and enriching one's own personality.

THE AFFECTIVE THEORY

Finally, there is the affective theory of art, which holds that a work of art ought to arouse a particular emotion, or affect (to use the psychologist's term), in the perceiver. This theory is often closely related to the expressive theory: the artist allegedly expresses an emotion, embodying it in a work of art, and this work evokes in the perceiver a similar or identical emotion. Presumably by describing certain things in a certain way the writer can evoke the proper response. The most famous presentation of this theory is Tolstoi's *What Is Art?*, a sentence of which is here quoted:

> Art is a human activity consisting in this, that one man consciously, by means of certain external signs, hands on to others feelings he has lived through, and that others are infected by these feelings, and also experience them.

In Alexander Pope's words, the artist

> . . . gives my breast a thousand pains,
> Can make me feel each passion that he feigns;
> Enrage, compose, with more than magic art,
> With pity and with terror tear my heart;
> And snatch me o'er the earth or through the air,
> To Thebes, to Athens, when he will, and where.

Affective theories hold that the stimulation of certain emotions is, for some reason, good: we need an occasional release (a good cry), or we need to have our emotions organized into a pleasant pattern (as the fretful child needs his mother's smile, to induce in him good spirits). That some readers seek emotional stimulus from books is beyond doubt; they want to identify themselves with the central character, experiencing bursts of love, sorrow, and so forth. But a good work of art neither invites this identification nor triggers stereotyped emotions. How many people have felt totally at one with Hamlet, Macbeth, Brutus?

Usually the affective theory insists that the aim is not to induce a temporary emotional state, but to induce an emotional state that will lead to action. Such a theory might hold that the artist should stimulate in people an awareness of the horror of war so that they will go out and do something about stopping wars. Tolstoi, who held such a view, regarded the evocation of emotion not as an end but as a means:

> The task of art is enormous. Through the influence of real art, aided by science, guided by religion, that peaceful cooperation of man which is now maintained by external means — by our lawcourts, police, charitable institutions, factory inspection, and so forth — should be obtained by man's free and joyous activity. Art should cause violence to be set aside.

Jean Pierre Gorin, close associate of film director Jean-Luc Godard, put the matter quite simply when asked, "What is the function of cinema?" "Cinema is part of the ideological struggle. And a revolutionary film is on the side of revolution." Ezekiel Mphahlele, an exiled South African black writer, has said that the best poetry is a "memorable" expression of "revolutionary passion and ideas," and Imamu Amiri Baraka (LeRoi Jones) has said that revolutionary writing must "transform reality." But against the view that a good work of art prompts us to action, one can put Robert Frost's deceptively simple question: "How soon?"

SOME TENTATIVE CONCLUSIONS

This chapter opened with the query, "What is literature?" and it has not yet given a satisfactory answer. Nor will it. No one has come up with a satisfactory answer so far. Textbooks and theoretical treatises are filled with neat definitions, but no definition has yet withstood all criticism. It would be nice to say that literature evokes emotion, but so does a good deal of nonliterature (for example, a documentary account of the bombing of Hiroshima), and perhaps much literature evokes "attention" rather than "emotion." It would be nice to say that literature is essentially fictional, but is a poem on, say, the power of God fictional? Is such a poem fictional to the believer who composes it or to the believer who reads it? Moreover, it can be argued that although works of art are superficially fictional, they are essentially true. It would be nice to say that in literature there is complexity and unity, but these are characteristics of a telephone book as well as of *Hamlet*. And so it goes, definition after definition failing when applied to specific works that we know are works of art.

The brief sketch of critical theories in the preceding pages, however, may help a reader toward a tentative definition. Surely we can agree that a piece of literature is a performance in words; it strongly holds our attention, seeming complete in itself; it is not primarily regarded as a source of factual information; it offers a unique delight or satisfaction. To these, most people would add that literature offers some sort of truth, though not the sort of truth found in factual propositions such as $E = mc^2$. Finally, most people would say that it has a beneficial effect on the perceiver. Tolstoi may be claiming too much for the arts, but is it absurd to believe that they can play a role in civilizing man? Music has beneficial effects on animals: cows are said to give more milk when music is played in barns, race horses are soothed by music at the starting gate at Aqueduct, and wolves reduce their howling when they hear classical music. Is there nothing in the following lines from *The Merchant of Venice*?

> *Jessica.* I am never merry when I hear sweet music.
> *Lorenzo.* The reason is your spirits are attentive;
>   For do but note a wild and wanton herd,
>   Or race of youthful and unhandled colts,
>   Fetching mad bounds, bellowing and neighing loud,
>   Which is the hot condition of their blood —
>   If they but hear perchance a trumpet sound,
>   Or any air of music touch their ears,
>   You shall perceive them make a mutual stand,
>   Their savage eyes turned to a modest gaze
>   By the sweet power of music. Therefore the poet
>   Did feign that Orpheus drew trees, stones, and floods,
>   Since nought so stockish, hard, and full of rage,
>   But music for the time doth change his nature.
>   The man that hath no music in himself,
>   Nor is not moved with concord of sweet sounds,
>   Is fit for treasons, stratagems, and spoils.

Is it not possible that works of art give us an insight into reality (as the imitative theory usually holds), that they broaden our awareness of the possibilities of experience (as the expressive theory usually holds), and that they valuably affect our nervous system (as the affective theory usually holds)? This is not to say that every work of art does all these things, but only that all these theories may have something to contribute to a deeper and more conscious awareness of what is valuable in the works we read. If we look back into our experiences, can we not find moments that seem to verify aspects of each theory? This book will offer further experiences; as you encounter them, you are invited to test these theories.

2
Reading and Responding to Literature

In a letter written in 1799, the English poet and painter William Blake made the following remark:

> The tree which moves some to tears of joy is in the eyes of others only a green thing that stands in the way. . . . As a man is, so he sees.

And in an essay of 1810, commenting on his visionary painting of the Last Judgment, he made a somewhat similar remark. (The reference to a guinea is to a gold British coin.)

> "What," it will be questioned, "when the sun rises do you not see a round disk of fire somewhat like a guinea?" Oh no, no; I see an innumerable company of the heavenly host crying, "Holy, holy, holy is the Lord God Almighty."

A third quotation, this one by William Wordsworth, Blake's contemporary, will complete this mini-anthology of remarks about strongly imaginative responses; or rather, in this case, a remark about an unimaginative viewer:

> A primrose by a river's brim
> A yellow primrose was to him,
> And it was nothing more.

All of us, of course, respond in our own individual ways, whether to a poem, a political candidate, or a slice of apple pie. We inevitably bring our selves — our conscious and unconscious assumptions, expectations, biases, values, histories — to all new experiences. When we look at something new, we may try to be objective, but we see, in large measure, what our ideology has conditioned us to see. We are all rather like the seven blind men who, in the fable, touched different parts of the elephant. One, feeling the tail, said, "The elephant is like a rope," Another, feeling the leg, said, "No, the elephant is like a tree." And so on.

When we read a literary work, say *Hamlet,* we are not reading something fixed "out there"; in some degree the work becomes what the reader sees in it. For instance, one reader of *Hamlet* sees a noble tragic hero, but another (Bernard Shaw in this case) sees an unpleasant young man who kills seven people and goes on griping (until late in the play) that he hasn't killed an eighth. How, then, can we hope to talk about literature, if all of us perceive what we read in our own way?

CAN WE KNOW THE AUTHOR'S INTENTIONS?

It is sometimes said that we should try to see the work of literature as the author intended it. But, to take only one objection, for most literature we do not know what the author intended. We have only the work itself; Shakespeare, for instance, has left no comments about what he intended *Hamlet* to mean. The best we can do is to read *Hamlet* and draw some conclusions about what (in our opinion) the author must have intended. Is it really possible to find the author's intention? Probably not; or rather, not entirely. We are readers of the late twentieth century, and we can probably never recover the exact feelings and ideas of a writer of the early seventeenth century. Historical research can tell us that the Elizabethans believed in ghosts (there is a ghost in *Hamlet*), but it is doubtful if we, living in the late twentieth century, can ever feel toward ghosts exactly as Shakespeare and his audience felt.

In technical language, Shakespeare's **repertoire** — the assumptions and attitudes and other aspects of his ideology that went into the writing of *Hamlet* — differs from our repertoire, that is, differs from the ideology that we bring to the play. It is even likely that not everyone in Shakespeare's audience shared his repertoire, or felt as he did about ghosts or revenge or kings or death or anything else. At least so far as certain parts of the play go, the Roman Catholics probably felt differently from the Protestants, young people probably felt differently from older people, rich people differently from poor people, and women differently from men.

Still, having said this, we at least can try to read the work closely and can try to respond to the whole of the work, rather than only to some isolated bit that appeals to us or repels us. That is, we can, at least for a start,

1. Pay close attention to all of the words.
2. Examine our responses and try to account for them.

If we do this, we may find that instead of reducing the work to fit our prejudices, the work enlarges our ideas.

Consider, for a moment, the story of Little Red Riding Hood. In Nazi Germany, the story of Red Riding Hood was interpreted as showing the German people victimized by the Jewish wolf. One cannot prove that this interpretation is wrong, but at least today, to Americans in the late twentieth century, it seems eccentric and, indeed, far out of touch with the text of the story. One can hardly find a clearer instance of reading a text with a predetermined idea or, to put it another way, of shutting one's eyes to the text and asserting one's own ideas. But what are we to make of a psychologist's interpretation of the same story as showing male envy of pregnancy: the wolf wants a living creature in his belly. Is this view as private (and as out of touch with the text) as the Nazi view? Certainly one cannot prove it true or false, and almost as certainly, it strikes one at first as odd. But is it a private interpretation imposed on the story? You may well feel there is something to it, even if you also feel that this interpretation does not offer *the exclusive meaning* of the story. It may account for part of the appeal of the story, but clearly it also leaves out much of the appeal — for instance, our pleasure in seeing an innocent child rescued.

In the technical language of literary specialists, this story — like most works of literature — is marked by **blanks** or **gaps** or **indeterminacies,** which active readers must fill for themselves. Perhaps the largest blank here concerns the theme; the storyteller does not explicitly tell us what the story adds up to, and so we fill in the blank as best we can, according to our experiences.

RESPONDING TO A STORY

The Parable of the Prodigal Son

Now let's look at a story, one told by Jesus, and reported in the fifteenth chapter of the Gospel according to St. Luke. Jesus here tells a **parable,** a short story from which a lesson is to be drawn. Luke reports that just before Jesus tells the story, the Pharisees and scribes — persons whom the Gospels depict as opposed to Jesus because he sometimes found their traditions and teachings inadequate — complained that Jesus was a man of loose morals, one who "receives sinners and eats with them." According to Luke, Jesus responded thus:

And he said, "A certain man had two sons: and the younger of them said to his father, 'Father, give me the portion of goods that falleth to me.' And he divided unto them his living. And not many days after, the younger son gathered all together, and took his journey into a far country, and there wasted his substance with riotous living.

And when he had spent all, there arose a mighty famine in that land, and he began to be in want. And he went and joined himself to a citizen of that country, and he sent him into his fields to feed swine. And he would fain have filled his belly with the husks that the swine did eat: and no man gave unto him.

And when he came to himself he said, 'How many hired servants of my father's have bread enough and to spare, and I perish with hunger? I will arise and go to my father, and will say unto him, "Father, I have sinned against heaven, and before thee. And am no more worthy to be called thy son: make me as one of thy hired servants." '

And he arose, and came to his father. But when he was a great way off, his father saw him, and had compassion, and ran, and fell on his neck, and kissed him. And the son said unto the father, 'Father, I have sinned against heaven, and in thy sight, and am no more worthy to be called thy son.' But the father said to his servants, 'Bring forth the best robe, and put it on him, and put a ring on his hand, and shoes on his feet. And bring hither the fatted calf and kill it, and let us eat, and be merry. For this my son was dead, and is alive again; he was lost, and is found.' And they began to be merry.

Now his elder son was in the field, and as he came and drew nigh to the house, he heard music and dancing. And he called one of the servants, and asked what these things meant. And he said unto him, 'Thy brother is come, and thy father hath killed the fatted calf, because he hath received him safe and sound.' And he was angry, and would not go in: therefore his father came out, and entreated him. And he answering said to his father, 'Lo, these many years do I serve thee, neither transgressed I at any time thy commandment, and yet thou never gavest me a kid, that I might make merry with my friends: but as soon as this thy son was come, which hath devoured thy living with harlots, thou has killed for him the fatted calf.' And he said unto him, 'Son, thou art ever with me, and all that I have is thine. It was meet that we should make merry, and be glad: for this thy brother was dead, and is alive again: and was lost, and is found.' "

Now, to begin with a small point, it is not likely that any but strictly observant Jews, or perhaps Moslems (who, like these Jews, do not eat pork), can feel the disgust that Jesus' audience must have felt at the thought that the son was reduced to feeding swine and that he even envied the food that swine ate. This disgust, then, is not part of the repertoire (to use the specialist's word) of most readers. Further, some of us may be vegetarians; if so, we are not at all delighted at the thought that the father kills the fatted calf (probably the wretched beast has been force-fed) in order to celebrate the son's return. And, of course, some of us do not believe in God, and hence are not prepared to fill in the blank or gap and to take the story, as many people take it, as a story whose message is that we, like God (the father in this parable is usually taken to stand for God), ought to rejoice in the restoration of the sinner. Probably, then, for all sorts of obvious reasons none of us can put ourselves back into the first century A.D. and hear the story exactly as Jesus' hearers heard it.

Still, it seems clear enough that all of us should be able to get the gist of the story and, more important, should enjoy the skillful way in which it is told. This skill will become apparent, however, only after several sympathetic readings. A single reading, and especially one that rejects the story because (for example) it apparently endorses the eating of animals, of course produces a response, but it is not a response that will be of much interest to others, nor, for that matter, will it be of much value to the reader, since it leaves the reader exactly where he or she was before reading the story.

What are some examples of superb storytelling here, and what can a reader gain from a sympathetic, thoughtful reading? We can begin by noting a few points:

1. Although the story is customarily called "The Parable of the Prodigal Son" or "The Parable of the Lost Son," it tells of

two sons, not of one. When we reread the story, we increasingly see that these brothers are compared and contrasted: the prodigal leaves his father's house for a different way of life — he thus seems lost to the father — but then he repents and returns to the father, whereas the older son, who physically remains with the father, is spiritually remote from the father, or is lost in a different way. By virtue of his self-centeredness he is remote from the father in feeling or spirit.

    2. Again, reading and rereading reveal small but telling details. For instance, when the prodigal plans to return home, he thinks of what he will say to his father. But, though he has come to his senses and repudiated his folly, he still does not understand his father, for we will see in a moment that the prodigal has no need of this speech. Jesus tells us that as soon as the father saw the prodigal returning, he "had compassion, and ran, and fell on his neck, and kissed him." And (another very human touch) the prodigal — although already forgiven — nevertheless cannot refrain from uttering his heartfelt but, under the circumstances, unnecessary speech of repentance.

    3. The elder brother, learning that the merrymaking is for the returning prodigal, "was angry, and would not go in." This character is sketched only briefly, but a reader immediately recognizes the type: self-centered, unforgiving, and petulant. The older son does not realize it, but he is as far from his father as the younger son had been. What is the father's response to this son, who is so different from the forgiving father? "Therefore came his father out, and entreated him." The father goes out to the dutiful son, just as he had gone out to the prodigal son. Notice, too, speaking of sons, that the older son, talking to the father, somewhat disdainfully speaks of "this thy son." And what is the father's response? To the elder son's "this thy son," the father replies, "this thy brother."

No matter how closely we look, however, certain blanks or gaps remain: we will not find out if the older brother learns a lesson and, following the younger brother, repents of his nasty behavior. We can offer guesses, based on our understanding of others and based on our own nature. We can, if we are so inclined, even say that the father was sentimental and foolish to forgive his younger son so easily, and we may say that the older brother makes a very good point: Why has the father never given a gift to the older brother? Perhaps we can even say that the father is not quite accurate when he soothes the older brother by saying, "All that I have is thine," for he has just killed the fatted calf for the younger brother, thus diminishing the property that he claims he is willing to give to the older brother. And — a very large issue — we may even question the historical accuracy of the picture of the Pharisees and scribes, for sources other than the Gospels depict them more sympathetically.

Thoughts of this sort may come to mind, because, again, we inevitably bring ourselves — our limited repertoires — to all that we experience (and reading is an experience). It may well turn out that, finally, we will (so to speak) go against the story. We may feel that the prodigal should show his repentance in more than words, or we may feel that the father has neglected the dutiful older son, or that this whole story of a father and his two sons is an example of the sort of patriarchal thinking that (one might argue) does not even consider women as worthy of mention. Responses of this sort can be interesting, and it can be interesting to set them forth in writing so that we share them with our colleagues. But if we let the work of literature merely trigger our stock responses, rather than try to let it induce new responses, we may be the losers. We may, to put it bluntly, simply retain our prejudices and miss the experience of encountering something more important, more substantial.

Put it this way: we can agree that readers today cannot set themselves back some two thousand years and hear the story exactly as Jesus told it. Readers in the twentieth century bring to the story experiences that Jesus' audience did not have. In some ways we must see the story differently, and must fill in the blanks in our own ways. But, on the other hand, we can make an effort to submit ourselves to the story. That is, we can tentatively assume that Jesus had something in mind in telling the story, and that he arranged the words so that they would guide our responses in a certain direction. After we have tried to let the story guide us, we can still hold to our own view, though certainly most of us hope that the older brother — a perfectly normal fellow, apparently — listened attentively to his father, opened himself to his father's words, and broke through the ice that surrounded his heart.

ANOTHER LOOK AT INTENTIONS

But it may still be asked, how do we know how the teller wanted us to respond? We have already mentioned that for much writing, such as *Hamlet,* we have only the writing itself, not a statement about intention. (And, of course, even if we had a writer's statement about his or her intention, it might be inaccurate or in some way inadequate. For instance, a writer might honestly say that she wrote a book merely to make money, or to prove to herself that she could break into print, or to kill time, and yet the book might compel our interest and strike us as more important than these intentions suggest.) Our only advice at this point is to urge you to practice two more or less opposed activities already hinted at:

1. Submit yourself to the text.
2. Trust your feelings.

By "Submit yourself to the text," we mean, for a start, read attentively, paying attention to every word and trying (insofar as is possible) to let the work do its work on you. Assume, at least for the moment, that the author is a person of intelligence, skill, and goodwill, and try to hear what this author has to say. (There will be ample time, later, to complain.) Jesus assumed that his parables would be properly understood by "those who have ears to hear." With a short work, especially if it is a poem, you may want to memorize it, or you may want to write out a complete copy, or at least a summary. Probably there is no better way of getting a work into your bones than copying it word for word, commas and all. (We have typed out the prodigal son parable several times, and have always felt that we were spending our time well.)

By "Trust your feelings," we mean that if you are moved one way or the other — if you strongly like or dislike something — begin with the assumption that you are on to something, but also spend a few moments thinking about why you feel this way or that. What assumptions do you hold that led you to respond this way to the text?

ANOTHER LOOK AT RESPONSES

Also keep this principle in mind: the reader of a work of literature must spend some time before getting to the end, and not until the end can the gist of the work be grasped. When we read even a very short story, such as the parable of the sons, it takes a minute or so just to get from the beginning to the end. In practice, this means that authors work by revealing things bit by bit. Something is said, we find it of interest, and we want to hear more. When the writer writes a sentence, that sentence reveals something, but in a sense it also conceals something and makes us eager to find out about what has been concealed. Take the beginning of the parable:

> A certain man had two sons: and the younger of them said to his father, "Father, give me the portion of goods that falleth to me."

"Two sons." We are told what the younger said, but we may wonder what the older will say. And surely when we hear the younger son's request, we wonder what the father's response will be, and what the son then will do. And thus a story proceeds, revealing (and thus satisfying) and at the same time raising questions, stimulating responses which we hope to satisfy by reading further. As we read, we more or less keep saying, "Oh? Ah, now I see. But what next? Ah, yes, of course." We respond, so to speak, to each sentence or each episode somewhat as we might respond when we see someone approaching us in the street. We try to grasp the intention, as revealed in the gait, the eyes, the clothing, the gestures, and we proceed by moving a bit to the right or the left, or perhaps we stop and talk. We "read" faces and gestures, and similarly as active readers we study written words for information about how to feel about them, how to respond appropriately to them. As we go along, we engage in what Wolfgang Iser in *The Act of Reading* (1978) calls **consistency building;** after experiencing uncertainties, we combine (or try to combine) into a meaningful whole the details we have thus far encountered. We periodically or even continually keep taking stock, but only when we get to the end of the work are we in a position to connect all the details. When we finish The Parable of the Prodigal Son, we see why the story includes two brothers. Our explanation may include the statement that by contrasting the two brothers Jesus apparently sought to stimulate his audience at the end to think (and act) a certain way.

    In the previous chapter, in discussing the affective theory, we quoted some passages to the effect that literature induces an emotion, and the emotion then causes the perceiver to act a certain way. Shakespeare attributes such a view to Hamlet, who in the second scene of the second act decides to stage a play about a murder in order to drive the real murderer to a confession:

> I have heard that guilty creatures sitting at a play
> Have by the very cunning of the scene
> Been struck so to the soul that presently
> They have proclaimed their malefactions.

In this instance, one notices, Hamlet assumes that although the literary work will serve to trap the murderer, it will serve also to free him from his guilt, to release him from his paralyzing state. Many authors could be cited who similarly have expressed the view that literature in one way or another opens our eyes to ourselves, but one of the most powerful statements to that effect was made by Franz Kafka, in a letter written in 1904:

> If the book we are reading does not wake us, as with a fist hammering on our skull, why then do we read it? So that it shall make us happy? Good God, we would also be happy if we had no books, and such books as make us happy we could, if need be, write ourselves. But what we must have are those books which come upon us like ill-fortune, and distress us deeply, like the death of one we love better than ourselves. . . . A book must be an ice-axe to break the sea frozen inside us.

Jesus' parable of the two sons was told not only as a heart-warming and comforting story about a father who forgives his prodigal son; it was told in order (in Kafka's words) to hammer on the skulls of those who had rebuked Jesus for associating with sinners; that is, it was told in order to break the sea frozen inside them (and us). We may think we want nice stories with attractive heroes and heroines — persons whom we can fantasize as ourselves — and with lots of action and a happy ending and a reassuring moral, but what we are more likely to get from the great storytellers is a subversive story, a story that does *not* confirm the values we already hold but that, rather, seeks to induce new values in us. As the writer Elizabeth Bowen put it, a work of art "is the only thing that can go on mattering once it has stopped hurting."

We have already suggested the limitations of turning to an author and asking what was the intention behind a literary work. Still, it may be valuable to have a sense of what some authors think they are doing when they write. Consider two comments made by writers of our day. When asked "How would you like for your stories to be read?" Eudora Welty replied:

> I would like to feel they gave pleasure. . . . I'd like people to be moved, to feel that they have passed through some experience with me.

Talking about writing, Raymond Carver said:

> Talent, even genius, is . . . the gift of seeing what everyone else has seen, but seeing it more clearly, from all sides.

These quotations imply that writers see or experience something, and that they hope their readers will share in the experiences recounted. Again, readers cannot help but bring their own experience (as they bring their own eyes and brains and hearts) to the writer's work, but readers also can try, at least for a start, to enter into the writer's experience or repertoire. Later they surely will want to test the writer's story against their own experience, but for a start they may find it most rewarding to try to let the writer guide their responses, that is, to try to read attentively and sympathetically.

RESPONDING TO A STORY

Jesus and the Woman Taken in Adultery

Early in this chapter we looked at a story told by Jesus, "The Parable of the Prodigal Son." Now let's look at a story told not by Jesus, but about Jesus, or rather, about his response to certain people who confronted him with a woman taken in adultery. The story appears in the eighth chapter of the Gospel according to St. John.

> Jesus went unto the Mount of Olives. And early in the morning he came again into the temple, and all the people came unto him; and he sat down, and taught them.
> And the scribes and Pharisees brought unto him a woman taken in adultery; and when they had set her in the midst, they said unto him, "Master, this woman was taken in adultery, in the very act. Now Moses in the law commanded us that such should be stoned: but what sayest thou?" This they said, tempting him, that they might have to accuse him. But Jesus stooped down, and with his finger wrote on the ground, as though he heard them not. So when they continued asking him, he lifted up himself, and said unto them, "He that is without sin among you, let him first cast a stone at her." And again he stooped down, and wrote on the ground. And they which heard it, being convicted by their own conscience, went out one by one, beginning at the eldest, even unto the last: and Jesus was left alone, and the woman standing in the midst.
> When Jesus had lifted up himself, and saw none but the woman, he said unto her, "Woman, where are those thine accusers? Hath no man condemned thee?" She said, "No man, Lord." And Jesus said unto her, "Neither do I condemn thee; go, and sin no more."

Again, it is impossible for us to hear this story, and to respond to it, exactly as Jesus' hearers did. For one thing, there are large blanks; we probably aren't quite clear about exactly what is happening. Perhaps the scribes and Pharisees are trying to get Jesus to disagree with Moses, so that they can then discredit Jesus as a spiritual leader. For instance, they might say that he condoned what Jewish law regarded as a great sin. Or maybe they are trying to get him to say that indeed the woman deserves to be stoned, a statement that the Roman authorities would take as illegally inciting others to violence. And what do we make of Jesus' writing on the ground? Is it perhaps a physical action that is made partly to relieve the strain of distress caused by the mean behavior of the self-righteous accusers? Does Jesus stoop and turn his eyes toward the ground in an effort to avoid embarrassing the tormented woman?

Despite these blanks or gaps, certain things are clear enough, partly because — however great the changes between Jesus' day and our own — some aspects of human nature have not changed. We easily recognize the nastiness of these scribes and Pharisees when they take the woman "and set her in the midst," and when to their statement that "this woman was taken in adultery" they gratuitously add, "in the very act." We have heard voices like these in our own day, perhaps issuing from our own throats. What is especially interesting, however, is that even these unfeeling men, so self-righteous at the beginning of the narrative, are moved by Jesus' words, for "convicted by their own conscience," they "went out one by one." (Why the eldest left first, however, is yet another blank, which we may fill in according to our individual responses.) Jesus' words apparently have provided them with the ice-axe that Kafka spoke of when he said that books "break the sea frozen inside us." Or we may imagine that the teller of this narrative might have felt, with Eudora Welty, that he wanted people "to feel that they have passed through some experience with me." Or, finally, we may imagine that the teller of this part of the story of Jesus' life had what Raymond Carver calls "the gift of seeing what everyone else has seen, but seeing it more clearly, from all sides."

We can, if we like, still question the story. We can still see it as told by a partisan of Jesus. Or we can see it as implying that adultery need not deserve punishment. Or we can see it as asserting the debatable idea that judges cannot pass judgment if they themselves are sinners. Our own experiences, our own repertoire, will color our responses and will make us see the story in our own way. But we can try to account for our responses. Finally, and really first, it is our duty to try to see the entire work as clearly as we can. Perhaps the best way to do this is to assume, at least at the start, that the work has value, and that the creator of the work

may himself or herself have had responses that are worth trying
to share.

RESPONDING TO POEMS

Edwin Arlington Robinson, "Richard Cory" and Hal Summers, "My Old Cat"

Let's look first at a short poem with which you perhaps are already
familiar, Edwin Arlington Robinson's "Richard Cory."

> Whenever Richard Cory went down town
> We people on the pavement looked at him:
> He was a gentleman from sole to crown,
> Clean favored, and imperially slim.
>
> And he was always quietly arrayed,
> And he was always human when he talked;
> But still he fluttered pulses when he said,
> "Good morning," and he glittered when he walked.
>
> And he was rich — yes, richer than a king —
> And admirably schooled in every grace:
> In fine, we thought that he was everything
> To make us wish that we were in his place.
>
> So on we worked, and waited for the light,
> And went without the meat, and cursed the bread;
> And Richard Cory, one calm summer night,
> Went home and put a bullet through his head.

If you have just read the poem for the first time, you may want
to take a moment now to read it again.

A poem, though written by a poet — in this case Edwin
Arlington Robinson — is spoken by a speaker whom the poet
creates. As one reads the poem, one usually develops an increasingly
strong impression of what sort of person the speaker is, though
obviously different readers will, in varying degrees, differ on exactly
how the speaker is to be regarded. But probably all readers would
agree that

1. The speaker of "Richard Cory" is an ordinary hard-working
    person who admired Cory.

And most readers, whatever their backgrounds or repertoires, would
probably agree with at least two additional statements:

2. The speaker recounts the suicide of a man named Richard Cory.

3. The speaker says that others regarded Cory as he did. For instance, he says that Cory "fluttered pulses," and that "We people on the pavement" regarded Cory as a "gentleman," and that "we thought that he was everything / To make us wish that we were in his place."

Probably we could make some other assertions with which almost everyone would agree. But now let's consider some responses that may be more personal, even eccentric. Suppose, for instance, someone says that she cannot stand the poem because she is married to a man named Richard Cory, who is a very nice fellow, and she can't bear to think of him committing suicide. Further, she says, he simply would *not* commit suicide. She knows him quite well — he is immensely important in her repertoire or thought — and she can't imagine him doing such a thing. This reader is responding, yes, but we probably would agree — indeed, even she probably would agree — that her response is extremely personal and that it gets in the way of whatever the poem has to offer.

None of us can claim that we have the "right" responses — we recognize that different people will respond (to a degree) differently, but we can try to listen to Robinson, and not slam the door in his face.

Now let's take a less extreme case. Someone says that he likes the poem because its moral is this: Money can't buy everything. This view, part of a widely held repertoire, is something we can discuss, in a way that we probably can't usefully discuss the response of a reader married to a man named Richard Cory or the response of a reader named Richard Cory. We can, for example, look in the poem for evidence that the moral is that money can't buy everything. That Richard Cory committed suicide is probably evidence of his unhappiness. (Nothing in the poem suggests, for instance, that he was happy but he committed suicide so that his wife would get his insurance money.) There is also conclusive evidence that Cory did not lack money: "And he was rich — yes, richer than a king." But suppose someone points out that the poem is not only about the unhappiness of a rich man. It is also about the unhappiness of a highly civilized man, a man "admirably schooled in every grace," a man who "was always human when he talked," a man whose "Good morning" excited and inspired those who saw him.

Perhaps, then, we might agree that the poem is not quite about the idea that money can't buy happiness. Perhaps it is true to say that if the poem has an underlying idea, the idea may be that we can never understand the thoughts of another, and that even possession of the most civilized virtues (as well as money) cannot assure one of happiness. The speaker of the poem, and the townspeople, wished they were in Cory's place:

> So on we worked, and waited for the light,
> And went without the meat, and cursed the bread. . . .

They see themselves as self-denying persons who strove to be like Richard Cory — and then Cory killed himself, bafflingly, it seems, since they think Cory had everything. Perhaps, then, the poem is about the townspeople as well as Richard Cory, and perhaps it suggests that despite their vision of themselves as self-denying almost to the point of saintliness ("waited for the light, / And went without the meat"), they are in fact rather vulgarly materialistic, for apparently it is these hard-working people, puzzled by Cory's suicide, who believe that good manners combined with money will buy happiness.

We could, of course, discuss many other things — many other possible responses to the poem. For instance, we could discuss a first response (when one first reads the poem one is surprised to learn at the end that Cory killed himself) and compare it with a second response (perhaps the poem is even more interesting when one already knows how it will end). Or we could discuss this Richard Cory, whom the speaker so admires. How does he strike us? How, that is, do we fill in this blank? As perhaps a bit stuffy? If this is your response, you might try to explain why you respond thus — what in the poem (and what in your experience) makes you feel this way about Cory?

We'll end this chapter by printing a short poem by a contemporary writer and following it with a few questions that may help to stimulate responses.

Hal Summers (b. *1911*)

My Old Cat

My old cat is dead
Who would butt me with his head.
He had the sleekest fur,
He had the blackest purr.

Always gentle with us
Was this black puss,
But when I found him today
Stiff and cold where he lay,
His look was a lion's,
Full of rage, defiance:
O! he would not pretend
That what came was a friend
But met it in pure hate.
Well died, my old cat.

QUESTIONS

1. What did you especially like about the poem? What did you especially dislike about it?
2. Exactly why, in your opinion, does the speaker say, "Well died, my old cat"? What do you think the speaker's attitude is toward death? How does this attitude strike you?
3. Do you have any feelings about cats, one way or the other, that you think are not widely shared? If so, do you think these feelings help you to enjoy the poem, or get in the way?

Fiction

3
Stories and Meanings

People tell stories for many reasons, including the sheer egotistical delight of talking, but probably most of the best storytelling proceeds from one of two more commendable desires: a desire to entertain or a desire to instruct. Among the most famous of the stories designed to instruct are the parables that Jesus told, for instance, The Parable of the Prodigal Son, which we discussed in the previous chapter. (*Parable* comes from the Greek word meaning "to throw beside," that is, "to compare," and we are to compare these little stories with our own behavior.) We can say that the parable is told for the sake of the point; we also can say that it is told for our sake, because we are implicitly invited to see ourselves in the story, and to live our lives in accordance with it. This simple but powerful story, with its memorable characters — though nameless and briefly sketched — makes us feel the point in our hearts.

Even older than Jesus' parables are the fables attributed to Aesop, some of which go back to the seventh century before Christ. These stories also teach lessons by telling brief incidents from which homely morals may easily be drawn, even though the stories are utterly fanciful. Among famous examples are the stories of the hare and the tortoise, the boy who cried "Wolf," the ant and the grasshopper, and a good many others that stick in the mind because of the sharply contrasted characters in sharply imagined situations. The fables just mentioned take only four or five sentences apiece, but, brief as they are, Aesop told some briefer ones. Here is the briefest of all:

> A vixen sneered at a lioness because she never bore more than one cub. "Only one," the lioness replied, "but a lion."

Just that: a situation with a conflict (the mere confrontation of a fox and a lion brings together the ignoble and the noble) and a resolution (*something* must come out of such a confrontation). There is no setting (we are not told that "one day in June a vixen, walking down a road, met a lioness"), but none is needed here. What there is — however briefly set forth — is characterization. The fox's baseness is effectively communicated through the verb "sneered" and through her taunt, and the lioness's nobility is even more effectively communicated through the brevity and decisiveness of her reply. This reply at first seems to agree with the fox ("Only one") and then, after a suspenseful delay provided by the words "the lioness replied," the reply is tersely and powerfully completed ("but a lion"), placing the matter firmly in a new light. Granted that the story is not much of a story, still, it is finely told, and more potent — more memorable, more lively, we might even say more real, despite its talking animals — than the mere moral, "Small-minded people confuse quantity with quality."

Here is a much later short tale, from nineteenth-century Japan. It is said to be true, but whether it really occurred or not is scarcely of any importance. It is the story, not the history, that counts.

> Two monks, Tanzan and Ekido, were once traveling together down a muddy road. A heavy rain was still falling.
>
> Coming around a bend, they met a lovely girl in a silk kimono and sash, unable to cross the intersection.
>
> "Come on, girl," said Tanzan at once. Lifting her in his arms, he carried her over the mud.
>
> Ekido did not speak again until that night when they reached a lodging temple. Then he no longer could restrain himself. "We monks don't go near females," he told Tanzan, "especially not young and lovely ones. It is dangerous. Why did you do that?"
>
> "I left the girl there," said Tanzan. "Are you still carrying her?"

A superb story. The opening paragraph, though simple and matter-of-fact, holds our attention: we sense that something interesting is going to happen during this journey along a muddy road on a rainy day. Perhaps we even sense, somehow, by virtue of the references to the mud and the rain, that the journey itself rather than the travelers' destination will be the heart of the story: getting there will be more than half the fun. And then, after the introduction of the two **characters** and the **setting,** we quickly get the **complication,** the encounter with the girl. Still there is apparently no **conflict,** though in "Ekido did not speak again until that night" we sense an unspoken conflict, an action (or, in this case, an inaction) that must be explained, an imbalance that must be righted before we are finished. At last Ekido, no longer able to contain his thoughts, lets his indignation burst out: "We monks don't go near females . . . , especially not young and lovely ones. It is dangerous. Why did you do that?" His statement and his question reveal not only his moral principles, but also his insecurity and the anger that grows from it. And now, when the conflict is out in the open, comes the brief reply that reveals Tanzan's very different character as clearly as the outburst revealed Ekido's. This reply — though we could not have predicted it — strikes us as exactly right, bringing the story to a perfect end, i.e., to a point (like the ends of Christ's parable and Aesop's fable) at which there is no more to be said. It provides the **dénouement** (literally, "unknotting"), or resolution.

Let's look now at another short piece, though this one is somewhat longer than the stories we have just read, and it is less concerned than they are with teaching a lesson.

Anton Chekhov (*Russian. 1860–1904*)

Misery

Translated by Constance Garnett

"To Whom Shall I Tell My Grief?"

The twilight of evening. Big flakes of wet snow are whirling lazily about the street lamps, which have just been lighted, and lying in a thin soft layer on roofs, horses' backs, shoulders, caps. Iona Potapov, the sledge-driver, is all white like a ghost. He sits on the box without stirring, bent as double as the living body can be bent. If a regular snowdrift fell on him it seems as though even then he would not think it necessary to shake it off. . . . His little mare is white and motionless too. Her stillness, the angularity of her lines, and the stick-like straightness of her legs make her look like a halfpenny gingerbread horse. She is probably lost in thought. Anyone who has been torn away from the plough, from the familiar gray landscapes, and cast into this slough, full of monstrous lights, of unceasing uproar and hurrying people, is bound to think.

It is a long time since Iona and his nag have budged. They came out of the yard before dinner-time and not a single fare yet.

But now the shades of evening are falling on the town. The pale light of the street lamps changes to a vivid color, and the bustle of the street grows noisier.

"Sledge to Vyborgskaya!" Iona hears. "Sledge!"

Iona starts, and through his snow-plastered eyelashes sees an officer in a military overcoat with a hood over his head.

"To Vyborgskaya," repeats the officer. "Are you asleep? To Vyborgskaya!"

In token of assent Iona gives a tug at the reins which sends cakes of snow flying from the horse's back and shoulders. The officer gets into the sledge. The sledge-driver clicks to the horse, cranes his neck like a swan, rises in his seat, and more from habit than necessity brandishes his whip. The mare cranes her neck, too, crooks her stick-like legs, and hesitatingly sets off. . . .

"Where are you shoving, you devil?" Iona immediately hears shouts from the dark mass shifting to and fro before him. "Where the devil are you going? Keep to the r-right!"

"You don't know how to drive! Keep to the right," says the officer angrily.

A coachman driving a carriage swears at him; a pedestrian crossing the road and brushing the horse's nose with his shoulder looks at him angrily and shakes the snow off his sleeve. Iona fidgets on the box as though he were sitting on thorns, jerks his elbows, and turns his eyes about like one possessed, as though he did not know where he was or why he was there.

"What rascals they all are!" says the officer jocosely. "They are simply doing their best to run up against you or fall under the horse's feet. They must be doing it on purpose."

Iona looks at his fare and moves his lips. . . . Apparently he means to say something, but nothing comes out but a sniff.

"What?" inquires the officer.

Iona gives a wry smile, and straining his throat, brings out huskily: "My son . . . , er . . . my son died this week, sir."

"H'm! What did he die of?"

Iona turns his whole body round to his fare, and says:

"Who can tell! It must have been from fever. . . . He lay three days in the hospital and then he died. . . . God's will."

"Turn round, you devil!" comes out of the darkness. "Have you gone cracked, you old dog? Look where you are going!"

"Drive on! drive on! . . ." says the officer. "We shan't get there till tomorrow going on like this. Hurry up!"

The sledge-driver cranes his neck again, rises in his seat, and with heavy grace swings his whip. Several times he looks round at the officer, but the latter keeps his eyes shut and is apparently disinclined to listen. Putting his fare down at Vyborgskaya, Iona stops by a restaurant, and again sits huddled up on the box. . . . Again the wet snow paints him and his horse white. One hour passes, and then another. . . .

Three young men, two tall and thin, one short and hunchbacked, come up, railing at each other and loudly stamping on the pavement with their goloshes.

"Cabby, to the Police Bridge!" the hunchback cries in a cracked voice. "The three of us, . . . twenty kopecks!"

Iona tugs at the reins and clicks to his horse. Twenty kopecks is not a fair price, but he has no thoughts for that. Whether it is a rouble or whether it is five kopecks does not matter to him now so long as he has a fare. . . . The three young men, shoving each other and using bad language, go up to the sledge, and all three try to sit down at once. The question remains to be settled: Which are to sit down and which one is to stand? After a long altercation, ill-temper, and abuse, they come to the conclusion that the hunchback must stand because he is the shortest.

"Well, drive on," says the hunchback in his cracked voice, settling himself and breathing down Iona's neck. "Cut along! What a cap you've got, my friend! You wouldn't find a worse one in all Petersburg. . . ."

"He-he! . . . he-he! . . ." laughs Iona. "It's nothing to boast of!"

"Well, then, nothing to boast of, drive on! Are you going to drive like this all the way? Eh? Shall I give you one in the neck?"

"My head aches," says one of the tall ones. "At the Dukmasovs' yesterday Vaska and I drank four bottles of brandy between us."

"I can't make out why you talk such stuff," says the other tall one angrily. "You lie like a brute."

"Strike me dead, it's the truth! . . ."

"It's about as true as that a louse coughs."

"He-he!" grins Iona. "Me-er-ry gentlemen!"

"Tfoo! the devil take you!" cries the hunchback indignantly. "Will you get on, you old plague, or won't you? Is that the way to drive? Give her one with the whip. Hang it all, give it her well."

Iona feels behind his back the jolting person and quivering voice of the hunchback. He hears abuse addressed to him, he sees people, and the feeling of loneliness begins little by little to be less heavy on his heart. The hunchback swears at him, till he chokes over some elaborately whimsical string of epithets and is overpowered by his cough. His tall companions begin talking of a certain Nadyezhda Petrovna. Iona looks round at them. Waiting till there is a brief pause, he looks round once more and says:

"This week . . . er . . . my . . . er . . . son died!"

"We shall all die, . . ." says the hunchback with a sigh, wiping his lips after coughing. "Come, drive on! drive on! My friends, I simply cannot stand crawling like this! When will he get us there?"

"Well, you give him a little encouragement . . . one in the neck!"

"Do you hear, you old plague? I'll make you smart. If one stands on ceremony with fellows like you one may as well walk. Do you hear, you old dragon? Or don't you care a hang what we say?"

And Iona hears rather than feels a slap on the back of his neck.

"He-he! . . ." he laughs. "Merry gentlemen . . . God give you health!"

"Cabman, are you married?" asks one of the tall ones.

"I? He-he! Me-er-ry gentlemen. The only wife for me now is the damp earth. . . . He-ho-ho! . . . The grave that is! . . . Here my son's dead and I am alive. . . . It's a strange thing, death has come in at the wrong door. . . . Instead of coming for me it went for my son. . . ."

And Iona turns round to tell them how his son died, but at that point the hunchback gives a faint sigh and announces that, thank God! they have arrived at last. After taking his twenty kopecks, Iona gazes for a long while after the revelers, who disappear into a dark entry. Again he is alone and again there is silence for him. . . . The misery which has been for a brief space eased comes back again and tears his heart more cruelly than ever. With a look of anxiety and suffering Iona's eyes stray restlessly among the crowds moving to and fro on both sides of the street: can he not find among those thousands someone who will listen to him? But the crowds flit by heedless of him and his misery. . . . His misery is immense, beyond all bounds. If Iona's heart were to burst and his misery to flow out, it would flood the whole world, it seems, but yet it is not seen. It has found a hiding-place in such an insignificant shell that one would not have found it with a candle by daylight. . . .

Iona sees a house-porter with a parcel and makes up his mind to address him.

"What time will it be, friend?" he asks.

"Going on for ten. . . . Why have you stopped here? Drive on!"

Iona drives a few paces away, bends himself double, and gives himself up to his misery. He feels it is no good to appeal to people. But before five minutes have passed he draws himself up, shakes his head as though he feels a sharp pain, and tugs at the reins. . . . He can bear it no longer.

"Back to the yard!" he thinks. "To the yard!"

And his little mare, as though she knew his thoughts, falls to trotting. An hour and a half later Iona is sitting by a big dirty stove. On the stove, on the floor, and on the benches are people snoring. The air is full of smells and stuffiness. Iona looks at the sleeping figures, scratches himself, and regrets that he has come home so early. . . .

"I have not earned enough to pay for the oats, even," he thinks. "That's why I am so miserable. A man who knows how to do his work, . . . who has had enough to eat, and whose horse has had enough to eat, is always at ease. . . ."

In one of the corners a young cabman gets up, clears his throat sleepily, and makes for the waterbucket.

"Want a drink?" Iona asks him.

"Seems so."

"May it do you good. . . . But my son is dead, mate. . . . Do you hear? This week in the hospital. . . . It's queer business. . . ."

Iona looks to see the effect produced by his words, but he sees nothing. The young man has covered his head over and is already asleep. The old man sighs and scratches himself. . . . Just as the young man had been thirsty for water, he thirsts for speech. His son will soon have been dead a week, and he has not really talked to anybody yet. . . . He wants to talk of it properly, with deliberation. . . . He wants to tell how his son was taken ill, how he suffered, what he said before he died, how he died. . . . He wants to describe the funeral, and how he went to the hospital to get his son's clothes. He still has his daughter Anisya in the country. . . . And he wants to talk about her too. . . . Yes, he has plenty to talk about now. His listener ought to sigh and exclaim and lament. . . . It would be even better to talk to women. Though they are silly creatures, they blubber at the first word.

"Let's go out and have a look at the mare," Iona thinks. "There is always time for sleep. . . . You'll have sleep enough, no fear. . . ."

He puts on his coat and goes into the stables where his mare is standing. He thinks about oats, about hay, about the weather. . . . He cannot think about his son when he is alone. . . . To talk about him with someone is possible, but to think of him and picture him is insufferable anguish. . . .

"Are you munching?" Iona asks his mare, seeing her shining eyes. "There, munch away, munch away. . . . Since we have not earned enough for oats, we will eat hay. . . . Yes, . . . I have grown too old to drive. . . . My son ought to be driving, not I. . . . He was a real cabman. . . . He ought to have lived. . . ."

Iona is silent for a while, and then he goes on:

"That's how it is, old girl. . . . Kuzma Ionitch is gone. . . . He said good-by to me. . . . He went and died for no reason. . . . Now, suppose you had a little colt, and you were own mother to that little colt. . . . And all at once that same little colt went and died. . . . You'd be sorry, wouldn't you? . . ."

The little mare munches, listens, and breathes on her master's hands. Iona is carried away and tells her all about it.

Let's look at Chekhov's "Misery" as a piece of craftsmanship. The happenings (here, a cabman seeks to tell his grief to several people, but is rebuffed and finally tells it to his horse) are the **plot;** the participants (cabman, officer, drunks, etc.) are the **characters;** the locale, time, and social circumstances (a snowy city in Russia, in the late nineteenth century) are the **setting;** and (though, as we will urge later, this word should be used with special caution) the meaning or point is the **theme.**

The traditional plot has this structure:

1. **Exposition** (setting forth of the initial situation)
2. **Conflict** (a complication that moves to a climax)
3. **Dénouement** (the outcome of the conflict; the resolution)

Chekhov's first paragraph begins by introducing a situation that seems to be static: it briefly describes a motionless cabdriver, who "is all white like a ghost," and the cabdriver's mare, whose immobility and angularity "make her look like a halfpenny gingerbread horse." A reader probably anticipates that something will intrude into this apparently static situation; some sort of conflict will be established, and then in all probability will be (in one way or another) resolved. In fact, the inertia described at the very beginning is disturbed even before the paragraph ends, when Chekhov rather surprisingly takes us into the mind not of the cabdriver but of the horse, telling us that if we were in such a situation as the horse finds itself, we "too would find it difficult not to think."

By the middle of the first paragraph, we have been given a brief but entirely adequate view of the setting: a Russian city in the days of horse-drawn sleighs, that is, in Chekhov's lifetime.

Strictly speaking, of course, the paragraph does not specifiy Russia or the period, but the author is a Russian writing in the late nineteenth century, the character has a Russian name, and there is lots of snow, so one concludes that the story is set in Russia. (A reader somewhat familiar with Chekhov does not even have to read the first paragraph of this story to know the setting, since all of Chekhov's work is set in the Russia of his day.)

One might almost say that by the end of the first paragraph we have met all the chief characters — though, of course, we can't know this until we finish the story. In later paragraphs we will meet additional figures, but the chief characters — the characters whose fates we are concerned with, one might say — are simply the cabdriver and the horse. It's odd, of course, to call the horse a character, but, as we noticed, even in the first paragraph Chekhov takes us into the mind of the horse. Notice, too, how Chekhov establishes connections between the man and the horse; for instance, when the first fare gets into the sleigh, the driver "cranes his neck" and then "the mare cranes her neck, too." By the end of the story, the horse seems almost a part of Iona. Perhaps the horse will be the best possible listener, since perhaps grief of Iona's sort can be told only to the self.

Before talking further about the characters, we should point out that the word "character" has two chief meanings: (1) a figure in a literary work (thus Iona is a character, the officer who hires the cab is another character, and the drunks are additional characters) and (2) personality, as when we say that Iona's character is described only briefly, or that Hamlet's character is complex, or that So-and-So's character is unpleasant. Usually the context makes clear the sense in which the word is used, but in your own writing, make sure that there is no confusion.

It is sometimes said that figures in literature are either **flat characters** (one-dimensional figures, figures with simple person-alities) or **round characters** (complex figures). The usual implication is that good writers give us round characters, believable figures who are more than cardboard cutouts holding up signs saying "jealous lover," "cruel landlord," "kind mother," and so forth. But a short story scarcely has space to show the complexity or roundness of several characters, and in fact, many good stories do not give even their central characters much complexity. In "Misery," for instance, Iona is shown chiefly as a grieving father aching to speak of the death of his son. We don't know what sort of food he likes, whether he ever gets drunk, what he thinks of the Czar, or whether he belongs to the church. But it is hard to imagine that knowing any of these things would be relevant and would increase our interest in him. Similarly, the other characters in the story are drawn with a few simple lines. The officer who first hires the cab is arrogant ("Sledge to Vyborgskaya! . . . Are you asleep? To Vyborgskaya!"), and though he at first makes a little joke that leads Iona to think the officer will listen to his story, the officer quickly changes the subject. We know of him only that he wants to get to Vyborg. The three noisy drunks whom Iona next picks up can probably be fairly characterized as just that — three noisy drunks. Again, we can hardly imagine that the story would be better if we knew much more about these drunks.

On the other hand, Iona is not quite so flat as we have perhaps implied. A careful reader notices, for instance, that Iona reveals other things about himself in addition to his need to express his grief. For instance, he treats his horse as kindly as possible. When the officer gets into the cab, Iona "more from habit than necessity brandishes his whip" — but he gets the horse moving by making a clicking sound, and he actually whips the horse only when the officer tells him to hurry. Later the hunchback will say of the mare, "Give her one with the whip. Hang it all, give it her well," but we feel that Iona uses his horse as gently as is possible. It should be noted, however, that the drunks, though they are not much more than drunks, are not less than drunks either. They are quarrelsome and they even display touches of cruelty, but we cannot call them villains. In some degree, the fact that they are drunk excuses their "bad language," their "ill-tempers," and even their displays of cruelty. If these characters are fairly flat, they nevertheless are thoroughly believable, and we know as much about them as we need to know for the purposes of the story. Furthermore, the characters in a story help to characterize other characters, by their resemblances or their differences. How Iona might behave if he were an officer, or if he were drunk, we do not know, but he is in some degree contrasted with the other characters and thus gains some complexity, to the extent that we can at least say that he is *not* drunk, arrogant, or quarrelsome.

We need hardly ask if there is **motivation** (a basis in personality) for Iona's final action. He has tried to express his grief to the officer, and then to the drunks. Next, his eyes search the crowds to "find someone who will listen to him." After speaking to the house-porter, Iona sees, Chekhov tells us, that "it is no good to appeal to people." When we read this line, we probably do not think, or at least do not think consciously, that he will turn from people to the mare, but when at the end of the story he does turn to the mare, the action seems entirely natural, inevitable.

In some stories, of course, we are chiefly interested in plot (the arrangement of happenings or doings), in others we are chiefly interested in character (the personalities of the doers), but on the whole the two are so intertwined that interest in one involves interest in the other. Happenings occur (people cross paths), and personalities respond, engendering further happenings. As Henry James rhetorically asked, "What is character but the determination of incident? What is incident but the illustration of character?" Commonly, as a good story proceeds and we become increasingly familiar with the characters, we get intimations of what they may do in the future. We may not know precisely how they will act, but we have a fairly good idea, and when in fact we see their subsequent actions, we usually recognize the appropriateness. Sometimes there are hints of what is to come, and because of this **foreshadowing,** we are not shocked by what happens later, but rather we experience suspense as we wait for the expected to come about. Coleridge had Shakespeare's use of foreshadowing in mind when he praised him for giving us not surprise, but expectation — the active reader participates in the work by reading it responsively — and then the fulfillment of expectation. E. M. Forster, in *Aspects of the Novel,* has a shrewd comment on the importance of both fulfilling expectation and offering a slight surprise: "Shock, followed by the feeling, 'Oh, that's all right,' is a sign that all is well with plot: characters, to be real, ought to run smoothly, but a plot ought to cause surprise."

Finally, a few words about **theme.** Usually we feel that a story is about something, it has a point — a theme. (What happens is the plot; what the happenings add up to is the theme.) But a word of caution is needed here. What is the theme of "Misery"? One student formulated the theme thus: "Human beings must utter their grief, even if only to an animal." Another student formulated it thus: "Human beings are indifferent to the sufferings of others." Still another student offered this: "Deep suffering is incommunicable, but the sufferer must try to find an outlet." And, of course, many other formulations are possible. Probably there is no "right" statement of the theme of "Misery" or of any other good story: a story is not simply an illustration of an abstract statement of theme. A story has a complex variety of details that modify any summary statement we may offer when we try to say what it is about. And what lives in our memory is not an abstract statement — certainly not a thesis, i.e., a proposition offered and argued, such as "We should pay attention to the suffering of others." What lives is an image that by every word in the story has convinced us that it is a representation, if not of "reality," of at least an aspect of reality.

Still, the writer is guided by a theme in the choice of details; of many possible details, Chekhov decided to present only a few.

The musical sense of the word "theme" can help us to understand what a theme in literature is: "a melody constituting the basis of variation, development, or the like." The variations and the development cannot be random, but must have a basis. (We have already suggested that the episodes in "Misery" — the movement from the officer to the drunks and then to the house-porter and the other cabman — are not random, but somehow seem exactly "right," just as the remarks about the man and the horse both stretching their necks seems "right.") What is it, Robert Frost asks, that prevents the writer from jumping "from one chance suggestion to another in all directions as of a hot afternoon in the life of a grasshopper?" Frost's answer: "Theme alone can steady us down."

We can, then, talk about the theme — again, what the story adds up to — as long as we do not think a statement of the theme is equivalent to or is a substitute for the whole story. As Flannery O'Connor said, "Some people have the notion that you can read the story and then climb out of it into the meaning, but for the fiction writer himself the whole story is the meaning." A theme, she said, is not like a string tying a sack of chicken feed, to be pulled out so that the feed can be got at. "A story is a way to say something that can't be said any other way." That "something" — which can't be said in any other way — is the theme. (On theme, see also page 101.)

QUESTIONS

1. What do you like or not like about Chekhov's story? Why?
2. Try to examine in detail your response to the ending. Do you think the ending is, in a way, a happy ending? Would you prefer a different ending? For instance, should the story end when the young cabman falls asleep? Or when Iona sets out for the stable? Or can you imagine a better ending? If so, what?

Finally, here are two stories by Kate Chopin (1851–1904). Katherine O'Flaherty was born in St. Louis; her father was an immigrant from Ireland, and her mother was descended from an old Creole family. At the age of nineteen she married Oscar Chopin, a cotton broker in New Orleans. They had six children, and though Kate Chopin had contemplated a literary career, she did not turn seriously to writing until after her husband's death in 1883. Most of her fiction concerns the lives of the descendants of the French who had settled in Louisiana.

Kate Chopin (American. 1851–1904)

The Story of an Hour

Knowing that Mrs. Mallard was afflicted with a heart trouble, great care was taken to break to her as gently as possible the news of her husband's death.

It was her sister Josephine who told her, in broken sentences, veiled hints that revealed in half concealing. Her husband's friend Richards was there, too, near her. It was he who had been in the newspaper office when intelligence of the railroad disaster was received, with Brently Mallard's name leading the list of "killed." He had only taken the time to assure himself of its truth by a second telegram, and had hastened to forestall any less careful, less tender friend in bearing the sad message.

She did not hear the story as many women have heard the same, with a paralyzed inability to accept its significance. She wept at once, with sudden, wild abandonment, in her sister's arms. When the storm of grief had spent itself she went away to her room alone. She would have no one follow her.

There stood, facing the open window, a comfortable, roomy armchair. Into this she sank, pressed down by a physical exhaustion that haunted her body and seemed to reach into her soul.

She could see in the open square before her house the tops of trees that were all aquiver with the new spring life. The delicious breath of rain was in the air. In the street below a peddler was crying his wares. The notes of a distant song which some one was singing reached her faintly, and countless sparrows were twittering in the eaves.

There were patches of blue sky showing here and there through the clouds that had met and piled above the other in the west facing her window.

She sat with her head thrown back upon the cushion of the chair quite motionless, except when a sob came up into her throat and shook her, as a child who has cried itself to sleep continues to sob in its dreams.

She was young, with a fair, calm face, whose lines bespoke repression and even a certain strength. But now there was a dull stare in her eyes, whose gaze was fixed away off yonder on one of those patches of blue sky. It was not a glance of reflection, but rather indicated a suspension of intelligent thought.

There was something coming to her and she was waiting for it, fearfully. What was it? She did not know; it was too subtle and elusive to name. But she felt it, creeping out of the sky, reaching toward her through the sounds, the scents, the color that filled the air.

Now her bosom rose and fell tumultuously. She was beginning to recognize this thing that was approaching to possess her, and she was striving to beat it back with her will — as powerless as her two white slender hands would have been.

When she abandoned herself a little whispered word escaped her slightly parted lips. She said it over and over under her breath: "Free, free, free!" The vacant stare and the look of terror that had followed it went from her eyes. They stayed keen and bright. Her pulses beat fast, and the coursing blood warmed and relaxed every inch of her body.

She did not stop to ask if it were not a monstrous joy that held her. A clear and exalted perception enabled her to dismiss the suggestion as trivial.

She knew that she would weep again when she saw the kind, tender hands folded in death; the face that had never looked save with love upon her, fixed and gray and dead. But she saw beyond that bitter moment a long procession of years to come that would belong to her absolutely. And she opened and spread her arms out to them in welcome.

There would be no one to live for during those coming years; she would live for herself. There would be no powerful will bending her in that blind persistence with which men and women believe they have a right to impose a private will upon a fellow creature. A kind intention or a cruel intention made the act seem no less a crime as she looked upon it in that brief moment of illumination.

And yet she had loved him — sometimes. Often she had not. What did it matter! What could love, the unsolved mystery, count for in face of this possession of self-assertion which she suddenly recognized as the strongest impulse of her being.

"Free! Body and soul free!" she kept whispering.

Josephine was kneeling before the closed door with her lips to the keyhole, imploring for admission. "Louise, open the door! I beg; open the door — you will make yourself ill. What are you doing, Louise? For heaven's sake open the door."

"Go away. I am not making myself ill." No; she was drinking in a very elixir of life through that open window.

Her fancy was running riot along those days ahead of her. Spring days, and summer days, and all sorts of days that would be her own. She breathed a quick prayer that life might be long. It was only yesterday she had thought with a shudder that life might be long.

She arose at length and opened the door to her sister's importunities. There was a feverish triumph in her eyes, and she carried herself unwittingly like a goddess of Victory. She clasped her sister's waist, and together they descended the stairs. Richards stood waiting for them at the bottom.

Some one was opening the front door with a latchkey. It was Brently Mallard who entered, a little travel-stained, composedly carrying his grip-sack and umbrella. He had been far from the scene of accident, and did not even know there had been one. He stood amazed at Josephine's piercing cry; at Richards' quick motion to screen him from the view of his wife.

But Richards was too late.

When the doctors came they said she had died of heart disease — of joy that kills.

QUESTIONS

1. Is Mrs. Mallard's grief sincere?
2. In the first half of the story, how does Chopin help to prepare for Mrs. Mallard's words, "Free, free, free"?
3. How accurate is the doctors' final diagnosis?

Kate Chopin (*American. 1851–1904*)

The Storm

I

The leaves were so still that even Bibi thought it was going to rain. Bobinôt, who was accustomed to converse on terms of perfect equality with his little son, called the child's attention to certain somber clouds that were rolling with sinister intention from the west, accompanied by a sullen, threatening roar. They were at Friedheimer's store and decided to remain there till the storm had passed. They sat within the door on two empty kegs. Bibi was four years old and looked very wise.

"Mama'll be 'afraid, yes," he suggested with blinking eyes.

"She'll shut the house. Maybe she got Sylvie helpin' her this evenin'," Bobinôt responded reassuringly.

"No; she ent got Sylvie. Sylvie was helpin' her yistiday," piped Bibi.

Bobinôt arose and going across to the counter purchased a can of shrimps, of which Calixta was very fond. Then he returned to his perch on the keg and sat stolidly holding the can of shrimps while the storm burst. It shook the wooden store and seemed to be ripping great furrows in the distant field. Bibi laid his little hand on his father's knee and was not afraid.

II

Calixta, at home, felt no uneasiness for their safety. She sat at a side window sewing furiously on a sewing machine. She was greatly occupied and did not notice the approaching storm. But she felt very warm and often stopped to mop her face on which the perspiration gathered in beads. She unfastened her white sacque at the throat. It began to grow dark, and suddenly realizing the situation she got up hurriedly and went about closing windows and doors.

Out on the small front gallery she had hung Bobinôt's Sunday clothes to air and she hastened out to gather them before the rain fell. As she stepped outside, Alcée Labellière rode in at the gate. She had not seen him very often since her marriage, and never alone. She stood there with Bobinôt's coat in her hands, and the big rain drops began to fall. Alcée rode his horse under the shelter of a side projection where the chickens had huddled and there were plows and a harrow piled up in the corner.

"May I come and wait on your gallery till the storm is over, Calixta?" he asked.

"Come 'long in, M'sieur Alcée."

His voice and her own startled her as if from a trance, and she seized Bobinôt's vest. Alcée, mounting to the porch, grabbed the trousers and snatched Bibi's braided jacket that was about to be carried away by a sudden gust of wind. He expressed an intention to remain outside, but it was soon apparent that he might as well have been out in the open: the water beat in upon the boards in driving sheets, and he went inside, closing the door after him. It was even necessary to put something beneath the door to keep the water out.

"My! what a rain! It's good two years since it rain' like that," exclaimed Calixta as she rolled up a piece of bagging and Alcée helped her to thrust it beneath the crack.

She was a little fuller of figure than five years before when she married; but she had lost nothing of her vivacity. Her blue eyes still retained their melting quality; and her yellow hair, dishevelled by the wind and rain, kinked more stubbornly than ever about her ears and temples.

The rain beat upon the low, shingled roof with a force and clatter that threatened to break an entrance and deluge them there. They were in the dining room — the sitting room — the general utility room. Adjoining was her bed room, with Bibi's couch along side her own. The door stood open, and the room with its white, monumental bed, its closed shutters, looked dim and mysterious.

Alcée flung himself into a rocker and Calixta nervously began to gather up from the floor the lengths of a cotton sheet which she had been sewing.

"If this keeps up, *Dieu sait*° if the levees goin' to stan' it!" she exclaimed.

"What have you got to do with the levees?"

"I got enough to do! An' there's Bobinôt with Bibi out in that storm — if he only didn' left Friedheimer's!"

"Let us hope, Calixta, that Bobinôt's got sense enough to come in out of a cyclone."

She went and stood at the window with a greatly disturbed look on her face. She wiped the frame that was clouded with moisture. It was stiflingly hot. Alcée got up and joined her at the window, looking over her shoulder. The rain was coming down in sheets obscuring the view of far-off cabins and enveloping the distant wood in a gray mist. The playing of the lightning was incessant. A bolt struck a tall chinaberry tree at the edge of the field. It filled all visible space with a blinding glare and the crash seemed to invade the very boards they stood upon.

Calixta put her hands to her eyes, and with a cry, staggered backward. Alcée's arm encircled her, and for an instant he drew her close and spasmodically to him.

"*Bonte!*"° she cried, releasing herself from his encircling arm and retreating from the window, "the house'll go next! If I only knew w'ere Bibi was!" She would not compose herself; she would not be seated. Alcée clasped her shoulders and looked into her face. The contact of her warm, palpitating body when he had unthinkingly drawn her into his arms, had aroused all the old-time infatuation and desire for her flesh.

"Calixta," he said, "don't be frightened. Nothing can happen. The house is too low to be struck, with so many tall trees standing about. There! aren't you going to be quiet? say, aren't you?" He pushed her hair back from her face that was warm and steaming. Her lips were as red and moist as pomegranate seed. Her white

Dieu sait God only knows
Bonte! Heavens

neck and a glimpse of her full, firm bosom disturbed him powerfully. As she glanced up at him the fear in her liquid blue eyes had given place to a drowsy gleam that unconsciously betrayed a sensuous desire. He looked down into her eyes and there was nothing for him to do but to gather her lips in a kiss. It reminded him of Assumption.°

"Do you remember — in Assumption, Calixta?" he asked in a low voice broken by passion. Oh! she remembered; for in Assumption he had kissed her and kissed and kissed her; until his senses would well nigh fail, and to save her he would resort to a desperate flight. If she was not an immaculate dove in those days, she was still inviolate; a passionate creature whose very defenselessness had made her defense, against which his honor forbade him to prevail. Now — well, now — her lips seemed in a manner free to be tasted, as well as her round, white throat and her whiter breasts.

They did not heed the crashing torrents, and the roar of the elements made her laugh as she lay in his arms. She was a revelation in that dim, mysterious chamber; as white as the couch she lay upon. Her firm, elastic flesh that was knowing for the first time its birthright, was like a creamy lily that the sun invites to contribute its breath and perfume to the undying life of the world.

The generous abundance of her passion, without guile or trickery, was like a white flame which penetrated and found response in depths of his own sensuous nature that had never yet been reached.

When he touched her breasts they gave themselves up in quivering ecstasy, inviting his lips. Her mouth was a fountain of delight. And when he possessed her, they seemed to swoon together at the very borderland of life's mystery.

He stayed cushioned upon her, breathless, dazed, enervated, with his heart beating like a hammer upon her. With one hand she clasped his head, her lips lightly touching his forehead. The other hand stroked with a soothing rhythm his muscular shoulders.

The growl of the thunder was distant and passing away. The rain beat softly upon the shingles, inviting them to drowsiness and sleep. But they dared not yield.

The rain was over; and the sun was turning the glistening green world into a palace of gems. Calixta, on the gallery, watched Alcée ride away. He turned and smiled at her with a beaming face; and she lifted her pretty chin in the air and laughed aloud.

Assumption   a church feast on 15 August celebrating Mary's bodily ascent to heaven

III

Bobinôt and Bibi, trudging home, stopped without at the cistern to make themselves presentable.

"My! Bibi, w'at will yo' mama say! You ought to be ashame'. You oughtn' put on those good pants. Look at 'em! An' that mud on yo' collar! How you got that mud on yo' collar, Bibi? I never saw such a boy!" Bibi was the picture of pathetic resignation. Bobinôt was the embodiment of serious solicitude as he strove to remove from his own person and his son's the signs of their tramp over heavy roads and through wet fields. He scraped the mud off Bibi's bare legs and feet with a stick and carefully removed all traces from his heavy brogans. Then, prepared for the worst — the meeting with an over-scrupulous housewife, they entered cautiously at the back door.

Calixta was preparing supper. She had set the table and was dripping coffee at the hearth. She sprang up as they came in.

"Oh, Bobinôt! You back! My! but I was uneasy. W'ere you been during the rain? An' Bibi? he ain't wet? he ain't hurt?" She had clasped Bibi and was kissing him effusively. Bobinôt's explanations and apologies which he had been composing all along the way, died on his lips as Calixta felt him to see if he were dry, and seemed to express nothing but satisfaction at their safe return.

"I brought you some shrimps, Calixta," offered Bobinôt, hauling the can from his ample side pocket and laying it on the table.

"Shrimps! Oh, Bobinôt! you too good fo' anything!" and she gave him a smacking kiss on the cheek that resounded. *"J'vous reponds*,° we'll have a feas' to night! umph-umph!"

Bobinôt and Bibi began to relax and enjoy themselves, and when the three seated themselves at table they laughed much and so loud that anyone might have heard them as far away as Laballière's.

IV

Alcée Laballière wrote to his wife, Clarisse, that night. It was a loving letter, full of tender solicitude. He told her not to hurry back, but if she and the babies liked it at Biloxi, to stay a month longer. He was getting on nicely; and though he missed them, he was willing to bear the separation a while longer — realizing that their health and pleasure were the first things to be considered.

J'vous reponds   Take my word; let me tell you

V

As for Clarisse, she was charmed upon receiving her husband's letter. She and the babies were doing well. The society was agreeable; many of her old friends and acquaintances were at the bay. And the first free breath since her marriage seemed to restore the pleasant liberty of her maiden days. Devoted as she was to her husband, their intimate conjugal life was something which she was more than willing to forego for a while.

So the storm passed and everyone was happy.

QUESTIONS

1. How would you characterize Calixta?
2. In Part III do you think Calixta is insincere in her expressions of solicitude for Bobinôt? Why, or why not?
3. Do you take Part IV to imply that Alcée and Calixta will continue their affair for another month?
4. Why does Chopin bother, in Part V, to tell us about Clarisse? And exactly what do you make of the last line of the story?
5. Do you think it is fair to say that the story is cynical? Explain.

4
Narrative Point of View

Every story is told by someone. Mark Twain wrote *The Adventures of Huckleberry Finn,* but he does not tell the story; Huck tells the story, and he begins thus:

> You don't know about me without you have read a book by the name of *The Adventures of Tom Sawyer,* but that ain't no matter. That book was made by Mr. Mark Twain, and he told the truth, mainly. There was things which he stretched, but mainly he told the truth.

Similarly, Edgar Allan Poe wrote "The Cask of Amontillado," but the story is told by a man whose name, we learn later, is Montresor. Here is the opening:

> The thousand injuries of Fortunato I had borne as best I could, but when he ventured upon insult, I vowed revenge.

Each of these passages gives a reader a very strong sense of the narrator, that is, of the person who tells the story, and it turns out that the works are chiefly about the speakers. Compare those opening passages, however, with two others, which sound far more objective. The first comes from Chekhov's "Misery" (page 31):

> The twilight of evening. Big flakes of wet snow are whirling lazily about the street lamps, which have just been lighted, and lying in a thin soft layer on roofs, horses' backs, shoulders, caps. Iona Potapov, the sledge-driver, is all white like a ghost. He sits on the box without stirring, bent as double as the living body can be bent.

And another example, this one from Hawthorne's "Young Goodman Brown" (page 105):

> Young Goodman Brown came forth at sunset into the street at Salem village; but put his head back, after crossing the threshold, to exchange a parting kiss with his young wife. And Faith, as the wife was aptly named, thrust her own pretty head into the street, letting the wind play with the pink ribbons of her cap while she called to Goodman Brown.

In each of these two passages, a reader is scarcely aware of the personality of the narrator; our interest is almost entirely in the scene that each speaker reveals, not in the speaker's response to the scene.

The narrators of *Huckleberry Finn* and of "The Cask of Amontillado" immediately impress us with their distinctive personalities. We realize that whatever happenings they report will be colored by the special ways in which such personalities see things. But what can we say about the narrators of "Misery" and of "Young Goodman Brown"? A reader is scarcely aware of them, at least in comparison with Huck and Montresor. We look, so to speak, not *at* these narrators, but at others (the cabman and Goodman Brown and Faith). Of course, it is true that as we read "Misery" and "Young Goodman Brown" we are looking through the eyes of the narrators, but these narrators seem (unlike Huck and Montresor) to have 20/20 vision. This is not to say that these apparently colorless narrators really are colorless or invisible. For instance, the narrator of "Misery" seems, at least if we judge from the opening sentences, to want to evoke an atmosphere. He describes the setting in some detail, whereas the narrator of "Young Goodman Brown" seems chiefly concerned with reporting the actions of people whom he sees. Moreover, if we listen carefully to Hawthorne's narrator, perhaps we can say that when he mentions that Faith was "aptly" named, he makes a judgment. Still, it is clear that the narrative voices we hear in "Misery" and "Young Goodman Brown" are at least relatively impartial and relatively inconspicuous; when we hear them, we feel, for the most part, that they are chiefly talking about something objective, about something "out there." These narrative voices will produce stories very different from the narrative voices used by Twain and Poe. The voice that the writer chooses, then, will in large measure shape the story; different voices, different stories.

The narrative point of view of *Huckleberry Finn* and of "The Cask of Amontillado" (and of any other story in which a character in the story tells the story) is a **participant** (or **first-person**) point of view. The point of view of "Young Goodman Brown" (and of any other story in which a nearly invisible outsider tells the story) is a **nonparticipant** (or **third-person**) point of view. Each of these two divisions can be subdivided:

I. Participant (first person)
   A. Narrator as a major character
   B. Narrator as a minor character
II. Nonparticipant (third person)
   A. Omniscient
   B. Selective omniscient
   C. Objective

PARTICIPANT POINTS OF VIEW

In the story by Toni Cade Bambara at the end of this chapter, the narrator is, like Mark Twain's Huck and Poe's Montresor, a major character. Bambara has invented a young black girl who undergoes certain experiences, and who comes to the conclusion that "ain't nobody gonna beat me at nuthin." Since the story is narrated by one of its characters, we can say that the author uses a first-person (or participant) point of view.

It happens that in Bambara's "The Lesson" the narrator is the central character, the character whose actions — whose life, we might say — most interests the reader. But sometimes a first-person narrator tells a story that focuses on another character; the narrator still says "I" (thus the point of view is first person), but the reader feels that the story is not chiefly about this "I" but is about some other figure. For instance, the narrator may be a witness to a story about Jones, and our interest is chiefly in what happens to Jones, though we get the story of Jones filtered through, say, the eyes of Jones's friend, or brother, or cat.

One special kind of first-person narrator (whether major or minor) is the **innocent eye:** the narrator is naive (usually a child, an idiot, or a not-too-bright adult), telling what he or she sees and feels; the contrast between what the narrator perceives and what the reader understands produces an ironic effect. Such a story, in which the reader understands more than the teller himself does, is Ring Lardner's "Haircut," a story told by a garrulous barber who does not perceive that the "accident" he is describing is in fact a murder.

NONPARTICIPANT POINTS OF VIEW

In a nonparticipant (third-person) point of view, the teller of the tale is not a character in the tale. The narrator has receded from the story. If the point of view is **omniscient,** the narrator relates what he or she wishes about the thoughts as well as the deeds of the characters. The omniscient teller can at any time enter the mind of any or all of the characters; whereas the first-person narrator can only say, "I was angry," or "Jones seemed angry to me," the omniscient narrator can say, "Jones was inwardly angry but gave no sign; Smith continued chatting, but he sensed Jones's anger."

Furthermore, a distinction can be made between **neutral omniscience** (the narrator recounts deeds and thoughts, but does not judge) and **editorial omniscience** (the narrator not only recounts, but also judges). The narrator in Hawthorne's "Young Goodman Brown" knows what goes on in the mind of Brown, and he comments approvingly or disapprovingly: "With this excellent resolve for the future, Goodman Brown felt himself justified in making more haste on his present evil purpose."

Because a short story can scarcely hope to develop effectively a picture of several minds, an author may prefer to limit his or her omniscience to the minds of only a few of the characters, or even to that of one of the characters; that is, the author may use **selective omniscience** as the point of view. Selective omniscience provides a focus, especially if it is limited to a single character. When thus limited, the author hovers over the shoulder of one character, seeing him or her from outside and from inside and seeing other characters only from the outside and from the impact they make on the mind of this selected receptor. In "Young Goodman Brown" the reader sees things mostly as they make their impact on the protagonist's mind:

> He could have well-nigh sworn that the shape of his own dead father beckoned him to advance, looking downward from a smoke wreath, while a woman, with dim features of despair, threw out her hand to warn him back. Was it his mother? But he had no power to retreat one step, nor to resist, even in thought, when the minister and good old Deacon Gookin seized his arms and led him to the blazing rock.

When selective omniscience attempts to record mental activity ranging from consciousness to the unconscious, from clear perceptions to confused longings, it is sometimes labeled the **stream-**

of-consciousness point of view. The following example is from Katherine Anne Porter's "The Jilting of Granny Weatherall":

> Her eyelids wavered and let in streamers of blue-gray light like tissue paper over her eyes. She must get up and pull the shades down or she'd never sleep. She was in bed again and the shades were not down. How could that happen? Better turn over, hide from the light, sleeping in the light gave you nightmares. "Mother, how do you feel now?" and a stinging wetness on her forehead. But I don't like having my face washed in cold water!

In an effort to reproduce the unending activity of the mind, some authors who use the stream-of-consciousness point of view dispense with conventional syntax, punctuation, and logical transitions. The last forty-six pages in James Joyce's *Ulysses* are an unpunctuated flow of one character's thoughts.

Finally, sometimes a third-person narrator does not enter even a single mind, but records only what crosses a dispassionate eye and ear. Such a point of view is **objective** (sometimes called **the camera** or **fly-on-the-wall**). The absence of editorializing and of dissection of the mind often produces the effect of a play; we see and hear the characters in action. Much of Hemingway's "Hills Like White Elephants" is objective, consisting of bits of dialogue that make the story look like a play:

> "What should we drink?" the girl asked. She had taken off her hat and put it on the table.
> "It's pretty hot," the man said.
> "Let's drink beer."
> "Dos cervezas," the man said into the curtain.
> "Big ones?" a woman asked from the doorway.
> "Yes. Two big ones."
> The woman brought two glasses of beer and two felt pads.

But the word "objective" is almost a misnomer, for to describe happenings is — by one's choice of words — to comment on them too, however unobtrusively. How objective is the point of view if a man is described as "fat" instead of "stout" or "stout" instead of "heavy" or "heavy" instead of "two hundred and fifty pounds in weight"? The objective point of view, even though it expressly enters no mind, often is a camouflaged version of the selective omniscient point of view.

THE POINT OF A POINT OF VIEW

Generalizations about the effect of a point of view are risky, but two have already been made: that the innocent eye can achieve an ironic effect otherwise unattainable, and that an objective point of view is dramatic. Three other generalizations are often made: (1) that a first-person point of view lends a sense of immediacy or reality, (2) that an omniscient point of view suggests human littleness, and (3) that the point of view must be consistent.

To take the first of these: it is true that when Poe begins a story "The thousand injuries of Fortunato I had borne as I best could, but when he ventured upon insult, I vowed revenge," we feel that the author has gripped us by the lapels; but, on the other hand, we know that we are only reading a piece of fiction, and we do not really believe in the existence of the "I" or of Fortunato; and furthermore, when we pick up a story that begins with *any* point of view, we agree (by picking up the book) to pretend to believe the fictions we are being told. That is, all fiction — whether in the first person or not — is known to be literally false but is read with the pretense that it is true. The writer must hold our attention, and make us feel that the fiction is meaningful, but the use of the first-person pronoun does not of itself confer reality. The second generalization, that an omniscient point of view can make puppets of its characters, is equally misleading; this point of view also can reveal in them a depth and complexity quite foreign to the idea of human littleness. The third generalization, that the narrator's point of view must be consistent lest the illusion of reality be shattered, has been much preached by the followers of Henry James. But E. M. Forster has suggested, in *Aspects of the Novel,* that what is important is not consistency but "the power of the writer to bounce the reader into accepting what he says." Forster notes that in *Bleak House* Dickens uses in Chapter I an omniscient point of view, in Chapter II a selective omniscient point of view, and in Chapter III a first-person point of view. "Logically," Forster says, "*Bleak House* is all to pieces, but Dickens bounces us, so that we do not mind the shiftings of the viewpoint."

Perhaps the only sound generalizations possible are that (1) because point of view is one of the things that gives form to a story, a good author chooses the point (or points) of view that he or she feels best for the particular story, and (2) the use of any other point of view would turn the story into a different story.

Toni Cade Bambara (American. b. 1939)

The Lesson

Back in the days when everyone was old and stupid or young and foolish and me and Sugar were the only ones just right, this lady moved on our block with nappy hair and proper speech and no makeup. And quite naturally we laughed at her, laughed the way we did at the junk man who went about his business like he was some big-time president and his sorry-ass horse his secretary. And we kinda hated her too, hated the way we did the winos who cluttered up our parks and pissed on our handball walls and stank up our hallways and stairs so you couldn't halfway play hide-and-seek without a goddamn gas mask. Miss Moore was her name. The only woman on the block with no first name. And she was black as hell, cept for her feet, which were fish-white and spooky. And she was always planning these boring-ass things for us to do, us being my cousins, mostly, who lived on the block cause we all moved North the same time and to the same apartment then spread out gradual to breathe. And our parents would yank our heads into some kinda shape and crisp up our clothes so we'd be presentable for travel with Miss Moore, who always looked like she was going to church, though she never did. Which is just one of the things the grownups talked about when they talked behind her back like a dog. But when she came calling with some sachet she'd sewed up or some gingerbread she'd made or some book, why then they'd all be too embarrassed to turn her down and we'd get handed over all spruced up. She'd been to college and said it was only right that she should take responsibility for the young ones' education, and she not even related by marriage or blood. So they'd go for it. Specially Aunt Gretchen. She was the main gofer in the family. You got some ole dumb shit foolishness you want somebody to go for, you send for Aunt Gretchen. She been screwed into the go-along for so long, it's a blood-deep natural thing with her. Which is how she got saddled with me and Sugar and Junior in the first place while our mothers were in a la-de-da apartment up the block having a good ole time.

So this one day Miss Moore rounds us all up at the mailbox and it's puredee hot and she's knockin herself out about arithmetic. And school suppose to let up in summer I heard, but she don't never let up. And the starch in my pinafore scratching the shit outta me and I'm really hating this nappy-head bitch and her goddamn college degree. I'd much rather go to the pool or to the show where it's cool. So me and Sugar leaning on the mailbox being surly, which is a Miss Moore word. And Flyboy checking out what everybody brought for lunch. And Fat Butt already wasting his peanut-butter-and-jelly sandwich like the pig he is. And Junebug punchin on Q.T.'s arm for potato chips. And Rosie Giraffe shifting from one hip to the other waiting for somebody to step on her foot or ask her if she from Georgia so she can kick ass, preferably Mercedes'. And Miss Moore asking us do we know what money is, like we a bunch of retards. I mean real money, she say, like it's only poker chips or monopoly papers we lay on the grocer. So right away I'm tired of this and say so. And would much rather snatch Sugar and go to the Sunset and terrorize the West Indian kids and take their hair ribbons and their money too. And Miss Moore files that remark away for next week's lesson on brotherhood, I can tell. And finally I say we oughta get to the subway cause it's cooler and besides we might meet some cute boys. Sugar done swiped her mama's lipstick, so we ready.

So we heading down the street and she's boring us silly about what things cost and what our parents make and how much goes for rent and how money ain't divided up right in this country. And then she gets to the part about we all poor and live in the slums, which I don't feature. And I'm ready to speak on that, but she steps out in the street and hails two cabs just like that. Then she hustles half the crew in with her and hands me a five-dollar bill and tells me to calculate 10 percent tip for the driver. And we're off. Me and Sugar and Junebug and Flyboy hangin out the window and hollering to everybody, putting lipstick on each other cause Flyboy a faggot anyway, and making farts with our sweaty armpits. But I'm mostly trying to figure how to spend this money. But they all fascinated with the meter ticking and Junebug starts laying bets as to how much it'll read when Flyboy can't hold his breath no more. Then Sugar lays bets as to how much it'll be when we get there. So I'm stuck. Don't nobody want to go for my plan, which is to jump out at the next light and run off to the first bar-b-que we can find. Then the driver tells us to get the hell out cause we there already. And the meter reads eighty-five cents. And I'm stalling to figure out the tip and Sugar say give him a dime. And I decide he don't need it bad as I do, so later for him. But then he tries to take off with Junebug foot still in the door so we talk about his mama something ferocious. Then we check out that we on Fifth Avenue and everybody dressed up in stockings. One lady in a fur coat, hot as it is. White folks crazy.

"This is the place," Miss Moore say, presenting it to us in

the voice she uses at the museum. "Let's look in the windows before we go in."

"Can we steal?" Sugar asks very serious like she's getting the ground rules squared away before she plays. "I beg your pardon," say Miss Moore, and we fall out. So she leads us around the windows of the toy store and me and Sugar screamin, "This is mine, that's mine, I gotta have that, that was made for me, I was born for that," till Big Butt drowns us out.

"Hey, I'm goin to buy that there."

"That there? You don't even know what it is, stupid."

"I do so," he say punchin on Rosie Giraffe. "It's a microscope."

"Whatcha gonna do with a microscope, fool?"

"Look at things."

"Like what, Ronald?" ask Miss Moore. And Big Butt ain't got the first notion. So here go Miss Moore gabbing about the thousands of bacteria in a drop of water and the somethinorother in a speck of blood and the million and one living things in the air around us is invisible to the naked eye. And what she say that for? Junebug go to town on that "naked" and we rolling. Then Miss Moore ask what it cost. So we all jam into the window smudgin it up and the price tag say $300. So then she ask how long'd take for Big Butt and Junebug to save up their allowances. "Too long," I say. "Yeh," adds Sugar, "outgrown it by that time." And Miss Moore say no, you never outgrow learning instruments. "Why, even medical students and interns and," blah, blah, blah. And we ready to choke Big Butt for bringing it up in the first damn place.

"This here costs four hundred eighty dollars," say Rosie Giraffe. So we pile up all over her to see what she pointin out. My eyes tell me it's a chunk of glass cracked with something heavy, and different-color inks dripped into the splits, then the whole thing put into a oven or something. But for $480 it don't make sense.

"That's a paperweight made of semi-precious stones fused together under tremendous pressure," she explains slowly, with her hands doing the mining and all the factory work.

"So what's a paperweight?" asks Rosie Giraffe.

"To weigh paper with, dumbbell," say Flyboy, the wise man from the East.

"Not exactly," say Miss Moore, which is what she say when you warm or way off too. "It's to weigh paper down so it won't scatter and make your desk untidy." So right away me and Sugar curtsy to each other and then to Mercedes who is more the tidy type.

"We don't keep paper on top of the desk in my class," say Junebug, figuring Miss Moore crazy or lyin one.

"At home, then," she say. "Don't you have a calendar and a pencil case and a blotter and a letter-opener on your desk at home where you do your homework?" And she know damn well what our homes look like cause she nosys around in them every chance she gets.

"I don't even have a desk," say Junebug. "Do we?"

"No. And I don't get no homework neither," says Big Butt.

"And I don't even have a home," say Flyboy like he do at school to keep the white folks off his back and sorry for him. Send this poor kid to camp posters, is his specialty.

"I do," says Mercedes. "I have a box of stationery on my desk and a picture of my cat. My godmother bought the stationery and the desk. There's a big rose on each sheet and the envelopes smell like roses."

"Who wants to know about your smelly-ass stationery," say Rosie Giraffe fore I can get my two cents in.

"It's important to have a work area all your own so that . . ."

"Will you look at this sailboat, please," say Flyboy, cuttin her off and pointin to the thing like it was his. So once again we tumble all over each other to gaze at this magnificent thing in the toy store which is just big enough to maybe sail two kittens across the pond if you strap them to the posts tight. We all start reciting the price tag like we in assembly. "Handcrafted sailboat of fiberglass at one thousand one hundred ninety-five dollars."

"Unbelievable," I hear myself say and am really stunned. I read it again for myself just in case the group recitation put me in a trance. Same thing. For some reason this pisses me off. We look at Miss Moore and she lookin at us, waiting for I dunno what.

"Who'd pay all that when you can buy a sailboat set for a quarter at Pop's, a tube of glue for a dime, and a ball of string for eight cents? It must have a motor and a whole lot else besides," I say. "My sailboat cost me about fifty cents."

"But will it take water?" say Mercedes with her smart ass.

"Took mine to Alley Pond Park once," say Flyboy. "String broke. Lost it. Pity."

"Sailed mine in Central Park and it keeled over and sank. Had to ask my father for another dollar."

"And you got the strap," laugh Big Butt. "The jerk didn't even have a string on it. My old man wailed on his behind."

Little Q.T. was staring hard at the sailboat and you could

see he wanted it bad. But he too little and somebody'd just take
it from him. So what the hell. "This boat for kids, Miss Moore?"

"Parents silly to buy something like that just to get all broke
up," say Rosie Giraffe.

"That much money it should last forever," I figure.

"My father'd buy it for me if I wanted it."

"Your father, my ass," say Rosie Giraffe getting a chance
to finally push Mercedes.

"Must be rich people shop here," say Q.T.

"You are a very bright boy," say Flyboy. "What was your
first clue?" And he rap him on the head with the back of his
knuckles, since Q.T. the only one he could get away with. Though
Q.T. liable to come up behind you years later and get his licks
in when you half expect it.

"What I want to know is," I says to Miss Moore though I
never talk to her, I wouldn't give the bitch that satisfaction, "is
how much a real boat costs? I figure a thousand'd get you a yacht
any day."

"Why don't you check that out," she says, "and report back
to the group?" Which really pains my ass. If you gonna mess up
a perfectly good swim day least you could do is have some answers.
"Let's go in," she say like she got something up her sleeve. Only
she don't lead the way. So me and Sugar turn the corner to where
the entrance is, but when we get there I kinda hang back. Not
that I'm scared, what's there to be afraid of, just a toy store. But
I feel funny, shame. But what I got to be shamed about? Got as
much right to go in as anybody. But somehow I can't seem to
get hold of the door, so I step away for Sugar to lead. But she
hangs back too. And I look at her and she looks at me and this
is ridiculous. I mean, damn, I have never ever been shy about
doing nothing or going nowhere. But then Mercedes steps up and
then Rosie Giraffe and Big Butt crowd in behind and shove, and
next thing we all stuffed into the doorway with only Mercedes
squeezing past us, smoothing out her jumper and walking right
down the aisle. Then the rest of us tumble in like a glued-together
jigsaw done all wrong. And people lookin at us. And it's like the
time me and Sugar crashed into the Catholic church on a dare.
But once we got in there and everything so hushed and holy and
the candles and the bowin and the handkerchiefs on all the drooping
heads, I just couldn't go through with the plan. Which was for
me to run up to the altar and do a tap dance while Sugar played
the nose flute and messed around in the holy water. And Sugar
kept givin me the elbow. Then later teased me so bad I tied her
up in the shower and turned it on and locked her in. And she'd

be there till this day if Aunt Gretchen hadn't finally figured I was lyin about the boarder takin a shower.

Same thing in the store. We all walkin on tiptoe and hardly touchin the games and puzzles and things. And I watched Miss Moore who is steady watchin us like she waitin for a sign. Like Mama Drewery watches the sky and sniffs the air and takes note of just how much slant is in the bird formation. Then me and Sugar bump smack into each other, so busy gazing at the toys, 'specially the sailboat. But we don't laugh and go into our fat-lady bump-stomach routine. We just stare at that price tag. Then Sugar run a finger over the whole boat. And I'm jealous and want to hit her. Maybe not her, but I sure want to punch somebody in the mouth.

"Watcha bring us here for, Miss Moore?"

"You sound angry, Sylvia. Are you mad about something?" Givin me one of them grins like she tellin a grown-up joke that never turns out to be funny. And she's lookin very closely at me like maybe she plannin to do my portrait from memory. I'm mad, but I won't give her that satisfaction. So I slouch around the store bein very bored and say, "Let's go."

Me and Sugar at the back of the train watchin the tracks whizzin by large then small then gettin gobbled up in the dark. I'm thinkin about this tricky toy I saw in the store. A clown that somersaults on a bar then does chin-ups just cause you yank lightly at his leg. Cost $35. I could see me askin my mother for a $35 birthday clown. "You wanna who that costs what?" she'd say, cocking her head to the side to get a better view of the hole in my head. Thirty-five dollars could buy new bunk beds for Junior and Gretchen's boy. Thirty-five dollars and the whole household could go visit Granddaddy Nelson in the country. Thirty-five dollars would pay for the rent and the piano bill too. Who are these people that spend that much for performing clowns and $1000 for toy sailboats? What kinda work they do and how they live and how come we ain't in on it? Where we are is who we are, Miss Moore always pointin out. But it don't necessarily have to be that way, she always adds then waits for somebody to say that poor people have to wake up and demand their share of the pie and don't none of us know what kind of pie she talkin about in the first damn place. But she ain't so smart cause I still got her four dollars from the taxi and she sure ain't gettin it. Messin up my day with this shit. Sugar nudges me in my pocket and winks.

Miss Moore lines us up in front of the mailbox where we started from, seem like years ago, and I got a headache for thinkin so hard. And we lean all over each other so we can hold up under the draggy-ass lecture she always finishes us off with at the end before we thank her for borin us to tears. But she just looks at us like she readin tea leaves. Finally she say, "Well, what did you think of F. A. O. Schwarz?"

Rosie Giraffe mumbles, "White folks crazy."

"I'd like to go there again when I get my birthday money," says Mercedes, and we shove her out the pack so she has to lean on the mailbox by herself.

"I'd like a shower. Tiring day," say Flyboy.

Then Sugar surprises me by sayin, "You know, Miss Moore, I don't think all of us here put together eat in a year what that sailboat costs." And Miss Moore lights up like somebody goosed her. "And?" she say, urging Sugar on. Only I'm standin on her foot so she don't continue.

"Imagine for a minute what kind of society it is in which some people can spend on a toy what it would cost to feed a family of six or seven. What do you think?"

"I think," say Sugar pushing me off her feet like she never done before, cause I whip her ass in a minute, "that this is not much of a democracy if you ask me. Equal chance to pursue happiness means an equal crack at the dough, don't it?" Miss Moore is besides herself and I am disgusted with Sugar's treachery. So I stand on her foot one more time to see if she'll shove me. She shuts up, and Miss Moore looks at me, sorrowfully I'm thinkin. And somethin weird is goin on, I can feel it in my chest.

"Anybody else learn anything today?" lookin dead at me. I walk away and Sugar has to run to catch up and don't even seem to notice when I shrug her arm off my shoulder.

"Well, we got four dollars anyway," she says.

"Uh hunh."

"We could go to Hascombs and get half a chocolate layer and then go to the Sunset and still have plenty money for potato chips and ice cream sodas."

"Uh hunh."

"Race you to Hascombs," she say.

We start down the block and she gets ahead which is O.K. by me cause I'm going to the West End and then over to the Drive to think this day through. She can run if she want to and even run faster. But ain't nobody gonna beat me at nuthin.

QUESTIONS

1. In a paragraph or two characterize the narrator.
2. Let's suppose Bambara had decided to tell the story through

the eyes of Miss Moore. Write the first 250 words of such a story.

3. What is the point of Miss Moore's lesson? Why does Sylvia resist it?

4. Describe the relationship between Sugar and Sylvia. What is Sugar's function in the story?

5
Allegory and Symbolism

In Chapter 2 we looked at "The Parable of the Prodigal Son," and in Chapter 3 we looked at some fables, short fictions that were evidently meant to teach us: the characters clearly stood for principles of behavior, and the fictions as a whole evidently taught us lessons. Closely related to these forms is the **allegory,** which presents items that are understood to have equivalents: Bunyan's allegory, *The Pilgrim's Progress,* tells of a man named Christian, who, on the road to the Celestial City, encounters, among others, Giant Despair, Mr. Worldly Wiseman, and Faithful. What these are equivalent to is clear from their names, and it is clear that Christian's journey stands for the trials of a soul in this world.

Modern short stories rarely have either the parable's explicit moral or the allegory's clear system of equivalents, but they nevertheless can be said to be about something. As Robert Frost once said,

> There is no story written that has any value at all, however straightforward it looks and free from doubleness, double entendre, and duplicity and double play, that you'd value at all if it didn't have intimations of something more than itself.

Such a detailed, realistic story as "The Lesson" (in the preceding chapter) may be a very good picture of one kind of urban life, but it also implies or suggests things not limited to that subject. This is not to say that after reading the story we discard the richly detailed narrative in favor of some abstraction that it implies — we do not throw away the narrative and cling to the implication. Frost went on to say, "The anecdote, the parable, the surface meaning has got to be good and got to be sufficient in itself."

We feel that the narrative is meaningful. "The Lesson" presents abundant precise details, and these details somehow add up to give the story a generality or universality. The numerous details are so interrelated that they are a revelation of what is otherwise inexpressible.

In "The Lesson" the narrative forces into the edges of our minds thoughts of the exuberance of children, their insensitivity and their sensitivity, economic inequities, the power of education, and a good deal more. These thoughts are sharply controlled by the details of the story, and they do not separate themselves from the details. But the thoughts are there, though we scarcely think of them; in the story they are just under the surface. Quite properly we take small notice of the substratum and concentrate on the surface details. But in other stories — such as parables and allegories — the details are so presented that we are forced to look from them to their implied equivalents.

Between these two extremes — on the one hand writing that is almost all surface and on the other hand writing that is almost all implication — are stories in which we strongly feel both the surface happenings and their implication. In *Place in Fiction,* Eudora Welty uses an image of a china lamp that unlit showed London and lit showed the Great Fire of London to explain literature that presents an interesting surface texture filled with rich significance. Though she is talking about the novel, her words apply equally to the short story, as a reading of her story "Livvie" (page 85) will show. Like a painted porcelain lamp which, when illuminated, reveals an inner picture shining through the outer, the physical details in a work are illuminated from within by the author's imaginative vision. The outer painting, the literal details, presents "a continuous, shapely, pleasing, and finished surface to the eye," but this surface is not the whole: "The lamp alight is the combination of internal and external, glowing at the imagination as one; and so is the good novel. . . . The good novel should be steadily alight, revealing."

The unified picture, the details and what they suggest by virtue of the inner illumination with which the artist endows them, constitutes the symbolic level of a piece of literature. Here is Ishmael, in *Moby Dick,* perceiving the symbolic meaning of Father Mapple's ascent into the pulpit:

> I was not prepared to see Father Mapple after gaining the height, slowly turn round, and stooping over the pulpit, deliberately drag up the ladder step by step, till the whole was deposited within, leaving him impregnable in his little Quebec.

> I pondered some time without fully comprehending the reason for this. Father Mapple enjoyed such a wide reputation for sincerity and sanctity, that I could not suspect him of courting notoriety by any mere tricks of the stage. No, thought I, there must be some sober reason for this thing; furthermore, it must symbolize something unseen. Can it be, then, that by that act of physical isolation, he signifies his spiritual withdrawal from the time, from all outward worldly ties and connections? Yes, for replenished with the meat and wine of the world, to the faithful man of God, this pulpit, I see, is a self-containing stronghold — a lofty Ehrenbreitstein, with a perennial well of water within the walls.

Ishmael's interpretation strikes the reader as well-stated and convincing, but many symbolic interpretations of literature (especially of *Moby Dick*) are neither. An ingenious reader may overcomplicate or overemphasize the symbolism of a work or may distort it by omitting some of the details and by unduly focusing on others. In many works the details glow, but the glow is so gentle and subtle that even to talk about the details is to overstate them and to understate other equally important aspects of the work.

Yet if it is false to overstate the significance of a detail, it is also false to understate a significant detail. For example, the let's-have-no-nonsense literal reader who holds that Faulkner's "The Bear" (which appears later in this chapter) is only an adventure story about a bear hunt impoverishes the story by neglecting the rich symbolic meaning just as much as the symbol-hunter impoverishes Bambara's "The Lesson" by slighting the literal meaning. Faulkner's insistence on the bear's magnificence (the beast is compared to King Priam, to a locomotive, to an immortal creature) compels the reader to attend to its symbolic meaning, as does his insistence that not until "the three lifeless mechanicals" (the watch, the compass, and the stick) are surrendered can the bear be fully seen. Near the end of the story Faulkner underlines the symbolic quality by having the boy's father explain that Keats's "Ode on a Grecian Urn" is not (as the son says) only "about a girl"; the talk about a girl, the father goes on, is a vehicle by which Keats communicates an insight about truth. "He had to talk about something. . . . He was talking about truth." Faulkner, too, had to talk about something in order to communicate his insight, so he chose as a meaningful vehicle a bear hunt.

There has been a tendency, for about a century and a half now, to call **allegoric** those works whose images have precise equivalents that can be paraphrased with some accuracy, and to call **symbolic** those works whose images cast long shadows, give off multiple suggestions that do not allow for easy substitutions.

This view might turn Father Mapple's gesture into an allegory and *Moby Dick* (which Melville called an allegory) into a symbolic work. D. H. Lawrence's pronouncement can serve as an example of modern usage:

> You can't give a great symbol a "meaning," any more than you can give a cat a "meaning." Symbols are organic units of consciousness with a life of their own, and you can never explain them away, because their value is dynamic, emotional, belonging to the sense-consciousness of the body and soul, and not simply mental. An allegorical image has a *meaning*. Mr. Facing-both-ways has a meaning. But I defy you to lay your finger on the full meaning of Janus, who is a symbol.

Whether or not we like the modern distinction between allegory and symbol (much that today is called symbolic was in the Middle Ages called allegorical), the distinction seems here to stay. But we should recall that every piece of art — including allegory as well as writing that might be called "realistic" — is, in Robert Frost's words, "a symbol small or great of the way the will has to pitch into commitments deeper and deeper to a rounded conclusion."

A NOTE ON SETTING

The **setting** of a story — not only the physical locale but also the time of day or year or century — may or may not be symbolic. Sometimes the setting is lightly sketched, presented only because the story had to take place somewhere and at some time. Often, however, the setting is more important, giving us the feel of the people who move through it. But if scenery is drawn in detail, yet adds up to nothing, we share the impatience Robert Louis Stevenson expressed in a letter: "'Roland approached the house; it had green doors and window blinds; and there was a scraper on the upper step.' To hell with Roland and the scraper." Yes, of course; but if the green doors and the scraper were to tell us something about the tenant, they could be important. As the novelist Elizabeth Bowen has said, "Nothing can happen nowhere. The locale of the happening always colors the happening, and often, to a degree, shapes it." A rocky New England farm may be an analogue to the farmer who cultivates it, and the story may be as much about the farm as about the farmer. (As Henry James neatly said, in fiction "landscape is character.") Though the wilderness in "The Bear" is described in little detail, it is not mere background but an important part of what the story is about. Take, for example, the following passage:

> On the second day he even found the gutted log where he
> had first seen the crooked print. It was almost completely
> crumbled now, healing with unbelievable speed, a passionate
> and almost visible relinquishment, back into the earth from
> which the tree had grown.

This is not just local color: it is also one of the ways by which
Faulkner talks about the importance of contact with nature; it helps
us understand what is involved when (a page or two later) the
boy

> . . . stood for a moment, alien and small in the green and
> topless solitude. . . . He hung the watch and compass care-
> fully on a bush and leaned the stick beside them and relinquished
> completely to it.

It is no accident that "relinquish" appears in both passages; like
the gutted log, the boy derives his vitality by merging himself
with the wilderness. What the wilderness stands for is something
that can be grasped only by reading the story.

William Faulkner (*American. 1897–1962*)

The Bear

He was ten. But it had already begun, long before that day when
at last he wrote his age in two figures and he saw for the first
time the camp where his father and Major de Spain and old General
Compson and the others spent two weeks each November and
two weeks again each June. He had already inherited then, without
ever having seen it, the tremendous bear with one trap-ruined foot
which, in an area almost a hundred miles deep, had earned itself
a name, a definite designation like a living man.

He had listened to it for years: the long legend of corncribs
rifled, of shotes and grown pigs and even calves carried bodily
into the woods and devoured, of traps and deadfalls overthrown
and dogs mangled and slain, and shotgun and even rifle charges
delivered at point-blank range and with no more effect than so
many peas blown through a tube by a boy — a corridor of wreckage
and destruction beginning back before he was born, through which
sped, not fast but rather with the ruthless and irresistible deliberation
of a locomotive, the shaggy tremendous shape.

It ran in his knowledge before he ever saw it. It loomed and towered in his dreams before he even saw the unaxed woods where it left its crooked print, shaggy, huge, red-eyed, not malevolent but just big — too big for the dogs which tried to bay it, for the horses which tried to ride it down, for the men and the bullets they fired into it, too big for the very country which was its constricting scope. He seemed to see it entire with a child's complete divination before he ever laid eyes on either — the doomed wilderness whose edges were being constantly and punily gnawed at by men with axes and plows who feared it because it was wilderness, men myriad and nameless even to one another in the land where the old bear had earned a name, through which ran not even a mortal animal but an anachronism, indomitable and invincible, out of an old dead time, a phantom, epitome and apotheosis of the old wild life at which the puny humans swarmed and hacked in a fury of abhorrence and fear, like pygmies about the ankles of a drowsing elephant: the old bear solitary, indomitable and alone, widowered, childless, and absolved of mortality — old Priam reft of his old wife and having outlived all his sons.

Until he was ten, each November he would watch the wagon containing the dogs and the bedding and food and guns and his father and Tennie's Jim, the Negro, and Sam Fathers, the Indian, son of a slave woman and a Chickasaw chief, depart on the road to town, to Jefferson, where Major de Spain and the others would join them. To the boy, at seven, eight, and nine, they were not going into the Big Bottom to hunt bear and deer, but to keep yearly rendezvous with the bear which they did not even intend to kill. Two weeks later they would return, with no trophy, no head and skin. He had not expected it. He had not even been afraid it would be in the wagon. He believed that even after he was ten and his father would let him go too, for those two weeks in November, he would merely make another one, along with his father and Major de Spain and General Compson and the others, the dogs which feared to bay at it and the rifles and shotguns which failed even to bleed it, in the yearly pageant of the old bear's furious immortality.

Then he heard the dogs. It was in the second week of his first time in the camp. He stood with Sam Fathers against a big oak beside the faint crossing where they had stood each dawn for nine days now, hearing the dogs. He had heard them once before, one morning last week — a murmur, sourceless, echoing through the wet woods, swelling presently into separate voices which he could recognize and call by name. He had raised and cocked the gun as Sam told him and stood motionless again while the uproar, the invisible course, swept up and past and faded; it seemed to him that he could actually see the deer, the buck, blond, smoke-colored, elongated with speed, fleeing, vanishing, the woods, the gray solitude, still ringing even when the cries of the dogs had died away.

"Now let the hammers down," Sam said.

"You knew they were not coming here too," he said.

"Yes," Sam said. "I want you to learn how to do when you didn't shoot. It's after the chance for the bear or the deer has done already come and gone that men and dogs get killed."

"Anyway," he said, "it was just a deer."

Then on the tenth morning he heard the dogs again. And he readied the too-long, too-heavy gun as Sam had taught him, before Sam even spoke. But this time it was no deer, no ringing chorus of dogs running strong on a free scent, but a moiling yapping an octave too high, with something more than indecision and even abjectness in it, not even moving very fast, taking a long time to pass completely out of hearing, leaving then somewhere in the air that echo, thin, slightly hysterical, abject, almost grieving, with no sense of a fleeting, unseen, smoke-colored, grass-eating shape ahead of it, and Sam, who had taught him first of all to cock the gun and take position where he could see everywhere and then never move again, had himself moved up beside him; he could hear Sam breathing at his shoulder, and he could see the arched curve of the old man's inhaling nostrils.

"Hah," Sam said. "Not even running. Walking."

"Old Ben!" the boy said. "But up here!" he cried. "Way up here!"

"He do it every year," Sam said. "Once. Maybe to see who in camp this time, if he can shoot or not. Whether we got the dog yet that can bay and hold him. He'll take them to the river, then he'll send them back home. We may as well go back too; see how they look when they come back to camp."

When they reached the camp the hounds were already there, ten of them crouching back under the kitchen, the boy and Sam squatting to peer back into the obscurity where they had huddled, quiet, the eyes luminous, glowing at them and vanishing, and no sound, only that effluvium of something more than dog, stronger than dog and not just animal, just beast, because still there had been nothing in front of that abject and almost painful yapping save the solitude, the wilderness, so that when the eleventh hound came in at noon and with all the others watching — even old Uncle Ash, who called himself first a cook — Sam daubed the tattered ear and the raked shoulder with turpentine and axle grease, to the boy it was still no living creature, but the wilderness which, leaning for the moment down, had patted lightly once the hound's temerity.

"Just like a man," Sam said. "Just like folks. Put off as long as she could having to be brave, knowing all the time that sooner or later she would have to be brave to keep on living with herself, and knowing all the time beforehand what was going to happen to her when she done it."

That afternoon, himself on the one-eyed wagon mule which did not mind the smell of blood nor, as they told him, of bear, and with Sam on the other one, they rode for more than three hours through the rapid, shortening winter day. They followed no path, no trail even that he could see; almost at once they were in a country which he had never seen before. Then he knew why Sam had made him ride the mule which would not spook. The sound one stopped short and tried to whirl and bolt even as Sam got down, blowing its breath, jerking and wrenching at the rein, while Sam held it, coaxing it forward with his voice, since he could not risk tying it, drawing it forward while the boy got down from the marred one.

Then, standing beside Sam in the gloom of the dying afternoon, he looked down at the rotted over-turned log, gutted and scored with claw marks and, in the wet earth beside it, the print of the enormous warped two-toed foot. He knew now what he had smelled when he peered under the kitchen where the dogs huddled. He realized for the first time that the bear which had run in his listening and loomed in his dreams since before he could remember to the contrary, and which, therefore, must have existed in the listening and dreams of his father and Major de Spain and even old General Compson, too, before they began to remember in their turn, was a mortal animal, and that if they had departed for the camp each November without any actual hope of bringing its trophy back, it was not because it could not be slain, but because so far they had had no actual hope to.

"Tomorrow," he said.

"We'll try tomorrow," Sam said. "We ain't got the dog yet."

"We've got eleven. They ran him this morning."

"It won't need but one," Sam said. "He ain't here. Maybe he ain't nowhere. The only other way will be for him to run by accident over somebody that has a gun."

"That wouldn't be me," the boy said. "It will be Walter or Major or ——"

"It might," Sam said. "You watch close in the morning. Because he's smart. That's how come he has lived this long. If he gets hemmed up and has to pick out somebody to run over, he will pick out you."

"How?" the boy said. "How will he know — " He ceased. "You mean he already knows me, that I ain't never been here before, ain't had time to find out yet whether I — " He ceased again, looking at Sam, the old man whose face revealed nothing until it smiled. He said humbly, not even amazed, "It was me he was watching. I don't reckon he did need to come but once."

The next morning they left the camp three hours before daylight. They rode this time because it was too far to walk, even the dogs in the wagon; again the first gray light found him in a place which he had never seen before, where Sam had placed him and told him to stay and then departed. With the gun which was too big for him, which did not even belong to him, but to Major de Spain, and which he had fired only once — at a stump on the first day, to learn the recoil and how to reload it — he stood against a gum tree beside a little bayou whose black still water crept without movement out of a canebrake and crossed a small clearing and into cane again, where, invisible, a bird — the big woodpecker called Lord-to-God by Negroes — clattered at a dead limb.

It was a stand like any other, dissimilar only in incidentals to the one where he had stood each morning for ten days; a territory new to him, yet no less familiar than that other one which, after almost two weeks, he had come to believe he knew a little — the same solitude, the same loneliness through which human beings had merely passed without altering it, leaving no mark, no scar, which looked exactly as it must have looked when the first ancestor of Sam Fathers' Chickasaw predecessors crept into it and looked about, club or stone ax or bone arrow drawn and poised; different only because, squatting at the edge of the kitchen, he smelled the hounds huddled and cringing beneath it and saw the raked ear and shoulder of the one who, Sam said, had had to be brave once in order to live with herself, and saw yesterday in the earth beside the gutted log the print of the living foot.

He heard no dogs at all. He never did hear them. He only heard the drumming of the woodpecker stop short off and knew that the bear was looking at him. He never saw it. He did not know whether it was in front of him or behind him. He did not move, holding the useless gun, which he had not even had warning

to cock and which even now he did not cock, tasting in his saliva
that taint as of brass which he knew now because he had smelled
it when he peered under the kitchen at the huddled dogs.

Then it was gone. As abruptly as it had ceased, the woodpecker's dry, monotonous clatter set up again, and after a while
he even believed he could hear the dogs — a murmur, scarce a
sound even, which he had probably been hearing for some time
before he even remarked it, drifting into hearing and then out
again, dying away. They came nowhere near him. If it was a bear
they ran, it was another bear. It was Sam himself who came out
of the cane and crossed the bayou, followed by the injured bitch
of yesterday. She was almost at heel, like a bird dog, making no
sound. She came and crouched against his leg, trembling, staring
off into the cane.

"I didn't see him," he said. "I didn't, Sam!"

"I know it," Sam said. "He done the looking. You didn't
hear him neither, did you?"

"No," the boy said. "I ——"

"He's smart," Sam said. "Too smart." He looked down at
the hound, trembling faintly and steadily against the boy's knee.
From the raked shoulder a few drops of fresh blood oozed and
clung. "Too big. We ain't got the dog yet. But maybe someday.
Maybe not next time. But someday."

So I must see him, he thought. *I must look at him.* Otherwise,
it seemed to him that it would go on like this forever, as it had
gone on with his father and Major de Spain, who was older than
his father, and even with old General Compson, who had been
old enough to be a brigade commander in 1865. Otherwise, it
would go on so forever, next time and next time, after and after
and after. It seemed to him that he could never see the two of
them, himself and the bear, shadowy in the limbo from which
time emerged, becoming time; the old bear absolved of mortality
and himself partaking, sharing a little of it, enough of it. And he
knew now what he had smelled in the huddled dogs and tasted
in his saliva. He recognized fear. *So I will have to see him,* he
thought, without dread or even hope. *I will have to look at him.*

It was in June of the next year. He was eleven. They were
in camp again, celebrating Major de Spain's and General Compson's
birthdays. Although the one had been born in September and the
other in the depth of winter and in another decade, they had met
for two weeks to fish and shoot squirrels and turkey and run coons
and wildcats with the dogs at night. That is, he and Boon Hoggenbeck and the Negroes fished and shot squirrels and ran the
coons and cats, because the proved hunters, not only Major de

Spain and old General Compson, who spent those two weeks
sitting in a rocking chair before a tremendous iron pot of Brunswick
stew, stirring and tasting, with old Ash to quarrel with about how
he was making it and Tennie's Jim to pour whiskey from the
demijohn into the tin dipper from which he drank it, but even
the boy's father and Walter Ewell, who were still young enough,
scorned such, other than shooting the wild gobblers with pistols
for wagers on their marksmanship.

Or, that is, his father and the others believed he was hunting
squirrels. Until the third day, he thought that Sam Fathers believed
that too. Each morning he would leave the camp right after breakfast.
He had his own gun now, a Christmas present. He went back to
the tree beside the bayou where he had stood that morning. Using
the compass which old General Compson had given him, he ranged
from that point; he was teaching himself to be a better-than-fair
woodsman without knowing he was doing it. On the second day
he even found the gutted log where he had first seen the crooked
print. It was almost completely crumbled now, healing with unbelievable speed, a passionate and almost visible relinquishment,
back into the earth from which the tree had grown.

He ranged the summer woods now, green with gloom; if
anything, actually dimmer than in November's gray dissolution,
where, even at noon, the sun fell only in intermittent dappling
upon the earth, which never completely dried out and which crawled
with snakes — moccasins and water snakes and rattlers, themselves
the color of the dappling gloom, so that he would not always see
them until they moved, returning later and later, first day, second
day, passing in the twilight of the third evening the little log pen
enclosing the log stable where Sam was putting up the horses for
the night.

"You ain't looked right yet," Sam said.

He stopped. For a moment he didn't answer. Then he said
peacefully, in a peaceful rushing burst as when a boy's miniature
dam in a little brook gives way, "All right. But how? I went to
the bayou. I even found that log again. I ——"

"I reckon that was all right. Likely he's been watching you.
You never saw his foot?"

"I," the boy said — "I didn't — I never thought ——"

"It's the gun," Sam said. He stood beside the fence motionless
— the old man, the Indian, in the battered faded overalls and the
five-cent straw hat which in the Negro's race had been the badge
of his enslavement and was now the regalia of his freedom. The
camp — the clearing, the house, the barn and its tiny lot with
which Major de Spain in his turn had scratched punily and eva-

nescently at the wilderness — faded in the dusk, back into the immemorial darkness of the woods. *The gun,* the boy thought. *The gun.*

"Be scared," Sam said. "You can't help that. But don't be afraid. Ain't nothing in the woods going to hurt you unless you corner it, or it smells that you are afraid. A bear or a deer, too, has got to be scared of a coward the same as a brave man has got to be."

The gun, the boy thought.

"You will have to choose," Sam said.

He left the camp before daylight, long before Uncle Ash would wake in his quilts on the kitchen floor and start the fire for breakfast. He had only the compass and a stick for snakes. He could go almost a mile before he would begin to need the compass. He sat on a log, the invisible compass in his invisible hand, while the secret night sounds, fallen still at his movements, scurried again and then ceased for good, and the owls ceased and gave over to the waking of day birds, and he could see the compass. Then he went fast yet still quietly; he was becoming better and better as a woodsman, still without having yet realized it.

He jumped a doe and a fawn at sunrise, walked them out of the bed, close enough to see them — the crash of undergrowth, the white scut, the fawn scudding behind her faster than he had believed it could run. He was hunting right, upwind, as Sam had taught him; not that it mattered now. He had left the gun; of his own will and relinquishment he had accepted not a gambit, not a choice, but a condition in which not only the bear's heretofore inviolable anonymity but all the old rules and balances of hunter and hunted had been abrogated. He would not even be afraid, not even in the moment when the fear would take him completely — blood, skin, bowels, bones, memory from the long time before it became his memory — all save that thin, clear, immortal lucidity which alone differed him from this bear and from all the other bear and deer he would ever kill in the humility and pride of his skill and endurance, to which Sam had spoken when he leaned in the twilight on the lot fence yesterday.

By noon he was far beyond the little bayou, farther into the new and alien country than he had ever been. He was traveling now not only by the compass but by the old, heavy, biscuit-thick silver watch which had belonged to his grandfather. When he stopped at last, it was for the first time since he had risen from the log at dawn when he could see the compass. It was far enough. He had left the camp nine hours ago; nine hours from now, dark would have already been an hour old. But he didn't think that.

He thought, *All right. Yes. But what?* and stood for a moment, alien and small in the green and topless solitude, answering his own question before it had formed and ceased. It was the watch, the compass, the stick — the three lifeless mechanicals with which for nine hours he had fended the wilderness off; he hung the watch and compass carefully on a bush and leaned the stick beside them and relinquished completely to it.

He had not been going very fast for the last two or three hours. He went no faster now, since distance would not matter even if he could have gone fast. And he was trying to keep a bearing on the tree where he had left the compass, trying to complete a circle which would bring him back to it or at least intersect itself, since direction would not matter now either. But the tree was not here, and he did as Sam had schooled him — made the next circle in the opposite direction, so that the two patterns would bisect somewhere, but crossing no print of his own feet, finding the tree at last, but in the wrong place — no bush, no compass, no watch — and the tree not even the tree, because there was a down log beside it and he did what Sam Fathers had told him was the next thing and the last.

As he sat down on the log he saw the crooked print — the warped, tremendous, two-toed indentation which, even as he watched it, filled with water. As he looked up, the wilderness coalesced, solidified — the glade, the tree he sought, the bush, the watch and the compass glinting where the ray of sunshine touched them. Then he saw the bear. It did not emerge, appear; it was just there, immobile, solid, fixed in the hot dappling of the green and windless noon, not as big as he had dreamed it, but as big as he had expected it, bigger, dimensionless, against the dappled obscurity, looking at him where he sat quietly on the log and looked back at it.

Then it moved. It made no sound. It did not hurry. It crossed the glade, walking for an instant into the full glare of the sun; when it reached the other side it stopped again and looked back at him across one shoulder while his quiet breathing inhaled and exhaled three times.

Then it was gone. It didn't walk into the woods, the undergrowth. It faded, sank back into the wilderness as he had watched a fish, a huge old bass, sink and vanish into the dark depths of its pool without even any movement of its fins.

He thought, *It will be next fall.* But it was not next fall, nor the next nor the next. He was fourteen then. He had killed his buck, and Sam Fathers had marked his face with the hot blood,

and in the next year he killed a bear. But even before that accolade
he had become as competent in the woods as many grown men
with the same experience; by his fourteenth year he was a better
woodsman than most grown men with more. There was no territory
within thirty miles of the camp that he did not know — bayou,
ridge, brake, landmark, tree and path. He could have led anyone
to any point in it without deviation, and brought them out again.
He knew the game trails that even Sam Fathers did not know; in
his thirteenth year he found a buck's bedding place, and unbeknown
to his father he borrowed Walter Ewell's rifle and lay in wait at
dawn and killed the buck when it walked back to the bed, as Sam
had told him how the old Chickasaw fathers did.

But not the old bear, although by now he knew its footprints
better than he did his own, and not only the crooked one. He
could see any one of three sound ones and distinguish it from any
other, and not only by its size. There were other bears within
these thirty miles which left tracks almost as large, but this was
more than that. If Sam Fathers had been his mentor and the backyard rabbits and squirrels at home his kindergarten, then the wilderness the old bear ran was his college, the old male bear itself,
so long unwifed and childless as to have become its own ungendered
progenitor, was his alma mater. But he never saw it.

He could find the crooked print now almost whenever he
liked, fifteen or ten or five miles, or sometimes nearer the camp
than that. Twice while on stand during the three years he heard
the dogs strike its trail by accident; on the second time they jumped
it seemingly, the voices high, abject, almost human in hysteria,
as on that first morning two years ago. But not the bear itself.
He would remember that noon three years ago, the glade, himself
and the bear fixed during that moment in the windless and dappled
blaze, and it would seem to him that it had never happened, that
he had dreamed that too. But it had happened. They had looked
at each other, they had emerged from the wilderness old as earth,
synchronized to the instant by something more than the blood
that moved the flesh and bones which bore them, and touched,
pledged something, affirmed, something more lasting than the
frail web of bones and flesh which any accident could obliterate.

Then he saw it again. Because of the very fact that he thought
of nothing else, he had forgotten to look for it. He was still hunting
with Walter Ewell's rifle. He saw it cross the end of a long blow-
down, a corridor where a tornado had swept, rushing through
rather than over the tangle of trunks and branches as a locomotive
would have, faster than he had ever believed it could move, almost
as fast as a deer even, because a deer would have spent most of

that time in the air, faster than he could bring the rifle sights up with it. And now he knew what had been wrong during all the three years. He sat on a log, shaking and trembling as if he had never seen the woods before nor anything that ran them, wondering with incredulous amazement how he could have forgotten the very thing which Sam Fathers had told him and which the bear itself had proved the next day and had now returned after three years to reaffirm.

And now he knew what Sam Fathers had meant about the right dog, a dog in which size would mean less than nothing. So when he returned alone in April — school was out then, so that the sons of farmers could help with the land's planting, and at last his father had granted him permission, on his promise to be back in four days — he had the dog. It was his own, a mongrel of the sort called by Negroes a fyce, a ratter, itself not much bigger than a rat and possessing that bravery which had long since stopped being courage and had become foolhardiness.

It did not take four days. Alone again, he found the trail on the first morning. It was not a stalk; it was an ambush. He timed the meeting almost as if it were an appointment with a human being. Himself holding the fyce muffled in a feed sack and Sam Fathers with two of the hounds on a piece of a plowline rope, they lay down wind of the trail at dawn of the second morning. They were so close that the bear turned without even running, as if in surprised amazement at the shrill and frantic uproar of the released fyce, turning at bay against the trunk of a tree, on its hind feet; it seemed to the boy that it would never stop rising, taller and taller, and even the two hounds seemed to take a desperate and despairing courage from the fyce, following it as it went in.

Then he realized that the fyce was actually not going to stop. He flung, threw the gun away, and ran; when he overtook and grasped the frantically pin-wheeling little dog, it seemed to him that he was directly under the bear.

He could smell it, strong and hot and rank. Sprawling, he looked up to where it loomed and towered over him like a cloudburst and colored like a thunderclap, quite familiar, peacefully and even lucidly familiar, until he remembered: This was the way he had used to dream about it. Then it was gone. He didn't see it go. He knelt, holding the frantic fyce with both hands, hearing the abashed wailing of the hounds drawing farther and farther away, until Sam came up. He carried the gun. He laid it down quietly beside the boy and stood looking down at him.

"You've done seed him twice now with a gun in your hands," he said. "This time you couldn't have missed him."

The boy rose. He still held the fyce. Even in his arms and clear of the ground, it yapped frantically, straining and surging after the fading uproar of the two hounds like a tangle of wire springs. He was panting a little but he was neither shaking nor trembling now.

"Neither could you!" he said. "You had the gun! Neither did you!"

"And you didn't shoot," his father said. "How close were you?"

"I don't know, sir," he said. "There was a big wood tick inside his right hind leg. I saw that. But I didn't have the gun then."

"But you didn't shoot when you had the gun," his father said. "Why?"

But he didn't answer, and his father didn't wait for him to, rising and crossing the room, across the pelt of the bear which the boy had killed two years ago and the larger one which his father had killed before he was born, to the bookcase beneath the mounted head of the boy's first buck. It was the room which his father called the office, from which all the plantation business was transacted; in it for the fourteen years of his life he had heard the best of all talking. Major de Spain would be there and sometimes old General Compson, and Walter Ewell and Boon Hoggenbeck and Sam Fathers and Tennie's Jim, too, were hunters, knew the woods and what ran them.

He would hear it, not talking himself but listening — the wilderness, the big woods, bigger and older than any recorded document of white man fatuous enough to believe he had bought any fragment of it or Indian ruthless enough to pretend that any fragment of it had been his to convey. It was of the men, not white nor black nor red, but men, hunters with the will and hardihood to endure and the humility and skill to survive, and the dogs and the bear and deer juxtaposed and reliefed against it, ordered and compelled by and within the wilderness in the ancient and unremitting contest by the ancient and immitigable rules which voided all regrets and brooked no quarter, the voices quiet and weighty and deliberate for retrospection and recollection and exact remembering, while he squatted in the blazing firelight as Tennie's Jim squatted, who stirred only to put more wood on the fire and to pass the bottle from one glass to another. Because the bottle was always present, so that after a while it seemed to him that those fierce instants of heart and brain and courage and wiliness and speed were concentrated and distilled into that brown liquor

which not women, not boys and children, but only hunters drank,
drinking not of the blood they had spilled but some condensation
of the wild immortal spirit, drinking it moderately, humbly even,
not with the pagan's base hope of acquiring the virtues of cunning
and strength and speed, but in salute to them.

His father returned with the book and sat down again and
opened it. "Listen," he said. He read the five stanzas aloud, his
voice quiet and deliberate in the room where there was no fire
now because it was already spring. Then he looked up. The boy
watched him. "All right," his father said. "Listen." He read again,
but only the second stanza this time, to the end of it, the last two
lines, and closed the book and put it on the table beside him. "She
cannot fade, though thou hast not thy bliss, forever wilt thou love,
and she be fair," he said.

"He's talking about a girl," the boy said.

"He had to talk about something," his father said. Then he
said, "He was talking about truth. Truth doesn't change. Truth
is one thing. It covers all things which touch the heart — honor
and pride and pity and justice and courage and love. Do you see
now?"

He didn't know. Somehow it was simpler than that. There
was an old bear, fierce and ruthless, not merely just to stay alive,
but with the fierce pride of liberty and freedom, proud enough
of the liberty and freedom to see it threatened without fear or
even alarm; nay, who at times even seemed deliberately to put
that freedom and liberty in jeopardy in order to savor them, to
remind his old strong bones and flesh to keep supple and quick
to defend and preserve them. There was an old man, son of a
Negro slave and an Indian king, inheritor on the one side of the
long chronicle of a people who had learned humility through
suffering, and pride through the endurance which survived the
suffering and injustice, and on the other side, the chronicle of a
people even longer in the land than the first, yet who no longer
existed in the land at all save in the solitary brotherhood of an
old Negro's alien blood and the wild and invincible spirit of an
old bear. There was a boy who wished to learn humility and pride
in order to become skillful and worthy in the woods, who suddenly
found himself becoming so skillful so rapidly that he feared he
would never become worthy because he had not learned humility
and pride, although he had tried to, until one day and as suddenly
he discovered that an old man who could not have defined either
had led him, as though by the hand, to that point where an old
bear and a little mongrel of a dog showed him that, by possessing
one thing other, he would possess them both.

And a little dog, nameless and mongrel and many-fathered, grown, yet weighing less than six pounds, saying as if to itself, "I can't be dangerous, because there's nothing much smaller than I am; I can't be fierce, because they would call it just a noise; I can't be humble, because I'm already too close to the ground to genuflect; I can't be proud, because I wouldn't be near enough to it for anyone to know who was casting the shadow, and I don't even know that I'm not going to heaven, because they have already decided that I don't possess an immortal soul. So all I can be is brave. But it's all right. I can be that, even if they still call it just noise."

That was all. It was simple, much simpler than somebody talking in a book about youth and a girl he would never need to grieve over, because he could never approach any nearer her and would never have to get any farther away. He had heard about a bear, and finally got big enough to trail it, and he trailed it four years and at last met it with a gun in his hands and he didn't shoot. Because a little dog — But he could have shot long before the little dog covered the twenty yards to where the bear waited, and Sam Fathers could have shot at any time during that interminable minute while Old Ben stood on his hind feet over them. He stopped. His father was watching him gravely across the spring-rife twilight of the room; when he spoke, his words were as quiet as the twilight, too, not loud, because they did not need to be because they would last. "Courage, and honor, and pride," his father said, "and pity, and love of justice and of liberty. They all touch the heart, and what the heart holds to becomes truth, as far as we know the truth. Do you see now?"

Sam, and Old Ben, and Nip, he thought. And himself too. He had been all right too. His father had said so. "Yes, sir," he said.

Several of Faulkner's comments on "The Bear," made during interviews at the University of Virginia (printed in *Faulkner in the University,* ed. F. L. Gwynn and J. W. Blotner, 1959), though not necessarily definitive, are suggestive:

> One symbol was the bear represented the vanishing wilderness. The little dog that wasn't scared of the bear represented the indomitable spirit of man. I'll have to dig back and get up some more of those symbols, because I have learned around an even dozen that I put into that story without knowing it. But there are two pretty good ones that you can hold to.

Asked the significance of the fyce, Faulkner said that it is

> . . . the antithesis of the bear. The bear represented the obsolete primitive. The fyce represents the creature who has coped

with environment and is still on top of it, you might say. That he has — instead of sticking to his breeding and becoming a decadent degenerate creature, he has mixed himself up with the good stock where he picked and chose. And he's quite smart, he's quite brave. All's against him is his size. But I never knew a fyce yet that realized that he wasn't big as anything else he ever saw, even a bear.

Asked to explain what the "one thing" was that would enable the boy to learn "humility and pride," Faulkner replied: "Courage, it was. A little dog that never saw a bear bigger than he was."

QUESTIONS

1. In the opening three paragraphs of the story, the pronoun "it" usually refers to Old Ben. But does "it" always have the same referent in this opening section of the story? How might the "it" be said to function ambiguously and thus prepare the reader for the symbolism in the story? What do you make out of the fact that the boy is nameless throughout the story? Does this fact somehow add to the symbolic meaning?

2. Compare the characterizations of the bear in the second and third paragraphs. How do they affect your attitude toward the bear? Does the fact that it is given a name and does the name itself affect your attitude toward Old Ben?

3. Sam Fathers makes a distinction between being "scared" and being "afraid." Is the distinction clear to you?

4. The boy relinquishes the three lifeless mechanicals before he is permitted to see the bear. Why? Is Faulkner making some social comment about modern man that goes beyond the limits of a bear hunt? Is the following letter, written by Faulkner to *The New York Times* (December 26, 1954), relevant to "The Bear"?

> This is about the Italian airliner which undershot the runway and crashed at Idlewild after failing three times to hold the instrument glide-path which would have brought it down to the runway.
>   It is written on the idea (postulate, if you like) that the instrument or instruments — altimeter-cum-drift-indicator — failed or had failed, was already out of order or incorrect before the moment when the pilot committed irrevocably the aircraft to it.
>   It is written in grief. Not just for the sorrow of the bereaved ones of those who died in the crash, and for the airline, the public carrier which, in selling the

tickets, promised or anyway implied security for the trip, but for the crew, the pilot himself, who will be blamed for the crash and whose record and memory will be tarnished by it; who, along with his unaware passengers, was victim not even of the failed instruments but victim of that mystical, unquestioning, almost religious awe and veneration in which our culture has trained us to hold gadgets — any gadget, if it is only complex enough and cryptic enough and costs enough.

I imagine that even after the first failure to hold the glide-path, certainly after the second one, his instinct — the seat of his pants, call it what you will — after that many hours in the air, told him that something was wrong. And his seniority as a four-engine over-water captain probably told him where the trouble was. But he dared not accept that knowledge and (this presumes that even after the second failure he still had enough fuel left to reach a field which he could see) act on it.

Possibly at some time during the four attempts to land, very likely at some one of the final rapid seconds before he had irrevocably committed the aircraft — that compounding of mass and weight by velocity — to the ground, his co-pilot (or flight engineer or whoever else might have been in the cockpit at the time) probably said to him: "Look. We're wrong. Get the flaps and gear up and let's get to hell out of here." But he dared not. He dared not so flout and affront, even with his own life too at stake, our cultural postulate of the infallibility of machines, instruments, gadgets — a Power more ruthless even than the old Hebrew concept of its God, since ours is not even jealous and vengeful, caring nothing about individuals.

He dared not commit that sacrilege. If he had, nothing would have remained to him save to open the cockpit hatch and (a Roman) cast himself onto the turning blades of one of the inboard air-screws. I grieve for him, for that moment's victims. We all had better grieve for all people beneath a culture which holds any mechanical superior to any man simply because the one, being mechanical, is infallible, while the other, being nothing but man, is not just subject to failure but doomed to it.

5. On page 78 the hunters pass around a bottle. What do you make out of this action?
6. Why doesn't the boy kill the bear?
7. A careful reading of Keats's "Ode on a Grecian Urn" (pages 419–420) may illuminate the father's comments to his son. What do you think is the particular relevance of the second stanza?

6
Style

"Style" comes from the Latin word *stilus,* a pointed instrument used to engrave or write. The meaning has been transferred from the instrument to the product, so we talk of the style of a piece of writing, or, more generally, of an author's style, or, for that matter, of anyone's style — way of hitting a tennis ball, of dancing, of dealing with people, or whatever.

What style shall a writer use?

Put this way, it is clear that there is no simple answer; anything can be right or wrong, depending on what effect is sought. James Joyce, in *A Portrait of the Artist as a Young Man,* uses a variety of styles, and each of them is right. Here are three passages from the novel — the opening sentence, a sentence from the middle, and the closing sentence:

> Once upon a time and a very good time it was there was a moocow coming down along the road and this moocow that was down along the road met a nicens little boy named baby tuckoo. . . .

> Only at times, in the pauses of his desire, when the luxury that was wasting him gave room to a softer languor, the image of Mercedes traversed the background of his memory.

> April 27. Old father, old artificer, stand me now and ever in good stead.

The first of these, in a childlike style, describes the protagonist's infancy. The second, in a luxurious style, describes the fantasies of his adolescence. And the third, in a spare style, describes his preparation for self-exile.

The following are the first two sentences in the opening paragraph of Eudora Welty's "Livvie":

> Solomon carried Livvie twenty-one miles away from her home when he married her. He carried her away up on the Old Natchez Trace into the deep country to live in his house.

These sentences can easily be transposed and combined into:

> When Solomon married Livvie, he carried her away up on
> the Old Natchez Trace into the deep country to live in his
> house, twenty-one miles away.

The words are the same, but everything is changed. By failing to
repeat the structure of subject-verb ("Solomon carried," "He carried"), the suggestion of Livvie's own voice is lost. Though the
lines, as Miss Welty wrote them, are not spoken by Livvie, they
carry within them a suggestion of her simplicity. Take the first
two sentences of the second paragraph:

> It was a nice house, inside and outside both. In the first place,
> it had three rooms.

These can be combined into:

> The three-room house was nice, inside and out.

Again, the innocence of Livvie's voice is missing. In these lines,
Miss Welty is not communicating information only about Livvie's
house; she is also giving us an image of Livvie's mind, and the
paraphrase does not.

A more subtle example may be useful. When Miss Welty
first published "Livvie," the third sentence of the opening paragraph
was simply:

> She was sixteen then.

But in the revision, printed in this book, the sentence runs:

> She was sixteen — an only girl, then.

Of course the revision has an additional piece of information, but
what is important for our present purpose is the difference in style.
"She was sixteen then" is a quite ordinary sentence, such as any
of us might write. But "She was sixteen — an only girl, then"
presents us with a special mind. It almost seems to suggest that
Livvie is no longer an only girl, yet this point is never made.
What the revision adds is a hint of Livvie's slightly wistful, disjointed
view of the past. Ordinarily the sentence might run, "She was
sixteen then, an only girl"; by being placed at the end of the
sentence, after some material that it does not logically follow,
"then" is somewhat unexpected, rather like the last step down to
the cellar. The slight jolt we feel in "then" both reveals Livvie's
special way of thinking and gives the past an emphasis lacking in
the original "She was sixteen then" and lacking in "She was sixteen
then, an only girl."

These comments do not come near to revealing the special

power of Miss Welty's sentences, but perhaps they have made clear that in good writing words cannot be rearranged without change in meaning. "I began to speak of style," Isaac Babel writes in one of his stories, "of the army of words, of the army in which all kinds of weapons may come into play. No iron can stab the heart with such force as a period put just at the right place."

A NOTE ON TONE

A speaker's tone of voice conveys part of the meaning: "Good Lord" can be a pious invocation; it also can be a blasphemous expletive, and the tone, quite as well as the context, can tell us which it is. **Tone** in a story is commonly defined as the author's voice (in distinction from the voices of the characters); it is, let us say, the author's attitude as the reader infers it. The characters may speak angrily, but the reader may rightly detect that the author's tone is gentle and compassionate. The characters may speak gaily and wittily, but the reader may rightly detect that the author's tone is scornful. When we talk about the author's sympathies and antipathies, his or her cynicism or solemnity or flippancy, we are talking about the author's tone. And it is through a pervasive style that the author's tone is heard.*

Eudora Welty (American. b. 1909)

Livvie

Solomon carried Livvie twenty-one miles away from her home when he married her. He carried her away up on the Old Natchez Trace into the deep country to live in his house. She was sixteen — an only girl, then. Once people said he thought nobody would ever come along there. He told her himself that it had been a long time, and a day she did not know about, since that road was a traveled road with *people* coming and going. He was good to her, but he kept her in the house. She had not thought that she could

* Although Chapter 10, "The Speaking Tone of Voice," draws its illustrative material from poems, the points it makes are relevant here. The reader may find it useful to consult the first half-dozen pages of that chapter now.

not get back. Where she came from, people said an old man did
not want anybody in the world to ever find his wife, for fear they
would steal her back from him. Solomon asked her before he took
her, "Would she be happy?" — very dignified, for he was a colored
man that owned his land and had it written down in the courthouse;
and she said, "Yes, sir," since he was an old man and she was
young and just listened and answered. He asked her, if she was
choosing winter, would she pine for spring, and she said, "No
indeed." Whatever she said, always, was because he was an old
man . . . while nine years went by. All the time, he got old, and
he got so old he gave out. At least he slept the whole day in bed,
and she was young still.

It was a nice house, inside and outside both. In the first
place, it had three rooms. The front room was papered in holly
paper, with green palmettos from the swamp spaced at careful
intervals over the walls. There was fresh newspaper cut with fancy
borders on the mantleshelf, on which were propped photographs
of old or very young men printed in faint yellow — Solomon's
people. Solomon had a houseful of furniture. There was a double
settee, a tall scrolled rocker and an organ in the front room, all
around a three-legged table with a pink marble top, on which was
set a lamp with three gold feet, beside a jelly glass with pretty
hen feathers in it. Behind the front room, the other room had the
bright iron bed with the polished knobs like a throne, in which
Solomon slept all day. There were snow-white curtains of wiry
lace at the window, and a lace bedspread belonged on the bed.
But what old Solomon slept sound under was a big feather-stitched
piece-quilt in the pattern "Trip Around the World," which had
twenty-one different colors, four hundred and forty pieces, and a
thousand yards of thread, and that was what Solomon's mother
made in her life and old age. There was a table holding the Bible,
and a trunk with a key. On the wall were two calendars, and a
diploma from somewhere in Solomon's family, and under that
Livvie's one possession was nailed, a picture of the little white
baby of the family she worked for, back in Natchez before she
was married. Going through that room and on to the kitchen,
there was a big wood stove and a big round table always with a
wet top and with the knives and forks in one jelly glass and the
spoons in another, and a cut-glass vinegar bottle between, and
going out from those, many shallow dishes of pickled peaches,
fig preserves, watermelon pickles and blackberry jam always sitting
there. The churn sat in the sun, the doors of the safe were always
both shut, and there were four baited mouse-traps in the kitchen,
one in every corner.

The outside of Solomon's house looked nice. It was not painted, but across the porch was an even balance. On each side there was one easy chair with high springs, looking out, and a fern basket hanging over it from the ceiling, and a dishpan of zinnia seedlings growing at its foot on the floor. By the door was a plow-wheel, just a pretty iron circle, nailed up on one wall and a square mirror on the other, a turquoise-blue comb stuck up in the frame, with the wash stand beneath it. On the door was a wooden knob with a pearl in the end, and Solomon's black hat hung on that, if he was in the house.

Out front was a clean dirt yard with every vestige of grass patiently uprooted and the ground scarred in deep whorls from the strike of Livvie's broom. Rose bushes with tiny blood-red roses blooming every month grew in threes on either side of the steps. On one side was a peach tree, on the other a pomegranate. Then coming around up the path from the deep cut of the Natchez Trace below was a line of bare crape-myrtle trees with every branch of them ending in a colored bottle, green or blue. There was no word that fell from Solomon's lips to say what they were for, but Livvie knew that there could be a spell put in trees, and she was familiar from the time she was born with the way bottle trees kept evil spirits from coming into the house — by luring them inside the colored bottles, where they cannot get out again. Solomon had made the bottle trees with his own hands over the nine years, in labor amounting to about a tree a year, and without a sign that he had any uneasiness in his heart, for he took as much pride in his precautions against spirits coming in the house as he took in the house, and sometimes in the sun the bottle trees looked prettier than the house did.

It was a nice house. It was in a place where the days would go by and surprise anyone that they were over. The lamplight and the firelight would shine out the door after dark, over the still and breathing country, lighting the roses and the bottle trees, and all was quiet there.

But there was nobody, nobody at all, not even a white person. And if there had been anybody, Solomon would not have let Livvie look at them, just as he would not let her look at a field hand, or a field hand look at her. There was no house near, except for the cabins of the tenants that were forbidden to her, and there was no house as far as she had been, stealing away down the still, deep Trace. She felt as if she waded a river when she went, for the dead leaves on the ground reached as high as her knees, and when she was all scratched and bleeding she said it was not like a road that went anywhere. One day, climbing up the high bank, she had found a graveyard without a church; with ribbon-grass growing about the foot of an angel (she had climbed up because she thought she saw angel wings), and in the sun, trees shining like burning flames through the great caterpillar nets which enclosed them. Scarey thistles stood looking like the prophets in the Bible in Solomon's house. Indian paint brushes grew over her head, and the mourning dove made the only sound in the world. Oh for a stirring of the leaves, and a breaking of the nets! But not by a ghost, prayed Livvie, jumping down the bank. After Solomon took to his bed, she never went out, except one more time.

Livvie knew she made a nice girl to wait on anybody. She fixed things to eat on a tray like a surprise. She could keep from singing when she ironed, and to sit by a bed and fan away the flies, she could be so still she could not hear herself breathe. She could clean up the house and never drop a thing, and wash the dishes without a sound, and she would step outside to churn, for churning sounded too sad to her, like sobbing, and if it made her home-sick and not Solomon, she did not think of that.

But Solomon scarcely opened his eyes to see her, and scarcely tasted his food. He was not sick or paralyzed or in any pain that he mentioned, but he was surely wearing out in the body, and no matter what nice hot thing Livvie would bring him to taste, he would only look at it now, as if he was past seeing how he could add anything more to himself. Before she could beg him, he would go fast asleep. She could not surprise him any more, if he would not taste, and she was afraid that he was never in the world going to taste another thing she brought him — and so how could he last?

But one morning it was breakfast time and she cooked his eggs and grits, carried them in on a tray, and called his name. He was sound asleep. He lay in a dignified way with his watch beside him, on his back in the middle of the bed. One hand drew the quilt up high, though it was the first day of spring. Through the white lace curtains a little puffy wind was blowing as if it came from round cheeks. All night the frogs had sung out in the swamp, like a commotion in the room, and he had not stirred, though she lay wide awake and saying, "Shh, frogs!" for fear he would mind them.

He looked as if he would like to sleep a little longer, and so she put back the tray and waited a little. When she tiptoed and stayed so quiet, she surrounded herself with a little reverie, and sometimes it seemed to her when she was so stealthy that the quiet she kept was for a sleeping baby, and that she had a baby and was its mother. When she stood at Solomon's bed and looked down at him, she would be thinking, "He sleeps so well,' and she would hate to wake him up. And in some other way, too, she was afraid to wake him up because even in his sleep he seemed to be such a strict man.

Of course, nailed to the wall over the bed — only she would forget who it was — there was a picture of him when he was young. Then he had a fan of hair over his forehead like a king's crown. Now his hair lay down on his head, the spring had gone out of it. Solomon had a lightish face, with eyebrows scattered but rugged, the way privet grows, strong eyes, with second sight, a strict mouth, and a little gold smile. This was the way he looked in his clothes, but in bed in the daytime he looked like a different and smaller man, even when he was wide awake, and holding the Bible. He looked like somebody kin to himself. And then sometimes when he lay in sleep and she stood fanning the flies away, and the light came in, his face was like new, so smooth and clear that it was like a glass of jelly held to the window, and she could almost look through his forehead and see what he thought.

She fanned him and at length he opened his eyes and spoke her name, but he would not taste the nice eggs she had kept warm under a pan.

Back in the kitchen she ate heartily, his breakfast and hers, and looked out the open door at what went on. The whole day, and the whole night before, she had felt the stir of spring close to her. It was as present in the house as a young man would be. The moon was in the last quarter and outside they were turning the sod and planting peas and beans. Up and down the red fields, over which smoke from the brush-burning hung showing like a little skirt of sky, a white horse and a white mule pulled the plow. At intervals hoarse shouts came through the air and roused her as if she dozed neglectfully in the shade, and they were telling her, "Jump up!" She could see how over each ribbon of field were moving men and girls, on foot and mounted on mules, with hats set on their heads and bright with tall hoes and forks as if they carried streamers on them and were going to some place on a journey — and how as if at a signal now and then they would all start at once shouting, hollering, cajoling, calling and answering back, running, being leaped on and breaking away, flinging to earth with a shout and lying motionless in the trance of twelve o'clock. The old women came out of the cabins and brought them food they had ready for them, and then all worked together, spread evenly out. The little children came too, like a bouncing stream overflowing the fields, and set upon the men, the women, the dogs, the rushing birds, and the wave-like rows of earth, their little voices almost too high to be heard. In the middle distance like some white-and-gold towers were the haystacks, with black cows coming around to eat their edges. High above everything, the wheel of fields, house, and cabins, and the deep road surrounding like a moat to keep them in, was the turning sky, blue with long, far-flung white mare's tail clouds, serene and still as high flames. And sound asleep while all this went around him that was his, Solomon was like a little still spot in the middle.

Even in the house the earth was sweet to breathe. Solomon had never let Livvie go any farther than the chicken house and the well. But what if she would walk now into the heart of the fields and take a hoe and work until she fell stretched out and drenched with her efforts, like other girls, and laid her cheek against the laid-open earth, and shamed the old man with her humbleness and delight? To shame him! A cruel wish would come in uninvited and so fast while she looked out the back door. She washed the dishes and scrubbed the table. She could hear the cries of the little lambs. Her mother, that she had not seen since her wedding day, had said one time, "I rather a man be anything, than a woman be mean."

So all morning she kept tasting the chicken broth on the stove, and when it was right she poured off a nice cupful. She carried it in to Solomon, and there he lay having a dream. Now what did he dream about? For she saw him sigh gently as if not to disturb some whole thing he held round in his mind, like a fresh egg. So even an old man dreamed about something pretty. Did he dream of her, while his eyes were shut and sunken, and his small hand with the wedding ring curled close in sleep around the quilt? He might be dreaming of what time it was, for even through his sleep he kept track of it like a clock, and knew how much of it went by, and waked up knowing where the hands were even before he consulted the silver watch that he never let go. He would sleep with the watch in his palm, and even holding it to his cheek like a child that loves a plaything. Or he might dream of journeys and travels on a steamboat to Natchez. Yet she thought he dreamed of her; but even while she scrutinized him, the rods of the foot of the bed seemed to rise up like a rail fence between them, and she could see that people never could be sure of anything as long as one of them was asleep and the other awake. To look at him dreaming of her when he might be going to die frightened her a little, as if he might carry her with him that way, and she wanted to run out of the room. She took hold of the bed and held on, and Solomon opened his eyes and called her name, but he did not want anything. He would not taste the good broth.

Just a little after that, as she was taking up the ashes in the front room for the last time in the year, she heard a sound. It was somebody coming. She pulled the curtains together and looked through the slit.

Coming up the path under the bottle trees was a white lady. At first she looked young, but then she looked old. Marvelous to see, a little car stood steaming like a kettle out in the field-track — it had come without a road.

Livvie stood listening to the long, repeated knockings at the door, and after a while she opened it just a little. The lady came in through the crack, though she was more than middle-sized and wore a big hat.

"My name is Miss Baby Marie," she said.

Livvie gazed respectfully at the lady and at the little suitcase she was holding close to her by the handle until the proper moment. The lady's eyes were running over the room, from palmetto to palmetto, but she was saying, "I live at home . . . out from Natchez . . . and get out and show these pretty cosmetic things to the white people and the colored people both . . . all around . . . years and years. . . . Both shades of powder and rouge. . . . It's the kind of work a girl can do and not go clear 'way from home. . . ." And the harder she looked, the more she talked. Suddenly she turned up her nose and said, "It's not Christian or sanitary to put feathers in a vase," and then she took a gold key out of the front of her dress and began unlocking the locks on her suitcase. Her face drew the light, the way it was covered with intense white and red, with a little patty-cake of white between the wrinkles by her upper lip. Little red tassels of hair bobbed under the rusty wires of her picture-hat, as with an air of triumph and secrecy she now drew open her little suitcase and brought out bottle after bottle and jar after jar, which she put down on the table, the mantlepiece, the settee, and the organ.

"Did you ever see so many cosmetics in your life?" cried Miss Baby Marie.

"No'm," Livvie tried to say, but the cat had her tongue.

"Have you ever applied cosmetics?" asked Miss Baby Marie next.

"No'm," Livvie tried to say.

"Then look!" she said, and pulling out the last thing of all, "Try this!" she said. And in her hand was unclenched a golden lipstick which popped open like magic. A fragrance came out of it like incense, and Livvie cried out suddenly, "Chinaberry flowers!"

Her hand took the lipstick, and in an instant she was carried away in the air through the spring, and looking down with a half-drowsy smile from a purple cloud she saw from above a chinaberry tree, dark and smooth and neatly leaved, neat as a guinea hen in the dooryard, and there was her home that she had left. On one side of the tree was her mama holding up her heavy apron, and she could see it was loaded with ripe figs, and on the other side was her papa holding a fish-pole over the pond, and she could see it transparently, the little clear fishes swimming up to the brim.

"Oh, no, not chinaberry flowers — secret ingredients," said Miss Baby Marie. "My cosmetics have secret ingredients — not chinaberry flowers."

"It's purple," Livvie breathed, and Miss Baby Marie said, "Use it freely. Rub it on."

Livvie tiptoed out to the wash stand on the front porch and before the mirror put the paint on her mouth. In the wavery surface her face danced before her like a flame. Miss Baby Marie followed her out, took a look at what she had done, and said, "That's it."

Livvie tried to say "Thank you" without moving her parted lips where the paint lay so new.

By now Miss Baby Marie stood behind Livvie and looked in the mirror over her shoulder, twisting up the tassels of her hair. "The lipstick I can let you have for only two dollars," she said, close to her neck.

"Lady, but I don't have no money, never did have," said Livvie.

"Oh, but you don't pay the first time. I make another trip, that's the way I do. I come back again — later."

"Oh," said Livvie, pretending she understood everything so as to please the lady.

"But if you don't take it now, this may be the last time I'll call at your house," said Miss Baby Marie sharply. "It's far away from anywhere, I'll tell you that. You don't live close to anywhere."

"Yes'm. My husband, he keep the *money,*" said Livvie, trembling. "He is strict as he can be. He don't know *you* walk in here — Miss Baby Marie!"

"Where is he?"

"Right now, he in yonder sound asleep, an old man. I wouldn't ever ask him for anything."

Miss Baby Marie took back the lipstick and packed it up. She gathered up the jars for both black and white and got them all inside the suitcase, with the same little fuss of triumph with which she had brought them out. She started away.

"Goodbye," she said, making herself look grand from the back, but at the last minute she turned around in the door. Her old hat wobbled as she whispered, "Let me see your husband."

Livvie obediently went on tiptoe and opened the door to the other room. Miss Baby Marie came behind her and rose on her toes and looked in.

"My, what a little tiny old, old man!" she whispered, clasping her hands and shaking her head over them. "What a beautiful quilt! What a tiny old, old man!"

"He can sleep like that all day," whispered Livvie proudly.

They looked at him awhile so fast asleep, and then all at once they looked at each other. Somehow that was as if they had a secret, for he had never stirred. Livvie then politely, but all at once, closed the door.

"Well! I'd certainly like to leave you with a lipstick!" said Miss Baby Marie vivaciously. She smiled in the door.

"Lady, but I told you I don't have no money, and never did have."

"And never will?" In the air and all around, like a bright halo around the white lady's nodding head, it was a true spring day.

"Would you take eggs, lady?" asked Livvie softly.

"No, I have plenty of eggs — plenty," said Miss Baby Marie.

"I still don't have no money," said Livvie, and Miss Baby Marie took her suitcase and went on somewhere else.

Livvie stood watching her go, and all the time she felt her heart beating in her left side. She touched the place with her hand. It seemed as if her heart beat and her whole face flamed from the pulsing color of her lips. She went to sit by Solomon and when he opened his eyes he could not see a change in her. "He's fixin' to die," she said inside. That was the secret. That was when she went out of the house for a little breath of air.

She went down the path and down the Natchez Trace a way, and she did not know how far she had gone, but it was not far, when she saw a sight. It was a man, looking like a vision — she standing on one side of the Old Natchez Trace and he standing on the other.

As soon as this man caught sight of her, he began to look himself over. Starting at the bottom with his pointed shoes, he began to look up, lifting his peg-top pants the higher to see fully his bright socks. His coat long and wide and leaf-green he opened like doors to see his high-up tawny pants and his pants he smoothed downward from the points of his collar, and he wore a luminous baby-pink satin shirt. At the end, he reached gently above his wide platter-shaped round hat, the color of a plum, and one finger touched at the feather, emerald green, blowing in the spring winds.

No matter how she looked, she could never look so fine as he did, and she was not sorry for that, she was pleased.

He took three jumps, one down and two up, and was by her side.

"My name is Cash," he said.

He had a guinea pig in his pocket. They began to walk along. She stared on and on at him, as if he were doing some daring spectacular thing, instead of just walking beside her. It was not simply the city way he was dressed that made her look at him and see hope in its insolence looking back. It was not only the way he moved along kicking the flowers as if he could break through everything in the way and destroy anything in the world, that made her eyes grow bright. It might be, if he had not appeared the way he did appear that day she would never have looked so closely at him, but the time people come makes a difference.

They walked through the still leaves of the Natchez Trace, the light and the shade falling through trees about them, the white irises shining like candles on the banks and the new ferns shining like green stars up in the oak branches. They came out at Solomon's house, bottle trees and all. Livvie stopped and hung her head.

Cash began whistling a little tune. She did not know what it was, but she had heard it before from a distance, and she had a revelation. Cash was a field hand. He was a transformed field hand. Cash belonged to Solomon. But he had stepped out of his overalls into this. There in front of Solomon's house he laughed. He had a round head, a round face, all of him was young, and he flung his head up, rolled it against the mare's-tail sky in his round hat, and he could laugh just to see Solomon's house sitting there. Livvie looked at it, and there was Solomon's black hat hanging on the peg on the front door, the blackest thing in the world.

"I been to Natchez," Cash said, wagging his head around the sky. "*I* taken a trip, *I* ready for Easter!"

How was it possible to look so fine before the harvest? Cash must have stolen the money, stolen it from Solomon. He stood in the path and lifted his spread hand high and brought it down again and again in his laughter. He kicked up his heels. A little chill went through her. It was as if Cash was bringing that strong hand down to beat a drum or to rain blows upon a man, such an abandon and menace were in his laugh. Frowning, she went closer to him and his swinging arm drew her in at once and the fright was crushed from her body, as a little match-flame might be smothered out by what it lighted. She gathered the folds of his coat behind him and fastened her red lips to his mouth, and she was dazzled by herself then, the way he had been dazzled with himself to begin with.

In that instant she felt something that could not be told — that Solomon's death was at hand, that he was the same to her as if he were dead now. She cried out, and uttering little cries turned and ran for the house.

At once Cash was coming, following after, he was running behind her. He came close, and half-way up the path he laughed and passed her. He even picked up a stone and sailed it into the bottle trees. She put her hands over her head, and sounds clattered through the bottle trees like cries of outrage. Cash stamped and plunged zigzag up the front steps and in at the door.

When she got there, he had stuck his hands in his pockets and was turning slowly about in the front room. The little guinea pig peeped out. Around Cash, the pinned-up palmettos looked as if a lazy green monkey had walked up and down and around the walls leaving green prints of his hands and feet.

She got through the room and his hands were still in his pockets, and she fell upon the closed door to the other room and pushed it open. She ran to Solomon's bed, calling "Solomon! Solomon!" The little shape of the old man never moved at all, wrapped under the quilt as if it were winter still.

"Solomon!" She pulled the quilt away, but there was another one under that, and she fell on her knees beside him. He made no sound except a sigh, and then she could hear in the silence the light springy steps of Cash walking and walking in the front room, and the ticking of Solomon's silver watch, which came from the bed. Old Solomon was far away in his sleep, his face looked small, relentless, and devout, as if he were walking somewhere where she could imagine the snow falling.

Then there was a noise like a hoof pawing the floor, and the door gave a creak, and Cash appeared beside her. When she looked up, Cash's face was so black it was bright, and so bright and bare of pity that it looked sweet to her. She stood up and held up her head. Cash was so powerful that his presence gave her strength even when she did not need any.

Under their eyes Solomon slept. People's faces tell of things and places not known to the one who looks at them while they sleep, and while Solomon slept under the eyes of Livvie and Cash his face told them like a mythical story that all his life he had built, little scrap by little scrap, respect. A beetle could not have been more laborious or more ingenious in the task of its destiny. When Solomon was young, as he was in his picture overhead, it was the infinite thing with him, and he could see no end to the respect he would contrive and keep in a house. He had built a

lonely house, the way he would make a cage, but it grew to be
the same with him as a great monumental pyramid and sometimes
in his absorption of getting it erected he was like the builder-slaves
of Egypt who forgot or never knew the origin and meaning of
the thing to which they gave all their strength of their bodies and
used up all their days. Livvie and Cash could see that as a man
might rest from a life-labor he lay in his bed, and they could hear
how, wrapped in his quilt, he sighed to himself comfortably in
sleep, while in his dreams he might have been an ant, a beetle, a
bird, an Egyptian, assembling and carrying on his back and building
with his hands, or he might have been an old man of India or a
swaddled baby, about to smile and brush all away.

Then without warning old Solomon's eyes flew wide open
under the hedgelike brows. He was wide awake.

And instantly Cash raised his quick arm. A radiant sweat
stood on his temples. But he did not bring his arm down — it
stayed in the air, as if something might have taken hold.

It was not Livvie — she did not move. As if something said
"Wait," she stood waiting. Even while her eyes burned under
motionless lids, her lips parted in a stiff grimace, and with her
arms stiff at her sides she stood above the prone old man and the
panting young one, erect and apart.

Movement when it came came in Solomon's face. It was an
old and strict face, a frail face, but behind it, like a covered light,
came an animation that could play hide and seek, that would dart
and escape, had always escaped. The mystery flickered in him,
and invited from his eyes. It was that very mystery that Cash with
his quick arm would have to strike, and that Livvie could not
weep for. But Cash only stood holding his arm in the air, when
the gentlest flick of his great strength, almost a puff of his breath,
would have been enough, if he had known how to give it, to
send the old man over the obstruction that kept him away from
death.

If it could not be that the tiny illumination in the fragile and
ancient face caused a crisis, a mystery in the room that would not
permit a blow to fall, at least it was certain that Cash, throbbing
in his Easter clothes, felt a pang of shame that the vigor of a man
would come to such an end that he could not be struck without
warning. He took down his hand and stepped back behind Livvie,
like a round-eyed schoolboy on whose unsuspecting head the dunce
cap has been set.

"Young ones can't wait," said Solomon.

Livvie shuddered violently, and then in a gush of tears she

stooped for a glass of water and handed it to him, but he did not see her.

"So here come the young man Livvie wait for. Was no prevention. No prevention. Now I lay eyes on young man and it come to be somebody I know all the time, and been knowing since he were born in a cotton patch, and watched grow up year to year, Cash McCord, growed to size, growed up to come in my house in the end — ragged and barefoot."

Solomon gave a cough of distaste. Then he shut his eyes vigorously, and his lips began to move like a chanter's.

"When Livvie married, her husband were already somebody. He had paid great cost for his land. He spread sycamore leaves over the ground from wagon to door, day he brought her home, so her foot would not have to touch ground. He carried her through his door. Then he growed old and could not lift her, and she were still young."

Livvie's sobs followed his words like a soft melody repeating each thing as he stated it. His lips moved for a little without sound, or she cried too fervently, and unheard he might have been telling his whole life, and then he said, "God forgive Solomon for sins great and small. God forgive Solomon for carrying away too young girl for wife and keeping her away from her people and from all the young people would clamor for her back."

Then he lifted up his right hand toward Livvie where she stood by the bed and offered her his silver watch. He dangled it before her eyes, and she hushed crying; her tears stopped. For a moment the watch could be heard ticking as it always did, precisely in his proud hand. She lifted it away. Then he took hold of the quilt; then he was dead.

Livvie left Solomon dead and went out of the room. Stealthily, nearly without noise, Cash went beside her. He was like a shadow, but his shiny shoes moved over the floor in spangles, and the green downy feather shone like a light in his hat. As they reached the front room, he seized her deftly as a long black cat and dragged her hanging by the waist round and round him, while he turned in a circle, his face bent down to hers. The first moment, she kept one arm and its hand stiff and still, the one that held Solomon's watch. Then the fingers softly let go, all of her was limp, and the watch fell somewhere on the floor. It ticked away in the still room, and all at once there began outside the full song of a bird.

They moved around and around the room and into the brightness of the open door, then he stopped and shook her once.

She rested in silence in his trembling arms, unprotesting as a bird
on a nest. Outside the redbirds were flying and criss-crossing, the
sun was in all the bottles on the prisoned trees, and the young
peach was shining in the middle of them with the bursting light
of spring.

QUESTIONS

1. Of another of her stories, Eudora Welty wrote:

   > Above all I had no wish to sound mystical, but did expect
   > to sound mysterious now and then, if I could: this was a
   > circumstantial realistic story in which the reality *was* mystery.

   "Livvie," too, can be described as a "realistic story in which
   the reality *was* mystery." Which details do you find that
   make the story both "realistic" and mysterious? Why does
   the story take place shortly before Easter? Why are Cash's
   clothes "luminous" and green and brown? What do you
   make out of the fact that Cash is described as "looking like
   a vision" (page 93)?
2. To a large extent the story is one of contrast, both explicit
   and implicit. What are some of the contrasting elements? In
   your opinion, how do they reflect or illuminate the story's
   theme? Compare and contrast the four characters. Are any
   of their names significant? How?
3. Do you think Livvie feels confined? Do you feel that Livvie
   is confined? Explain.
4. Though there is a basic conflict between young Livvie and
   old Solomon, how does Miss Welty avoid a simple "good-
   bad" dichotomy?
5. What do you make of the appearance of Miss Baby Marie?
   Do you think she is introduced merely for comic relief?
6. What do you make of the bottle trees and Solomon's watch?

7
Summing Up: Reading Fiction Responsively

PLOT

1. Does the plot grow out of the characters, or does it depend on chance or coincidence? Did something relevant at first strike you as irrelevant? Do some parts continue to strike you as irrelevant? Does surprise play an important role, or does foreshadowing?
2. What was your first response to the title? What do you now think of the title?
3. How is the gist of the story embodied in the structure? For example, are certain episodes told out of chronological order? If so, were you puzzled? Annoyed? On reflection, does the arrangement of episodes seem effective? And are certain juxtapositions of happenings especially suggestive? Are certain situations repeated? If so, what do you make of the repetitions?

CHARACTER

4. Which character chiefly engages your interest?
5. What purposes do minor characters serve? Do you find some who by their similarities and differences define each other? How else is a particular character defined (words, actions — including thoughts and emotions — dress, setting, narrative point of view)? Do certain characters act differently in the same, or in a similar, situation?

6. To what extent does a character change, and (so far as you can tell) what causes the change? Or did you change your attitude toward a character not because the character changed, but because you came to know the character better? If the characters change, why and how do they change?
7. Would you say that the characters are highly individualized or, rather, highly typical (e.g., representatives of a social class or age)? Are you chiefly interested in a character's psychology, or does the character strike you as an allegorical representation?

POINT OF VIEW

8. Who tells the story? How much does the narrator know? Does the narrator strike you as reliable?
9. How does the point of view help shape the theme? After all, the basic story of "Little Red Riding Hood" remains unchanged whether told from the wolf's point of view or the girl's , but (to simplify grossly) if we hear the story from the wolf's point of view, we may feel that the story is about terrifying yet pathetic compulsive behavior; if from the girl's point of view, about terrified innocence.
10. Does the language help you to construct a picture of the narrator's attitude, strengths, and limitations? (Notice especially any figurative language, patterns of imagery.) How far can you trust the narrator? Why?

SETTING

11. Do you have a strong sense of the time and place? If not, do you think that the author should have made the setting more evident?
12. What is the relation of the setting to the plot and the characters? Would anything be lost if the setting were changed?

STYLE

13. Do you think that the style is consistent? If it isn't, what do you make out of the inconsistency?

14. How would you characterize the style? Simple? Understated? Figurative? Or what, and why?
15. How would you characterize the author's tone? Whimsical? Bitter? Cold? Or what?

THEME

16. Do you think that the title of the story is significant? Does it help you to formulate a theme?
17. Do certain passages — dialogue or description — seem to you to point especially toward the theme? Do you find certain repetitions or juxtapositions highly suggestive and helpful in directing your thoughts toward stating a theme?
18. Suppose someone asked you to state the point — the theme — of the story. Could you? And if you could, would you say that the theme of a particular story reinforces values you hold, or does it to some degree challenge them?

8
A Collection of Short Fiction

The stories of Ruth, Samson, and Joseph in the Old Testament and the parables of Jesus in the New Testament are sufficient evidence that brief narratives existed in ancient times. The short tales in Boccaccio's *Decameron* and Chaucer's *Canterbury Tales* (the latter an amazing variety of narrative poems ranging from bawdy stories to legends of saints) are medieval examples of the ancient form. But, speaking generally, short narratives before the nineteenth century were either didactic pieces, with the narrative existing for the sake of a moral point, or they were "curious and striking" tales (to use Maugham's words for his favorite kind of story) recounted in order to entertain. The contemporary short story is rather different from both these genres, which can be called the **parable** and the **anecdote.** Like the parable, the contemporary short story has a point, a meaning; but unlike the parable, it has a richness of surface as well as depth, so that it is interesting whether or not the reader goes on to ponder "the meaning." The short story, like the anecdote, relates a happening, but whereas the happening in the anecdote is curious and is the center of interest, the happening in the contemporary story often is less interesting in itself than as a manifestation of a character's state of mind. A good short story usually has a psychological interest that an anecdote lacks.

The anecdotal story is what "story" means for most readers. It is an interesting happening or series of happenings, usually with a somewhat surprising ending. The anecdotal story, however, is quite different from most of the contemporary short stories in this book. The anecdote is good entertainment, and good entertainment should not be lightly dismissed. But it has two elements within it that prevent it (unless it is something in addition to an anecdote) from taking a high place among the world's literature. First, it cannot be reread with increasing or even continued pleasure. Even when it is well told, once we know the happening we may lose patience with the telling. Second, effective anecdotes are often highly implausible. Now, implausible anecdotes alleged to be true have a special impact by virtue of their alleged truth: they make us say to ourselves, "Truth is stranger than fiction." But the invented anecdote lacks this power; its unlikely coincidence, its unconvincing ironic situation, its surprise ending, are both untrue and unbelievable. It is entertaining but it is usually not especially meaningful.

The modern short story is not an anecdote and is not an abbreviated novel. If it were the latter, *Reader's Digest* condensations of novels would be short stories. But they aren't; they are only eviscerated novels. The novelist usually covers a long period of time, presenting not only a few individuals but also something of a society. He often tells of the development of several many-sided figures. In contrast, the short-story writer, having only a few pages, usually focuses on a single figure in a single episode, revealing his character rather than recording his development. Whereas the novel is narrative, the contemporary short story often seems less narrative than lyric or dramatic: in the short story we have a sense of a present mood or personality revealed, rather than the sense of a history reported. The revelation in a story is presented through incidents, of course, but the interest commonly resides in the character revealed through the incidents, rather than in the incidents themselves. Little "happens," in the sense that there is little rushing from place to place. What does "happen" is usually a mental reaction to an experience, and the mental reaction, rather than the external experience, is the heart of the story. In older narratives the plot usually involves a conflict that is resolved, bringing about a change in the protagonist's condition; in contemporary stories the plot usually is designed to reveal a protagonist's state of mind. This de-emphasis of overt actions results in an affinity with the lyric and the drama.

The de-emphasis on narrative in the contemporary short story is not an invention of the twentieth-century mind. It goes back at least to three important American writers of the early nineteenth century — Washington Irving, Nathaniel Hawthorne, and Edgar Allan Poe. In 1824 Irving wrote:

> I fancy much of what I value myself upon in writing, escapes the observation of the great mass of my readers: who are

intent more upon the story than the way in which it is told. For my part I consider a story merely as a frame on which to stretch my materials. It is the play of thought, and sentiments and language; the weaving in of characters, lightly yet expressively delineated; the familiar and faithful exhibition of scenes in common life; and the half-concealed vein of humor that is often playing through the whole — these are among what I aim at, and upon which I felicitate myself in proportion as I think I succeed.

Hawthorne and Poe may seem stranger than Irving as forebears of the contemporary short story: both are known for their fantastic narratives (and, in addition, Poe is known as the inventor of the detective story, a genre in which there is strong interest in curious happenings). But because Hawthorne's fantastic narratives are, as he said, highly allegorical, the reader's interest is pushed beyond the narrative to the moral significance. Poe's "arabesques," as he called his fanciful tales (in distinction from his detective tales of "ratiocination"), are aimed at revealing and arousing unusual mental states. The weird happenings and personages are symbolic representations of the mind or soul. In "The Fall of the House of Usher" the twins Roderick and Madeline probably represent complementary parts of a single personality, just as the house described in the poem within this story represents a person: the "banners yellow" are hair, the "two luminous windows" are eyes, the "fair palace door" of "pearl and ruby" is a mouth, and so on. But, it must be noted, in both Hawthorne and Poe we usually get what is commonly called the **tale** rather than the **short story**: we get short prose fiction dealing with the strange rather than the usual. (This distinction between the wondrous and the ordinary is discussed at some length in Chapter 8, "Observations on the Novel," page 400.)

   A paragraph from Poe's review (1842) of Hawthorne's *Twice Told Tales,* though more useful in revealing Poe's theory of fiction than Hawthorne's, illuminates something of the kinship between the contemporary short story and the best short fictions of the earlier nineteenth century. In the review Poe has been explaining that because "unity of effect or impression" is essential, a tale (Poe doubtless uses "tale" to mean short fiction in general, rather than the special type just discussed) that can be read at a single sitting has an advantage over the novel:

> A skillful artist has constructed a tale. He has not fashioned his thoughts to accommodate his incidents, but having deliberately conceived a certain single effect to be wrought, he then invents such incidents, he then combines such events,

and discusses them in such tone as may best serve him in establishing this preconceived effect. If his very first sentence tends not to the outbringing of this effect, then in his very first step has he committed a blunder. In the whole composition there should be no word written of which the tendency, direct or indirect, is not to the one pre-established design. And by such means, with such care and skill a picture is at length painted which leaves in the mind of him who contemplates it with a kindred art, a sense of the fullest satisfaction. The idea of the tale, its thesis, has been presented unblemished, because undisturbed — an end absolutely demanded, yet, in the novel, altogether unattainable.

Nothing that has been said here should be construed as suggesting that contemporary short stories are necessarily better than older short narratives. The object of these comments has not been to evaluate, but to call attention to the characteristics dominating most good contemporary brief fiction. Furthermore, it should not be thought that contemporary fiction is all of a piece; the preceding stories have already demonstrated its variety. The following are also varied; if the reader does not like one, he or she need not despair; he or she need only (in Chaucer's words) "turne over the leef and chese another tale."

Nathaniel Hawthorne (*American. 1804–1864*)

Young Goodman Brown

Young Goodman Brown came forth at sunset into the street at Salem village; but put his head back, after crossing the threshold, to exchange a parting kiss with his young wife. And Faith, as the wife was aptly named, thrust her own pretty head into the street, letting the wind play with the pink ribbons of her cap while she called to Goodman Brown.

"Dearest heart," whispered she, softly and rather sadly, when her lips were close to his ear, "prithee put off your journey until sunrise and sleep in your own bed to-night. A lone woman is troubled with such dreams and such thoughts that she's afeared of herself sometimes. Pray tarry with me this night, dear husband, of all nights in the year."

"My love and my Faith," replied young Goodman Brown, "of all nights in the year, this one night must I tarry away from thee. My journey, as thou callest it, forth and back again, must needs be done 'twixt now and sunrise. What, my sweet, pretty wife, dost thou doubt me already, and we but three months married?"

"Then God bless you!" said Faith, with the pink ribbons; "and may you find all well when you come back."

"Amen!" cried Goodman Brown. "Say thy prayers, dear Faith, and go to bed at dusk, and no harm will come to thee."

So they parted; and the young man pursued his way until, being about to turn the corner by the meeting-house, he looked back and saw the head of Faith still peeping after him with a melancholy air, in spite of her pink ribbons.

"Poor little Faith!" thought he, for his heart smote him. "What a wretch am I to leave her on such an errand! She talks of dreams, too. Methought as she spoke there was trouble in her face, as if a dream had warned her what work is to be done to-night. But no, no; 'twould kill her to think it. Well, she's a blessed angel on earth; and after this one night I'll cling to her skirts and follow her to heaven."

With this excellent resolve for the future, Goodman Brown felt himself justified in making more haste on his present evil purpose. He had taken a dreary road, darkened by all the gloomiest trees of the forest, which barely stood aside to let the narrow path creep through, and closed immediately behind. It was all as lonely as could be; and there is this peculiarity in such a solitude, that the traveller knows not who may be concealed by the innumerable trunks and the thick boughs overhead; so that with lonely footsteps he may yet be passing through an unseen multitude.

"There may be a devilish Indian behind every tree," said Goodman Brown to himself and he glanced fearfully behind him as he added, "What if the devil himself should be at my very elbow!"

His head being turned back, he passed a crook of the road, and, looking forward again, beheld the figure of a man, in grave and decent attire, seated at the foot of an old tree. He arose at Goodman Brown's approach and walked onward side by side with him.

"You are late, Goodman Brown," said he. "The clock of the Old South was striking as I came through Boston, and that is full fifteen minutes agone."

"Faith kept me back a while," replied the young man, with a tremor in his voice, caused by the sudden appearance of his companion, though not wholly unexpected.

It was now deep dusk in the forest, and deepest in that part of it where these two were journeying. As nearly as could be discerned, the second traveller was about fifty years old, apparently in the same rank of life as Goodman Brown, and bearing a considerable resemblance to him, though perhaps more in expression than features. Still they might have been taken for father and son. And yet, though the elder person was as simply clad as the younger, and as simple in manner too, he had an indescribable air of one who knew the world, and who would not have felt abashed at the governor's dinner table or in King William's court, were it possible that his affairs should call him thither. But the only thing about him that could be fixed upon as remarkable was his staff, which bore the likeness of a great black snake, so curiously wrought that it might almost be seen to twist and wriggle itself like a living serpent. This, of course, must have been an ocular deception, assisted by the uncertain light.

"Come, Goodman Brown," cried his fellow-traveller, "this is a dull pace for the beginning of a journey. Take my staff, if you are so soon weary."

"Friend," said the other, exchanging his slow pace for a full stop, "having kept covenant by meeting thee here, it is my purpose now to return whence I came. I have scruples touching the matter thou wot'st of."

"Sayest thou so?" replied he of the serpent, smiling apart. "Let us walk on, nevertheless, reasoning as we go; and if I convince thee not thou shalt turn back. We are but a little way in the forest yet."

"Too far! too far!" exclaimed the goodman, unconsciously resuming his walk. "My father never went into the woods on such an errand, nor his father before him. We have been a race of honest men and good Christians since the days of the martyrs; and shall I be the first of the name of Brown that ever took this path and kept —"

"Such company, thou wouldst say," observed the elder person, interpreting his pause. "Well said, Goodman Brown! I have been as well acquainted with your family as with ever a one among the Puritans; and that's no trifle to say. I helped your grandfather, the constable, when he lashed the Quaker woman so smartly through the streets of Salem; and it was I that brought your father a pitch-pine knot, kindled at my own hearth, to set fire to an Indian village, in King Philip's war. They were my good friends, both; and many a pleasant walk have we had along this path, and returned merrily after midnight. I would fain be friends with you for their sake."

"If it be as thou sayest," replied Goodman Brown, "I marvel

they never spoke of these matters; or, verily, I marvel not, seeing that the least rumor of the sort would have driven them from New England. We are a people of prayer, and good works to boot, and abide no such wickedness."

"Wickedness or not," said the traveller with the twisted staff, "I have a very general acquaintance here in New England. The deacons of many a church have drunk the communion wine with me; the selectmen of divers towns make me their chairman; and a majority of the Great and General Court are firm supporters of my interest. The governor and I, too — But these are state secrets."

"Can this be so?" cried Goodman Brown, with a stare of amazement at his undisturbed companion. "Howbeit, I have nothing to do with the governor and council; they have their own ways, and are no rule for a simple husbandman like me. But, were I to go on with thee, how should I meet the eye of that good old man, or minister, at Salem village? Oh, his voice would make me tremble both Sabbath day and lecture day."

Thus far the elder traveller had listened with due gravity; but now burst into a fit of irrepressible mirth, shaking himself so violently that his snake-like staff actually seemed to wriggle in sympathy.

"Ha! ha! ha!" shouted he again and again; then composing himself, "Well, go on, Goodman Brown, go on; but, prithee, don't kill me with laughing."

"Well, then, to end the matter at once," said Goodman Brown, considerably nettled, "there is my wife, Faith. It would break her dear little heart; and I'd rather break my own."

"Nay, if that be the case," answered the other, "e'en go thy ways, Goodman Brown. I would not for twenty old women like the one hobbling before us that Faith should come to any harm."

As he spoke he pointed his staff at a female figure on the path, in whom Goodman Brown recognized a very pious and exemplary dame, who had taught him his catechism in youth, and was still his moral and spiritual adviser, jointly with the minister and Deacon Gookin.

"A marvel, truly, that Goody Cloyse should be so far in the wilderness at nightfall," said he. "But with your leave, friend, I shall take a cut through the woods until we have left this Christian woman behind. Being a stranger to you, she might ask whom I was consorting with and whither I was going."

"Be it so," said his fellow-traveller. "Betake you the woods, and let me keep the path."

Accordingly the young man turned aside, but took care to

watch his companion, who advanced softly along the road until he had come within a staff's length of the old dame. She, meanwhile, was making the best of her way, with singular speed for so aged a woman, and mumbling some indistinct words — a prayer, doubtless — as she went. The traveller put forth his staff and touched her withered neck with what seemed the serpent's tail.

"The devil!" screamed the pious old lady.

"Then Goody Cloyse knows her old friend?" observed the traveller, confronting her and leaning on his writing stick.

"Ah, forsooth, and is it your worship indeed?" cried the good dame. "Yea, truly is it, and in the very image of my old gossip, Goodman Brown, the grandfather of the silly fellow that now is. But — would your worship believe it? — my broomstick hath strangely disappeared, stolen, as I suspect, by that unhanged witch, Goody Cory, and that, too, when I was all anointed with the juice of smallage, and cinquefoil, and wolf's bane —"

"Mingled with fine wheat and the fat of a new-born babe," said the shape of old Goodman Brown.

"Ah, your worship knows the recipe," cried the old lady, cackling aloud. "So, as I was saying, being all ready for the meeting, and no horse to ride on, I made up my mind to foot it; for they tell me there is a nice young man to be taken into communion tonight. But now your good worship will lend me your arm, and we shall be there in a twinkling."

"That can hardly be," answered her friend. "I may not spare you my arm, Goody Cloyse; but here is my staff, if you will."

So saying, he threw it down at her feet, where, perhaps, it assumed life, being one of the rods which its owner had formerly lent to the Egyptian magi. Of this fact, however, Goodman Brown could not take cognizance. He had cast up his eyes in astonishment, and, looking down again, beheld neither Goody Cloyse nor the serpentine staff but his fellow-traveller alone, who waited for him as calmly as if nothing had happened.

"That old woman taught me my catechism," said the young man; and there was a world of meaning in this simple comment.

They continued to walk onward, while the elder traveller exhorted his companion to make good speed and persevere in the path, discoursing so aptly that his arguments seemed rather to spring up in the bosom of his auditor than to be suggested by himself. As they went, he plucked a branch of maple to serve for a walking stick, and began to strip it of the twigs and little boughs, which were wet with evening dew. The moment his fingers touched them they became strangely withered and dried up as with a week's sunshine. Thus the pair proceeded, at a good free pace, until suddenly, in a gloomy hollow of the road, Goodman Brown sat himself down on the stump of a tree and refused to go any farther.

"Friend," said he, stubbornly, "my mind is made up. Not another step will I budge on this errand. What if a wretched old woman do choose to go to the devil when I thought she was going to heaven: is that any reason why I should quit my dear Faith and go after her?"

"You will think better of this by and by," said his acquaintance, composedly. "Sit here and rest yourself a while; and when you feel like moving again, there is my staff to help you along."

Without more words, he threw his companion the maple stick, and was as speedily out of sight as if he had vanished into the deepening gloom. The young man sat a few moments by the roadside, applauding himself greatly, and thinking with how clear a conscience he should meet the minister in his morning walk, nor shrink from the eye of good old Deacon Gookin. And what calm sleep would be his that very night, which was to have been spent so wickedly, but so purely and sweetly now, in the arms of Faith! Amidst these pleasant and praiseworthy meditations, Goodman Brown heard the tramp of horses along the road, and deemed it advisable to conceal himself within the verge of the forest, conscious of the guilty purpose that had brought him thither, though now so happily turned from it.

On came the hoof tramps and the voices of the riders, two grave old voices, conversing soberly as they drew near. These mingled sounds appeared to pass along the road, within a few yards of the young man's hiding-place; but, owing doubtless to the depth of the gloom at that particular spot, neither the travellers nor their steeds were visible. Though their figures brushed the small boughs by the wayside, it could not be seen that they intercepted, even for a moment, the faint gleam from the strip of bright sky athwart which they must have passed. Goodman Brown alternately crouched and stood on tiptoe, pulling aside the branches and thrusting forth his head as far as he durst without discerning so much as a shadow. It vexed him the more, because he could have sworn, were such a thing possible, that he recognized the voices of the minister and Deacon Gookin, jogging along quietly, as they were wont to do, when bound to some ordination or ecclesiastical council. While yet within hearing, one of the riders stopped to pluck a switch.

"Of the two, reverend sir," said the voice like the deacon's, "I had rather miss an ordination dinner than to-night's meeting. They tell me that some of our community are to be here from

Falmouth and beyond, and others from Connecticut and Rhode Island, besides several of the Indian powwows, who, after their fashion, know almost as much deviltry as the best of us. Moreover, there is a goodly young woman to be taken into communion."

"Mighty well, Deacon Gookin!" replied the solemn old tones of the minister. "Spur up, or we shall be late. Nothing can be done, you know, until I get on the ground."

The hoofs clattered again; and the voices, talking so strangely in the empty air, passed on through the forest, where no church had ever been gathered or solitary Christian prayed. Whither, then, could these holy men be journeying so deep into the heathen wilderness? Young Goodman Brown caught hold of a tree for support, being ready to sink down on the ground, faint and over-burdened with the heavy sickness of his heart. He looked up to the sky, doubting whether there really was a heaven above him. Yet there was the blue arch, and the stars brightening in it.

"With heaven above and Faith below, I will yet stand firm against the devil!" cried Goodman Brown.

While he still gazed upward into the deep arch of the firmament and had lifted his hands to pray, a cloud, though no wind was stirring, hurried across the zenith and hid the brightening stars. The blue sky was still visible, except directly overhead, where this black mass of cloud was sweeping swiftly northward. Aloft in the air, as if from the depths of the cloud, came a confused and doubtful sound of voices. Once the listener fancied that he could distinguish the accents of townspeople of his own, men and women, both pious and ungodly, many of whom he had met at the com-munion table, and had seen others rioting at the tavern. The next moment, so indistinct were the sounds, he doubted whether he had heard aught but the murmur of the old forest, whispering without a wind. Then came a stronger swell of those familiar tones, heard daily in the sunshine at Salem village, but never until now from a cloud of night. There was one voice, of a young woman, uttering lamentations, yet with an uncertain sorrow, and entreating for some favor, which, perhaps, it would grieve her to obtain; and all the unseen multitude, both saints and sinners, seemed to encourage her onward.

"Faith!" shouted Goodman Brown, in a voice of agony and desperation; and the echoes of the forest mocked him, crying, "Faith! Faith!" as if bewildered wretches were seeking her all through the wilderness.

The cry of grief, rage, and terror was yet piercing the night, when the unhappy husband held his breath for a response. There was a scream, drowned immediately in a louder murmur of voices,

fading into far-off laughter, as the dark cloud swept away, leaving
the clear and silent sky above Goodman Brown. But something
fluttered lightly down through the air and caught on the branch
of a tree. The young man seized it, and beheld a pink ribbon.

"My Faith is gone!" cried he, after one stupefied moment.
"There is no good on earth; and sin is but a name. Come, devil;
for to thee is this world given."

And, maddened with despair, so that he laughed loud and
long, did Goodman Brown grasp his staff and set forth again, at
such a rate that he seemed to fly along the forest path rather than
to walk or run. The road grew wilder and drearier and more
faintly traced, and vanished at length, leaving him in the heart of
the dark wilderness, still rushing onward with the instinct that
guides mortal man to evil. The whole forest was peopled with
frightful sounds — the creaking of the trees, the howling of wild
beasts, and the yell of Indians; while sometimes the wind tolled
like a distant church bell, and sometimes gave a broad roar around
the traveller, as if all Nature were laughing him to scorn. But he
was himself the chief horror of the scene, and shrank not from
its other horrors.

"Ha! ha! ha!" roared Goodman Brown when the wind laughed
at him. "Let us hear which will laugh loudest. Think not to
frighten me with your deviltry. Come witch, come wizard, come
Indian powwow, come devil himself, and here comes Goodman
Brown. You may as well fear him as he fear you."

In truth, all through the haunted forest there could be nothing
more frightful than the figure of Goodman Brown. On he flew
among the black pines, brandishing his staff with frenzied gestures,
now giving vent to an inspiration of horrid blasphemy, and now
shouting forth such laughter as set all the echoes of the forest
laughing like demons around him. The fiend in his own shape is
less hideous than when he rages in the breast of man. Thus sped
the demoniac on his course, until, quivering among the trees, he
saw a red light before him, as when the felled trunks and branches
of a clearing have been set on fire, and throw up their lurid blaze
against the sky, at the hour of midnight. He paused, in a lull of
the tempest that had driven him onward, and heard the swell of
what seemed a hymn, rolling solemnly from a distance with the
weight of many voices. He knew the tune; it was a familiar one
in the choir of the village meeting-house. The verse died heavily
away, and was lengthened by a chorus, not of human voices, but
of all the sounds of the benighted wilderness pealing in awful
harmony together. Goodman Brown cried out, and his cry was
lost to his own ear by its unison with the cry of the desert.

In the interval of silence he stole forward until the light glared full upon his eyes. At one extremity of an open space, hemmed in by the dark wall of the forest, arose a rock, bearing some rude, natural resemblance either to an altar or a pulpit, and surrounded by four blazing pines, their tops aflame, their stems untouched, like candles at an evening meeting. The mass of foliage that had overgrown the summit of the rock was all on fire, blazing high into the night and fitfully illuminating the whole field. Each pendent twig and leafy festoon was in a blaze. As the red light arose and fell, a numerous congregation alternately shone forth, then disappeared in shadow, and again grew, as it were, out of the darkness, peopling the heart of the solitary woods at once.

"A grave and dark-clad company," quoth Goodman Brown.

In truth they were such. Among them, quivering to and fro between gloom and splendor, appeared faces that would be seen next day at the council board of the province, and others which, Sabbath after Sabbath, looked devoutly heavenward, and benignantly over the crowded pews, from the holiest pulpits in the land. Some affirm that the lady of the governor was there. At least there were high dames well known to her, and wives of honored husbands, and widows, a great multitude, and ancient maidens, all of excellent repute, and fair young girls, who trembled lest their mothers should espy them. Either the sudden gleams of light flashing over the obscure field bedazzled Goodman Brown, or he recognized a score of the church members of Salem village famous for their especial sanctity. Good old Deacon Gookin had arrived, and waited at the skirts of that venerable saint, his revered pastor. But, irreverently consorting with these grave, reputable, and pious people, these elders of the church, these chaste dames and dewy virgins, there were men of dissolute lives and women of spotted fame, wretches given over to all mean and filthy vice, and suspected even of horrid crimes. It was strange to see that the good shrank not from the wicked, nor were the sinners abashed by the saints. Scattered also among their pale-faced enemies were the Indian priests, or powwows, who had often scared their native forest with more hideous incantations than any known to English witchcraft.

"But where is Faith?" thought Goodman Brown; and, as hope came into his heart, he trembled.

Another verse of the hymn arose, a slow and mournful strain, such as the pious love, but joined to words which expressed all that our nature can conceive of sin, and darkly hinted at far more. Unfathomable to mere mortals is the lore of fiends. Verse after verse was sung; and still the chorus of the desert swelled between like the deepest tone of a mighty organ; and with the final peal of that dreadful anthem there came a sound, as if the roaring wind, the rushing streams, the howling beasts, and every other voice of the unconcerted wilderness were mingling and according with the voice of guilty man in homage to the prince of all. The four blazing pines threw up a loftier flame, and obscurely discovered shapes and visages of horror on the smoke wreaths above the impious assembly. At the same moment the fire on the rock shot redly forth and formed a glowing arch above its base, where now appeared a figure. With reverence be it spoken, the figure bore no slight similitude, both in garb and manner, to some grave divine of the New England churches.

"Bring forth the converts!" cried a voice that echoed through the field and rolled into the forest.

At the word, Goodman Brown stepped forth from the shadow of the trees and approached the congregation, with whom he felt a loathful brotherhood by the sympathy of all that was wicked in his heart. He could have well-nigh sworn that the shape of his own dead father beckoned him to advance, looking downward from a smoke wreath, while a woman, with dim features of despair, threw out her hand to warn him back. Was it his mother? But he had no power to retreat one step, nor to resist, even in thought, when the minister and good old Deacon Gookin seized his arms and led him to the blazing rock. Thither came also the slender form of a veiled female, led between Goody Cloyse, that pious teacher of the catechism, and Martha Carrier, who had received the devil's promise to be queen of hell. A rampant hag was she. And there stood the proselytes beneath the canopy of fire.

"Welcome, my children," said the dark figure, "to the communion of your race. Ye have found thus young your nature and your destiny. My children, look behind you!"

They turned; and flashing forth, as it were, in a sheet of flame, the fiend worshippers were seen; the smile of welcome gleamed darkly on every visage.

"There," resumed the sable form, "are all whom ye have reverenced from youth. Ye deemed them holier than yourselves, and shrank from your own sin, contrasting it with their lives of righteousness and prayerful aspirations heavenward. Yet here are they all in my worshipping assembly. This night it shall be granted you to know their secret deeds: how hoary-bearded elders of the church have whispered wanton words to the young maids of their households; how many a woman, eager for widows' weeds, has given her husband a drink at bedtime and let him sleep his last sleep in her bosom; how beardless youths have made haste to inherit their fathers' wealth; and how fair damsels — blush not, sweet ones — have dug little graves in the garden, and bidden me, the sole guest, to an infant's funeral. By the sympathy of your human hearts for sin ye shall scent out all the places — whether in church, bed-chamber, street, field, or forest — where crime has been committed, and shall exult to behold the whole earth one stain of guilt, one mighty blood spot. Far more than this. It shall be yours to penetrate, in every bosom, the deep mystery of sin, the fountain of all wicked arts, and which inexhaustibly supplies more evil impulses than human power — than my power at its utmost — can make manifest in deeds. And now, my children, look upon each other."

They did so; and, by the blaze of the hell-kindled torches, the wretched man beheld his Faith, and the wife her husband, trembling before that unhallowed altar.

"Lo, there ye stand, my children," said the figure, in a deep and solemn tone, almost sad with its despairing awfulness, as if his once angelic nature could yet mourn for our miserable race. "Depending upon one another's hearts, ye had still hoped that virtue were not all a dream. Now are ye undeceived. Evil is the nature of mankind. Evil must be your only happiness. Welcome again, my children, to the communion of your race."

"Welcome," repeated the fiend worshippers, in one cry of despair and triumph.

And there they stood, the only pair, as it seemed, who were yet hesitating on the verge of wickedness in this dark world. A basin was hollowed, naturally, in the rock. Did it contain water, reddened by the lurid light! or was it blood? or, perchance, a liquid flame? Herein did the shape of evil dip his hand and prepare to lay the mark of baptism upon their foreheads, that they might be partakers of the mystery of sin, more conscious of the secret guilt of others, both in deed and thought, than they could now be of their own. The husband cast one look at his pale wife, and Faith at him. What polluted wretches would the next glance show them to each other, shuddering alike at what they disclosed and what they saw!

"Faith! Faith!" cried the husband, "look up to heaven, and resist the wicked one."

Whether Faith obeyed he knew not. Hardly had he spoken when he found himself amid calm night and solitude, listening to a roar of the wind which died heavily away through the forest. He staggered against the rock, and felt it chill and damp; while a hanging twig, that had been all on fire, besprinkled his cheek with the coldest dew.

The next morning young Goodman Brown came slowly into the street of Salem village, staring around him like a bewildered man. The good old minister was taking a walk along the graveyard to get an appetite for breakfast and meditate his sermon, and bestowed a blessing, as he passed, on Goodman Brown. He shrank from the venerable saint as if to avoid an anathema. Old Deacon Gookin was at domestic worship, and the holy words of his prayer were heard through the open window. "What God doth the wizard pray to?" quoth Goodman Brown. Goody Cloyse, that excellent old Christian, stood in the early sunshine at her own lattice, catechizing a little girl who had brought her a pint of morning's milk. Goodman Brown snatched away the child as from the grasp of the fiend himself. Turning the corner by the meeting-house, he spied the head of Faith, with the pink ribbons, gazing anxiously forth, and bursting into such joy at sight of him that she skipped along the street and almost kissed her husband before the whole village. But Goodman Brown looked sternly and sadly into her face, and passed on without a greeting.

Had Goodman Brown fallen asleep in the forest and only dreamed a wild dream of a witch-meeting?

Be it so if you will; but, alas! it was a dream of evil omen for young Goodman Brown. A stern, a sad, a darkly meditative, a distrustful, if not a desperate man did he become from the night of that fearful dream. On the Sabbath day, when the congregation were singing a holy psalm, he could not listen because an anthem of sin rushed loudly upon his ear and drowned all the blessed strain. When the minister spoke from the pulpit with power and fervid eloquence, and, with his hand on the open Bible, of the sacred truths of our religion, and of saint-like lives and triumphant deaths, and of future bliss or misery unutterable, then did Goodman Brown turn pale, dreading lest the roof should thunder down upon the gray blasphemer and his hearers. Often, awaking suddenly at midnight, he shrank from the bosom of Faith; and at morning or eventide, when the family knelt down at prayer, he scowled and muttered to himself, and gazed sternly at his wife, and turned away. And when he had lived long, and was borne to his grave a hoary corpse, followed by Faith, an aged woman, and children and grandchildren, a goodly procession, besides neighbors not a few, they carved no hopeful verse upon his tombstone, for his dying hour was gloom.

Edgar Allan Poe (American. 1809–1849)

The Cask of Amontillado

The thousand injuries of Fortunato I had borne as I best could, but when he ventured upon insult, I vowed revenge. You, who so well know the nature of my soul, will not suppose, however, that I gave utterance to a threat. *At length* I would be avenged; this was a point definitely settled — but the very definitiveness with which it was resolved precluded the idea of risk. I must not only punish, but punish with impunity. A wrong is unredressed when retribution overtakes its redresser. It is equally unredressed when the avenger fails to make himself felt as such to him who has done the wrong.

It must be understood that neither by word nor deed had I given Fortunato cause to doubt my good will. I continued, as was my wont, to smile in his face, and he did not perceive that my smile *now* was at the thought of his immolation.

He had a weak point — this Fortunato — although in other regards he was a man to be respected and even feared. He prided himself on his connoisseurship in wine. Few Italians have the true virtuoso spirit. For the most part their enthusiasm is adopted to suit the time and opportunity to practice imposture upon the British and Austrian *millionaires*. In painting and gemmary Fortunato, like his countrymen, was a quack, but in the matter of old wines he was sincere. In this respect I did not differ from him materially; — I was skillful in the Italian vintages myself, and bought largely whenever I could.

It was about dusk, one evening during the supreme madness of the carnival season, that I encountered my friend. He accosted me with excessive warmth, for he had been drinking much. The man wore motley. He had on a tight-fitting parti-striped dress, and his head was surmounted by the conical cap and bells. I was so pleased to see him, that I thought I should never have done wringing his hand.

I said to him — "My dear Fortunato, you are luckily met. How remarkably well you are looking to-day! But I have received a pipe° of what passes for Amontillado, and I have my doubts."

"How?" said he, "Amontillado? A pipe? Impossible! And in the middle of the carnival?"

"I have my doubts," I replied; "and I was silly enough to

pipe wine cask

pay the full Amontillado price without consulting you in the matter. You were not to be found, and I was fearful of losing a bargain."

"Amontillado!"

"I have my doubts."

"Amontillado!"

"And I must satisfy them."

"Amontillado!"

"As you are engaged, I am on my way to Luchesi. If any one has a critical turn, it is he. He will tell me —"

"Luchesi cannot tell Amontillado from Sherry."

"And yet some fools will have it that his taste is a match for your own."

"Come, let us go."

"Whither?"

"To your vaults."

"My friend, no; I will not impose upon your good nature. I perceive you have an engagement. Luchesi —"

"I have no engagement; come."

"My friend, no. It is not the engagement, but the severe cold with which I perceive you are afflicted. The vaults are insufferably damp. They are encrusted with nitre."

"Let us go, nevertheless. The cold is merely nothing. Amontillado! You have been imposed upon; and as for Luchesi, he cannot distinguish Sherry from Amontillado."

Thus speaking, Fortunato possessed himself of my arm. Putting on a mask of black silk, and drawing a *roquelaure*° closely about my person, I suffered him to hurry me to my palazzo.

There were no attendants at home; they had absconded to make merry in honor of the time. I had told them that I should not return until the morning, and had given them explicit orders not to stir from the house. These orders were sufficient, I well knew, to insure their immediate disappearance, one and all, as soon as my back was turned.

I took from their sconces two flambeaux, and giving one to Fortunato, bowed him through several suites of rooms to the archway that led into the vaults. I passed down a long and winding staircase, requesting him to be cautious as he followed. We came at length to the foot of the descent, and stood together on the damp ground of the catacombs of the Montresors.

The gait of my friend was unsteady, and the bells upon his cap jingled as he strode.

"The pipe," said he.

---

roquelaure   short cloak

"It is farther on," said I; "but observe the white web-work which gleams from these cavern walls."

He turned towards me, and looked into my eyes with two filmy orbs that distilled the rheum of intoxication.

"Nitre?" he asked, at length.

"Nitre," I replied. "How long have you had that cough?"

"Ugh! ugh! ugh! — ugh! ugh! ugh! — ugh! ugh! ugh! — ugh! ugh! ugh! — ugh! ugh! ugh!"

My poor friend found it impossible to reply for many minutes.

"It is nothing," he said, at last.

"Come," I said, with decision, "we will go back; your health is precious. You are rich, respected, admired, beloved; you are happy, as once I was. You are a man to be missed. For me it is no matter. We will go back; you will be ill, and I cannot be responsible. Besides, there is Luchesi —"

"Enough," he said; "the cough is a mere nothing: it will not kill me. I shall not die of a cough."

"True — true," I replied; "and, indeed, I had no intention of alarming you unnecessarily — but you should use all proper caution. A draught of this Medoc will defend us from the damps."

Here I knocked off the neck of a bottle which I drew from a long row of its fellows that lay upon the mould.

"Drink," I said, presenting him the wine.

He raised it to his lips with a leer. He paused and nodded to me familiarly, while his bells jingled.

"I drink," he said, "to the buried that repose around us."

"And I to your long life."

He again took my arm, and we proceeded.

"These vaults," he said, "are extensive."

"The Montresors," I replied, "were a great and numerous family."

"I forget your arms."

"A huge human foot d'or, in a field azure; the foot crushes a serpent rampant whose fangs are imbedded in the heel."

"And the motto?"

"*Nemo me impune lacessit.*"°

"Good!" he said.

The wine sparkled in his eyes and the bells jingled. My own fancy grew warm with the Medoc. We had passed through walls of piled bones, with casks and puncheons intermingling, into the

---

Nemo me impune lacessit No one dare attack me with impunity (the motto of Scotland)

inmost recesses of the catacombs. I paused again, and this time I made bold to seize Fortunato by an arm above the elbow.

"The nitre!" I said; "see, it increases. It hangs like moss upon the vaults. We are below the river's bed. The drops of moisture trickle among the bones. Come, we will go back ere it is too late. Your cough —"

"It is nothing," he said; "let us go on. But first, another draught of the Medoc."

I broke and reached him a flagon of De Grâve. He emptied it at a breath. His eyes flashed with a fierce light. He laughed and threw the bottle upwards with a gesticulation I did not understand.

I looked at him in surprise. He repeated the movement — a grotesque one.

"You do not comprehend?" he said.

"Not I," I replied.

"Then you are not of the brotherhood."

"How?"

"You are not of the masons."

"Yes, yes," I said, "yes, yes."

"You? Impossible! A mason?"

"A mason," I replied.

"A sign," he said.

"It is this," I answered, producing a trowel from beneath the folds of my *roquelaure.*

"You jest," he exclaimed, recoiling a few paces. "But let us proceed to the Amontillado."

"Be it so," I said, replacing the tool beneath the cloak, and again offering him my arm. He leaned upon it heavily. We continued our route in search of the Amontillado. We passed through a range of low arches, descended, passed on, and descending again, arrived at a deep crypt, in which the foulness of the air caused our flambeaux rather to glow than flame.

At the most remote end of the crypt there appeared another less spacious. Its walls had been lined with human remains piled to the vault overhead, in the fashion of the great catacombs of Paris. Three sides of this interior crypt were still ornamented in this manner. From the fourth the bones had been thrown down, and lay promiscuously upon the earth, forming at one point a mound of some size. Within the wall thus exposed by the displacing of the bones, we perceived a still interior recess, in depth about four feet, in width three, in height six or seven. It seemed to have been constructed for no especial use within itself, but formed merely the interval between two of the colossal supports of the roof of the catacombs, and was backed by one of their circumscribing walls of solid granite.

It was in vain that Fortunato, uplifting his dull torch, endeavored to pry into the depths of the recess. Its termination the feeble light did not enable us to see.

"Proceed," I said; "herein is the Amontillado. As for Luchesi —"

"He is an ignoramus," interrupted my friend, as he stepped unsteadily forward, while I followed immediately at his heels. In an instant he had reached the extremity of the niche, and finding his progress arrested by the rock, stood stupidly bewildered. A moment more and I had fettered him to the granite. In its surface were two iron staples, distant from each other about two feet, horizontally. From one of these depended a short chain, from the other a padlock. Throwing the links about his waist, it was but the work of a few seconds to secure it. He was too much astounded to resist. Withdrawing the key I stepped back from the recess.

"Pass your hand," I said, "over the wall; you cannot help feeling the nitre. Indeed it is *very* damp. Once more let me *implore* you to return. No? Then I must positively leave you. But I must first render you all the little attentions in my power."

"The Amontillado!" ejaculated my friend, not yet recovered from his astonishment.

"True," I replied; "the Amontillado."

As I said these words I busied myself among the pile of bones of which I have before spoken. Throwing them aside, I soon uncovered a quantity of building-stone and mortar. With these materials and with the aid of my trowel, I began vigorously to wall up the entrance of the niche.

I had scarcely laid the first tier of masonry when I discovered that the intoxication of Fortunato had in a great measure worn off. The earliest indication I had of this was a low moaning cry from the depth of the recess. It was *not* the cry of a drunken man. There was then a long and obstinate silence. I laid the second tier, and the third, and the fourth; and then I heard the furious vibrations of the chain. The noise lasted for several minutes, during which, that I might hearken to it with the more satisfaction, I ceased my labors and sat down upon the bones. When at last the clanking subsided, I resumed the trowel, and finished without interruption the fifth, the sixth, and the seventh tier. The wall was now nearly upon a level with my breast. I again paused, and holding the flambeaux over the masonwork, threw a few feeble rays upon the figure within.

A succession of loud and shrill screams, bursting suddenly from the throat of the chained form, seemed to thrust me violently back. For a brief moment I hesitated — I trembled. Unsheathing my rapier, I began to grope with it about the recess; but the thought of an instant reassured me. I placed my hand upon the solid fabric of the catacombs, and felt satisfied. I reapproached the wall. I replied to the yells of him who clamored. I re-echoed — I aided — I surpassed them in volume and in strength. I did this, and the clamorer grew still.

It was now midnight, and my task was drawing to a close. I had completed the eighth, the ninth, and the tenth tier. I had finished a portion of the last and the eleventh; there remained but a single stone to be fitted and plastered in. I struggled with its weight; I placed it partially in its destined position. But now there came from out the niche a low laugh that erected the hairs upon my head. It was succeeded by a sad voice, which I had difficulty in recognizing as that of the noble Fortunato. The voice said —

"Ha! ha! ha! — he! he! he! — a very good joke indeed — an excellent jest. We will have many a rich laugh about it at the palazzo — he! he! he! — over our wine — he! he! he!"

"The Amontillado!" I said.

"He! he! he! — he! he! he! — yes, the Amontillado. But is it not getting late? Will not they be awaiting us at the palazzo, the Lady Fortunato and the rest? Let us be gone."

"Yes," I said, "let us be gone."

"For the love of God, Montresor!"

"Yes," I said, "for the love of God!"

But to these words I hearkened in vain for a reply. I grew impatient. I called aloud;

"Fortunato!"

No answer. I called again;

"Fortunato!"

No answer still, I thrust a torch through the remaining aperture and let it fall within. There came forth in return only a jingling of the bells. My heart grew sick — on account of the dampness of the catacombs. I hastened to make an end of my labor. I forced the last stone into its position; I plastered it up. Against the new masonry I reerected the old rampart of bones. For the half of a century no mortal has disturbed them. *In pace requiescat!*°

In pace requiescat!   May he rest in peace!

Anton Chekhov (*Russian. 1860–1904*)

The Lady with the Pet Dog

Translated by Avrahm Yarmolinsky

I

A new person, it was said, had appeared on the esplanade: a lady with a pet dog. Dmitry Dmitrich Gurov, who had spent a fortnight at Yalta and had got used to the place, had also begun to take an interest in new arrivals. As he sat in Vernet's confectionery shop, he saw, walking on the esplanade, a fair-haired young woman of medium height, wearing a beret; a white Pomeranian was trotting behind her.

And afterwards he met her in the public garden and in the square several times a day. She walked alone, always wearing the same beret and always with the white dog; no one knew who she was and everyone called her simply "the lady with the pet dog."

"If she is here alone without husband or friends," Gurov reflected, "it wouldn't be a bad thing to make her acquaintance."

He was under forty, but he already had a daughter twelve years old, and two sons at school. They had found a wife for him when he was very young, a student in his second year, and by now she seemed half as old again as he. She was a tall, erect woman with dark eyebrows, stately and dignified and, as she said of herself, intellectual. She read a great deal, used simplified spelling in her letters, called her husband, not Dmitry, but Dimitry, while he privately considered her of limited intelligence, narrow-minded, dowdy, was afraid of her, and did not like to be at home. He had begun being unfaithful to her long ago — had been unfaithful to her often and, probably for that reason, almost always spoke ill of women, and when they were talked of in his presence used to call them "the inferior race."

It seemed to him that he had been sufficiently tutored by bitter experience to call them what he pleased, and yet he could not have lived without "the inferior race" for two days together. In the company of men he was bored and ill at ease, he was chilly and uncommunicative with them; but when he was among women he felt free, and knew what to speak to them about and how to comport himself; and even to be silent with them was no strain on him. In his appearance, in his character, in his whole make-up there was something attractive and elusive that disposed women in his favor and allured them. He knew that, and some force seemed to draw him to them, too.

Oft-repeated and really bitter experience had taught him long ago that with decent people — particularly Moscow people — who are irresolute and slow to move, every affair which at first seems a light and charming adventure inevitably grows into a whole problem of extreme complexity, and in the end a painful situation is created. But at every new meeting wth an interesting woman this lesson of experience seemed to slip from his memory, and he was eager for life, and everything seemed so simple and diverting.

One evening while he was dining in the public garden the lady in the beret walked up without haste to take the next table. Her expression, her gait, her dress, and the way she did her hair told him that she belonged to the upper class, that she was married, that she was in Yalta for the first time and alone, and that she was bored there. The stories told of the immorality in Yalta are to a great extent untrue; he despised them, and knew that such stories were made up for the most part by persons who would have been glad to sin themselves if they had had the chance; but when the lady sat down at the next table three paces from him, he recalled these stories of easy conquests, of trips to the mountains, and the tempting thought of a swift, fleeting liaison, a romance with an unknown woman of whose very name he was ignorant suddenly took hold of him.

He beckoned invitingly to the Pomeranian, and when the dog approached him, shook his finger at it. The Pomeranian growled; Gurov threatened it again.

The lady glanced at him and at once dropped her eyes.

"He doesn't bite," she said and blushed.

"May I give him a bone?" he asked; and when she nodded he inquired affably, "Have you been in Yalta long?"

"About five days."

"And I am dragging out the second week here."

There was a short silence.

"Time passes quickly, and yet it is so dull here!" she said, not looking at him.

"It's only the fashion to say it's dull here. A provincial will live in Belyov or Zhizdra and not be bored, but when he comes here it's 'Oh, the dullness! Oh, the dust!' One would think he came from Granada."

She laughed. Then both continued eating in silence, like strangers, but after dinner they walked together and there sprang up between them the light banter of people who are free and contented, to whom it does not matter where they go or what they talk about. They walked and talked of the strange light on the sea: the water was a soft, warm, lilac color, and there was a golden band of moonlight upon it. They talked of how sultry it was after a hot day. Gurov told her that he was a native of Moscow, that he had studied languages and literature at the university, but had a post in a bank; that at one time he had trained to become an opera singer but had given it up, that he owned two houses in Moscow. And he learned from her that she had grown up in Petersburg, but had lived in S — since her marriage two years previously, that she was going to stay in Yalta for about another month, and that her husband, who needed a rest, too, might perhaps come to fetch her. She was not certain whether her husband was a member of a Government Board or served on a Zemstvo Council,° and this amused her. And Gurov learned too that her name was Anna Sergeyevna.

Afterwards in his room at the hotel he thought about her — and was certain that he would meet her the next day. It was bound to happen. Getting into bed he recalled that she had been a schoolgirl only recently, doing lessons like his own daughter; he thought how much timidity and angularity there was still in her laugh and her manner of talking with a stranger. It must have been the first time in her life that she was alone in a setting in which she was followed, looked at, and spoken to for one secret purpose alone, which she could hardly fail to guess. He thought of her slim, delicate throat, her lovely gray eyes.

"There's something pathetic about her, though," he thought, and dropped off.

II

A week had passed since they had struck up an acquaintance. It was a holiday. It was close indoors, while in the street the wind whirled the dust about and blew people's hats off. One was thirsty all day, and Gurov often went into the restaurant and offered Anna Sergeyevna a soft drink or ice cream. One did not know what to do with oneself.

In the evening when the wind had abated they went out on the pier to watch the steamer come in. There were a great many people walking about the dock; they had come to welcome someone and they were carrying bunches of flowers. And two peculiarities of a festive Yalta crowd stood out: the elderly ladies were dressed like young ones and there were many generals.

Owing to the choppy sea, the steamer arrived late, after

Zemstvo Council   county council

sunset, and it was a long time tacking about before it put in at
the pier. Anna Sergeyevna peered at the steamer and the passengers
through her lorgnette as though looking for acquaintances, and
whenever she turned to Gurov her eyes were shining. She talked
a great deal and asked questions jerkily, forgetting the next moment
what she had asked; then she lost her lorgnette in the crush.

The festive crowd began to disperse; it was now too dark
to see people's faces; there was no wind any more, but Gurov
and Anna Sergeyevna still stood as though waiting to see someone
else come off the steamer. Anna Sergeyevna was silent now, and
sniffed her flowers without looking at Gurov.

"The weather has improved this evening," he said. "Where
shall we go now? Shall we drive somewhere?"

She did not reply.

Then he looked at her intently, and suddenly embraced her
and kissed her on the lips, and the moist fragrance of her flowers
enveloped him; and at once he looked round him anxiously, wondering if anyone had seen them.

"Let us go to your place," he said softly. And they walked
off together rapidly.

The air in her room was close and there was the smell of
the perfume she had bought at the Japanese shop. Looking at her,
Gurov thought: "What encounters life offers!" From the past he
preserved the memory of carefree, good-natured women whom
love made gay and who were grateful to him for the happiness
he gave them, however brief it might be; and of women like his
wife who loved without sincerity, with too many words, affectedly,
hysterically, with an expression that it was not love or passion
that engaged them but something more significant; and of two or
three others, very beautiful, frigid women, across whose faces
would suddenly flit a rapacious expression — an obstinate desire
to take from life more than it could give, and these were women
no longer young, capricious, unreflecting, domineering, unintel-
ligent, and when Gurov grew cold to them their beauty aroused
his hatred, and the lace on their lingerie seemed to him to resemble
scales.

But here there was the timidity, the angularity of inexperienced
youth, a feeling of awkwardness; and there was a sense of embarrassment, as though someone had suddenly knocked at the
door. Anna Sergeyevna, "the lady with the pet dog," treated what
had happened in a peculiar way, very seriously, as though it were
her fall — so it seemed, and this was odd and inappropriate. Her
features drooped and faded, and her long hair hung down sadly

on either side of her face; she grew pensive and her dejected pose was that of a Magdalene in a picture by an old master.

"It's not right," she said. "You don't respect me now, you first of all."

There was a watermelon on the table. Gurov cut himself a slice and began eating it without haste. They were silent for at least half an hour.

There was something touching about Anna Sergeyevna; she had the purity of a well-bred, naive woman who has seen little of life. The single candle burning on the table barely illumined her face, yet it was clear that she was unhappy.

"Why should I stop respecting you, darling?" asked Gurov. "You don't know what you're saying."

"God forgive me," she said, and her eyes filled with tears. "It's terrible."

"It's as though you were trying to exonerate yourself."

"How can I exonerate myself? No. I am a bad, low woman; I despise myself and I have no thought of exonerating myself. It's not my husband but myself I have deceived. And not only just now; I have been deceiving myself for a long time. My husband may be a good, honest man, but he is a flunkey! I don't know what he does, what his work is, but I know he is a flunkey! I was twenty when I married him. I was tormented by curiosity; I wanted something better. 'There must be a different sort of life,' I said to myself. I wanted to live! To live, to live! Curiosity kept eating at me — you don't understand it, but I swear to God I could no longer control myself; something was going on in me; I could not be held back. I told my husband I was ill, and came here. And here I have been walking about as though in a daze, as though I were mad; and now I have become a vulgar, vile woman whom anyone may despise."

Gurov was already bored with her; he was irritated by her naive tone, by her repentance, so unexpected and so out of place, but for the tears in her eyes he might have thought she was joking or play-acting.

"I don't understand, my dear," he said softly. "What do you want?"

She hid her face on his breast and pressed close to him.

"Believe me, believe me, I beg you," she said, "I love honesty and purity, and sin is loathsome to me; I don't know what I'm doing. Simple people say, 'The Evil One has led me astray.' And I may say of myself now that the Evil One has led me astray."

"Quiet, quiet," he murmured.

He looked into her fixed, frightened eyes, kissed her, spoke to her softly and affectionately, and by degrees she calmed down, and her gaiety returned; both began laughing.

Afterwards when they went out there was not a soul on the esplanade. The town with its cypresses looked quite dead, but the sea was still sounding as it broke upon the beach; a single launch was rocking on the waves and on it a lantern was blinking sleepily.

They found a cab and drove to Oreanda.

"I found out your surname in the hall just now: it was written on the board — von Dideritz," said Gurov. "Is your husband German?"

"No; I believe his grandfather was German, but he is Greek Orthodox himself."

At Oreanda they sat on a bench not far from the church, looked down at the sea, and were silent. Yalta was barely visible through the morning mist; white clouds rested motionlessly on the mountaintops. The leaves did not stir on the trees, cicadas twanged, and the monotonous muffled sound of the sea that rose from below spoke of the peace, the eternal sleep awaiting us. So it rumbled below when there was no Yalta, no Oreanda here; so it rumbles now, and it will rumble as indifferently and as hollowly when we are no more. And in this constancy, in this complete indifference to the life and death of each of us, there lies, perhaps, a pledge of our eternal salvation, of the unceasing advance of life upon earth, of unceasing movement towards perfection. Sitting beside a young woman who in the dawn seemed so lovely, Gurov, soothed and spellbound by these magical surroundings — the sea, the mountains, the clouds, the wide sky — thought how everything is really beautiful in this world when one reflects: everything except what we think or do ourselves when we forget the higher aims of life and our own human dignity.

A man strolled up to them — probably a guard — looked at them and walked away. And this detail, too, seemed so mysterious and beautiful. They saw a steamer arrive from Feodosia, its lights extinguished in the glow of dawn.

"There is dew on the grass," said Anna Sergeyevna, after a silence.

"Yes, it's time to go home."

They returned to the city.

Then they met every day at twelve o'clock on the esplanade, lunched and dined together, took walks, admired the sea. She complained that she slept badly, that she had palpitations, asked the same questions, troubled now by jealousy and now by the fear that he did not respect her sufficiently. And often in the square or the public garden, when there was no one near them, he suddenly drew her to him and kissed her passionately. Complete idleness, these kisses in broad daylight exchanged furtively in dread of someone's seeing them, the heat, the smell of the sea, and the continual flitting before his eyes of idle, well-dressed, well-fed people, worked a complete change in him; he kept telling Anna Sergeyevna how beautiful she was, how seductive, was urgently passionate; he would not move a step away from her, while she was often pensive and continually pressed him to confess that he did not respect her, did not love her in the least, and saw in her nothing but a common woman. Almost every evening rather late they drove somewhere out of town, to Oreanda or to the waterfall; and the excursion was always a success, the scenery invariably impressed them as beautiful and magnificent.

They were expecting her husband, but a letter came from him saying that he had eye-trouble, and begging his wife to return home as soon as possible. Anna Sergeyevna made haste to go.

"It's a good thing I am leaving," she said to Gurov. "It's the hand of Fate!"

She took a carriage to the railway station, and he went with her. They were driving the whole day. When she had taken her place in the express, and when the second bell had rung, she said, "Let me look at you once more — let me look at you again. Like this."

She was not crying but was so sad that she seemed ill and her face was quivering.

"I shall be thinking of you — remembering you," she said. "God bless you; be happy. Don't remember evil against me. We are parting forever — it has to be, for we ought never to have met. Well, God bless you."

The train moved off rapidly, its lights soon vanished, and a minute later there was no sound of it, as though everything had conspired to end as quickly as possible that sweet trance, that madness. Left alone on the platform, and gazing into the dark distance, Gurov listened to the twang of the grasshoppers and the hum of the telegraph wires, feeling as though he had just waked up. And he reflected, musing, that there had now been another episode or adventure in his life, and it, too, was at an end, and nothing was left of it but a memory. He was moved, sad, and slightly remorseful: this young woman whom he would never meet again had not been happy with him; he had been warm and affectionate with her, but yet in his manner, his tone, and his caresses there had been a shade of light irony, the slightly coarse arrogance of a happy male who was, besides, almost twice her age. She had constantly called him kind, exceptional, high-minded; obviously he had seemed to her different from what he really was, so he had involuntarily deceived her.

Here at the station there was already a scent of autumn in the air; it was a chilly evening.

"It is time for me to go north, too," thought Gurov as he left the platform. "High time!"

III

At home in Moscow the winter routine was already established; the stoves were heated, and in the morning it was still dark when the children were having breakfast and getting ready for school, and the nurse would light the lamp for a short time. There were frosts already. When the first snow falls, on the first day the sleighs are out, it is pleasant to see the white earth, the white roofs; one draws easy, delicious breaths, and the season brings back the days of one's youth. The old limes and birches, white with hoar-frost, have a good-natured look; they are closer to one's heart than cypresses and palms, and near them one no longer wants to think of mountains and the sea.

Gurov, a native of Moscow, arrived there on a fine frosty day, and when he put on his fur coat and warm gloves and took a walk along Petrovka, and when on Saturday night he heard the bells ringing, his recent trip and the places he had visited lost all charm for him. Little by little he became immersed in Moscow life, greedily read three newspapers a day, and declared that he did not read the Moscow papers on principle. He already felt a longing for restaurants, clubs, formal dinners, anniversary celebrations, and it flattered him to entertain distinguished lawyers and actors, and to play cards with a professor at the physicians' club. He could eat a whole portion of meat stewed with pickled cabbage and served in a pan, Moscow style.

A month or so would pass and the image of Anna Sergeyevna, it seemed to him, would become misty in his memory, and ony from time to time he would dream of her with her touching smile as he dreamed of others. But more than a month went by, winter came into its own, and everything was still clear in his memory as though he had parted from Anna Sergeyevna only yesterday. And his memories glowed more and more vividly. When in the evening stillness the voices of his children preparing their lessons reached his study, or when he listened to a song or to an organ playing in a restaurant, or when the storm howled in the chimney, suddenly everything would rise up in his memory; what had happened on the pier and the early morning with the mist on the mountains, and the steamer coming from Feodosia, and the kisses. He would pace about his room a long time, remembering and smiling; then his memories passed into reveries, and in his imagination the past would mingle with what was to come. He did not dream of Anna Sergeyevna, but she followed him about everywhere and watched him. When he shut his eyes he saw her before him as though she were there in the flesh, and she seemed to him lovelier, younger, tenderer than she had been, and he imagined himself a finer man than he had been in Yalta. Of evenings she peered out at him from the bookcase, from the fireplace, from the corner — he heard her breathing, the caressing rustle of her clothes. In the street he followed the women with his eyes, looking for someone who resembled her.

Already he was tormented by a strong desire to share his memories with someone. But in his home it was impossible to talk of his love, and he had no one to talk to outside; certainly he could not confide in his tenants or in anyone at the bank. And what was there to talk about? He hadn't loved her then, had he? Had there been anything beautiful, poetical, edifying, or simply interesting in his relations with Anna Sergeyevna? And he was forced to talk vaguely of love, of women, and no one guessed what he meant; only his wife would twitch her black eyebrows and say, "The part of a philanderer does not suit you at all, Dimitry."

One evening, coming out of the physicians' club with an official with whom he had been playing cards, he could not resist saying:

"If you only knew what a fascinating woman I became acquainted with at Yalta!"

The official got into his sledge and was driving away, but turned suddenly and shouted:

"Dmitry Dmitrich!"

"What is it?"

"You were right this evening: the sturgeon was a bit high."

These words, so commonplace, for some reason moved Gurov to indignation, and struck him as degrading and unclean. What savage manners, what mugs! What stupid nights, what dull, humdrum days! Frenzied gambling, gluttony, drunkenness, continual talk always about the same thing! Futile pursuits and conversations always about the same topics take up the better part of one's time, the better part of one's strength, and in the end there is left a life clipped and wingless, an absurd mess, and there is no escaping or getting away from it — just as though one were in a madhouse or a prison.

Gurov, boiling with indignation, did not sleep all night. And he had a headache all the next day. And the following nights too he slept badly; he sat up in bed, thinking, or paced up and down his room. He was fed up with his children, fed up with the bank; he had no desire to go anywhere or to talk of anything.

In December during the holidays he prepared to take a trip and told his wife he was going to Petersburg to do what he could for a young friend — and he set off for S — . What for? He did not know, himself. He wanted to see Anna Sergeyevna and talk with her, to arrange a rendezvous if possible.

He arrived at S — in the morning, and at the hotel took the best room, in which the floor was covered with gray army cloth, and on the table there was an inkstand, gray with dust and topped by a figure on horseback, its hat in its raised hand and its head broken off. The porter gave him the necessary information: von Dideritz lived in a house of his own on Staro-Goncharnaya Street, not far from the hotel: he was rich and lived well and kept his own horses; everyone in the town knew him. The porter pronounced the name: "Dridiritz."

Without haste Gurov made his way to Staro-Goncharnaya Street and found the house. Directly opposite the house stretched a long gray fence studded with nails.

"A fence like that would make one run away," thought Gurov, looking now at the fence, now at the windows of the house.

He reflected: this was a holiday, and the husband was apt to be at home. And in any case, it would be tactless to go into the house and disturb her. If he were to send her a note, it might fall into her husband's hands, and that might spoil everything. The best thing was to rely on chance. And he kept walking up and down the street and along the fence, waiting for the chance. He saw a beggar go in at the gate and heard the dogs attack him; then an hour later he heard a piano, and the sound came to him faintly and indistinctly. Probably it was Anna Sergeyevna playing. The front door opened suddenly, and an old woman came out, followed by the familiar white Pomeranian. Gurov was on the point of calling to the dog, but his heart began beating violently, and in his excitement he could not remember the Pomeranian's name.

He kept walking up and down, and hated the gray fence more and more, and by now he thought irritably that Anna Sergeyevna had forgotten him, and was perhaps already diverting herself with another man, and that that was very natural in a young woman who from morning till night had to look at that damn fence. He went back to his hotel room and sat on the couch for a long while, not knowing what to do, then he had dinner and a long nap.

"How stupid and annoying all this is!" he thought when he woke and looked at the dark windows: it was already evening. "Here I've had a good sleep for some reason. What am I going to do at night?"

He sat on the bed, which was covered with a cheap gray blanket of the kind seen in hospitals, and he twitted himself in his vexation:

"So there's your lady with the pet dog. There's your adventure. A nice place to cool your heels in."

That morning at the station a playbill in large letters had caught his eye. *The Geisha* was to be given for the first time. He thought of this and drove to the theater.

"It's quite possible that she goes to first nights," he thought.

The theater was full. As in all provincial theaters, there was a haze above the chandelier, the gallery was noisy and restless; in the front row, before the beginning of the performance the local dandies were standing with their hands clasped behind their backs; in the Governor's box the Governor's daughter, wearing a boa, occupied the front seat, while the Governor himself hid modestly behind the portiere and only his hands were visible; the curtain swayed; the orchestra was a long time tuning up. While the audience was coming in and taking their seats, Gurov scanned the faces eagerly.

Anna Sergeyevna, too, came in. She sat down in the third row, and when Gurov looked at her his heart contracted, and he understood clearly that in the whole world there was no human being so near, so precious, and so important to him; she, this little, undistinguished woman, lost in a provincial crowd, with a vulgar lorgnette in her hand, filled his whole life now, was his sorrow and his joy, the only happiness that he now desired for himself, and to the sounds of the bad orchestra, of the miserable local violins, he thought how lovely she was. He thought and dreamed.

A young man with small side-whiskers, very tall and stooped, came in with Anna Sergeyevna and sat down beside her; he nodded his head at every step and seemed to be bowing continually. Probably this was the husband whom at Yalta, in an access of bitter feeling, she had called a flunkey. And there really was in his lanky figure, his side-whiskers, his small bald patch, something of a flunkey's retiring manner; his smile was mawkish, and in his buttonhole there was an academic badge like a waiter's number.

During the first intermission the husband went out to have a smoke; she remained in her seat. Gurov, who was also sitting in the orchestra, went up to her and said in a shaky voice, with a forced smile:

"Good evening!"

She glanced at him and turned pale, then looked at him again in horror, unable to believe her eyes, and gripped the fan and the lorgnette tightly together in her hands, evidently trying to keep herself from fainting. Both were silent. She was sitting, he was standing, frightened by her distress and not daring to take a seat beside her. The violins and the flute that were being tuned up sang out. He suddenly felt frightened: it seemed as if all the people in the boxes were looking at them. She got up and went hurriedly to the exit; he followed her, and both of them walked blindly along the corridors and up and down stairs, and figures in the uniforms prescribed for magistrates, teachers, and officials of the Department of Crown Lands, all wearing badges, flitted before their eyes, as did also ladies, and fur coats on hangers; they were consicious of drafts and the smell of stale tobacco. And Gurov, whose heart was beating violently, thought:

"Oh, Lord! Why are these people here and this orchestra!"

And at that instant he suddenly recalled how when he had seen Anna Sergeyevna off at the station he had said to himself that all was over between them and that they would never meet again. But how distant the end still was!

On the narrow, gloomy staircase over which it said "To the Amphitheatre," she stopped.

"How you frightened me!" she said, breathing hard, still pale and stunned. "Oh, how you frightened me! I am barely alive. Why did you come? Why?"

"But do understand, Anna, do understand — " he said hurriedly, under his breath. "I implore you, do understand — "

She looked at him with fear, with entreaty, with love; she looked at him intently, to keep his features more distinctly in her memory.

"I suffer so," she went on, not listening to him. "All this time I have been thinking of nothing but you; I live only by the thought of you. And I wanted to forget, to forget; but why, oh, why have you come?"

On the landing above them two high school boys were looking down and smoking, but it was all the same to Gurov; he drew Anna Sergeyevna to him and began kissing her face and hands.

"What are you doing, what are you doing!" she was saying in horror, pushing him away. "We have lost our senses. Go away today; go away at once — I conjure you by all that is sacred, I implore you — People are coming this way!"

Someone was walking up the stairs.

"You must leave," Anna Sergeyevna went on in a whisper. "Do you hear, Dmitry Dmitrich? I will come and see you in Moscow. I have never been happy; I am unhappy now, and I never, never shall be happy, never! So don't make me suffer still more! I swear I'll come to Moscow. But now let us part. My dear, good, precious one, let us part!"

She pressed his hand and walked rapidly downstairs, turning to look round at him, and from her eyes he could see that she really was unhappy. Gurov stood for a while, listening, then when all grew quiet, he found his coat and left the theater.

IV

And Anna Sergeyevna began coming to see him in Moscow. Once every two or three months she left S — telling her husband that she was going to consult a doctor about a woman's ailment from which she was suffering — and her husband did and did not believe her. When she arrived in Moscow she would stop at the Slavyansky Bazar Hotel, and at once send a man in a red cap to Gurov. Gurov came to see her, and no one in Moscow knew of it.

Once he was going to see her in this way on a winter morning (the messenger had come the evening before and not found him in). With him walked his daughter, whom he wanted to take to school; it was on the way. Snow was coming down in big wet flakes.

"It's three degrees above zero,° and yet it's snowing," Gurov was saying to his daughter. "But this temperature prevails only on the surface of the earth; in the upper layers of the atmosphere there is quite a different temperature."

"And why doesn't it thunder in winter, papa?"

He explained that, too. He talked, thinking all the while that he was on his way to a rendezvous, and no living soul knew of it, and probably no one would ever know. He had two lives, an open one, seen and known by all who needed to know it, full of conventional truth and conventional falsehood, exactly like the lives of his friends and acquaintances; and another life that went on in secret. And through some strange, perhaps accidental, combination of circumstances, everything that was of interest and

---

three degrees above zero Celsius—about thirty-seven degrees Fahrenheit

importance to him, everything that was essential to him, everything
about which he felt sincerely and did not deceive himself, everything
that constituted the core of his life, was going on concealed from
others; while all that was false, the shell in which he hid to cover
the truth — his work at the bank, for instance, his discussions at
the club, his references to the "inferior race," his appearances at
anniversary celebrations with his wife — all that went on in the
open. Judging others by himself, he did not believe what he saw,
and always fancied that every man led his real, most interesting
life under cover of secrecy as under cover of night. The personal
life of every individual is based on secrecy, and perhaps it is partly
for that reason that civilized man is so nervously anxious that
personal privacy should be respected.

Having taken his daughter to school, Gurov went on to the
Slavyansky Bazar Hotel. He took off his fur coat in the lobby,
went upstairs, and knocked gently at the door. Anna Sergeyevna,
wearing his favorite gray dress, exhausted by the journey and by
waiting, had been expecting him since the previous evening. She
was pale, and looked at him without a smile, and he had hardly
entered when she flung herself on his breast. That kiss was a long,
lingering one, as though they had not seen one another for two
years.

"Well, darling, how are you getting on there?" he asked.
"What news?"

"Wait; I'll tell you in a moment — I can't speak."

She could not speak; she was crying. She turned away from
him, and pressed her handkerchief to her eyes.

"Let her have her cry; meanwhile I'll sit down," he thought,
and he seated himself in an armchair.

Then he rang and ordered tea, and while he was having his
tea she remained standing at the window with her back to him.
She was crying out of sheer agitation, in the sorrowful consciousness
that their life was so sad; that they could only see each other in
secret and had to hide from people like thieves! Was it not a broken
life?

"Come, stop now, dear!" he said.

It was plain to him that this love of theirs would not be
over soon, that the end of it was not in sight. Anna Sergeyevna
was growing more and more attached to him. She adored him,
and it was unthinkable to tell her that their love was bound to
come to an end some day; besides, she would not have believed
it!

He went up to her and took her by the shoulders, to fondle

her and say something diverting, and at that moment he caught sight of himself in the mirror.

His hair was already beginning to turn gray. And it seemed odd to him that he had grown so much older in the last few years, and lost his looks. The shoulders on which his hands rested were warm and heaving. He felt compassion for this life, still so warm and lovely, but probably already about to begin to fade and wither like his own. Why did she love him so much? He always seemed to women different from what he was, and they loved in him not himself, but the man whom their imagination created and whom they had been eagerly seeking all their lives; and afterwards, when they saw their mistake, they loved him nevertheless. And not one of them had been happy with him. In the past he had met women, come together with them, parted from them, but he had never once loved; it was anything you please, but not love. And only now when his head was gray he had fallen in love, really, truly — for the first time in his life.

Anna Sergeyevna and he loved each other as people do who are very close and intimate, like man and wife, like tender friends; it seemed to them that Fate itself had meant them for one another, and they could not understand why he had a wife and she a husband; and it was as though they were a pair of migratory birds, male and female, caught and forced to live in different cages. They forgave each other what they were ashamed of in their past, they forgave everything in the present, and felt that this love of theirs had altered them both.

Formerly in moments of sadness he had soothed himself with whatever logical arguments came into his head, but now he no longer cared for logic; he felt profound compassion, he wanted to be sincere and tender.

"Give it up now, my darling," he said. "You've had your cry; that's enough. Let us have a talk now, we'll think up something."

Then they spent a long time taking counsel together, they talked of how to avoid the necessity for secrecy, for deception, for living in different cities, and not seeing one another for long stretches of time. How could they free themselves from these intolerable fetters?

"How? How?" he asked, clutching his head. "How?"

And it seemed as though in a little while the solution would be found, and then a new and glorious life would begin; and it was clear to both of them that the end was still far off, and that what was to be most complicated and difficult for them was only just beginning.

Charlotte Perkins Gilman (American. 1860–1935)

The Yellow Wallpaper

It is very seldom that mere ordinary people like John and myself secure ancestral halls for the summer.

A colonial mansion, a hereditary estate, I would say a haunted house, and reach the height of romantic felicity — but that would be asking too much of fate!

Still I will proudly declare that there is something queer about it.

Else, why should it be let so cheaply? And why have stood so long untenanted?

John laughs at me, of course, but one expects that in marriage.

John is practical in the extreme. He has no patience with faith, an intense horror of superstition, and he scoffs openly at any talk of things not to be felt and seen and put down in figures.

John is a physician, and *perhaps* — (I would not say it to a living soul, of course, but this is dead paper and a great relief to my mind) — *perhaps* that is one reason I do not get well faster.

You see he does not believe I am sick!

And what can one do?

If a physician of high standing, and one's own husband, assures friends and relatives that there is really nothing the matter with one but temporary nervous depression — a slight hysterical tendency — what is one to do?

My brother is also a physician, and also of high standing, and he says the same thing.

So I take phosphates or phosphites — whichever it is, and tonics, and journeys, and air, and exercise, and am absolutely forbidden to "work" until I am well again.

Personally, I disagree with their ideas.

Personally, I believe that congenial work, with excitement and change, would do me good.

But what is one to do?

I did write for a while in spite of them; but it *does* exhaust me a good deal — having to be so sly about it, or else meet with heavy opposition.

I sometimes fancy that in my condition if I had less opposition and more society and stimulus — but John says the very worst thing I can do is to think about my condition, and I confess it always makes me feel bad.

So I will let it alone and talk about the house.

The most beautiful place! It is quite alone, standing well back from the road, quite three miles from the village. It makes me think of English places that you read about, for there are hedges and walls and gates that lock, and lots of separate little houses for the gardeners and people.

There is a *delicious* garden! I never saw such a garden — large and shady, full of box-bordered paths, and lined with long grapecovered arbors with seats under them.

There were greenhouses, too, but they are all broken now. There was some legal trouble, I believe, something about the heirs and coheirs; anyhow, the place has been empty for years.

That spoils my ghostliness, I am afraid, but I don't care — there is something strange about the house — I can feel it.

I even said so to John one moonlight evening, but he said what I felt was a *draught,* and shut the window.

I get unreasonably angry with John sometimes. I'm sure I never used to be so sensitive. I think it is due to this nervous condition.

But John says if I feel so, I shall neglect proper self-control; so I take pains to control myself — before him, at least, and that makes me very tired.

I don't like our room a bit. I wanted one downstairs that opened on the piazza and had roses all over the window, and such pretty old-fashioned chintz hangings! but John would not hear of it.

He said there was only one window and not room for two beds, and no near room for him if he took another.

He is very careful and loving, and hardly lets me stir without special direction.

I have a schedule prescription for each hour in the day; he takes all care from me, and so I feel basely ungrateful not to value it more.

He said we came here solely on my account, that I was to have perfect rest and all the air I could get. "Your exercise depends on your strength, my dear," said he, "and your food somewhat on your appetite; but air you can absorb all the time." So we took the nursery at the top of the house.

It is a big, airy room, the whole floor nearly, with windows that look all ways, and air and sunshine galore. It was nursery first and then playroom and gymnasium, I should judge; for the windows are barred for little children, and there are rings and things in the walls.

The paint and paper look as if a boys' school had used it. It is stripped off — the paper — in great patches all around the head of my bed, about as far as I can reach, and in a great place on the other side of the room low down. I never saw a worse paper in my life.

One of those sprawling flamboyant patterns committing every artistic sin.

It is dull enough to confuse the eye in following, pronounced enough to constantly irritate and provoke study, and when you follow the lame uncertain curves for a little distance they suddenly commit suicide — plunge off at outrageous angles, destroy themselves in unheard of contradictions.

The color is repellent, almost revolting; a smouldering unclean yellow, strangely faded by the slow-turning sunlight.

It is a dull yet lurid orange in some places, a sickly sulphur tint in others.

No wonder the children hated it! I should hate it myself if I had to live in this room long.

There comes John, and I must put this away, — he hates to have me write a word.

We have been here two weeks, and I haven't felt like writing before, since that first day.

I am sitting by the window now, up in this atrocious nursery, and there is nothing to hinder my writing as much as I please, save lack of strength.

John is away all day, and even some nights when his cases are serious.

I am glad my case is not serious!

But these nervous troubles are dreadfully depressing.

John does not know how much I really suffer. He knows there is no *reason* to suffer, and that satisfies him.

Of course it is only nervousness. It does weigh on me so not to do my duty in any way!

I meant to be such a help to John, such a real rest and comfort, and here I am a comparative burden already!

Nobody would believe what an effort it is to do what little I am able, — to dress and entertain, and order things.

It is fortunate Mary is so good with the baby. Such a dear baby!

And yet I *cannot* be with him, it makes me so nervous.

I suppose John never was nervous in his life. He laughs at me so about this wallpaper!

At first he meant to repaper the room, but afterwards he said that I was letting it get the better of me, and that nothing was worse for a nervous patient than to give way to such fancies.

He said that after the wallpaper was changed it would be the heavy bedstead, and then the barred windows, and then that gate at the head of the stairs, and so on.

"You know the place is doing you good," he said, "and really, dear, I don't care to renovate the house just for a three months' rental."

"Then do let us go downstairs," I said, "there are such pretty rooms there."

Then he took me in his arms and called me a blessed little goose, and said he would go down to the cellar, if I wished, and have it whitewashed into the bargain.

But he is right enough about the beds and windows and things.

It is an airy and comfortable room as any one need wish, and, of course, I would not be so silly as to make him uncomfortable just for a whim.

I'm really getting quite fond of the big room, all but that horrid paper.

Out of one window I can see the garden, those mysterious deepshaded arbors, the riotous old-fashioned flowers, and bushes and gnarly trees.

Out of another I get a lovely view of the bay and a little private wharf belonging to the estate. There is a beautiful shaded lane that runs down there from the house. I always fancy I see people walking in these numerous paths and arbors, but John has cautioned me not to give way to fancy in the least. He says that with my imaginative power and habit of story-making, a nervous weakness like mine is sure to lead to all manner of excited fancies, and that I ought to use my will and good sense to check the tendency. So I try.

I think sometimes that if I were only well enough to write a little it would relieve the press of ideas and rest me.

But I find I get pretty tired when I try.

It is so discouraging not to have any advice and companionship about my work. When I get really well, John says we will ask Cousin Henry and Julia down for a long visit; but he says he would as soon put fireworks in my pillow-case as to let me have those stimulating people about now.

I wish I could get well faster.

But I must not think about that. This paper looks to me as if it *knew* what a vicious influence it had!

There is a recurrent spot where the pattern lolls like a broken neck and two bulbous eyes stare at you upside down.

I get positively angry with the impertinence of it and the

everlastingness. Up and down and sideways they crawl, and those absurd, unblinking eyes are everywhere. There is one place where two breadths didn't match, and the eyes go all up and down the line, one a little higher than the other.

I never saw so much expression in an inanimate thing before, and we all know how much expression they have! I used to lie awake as a child and get more entertainment and terror out of blank walls and plain furniture than most children could find in a toystore.

I remember what a kindly wink the knobs of our big, old bureau used to have, and there was one chair that always seemed like a strong friend.

I used to feel that if any of the other things looked too fierce I could always hop into that chair and be safe.

The furniture in this room is no worse than inharmonious, however, for we had to bring it all from downstairs. I suppose when this was used as a playroom they had to take the nursery things out, and no wonder! I never saw such ravages as the children have made here.

The wallpaper, as I said before, is torn off in spots, and it sticketh closer than a brother — they must have had perseverance as well as hatred.

Then the floor is scratched and gouged and splintered, the plaster itself is dug out here and there, and this great heavy bed which is all we found in the room, looks as if it had been through the wars.

But I don't mind it a bit — only the paper.

There comes John's sister. Such a dear girl as she is, and so careful of me! I must not let her find me writing.

She is a perfect and enthusiastic housekeeper, and hopes for no better profession. I verily believe she thinks it is the writing which made me sick!

But I can write when she is out, and see her a long way off from these windows.

There is one that commands the road, a lovely shaded winding road, and one that just looks off over the country. A lovely country, too, full of great elms and velvet meadows.

This wallpaper has a kind of sub-pattern in a different shade, a particularly irritating one, for you can only see it in certain lights, and not clearly then.

But in the places where it isn't faded and where the sun is just so — I can see a strange, provoking, formless sort of figure, that seems to skulk about behind that silly and conspicuous front design.

There's sister on the stairs!

Well, the Fourth of July is over! The people are all gone and I am tired out. John thought it might do me good to see a little company, so we just had mother and Nellie and the children down for a week.

Of course I didn't do a thing. Jennie sees to everything now. But it tired me all the same.

John says if I don't pick up faster he shall send me to Weir Mitchell in the fall.

But I don't want to go there at all. I had a friend who was in his hands once, and she says he is just like John and my brother, only more so!

Besides, it is such an undertaking to go so far.

I don't feel as if it was worth while to turn my hand over for anything, and I'm getting dreadfully fretful and querulous.

I cry at nothing, and cry most of the time.

Of course I don't when John is here, or anybody else, but when I am alone.

And I am alone a good deal just now. John is kept in town very often by serious cases, and Jennie is good and lets me alone when I want her to.

So I walk a little in the garden or down that lovely lane, sit on the porch under the roses, and lie down up here a good deal.

I'm getting really fond of the room in spite of the wallpaper. Perhaps *because* of the wallpaper.

It dwells in my mind so!

I lie here on this great immovable bed — it is nailed down, I believe — and follow that pattern about by the hour. It is as good as gymnastics, I assure you. I start, we'll say, at the bottom, down in the corner over there where it has not been touched, and I determine for the thousandth time that I *will* follow that pointless pattern to some sort of a conclusion.

I know a little of the principle of design, and I know this thing was not arranged on any laws of radiation, or alternation, or repetition, or symmetry, or anything else that I ever heard of.

It is repeated, of course, by the breadths, but not otherwise.

Looked at in one way each breadth stands alone, the bloated curves and flourishes — a kind of "debased Romanesque" with *delirium tremens* — go waddling up and down in isolated columns of fatuity.

But, on the other hand, they connect diagonally, and the sprawling outlines run off in great slanting waves of optic horror, like a lot of wallowing seaweeds in full chase.

The whole thing goes horizontally, too, at least it seems so, and I exhaust myself in trying to distinguish the order of its going in that direction.

They have used a horizontal breadth for a frieze, and that adds wonderfully to the confusion.

There is one end of the room where it is almost intact, and there, when the crosslights fade and the low sun shines directly upon it, I can almost fancy radiation after all, — the interminable grotesques seem to form around a common center and rush off in headlong plunges of equal distraction.

It makes me tired to follow it. I will take a nap I guess.

I don't know why I should write this.

I don't want to.

I don't feel able.

And I know John would think it absurd. But I *must* say what I feel and think in some way — it is such a relief

But the effort is getting to be greater than the relief!

Half the time now I am awfully lazy, and lie down ever so much.

John says I mustn't lose my strength, and has me take cod liver oil and lots of tonics and things, to say nothing of ale and wine and rare meat.

Dear John! He loves me very dearly, and hates to have me sick. I tried to have a real earnest reasonable talk with him the other day, and tell him how I wish he would let me go and make a visit to Cousin Henry and Julia.

But he said I wasn't able to go, nor able to stand it after I got there; and I did not make out a very good case for myself, for I was crying before I had finished.

It is getting to be a great effort for me to think straight. Just this nervous weakness I suppose.

And dear John gathered me up in his arms, and just carried me upstairs and laid me on the bed, and sat by me and read to me till it tired my head.

He said I was his darling and his comfort and all he had, and that I must take care of myself for his sake, and keep well.

He says no one but myself can help me out of it, that I must use my will and self-control and not let any silly fancies run away with me.

There's one comfort, the baby is well and happy, and does not have to occupy this nursery with the horrid wallpaper.

If we had not used it, that blessed child would have! What a fortunate escape! Why, I wouldn't have a child of mine, an impressionable little thing, live in such a room for worlds.

I never thought of it before, but it is lucky that John kept me here after all, I can stand it so much easier than a baby, you see.

Of course I never mention it to them any more — I am too wise, — but I keep watch of it all the same.

There are things in that paper that nobody knows but me, or ever will.

Behind that outside pattern the dim shapes get clearer every day.

It is always the same shape, only very numerous.

And it is like a woman stooping down and creeping about behind that pattern. I don't like it a bit. I wonder — I begin to think — I wish John would take me away from here!

It is so hard to talk with John about my case, because he is so wise, and because he loves me so.

But I tried it last night.

It was moonlight. The moon shines in all around just as the sun does.

I hate to see it sometimes, it creeps so slowly, and always comes in by one window or another.

John was asleep and I hated to waken him, so I kept still and watched the moonlight on that undulating wallpaper till I felt creepy.

The faint figure behind seemed to shake the pattern, just as if she wanted to get out.

I got up softly and went to feel and see if the paper *did* move, and when I came back John was awake.

"What is it, little girl?" he said. "Don't go walking about like that — you'll get cold."

I thought it was a good time to talk, so I told him that I really was not gaining here, and that I wished he would take me away.

"Why darling!" said he, "our lease will be up in three weeks, and I can't see how to leave before.

"The repairs are not done at home, and I cannot possibly leave town just now. Of course if you were in any danger, I could and would, but you really are better, dear, whether you can see it or not. I am a doctor, dear, and I know. You are gaining flesh and color, your appetite is better, I feel really much easier about you."

"I don't weigh a bit more," said I, "nor as much; and my appetite may be better in the evening when you are here, but it is worse in the morning when you are away!"

"Bless her little heart!" said he with a big hug, "she shall be as sick as she pleases! But now let's improve the shining hours by going to sleep, and talk about it in the morning!"

"And you won't go away?" I asked gloomily.

"Why, how can I, dear? It is only three weeks more and then we will take a nice little trip of a few days while Jennie is getting the house ready. Really dear you are better!"

"Better in body perhaps — " I began, and stopped short, for he sat up straight and looked at me with such a stern, reproachful look that I could not say another word.

"My darling," said he, "I beg of you, for my sake and for our child's sake, as well as for your own, that you will never for one instant let that idea enter your mind! There is nothing so dangerous, so fascinating, to a temperament like yours. It is a false and foolish fancy. Can you not trust me as a physician when I tell you so?"

So of course I said no more on that score, and we went to sleep before long. He thought I was asleep first, but I wasn't, and lay there for hours trying to decide whether that front pattern and the back pattern really did move together or separately.

On a pattern like this, by daylight, there is a lack of sequence, a defiance of law, that is a constant irritant to a normal mind.

The color is hideous enough, and unreliable enough, and infuriating enough, but the pattern is torturing.

You think you have mastered it, but just as you get well underway in following, it turns a back-somersault and there you are. It slaps you in the face, knocks you down, and tramples upon you. It is like a bad dream.

The outside pattern is a florid arabesque, reminding one of a fungus. If you can imagine a toadstool in joints, an interminable string of toadstools, budding and sprouting in endless convolutions — why, that is something like it.

That is, sometimes!

There is one marked peculiarity about this paper, a thing nobody seems to notice but myself, and that is that it changes as the light changes.

When the sun shoots in through the east window — I always watch for that first long, straight ray — it changes so quickly that I never can quite believe it.

That is why I watch it always.

By moonlight — the moon shines in all night when there is a moon — I wouldn't know it was the same paper.

At night in any kind of light, in twilight, candle light, lamplight, and worst of all by moonlight, it becomes bars! The outside pattern I mean, and the woman behind it is as plain as can be.

I didn't realize for a long time what the thing was that showed behind, that dim sub-pattern, but now I am quite sure it is a woman.

By daylight she is subdued, quiet. I fancy it is the pattern that keeps her so still. It is so puzzling. It keeps me quiet by the hour.

I lie down ever so much now. John says it is good for me, and to sleep all I can.

Indeed he started the habit by making me lie down for an hour after each meal.

It is a very bad habit I am convinced, for you see I don't sleep.

And that cultivates deceit, for I don't tell them I'm awake — O no!

The fact is I am getting a little afraid of John.

He seems very queer sometimes, and even Jennie has an inexplicable look.

It strikes me occasionally, just as a scientific hypothesis, — that perhaps it is the paper!

I have watched John when he did not know I was looking, and come into the room suddenly on the most innocent excuses, and I've caught him several times *looking at the paper!* And Jennie too. I caught Jennie with her hand on it once.

She didn't know I was in the room, and when I asked her in a quiet, a very quiet voice, with the most restrained manner possible, what she was doing with the paper — she turned around as if she had been caught stealing, and looked quite angry — asked me why I should frighten her so!

Then she said that the paper stained everything it touched, that she had found yellow smooches on all my clothes and John's, and she wished we would be more careful!

Did not that sound innocent? But I know she was studying that pattern, and I am determined that nobody shall find it out but myself!

Life is very much more exciting now than it used to be. You see I have something more to expect, to look forward to, to watch. I really do eat better, and am more quiet than I was.

John is so pleased to see me improve! He laughed a little the other day, and said I seemed to be flourishing in spite of my wallpaper.

I turned it off with a laugh. I had no intention of telling

him it was *because* of the wallpaper — he would make fun of me. He might even want to take me away.

I don't want to leave now until I have found it out. There is a week more, and I think that will be enough.

I'm feeling ever so much better! I don't sleep much at night, for it is so interesting to watch developments; but I sleep a good deal in the daytime.

In the daytime it is tiresome and perplexing.

There are always new shoots on the fungus, and new shades of yellow all over it. I cannot keep count of them, though I have tried conscientiously.

It is the strangest yellow, that wallpaper! It makes me think of all the yellow things I ever saw — not beautiful ones like buttercups, but old foul, bad yellow things.

But there is something else about that paper — the smell! I noticed it the moment we came into the room, but with so much air and sun it was not bad. Now we have had a week of fog and rain, and whether the windows are open or not, the smell is here.

It creeps all over the house.

I find it hovering in the dining-room, skulking in the parlor, hiding in the hall, lying in wait for me on the stairs.

It gets into my hair.

Even when I go to ride, if I turn my head suddenly and surprise it — there is that smell!

Such a peculiar odor, too! I have spent hours in trying to analyze it, to find what it smelled like.

It is not bad — at first, and very gentle, but quite the subtlest, most enduring odor I ever met.

In this damp weather it is awful, I wake up in the night and find it hanging over me.

It used to disturb me at first. I thought seriously of burning the house — to reach the smell.

But now I am used to it. The only thing I can think of that it is like is the *color* of the paper! A yellow smell.

There is a very funny mark on this wall, low down, near the mopboard. A streak that runs round the room. It goes behind every piece of furniture, except the bed, a long, straight, even *smooch*, as if it had been rubbed over and over.

I wonder how it was done and who did it, and what they did it for. Round and round and round — round and round and round — it makes me dizzy!

I really have discovered something at last.

Through watching so much at night, when it changes so, I have finally found out.

The front pattern *does* move — and no wonder! The woman behind shakes it!

Sometimes I think there are a great many women behind, and sometimes only one, and she crawls around fast, and her crawling shakes it all over.

Then in the very bright spots she keeps still, and in the very shady spots she just takes hold of the bars and shakes them hard.

And she is all the time trying to climb through. But nobody could climb through that pattern — it strangles so; I think that is why it has so many heads.

They get through, and then the pattern strangles them off and turns them upside down, and makes their eyes white!

If those heads were covered or taken off it would not be half so bad.

I think that woman gets out in the daytime!

And I'll tell you why — privately — I've seen her!

I can see her out of every one of my windows!

It is the same woman, I know, for she is always creeping, and most women do not creep by daylight.

I see her on that long road under the trees, creeping along, and when a carriage comes she hides under the blackberry vines.

I don't blame her a bit. It must be very humiliating to be caught creeping by daylight!

I always lock the door when I creep by daylight. I can't do it at night, for I know John would suspect something at once.

And John is so queer now, that I don't want to irritate him. I wish he would take another room! Besides, I don't want anybody to get that woman out at night but myself.

I often wonder if I could see her out of all the windows at once.

But, turn as fast as I can, I can only see out of one at one time. And though I always see her, she *may* be able to creep faster than I can turn!

I have watched her sometimes away off in the open country, creeping as fast as a cloud shadow in a high wind.

If only that top pattern could be gotten off from the under one! I mean to try it, little by little.

I have found out another funny thing, but I shan't tell it this time! It does not do to trust people too much.

There are only two more days to get this paper off, and I

believe John is beginning to notice. I don't like the look in his eyes.

And I heard him ask Jennie a lot of professional questions about me. She had a very good report to give.

She said I slept a good deal in the daytime.

John knows I don't sleep very well at night, for all I'm so quiet!

He asked me all sorts of questions, too, and pretended to be very loving and kind.

As if I couldn't see through him!

Still, I don't wonder he acts so, sleeping under this paper for three months.

It only interests me, but I feel sure John and Jennie are secretly affected by it.

Hurrah! This is the last day, but it is enough. John to stay in town over night, and won't be out until this evening.

Jennie wanted to sleep with me — the sly thing! But I told her I should undoubtedly rest better for a night all alone.

That was clever, for really I wasn't alone a bit! As soon as it was moonlight and that poor thing began to crawl and shake the pattern, I got up and ran to help her.

I pulled and she shook, I shook and she pulled, and before morning we had peeled off yards of that paper.

A strip about as high as my head and half around the room. And then when the sun came and that awful pattern began to laugh at me, I declared I would finish it to-day!

We go away to-morrow, and they are moving all my furniture down again to leave things as they were before.

Jennie looked at the wall in amazement, but I told her merrily that I did it out of pure spite at the vicious thing.

She laughed and said she wouldn't mind doing it herself, but I must not get tired.

How she betrayed herself that time!

But I am here, and no person touches this paper but me — not *alive!*

She tried to get me out of the room — it was too patent! But I said it was so quiet and empty and clean now that I believed I would lie down again and sleep all I could; and not to wake me even for dinner — I would call when I woke.

So now she is gone, and the servants are gone, and the things are gone, and there is nothing left but that great bedstead nailed down, with the canvas mattress we found on it.

We shall sleep downstairs to-night, and take the boat home to-morrow.

I quite enjoy the room, now it is bare again.

How those children did tear about here!

This bedstead is fairly gnawed!

But I must get to work.

I have locked the door and thrown the key down into the front path.

I don't want to go out, and I don't want to have anybody come in, till John comes.

I want to astonish him.

I've got a rope up here that even Jennie did not find. If that woman does get out, and tries to get away, I can tie her!

But I forgot I could not reach far without anything to stand on! This bed will *not* move!

I tried to lift and push it until I was lame, and then I got so angry I bit off a little piece at one corner — but it hurt my teeth.

Then I peeled off all the paper I could reach standing on the floor. It sticks horribly and the pattern just enjoys it! All those strangled heads and bulbous eyes and waddling fungus growths just shriek with derision!

I am getting angry enough to do something desperate. To jump out of the window would be admirable exercise, but the bars are too strong even to try.

Besides I wouldn't do it. Of course not. I know well enough that a step like that is improper and might be misconstrued.

I don't like to *look* out of the windows even — there are so many of those creeping women, and they creep so fast.

I wonder if they all come out of that wallpaper as I did?

But I am securely fastened now by my well-hidden rope — you don't get *me* out in the road there!

I suppose I shall have to get back behind the pattern when it comes night, and that is hard!

It is so pleasant to be out in this great room and creep around as I please!

I don't want to go outside. I won't, even if Jennie asks me to.

For outside you have to creep on the ground, and everything is green instead of yellow.

But here I can creep smoothly on the floor, and my shoulder just fits in that long smooch around the wall, so I cannot lose my way.

Why there's John at the door!

It is no use, young man, you can't open it!

How he does call and pound!

Now he's crying for an axe.

It would be a shame to break down that beautiful door!

"John dear!" said I in the gentlest voice, "the key is down by the front steps, under a plantain leaf!"

That silenced him for a few moments.

Then he said — very quietly indeed, "Open the door, my darling!"

"I can't," said I. "The key is down by the front door under a plantain leaf!"

And then I said it again, several times, very gently and slowly, and said it so often that he had to go and see, and he got it of course, and came in. He stopped short by the door.

"What is the matter?" he cried. "For God's sake, what are you doing!"

I kept on creeping just the same, but I looked at him over my shoulder.

"I've got out at last," said I, "in spite of you and Jennie. And I've pulled off most of the paper, so you can't put me back!"

Now why should that man have fainted? But he did, and right across my path by the wall, so that I had to creep over him every time!

James Joyce (Irish. 1882–1941)

Araby

North Richmond Street, being blind,° was a quiet street except at the hour when the Christian Brothers' School set the boys free. An uninhabited house of two storeys stood at the blind end, detached from its neighbours in a square ground. The other houses of the street, conscious of decent lives within them, gazed at one another with brown imperturbable faces.

The former tenant of our house, a priest, had died in the back drawing-room. Air, musty from having been long enclosed, hung in all the rooms, and the waste room behind the kitchen was littered with old useless papers. Among these I found a few papercovered books, the pages of which were curled and damp:

---

blind   a dead-end street

The Abbot, by Walter Scott, *The Devout Communicant* and *The Memoirs of Vidocq.** I liked the last best because its leaves were yellow. The wild garden behind the house contained a central apple-tree and a few straggling bushes under one of which I found the late tenant's rusty bicycle-pump. He had been a very charitable priest; in his will he had left all his money to institutions and the furniture of his house to his sister.

When the short days of winter came dusk fell before we had well eaten our dinners. When we met in the street the houses had grown sombre. The space of sky above us was the colour of everchanging violet and towards it the lamps of the street lifted their feeble lanterns. The cold air stung us and we played till our bodies glowed. Our shouts echoed in the silent street. The career of our play brought us through the dark muddy lanes behind the houses where we ran the gauntlet of the rough tribes from the cottages, to the back doors of the dark dripping gardens where odours arose from the ashpits, to the dark odorous stables where a coachman smoothed and combed the horse or shook music from the buckled harness. When we returned to the street light from the kitchen windows had filled the areas. If my uncle was seen turning the corner we hid in the shadow until we had seen him safely housed. Or if Mangan's sister came out on the doorstep to call her brother in to his tea we watched her from our shadow peer up and down the street. We waited to see whether she would remain or go in and, if she remained, we left our shadow and walked up to Mangan's steps resignedly. She was waiting for us, her figure defined by the light from the half-opened door. Her brother always teased her before he obeyed and I stood by the railings looking at her. Her dress swung as she moved her body and the soft rope of her hair tossed from side to side.

Every morning I lay on the floor in the front parlour watching her door. The blind was pulled down to within an inch of the sash so that I could not be seen. When she came out on the doorstep my heart leaped. I ran to the hall, seized my books and followed her. I kept her brown figure always in my eye and, when we came near the point at which our ways diverged, I quickened my pace and passed her. This happened morning after morning. I had never spoken to her, except for a few casual words, and yet her name was like a summons to all my foolish blood.

Her image accompanied me even in places the most hostile

---

* *The Abbot* was one of Scott's popular historical romances; *The Devout Communicant* was a Catholic religious manual; *The Memoirs of Vidocq* were the memoirs of the chief of the French detective force.

to romance. On Saturday evenings when my aunt went marketing I had to go to carry some of the parcels. We walked through the flaring streets, jostled by drunken men and bargaining women, amid the curses of labourers, the shrill litanies of shop-boys who stood on guard by the barrels of pigs' cheeks, the nasal chanting of street-singers, who sang a *come-all-you* about O'Donovan Rossa,* or a ballad about the troubles in our native land. These noises converged in a single sensation of life for me: I imagined that I bore my chalice safely through a throng of foes. Her name sprang to my lips at moments in strange prayers and praises which I myself did not understand. My eyes were often full of tears (I could not tell why) and at times a flood from my heart seemed to pour itself out into my bosom. I thought little of the future. I did not know whether I would ever speak to her or not or, if I spoke to her, how I could tell her of my confused adoration. But my body was like a harp and her words and gestures were like fingers running upon the wires.

One evening I went into the back drawing-room in which the priest had died. It was a dark rainy evening and there was no sound in the house. Through one of the broken panes I heard the rain impinge upon the earth, the fine incessant needles of water playing in the sodden beds. Some distant lamp or lighted window gleamed below me. I was thankful that I could see so little. All my senses seemed to desire to veil themselves and, feeling that I was about to slip from them, I pressed the palms of my hands together until they trembled, murmuring: *O love! O love!* many times.

At last she spoke to me. When she addressed the first words to me I was so confused that I did not know what to answer. She asked me was I going to Araby. I forget whether I answered yes or no. It would be a splendid bazaar, she said; she would love to go.

— And why can't you? I asked.

While she spoke she turned a silver bracelet round and round her wrist. She could not go, she said, because there would be a retreat that week in her convent. Her brother and two other boys were fighting for their caps and I was alone at the railings. She held one of the spikes, bowing her head towards me. The light from the lamp opposite our door caught the white curve of her

* Jeremiah O'Donovan (1831–1915) was a popular Irish leader who was jailed by the British for advocating violent rebellion. A "come-all-you" was a topical song that began "Come all you gallant Irishmen."

neck, lit up her hair that rested there and, falling, lit up the hand
upon the railing. It fell over one side of her dress and caught the
white border of a petticoat, just visible as she stood at ease.

— It's well for you, she said.

— If I go, I said, I will bring you something.

What innumerable follies laid waste my waking and sleeping
thoughts after that evening! I wished to annihilate the tedious
intervening days. I chafed against the work of school. At night
in my bedroom and by day in the classroom her image came
between me and the page I strove to read. The syllables of the
word *Araby* were called to me through the silence in which my
soul luxuriated and cast an Eastern enchantment over me. I asked
for leave to go to the bazaar on Saturday night. My aunt was
surprised and hoped it was not some Freemason* affair. I answered
few questions in class, I watched my master's face pass from
amiability to sternness; he hoped I was not beginning to idle. I
could not call my wandering thoughts together. I had hardly any
patience with the serious work of life which, now that it stood
between me and my desire, seemed to me child's play, ugly monotonous child's play.

On Saturday morning I reminded my uncle that I wished
to go to the bazaar in the evening. He was fussing at the hallstand,
looking for the hat-brush, and answered me curtly:

— Yes, boy, I know.

As he was in the hall I could not go into the front parlour
and lie at the window. I left the house in bad humour and walked
slowly towards the school. The air was pitilessly raw and already
my heart misgave me.

When I came home to dinner my uncle had not yet been
home. Still it was early. I sat staring at the clock for some time
and, when its ticking began to irritate me, I left the room. I
mounted the staircase and gained the upper part of the house. The
high cold empty gloomy rooms liberated me and I went from
room to room singing. From the front window I saw my companions playing below in the street. Their cries reached me weakened
and indistinct and, leaning my forehead against the cool glass, I
looked over at the dark house where she lived. I may have stood
there for an hour, seeing nothing but the brown-clad figure cast
by my imagination, touched discreetly by the lamplight at the
curved neck, at the hand upon the railings and at the border below
the dress.

---

* Irish Catholics viewed the Masons as their Protestant enemies.

When I came downstairs again I found Mrs Mercer sitting at the fire. She was an old garrulous woman, a pawnbroker's widow, who collected used stamps for some pious purpose. I had to endure the gossip of the tea-table. The meal was prolonged beyond an hour and still my uncle did not come. Mrs Mercer stood up to go: she was sorry she couldn't wait any longer, but it was after eight o'clock and she did not like to be out late, as the night air was bad for her. When she had gone I began to walk up and down the room, clenching my fists. My aunt said:

— I'm afraid you may put off your bazaar for this night of Our Lord.

At nine o'clock I heard my uncle's latchkey in the halldoor. I heard him talking to himself and heard the hallstand rocking when it had received the weight of his overcoat. I could interpret these signs. When he was midway through his dinner I asked him to give me the money to go to the bazaar. He had forgotten.

— The people are in bed and after their first sleep now, he said.

I did not smile. My aunt said to him energetically:

— Can't you give him the money and let him go? You've kept him late enough as it is.

My uncle said he was very sorry he had forgotten. He said he believed in the old saying: *All work and no play makes Jack a dull boy.* He asked me where I was going and, when I had told him a second time he asked me did I know *The Arab's Farewell to his Steed.** When I left the kitchen he was about to recite the opening lines of the piece to my aunt.

I held a florin tightly in my hand as I strode down Buckingham Street towards the station. The sight of the streets thronged with buyers and glaring with gas recalled to me the purpose of my journey. I took my seat in a third-class carriage of a deserted train. After an intolerable delay the train moved out of the station slowly. It crept onward among ruinous houses and over the twinkling river. At Westland Row Station a crowd of people pressed to the carriage doors; but the porters moved them back, saying that it was a special train for the bazaar. I remained alone in the bare carriage. In a few minutes the train drew up beside an improvised wooden platform. I passed out on to the road and saw by the lighted dial of a clock that it was ten minutes to ten. In front of me was a large building which displayed the magical name.

* "The Arab to His Favorite Steed" was a popular sentimental poem by Caroline Norton (1808–1877).

I could not find any sixpenny entrance and, fearing that the bazaar would be closed, I passed in quickly through a turnstile, handing a shilling to a weary-looking man. I found myself in a big hall girdled at half its height by a gallery. Nearly all the stalls were closed and the greater part of the hall was in darkness. I recognised a silence like that which pervades a church after a service. I walked into the centre of the bazaar timidly. A few people were gathered about the stalls which were still open. Before a curtain, over which the words *Café Chantant* were written in coloured lamps, two men were counting money on a salver. I listened to the fall of the coins.

Remembering with difficulty why I had come I went over to one of the stalls and examined porcelain vases and flowered teasets. At the door of the stall a young lady was talking and laughing with two young gentlemen. I remarked their English accents and listened vaguely to their conversation.

— O, I never said such a thing!
— O, but you did!
— O, but I didn't!
— Didn't she say that?
— Yes! I heard her.
— O, there's a . . . fib!

Observing me the young lady came over and asked me did I wish to buy anything. The tone of her voice was not encouraging; she seemed to have spoken to me out of a sense of duty. I looked humbly at the great jars that stood like eastern guards at either side of the dark entrance to the stall and murmured:

— No, thank you.

The young lady changed the position of one of the vases and went back to the two young men. They began to talk of the same subject. Once or twice the young lady glanced at me over her shoulder.

I lingered before her stall, though I knew my stay was useless, to make my interest in her wares seem the more real. Then I turned away slowly and walked down the middle of the bazaar. I allowed the two pennies to fall against the sixpence in my pocket. I heard a voice call from one end of the gallery that the light was out. The upper part of the hall was now completely dark.

Gazing up into darkness I saw myself as a creature driven and derided by vanity; and my eyes burned with anguish and anger.

Franz Kafka (*Austrian-Czechoslovakian. 1883–1924*)

A Hunger Artist

Translated by Willa and Edwin Muir

During these last decades the interest in professional fasting has markedly diminished. It used to pay very well to stage such great performances under one's own management, but today that is quite impossible. We live in a different world now. At one time the whole town took a lively interest in the hunger artist; from day to day of his fast the excitement mounted; everybody wanted to see him at least once a day; there were people who bought season tickets for the last few days and sat from morning till night in front of his small barred cage; even in the nighttime there were visiting hours, when the whole effect was heightened by torch flares; on fine days the cage was set out in the open air, and then it was the children's special treat to see the hunger artist; for their elders he was often just a joke that happened to be in fashion, but the children stood open-mouthed, holding each other's hands for greater security, marveling at him as he sat there pallid in black tights, with his ribs sticking out so prominently, not even on a seat but down among straw on the ground, sometimes giving a courteous nod, answering questions with a constrained smile, or perhaps stretching an arm through the bars so that one might feel how thin it was, and then again withdrawing deep into himself, paying no attention to anyone or anything, not even to the all-important striking of the clock that was the only piece of furniture in his cage, but merely staring into vacancy with half-shut eyes, now and then taking a sip from a tiny glass of water to moisten his lips.

Besides casual onlookers there were also relays of permanent watchers selected by the public, usually butchers, strangely enough, and it was their task to watch the hunger artist day and night, three of them at a time, in case he should have some secret recourse to nourishment. This was nothing but a formality, instituted to reassure the masses, for the initiates knew well enough that during his fast the artist would never in any circumstances, not even under forcible compulsion, swallow the smallest morsel of food; the honor of his profession forbade it. Not every watcher, of course, was capable of understanding this, there were often groups of night watchers who were very lax in carrying out their duties and deliberately huddled together in a retired corner to play cards with great absorption, obviously intending to give the hunger artist the chance of a little refreshment, which they supposed he could draw from some private hoard. Nothing annoyed the artist more than such watchers; they made him miserable; they made his fast seem unendurable; sometimes he mastered his feebleness sufficiently to sing during their watch for as long as he could keep going, to show them how unjust their suspicions were. But that was of little use; they only wondered at his cleverness in being able to fill his mouth even while singing. Much more to his taste were the watchers who sat close up to the bars, who were not content with the dim night lighting of the hall but focused him in the full glare of the electric pocket torch given them by the impresario. The harsh light did not trouble him at all. In any case he could never sleep properly, and he could always drowse a little, whatever the light, at any hour, even when the hall was thronged with noisy onlookers. He was quite happy at the prospect of spending a sleepless night with such watchers; he was ready to exchange jokes with them, to tell them stories out of his nomadic life, anything at all to keep them awake and demonstrate to them again that he had no eatables in his cage and that he was fasting as not one of them could fast. But his happiest moment was when the morning came and an enormous breakfast was brought them, as his expense, on which they flung themselves with the keen appetite of healthy men after a weary night of wakefulness. Of course there were people who argued that this breakfast was an unfair attempt to bribe the watchers, but that was going rather too far, and when they were invited to take on a night's vigil without a breakfast, merely for the sake of the cause, they made themselves scarce, although they stuck stubbornly to their suspicions.

Such suspicions, anyhow, were a necessary accompaniment to the profession of fasting. No one could possibly watch the hunger artist continuously, day and night, and so no one could produce first-hand evidence that the fast had really been rigorous and continuous; only the artist himself could know that; he was therefore bound to be the sole completely satisfied spectator of his own fast. Yet for other reasons he was never satisfied; it was not perhaps mere fasting that had brought him to such skeleton thinness that many people had regretfully to keep away from his exhibitions, because the sight of him was too much for them, perhaps it was dissatisfaction with himself that had worn him down. For he alone knew, what no other initiate knew, how easy it was to fast. It was the easiest thing in the world. He made no secret of this, yet people did not believe him; at the best they set

him down as modest, most of them, however, thought he was
out for publicity or else was some kind of cheat who found it
easy to fast because he had discovered a way of making it easy,
and then had the impudence to admit the fact, more or less. He
had to put up with all that, and in the course of time had got
used to it, but his inner dissatisfaction always rankled, and never
yet, after any term of fasting — this must be granted to his credit
— had he left the cage of his own free will. The longest period
of fasting was fixed by his impresario at forty days, beyond that
term he was not allowed to go, not even in great cities, and there
was good reason for it, too. Experience had proved that for about
forty days the interest of the public could be stimulated by a
steadily increasing pressure of advertisement, but after that the
town began to lose interest, sympathetic support began notably
to fall off; there were of course local variations as between one
town and another or one country and another, but as a general
rule forty days marked the limit. So on the fortieth day the flower-
bedecked cage was opened, enthusiastic spectators filled the hall,
a military band played, two doctors entered the cage to measure
the results of the fast, which were announced through a megaphone,
and finally two young ladies appeared, blissful at having been
selected for the honor, to help the hunger artist down the few
steps leading to a small table on which was spread a carefully
chosen invalid repast. And at this very moment the artist always
turned stubborn. True, he would entrust his bony arms to the
outstretched helping hands of the ladies bending over him, but
stand up he would not. Why stop fasting at this particular moment,
after forty days of it? He had held out for a long time, an illimitably
long time; why stop now, when he was in his best fasting form,
or rather, not yet quite in his best fasting form? Why should he
be cheated of the fame he would get for fasting longer, for being
not only the record hunger artist of all time, which presumably
he was already, but for beating his own record by a performance
beyond human imagination, since he felt that there were no limits
to his capacity for fasting? His public pretended to admire him so
much, why should it have so little patience with him; if he could
endure fasting longer, why shouldn't the public endure it? Besides,
he was tired, he was comfortable sitting in the straw, and now
he was supposed to lift himself to his full height and go down to
a meal the very thought of which gave him a nausea that only
the presence of the ladies kept him from betraying, and even that
with an effort. And he looked up into the eyes of the ladies who
were apparently so friendly and in reality so cruel, and shook his
head, which felt too heavy on its strengthless neck. But then there

happened yet again what always happened. The impresario came forward, without a word — for the band made speech impossible — lifted his arms in the air above the artist, as if inviting Heaven to look down upon its creature here in the straw, this suffering martyr, which indeed he was, although in quite another sense; grasped him around the emaciated waist, with exaggerated caution, so that the frail condition he was in might be appreciated; and committed him to the care of the blenching ladies, not without secretly giving him a shaking so that his legs and body tottered and swayed. The artist now submitted completely; his head rolled on his breast as if it had landed there by chance; his body was hollowed out; his legs in a spasm of self-preservation clung close to each other at the knees, yet scraped on the ground as if it were not really solid ground, as if they were only trying to find solid ground; and the whole weight of his body, a featherweight after all, relapsed onto one of the ladies, who, looking round for help and panting a little — this post of honor was not at all what she had expected it to be — first stretched her neck as far as she could to keep her face at least free from contact with the artist, then finding this impossible, and her more fortunate companion not coming to her aid but merely holding extended on her own trembling hand the little bunch of knucklebones that was the artist's, to the great delight of the spectators burst into tears and had to be replaced by an attendant who had long been stationed in readiness. Then came the food, a little of which the impresario managed to get between the artist's lips, while he sat in a kind of half-fainting trance, to the accompaniment of cheerful patter designed to distract the public's attention from the artist's condition; after that, a toast was drunk to the public, supposedly prompted by a whisper from the artist in the impresario's ear; the band confirmed it with a mightly flourish, the spectators melted away, and no one had any cause to be dissatisfied with the proceedings, no one except the hunger artist himself, he only, as always.

So he lived for many years, with small regular intervals of recuperation, in visible glory, honored by the world, yet in spite of that troubled in spirit, and all the more troubled because no one would take his trouble seriously. What comfort could he possibly need? What more could he possibly wish for? And if some good-natured person, feeling sorry for him, tried to console him by pointing out that his melancholy was probably caused by fasting, it could happen, especially when he had been fasting for some time, that he reacted with an outburst of fury and to the general alarm began to shake the bars of his cage like a wild animal. Yet the impresario had a way of punishing these outbreaks which he rather enjoyed putting into operation. He would apologize publicly for the artist's behavior, which was only to be excused, he admitted, because of the irritability caused by fasting; a condition hardly to be understood by well-fed people; then by natural transition he went on to mention the artist's equally incomprehensible boast that he could fast for much longer than he was doing; he praised the high ambition, the good will, the great self-denial undoubtedly implicit in such a statement; and then quite simply countered it by bringing out photographs, which were also on sale to the public, showing the artist on the fortieth day of a fast lying in bed almost dead from exhaustion. This perversion of the truth, familiar to the artist though it was, always unnerved him afresh and proved too much for him. What was a consequence of the premature ending of his fast was here presented as the cause of it! To fight against this lack of understanding, against a whole world of non-understanding, was impossible. Time and again in good faith he stood by the bars listening to the impresario, but as soon as the photographs appeared he always let go and sank with a groan back on to his straw, and the reassured public could once more come close and gaze at him.

A few years later when the witnesses of such scenes called them to mind, they often failed to understand themselves at all. For meanwhile the aforementioned change in public interest had set in; it seemed to happen almost overnight; there may have been profound causes for it, but who was going to bother about that; at any rate the pampered hunger artist suddenly found himself deserted one fine day by the amusement seekers, who went streaming past him to other more favored attractions. For the last time the impresario hurried him over half Europe to discover whether the old interest might still survive here and there; all in vain; everywhere, as if by secret agreement, a positive revulsion from professional fasting was in evidence. Of course it could not really have sprung up so suddenly as all that, and many premonitory symptoms which had not been sufficiently remarked or suppressed during the rush and glitter of success now came retrospectively to mind, but it was now too late to take any countermeasures. Fasting would surely come into fashion again at some future date, yet that was no comfort for those living in the present. What, then, was the hunger artist to do? He had been applauded by thousands in his time and could hardly come down to showing himself in a street booth at village fairs, and as for adopting another profession, he was not only too old for that but too fanatically devoted to fasting. So he took leave of the impresario, his partner in an unparalleled career, and hired himself to a large circus; in order to spare his own feelings he avoided reading the conditions of his contract.

A large circus with its enormous traffic in replacing and recruiting men, animals and apparatus can always find a use for people at any time, even for a hunger artist, provided of course that he does not ask too much, and in this particular case anyhow it was not only the artist who was taken on but his famous and long-known name as well; indeed considering the peculiar nature of his performance, which was not impaired by advancing age, it could not be objected that here was an artist past his prime, no longer at the height of his professional skill, seeking a refuge in some quiet corner of a circus; on the contrary, the hunger artist averred that he could fast as well as ever, which was entirely credible; he even alleged that if he were allowed to fast as he liked, and this was at once promised him without more ado, he could astound the world by establishing a record never yet achieved, a statement which certainly provoked a smile among the other professionals, since it left out of account the change in public opinion, which the hunger artist in his zeal conveniently forgot.

He had not, however, actually lost his sense of the real situation and took it as a matter of course that he and his cage should be stationed, not in the middle of the ring as a main attraction, but outside, near the animal cages, on a site that was after all easily accessible. Large and gaily painted placards made a frame for the cage and announced what was to be seen inside it. When the public came thronging out in the intervals to see the animals, they could hardly avoid passing the hunger artist's cage and stopping there for a moment; perhaps they might even have stayed longer had not those pressing behind them in the narrow gangway, who did not understand why they should be held up on their way towards the excitements of the menagerie, made it impossible for anyone to stand gazing quietly for any length of time. And that was the reason why the hunger artist, who had of course been looking forward to these visiting hours as the main achievement of his life, began instead to shrink from them. At first he could hardly wait for the intervals; it was exhilarating to watch the crowds come streaming his way, until only too soon — not even the most obstinate self-deception, clung to almost consciously, could hold out against the fact — the conviction was borne in upon him that these people, most of them, to judge from their actions, again and again, without exception, were all on their way to the menagerie. And the first sight of them from the distance remained the best. For when they reached his cage he was at once

deafened by the storm of shouting and abuse that arose from the
two contending factions, which renewed themselves continuously,
of those who wanted to stop and stare at him — he soon began
to dislike them more than the others — not out of real interest
but only out of obstinate self-assertiveness, and those who wanted
to go straight on to the animals. When the first great rush was
past, the stragglers came along, and these, whom nothing could
have prevented from stopping to look at him as long as they had
breath, raced past with long strides, hardly even glancing at him,
in their haste to get to the menagerie in time. And all too rarely
did it happen that he had a stroke of luck, when some father of
a family fetched up before him with his children, pointed a finger
at the hunger artist and explained at length what the phenomenon
meant, telling stories of earlier years when he himself had watched
similar but much more thrilling performances, and the children,
still rather uncomprehending, since neither inside nor outside school
had they been sufficiently prepared for this lesson — what did
they care about fasting? — yet showed by the brightness of their
intent eyes that new and better times might be coming. Perhaps,
said the hunger artist to himself many a time, things would be a
little better if his cage were set not quite so near the menagerie.
That made it too easy for people to make their choice, to say
nothing of what he suffered from the stench of the menagerie,
the animals' restlessness by night, the carrying past of raw lumps
of flesh for the beasts of prey, the roaring at feeding times, which
depressed him continually. But he did not dare to lodge a complaint
with the management; after all, he had the animals to thank for
the troops of people who passed his cage, among whom there
might always be one here and there to take an interst in him, and
who could tell where they might seclude him if he called attention
to his existence and thereby to the fact that, strictly speaking, he
was only an impediment on the way to the menagerie.

A small impediment, to be sure, one that grew steadily less.
People grew familiar with the strange idea that they could be
expected, in times like these, to take an interest in a hunger artist,
and with this familiarity the verdict went out against him. He
might fast as much as he could, and he did so; but nothing could
save him now, people passed him by. Just try to explain to anyone
the art of fasting! Anyone who has no feeling for it cannot be
made to understand it. The fine placards grew dirty and illegible,
they were torn down; the little notice board telling the number
of fast days achieved, which at first was changed carefully every
day, had long stayed at the same figure, for after the first few
weeks even this small task seemed pointless to the staff; and so

the artist simply fasted on and on, as he had once dreamed of doing, and it was no trouble to him, just as he had always foretold, but no one counted the days, no one, not even the artist himself, knew what records he was already breaking, and his heart grew heavy. And when once in a time some leisurely passer-by stopped, made merry over the old figure on the board and spoke of swindling, that was in its way the stupidest lie ever invented by indifference and inborn malice, since it was not the hunger artist who was cheating; he was working honestly, but the world was cheating him of his reward.

Many more days went by, however, and that too came to an end. An overseer's eye fell on the cage one day and he asked the attendants why this perfectly good cage should be left standing there unused with dirty straw inside it; nobody knew, until one man, helped out by the notice board, remembered about the hunger artist. They poked into the staw with sticks and found him in it. "Are you still fasting?" asked the overseer. "When on earth do you mean to stop?" "Forgive me, everybody," whispered the hunger artist; only the overseer, who had his ear to the bars, understood him. "Of course," said the overseer, and tapped his forehead with a finger to let the attendants know what state the man was in, "we forgive you." "I always wanted you to admire my fasting," said the hunger artist. "We do admire it," said the overseer, affably. "But you shouldn't admire it," said the hunger artist. "Well, then we don't admire it," said the overseer, "but why shouldn't we admire it?" "Because I have to fast, I can't help it," said the hunger artist. "What a fellow you are," said the overseer; "and why can't you help it?" "Because," said the hunger artist, lifting his head a little and speaking, with his lips pursed, as if for a kiss, right into the overseer's ear, so that no syllable might be lost, "because I couldn't find the food I liked. If I had found it, believe me, I should have made no fuss and stuffed myself like you or anyone else." These were his last words, but in his dimming eyes remained the firm though no longer proud persuasion that he was still continuing to fast.

"Well, clear this out now!" said the overseer, and they buried the hunger artist, straw and all. Into the cage they put a young panther. Even the most insensitive felt it refreshing to see this wild creature leaping around the cage that had so long been dreary. The panther was all right. The food he liked was brought him without hesitation by the attendants; he seemed not even to miss his freedom; his noble body, furnished almost to the bursting point with all that it needed, seemed to carry freedom around with it too; somewhere in his jaws it seemed to lurk; and the joy of life streamed with such ardent passion from his throat that for the onlookers it was not easy to stand the shock of it. But they braced themselves, crowded round the cage, and did not want ever to move away.

Franz Kafka (*Austrian-Czechoslovakian. 1883–1924*)

The Metamorphosis

Translated by Willa and Edwin Muir

I

As Gregor Samsa awoke one morning from uneasy dreams he found himself transformed in his bed into a gigantic insect. He was lying on his hard, as it were armor-plated, back and when he lifted his head a little he could see his dome-like brown belly divided into stiff arched segments on top of which the bed quilt could hardly keep in position and was about to slide off completely. His numerous legs, which were pitifully thin compared to the rest of his bulk, waved helplessly before his eyes.

What has happened to me? he thought. It was no dream. His room, a regular human bedroom, only rather too small, lay quiet between the four familiar walls. Above the table on which a collection of cloth samples was unpacked and spread out — Samsa was a commercial traveler — hung the picture which he had recently cut out of an illustrated magazine and put into a pretty gilt frame. It showed a lady, with a fur cap on and a fur stole, sitting upright and holding out to the spectator a huge fur muff into which the whole of her forearm had vanished!

Gregor's eyes turned next to the window, and the overcast sky — one could hear rain drops beating on the window gutter — made him quite melancholy. What about sleeping a little longer and forgetting all this nonsense, he thought, but it could not be done, for he was accustomed to sleep on his right side and in his present condition he could not turn himself over. However violently he forced himself towards his right side he always rolled on to his back again. He tried it at least a hundred times, shutting his eyes to keep from seeing his struggling legs, and only desisted when he began to feel in his side a faint dull ache he had never experienced before.

Oh God, he thought, what an exhausting job I've picked on! Traveling about day in, day out. It's much more irritating work than doing the actual business in the office, and on top of that there's the trouble of constant traveling, of worrying about train connections, the bed and irregular meals, casual acquaintances that are always new and never become intimate friends. The devil take it all! He felt a slight itching up on his belly; slowly pushed himself on his back nearer to the top of the bed so that he could lift his head more easily; identified the itching place which was surrounded by many small white spots the nature of which he could not understand and made to touch it with a leg, but drew the leg back immediately, for the contact made a cold shiver run through him.

He slid down again into his former position. This getting up early, he thought, makes one quite stupid. A man needs his sleep. Other commercials live like harem women. For instance, when I come back to the hotel of a morning to write up the orders I've got, these others are only sitting down to breakfast. Let me just try that with my chief; I'd be sacked on the spot. Anyhow, that might be quite a good thing for me, who can tell? If I didn't have to hold my hand because of my parents I'd have given notice long ago, I'd have gone to the chief and told him exactly what I think of him. That would knock him endways from his desk! It's a queer way of doing, too, this sitting on high at a desk and talking down to employees, especially when they have to come quite near because the chief is hard of hearing. Well, there's still hope; once I've saved enough money to pay back my parents' debts to him — that should take another five or six years — I'll do it without fail. I'll cut myself completely loose then. For the moment, though, I'd better get up, since my train goes at five.

He looked at the alarm clock ticking on the chest. Heavenly Father! he thought. It was half-past six o'clock and the hands were quietly moving on, it was even past the half-hour, it was getting on toward a quarter to seven. Had the alarm clock not gone off? From the bed one could see that it had been properly set for four o'clock; of course it must have gone off. Yes, but was it possible to sleep quietly through that ear-splitting noise? Well, he had not slept quietly, yet apparently all the more soundly for that. But what was he to do now? The next train went at seven o'clock; to catch that he would need to hurry like mad and his samples weren't even packed up, and he himself wasn't feeling particularly fresh and active. And even if he did catch the train he wouldn't avoid a row with the chief, since the firm's porter would have been waiting for the five o'clock train and would have long since reported his failure to turn up. The porter was a creature of the chief's, spineless and stupid. Well, supposing he were to say he was sick? But that would be most unpleasant and would look suspicious, since during his five years' employment he had not been ill once. The chief himself would be sure to come with the sick-insurance doctor, would reproach his parents with their son's laziness and would cut all excuses short by referring to the insurance doctor, who of course regarded all mankind as perfectly healthy malingerers. And would he be so far wrong on this occasion? Gregor really felt quite well, apart from a drowsiness that was utterly superfluous after such a long sleep, and he was even unusually hungry.

As all this was running through his mind at top speed without his being able to decide to leave his bed — the alarm clock had just struck a quarter to seven — there came a cautious tap at the door behind the head of his bed. "Gregor," said a voice — it was his mother's — "it's a quarter to seven. Hadn't you a train to catch?" That gentle voice! Gregor had a shock as he heard his own voice answering hers, unmistakably his own voice, it was true, but with a persistent horrible twittering squeak behind it like an undertone, that left the words in their clear shape only for the first moment and then rose up reverberating round them to destroy their sense, so that one could not be sure one had heard them rightly. Gregor wanted to answer at length and explain everything, but in the circumstances he confined himself to saying: "Yes, yes, thank you, Mother, I'm getting up now." The wooden door between them must have kept the change in his voice from being noticeable outside, for his mother contented herself with this statement and shuffled away. Yet this brief exchange of words had made the other members of the family aware that Gregor was still in the house, as they had not expected, and at one of the side doors his father was already knocking, gently, yet with his fist. "Gregor, Gregor," he called, "what's the matter with you?" And after a little while he called again in a deeper voice: "Gregor! Gregor!" At the other side door his sister was saying in a low, plaintive tone: "Gregor? Aren't you well? Are you needing anything?" He answered them both at once: "I'm just ready," and did his best to make his voice sound as normal as possible by enunciating the words very clearly and leaving long pauses between them. So his father went back to his breakfast, but his sister whispered: "Gregor, open the door, do." However, he was not thinking of opening the door, and felt thankful for the prudent habit he had acquired in traveling of locking all doors during the night, even at home.

His immediate intention was to get up quietly without being disturbed, to put on his clothes and above all eat his breakfast, and only then to consider what else was to be done, since in bed, he was well aware, his meditations would come to no sensible conclusion. He remembered that often enough in bed he had felt small aches and pains, probably caused by awkward postures, which had proved purely imaginary once he got up, and he looked forward eagerly to seeing this morning's delusions gradually fall away. That the change in his voice was nothing but the precursor of a severe chill, a standing ailment of commercial travelers, he had not the least possible doubt.

To get rid of the quilt was quite easy; he had only to inflate himself a little and it fell off by itself. But the next move was difficult, especially because he was so uncommonly broad. He would have needed arms and hands to hoist himself up; instead he had only the numerous little legs which never stopped waving in all directions and which he could not control in the least. When he tried to bend one of them it was the first to stretch itself straight; and did he succeed at last in making it do what he wanted, all the other legs meanwhile waved the more wildly in a high degree of unpleasant agitation. "But what's the use of lying idle in bed," said Gregor to himself.

He thought that he might get out of bed with the lower part of his body first, but this lower part, which he had not yet seen and of which he could form no clear conception, proved too difficult to move; it shifted so slowly; and when finally, almost wild with annoyance, he gathered his forces together and thrust out recklessly, he had miscalculated the direction and bumped heavily against the lower end of the bed, and the stinging pain he felt informed him that precisely this lower part of his body was at the moment probably the most sensitive.

So he tried to get the top part of himself out first, and cautiously moved his head towards the edge of the bed. That proved easy enough, and despite its breadth and mass the bulk of his body at last slowly followed the movement of his head. Still, when he finally got his head free over the edge of the bed he felt too scared to go on advancing, for after all if he let himself fall in this way it would take a miracle to keep his head from being injured. And at all costs he must not lose consciousness now, precisely now; he would rather stay in bed.

But when after a repetition of the same efforts he lay in his former position again, sighing, and watched his little legs struggling against each other more wildly than ever, if that were possible, and saw no way of bringing any order into this arbitrary confusion, he told himself again that it was impossible to stay in bed and that the most sensible course was to risk everything for the smallest hope of getting away from it. At the same time he did not forget meanwhile to remind himself that cool reflection, the coolest possible, was much better than desperate resolves. In such moments he focused his eyes as sharply as possible on the window, but, unfortunately, the prospect of the morning fog, which muffled even the other side of the narrow street, brought him little encouragement and comfort. "Seven o'clock already," he said to himself when the alarm clock chimed again, "seven o'clock already and still such a thick fog." And for a little while he lay quiet, breathing lightly, as if perhaps expecting such complete repose to restore all things to their real and normal condition.

But then he said to himself: "Before it strikes a quarter past seven I must be quite out of this bed, without fail. Anyhow, by that time someone will have come from the office to ask for me, since it opens before seven." And he set himself to rocking his whole body at once in a regular rhythm, with the idea of swinging it out of the bed. If he tipped himself out in that way he could keep his head from injury by lifting it at an acute angle when he fell. His back seemed to be hard and was not likely to suffer from a fall on the carpet. His biggest worry was the loud crash he would not be able to help making, which would probably cause anxiety, if not terror, behind all the doors. Still, he must take the risk.

When he was already half out of the bed — the new method was more a game than an effort, for he needed only to hitch himself across by rocking to and fro — it struck him how simple it would be if he could get help. Two strong people — he thought of his father and the servant girl — would be amply sufficient; they would only have to thrust their arms under his convex back, lever him out of the bed, bend down with their burden and then be patient enough to let him turn himself right over on to the floor, where it was to be hoped his legs would then find their proper function. Well, ignoring the fact that the doors were all locked, ought he really to call for help? In spite of his misery he could not suppress a smile at the very idea of it.

He had got so far that he could barely keep his equilibrium when he rocked himself strongly, and he would have to nerve himself very soon for the final decision since in five minutes' time it would be a quarter past seven — when the front doorbell rang. "That's someone from the office," he said to himself, and grew almost rigid, while his little legs only jigged about all the faster.

For a moment everything stayed quiet. "They're not going to open the door," said Gregor to himself, catching at some kind of irrational hope. But then of course the servant girl went as usual to the door with her heavy tread and opened it. Gregor needed only to hear the first good morning of the visitor to know immediately who it was — the chief clerk himself. What a fate, to be condemned to work for a firm where the smallest omission at once gave rise to the gravest suspicion! Were all employees in a body nothing but scoundrels, was there not among them one single loyal devoted man who, had he wasted only an hour or so of the firm's time in a morning, was so tormented by conscience as to be driven out of his mind and actually incapable of leaving his bed? Wouldn't it really have been sufficient to send an apprentice to inquire — if any inquiry were necessary at all — did the chief clerk himself have to come and thus indicate to the entire family, an innocent family, that this suspicious circumstance could be investigated by no one less versed in affairs than himself? And more through the agitation caused by these reflections than through any act of will Gregor swung himself out of bed with all his strength. There was a loud thump, but it was not really a crash. His fall was broken to some extent by the carpet, his back, too, was less stiff than he thought, and so there was merely a dull thud, not so very startling. Only he had not lifted his head carefully enough and had hit it; he turned it and rubbed it on the carpet in pain and irritation.

"That was something falling down in there," said the chief clerk in the next room to the left. Gregor tried to suppose to himself that something like what had happened to him today might some day happen to the chief clerk; one really could not deny that it was possible. But as if in brusque reply to this supposition the chief clerk took a couple of firm steps in the next-door room and his patent leather boots creaked. From the right-hand room his sister was whispering to inform him of the situation: "Gregor, the chief clerk's here." "I know," muttered Gregor to himself; but he didn't dare to make his voice loud enough for his sister to hear it.

"Gregor," said his father now from the left-hand room, "the chief clerk has come and wants to know why you didn't catch the early train. We don't know what to say to him. Besides, he wants to talk to you in person. So open the door, please. He will be good enough to excuse the untidiness of your room." "Good morning, Mr. Samsa," the chief clerk was calling amiably meanwhile. "He's not well," said his mother to the visitor, while his father was still speaking through the door, "he's not well, sir,

believe me. What else would make him miss a train! The boy
thinks about nothing but his work. It makes me almost cross the
way he never goes out in the evenings; he's been here the last
eight days and has stayed at home every single evening. He just
sits there quietly at the table reading a newspaper or looking
through railway timetables. The only amusement he gets is doing
fretwork. For instance, he spent two or three evenings cutting out
a little picture frame; you would be surprised to see how pretty
it is; it's hanging in his room; you'll see it in a minute when
Gregor opens the door. I must say I'm glad you've come, sir; we
should never have got him to unlock the door by ourselves; he's
so obstinate; and I'm sure he's unwell, though he wouldn't have
it to be so this morning." "I'm just coming," said Gregor slowly
and carefully, not moving an inch for fear of losing one word of
the conversation. "I can't think of any other explanation, madam,"
said the chief clerk, "I hope it's nothing serious. Although on the
other hand I must say that we men of business — fortunately or
unfortunately — very often simply have to ignore any slight indisposition, since business must be attended to." "Well, can the
chief clerk come in now?" asked Gregor's father impatiently, again
knocking on the door. "No," said Gregor. In the left-hand room
a painful silence followed this refusal, in the right-hand room his
sister began to sob.

Why didn't his sister join the others? She was probably newly
out of bed and hadn't even begun to put on her clothes yet. Well,
why was she crying? Because he wouldn't get up and let the chief
clerk in, because he was in danger of losing his job, and because
the chief would begin dunning his parents again for the old debts?
Surely these were things one didn't need to worry about for the
present. Gregor was still at home and not in the least thinking of
deserting the family. At the moment, true, he was lying on the
carpet and no one who knew the condition he was in could seriously
expect him to admit the chief clerk. But for such a small discourtesy,
which could plausibly be explained away somehow later on, Gregor
could hardly be dismissed on the spot. And it seemed to Gregor
that it would be much more sensible to leave him in peace for
the present than to trouble him with tears and entreaties. Still, of
course, their uncertainty bewildered them all and excused their
behavior.

"Mr. Samsa," the chief clerk called now in a louder voice,
"what's the matter with you? Here you are, barricading yourself
in your room, giving only 'yes' and 'no' for answers, causing your
parents a lot of unnecessary trouble and neglecting — I mention
this only in passing — neglecting your business duties in an incredible

fashion. I am speaking here in the name of your parents and of your chief, and I beg you quite seriously to give me an immediate and precise explanation. You amaze me, you amaze me. I thought you were a quiet, dependable person, and now all at once you seem bent on making a disgraceful exhibition of yourself. The chief did hint to me early this morning a possible explanation for your disappearance — with reference to the cash payments that were entrusted to you recently — but I almost pledged my solemn word of honor that this could not be so. But now that I see how incredibly obstinate you are, I no longer have the slightest desire to take your part at all. And your position in the firm is not so unassailable. I came with the intention of telling you all this in private, but since you are wasting my time so needlessly I don't see why your parents shouldn't hear it too. For some time past your work has been most unsatisfactory; this is not the season of the year for a business boom, of course, we admit that, but a season of the year for doing no business at all, that does not exist, Mr. Samsa, must not exist."

"But, sir," cried Gregor, beside himself and in his agitation forgetting everything else, "I'm just going to open the door this very minute. A slight illness, an attack of giddiness, has kept me from getting up. I'm still lying in bed. But I feel all right again. I'm getting out of bed now. Just give me a moment or two longer! I'm not quite so well as I thought. But I'm all right, really. How a thing like that can suddenly strike one down! Only last night I was quite well, my parents can tell you, or rather I did have a slight presentiment. I must have showed some sign of it. Why didn't I report it at the office! But one always thinks that an indisposition can be got over without staying in the house. Oh sir, do spare my parents! All that you're reproaching me with now has no foundation; no one has ever said a word to me about it. Perhaps you haven't looked at the last orders I sent in. Anyhow, I can still catch the eight o'clock train, I'm much the better for my few hours' rest. Don't let me detain you here, sir; I'll be attending to business very soon, and do be good enough to tell the chief so and to make my excuses to him!"

And while all this was tumbling out pell-mell and Gregor hardly knew what he was saying, he had reached the chest quite easily, perhaps because of the practice he had had in bed, and was now trying to lever himself upright by means of it. He meant actually to open the door, actually to show himself and speak to the chief clerk; he was eager to find out what the others, after all their insistence, would say at the sight of him. If they were horrified then the responsibility was no longer his and he could stay quiet.

But if they took it calmly, then he had no reason either to be upset, and could really get to the station for the eight o'clock train if he hurried. At first he slipped down a few times from the polished surface of the chest, but at length with a last heave he stood upright; he paid no more attention to the pains in the lower part of his body, however they smarted. Then he let himself fall against the back of a nearby chair, and clung with his little legs to the edges of it. That brought him into control of himself again and he stopped speaking, for now he could listen to what the chief clerk was saying.

"Did you understand a word of it?" the chief clerk was asking; "surely he can't be trying to make fools of us?" "Oh dear," cried his mother, in tears, "perhaps he's terribly ill and we're tormenting him. Grete! Grete!" she called out then. "Yes Mother?" called his sister from the other side. They were calling to each other across Gregor's room. "You must go this minute for the doctor. Gregor is ill. Go for the doctor, quick. Did you hear how he was speaking?" "That was no human voice," said the chief clerk in a voice noticeably low beside the shrillness of the mother's. "Anna! Anna!" his father was calling through the hall to the kitchen, clapping his hands, "get a locksmith at once!" And the two girls were already running through the hall with a swish of skirts — how could his sister have got dressed so quickly? — and were tearing the front door open. There was no sound of its closing again; they had evidently left it open as one does in houses where some great misfortune has happened.

But Gregor was now much calmer. The words he uttered were no longer understandable, apparently, although they seemed clear enough to him, even clearer than before, perhaps because his ear had grown accustomed to the sound of them. Yet at any rate people now believed that something was wrong with him, and were ready to help him. The positive certainty with which these first measures had been taken comforted him. He felt himself drawn once more into the human circle and hoped for great and remarkable results from both the doctor and the locksmith, without really distinguishing precisely between them. To make his voice as clear as possible for the decisive conversation that was now imminent he coughed a little, as quietly as he could, of course, since this noise too might not sound like a human cough for all he was able to judge. In the next room meanwhile there was complete silence. Perhaps his parents were sitting at the table with the chief clerk, whispering, perhaps they were all leaning against the door and listening.

Slowly Gregor pushed the chair towards the door, then let

go of it, caught hold of the door for support — the soles at the end of his little legs were somewhat sticky — and rested against it for a moment after his efforts. Then he set himself to turning the key in the lock with his mouth. It seemed, unhappily, that he hadn't really any teeth — what could he grip the key with? — but on the other hand his jaws were certainly very strong; with their help he did manage to set the key in motion, heedless of the fact that he was undoubtedly damaging them somewhere, since a brown fluid issued from his mouth, flowed over the key and dripped on the floor. "Just listen to that," said the chief clerk next door; "he's turning the key." That was a great encouragement to Gregor; but they should all have shouted encouragement to him, his father and mother too: "Go on, Gregor," they should have called out, "keep going, hold on to that key!" And in the belief that they were all following his efforts intently, he clenched his jaws recklessly on the key with all the force at his command. As the turning of the key progressed he circled round the lock, holding on now only with his mouth, pushing on the key, as required, or pulling it down again with all the weight of his body. The louder click of the finally yielding lock literally quickened Gregor. With a deep breath of relief he said to himself. "So I didn't need the locksmith," and laid his head on the handle to open the door wide.

Since he had to pull the door towards him, he was still invisible when it was really wide open. He had to edge himself very slowly round the near half of the double door, and to do it very carefully if he was not to fall plump upon his back just on the threshold. He was still carrying out this difficult manoeuvre, with no time to observe anything else, when he heard the chief clerk utter a loud "Oh!" — it sounded like a gust of wind — and now he could see the man, standing as he was nearest to the door, clapping one hand before his open mouth and slowly backing away as if driven by some invisible steady pressure. His mother — in spite of the chief clerk's being there her hair was still undone and sticking up in all directions — first clasped her hands and looked at his father, then took two steps towards Gregor and fell on the floor among her outspread skirts, her face quite hidden on her breast. His father knotted his fist with a fierce expression on his face as if he meant to knock Gregor back into his room, then looked uncertainly round the living room, covered his eyes with his hands and wept till his great chest heaved.

Gregor did not go now into the living room, but leaned against the inside of the firmly shut wing of the door, so that only half his body was visible and his head above it bending sideways to look at the others. The light had meanwhile strengthened; on the other side of the street one could see clearly a section of the endlessly long, dark gray building opposite — it was a hospital — abruptly punctuated by its row of regular windows; the rain was still falling, but only in large singly discernible and literally singly splashing drops. The breakfast dishes were set out on the table lavishly, for breakfast was the most important meal of the day to Gregor's father, who lingered it out for hours over various newspapers. Right opposite Gregor on the wall hung a photograph of himself on military service, as a lieutenant, hand on sword, a carefree smile on his face, inviting one to respect his uniform and military bearing. The door leading to the hall was open, and one could see that the front door stood open too, showing the landing beyond and the beginning of the stairs going down.

"Well," said Gregor, knowing perfectly that he was the only one who had retained any composure, "I'll put my clothes on at once, pack up my samples and start off. Will you only let me go? You see, sir, I'm not obstinate, and I'm willing to work; traveling is a hard life, but I couldn't live without it. Where are you going, sir? To the office? Yes? Will you give a true account of all this? One can be temporarily incapacitated, but that's just the moment for remembering former services and bearing in mind that later on, when the incapacity has been got over, one will certainly work with all the more industry and concentration. I'm loyally bound to serve the chief, you know that very well. Besides, I have to provide for my parents and my sister. I'm in great difficulties, but I'll get out of them again. Don't make things any worse for me than they are. Stand up for me in the firm. Travelers are not popular there, I know. People think they earn sacks of money and just have a good time. A prejudice there's no particular reason for revising. But you, sir, have a more comprehensive view of affairs than the rest of the staff, yes, let me tell you in confidence, a more comprehensive view than the chief himself, who, being the owner, lets his judgment easily be swayed against one of his employees. And you know very well that the traveler, who is never seen in the office almost the whole year round, can so easily fall a victim to gossip and ill luck and unfounded complaints, which he mostly knows nothing about, except when he comes back exhausted from his rounds, and only then suffers in person from their evil consequences, which he can no longer trace back to the original causes. Sir, sir, don't go away without a word to me to show that you think me in the right at least to some extent!"

But at Gregor's very first words the chief clerk had already backed away and only stared at him with parted lips over one twitching shoulder. And while Gregor was speaking he did not stand still one moment but stole away towards the door, without taking his eyes off Gregor, yet only an inch at a time, as if obeying some secret injunction to leave the room. He was already at the hall, and the suddenness with which he took his last step out of the living room would have made one believe he had burned the sole of his foot. Once in the hall he stretched his right arm before him towards the staircase, as if some supernatural power were waiting there to deliver him.

Gregor perceived that the chief clerk must on no account be allowed to go away in this frame of mind if his position in the firm were not to be endangered to the utmost. His parents did not understand this so well; they had convinced themselves in the course of years that Gregor was settled for life in this firm, and besides they were so occupied with their immediate troubles that all foresight had forsaken them. Yet Gregor had this foresight. The chief clerk must be detained, soothed, persuaded and finally won over; the whole future of Gregor and his family depended on it! If only his sister had been there! She was intelligent; she had begun to cry while Gregor was still lying quietly on his back. And no doubt the chief clerk, so partial to ladies, would have been guided by her; she would have shut the door of the flat and in the hall talked him out of his horror. But she was not there, and Gregor would have to handle the situation himself. And without remembering that he was still unaware what powers of movement he possessed, without even remembering that his words in all possibility, indeed in all likelihood, would again be unintelligible, he let go the wing of the door, pushed himself through the opening, started to walk towards the chief clerk, who was already ridiculously clinging with both hands to the railing on the landing; but immediately, as he was feeling for a support, he fell down with a little cry upon all his numerous legs. Hardly was he down when he experienced for the first time this morning a sense of physical comfort; his legs had firm ground under them; they were completely obedient, as he noted with joy; they even strove to carry him forward in whatever direction he chose; and he was inclined to believe that a final relief from all his sufferings was at hand. But in the same moment as he found himself on the floor, rocking with suppressed eagerness to move, not far from his mother, indeed just in front of her, she, who had seemed so completely crushed, sprang all at once to her feet, her arms and fingers outspread, cried: "Help, for God's sake, help!" bent her head down as if to see Gregor better, yet on the contrary kept backing senselessly away; had quite forgotten that the laden table stood behind her;

sat upon it hastily, as if in absence of mind, when she bumped
into it; and seemed altogether unaware that the big coffee pot
beside her was upset and pouring coffee in a flood over the carpet.

"Mother, Mother," said Gregor in a low voice, and looked
up at her. The chief clerk, for the moment, had quite slipped from
his mind; instead he could not resist snapping his jaws together
at the sight of the streaming coffee. That made his mother scream
again, she fled from the table and fell into the arms of his father,
who hastened to catch her. But Gregor had now no time to spare
for his parents; the chief clerk was already on the stairs; with his
chin on the banisters he was taking one last backward look. Gregor
made a spring, to be as sure as possible of overtaking him; the
chief clerk must have divined his intention, for he leaped down
several steps and vanished; he was still yelling "Ugh!" and it
echoed through the whole staircase.

Unfortunately, the flight of the chief clerk seemed completely
to upset Gregor's father, who had remained relatively calm until
now, for instead of running after the man himself, or at least not
hindering Gregor in his pursuit, he seized in his right hand the
walking stick which the chief clerk had left behind on a chair,
together with a hat and greatcoat, snatched in his left hand a large
newspaper from the table and began stamping his feet and flourishing
the stick and the newspaper to drive Gregor back into his room.
No entreaty of Gregor's availed, indeed no entreaty was even
understood; however humbly he bent his head his father only
stamped on the floor the more loudly. Behind his father his mother
had torn open a window, despite the cold weather, and was leaning
far out of it with her face in her hands. A strong draught set in
from the street to the staircase, the window curtain blew in, the
newspapers on the table fluttered, stray pages whisked over the
floor. Pitilessly Gregor's father drove him back, hissing and crying
"Shoo!" like a savage. But Gregor was quite unpracticed in walking
backwards, it really was a slow business. If he only had a chance
to turn round he could get back to his room at once, but he was
afraid of exasperating his father by the slowness of such a rotation
and at any moment the stick in his father's hand might hit him a
fatal blow on the back or on the head. In the end, however, nothing
else was left for him to do since to his horror he observed that
in moving backwards he could not even control the direction he
took; and so, keeping an anxious eye on his father all the time
over his shoulder, he began to turn round as quickly as he could,
which was in reality very slowly. Perhaps his father noted his
good intentions, for he did not interfere except every now and
then to help him in the manoeuvre from a distance with the point

of the stick. If only he would have stopped making that unbearable hissing noise! It made Gregor quite lose his head. He had turned almost completely round when the hissing noise so distracted him that he even turned a little the wrong way again. But when at last his head was fortunately right in front of the doorway, it appeared that his body was too broad simply to get through the opening. His father, of course, in his present mood was far from thinking of such a thing as opening the other half of the door, to let Gregor have enough space. He had merely the fixed idea of driving Gregor back into his room as quickly as possible. He would have never suffered Gregor to make the circumstantial preparations for standing up on end and perhaps slipping his way through the door. Maybe he was now making more noise than ever to urge Gregor forward, as if no obstacle impeded him; to Gregor, anyhow, the noise in his rear sounded no longer like the voice of one single father; this was really no joke, and Gregor thrust himself — come what might — into the doorway. One side of his body rose up, he was tilted at an angle in the doorway, his flank was quite bruised, horrid blotches stained the white door, soon he was stuck fast and, left to himself, could not have moved at all, his legs on one side fluttered trembling in the air, those on the other were crushed painfully to the floor — when from behind his father gave him a strong push which was literally a deliverance and he flew far into the room, bleeding freely. The door was slammed behind him with the stick, and then at last there was silence.

II

Not until it was twilight did Gregor awake out of a deep sleep, more like a swoon than a sleep. He would certainly have waked up of his own accord not much later, for he felt himself sufficiently rested and well-slept, but it seemed to him as if a fleeting step and a cautious shutting of the door leading into the hall had aroused him. The electric lights in the street cast a pale sheen here and there on the ceiling and the upper surfaces of the furniture, but down below, where he lay, it was dark. Slowly, awkwardly trying out his feelers, which he now first learned to appreciate, he pushed his way to the door to see what had been happening there. His left side felt like one single long, unpleasantly tense scar, and he had actually to limp on his two rows of legs. One little leg, moreover, had been severely damaged in the course of that morning's events — it was almost a miracle that only one had been damaged — and trailed uselessly behind him.

He had reached the door before he discovered what had really drawn him to it: the smell of food. For there stood a basin filled with fresh milk in which floated little sops of white bread. He could almost have laughed with joy, since he was now still hungrier than in the morning, and dipped his head almost over the eyes straight into the milk. But soon in disappointment he withdrew it again; not only did he find it difficult to feed because of his tender left side — and he could only feed with the palpitating collaboration of his whole body — he did not like the milk either, although milk had been his favorite drink and that was certainly why his sister had set it there for him, indeed it was almost with repulsion that he turned away from the basin and crawled back to the middle of the room.

He could see through the crack of the door that the gas was turned on in the living room, but while usually at this time his father made a habit of reading the afternoon newspaper in a loud voice to his mother and occasionally to his sister as well, not a sound was now to be heard. Well, perhaps his father had recently given up this habit of reading aloud, which his sister had mentioned so often in conversation and in her letters. But there was the same silence all around, although the flat was certainly not empty of occupants. "What a quiet life our family has been leading," said Gregor to himself, and as he sat there motionless staring into the darkness he felt great pride in the fact that he had been able to provide such a life for his parents and sister in such a fine flat. But what if all the quiet, the comfort, the contentment were now to end in horror? To keep himself from being lost in such thoughts Gregor took refuge in movement and crawled up and down the room.

Once during the long evening one of the side doors was opened a little and quickly shut again, later the other side door too; someone had apparently wanted to come in and then thought better of it. Gregor now stationed himself immediately before the living room door, determined to persuade any hesitating visitor to come in or at least to discover who it might be; but the door was not opened again and he waited in vain. In the early morning, when the doors were locked, they had all wanted to come in, now that he had opened one door and the other had apparently been opened during the day, no one came in and even the keys were on the other side of the doors.

It was late at night before the gas went out in the living room, and Gregor could easily tell that his parents and his sister had all stayed awake until then, for he could clearly hear the three of them stealing away on tiptoe. No one was likely to visit him, not until the morning, that was certain; so he had plenty of time to meditate at his leisure on how he was to arrange his life afresh.

But the lofty, empty room in which he had to lie flat on the floor filled him with an apprehension he could not account for, since it had been his very own room for the past five years — and with a half-unconscious action, not without a slight feeling of shame, he scuttled under the sofa, where he felt comfortable at once, although his back was a little cramped and he could not lift his head up, and his only regret was that his body was too broad to get the whole of it under the sofa.

He stayed there all night, spending the time partly in a light slumber, from which his hunger kept waking him up with a start, and partly in worrying and sketching vague hopes, which all led to the same conclusion, that he must lie low for the present and, by exercising patience and the utmost consideration, help the family to bear the inconvenience he was bound to cause them in his present condition.

Very early in the morning, it was still almost night, Gregor had the chance to test the strength of his new resolutions, for his sister, nearly fully dressed, opened the door from the hall and peered in. She did not see him at once, yet when she caught sight of him under the sofa — well, he had to be somewhere, he couldn't have flown away, could he? — she was so startled that without being able to help it she slammed the door shut again. But as if regretting her behavior she opened the door again immediately and came in on tiptoe, as if she were visiting an invalid or even a stranger. Gregor had pushed his head forward to the very edge of the sofa and watched her. Would she notice that he had left the milk standing, and not for lack of hunger, and would she bring in some other kind of food more to his taste? If she did not do it of her own accord, he would rather starve than draw her attention to the fact, although he felt a wild impulse to dart out from under the sofa, throw himself at her feet and beg her for something to eat. But his sister at once noticed, with surprise, that the basin was still full, except for a little milk that had been spilt all around it, she lifted it immediately, not with her bare hands, true, but with a cloth and carried it away. Gregor was wildly curious to know what she would bring instead, and made various speculations about it. Yet what she actually did next, in the goodness of her heart, he could never have guessed at. To find out what he liked she brought him a whole selection of food, all set out on an old newspaper. There were old, half-decayed vegetables, bones from last night's supper covered with a white sauce that had thickened; some raisins and almonds; a piece of cheese that Gregor would have called uneatable two days ago; a dry roll of bread, a buttered roll, and a roll both buttered and salted. Besides all that, she set down again the same basin, into which she had poured some water, and which was apparently to be reserved for his exclusive use. And with fine tact, knowing that Gregor would not eat in her presence, she withdrew quickly and even turned the key, to let him understand that he could take his ease as much as he liked. Gregor's legs all whizzed towards the food. His wounds must have healed completely, moreover, for he felt no disability, which amazed him and made him reflect how more than a month ago he had cut one finger a little with a knife and had still suffered pain from the wound only the day before yesterday. Am I less sensitive now? he thought, and sucked greedily at the cheese, which above all the other edibles attracted him at once and strongly. One after another and with tears of satisfaction in his eyes he quickly devoured the cheese, the vegetables and the sauce; the fresh food, on the other hand, had no charms for him, he could not even stand the smell of it and actually dragged away to some little distance the things he could eat. He had long finished his meal and was only lying lazily on the same spot when his sister turned the key slowly as a sign for him to retreat. That roused him at once, although he was nearly asleep, and he hurried under the sofa again. But it took considerable self-control for him to stay under the sofa, even for the short time his sister was in the room, since the large meal had swollen his body somewhat and he was so cramped he could hardly breathe. Slight attacks of breathlessness afflicted him and his eyes were starting a little out of his head as he watched his unsuspecting sister sweeping together with a broom not only the remains of what he had eaten but even the things he had not touched, as if these were now of no use to anyone, and hastily shoveling it all into a bucket, which she covered with a wooden lid and carried away. Hardly had she turned her back when Gregor came from under the sofa and stretched and puffed himself out.

In this manner Gregor was fed, once in the early morning while his parents and the servant girl were still asleep, and a second time after they had all had their midday dinner, for then his parents took a short nap and the servant girl could be sent out on some errand or other by his sister. Not that they would have wanted him to starve, of course, but perhaps they could not have borne to know more about his feeding than from hearsay, perhaps too his sister wanted to spare them such little anxieties wherever possible, since they had quite enough to bear as it was.

Under what pretext the doctor and the locksmith had been got rid of on that first morning Gregor could not discover, for since what he said was not understood by the others it never struck any of them, not even his sister, that he could understand what they said, and so whenever his sister came into his room he had to content himself with hearing her utter only a sigh now and then and an occasional appeal to the saints. Later on, when she had got a little used to the situation — of course she could never get completely used to it — she sometimes threw out a remark which was kindly meant or could be so interpreted. "Well, he liked his dinner today," she would say when Gregor had made a good clearance of his food; and when he had not eaten, which gradually happened more and more often, she would say almost sadly: "Everything's been left standing again."

But although Gregor could get no news directly, he overheard a lot from the neighboring rooms, and as soon as voices were audible, he would run to the door of the room concerned and press his whole body against it. In the first few days especially there was no conversation that did not refer to him somehow, even if only indirectly. For two whole days there were family consultations at every mealtime about what should be done; but also between meals the same subject was discussed, for there were always at least two members of the family at home, since no one wanted to be alone in the flat and to leave it quite empty was unthinkable. And on the very first of these days the household cook — it was not quite clear what and how much she knew of the situation — went down on her knees to his mother and begged leave to go, and when she departed, a quarter of an hour later, gave thanks for her dismissal with tears in her eyes as if for the greatest benefit that could have been conferred on her, and without any prompting swore a solemn oath that she would never say a single word to anyone about what had happened.

Now Gregor's sister had to cook too, helping her mother; true, the cooking did not amount to much, for they ate scarcely anything. Gregor was always hearing one of the family vainly urging another to eat and getting no answer but: "Thanks, I've had all I want," or something similar. Perhaps they drank nothing either. Time and again his sister kept asking his father if he wouldn't like some beer and offered kindly to go and fetch it herself, and when he made no answer suggested that she could ask the concierge to fetch it, so that he need feel no sense of obligation, but then a round "No" came from his father and no more was said about it.

In the course of that very first day Gregor's father explained the family's financial position and prospects to both his mother and his sister. Now and then he rose from the table to get some voucher or memorandum out of the small safe he had rescued from the collapse of his business five years earlier. One could hear him opening the complicated lock and rustling papers out and shutting it again. This statement made by his father was the first cheerful information Gregor had heard since his imprisonment. He had been of the opinion that nothing at all was left over from his father's business, at least his father had never said anything to the contrary, and of course he had not asked him directly. At that time Gregor's sole desire was to do his utmost to help the family to forget as soon as possible the catastrophe which had overwhelmed the business and thrown them all into a state of complete despair. And so he had set to work with unusual ardor and almost overnight had become a commercial traveler instead of a little clerk, with of course much greater chances of earning money, and his success was immediately translated into good round coin which he could lay on the table for his amazed and happy family. These had been fine times, and they had never recurred, at least not with the same sense of glory, although later on Gregor had earned so much money that he was able to meet the expenses of the whole household and did so. They had simply got used to it, both the family and Gregor; the money was gratefully accepted and gladly given, but there was no special uprush of warm feeling. With his sister alone had he remained intimate, and it was a secret plan of his that she, who loved music, unlike himself, and could play movingly on the violin, should be sent next year to study at the Conservatorium, despite the great expense that would entail, which must be made up in some other way. During his brief visits home the Conservatorium was often mentioned in the talks he had with his sister, but always merely as a beautiful dream which could never come true, and his parents discouraged even these innocent references to it; yet Gregor had made up his mind firmly about it and meant to announce the fact with due solemnity on Christmas Day.

Such were the thoughts, completely futile in his present condition, that went through his head as he stood clinging upright to the door and listening. Sometimes out of sheer weariness he had to give up listening and let his head fall negligently against the door, but he always had to pull himself together again at once, for even the slight sound his head made was audible next door and brought all conversation to a stop. "What can he be doing now?" his father would say after a while, obviously turning towards the door, and only then would the interrupted conversation gradually be set going again.

Gregor was now informed as amply as he could wish — for his father tended to repeat himself in his explanations, partly because it was a long time since he had handled such matters and partly because his mother could not always grasp things at once — that a certain amount of investments, a very small amount it was true, had survived the wreck of their fortunes and had even increased a little because the dividends had not been touched meanwhile. And besides that, the money Gregor brought home every month — he had kept only a few dollars for himself — had never been quite used up and now amounted to a small capital sum. Behind the door Gregor nodded his head eagerly, rejoiced at this evidence of unexpected thrift and foresight. True, he could really have paid off some more of his father's debts to the chief with this extra money, and so brought much nearer the day on which he could quit his job, but doubtless it was better the way his father had arranged it.

Yet this capital was by no means sufficient to let the family live on the interest of it; for one year, perhaps, or at the most two, they could live on the principal, that was all. It was simply a sum that ought not to be touched and should be kept for a rainy day; money for living expenses would have to be earned. Now his father was still hale enough but an old man, and he had done no work for the past five years and could not be expected to do much; during these five years, the first years of leisure in his laborious though unsuccessful life, he had grown rather fat and become sluggish. And Gregor's old mother, how was she to earn a living with her asthma, which troubled her even when she walked through the flat and kept her lying on a sofa every other day panting for breath beside an open window? And was his sister to earn her bread, she who was still a child of seventeen and whose life hitherto had been so pleasant, consisting as it did in dressing herself nicely, sleeping long, helping in the housekeeping, going out to a few modest entertainments and above all playing the violin? At first whenever the need for earning money was mentioned Gregor let go his hold on the door and threw himself down on the cool leather sofa beside it, he felt so hot with shame and grief.

Often he just lay there the long nights through without sleeping at all, scrabbling for hours on the leather. Or he nerved himself to the great effort of pushing an armchair to the window, then crawled up over the window sill and, braced against the chair, leaned against the window panes, obviously in some recollection of the sense of freedom that looking out of a window always used to give him. For in reality day by day things that were even a little way off were growing dimmer to his sight; the hospital across the street, which he used to execrate for being all too often before his eyes, was not quite beyond his range of vision, and if he had not known that he lived in Charlotte Street, a quiet street but still a city street, he might have believed that his window gave on a desert waste where gray sky and gray land blended indistinguishably into each other. His quick-witted sister only needed to observe twice that the armchair stood by the window; after that whenever she had tidied the room she always pushed the chair back to the same place at the window and even left the inner casements open.

If he could have spoken to her and thanked her for all she had to do for him, he could have borne her ministrations better; as it was, they oppressed him. She certainly tried to make as light as possible of whatever was disagreeable in her task, and as time went on she succeeded, of course, more and more, but time brought more enlightenment to Gregor too. The very way she came in distressed him. Hardly was she in the room when she rushed to the window, without even taking time to shut the door, careful as she was usually to shield the sight of Gregor's room from the others, and as if she were almost suffocating tore the casements open with hasty fingers, standing then in the open draught for a while even in the bitterest cold and drawing deep breaths. This noisy scurry of hers upset Gregor twice a day; he would crouch trembling under the sofa all the time, knowing quite well that she would certainly have spared him such a disturbance had she found it at all possible to stay in his presence without opening the window.

On one occasion, about a month after Gregor's metamorphosis, when there was surely no reason for her to be still startled at his appearance, she came a little earlier than usual and found him gazing out of the window, quite motionless, and thus well placed to look like a bogey. Gregor would not have been surprised had she not come in at all, for she could not immediately open the window while he was there, but not only did she retreat, she jumped back as if in alarm and banged the door shut; a stranger might well have thought that he had been lying in wait for her there meaning to bite her. Of course he hid himself under the sofa at once, but he had to wait until midday before she came again, and she seemed more ill at ease than usual. This made him realize how repulsive the sight of him still was to her, and that it was bound to go on being repulsive, and what an effort it must cost her not to run away even from the sight of the small portion of his body that stuck out from under the sofa. In order to spare her that, therefore, one day he carried a sheet on his back to the sofa — it cost him four hours' labor — and arranged it there in such a way as to hide him completely, so that even if she were to bend down she could not see him. Had she considered the sheet unnecessary, she would certainly have stripped it off the sofa again, for it was clear enough that this curtaining and confining of himself was not likely to conduce Gregor's comfort, but she left it where it was, and Gregor even fancied that he caught a thankful glance from her eye when he lifted the sheet carefully a very little with his head to see how she was taking the new arrangement.

For the first fortnight his parents could not bring themselves to the point of entering his room, and he often heard them expressing their appreciation of his sister's activities, whereas formerly they had frequently scolded her for being as they thought a somewhat useless daughter. But now, both of them often waited outside the door, his father and his mother, while his sister tidied his room, and as soon as she came out she had to tell them exactly how things were in the room, what Gregor had eaten, how he had conducted himself this time and whether there was not perhaps some slight improvement in his condition. His mother, moreover, began relatively soon to want to visit him, but his father and sister dissuaded her at first with arguments which Gregor listened to very attentively and altogether approved. Later, however, she had to be held back by main force, and when she cried out: "Do let me in to Gregor, he is my unfortunate son! Can't you understand that I must go to him?" Gregor thought that it might be well to have her come in, not every day, of course, but perhaps once a week; she understood things, after all, much better than his sister, who was only a child despite the efforts she was making and had perhaps taken on so difficult a task merely out of childish thoughtlessness.

Gregor's desire to see his mother was soon fulfilled. During the daytime he did not want to show himself at the window, out of consideration for his parents, but he could not crawl very far around the few square yards of floor space he had, nor could he bear lying quietly at rest all during the night, while he was fast losing any interest he had ever taken in food, so that for mere recreation he had formed the habit of crawling crisscross over the walls and ceiling. He especially enjoyed hanging suspended from the ceiling; it was much better than lying on the floor. One could breathe more freely; one's body swung and rocked lightly; and in the almost blissful absorption induced by this suspension it could happen to his own surprise that he let go and fell plump on the floor. Yet he now had his body much better under control than formerly, and even such a big fall did him no harm. His sister at once remarked the new distraction Gregor had found for himself — he left traces behind him of the sticky stuff on his soles wherever he crawled — and she got the idea in her head of giving him as wide a field as possible to crawl in and of removing the pieces of furniture that hindered him, above all the chest of drawers and

the writing desk. But that was more than she could manage all
by herself, she did not dare ask her father to help her; and as for
the servant girl, a young creature of sixteen who had had the
courage to stay on after the cook's departure, she could not be
asked to help, for she had begged as an especial favor that she
might keep the kitchen door locked and open it only on a definite
summons; so there was nothing left but to apply to her mother
at an hour when her father was out. And the old lady did come,
with exclamations of joyful eagerness, which, however, died away
at the door of Gregor's room. Gregor's sister, of course, went in
first, to see that everything was in order before letting his mother
enter. In great haste Gregor pulled the sheet lower and tucked it
more in folds so that it really looked as if it had been thrown
accidentally over the sofa. And this time he did not peer out from
under it; he renounced the pleasure of seeing his mother on this
occasion and was only glad that she had come at all. "Come in,
he's out of sight," said his sister, obviously leading her mother
by the hand. Gregor could now hear the two women struggling
to shift the heavy old chest from its place, and his sister claiming
the greater part of the labor for herself, without listening to the
admonitions of her mother who feared she might overstrain herself.
It took a long time. After at least a quarter of an hour's tugging
his mother objected that the chest had better be left where it was,
for in the first place it was too heavy and could never be got out
before his father came home, and standing in the middle of the
room like that it would only hamper Gregor's movements, while
in the second place it was not at all certain that removing the
furniture would be doing a service to Gregor. She was inclined
to think to the contrary; the sight of the naked walls made her
own heart heavy, and why shouldn't Gregor have the same feeling,
considering that he had been used to his furniture for so long and
might feel forlorn without it. "And doesn't it look," she concluded
in a low voice — in fact she had been almost whispering all the
time as if to avoid letting Gregor, whose exact whereabouts she
did not know, hear even the tones of her voice, for she was
convinced that he could not understand her words — "doesn't it
look as if we were showing him, by taking away his furniture,
that we have given up hope of his ever getting better and are just
leaving him coldly to himself? I think it would be best to keep
his room exactly as it has always been, so that when he comes
back to us he will find everything unchanged and be able all the
more easily to forget what has happened in between."

On hearing these words from his mother Gregor realized
that the lack of all direct human speech for the past two months

together with the monotony of family life must have confused his mind, otherwise he could not account for the fact that he had quite earnestly looked forward to having his room emptied of furnishing. Did he really want his warm room, so comfortably fitted with old family furniture, to be turned into a naked den in which he would certainly be able to crawl unhampered in all directions but at the price of shedding simultaneously all recollection of his human background? He had indeed been so near the brink of forgetfulness that only the voice of his mother, which he had not heard for so long, had drawn him back from it. Nothing should be taken out of his room; everything must stay as it was; he could not dispense with the good influence of the furniture on his state of mind; and even if the furniture did hamper him in his senseless crawling round and round, that was no drawback but a great advantage.

Unfortunately his sister was of the contrary opinion; she had grown accustomed, and not without reason, to consider herself an expert in Gregor's affairs as against her parents, and so her mother's advice was now enough to make her determined on the removal not only of the chest and the writing desk, which had been her first intention, but of all the furniture except the indispensable sofa. This determination was not, of course, merely the outcome of childish recalcitrance and of the self-confidence she had recently developed so unexpectedly and at such cost; she had in fact perceived that Gregor needed a lot of space to crawl about in, while on the other hand he never used the furniture at all, so far as could be seen. Another factor might have been also the enthusiastic temperament of an adolescent girl, which seeks to indulge itself on every opportunity and which now tempted Grete to exaggerate the horror of her brother's circumstances in order that she might do all the more for him. In a room where Gregor lorded it all alone over empty walls no one save herself was likely ever to set foot.

And so she was not to be moved from her resolve by her mother who seemed moreover to be ill at ease in Gregor's room and therefore unsure of herself, was soon reduced to silence and helped her daughter as best she could to push the chest outside. Now, Gregor could do without the chest, if need be, but the writing desk he must retain. As soon as the two women had got the chest out of his room, groaning as they pushed it, Gregor stuck his head out from under the sofa to see how he might intervene as kindly and cautiously as possible. But as bad luck would have it, his mother was the first to return, leaving Grete clasping the chest in the room next door where she was trying to shift it all by herself, without of course moving it from the spot. His mother however was not accustomed to the sight of him, it might sicken her and so in alarm Gregor backed quickly to the other end of the sofa, yet could not prevent the sheet from swaying a little in front. That was enough to put her on the alert. She paused, stood still for a moment and then went back to Grete.

Although Gregor kept reassuring himself that nothing out of the way was happening, but only a few bits of furniture were being changed round, he soon had to admit that all this trotting to and fro of the two women, their little ejaculations and the scraping of furniture along the floor affected him like a vast disturbance coming from all sides at once, and however much he tucked in his head and legs and cowered to the very floor he was bound to confess that he would not be able to stand it for long. They were clearing his room out; taking away everything he loved; the chest in which he kept his fret saw and other tools was already dragged off; they were now loosening the writing desk which had almost sunk into the floor, the desk at which he had done all his homework when he was at the commercial academy, at the grammar school before that, and, yes, even at the primary school — he had no more time to waste in weighing the good intentions of the two women, whose existence he had by now almost forgotten, for they were so exhausted that they were laboring in silence and nothing could be heard but the heavy scuffling of their feet.

And so he rushed out — the women were just leaning against the writing desk in the next room to give themselves a breather — and four times changed his direction, since he really did not know what to rescue first, then on the wall opposite, which was already otherwise cleared, he was struck by the picture of the lady muffled in so much fur and quickly crawled up to it and pressed himself to the glass, which was a good surface to hold on to and comforted his hot belly. This picture at least, which was entirely hidden beneath him, was going to be removed by nobody. He turned his head towards the door of the living room so as to observe the women when they came back.

They had not allowed themselves much of a rest and were already coming; Grete had twined her arm round her mother and was almost supporting her. "Well, what shall we take now?" said Grete, looking round. Her eyes met Gregor's from the wall. She kept her composure, presumably because of her mother, bent her head down to her mother, to keep her from looking up, and said, although in a fluttering, unpremeditated voice: "Come, hadn't we better go back to the living room for a moment?" Her intentions were clear enough to Gregor, she wanted to bestow her mother

in safety and then chase him down from the wall. Well, just let
her try it! He clung to his picture and would not give it up. He
would rather fly in Grete's face.

But Grete's words had succeeded in disquieting her mother,
who took a step to one side, caught sight of the huge brown mass
on the flowered wallpaper, and before she was really conscious
that what she saw was Gregor screamed in a loud, hoarse voice:
"Oh God, oh God!" fell with outspread arms over the sofa as if
giving up and did not move. "Gregor!" cried his sister, shaking
her fist and glaring at him. This was the first time she had directly
addressed him since his metamorphosis. She ran into the next
room for some aromatic essence with which to rouse her mother
from her fainting fit. Gregor wanted to help too — there was still
time to rescue the picture — but he was stuck fast to the glass
and had to tear himself loose; he then ran after his sister into the
next room as if he could advise her, as he used to do; but then
had to stand helplessly behind her; she meanwhile searched among
various small bottles and when she turned round started in alarm
at the sight of him; one bottle fell on the floor and broke; a splinter
of glass cut Gregor's face and some kind of corrosive medicine
splashed him; without pausing a moment longer Grete gathered
up all the bottles she could carry and ran to her mother with them;
she banged the door shut with her foot. Gregor was now cut off
from his mother, who was perhaps nearly dying because of him;
he dared not open the door for fear of frightening away his sister,
who had to stay with her mother; there was nothing he could do
but wait; and harassed by self-reproach and worry he began now
to crawl to and fro, over everything, walls, furniture and ceiling,
and finally in his despair, when the whole room seemed to be
reeling round him, fell down on to the middle of the big table.

A little while elapsed, Gregor was still lying there feebly and
all around was quiet, perhaps that was a good omen. Then the
doorbell rang. The servant girl was of course locked in her kitchen,
and Grete would have to open the door. It was his father. "What's
been happening?" were his first words; Grete's face must have
told him everything. Grete answered in a muffled voice, apparently
hiding her head on his breast: "Mother has been fainting, but she's
better now. Gregor's broken loose." "Just what I expected," said
his father, "just what I've been telling you, but you women would
never listen." It was clear to Gregor that his father had taken the
worst interpretation of Grete's all too brief statement and was
assuming that Gregor had been guilty of some violent act. Therefore
Gregor must now try to propitiate his father, since he had neither
time nor means for an explanation. And so he fled to the door of

his own room and crouched against it, to let his father see as soon
as he came in from the hall that his son had the good intention
of getting back into his room immediately and that it was not
necessary to drive him there, but that if only the door were opened
he would disappear at once.

Yet his father was not in the mood to perceive such fine
distinctions. "Ah!" he cried as soon as he appeared, in a tone
which sounded at once angry and exultant. Gregor drew his head
back from the door and lifted it to look at his father. Truly, this
was not the father he had imagined to himself, admittedly he had
been too absorbed of late in his new recreation of crawling over
the ceiling to take the same interest as before in what was happening
elsewhere in the flat, and he ought really to be prepared for some
changes. And yet, and yet, could that be his father? The man who
used to lie wearily sunk in bed whenever Gregor set out on a
business journey; who welcomed him back of an evening lying
in a long chair in a dressing gown; who could not really rise to
his feet but only lifted his arms in greeting, and on the rare occasions
when he did go out with his family, on one or two Sundays a
year and on high holidays, walked between Gregor and his mother,
who were slow walkers anyhow, even more slowly than they did,
muffled in his old greatcoat, shuffling laboriously forward with
the help of his crook-handled stick which he set down most cautiously at every step and, whenever he wanted to say anything,
nearly always came to a full stop and gathered his escort around
him? Now he was standing there in fine shape; dressed in a smart
blue uniform with gold buttons, such as bank messengers wear;
his strong double chin bulged over the stiff high collar of his
jacket; from under his bushy eyebrows his black eyes darted fresh
and penetrating glances; his one-time tangled white hair had been
combed flat on either side of a shining and carefully exact parting.
He pitched his cap, which bore a gold monogram, probably the
badge of some bank, in a wide sweep across the whole room on
to a sofa and with the tail-ends of his jacket thrown back, his
hands in his trouser pockets, advanced with a grim visage towards
Gregor. Likely enough he did not himself know what he meant
to do; at any rate he lifted his feet uncommonly high, and Gregor
was dumbfounded at the enormous size of his shoe soles. But
Gregor could not risk standing up to him, aware as he had been
from the very first day of his new life that his father believed only
the severest measures suitable for dealing with him. And so he
ran before his father, stopping when he stopped and scuttling
forward again when his father made any kind of move. In this
way they circled the room several times without anything decisive

happening, indeed the whole operation did not even look like a pursuit because it was carried out so slowly. And so Gregor did not leave the floor, for he feared that his father might take as a piece of peculiar wickedness any excursion of his over the walls or the ceiling. All the same, he could not stay this course much longer, for while his father took one step he had to carry out a whole series of movements. He was already beginning to feel breathless, just as in his former life his lungs had not been very dependable. As he was staggering along, trying to concentrate his energy on running, hardly keeping his eyes open; in his dazed state never even thinking of any other escape than simply going forward; and having almost forgotten that the walls were free to him, which in this room were well provided with finely carved pieces of furniture full of knobs and crevices — suddenly something lightly flung landed close behind him and rolled before him. It was an apple; a second apple followed immediately; Gregor came to a stop in alarm; there was no point in running on, for his father was determined to bombard him. He had filled his pockets with fruit from the dish on the sideboard and was now shying apple after apple, without taking particularly good aim for the moment. The small red apples rolled about the floor as if magnetized and cannoned into each other. An apple thrown without much force grazed Gregor's back and glanced off harmlessly. But another following immediately landed right on his back and sank in; Gregor wanted to drag himself forward, as if this startling, incredible pain could be left behind him; but he felt as if nailed to the spot and flattened himself out in a complete derangement of all his senses. With his last conscious look he saw the door of his room being torn open and his mother rushing out ahead of his screaming sister, in her underbodice, for her daughter had loosened her clothing to let her breathe more freely and recover from her swoon, he saw his mother rushing towards his father, leaving one after another behind her on the floor her loosened petticoats, stumbling over her petticoats straight to his father and embracing him, in complete union with him — but here Gregor's sight began to fail — with her hands clasped round his father's neck as she begged for her son's life.

III

The serious injury done to Gregor, which disabled him for more than a month — the apple went on sticking in his body as a visible reminder, since no one ventured to remove it — seemed to have made even his father recollect that Gregor was a member of the family, despite his present unfortunate and repulsive shape, and ought not to be treated as an enemy, that, on the contrary, family duty required the suppression of disgust and the exercise of patience, nothing but patience.

And although his injury had impaired, probably for ever, his power of movement, and for the time being it took him long, long minutes to creep across his room like an old invalid — there was no question now of crawling up the wall — yet in his own opinion he was sufficiently compensated for this worsening of his condition by the fact that towards evening the living-room door, which he used to watch intently for an hour or two beforehand, was always thrown open, so that lying in the darkness of his room, invisible to the family, he could see them all at the lamp-lit table and listen to their talk, by general consent as it were, very different from his earlier eavesdropping.

True, their intercourse lacked the lively character of former times, which he had always called to mind with a certain wistfulness in the small hotel bedrooms where he had been wont to throw himself down, tired out, on damp bedding. They were now mostly very silent. Soon after supper his father would fall asleep in his armchair; his mother and sister would admonish each other to be silent; his mother, bending low over the lamp, stitched at fine sewing for an underwear firm; his sister, who had taken a job as a salesgirl, was learning shorthand and French in the evenings on the chance of bettering herself. Sometimes his father woke up, and as if quite unaware that he had been sleeping said to his mother: "What a lot of sewing you're doing today!" and at once fell asleep again, while the two women exchanged a tired smile.

With a kind of mulishness his father persisted in keeping his uniform on even in the house; his dressing gown hung uselessly on its peg and he slept fully dressed where he sat, as if he were ready for service at any moment and even here only at the beck and call of his superior. As a result, his uniform, which was not brand-new to start with, began to look dirty, despite all the loving care of the mother and sister to keep it clean, and Gregor often spent whole evenings gazing at the many greasy spots on the garment, gleaming with gold buttons always in a high state of polish, in which the old man sat sleeping in extreme discomfort and yet quite peacefully.

As soon as the clock struck ten his mother tried to rouse his father with gentle words and to persuade him after that to get into bed, for sitting there he could not have a proper sleep and that was what he needed most, since he had to go to duty at six. But with the mulishness that had obsessed him since he became a bank messenger he always insisted on staying longer at the table, although he regularly fell asleep again and in the end only with the greatest trouble could be got out of his armchair and into his bed. However insistently Gregor's mother and sister kept urging him with gentle reminders, he would go on slowly shaking his head for a quarter of an hour, keeping his eyes shut, and refuse to get to his feet. The mother plucked at his sleeve, whispering endearments in his ear, the sister left her lessons to come to her mother's help, but Gregor's father was not to be caught. He would only sink down deeper in his chair. Not until the two women hoisted him up by the armpits did he open his eyes and look at them both, one after the other, usually with the remark: "This is a life. This is the peace and quiet of my old age." And leaning on the two of them he would heave himself up, with difficulty, as if he were a great burden to himself, suffer them to lead him as far as the door and then wave them off and go on alone, while the mother abandoned her needlework and the sister her pen in order to run after him and help him farther.

Who could find time, in this overworked and tired-out family, to bother about Gregor more than was absolutely needful? The household was reduced more and more; the servant girl was turned off; a gigantic bony charwoman with white hair flying round her head came in morning and evening to do the rough work; everything else was done by Gregor's mother, as well as great piles of sewing. Even various family ornaments, which his mother and sister used to wear with pride at parties and celebrations, had to be sold, as Gregor discovered of an evening from hearing them all discuss the prices obtained. But what they lamented most was the fact that they could not leave the flat which was much too big for their present circumstances, because they could not think of any way to shift Gregor. Yet Gregor saw well enough that consideration for him was not the main difficulty preventing the removal, for they could have easily shifted him in some suitable box with a few air holes in it; what really kept them from moving into another flat was rather their own complete hopelessness and the belief that they had been singled out for a misfortune such as had never happened to any of their relations or acquaintances. They fulfilled to the uttermost all that the world demands of poor people, the father fetched breakfast for the small clerks in the bank, the mother devoted her energy to making underwear for strangers, the sister trotted to and fro behind the counter at the behest of customers, but more than this they had not the strength to do. And the wound in Gregor's back began to nag at him afresh when his mother and sister, after getting his father into bed, came back again, left their work lying, drew close to each other and sat cheek by cheek; when his mother, pointing towards his room, said: "Shut that door now, Grete," and he was left again in darkness, while next door the women mingled their tears or perhaps sat dry-eyed staring at the table.

Gregor hardly slept at all by night or by day. He was often haunted by the idea that next time the door opened he would take the family's affairs in hand again just as he used to do; once more, after this long interval, there appeared in his thoughts the figures of the chief and the chief clerk, the commercial travelers and the apprentices, the porter who was so dull-witted, two or three friends in other firms, a chambermaid in one of the rural hotels, a sweet and fleeting memory, a cashier in a milliner's shop, whom he had wooed earnestly but too slowly — they all appeared, together with strangers or people he had quite forgotten, but instead of helping him and his family they were one and all unapproachable and he was glad when they vanished. At other times he would not be in the mood to bother about his family, he was only filled with rage at the way they were neglecting him, and although he had no clear idea of what he might care to eat he would make plans for getting into the larder to take the food that was after all his due, even if he were not hungry. His sister no longer took thought to bring him what might especially please him, but in the morning and at noon before she went to business hurriedly pushed into his room with her foot any food that was available, and in the evening cleared it out again with one sweep of the broom, heedless of whether it had been merely tasted, or — as most frequently happened — left untouched. The cleaning of his room, which she now did always in the evenings, could not have been more hastily done. Streaks of dirt stretched along the walls, here and there lay balls of dust and filth. At first Gregor used to station himself in some particularly filthy corner when his sister arrived, in order to reproach her with it, so to speak. But he could have sat there for weeks without getting her to make any improvements; she could see the dirt as well as he did, but she had simply made up her mind to leave it alone. And yet, with a touchiness that was new to her, which seemed anyhow to have infected the whole family, she jealously guarded her claim to be the sole caretaker of Gregor's room. His mother once subjected his room to a thorough cleaning, which was achieved only by means of several buckets of water — all this dampness of course upset Gregor too and he lay widespread, sulky and motionless on the sofa — but she was well punished for it. Hardly had his sister noticed the changed aspect of his room that evening than she rushed in high dudgeon into the living room and, despite the imploringly raised hands of her mother, burst into a storm of weeping, while her parents — her father had of course been startled out of his chair — looked on at first in helpless amazement; then they too began to go into action; the father reproached the mother on his right for not having left the cleaning of Gregor's room to his sister; shrieked at the sister on his left that never again was she to be allowed to clean Gregor's room; while the mother tried to pull the father into his bedroom, since he was beyond himself with agitation; the sister, shaken with sobs, then beat upon the table with her small fists; and Gregor hissed loudly with rage because not one of them thought of shutting the door to spare him such a spectacle and so much noise.

Still, even if the sister, exhausted by her daily work, had grown tired of looking after Gregor as she did formerly, there was no need for his mother's intervention or for Gregor's being neglected at all. The charwoman was there. This old widow, whose strong bony frame had enabled her to survive the worst a long life could offer, by no means recoiled from Gregor. Without being in the least curious she had once by chance opened the door of his room and at the sight of Gregor, who, taken by surprise, began to rush to and fro although no one was chasing him, merely stood there with her arms folded. From that time she never failed to open his door a little for a moment, morning and evening, to have a look at him. At first she even used to call him to her, with words which apparently she took to be friendly; such as: "Come along, then, you old dung beetle!" or "Look at the old dung beetle, then!" To such allocutions Gregor made no answer, but stayed motionless where he was, as if the door had never been opened. Instead of being allowed to disturb him so senselessly whenever the whim took her, she should rather have been ordered to clean out his room daily, that charwoman! Once, early in the morning — heavy rain was lashing on the windowpanes, perhaps a sign that spring was on the way — Gregor was so exasperated when she began addressing him again that he ran for her, as if to attack her, although slowly and feebly enough. But the charwoman instead of showing fright merely lifted high a chair that happened to be beside the door, and as she stood there with her mouth wide open it was clear that she meant to shut it only when she brought the chair down on Gregor's back. "So you're not coming any nearer?" she asked, as Gregor turned away again, and quietly put the chair back into the corner.

Gregor was now eating hardly anything. Only when he happened to pass the food laid out for him did he take a bit of something in his mouth as a pastime, kept it there for an hour at

a time and usually spat it out again. At first he thought it was
chagrin over the state of his room that prevented him from eating,
yet he soon got used to the various changes in his room. It had
become a habit in the family to push into his room things there
was no room for elsewhere, and there were plenty of these now,
since one of the rooms had been let to three lodgers. These serious
gentlemen — all three of them with full beards, as Gregor once
observed through a crack in the door — had a passion for order,
not only in their own room but, since they were now members
of the household, in all its arrangements, especially in the kitchen.
Superfluous, not to say dirty, objects they could not bear. Besides,
they had brought with them most of the furnishings they needed.
For this reason many things could be dispensed with that it was
no use trying to sell but that should not be thrown away either.
All of them found their way into Gregor's room. The ash can
likewise and the kitchen garbage can. Anything that was not needed
for the moment was simply flung into Gregor's room by the
charwoman, who did everything in a hurry; fortunately Gregor
usually saw only the object, whatever it was, and the hand that
held it. Perhaps she intended to take the things away again as time
and opportunity offered, or to collect them until she could throw
them all out in a heap, but in fact they just lay wherever she
happened to throw them, except when Gregor pushed his way
through the junk heap and shifted it somewhat, at first out of
necessity, because he had not room enough to crawl, but later
with increasing enjoyment, although after such excursions, being
sad and weary to death, he would lie motionless for hours. And
since the lodgers often ate their supper at home in the common
living room, the living-room door stayed shut many an evening,
yet Gregor reconciled himself quite easily to the shutting of the
door, for often enough on evenings when it was opened he had
disregarded it entirely and lain in the darkest corner of his room,
quite unnoticed by the family. But on one occasion the charwoman
left the door open a little and it stayed ajar even when the lodgers
came in for supper and the lamp was lit. They set themselves at
the top end of the table where formerly Gregor and his father and
mother had eaten their meals, unfolded their napkins and took
knife and fork in hand. At once his mother appeared in the doorway
with a dish of meat and close behind her his sister with a dish of
potatoes piled high. The food steamed with a thick vapor. The
lodgers bent over the food set before them as if to scrutinize it
before eating, in fact the man in the middle, who seemed to pass
for an authority with the other two, cut a piece of meat as it lay
on the dish, obviously to discover if it were tender or should be

sent back to the kitchen. He showed satisfaction, and Gregor's mother and sister, who had been watching anxiously, breathed freely and began to smile.

The family itself took its meals in the kitchen. None the less, Gregor's father came into the living room before going into the kitchen and with one prolonged bow, cap in hand, made a round of the table. The lodgers all stood up and murmured something in their beards. When they were alone again they ate their food in almost complete silence. It seemed remarkable to Gregor that among the various noises coming from the table he could always distinguish the sound of their masticating teeth, as if this were a sign to Gregor that one needed teeth in order to eat, and that with toothless jaws even of the finest make one could do nothing. "I'm hungry enough," said Gregor sadly to himself, "but not for that kind of food. How these lodgers are stuffing themselves, and here am I dying of starvation!"

On that very evening — during the whole of his time there Gregor could not remember ever having heard the violin — the sound of violin-playing came from the kitchen. The lodgers had already finished their supper, the one in the middle had brought out a newspaper and given the other two a page apiece, and now they were leaning back at ease reading and smoking. When the violin began to play they pricked up their ears, got to their feet, and went on tiptoe to the hall door where they stood huddled together. Their movements must have been heard in the kitchen, for Gregor's father called out: "Is the violin-playing disturbing you gentlemen? It can be stopped at once." "On the contrary," said the middle lodger, "could not Fräulein Samsa come and play in this room, beside us, where it is much more convenient and comfortable?" "Oh certainly," cried Gregor's father, as if he were the violin player. The lodgers came back into the living room and waited. Presently Gregor's father arrived with the music stand, his mother carrying the music and his sister with the violin. His sister quietly made everything ready to start playing; his parents, who had never let rooms before and so had an exaggerated idea of the courtesy due to lodgers, did not venture to sit down on their own chairs; his father leaned against the door, the right hand thrust between two buttons of his livery coat, which was formally buttoned up; but his mother was offered a chair by one of the lodgers and, since she left the chair just where he had happened to put it, sat down in a corner to one side.

Gregor's sister began to play; the father and mother, from either side, intently watched the movements of her hands. Gregor, attracted by the playing, ventured to move forward a little until his head was actually inside the living room. He felt hardly any surprise at his growing lack of consideration for the others; there had been a time when he prided himself on being considerate. And yet just on this occasion he had more reason than ever to hide himself, since owing to the amount of dust which lay thick in his room and rose into the air at the slightest movement, he too was covered with dust; fluff and hair and remnants of food trailed with him, caught on his back and along his sides; his indifference to everything was much too great for him to turn on his back and scrape himself clean on the carpet, as once he had done several times a day. And in spite of his condition, no shame deterred him from advancing a little over the spotless floor of the living room.

To be sure, no one was aware of him. The family was entirely absorbed in the violin-playing; the lodgers, however, who first of all had stationed themselves, hands in pockets, much too close behind the music stand so that they could all have read the music, which must have bothered his sister, had soon retreated to the window, half-whispering with downbent heads, and stayed there while his father turned an anxious eye on them. Indeed, they were making it more than obvious that they had been disappointed in their expectation of hearing good or enjoyable violin-playing, that they had had more than enough of the performance and only out of courtesy suffered a continued disturbance of their peace. From the way they all kept blowing the smoke of their cigars high in the air through nose and mouth one could divine their irritation. And yet Gregor's sister was playing so beautifully. Her face leaned sideways, intently and sadly her eyes followed the notes of music. Gregor crawled a little farther forward and lowered his head to the ground so that it might be possible for his eyes to meet hers. Was he an animal, that music had such an effect upon him? He felt as if the way were opening before him to the unknown nourishment he craved. He was determined to push forward till he reached his sister, to pull at her skirt and so let her know that she was to come into his room with her violin, for no one here appreciated her playing as he would appreciate it. He would never let her out of his room, at least, not so long as he lived; his frightful appearance would become, for the first time, useful to him; he would watch all the doors of his room at once and spit at intruders; but his sister should need no constraint, she should stay with him of her own free will; she should sit beside him on the sofa, bend down her ear to him and hear him confide that he had had the firm intention of sending her to the Conservatorium, and that, but for his mishap, last Christmas — surely

Christmas was long past? — he would have announced it to everybody without allowing a single objection. After this confession
his sister would be so touched that she would burst into tears,
and Gregor would then raise himself to her shoulder and kiss her
on the neck, which, now that she went to business, she kept free
of any ribbon or collar.

"Mr. Samsa!" cried the middle lodger, to Gregor's father,
and pointed, without wasting any more words, at Gregor, now
working himself slowly forwards. The violin fell silent, the middle
lodger first smiled to his friends with a shake of the head and then
looked at Gregor again. Instead of driving Gregor out, his father
seemed to think it more needful to begin by soothing down the
lodgers, although they were not at all agitated and apparently
found Gregor more entertaining than the violin-playing. He hurried
towards them and, spreading out his arms, tried to urge them
back into their own room and at the same time to block their
view of Gregor. They now began to be really a little angry, one
could not tell whether because of the old man's behavior or because
it just dawned on them that all unwittingly they had such a neighbor
as Gregor next door. They demanded explanations of his father,
they waved their arms like him, tugged uneasily at their beards,
and only with reluctance backed towards their room. Meanwhile
Gregor's sister, who stood there as if lost when her playing was
so abruptly broken off, came to life again, pulled herself together
all at once after standing for a while holding violin and bow in
nervelessly hanging hands and staring at her music, pushed her
violin into the lap of her mother, who was still sitting in her chair
fighting asthmatically for breath, and ran into the lodgers' room
to which they were now being shepherded by her father rather
more quickly than before. One could see the pillows and blankets
on the beds flying under her accustomed fingers and being laid in
order. Before the lodgers had actually reached their room she had
finished making the beds and slipped out.

The old man seemed once more to be so possessed by his
mulish self-assertiveness that he was forgetting all the respect he
should show to his lodgers. He kept driving them on and driving
them on until in the very door of the bedroom the middle lodger
stamped his foot loudly on the floor and so brought him to a halt.
"I beg to announce," said the lodger, lifting one hand and looking
also at Gregor's mother and sister, "that because of the disgusting
conditions prevailing in this household and family" — here he
spat on the floor with emphatic brevity — "I give you notice on
the spot. Naturally I won't pay you a penny for the days I have
lived here, on the contrary I shall consider bringing an action for

damages against you, based on claims — believe me — that will
be easily susceptible of proof." He ceased and stared straight in
front of him, as if he expected something. In fact his two friends
at once rushed into the breach with these words: "And we too
give notice on the spot." On that he seized the door-handle and
shut the door with a slam.

Gregor's father, groping with his hands, staggered forward
and fell into his chair; it looked as if he were stretching himself
there for his ordinary evening nap, but the marked jerkings of his
head, which was as if uncontrollable, showed that he was far from
asleep. Gregor had simply stayed quietly all the time on the spot
where the lodgers had espied him. Disappointment at the failure
of his plan, perhaps also the weakness arising from extreme hunger,
made it impossible for him to move. He feared, with a fair degree
of certainty, that at any moment the general tension would discharge
itself in a combined attack upon him, and he lay waiting. He did
not react even to the noise made by the violin as it fell off his
mother's lap from under her trembling fingers and gave out a
resonant note.

"My dear parents," said his sister, slapping her hand on the
table by way of introduction, "things can't go on like this. Perhaps
you don't realize that, but I do. I won't utter my brother's name
in the presence of this creature, and so all I say is: we must try
to get rid of it. We've tried to look after it and to put up with it
as far as is humanly possible, and I don't think anyone could
reproach us in the slightest."

"She is more than right," said Gregor's father to himself.
His mother, who was still choking for lack of breath, began to
cough hollowly into her hand with a wild look in her eyes.

His sister rushed over to her and held her forehead. His
father's thoughts seemed to have lost their vagueness at Grete's
words, he sat more upright, fingering his service cap that lay
among the plates still lying on the table from the lodgers' supper,
and from time to time looked at the still form of Gregor.

"We must try to get rid of it," his sister now said explicitly
to her father, since her mother was coughing too much to hear a
word, "it will be the death of both of you, I can see that coming.
When one has to work as hard as we do, all of us, one can't stand
this continual torment at home on top of it. At least I can't stand
it any longer." And she burst into such a passion of sobbing that
her tears dropped on her mother's face, where she wiped them
off mechanically.

"My dear," said the old man sympathetically, and with evident
understanding, "but what can we do?"

Gregor's sister merely shrugged her shoulders to indicate the feeling of helplessness that had now overmastered her during her weeping fit, in contrast to her former confidence.

"If he could understand us," said her father, half questioningly; Grete, still sobbing, vehemently waved a hand to show how unthinkable that was.

"If he could understand us," repeated the old man, shutting his eyes to consider his daughter's conviction that understanding was impossible, "then perhaps we might come to some agreement with him. But as it is —"

"He must go," cried Gregor's sister, "that's the only solution, Father. You must just try to get rid of the idea that this is Gregor. The fact that we've believed it for so long is the root of all our trouble. But how can it be Gregor? If this were Gregor, he would have realized long ago that human beings can't live with such a creature, and he'd have gone away on his own accord. Then we wouldn't have any brother, but we'd be able to go on living and keep his memory in honor. As it is, this creature persecutes us, drives away our lodgers, obviously wants the whole apartment to himself and would have us all sleep in the gutter. Just look, Father," she shrieked all at once, "he's at it again!" And in an access of panic that was quite incomprehensible to Gregor she even quitted her mother, literally thrusting the chair from her as if she would rather sacrifice her mother than stay so near to Gregor, and rushed behind her father, who also rose up, being simply upset by her agitation, and half-spread his arms out as if to protect her.

Yet Gregor had not the slightest intention of frightening anyone, far less his sister. He had only begun to turn round in order to crawl back to his room, but it was certainly a startling operation to watch, since because of his disabled condition he could not execute the difficult turning movements except by lifting his head and then bracing it against the floor over and over again. He paused and looked round. His good intentions seemed to have been recognized; the alarm had only been momentary. Now they were all watching him in melancholy silence. His mother lay in her chair, her legs stiffly outstretched and pressed together, her eyes almost closing for sheer weariness; his father and his sister were sitting beside each other, his sister's arm around the old man's neck.

Perhaps I can go on turning round now, thought Gregor, and began his labors again. He could not stop himself from panting with the effort, and had to pause now and then to take breath. Nor did anyone harass him, he was left entirely to himself. When he had completed the turn-round he began at once to crawl straight back. He was amazed at the distance separating him from his room and could not understand how in his weak state he had managed to accomplish the same journey so recently, almost without re-marking it. Intent on crawling as fast as possible, he barely noticed that not a single word, not an ejaculation from his family, interfered with his progress. Only when he was already in the doorway did he turn his head round, not completely, for his neck muscles were getting stiff, but enough to see that nothing had changed behind him except that his sister had risen to her feet. His last glance fell on his mother, who was not quite overcome by sleep.

Hardly was he well inside his room when the door was hastily pushed shut, bolted and locked. The sudden noise in his rear startled him so much that his little legs gave beneath him. It was his sister who had shown such haste. She had been standing ready waiting and had made a light spring forward. Gregor had not even heard her coming, and she cried "At last!" to her parents as she turned the key in the lock.

"And what now?" said Gregor to himself, looking round in the darkness. Soon he made the discovery that he was now unable to stir a limb. This did not surprise him, rather it seemed unnatural that he should ever actually have been able to move on these feeble little legs. Otherwise he felt relatively comfortable. True, his whole body was aching, but it seemed that the pain was gradually growing less and would finally pass away. The rotting apple in his back and the inflamed area around it, all covered with soft dust, already hardly troubled him. He thought of his family with tenderness and love. The decision that he must disappear was one that he held to even more strongly than his sister, if that were possible. In this state of vacant and peaceful meditation he remained until the tower clock struck three in the morning. The first broadening of light in the world outside the window entered his consciousness once more. Then his head sank to the floor of its own accord and from his nostrils came the last faint flicker of his breath.

When the charwoman arrived early in the morning — what between her strength and her impatience she slammed all the doors so loudly, never mind how often she had been begged not to do so, that no one in the whole apartment could enjoy any quiet sleep after her arrival — she noticed nothing unusual as she took her customary peep into Gregor's room. She thought he was lying motionless on purpose, pretending to be in the sulks; she credited him with every kind of intelligence. Since she happened to have the longhandled broom in her hand she tried to tickle him up with it from the doorway. When that too produced no reaction she felt

provoked and poked at him a little harder, and only when she
had pushed him along the floor without meeting any resistance
was her attention aroused. It did not take her long to establish
the truth of the matter, and her eyes widened, she let out a whistle,
yet did not waste much time over it but tore open the door of
the Samsas' bedroom and yelled into the darkness at the top of
her voice: "Just look at this, it's dead; it's lying here dead and
done for!"

Mr. and Mrs. Samsa started up in their double bed and before
they realized the nature of the charwoman's announcement had
some difficulty in overcoming the shock of it. But then they got
out of bed quickly, one on either side, Mr. Samsa throwing a
blanket over his shoulders, Mrs. Samsa in nothing but her nightgown; in this array they entered Gregor's room. Meanwhile the
door of the living room opened, too, where Grete had been sleeping
since the advent of the lodgers; she was completely dressed as if
she had not been to bed, which seemed to be confirmed also by
the paleness of her face. "Dead?" said Mrs. Samsa, looking questioningly at the charwoman, although she could have investigated
for herself, and the fact was obvious enough without investigation.
"I should say so," said the charwoman, proving her words by
pushing Gregor's corpse a long way to one side with her broomstick.
Mrs. Samsa made a movement as if to stop her, but checked it.
"Well," said Mr. Samsa, "now thanks be to God." He crossed
himself, and the three women followed his example. Grete, whose
eyes never left the corpse, said: "Just see how thin he was. It's
such a long time since he's eaten anything. The food came out
again just as it went in." Indeed, Gregor's body was completely
flat and dry, as could only now be seen when it was no longer
supported by the legs and nothing prevented one from looking
closely at it.

"Come in beside us, Grete, for a little while," said Mrs.
Samsa with a tremulous smile, and Grete, not without looking
back at the corpse, followed her parents into their bedroom. The
charwoman shut the door and opened the window wide. Although
it was so early in the morning a certain softness was perceptible
in the fresh air. After all, it was already the end of March.

The three lodgers emerged from their room and were surprised
to see no breakfast; they had been forgotten. "Where's our breakfast?"
said the middle lodger peevishly to the charwoman. But she put
her finger to her lips and hastily, without a word, indicated by
gestures that they should go into Gregor's room. They did so and
stood, their hands in the pockets of their somewhat shabby coats,
around Gregor's corpse in the room where it was now fully light.

At that the door of the Samsas' bedroom opened and Mr. Samsa appeared in his uniform, his wife on one arm, his daughter on the other. They all looked a little as if they had been crying; from time to time Grete hid her face on her father's arm.

"Leave my house at once!" said Mr. Samsa, and pointed to the door without disengaging himself from the women. "What do you mean by that?" said the middle lodger, taken somewhat aback, with a feeble smile. The two others put their hands behind them and kept rubbing them together, as if in gleeful expectation of a fine set-to in which they were bound to come off the winners. "I mean just what I say," answered Mr. Samsa, and advanced in a straight line with his two companions towards the lodger. He stood his ground at first quietly, looking at the floor as if his thoughts were taking a new pattern in his head. "Then let us go, by all means," he said and looked up at Mr. Samsa as if in a sudden access of humility he were expecting some renewed sanction for this decision. Mr. Samsa merely nodded briefly once or twice with meaning eyes. Upon that the lodger really did go with long strides into the hall, his two friends had been listening and had quite stopped rubbing their hands for some moments and now went scuttling after him as if afraid that Mr. Samsa might get into the hall before them and cut them off from their leader. In the hall they all three took their hats from the rack, their sticks from the umbrella stand, bowed in silence and quitted the apartment. With a suspiciousness which proved quite unfounded Mr. Samsa and the two women followed them out to the landing; leaning over the banister they watched the three figures slowly but surely going down the long stairs, vanishing from sight at a certain turn of the staircase on every floor and coming into view again after a moment or so; the more they dwindled, the more the Samsa family's interest in them dwindled, and when a butcher's boy met them and passed them on the stairs coming up proudly with a tray on his head, Mr. Samsa and the two women soon left the landing and as if a burden had been lifted from them went back into their apartment.

They decided to spend this day in resting and going for a stroll; they had not only deserved such a respite from work, but absolutely needed it. And so they sat down at the table and wrote three notes of excuse, Mr. Samsa to his board of management, Mrs. Samsa to her employer and Grete to the head of her firm. While they were writing, the charwoman came in to say that she was going now, since her morning's work was finished. At first they only nodded without looking up, but as she kept hovering there they eyed her irritably. "Well?" said Mr. Samsa. The charwoman stood grinning in the doorway as if she had good news to impart to the family but meant not to say a word unless properly questioned. The small ostrich feather standing upright on her hat, which had annoyed Mr. Samsa ever since she was engaged, was waving gaily in all directions. "Well, what is it then?" asked Mrs. Samsa, who obtained more respect from the charwoman than the others. "Oh," said the charwoman, giggling so amiably that she could not at once continue, "just this, you don't need to bother about how to get rid of the thing next door. It's been seen to already." Mrs. Samsa and Grete bent over their letters again, as if preoccupied; Mr. Samsa, who perceived that she was eager to begin describing it all in detail, stopped her with a decisive hand. But since she was not allowed to tell her story, she remembered the great hurry she was in, being obviously deeply huffed: "Bye, everybody," she said, whirling off violently, and departed with a frightful slamming of doors.

"She'll be given notice tonight," said Mr. Samsa, but neither from his wife nor his daughter did he get any answer, for the charwoman seemed to have shattered again the composure they had barely achieved. They rose, went to the window and stayed there, clasping each other tight. Mr. Samsa turned in his chair to look at them and quietly observed them for a little. Then he called out: "Come along, now, do. Let bygones be bygones. And you might have some consideration for me." The two of them complied at once, hastened to him, caressed him and quickly finished their letters.

Then they all three left the apartment together, which was more than they had done for months, and went by tram into the open country outside the town. The tram, in which they were the only passengers, was filled with warm sunshine. Leaning comfortably back in their seats they canvassed their prospects for the future, and it appeared on closer inspection that these were not at all bad, for the jobs they had got, which so far they had never really discussed with each other, were all three admirable and likely to lead to better things later on. The greatest immediate improvement in their condition would of course arise from moving to another house; they wanted to take a smaller and cheaper but also better situated and more easily run apartment than the one they had, which Gregor had selected. While they were thus conversing, it struck both Mr. and Mrs. Samsa, almost at the same moment, as they became aware of their daughter's increasing vivacity, that in spite of all the sorrow of recent times, which had made her cheeks pale, she had bloomed into a pretty girl with a good figure. They grew quieter and half unconsciously exchanged glances of complete agreement, having come to the conclusion that it would soon be time to find a good husband for her. And it was like a confirmation of their new dreams and excellent intentions that at the end of their journey their daughter sprang to her feet first and stretched her young body.

D. H. Lawrence (*English. 1885–1930*)

The Horse Dealer's Daughter

"Well, Mabel, and what are you going to do with yourself?" asked Joe, with foolish flippancy. He felt quite safe himself. Without listening for an answer, he turned aside, worked a grain of tobacco to the tip of his tongue and spat it out. He did not care about anything, since he felt safe himself.

The three brothers and the sister sat round the desolate breakfast table, attempting some sort of desultory consultation. The morning's post had given the final tap to the family fortune, and all was over. The dreary dining room itself, with its heavy mahogany furniture, looked as if it were waiting to be done away with.

But the consultation amounted to nothing. There was a strange air of ineffectuality about the three men, as they sprawled at table, smoking and reflecting vaguely on their own condition. The girl was alone, a rather short, sullen-looking young woman of twenty-seven. She did not share the same life as her brothers. She would have been good-looking, save for the impassive fixity of her face, "bull-dog," as her brothers called it.

There was a confused tramping of horses' feet outside. The three men all sprawled round in their chairs to watch. Beyond the dark holly bushes that separated the strip of lawn from the highroad, they could see a cavalcade of shire horses swinging out of their own yard, being taken for exercise. This was the last time. These were the last horses that would go through their hands. The young men watched with critical, callous looks. They were all frightened at the collapse of their lives, and the sense of disaster in which they were involved left them no inner freedom.

Yet they were three fine, well-set fellows enough. Joe, the eldest, was a man of thirty-three, broad and handsome in a hot, flushed way. His face was red, he twisted his black moustache over a thick finger, his eyes were shallow and restless. He had a sensual way of uncovering his teeth when he laughed, and his bearing was stupid. Now he watched the horses with a glazed look of helplessness in his eyes, a certain stupor of downfall.

The great draught-horses swung past. They were tied head to tail, four of them, and they heaved along to where a lane branched off from the highroad, planting their great hoofs floutingly in the fine black mud, swinging their great rounded haunches sumptuously, and trotting a few sudden steps as they were led into the lane, round the corner. Every movement showed a massive, slumbrous strength, and a stupidity which held them in subjection. The groom at the head looked back, jerking the leading rope. And the cavalcade moved out of sight up the lane, the tail of the last horse, bobbed up tight and stiff, held out taut from the swinging great haunches as they rocked behind the hedges in a motion-like sleep.

Joe watched with glazed hopeless eyes. The horses were almost like his own body to him. He felt he was done for now. Luckily he was engaged to a woman as old as himself, and therefore her father, who was steward of a neighboring estate, would provide him with a job. He would marry and go into harness. His life was over, he would be a subject animal now.

He turned uneasily aside, the retreating steps of the horses echoing in his ears. Then, with foolish restlessness, he reached for the scraps of bacon rind from the plates, and making a faint whistling sound, flung them to the terrier that lay against the fender. He watched the dog swallow them, and waited till the creature looked into his eyes. Then a faint grin came on his face, and in a high, foolish voice he said:

"You won't get much more bacon, shall you, you little bitch?"

The dog faintly and dismally wagged its tail, then lowered its haunches, circled round, and lay down again.

There was another helpless silence at the table. Joe sprawled uneasily in his seat, not willing to go till the family conclave was dissolved. Fred Henry, the second brother, was erect, cleanlimbed, alert. He had watched the passing of the horses with more sang-froid. If he was an animal, like Joe, he was an animal which controls, not one which is controlled. He was master of any horse, and he carried himself with a well-tempered air of mastery. But he was not master of the situations of life. He pushed his coarse brown moustache upwards, off his lip, and glanced irritably at his sister, who sat impassive and inscrutable.

"You'll go and stop with Lucy for a bit, shan't you?" he asked. The girl did not answer.

"I don't see what else you can do," persisted Fred Henry.

"Go as a skivvy," Joe interpolated laconically.

The girl did not move a muscle.

"If I was her, I should go in for training for a nurse," said Malcolm, the youngest of them all. He was the baby of the family, a young man of twenty-two, with a fresh, jaunty *museau*.°

But Mabel did not take any notice of him. They had talked at her and round her for so many years, that she hardly heard them at all.

The marble clock on the mantelpiece softly chimed the half-hour, the dog rose uneasily from the hearthrug and looked at the party at the breakfast table. But still they sat on in effectual conclave.

"Oh, all right," said Joe suddenly, apropos of nothing. "I'll get a move on."

He pushed back his chair, straddled his knees with a downward jerk, to get them free, in horsey fashion, and went to the fire. Still he did not go out of the room; he was curious to know what the others would do or say. He began to charge his pipe, looking down at the dog and saying, in a high, affected voice:

"Going wi' me? Going wi' me are ter? Tha'rt goin' further tha that counts on just now, dost hear?"

The dog faintly wagged its tail, the man stuck out his jaw and covered his pipe with his hands, and puffed intently, losing himself in the tobacco, looking down all the while at the dog with an absent brown eye. The dog looked at him in mournful distrust. Joe stood with his knees stuck out, in real horsey fashion.

"Have you had a letter from Lucy?" Fred Henry asked of his sister.

"Last week," came the neutral reply.

"And what does she say?"

There was no answer.

"Does she *ask* you to go and stop there?" persisted Fred Henry.

"She says I can if I like."

"Well, then, you'd better. Tell her you'll come on Monday." This was received in silence.

"That's what you'll do then, is it?" said Fred Henry, in some exasperation.

But she made no answer. There was a silence of futility and irritation in the room. Malcolm grinned fatuously.

"You'll have to make up your mind between now and next Wednesday," said Joe loudly, "or else find yourself lodgings on the curbstone."

The face of the young woman darkened, but she sat on immutable.

museau   jaw (literally muzzle or snout of a beast)

"Here's Jack Fergusson!" exclaimed Malcolm, who was looking aimlessly out of the window.

"Where?" exclaimed Joe, loudly.

"Just gone past."

"Coming in?"

Malcolm craned his neck to see the gate.

"Yes," he said.

There was a silence. Mabel sat on like one condemned, at the head of the table. Then a whistle was heard from the kitchen. The dog got up and barked sharply. Joe opened the door and shouted:

"Come on."

After a moment a young man entered. He was muffled up in overcoat and a purple woolen scarf, and his tweed cap, which he did not remove, was pulled down on his head. He was of medium height, his face was rather long and pale, his eyes looked tired.

"Hello, Jack! Well, Jack!" exclaimed Malcolm and Joe. Fred Henry merely said, "Jack."

"What's doing?" asked the newcomer, evidently addressing Fred Henry.

"Same. We've got to be out by Wednesday. Got a cold?"

"I have — got it bad, too."

"Why don't you stop in?"

"*Me* stop in? When I can't stand on my legs, perhaps I shall have a chance." The young man spoke huskily. He had a slight Scotch accent.

"It's a knock-out, isn't it," said Joe, boisterously, "if a doctor goes round croaking with a cold. Looks bad for the patients, doesn't it?"

The young doctor looked at him slowly.

"Anything the matter with *you*, then?" he asked sarcastically.

"Not as I know of. Damn your eyes, I hope not. Why?"

"I thought you were very concerned about the patients, wondered if you might be one yourself."

"Damn it, no, I've never been patient to no flaming doctor, and hope I never shall be," returned Joe.

At this point Mabel rose from the table, and they all seemed to become aware of her existence. She began putting the dishes together. The young doctor looked at her, but did not address her. He had not greeted her. She went out of the room with the tray, her face impassive and unchanged.

"When are you off then, all of you?" asked the doctor.

"I'm catching the eleven-forty," replied Malcolm. "Are you goin' down wi' th' trap, Joe?"

"Yes, I've told you I'm going down wi' th' trap, haven't I?"

"We'd better be getting her in then. So long, Jack, if I don't see you before I go," said Malcolm, shaking hands.

He went out, followed by Joe, who seemed to have his tail between his legs.

"Well, this is the devil's own," exclaimed the doctor, when he was left alone with Fred Henry. "Going before Wednesday, are you?"

"That's the orders," replied the other.

"Where, to Northampton?"

"That's it."

"The devil!" exclaimed Fergusson, with quiet chagrin.

And there was silence between the two.

"All settled up, are you?" asked Fergusson.

"About."

There was another pause.

"Well, I shall miss yer, Freddy, boy," said the young doctor.

"And I shall miss thee, Jack," returned the other.

"Miss you like hell," mused the doctor.

Fred Henry turned aside. There was nothing to say. Mabel came in again, to finish clearing the table.

"What are *you* going to do, then, Miss Pervin?" asked Fergusson. "Going to your sister's, are you?"

Mabel looked at him with her steady, dangerous eyes, that always made him uncomfortable, unsettling his superficial ease.

"No," she said.

"Well, what in the name of fortune *are* you going to do? Say what you mean to do," cried Fred Henry, with futile intensity.

But she only averted her head, and continued her work. She folded the white table-cloth, and put on the chenille cloth.

"The sulkiest bitch that ever trod!" muttered her brother.

But she finished her task with perfectly impassive face, the young doctor watching her interestedly all the while. Then she went out.

Fred Henry stared after her, clenching his lips, his blue eyes fixing in sharp antagonism, as he made a grimace of sour exasperation.

"You could bray her into bits, and that's all you'd get out of her," he said in a small, narrowed tone.

The doctor smiled faintly.

"What's she *going* to do, then?" he asked.

"Strike me if *I* know!" returned the other.

There was a pause. Then the doctor stirred.

"I'll be seeing you to-night, shall I?" he said to his friend.
"Ay — where's it to be? Are we going over to Jessdale?"
"I don't know. I've got such a cold on me. I'll come round
to the Moon and Stars, anyway."
"Let Lizzie and May miss their night for once, eh?"
"That's it — if I feel as I do now."
"All's one —"
The two young men went through the passage and down
to the back door together. The house was large, but it was servantless
now, and desolate. At the back was a small bricked house-yard,
and beyond that a big square, graveled fine and red, and having
stables on two sides. Sloping, dank, winter-dark fields stretched
away on the open sides.

But the stables were empty. Joseph Pervin, the father of the
family, had been a man of no education, who had become a fairly
large horse dealer. The stables had been full of horses, there was
a great turmoil and come-and-go of horses and of dealers and
grooms. Then the kitchen was full of servants. But of late things
had declined. The old man had married a second time, to retrieve
his fortunes. Now he was dead and everything was gone to the
dogs, there was nothing but debt and threatening.

For months, Mabel had been servantless in the big house,
keeping the home together in penury for her ineffectual brothers.
She had kept house for ten years. But previously it was with
unstinted means. Then, however brutal and coarse everything was,
the sense of money had kept her proud, confident. The men might
be foul-mouthed, the women in the kitchen might have bad rep-
utations, her brothers might have illegitimate children. But so long
as there was money, the girl felt herself established, and brutally
proud, reserved.

No company came to the house, save dealers and coarse
men. Mabel had no associates of her own sex, after her sister went
away. But she did not mind. She went regularly to church, she
attended to her father. And she lived in the memory of her mother,
who had died when she was fourteen, and whom she had loved.
She had loved her father, too, in a different way, depending upon
him, and feeling secure in him, until at the age of fifty-four he
married again. And then she had set hard against him. Now he
had died and left them all hopelessly in debt.

She had suffered badly during the period of poverty. Nothing,
however, could shake the curious sullen, animal pride that dominated
each member of the family. Now, for Mabel, the end had come.
Still she would not cast about her. She would follow her own
way just the same. She would always hold the keys of her own

situation. Mindless and persistent, she endured from day to day. Why should she think? Why should she answer anybody? It was enough that this was the end, and there was no way out. She need not pass any more darkly along the main street of the small town, avoiding every eye. She need not demean herself any more, going into the shops and buying the cheapest food. This was at an end. She thought of nobody, not even of herself. Mindless and persistent, she seemed in a sort of ecstasy to be coming nearer to her fulfillment, her own glorification, approaching her dead mother, who was glorified.

In the afternoon she took a little bag, with shears and sponge and a small scrubbing brush, and went out. It was a gray, wintry day, with saddened, dark green fields and an atmosphere blackened by the smoke of foundries not far off. She went quickly, darkly along the causeway, heeding nobody, through the town to the churchyard.

There she always felt secure, as if no one could see her, although as a matter of fact she was exposed to the stare of every one who passed along under the churchyard wall. Nevertheless, once under the shadow of the great looming church, among the graves, she felt immune from the world, reserved within the thick churchyard wall as in another country.

Carefully she clipped the grass from the grave, and arranged the pinky white, small chrysanthemums in the tin cross. When this was done, she took an empty jar from a neighboring grave, brought water, and carefully, most scrupulously sponged the marble headstone and the coping-stone. It gave her sincere satisfaction to do this. She felt in immediate contact with the world of her mother. She took minute pains, went through the park in a state bordering on pure happiness, as if in performing this task she came into a subtle, intimate connection with her mother. For the life she followed here in the world was far less real than the world of death she inherited from her mother.

The doctor's house was just by the church. Fergusson, being a mere hired assistant, was slave to the countryside. As he hurried now to attend to the outpatients in the surgery, glancing across the graveyard with his quick eyes, he saw the girl at her task at the grave. She seemed so intent and remote, it was like looking into another world. Some mystical element was touched in him. He slowed down as he walked, watching her as if spellbound.

She lifted her eyes, feeling him looking. Their eyes met. And each looked away again at once, each feeling, in some way, found out by the other. He lifted his cap and passed on down the road. There remained distinct in his consciousness, like a vision, the memory of her face, lifted from the tombstone in the churchyard, and looking at him with slow, large, portentous eyes. It *was* portentous, her face. It seemed to mesmerize him. There was a heavy power in her eyes which laid hold of his whole being, as if he had drunk some powerful drug. He had been feeling weak and done before. Now the life came back into him, he felt delivered from his own fretted, daily self.

He finished his duties at the surgery as quickly as might be, hastily filling up the bottles of the waiting people with cheap drugs. Then, in perpetual haste, he set off again to visit several cases in another part of his round, before teatime. At all times he preferred to walk if he could, but particularly when he was not well. He fancied the motion restored him.

The afternoon was falling. It was gray, deadened, and wintry, with a slow, moist, heavy coldness sinking in and deadening all the faculties. But why should he think or notice? He hastily climbed the hill and turned across the dark green fields, following the black cindertrack. In the distance, across a shallow dip in the country, the small town was clustered like smouldering ash, a tower, a spire, a heap of low, raw, extinct houses. And on the nearest fringe of the town, sloping into the dip, was Oldmeadow, the Pervins's house. He could see the stables and the outbuildings distinctly, as they lay towards him on the slope. Well, he would not go there many more times! Another resource would be lost to him, another place gone: the only company he cared for in the alien, ugly little town he was losing. Nothing but work, drudgery, constant hastening from dwelling to dwelling among the colliers and the iron-workers. It wore him out, but at the same time he had a craving for it. It was a stimulant to him to be in the homes of the working people, moving as it were through the innermost body of their life. His nerves were excited and gratified. He could come so near, into the very lives of the rough, inarticulate, powerfully emotional men and women. He grumbled, he said he hated the hellish hole. But as a matter of fact it excited him, the contact with the rough, strongly-feeling people was a stimulant applied direct to his nerves.

Below Oldmeadow, in the green, shallow, soddened hollow of fields, lay a square, deep pond. Roving across the landscape, the doctor's quick eye detected a figure in black passing through the gate of the field, down towards the pond. He looked again. It would be Mabel Pervin. His mind suddenly became alive and attentive.

Why was she going down there? He pulled up on the path on the slope above, and stood staring. He could just make sure of the small black figure moving in the hollow of the failing day. He seemed to see her in the midst of such obscurity, that he was like a clairvoyant, seeing rather with the mind's eye than with ordinary sight. Yet he could see her positively enough, while he kept his eye attentive. He felt, if he looked away from her, in the thick, ugly falling dusk, he would lose her altogether.

He followed her minutely as she moved, direct and intent, like something transmitted rather than stirring in voluntary activity, straight down the field towards the pond. There she stood on the bank for a moment. She never raised her head. Then she waded slowly into the water.

He stood motionless as the small black figure walked slowly and deliberately towards the center of the pond, very slowly, gradually moving deeper into the motionless water, and still moving forward as the water got up to her breast. Then he could see her no more in the dusk of the dead afternoon.

"There!" he exclaimed. "Would you believe it?"

And he hastened straight down, running over the wet, soddened fields, pushing through the hedges, down into the depression of callous wintry obscurity. It took him several minutes to come to the pond. He stood on the bank, breathing heavily. He could see nothing. His eyes seemed to penetrate the dead water. Yes, perhaps that was the dark shadow of her black clothing beneath the surface of the water.

He slowly ventured into the pond. The bottom was deep, soft clay, he sank in, and the water clasped dead cold round his legs. As he stirred he could smell the cold, rotten clay that fouled up into the water. It was objectionable in his lungs. Still, repelled and yet not heeding, he moved deeper into the pond. The cold water rose over his thighs, over his loins, upon his abdomen. The lower part of his body was all sunk in the hideous cold element. And the bottom was so deeply soft and uncertain he was afraid of pitching with his mouth underneath. He could not swim, and was afraid.

He crouched a little, spreading his hands under the water and moving them round, trying to feel for her. The dead cold pond swayed upon his chest. He moved again, a little deeper, and again, with his hands underneath, he felt all around under the water. And he touched her clothing. But it evaded his fingers. He made a desperate effort to grasp it.

And so doing he lost his balance and went under, horribly, suffocating in the foul earthy water, struggling madly for a few moments. At last, after what seemed an eternity, he got his footing, rose again into the air and looked around. He gasped, and knew he was in the world. Then he looked at the water. She had risen near him. He grasped her clothing, and drawing her nearer, turned to take his way to land again.

He went very slowly, carefully, absorbed in the slow progress. He rose higher, climbing out of the pond. The water was now only about his legs; he was thankful, full of relief to be out of the clutches of the pond. He lifted her and staggered on to the bank, out of the horror of wet, gray clay.

He laid her down on the bank. She was quite unconscious and running with water. He made the water come from her mouth, he worked to restore her. He did not have to work very long before he could feel the breathing begin again in her; she was breathing naturally. He worked a little longer. He could feel her live beneath his hands; she was coming back. He wiped her face, wrapped her in his overcoat, looked round into the dim, dark gray world, then lifted her and staggered down the bank and across the fields.

It seemed an unthinkably long way, and his burden so heavy he felt he would never get to the house. But at last he was in the stableyard, and then in the house-yard. He opened the door and went into the house. In the kitchen he laid her down on the hearthrug, and called. The house was empty. But the fire was burning in the grate.

Then again he kneeled to attend to her. She was breathing regularly, her eyes were wide open and as if conscious, but there seemed something missing in her look. She was conscious in herself, but unconscious of her surroundings.

He ran upstairs, took blankets from a bed, and put them before the fire to warm. Then he removed her saturated, earthy-smelling clothing, rubbed her dry with a towel, and wrapped her naked in the blankets. Then he went into the dining-room, to look for spirits. There was a little whisky. He drank a gulp himself, and put some into her mouth.

The effect was instantaneous. She looked full into his face, as if she had been seeing him for some time, and yet had only just become conscious of him.

"Dr. Fergusson?" she said.

"What?" he answered.

He was divesting himself of his coat, intending to find some dry clothing upstairs. He could not bear the smell of the dead, clayey water, and he was mortally afraid of his own health.

"What did I do?" she asked.

"Walked into the pond," he replied. He had begun to shudder like one sick, and could hardly attend to her. Her eyes remained

full on him, he seemed to be going dark in his mind, looking
back at her helplessly. The shuddering became quieter in him, his
life came back in him, dark and unknowing, but strong again.

"Was I out of my mind?" she asked, while her eyes were
fixed on him all the time.

"Maybe, for the moment," he replied. He felt quiet, because
his strength came back. The strange fretful strain had left him.

"Am I out of my mind now?" she asked.

"Are you?" he reflected a moment. "No," he answered
truthfully, "I don't see that you are." He turned his face aside.
He was afraid now, because he felt dazed, and felt dimly that her
power was stronger than his, in this issue. And she continued to
look at him fixedly all the time. "Can you tell me where I shall
find some dry things to put on?" he asked.

"Did you dive into the pond for me?" she asked.

"No," he answered. "I walked in. But I went in overhead
as well."

There was silence for a moment. He hesitated. He very much
wanted to go upstairs to get into dry clothing. But there was
another desire in him. And she seemed to hold him. His will
seemed to have gone to sleep, and left him, standing there slack
before her. But he felt warm inside himself. He did not shudder
at all, though his clothes were sodden on him.

"Why did you?" she asked.

"Because I didn't want you to do such a foolish thing," he
said.

"It wasn't foolish," she said, still gazing at him as she lay
on the floor, with a sofa cushion under her head. "It was the right
thing to do. *I* knew best, then."

"I'll go and shift these wet things," he said. But still he had
not the power to move out of her presence, until she sent him.
It was as if she had the life of his body in her hands, and he could
not extricate himself. Or perhaps he did not want to.

Suddenly she sat up. Then she became aware of her own
immediate condition. She felt the blankets about her, she knew
her own limbs. For a moment it seemed as if her reason were
going. She looked round, with wild eye, as if seeking something.
He stood still with fear. She saw her clothing lying scattered.

"Who undressed me?" she asked, her eyes resting full and
inevitable on his face.

"I did," he replied, "to bring you round."

For some moments she sat and gazed at him awfully, her
lips parted.

"Do you love me, then?" she asked.

He only stood and stared at her, fascinated. His soul seemed to melt.

She shuffled forward on her knees, and put her arms round him, round his legs, as he stood there, pressing her breasts against his knees and thighs, clutching him with strange, convulsive certainty, pressing his thighs against her, drawing him to her face, her throat, as she looked up at him with flaring, humble eyes of transfiguration, triumphant in first possession.

"You love me," she murmured, in strange transport, yearning and triumphant and confident. "You love me. I know you love me, I know."

And she was passionately kissing his knees, through the wet clothing, passionately and indiscriminately kissing his knees, his legs, as if unaware of everything.

He looked down at the tangled wet hair, the wild, bare, animal shoulders. He was amazed, bewildered, and afraid. He had never thought of loving her. He had never wanted to love her. When he rescued her and restored her, he was a doctor, and she was a patient. He had had no single personal thought of her. Nay, this introduction of the personal element was very distasteful to him, a violation of his professional honor. It was horrible to have her there embracing his knees. It was horrible. He revolted from it, violently. And yet — and yet — he had not the power to break away.

She looked at him again, with the same supplication of powerful love, and that same transcendent, frightening light of triumph. In view of the delicate flame which seemed to come from her face like a light, he was powerless. And yet he had never intended to love her. He had never intended. And something stubborn in him could not give way.

"You love me," she repeated, in a murmur of deep, rhapsodic assurance. "You love me."

Her hands were drawing him, drawing him down to her. He was afraid, even a little horrified. For he had, really, no intention of loving her. Yet her hands were drawing him towards her. He put out his hand quickly to steady himself, and grasped her bare shoulder. A flame seemed to burn the hand that grasped her soft shoulder. He had no intention of loving her: his whole will was against his yielding. It was horrible. And yet wonderful was the touch of her shoulders, beautiful the shining of her face. Was she perhaps mad? He had a horror of yielding to her. Yet something in him ached also.

He had been staring away at the door, away from her. But his hand remained on her shoulder. She had gone suddenly very still. He looked down at her. Her eyes were now wide with fear, with doubt, the light was dying from her face, a shadow of terrible grayness was returning. He could not bear the touch of her eyes' question upon him, and the look of death behind the question.

With an inward groan he gave way, and let his heart yield towards her. A sudden gentle smile came on his face. And her eyes, which never left his face, slowly, slowly filled with tears. He watched the strange water rise in her eyes, like some slow fountain coming up. And his heart seemed to burn and melt away in his breast.

He could not bear to look at her any more. He dropped on his knees and caught her head with his arms and pressed her face against his throat. She was very still. His heart, which seemed to have broken, was burning with a kind of agony in his breast. And he felt her slow, hot tears wetting his throat. But he could not move.

He felt the hot tears wet his neck and the hollows of his neck, and he remained motionless, suspended through one of man's eternities. Only now it had become indispensable to him to have her face pressed close to him; he could never let her go again. He could never let her head go away from the close clutch of his arm. He wanted to remain like that for ever, with his heart hurting him in a pain that was also life to him. Without knowing, he was looking down on her damp, soft brown hair.

Then, as it were suddenly, he smelt the horrid stagnant smell of that water. And at the same moment she drew away from him and looked at him. Her eyes were wistful and unfathomable. He was afraid of them, and he fell to kissing her, not knowing what he was doing. He wanted her eyes not to have that terrible, wistful, unfathomable look.

When she turned her face to him again, a faint delicate flush was glowing, and there was again dawning that terrible shining of joy in her eyes, which really terrified him, and yet which he now wanted to see, because he feared the look of doubt still more.

"You love me?" she said, rather faltering.

"Yes." The word cost him a painful effort. Not because it wasn't true. But because it was too newly true, the *saying* seemed to tear open again his newly torn heart. And he hardly wanted it to be true, even now.

She lifted her face to him, and he bent forward and kissed her on the mouth, gently, with the one kiss that is an eternal pledge. And as he kissed her his heart strained again in his breast. He never intended to love her. But now it was over. He had crossed over the gulf to her, and all that he had left behind had shriveled and become void.

After the kiss, her eyes again slowly filled with tears. She sat still, away from him, with her face drooped aside, and her hands folded in her lap. The tears fell very slowly. There was complete silence. He too sat there motionless and silent on the hearthrug. The strange pain of his heart that was broken seemed to consume him. That he should love her? That this was love! That he should be ripped open in this way! Him, a doctor! How they would all jeer if they knew! It was agony to him to think they might know.

In the curious naked pain of the thought he looked again to her. She was sitting there drooped into a muse. He saw a tear fall, and his heart flared hot. He saw for the first time that one of her shoulders was quite uncovered, one arm bare, he could see one of her small breasts; dimly, because it had become almost dark in the room.

"Why are you crying?" he asked, in an altered voice.

She looked up at him, and behind her tears the consciousness of her situation for the first time brought a dark look of shame to her eyes.

"I'm not crying, really," she said, watching him half frightened.

He reached his hand, and softly closed it on her bare arm.

"I love you! I love you!" he said in a soft, low vibrating voice, unlike himself.

She shrank, and dropped her head. The soft, penetrating grip of his hand on her arm distressed her. She looked up at him.

"I want to go," she said. "I want to go and get you some dry things."

"Why?" he said. "I'm all right."

"But I want to go," she said. "And I want you to change your things."

He released her arm, and she wrapped herself in the blanket, looking at him rather frightened. And still she did not rise.

"Kiss me," she said wistfully.

He kissed her, but briefly, half in anger.

Then, after a second, she rose nervously, all mixed up in the blanket. He watched her in her confusion, as she tried to extricate herself and wrap herself up so that she could walk. He watched her relentlessly, as she knew. And as she went, the blanket trailing, and as he saw a glimpse of her feet and her white leg, he tried to remember her as she was when he had wrapped her in the blanket. But then he didn't want to remember, because she had been nothing to him then, and his nature revolted from remembering her as she was when she was nothing to him.

A tumbling, muffled noise from within the dark house startled him. Then he heard her voice: — "There are clothes." He rose and went to the foot of the stairs, and gathered up the garments she had thrown down. Then he came back to the fire, to rub himself down and dress. He grinned at his own appearance when he had finished.

The fire was sinking, so he put on coal. The house was now quite dark, save for the light of a street-lamp that shone in faintly from beyond the holly trees. He lit the gas with matches he found on the mantelpiece. Then he emptied the pockets of his own clothes, and threw all his wet things in a heap into the scullery. After which he gathered up her sodden clothes, gently, and put them in a separate heap on the copper-top in the scullery.

It was six o'clock on the clock. His own watch had stopped. He ought to go back to the surgery. He waited, and still she did not come down. So he went to the foot of the stairs and called:

"I shall have to go."

Almost immediately he heard her coming down. She had on her best dress of black voile, and her hair was tidy, but still damp. She looked at him — and in spite of herself, smiled.

"I don't like you in those clothes," she said.

"Do I look a sight?" he answered.

They were shy of one another.

"I'll make you some tea," she said.

"No, I must go."

"Must you?" And she looked at him again with the wide, strained, doubtful eyes. And again, from the pain of his breast, he knew how he loved her. He went and bent to kiss her, gently, passionately, with his heart's painful kiss.

"And my hair smells so horrible," she murmured in distraction. "And I'm so awful, I'm so awful! Oh, no, I'm too awful." And she broke into bitter, heart-broken sobbing. "You can't want to love me, I'm horrible."

"Don't be silly, don't be silly," he said, trying to comfort her, kissing her, holding her in his arms. "I want you, I want to marry you, we're going to be married, quickly, quickly — tomorrow if I can."

But she only sobbed terribly, and cried:

"I feel awful. I feel awful. I feel I'm horrible to you."

"No, I want you, I want you," was all he answered, blindly, with that terrible intonation which frightened her almost more than her horror lest he should *not* want her.

Katherine Anne Porter (*American. 1890–1980*)

The Jilting of Granny Weatherall

She flicked her wrist neatly out of Doctor Harry's pudgy careful fingers and pulled the sheet up to her chin. The brat ought to be in knee breeches. Doctoring around the country with spectacles on his nose! "Get along now, take your schoolbooks and go. There's nothing wrong with me."

Doctor Harry spread a warm paw like a cushion on her forehead where the forked green vein danced and made her eyelids twitch. "Now, now, be a good girl, and we'll have you up in no time."

"That's no way to speak to a woman nearly eighty years old just because she's down. I'd have you respect your elders, young man."

"Well, Missy, excuse me." Doctor Harry patted her cheek. "But I've got to warn you, haven't I? You're a marvel, but you must be careful or you're going to be good and sorry."

"Don't tell me what I'm going to be. I'm on my feet now, morally speaking. It's Cornelia. I had to go to bed to get rid of her."

Her bones felt loose, and floated around in her skin, and Doctor Harry floated like a balloon around the foot of the bed. He floated and pulled down his waistcoat and swung his glasses on a cord. "Well, stay where you are, it certainly can't hurt you."

"Get along and doctor your sick," said Granny Weatherall. "Leave a well woman alone. I'll call for you when I want you. . . . Where were you forty years ago when I pulled through milk-leg and double pneumonia? You weren't even born. Don't let Cornelia lead you on," she shouted, because Doctor Harry appeared to float up to the ceiling and out. "I pay my own bills, and I don't throw my money away on nonsense!"

She meant to wave good-by, but it was too much trouble. Her eyes closed of themselves, it was like a dark curtain drawn around the bed. The pillow rose and floated under her, pleasant as a hammock in a light wind. She listened to the leaves rustling outside the window. No, somebody was swishing newspapers: no, Cornelia and Doctor Harry were whispering together. She leaped broad awake, thinking they whispered in her ear.

"She was never like this, *never* like this!" "Well, what can we expect?" "Yes, eighty years old. . . ."

Well, and what if she was? She still had ears. It was like Cornelia to whisper around doors. She always kept things secret in such a public way. She was always being tactful and kind. Cornelia was dutiful; that was the trouble with her. Dutiful and good: "So good and dutiful," said Granny, "and I'd like to spank her." She saw herself spanking Cornelia and making a fine job of it.

"What'd you say, Mother?"

Granny felt her face tying up in hard knots.

"Can't a body think, I'd like to know?"

"I thought you might want something."

"I do. I want a lot of things. First off, go away and don't whisper."

She lay and drowsed, hoping in her sleep that the children would keep out and let her rest a minute. It had been a long day. Not that she was tired. It was always pleasant to snatch a minute now and then. There was always so much to be done, let me see: tomorrow.

Tomorrow was far away and there was nothing to trouble about. Things were finished somehow when the time came; thank God there was always a little margin over for peace: then a person could spread out the plan of life and tuck in the edges orderly. It was good to have everything clean and folded away, with the hair brushes and tonic bottles sitting straight on the white embroidered linen: the day started without fuss and the pantry shelves laid out with rows of jelly glasses and brown jugs and white stone-china jars with blue whirligigs and words painted on them: coffee, tea, sugar, ginger, cinnamon, allspice: and the bronze clock with the lion on top nicely dusted off. The dust that lion could collect in twenty-four hours! The box in the attic with all those letters tied up, well, she'd have to go through that tomorrow. All those letters — George's letters and John's letters and her letters to them both — lying around for the children to find afterwards made her uneasy. Yes, that would be tomorrow's business. No use to let them know how silly she had been once.

While she was rummaging around she found death in her mind and it felt clammy and unfamiliar. She had spent so much time preparing for death there was no need for bringing it up again. Let it take care of itself now. When she was sixty she had felt very old, finished, and went around making farewell trips to see her children and grandchildren, with a secret in her mind: This is the very last of your mother, children! Then she made her will and came down with a long fever. That was all just a notion like a lot of other things, but it was lucky too, for she had once for all got over the idea of dying for a long time. Now she couldn't be worried. She hoped she had better sense now. Her father had lived to be one hundred and two years old and had drunk a noggin of strong hot toddy on his last birthday. He told the reporters it was his daily habit, and he owed his long life to that. He had made quite a scandal and was very pleased about it. She believed she'd just plague Cornelia a little.

"Cornelia! Cornelia!" No footsteps, but a sudden hand on her cheek. "Bless you, where have you been?"

"Here, Mother."

"Well, Cornelia, I want a noggin of hot toddy."

"Are you cold, darling?"

"I'm chilly, Cornelia. Lying in bed stops the circulation. I must have told you that a thousand times."

Well, she could just hear Cornelia telling her husband that Mother was getting a little childish and they'd have to humor her. The thing that most annoyed her was that Cornelia thought she was deaf, dumb, and blind. Little hasty glances and tiny gestures tossed around her and over her head saying, "Don't cross her, let her have her way, she's eighty years old," and she sitting there as if she lived in a thin glass cage. Sometimes Granny almost made up her mind to pack up and move back to her own house where nobody could remind her every minute that she was old. Wait, wait, Cornelia, till your own children whisper behind your back!

In her day she had kept a better house and had got more work done. She wasn't too old yet for Lydia to be driving eighty miles for advice when one of the children jumped the track, and Jimmy still dropped in and talked things over: "Now, Mammy, you've a good business head, I want to know what you think of this? . . ." Old. Cornelia couldn't change the furniture around without asking. Little things, little things! They had been so sweet when they were little. Granny wished the old days were back again with the children young and everything to be done over. It had been a hard pull, but not too much for her. When she thought of all the food she had cooked, and all the clothes she had cut and sewed, and all the gardens she had made — well, the children showed it. There they were, made out of her, and they couldn't get away from that. Sometimes she wanted to see John again and point to them and say, Well, I didn't do so badly, did I? But that would have to wait. That was for tomorrow. She used to think of him as a man, but now all the children were older than their father, and he would be a child beside her if she saw him now.

It seemed strange and there was something wrong in the idea. Why, he couldn't possibly recognize her. She had fenced in a hundred acres once, digging the post holes herself and clamping the wires with just a negro boy to help. That changed a woman. John would be looking for a young woman with the peaked Spanish comb in her hair and the painted fan. Digging post holes changed a woman. Riding country roads in the winter when women had their babies was another thing: sitting up nights with sick horses and sick negroes and sick children and hardly ever losing one. John, I hardly ever lost one of them! John would see that in a minute, that would be something he could understand, she wouldn't have to explain anything!

It made her feel like rolling up her sleeves and putting the whole place to rights again. No matter if Cornelia was determined to be everywhere at once, there were a great many things left undone on this place. She would start tomorrow and do them. It was good to be strong enough for everything, even if all you made melted and changed and slipped under your hands, so that by the time you finished you almost forgot what you were working for. What was it I set out to do? she asked herself intently, but she could not remember. A fog rose over the valley, she saw it marching across the creek swallowing the trees and moving up the hill like an army of ghosts. Soon it would be at the near edge of the orchard, and then it was time to go in and light the lamps. Come in, children, don't stay out in the night air.

Lighting the lamps had been beautiful. The children huddled up to her and breathed like little calves waiting at the bars in the twilight. Their eyes followed the match and watched the flame rise and settle in a blue curve, then they moved away from her. The lamp was lit, they didn't have to be scared and hang on to mother any more. Never, never, never more. God, for all my life I thank Thee. Without Thee, my God, I could never have done it. Hail, Mary, full of grace.

I want you to pick all the fruit this year and see that nothing is wasted. There's always someone who can use it. Don't let good things rot for want of using. You waste life when you waste good food. Don't let things get lost. It's bitter to lose things. Now, don't let me get to thinking, not when I am tired and taking a little nap before supper. . . .

The pillow rose about her shoulders and pressed against her heart and the memory was being squeezed out of it: oh, push down the pillow, somebody: it would smother her if she tried to hold it. Such a fresh breeze blowing and such a green day with no threats in it. But he had not come, just the same. What does a woman do when she has put on the white veil and set out the white cake for a man and he doesn't come? She tried to remember. No, I swear he never harmed me but in that. He never harmed me but in that . . . and what if he did? There was the day, the day, but a whirl of dark smoke rose and covered it, crept up and over into the bright field where everything was planted so carefully in orderly rows. That was hell, she knew hell when she saw it. For sixty years she had prayed against remembering him and against losing her soul in the deep pit of hell, and now the two things were mingled in one and the thought of him was a smoky cloud from hell that moved and crept in her head when she had just got rid of Doctor Harry and was trying to rest a minute. Wounded vanity, Ellen, said a sharp voice in the top of her mind. Don't let your wounded vanity get the upper hand of you. Plenty of girls get jilted. You were jilted, weren't you? Then stand up to it. Her eyelids wavered and let in streamers of blue-gray light like tissue paper over her eyes. She must get up and pull the shades down or she'd never sleep. She was in bed again and the shades were not down. How could that happen? Better turn over, hide from the light, sleeping in the light gave you nightmares. "Mother, how do you feel now?" and a stinging wetness on her forehead. But I don't like having my face washed in cold water!

Hapsy? George? Lydia? Jimmy? No, Cornelia, and her features were swollen and full of little puddles. "They're coming, darling, they'll all be here soon." Go wash your face, child, you look funny.

Instead of obeying, Cornelia knelt down and put her head on the pillow. She seemed to be talking but there was no sound. "Well, are you tongue-tied? Whose birthday is it? Are you going to give a party?"

Cornelia's mouth moved urgently in strange shapes. "Don't do that, you bother me, daughter."

"Oh, no, Mother. Oh, no. . . ."

Nonsense. It was strange about children. They disputed your every word. "No what, Cornelia?"

"Here's Doctor Harry."

"I won't see that boy again. He just left five minutes ago."

"That was this morning, Mother. It's night now. Here's the nurse."

"This is Doctor Harry, Mrs. Weatherall. I never saw you look so young and happy!"

"Ah, I'll never be young again — but I'd be happy if they'd let me lie in peace and get rested."

She thought she spoke up loudly, but no one answered. A

warm weight on her forehead, a warm bracelet on her wrist, and a breeze went on whispering, trying to tell her something. A shuffle of leaves in the everlasting hand of God. He blew on them and they danced and rattled. "Mother, don't mind, we're going to give you a little hypodermic." "Look here, daughter, how do ants get in this bed? I saw sugar ants yesterday." Did you send for Hapsy too?

It was Hapsy she really wanted. She had to go a long way back through a great many rooms to find Hapsy standing with a baby on her arm. She seemed to herself to be Hapsy also, and the baby on Hapsy's arm was Hapsy and himself and herself, all at once, and there was no surprise in the meeting. Then Hapsy melted from within and turned flimsy as gray gauze and the baby was a gauzy shadow, and Hapsy came up close and said, "I thought you'd never come," and looked at her very searchingly and said, "You haven't changed a bit!" They leaned forward to kiss, when Cornelia began whispering from a long way off, "Oh, is there anything you want to tell me? Is there anything I can do for you?"

Yes, she had changed her mind after sixty years and she would like to see George. I want you to find George. Find him and be sure to tell him I forgot him. I want him to know I had my husband just the same and my children and my house like any other woman. A good house too and a good husband that I loved and fine children out of him. Better than I hoped for even. Tell him I was given back everything he took away and more. Oh, no, oh, God, no, there was something else besides the house and the man and the children. Oh, surely they were not all? What was it? Something not given back. . . . Her breath crowded down under her ribs and grew into a monstrous frightening shape with cutting edges; it bored up into her head, and the agony was unbelievable: Yes, John, get the doctor now, no more talk, my time has come.

When this one was born it should be the last. The last. It should have been born first, for it was the one she had truly wanted. Everything came in good time. Nothing left out, left over. She was strong, in three days she would be as well as ever. Better. A woman needed milk in her to have her full health.

"Mother, do you hear me?"

"I've been telling you —"

"Mother, Father Connolly's here."

"I went to Holy Communion only last week. Tell him I'm not so sinful as all that."

"Father just wants to speak to you."

He could speak as much as he pleased. It was like him to drop in and inquire about her soul as if it were a teething baby, and then stay on for a cup of tea and a round of cards and gossip. He always had a funny story of some sort, usually about an Irishman who made his little mistakes and confessed them, and the point lay in some absurd thing he would blurt out in the confessional showing his struggles between native piety and original sin. Granny felt easy about her soul. Cornelia, where are your manners? Give Father Connolly a chair. She had her secret comfortable understanding with a few favorite saints who cleared a straight road to God for her. All as surely signed and sealed as the papers for the new Forty Acres. Forever . . . heirs and assigns forever. Since the day the wedding cake was not cut, but thrown out and wasted. The whole bottom dropped out of the world, and there she was blind and sweating with nothing under her feet and the walls falling away.

His hand had caught her under the breast, she had not fallen, there was the freshly polished floor with the green rug on it, just as before. He had cursed like a sailor's parrot and said, "I'll kill him for you." Don't lay a hand on him, for my sake leave something to God. "Now, Ellen, you must believe what I tell you. . . ."

So there was nothing, nothing to worry about any more, except sometimes in the night one of the children screamed in a nightmare, and they both hustled out shaking and hunting for the matches and calling, "There, wait a minute, here we are!" John, get the doctor now, Hapsy's time has come. But there was Hapsy standing by the bed in a white cap. "Cornelia, tell Hapsy to take off her cap. I can't see her plain."

Her eyes opened very wide and the room stood out like a picture she had seen somewhere. Dark colors with the shadows rising towards the ceiling in long angles. The tall black dresser gleamed with nothing on it but John's picture, enlarged from a little one, with John's eyes very black when they should have been blue. You never saw him, so how do you know how he looked? But the man insisted the copy was perfect, it was very rich and handsome. For a picture, yes, but it's not my husband. The table by the bed had a linen cover and a candle and a crucifix. The light was blue from Cornelia's silk lampshades. No sort of light at all, just frippery. You had to live forty years with kerosene lamps to appreciate honest electricity. She felt very strong and she saw Doctor Harry with a rosy nimbus around him.

"You look like a saint, Doctor Harry, and I vow that's as near as you'll ever come to it."

"She's saying something."

"I heard you, Cornelia. What's all this carrying on?"

"Father Connolly's saying —"

Cornelia's voice staggered and bumped like a cart in a bad road. It rounded corners and turned back again and arrived nowhere. Granny stepped up in the cart very lightly and reached for the reins, but a man sat beside her and she knew him by his hands, driving the cart. She did not look in his face, for she knew without seeing, but looked instead down the road where the trees leaned over and bowed to each other and a thousand birds were singing a Mass. She felt like singing too, but she put her hand in the bosom of her dress and pulled out a rosary, and Father Connolly murmured Latin in a very solemn voice and tickled her feet. My God, will you stop that nonsense? I'm a married woman. What if he did run away and leave me to face the priest by myself? I found another a whole world better. I wouldn't have exchanged my husband for anybody except St. Michael himself, and you may tell him that for me with a thank you in the bargain.

Light flashed on her closed eyelids, and a deep roaring shook her. Cornelia, is that lightning? I hear thunder. There's going to be a storm. Close all the windows. Call the children in. . . . "Mother, here we are, all of us." "Is that you, Hapsy?" "Oh, no, I'm Lydia. We drove as fast as we could." Their faces drifted above her, drifted away. The rosary fell out of her hands and Lydia put it back. Jimmy tried to help, their hands fumbled together, and Granny closed two fingers around Jimmy's thumb. Beads wouldn't do, it must be something alive. She was so amazed her thoughts ran round and round. So, my dear Lord, this is my death and I wasn't even thinking about it. My children have come to see me die. But I can't, it's not time. Oh, I always hated surprises. I wanted to give Cornelia the amethyst set — Cornelia, you're to have the amethyst set, but Hapsy's to wear it when she wants, and, Doctor Harry, do shut up. Nobody sent for you. Oh, my dear Lord, do wait a minute. I meant to do something about the Forty Acres, Jimmy doesn't need it and Lydia will later on, with that worthless husband of hers. I meant to finish the altar cloth and send six bottles of wine to Sister Borgia for her dyspepsia. I want to send six bottles of wine to Sister Borgia, Father Connolly, now don't let me forget.

Cornelia's voice made short turns and tilted over and crashed. "Oh, Mother, oh, Mother, oh, Mother. . . ."

"I'm not going, Cornelia. I'm taken by surprise. I can't go."

You'll see Hapsy again. What about her? "I thought you'd never come." Granny made a long journey outward, looking for

Hapsy. What if I don't find her? What then? Her heart sank down and down, there was no bottom to death, she couldn't come to the end of it. The blue light from Cornelia's lampshade drew into a tiny point in the center of her brain, it flickered and winked like an eye, quietly it fluttered and dwindled. Granny lay curled down within herself, amazed and watchful, staring at the point of light that was herself, her body was now only a deeper mass of shadow in an endless darkness and this darkness would curl around the light and swallow it up. God, give a sign!

For the second time there was no sign. Again no bridegroom and the priest in the house. She could not remember any other sorrow because this grief wiped them all away. Oh, no, there's nothing more cruel than this — I'll never forgive it. She stretched herself with a deep breath and blew out the light.

James Thurber (American. 1894–1961)

The Secret Life of Walter Mitty

"We're going through!" The Commander's voice was like thin ice breaking. He wore his full-dress uniform, with the heavily braided white cap pulled down rakishly over one cold gray eye. "We can't make it, sir. It's spoiling for a hurricane, if you ask me." "I'm not asking you, Lieutenant Berg," said the Commander. "Throw on the power lights! Rev her up to 8500! We're going through!" The pounding of the cylinders increased; ta-pocketa-pocketa-pocketa-*pocketa-pocketa*. The Commander stared at the ice forming on the pilot window. He walked over and twisted a row of complicated dials. "Switch on No. 8 auxiliary!" he shouted. "Switch on No. 8 auxiliary!" repeated Lieutenant Berg. "Full strength in No. 3 turret!" shouted the Commander. "Full strength in No. 3 turret!" The crew, bending to their various tasks in the huge, hurtling eight-engined Navy hydroplane, looked at each other and grinned. "The Old Man'll get us through," they said to one another. "The Old Man ain't afraid of Hell!". . .

"Not so fast! You're driving too fast!" said Mrs. Mitty. "What are you driving so fast for?"

"Hmm?" said Walter Mitty. He looked at his wife, in the
seat beside him, with shocked astonishment. She seemed grossly
unfamiliar, like a strange woman who had yelled at him in a crowd.
"You were up to fifty-five," she said. "You know I don't like to
go more than forty. You were up to fifty-five." Walter Mitty
drove on toward Waterbury in silence, the roaring of the SN202
through the worst storm in twenty years of Navy flying fading
in the remote, intimate airways of his mind. "You're tensed up
again," said Mrs. Mitty. "It's one of your days. I wish you'd let
Dr. Renshaw look you over."

Walter Mitty stopped the car in front of the building where
his wife went to have her hair done. "Remember to get those
overshoes while I'm having my hair done," she said. "I don't need
overshoes," said Mitty. She put her mirror back into her bag.
"We've been all through that," she said, getting out of the car.
"You're not a young man any longer." He raced the engine a
little. "Why don't you wear your gloves? Have you lost your
gloves?" Walter Mitty reached in a pocket and brought out the
gloves. He put them on, but after she had turned and gone into
the building and he had driven on to a red light, he took them
off again. "Pick it up, brother," snapped a cop as the light changed,
and Mitty hastily pulled on his gloves and lurched ahead. He drove
around the streets aimlessly for a time, and then he drove past
the hospital on his way to the parking lot.

. . . "It's the millionaire banker, Wellington McMillan," said
the pretty nurse. "Yes?" said Walter Mitty, removing his gloves
slowly. "Who has the case?" "Dr. Renshaw and Dr. Benbow,
but there are two specialists here, Dr. Remington from New York
and Dr. Pritchard-Mitford from London. He flew over." A door
opened down a long, cool corridor and Dr. Renshaw came out.
He looked distraught and haggard. "Hello, Mitty," he said. "We're
having the devil's own time with McMillan, the millionaire banker
and close personal friend of Roosevelt. Obstreosis of the ductal
tract. Tertiary. Wish you'd take a look at him." "Glad to," said
Mitty.

In the operating room there were whispered introductions:
"Dr. Remington, Dr. Mitty, Dr. Pritchard-Mitford, Dr. Mitty."
"I've read your book on streptothricosis," said Pritchard-Mitford,
shaking hands. "A brilliant performance, sir." "Thank you," said
Walter Mitty. "Didn't know you were in the States, Mitty," grumbled Remington. "Coals to Newcastle, bringing Mitford and me
up here for a tertiary." "You are very kind," said Mitty. A huge,
complicated machine, connected to the operating table, with many

tubes and wires, began at this moment to go pocketa-pocketa-pocketa. "The new anaesthetizer is giving away!" shouted an intern. "There is no one in the East who knows how to fix it!" "Quiet, man!" said Mitty, in a low, cool voice. He sprang to the machine, which was now going pocketa-pocketa-queep-pocketa-queep. He began fingering delicately a row of glistening dials. "Give me a fountain pen!" he snapped. Someone handed him a fountain pen. He pulled a faulty piston out of the machine and inserted the pen in its place. "That will hold for ten minutes," he said. "Get on with the operation." A nurse hurried over and whispered to Renshaw, and Mitty saw the man turn pale. "Coreopsis has set in," said Renshaw nervously. "If you would take over, Mitty?" Mitty looked at him and at the craven figure of Benbow, who drank, and at the grave, uncertain faces of the two great specialists. "If you wish," he said. They slipped a white gown on him; he adjusted a mask and drew on thin gloves; nurses handed him shining . . .

"Back it up, Mac! Look out for that Buick!" Walter Mitty jammed on the brakes. "Wrong lane, Mac," said the parking-lot attendant, looking at Mitty closely. "Gee. Yeh," muttered Mitty. He began cautiously to back out of the lane marked Exit Only. "Leave her sit there," said the attendant. "I'll put her away." Mitty got out of the car. "Hey, better leave the key." "Oh," said Mitty, handing the man the ignition key. The attendant vaulted into the car, backed it up with insolent skill, and put it where it belonged.

They're so damn cocky, thought Walter Mitty, walking along Main Street; they think they know everything. Once he had tried to take his chains off, outside New Milford, and he had got them wound around the axles. A man had had to come out in a wrecking car and unwind them, a young, grinning garage man. Since then Mrs. Mitty always made him drive to a garage to have the chains taken off. The next time, he thought, I'll wear my right arm in a sling; they won't grin at me then. I'll have my right arm in a sling and they'll see I couldn't possibly take the chains off myself. He kicked at the slush on the sidewalk. "Overshoes," he said to himself, and he began looking for a shoe store.

When he came out into the street again, with the overshoes in a box under his arm, Walter Mitty began to wonder what the other thing was his wife had told him to get. She had told him, twice before they set out from their house for Waterbury. In a way he hated these weekly trips to town — he was always getting something wrong. Kleenex, he thought, Squibb's, razor blades? No. Toothpaste, toothbrush, bicarbonate, carborundum, initiative and referendum? He gave it up. But she would remember it.

"Where's the what's-its-name?" she would ask. "Don't tell me you forgot the what's-its-name." A newsboy went by shouting something about the Waterbury trial.

. . . "Perhaps this will refresh your memory." The District Attorney suddenly thrust a heavy automatic at the quiet figure on the witness stand. "Have you ever seen this before?" Walter Mitty took the gun and examined it expertly. "This is my Webley-Vickers 50.80," he said calmly. An excited buzz ran around the courtroom. The judge rapped for order. "You are a crack shot with any sort of firearms, I believe?" said the District Attorney, insinuatingly. "Objection!" shouted Mitty's attorney. "We have shown that the defendant could not have fired the shot. We have shown that he wore his right arm in a sling on the night of the fourteenth of July." Walter Mitty raised his hand briefly and the bickering attorneys were stilled. "With any known make of gun," he said evenly, "I could have killed Gregory Fitzhurst at three hundred feet *with my left hand*." Pandemonium broke loose in the courtroom. A woman's scream rose above the bedlam and suddenly a lovely, dark-haired girl was in Walter Mitty's arms. The District Attorney struck at her savagely. Without rising from his chair, Mitty let the man have it on the point of the chin. "You miserable cur!" . . .

"Puppy biscuit," said Walter Mitty. He stopped walking and the buildings of Waterbury rose up out of the misty courtroom and surrounded him again. A woman who was passing laughed. "He said 'Puppy biscuit,'" she said to her companion. "That man said 'Puppy biscuit' to himself." Walter Mitty hurried on. He went into an A. & P., not the first one he came to but a smaller one farther up the street. "I want some biscuit for small, young dogs," he said to the clerk. "Any special brand, sir?" The greatest pistol shot in the world thought a moment. "It says 'Puppies Bark for It' on the box," said Walter Mitty.

His wife would be through at the hairdresser's in fifteen minutes, Mitty saw in looking at his watch, unless they had trouble drying it; sometimes they had trouble drying it. She didn't like to get to the hotel first; she would want him to be there waiting for her as usual. He found a big leather chair in the lobby, facing a window, and he put the overshoes and the puppy biscuit on the floor beside it. He picked up an old copy of *Liberty* and sank down into the chair. "Can Germany Conquer the World through the Air?" Walter Mitty looked at the pictures of bombing planes and of ruined streets.

. . . "The cannonading has got the wind up in young Raleigh, sir," said the sergeant. Captain Mitty looked up at him through tousled hair. "Get him to bed," he said wearily, "with the others. I'll fly alone." "But you can't, sir," said the sergeant anxiously. "It takes two men to handle that bomber and the Archies are pounding hell out of the air. Von Richtman's circus is between here and Saulier." "Somebody's got to get that ammunition dump," said Mitty. "I'm going over. Spot of brandy?" He poured a drink for the sergeant and one for himself. War thundered and whined around the dugout and battered at the door. There was a rending of wood and splinters flew through the room. "A bit of a near thing," said Captain Mitty carelessly. "The box barrage is closing in," said the sergeant. "We only live once, sergeant," said Mitty, with his faint, fleeting smile. "Or do we?" He poured another brandy and tossed it off. "I never see a man could hold his brandy like you, sir," said the sergeant. "Begging your pardon, sir." Captain Mitty stood up and strapped on his huge Webley-Vickers automatic. "It's forty kilometers through hell, sir," said the sergeant. Mitty finished one last brandy. "After all," he said softly, "what isn't?" The pounding of the cannon increased; there was the rat-tat-tatting of machine guns, and from somewhere came the menacing pocketa-pocketa-pocketa of the new flame-throwers. Walter Mitty walked to the door of the dugout humming "*Auprès de Ma Blonde.*" He turned and waved to the sergeant. "Cheerio!" he said. . . .

Something struck his shoulder. "I've been looking all over this hotel for you," said Mrs. Mitty. "Why do you have to hide in this old chair? How did you expect me to find you?" "Things close in," said Walter Mitty vaguely. "What?" Mrs. Mitty said. "Did you get the what's-its-name? The puppy biscuit? What's in that box?" "Overshoes," said Mitty. "Couldn't you have put them on in the store?" "I was thinking," said Walter Mitty. "Does it ever occur to you that I am sometimes thinking?" She looked at him. "I'm going to take your temperature when I get you home," she said.

They went out through the revolving doors that made a faintly derisive whistling sound when you pushed them. It was two blocks to the parking lot. At the drugstore on the corner she said, "Wait here for me. I forgot something. I won't be a minute." She was more than a minute. Walter Mitty lighted a cigarette. It began to rain, rain with sleet in it. He stood up against the wall of the drugstore, smoking. . . . He put his shoulders back and his heels together. "To hell with the handkerchief," said Walter Mitty scornfully. He took one last drag on his cigarette and snapped it away. Then, with that faint, fleeting smile playing about his lips, he faced the firing squad; erect and motionless, proud and disdainful, Walter Mitty the Undefeated, inscrutable to the last.

William Faulkner (American. 1897–1962)

A Rose for Emily

I

When Miss Emily Grierson died, our whole town went to her funeral: the men through a sort of respectful affection for a fallen monument, the women mostly out of curiosity to see the inside of her house, which no one save an old manservant — a combined gardener and cook — had seen in at least ten years.

It was a big, squarish frame house that had once been white, decorated with cupolas and spires and scrolled balconies in the heavily lightsome style of the seventies, set on what had once been our most select street. But garages and cotton gins had encroached and obliterated even the august names of that neighborhood; only Miss Emily's house was left, lifting its stubborn and coquettish decay above the cotton wagons and the gasoline pumps — an eyesore among eyesores. And now Miss Emily had gone to join the representatives of those august names where they lay in the cedar-bemused cemetery among the ranked and anonymous graves of Union and Confederate soldiers who fell at the battle of Jefferson.

Alive, Miss Emily had been a tradition, a duty, and a care; a sort of hereditary obligation upon the town, dating from that day in 1894 when Colonel Sartoris, the mayor — he who fathered the edict that no Negro woman should appear on the streets without an apron — remitted her taxes, the dispensation dating from the death of her father on into perpetuity. Not that Miss Emily would have accepted charity. Colonel Sartoris invented an involved tale to the effect that Miss Emily's father had loaned money to the town, which the town, as a matter of business, preferred this way of repaying. Only a man of Colonel Sartoris' generation and thought could have invented it, and only a woman could have believed it.

When the next generation, with its more modern ideas, became mayors and aldermen, this arrangement created some little dissatisfaction. On the first of the year they mailed her a tax notice. February came, and there was no reply. They wrote her a formal letter, asking her to call at the sheriff's office at her convenience. A week later the mayor wrote her himself, offering to call or to send his car for her, and received in reply a note on paper of an archaic shape, in a thin, flowing calligraphy in faded ink, to the effect that she no longer went out at all. The tax notice was also enclosed, without comment.

They called a special meeting of the Board of Aldermen. A

deputation waited upon her, knocked at the door through which no visitor had passed since she ceased giving china-painting lessons eight or ten years earlier. They were admitted by the old Negro into a dim hall from which a staircase mounted into still more shadow. It smelled of dust and disuse — a close, dank smell. The Negro led them into the parlor. It was furnished in heavy, leather-covered furniture. When the Negro opened the blinds of one window, a faint dust rose sluggishly about their thighs, spinning with slow notes in the single sunray. On a tarnished gilt easel before the fireplace stood a crayon portrait of Miss Emily's father.

They rose when she entered — a small, fat woman in black, with a thin gold chain descending to her waist and vanishing into her belt, leaning on an ebony cane with a tarnished gold head. Her skeleton was small and spare; perhaps that was why what would have been merely plumpness in another was obesity in her. She looked bloated, like a body long submerged in motionless water, and of that pallid hue. Her eyes, lost in the fatty ridges of her face, looked like two small pieces of coal pressed into a lump of dough as they moved from one face to another while the visitors stated their errand.

She did not ask them to sit. She just stood in the door and listened quietly until the spokesman came to a stumbling halt. Then they could hear the invisible watch ticking at the end of the gold chain.

Her voice was dry and cold. "I have no taxes in Jefferson. Colonel Sartoris explained it to me. Perhaps one of you can gain access to the city records and satisfy yourselves."

"But we have. We are the city authorities, Miss Emily. Didn't you get a notice from the sheriff, signed by him?"

"I received a paper, yes," Miss Emily said. "Perhaps he considers himself the sheriff. . . . I have no taxes in Jefferson."

"But there is nothing on the books to show that, you see. We must go by the —"

"See Colonel Sartoris. I have no taxes in Jefferson."

"But, Miss Emily —"

"See Colonel Sartoris." (Colonel Sartoris had been dead almost ten years.) "I have no taxes in Jefferson. Tobe!" The Negro appeared. "Show these gentlemen out."

II

So she vanquished them, horse and foot, just as she had vanquished their fathers thirty years before about the smell. That was two years after her father's death and a short time after her sweetheart — the one we believed would marry her — had deserted her. After her father's death she went out very little; after her sweetheart went away, people hardly saw her at all. A few of the ladies had the temerity to call, but were not received, and the only sign of life about the place was the Negro man — a young man then — going in and out with a market basket.

"Just as if a man — any man — could keep a kitchen properly," the ladies said; so they were not surprised when the smell developed. It was another link between the gross, teeming world and the high and mighty Griersons.

A neighbor, a woman, complained to the mayor, Judge Stevens, eighty years old.

"But what will you have me do about it, madam?" he said.

"Why, send her word to stop it," the woman said. "Isn't there a law?"

"I'm sure that won't be necessary," Judge Stevens said. "It's probably just a snake or a rat that nigger of hers killed in the yard. I'll speak to him about it."

The next day he received two more complaints, one from a man who came in diffident deprecation. "We really must do something about it, Judge. I'd be the last one in the world to bother Miss Emily, but we've got to do something." That night the Board of Aldermen met — three gray-beards and one younger man, a member of the rising generation.

"It's simple enough," he said. "Send her word to have her place cleaned up. Give her a certain time to do it in, and if she don't . . ."

"Dammit, sir," Judge Stevens said, "will you accuse a lady to her face of smelling bad?"

So the next night, after midnight, four men crossed Miss Emily's lawn and slunk about the house like burglars, sniffing along the base of the brickwork and at the cellar openings while one of them performed a regular sowing motion with his hand out of a sack slung from his shoulder. They broke open the cellar door and sprinkled lime there, and in all the out-buildings. As they recrossed the lawn, a window that had been dark was lighted and Miss Emily sat in it, the light behind her, and her upright torso motionless as that of an idol. They crept quietly across the lawn and into the shadow of the locusts that lined the street. After a week or two the smell went away.

That was when people had begun to feel really sorry for her. People in our town remembering how old lady Wyatt, her great-aunt, had gone completely crazy at last, believed that the Griersons held themselves a little too high for what they really were. None of the young men were quite good enough for Miss

Emily and such. We had long thought of them as a tableau; Miss Emily a slender figure in white in the background, her father a spraddled silhouette in the foreground, his back to her and clutching a horsewhip, the two of them framed by the back-flung front door. So when she got to be thirty and was still single, we were not pleased exactly, but vindicated; even with insanity in the family she wouldn't have turned down all of her chances if they had really materialized.

When her father died, it got about that the house was all that was left to her; and in a way, people were glad. At last they could pity Miss Emily. Being left alone, and a pauper, she had become humanized. Now she too would know the old thrill and the old despair of a penny more or less.

The day after his death all the ladies prepared to call at the house and offer condolence and aid, as is our custom. Miss Emily met them at the door, dressed as usual and with no trace of grief on her face. She told them that her father was not dead. She did that for three days, with the ministers calling on her, and the doctors, trying to persuade her to let them dispose of the body. Just as they were about to resort to law and force, she broke down, and they buried her father quickly.

We did not say she was crazy then. We believed she had to do that. We remembered all the young men her father had driven away, and we knew that with nothing left, she would have to cling to that which had robbed her, as people will.

III

She was sick for a long time. When we saw her again, her hair was cut short, making her look like a girl, with a vague resemblance to those angels in colored church windows — sort of tragic and serene.

The town had just let the contracts for paving the sidewalks, and in the summer after her father's death they began to work. The construction company came with niggers and mules and machinery, and a foreman named Homer Barron, a Yankee — a big, dark, ready man, with a big voice and eyes lighter than his face. The little boys would follow in groups to hear him cuss the niggers, and the niggers singing in time to the rise and fall of picks. Pretty soon he knew everybody in town. Whenever you heard a lot of laughing anywhere about the square, Homer Barron would be in the center of the group. Presently we began to see him and Miss Emily on Sunday afternoons driving in the yellow-wheeled buggy and the matched team of bays from the livery stable.

At first we were glad that Miss Emily would have an interest, because the ladies all said, "Of course a Grierson would not think seriously of a Northerner, a day laborer." But there were still others, older people, who said that even grief could not cause a real lady to forget *noblesse oblige* — without calling it *noblesse oblige.* They just said, "Poor Emily. Her kinsfolk should come to her." She had some kin in Alabama; but years ago her father had fallen out with them over the estate of old lady Wyatt, the crazy woman, and there was no communication between the two families. They had not even been represented at the funeral.

And as soon as the old people said, "Poor Emily," the whispering began. "Do you suppose it's really so?" they said to one another. "Of course it is. What else could . . ." This behind their hands; rustling of craned silk and satin behind jalousies closed upon the sun of Sunday afternoon as the thin, swift clop-clop-clop of the matched team passed: "Poor Emily."

She carried her head high enough — even when we believed that she was fallen. It was as if she demanded more than ever the recognition of her dignity as the last Grierson; as if it had wanted that touch of earthiness to reaffirm her imperviousness. Like when she bought the rat poison, the arsenic. That was over a year after they had begun to say "Poor Emily," and while the two female cousins were visiting her.

"I want some poison," she said to the druggist. She was over thirty then, still a slight woman, though thinner than usual, with cold, haughty black eyes in a face the flesh of which was strained across the temples and about the eyesockets as you imagine a lighthousekeeper's face ought to look. "I want some poison," she said.

"Yes, Miss Emily. What kind? For rats and such? I'd recom —"

"I want the best you have. I don't care what kind."

The druggist named several. "They'll kill anything up to an elephant. But what you want is —"

"Arsenic," Miss Emily said. "Is that a good one?"

"Is . . . arsenic? Yes ma'am. But what you want —"

"I want arsenic."

The druggist looked down at her. She looked back at him, erect, her face like a strained flag. "Why, of course," the druggist said. "If that's what you want. But the law requires you to tell what you are going to use it for."

Miss Emily just stared at him, her head tilted back in order to look him eye for eye, until he looked away and went and got the arsenic and wrapped it up. The Negro delivery boy brought her the package; the druggist didn't come back. When she opened the package at home there was written on the box, under the skull and bones: "For rats."

IV

So the next day we all said, "She will kill herself"; and we said it would be the best thing. When she had first begun to be seen with Homer Barron, we had said, "She will marry him." Then we said, "She will persuade him yet," because Homer himself had remarked — he liked men, and it was known that he drank with the younger men in the Elk's Club — that he was not a marrying man. Later we said, "Poor Emily," behind the jalousies as they passed on Sunday afternoon in the glittering buggy, Miss Emily with her head high and Homer Barron with his hat cocked and a cigar in his teeth, reins and whip in a yellow glove.

Then some of the ladies began to say that it was a disgrace to the town and a bad example to the young people. The men did not want to interfere, but at last the ladies forced the Baptist minister — Miss Emily's people were Episcopal — to call upon her. He would never divulge what happened during that interview, but he refused to go back again. The next Sunday they again drove about the streets, and the following day the minister's wife wrote to Miss Emily's relations in Alabama.

So she had blood-kin under her roof again and we sat back to watch developments. At first nothing happened. Then we were sure that they were to be married. We learned that Miss Emily had been to the jeweler's and ordered a man's toilet set in silver, with the letters H.B. on each piece. Two days later we learned that she had bought a complete outfit of men's clothing, including a nightshirt, and we said, "They are married." We were really glad. We were glad because the two female cousins were even more Grierson than Miss Emily had ever been.

So we were surprised when Homer Barron — the streets had been finished some time since — was gone. We were a little disappointed that there was not a public blowing-off, but we believed that he had gone on to prepare for Miss Emily's coming, or to give a chance to get rid of the cousins. (By that time it was a cabal, and we were all Miss Emily's allies to help circumvent the cousins.) Sure enough, after another week they departed. And, as we had expected all along, within three days Homer Barron was back in town. A neighbor saw the Negro man admit him at the kitchen door at dusk one evening.

And that was the last we saw of Homer Barron. And of Miss Emily for some time. The Negro man went in and out with the market basket, but the front door remained closed. Now and then we would see her at a window for a moment, as the men did that night when they sprinkled the lime, but for almost six months she did not appear on the streets. Then we knew that this was to be expected too; as if that quality of her father which had thwarted her woman's life so many times had been too virulent and too furious to die.

When we next saw Miss Emily, she had grown fat and her hair was turning gray. During the next few years it grew grayer and grayer until it attained an even pepper-and-salt iron-gray, when it ceased turning. Up to the day of her death at seventy-four it was still that vigorous iron-gray, like the hair of an active man.

From that time on her front door remained closed, save for a period of six or seven years, when she was about forty, during which she gave lessons in china-painting. She fitted up a studio in one of the downstairs rooms, where the daughters and grand-daughters of Colonel Sartoris' contemporaries were sent to her with the same regularity and in the same spirit that they were sent on Sundays with a twenty-five cent piece for the collection plate. Meanwhile her taxes had been remitted.

Then the newer generation became the backbone and the spirit of the town, and the painting pupils grew up and fell away and did not send their children to her with boxes of color and tedious brushes and pictures cut from the ladies' magazines. The front door closed upon the last one and remained closed for good. When the town got free postal delivery Miss Emily alone refused to let them fasten the metal numbers above her door and attach a mailbox to it. She would not listen to them.

Daily, monthly, yearly we watched the Negro grow grayer and more stooped, going in and out with the market basket. Each December we sent her a tax notice, which would be returned by the post office a week later, unclaimed. Now and then we would see her in one of the downstairs windows — she had evidently shut up the top floor of the house — like the carven torso of an idol in a niche, looking or not looking at us, we could never tell which. Thus she passed from generation to generation — dear, inescapable, impervious, tranquil, and perverse.

And so she died. Fell ill in the house filled with dust and shadows, with only a doddering Negro man to wait on her. We did not even know she was sick; we had long since given up trying to get any information from the Negro. He talked to no one, probably not even to her, for his voice had grown harsh and rusty, as if from disuse.

She died in one of the downstairs rooms, in a heavy walnut bed with a curtain, her gray head propped on a pillow yellow and moldy with age and lack of sunlight.

V

The Negro met the first of the ladies at the front door and let them in, with their hushed, sibilant voices and their quick, curious glances, and then he disappeared. He walked right through the house and out the back and was not seen again.

The two female cousins came at once. They held the funeral on the second day, with the town coming to look at Miss Emily beneath a mass of bought flowers, with the crayon face of her father musing profoundly above the bier and the ladies sibilant and macabre; and the very old men — some in their brushed Confederate uniforms — on the porch and the lawn, talking of Miss Emily as if she had been a contemporary of theirs, believing that they had danced with her and courted her perhaps, confusing time with its mathematical progression, as the old do, to whom all the past is not a diminishing road, but, instead, a huge meadow which no winter ever quite touches, divided from them now by the narrow bottleneck of the most recent decade of years.

Already we knew that there was one room in that region above stairs which no one had seen in forty years, and which would have to be forced. They waited until Miss Emily was decently in the ground before they opened it.

The violence of breaking down the door seemed to fill this room with pervading dust. A thin, acrid pall as of the tomb seemed to lie everywhere upon this room decked and furnished as for a bridal: upon the valance curtains of faded rose color, upon the rose-shaded lights, upon the dressing table, upon the delicate array of crystal and the man's toilet things backed with tarnished silver, silver so tarnished that the monogram was obscured. Among them lay a collar and tie, as if they had just been removed, which, lifted, left upon the surface a pale crescent in the dust. Upon a chair hung the suit, carefully folded; beneath it the two mute shoes and the discarded socks.

The man himself lay in the bed.

For a long while we just stood there, looking down at the profound and fleshless grin. The body had apparently once lain in the attitude of an embrace, but now the long sleep that outlasts love, that conquers even the grimace of love, had cuckolded him. What was left of him, rotted beneath what was left of the nightshirt, had become inextricable from the bed in which he lay; and upon him and upon the pillow beside him lay that even coating of the patient and biding dust.

Then we noticed that in the second pillow was the indentation of a head. One of us lifted something from it, and leaning forward, that faint and invisible dust dry and acrid in the nostrils, we saw a long strand of iron-gray hair.

Ernest Hemingway (*American. 1899–1961*)

Hills Like White Elephants

The hills across the valley of the Ebro were long and white. On this side there was no shade and no trees and the station was between two lines of rails in the sun. Close against the side of the station there was the warm shadow of the building and a curtain, made of strings of bamboo beads, hung across the open door into the bar, to keep out flies. The American and the girl with him sat at a table in the shade, outside the building. It was very hot and the express from Barcelona would come in forty minutes. It stopped at this junction for two minutes and went on to Madrid.

"What should we drink?" the girl asked. She had taken off her hat and put it on the table.

"It's pretty hot," the man said.

"Let's drink beer."

"Dos cervezas,"° the man said into the curtain.

"Big ones?" a woman asked from the doorway.

"Yes. Two big ones."

The woman brought two glasses of beer and two felt pads. She put the felt pads and the beer glasses on the table and looked at the man and the girl. The girl was looking off at the line of hills. They were white in the sun and the country was brown and dry.

"They look like white elephants," she said.

"I've never seen one," the man drank his beer.

"No, you wouldn't have."

Dos cervezas   two beers (Spanish). Later they pay four reales, i.e., Spanish coins.

"I might have," the man said. "Just because you say I wouldn't have doesn't prove anything."

The girl looked at the bead curtain. "They've painted something on it," she said. "What does it say?"

"Anis del Toro. It's a drink."

"Could we try it?"

The man called "Listen" through the curtain. The woman came out from the bar.

"Four reales."

"We want two Anis del Toro."

"With water?"

"Do you want it with water?"

"I don't know," the girl said. "Is it good with water?"

"It's all right."

"You want them with water?" asked the woman.

"Yes, with water."

"It tastes like licorice," the girl said and put the glass down.

"That's the way with everything."

"Yes," said the girl. "Everything tastes of licorice. Especially all the things you've waited so long for, like absinthe."

"Oh, cut it out."

"You started it," the girl said. "I was being amused. I was having a fine time."

"Well, let's try and have a fine time."

"All right. I was trying. I said the mountains looked like white elephants. Wasn't that bright?"

"That was bright."

"I wanted to try this new drink. That's all we do, isn't it — look at things and try new drinks?"

"I guess so."

The girl looked across at the hills.

"They're lovely hills," she said. "They don't really look like white elephants. I just meant the coloring of their skin through the trees."

"Should we have another drink?"

"All right."

The warm wind blew the bead curtain against the table.

"The beer's nice and cool," the man said.

"It's lovely," the girl said.

"It's really an awfully simple operation, Jig," the man said. "It's not really an operation at all."

The girl looked at the ground the table legs rested on.

"I know you wouldn't mind it, Jig. It's really not anything. It's just to let the air in."

The girl did not say anything.

"I'll go with you and I'll stay with you all the time. They just let the air in and then it's all perfectly natural."

"Then what will we do afterward?"

"We'll be fine afterward. Just like we were before."

"What makes you think so?"

"That's the only thing that bothers us. It's the only thing that's made us unhappy."

The girl looked at the bead curtain, put her hand out and took hold of two of the strings of beads.

"And you think then we'll be all right and be happy."

"I know we will. You don't have to be afraid. I've known lots of people that have done it."

"So have I," said the girl. "And afterward they were all so happy."

"Well," the man said, "if you don't want to you don't have to. I wouldn't have you do it if you didn't want to. But I know it's perfectly simple."

"And you really want to?"

"I think it's the best thing to do. But I don't want you to do it if you don't really want to."

"And if I do it you'll be happy and things will be like they were and you'll love me?"

"I love you now. You know I love you."

"I know. But if I do it, then it will be nice again if I say things are like white elephants, and you'll like it?"

"I'll love it. I love it now but I just can't think about it. You know how I get when I worry."

"If I do it you won't ever worry?"

"I won't worry about that because it's perfectly simple."

"Then I'll do it. Because I don't care about me."

"What do you mean?"

"I don't care about me."

"Well, I care about you."

"Oh, yes. But I don't care about me. And I'll do it and then everything will be fine."

"I don't want you to do it if you feel that way."

The girl stood up and walked to the end of the station. Across, on the other side, were fields of grain and trees along the banks of the Ebro. Far away, beyond the river, were mountains. The shadow of a cloud moved across the field of grain and she saw the river through the trees.

"And we could have all this," she said. "And we could have everything and every day we make it more impossible."

"What did you say?"

"I said we could have everything."

"We can have everything."

"No, we can't."

"We can have the whole world."

"No, we can't."

"We can go everywhere."

"No, we can't. It isn't ours any more."

"It's ours."

"No, it isn't. And once they take it away, you never get it back."

"But they haven't taken it away."

"We'll wait and see."

"Come on back in the shade," he said. "You mustn't feel that way."

"I don't feel any way," the girl said. "I just know things."

"I don't want you to do anything that you don't want to do —"

"Nor that isn't good for me," she said. "I know. Could we have another beer?"

"All right. But you've got to realize —"

"I realize," the girl said. "Can't we maybe stop talking?"

They sat down at the table and the girl looked across at the hills on the dry side of the valley and the man looked at her and at the table.

"You've got to realize," he said, "that I don't want you to do it if you don't want to. I'm perfectly willing to go through with it if it means anything to you."

"Doesn't it mean anything to you? We could get along."

"Of course it does. But I don't want anybody but you. I don't want any one else. And I know it's perfectly simple."

"Yes, you know it's perfectly simple."

"It's all right for you to say that, but I do know it."

"Would you do something for me now?"

"I'd do anything for you."

"Would you please please please please please please please stop talking?"

He did not say anything but looked at the bags against the wall of the station. There were labels on them from all the hotels where they had spent nights.

"But I don't want you to," he said, "I don't care anything about it."

"I'll scream," the girl said.

The woman came out through the curtains with two glasses

of beer and put them down on the damp felt pads. "The train comes in five minutes," she said.

"What did she say?" asked the girl.

"That the train is coming in five minutes."

The girl smiled brightly at the woman, to thank her.

"I'd better take the bags over to the other side of the station," the man said. She smiled at him.

"All right. Then come back and we'll finish the beer."

He picked up the two heavy bags and carried them around the station to the other tracks. He looked up the tracks but could not see the train. Coming back, he walked through the barroom, where people waiting for the train were drinking. He drank an Anis at the bar and looked at the people. The were all waiting reasonably for the train. He went out through the bead curtain. She was sitting at the table and smiled at him. "Do you feel better?" he asked.

"I feel fine," she said. "There's nothing wrong with me. I feel fine."

Frank O'Connor (Irish. 1903–1966)

Guests of the Nation

I

At dusk the big Englishman, Belcher, would shift his long legs out of the ashes and say "Well, chums, what about it?" and Noble or me would say "All right, chum" (for we had picked up some of their curious expressions), and the little Englishman, Hawkins, would light the lamp and bring out the cards. Sometimes Jeremiah Donovan would come up and supervise the game and get excited over Hawkins's cards, which he always played badly, and shout at him as if he was one of our own "Ah, you divil, you, why didn't you play the tray?"

But ordinarily Jeremiah was a sober and contented poor devil like the big Englishman, Belcher, and was looked up to only because he was a fair hand at documents, though he was slow enough even with them. He wore a small cloth hat and big gaiters over his long pants, and you seldom saw him with his hands out of his pockets. He reddened when you talked to him, tilting from toe to heel and back, and looking down all the time at his big farmer's feet. Noble and me used to make fun of his broad accent, because we were from the town.

I couldn't at the time see the point of me and Noble guarding Belcher and Hawkins at all, for it was my belief that you could have planted that pair down anywhere from ·this to Claregalway and they'd have taken root there like a native weed. I never in my short experience seen two men to take to the country as they did.

They were handed on to us by the Second Battalion when the search for them became too hot, and Noble and myself, being young, took over with a natural feeling of responsibility, but Hawkins made us look like fools when he showed that he knew the country better than we did.

"You're the bloke they calls Bonaparte," he says to me. "Mary Brigid O'Connell told me to ask you what you done with the pair of her brother's socks you borrowed."

For it seemed, as they explained it, that the Second used to have little evenings, and some of the girls of the neighborhood turned in, and, seeing they were such decent chaps, our fellows couldn't leave the two Englishmen out of them. Hawkins learned to dance "The Walls of Limerick," "The Siege of Ennis," and "The Waves of Tory" as well as any of them, though, naturally, we couldn't return the compliment, because our lads at that time did not dance foreign dances on principle.

So whatever privileges Belcher and Hawkins had with the Second they just naturally took with us, and after the first day or two we gave up all pretense of keeping a close eye on them. Not that they could have got far, for they had accents you could cut with a knife and wore khaki tunics and overcoats with civilian boots. But it's my belief that they never had any idea of escaping and were quite content to be where they were.

It was a treat to see how Belcher got off with the old woman of the house where we were staying. She was a great warrant to scold, and cranky even with us, but before ever she had a chance of giving our guests, as I may call them, a lick of her tongue, Belcher had made her his friend for life. She was breaking sticks, and Belcher, who hadn't been more than ten minutes in the house, jumped up from his seat and went over to her.

"Allow me, madam," he says, smiling his queer little smile, "please allow me"; and he takes the bloody hatchet. She was struck too paralytic to speak, and after that, Belcher would be at her heels, carrying a bucket, a basket, or a load of turf as the case might be. As Noble said, he got into looking before she leapt,

and hot water, or any little thing she wanted, Belcher would have
it ready for her. For such a huge man (and though I am five foot
ten myself I had to look up at him) he had an uncommon shortness
— or should I say lack? — of speech. It took us some time to get
used to him, walking in and out, like a ghost, without a word.
Especially because Hawkins talked enough for a platoon, it was
strange to hear big Belcher with his toes in the ashes come out
with a solitary "Excuse me, chum," or "That's right, chum." His
one and only passion was cards, and I will say for him that he
was a good cardplayer. He could have fleeced myself and Noble,
but whatever we lost to him Hawkins lost to us, and Hawkins
played with the money Belcher gave him.

Hawkins lost to us because he had too much old gab, and
we probably lost to Belcher for the same reason. Hawkins and
Noble would spit at one another about religion into the early
hours of the morning, and Hawkins worried the soul out of Noble,
whose brother was a priest, with a string of questions that would
puzzle a cardinal. To make it worse, even in treating of holy
subjects, Hawkins had a deplorable tongue. I never in all my career
met a man who could mix such a variety of cursing and bad
language into an argument. He was a terrible man, and a fright
to argue. He never did a stroke of work, and when he had no
one else to talk to, he got stuck in the old woman.

He met his match in her, for one day when he tried to get
her to complain profanely of the drought, she gave him a great
come-down by blaming it entirely on Jupiter Pluvius (a deity
neither Hawkins nor I had ever heard of, though Noble said that
among the pagans it was believed that he had something to do
with the rain). Another day he was swearing at the capitalists for
starting the German war when the old lady laid down her iron,
puckered up her little crab's mouth, and said: "Mr. Hawkins, you
can say what you like about the war, and think you'll deceive me
because I'm only a simple poor countrywoman, but I know what
started the war. It was the Italian Count that stole the heathen
divinity out of the temple in Japan. Believe me, Mr. Hawkins,
nothing but sorrow and want can follow the people that disturb
the hidden powers."

A queer old girl, all right.

II

We had our tea one evening, and Hawkins lit the lamp and
we all sat into cards. Jeremiah Donovan came in too, and sat down
and watched us for a while, and it suddenly struck me that he

had no great love for the two Englishmen. It came as a great surprise to me, because I hadn't noticed anything about him before.

Late in the evening a really terrible argument blew up between Hawkins and Noble, about capitalists and priests and love of your country.

"The capitalists," says Hawkins with an angry gulp, "pays the priests to tell you about the next world so as you won't notice what the bastards are up to in this."

"Nonsense, man!" says Noble, losing his temper. "Before ever a capitalist was thought of, people believed in the next world."

Hawkins stood up as though he was preaching a sermon. "Oh, they did, did they?" he says with a sneer. "They believed all the things you believe, isn't that what you mean? And you believe that God created Adam, and Adam created Shem, and Shem created Jehoshaphat. You believe all that silly old fairytale about Eve and Eden and the apple. Well, listen to me, chum. If you're entitled to hold a silly belief like that, I'm entitled to hold my silly belief — which is that the first thing your God created was a bleeding capitalist, with morality and Rolls-Royce complete. Am I right, chum?" he says to Belcher.

"You're right, chum," says Belcher with his amused smile, and got up from the table to stretch his long legs into the fire and stroke his moustache. So, seeing that Jeremiah Donovan was going, and that there was no knowing when the argument about religion would be over, I went out with him. We strolled down to the village together, and then he stopped and started blushing and mumbling and saying I ought to be behind, keeping guard on the prisoners. I didn't like the tone he took with me, and anyway I was bored with life in the cottage, so I replied by asking him what the hell we wanted guarding them at all for. I told him I'd talked it over with Noble, and that we'd both rather be out with a fighting column.

"What use are those fellows to us?" says I.

He looked at me in surprise and said: "I thought you knew we were keeping them as hostages."

"Hostages?" I said.

"The enemy have prisoners belonging to us," he says, "and now they're talking of shooting them. If they shoot our prisoners, we'll shoot theirs."

"Shoot them?" I said.

"What else did you think we were keeping them for?" he says.

"Wasn't it very unforeseen of you not to warn Noble and myself of that in the beginning?" I said.

"How was it?" says he. "You might have known it."

"We couldn't know it, Jeremiah Donovan," says I. "How could we when they were on our hands so long?"

"The enemy have our prisoners as long and longer," says he.

"That's not the same thing at all," says I.

"What difference is there?" says he.

I couldn't tell him, because I knew he wouldn't understand. If it was only an old dog that was going to the vet's, you'd try and not get too fond of him, but Jeremiah Donovan wasn't a man that would ever be in danger of that.

"And when is this thing going to be decided?" says I.

"We might hear tonight," he says. "Or tomorrow or the next day at latest. So if it's only hanging round here that's a trouble to you, you'll be free soon enough."

It wasn't the hanging round that was a trouble to me at all by this time. I had worse things to worry about. When I got back to the cottage the argument was still on. Hawkins was holding forth in his best style, maintaining that there was no next world, and Noble was maintaining that there was; but I could see that Hawkins had had the best of it.

"Do you know what, chum?" he was saying with a saucy smile. "I think you're just as big a bleeding unbeliever as I am. You say you believe in the next world, and you know just as much about the next world as I do, which is sweet damn-all. What's heaven? You don't know. Where's heaven? You don't know. You know sweet damn-all! I ask you again, do they wear wings?"

"Very well, then," says Noble, "they do. Is that enough for you? They do wear wings."

"Where do they get them, then? Who makes them? Have they a factory for wings? Have they a sort of store where you hands in your chit and takes your bleeding wings?"

"You're an impossible man to argue with," says Noble. "Now, listen to me —" And they were off again.

It was long after midnight when we locked up and went to bed. As I blew out the candle I told Noble what Jeremiah Donovan was after telling me. Noble took it very quietly. When we'd been in bed about an hour he asked me did I think we ought to tell the Englishmen. I didn't think we should, because it was more than likely that the English wouldn't shoot our men, and even if they did, the brigade officers, who were always up and down with the Second Battalion and knew the Englishmen well, wouldn't be likely to want them plugged. "I think so too," says Noble. "It would be great cruelty to put the wind up them now."

"It was very unforeseen of Jeremiah Donovan anyhow," says I.

It was next morning that we found it so hard to face Belcher and Hawkins. We went about the house all day scarcely saying a word. Belcher didn't seem to notice; he was stretched into the ashes as usual, with his usual look of waiting in quietness for something unforeseen to happen, but Hawkins noticed and put it down to Noble's being beaten in the argument of the night before.

"Why can't you take a discussion in the proper spirit?" he says severely. "You and your Adam and Eve! I'm a Communist, that's what I am. Communist or anarchist, it all comes to much the same thing." And for hours he went round the house, muttering when the fit took him. "Adam and Eve! Adam and Eve! Nothing better to do with their time than picking bleeding apples!"

III

I don't know how we got through that day, but I was very glad when it was over, the tea things were cleared away, and Belcher said in his peaceable way: "Well, chums, what about it?" We sat round the table and Hawkins took out the cards, and just then I heard Jeremiah Donovan's footstep on the path and a dark presentiment crossed my mind. I rose from the table and caught him before he reached the door.

"What do you want?" I asked.

"I want those two soldier friends of yours," he says, getting red.

"Is that the way, Jeremiah Donovan?" I asked.

"That's the way. There were four of our lads shot this morning, one of them a boy of sixteen."

"That's bad," I said.

At that moment Noble followed me out, and the three of us walked down the path together, talking in whispers. Feeney, the local intelligence officer, was standing by the gate.

"What are you going to do about it?" I asked Jeremiah Donovan.

"I want you and Noble to get them out; tell them they're being shifted again; that'll be the quietest way."

"Leave me out of that," says Noble under his breath.

Jeremiah Donovan looks at him hard.

"All right," he says. "You and Feeney get a few tools from the shed and dig a hole by the far end of the bog. Bonaparte and

myself will be after you. Don't let anyone see you with the tools.
I wouldn't like it to go beyond ourselves."

We saw Feeney and Noble go round to the shed and went
in ourselves. I left Jeremiah Donovan to do the explanations. He
told them that he had orders to send them back to the Second
Battalion. Hawkins let out a mouthful of curses, and you could
see that though Belcher didn't say anything, he was a bit upset
too. The old woman was for having them stay in spite of us, and
she didn't stop advising them until Jeremiah Donovan lost his
temper and turned on her. He had a nasty temper, I noticed. It
was pitch-dark in the cottage by this time, but no one thought
of lighting the lamp, and in the darkness the two Englishmen
fetched their topcoats and said good-bye to the old woman.

"Just as a man makes a home of a bleeding place, some
bastard at headquarters thinks you're too cushy and shunts you
off," says Hawkins, shaking her hand.

"A thousand thanks, madam," says Belcher. "A thousand
thanks for everything" — as though he'd made it up.

We went round to the back of the house and down towards
the bog, it was only then that Jeremiah Donovan told them. He
was shaking with excitement.

"There were four of our fellows shot in Cork this morning
and now you're to be shot as a reprisal."

"What are you talking about?" snaps Hawkins. "It's bad
enough being mucked about as we are without having to put up
with your funny jokes."

"It isn't a joke," says Donovan. "I'm sorry, Hawkins, but
it's true," and begins on the usual rigmarole about duty and how
unpleasant it is.

I never noticed that people who talk a lot about duty find
it much of a trouble to them.

"Oh, cut it out!" says Hawkins.

"Ask Bonaparte," says Donovan, seeing that Hawkins isn't
taking him seriously. "Isn't it true, Bonaparte?"

"It is," I say, and Hawkins stops.

"Ah, for Christ's sake, chum."

"I mean it, chum," I say.

"You don't sound as if you meant it."

"If he doesn't mean it, I do," says Donovan, working himself
up.

"What have you against me, Jeremiah Donovan?"

"I never said I had anything against you. But why did your
people take out four of our prisoners and shoot them in cold
blood?"

He took Hawkins by the arm and dragged him on, but it was impossible to make him understand that we were in earnest. I had the Smith and Wesson in my pocket and I kept fingering it and wondering what I'd do if they put up a fight for it or ran, and wishing to God they'd do one or the other. I knew if they did run for it, that I'd never fire on them. Hawkins wanted to know was Noble in it, and when we said yes, he asked us why Noble wanted to plug him. Why did any of us want to plug him? What had he done to us? Weren't we all chums? Didn't we understand him and didn't he understand us? Did we imagine for an instant that he'd shoot us for all the so-and-so officers in the so-and-so British Army?

By this time we'd reached the bog, and I was so sick I couldn't even answer him. We walked along the edge of it in the darkness, and every now and then Hawkins would call a halt and begin all over again, as if he was wound up, about our being chums, and I knew that nothing but the sight of the grave would convince him that we had to do it. And all the time I was hoping that something would happen; that they'd run for it or that Noble would take over the responsibility from me. I had the feeling that it was worse on Noble than on me.

IV

At last we saw the lantern in the distance and made towards it. Noble was carrying it, and Feeney was standing somewhere in the darkness behind him, and the picture of them so still and silent in the bogland brought it home to me that we were in earnest, and banished the last bit of hope I had.

Belcher, on recognizing Noble, said: "Hallo, chum," in his quiet way, but Hawkins flew at him at once, and the argument began all over again, only this time Noble had nothing to say for himself and stood with his head down, holding the lantern between his legs.

It was Jeremiah Donovan who did the answering. For the twentieth time, as though it was haunting his mind, Hawkins asked if anybody thought he'd shoot Noble.

"Yes, you would," says Jeremiah Donovan.

"No, I wouldn't, damn you!"

"You would, because you'd know you'd be shot for not doing it."

"I wouldn't, not if I was to be shot twenty times over. I wouldn't shoot a pal. And Belcher wouldn't — isn't that right, Belcher?"

"That's right, chum," Belcher said, but more by way of

answering the question than of joining in the argument. Belcher
sounded as though whatever unforeseen thing he'd always been
waiting for had come at last.

"Anyway, who says Noble would be shot if I wasn't? What
do you think I'd do if I was in his place, out in the middle of a
blasted bog?"

"What would you do?" asks Donovan.

"I'd go with him wherever he was going, of course. Share
my last bob with him and stick by him through thick and thin.
No one can ever say of me that I let down a pal."

"We had enough of this," says Jeremiah Donovan, cocking
his revolver. "Is there any message you want to send?"

"No, there isn't."

"Do you want to say your prayers?"

Hawkins came out with a cold-blooded remark that even
shocked me and turned on Noble again.

"Listen to me, Noble," he says. "You and me are chums.
You can't come over to my side, so I'll come over to your side.
That show you I mean what I say? Give me a rifle and I'll go
along with you and the other lads."

Nobody answered him. We knew that was no way out.

"Hear what I'm saying?" he says. "I'm through with it. I'm
a deserter or anything else you like. I don't believe in your stuff,
but it's no worse than mine. That satisfy you?"

Noble raised his head, but Donovan began to speak and he
lowered it again without replying.

"For the last time, have you any messages to send?" says
Donovan in a cold, excited sort of voice.

"Shut up, Donovan! You don't understand me, but these
lads do. They're not the sort to make a pal and kill a pal. They're
not the tools of any capitalist."

I alone of the crowd saw Donovan raise his Webley to the
back of Hawkins's neck, and as he did so I shut my eyes and tried
to pray. Hawkins had begun to say something else when Donovan
fired, and as I opened my eyes at the bang, I saw Hawkins stagger
at the knees and lie out flat at Noble's feet, slowly and as quiet
as a kid falling asleep, with the lantern-light on his lean legs and
bright farmer's boots. We all stood very still, watching him settle
out in the last agony.

Then Belcher took out a handkerchief and began to tie it
about his own eyes (in our excitement we'd forgotten to do the
same for Hawkins), and, seeing it wasn't big enough, turned and
asked for the loan of mine. I gave it to him and he knotted the
two together and pointed with his foot at Hawkins.

"He's not quite dead," he says. "Better give him another."
Sure enough, Hawkins's left knee is beginning to rise. I bend
down and put my gun to his head; then, recollecting myself, I
get up again. Belcher understands what's in my mind.
"Give him his first," he says. "I don't mind. Poor bastard,
we don't know what's happening to him now."
I knelt and fired. By this time I didn't seem to know what
I was doing. Belcher, who was fumbling a bit awkwardly with
the handkerchiefs, came out with a laugh as he heard the shot. It
was the first time I heard him laugh and it sent a shudder down
my back; it sounded so unnatural.
"Poor bugger!" he said quietly. "And last night he was so
curious about it all. It's very queer, chums, I always think. Now
he knows as much about it as they'll ever let him know, and last
night he was all in the dark."
Donovan helped him to tie the handkerchiefs about his eyes.
"Thanks, chum," he said. Donovan asked if there were any messages
he wanted sent.
"No, chum," he says. "Not for me. If any of you would
like to write to Hawkins's mother, you'll find a letter from her
in his pocket. He and his mother were great chums. But my missus
left me eight years ago. Went away with another fellow and took
the kid with her. I like the feeling of a home, as you may have
noticed, but I couldn't start again after that."
It was an extraordinary thing, but in those few minutes
Belcher said more than in all the weeks before. It was just as if
the sound of the shot had started a flood of talk in him and he
could go on the whole night like that, quite happily, talking about
himself. We stood round like fools now that he couldn't see us
any longer. Donovan looked at Noble, and Noble shook his head.
Then Donovan raised his Webley, and at that moment Belcher
gives his queer laugh again. He may have thought we were talking
about him, or perhaps he noticed the same thing I'd noticed and
couldn't understand it.
"Excuse me, chums," he says. "I feel I'm talking the hell
of a lot, and so silly, about my being so handy about a house and
things like that. But this thing came on me suddenly. You'll
forgive me, I'm sure."
"You don't want to say a prayer?" asked Donovan.
"No, chum," he says. "I don't think it would help. I'm
ready, and you boys want to get it over."
"You understand that we're only doing our duty?" says
Donovan.
Belcher's head was raised like a blind man's, so that you

could only see his chin and the tip of his nose in the lantern-light.
"I never could make out what duty was myself," he said.
"I think you're all good lads, if that's what you mean. I'm not
complaining."

Noble, just as if he couldn't bear any more of it, raised his
fist at Donovan, and in a flash Donovan raised his gun and fired.
The big man went over like a sack of meal, and this time there
was no need of a second shot.

I don't remember much about the burying, but that it was
worse than all the rest because we had to carry them to the grave.
It was all mad lonely with nothing but a patch of lantern-light
between ourselves and the dark, and birds hooting and screeching
all round, disturbed by the guns. Noble went through Hawkins's
belongings to find the letter from his mother, and then joined his
hands together. He did the same with Belcher. Then, when we'd
filled in the grave, we separated from Jeremiah Donovan and
Feeney and took our tools back to the shed. All the way we didn't
speak a word. The kitchen was dark and cold as we'd left it, and
the old woman was sitting over the hearth, saying her beads. We
walked past her into the room, and Noble struck a match to light
the lamp. She rose quietly and came to the doorway with all her
cantankerousness gone.

"What did ye do with them?" she asked in a whisper, and
Noble started so that the match went out in his hand.

"What's that?" he asked without turning round.

"I heard ye," she said.

"What did you hear?" asked Noble.

"I heard ye. Do ye think I didn't hear ye, putting the spade
back in the houseen?"

Noble struck another match and this time the lamp lit for
him.

"Was that what ye did to them?" she asked.

Then, by God, in the very doorway, she fell on her knees
and began praying, and after looking at her for a minute or two
Noble did the same by the fireplace. I pushed my way out past
her and left them at it. I stood at the door, watching the stars and
listening to the shrieking of the birds dying out over the bogs. It
is so strange what you feel at times like that you can't describe
it. Noble says he saw everything ten times the size, as though
there were nothing in the whole world but that little patch of bog
with the two Englishmen stiffening into it, but with me it was
as if the patch of bog where the Englishmen were was a million

miles away, and even Noble and the old woman, mumbling behind me, and the birds and the bloody stars were all far away, and I was somehow very small and very lost and lonely like a child astray in the snow. And anything that happened to me afterwards, I never felt the same about again.

Eudora Welty (*American. b. 1909*)

A Worn Path

It was December — a bright frozen day in the early morning. Far out in the country there was an old Negro woman with her head tied in a red rag, coming along a path through the pinewoods. Her name was Phoenix Jackson. She was very old and small and she walked slowly in the dark pine shadows, moving a little from side to side in her steps, with the balanced heaviness and lightness of a pendulum in a grandfather clock. She carried a thin, small cane made from an umbrella, and with this she kept tapping the frozen earth in front of her. This made a grave and persistent noise in the still air, that seemed meditative like the chirping of a solitary little bird.

She wore a dark striped dress reaching down to her shoe tops, and an equally long apron of bleached sugar sacks, with a full pocket: all neat and tidy, but every time she took a step she might have fallen over her shoe-laces, which dragged from her unlaced shoes. She looked straight ahead. Her eyes were blue with age. Her skin had a pattern all its own of numberless branching wrinkles and as though a whole little tree stood in the middle of her forehead, but a golden color ran underneath, and the two knobs of her cheeks were illuminated by a yellow burning under the dark. Under the red rag her hair came down on her neck in the frailest of ringlets, still black, and with an odor like copper.

Now and then there was a quivering in the thicket. Old Phoenix said, "Out of my way, all you foxes, owls, beetles, jack rabbits, coons, and wild animals! . . . Keep out from under these feet, little bob-whites. . . . Keep the big wild hogs out of my path. Don't let none of those come running my direction. I got a long way." Under her small black-freckled hand her cane, limber as a buggy whip, would switch at the brush as if to rouse up any hiding things.

On she went. The woods were deep and still. The sun made the pine needles almost too bright to look at, up where the wind rocked. The cones dropped as light as feathers. Down in the hollow was the mourning dove — it was not too late for him.

The path ran up a hill. "Seem like there is chains about my feet, time I get this far," she said, in the voice of argument old people keep to use with themselves. "Something always take a hold of me on this hill — pleads I should stay."

After she got to the top she turned and gave a full, severe look behind her where she had come. "Up through pines," she said at length. "Now down through oaks."

Her eyes opened their widest, and she started down gently. But before she got to the bottom of the hill a bush caught her dress.

Her fingers were busy and intent, but her skirts were full and long, so that before she could pull them free in one place they were caught in another. It was not possible to allow the dress to tear. "I in the thorny bush," she said. "Thorns, you doing your appointed work. Never want to let folks pass — no sir. Old eyes thought you was a pretty little *green* bush."

Finally, trembling all over, she stood free, and after a moment dared to stoop for her cane.

"Sun so high!" she cried, leaning back and looking, while the thick tears went over her eyes. "The time getting all gone here."

At the foot of this hill was a place where a log was laid across the creek.

"Now comes the trial," said Phoenix.

Putting her right foot out, she mounted the log and shut her eyes. Lifting her skirt, levelling her cane fiercely before her, like a festival figure in some parade, she began to march across. Then she opened her eyes and she was safe on the other side.

"I wasn't as old as I thought," she said.

But she sat down to rest. She spread her skirts on the bank around her and folded her hands over her knees. Up above her was a tree in a pearly cloud of mistletoe. She did not dare to close her eyes, and when a little boy brought her a little plate with a slice of marble-cake on it she spoke to him. "That would be acceptable," she said. But when she went to take it there was just her own hand in the air.

So she left that tree, and had to go through a barbed-wire fence. There she had to creep and crawl, spreading her knees and stretching her fingers like a baby trying to climb the steps. But she talked loudly to herself: she could not let her dress be torn now, so late in the day, and she could not pay for having her arm or her leg sawed off if she got caught fast where she was.

At last she was safe through the fence and risen up out in the clearing. Big dead trees, like black men with one arm, were standing in the purple stalks of the withered cotton field. There sat a buzzard.

"Who you watching?"

In the furrow she made her way along.

"Glad this not the season for bulls," she said, looking sideways, "and the good Lord made his snakes to curl up and sleep in the winter. A pleasure I don't see no two-headed snake coming around that tree, where it come once. It took a while to get by him, back in the summer."

She passed through the old cotton and went into a field of dead corn. It whispered and shook and was taller than her head. "Through the maze now," she said, for there was no path.

Then there was something tall, black, and skinny there, moving before her.

At first she took it for a man. It could have been a man dancing in the field. But she stood still and listened, and it did not make a sound. It was as silent as a ghost.

"Ghost," she said sharply, "who be you the ghost of? For I have heard of nary death close by."

But there was no answer — only the ragged dancing in the wind.

She shut her eyes, reached out her hand, and touched a sleeve. She found a coat and inside that an emptiness, cold as ice.

"You scarecrow," she said. Her face lighted. "I ought to be shut up for good," she said with laughter. "My senses is gone, I too old. I the oldest people I ever know. Dance, old scarecrow," she said, "while I dancing with you." She kicked her foot over the furrow, and with mouth drawn down, shook her head once or twice in a little strutting way. Some husks blew down and whirled in streamers about her skirts.

Then she went on, parting her way from side to side with the cane, through the whispering field. At last she came to the end, to a wagon track where the silver grass blew between the red ruts. The quail were walking around like pullets, seeming all dainty and unseen.

"Walk pretty," she said. "This the easy place. This the easy going."

She followed the track, swaying through the quiet bare fields, through the little strings of trees silver in their dead leaves, past cabins silver from weather, with the doors and windows boarded shut, all like old women under a spell sitting there. "I walking in their sleep," she said, nodding her head vigorously.

In a ravine she went where a spring was silently flowing through a hollow log. Old Phoenix bent and drank. "Sweet-gum makes the water sweet," she said, and drank more. "Nobody know who made this well, for it was here when I was born."

The track crossed a swampy part where the moss hung as white as lace from every limb. "Sleep on, alligators, and blow your bubbles." Then the track went into the road.

Deep, deep the road went down between the high green-colored banks. Overhead the live-oaks met, and it was as dark as a cave.

A black dog with a lolling tongue came up out of the weeds by the ditch. She was meditating, and not ready, and when he came at her she only hit him a little with her cane. Over she went in the ditch, like a little puff of milk-weed.

Down there, her senses drifted away. A dream visited her, and she reached her hand up, but nothing reached down and gave her a pull. So she lay there and presently went to talking. "Old woman," she said to herself, "that black dog come up out of the weeds to stall you off, and now there he sitting on his fine tail, smiling at you."

A white man finally came along and found her — a hunter, a young man, with his dog on a chain.

"Well, Granny!" he laughed, "what are you doing there?"

"Lying on my back like a June-bug waiting to be turned over, mister," she said, reaching up her hand.

He lifted her up, gave her a swing in the air, and set her down. "Anything broken, Granny?"

"No sir, them old dead weeds is springy enough," said Phoenix, when she had got her breath. "I thank you for your trouble."

"Where do you live, Granny?" he asked, while the two dogs were growling at each other.

"Away back yonder, sir, behind the ridge. You can't even see it from here."

"On your way home?"

"No, sir, I going to town."

"Why, that's too far! That's as far as I walk when I come out myself, and I get something for my trouble." He patted the stuffed bag he carried, and there hung down a little closed claw. It was one of the bob-whites, with its beak hooked bitterly to show it was dead. "Now you go on home, Granny!"

"I bound to go to town, mister," said Phoenix. "The time come around."

He gave another laugh, filling the whole landscape. "I know you old colored people! Wouldn't miss going to town to see Santa Claus!"

But something held Old Phoenix very still. The deep lines in her face went into a fierce and different radiation. Without warning, she had seen with her own eyes a flashing nickel fall out of the man's pocket onto the ground.

"How old are you, Granny?" he was saying.

"There is no telling, mister," she said, "no telling."

Then she gave a little cry and clapped her hands and said, "Git on away from here, dog! Look! Look at that dog!" She laughed as if in admiration. "He ain't scared of nobody. He a big black dog." She whispered, "Sic him!"

"Watch me get rid of that cur," said the man. "Sic him, Pete! Sic him!"

Phoenix heard the dogs fighting, and heard the man running and throwing sticks. She even heard a gunshot. But she was slowly bending forward by that time, further and further forward, the lids stretched down over her eyes, as if she were doing this in her sleep. Her chin was lowered almost to her knees. The yellow palm of her hand came out from the fold of her apron. Her fingers slid down and along the ground under the piece of money with the grace and care they would have in lifting an egg from under a sitting hen. Then she slowly straightened up, she stood erect, and the nickel was in her apron pocket. A bird flew by. Her lips moved. "God watching me the whole time. I come to stealing."

The man came back, and his own dog panted about them. "Well, I scared him off that time," he said, and then he laughed and lifted his gun and pointed it at Phoenix.

She stood straight and faced him.

"Doesn't the gun scare you?" he said, still pointing it.

"No, sir, I seen plenty go off closer by, in my day, and for less than what I done," she said, holding utterly still.

He smiled, and shouldered the gun. "Well, Granny," he said, "You must be a hundred years old, and scared of nothing. I'd give you a dime if I had any money with me. But you take my advice and stay home, and nothing will happen to you."

"I bound to go on my way, mister," said Phoenix. She inclined her head in the red rag. Then they went in different directions, but she could hear the gun shooting again and again over the hill.

She walked on. The shadows hung from the oak trees to the road like curtains. Then she smelled wood-smoke, and smelled the river, and she saw a steeple and the cabins on their steep steps. Dozens of little black children whirled around her. There ahead was Natchez shining. Bells were ringing. She walked on.

In the paved city it was Christmas time. There were red and green electric lights strung and crisscrossed everywhere, and all turned on in the daytime. Old Phoenix would have been lost if she had not distrusted her eyesight and depended on her feet to know where to take her.

She paused quietly on the sidewalk where people were passing by. A lady came along in the crowd, carrying an armful of red-, green-, and silver-wrapped presents; she gave off perfume like the red roses in hot summer, and Phoenix stopped her.

"Please, missy, will you lace up my shoe?" She held up her foot.

"What do you want, Grandma?"

"See my shoe," said Phoenix. "Do all right for out in the country, but wouldn't look right to go in a big building."

"Stand still then, Grandma," said the lady. She put her packages down on the sidewalk beside her and laced and tied both shoes tightly.

"Can't lace 'em with a cane," said Phoenix. "Thank you, missy. I doesn't mind asking a nice lady to tie up my shoe, when I gets out on the street."

Moving slowly and from side to side, she went into the big building and into a tower of steps, where she walked up and around and around until her feet knew to stop.

She entered a door, and there she saw nailed up on the wall the document that had been stamped with the gold seal and framed in the gold frame, which matched the dream that was hung up in her head.

"Here I be," she said. There was a fixed and ceremonial stiffness over her body.

"A charity case, I suppose," said an attendant who sat at the desk before her.

But Phoenix only looked above her head. There was sweat on her face, the wrinkles in her skin shone like a bright net.

"Speak up, Grandma," the woman said. "What's your name? We must have your history, you know. Have you been here before? What seems to be the trouble with you?"

Old Phoenix only gave a twitch to her face as if a fly were bothering her.

"Are you deaf?" cried the attendant.

But then the nurse came in.

"Oh, that's just old Aunt Phoenix," she said. "She doesn't

come for herself — she has a little grandson. She makes these trips just as regular as clockwork. She lives away back off the old Natchez Trace." She bent down. "Well, Aunt Phoenix, why don't you just take a seat? We won't keep you standing after your long trip." She pointed.

The old woman sat down, bolt upright in the chair.

"Now, how is the boy?" asked the nurse.

Old Phoenix did not speak.

"I said, how is the boy?"

But Phoenix only waited and stared straight ahead, her face very solemn and withdrawn into rigidity.

"Is his throat any better?" asked the nurse. "Aunt Phoenix, don't you hear me? Is your grandson's throat any better since the last time you came for the medicine?"

With her hands on her knees, the old woman waited, silent, erect and motionless, just as if she were in armor.

"You mustn't take up our time this way, Aunt Phoenix," the nurse said. "Tell us quickly about your grandson, and get it over. He isn't dead, is he?"

At last there came a flicker and then a flame of comprehension across her face, and she spoke.

"My grandson. It was my memory had left me. There I sat and forgot why I made my long trip."

"Forgot?" The nurse frowned. "After you came so far?"

Then Phoenix was like an old woman begging a dignified forgiveness for waking up frightened in the night. "I never did go to school, I was too old at the Surrender," she said in a soft voice. "I'm an old woman without an education. It was my memory fail me. My little grandson, he is just the same, and I forgot it in the coming."

"Throat never heals, does it?" said the nurse, speaking in a loud, sure voice to Old Phoenix. By now she had a card with something written on it, a little list. "Yes. Swallowed lye. When was it — January — two-three years ago —"

Phoenix spoke unasked now. "No, missy, he not dead, he just the same. Every little while his throat begin to close up again, and he not able to swallow. He not get his breath. He not able to help himself. So the time come around, and I go on another trip for the soothing medicine."

"All right. The doctor said as long as you came to get it, you could have it," said the nurse. "But it's an obstinate case."

"My little grandson, he sit up there in the house all wrapped up, waiting by himself," Phoenix went on. "We is the only two left in the world. He suffer and it don't seem to put him back at all. He got a sweet look. He going to last. He wear a little patch quilt and peep out holding his mouth open like a little bird. I remembers so plain now. I not going to forget him again, no, the whole enduring time. I could tell him from all the others in creation."

"All right." The nurse was trying to hush her now. She brought her a bottle of medicine. "Charity," she said, making a check mark in a book.

Old Phoenix held the bottle close to her eyes and then carefully put it into her pocket.

"I thank you," she said.

"It's Christmas time, Grandma," said the attendant. "Could I give you a few pennies out of my purse?"

"Five pennies is a nickel," said Phoenix stiffly.

"Here's a nickel," said the attendant.

Phoenix rose carefully and held out her hand. She received the nickel and then fished the other nickel out of her pocket and laid it beside the new one. She stared at her palm closely, with her head on one side.

Then she gave a tap with her cane on the floor.

"This is what come to me to do," she said. "I going to the store and buy my child a little windmill they sells, made out of paper. He going to find it hard to believe there such a thing in the world. I'll march myself back where he waiting, holding it straight up in this hand."

She lifted her free hand, gave a little nod, turned round, and walked out of the doctor's office. Then her slow step began on the stairs, going down.

Shirley Jackson (*American. 1919–1965*)

The Lottery

The morning of June 27th was clear and sunny, with the fresh warmth of a full-summer day; the flowers were blossoming profusely and the grass was richly green. The people of the village began to gather in the square, between the post office and the bank, around ten o'clock; in some towns there were so many people that the lottery took two days and had to be started on June 26th, but in this village, where there were only about three hundred people, the whole lottery took less than two hours, so it could begin at ten o'clock in the morning and still be through in time to allow the villagers to get home for noon dinner.

The children assembled first, of course. School was recently over for the summer, and the feeling of liberty sat uneasily on most of them; they tended to gather together quietly for a while before they broke into boisterous play, and their talk was still of the classroom and the teacher, of books and reprimands. Bobby Martin had already stuffed his pockets full of stones, and the other boys soon followed his example, selecting the smoothest and roundest stones; Bobby and Harry Jones and Dickie Delacroix — the villagers pronounced this name "Dellacroy" — eventually made a great pile of stones in one corner of the square and guarded it against the raids of the other boys. The girls stood aside, talking among themselves, looking over their shoulders at the boys, and the very small children rolled in the dust or clung to the hands of their older brothers or sisters.

Soon the men began to gather, surveying their own children, speaking of planting and rain, tractors and taxes. They stood together, away from the pile of stones in the corner, and their jokes were quiet and they smiled rather than laughed. The women, wearing faded house dresses and sweaters, came shortly after their menfolk. They greeted one another and exchanged bits of gossip as they went to join their husbands. Soon the women, standing by their husbands, began to call to their children, and the children came reluctantly, having to be called four or five times. Bobby Martin ducked under his mother's grasping hand and ran, laughing, back to the pile of stones. His father spoke up sharply, and Bobby came quickly and took his place between his father and his oldest brother.

The lottery was conducted — as were the square dances, the teenage club, the Halloween program — by Mr. Summers, who had time and energy to devote to civic activities. He was a round-faced, jovial man and he ran the coal business, and people were sorry for him, because he had no children and his wife was a scold. When he arrived in the square, carrying the black wooden box, there was a murmur of conversation among the villagers and he waved and called, "Little late today, folks." The postmaster, Mr. Graves, followed him, carrying a three-legged stool, and the stool was put in the center of the square and Mr. Summers set the black box down on it. The villagers kept their distance, leaving a space between themselves and the stool, and when Mr. Summers said, "Some of you fellows want to give me a hand?" there was a hesitation before two men, Mr. Martin and his oldest son, Baxter, came forward to hold the box steady on the stool while Mr. Summers stirred up the papers inside it.

The original paraphernalia for the lottery had been lost long ago, and the black box now resting on the stool had been put into use even before Old Man Warner, the oldest man in town, was born. Mr. Summers spoke frequently to the villagers about making a new box, but no one liked to upset even as much tradition as was represented by the black box. There was a story that the present box had been made with some pieces of the box that had preceded it, the one that had been constructed when the first people settled down to make a village here. Every year, after the lottery, Mr. Summers began talking again about a new box, but every year the subject was allowed to fade off without anything's being done. The black box grew shabbier each year; by now it was no longer completely black but splintered badly along one side to show the original wood color, and in some places faded or stained.

Mr. Martin and his oldest son, Baxter, held the black box securely on the stool until Mr. Summers had stirred the papers thoroughly with his hand. Because so much of the ritual had been forgotten or discarded, Mr. Summers had been successful in having slips of paper substituted for the chips of wood that had been used for generations. Chips of wood, Mr. Summers had argued, had been all very well when the village was tiny, but now that the population was more than three hundred and likely to keep on growing, it was necessary to use something that would fit more easily into the black box. The night before the lottery, Mr. Summers and Mr. Graves made up the slips of paper and put them in the box, and it was then taken to the safe of Mr. Summers's coal company and locked up until Mr. Summers was ready to take it to the square next morning. The rest of the year, the box was put away, sometimes one place, sometimes another; it had spent one year in Mr. Graves's barn and another year underfoot in the post office, and sometimes it was set on a shelf in the Martin grocery and left there.

There was a great deal of fussing to be done before Mr. Summers declared the lottery open. There were lists to make up — of heads of families, heads of households in each family, members of each household in each family. There was the proper swearing-in of Mr. Summers by the postmaster, as the official of the lottery; at one time, some people remembered, there had been a recital of some sort, performed by the official of the lottery, a perfunctory, tuneless chant that had been rattled off duly each year; some people believed that the official of the lottery used to stand just so when he said or sang it, others believed that he was supposed to walk among the people, but years and years ago this part of the ritual had been allowed to lapse. There had been, also, a ritual salute, which the official of the lottery had had to use in addressing each person who came up to draw from the box, but this also had changed with time, until now it was felt necessary only for the official to speak to each person approaching. Mr. Summers was very good at all this; in his clean white shirt and blue jeans, with one hand resting carelessly on the black box, he seemed very proper and important as he talked interminably to Mr. Graves and the Martins.

Just as Mr. Summers finally left off talking and turned to the assembled villagers, Mrs. Hutchinson came hurriedly along the path to the square, her sweater thrown over her shoulders, and slid into place in the back of the crowd. "Clean forgot what day it was," she said to Mrs. Delacroix, who stood next to her, and they both laughed softly. "Thought my old man was out back stacking wood," Mrs. Hutchinson went on, "and then I looked out the window and the kids were gone, and then I remembered it was the twenty-seventh and came a-running." She dried her hands on her apron, and Mrs. Delacroix said, "You're in time, though. They're still talking away up there."

Mrs. Hutchinson craned her neck to see through the crowd and found her husband and children standing near the front. She tapped Mrs. Delacroix on the arm as a farewell and began to make her way through the crowd. The people separated goodhumoredly to let her through; two or three people said, in voices just loud enough to be heard across the crowd, "Here comes your Missus, Hutchinson," and "Bill, she made it after all." Mrs. Hutchinson reached her husband, and Mr. Summers, who had been waiting, said cheerfully, "Thought we were going to have to get on without you, Tessie." Mrs. Hutchinson said, grinning, "Wouldn't have me leave m'dishes in the sink, now would you, Joe?," and soft laughter ran through the crowd as the people stirred back into position after Mrs. Hutchinson's arrival.

"Well, now," Mr. Summers said soberly, "guess we better get started, get this over with, so's we can go back to work. Anybody ain't here?"

"Dunbar," several people said. "Dunbar, Dunbar."

Mr. Summers consulted his list. "Clyde Dunbar," he said. "That's right. He's broke his leg, hasn't he? Who's drawing for him?"

"Me, I guess," a woman said, and Mr. Summers turned to look at her. "Wife draws for her husband," Mr. Summers said.

"Don't you have a grown boy to do it for you, Janey?" Although Mr. Summers and everyone else in the village knew the answer perfectly well, it was the business of the official of the lottery to ask such questions formally. Mr. Summers waited with an expression of polite interest while Mrs. Dunbar answered.

"Horace's not but sixteen yet," Mrs. Dunbar said regretfully. "Guess I gotta fill in for the old man this year."

"Right," Mr. Summers said. He made a note on the list he was holding. Then he asked, "Watson boy drawing this year?"

A tall boy in the crowd raised his hand. "Here," he said. "I'm drawing for m'mother and me." He blinked his eyes nervously and ducked his head as several voices in the crowd said things like "Good fellow, Jack," and "Glad to see your mother's got a man to do it."

"Well," Mr. Summers said, "guess that's everyone. Old Man Warner make it?"

"Here," a voice said, and Mr. Summers nodded.

A sudden hush fell on the crowd as Mr. Summers cleared his throat and looked at the list. "All ready?" he called. "Now, I'll read the names — heads of families first — and the men come up and take a paper out of the box. Keep the paper folded in your hand without looking at it until everyone has had a turn. Everything clear?"

The people had done it so many times that they only half listened to the directions, most of them were quiet, wetting their lips, not looking around. Then Mr. Summers raised one hand high and said, "Adams." A man disengaged himself from the crowd and came forward. "Hi, Steve," Mr. Summers said, and Mr. Adams said, "Hi, Joe." They grinned at one another humorlessly and nervously. Then Mr. Adams reached into the black box and took out a folded paper. He held it firmly by one corner as he turned and went hastily back to his place in the crowd, where he stood a little apart from his family, not looking down at his hand.

"Allen," Mr. Summers said. "Anderson. . . . Bentham."

"Seems like there's no time at all between lotteries any more," Mrs. Delacroix said to Mrs. Graves in the back row. "Seems like we got through with the last one only last week."

"Time sure goes fast," Mrs. Graves said.

"Clark. . . . Delacroix."

"There goes my old man," Mrs. Delacroix said. She held her breath while her husband went forward.

"Dunbar," Mr. Summers said, and Mrs. Dunbar went steadily to the box while one of the women said, "Go on, Janey," and another said, "There she goes."

"We're next," Mrs. Graves said. She watched while Mr. Graves came around from the side of the box, greeted Mr. Summers gravely, and selected a slip of paper from the box. By now, all through the crowd there were men holding the small folded papers in their large hands, turning them over and over nervously. Mrs. Dunbar and her two sons stood together, Mrs. Dunbar holding the slip of paper.

"Harburt. . . . Hutchinson."

"Get up there, Bill," Mrs. Hutchinson said, and the people near her laughed.

"Jones."

"They do say," Mr. Adams said to Old Man Warner, who stood next to him, "that over in the north village they're talking of giving up the lottery."

Old Man Warner snorted, "Pack of crazy fools," he said. "Listening to the young folks, nothing's good enough for *them.* Next thing you know, they'll be wanting to go back to living in caves, nobody work any more, live *that* way for a while. Used to be a saying about 'Lottery in June, corn be heavy soon.' First thing you know, we'd all be eating stewed chickweed and acorns. There's *always* been a lottery," he added petulantly. "Bad enough to see young Joe Summers up there joking with everybody."

"Some places have already quit lotteries," Mrs. Adams said.

"Nothing but trouble in *that,*" Old Man Warner said stoutly. "Pack of young fools."

"Martin." And Bobby Martin watched his father go forward. "Overdyke. . . . Percy."

"I wish they'd hurry," Mrs. Dunbar said to her older son. "I wish they'd hurry."

"They're almost through," her son said.

"You get ready to run tell Dad," Mrs. Dunbar said.

Mr. Summers called his own name and then stepped forward precisely and selected a slip from the box. Then he called, "Warner."

"Seventy-seventh year I been in the lottery," Old Man Warner said as he went through the crowd. "Seventy-seventh time."

"Watson." The tall boy came awkwardly through the crowd. Someone said, "Don't be nervous, Jack," and Mr. Summers said, "Take your time, son."

"Zanini."

After that, there was a long pause, a breathless pause, until Mr. Summers, holding his slip of paper in the air, said, "All right, fellows." For a minute, no one moved, and then all the slips of paper were opened. Suddenly, all the women began to speak at

once, saying, "Who is it?," "Who's got it?," "Is it the Dunbars?,"
"Is it the Watsons?" Then the voices began to say, "It's Hutchinson.
It's Bill." "Bill Hutchinson's got it."

"Go tell your father," Mrs. Dunbar said to her older son.

People began to look around to see the Hutchinsons. Bill
Hutchinson was standing quiet, staring down at the paper in his
hand. Suddenly, Tessie Hutchinson shouted to Mr. Summers,
"You didn't give him time enough to take any paper he wanted.
I saw you. It wasn't fair!"

"Be a good sport, Tessie," Mrs. Delacroix called, and Mrs.
Graves said, "All of us took the same chance."

"Shut up, Tessie," Bill Hutchinson said.

"Well, everyone," Mr. Summers said, "that was done pretty
fast, and now we've got to be hurrying a little more to get done
in time." He consulted his next list. "Bill," he said, "you draw
for the Hutchinson family. You got any other households in the
Hutchinsons?"

"There's Don and Eva," Mrs. Hutchinson yelled. "Make
them take their chance!"

"Daughters draw with their husbands' families, Tessie," Mr.
Summers said gently. "You know that as well as anyone else."

"It wasn't fair," Tessie said.

"I guess not, Joe," Bill Hutchinson said regretfully. "My
daughter draws with her husband's family, that's only fair. And
I've got no other family except the kids."

"Then, as far as drawing for families is concerned, it's you,"
Mr. Summers said in explanation, "and as far as drawing for
households is concerned, that's you, too. Right?"

"Right," Bill Hutchinson said.

"How many kids, Bill?" Mr. Summers asked formally.

"Three," Bill Hutchinson said. "There's Bill, Jr., and Nancy,
and little Dave. And Tessie and me."

"All right, then," Mr. Summers said. "Harry, you got their
tickets back?"

Mr. Graves nodded and held up the slips of paper. "Put
them in the box, then," Mr. Summers directed. "Take Bill's and
put it in."

"I think we ought to start over," Mrs. Hutchinson said, as
quietly as she could. "I tell you it wasn't *fair*. You didn't give
him time enough to choose. *Every*body saw that."

Mr. Graves had selected the five slips and put them in the
box, and he dropped all the papers but those onto the ground,
where the breeze caught them and lifted them off.

"Listen, everybody," Mrs. Hutchinson was saying to the people around her.

"Ready, Bill?" Mr. Summers asked, and Bill Hutchinson, with one quick glance around at his wife and children, nodded.

"Remember," Mr. Summers said, "take the slips and keep them folded until each person has taken one. Harry, you help little Dave." Mr. Graves took the hand of the little boy, who came willingly with him up to the box. "Take a paper out of the box, Davy," Mr. Summers said. Davy put his hand into the box and laughed. "Take just *one* paper," Mr. Summers said. "Harry, you hold it for him." Mr. Graves took the child's hand and removed the folded paper from the tight fist and held it while little Dave stood next to him and looked up at him wonderingly.

"Nancy next," Mr. Summers said. Nancy was twelve, and her school friends breathed heavily as she went forward, switching her skirt, and took a slip daintily from the box. "Bill, Jr.," Mr. Summers said, and Billy, his face red and his feet over-large, nearly knocked the box over as he got a paper out. "Tessie," Mr. Summers said. She hesitated for a minute, looking around defiantly, and then set her lips and went up to the box. She snatched a paper out and held it behind her.

"Bill," Mr. Summers said, and Bill Hutchinson reached into the box and felt around, bringing his hand out at last with the slip of paper in it.

The crowd was quiet. A girl whispered, "I hope it's not Nancy," and the sound of the whisper reached the edges of the crowd.

"It's not the way it used to be," Old Man Warner said clearly. "People ain't the way they used to be."

"All right," Mr. Summers said. "Open the papers. Harry, you open little Dave's."

Mr. Graves opened the slip of paper and there was a general sigh through the crowd as he held it up and everyone could see that it was blank. Nancy and Bill, Jr., opened theirs at the same time, and both beamed and laughed, turning around to the crowd and holding their slips of paper above their heads.

"Tessie," Mr. Summers said. There was a pause, and then Mr. Summers looked at Bill Hutchinson, and Bill unfolded his paper and showed it. It was blank.

"It's Tessie," Mr. Summers said, and his voice was hushed. "Show us her paper, Bill."

Bill Hutchinson went over to his wife and forced the slip of paper out of her hand. It had a black spot on it, the black spot

Mr. Summers had made the night before with the heavy pencil in the coal-company office. Bill Hutchinson held it up, and there was a stir in the crowd.

"All right, folks," Mr. Summers said, "let's finish quickly."

Although the villagers had forgotten the ritual and lost the original black box, they still remembered to use stones. The pile of stones the boys had made earlier was ready; there were stones on the ground with the blowing scraps of paper that had come out of the box. Mrs. Delacroix selected a stone so large she had to pick it up with both hands and turned to Mrs. Dunbar. "Come on," she said. "Hurry up."

Mrs. Dunbar had small stones in both hands, and she said, gasping for breath, "I can't run at all. You'll have to go ahead and I'll catch up with you."

The children had stones already, and someone gave little Davy Hutchinson a few pebbles.

Tessie Hutchinson was in the center of a cleared space by now, and she held her hands out desperately as the villagers moved in on her. "It isn't fair," she said. A stone hit her on the side of the head.

Old Man Warner was saying, "Come on, come on, everyone." Steve Adams was in the front of the crowd of villagers, with Mrs. Graves beside him.

"It isn't fair, it isn't right," Mrs. Hutchinson screamed, and then they were upon her.

Flannery O'Connor (*American. 1925–1964*)

A Good Man Is Hard to Find

The grandmother didn't want to go to Florida. She wanted to visit some of her connections in east Tennessee and she was seizing at every chance to change Bailey's mind. Bailey was the son she lived with, her only boy. He was sitting on the edge of his chair at the table, bent over the orange sports section of the *Journal*. "Now look here, Bailey," she said, "see here, read this," and she stood with one hand on her thin hip and the other rattling the newspaper at his bald head. "Here this fellow that calls himself The Misfit is aloose from the Federal Pen and headed toward

Florida and you read here what it says he did to these people. Just you read it. I wouldn't take my children in any direction with a criminal like that aloose in it. I couldn't answer to my conscience if I did."

Bailey didn't look up from his reading so she wheeled around then and faced the children's mother, a young woman in slacks, whose face was as broad and innocent as a cabbage and was tied round with a green head-kerchief that had two points on the top like rabbit's ears. She was sitting on the sofa, feeding the baby his apricots out of a jar. "The children have been to Florida before," the old lady said. "You all ought to take them somewhere else for a change so they would see different parts of the world and be broad. They never have been to east Tennessee."

The children's mother didn't seem to hear her but the eight-year-old boy, John Wesley, a stocky child with glasses, said, "If you don't want to go to Florida, why dontcha stay at home?" He and the little girl, June Star, were reading the funny papers on the floor.

"She wouldn't stay at home to be queen for a day," June Star said without raising her yellow head.

"Yes and what would you do if this fellow, The Misfit, caught you?" the grandmother asked.

"I'd smack his face," John Wesley said.

"She wouldn't stay at home for a million bucks," June Star said. "Afraid she'd miss something. She has to go everywhere we go."

"All right, Miss," the grandmother said. "Just remember that the next time you want me to curl your hair."

June Star said her hair was naturally curly.

The next morning the grandmother was the first one in the car, ready to go. She had her big black valise that looked like the head of a hippopotamus in one corner, and underneath it she was hiding a basket with Pitty Sing, the cat, in it. She didn't intend for the cat to be left alone in the house for three days because he would miss her too much and she was afraid he might brush against one of the gas burners and accidentally asphyxiate himself. Her son, Bailey, didn't like to arrive at a motel with a cat.

She sat in the middle of the back seat with John Wesley and June Star on either side of her. Bailey and the children's mother and the baby sat in the front and they left Atlanta at eight forty-five with the mileage on the car at 55890. The grandmother wrote this down because she thought it would be interesting to say how many miles they had been when they got back. It took them twenty minutes to reach the outskirts of the city.

The old lady settled herself comfortably, removing her white cotton gloves and putting them up with her purse on the shelf in front of the back window. The children's mother still had on slacks and still had her head tied up in a green kerchief, but the grandmother had on a navy blue straw sailor hat with a bunch of white violets on the brim and a navy blue dress with a small white dot in the print. Her collar and cuffs were white organdy trimmed with lace and at her neckline she had pinned a purple spray of cloth violets containing a sachet. In case of an accident, anyone seeing her dead on the highway would know at once that she was a lady.

She said she thought it was going to be a good day for driving, neither too hot nor too cold, and she cautioned Bailey that the speed limit was fifty-five miles an hour and that the patrolmen hid themselves behind billboards and small clumps of trees and sped out after you before you had a chance to slow down. She pointed out interesting details of the scenery: Stone Mountain; the blue granite that in some places came up to both sides of the highway; the brilliant red clay banks slightly streaked with purple; and the various crops that made rows of green lace-work on the ground. The trees were full of silver-white sunlight and the meanest of them sparkled. The children were reading comic magazines and their mother had gone back to sleep.

"Let's go through Georgia fast so we won't have to look at it much," John Wesley said.

"If I were a little boy," said the grandmother, "I wouldn't talk about my native state that way. Tennessee has the mountains and Georgia has the hills."

"Tennessee is just a hillbilly dumping ground," John Wesley said, "and Georgia is a lousy state too."

"You said it," June Star said.

"In my time," said the grandmother, folding her thin veined fingers, "children were more respectful of their native states and their parents and everything else. People did right then. Oh look at the cute little pickaninny!" she said and pointed to a Negro child standing in the door of a shack. "Wouldn't that make a picture, now?" she asked and they all turned and looked at the little Negro out of the back window. He waved.

"He didn't have any britches on," June Star said.

"He probably didn't have any," the grandmother explained. "Little niggers in the country don't have things like we do. If I could paint, I'd paint that picture," she said.

The children exchanged comic books.

The grandmother offered to hold the baby and the children's mother passed him over the front seat to her. She set him on her knee and bounced him and told him about the things they were passing. She rolled her eyes and screwed up her mouth and stuck her leathery thin face into his smooth bland one. Occasionally he gave her a faraway smile. They passed a large cotton field with five or six graves fenced in the middle of it, like a small island. "Look at the graveyard!" the grandmother said, pointing it out. "That was the old family burying ground. That belonged to the plantation."

"Where's the plantation?" John Wesley asked.

"Gone With the Wind," said the grandmother. "Ha. Ha."

When the children finished all the comic books they had brought, they opened the lunch and ate it. The grandmother ate a peanut butter sandwich and an olive and would not let the children throw the box and the paper napkins out the window. When there was nothing else to do they played a game by choosing a cloud and making the other two guess what shape it suggested. John Wesley took one the shape of a cow and June Star guessed a cow and John Wesley said, no, an automobile, and June Star said he didn't play fair, and they began to slap each other over the grandmother.

The grandmother said she would tell them a story if they would keep quiet. When she told a story, she rolled her eyes and waved her head and was very dramatic. She said once when she was a maiden lady she had been courted by a Mr. Edgar Atkins Teagarden from Jasper, Georgia. She said he was a very good-looking man and a gentleman and that he brought her a watermelon every Saturday afternoon with his initials cut in it, E. A. T. Well, one Saturday, she said, Mr. Teagarden brought the watermelon and there was nobody at home and he left it on the front porch and returned in his buggy to Jasper, but she never got the watermelon, she said, because a nigger boy ate it when he saw the initials, E. A. T.! This story tickled John Wesley's funny bone and he giggled and giggled but June Star didn't think it was any good. She said she wouldn't marry a man that just brought her a watermelon on Saturday. The grandmother said she would have done well to marry Mr. Teagarden because he was a gentleman and had bought Coca-Cola stock when it first came out and that he had died only a few years ago, a very wealthy man.

They stopped at The Tower for barbecued sandwiches. The Tower was a part stucco and part wood filling station and dance hall set in a clearing outside of Timothy. A fat man named Red

Sammy Butts ran it and there were signs stuck here and there on the building and for miles up and down the highway saying, TRY RED SAMMY'S FAMOUS BARBECUE. NONE LIKE FAMOUS RED SAMMY'S! RED SAM! THE FAT BOY WITH THE HAPPY LAUGH. A VETERAN! RED SAMMY'S YOUR MAN!

Red Sammy was lying on the bare ground outside The Tower with his head under a truck while a gray monkey about a foot high, chained to a small chinaberry tree, chattered nearby. The monkey sprang back into the tree and got on the highest limb as soon as he saw the children jump out of the car and run toward him.

Inside, The Tower was a long dark room with a counter at one end and tables at the other and dancing space in the middle. They all sat down at a broad table next to the nickelodeon and Red Sam's wife, a tall burnt-brown woman with hair and eyes lighter than her skin, came and took their order. The children's mother put a dime in the machine and played "The Tennessee Waltz," and the grandmother said that tune always made her want to dance. She asked Bailey if he would like to dance but he only glared at her. He didn't have a naturally sunny disposition like she did and trips made him nervous. The grandmother's brown eyes were very bright. She swayed her head from side to side and pretended she was dancing in her chair. June Star said play something she could tap to so the children's mother put in another dime and played a fast number and June Star stepped out onto the dance floor and did her tap routine.

"Ain't she cute?" Red Sam's wife said, leaning over the counter. "Would you like to come be my little girl?"

"No I certainly wouldn't," June Star said. "I wouldn't live in a broken-down place like this for a million bucks!" and she ran back to the table.

"Ain't she cute?" the woman repeated, stretching her mouth politely.

"Aren't you ashamed?" hissed the grandmother.

Red Sam came in and told his wife to quit lounging on the counter and hurry with these people's order. His khaki trousers reached just to his hip bones and his stomach hung over them like a sack of meal swaying under his shirt. He came over and sat down at a table nearby and let out a combination sigh and yodel. "You can't win," he said. "You can't win," and he wiped his sweating red face off with a gray handkerchief. "These days you don't know who to trust," he said. "Ain't that the truth?"

"People are certainly not nice like they used to be," said the grandmother.

"Two fellers come in here last week," Red Sammy said, "driving a Chrysler. It was a old beat-up car but it was a good one and these boys looked all right to me. Said they worked at the mill and you know I let them fellers charge the gas they bought? Now why did I do that?"

"Because you're a good man!" the grandmother said at once.

"Yes'm, I suppose so," Red Sam said as if he were struck with the answer.

His wife brought the orders, carrying the five plates all at once without a tray, two in each hand and one balanced on her arm. "It isn't a soul in this green world of God's that you can trust," she said. "And I don't count anybody out of that, not nobody," she repeated, looking at Red Sammy.

"Did you read about that criminal, The Misfit, that's escaped?" asked the grandmother.

"I wouldn't be a bit surprised if he didn't attack this place right here," said the woman. "If he hears about it being here, I wouldn't be none surprised to see him. If he hears it's two cent in the cash register, I wouldn't be a tall surprised if he . . ."

"That'll do," Red Sam said. "Go bring these people their Co'Colas," and the woman went off to get the rest of the order.

"A good man is hard to find," Red Sammy said. "Everything is getting terrible. I remember the day you could go off and leave your screen door unlatched. Not no more."

He and the grandmother discussed better times. The old lady said that in her opinion Europe was entirely to blame for the way things were now. She said the way Europe acted you would think we were made of money and Red Sam said it was no use talking about it, she was exactly right. The children ran outside into the white sunlight and looked at the monkey in the lacy chinaberry tree. He was busy catching fleas on himself and biting each one carefully between his teeth as if it were a delicacy.

They drove off again into the hot afternoon. The grandmother took cat naps and woke up every few minutes with her own snoring. Outside of Toombsboro she woke up and recalled an old plantation that she had visited in this neighborhood once when she was a young lady. She said the house had six white columns across the front and that there was an avenue of oaks leading up to it and two little wooden trellis arbors on either side in front where you sat down with your suitor after a stroll in the garden. She recalled exactly which road to turn off to get to it. She knew that Bailey would not be willing to lose any time looking at an old house, but the more she talked about it, the more she wanted to see it once again and find out if the little twin arbors were still standing. "There was a secret panel in this house," she said craftily, not telling the truth but wishing that she were, "and the story went that all the family silver was hidden in it when Sherman came through but it was never found . . ."

"Hey!" John Wesley said. "Let's go see it! We'll find it! We'll poke all the woodwork and find it! Who lives there? Where do you turn off at? Hey Pop, can't we turn off there?"

"We never have seen a house with a secret panel!" June Star shrieked. "Let's go to the house with the secret panel! Hey, Pop, can't we go see the house with the secret panel!"

"It's not far from here, I know," the grandmother said. "It wouldn't take over twenty minutes."

Bailey was looking straight ahead. His jaw was as rigid as a horseshoe. "No," he said.

The children began to yell and scream that they wanted to see the house with the secret panel. John Wesley kicked the back of the front seat and June Star hung over her mother's shoulder and whined desperately into her ear that they never had any fun even on their vacation, and that they could never do what THEY wanted to do. The baby began to scream and John Wesley kicked the back of the seat so hard that his father could feel the blows in his kidney.

"All right!" he shouted, and drew the car to a stop at the side of the road. "Will you all shut up? Will you all just shut up for one second? If you don't shut up, we won't go anywhere."

"It would be very educational for them," the grandmother murmured.

"All right," Bailey said, "but get this: this is the only time we're going to stop for anything like this. This is the one and only time."

"The dirt road that you have to turn down is about a mile back," the grandmother directed. "I marked it when we passed."

"A dirt road," Bailey groaned.

After they had turned around and were headed toward the dirt road, the grandmother recalled other points about the house, the beautiful glass over the front doorway and the candle-lamp in the hall. John Wesley said that the secret panel was probably in the fireplace.

"You can't go inside this house," Bailey said. "You don't know who lives there."

"While you all talk to the people in front, I'll run around behind and get in a window," John Wesley suggested.

"We'll all stay in the car," his mother said.

They turned onto the dirt road and the car raced roughly along in a swirl of pink dust. The grandmother recalled the times when there were no paved roads and thirty miles was a day's journey. The dirt road was hilly and there were sudden washes in it and sharp curves on dangerous embankments. All at once they would be on a hill, looking down over the blue tops of trees for miles around, then the next minute, they would be in a red depression with the dust-coated trees looking down on them.

"This place had better turn up in a minute," Bailey said, "or I'm going to turn around."

The road looked as if no one had traveled on it in months.

"It's not much farther," the grandmother said and just as she said it, a horrible thought came to her. The thought was so embarrassing that she turned red in the face and her eyes dilated and her feet jumped up, upsetting her valise in the corner. The instant the valise moved, the newspaper top she had over the basket under it rose with a snarl and Pitty Sing, the cat, sprang onto Bailey's shoulder.

The children were thrown to the floor and their mother, clutching the baby, was thrown out of the door onto the ground, the old lady was thrown into the front seat. The car turned over once and landed rightside up in a gulch on the side of the road. Bailey remained in the driver's seat with the cat — gray-striped with a broad white face and an orange nose — clinging to his neck like a caterpillar.

As soon as the children saw they could move their arms and legs, they scrambled out of the car, shouting, "We've had an ACCIDENT!" The grandmother was curled up under the dashboard, hoping she was injured so that Bailey's wrath would not come down on her all at once. The horrible thought she had had before the accident was that the house she had remembered so vividly was not in Georgia but in Tennessee.

Bailey removed the cat from his neck with both hands and flung it out the window against the side of a pine tree. Then he got out of the car and started looking for the children's mother. She was sitting against the side of the red gutted ditch, holding the screaming baby, but she only had a cut down her face and a broken shoulder. "We've had an ACCIDENT!" the children screamed in a frenzy of delight.

"But nobody's killed," June Star said with disappointment as the grandmother limped out of the car, her hat still pinned to her head but the broken front brim standing up at a jaunty angle and the violet spray hanging off the side. They all sat down in the ditch, except the children, to recover from the shock. They were all shaking.

"Maybe a car will come along," said the children's mother hoarsely.

"I believe I have injured an organ," said the grandmother, pressing her side, but no one answered her. Bailey's teeth were clattering. He had on a yellow sport shirt with bright blue parrots designed in it and his face was as yellow as the shirt. The grandmother decided that she would not mention that the house was in Tennessee.

The road was about ten feet above and they could see only the tops of the trees on the other side of it. Behind the ditch they were sitting in there were more woods, tall and dark and deep. In a few minutes they saw a car some distance away on top of a hill, coming slowly as if the occupants were watching them. The grandmother stood up and waved both arms dramatically to attract their attention. The car continued to come on slowly, disappeared around a bend and appeared again, moving even slower, on top of the hill they had gone over. It was a big black battered hearselike automobile. There were three men in it.

It came to a stop just over them and for some minutes, the driver looked down with a steady expressionless gaze to where they were sitting, and didn't speak. Then he turned his head and muttered something to the other two and they got out. One was a fat boy in black trousers and a red sweat shirt with a silver stallion embossed on the front of it. He moved around on the right side of them and stood staring, his mouth partly open in a kind of loose grin. The other had on khaki pants and a blue striped coat and a gray hat pulled down very low, hiding most of his face. He came around slowly on the left side. Neither spoke.

The driver got out of the car and stood by the side of it, looking down at them. He was an older man than the other two. His hair was just beginning to gray and he wore silver-rimmed spectacles that gave him a scholarly look. He had a long creased face and didn't have on any shirt or undershirt. He had on blue jeans that were too tight for him and was holding a black hat and a gun. The two boys also had guns.

"We've had an ACCIDENT!" the children screamed.

The grandmother had the peculiar feeling that the bespectacled man was someone she knew. His face was as familiar to her as if she had known him all her life, but she could not recall who he was. He moved away from the car and began to come down the embankment, placing his feet carefully so that he wouldn't slip. He had on tan and white shoes and no socks, and his ankles were red and thin. "Good afternoon," he said. "I see you all had you a little spill."

"We turned over twice!" said the grandmother.

"Oncet," he corrected. "We seen it happen. Try their car and see will it run, Hiram," he said quietly to the boy with the gray hat.

"What you got that gun for?" John Wesley asked. "Watcha gonna do with that gun?"

"Lady," the man said to the children's mother, "would you mind calling them children to set down by you? Children make me nervous. I want all you all to sit down right together there where you're at."

"What are you telling us what to do for?" June Star asked.

Behind them the line of woods gaped like a dark open mouth. "Come here," said their mother.

"Look here now," Bailey began suddenly, "we're in a predicament! We're in . . ."

The grandmother shrieked. She scrambled to her feet and stood staring. "You're The Misfit!" she said. "I recognized you at once."

"Yes'm," the man said, smiling slightly as if he were pleased in spite of himself to be known, "but it would have been better for all of you, lady, if you hadn't of recognized me."

Bailey turned his head sharply and said something to his mother that shocked even the children. The old lady began to cry and The Misfit reddened.

"Lady," he said, "don't you get upset. Sometimes a man says things he don't mean. I don't reckon he meant to talk to you thataway."

"You wouldn't shoot a lady, would you?" the grandmother said and removed a clean handkerchief from her cuff and began to slap at her eyes with it.

The Misfit pointed the toe of his shoe into the ground and made a little hole and then covered it up again. "I would hate to have to," he said.

"Listen," the grandmother almost screamed, "I know you're a good man. You don't look a bit like you have common blood. I know you must come from nice people!"

"Yes ma'm," he said, "finest people in the world." When he smiled he showed a row of strong white teeth. "God never made a finer woman than my mother and my daddy's heart was pure gold," he said. The boy with the red sweat shirt had come around behind them and was standing with his gun at his hip.

The Misfit squatted down on the ground. "Watch them children, Bobby Lee," he said. "You know they make me nervous." He looked at the six of them huddled together in front of him and he seemed to be embarrassed as if he couldn't think of anything to say. "Ain't a cloud in the sky," he remarked, looking up at it. "Don't see no sun but don't see no cloud neither."

"Yes, it's a beautiful day," said the grandmother. "Listen," she said, "you shouldn't call yourself The Misfit because I know you're a good man at heart. I can just look at you and tell."

"Hush!" Bailey yelled. "Hush! Everybody shut up and let me handle this!" He was squatting in the position of a runner about to sprint forward but he didn't move.

"I pre-chate that, lady," The Misfit said and drew a little circle in the ground with the butt of his gun.

"It'll take a half a hour to fix this here car," Hiram called, looking over the raised hood of it.

"Well, first you and Bobby Lee get him and that little boy to step over yonder with you," The Misfit said, pointing to Bailey and John Wesley. "The boys want to ask you something," he said to Bailey. "Would you mind stepping back in them woods there with them?"

"Listen," Bailey began, "we're in a terrible predicament. Nobody realizes what this is," and his voice cracked. His eyes were as blue and intense as the parrots in his shirt and he remained perfectly still.

The grandmother reached up to adjust her hat brim as if she were going to the woods with him but it came off in her hand. She stood staring at it and after a second she let it fall on the ground. Hiram pulled Bailey up by the arm as if he were assisting an old man. John Wesley caught hold of his father's hand and Bobby Lee followed. They went off toward the woods and just as they reached the dark edge, Bailey turned and supporting himself against a gray naked pine trunk, he shouted, "I'll be back in a minute, Mamma, wait on me!"

"Come back this instant!" his mother shrilled but they all disappeared into the woods.

"Bailey Boy!" the grandmother called in a tragic voice but she found she was looking at The Misfit squatting on the ground in front of her. "I just know you're a good man," she said desperately. "You're not a bit common!"

"Nome, I ain't a good man," The Misfit said after a second as if he had considered her statement carefully, "but I ain't the worst in the world neither. My daddy said I was a different breed of dog from my brothers and sisters. 'You know,' Daddy said, 'it's some that can live their whole life out without asking about it and it's others has to know why it is, and this boy is one of the latters. He's going to be into everything!'" He put on his black hat and looked up suddenly and then away deep into the woods as if he were embarrassed again. "I'm sorry I don't have on a shirt before you ladies," he said, hunching his shoulders slightly. "We buried our clothes that we had on when we escaped and we're just making do until we can get better. We borrowed these from some folks we met," he explained.

"That's perfectly all right," the grandmother said. "Maybe Bailey has an extra shirt in his suitcase."

"I'll look and see terrectly," The Misfit said.

"Where are they taking him?" the children's mother screamed.

"Daddy was a card himself," The Misfit said. "You couldn't put anything over on him. He never got in trouble with the Authorities though. Just had the knack of handling them."

"You could be honest too if you'd only try," said the grandmother. "Think how wonderful it would be to settle down and live a comfortable life and not have to think about somebody chasing you all the time."

The Misfit kept scratching in the ground with the butt of his gun as if he were thinking about it. "Yes'm, somebody is always after you," he murmured.

The grandmother noticed how thin his shoulder blades were just behind his hat because she was standing up looking down on him. "Do you ever pray?" she asked.

He shook his head. All she saw was the black hat wiggle between shoulder blades. "Nome," he said.

There was a pistol shot from the woods, followed closely by another. Then silence. The old lady's head jerked around. She could hear the wind move through the tree tops like a long satisfied insuck of breath. "Bailey Boy!" she called.

"I was a gospel singer for a while," The Misfit said. "I been most everything. Been in the arm service, both land and sea, at home and abroad, been twict married, been an undertaker, been with the railroads, plowed Mother Earth, been in a tornado, seen a man burnt alive oncet," and he looked up at the children's mother and the little girl who were sitting close together, their faces white and their eyes glassy; "I even seen a woman flogged," he said.

"Pray, pray," the grandmother began, "pray, pray . . ."

"I never was a bad boy that I remember of," The Misfit said in an almost dreamy voice, "but somewheres along the line

I done something wrong and got sent to the penitentiary. I was buried alive," and he looked up and held her attention to him by a steady stare.

"That's when you should have started to pray," she said. "What did you do to get sent to the penitentiary that first time?"

"Turn to the right, it was a wall," The Misfit said, looking up again at the cloudless sky. "Turn to the left, it was a wall. Look up it was a ceiling, look down it was a floor. I forget what I done, lady. I set there and set there, trying to remember what it was I done and I ain't recalled it to this day. Oncet in a while, I would think it was coming to me, but it never come."

"Maybe they put you in by mistake," the old lady said vaguely.

"Nome," he said. "It wasn't no mistake. They had the papers on me."

"You must have stolen something," she said.

The Misfit sneered slightly. "Nobody had nothing I wanted," he said. "It was a head-doctor at the penitentiary said what I had done was kill my daddy but I know that for a lie. My daddy died in nineteen ought nineteen of the epidemic flu and I never had a thing to do with it. He was buried in the Mount Hopewell Baptist churchyard and you can go there and see for yourself."

"If you would pray," the old lady said, "Jesus would help you."

"That's right," The Misfit said.

"Well then, why don't you pray?" she asked trembling with delight suddenly.

"I don't want no hep," he said. "I'm doing all right by myself."

Bobby Lee and Hiram came ambling back from the woods. Bobby Lee was dragging a yellow shirt with bright blue parrots in it.

"Throw me that shirt, Bobby Lee," The Misfit said. The shirt came flying at him and landed on his shoulder and he put it on. The grandmother couldn't name what the shirt reminded her of. "No, lady," The Misfit said while he was buttoning it up. "I found out the crime don't matter. You can do one thing or you can do another, kill a man or take a tire off his car, because sooner or later you're going to forget what it was you done and just be punished for it."

The children's mother had begun to make heaving noises as if she couldn't get her breath. "Lady," he asked, "would you and that little girl like to step off yonder with Bobby Lee and Hiram and join your husband?"

"Yes, thank you," the mother said faintly. Her left arm dangled helplessly and she was holding the baby, who had gone to sleep, in the other. "Hep that lady up, Hiram," The Misfit said as she struggled to climb out of the ditch, "and Bobby Lee, you hold onto that little girl's hand."

"I don't want to hold hands with him," June Star said. "He reminds me of a pig."

The fat boy blushed and laughed and caught her by the arm and pulled her off into the woods after Hiram and her mother.

Alone with The Misfit, the grandmother found that she had lost her voice. There was not a cloud in the sky nor any sun. There was nothing around her but woods. She wanted to tell him that he must pray. She opened and closed her mouth several times before anything came out. Finally she found herself saying, "Jesus, Jesus," meaning Jesus will help you, but the way she was saying it, it sounded as if she might be cursing.

"Yes'm," The Misfit said as if he agreed. "Jesus thown everything off balance. It was the same case with Him as with me except He hadn't committed any crime and they could prove I had committed one because they had the papers on me. Of course," he said, "they never shown me my papers. That's why I sign myself now. I said long ago, you get you a signature and sign everything you do and keep a copy of it. Then you'll know what you done and you can hold up the crime to the punishment and see do they match and in the end you'll have something to prove you ain't been treated right. I call myself The Misfit," he said, "because I can't make what all I done wrong fit what all I gone through in punishment."

There was a piercing scream from the woods, followed closely by a pistol report. "Does it seem right to you, lady, that one is punished a heap and another ain't punished at all?"

"Jesus!" the old lady cried. "You've got good blood! I know you wouldn't shoot a lady! I know you come from nice people! Pray! Jesus, you ought not to shoot a lady. I'll give you all the money I've got!"

"Lady," The Misfit said, looking beyond her far into the woods, "there never was a body that give the undertaker a tip."

There were two more pistol reports and the grandmother raised her head like a parched old turkey hen crying for water and called, "Bailey Boy, Bailey Boy!" as if her heart would break.

"Jesus was the only One that ever raised the dead." The Misfit continued, "and He shouldn't have done it. He thown everything off balance. If He did what He said, then it's nothing for you to do but thow away everything and follow Him, and if

He didn't, then it's nothing for you to do but enjoy the few minutes you got left the best way you can — by killing somebody or burning down his house or doing some other meanness to him. No pleasure but meanness," he said and his voice had become almost a snarl.

"Maybe He didn't raise the dead," the old lady mumbled, not knowing what she was saying and feeling so dizzy that she sank down in the ditch with her legs twisted under her.

"I wasn't there so I can't say He didn't," The Misfit said. "I wisht I had of been there," he said, hitting the ground with his fist. "It ain't right I wasn't there because if I had of been there I would of known. Listen lady," he said in a high voice, "if I had of been there I would of known and I wouldn't be like I am now." His voice seemed about to crack and the grandmother's head cleared for an instant. She saw the man's face twisted close to her own as if he were going to cry and she murmured, "Why you're one of my babies. You're one of my own children!" She reached out and touched him on the shoulder. The Misfit sprang back as if a snake had bitten him and shot her three times through the chest. Then he put his gun down on the ground and took off his glasses and began to clean them.

Hiram and Bobby Lee returned from the woods and stood over the ditch, looking down at the grandmother who half sat and half lay in a puddle of blood with her legs crossed under her like a child's and her face smiling up at the cloudless sky.

Without his glasses, The Misfit's eyes were red-rimmed and pale and defenseless-looking. "Take her off and thow her where you thown the others," he said, picking up the cat that was rubbing itself against his leg.

"She was a talker, wasn't she?" Bobby Lee said, sliding down the ditch with a yodel.

"She would of been a good woman," The Misfit said, "if it had been somebody there to shoot her every minute of her life."

"Some fun!" Bobby Lee said.

"Shut up, Bobby Lee," The Misfit said. "It's no real pleasure in life."

Flannery O'Connor (*American. 1925–1964*)

Revelation

The doctor's waiting room, which was very small, was almost full when the Turpins entered and Mrs. Turpin, who was very large, made it look even smaller by her presence. She stood looming at the head of the magazine table set in the center of it, a living demonstration that the room was inadequate and ridiculous. Her little bright black eyes took in all the patients as she sized up the seating situation. There was one vacant chair and a place on the sofa occupied by a blond child in a dirty blue romper who should have been told to move over and make room for the lady. He was five or six, but Mrs. Turpin saw at once that no one was going to tell him to move over. He was slumped down in the seat, his arms idle at his sides and his eyes idle in his head; his nose ran unchecked.

Mrs. Turpin put a firm hand on Claud's shoulder and said in a voice that included everyone that wanted to listen, "Claud, you sit in that chair there," and gave him a push down into the vacant one. Claud was florid and bald and sturdy, somewhat shorter than Mrs. Turpin, but he sat down as if he were accustomed to doing what she told him to.

Mrs. Turpin remained standing. The only man in the room besides Claud was a lean stringy old fellow with a rusty hand spread out on each knee, whose eyes were closed as if he were asleep or dead or pretending to be so as not to get up and offer her his seat. Her gaze settled agreeably on a well-dressed gray-haired lady whose eyes met hers and whose expression said: If that child belonged to me, he would have some manners and move over — there's plenty of room there for you and him too.

Claud looked up with a sigh and made as if to rise.

"Sit down," Mrs. Turpin said. "You know you're not supposed to stand on that leg. He has an ulcer on his leg," she explained.

Claud lifted his foot onto the magazine table and rolled his trouser leg up to reveal a purple swelling on a plump marble-white calf.

"My!" the pleasant lady said. "How did you do that?"

"A cow kicked him," Mrs. Turpin said.

"Goodness!" said the lady.

Claud rolled his trouser leg down.

"Maybe the little boy would move over," the lady suggested, but the child did not stir.

"Somebody will be leaving in a minute," Mrs. Turpin said. She could not understand why a doctor — with as much money as they made charging five dollars a day just to stick their head in the hospital door and look at you — couldn't afford a decent-sized waiting room. This one was hardly bigger than a garage. The table was cluttered with limp-looking magazines and at one end of it there was a big green glass ash tray full of cigaret butts and cotton wads with little blood spots on them. If she had had anything to do with the running of the place, that would have been emptied every so often. There were no chairs against the wall at the head of the room. It had a rectangular-shaped panel in it that permitted a view of the office where the nurse came and went and the secretary listened to the radio. A plastic fern in a gold pot sat in the opening and trailed its fronds down almost to the floor. The radio was softly playing gospel music.

Just then the inner door opened and a nurse with the highest stack of yellow hair Mrs. Turpin had ever seen put her face in the crack and called for the next patient. The woman sitting beside Claud grasped the two arms of her chair and hoisted herself up; she pulled her dress free from her legs and lumbered through the door where the nurse had disappeared.

Mrs. Turpin eased into the vacant chair, which held her tight as a corset. "I wish I could reduce," she said, and rolled her eyes and gave a comic sigh.

"Oh, *you* aren't fat," the stylish lady said.

"Ooooo I am too," Mrs. Turpin said. "Claud he eats all he wants to and never weighs over one hundred and seventy-five pounds, but me I just look at something good to eat and I gain some weight," and her stomach and shoulders shook with laughter. "You can eat all you want to, can't you, Claud?" she asked turning to him.

Claud only grinned.

"Well, as long as you have such a good disposition," the stylish lady said, "I don't think it makes a bit of difference what size you are. You just can't beat a good disposition."

Next to her was a fat girl of eighteen or nineteen, scowling into a thick blue book which Mrs. Turpin saw was entitled *Human Development*. The girl raised her head and directed her scowl at Mrs. Turpin as if she did not like her looks. She appeared annoyed that anyone should speak while she tried to read. The poor girl's face was blue with acne and Mrs. Turpin thought how pitiful it was to have a face like that at that age. She gave the girl a friendly smile but the girl only scowled the harder. Mrs. Turpin herself was fat but she had always had good skin, and, though she was forty-seven years old, there was not a wrinkle in her face except around her eyes from laughing too much.

Next to the ugly girl was the child, still in exactly the same position, and next to him was a thin leathery old woman in a cotton print dress. She and Claud had three sacks of chicken feed in their pump house that was in the same print. She had seen from the first that the child belonged with the old woman. She could tell by the way they sat — kind of vacant and white-trashy, as if they would sit there until Doomsday if nobody called and told them to get up. And at right angles but next to the well-dressed pleasant lady was a lank-faced woman who was certainly the child's mother. She had on a yellow sweat shirt and wine-colored slacks, both gritty-looking, and the rims of her lips were stained with snuff. Her dirty yellow hair was tied behind with a little piece of red paper ribbon. Worse than niggers any day, Mrs. Turpin thought.

The gospel hymn playing was, "When I looked up and He looked down," and Mrs. Turpin, who knew it, supplied the last line mentally, "And wona these days I know I'll we-eara crown."

Without appearing to, Mrs. Turpin always noticed people's feet. The well-dressed lady had on red and gray suede shoes to match her dress. Mrs. Turpin had on her good black patent leather pumps. The ugly girl had on Girl Scout shoes and heavy socks. The old woman had on tennis shoes and the white-trashy mother had on what appeared to be bedroom slippers, black straw with gold braid threaded through them — exactly what you would have expected her to have on.

Sometimes at night when she couldn't go to sleep, Mrs. Turpin would occupy herself with the question of who she would have chosen to be if she couldn't have been herself. If Jesus had said to her before he made her, "There's only two places available for you. You can either be a nigger or white-trash," what would she have said? "Please, Jesus, please," she would have said, "just let me wait until there's another place available," and he would have said, "No, you have to go right now and I have only those two places so make up your mind." She would have wiggled and squirmed and begged and pleaded but it would have been no use and finally she would have said, "All right, make me a nigger then — but that don't mean a trashy one." And he would have made her a neat clean respectable Negro woman, herself but black.

Next to the child's mother was a red-headed youngish woman, reading one of the magazines and working a piece of chewing gum, hell for leather, as Claud would say. Mrs. Turpin could not see the woman's feet. She was not white-trash, just common. Sometimes Mrs. Turpin occupied herself at night naming the classes of people. On the bottom of the heap were most colored people, not the kind she would have been if she had been one, but most of them; then next to them — not above, just away from — were the white-trash; then above them were the homeowners, and above them the home-and-land owners, to which she and Claud belonged. Above she and Claud were people with a lot of money and much bigger houses and much more land. But here the complexity of it would begin to bear in on her, for some of the people with a lot of money were common and ought to be below she and Claud and some of the people who had good blood had lost their money and had to rent and then there were colored people who owned their homes and land as well. There was a colored dentist in town who had two red Lincolns and a swimming pool and a farm with registered white-face cattle on it. Usually by the time she had fallen asleep all the classes of people were moiling and roiling around in her head, and she would dream they were all crammed in together in a box car, being ridden off to be put in a gas oven.

"That's a beautiful clock," she said and nodded to her right. It was a big wall clock, the face encased in a brass sunburst.

"Yes, it's very pretty," the stylish lady said agreeably. "And right on the dot too," she added, glancing at her watch.

The ugly girl beside her cast an eye upward at the clock, smirked, then looked directly at Mrs. Turpin and smirked again. Then she returned her eyes to her book. She was obviously the lady's daughter because, although they didn't look anything alike as to disposition, they both had the same shape of face and the same blue eyes. On the lady they sparkled pleasantly but in the girl's seared face they appeared alternately to smolder and to blaze.

What if Jesus had said, "All right, you can be white-trash or a nigger or ugly"!

Mrs. Turpin felt an awful pity for the girl, though she thought it was one thing to be ugly and another to act ugly.

The woman with the snuff-stained lips turned around in her chair and looked up at the clock. Then she turned back and appeared to look a little to the side of Mrs. Turpin. There was a cast in one of her eyes. "You want to know wher you can get one of themther clocks?" she asked in a loud voice.

"No, I already have a nice clock," Mrs. Turpin said. Once somebody like her got a leg in the conversation, she would be all over it.

"You can get you one with green stamps," the woman said.

"That's most likely wher he got hisn. Save you up enough, you can get you most anythang. I got me some joo'ry."

Ought to have got you a wash rag and some soap, Mrs. Turpin thought.

"I get contour sheets with mine," the pleasant lady said.

The daughter slammed her book shut. She looked straight in front of her, directly through Mrs. Turpin and on through the yellow curtain and the plate glass window which made the wall behind her. The girl's eyes seemed lit all of a sudden with a peculiar light, an unnatural light like night road signs give. Mrs. Turpin turned her head to see if there was anything going on outside that she should see, but she could not see anything. Figures passing cast only a pale shadow through the curtain. There was no reason the girl should single her out for her ugly looks.

"Miss Finley," the nurse said, cracking the door. The gum-chewing woman got up and passed in front of her and Claud and went into the office. She had on red high-heeled shoes.

Directly across the table, the ugly girl's eyes were fixed on Mrs. Turpin as if she had some very special reason for disliking her.

"This is wonderful weather, isn't it?" the girl's mother said.

"It's good weather for cotton if you can get the niggers to pick it," Mrs. Turpin said, "but niggers don't want to pick cotton any more. You can't get the white folks to pick it and now you can't get the niggers — because they got to be right up there with the white folks."

"They gonna *try* anyways," the white-trash woman said, leaning forward.

"Do you have one of those cotton-picking machines?" the pleasant lady asked.

"No," Mrs. Turpin said, "they leave half the cotton in the field. We don't have much cotton anyway. If you want to make it farming now, you have to have a little of everything. We got a couple of acres of cotton and a few hogs and chickens and just enough white-face that Claud can look after them himself."

"One thang I don't want," the white-trash woman said, wiping her mouth with the back of her hand. "Hogs. Nasty stinking things, a-gruntin and a-rootin all over the place."

Mrs. Turpin gave her the merest edge of her attention. "Our hogs are not dirty and they don't stink," she said. "They're cleaner than some children I've seen. Their feet never touch the ground. We have a pig-parlor — that's where you raise them on concrete," she explained to the pleasant lady, "and Claud scoots them down with the hose every afternoon and washes off the floor." Cleaner by far than that child right there, she thought. Poor nasty little thing. He had not moved except to put the thumb of his dirty hand into his mouth.

The woman turned her face away from Mrs. Turpin. "I know I wouldn't scoot down no hog with no hose," she said to the wall.

You wouldn't have no hog to scoot down, Mrs. Turpin said to herself.

"A-gruntin and a-rootin and a-groanin," the woman muttered.

"We got a little of everything," Mrs. Turpin said to the pleasant lady. "It's no use in having more than you can handle yourself with help like it is. We found enough niggers to pick our cotton this year but Claud he has to go after them and take them home again in the evening. They can't walk that half a mile. No they can't. I tell you," she said and laughed merrily, "I sure am tired of buttering up niggers, but you got to love em if you want em to work for you. When they come in the morning, I run out and I say, 'Hi yawl this morning?' and when Claud drives them off to the field I just wave to beat the band and they just wave back." And she waved her hand rapidly to illustrate.

"Like you read out of the same book," the lady said, showing she understood perfectly.

"Child, yes," Mrs. Turpin said. "And when they come in from the field, I run out with a bucket of icewater. That's the way it's going to be from now on," she said. "You may as well face it."

"One thang I know," the white-trash woman said. "Two thangs I ain't going to do: love no niggers or scoot down no hog with no hose." And she let out a bark of contempt.

The look that Mrs. Turpin and the pleasant lady exchanged indicated they both understood that you had to *have* certain things before you could *know* certain things. But every time Mrs. Turpin exchanged a look with the lady, she was aware that the ugly girl's peculiar eyes were still on her, and she had trouble bringing her attention back to the conversation.

"When you got something," she said, "you got to look after it." And when you ain't got a thing but breath and britches, she added to herself, you can afford to come to town every morning and just sit on the Court House coping and spit.

A grotesque revolving shadow passed across the curtain behind her and was thrown palely on the opposite wall. Then a bicycle clattered down against the outside of the building. The door opened and a colored boy glided in with a tray from the drug store. It had two large red and white paper cups on it with tops on them. He was a tall, very black boy in discolored white pants and a green nylon shirt. He was chewing gum slowly, as if to music. He set the tray down in the office opening next to the fern and stuck his head through to look for the secretary. She was not in there. He rested his arms on the ledge and waited, his narrow bottom stuck out, swaying slowly to the left and right. He raised a hand over his head and scratched the base of his skull.

"You see that button there, boy?" Mrs. Turpin said. "You can punch that and she'll come. She's probably in the back somewhere."

"Is thas right?" the boy said agreeably, as if he had never seen the button before. He leaned to the right and put his finger on it. "She sometime out," he said and twisted around to face his audience, his elbows behind him on the counter. The nurse appeared and he twisted back again. She handed him a dollar and he rooted in his pocket and made the change and counted it out to her. She gave him fifteen cents for a tip and he went out with the empty tray. The heavy door swung to slowly and closed at length with the sound of suction. For a moment no one spoke.

"They ought to send all them niggers back to Africa," the white-trash woman said. "That's wher they come from in the first place."

"Oh, I couldn't do without my good colored friends," the pleasant lady said.

"There's a heap of things worse than a nigger," Mrs. Turpin agreed. "It's all kinds of them just like it's all kinds of us."

"Yes, and it takes all kinds to make the world go round," the lady said in her musical voice.

As she said it, the raw-complexioned girl snapped her teeth together. Her lower lip turned downwards and inside out, revealing the pale pink inside of her mouth. After a second it rolled back up. It was the ugliest face Mrs. Turpin had ever seen anyone make and for a moment she was certain that the girl had made it at her. She was looking at her as if she had known and disliked her all her life — all of Mrs. Turpin's life, it seemed too, not just all the girl's life. Why, girl, I don't even know you, Mrs. Turpin said silently.

She forced her attention back to the discussion. "It wouldn't be practical to send them back to Africa," she said. "They wouldn't want to go. They got it too good here."

"Wouldn't be what they wanted — if I had anythang to do with it," the woman said.

"It wouldn't be a way in the world you could get all the

niggers back over there," Mrs. Turpin said. "They'd be hiding out and lying down and turning sick on you and wailing and hollering and raring and pitching. It wouldn't be a way in the world to get them over there."

"They got over here," the trashy woman said. "Get back like they got over."

"It wasn't so many of them then," Mrs. Turpin explained.

The woman looked at Mrs. Turpin as if here was an idiot indeed but Mrs. Turpin was not bothered by the look, considering where it came from.

"Nooo," she said, "they're going to stay here where they can go to New York and marry white folks and improve their color. That's what they all want to do, every one of them, improve their color."

"You know what comes of that, don't you?" Claud asked.

"No, Claud, what?" Mrs. Turpin said.

Claud's eyes twinkled. "White-faced niggers," he said with never a smile.

Everybody in the office laughed except the white-trash and the ugly girl. The girl gripped the book in her lap with white fingers. The trashy woman looked around her from face to face as if she thought they were all idiots. The old woman in the feed sack dress continued to gaze expressionless across the floor at the high-top shoes of the man opposite her, the one who had been pretending to be asleep when the Turpins came in. He was laughing heartily, his hands still spread out on his knees. The child had fallen to the side and was lying now almost face down in the old woman's lap.

While they recovered from their laughter, the nasal chorus on the radio kept the room from silence.

> You go to blank blank
> And I'll go to mine
> But we'll all blank along
> To-geth-ther
> And all along the blank
> We'll hep each other out
> Smile-ling in any kind of
> Weath-ther!

Mrs. Turpin didn't catch every word but she caught enough to agree with the spirit of the song and it turned her thoughts sober. To help anybody out that needed it was her philosophy of life. She never spared herself when she found somebody in need, whether they were white or black, trash or decent. And of all she had to be thankful for, she was most thankful that this was so. If Jesus had said, "You can be high society and have all the money you want and be thin and svelte-like, but you can't be a good woman with it," she would have had to say, "Well don't make me that then. Make me a good woman and it don't matter what else, how fat or how ugly or how poor!" Her heart rose. He had not made her a nigger or white-trash or ugly! He had made her herself and given her a little of everything. Jesus, thank you! she said. Thank you thank you thank you! Whenever she counted her blessings she felt as buoyant as if she weighed one hundred and twenty-five pounds instead of one hundred and eighty.

"What's wrong with your little boy?" the pleasant lady asked the white-trashy woman.

"He has a ulcer," the woman said proudly. "He ain't give me a minute's peace since he was born. Him and her are just alike," she said, nodding at the old woman, who was running her leathery fingers through the child's pale hair. "Look like I can't get nothing down them two but Co'Cola and candy."

That's all you try to get down em, Mrs. Turpin said to herself. Too lazy to light the fire. There was nothing you could tell her about people like them that she didn't know already. And it was not just that they didn't have anything. Because if you gave them everything, in two weeks it would all be broken or filthy or they would have chopped it up for lightwood. She knew all this from her own experience. Help them you must, but help them you couldn't.

All at once the ugly girl turned her lips inside out again. Her eyes were fixed like two drills on Mrs. Turpin. This time there was no mistaking that there was something urgent behind them.

Girl, Mrs. Turpin exclaimed silently, I haven't done a thing to you! The girl might be confusing her with somebody else. There was no need to sit by and let herself be intimidated. "You must be in college," she said boldly, looking directly at the girl. "I see you reading a book there."

The girl continued to stare and pointedly did not answer.

Her mother blushed at this rudeness. "The lady asked you a question, Mary Grace," she said under her breath.

"I have ears," Mary Grace said.

The poor mother blushed again. "Mary Grace goes to Wellesley College," she explained. She twisted one of the buttons on her dress. "In Massachusetts," she added with a grimace. "And in the summer she just keeps right on studying. Just reads all the time, a real book worm. She's done real well at Wellesley; she's taking English and Math and History and Psychology and Social Studies," she rattled on, "and I think it's too much. I think she ought to get out and have fun."

The girl looked as if she would like to hurl them all through the plate glass window.

"Way up north," Mrs. Turpin murmured and thought, well, it hasn't done much for her manners.

"I'd almost rather to have him sick," the white-trash woman said, wrenching the attention back to herself. "He's so mean when he ain't. Look like some children just take natural to meanness. It's some gets bad when they get sick but he was the opposite. Took sick and turned good. He don't give me no trouble now. It's me waitin to see the doctor," she said.

If I was going to send anybody back to Africa, Mrs. Turpin thought, it would be your kind, woman. "Yes, indeed," she said aloud, but looking up at the ceiling, "it's a heap of things worse than a nigger." And dirtier than a hog, she added to herself.

"I think people with bad dispositions are more to be pitied than anyone on earth," the pleasant lady said in a voice that was decidedly thin.

"I thank the Lord he has blessed me with a good one," Mrs. Turpin said. "The day has never dawned that I couldn't find something to laugh at."

"Not since she married me anyways," Claud said with a comical straight face.

Everybody laughed except the girl and the white-trash.

Mrs. Turpin's stomach shook. "He's such a caution," she said, "that I can't help but laugh at him."

The girl made a loud ugly noise through her teeth.

Her mother's mouth grew thin and tight. "I think the worst thing in the world," she said, "is an ungrateful person. To have everything and not appreciate it. I know a girl," she said, "who has parents who would give her anything, a little brother who loves her dearly, who is getting a good education, who wears the best clothes, but who can never say a kind word to anyone, who never smiles, who just criticizes and complains all day long."

"Is she too old to paddle?" Claud asked.

The girl's face was almost purple.

"Yes," the lady said, "I'm afraid there's nothing to do but leave her to her folly. Some day she'll wake up and it'll be too late."

"It never hurt anyone to smile," Mrs. Turpin said. "It just makes you feel better all over."

"Of course," the lady said sadly, "but there are just some people you can't tell anything to. They can't take criticism."

"If it's one thing I am," Mrs. Turpin said with feeling, "it's grateful. When I think who all I could have been besides myself and what all I got, a little of everything, and a good disposition besides, I just feel like shouting, 'Thank you, Jesus, for making everything the way it is!' It could have been different!" For one thing, somebody else could have got Claud. At the thought of this, she was flooded with gratitude and a terrible pang of joy ran through her. "Oh thank you, Jesus, Jesus, thank you!" she cried aloud.

The book struck her directly over her left eye. It struck almost at the same instant that she realized the girl was about to hurl it. Before she could utter a sound, the raw face came crashing across the table toward her, howling. The girl's fingers sank like clamps into the soft flesh of her neck. She heard the mother cry out and Claud shout, "Whoa!" There was an instant when she was certain that she was about to be in an earthquake.

All at once her vision narrowed and she saw everything as if it were happening in a small room far away, or as if she were looking at it through the wrong end of a telescope. Claud's face crumpled and fell out of sight. The nurse ran in, then out, then in again. Then the gangling figure of the doctor rushed out of the inner door. Magazines flew this way and that as the table turned over. The girl fell with a thud and Mrs. Turpin's vision suddenly reversed itself and she saw everything large instead of small. The eyes of the white-trashy woman were staring hugely at the floor. There the girl, held down on one side by the nurse and on the other by her mother, was wrenching and turning in their grasp. The doctor was kneeling astride her, trying to hold her arm down. He managed after a second to sink a long needle into it.

Mrs. Turpin felt entirely hollow except for her heart which swung from side to side as if it were agitated in a great empty drum of flesh.

"Somebody that's not busy call for the ambulance," the doctor said in the off-hand voice young doctors adopt for terrible occasions.

Mrs. Turpin could not have moved a finger. The old man who had been sitting next to her skipped nimbly into the office and made the call, for the secretary still seemed to be gone.

"Claud!" Mrs. Turpin called.

He was not in his chair. She knew she must jump up and find him but she felt like some one trying to catch a train in a dream, when everything moves in slow motion and the faster you try to run the slower you go.

"Here I am," a suffocated voice, very unlike Claud's, said. He was doubled up in the corner on the floor, pale as paper,

holding his leg. She wanted to get up and go to him but she could
not move. Instead, her gaze was drawn slowly downward to the
churning face on the floor, which she could see over the doctor's
shoulder.

The girl's eyes stopped rolling and focused on her. They
seemed a much lighter blue than before, as if a door that had been
tightly closed behind them was now open to admit light and air.

Mrs. Turpin's head cleared and her power of motion returned.
She leaned forward until she was looking directly into the fierce
brilliant eyes. There was no doubt in her mind that the girl did
know her, knew her in some intense and personal way, beyond
time and place and condition. "What you got to say to me?" she
asked hoarsely and held her breath, waiting, as for a revelation.

The girl raised her head. Her gaze locked with Mrs. Turpin's.
"Go back to hell where you came from, you old wart hog," she
whispered. Her voice was low but clear. Her eyes burned for a
moment as if she saw with pleasure that her message had struck
its target.

Mrs. Turpin sank back in her chair.

After a moment the girl's eyes closed and she turned her
head wearily to the side.

The doctor rose and handed the nurse the empty syringe.
He leaned over and put both hands for a moment on the mother's
shoulders, which were shaking. She was sitting on the floor, her
lips pressed together, holding Mary Grace's hand in her lap. The
girl's fingers were gripped like a baby's around her thumb. "Go
on to the hospital," he said. "I'll call and make the arrangements."

"Now let's see that neck," he said in a jovial voice to Mrs.
Turpin. He began to inspect her neck with his first two fingers.
Two little moon-shaped lines like pink fish bones were indented
over her windpipe. There was the beginning of an angry red
swelling above her eye. His fingers passed over this also.

"Lea' me be," she said thickly and shook him off. "See about
Claud. She kicked him."

"I'll see about him in a minute," he said and felt her pulse.
He was a thin gray-haired man, given to pleasantries. "Go home
and have yourself a vacation the rest of the day," he said and
patted her on the shoulder.

Quit your pattin me, Mrs. Turpin growled to herself.

"And put an ice pack over that eye," he said. Then he went
and squatted down beside Claud and looked at his leg. After a
moment he pulled him up and Claud limped after him into the
office.

Until the ambulance came, the only sounds in the room
were the tremulous moans of the girl's mother, who continued

to sit on the floor. The white-trash woman did not take her eyes off the girl. Mrs. Turpin looked straight ahead at nothing. Presently the ambulance drew up, a long dark shadow, behind the curtain. The attendants came in and set the stretcher down beside the girl and lifted her expertly onto it and carried her out. The nurse helped the mother gather up her things. The shadow of the ambulance moved silently away and the nurse came back in the office.

"That ther girl is going to be a lunatic, ain't she?" the white-trash woman asked the nurse, but the nurse kept on to the back and never answered her.

"Yes, she's going to be a lunatic," the white-trash woman said to the rest of them.

"Po' critter," the old woman murmured. The child's face was still in her lap. His eyes looked idly out over her knees. He had not moved during the disturbance except to draw one leg up under him.

"I thank Gawd," the white-trash woman said fervently, "I ain't a lunatic."

Claud came limping out and the Turpins went home.

As their pick-up truck turned into their own dirt road and made the crest of the hill, Mrs. Turpin gripped the window ledge and looked out suspiciously. The land sloped gracefully down through a field dotted with lavender weeds and at the start of the rise their small yellow frame house, with its little flower beds spread out around it like a fancy apron, sat primly in its accustomed place between two giant hickory trees. She would not have been startled to see a burnt wound between two blackened chimneys.

Neither of them felt like eating so they put on their house clothes and lowered the shade in the bedroom and lay down, Claud with his leg on a pillow and herself with a damp washcloth over her eye. The instant she was flat on her back, the image of a razorbacked hog with warts on its face and horns coming out behind its ears snorted into her head. She moaned, a low quiet moan.

"I am not," she said tearfully, "a wart hog. From hell." But the denial had no force. The girl's eyes and her words, even the tone of her voice, low but clear, directed only to her, brooked no repudiation. She had been singled out for the message, though there was trash in the room to whom it might justly have been applied. The full force of this fact struck her only now. There was a woman there who was neglecting her own child but she had been overlooked. The message had been given to Ruby Turpin, a respectable, hard-working, church-going woman. The tears dried. Her eyes began to burn instead with wrath.

She rose on her elbow and the washcloth fell into her hand.

Claud was lying on his back, snoring. She wanted to tell him what the girl had said. At the same time, she did not wish to put the image of herself as a wart hog from hell into his mind.

"Hey, Claud," she muttered and pushed his shoulder.

Claud opened one pale baby blue eye.

She looked into it warily. He did not think about anything. He just went his way.

"Wha, whasit?" he said and closed the eye again.

"Nothing," she said. "Does your leg pain you?"

"Hurts like hell," Claud said.

"It'll quit terreckly," she said and lay back down. In a moment Claud was snoring again. For the rest of the afternoon they lay there. Claud slept. She scowled at the ceiling. Occasionally she raised her fist and made a small stabbing motion over her chest as if she was defending her innocence to invisible guests who were like the comforters of Job, reasonable-seeming but wrong.

About five-thirty Claud stirred. "Got to go after those niggers," he sighed, not moving.

She was looking straight up as if there were unintelligible handwriting on the ceiling. The protuberance over her eye had turned a greenish-blue. "Listen here," she said.

"What?"

"Kiss me."

Claud leaned over and kissed her loudly on the mouth. He pinched her side and their hands interlocked. Her expression of ferocious concentration did not change. Claud got up, groaning and growling, and limped off. She continued to study the ceiling.

She did not get up until she heard the pick-up truck coming back with the Negroes. Then she rose and thrust her feet in her brown oxfords, which she did not bother to lace, and stumped out onto the back porch and got her red plastic bucket. She emptied a tray of ice cubes into it and filled it half full of water and went out into the back yard. Every afternoon after Claud brought the hands in, one of the boys helped him put out hay and the rest waited in the back of the truck until he was ready to take them home. The truck was parked in the shade under one of the hickory trees.

"Hi yawl this evening?" Mrs. Turpin asked grimly, appearing with the bucket and the dipper. There were three women and a boy in the truck.

"Us doin nicely," the oldest woman said. "Hi you doin?" and her gaze stuck immediately on the dark lump on Mrs. Turpin's forehead. "You done fell down, ain't you?" she asked in a solicitous voice. The old woman was dark and almost toothless. She had on an old felt hat of Claud's set back on her head. The other two women were younger and lighter and they both had new bright green sun hats. One of them had hers on her head; the other had taken hers off and the boy was grinning beneath it.

Mrs. Turpin set the bucket down on the floor of the truck. "Yawl hep yourselves," she said. She looked around to make sure Claud had gone. "No. I didn't fall down," she said, folding her arms. "It was something worse than that."

"Ain't nothing bad happen to you!" the old woman said. She said it as if they all knew that Mrs. Turpin was protected in some special way by Divine Providence. "You just had you a little fall."

"We were in town at the doctor's office for where the cow kicked Mr. Turpin," Mrs. Turpin said in a flat tone that indicated they could leave off their foolishness. "And there was this girl there. A big fat girl with her face all broke out. I could look at that girl and tell she was peculiar but I couldn't tell how. And me and her mama were just talking and going along and all of a sudden WHAM! She throws this big book she was reading at me and . . ."

"Naw!" the old woman cried out.

"And then she jumps over the table and commences to choke me."

"Naw!" they all exclaimed, "naw!"

"Hi come she do that?" the old woman asked. "What ail her?"

Mrs. Turpin only glared in front of her.

"Somethin ail her," the old woman said.

"They carried her off in an ambulance," Mrs. Turpin continued, "but before she went she was rolling on the floor and they were trying to hold her down to give her a shot and she said something to me." She paused. "You know what she said to me?"

"What she say?" they asked.

"She said," Mrs. Turpin began, and stopped, her face very dark and heavy. The sun was getting whiter and whiter, blanching the sky overhead so that the leaves of the hickory tree were black in the face of it. She could not bring forth the words. "Something real ugly," she muttered.

"She sho shouldn't said nothing ugly to you," the old woman said. "You so sweet. You the sweetest lady I know."

"She pretty too," the one with the hat on said.

"And stout," the other one said. "I never knowed no sweeter white lady."

"That's the truth befo' Jesus," the old woman said. "Amen! You des as sweet and pretty as you can be."

Mrs. Turpin knew just exactly how much Negro flattery

was worth and it added to her rage. "She said," she began again and finished this time with a fierce rush of breath, "that I was an old wart hog from hell."

There was an astounded silence.

"Where she at?" the youngest woman cried in a piercing voice.

"Lemme see her. I'll kill her!"

"I'll kill her with you!" the other one cried.

"She b'long in the sylum," the old woman said emphatically. "You the sweetest white lady I know."

"She pretty too," the other two said. "Stout as she can be and sweet. Jesus satisfied with her!"

"Deed he is," the old woman declared.

Idiots! Mrs. Turpin growled to herself. You could never say anything intelligent to a nigger. You could talk at them but not with them. "Yawl ain't drunk your water," she said shortly. "Leave the bucket in the truck when you're finished with it. I got more to do than just stand around and pass the time of day," and she moved off and into the house.

She stood for a moment in the middle of the kitchen. The dark protuberance over her eye looked like a miniature tornado cloud which might any moment sweep across the horizon of her brow. Her lower lip protruded dangerously. She squared her massive shoulders. Then she marched into the front of the house and out the side door and started down the road to the pig parlor. She had the look of a woman going single-handed, weaponless, into battle.

The sun was a deep yellow now like a harvest moon and was riding westward very fast over the far tree line as if it meant to reach the hogs before she did. The road was rutted and she kicked several good-sized stones out of her path as she strode along. The pig parlor was on a little knoll at the end of a lane that ran off from the side of the barn. It was a square of concrete as large as a small room, with a board fence about four feet high around it. The concrete floor sloped slightly so that the hog wash could drain off into a trench where it was carried to the field for fertilizer. Claud was standing on the outside, on the edge of the concrete, hanging onto the top board, hosing down the floor inside. The hose was connected to the faucet of a water trough nearby.

Mrs. Turpin climbed up beside him and glowered down at the hogs inside. There were seven long-snouted bristly shoats in it — tan with liver-colored spots — and an old sow a few weeks off from farrowing. She was lying on her side grunting. The shoats were running about shaking themselves like idiot children, their little slit pig eyes searching the floor for anything left. She had read that pigs were the most intelligent animal. She doubted it. They were supposed to be smarter than dogs. There had even been a pig astronaut. He had performed his assignment perfectly but died of a heart attack afterwards because they left him in his electric suit, sitting upright throughout his examination when naturally a hog should be on all fours.

A-gruntin and a-rootin and a-groanin.

"Gimme that hose," she said, yanking it away from Claud. "Go on and carry them niggers home and then get off that leg."

"You look like you might have swallowed a mad dog," Claud observed, but he got down and limped off. He paid no attention to her humors.

Until he was out of earshot, Mrs. Turpin stood on the side of the pen, holding the hose and pointing the stream of water at the hind quarter of any shoat that looked as if it might try to lie down. When he had had time to get over the hill, she turned her head slightly and her wrathful eyes scanned the path. He was nowhere in sight. She turned back again and seemed to gather herself up. Her shoulders rose and she drew in her breath.

"What do you send me a message like that for?" she said in a low fierce voice, barely above a whisper but with the force of a shout in its concentrated fury. "How am I a hog and me both? How am I saved and from hell too?" Her free fist was knotted and with the other she gripped the hose, blindly pointing the stream of water in and out of the eye of the old sow whose outraged squeal she did not hear.

The pig parlor commanded a view of the back pasture where their twenty beef cows were gathered around the hay-bales Claud and the boy had put out. The freshly cut pasture sloped down to the highway. Across it was their cotton field and beyond that a dark green dusty wood which they owned as well. The sun was behind the wood, very red, looking over the paling of trees like a farmer inspecting his own hogs.

"Why me?" she rumbled. "It's no trash around here, black or white, that I haven't given to. And break my back to the bone every day working. And do for the church."

She appeared to be the right size woman to command the arena before her. "How am I a hog?" she demanded. "Exactly how am I like them?" and she jabbed the stream of water at the shoats. "There was plenty of trash there. It didn't have to be me."

"If you like trash better, go get yourself some trash then," she railed. "You could have made me trash. Or a nigger. If trash is what you wanted why didn't you make me trash?" She shook her fist with the hose in it and a watery snake appeared momentarily in the air. "I could quit working and take it easy and be filthy," she growled. "Lounge about the sidewalks all day drinking root beer. Dip snuff and spit in every puddle and have it all over my face. I could be nasty."

"Or you could have made me a nigger. It's too late for me to be a nigger," she said with deep sarcasm, "but I could act like one. Lay down in the middle of the road and stop traffic. Roll on the ground."

In the deepening light everything was taking on a mysterious hue. The pasture was growing a peculiar glassy green and the streak of highway had turned lavender. She braced herself for a final assault and this time her voice rolled out over the pasture. "Go on," she yelled, "call me a hog! Call me a hog again. From hell. Call me a wart hog from hell. Put that bottom rail on top. There'll still be a top and bottom!"

A garbled echo returned to her.

A final surge of fury shook her and she roared, "Who do you think you are?"

The color of everything, field and crimson sky, burned for a moment with a transparent intensity. The question carried over the pasture and across the highway and the cotton field and returned to her clearly like an answer from beyond the wood.

She opened her mouth but no sound came out of it.

A tiny truck, Claud's, appeared on the highway, heading rapidly out of sight. Its gears scraped thinly. It looked like a child's toy. At any moment a bigger truck might smash into it and scatter Claud's and the niggers' brains all over the road.

Mrs. Turpin stood there, her gaze fixed on the highway, all her muscles rigid, until in five or six minutes the truck reappeared, returning. She waited until it had had time to turn into their own road. Then like a monumental statue coming to life, she bent her head slowly and gazed, as if through the very heart of the mystery, down into the pig parlor at the hogs. They had settled all in one corner around the old sow who was grunting softly. A red glow suffused them. They appeared to pant with a secret life.

Until the sun slipped finally behind the tree line, Mrs. Turpin remained there with her gaze bent to them as if she were absorbing some abysmal life-giving knowledge. At last she lifted her head. There was only a purple streak in the sky, cutting through a field of crimson and leading, like an extension of the highway, into the descending dusk. She raised her hands from the side of the pen in a gesture hieratic and profound. A visionary light settled in her eyes. She saw the streak as a vast swinging bridge extending upward from the earth through a field of living fire. Upon it a vast horde of souls were rumbling toward heaven. There were whole companies of white-trash, clean for the first time in their lives, and bands of black niggers in white robes, and battalions of freaks and lunatics shouting and clapping and leaping like frogs. And bringing up the end of the procession was a tribe of people whom she recognized at once as those who, like herself and Claud, had always had a little of everything and the God-given wit to use it right. She leaned forward to observe them closer. They were marching behind the others with great dignity, accountable as they had always been for good order and common sense and respectable behavior. They alone were on key. Yet she could see by their shocked and altered faces that even their virtues were being burned away. She lowered her hands and gripped the rail of the hog pen, her eyes small but fixed unblinkingly on what lay ahead. In a moment the vision faded but she remained where she was, immobile.

At length she got down and turned off the faucet and made her slow way on the darkening path to the house. In the woods around her the invisible cricket choruses had struck up, but what she heard were the voices of the souls climbing upward into the starry field and shouting hallelujah.

Donald Hall (American. b.1928)

The Fifty-Dollar Bill

I am a lawyer in Akron, Ohio. I am respected in my profession and in my community. Among my associates respect is not accorded easily. I have never asked the judge who is my best friend to fix a traffic ticket for the son of my liquor dealer. I have never promised a favor to a detective in order to hide evidence unfavorable to my client. Many lawyers I meet in the courts have done these things and live on intimate terms with dishonesty. I call myself an honest man.

In 1942, just after Pearl Harbor, I was in my last year of law school and my wife was pregnant. We had seen the war coming and were married in June at the end of my second year.

I had been deferred from the peacetime draft in order to finish school. I had no intention of avoiding service to my country and I expected, even before the Japanese attack, to go into the office of the judge advocate general in June, 1942.

The Japanese attack on December 7, 1941, changed everyone's plans. There was great confusion then about the draft, as anyone my age will remember. Some first- and second-year men quit law school to enlist, but we third-year students were determined to finish our degrees. For a while there were rumors, sometimes printed in the papers, that we would be drafted out of the classroom and into the infantry. For a while I must admit that I was anxious: In sight of my degree and my first child, I was to exchange my studies for basic training; after six and a half years of college and graduate school, I would be a private like the drugstore cowboys from high school. I had a dream at that time that surprised me, because it showed that I feared dying. It was not exactly a dream but a repeated sequence that I saw in my mind's eye even while I was awake, a film clip of my death. I was wading ashore from a landing craft, my rifle held over my head. Ahead of me was a small island of palm trees and tall grass. A shell exploded near me and shrapnel hit my legs. I was not badly hurt, but I could not stand up. I sank under the weight of my equipment, shouting for help that no one could give me, drowning in shallow green waters.

My father, who owned a department store in Canton, suggested that I write our congressman. Our family was prominent in politics and my name would be known as belonging to a good Republican family. Our representative redirected my letter to the army and the J.A.G.'s headquarters. I should say that I was interested in getting the J.A.G.'s office to request my deferment until graduation. Because my grades were good and I was an editor of the *Law Review,* I had something to say for myself.

Now I must go backward in time, because in January of 1942 I had forgotten something from the summer of 1941. That summer, after our marriage, I worked part-time in the law office of my wife's uncle. The rest of the time I was preparing the first issue of the *Law Review,* studying, and honeymooning. My wife wasn't working. Her uncle paid me a wage that was fair but insufficient and in order to get by we dipped into wedding-present money. My wife's grandfather had given us $500. Whenever we ran low that summer, we pulled out another of his fresh fifty-dollar bills. We hid the money under our bed, in the last envelope in a box of envelopes. When school started in the fall, Marion began to work as a university secretary, and we were able to live on her salary.

The J.A.G.'s office sent me a form letter that confused me and everyone to whom I showed it. I wrote to the man whose name was printed at the bottom, set forth my achievements, and said what I wanted. I drafted the letter a dozen times, typed it in a hurry, stuffed it into an envelope, and ran to catch the evening mail.

Four days later my father called from Canton, in such a rage that I could hardly understand him. I finally made out what he was saying, and understood what is obvious from the details of my story: I had enclosed my letter in the last envelope of the box under our bed, and the last fifty-dollar bill was still in it. To the man in Washington, my letter was an open, stupid, insulting attempt at bribery. He had called our congressman in a fury: Only personal regard for Congressman Morgan kept him from taking my letter to the FBI; the young man was not fit for the bar, much less the J.A.G.'s office. Whereupon Morgan called my father.

I convinced my father, finally, that it was merely an unfortunate coincidence. Of course I wrote letters to our representative — who died a year later, I suppose luckily for me — and the man at the J.A.G.'s office, but I never heard from them. If I had been they, I would never have believed this farfetched story. But the incident disturbed me deeply. I found that I had to tell the story over and over. In the navy — I was automatically deferred until graduation and found a commission without difficulty — I told everyone I met. Even after I came home and started practicing law in Akron, I told people. I suppose most of them believed me simply because I told them. Besides, as I emphasized earlier, I have a reputation for honesty. No one could believe I had been so corrupt or so stupid. Finaly I grew tired of the story and stopped telling it.

But I did not forget it entirely. My son is twenty and a sophomore at the university. Last month he talked about transferring to the Air Force Academy if he could get in. He asked me to write our congressman. That night I had the most extraordinary dream. I was back in the apartment of our first year of marriage. Marion was wearing the brooch that she lost when I was in the Pacific; I saw myself in the mirror as I was at that time. Then I stooped under the bed to find an envelope for the letter I held in my hand. Then I licked the envelope and shut it, and saw, for a fraction of a second but clearly, a delicate line of green frothing upward against white paper like a sea made tiny but a sea in which I could drown.

Gabriel García Márquez (Colombian. b. 1928)

A Very Old Man with Enormous Wings

A Tale for Children

Translated by Gregory Rabassa

On the third day of rain they had killed so many crabs inside the house that Pelayo had to cross his drenched courtyard and throw them into the sea, because the newborn child had a temperature all night and they thought it was due to the stench. The world had been sad since Tuesday. Sea and sky were a single ash-gray thing and the sands of the beach, which on March nights glimmered like powdered light, had become a stew of mud and rotten shellfish. The light was so weak at noon that when Pelayo was coming back to the house after throwing away the crabs, it was hard for him to see what it was that was moving and groaning in the rear of the courtyard. He had to go very close to see that it was an old man, a very old man, lying face down in the mud, who, in spite of his tremendous efforts, couldn't get up, impeded by his enormous wings.

Frightened by that nightmare, Pelayo ran to get Elisenda, his wife, who was putting compresses on the sick child, and he took her to the rear of the courtyard. They both looked at the fallen body with mute stupor. He was dressed like a ragpicker. There were only a few faded hairs left on his bald skull and very few teeth in his mouth, and his pitiful condition of a drenched great-grandfather had taken away any sense of grandeur he might have had. His huge buzzard wings, dirty and half-plucked, were forever entangled in the mud. The looked at him so long and so closely that Pelayo and Elisenda very soon overcame their surprise and in the end found him familiar. Then they dared speak to him, and he answered in an incomprehensible dialect with a strong sailor's voice. That was how they skipped over the inconvenience of the wings and quite intelligently concluded that he was a lonely castaway from some foreign ship wrecked by the storm. And yet, they called in a neighbor woman who knew everything about life and death to see him, and all she needed was one look to show them their mistake.

"He's an angel," she told them. "He must have been coming for the child, but the poor fellow is so old that the rain knocked him down."

On the following day everyone knew that a flesh-and-blood angel was held captive in Pelayo's house. Against the judgment of the wise neighbor woman, for whom angels in those times were the fugitive survivors of a celestial conspiracy, they did not have the heart to club him to death. Pelayo watched over him all afternoon from the kitchen, armed with his bailiff's club, and before going to bed he dragged him out of the mud and locked him up with the hens in the wire chicken coop. In the middle of the night, when the rain stopped, Pelayo and Elisenda were still killing crabs. A short time afterward the child woke up without a fever and with a desire to eat. Then they felt magnanimous and decided to put the angel on a raft with fresh water and provisions for three days and leave him to his fate on the high seas. But when they went out into the courtyard with the first light of dawn, they found the whole neighborhood in front of the chicken coop having fun with the angel, without the slightest reverence, tossing him things to eat through the openings in the wire as if he weren't a supernatural creature but a circus animal.

Father Gonzaga arrived before seven o'clock, alarmed at the strange news. By that time onlookers less frivolous than those at dawn had already arrived and they were making all kinds of conjectures concerning the captive's future. The simplest among them thought that he should be named mayor of the world. Others of sterner mind felt that he should be promoted to the rank of five-star general in order to win all wars. Some visionaries hoped that he could be put to stud in order to implant on earth a race of winged wise men who could take charge of the universe. But Father Gonzaga, before becoming a priest, had been a robust woodcutter. Standing by the wire, he reviewed his catechism in an instant and asked them to open the door so that he could take a close look at that pitiful man who looked more like a huge decrepit hen among the fascinated chickens. He was lying in a corner drying his open wings in the sunlight among the fruit peels and breakfast leftovers that the early risers had thrown him. Alien to the impertinences of the world, he only lifted his antiquarian eyes and murmured something in his dialect when Father Gonzaga went into the chicken coop and said good morning to him in Latin. The parish priest had his first suspicion of an imposter when he saw that he did not understand the language of God or know how to greet His ministers. Then he noticed that seen close up he was much too human: he had an unbearable smell of the outdoors, the back side of his wings was strewn with parasites and his main feathers had been mistreated by terrestrial winds, and nothing about him measured up to the proud dignity of angels. Then he came out of the chicken coop and in a brief sermon warned the curious against the risks of being ingenuous. He reminded them that the devil had the bad habit of making use of carnival tricks in order to confuse the unwary. He argued that if wings were not the essential element in determining the difference between a hawk and an airplane, they were even less so in the recognition of angels. Nevertheless, he promised to write a letter to his bishop so that the latter would write to his primate so that the latter would write to the Supreme Pontiff in order to get the final verdict from the highest courts.

His prudence fell on sterile hearts. The news of the captive angel spread with such rapidity that after a few hours the courtyard had the bustle of a marketplace and they had to call in troops with fixed bayonets to disperse the mob that was about to knock the house down. Elisenda, her spine all twisted from sweeping up so much marketplace trash, then got the idea of fencing in the yard and charging five cents admission to see the angel.

The curious came from far away. A traveling carnival arrived with a flying acrobat who buzzed over the crowd several times, but no one paid any attention to him because his wings were not those of an angel but, rather, those of a sidereal bat. The most unfortunate invalids on earth came in search of health: a poor woman who since childhood had been counting her heartbeats and had run out of numbers; a Portuguese man who couldn't sleep because the noise of the stars disturbed him; a sleepwalker who got up at night to undo the things he had done while awake; and many others with less serious ailments. In the midst of that shipwreck disorder that made the earth tremble, Pelayo and Elisenda were happy with fatigue, for in less than a week they had crammed their rooms with money and the line of pilgrims waiting their turn to enter still reached beyond the horizon.

The angel was the only one who took no part in his own act. He spent his time trying to get comfortable in his borrowed nest, befuddled by the hellish heat of the oil lamps and sacramental candles that had been placed along the wire. At first they tried to make him eat some mothballs, which, according to the wisdom of the wise neighbor woman, were the food prescribed for angels. But he turned them down, just as he turned down the papal lunches that the penitents brought him, and they never found out whether it was because he was an angel or because he was an old man that in the end he ate nothing but eggplant mush. His only supernatural virtue seemed to be patience. Especially during the first days, when the hens pecked at him, searching for the stellar parasites that proliferated in his wings, and the cripples pulled out feathers to touch their defective parts with, and even the most merciful threw stones at him, trying to get him to rise so they could see him standing. The only time they succeeded in arousing him was when they burned his side with an iron for branding steers, for he had been motionless for so many hours that they thought he was dead. He awoke with a start, ranting in his hermetic language and with tears in his eyes, and he flapped his wings a couple of times, which brought on a whirlwind of chicken dung and lunar dust and a gale of panic that did not seem to be of this world. Although many thought that his reaction had been one not of rage but of pain, from then on they were careful not to annoy him, because the majority understood that his passivity was not that of a hero taking his ease but that of a cataclysm in repose.

Father Gonzaga held back the crowd's frivolity with formulas of maidservant inspiration while awaiting the arrival of a final judgment on the nature of the captive. But the mail from Rome showed no sense of urgency. They spent their time finding out if the prisoner had a navel, if his dialect had any connection with Aramaic, how many times he could fit on the head of a pin, or whether he wasn't just a Norwegian with wings. Those meager letters might have come and gone until the end of time if a providential event had not put an end to the priest's tribulations.

It so happened that during those days, among so many other carnival attractions, there arrived in town the traveling show of the woman who had been changed into a spider for having disobeyed her parents. The admission to see her was not only less than the admission to see the angel, but people were permitted to ask her all manner of questions about her absurd state and to examine her up and down so that no one would ever doubt the truth of her horror. She was a frightful tarantula the size of a ram and with the head of a sad maiden. What was most heart-rending, however, was not her outlandish shape but the sincere affliction with which she recounted the details of her misfortune. While still practically a child she had sneaked out of her parents' house to go to a dance, and while she was coming back through the woods after having danced all night without permission, a fearful thunderclap rent the sky in two and through the crack came the lightning bolt of brimstone that changed her into a spider. Her only nourishment came from the meatballs that charitable souls chose to toss into her mouth. A spectacle like that, full of so much human truth and with such a fearful lesson, was bound to defeat without even trying that of a haughty angel who scarcely deigned to look at mortals. Besides, the few miracles attributed to the angel showed a certain mental disorder, like the blind man who didn't recover his sight but grew three new teeth, or the paralytic who didn't get to walk but almost won the lottery, and the leper whose sores sprouted sunflowers. Those consolation miracles, which were more like mocking fun, had already ruined the angel's reputation when the woman who had been changed into a spider finally crushed him completely. That was how Father Gonzaga was cured forever of his insomnia and Pelayo's courtyard went back to being as empty as during the time it had rained for three days and crabs walked through the bedrooms.

The owners of the house had no reason to lament. With the money they saved they built a two-story mansion with balconies and gardens and high netting so that crabs wouldn't get in during the winter, and with iron bars on the windows so that angels wouldn't get in. Pelayo also set up a rabbit warren close to town and gave up his job as bailiff for good, and Elisenda bought some satin pumps with high heels and many dresses of iridescent silk, the kind worn on Sunday by the most desirable women in those times. The chicken coop was the only thing that didn't receive any attention. If they washed it down with creolin and burned tears of myrrh inside it every so often, it was not in homage to the angel but to drive away the dungheap stench that still hung everywhere like a ghost and was turning the new house into an old one. At first, when the child learned to walk, they were careful that he not get too close to the chicken coop. But then they began to lose their fears and got used to the smell, and before the child got his second teeth he'd gone inside the chicken coop to play, where the wires were falling apart. The angel was no less standoffish with him than with other mortals, but he tolerated the most ingenious infamies with the patience of a dog who had no illusions. They both came down with chicken pox at the same time. The doctor who took care of the child couldn't resist the temptation to listen to the angel's heart, and he found so much whistling in the heart and so many sounds in his kidneys that it seemed impossible for him to be alive. What surprised him most, however, was the logic of his wings. They seemed so natural on that completely human organism that he couldn't understand why other men didn't have them too.

When the child began school it had been some time since the sun and rain had caused the collapse of the chicken coop. The angel went dragging himself about here and there like a stray dying man. They would drive him out of the bedroom with a broom and a moment later find him in the kitchen. He seemed to be in so many places at the same time that they grew to think that he'd been duplicated, that he was reproducing himself all through the house, and the exasperated and unhinged Elisenda shouted that it was awful living in that hell full of angels. He could scarcely eat and his antiquarian eyes had also become so foggy that he went about bumping into posts. All he had left were the bare cannulae of his last feathers. Pelayo threw a blanket over him and extended him the charity of letting him sleep in the shed, and only then did they notice that he had a temperature at night, and was delirious with the tongue twisters of an old Norwegian. That was one of the few times they became alarmed, for they thought he was going to die and not even the wise neighbor woman had been able to tell them what to do with dead angels.

And yet he not only survived his worst winter, but seemed improved with the first sunny days. He remained motionless for several days in the farthest corner of the courtyard, where no one would see him, and at the beginning of December some large, stiff feathers began to grow on his wings, the feathers of a scarecrow, which looked more like another misfortune of decrepitude. But he must have known the reason for those changes, for he was quite careful that no one should notice them, that no one should hear the sea chanteys that he sometimes sang under the stars. One morning Elisenda was cutting some bunches of onions for lunch when a wind that seemed to come from the high seas blew into the kitchen. Then she went to the window and caught the angel in his first attempts at flight. They were so clumsy that his fingernails opened a furrow in the vegetable patch and he was on the point of knocking the shed down with the ungainly flapping that slipped on the light and couldn't get a grip on the air. But he did manage to gain altitude. Elisenda let out a sigh of relief, for herself and for him, when she saw him pass over the last houses, holding himself up in some way with the risky flapping of a senile vulture. She kept watching him even when she was through cutting the onions and she kept on watching until it was no longer possible for her to see him, because then he was no longer an annoyance in her life but an imaginary dot on the horizon of the sea.

Donald Barthelme (*American. b. 1931*)

The Balloon

The balloon, beginning at a point on Fourteenth Street, the exact location of which I cannot reveal, expanded northward all one night, while people were sleeping, until it reached the Park. There,

I stopped it; at dawn the northernmost edges lay over the Plaza; the free-hanging motion was frivolous and gentle. But experiencing a faint irritation at stopping, even to protect the trees, and seeing no reason the balloon should not be allowed to expand upward, over the parts of the city it was already covering, into the "air space" to be found there, I asked the engineers to see to it. This expansion took place throughout the morning, soft imperceptible sighing of gas through the valves. The balloon then covered forty-five blocks north-south on either side of the Avenue in some places. That was the situation, then.

But it is wrong to speak of "situations," implying sets of circumstances leading to some resolution, some escape of tension; there were no situations, simply the balloon hanging there — muted heavy grays and browns for the most part, contrasting with walnut and soft yellows. A deliberate lack of finish, enhanced by skillful installation, gave the surface a rough, forgotten quality; sliding weights on the inside, carefully adjusted, anchored the great, vari-shaped mass at a number of points. Now we have had a flood of original ideas in all media, works of singular beauty as well as significant milestones in the history of inflation, but at that moment there was only *this balloon,* concrete particular, hanging there.

There were reactions. Some people found the balloon "interesting." As a response this seemed inadequate to the immensity of the balloon, the suddenness of its appearance over the city; on the other hand, in the absence of hysteria or other societally induced anxiety, it must be judged a calm, "mature" one. There was a certain amount of initial argumentation about the "meaning" of the balloon; this subsided, because we have learned not to insist on meanings, and they are rarely even looked for now, except in cases involving the simplest, safest phenomena. It was agreed that since the meaning of the balloon could never be known absolutely, extended discussion was pointless, or at least less purposeful than the activities of those who, for example, hung green and blue paper lanterns from the warm gray underside, in certain streets, or seized the occasion to write messages on the surface, announcing their availability for the performance of unnatural acts, or the availability of acquaintances.

Daring children jumped, especially at those points where the balloon hovered close to a building, so that the gap between balloon and building was a matter of a few inches, or points where the balloon actually made contact, exerting an ever-so-slight pressure against the side of a building, so that balloon and building seemed a unity. The upper surface was so structured that a "landscape" was presented, small valleys as well as slight knolls, or mounds; once atop the balloon, a stroll was possible, or even a trip, from one place to another. There was pleasure in being able to run down an incline, then up the opposing slope, both gently graded, or in making a leap from one side to the other. Bouncing was possible, because of the pneumaticity of the surface, and even falling, if that was your wish. That all these varied motions, as well as others, were within one's possibilities, in experiencing the "up" side of the balloon, was extremely exciting for children, accustomed to the city's flat, hard skin. But the purpose of the balloon was not to amuse children.

Too, the number of people, children and adults, who took advantage of the opportunities described was not so large as it might have been: a certain timidity, lack of trust in the balloon, was seen. There was, furthermore, some hostility. Because we had hidden the pumps, which fed helium to the interior, and because the surface was so vast that the authorities could not determine the point of entry — that is, the point at which the gas was injected—a degree of frustration was evidenced by those city officers into whose province such manifestations normally fell. The apparent purposelessness of the balloon was vexing (as was the fact that it was "there" at all). Had we painted, in great letters, "LABORATORY TESTS PROVE" or "18% MORE EFFECTIVE!" on the sides of the balloon, this difficulty would have been circumvented. But I could not bear to do so. On the whole, these officers were remarkably tolerant, considering the dimensions of the anomaly, this tolerance being the result of, first, secret tests conducted by night that convinced them that little or nothing could be done in the way of removing or destroying the balloon, and, secondly, a public warmth that arose (not uncolored by touches of the afore-mentioned hostility) toward the balloon, from ordinary citizens.

As a single balloon must stand for a lifetime of thinking about balloons, so each citizen expressed, in the attitude he chose, a complex of attitudes. One man might consider that the balloon had to do with the notion *sullied,* as in the sentence *The big balloon sullied the otherwise clear and radiant Manhattan sky.* That is, the balloon was, in this man's view, an imposture, something inferior to the sky that had formerly been there, something interposed between the people and their "sky." But in fact it was January, the sky was dark and ugly; it was not a sky you could look up into, lying on your back in the street, with pleasure, unless pleasure, for you, proceeded from having been threatened, from having been misused. And the underside of the balloon was a pleasure to look up into, we had seen to that, muted grays and browns for the most part, contrasted with walnut and soft, forgotten yellows. And so, while this man was thinking *sullied,* still there was an admixture of pleasurable cognition in his thinking, struggling with the original perception.

Another man, on the other hand, might view the balloon as if it were part of a system of unanticipated rewards, as when one's employer walks in and says, "Here, Henry, take this package of money I have wrapped for you, because we have been doing so well in the business here, and I admire the way you bruise the tulips, without which bruising your department would not be a success, or at least not the success that it is." For this man the balloon might be a brilliantly heroic "muscle and pluck" experience, even if an experience poorly understood.

Another man might say, "Without the example of ——, it is doubtful that —— would exist today in its present form," and find many to agree with him, or to argue with him. Ideas of "bloat" and "float" were introduced, as well as concepts of dream and responsibility. Others engaged in remarkably detailed fantasies having to do with a wish either to lose themselves in the balloon, or to engorge it. The private character of these wishes, of their origins, deeply buried and unknown, was such that they were not much spoken of; yet there is evidence that they were widespread. It was also argued that what was important was what you felt when you stood under the balloon; some people claimed that they felt sheltered, warmed, as never before, while enemies of the balloon felt, or reported feeling, constrained, a "heavy" feeling.

Critical opinion was divided:

"monstrous pourings"

                                                                    "harp"

XXXXXXX *"certain contrasts with darker portions"*
                              "inner joy"
"large, square corners"
"conservative eclecticism that has so far governed modern balloon design"
        :::::: *"abnormal vigor"*
"warm, soft, lazy passages"

The Balloon

"Has unity been sacrificed for a sprawling quality?"
"Quelle catastrophe!"
"munching"

People began, in a curious way, to locate themselves in relation to aspects of the balloon: "I'll be at that place where it dips down into Forty-seventh Street almost to the sidewalk, near the Alamo Chile House," or, "Why don't we go stand on top, and take the air, and maybe walk about a bit, where it forms a tight, curving line with the façade of the Gallery of Modern Art—" Marginal intersections offered entrances with a given time duration, as well as "warm, soft, lazy passages" in which . . . But it is wrong to speak of "marginal intersections," each intersection was crucial, none could be ignored (as if, walking there, you might not find someone capable of turning your attention, in a flash, from old exercises to new exercises, risks and escalations). Each intersection was crucial, meeting of balloon and building, meeting of balloon and man, meeting of balloon and balloon.

It was suggested that what was admired about the balloon was finally this: that it was not limited, or defined. Sometimes a bulge, blister, or sub-section would carry all the way east to the river on its own initiative, in the manner of an army's movements on a map, as seen in a headquarters remote from the fighting. Then that part would be, as it were, thrown back again, or would withdraw into new dispositions; the next morning, that part would have made another sortie, or disappeared altogether. This ability of the balloon to shift its shape, to change, was very pleasing, especially to people whose lives were rather rigidly patterned, persons to whom change, although desired, was not available. The balloon, for the twenty-two days of its existence, offered the possibility, in its randomness, of mislocation of the self, in contradistinction to the grid of precise, rectangular pathways under our feet. The amount of specialized training currently needed, and the consequent desirability of long-term commitments, has been occasioned by the steadily growing importance of complex machinery, in virtually all kinds of operations; as this tendency increases, more and more people will turn, in bewildered inadequacy, to solutions for which the balloon may stand as a prototype, or "rough draft."

I met you under the balloon, on the occasion of your return from Norway; you asked if it was mine; I said it was. The balloon, I said, is a spontaneous autobiographical disclosure, having to do with the unease I felt at your absence, and with sexual deprivation, but now that your visit to Bergen has been terminated, it is no longer necessary or appropriate. Removal of the balloon was easy; trailer trucks carried away the depleted fabric, which is now stored in West Virginia, awaiting some other time of unhappiness, sometime, perhaps, when we are angry with one another.

Alice Munro (*Canadian. b. 1931*)

Boys and Girls

My father was a fox farmer. That is, he raised silver foxes, in pens; and in the fall and early winter, when their fur was prime, he killed them and skinned them and sold their pelts to the Hudson's Bay Company or the Montreal Fur Traders. These companies supplied us with heroic calendars to hang, one on each side of the kitchen door. Against a background of cold blue sky and black pine forests and treacherous northern rivers, plumed adventurers planted the flags of England or of France; magnificent savages bent their backs to the portage.

For several weeks before Christmas, my father worked after supper in the cellar of our house. The cellar was whitewashed, and lit by a hundred-watt bulb over the worktable. My brother Laird and I sat on the top step and watched. My father removed the pelt inside-out from the body of the fox, which looked surprisingly small, mean and rat-like, deprived of its arrogant weight of fur. The naked, slippery bodies were collected in a sack and buried at the dump. One time the hired man, Henry Bailey, had taken a swipe at me with this sack, saying, "Christmas present!" My mother thought that was not funny. In fact she disliked the whole pelting operation — that was what the killing, skinning, and preparation of the furs was called — and wished it did not have to take place in the house. There was the smell. After the pelt had been stretched inside-out on a long board my father scraped away delicately, removing the little clotted webs of blood vessels, the bubbles of fat; the smell of blood and animal fat, with the strong primitive odor of the fox itself, penetrated all parts of the house. I found it reassuringly seasonal, like the smell of oranges and pine needles.

Henry Bailey suffered from bronchial troubles. He would cough and cough until his narrow face turned scarlet, and his light blue, derisive eyes filled up with tears; then he took the lid off the stove, and, standing well back, shot out a great clot of phlegm — hsss — straight into the heart of the flames. We admired him for this performance and for his ability to make his stomach growl at will, and for his laughter, which was full of high whistlings and gurglings and involved the whole faulty machinery of his chest. It was sometimes hard to tell what he was laughing at, and always possible that it might be us.

After we had been sent to bed we could still smell fox and still hear Henry's laugh, but these things, reminders of the warm, safe, brightly lit downstairs world, seemed lost and diminished, floating on the stale cold air upstairs. We were afraid at night in the winter. We were not afraid of *outside* though this was the time of year when snowdrifts curled around our house like sleeping whales and the wind harassed us all night, coming up from the buried fields, the frozen swamp, with its old bugbear chorus of threats and misery. We were afraid of *inside,* the room where we slept. At this time the upstairs of our house was not finished. A brick chimney went up one wall. In the middle of the floor was a square hole, with a wooden railing around it; that was where the stairs came up. On the other side of the stairwell were the things that nobody had any use for any more — a soldiery roll of linoleum, standing on end, a wicker baby carriage, a fern basket, china jugs and basins with cracks in them, a picture of the Battle of Balaclava, very sad to look at. I had told Laird, as soon as he was old enough to understand such things, that bats and skeletons lived over there; whenever a man escaped from the county jail, twenty miles away, I imagined that he had somehow let himself in the window and was hiding behind the linoleum. But we had rules to keep us safe. When the light was on, we were safe as long as we did not step off the square of worn carpet which defined our bedroom-space; when the light was off no place was safe but the beds themselves. I had to turn out the light kneeling on the end of my bed, and stretching as far as I could to reach the cord.

In the dark we lay on our beds, our narrow life rafts, and fixed our eyes on the faint light coming up the stairwell, and sang songs. Laird sang "Jingle Bells," which he would sing any time, whether it was Christmas or not, and I sang "Danny Boy." I loved the sound of my own voice, frail and supplicating, rising in the dark. We could make out the tall frosted shapes of the windows now, gloomy and white. When I came to the part, *When I am dead, as dead I well may be* — a fit of shivering caused not by the cold sheets but by pleasurable emotion almost silenced me. *You'll kneel and say, an Ave there above me* — What was an Ave? Every day I forgot to find out.

Laird went straight from singing to sleep. I could hear his long, satisfied, bubbly breaths. Now for the time that remained to me, the most perfectly private and perhaps the best time of the whole day, I arranged myself tightly under the covers and went on with one of the stories I was telling myself from night to night. These stories were about myself, when I had grown a little older; they took place in a world that was recognizably mine, yet one that presented opportunities for courage, boldness and self-sacrifice, as mine never did. I rescued people from a bombed building (it discouraged me that the real war had gone on so far away from Jubilee). I shot two rabid wolves who were menacing the schoolyard (the teachers cowered terrified at my back). I rode a fine horse spiritedly down the main street of Jubilee, acknowledging the townspeople's gratitude for some yet-to-be-worked-out piece of heroism (nobody ever rode a horse there, except King Billy in the Orangemen's Day* parade). There was always riding and shooting in these stores, though I had only been on a horse twice —bareback because we did not own a saddle — and the second time I had slid right around and dropped under the horse's feet; it had stepped placidly over me. I really was learning to shoot, but I could not hit anything yet, not even tin cans on fence posts.

★   ★   ★   ★   ★

Alive, the foxes inhabited a world my father made for them. It was surrounded by a high guard fence, like a medieval town, with a gate that was padlocked at night. Along the streets of this town were ranged large, sturdy pens. Each of them had a real door that a man could go through, a wooden ramp along the wire, for the foxes to run up and down on, and a kennel — something like a clothes chest with airholes — where they slept and stayed in winter and had their young. There were feeding and watering dishes attached to the wire in such a way that they could be emptied and cleaned from the outside. The dishes were made of old tin cans, and the ramps and kennels of odds and ends of old lumber. Everything was tidy and ingenious; my father was tirelessly inventive and his favorite book in the world was Robinson Crusoe. He had fitted a tin drum on a wheelbarrow, for bringing water down to the pens. This was my job in summer, when the foxes had to have water twice a day. Between nine and ten o'clock in the morning, and again after supper, I filled the drum at the pump and trundled in down through the barnyard to the pens, where I parked it, and filled my watering can and went along the streets. Laird came too, with his little cream and green gardening can, filled too full and knocking against his legs and slopping water on his canvas shoes. I had the real watering can, my father's, though I could only carry it three-quarters full.

* The Orange Society is named for William of Orange, who, as King William III of England, defeated James II of England at the Battle of the Boyne on July 12, 1609. It sponsors an annual procession on July 12. (Notes to this selection are by the editors.)

The foxes all had names, which were printed on a tin plate and hung beside their doors. They were not named when they were born, but when they survived the first year's pelting and were added to the breeding stock. Those my father had named were called names like Prince, Bob, Wally and Betty. Those I had named were called Star or Turk, or Maureen or Diana. Laird named one Maud after a hired girl we had when he was little, one Harold after a boy at school, and one Mexico, he did not say why.

Naming them did not make pets out of them, or anything like it. Nobody but my father ever went into the pens, and he had twice had blood-poisoning from bites. When I was bringing them their water they prowled up and down on the paths they had made inside their pens, barking seldom — they saved that for nighttime, when they might get up a chorus of community frenzy — but always watching me, their eyes burning, clear gold, in their pointed, malevolent faces. They were beautiful for their delicate legs and heavy, aristocratic tails and the bright fur sprinkled on dark down their backs — which gave them their name — but especially for their faces, drawn exquisitely sharp in pure hostility, and their golden eyes.

Besides carrying water I helped my father when he cut the long grass, and the lamb's quarter and flowering money-musk, that grew between the pens. He cut with the scythe and I raked into piles. Then he took a pitchfork and threw fresh-cut grass all over the top of the pens to keep the foxes cooler and shade their coats, which were browned by too much sun. My father did not talk to me unless it was about the job we were doing. In this he was quite different from my mother, who, if she was feeling cheerful, would tell me all sorts of things — the name of a dog she had had when she was a little girl, the names of boys she had gone out with later on when she was grown up, and what certain dresses of hers had looked like — she could not imagine now what had become of them. Whatever thoughts and stories my father had were private, and I was shy of him and would never ask him questions. Nevertheless I worked willingly under his eyes, and with a feeling of pride. One time a feed salesman came down into the pens to talk to him and my father said, "Like to have you meet my new hired man." I turned away and raked furiously, red in the face with pleasure.

"Could of fooled me," said the salesman. "I thought it was only a girl."

After the grass was cut, it seemed suddenly much later in

the year. I walked on stubble in the earlier evening, aware of the reddening skies, the entering silences, of fall. When I wheeled the tank out of the gate and put the padlock on, it was almost dark. One night at this time I saw my mother and father standing talking on the little rise of ground we called the gangway, in front of the barn. My father had just come from the meathouse; he had his stiff bloody apron on, and a pail of cut-up meat in his hand.

It was an odd thing to see my mother down at the barn. She did not often come out of the house unless it was to do something — hang out the wash or dig potatoes in the garden. She looked out of place, with her bare lumpy legs, not touched by the sun, her apron still on and damp across the stomach from the supper dishes. Her hair was tied up in a kerchief, wisps of it falling out. She would tie her hair up like this in the morning, saying she did not have time to do it properly, and it would stay tied up all day. It was true, too; she really did not have time. These days our back porch was piled with baskets of peaches and grapes and pears, bought in town, and onions and tomatoes and cucumbers grown at home, all waiting to be made into jelly and jam and preserves, pickles and chili sauce. In the kitchen there was a fire in the stove all day, jars clinked in boiling water, sometimes a cheesecloth bag was strung on a pole between two chairs straining blue-black grape pulp for jelly. I was given jobs to do and I would sit at the table peeling peaches that had been soaked in the hot water, or cutting up onions, my eyes smarting and streaming. As soon as I was done I ran out of the house, trying to get out of earshot before my mother thought of what she wanted me to do next. I hated the hot dark kitchen in summer, the green blinds and the flypapers, the same old oilcloth table and wavy mirror and bumpy linoleum. My mother was too tired and preoccupied to talk to me, she had no heart to tell about the Normal School Graduation Dance; sweat trickled over her face and she was always counting under her breath, pointing at jars, dumping cups of sugar. It seemed to me that work in the house was endless, dreary and peculiarly depressing; work done out of doors, and in my father's service, was ritualistically important.

I wheeled the tank up to the barn, where it was kept, and I heard my mother saying, "Wait till Laird gets a little bigger, then you'll have a real help."

What my father said I did not hear. I was pleased by the way he stood listening, politely as he would to a salesman or a stranger, but with an air of wanting to get on with his real work. I felt my mother had no business down here and I wanted him to feel the same way. What did she mean about Laird? He was no help to anybody. Where was he now? Swinging himself sick on the swing, going around in circles, or trying to catch caterpillars. He never once stayed with me till I was finished.

"And then I can use her more in the house," I heard my mother say. She had a dead-quiet, regretful way of talking about me that always made me uneasy. "I just get my back turned and she runs off. It's not like I had a girl in the family at all."

I went and sat on a feed bag in the corner of the barn, not wanting to appear when this conversation was going on. My mother, I felt, was not to be trusted. She was kinder than my father and more easily fooled, but you could not depend on her, and the real reasons for the things she said and did were not to be known. She loved me, and she sat up late at night making a dress of the difficult style I wanted, for me to wear when school started, but she was also my enemy. She was always plotting. She was plotting now to get me to stay in the house more, although she knew I hated it (*because* she knew I hated it) and keep me from working for my father. It seemed to me she would do this simply out of perversity, and to try her power. It did not occur to me that she could be lonely, or jealous. No grown-up could be; they were too fortunate. I sat and kicked my heels monotonously against a feed bag, raising dust, and did not come out till she was gone.

At any rate, I did not expect my father to pay any attention to what she said. Who could imagine Laird doing my work — Laird remembering the padlock and cleaning out the watering dishes with a leaf on the end of a stick, or even wheeling the tank without it tumbling over? It showed how little my mother knew about the way things really were.

I have forgotten to say what the foxes were fed. My father's bloody apron reminded me. They were fed horsemeat. At this time most farmers still kept horses, and when a horse got too old to work, or broke a leg or got down and would not get up, as they sometimes did, the owner would call my father, and he and Henry went out to the farm in the truck. Usually they shot and butchered the horse there, paying the farmer from five to twelve dollars. If they had already too much meat on hand, they would bring the horse back alive, and keep it for a few days or weeks in our stable, until the meat was needed. After the war the farmers were buying tractors and gradually getting rid of horses altogether, so it sometimes happened that we got a good healthy horse, that there was just no use for any more. If this happened in the winter we might keep the horse in our stable till spring, for we had plenty

of hay and if there was a lot of snow — and the plow did not
always get our road cleared — it was convenient to be able to go
to town with a horse and cutter.°

The winter I was eleven years old we had two horses in the
stable. We did not know what names they had had before, so we
called them Mack and Flora. Mack was an old black workhorse,
sooty and indifferent. Flora was a sorrel mare, a driver. We took
them both out in the cutter. Mack was slow and easy to handle.
Flora was given to fits of violent alarm, veering at cars and even
at other horses, but we loved her speed and high-stepping, her
general air of gallantry and abandon. On Saturdays we went
to the stable and as soon as we opened the door on its cosy,
animal-smelling darkness Fora threw up her head, rolled her eyes,
whinnied despairingly and pulled herself through a crisis of nerves
on the spot. It was not safe to go into her stall; she would kick.

This winter also I began to hear a great deal more on the
theme my mother had sounded when she had been talking in front
of the barn. I no longer felt safe. It seemed that in the minds of
the people around me there was a steady undercurrent of thought,
not to be deflected, on this one subject. The word *girl* had formerly
seemed to me innocent and unburdened, like the work *child*; now
it appeared that it was no such thing. A girl was not, as I had
supposed, simply what I was; it was what I had to become. It
was a definition, always touched with emphasis, with reproach
and disappointment. Also it was a joke on me. Once Laird and I
were fighting, and for the first time ever I had to use all my
strength against him; even so, he caught and pinned my arm for
a moment, really hurting me. Henry saw this, and laughed, saying,
"Oh, that there Laird's gonna show you, one of these days!" Laird
was getting a lot bigger. But I was getting bigger too.

My grandmother came to stay with us for a few weeks and
I heard other things. "Girls don't slam doors like that." "Girls
keep their knees together when they sit down." And worse still,
when I asked some questions, "That's none of girls' business." I
continued to slam the doors and sit as awkwardly as possible,
thinking that by such measures I kept myself free.

When spring came, the horses were let out in the barnyard.
Mack stood against the barn wall trying to scratch his neck and
haunches, but Flora trotted up and down and reared at the fences,
clattering her hooves against the rails. Snow drifts dwindled quickly,
revealing the hard gray and brown earth, the familiar rise and fall

cutter a small sleigh

of the ground, plain and bare after the fantastic landscape of winter. There was a great feeling of opening-out, of release. We just wore rubbers now, over our shoes; our feet felt ridiculously light. One Saturday we went to the stable and found all the doors open, letting in the unaccustomed sunlight and fresh air. Henry was there, just idling around looking at his collection of calendars which were tacked up behind the stalls in a part of the stable my mother had probably never seen.

"Come to say goodbye to your old friend Mack?" Henry said. "Here, you give him a taste of oats." He poured some oats into Laird's cupped hands and Laird went to feed Mack. Mack's teeth were in bad shape. He ate very slowly, patiently shifting the oats around in his mouth, trying to find a stump of a molar to grind it on. "Poor old Mack," said Henry mournfully. "When a horse's teeth's gone, he's gone. That's about the way."

"Are you going to shoot him today?" I said. Mack and Flora had been in the stable so long I had almost forgotten they were going to be shot.

Henry didn't answer me. Instead he started to sing in a high, trembly, mocking-sorrowful voice. *Oh, there's no more work, for poor Uncle Ned, he's gone where the good darkies go.* Mack's thick, blackish tongue worked diligently at Laird's hand. I went out before the song was ended and sat down on the gangway.

I had never seen them shoot a horse, but I knew where it was done. Last summer Laird and I had come upon a horse's entrails before they were buried. We had thought it was a big black snake, coiled up in the sun. That was around in the field that ran up beside the barn. I thought that if we went inside the barn, and found a wide crack or a knothole to look through, we would be able to see them do it. It was not something I wanted to see; just the same, if a thing really happened, it was better to see, and know.

My father came down from the house, carrying the gun.

"What are you doing here?" he said.

"Nothing."

'Go on up and play around the house."

He sent Laird out of the stable. I said to Laird, "Do you want to see them shoot Mack?" and without waiting for an answer led him around to the front door of the barn, opened it carefully, and went in. "Be quiet or they'll hear us," I said. We could hear Henry and my father talking in the stable; then the heavy, shuffling steps of Mack being backed out of his stall.

In the loft it was cold and dark. Thin crisscrossed beams of sunlight fell through the cracks. The hay was low. It was a rolling country, hills and hollows, slipping under our feet. About four feet up was a beam going around the walls. We piled hay up in one corner and I boosted Laird up and hoisted myself. The beam was not very wide; we crept along it with our hands flat on the barn walls. There were plenty of knotholes, and I found one that gave me the view I wanted — a corner of the barnyard, the gate, part of the field. Laird did not have a knothole and began to complain.

I showed him a widened crack between two boards. "Be quiet and wait. If they hear you you'll get us in trouble."

My father came in sight carrying the gun. Henry was leading Mack by the halter. He dropped it and took out his cigarette papers and tobacco; he rolled cigarettes for my father and himself. While this was going on Mack nosed around in the old, dead grass along the fence. Then my father opened the gate and they took Mack through. Henry led Mack away from the path to a patch of ground and they talked together, not loud enough for us to hear. Mack again began searching for a mouthful of fresh grass, which was not to be found. My father walked away in a straight line, and stopped short at a distance which seemed to suit him. Henry was walking away from Mack too, but sideways, still negligently holding on to the halter. My father raised the gun and Mack looked up as if he had noticed something and my father shot him.

Mack did not collapse at once but swayed, lurched sideways and fell, first on his side; then he rolled over on his back and, amazingly, kicked his legs for a few seconds in the air. At this Henry laughed, as if Mack had done a trick for him. Laird, who had drawn a long, groaning breath of surprise when the shot was fired, said out loud, "He's not dead." And it seemed to me it might be true. But his legs stopped, he rolled on his side again, his muscles quivered and sank. The two men walked over and looked at him in a businesslike way; they bent down and examined his forehead where the bullet had gone in, and now I saw his blood on the brown grass.

"Now they just skin him and cut him up," I said. "Let's go." My legs were a little shaky and I jumped gratefully down into the hay. "Now you've seen how they shoot a horse," I said in a congratulatory way, as if I had seen it many times before. "Let's see if any barn cat's had kittens in the hay." Laird jumped. He seemed young and obedient again. Suddenly I remembered how, when he was little, I had brought him into the barn and told him to climb the ladder to the top beam. That was in the spring, too, when the hay was low. I had done it out of a need for excitement, a desire for something to happen so that I could tell about it. He was wearing a little bulky brown and white checked coat, made down from one of mine. He went all the way up just as I told him, and sat down on the top beam with the hay far below him on one side, and the barn floor and some old machinery on the other. Then I ran screaming to my father, "Laird's up on the top beam!" My father came, my mother came, my father went up the ladder talking very quietly and brought Laird down under his arm, at which my mother leaned against the ladder and began to cry. They said to me, "Why weren't you watching him?" but nobody ever knew the truth. Laird did not know enough to tell. But whenever I saw the brown and white checked coat hanging in the closet, or at the bottom of the rag bag, which was where it ended up, I felt a weight in my stomach, the sadness of unexorcised guilt.

I looked at Laird, who did not even remember this, and I did not like the look on this thin, winter-pale face. His expression was not frightened or upset, but remote, concentrating. "Listen," I said, in an unusually bright and friendly voice, "you aren't going to tell, are you?"

"No," he said absently.

"Promise."

"Promise," he said. I grabbed the hand behind his back to make sure he was not crossing his fingers. Even so, he might have a nightmare; it might come out that way. I decided I had better work hard to get all thoughts of what he had seen out of his mind — which, it seemed to me, could not hold very many things at a time. I got some money I had saved and that afternoon we went into Jubilee and saw a show, with Judy Canova,* at which we both laughed a great deal. After that I thought it would be all right.

Two weeks later I knew they were going to shoot Flora. I knew from the night before, when I heard my mother ask if the hay was holding out all right, and my father said, "Well, after tomorrow there'll just be the cow, and we should be able to put her out to grass in another week." So I knew it was Flora's turn in the morning.

This time I didn't think of watching it. That was something to see just one time. I had not thought about it very often since, but sometimes when I was busy, working at school, or standing in front of the mirror combing my hair and wondering if I would be pretty when I grew up, the whole scene would flash into my mind: I would see the easy, practiced way my father raised the

* American comedian, popular in films of the 1940s.

gun, and hear Henry laughing when Mack kicked his legs in the air. I did not have any great feeling of horror and opposition, such as a city child might have had; I was too used to seeing the death of animals as a necessity by which we lived. Yet I felt a little ashamed, and there was a new wariness, a sense of holding-off, in my attitude to my father and his work.

It was a fine day, and we were going around the yard picking up tree branches that had been torn off in winter storms. This was something we had been told to do, and also we wanted to use them to make a teepee. We heard Flora whinny, and then my father's voice and Henry's shouting, and we ran down to the barnyard to see what was going on.

The stable door was open. Henry had just brought Flora out, and she had broken away from him. She was running free in the barnyard, from one end to the other. We climbed up on the fence. It was exciting to see her running, whinnying, going up on her hind legs, prancing and threatening like a horse in a Western movie, an unbroken ranch horse, though she was just an old driver, an old sorrel mare. My father and Henry ran after her and tried to grab the dangling halter. They tried to work her into a corner, and they had almost succeeded when she made a run between them, wild-eyed, and disappeared around the corner of the barn. We heard the rails clatter down as she got over the fence, and Henry yelled. "She's into the field now!"

That meant she was in the long L-shaped field that ran up by the house. If she got around the center, heading towards the lane, the gate was open; the truck had been driven into the field this morning. My father shouted to me, because I was on the other side of the fence, nearest the lane, "Go shut the gate!"

I could run very fast. I ran across the garden, past the tree where our swing was hung, and jumped across a ditch into the lane. There was the open gate. She had not got out, I could not see her up on the road; she must have run to the other end of the field. The gate was heavy. I lifted it out of the gravel and carried it across the roadway. I had it halfway across when she came in sight, galloping straight toward me. There was just time to get the chain on. Laird came scrambling through the ditch to help me.

Instead of shutting the gate, I opened it as wide as I could. I did not make any decision to do this, it was just what I did. Flora never slowed down; she galloped straight past me, and Laird jumping up and down, yelling, "Shut it, shut it!" even after it was too late. My father and Henry appeared in the field a moment too late to see what I had done. They only saw Flora heading for the township road. They would think I had not got there in time.

They did not waste any time asking about it. They went back to the barn and got the gun and the knives they used, and put these in the truck; then they turned the truck around and came bouncing up the field toward us. Laird called to them, "Let me go too, let me go too!" and Henry stopped the truck and they took him in. I shut the gate after they were all gone.

I supposed Laird would tell. I wondered what would happen to me. I had never disobeyed my father before, and I could not understand why I had done it. Flora would not really get away. They would catch up with her in the truck. Or if they did not catch her this morning somebody would see her and telephone us this afternoon or tomorrow. There was no wild country here for her to run to, only farms. What was more, my father had paid for her, we needed the meat to feed the foxes, we needed the foxes to make our living. All I had done was make more work for my father who worked hard enough already. And when my father found out about it he was not going to trust me any more; he would know that I was not entirely on his side. I was on Flora's side, and that made me no use to anybody, not even to her. Just the same, I did not regret it; when she came running at me and I held the gate open, that was the only thing I could do.

I went back to the house, and my mother said, "What's all the commotion?" I told her that Flora had kicked down the fence and got away. "Your poor father," she said, "now he'll have to go chasing over the countryside. Well, there isn't any use planning dinner before one." She put up the ironing board. I wanted to tell her, but thought better of it and went upstairs and sat on my bed.

Lately I had been trying to make my part of the room fancy, spreading the bed with old lace curtains, and fixing myself a dressing table with some leftovers of cretonne for a skirt. I planned to put up some kind of barricade between my bed and Laird's, to keep my section separate from his. In the sunlight, the lace curtains were just dusty rags. We did not sing at night any more. One night when I was singing Laird said, "You sound silly," and I went right on but the next night I did not start. There was not so much need to anyway, we were no longer afraid. We knew it was just old furniture over there, old jumble and confusion. We did not keep to the rules. I still stayed awake after Laird was asleep and told myself stories, but even in these stories something different was happening, mysterious alterations took place. A story might start off in the old way, with a spectacular danger, a fire or wild animals, and for a while I might rescue people; then things would change around, and instead, somebody would be rescuing me. It might be a boy from our class at school, or even Mr. Campbell, our teacher, who tickled girls under the arms. And at this point the story concerned itself at great length with what I looked like — how long my hair was, and what kind of dress I had on; by the time I had these details worked out the real excitement of the story was lost.

It was later than one o'clock when the truck came back. The tarpaulin was over the back, which meant there was meat in it. My mother had to heat dinner up all over again. Henry and my father had changed from their bloody overalls into ordinary working overalls in the barn, and they washed their arms and necks and faces at the sink, and splashed water on their hair and combed it. Laird lifted his arm to show off a streak of blood. "We shot old Flora," he said, "and cut her up in fifty pieces."

"Well I don't want to hear about it," my mother said. "And don't come to my table like that."

My father made him go and wash the blood off.

We sat down and my father said grace and Henry pasted his chewing gum on the end of his fork, the way he always did; when he took it off he would have us admire the pattern. We began to pass the bowls of steaming, overcooked vegetables. Laird looked across the table at me and said proudly, distinctly, "Anyway it was her fault Flora got away."

"What?" my father said.

"She could of shut the gate and she didn't. She just open' it up and Flora run out."

"Is that right?" my father said.

Everybody at the table was looking at me. I nodded, swallowing food with great difficulty. To my shame, tears flooded my eyes.

My father made a curt sound of disgust. "What did you do that for?"

I did not answer. I put down my fork and waited to be sent from the table, still not looking up.

But this did not happen. For some time nobody said anything, then Laird said matter-of-factly, "She's crying."

"Never mind," my father said. He spoke with resignation, even good humor, the words which absolved and dismissed me for good. "She's only a girl," he said.

I didn't protest that, even in my heart. Maybe it was true.

John Updike (*American. b. 1932*)

A & P

In walks these three girls in nothing but bathing suits. I'm in the third checkout slot, with my back to the door, so I don't see them until they're over by the bread. The one that caught my eye first was the one in the plaid green two-piece. She was a chunky kid, with a good tan and a sweet broad soft-looking can with those two crescents of white just under it, where the sun never seems to hit, at the top of the backs of her legs. I stood there with my hand on a box of HiHo crackers trying to remember if I rang it up or not. I ring it up again and the customer starts giving me hell. She's one of these cash-register-watchers, a witch about fifty with rouge on her cheekbones and no eyebrows, and I know it made her day to trip me up. She'd been watching cash registers for fifty years and probably never seen a mistake before.

By the time I got her feathers smoothed and her goodies into a bag — she gives me a little snort in passing, if she'd been born at the right time they would have burned her over in Salem — by the time I get her on her way the girls had circled around the bread and were coming back, without a pushcart, back my way along the counters, in the aisle between the checkouts and the Special bins. They didn't even have shoes on. There was this chunky one, with the two-piece — it was bright green and the seams on the bra were still sharp and her belly was still pretty pale so I guessed she just got it (the suit) — there was this one, with one of those chubby berry-faces, the lips all bunched together under her nose, this one, and a tall one, with black hair that hadn't quite frizzed right, and one of these sunburns right across under the eyes, and a chin that was too long — you know, the kind of girl other girls think is very "striking" and "attractive" but never quite makes it, as they very well know, which is why they like her so much — and then the third one, that wasn't quite so tall. She was the queen. She kind of led them, the other two peeking around and making their shoulders round. She didn't look around, not this queen, she just walked straight on slowly, on these long white prima-donna legs. She came down a little hard on her heels, as if she didn't walk in her bare feet that much, putting down her heels and then letting the weight move along to her toes as if she was testing the floor with every step, putting a little deliberate extra action into it. You never know for sure how girls' minds work (do you really think it's a mind in there or just a little buzz like a bee in a glass jar?) but you got the idea she had talked the other two into coming in here with her, and now she was showing them how to do it, walk slow and hold yourself straight.

She had on a kind of dirty-pink — beige maybe, I don't know — bathing suit with a little nubble all over it and, what got me, the straps were down. They were off her shoulders looped loose around the cool tops of her arms, and I guess as a result the suit had slipped a little on her, so all around the top of the cloth there was this shining rim. If it hadn't been there you wouldn't have known there could have been anything whiter than those shoulders. With the straps pushed off, there was nothing between the top of the suit and the top of her head except just *her,* this clean bare plane of the top of her chest down from the shoulder bones like a dented sheet of metal tilted in the light. I mean, it was more than pretty.

She had sort of oaky hair that the sun and salt had bleached, done up in a bun that was unravelling, and a kind of prim face. Walking into the A & P with your straps down, I suppose it's the only kind of face you *can* have. She held her head so high her neck, coming up out of those white shoulders, looked kind of stretched, but I didn't mind. The longer her neck was, the more of her there was.

She must have felt in the corner of her eye me and over my shoulder Stokesie in the second slot watching, but she didn't tip. Not this queen. She kept her eyes moving across the racks, and stopped, and turned so slow it made my stomach rub the inside of my apron, and buzzed to the other two, who kind of huddled against her for relief, and then they all three of them went up the cat and dog food-breakfast cereal-macaroni-rice-raisins-seasonings-spreads-spaghetti-soft drinks-crackers-and-cookies aisle. From the third slot I look straight up this aisle to the meat counter, and I watched them all the way. The fat one with the tan sort of fumbled with the cookies, but on second thought she put the package back. The sheep pushing their carts down the aisle — the girls were walking against the usual traffic (not that we have one-way signs or anything) — were pretty hilarious. You could see them, when Queenie's white shoulders dawned on them, kind of jerk, or hop, or hiccup, but their eyes snapped back to their own baskets and on they pushed. I bet you could set off dynamite in an A & P and the people would by and large keep reaching and checking oatmeal off their lists and muttering "Let me see, there was a third thing, began with A, asparagus, no, ah, yes, applesauce!" or whatever it is they do mutter. But there was no doubt, this jiggled them. A few house slaves in pin curlers even look around after pushing their carts past to make sure what they had seen was correct.

You know, it's one thing to have a girl in a bathing suit down on the beach, where what with the glare nobody can look at each other much anyway, and another thing in the cool of the A & P, under the fluorescent lights, against all those stacked packages, with her feet paddling along naked over our checker-board green-and-cream rubber-tile floor.

"Oh, Daddy," Stokesie said beside me. "I feel so faint."

"Darling," I said. "Hold me tight." Stokesie's married, with two babies chalked up on his fuselage already, but as far as I can tell that's the only difference. He's twenty-two, and I was nineteen this April.

"Is it done?" he asks, the responsible married man finding his voice. I forgot to say he thinks he's going to be manager some sunny day, maybe in 1990 when it's called the Great Alexandrov and Petrooshki Tea Company or something.

What he meant was, our town is five miles from a beach, with a big summer colony out on the Point, but we're right in the middle of town, and the women generally put on a shirt or shorts or something before they get out of the car into the street. And anyway these are usually women with six children and varicose veins mapping their legs and nobody, including them, could care less. As I say, we're right in the middle of town, and if you stand at our front doors you can see two banks and the Congregational church and the newspaper store and three real estate offices and about twenty-seven old freeloaders tearing up Central Street because the sewer broke again. It's not as if we're on the Cape; we're north of Boston and there's people in this town haven't seen the ocean for twenty years.

The girls had reached the meat counter and were asking McMahon something. He pointed, they pointed, and they shuffled out of sight behind a pyramid of Diet Delight peaches. All that was left for us to see was old McMahon patting his mouth and looking after them sizing up their joints. Poor kids, I began to feel sorry for them, they couldn't help it.

Now here comes the sad part of the story, at least my family says it's sad, but I don't think it's so sad myself. The store's pretty empty, it being Thursday afternoon, so there was nothing much to do except lean on the register and wait for the girls to show up again. The whole store was like a pinball machine and I didn't know which tunnel they'd come out of. After a while they come around out of the far aisle, around the light bulbs, records at discount of the Caribbean Six or Tony Martin Sings or some such gunk you wonder they waste the wax on, sixpacks of candy bars, and plastic toys done up in cellophane that fall apart when a kid looks at them anyway. Around they come, Queenie still leading

the way, and holding a little gray jar in her hand. Slots Three
through Seven are unmanned and I could see her wondering between
Stokes and me, but Stokesie with his usual luck draws an old
party in baggy gray pants who stumbles up with four giant cans
of pineapple juice (what do these bums *do* with all that pineapple
juice? I've often asked myself) so the girls come to me. Queenie
puts down the jar and I take it into my fingers icy cold. Kingfish
Fancy Herring Snacks in Pure Sour Cream: 49¢. Now her hands
are empty, not a ring or a bracelet, bare as God made them, and
I wonder where the money's coming from. Still with that prim
look she lifts a folded dollar bill out of the hollow at the center
of her nubbled pink top. The jar went heavy in my hand. Really,
I thought that was so cute.

Then everybody's luck begins to run out. Lengel comes in
from haggling with a truck full of cabbages on the lot and is about
to scuttle into the door marked MANAGER behind which he hides
all day when the girls touch his eye. Lengel's pretty dreary, teaches
Sunday school and the rest, but he doesn't miss that much. He
comes over and says, "Girls, this isn't the beach."

Queenie blushes, though maybe it's just a brush of sunburn
I was noticing for the first time, now that she was so close. "My
mother asked me to pick up a jar of herring snacks." Her voice
kind of startled me, the way voices do when you see the people
first, coming out so flat and dumb yet kind of tony, too, the way
it ticked over "pick up" and "snacks." All of a sudden I slid right
down her voice into her living room. Her father and the other
men were standing around in ice-cream coats and bow ties and
the women were in sandals picking up herring snacks on toothpicks
off a big glass plate and they were all holding drinks the color of
water with olives and sprigs of mint in them. When my parents
have somebody over they get lemonade and if it's a real racy affair
Schlitz in tall glasses with "They'll Do It Every Time" cartoons
stencilled on.

"That's all right," Lengel said. "But this isn't the beach."
His repeating this struck me as funny, as if it had just occurred
to him, and he had been thinking all these years the A & P was
a great big dune and he was the head lifeguard. He didn't like my
smiling — as I say he doesn't miss much — but he concentrates
on giving the girls that sad Sunday-school-superintendent stare.

Queenie's blush is no sunburn now, and the plump one in
plaid, that I liked better from the back — a really sweet can —
pipes up, "We weren't doing any shopping. We just came in for
the one thing."

"That makes no difference," Lengel tells her, and I could

see from the way his eyes went that he hadn't noticed she was wearing a two-piece before. "We want you decently dressed when you come in here."

"We *are* decent," Queenie says suddenly, her lower lip pushing, getting sore now that she remembers her place, a place from which the crowd that runs the A & P must look pretty crummy. Fancy Herring Snacks flashed in her very blue eyes.

"Girls, I don't want to argue with you. After this come in here with your shoulders covered. It's our policy." He turns his back. That's policy for you. Policy is what the kingpins want. What the others want is juvenile delinquency.

All this while, the customers had been showing up with their carts but, you know, sheep, seeing a scene, they had all bunched up on Stokesie, who shook open a paper bag as gently as peeling a peach, not wanting to miss a word. I could feel in the silence everybody getting nervous, most of all Lengel, who asks me, "Sammy, have you rung up this purchase?"

I thought and said "No" but it wasn't about that I was thinking. I go through the punches, 4, 9, GROC, TOT — it's more complicated than you think and after you do it often enough, it begins to make a little song, that you hear words to, in my case "Hello (*bing*) there, you (*gung*) hap-py *pee*pul (*splat*)!" — the *splat* being the drawer flying out. I uncrease the bill, tenderly as you may imagine, it just having come from between the two smoothest scoops of vanilla I had ever known were there, and pass a half and a penny into her narrow pink palm, and nestle the herrings in a bag and twist its neck and hand it over, all the time thinking.

The girls, and who'd blame them, are in a hurry to get out, so I say "I quit" to Lengel quick enough for them to hear, hoping they'll stop and watch me, their unsuspected hero. They keep right on going, into the electric eye; the door flies open and they flicker across the lot to their car, Queenie and Plaid and Big Tall Goony-Goony (not that as raw material she was so bad), leaving me with Lengel and a kink in his eyebrow.

"Did you say something, Sammy?"

"I said I quit."

"I thought you did."

"You didn't have to embarrass them."

"It was they who were embarrassing us."

I started to say something that came out "Fiddle-de-doo." It's a saying of my grandmother's, and I know she would have been pleased.

"I don't think you know what you're saying," Lengel said.

"I know you don't," I said. "But I do." I pull the bow at

the back of my apron and start shrugging it off my shoulders. A couple customers that had been heading for my slot begin to knock against each other, like scared pigs in a chute.

Lengel sighs and begins to look very patient and old and gray. He's been a friend of my parents for years. "Sammy, you don't want to do this to your Mom and Dad," he tells me. It's true, I don't. But it seems to me that once you begin a gesture it's fatal not to go through with it. I fold the apron, "Sammy" stitched in red on the pocket, and put it on the counter, and drop the bow tie on top of it. The bow tie is theirs, if you've ever wondered. "You'll feel this for the rest of your life," Lengel says, and I know that's true, too, but remembering how he made that pretty girl blush makes me so scrunchy inside I punch the No Sale tab and the machine whirs "pee-pul" and the drawer splats out. One advantage to this scene taking place in summer, I can follow this up with a clean exit, there's no fumbling around getting your coat and galoshes, I just saunter into the electric eye in my white shirt that my mother ironed the night before, and the door heaves itself open, and outside the sunshine is skating around on the asphalt.

I look around for my girls, but they're gone, of course. There wasn't anybody but some young married screaming with her children about some candy they didn't get by the door of a powder-blue Falcon station wagon. Looking back in the big windows, over the bags of peat moss and aluminum lawn furniture stacked on the pavement, I could see Lengel in my place in the slot, checking the sheep through. His face was dark gray and his back stiff, as if he'd just had an injection of iron, and my stomach kind of fell as I felt how hard the world was going to be to me hereafter.

Joyce Carol Oates (*American. b. 1938*)

Where Are You Going, Where Have You Been?

To Bob Dylan

Her name was Connie. She was fifteen and she had a quick nervous giggling habit of craning her neck to glance into mirrors or checking other people's faces to make sure her own was all right. Her mother, who noticed everything and knew everything and who hadn't much reason any longer to look at her own face, always scolded Connie about it. "Stop gawking at yourself, who are you? You think you're so pretty?" she would say. Connie would raise her eyebrows at these familiar complaints and look right through her mother, into a shadowy vision of herself as she was right at that moment: she knew she was pretty and that was everything. Her mother had been pretty once too, if you could believe those old snapshots in the album, but now her looks were gone and that was why she was always after Connie.

"Why don't you keep your room clean like your sister? How've you got your hair fixed — what the hell stinks? Hair spray? You don't see your sister using that junk."

Her sister June was twenty-four and still lived at home. She was a secretary in the high school Connie attended, and if that wasn't bad enough — with her in the same building — she was so plain and chunky and steady that Connie had to hear her praised all the time by her mother and her mother's sisters. June did this, June did that, she saved money and helped clean the house and cooked and Connie couldn't do a thing, her mind was all filled with trashy daydreams. Their father was away at work most of the time and when he came home he wanted supper and he read the newspaper at supper and after supper he went to bed. He didn't bother talking much to them, but around his bent head Connie's mother kept picking at her until Connie wished her mother were dead and she herself were dead and it were all over. "She makes me want to throw up sometimes," she complained to her friends. She had a high, breathless, amused voice which made everything she said sound a little forced, whether it was sincere or not.

There was one good thing: June went places with girlfriends of hers, girls who were just as plain and steady as she, and so when Connie wanted to do that her mother had no objections. The father of Connie's best girlfriend drove the girls the three miles to town and left them off at a shopping plaza, so that they could walk through the stores or go to a movie, and when he came to pick them up again at eleven he never bothered to ask what they had done.

They must have been familiar sights, walking around that shopping plaza in their shorts and flat ballerina slippers that always scuffed the sidewalk, with charm bracelets jingling on their thin wrists; they would lean together to whisper and laugh secretly if someone passed by who amused or interested them. Connie had long dark blond hair that drew anyone's eye to it, and she wore part of it pulled up on her head and puffed out and the rest of it she let fall down her back. She wore a pullover jersey blouse that looked one way when she was at home and another way when she was away from home. Everything about her had two sides to it, one for home and one for anywhere that was not home: her walk that could be childlike and bobbing, or languid enough to make anyone think she was hearing music in her head, her mouth which was pale and smirking most of the time, but bright and pink on these evenings out, her laugh which was cynical and drawling at home — "Ha, ha, very funny" — but high-pitched and nervous anywhere else, like the jingling of the charms on her bracelet.

Sometimes they did go shopping or to a movie, but sometimes they went across the highway, ducking fast across the busy road, to a drive-in restaurant where older kids hung out. The restaurant was shaped like a big bottle, though squatter than a real bottle, and on its cap was a revolving figure of a grinning boy who held a hamburger aloft. One night in midsummer they ran across, breathless with daring, and right away someone leaned out a car window and invited them over, but it was just a boy from high school they didn't like. It made them feel good to be able to ignore him. They went up through the maze of parked and cruising cars to the bright-lit, fly-infested restaurant, their faces pleased and expectant as if they were entering a sacred building that loomed out of the night to give them what haven and what blessing they yearned for. They sat at the counter and crossed their legs at the ankles, their thin shoulders rigid with excitement, and listened to the music that made everything so good: the music was always in the background like music at a church service, it was something to depend upon.

A boy named Eddie came in to talk with them. He sat backward on his stool, turning himself jerkily around in semicircles and then stopping and turning again, and after a while he asked Connie if she would like something to eat. She said she did and so she tapped her friend's arm on her way out — her friend pulled her face up into a brave droll look — and Connie said she would meet her at eleven, across the way. "I just hate to leave her like that," Connie said earnestly, but the boy said that she wouldn't be alone for long. So they went out to his car and on the way Connie couldn't help but let her eyes wander over the windshields and faces all around her, her face gleaming with a joy that had nothing to do with Eddie or even this place; it might have been the music. She drew her shoulders up and sucked in her breath with the pure pleasure of being alive, and just at that moment she happened to glance at a face just a few feet from hers. It was a boy with shaggy black hair, in a convertible jalopy painted gold. He stared at her and then his lips widened into a grin. Connie slit her eyes at him and turned away, but she couldn't help glancing back and there he was still watching her. He wagged a finger and laughed and said, "Gonna get you, baby," and Connie turned away again without Eddie noticing anything.

She spent three hours with him, at the restaurant where they ate hamburgers and drank Cokes in wax cups that were always sweating, and then down an alley a mile or so away, and when he left her off at five to eleven only the movie house was still open at the plaza. Her girlfriend was there, talking with a boy. When Connie came up the two girls smiled at each other and Connie said, "How was the movie?" and the girl said, "*You* should know." They rode off with the girl's father, sleepy and pleased, and Connie couldn't help but look at the darkened shopping plaza with its big empty parking lot and its signs that were faded and ghostly now, and over at the drive-in restaurant where cars were still circling tirelessly. She couldn't hear the music at this distance.

Next morning June asked her how the movie was and Connie said, "So-so."

She and that girl and occasionally another girl went out several times a week that way, and the rest of the time Connie spent around the house — it was summer vacation — getting in her mother's way and thinking, dreaming, about the boys she met. But all the boys fell back and dissolved into a single face that was not even a face, but an idea, a feeling, mixed up with the urgent insistent pounding of the music and the humid night air of July. Connie's mother kept dragging her back to the daylight by finding things for her to do or saying, suddenly, "What's this about the Pettinger girl?"

And Connie would say nervously, "Oh, her. That dope." She always drew thick clear lines between herself and such girls, and her mother was simple and kindly enough to believe her. Her mother was so simple, Connie thought, that it was maybe cruel to fool her so much. Her mother went scuffling around the house in old bedroom slippers and complained over the telephone to one sister about the other, then the other called up and the two of them complained about the third one. If June's name was mentioned her mother's tone was approving, and if Connie's name was mentioned it was disapproving. This did not really mean she disliked Connie and actually Connie thought that her mother preferred her to June because she was prettier, but the two of them kept up a pretense of exasperation, a sense that they were tugging and struggling over something of little value to either of them. Sometimes, over coffee, they were almost friends, but something would come up — some vexation that was like a fly buzzing suddenly around their heads — and their faces went hard with contempt.

One Sunday Connie got up at eleven — none of them bothered with church — and washed her hair so that it could dry all day long, in the sun. Her parents and sister were going to a barbecue at an aunt's house and Connie said no, she wasn't interested, rolling her eyes to let her mother know just what she thought of it. "Stay home alone then," her mother said sharply. Connie sat out back in a lawn chair and watched them drive away, her father quiet and bald, hunched around so that he could back the car out, her mother with a look that was still angry and not at all softened through the windshield, and in the back seat poor old June all dressed up as if she didn't know what a barbecue was, with all the running yelling kids and the flies. Connie sat with her eyes closed in the sun, dreaming and dazed with the warmth about her as if this were a kind of love, the caresses of love, and her mind slipped over onto thoughts of the boy she had been with the night before and how nice he had been, how sweet it always was, not the way someone like June would suppose but sweet, gentle, the way it was in movies and promised in songs; and when she opened her eyes she hardly knew where she was, the back yard ran off into weeds and a fence line of trees and behind it the sky was perfectly blue and still. The asbestos "ranch house" that was now three years old startled her — it looked small. She shook her head as if to get awake.

It was too hot. She went inside the house and turned on the radio to drown out the quiet. She sat on the edge of her bed, barefoot, and listened for an hour and a half to a program called XYZ Sunday Jamboree, record after record of hard, fast, shrieking songs she sang along with, interspersed by exclamations from "Bobby King": "An' look here you girls at Napoleon's — Son and Charley want you to pay real close attention to this song coming up!"

And Connie paid close attention herself, bathed in a glow of slow-pulsed joy that seemed to rise mysteriously out of the music itself and lay languidly about the airless little room, breathed in and breathed out with each gentle rise and fall of her chest.

After a while she heard a car coming up the drive. She sat up at once, startled, because it couldn't be her father so soon. The gravel kept crunching all the way in from the road — the driveway was long — and Connie ran to the window. It was a car she didn't know. It was an open jalopy, painted a bright gold that caught the sunlight opaquely. Her heart began to pound and her fingers snatched at her hair, checking it, and she whispered "Christ, Christ," wondering how bad she looked. The car came to a stop at the side door and the horn sounded four short taps as if this were a signal Connie knew.

She went into the kitchen and approached the door slowly, then hung out the screen door, her bare toes curling down off the step. There were two boys in the car and now she recognized the driver: he had shaggy, shabby black hair that looked crazy as a wig and he was grinning at her.

"I ain't late, am I?" he said.

"Who the hell do you think you are?" Connie said.

"Toldja I'd be out, didn't I?"

"I don't even know who you are."

She spoke sullenly, careful to show no interest or pleasure, and he spoke in a fast bright monotone. Connie looked past him to the other boy, taking her time. He had fair brown hair, with a lock that fell onto his forehead. His sideburns gave him a fierce, embarrassed look, but so far he hadn't even bothered to glance at her. Both boys wore sunglasses. The driver's glasses were metallic and mirrored everything in miniature.

"You wanta come for a ride?" he said.

Connie smirked and let her hair fall loose over one shoulder.

"Don'tcha like my car? New paint job," he said. "Hey."

"What?"

"You're cute."

She pretended to fidget, chasing flies away from the door.

"Don'tcha believe me, or what?" he said.

"Look, I don't even know who you are," Connie said in disgust.

"Hey, Ellie's got a radio, see. Mine's broke down." He lifted his friend's arm and showed her the little transistor the boy was holding, and now Connie began to hear the music. It was the same program that was playing inside the house.

"Bobby King?" she said.

"I listen to him all the time. I think he's great."

"He's kind of great," Connie said reluctantly.

"Listen, that guy's *great*. He knows where the action is."

Connie blushed a little, because the glasses made it impossible for her to see just what this boy was looking at. She couldn't decide if she liked him or if he was just a jerk, and so she dawdled in the doorway and wouldn't come down or go back inside. She said, "What's all that stuff painted on your car?"

"Can'tcha read it?" He opened the door very carefully, as if he was afraid it might fall off. He slid out just as carefully,

planting his feet firmly on the ground, the tiny metallic world in
his glasses slowing down like gelatine hardening and in the midst
of it Connie's bright green blouse. "This here is my name, to
begin with," he said. ARNOLD FRIEND was written in tarlike black
letters on the side, with a drawing of a round grinning face that
reminded Connie of a pumpkin, except it wore sunglasses. "I
wanta introduce myself, I'm Arnold Friend and that's my real
name and I'm gonna be your friend, honey, and inside the car's
Ellie Oscar, he's kinda shy." Ellie brought his transistor radio up
to his shoulder and balanced it there. "Now these numbers are a
secret code, honey," Arnold Friend explained. He read off the
numbers 33, 19, 17 and raised his eyebrows at her to see what
she thought of that, but she didn't think much of it. The left rear
fender had been smashed and around it was written, on the gleaming
gold background: DONE BY CRAZY WOMAN DRIVER. Connie had to
laugh at that. Arnold Friend was pleased at her laughter and looked
up at her. "Around the other side's a lot more — you wanta come
and see them?"

"No."

"Why not?"

"Why should I?"

"Don'tcha wanta see what's on the car? Don'tcha wanta go
for a ride?"

"I don't know."

"Why not?"

"I got things to do."

"Like what?"

"Things."

He laughed as if she had said something funny. He slapped
his thighs. He was standing in a strange way, leaning back against
the car as if he were balancing himself. He wasn't tall, only an
inch or so taller than she would be if she came down to him.
Connie liked the way he was dressed, which was the way all of
them dressed: tight faded jeans stuffed into black, scuffed boots,
a belt that pulled his waist in and showed how lean he was, and
a white pullover shirt that was a little soiled and showed the hard
small muscles of his arms and shoulders. He looked as if he probably
did hard work, lifting and carrying things. Even his neck looked
muscular. And his face was a familiar face, somehow: the jaw and
chin and cheeks slightly darkened, because he hadn't shaved for
a day or two, and the nose long and hawklike, sniffing as if she
were a treat he was going to gobble up and it was all a joke.

"Connie, you ain't telling the truth. This is your day set
aside for a ride with me and you know it," he said, still laughing.

The way he straightened and recovered from his fit of laughing showed that it had been all fake.

"How do you know what my name is?" she said suspiciously.

"It's Connie."

"Maybe and maybe not."

"I know my Connie," he said, wagging his finger. Now she remembered him even better, back at the restaurant, and her cheeks warmed at the thought of how she sucked in her breath just at the moment she passed him — how she must have looked at him. And he had remembered her. "Ellie and I come out here especially for you," he said. "Ellie can sit in back. How about it?"

"Where?"

"Where what?"

"Where're we going?"

He looked at her. He took off the sunglasses and she saw how pale the skin around his eyes was, like holes that were not in shadow but instead in light. His eyes were like chips of broken glass that catch the light in an amiable way. He smiled. It was as if the idea of going for a ride somewhere, to some place, was a new idea to him.

"Just for a ride, Connie sweetheart."

"I never said my name was Connie," she said.

"But I know what it is. I know your name and all about you, lots of things," Arnold Friend said. He had not moved yet but stood still leaning back against the side of his jalopy. "I took a special interest in you, such a pretty girl, and found out all about you like I know your parents and sister are gone somewheres and I know where and how long they're going to be gone, and I know who you were with last night, and your best girlfriend's name is Betty. Right?"

He spoke in a simple lilting voice, exactly as if he were reciting the words to a song. His smile assured her that everything was fine. In the car Ellie turned up the volume on his radio and did not bother to look around at them.

"Ellie can sit in the back seat," Arnold Friend said. He indicated his friend with a casual jerk of his chin, as if Ellie did not count and she should not bother with him.

"How'd you find out all that stuff?" Connie said.

"Listen: Betty Schultz and Tony Fitch and Jimmy Pettinger and Nancy Pettinger," he said, in a chant. "Raymond Stanley and Bob Hutter — "

"Do you know all those kids?"

"I know everybody."

"Look, you're kidding. You're not from around here."

"Sure."

"But — how come we never saw you before?"

"Sure you saw me before," he said. He looked down at his boots, as if he were a little offended. "You just don't remember."

"I guess I'd remember you," Connie said.

"Yeah?" He looked up at this, beaming. He was pleased. He began to mark time with the music from Ellie's radio, tapping his fists lightly together. Connie looked away from his smile to the car, which was painted so bright it almost hurt her eyes to look at it. She looked at that name. ARNOLD FRIEND. And up at the front fender was an expression that was familiar — MAN THE FLYING SAUCERS. It was an expression kids had used the year before, but didn't use this year. She looked at it for a while as if the words meant something to her that she did not yet know.

"What're you thinking about? Huh?" Arnold Friend demanded. "Not worried about your hair blowing around in the car, are you?"

"No."

"Think I maybe can't drive good?"

"How do I know?"

"You're a hard girl to handle. How come?" he said. "Don't you know I'm your friend? Didn't you see me put my sign in the air when you walked by?"

"What sign?"

"My sign." And he drew an X in the air, leaning out toward her. They were maybe ten feet apart. After his hand fell back to his side the X was still in the air, almost visible. Connie let the screen door close and stood perfectly still inside it, listening to the music from her radio and the boy's blend together. She stared at Arnold Friend. He stood there so stiffly relaxed, pretending to be relaxed, with one hand idly on the door handle as if he were keeping himself up that way and had no intention of ever moving again. She recognized most things about him, the tight jeans that showed his thighs and buttocks and the greasy leather boots and the tight shirt, and even that slippery friendly smile of his, that sleepy dreamy smile that all the boys used to get across ideas they didn't want to put into words. She recognized all this and also the singsong way he talked, slightly mocking, kidding, but serious and a little melancholy, and she recognized the way he tapped one fist against the other in homage of the perpetual music behind him. But all these things did not come together.

She said suddenly, "Hey, how old are you?"

His smile faded. She could see then that he wasn't a kid, he was much older — thirty, maybe more. At this knowledge her heart began to pound faster.

"That's a crazy thing to ask. Can'tcha see I'm your own age?"

"Like hell you are."

"Or maybe a coupla years older, I'm eighteen."

"Eighteen?" she said doubtfully.

He grinned to reassure her and lines appeared at the corners of his mouth. His teeth were big and white. He grinned so broadly his eyes became slits and she saw how thick the lashes were, thick and black as if painted with a black tarlike material. Then he seemed to become embarrassed, abruptly, and looked over his shoulder at Ellie. "*Him,* he's crazy," he said. "Ain't he a riot, he's a nut, a real character." Ellie was still listening to the music. His sunglasses told nothing about what he was thinking. He wore a bright orange shirt unbuttoned halfway to show his chest, which was a pale, bluish chest and not muscular like Arnold Friend's. His shirt collar was turned up all around and the very tips of the collar pointed out past his chin as if they were protecting him. He was pressing the transistor radio up against his ear and sat there in a kind of daze, right in the sun.

"He's kinda strange," Connie said.

"Hey, she says you're kinda strange! Kinda strange!" Arnold Friend cried. He pounded on the car to get Ellie's attention. Ellie turned for the first time and Connie saw with shock that he wasn't a kid either — he had a fair, hairless face, cheeks reddened slightly as if the veins grew too close to the surface of his skin, the face of a forty-year-old baby. Connie felt a wave of dizziness rise in her at this sight and she stared at him as if waiting for something to change the shock of the moment, make it all right again. Ellie's lips kept shaping words, mumbling along with the words blasting in his ear.

"Maybe you two better go away," Connie said faintly.

"What? How come?" Arnold Friend cried. "We come out here to take you for a ride. It's Sunday." He had the voice of the man on the radio now. It was the same voice, Connie thought. "Don'tcha know it's Sunday all day and honey, no matter who you were with last night today you're with Arnold Friend and don't you forget it! — Maybe you better step out here," he said, and this last was in a different voice. It was a little flatter, as if the heat was finally getting to him.

"No. I got things to do."

"Hey."

"You two better leave."

"We ain't leaving until you come with us."

"Like hell I am —"

"Connie, don't fool around with me. I mean, I mean, don't fool *around*," he said, shaking his head. He laughed incredulously. He placed his sunglasses on top of his head, carefully, as if he were indeed wearing a wig, and brought the stems down behind his ears. Connie stared at him, another wave of dizziness and fear rising in her so that for a moment he wasn't even in focus but was just a blur, standing there against his gold car, and she had the idea that he had driven up the driveway all right but had come from nowhere before that and belonged nowhere and that everything about him and even about the music that was so familiar to her was only half real.

"If my father comes and sees you —"

"He ain't coming. He's at a barbecue."

"How do you know that?"

"Aunt Tillie's. Right now they're — uh — they're drinking. Sitting around," he said vaguely, squinting as if he were staring all the way to town and over to Aunt Tillie's back yard. Then the vision seemed to get clear and he nodded energetically. "Yeah. Sitting around. There's your sister in a blue dress, huh? And high heels, the poor sad bitch — nothing like you, sweetheart! And your mother's helping some fat woman with the corn, they're cleaning the corn — husking the corn —"

"What fat woman?" Connie cried.

"How do I know what fat woman, I don't know every goddam fat woman in the world!" Arnold laughed.

"Oh, that's Mrs. Hornby . . . Who invited her?" Connie said. She felt a little light-headed. Her breath was coming quickly.

"She's too fat. I don't like them fat. I like them the way you are, honey," he said, smiling sleepily at her. They stared at each other for a while, through the screen door. He said softly, "Now what you're going to do is this: you're going to come out that door. You're going to sit up front with me and Ellie's going to sit in the back, the hell with Ellie, right? This isn't Ellie's date. You're my date. I'm your lover, honey."

"What? You're crazy —"

"Yes, I'm your lover. You don't know what that is, but you will," he said. "I know that too. I know all about you. But look: it's real nice and you couldn't ask for nobody better than me, or more polite. I always keep my word. I'll tell you how it is, I'm always nice at first, the first time. I'll hold you so tight you won't think you have to try to get away or pretend anything because you'll know you can't. And I'll come inside you where it's all secret and you'll give in to me and you'll love me —"

"Shut up! You're crazy!" Connie said. She backed away from the door. She put her hands against her ears as if she'd heard something terrible, something not meant for her. "People don't talk like that, you're crazy," she muttered. Her heart was almost too big now for her chest and its pumping made sweat break out all over her. She looked out to see Arnold Friend pause and then take a step toward the porch lurching. He almost fell. But, like a clever drunken man, he managed to catch his balance. He wobbled in his high boots and grabbed hold of one of the porch posts.

"Honey?" he said. "You still listening?"

"Get the hell out of here!"

"Be nice, honey. Listen."

"I'm going to call the police —"

He wobbled again and out of the side of his mouth came a fast spat curse, an aside not meant for her to hear. But even this "Christ!" sounded forced. Then he began to smile again. She watched this smile come, awkward as if he were smiling from inside a mask. His whole face was a mask, she thought wildly, tanned down onto his throat but then running out as if he had plastered makeup on his face but had forgotten about his throat.

"Honey — ? Listen, here's how it is. I always tell the truth and I promise you this: I ain't coming in that house after you."

"You better not! I'm going to call the police if you — if you don't —"

"Honey," he said, talking right through her voice, "honey, I'm not coming in there but you are coming out here. You know why?"

She was panting. The kitchen looked like a place she had never seen before, some room she had run inside but which wasn't good enough, wasn't going to help her. The kitchen window had never had a curtain, after three years, and there were dishes in the sink for her to do — probably — and if you ran your hand across the table you'd probably feel something sticky there.

"You listening, honey? Hey?"

" — going to call the police — "

"Soon as you touch the phone I don't need to keep my promise and can come inside. You won't want that."

She rushed forward and tried to lock the door. Her fingers were shaking. "But why lock it," Arnold Friend said gently, talking right into her face. "It's just a screen door. It's just nothing."

One of his boots was at a strange angle, as if his foot wasn't in it. It pointed out to the left, bent at the ankle. "I mean, anybody can break through a screen door and glass and wood and iron or anything else if he needs to, anybody at all and specially Arnold Friend. If the place got lit up with a fire honey you'd come runnin' out into my arms, right into my arms an' safe at home — like you knew I was your lover and'd stopped fooling around. I don't mind a nice shy girl but I don't like no fooling around." Part of those words were spoken with a slight rhythmic lilt, and Connie somehow recognized them — the echo of a song from last year, about a girl rushing into her boyfriend's arms and coming home again —

Connie stood barefoot on the linoleum floor, staring at him. "What do you want?" she whispered.

"I want you," he said.

"What?"

"Seen you that night and thought, that's the one, yes sir. I never needed to look any more."

"But my father's coming back. He's coming to get me. I had to wash my hair first —" She spoke in a dry, rapid voice, hardly raising it for him to hear.

"No, your Daddy is not coming and yes, you had to wash your hair and you washed it for me. It's nice and shining and all for me, I thank you, sweetheart," he said, with a mock bow, but again he almost lost his balance. He had to bend and adjust his boots. Evidently his feet did not go all the way down; the boots must have been stuffed with something so that he would seem taller. Connie stared out at him and behind him Ellie in the car, who seemed to be looking off toward Connie's right into nothing. This Ellie said, pulling the words out of the air one after another as if he were just discovering them, "You want me to pull out the phone?"

"Shut your mouth and keep it shut," Arnold Friend said, his face red from bending over or maybe from embarrassment because Connie had seen his boots. "This ain't none of your business."

"What — what are you doing? What do you want?" Connie said. "If I call the police they'll get you, they'll arrest you —"

"Promise was not to come in unless you touch that phone, and I'll keep that promise," he said. He resumed his erect position and tried to force his shoulders back. He sounded like a hero in a movie, declaring something important. He spoke too loudly and it was as if he were speaking to someone behind Connie. "I ain't made plans for coming in that house where I don't belong but just for you to come out to me, the way you should. Don't you know who I am?"

"You're crazy," she whispered. She backed away from the door but did not want to go into another part of the house, as if this would give him permission to come through the door. "What do you . . . You're crazy, you . . ."

"Huh? What're you saying, honey?"

Her eyes darted everywhere in the kitchen. She could not remember what it was, this room.

"This is how it is, honey: you come out and we'll drive away, have a nice ride. But if you don't come out we're gonna wait till your people come home and then they're all going to get it."

"You want that telephone pulled out?" Ellie said. He held the radio away from his ear and grimaced, as if without the radio the air was too much for him.

"I toldja shut up, Ellie," Arnold Friend said, "you're deaf, get a hearing aid, right? Fix yourself up. This little girl's no trouble and's gonna be nice to me, so Ellie keep to yourself, this ain't your date — right? Don't hem in on me. Don't hog. Don't crush. Don't bird dog. Don't trail me," he said in a rapid meaningless voice, as if he were running through all the expressions he'd learned but was no longer sure which one of them was in style, then rushing on to new ones, making them up with his eyes closed, "Don't crawl under my fence, don't squeeze in my chipmunk hole, don't sniff my glue, suck my popsicle, keep your own greasy fingers on yourself!" He shaded his eyes and peered in at Connie, who was backed against the kitchen table. "Don't mind him honey he's just a creep. He's a dope. Right? I'm the boy for you and like I said you come out here nice like a lady and give me your hand, and nobody else gets hurt, I mean, your nice old bald-headed daddy and your mummy and your sister in her high heels. Because listen: why bring them in this?"

"Leave me alone," Connie whispered.

"Hey, you know that old woman down the road, the one with the chickens and stuff — you know her?"

"She's dead!"

"Dead? What? You know her?" Arnold Friend said.

"She's dead —"

"Don't you like her?"

"She's dead — she's — she isn't here any more —"

"But don't you like her, I mean, you got something against her? Some grudge or something?" Then his voice dipped as if he were conscious of a rudeness. He touched the sunglasses perched on top of his head as if to make sure they were still there. "Now you be a good girl."

"What are you going to do?"

"Just two things, or maybe three," Arnold Friend said. "But I promise it won't last long and you'll like me the way you get to like people you're close to. You will. It's all over for you here, so come on out. You don't want your people in any trouble, do you?"

She turned and bumped against a chair or something, hurting her leg, but she ran into the back room and picked up the telephone. Something roared in her ear, a tiny roaring, and she was so sick with fear that she could do nothing but listen to it — the telephone was clammy and very heavy and her fingers groped down to the dial but were too weak to touch it. She began to scream into the phone, into the roaring. She cried out, she cried for her mother, she felt her breath start jerking back and forth in her lungs as if it were something Arnold Friend were stabbing her with again and again with no tenderness. A noisy sorrowful wailing rose all about her and she was locked inside it the way she was locked inside this house.

After a while she could hear again. She was sitting on the floor with her wet back against the wall.

Arnold Friend was saying from the door, "That's a good girl. Put the phone back."

She kicked the phone away from her.

"No, honey. Pick it up. Put it back right."

She picked it up and put it back. The dial tone stopped.

"That's a good girl. Now you come outside."

She was hollow with what had been fear, but what was now just an emptiness. All that screaming had blasted it out of her. She sat, one leg cramped under her, and deep inside her brain was something like a pinpoint of light that kept going and would not let her relax. She thought, I'm not going to see my mother again. She thought, I'm not going to sleep in my bed again. Her bright green blouse was all wet.

Arnold Friend said, in a gentle-loud voice that was like a stage voice. "The place where you came from ain't there any more, and where you had in mind to go is canceled out. This place you are now — inside your daddy's house — is nothing but a cardboard box I can knock down any time. You know that and always did know it. You hear me?"

She thought, I have got to think. I have to know what to do.

"We'll go out to a nice field, out in the country here where it smells so nice and it's sunny," Arnold Friend said. "I'll have my arms tight around you so you won't need to try to get away and I'll show you what love is like, what it does. The hell with this house! It looks solid all right," he said. He ran a fingernail down the screen and the noise did not make Connie shiver, as it would have the day before. "Now put your hand on your heart, honey. Feel that? That feels solid too, but we know better, be nice to me, be sweet like you can because what else is there for a girl like you but to be sweet and pretty and give in? — and get away before her people come back?"

She felt her pounding heart. Her hand seemed to enclose it. She thought for the first time in her life that it was nothing that was hers, that belonged to her, but just a pounding, living thing inside this body that wasn't really hers either.

"You don't want them to get hurt," Arnold Friend went on. "Now get up, honey. Get up all by yourself."

She stood.

"Now turn this way. That's right. Come over here to me — Ellie, put that away, didn't I tell you? You dope. You miserable creepy dope," Arnold Friend said. His words were not angry but only part of an incantation. The incantation was kindly. "Now come out through the kitchen to me honey, and let's see a smile, try it, you're a brave sweet little girl and now they're eating corn and hot dogs cooked to bursting over an outdoor fire, and they don't know one thing about you and never did and honey you're better than them because not a one of them would have done this for you."

Connie felt the linoleum under her feet; it was cool. She brushed her hair back out of her eyes. Arnold Friend let go of the post tentatively and opened his arms for her, his elbows pointing in toward each other and his wrists limp, to show that this was an embarrassed embrace and a little mocking, he didn't want to make her self-conscious.

She put out her hand against the screen. She watched herself push the door slowly open as if she were safe back somewhere in the other doorway, watching this body and this head of long hair moving out into the sunlight where Arnold Friend waited.

"My sweet little blue-eyed girl," he said, in a half-sung sigh that had nothing to do with her brown eyes but was taken up just the same by the vast sunlit reaches of the land behind him and on all sides of him, so much land that Connie had never seen before and did not recognize except to know that she was going to it.

Raymond Carver (*American. 1938–1988*)

Cathedral

This blind man, an old friend of my wife's, he was on his way to spend the night. His wife had died. So he was visiting the dead wife's relatives in Connecticut. He called my wife from his in-laws'. Arrangements were made. He would come by train, a five-hour trip, and my wife would meet him at the station. She hadn't seen him since she worked for him one summer in Seattle ten years ago. But she and the blind man had kept in touch. They made tapes and mailed them back and forth. I wasn't enthusiastic about his visit. He was no one I knew. And his being blind bothered me. My idea of blindness came from the movies. In the movies, the blind moved slowly and never laughed. Sometimes they were led by seeing-eye dogs. A blind man in my house was not something I looked forward to.

That summer in Seattle she had needed a job. She didn't have any money. The man she was going to marry at the end of the summer was in officers' training school. He didn't have any money, either. But she was in love with the guy, and he was in love with her, etc. She'd seen something in the paper: HELP WANTED — *Reading to Blind Man,* and a telephone number. She phoned and went over, was hired on the spot. She'd worked with this blind man all summer. She read stuff to him, case studies, reports, that sort of thing. She helped him organize his little office in the county social-service department. They'd become good friends, my wife and the blind man. How do I know these things? She told me. And she told me something else. On her last day in the office, the blind man asked if he could touch her face. She agreed to this. She told me he touched his fingers to every part of her face, her nose — even her neck! She never forgot it. She even tried to write a poem about it. She was always trying to write a poem. She wrote a poem or two every year, usually after something really important had happened to her.

When we first started going out together, she showed me the poem. In the poem, she recalled his fingers and the way they had moved around over her face. In the poem, she talked about what she had felt at the time, about what went through her mind when the blind man touched her nose and lips. I can remember I didn't think much of the poem. Of course, I didn't tell her that. Maybe I just don't understand poetry. I admit it's not the first thing I reach for when I pick up something to read.

Anyway, this man who'd first enjoyed her favors, the officer-to-be, he'd been her childhood sweeheart. So okay. I'm saying that at the end of the summer she let the blind man run his hands over her face, said goodbye to him, married her childhood etc., who was now a commissioned officer, and she moved away from Seattle. But they'd kept in touch, she and the blind man. She made the first contact after a year or so. She called him up one night from an Air Force base in Alabama. She wanted to talk. They talked. He asked her to send him a tape and tell him about her life. She did this. She sent the tape. On the tape, she told the blind man about her husband and about their life together in the military. She told the blind man she loved her husband but she didn't like it where they lived and she didn't like it that he was a part of the military-industrial thing. She told the blind man she'd written a poem and he was in it. She told him that she was writing a poem about what it was like to be an Air Force officer's wife. The poem wasn't finished yet. She was still writing it. The blind man made a tape. He sent her the tape. She made a tape. This went on for years. My wife's officer was posted to one base and then another. She sent tapes from Moody AFB, McGuire, McConnell, and finally Travis, near Sacramento, where one night she got to feeling lonely and cut off from people she kept losing in that moving-around life. She got to feeling she couldn't go it another step. She went in and swallowed all the pills and capsules in the medicine chest and washed them down with a bottle of gin. Then she got into a hot bath and passed out.

But instead of dying, she got sick. She threw up. Her officer — why should he have a name? he was the childhood sweetheart, and what more does he want? — came home from somewhere, found her, and called the ambulance. In time, she put it all on a tape and sent the tape to the blind man. Over the years, she put all kinds of stuff on tapes and sent the tapes off lickety-split. Next to writing a poem every year, I think it was her chief means of recreation. On one tape, she told the blind man she'd decided to live away from her officer for a time. On another tape, she told him about her divorce. She and I began going out, and of course she told her blind man about it. She told him everything, or so it seemed to me. Once she asked me if I'd like to hear the latest tape from the blind man. This was a year ago. I was on the tape, she said. So I said okay, I'd listen to it. I got us drinks and we settled down in the living room. We made ready to listen. First she inserted the tape into the player and adjusted a couple of dials. Then she pushed a lever. The tape squeaked and someone began to talk in this loud voice. She lowered the volume. After a few minutes of harmless chitchat, I heard my own name in the mouth of this stranger, this blind man I didn't even know! And then this: "From all you've said about him, I can only conclude — " But we were interrupted, a knock at the door, something, and we didn't ever get back to the tape. Maybe it was just as well. I'd heard all I wanted to.

Now this same blind man was coming to sleep in my house.

"Maybe I could take him bowling," I said to my wife. She was at the draining board doing scalloped potatoes. She put down the knife she was using and turned around.

"If you love me," she said, "you can do this for me. If you don't love me, okay. But if you had a friend, any friend, and the friend came to visit, I'd make him feel comfortable." She wiped her hands with the dish towel.

"I don't have any blind friends," I said.

"You don't have *any* friends," she said. "Period. Besides," she said, "goddamn it, his wife's just died! Don't you understand that? The man's lost his wife!"

I didn't answer. She'd told me a little about the blind man's wife. Her name was Beulah. Beulah! That's a name for a colored woman.

"Was his wife a Negro?" I asked.

"Are you crazy?" my wife said. "Have you just flipped or something?" She picked up a potato. I saw it hit the floor, then roll under the stove. "What's wrong with you?" she said. "Are you drunk?"

"I'm just asking," I said.

Right then my wife filled me in with more detail than I cared to know. I made a drink and sat at the kitchen table to listen. Pieces of the story began to fall into place.

Beulah had gone to work for the blind man the summer after my wife had stopped working for him. Pretty soon Beulah and the blind man had themselves a church wedding. It was a little wedding — who'd want to go to such a wedding in the first place? — just the two of them, plus the minister and the minister's wife. But it was a church wedding just the same. It was what Beulah had wanted, he'd said. But even then Beulah must have been carrying the cancer in her glands. After they had been inseparable for eight years — my wife's word, *inseparable* — Beaulah's health went into a rapid decline. She died in a Seattle hospital room, the blind man sitting beside the bed and holding on to her hand. They'd married, lived and worked together, slept together — had sex, sure — and then the blind man had to bury her. All this without his having ever seen what the goddamned woman looked like. It was beyond my understanding. Hearing this, I felt sorry for the blind man for a little bit. And then I found myself thinking what a pitiful life this woman must have led. Imagine a woman who could never see herself as she was seen in the eyes of her loved one. A woman who could go on day after day and never receive the smallest compliment from her beloved. A woman whose husband could never read the expression on her face, be it misery or something better. Someone who could wear makeup or not — what difference to him? She could, if she wanted, wear green eyeshadow around one eye, a straight pin in her nostril, yellow slacks and purple shoes, no matter. And then to slip off into death, the blind man's hand on her hand, his blind eyes streaming tears — I'm imagining now — her last thought maybe this: that he never even knew what she looked like, and she on an express to the grave. Robert was left with a small insurance policy and half of a twenty-peso Mexican coin. The other half of the coin went into the box with her. Pathetic.

So when the time rolled around, my wife went to the depot to pick him up. With nothing to do but wait — sure, I blamed him for that — I was having a drink and watching the TV when I heard the car pull into the drive. I got up from the sofa with my drink and went to the window to have a look.

I saw my wife laughing as she parked the car. I saw her get out of the car and shut the door. She was still wearing a smile. Just amazing. She went around to the other side of the car to where the blind man was already starting to get out. This blind man, feature this, he was wearing a full beard! A beard on a blind man! Too much, I say. The blind man reached into the back seat and dragged out a suitcase. My wife took his arm, shut the car door, and, talking all the way, moved him down the drive and then up the steps to the front porch. I turned off the TV. I finished my drink, rinsed the glass, dried my hands. Then I went to the door.

My wife said, "I want you to meet Robert. Robert, this is my husband. I've told you all about him." She was beaming. She had this blind man by his coat sleeve.

The blind man let go of his suitcase and up came his hand. I took it. He squeezed hard, held my hand, and then he let it go.

"I feel like we've already met," he boomed.

"Likewise," I said. I didn't know what else to say. Then I said. "Welcome. I've heard a lot about you." We began to move then, a little group, from the porch into the living room, my wife guiding him by the arm. The blind man was carrying his suitcase in his other hand. My wife said things like, "To your left here, Robert. That's right. Now watch it, there's a chair. That's it. Sit

down right here. This is the sofa. We just bought this sofa two
weeks ago."

I started to say something about the old sofa. I'd liked that
old sofa. But I didn't say anything. Then I wanted to say something
else, small-talk, about the scenic ride along the Hudson. How
going *to* New York, you should sit on the right-hand side of the
train, and coming *from* New York, the left-hand side.

"Did you have a good train ride?" I said, "Which side of
the train did you sit on, by the way?"

"What a question, which side!" my wife said. "What's it
matter which side?" she said.

"I just asked," I said.

"Right side," the blind man said. "I hadn't been on a train
in nearly forty years. Not since I was a kid. With my folks. That's
been a long time. I'd nearly forgotten the sensation. I have winter
in my beard now," he said. "So I've been told, anyway. Do I
look distinguished, my dear?" the blind man said to my wife.

"You look distinguished, Robert," she said. "Robert," she
said. "Robert, it's just so good to see you."

My wife finally took her eyes off the blind man and looked
at me. I had the feeling she didn't like what she saw. I shrugged.

I've never met, or personally known, anyone who was blind.
This blind man was late forties, a heavy-set, balding man with
stooped shoulders, as if he carried a great weight there. He wore
brown slacks, brown shoes, a light-brown shirt, a tie, a sports
coat. Spiffy. He also had this full beard. But he didn't use a cane
and he didn't wear dark glasses. I'd always thought dark glasses
were a must for the blind. Fact was, I wished he had a pair. At
first glance, his eyes looked like anyone else's eyes. But if you
looked close, there was something different about them. Too much
white in the iris, for one thing, and the pupils seemed to move
round in the sockets without his knowing it or being able to stop
it. Creepy. As I stared at his face, I saw the left pupil turn in
toward his nose while the other made an effort to keep in one
place. But it was only an effort, for that eye was on the roam
without knowing it or wanting it to be.

I said, "Let me get you a drink. What's your pleasure? We
have a little of everything. It's one of our pastimes."

"Bub, I'm a Scotch man myself," he said fast enough in this
big voice.

"Right," I said. Bub! "Sure you are. I knew it."

He let his fingers touch his suitcase, which was sitting alongside
the sofa. He was taking his bearings. I didn't blame him for that.

"I'll move that up to your room," my wife said.

"No, that's fine," the blind man said loudly. "It can go up when I go up."

"A little water with the Scotch?" I said.

"Very little," he said.

"I knew it," I said.

He said, "Just a tad. The Irish actor, Barry Fitzgerald? I'm like that fellow. When I drink water, Fitzgerald said, I drink water. When I drink whiskey, I drink whiskey." My wife laughed. The blind man brought his hand up under his beard. He lifted his beard slowly and let it drop.

I did the drinks, three big glasses of Scotch with a splash of water in each. Then we made ourselves comfortable and talked about Robert's travels. First the long flight from the West Coast to Connecticut, we covered that. Then from Connecticut up here by train. We had another drink concerning that leg of the trip.

I remembered having read somewhere that the blind didn't smoke because, as speculation had it, they couldn't see the smoke they exhaled. I thought I knew that much and that much only about blind people. But this blind man smoked his cigarette down to the nubbin and then lit another one. This blind man filled his ashtray and my wife emptied it.

When we sat down at the table for dinner, we had another drink. My wife heaped Robert's plate with cube steak, scalloped potatoes, green beans. I buttered him up two slices of bread. I said, "Here's bread and butter for you." I swallowed some of my drink. "Now let us pray," I said, and the blind man lowered his head. My wife looked at me, her mouth agape. "Pray the phone won't ring and the food doesn't get cold," I said.

We dug in. We ate everything there was to eat on the table. We ate like there was no tomorrow. We didn't talk. We ate. We scarfed. We grazed that table. We were into serious eating. The blind man had right away located his foods, he knew just where everything was on his plate. I watched with admiration as he used his knife and fork on the meat. He'd cut two pieces of meat, fork the meat into his mouth, and then go all out for the scalloped potatoes, the beans next, and then he'd tear off a hunk of buttered bread and eat that. He'd follow this up with a big drink of milk. It didn't seem to bother him to use his fingers once in a while, either.

We finished everything, including half a strawberry pie. For a few moments, we sat as if stunned. Sweat beaded on our faces. Finally, we got up from the table and left the dirty plates. We didn't look back. We took ourselves into the living room and sank into our places again. Robert and my wife sat on the sofa. I took the big chair. We had us two or three more drinks while they talked about the major things that had come to pass for them in the past ten years. For the most part, I just listened. Now and then I joined in. I didn't want him to think I'd left the room, and I didn't want her to think I was feeling left out. They talked of things that had happened to them — to them! — these past ten years. I waited in vain to hear my name on my wife's sweet lips: "And then my dear husband came into my life" — something like that. But I heard nothing of the sort. More talk of Robert. Robert had done a little of everything, it seemed, a regular blind jack-of-all-trades. But most recently he and his wife had had an Amway distributorship, from which, I gathered, they'd earned their living, such as it was. The blind man was also a ham radio operator. He talked in his loud voice about conversations he'd had with fellow operators in Guam, in the Philippines, in Alaska, and even in Tahiti. He said he'd have a lot of friends there if he ever wanted to go visit those places. From time to time, he'd turn his blind face toward me, put his hand under his beard, ask me something. How long had I been in my present position? (Three years.) Did I like my work? (I didn't.) Was I going to stay with it? (What were the options?) Finally, when I thought he was beginning to run down, I got up and turned on the TV.

My wife looked at me with irritation. She was heading toward a boil. Then she looked at the blind man and said, "Robert, do you have a TV?"

The blind man said, "My dear, I have two TVs. I have a color set and a black-and-white thing, an old relic. It's funny, but if I turn the TV on, and I'm always turning it on, I turn on the color set. It's funny, don't you think?"

I didn't know what to say to that. I had absolutely nothing to say to that. No opinion. So I watched the news program and tried to listen to what the announcer was saying.

"This is a color TV," the blind man said. "Don't ask me how, but I can tell."

"We traded up a while ago," I said.

The blind man had another taste of his drink. He lifted his beard, sniffed it, and let it fall. He leaned forward on the sofa. He positioned his ashtray on the coffee table, then put the lighter to his cigarette. He leaned back on the sofa and crossed his legs at the ankles.

My wife covered her mouth, and then she yawned. She stretched. She said, "I think I'll go upstairs and put on my robe. I think I'll change into something else. Robert, you make yourself comfortable," she said.

"I'm comfortable," the blind man said.

"I want you to feel comfortable in this house," she said.

"I am comfortable," the blind man said.

After she'd left the room, he and I listened to the weather report and then to the sports roundup. By that time, she'd been gone so long I didn't know if she was going to come back. I thought she might have gone to bed. I wished she'd come back downstairs. I didn't want to be left alone with a blind man. I asked him if he wanted another drink, and he said sure. Then I asked if he wanted to smoke some dope with me. I said I'd just rolled a number. I hadn't, but I planned to do so in about two shakes.

"I'll try some with you," he said.

"Damn right," I said. "That's the stuff."

I got our drinks and sat down on the sofa with him. Then I rolled us two fat numbers. I lit one and passed it. I brought it to his fingers. He took it and inhaled.

"Hold it as long as you can," I said. I could tell he didn't know the first thing.

My wife came back downstairs wearing her pink robe and her pink slippers.

"What do I smell?" she said.

"We thought we'd have us some cannabis," I said.

My wife gave me a savage look. Then she looked at the blind man and said, "Robert, I didn't know you smoked."

He said, "I do now, my dear. There's a first time for everything. But I don't feel anything yet."

"This stuff is pretty mellow," I said. "This stuff is mild. It's dope you can reason with," I said. "It doesn't mess you up."

"Not much it doesn't, bub," he said, and laughed.

My wife sat on the sofa between the blind man and me. I passed her the number. She took it and toked and then passed it back to me. "Which way is this going?" she said. Then she said, "I shouldn't be smoking this. I can hardly keep my eyes open as it is. That dinner did me in. I shouldn't have eaten so much."

"It was the strawberry pie," the blind man said. "That's what did it," he said, and he laughed his big laugh. Then he shook his head.

"There's more strawberry pie," I said.

"Do you want some more, Robert?" my wife said.

"Maybe in a little while," he said.

We gave our attention to the TV. My wife yawned again. She said, "Your bed is made up when you feel like going to bed,

Robert. I know you must have had a long day. When you're ready to go to bed, say so." She pulled his arm. "Robert?"

He came to and said, "I've had a real nice time. This beats tapes, doesn't it?"

I said, "Coming at you," and I put the number between his fingers. He inhaled, held the smoke, and then let it go. It was like he'd been doing it since he was nine years old.

"Thanks, bub," he said. "But I think this is all for me. I think I'm beginning to feel it," he said. He held the burning roach out for my wife.

"Same here," she said. "Ditto. Me, too." She took the roach and passed it to me. "I may just sit here for a while between you two guys with my eyes closed. But don't let me bother you, okay? Either one of you. If it bothers you, say so. Otherwise, I may just sit here with my eyes closed until you're ready to go to bed," she said. "Your bed's made up, Robert, when you're ready. It's right next to our room at the top of the stairs. We'll show you up when you're ready. You wake me up now, you guys, if I fall asleep." She said that and then she closed her eyes and went to sleep.

The news program ended. I got up and changed the channel. I sat back down on the sofa. I wished my wife hadn't pooped out. Her head lay across the back of the sofa, her mouth open. She'd turned so that her robe had slipped away from her legs, exposing a juicy thigh. I reached to draw her robe back over her, and it was then that I glanced at the blind man. What the hell! I flipped the robe open again.

"You say when you want some strawberry pie," I said.

"I will," he said.

I said, "Are you tired? Do you want me to take you up to your bed? Are you ready to hit the hay?"

"Not yet," he said. "No, I'll stay up with you, bub. If that's all right. I'll stay up until you're ready to turn in. We haven't had a chance to talk. Know what I mean? I feel like me and her monopolized the evening." He lifted his beard and he let it fall. He picked up his cigarettes and his lighter.

"That's all right," I said. Then I said, "I'm glad for the company."

And I guess I was. Every night I smoked dope and stayed up as long as I could before I fell asleep. My wife and I hardly ever went to bed at the same time. When I did go to sleep, I had these dreams. Sometimes I'd wake up from one of them, my heart going crazy.

Something about the church and the Middle Ages was on the TV. Not your run-of-the-mill TV fare. I wanted to watch something else. I turned to the other channels. But there was nothing on them, either. So I turned back to the first channel and apologized.

"Bub, it's all right," the blind man said. "It's fine with me. Whatever you want to watch is okay. I'm always learning something. Learning never ends. It won't hurt me to learn something tonight. I got ears," he said.

We didn't say anything for a time. He was leaning forward with his head turned at me, his right ear aimed in the direction of the set. Very disconcerting. Now and then his eyelids drooped and then they snapped open again. Now and then he put his fingers into his beard and tugged, like he was thinking about something he was hearing on the television.

On the screen, a group of men wearing cowls was being set upon and tormented by men dressed in skeleton costumes and men dressed as devils. The men dressed as devils wore devil masks, horns, and long tails. This pageant was part of a procession. The Englishman who was narrating the thing said it took place in Spain once a year. I tried to explain to the blind man what was happening.

"Skeletons," he said. "I know about skeletons," he said, and he nodded.

The TV showed this one cathedral. Then there was a long, slow look at another one. Finally, the picture switched to the famous one in Paris, with its flying buttresses and its spires reaching up to the clouds. The camera pulled away to show the whole of the cathedral rising above the skyline.

There were times when the Englishman who was telling the thing would shut up, would simply let the camera move around over the cathedrals. Or else the camera would tour the countryside, men in fields walking behind oxen. I waited as long as I could. Then I felt I had to say something. I said, "They're showing the outside of this cathedral now. Gargoyles. Little statues carved to look like monsters. Now I guess they're in Italy. Yeah, they're in Italy. There's paintings on the walls of this one church."

"Are those fresco paintings, bub?" he asked, and he sipped from his drink.

I reached for my glass. But it was empty. I tried to remember what I could remember. "You're asking me are those fresoces?" I said. "That's a good question. I don't know."

The camera moved to a cathedral outside Lisbon. The differences in the Portuguese cathedral compared with the French and Italian were not that great. But they were there. Mostly the interior stuff. Then something occurred to me, and I said, "Something has occurred to me. Do you have any idea what a cathedral is? What they look like, that is? Do you follow me? If somebody says cathedral to you, do you have any notion what they're talking about? Do you know the difference between that and a Baptist church, say?"

He let the smoke dribble from his mouth. "I know they took hundreds of workers fifty or a hundred years to build," he said. "I just heard the man say that, of course. I know generations of the same families worked on a cathedral. I heard him say that, too. The men who began their life's work on them, they never lived to see the completion of their work. In that wise, bub, they're no different from the rest of us, right?" He laughed. Then his eyelids drooped again. His head nodded. He seemed to be snoozing. Maybe he was imagining himself in Portugal. The TV was showing another cathedral now. This one was in Germany. The Englishman's voice droned on. "Cathedrals," the blind man said. He sat up and rolled his head back and forth. "If you want the truth, bub, that's about all I know. What I just said. What I heard him say. But maybe you could describe one to me? I wish you'd do it. I'd like that. If you want to know, I really don't have a good idea."

I stared hard at the shot of the cathedral on the TV. How could I even begin to describe it? But say my life depended on it. Say my life was being threatened by an insane guy who said I had to do it or else.

I stared some more at the cathedral before the picture flipped off into the countryside. There was no use. I turned to the blind man and said, "To begin with, they're very tall." I was looking around the room for clues. "They reach way up. Up and up. Toward the sky. They're so big, some of them, they have to have these supports. To help hold them up, so to speak. These supports are called buttresses. They remind me of viaducts, for some reason. But maybe you don't know viaducts, either? Sometimes the cathedrals have devils and such carved into the front. Sometimes lords and ladies. Don't ask me why this is," I said.

He was nodding. The whole upper part of his body seemed to be moving back and forth.

"I'm not doing so good, am I?" I said.

He stopped nodding and leaned forward on the edge of the sofa. As he listened to me, he was running his fingers through his beard. I wasn't getting through to him, I could see that. But he waited for me to go on just the same. He nodded, like he was trying to encourage me. I tried to think what else to say. "They're really big," I said. "They're massive. They're built of stone. Marble, too, sometimes. In those olden days, when they built cathedrals, men wanted to be close to God. In those olden days, God was an important part of everyone's life. You could tell this from their cathedral-building. I'm sorry," I said, "but it looks like that's the best I can do for you. I'm just no good at it."

"That's all right, bub," the blind man said. "Hey, listen. I hope you don't mind my asking you. Can I ask you something? Let me ask you a simple question, yes or no. I'm just curious and there's no offense. You're my host. But let me ask if you are in any way religious? You don't mind my asking?"

I shook my head. He couldn't see that, though. A wink is the same as a nod to a blind man. "I guess I don't believe in it. In anything. Sometimes it's hard. You know what I'm saying?"

"Sure, I do," he said.

"Right," I said.

The Englishman was still holding forth. My wife sighed in her sleep. She drew a long breath and went on with her sleeping.

"You'll have to forgive me," I said. "But I can't tell you what a cathedral looks like. It just isn't in me to do it. I can't do any more than I've done."

The blind man sat very still, his head down, as he listened to me.

I said, "The truth is, cathedrals don't mean anything special to me. Nothing. Cathedrals. They're something to look at on late-night TV. That's all they are."

It was then that the blind man cleared his thoat. He brought something up. He took a handkerchief from his back pocket. Then he said. "I get it, bub. It's okay. It happens. Don't worry about it," he said. "Hey, listen to me. Will you do me a favor? I got an idea. Why don't you find us some heavy paper? And a pen. We'll do something. We'll draw one together. Get us a pen and some heavy paper. Go on, bub, get the stuff," he said.

So I went upstairs. My legs felt like they didn't have any strength in them. They felt like they did after I'd done some running. In my wife's room, I looked around. I found some ballpoints in a little basket on her table. And then I tried to think where to look for the kind of paper he was talking about.

Downstairs, in the kitchen, I found a shopping bag with onion skins in the bottom of the bag. I emptied the bag and shook it. I brought it into the living room and sat down with it near his legs. I moved some things, smoothed the wrinkles from the bag, spread it out on the coffee table.

The blind man got down from the sofa and sat next to me on the carpet.

He ran his fingers over the paper. He went up and down the sides of the paper. The edges, even the edges. He fingered the corners.

"All right," he said. "All right, let's do her."

He found my hand, the hand with the pen. He closed his hand over my hand. "Go ahead, bub, draw," he said. "Draw. You'll see. I'll follow along with you. It'll be okay. Just begin now like I'm telling you. You'll see. Draw," the blind man said.

So I began. First I drew a box that looked like a house. It could have been the house I lived in. Then I put a roof on it. At either end of the roof, I drew spires. Crazy.

"Swell," he said. "Terrific. You're doing fine," he said. "Never thought anything like this could happen in your lifetime, did you, bub? Well, it's a strange life, we all know that. Go on now. Keep it up."

I put in windows with arches. I drew flying buttresses. I hung great doors. I couldn't stop. The TV station went off the air. I put down the pen and closed and opened my fingers. The blind man felt around over the paper. He moved the tips of his fingers over the paper, all over what I had drawn, and he nodded.

"Doing fine," the blind man said.

I took up the pen again, and he found my hand. I kept at it. I'm no artist. But I kept drawing just the same.

My wife opened up her eyes and gazed at us. She sat up on the sofa, her robe hanging open. She said, "What are you doing? Tell me, I want to know."

I didn't answer her.

The blind man said, "We're drawing a cathedral. Me and him are working on it. Press hard," he said to me. "That's right. That's good," he said. "Sure. You got it, bub. I can tell. You didn't think you could. But you can, can't you? You're cooking with gas now. You know what I'm saying? We're going to really have us something here in a minute. How's the old arm?" he said. "Put some people in there now. What's a cathedral without people?"

My wife said, "What's going on? Robert, what are you doing? What's going on?"

"It's all right," he said to her. "Close your eyes now," the blind man said to me.

I did it. I closed them just like he said.

"Are they closed?" he said. "Don't fudge."

"They're closed," I said.

"Keep them that way," he said. He said, "Don't stop now. Draw."

So we kept on with it. His fingers rode my fingers as my hand went over the paper. It was like nothing else in my life up to now.

Then he said, "I think that's it. I think you got it," he said. "Take a look. What do you think?"

But I had my eyes closed. I thought I'd keep them that way for a little longer. I thought it was something I ought to do.

"Well?" he said. "Are you looking?"

My eyes were still closed. I was in my house. I knew that. But I didn't feel like I was inside anything.

"It's really something," I said.

Bobbie Ann Mason (*American. b. 1940*)

Shiloh

Leroy Moffitt's wife, Norma Jean, is working on her pectorals. She lifts three-pound dumbbells to warm up, then progresses to a twenty-pound barbell. Standing with her legs apart, she reminds Leroy of Wonder Woman.

"I'd give anything if I could just get these muscles to where they're real hard," says Norma Jean. "Feel this arm. It's not as hard as the other one."

"That's 'cause you're right-handed," says Leroy, dodging as she swings the barbell in an arc.

"Do you think so?"

"Sure."

Leroy is a truckdriver. He injured his leg in a highway accident four months ago, and his physical therapy, which involves weights and a pulley, prompted Norma Jean to try building herself up. Now she is attending a body-building class. Leroy has been collecting temporary disability since his tractor-trailer jackknifed in Missouri, badly twisting his left leg in its socket. He has a steel pin in his hip. He will probably not be able to drive his rig again. It sits in the backyard, like a gigantic bird that has flown home to roost. Leroy has been home in Kentucky for three months, and his leg is almost healed, but the accident frightened him and he does not want to drive any more long hauls. He is not sure what to do next. In the meantime, he makes things from craft kits. He started by building a miniature log cabin from notched Popsicle sticks. He varnished it and placed it on the TV set, where it remains. It reminds him of a rustic Nativity scene. Then he tried string art (sailing ships on black velvet), a macramé owl kit, a snap-together B-17 Flying Fortress, and a lamp made out of a model truck, with a light fixture screwed in the top of the cab. At first the kits were diversions, something to kill time, but now he is thinking about building a full-scale log house from a kit. It would be considerably cheaper than building a regular house, and besides, Leroy has grown to appreciate how things are put together. He has begun to realize that in all the years he was on the road he never took time to examine anything. He was always flying past scenery.

"They won't let you build a log cabin in any of the new subdivisions," Norma Jean tells him.

"They will if I tell them it's for you," he says, teasing her. Ever since they were married, he has promised Norma Jean he would build her a new home one day. They have always rented, and the house they live in is small and nondescript. It does not even feel like a home, Leroy realizes now.

Norma Jean works at the Rexall drugstore, and she has acquired an amazing amount of information about cosmetics. When she explains to Leroy the three stages of complexion care, involving creams, toners, and moisturizers, he thinks happily of other petroleum products — axle grease, diesel fuel. This is a connection between him and Norma Jean. Since he has been home, he has felt unusually tender about his wife and guilty over his long absences. But he can't tell what she feels about him. Norma Jean has never complained about his traveling; she has never made hurt remarks, like calling his truck a "widow-maker." He is reasonably certain she has been faithful to him, but he wishes she would celebrate his permanent home-coming more happily. Norma Jean is often startled to find Leroy at home, and he thinks she seems a little disappointed about it. Perhaps he reminds her too much of the early days of their marriage, before he went on the road. They had a child who died as an infant, years ago. They never speak about their memories of Randy, which have almost faded, but now that Leroy is home all the time, they sometimes feel awkward around each other, and Leroy wonders if one of them should mention the child. He has the feeling that they are waking up out of a dream together — that they must create a new marriage, start afresh. They are lucky they are still married. Leroy has read that for most people losing a child destroys the marriage — or else he heard this on *Donahue.* He can't always remember where he learns things anymore.

At Christmas, Leroy bought an electric organ for Norma Jean. She used to play the piano when she was in high school. "It don't leave you," she told him once. "It's like riding a bicycle."

The new instrument had so many keys and buttons that she was bewildered by it at first. She touched the keys tentatively, pushed some buttons, then pecked out "Chopsticks." It came out in an amplified fox-trot rhythm, with marimba sounds.

"It's an orchestra!" she cried.

The organ had a pecan-look finish and eighteen preset chords, with optional flute, violin, trumpet, clarinet, and banjo accompaniments. Norma Jean mastered the organ almost immediately. At first she played Christmas songs. Then she bought *The Sixties Songbook* and learned every tune in it, adding variations to each with the rows of brightly colored buttons.

"I didn't like these old songs back then," she said. "But I have this crazy feeling I missed something."

"You didn't miss a thing," said Leroy.

Leroy likes to lie on the couch and smoke a joint and listen to Norma Jean play "Can't Take My Eyes Off You" and "I'll Be Back." He is back again. After fifteen years on the road, he is finally settling down with the woman he loves. She is still pretty. Her skin is flawless. Her frosted curls resemble pencil trimmings.

Now that Leroy has come home to stay, he notices how much the town has changed. Subdivisions are spreading across western Kentucky like an oil slick. The sign at the edge of town says "Pop: 11,500" — only seven hundred more than it said twenty years before. Leroy can't figure out who is living in all the new houses. The farmers who used to gather around the courthouse square on Saturday afternoons to play checkers and spit tobacco juice have gone. It has been years since Leroy has thought about the farmers, and they have disappeared without his noticing.

Leroy meets a kid named Stevie Hamilton in the parking lot at the new shopping center. While they pretend to be strangers meeting over a stalled car, Stevie tosses an ounce of marijuana under the front seat of Leroy's car. Stevie is wearing orange jogging shoes and a T-shirt that says CHATTAHOOCHEE SUPER-RAT. His father is a prominent doctor who lives in one of the expensive subdivisions in a new white-columned brick house that looks like a funeral

parlor. In the phone book under his name there is a separate
number, with the listing "Teenagers."

"Where do you get this stuff?" asks Leroy. "From your
pappy?"

"That's for me to know and you to find out," Stevie says.
He is slit-eyed and skinny.

"What else you got?"

"What you interested in?"

"Nothing special. Just wondered."

Leroy used to take speed on the road. Now he has to go
slowly. He needs to be mellow. He leans back against the car and
says, "I'm aiming to build me a log house, soon as I get time.
My wife, though, I don't think she likes the idea."

"Well, let me know when you want me again," Stevie says.
He has a cigarette in his cupped palm, as though sheltering it from
the wind. He takes a long drag, then stomps it on the asphalt and
slouches away.

Stevie's father was two years ahead of Leroy in high school.
Leroy is thirty-four. He married Norma Jean when they were both
eighteen, and their child Randy was born a few months later, but
he died at the age of four months and three days. He would be
about Stevie's age now. Norma Jean and Leroy were at the drive-
in, watching a double feature (*Dr. Strangelove* and *Lover Come
Back*), and the baby was sleeping in the back seat. When the first
movie ended, the baby was dead. It was the sudden infant death
syndrome. Leroy remembers handing Randy to a nurse at the
emergency room, as though he were offering her a large doll as
a present. A dead baby feels like a sack of flour. "It just happens
sometimes," said the doctor, in what Leroy always recalls as a
nonchalant tone. Leroy can hardly remember the child anymore,
but he still sees vividly a scene from *Dr. Strangelove* in which the
President of the United States was talking in a folksy voice on
the hot line to the Soviet premier about the bomber accidentally
headed toward Russia. He was in the War Room, and the world
map was lit up. Leroy remembers Norma Jean standing catatonically
beside him in the hospital and himself thinking: Who is this strange
girl? He had forgotten who she was. Now scientists are saying
that crib death is caused by a virus. Nobody knows anything,
Leroy thinks. The answers are always changing.

When Leroy gets home from the shopping center, Norma
Jeans' mother, Mable Beasley, is there. Until this year, Leroy has
not realized how much time she spends with Norma Jean. When
she visits, she inspects the closets and then the plants, informing
Norma Jean when a plant is droopy or yellow. Mable calls the

plants "flowers," although there are never any blooms. She always notices if Norma Jean's laundry is piling up. Mable is a short, overweight woman whose tight, brown-dyed curls look more like a wig than the actual wig she sometimes wears. Today she has brought Norma Jean an off-white dust ruffle she made for the bed; Mabel works in a custom-upholstery shop.

"This is the tenth one I made this year," Mabel says. "I got started and couldn't stop."

"It's real pretty," says Norma Jean.

"Now we can hide things under the bed," says Leroy, who get along with his mother-in-law primarily by joking with her. Mabel has never really forgiven him for disgracing her by getting Norma Jean pregnant. When the baby died, she said that fate was mocking her.

"What's that thing?" Mabel says to Leroy in a loud voice, pointing to a tangle of yarn on a piece of canvas.

Leroy holds it up for Mabel to see. "It's my needlepoint," he explains. "This is a *Star Trek* pillow cover."

"That's what a woman would do," says Mabel. "Great day in the morning!"

"All the big football players on TV do it," he says.

"Why, Leroy, you're always trying to fool me. I don't believe you for one minute. You don't know what to do with yourself — that's the whole trouble. Sewing!"

"I'm aiming to build us a log house," says Leroy. "Soon as my plans come."

"Like *heck* you are," says Norma Jean. She takes Leroy's needlepoint and shoves it into a drawer. "You have to find a job first. Nobody can afford to build now anyway."

Mabel straightens her girdle and says, "I still think before you get tied down y'all ought to take a little run to Shiloh."

"One of these days, Mama," Norma Jean says impatiently.

Mabel is talking about Shiloh, Tennessee. For the past few years, she has been urging Leroy and Norma Jean to visit the Civil War battleground there. Mabel went there on her honeymoon — the only real trip she ever took. Her husband died of a perforated ulcer when Norma Jean was ten, but Mabel, who was accepted into the United Daughters of the Confederacy in 1975, is still preoccupied with going back to Shiloh.

"I've been to kingdom come and back in that truck out yonder," Leroy says to Mabel, "but we never yet set foot in that battleground. Ain't that something? How did I miss it?"

"It's not even that far," Mabel says.

After Mabel leaves, Norma Jean reads to Leroy from a list

she has made. "Things you could do," she announces. "You could get a job as a guard at Union Carbide, where they'd let you set on a stool. You could get on at the lumberyard. You could do a little carpenter work, if you want to build so bad. You could —"

"I can't do something where I'd have to stand up all day."

"You ought to try standing up all day behind a cosmetics counter. It's amazing that I have strong feet, coming from two parents that never had strong feet at all." At the moment Norma Jean is holding on to the kitchen counter, raising her knees one at a time as she talks. She is wearing two-pound ankle weights.

"Don't worry," says Leroy. "I'll do something."

"You could truck calves to slaughter for somebody. You wouldn't have to drive any big old truck for that."

"I'm going to build you this house," says Leroy. "I want to make you a real home."

'I don't want to live in any log cabin."

"It's not a cabin. It's a house."

"I don't care. It looks like a cabin."

"You and me together could lift those logs. It's just like lifting weights."

Norma Jean doesn't answer. Under her breath, she is counting. Now she is marching through the kitchen. She is doing goose steps.

Before his accident, when Leroy came home he used to stay in the house with Norma Jean, watching TV in bed and playing cards. She would cook fried chicken, picnic ham, chocolate pie — all his favorites. Now he is home alone much of the time. In the mornings, Norma Jean disappears, leaving a cooling place in the bed. She eats a cereal called Body Buddies, and she leaves the bowl on the table, with the soggy tan balls floating in a milk puddle. He sees things about Norma Jean that he never realized before. When she chops onions, she stares off into a corner, as if she can't bear to look. She puts on her house slippers almost precisely at nine o'clock every evening and nudges her jogging shoes under the couch. She saves bread heels for the birds. Leroy watches the birds at the feeder. He notices the peculiar way goldfinches fly past the window. They close their wings, then fall, then spread their wings to catch and lift themselves. He wonders if they close their eyes when they fall. Norma Jean closes her eyes when they are in bed. She wants the lights turned out. Even then, he is sure she closes her eyes.

He goes for long drives around town. He tends to drive a car rather carelessly. Power steering and an automatic shift make a car feel so small and inconsequential that his body is hardly involved in the driving process. His injured leg stretches out comfortably. Once or twice he has almost hit something, but even the prospect of an accident seems minor in a car. He cruises the new subdivisions, feeling like a criminal rehearsing for a robbery. Norma Jean is probably right about a log house being inappropriate here in the new subdivisions. All the houses look grand and complicated. They depress him.

One day when Leroy comes home from a drive he finds Norma Jean in tears. She is in the kitchen making a potato and mushroom-soup casserole, with grated-cheese topping. She is crying because her mother caught her smoking.

"I didn't hear her coming. I was standing here puffing away pretty as you please," Norma Jean says, wiping her eyes.

"I knew it would happen sooner or later," says Leroy, putting his arm around her.

"She don't know the meaning of the word 'knock,' " says Norma Jean. "It's a wonder she hadn't caught me years ago."

"Think of it this way," Leroy says. "What if she caught me with a joint?"

"You better not let her!" Norma Jean shrieks. "I'm warning you, Leroy Moffitt!"

"I'm just kidding. Here, play me a tune. That'll help you relax."

Norma Jean puts the casserole in the oven and sets the timer. Then she plays a ragtime tune, with horns and banjo, as Leroy lights up a joint and lies on the couch, laughing to himself about Mabel's catching him at it. He thinks of Stevie Hamilton — a doctor's son pushing grass. Everything is funny. The whole town seems crazy and small. He is reminded of Virgil Mathis, a boastful policeman Leroy used to shoot pool with. Virgil recently led a drug bust in a back room at a bowling alley, where he seized ten thousand dollars' worth of marijuana. The newspaper had a picture of him holding up the bags of grass and grinning widely. Right now, Leroy can imagine Virgil breaking down the door and arresting him with a lungful of smoke. Virgil would probably have been alerted to the scene because of all the racket Norma Jean is making. Now she sounds like a hard-rock band. Norma Jean is terrific. When she switches to a Latin-rhythm version of "Sunshine Superman," Leroy hums along. Norma Jean's foot goes up and down, up and down.

"Well, what do you think?" Leroy says, when Norma Jean pauses to search through her music.

"What do I think about what?"

His mind had gone blank. Then he says, "I'll sell my rig and build us a house." That wasn't what he wanted to say. He wanted to know what she thought — what she *really* thought — about them.

"Don't start in on that again," says Norma Jean. She begins playing "Who'll Be the Next in Line?"

Leroy used to tell hitchhikers his whole life story — about his travels, his hometown, the baby. He would end with a question: "Well, what do you think?" It was just a rhetorical question. In time, he had the feeling that he'd been telling the same story over and over to the same hitchhikers. He quit talking to hitchhikers when he realized how his voice sounded — whining and self-pitying, like some teenage-tragedy song. Now Leroy has the sudden impulse to tell Norma Jean about himself, as if he had just met her. They have known each other so long they have forgotten a lot about each other. They could become reacquainted. But when the oven timer goes off and she runs to the kitchen, he forgets why he wants to do this.

The next day, Mabel drops by. It is Saturday and Norma Jean is cleaning. Leroy is studying the plans of his log house, which have finally come in the mail. He has them spread out on the table — big sheets of stiff blue paper, with diagrams and numbers printed in white. While Norma Jean runs the vacuum, Mabel drinks coffee. She sets her coffee cup on a blueprint.

"I'm just waiting for time to pass," she says to Leroy, drumming her fingers on the table.

As soon as Norma Jean switches off the vacuum, Mabel says in a loud voice, "Did you hear about the datsun dog that killed the baby?"

Norma Jean says, "The word is 'dachshund.' "

"They put the dog on trial. It chewed the baby's legs off. The mother was in the next room all the time." She raises her voice. "They thought it was neglect."

Norma Jean is holding her ears. Leroy manages to open the refrigerator and get some Diet Pepsi to offer Mabel. Mabel still has some coffee and she waves away the Pepsi.

"Datsuns are like that," Mabel says. "They're jealous dogs. They'll tear a place to pieces if you don't keep an eye on them."

"You better watch out what you're saying, Mabel," says Leroy.

"Well, facts is facts."

Leroy looks out the window at his rig. It is like a huge piece of furniture gathering dust in the backyard. Pretty soon it will be an antique. He hears the vacuum cleaner. Norma Jean seems to be cleaning the living room rug again.

Later, she says to Leroy, "She just said that about the baby because she caught me smoking. She's trying to pay me back."

"What are you talking about?" Leroy says, nervously shuffling blueprints.

"You know good and well," Norma Jean says. She is sitting in a kitchen chair with her feet up and her arms wrapped around her knees. She looks small and helpless. She says, "The very idea, her bringing up a subject like that! Saying it was neglect."

"She didn't mean that," Leroy says.

"She might not have *thought* she meant it. She always says things like that. You don't know how she goes on."

"But she didn't really mean it. She was just talking."

Leroy opens a king-sized bottle of beer and pours it into two glasses, dividing it carefully. He hands a glass to Norma Jean and she takes it from him mechanically. For a long time, they sit by the kitchen window watching the birds at the feeder.

Something is happening. Norma Jean is going to night school. She has graduated from her six-week body-building course and now she is taking an adult-education course in composition at Paducah Community College. She spends her evenings outlining paragraphs.

"First you have a topic sentence," she explains to Leroy. "Then you divide it up. Your secondary topic has to be connected to your primary topic."

To Leroy, this sounds intimidating. "I never was any good in English," he says.

"It makes a lot of sense."

"What are you doing this for, anyhow?"

She shrugs. "It's something to do." She stands up and lifts her dumbbells a few times.

"Driving a rig, nobody cared about my English."

"I'm not criticizing your English."

Norma Jean used to say, "If I lose ten minutes' sleep, I just drag all day." Now she stays up late, writing compositions. She got a B on her first paper — a how-to theme on soup-based casseroles. Recently Norma Jean has been cooking unusual foods — tacos, lasagna, Bombay chicken. She doesn't play the organ anymore, though her second paper was called "Why Music Is Important to Me." She sits at the kitchen table, concentrating on her outlines, while Leroy plays with his log house plans, practicing with a set of Lincoln Logs. The thought of getting a truckload of notched, numbered logs scares him, and he wants to be prepared. As he and Norma Jean work together at the kitchen table, Leroy has the hopeful thought that they are sharing something, but he knows he is a fool to think this. Norma Jean is miles away. He knows he is going to lose her. Like Mabel, he is just waiting for time to pass.

One day, Mabel is there before Norma Jean gets home from work, and Leroy finds himself confiding in her. Mabel, he realizes, must know Norma Jean better than he does.

"I don't know what's got into that girl," Mabel says. "She used to go to bed with the chickens. Now you say she's up all hours. Plus her a-smoking. I like to died."

"I want to make her this beautiful home," Leroy says, indicating the Lincoln Logs. "I don't think she even wants it. Maybe she was happier with me gone."

"She don't know what to make of you, coming home like this."

"Is that it?"

Mabel takes the roof off his Lincoln Log cabin. "You couldn't get *me* in a log cabin," she says. "I was raised in one. It's no picnic, let me tell you."

"They're different now," says Leroy.

"I tell you what," Mabel says, smiling oddly at Leroy.

"What?"

"Take her on down to Shiloh. Y'all need to get out together, stir a little. Her brain's all balled up over them books."

Leroy can see traces of Norma Jean's features in her mother's face. Mabel's worn face has the texture of crinkled cotton, but suddenly she looks pretty. It occurs to Leroy that Mabel has been hinting all along that she wants them to take her with them to Shiloh.

"Let's all go to Shiloh," he says. "You and me and her. Come Sunday."

Mabel throws up her hand in protest. "Oh, no, not me. Young folks want to be by theirselves."

When Norma Jean comes in with groceries, Leroy says excitedly, "Your mama here's been dying to go to Shiloh for thirty-five years. It's about time we went, don't you think?"

"I'm not going to butt in on anybody's second honeymoon," Mabel says.

"Who's going on a honeymoon, for Christ's sake?" Norma Jean says loudly.

"I never raised no daughter of mine to talk that-a-way," Mabel says.

"You ain't seen nothing yet," says Norma Jean. She starts putting away boxes and cans, slamming cabinet doors.

"There's a log cabin at Shiloh," Mabel says. "It was there during the battle. There's bullet holes in it."

"When are you going to *shut up* about Shiloh, Mama?" asks Norma Jean.

"I always thought Shiloh was the prettiest place, so full of history," Mabel goes on. "I just hoped y'all could see it once before I die, so you could tell me about it." Later, she whispers to Leroy, "You do what I said. A little change is what she needs."

"Your name means 'the king,' " Norma Jean says to Leroy that evening. He is trying to get her to go to Shiloh, and she is reading a book about another century.

"Well, I reckon I ought to be right proud."

"I guess so."

"Am I still king around here?"

Norma Jean flexes her biceps and feels them for hardness. "I'm not fooling around with anybody, if that's what you mean," she says.

"Would you tell me if you were?"

"I don't know."

"What does *your* name mean?"

"It was Marilyn Monroe's real name."

"No kidding!"

"Norma comes from the Normans. They were invaders," she says. She closes her book and looks hard at Leroy. "I'll go to Shiloh with you if you'll stop staring at me."

On Sunday, Norma Jean packs a picnic and they go to Shiloh. To Leroy's relief, Mabel says she does not want to come with them. Norma Jean drives, and Leroy, sitting beside her, feels like some boring hitchhiker she has picked up. He tries some conversation, but she answers him in monosyllables. At Shiloh, she drives aimlessly through the park, past bluffs and trails and steep ravines. Shiloh is an immense place, and Leroy cannot see it as a battleground. It is not what he expected. He thought it would look like a golf course. Monuments are everywhere, showing through the thick clusters of trees. Norma Jean passes the log cabin Mabel mentioned. It is surrounded by tourists looking for bullet holes.

"That's not the kind of log house I've got in mind," says Leroy apologetically.

"I know *that*."

"This is a pretty place. Your mama was right."

"It's O.K.," says Norma Jean. "Well, we've seen it. I hope she's satisfied."

They burst out laughing together.

At the park museum, a movie on Shiloh is shown every half hour, but they decide that they don't want to see it. They buy a souvenir Confederate flag for Mabel, and then they find a picnic spot near the cemetery. Norma Jean has brought a picnic cooler, with pimiento sandwiches, soft drinks, and Yodels. Leroy eats a sandwich and then smokes a joint, hiding it behind the picnic cooler. Norma Jean has quit smoking altogether. She is picking cake crumbs from the cellophane wrapper, like a fussy bird.

Leroy says, "So the boys in gray ended up in Corinth. The Union soldiers zapped 'em finally. April 7, 1862."

They both know that he doesn't know any history. He is just talking about some of the historical plaques they have read. He feels awkward, like a boy on a date with an older girl. They are still just making conversation.

"Corinth is where Mama eloped to," says Norma Jean.

They sit in silence and stare at the cemetery for the Union dead and, beyond, at a tall cluster of trees. Campers are parked nearby, bumper to bumper, and small children in bright clothing are cavorting and squealing. Norma Jean wads up the cake wrapper and squeezes it tightly in her hand. Without looking at Leroy, she says, "I want to leave you."

Leroy takes a bottle of Coke out of the cooler and flips off the cap. He holds the bottle poised near his mouth but cannot remember to take a drink. Finally he says, "No, you don't."

"Yes, I do."

"I won't let you."

"You can't stop me."

"Don't do me that way."

Leroy knows Norma Jean will have her own way. "Didn't I promise to be home from now on?" he says.

"In some ways, a woman prefers a man who wanders," says Norma Jean. "That sounds crazy, I know."

"You're not crazy."

Leroy remembers to drink from his Coke. Then he says, "Yes, you *are* crazy. You and me could start all over again. Right back at the beginning."

"We *have* started all over again," says Norma Jean. "And this is how it turned out."

"What did I do wrong?"

"Nothing."

"Is this one of those women's lib things?" Leroy asks.

"Don't be funny."

The cemetery, a green slope dotted with white markers, looks like a subdivision site. Leroy is trying to comprehend that his marriage is breaking up, but for some reason he is wondering about white slabs in a graveyard.

"Everything was fine till Mama caught me smoking," says Norma Jean, standing up. "That set something off."

"What are you talking about?"

"She won't leave me alone — *you* won't leave me alone." Norma Jean seems to be crying, but she is looking away from him. "I feel eighteen again. I can't face that all over again." She starts walking away. "No, it *wasn't* fine. I don't know what I'm saying. Forget it."

Leroy takes a lungful of smoke and closes his eyes as Norma Jean's words sink in. He tries to focus on the fact that thirty-five hundred soldiers died on the grounds around him. He can only think of that war as a board game with plastic soldiers. Leroy almost smiles, as he compares the Confederates' daring attack on the Union camps and Virgil Mathis's raid on the bowling alley. General Grant, drunk and furious, shoved the Southerners back to Corinth, where Mabel and Jet Beasley were married years later, when Mabel was still thin and good-looking. The next day, Mabel and Jet visited the battleground, and then Norma Jean was born, and then she married Leroy and they had a baby, which they lost, and now Leroy and Norma Jean are here at the same battleground. Leroy knows he is leaving out a lot. He is leaving out the insides of history. History was always just names and dates to him. It occurs to him that building a house out of logs is similarly empty — too simple. And the real inner workings of a marriage, like most of history, have escaped him. Now he sees that building a log house is the dumbest idea he could have had. It was clumsy of him to think Norma Jean would want a log house. It was a crazy idea. He'll have to think of something else, quickly. He will wad the blueprints into tight balls and fling them into the lake. Then he'll get moving again. He opens his eyes. Norma Jean has moved away and is walking through the cemetery, following a serpentine brick path.

Leroy gets up to follow his wife, but his good leg is asleep and his bad leg still hurts him. Norma Jean is far away, walking rapidly toward the bluff by the river, and he tries to hobble toward her. Some children run past him, screaming noisily. Norma Jean has reached the bluff, and she is looking out over the Tennessee River. Now she turns toward Leroy and waves her arms. Is she

beckoning to him? She seems to be doing an exercise for her chest
muscles. The sky is unusually pale — the color of the dust ruffle
Mabel made for their bed.

Alice Walker (American. b. 1944)

Everyday Use

For your grandmama

I will wait for her in the yard that Maggie and I made so clean
and wavy yesterday afternoon. A yard like this is more comfortable
than most people know. It is not just a yard. It is like an extended
living room. When the hard clay is swept clean as a floor and the
fine sand around the edges lined with tiny, irregular grooves anyone
can come and sit and look up into the elm tree and wait for the
breezes that never come inside the house.

Maggie will be nervous until after her sister goes: she will
stand hopelessly in corners homely and ashamed of the burn scars
down her arms and legs, eyeing her sister with a mixture of envy
and awe. She thinks her sister has held life always in the palm of
one hand, that "no" is a word the world never learned to say to
her.

You've no doubt seen those TV shows where the child who
has "made it" is confronted, as a surprise, by her own mother
and father, tottering in weakly from backstage. (A pleasant surprise,
of course: What would they do if parent and child came on the
show only to curse out and insult each other?) On TV mother
and child embrace and smile into each other's faces. Sometimes
the mother and father weep, the child wraps them in her arms
and leans across the table to tell how she would not have made
it without their help. I have seen these programs.

Sometimes I dream a dream in which Dee and I are suddenly
brought together on a TV program of this sort. Out of a dark
and soft-seated limousine I am ushered into a bright room filled
with many people. There I meet a smiling, gray, sporty man like
Johnny Carson who shakes my hand and tells me what a fine girl
I have. Then we are on the stage and Dee is embracing me with

tears in her eyes. She pins on my dress a large orchid, even though she has told me once that she thinks orchids are tacky flowers.

In real life I am a large, big-boned woman with rough, man-working hands. In the winter I wear flannel nightgowns to bed and overalls during the day. I can kill and clean a hog as mercilessly as a man. My fat keeps me hot in zero weather. I can work outside all day, breaking ice to get water for washing. I can eat pork liver cooked over the open fire minutes after it comes steaming from the hog. One winter I knocked a bull calf straight in the brain between the eyes with a sledge hammer and had the meat hung up to chill before nightfall. But of course all this does not show on television. I am the way my daughter would want me to be: a hundred pounds lighter, my skin like an uncooked barley pancake. My hair glistens in the hot bright lights. Johnny Carson has much to do to keep up with my quick and witty tongue.

But that is a mistake. I know even before I wake up. Who ever knew a Johnson with a quick tongue? Who can even imagine me looking a strange white man in the eye? It seems to me I have talked to them always with one foot raised in flight, with my head turned in whichever way is farthest from them. Dee, though. She would always look anyone in the eye. Hesitation was no part of her nature.

"How do I look, Mama?" Maggie says, showing just enough of her thin body enveloped in pink skirt and red blouse for me to know she's there, almost hidden by the door.

"Come out into the yard," I say.

Have you ever seen a lame animal, perhaps a dog run over by some careless person rich enough to own a car, sidle up to someone who is ignorant enough to be kind to him? That is the way my Maggie walks. She has been like this, chin on chest, eyes on ground, feet in shuffle, ever since the fire that burned the other house to the ground.

Dee is lighter than Maggie, with nicer hair and a fuller figure. She's a woman now, though sometimes I forget. How long ago was it that the other house burned? Ten, twelve years? Sometimes I can still hear the flames and feel Maggie's arms sticking to me, her hair smoking and her dress falling off her in little black papery flakes. Her eyes seemed stretched open, blazed open by the flames reflected in them. And Dee. I see her standing off under the sweet gum tree she used to dig gum out of; a look of concentration on her face as she watched the last dingy gray board of the house fall in toward the red-hot brick chimney. Why don't you do a dance around the ashes? I'd wanted to ask her. She had hated the house that much.

I used to think she hated Maggie, too. But that was before we raised the money, the church and me, to send her to Augusta to school. She used to read to us without pity; forcing words, lies, other folks' habits, whole lives upon us two, sitting trapped and ignorant underneath her voice. She washed us in a river of make-believe, burned us with a lot of knowledge we didn't necessarily need to know. Pressed us to her with the serious way she read, to shove us away at just the moment, like dimwits, we seemed about to understand.

Dee wanted nice things. A yellow organdy dress to wear to her graduation from high school; black pumps to match a green suit she'd made from an old suit somebody gave me. She was determined to stare down any disaster in her efforts. Her eyelids would not flicker for minutes at a time. Often I fought off the temptation to shake her. At sixteen she had a style of her own: and knew what style was.

I never had an education myself. After second grade the school was closed down. Don't ask me why: in 1927 colored asked fewer questions than they do now. Sometimes Maggie reads to me. She stumbles along good-naturedly but can't see well. She knows she is not bright. Like good looks and money, quickness passed her by. She will marry John Thomas (who has mossy teeth in an earnest face) and then I'll be free to sit here and I guess just sing church songs to myself. Although I never was a good singer. Never could carry a tune. I was always better at a man's job. I used to love to milk till I was hoofed in the side in '49. Cows are soothing and slow and don't bother you, unless you try to milk them the wrong way.

I have deliberately turned my back on the house. It is three rooms, just like the one that burned, except the roof is tin; they don't make shingle roofs any more. There are no real windows, just some holes cut in the sides, like the portholes in a ship, but not round and not square, with rawhide holding the shutters up on the outside. This house is in a pasture, too, like the other one. No doubt when Dee sees it she will want to tear it down. She wrote me once that no matter where we "choose" to live, she will manage to come see us. But she will never bring her friends. Maggie and I thought about this and Maggie asked me, "Mama, when did Dee ever *have* any friends?"

She had a few. Furtive boys in pink shirts hanging about on washday after school. Nervous girls who never laughed. Impressed with her they worshiped the well-turned phrase, the cute shape, the scalding humor that erupted like bubbles in lye. She read to them.

When she was courting Jimmy T she didn't have much time to pay to us, but turned all her faultfinding power on him. He *flew* to marry a cheap gal from a family of ignorant flashy people. She hardly had time to recompose herself.

When she comes I will meet — but there they are!

Maggie attempts to make a dash for the house, in her shuffling way, but I stay her with my hand. "Come back here," I say. And she stops and tries to dig a well in the sand with her toe.

It is hard to see them clearly through the strong sun. But even the first glimpse of leg out of the car tells me it is Dee. Her feet were always neat-looking, as if God himself had shaped them with a certain style. From the other side of the car comes a short, stocky man. Hair is all over his head a foot long and hanging from his chin like a kinky mule tail. I hear Maggie suck in her breath. "Uhnnnh," is what it sounds like. Like when you see the wriggling end of a snake just in front of your foot on the road. "Uhnnnh."

Dee next. A dress down to the ground, in this hot weather. A dress so loud it hurts my eyes. There are yellows and oranges enough to throw back the light of the sun. I feel my whole face warming from the heat waves it throws out. Earrings, too, gold and hanging down to her shoulders. Bracelets dangling and making noises when she moves her arm up to shake the folds of the dress out of her armpits. The dress is loose and flows, and as she walks closer, I like it. I hear Maggie go "Uhnnnh" again. It is her sister's hair. It stands straight up like the wool on a sheep. It is black as night and around the edges are two long pigtails that rope about like small lizards disappearing behind her ears.

"Wa-su-zo-Tean-o!" she says, coming on in that gliding way the dress makes her move. The short stocky fellow with the hair to his navel is all grinning and he follows up with "Asalamalakim, my mother and sister!" He moves to hug Maggie but she falls back, right up against the back of my chair. I feel her trembling there and when I look up I see the perspiration falling off her chin.

"Don't get up," says Dee. Since I am stout it takes something of a push. You can see me trying to move a second or two before I make it. She turns, showing white heels through her sandals, and goes back to the car. Out she peeks next with a Polaroid. She stoops down quickly and lines up picture after picture of me sitting there in front of the house with Maggie cowering behind me. She

never takes a shot without making sure the house is included.
When a cow comes nibbling around the edge of the yard she snaps
it and me and Maggie *and* the house. Then she puts the Polaroid
in the back seat of the car, and comes up and kisses me on the
forehead.

Meanwhile Asalamalakim is going through the motions with
Maggie's hand. Maggie's hand is as limp as a fish, and probably
as cold, despite the sweat, and she keeps trying to pull it back. It
looks like Asalamalakim wants to shake hands but wants to do it
fancy. Or maybe he don't know how people shake hands.
Anyhow, he soon gives up on Maggie.

"Well," I say. "Dee."

"No, Mama," she says. "Not 'Dee,' Wangero Leewanika
Kemanjo!"

"What happened to 'Dee'?" I wanted to know.

"She's dead," Wangero said. "I couldn't bear it any longer
being named after the people who oppress me."

"You know as well as me you was named after your aunt
Dicie," I said. Dicie is my sister. She named Dee. We called her
"Big Dee" after Dee was born.

"But who was *she* named after?" asked Wangero.

"I guess after Grandma Dee," I said.

"And who was she named after?" asked Wangero.

"Her mother," I said, and saw Wangero was getting tired.
"That's about as far back as I can trace it," I said. Though, in
fact, I probably could have carried it back beyond the Civil War
through the branches.

"Well," said Asalamalakim, "there you are."

"Uhnnnh," I heard Maggie say.

"There I was not," I said, "before 'Dicie' cropped up in our
family, so why should I try to trace it that far back?"

He just stood there grinning, looking down on me like somebody inspecting a Model A car. Every once in a while he and
Wangero sent eye signals over my head.

"How do you pronounce this name?" I asked.

"You don't have to call me by it if you don't want to," said
Wangero.

"Why shouldn't I?" I asked. "If that's what you want us to
call you, we'll call you."

"I know it might sound awkward at first," said Wangero.

"I'll get used to it," I said. "Ream it out again."

Well, soon we got the name out of the way. Asalamalakim
had a name twice as long and three times as hard. After I tripped
over it two or three times he told me to just call him Hakim-a-

barber. I wanted to ask him was he a barber, but I didn't really think he was, so I didn't ask.

"You must belong to those beef-cattle peoples down the road," I said. They said "Asalamalakim" when they met you, too, but they didn't shake hands. Always too busy: feeding the cattle, fixing the fences, putting up salt-lick shelters, throwing down hay. When the white folks poisoned some of the herd the men stayed up all night with rifles in their hands. I walked a mile and a half just to see the sight.

Hakim-a-barber said, "I accept some of their doctrines, but farming and raising cattle is not my style." (They didn't tell me, and I didn't ask, whether Wangero [Dee] had really gone and married him.)

We sat down to eat and right away he said he didn't eat collards and pork was unclean. Wangero, though, went on through the chitlins and corn bread, the greens and everything else. She talked a blue streak over the sweet potatoes. Everything delighted her. Even the fact that we still used the benches her daddy made for the table when we couldn't afford to buy chairs.

"Oh, Mama!" she cried. Then turned to Hakim-a-barber. "I never knew how lovely these benches are. You can feel the rump prints," she said, running her hands underneath her and along the bench. Then she gave a sigh and her hand closed over Grandma Dee's butter dish. "That's it!" she said. "I knew there was something I wanted to ask you if I could have." She jumped up from the table and went over in the corner where the churn stood, the milk in it clabber by now. She looked at the churn and looked at it.

"This churn top is what I need," she said. "Didn't Uncle Buddy whittle it out of a tree you all used to have?"

"Yes," I said.

"Uh huh," she said happily. "And I want the dasher, too."

"Uncle Buddy whittle that, too?" asked the barber.

Dee (Wangero) looked up at me.

"Aunt Dee's first husband whittled the dash," said Maggie so low you almost couldn't hear her. "His name was Henry, but they called him Stash."

"Maggie's brain is like an elephant's," Wangero said, laughing. "I can use the churn top as a centerpiece for the alcove table," she said, sliding a plate over the churn, "and I'll think of something artistic to do with the dasher."

When she finished wrapping the dasher the handle stuck out. I took it for a moment in my hands. You didn't even have to look close to see where hands pushing the dasher up and down to make butter had left a kind of sink in the wood. In fact, there were a lot of small sinks; you could see where thumbs and fingers had sunk into the wood. It was beautiful light yellow wood, from a tree that grew in the yard where Big Dee and Stash had lived.

After dinner Dee (Wangero) went to the trunk at the foot of my bed and started rifling through it. Maggie hung back in the kitchen over the dishpan. Out came Wangero with two quilts. They had been pieced by Grandma Dee and then Big Dee and me had hung them on the quilt frames on the front porch and quilted them. One was in the Lone Star pattern. The other was Walk Around the Mountain. In both of them were scraps of dresses Grandma Dee had worn fifty and more years ago. Bits and pieces of Grandpa Jarrell's paisley shirts. And one teeny faded blue piece, about the piece of a penny matchbox, that was from Great Grandpa Ezra's uniform that he wore in the Civil War.

"Mama," Wangero said sweet as a bird. "Can I have these old quilts?"

I heard something fall in the kitchen, and a minute later the kitchen door slammed.

"Why don't you take one or two of the others?" I asked. "These old things was just done by me and Big Dee from some tops your grandma pieced before she died."

"No," said Wangero. "I don't want those. They are stitched around the borders by machine."

"That's make them last better," I said.

"That's not the point," said Wangero. "These are all pieces of dresses Grandma used to wear. She did all this stitching by hand. Imagine!" She held the quilts securely in her arms, stroking them.

"Some of the pieces, like those lavender ones, come from old clothes her mother handed down to her," I said, moving up to touch the quilts. Dee (Wangero) moved back just enough so that I couldn't reach the quilts. They already belonged to her.

"Imagine!" she breathed again, clutching them closely to her bosom.

"The truth is," I said, "I promised to give them quilts to Maggie, for when she marries John Thomas."

She gasped like a bee had stung her.

"Maggie can't appreciate these quilts!" she said. "She'd probably be backward enough to put them to everyday use."

"I reckon she would," I said. "God knows I been saving 'em for long enough with nobody using 'em. I hope she will!" I didn't want to bring up how I had offered Dee (Wangero) a quilt when she went away to college. Then she had told me they were old-fashioned, out of style.

"But they're *priceless!*" she was saying now, furiously; for she has a temper. "Maggie would put them on the bed and in five years they'd be in rags. Less than that!"

"She can always make some more," I said. "Maggie knows how to quilt."

Dee (Wangero) looked at me with hatred. "You just will not understand. The point is these quilts, *these* quilts!"

"Well," I said, stumped. "What would *you* do with them?"

"Hang them," she said. As if that was the only thing you *could* do with quilts.

Maggie by now was standing in the door. I could almost hear the sound her feet made as they scraped over each other.

"She can have them, Mama," she said, like somebody used to never winning anything, or having anything reserved for her. "I can 'member Grandma Dee without the quilts."

I looked at her hard. She had filled her bottom lip with checkerberry snuff and it gave her face a kind of dopey, hangdog look. It was Grandma Dee and Big Dee who taught her how to quilt herself. She stood there with her scarred hands hidden in the folds of her skirt. She looked at her sister with something like fear but she wasn't mad at her. This was Maggie's portion. This was the way she knew God to work.

When I looked at her like that something hit me in the top of my head and ran down to the soles of my feet. Just like when I'm in church and the spirit of God touches me and I get happy and shout. I did something I never had done before: hugged Maggie to me, then dragged her on into the room, snatched the quilts out of Miss Wangero's hands and dumped them into Maggie's lap. Maggie just sat there on my bed with her mouth open.

"Take one or two of the others," I said to Dee.

But she turned without a word and went out to Hakim-a-barber.

"You just don't understand," she said, as Maggie and I came out to the car.

"What don't I understand?" I wanted to know.

"Your heritage," she said. And then she turned to Maggie, kissed her, and said, "You ought to try to make something of yourself, too, Maggie. It's really a new day for us. But from the way you and Mama still live you'd never know it."

She put on some sunglasses that hid everything above the tip of her nose and her chin.

Maggie smiled; maybe at the sunglasses. But a real smile, not scared. After we watched the car dust settle I asked Maggie to bring me a dip of snuff. And then the two of us sat there just enjoying, until it was time to go in the house and go to bed.

Louise Erdrich (American. b. 1954)

Fleur

The first time she drowned in the cold and glassy waters of Lake Turcot, Fleur Pillager was only a girl. Two men saw the boat tip, saw her struggle in the waves. They rowed over to the place she went down, and jumped in. When they dragged her over the gunwales, she was cold to the touch and stiff, so they slapped her face, shook her by the heels, worked her arms back and forth, and pounded her back until she coughed up lake water. She shivered all over like a dog, then took a breath. But it wasn't long afterward that those two men disappeared. The first wandered off, and the other, Jean Hat, got himself run over by a cart.

It went to show, my grandma said. It figured to her, all right. By saving Fleur Pillager, those two men had lost themselves.

The next time she fell in the lake, Fleur Pillager was twenty years old and no one touched her. She washed onshore, her skin a dull dead gray, but when George Many Women bent to look closer, he saw her chest move. Then her eyes spun open, sharp black riprock, and she looked at him. "You'll take my place," she hissed. Everybody scattered and left her there, so no one knows how she dragged herself home. Soon after that we noticed Many Women changed, grew afraid, wouldn't leave his house, and would not be forced to go near water. For his caution, he lived until the day that his sons brought him a new tin bathtub. Then the first time he used the tub he slipped, got knocked out, and breathed water while his wife stood in the other room frying breakfast.

Men stayed clear of Fleur Pillager after the second drowning. Even though she was good-looking, nobody dared to court her because it was clear that Misshepeshu, the waterman, the monster, wanted her for himself. He's a devil, that one, love-hungry with desire and maddened for the touch of young girls, the strong and daring especially, the ones like Fleur.

Our mothers warn us that we'll think he's handsome, for he appears with green eyes, copper skin, a mouth tender as a child's. But if you fall into his arms, he sprouts horns, fangs, claws, fins. His feet are joined as one and his skin, brass scales, rings to the touch. You're fascinated, cannot move. He casts a shell necklace at your feet, weeps gleaming chips that harden into mica on your breasts. He holds you under. Then he takes the body of a lion or a fat brown worm. He's made of gold. He's made of beach moss. He's a thing of dry foam, a thing of death by drowning, the death a Chippewa cannot survive.

Unless you are Fleur Pillager. We all knew she couldn't swim. After the first time, we thought she'd never go back to Lake Turcot. We thought she'd keep to herself, live quiet, stop killing men off by drowning in the lake. After the first time, we thought she'd keep the good ways. But then, after the second drowning, we knew that we were dealing with something much more serious. She was haywire, out of control. She messed with evil, laughed at the old women's advice, and dressed like a man. She got herself into some half-forgotten medicine, studied ways we shouldn't talk about. Some say she kept the finger of a child in her pocket and a powder of unborn rabbits in a leather thong around her neck. She laid the heart of an owl on her tongue so she could see at night, and went out, hunting, not even in her own body. We know for sure because the next morning, in the snow or dust, we followed the tracks of her bare feet and saw where they changed, where the claws sprang out, the pad broadened and pressed into the dirt. By night we heard her chuffing cough, the bear cough. By day her silence and the wide grin she threw to bring down our guard made us frightened. Some thought that Fleur Pillager should be driven off the reservation, but not a single person who spoke like this had the nerve. And finally, when people were just about to get together and throw her out, she left on her own and didn't come back all summer. That's what this story is about.

During that summer, when she lived a few miles south in Argus, things happened. She almost destroyed that town.

When she got down to Argus in the year of 1920, it was just a small grid of six streets on either side of the railroad depot. There were two elevators, one central, the other a few miles west. Two stores competed for the trade of the three hundred citizens, and three churches quarreled with one another for their souls. There was a frame building for Lutherans, a heavy brick one for Episcopalians, and a long narrow shingled Catholic church. This last had a tall slender steeple, twice as high as any building or tree.

No doubt, across the low, flat wheat, watching from the road as she came near Argus on foot, Fleur saw that steeple rise, a shadow thin as a needle. Maybe in that raw space it drew her the way a lone tree draws lightning. Maybe, in the end, the Catholics are to blame. For if she hadn't seen that sign of pride, that slim prayer, that marker, maybe she would have kept walking.

But Fleur Pillager turned, and the first place she went once she came into town was to the back door of the priest's residence attached to the landmark church. She didn't go there for a handout, although she got that, but to ask for work. She got that too, or the town got her. It's hard to tell which came out worse, her or the men or the town, although the upshot of it all was that Fleur lived.

The four men who worked at the butcher's had carved up about a thousand carcasses between them, maybe half of that steers and the other half pigs, sheep, and game animals like deer, elk, and bear. That's not even mentioning the chickens, which were beyond counting. Pete Kozka owned the place, and employed Lily Veddar, Tor Grunewald, and my stepfather, Dutch James, who had brought my mother down from the reservation the year before she disappointed him by dying. Dutch took me out of school to take her place. I kept house half the time and worked the other in the butcher shop, sweeping floors, putting sawdust down, running a hambone across the street to a customer's bean pot or a package of sausage to the corner. I was a good one to have around because until they needed me, I was invisible. I blended into the stained brown walls, a skinny, big-nosed girl with staring eyes. Because I could fade into a corner or squeeze beneath a shelf, I knew everything, what the men said when no one was around, and what they did to Fleur.

Kozka's Meats served farmers for a fifty-mile area, both to slaughter, for it had a stock pen and chute, and to cure the meat by smoking it or spicing it in sausage. The storage locker was a marvel, made of many thicknesses of brick, earth insulation, and Minnesota timber, lined inside with sawdust and vast blocks of ice cut from Lake Turcot, hauled down from home each winter by horse and sledge.

A ramshackle board building, part slaughterhouse, part store, was fixed to the low, thick square of the lockers. That's where Fleur worked. Kozka hired her for her strength. She could lift a haunch or carry a pole of sausages without stumbling, and she soon learned cutting from Pete's wife, a string-thin blonde who chain-smoked and handled the razor-sharp knives with nerveless precision, slicing close to her stained fingers. Fleur and Fritzie

Kozka worked afternoons, wrapping their cuts in paper, and Fleur hauled the packages to the lockers. The meat was left outside the heavy oak doors that were only opened at 5:00 each afternoon, before the men ate supper.

Sometimes Dutch, Tor, and Lily ate at the lockers, and when they did I stayed too, cleaned floors, restoked the fires in the front smokehouses, while the men sat around the squat cast-iron stove spearing slats of herring onto hardtack bread. They played long games of poker or cribbage on a board made from the planed end of a salt crate. They talked and I listened, although there wasn't much to hear since almost nothing ever happened in Argus. Tor was married, Dutch had lost my mother, and Lily read circulars. They mainly discussed about the auctions to come, equipment, or women.

Every so often, Pete Kozka came out front to make a whist, leaving Fritzie to smoke cigarettes and fry raised doughnuts in the back room. He sat and played a few rounds but kept his thoughts to himself. Fritzie did not tolerate him talking behind her back, and the one book he read was the New Testament. If he said something, it concerned weather or a surplus of sheep stomachs, a ham that smoked green or the markets for corn and wheat. He had a good-luck talisman, the opal-white lens of a cow's eye. Playing cards, he rubbed it between his fingers. That soft sound and the slap of cards was about the only conversation.

Fleur finally gave them a subject.

Her cheeks were wide and flat, her hands large, chapped, muscular. Fleur's shoulders were broad as beams, her hips fishlike, slippery, narrow. An old green dress clung to her waist, worn thin where she sat. Her braids were thick like the tails of animals, and swung against her when she moved, deliberately, slowly in her work, held in and half-tamed, but only half. I could tell, but the others never saw. They never looked into her sly brown eyes or noticed her teeth, strong and curved and very white. Her legs were bare, and since she padded around in beadwork moccasins they never saw that her fifth toes were missing. They never knew she'd drowned. They were blinded, they were stupid, they only saw her in the flesh.

And yet it wasn't just that she was a Chippewa, or even that she was a woman, it wasn't that she was good-looking or even that she was alone that made their brains hum. It was how she played cards.

Women didn't usually play with men, so the evening that Fleur drew a chair up to the men's table without being so much as asked, there was a shock of surprise.

"What's this," said Lily. He was fat, with a snake's cold pale eyes and precious skin, smooth and lily-white, which is how he got his name. Lily had a dog, a stumpy mean little bull of a thing with a belly drum-tight from eating pork rinds. The dog liked to play cards just like Lily, and straddled his barrel thighs through games of stud, rum poker, vingt-un. The dog snapped at Fleur's arm that first night, but cringed back, it's snarl frozen, when she took her place.

"I thought," she said, her voice soft and stroking, "you might deal me in."

There was a space between the heavy bin of spiced flour and the wall where I just fit. I hunkered down there, kept my eyes open, saw her black hair swing over the chair, her feet solid on the wood floor. I couldn't see up on the table where the cards slapped down, so after they were deep in their game I raised myself up in the shadows, and crouched on a sill of wood.

I watched Fleur's hands stack and ruffle, divide the cards, spill them to each player in a blur, rake them up and shuffle again. Tor, short and scrappy, shut one eye and squinted the other at Fleur. Dutch screwed his lips around a wet cigar.

"Gotta see a man," he mumbled, getting up to go out back to the privy. The others broke, put their cards down, and Fleur sat alone in the lamplight that glowed in a sheen across the push of her breasts. I watched her closely, then she paid me a beam of notice for the first time. She turned, looked straight at me, and grinned the white wolf grin a Pillager turns on its victims, except that she wasn't after me.

"Pauline there," she said, "how much money you got?"

We'd all been paid for the week that day. Eight cents was in my pocket.

"Stake me," she said, holding out her long fingers. I put the coins in her palm and then I melted back to nothing, part of the walls and tables. It was a long time before I understood that the men would not have seen me no matter what I did, how I moved. I wasn't anything like Fleur. My dress hung loose and my back was already curved, an old woman's. Work had roughened me, reading made my eyes sore, caring for my mother before she died had hardened my face. I was not much to look at, so they never saw me.

When the men came back and sat around the table, they had drawn together. They shot each other small glances, stuck their tongues in their cheeks, burst out laughing at odd moments, to rattle Fleur. But she never minded. They played their vingt-un staying even as Fleur slowly gained. Those pennies I had given her drew nickels and attracted dimes until there was a small pile in front of her.

Then she hooked them with five-card draw, nothing wild. She dealt, discarded, drew, and then she sighed and her cards gave a little shiver. Tor's eye gleamed, and Dutch straightened in his seat.

"I'll pay to see that hand," said Lily Veddar.

Fleur showed, and she had nothing there, nothing at all.

Tor's thin smile cracked open, and he threw his hand in too.

"Well, we know one thing," he said, leaning back in his chair, "the squaw can't bluff."

With that I lowered myself into a mound of swept sawdust and slept. I woke up during the night, but none of them had moved yet, so I couldn't either. Still later, the men must have gone out again, or Fritzie come out to break the game, because I was lifted, soothed, cradled in a woman's arms and rocked so quiet that I kept my eyes shut while Fleur rolled me into a closet of grimy ledgers, oiled paper, balls of string, and thick files that fit beneath me like a mattress.

The game went on after work the next evening. I got my eight cents back five times over, and Fleur kept the rest of the dollar she'd won for a stake. This time they didn't play so late, but they played regular, and then kept going at it night after night. They played poker now, or variations, for one week straight, and each time Fleur won exactly one dollar, no more and no less, too consistent for luck.

By this time, Lily and the other men were so lit with suspense that they got Pete to join the game with them. They concentrated, the fat dog sitting tense in Lily Veddar's lap, Tor suspicious, Dutch stroking his huge square brow, Pete steady. It wasn't that Fleur won that hooked them in so, because she lost hands too. It was rather that she never had a freak hand or even anything above a straight. She only took on her low cards, which didn't sit right. By chance, Fleur should have gotten a full or flush by now. The irritating thing was she beat with pairs and never bluffed, because she couldn't, and still she ended up each night with exactly one dollar. Lily couldn't believe, first of all, that a woman could be smart enough to play cards, but even if she was, that she would then be stupid enough to cheat for a dollar a night. By day I watched him turn the problem over, his hard white face dull, small fingers probing at his knuckles, until he finally thought he had Fleur figured out as a bit-time player, caution her game. Raising the stakes would throw her.

More than anything now, he wanted Fleur to come away

with something but a dollar. Two bits less or ten more, the sum didn't matter, just so he broke her streak.

Night after night she played, won her dollar, and left to stay in a place that just Fritzie and I knew about. Fleur bathed in the slaughtering tub, then slept in the unused brick smokehouse behind the lockers, a windowless place tarred on the inside with scorched fats. When I brushed against her skin I noticed that she smelled of the walls, rich and woody, slightly burnt. Since that night she put me in the closet I was no longer afraid of her, but followed her close, stayed with her, became her moving shadow that the men never noticed, the shadow that could have saved her.

August, the month that bears fruit, closed around the shop, and Pete and Fritzie left for Minnesota to escape the heat. Night by night, running, Fleur had won thirty dollars, and only Pete's presence had kept Lily at bay. But Pete was gone now, and one payday, with the heat so bad no one could move but Fleur, the men sat and played and waited while she finished work. The cards sweat, limp in their fingers, the table was slick with grease, and even the walls were warm to the touch. The air was motionless. Fleur was in the next room boiling heads.

Her green dress, drenched, wrapped her like a transparent sheet. A skin of lakeweed. Black snarls of veining clung to her arms. Her braids were loose, half-unraveled, tied behind her neck in a thick loop. She stood in steam, turning skulls through a vat with a wooden paddle. When scraps boiled to the surface, she bent with a round tin sieve and scooped them out. She'd filled two dishpans.

"Ain't that enough now?" called Lily. "We're waiting." The stump of a dog trembled in his lap, alive with rage. It never smelled me or noticed me above Fleur's smoky skin. The air was heavy in my corner, and pressed me down. Fleur sat with them.

"Now what do you say?" Lily asked the dog. It barked. That was the signal for the real game to start.

"Let's up the ante," said Lily, who had been stalking this night all month. He had a roll of money in his pocket. Fleur had five bills in her dress. The men had each saved their full pay.

"Ante a dollar then," said Fleur, and pitched hers in. She lost, but they let her scrape along, cent by cent. And then she won some. She played unevenly, as if chance was all she had. She reeled them in. The game went on. The dog was stiff now, poised on Lily's knees, a ball of vicious muscle with its yellow eyes slit in concentration. It gave advice, seemed to sniff the lay of Fleur's cards, twitched and nudged. Fleur was up, then down, saved by

a scratch. Tor dealt seven cards, three down. The pot grew, round
by round, until it held all the money. Nobody folded. Then it all
rode on one last card and they went silent. Fleur picked hers up
and blew a long breath. The heat lowered like a bell. Her card
shook, but she stayed in.

Lily smiled and took the dog's head tenderly between his
palms.

"Say, Fatso," he said, crooning the words, "you reckon that
girl's bluffing?"

The dog whined and Lily laughed. "Me too," he said, "let's
show." He swept his bills and coins into the pot and then they
turned their cards over.

Lily looked once, looked again, then he squeezed the dog
up like a fist of dough and slammed it on the table.

Fleur threw her arms out and drew the money over, grinning
that same wolf grin that she'd used on me, the grin that had them.
She jammed the bills in her dress, scooped the coins up in waxed
white paper that she tied with string.

"Let's go another round," said Lily, his voice choked with
burrs. But Fleur opened her mouth and yawned, then walked out
back to gather slops for the one big hog that was waiting in the
stock pen to be killed.

The men sat still as rocks, their hands spread on the oiled
wood table. Dutch had chewed his cigar to damp shreds, Tor's
eye was dull. Lily's gaze was the only one to follow Fleur. I didn't
move. I felt them gathering, saw my stepfather's veins, the ones
in his forehead that stood out in anger. The dog had rolled off
the table and curled in a knot below the counter, where none of
the men could touch it.

Lily rose and stepped out back to the closet of ledgers where
Pete kept his private stock. He brought back a bottle, uncorked
and tipped it between his fingers. The lump in his throat moved,
then he passed it on. They drank, quickly felt the whiskey's fire,
and planned with their eyes things they couldn't say out loud.

When they left, I followed. I hid out back in the clutter of
broken boards and chicken crates beside the stock pen, where they
waited. Fleur could not be seen at first, and then the moon broke
and showed her, slipping cautiously along the rough board chute
with a bucket in her hand. Her hair fell, wild and coarse, to her
waist, and her dress was a floating patch in the dark. She made
a pig-calling sound, rang the tin pail lightly against the wood,
froze suspiciously. But too late. In the sound of the ring Lily
moved, fat and nimble, stepped right behind Fleur and put out
his creamy hands. At his first touch, she whirled and doused him

with the bucket of sour slops. He pushed her against the big fence and the package of coins split, went clinking and jumping, winked against the wood. Fleur rolled over once and vanished in the yard.

The moon fell behind a curtain of ragged clouds, and Lily followed into the dark muck. But he tripped, pitched over the huge flank of the pig, who lay mired to the snout, heavily snoring. I sprang out of the weeds and climbed the side of the pen, stuck like glue. I saw the sow rise to her neat, knobby knees, gain her balance, and sway, curious, as Lily stumbled forward. Fleur had backed into the angle of rough wood just beyond, and when Lily tried to jostle past, the sow tipped up on her hind legs and struck, quick and hard as a snake. She plunged her head into Lily's thick side and snatched a mouthful of his shirt. She lunged again, caught him lower, so that he grunted in pained surprise. He seemed to ponder, breathing deep. Then he launched his huge body in a swimmer's dive.

The sow screamed as his body smacked over hers. She rolled, striking out with her knife-sharp hooves, and Lily gathered himself upon her, took her foot-long face by the ears and scraped her snout and cheeks against the trestles of the pen. He hurled the sow's tight skull against an iron post, but instead of knocking her dead, he merely woke her from her dream.

She reared, shrieked, drew him with her so that they posed standing upright. They bowed jerkily to each other, as if to begin. Then his arms swung and flailed. She sank her black fangs into his shoulder, clasping him, dancing him forward and backward through the pen. Their steps picked up pace, went wild. The two dipped as one, box-stepped, tripped each other. She ran her split foot through his hair. He grabbed her kinked tail. They went down and came up, the same shape and then the same color, until the men couldn't tell one from the other in that light and Fleur was able to launch herself over the gates, swing down, hit gravel.

The men saw, yelled, and chased her at a dead run to the smokehouse. And Lily too, once the sow gave up in disgust and freed him. That is where I should have gone to Fleur, saved her, thrown myself on Dutch. But I went stiff with fear and couldn't unlatch myself from the trestles or move at all. I closed my eyes and put my head in my arms, tried to hide, so there is nothing to describe but what I couldn't block out, Fleur's hoarse breath, so loud it filled me, her cry in the old language, and my name repeated over and over among the words.

The heat was still dense the next morning when I came back to work. Fleur was gone but the men were there, slack-faced, hung over. Lily was paler and softer than ever, as if his flesh had steamed on his bones. They smoked, took pulls off a bottle. It wasn't noon yet. I worked awhile, waiting shop and sharpening steel. But I was sick, I was smothered, I was sweating so hard that my hands slipped on the knives, and I wiped my fingers clean of the greasy touch of the customers' coins. Lily opened his mouth and roared once, not in anger. There was no meaning to the sound. His boxer dog, sprawled limp beside his foot, never lifted its head. Nor did the other men.

They didn't notice when I stepped outside, hoping for a clear breath. And then I forgot them because I knew that we were all balanced, ready to tip, to fly, to be crushed as soon as the weather broke. The sky was so low that I felt the weight of it like a yoke. Clouds hung down, witch teats, a tornado's green-brown cones, and as I watched one flicked out and became a delicate probing thumb. Even as I picked up my heels and ran back inside, the wind blew suddenly, cold, and then came rain.

Inside, the men had disappeared already and the whole place was trembling as if a huge hand was pinched at the rafters, shaking it. I ran straight through, screaming for Dutch or for any of them, and then I stopped at the heavy doors of the lockers, where they had surely taken shelter. I stood there a moment. Everything went still. Then I heard a cry building in the wind, faint at first, a whistle and then a shrill scream that tore through the walls and gathered around me, spoke plain so I understood that I should move, put my arms out, and slam down the great iron bar that fit across the hasp and lock.

Outside, the wind was stronger, like a hand held against me. I struggled forward. The bushes tossed, the awnings flapped off storefronts, the rails of porches rattled. The odd cloud became a fat snout that nosed along the earth and sniffled, jabbed, picked at things, sucked them up, blew them apart, rooted around as if it was following a certain scent, then stopped behind me at the butcher shop and bored down like a drill.

I went flying, landed somewhere in a ball. When I opened my eyes and looked, stranger things were happening.

A herd of cattle flew through the air like giant birds, dropping dung, their mouths opened in stunned bellows. A candle, still lighted, blew past, and tables, napkins, garden tools, a whole school of drifting eyeglasses, jackets on hangers, hams, a checkerboard, a lampshade, and at last the sow from behind the lockers, on the run, her hooves a blur, set free, swooping, diving, screaming as everything in Argus fell apart and got turned upside down, smashed, and thoroughly wrecked.

Days passed before the town went looking for the men.

They were bachelors, after all, except for Tor, whose wife had suffered a blow to the head that made her forgetful. Everyone was occupied with digging out, in high relief because even though the Catholic steeple had been torn off like a peaked cap and sent across five fields, those huddled in the cellar were unhurt. Walls had fallen, windows were demolished, but the stores were intact and so were the bankers and shop owners who had taken refuge in their safes or beneath their cash registers. It was a fair-minded disaster, no one could be said to have suffered much more than the next, at least not until Fritzie and Pete came home.

Of all the businesses in Argus, Kozka's Meats had suffered worst. The boards of the front building had been split to kindling, piled in a huge pyramid, and the shop equipment was blasted far and wide. Pete paced off the distance the iron bathtub had been flung — a hundred feet. The glass candy case went fifty, and landed without so much as a cracked pane. There were other surprises as well, for the back rooms where Fritzie and Pete lived were undisturbed. Fritzie said the dust still coated her china figures, and upon her kitchen table, in the ashtray, perched the last cigarette she'd put out in haste. She lit it up and finished it, looking through the window. From there, she could see that the old smokehouse Fleur had slept in was crushed to a reddish sand and the stockpens were completely torn apart, the rails stacked helter-skelter. Fritzie asked for Fleur. People shrugged. Then she asked about the others and, suddenly, the town understood that three men were missing.

There was a rally of help, a gathering of shovels and volunteers. We passed boards from hand to hand, stacked them, uncovered what lay beneath the pile of jagged splinters. The lockers, full of the meat that was Pete and Fritzie's investment, slowly came into sight, still intact. When enough room was made for a man to stand on the roof, there were calls, a general urge to hack through and see what lay below. But Fritzie shouted that she wouldn't allow it because the meat would spoil. And so the work continued, board by board, until at last the heavy oak doors of the freezer were revealed and people pressed to the entry. Everyone wanted to be the first, but since it was my stepfather lost, I was let go in when Pete and Fritzie wedged through into the sudden icy air.

Pete scraped a match on his boot, lit the lamp Fritzie held, and then the three of us stood still in its circle. Light glared off the skinned and hanging carcasses, the crates of wrapped sausages, the bright and cloudy blocks of lake ice, pure as winter. The cold bit into us, pleasant at first, then numbing. We must have stood there a couple of minutes before we saw the men, or more rightly, the humps of fur, the iced and shaggy hides they wore, the bearskins they had taken down and wrapped around themselves. We stepped closer and tilted the lantern beneath the flaps of fur into their faces. The dog was there, perched among them, heavy as a doorstop. The three had hunched around a barrel where the game was still laid out, and a dead lantern and an empty bottle, too. But they had thrown down their last hands and hunkered tight, clutching one another, knuckles raw from beating at the door they had also attacked with hooks. Frost stars gleamed off their eyelashes and the stubble of their beards. Their faces were set in concentration, mouths open as if to speak some careful thought, some agreement they'd come to in each other's arms.

★   ★   ★

Power travels in the bloodlines, handed out before birth. It comes down through the hands, which in the Pillagers were strong and knotted, big, spidery, and rough, with sensitive fingertips good at dealing cards. It comes through the eyes, too, belligerent, darkest brown, the eyes of those in the bear clan, impolite as they gaze directly at a person.

In my dreams, I look straight back at Fleur, at the men. I am no longer the watcher on the dark sill, the skinny girl.

The blood draws us back, as if it runs through a vein of earth. I've come home and, except for talking to my cousins, live a quiet life. Fleur lives quiet too, down on Lake Turcot with her boat. Some say she's married to the waterman, Misshepeshu, or that she's living in shame with white men or windigos, or that she's killed them all. I'm about the only one here who ever goes to visit her. Last winter, I went to help out in her cabin when she bore the child, whose green eyes and skin the color of an old penny made more talk, as no one could decide if the child was mixed blood or what, fathered in a smokehouse, or by a man with brass scales, or by the lake. The girl is bold, smiling in her sleep, as if she knows what people wonder, as if she hears the old men talk, turning the story over. It comes up different every time and has no ending, no beginning. They get the middle wrong too. They only know that they don't know anything.

9
Observations on the Novel

Most of what has been said about short stories (on probability, narrative point of view, style) is relevant to the novel. And just as the short story of the last hundred years or so is rather different from earlier short fiction (see page 102), the novel — though here we must say of the last few hundred years — is different from earlier long fiction.

The ancient epic is at best a distant cousin to the novel, for though a narrative, the epic is in verse, and deals with god-like men and even with gods themselves. One has only to think of the *Odyssey* or the *Iliad* or the *Aeneid* or *Beowulf* or *Paradise Lost* to recall that the epic does not deal with the sort of people one meets in *Tom Jones, David Copperfield, Crime and Punishment, The Return of the Native, The Portrait of a Lady, The Sun Also Rises,* or *The Catcher in the Rye.*

The romance is perhaps a closer relative to the novel. Ancient romances were even in prose. But the hallmark of the romance, whether the romance is by a Greek sophist (Longus's *Daphnis and Chloe*) or by a medieval English poet (Chaucer's "The Knight's Tale") or by an American (Hawthorne's *The House of the Seven Gables*), is a presentation of the remote or the marvelous, rather than the local and the ordinary. The distinction is the same as that between the tale and the short story. "Tale" has the suggestion of a yarn, of unreality or of wondrous reality. (A case can be made for excluding Hawthorne's "Young Goodman Brown" from a collection of short stories on the ground that its remoteness and its allegorical implications mark it as a tale rather than a short story. This is not to say that it is inferior to a story, but only different.) In his preface to *The House of the Seven Gables* Hawthorne himself distinguishes between the romance and the novel:

> The latter form of composition is presumed to aim at a very minute fidelity, not merely to the possible, but to the probable and ordinary course of man's experience. The former—while, as a work of art, it must rigidly subject itself to laws, and while it sins unpardonably so far as it may swerve aside from the truth of the human heart — has fairly a right to present that truth under circumstances, to a great extent, of the writer's own choosing or creation.

In his preface to *The Marble Faun* Hawthorne explains that he chose "Italy as the site of his Romance" because it afforded him "a sort of poetic or fairy precinct, where actualities would not be so terribly insisted upon as they are . . . in America."

"Actualities . . . insisted upon." That, in addition to prose and length, is the hallmark of the novel. The novel is a sort of long newspaper story; the very word "novel" comes from an Italian word meaning a little new thing, and is related to the French word that gives us "news." (It is noteworthy that the French cognate of Hawthorne's "actualities," *actualités,* means "news" or "current events.") It is no accident that many novelists have been newspapermen: Defoe, Dickens, Crane, Dreiser, Joyce, Hemingway, Camus. And this connection with reportage perhaps helps to account for the relatively low esteem in which the novel is occasionally held: to some college students, a course in the novel does not seem quite up to a course in poetry, and people who read novels but not poetry are not likely to claim an interest in "literature."

Though Defoe's *Robinson Crusoe* is set in a far-off place, and thus might easily have been a romance, in Defoe's day it was close to current events, for it is a fictionalized version of events that had recently made news — Alexander Selkirk's life on the island of Juan Fernandez. And the story is not about marvelous happenings, but about a man's struggle for survival in dismal surroundings. Crusoe is not armed with Arthur's Excalibur or with Gawain's supposedly magic girdle, nor does he struggle as does Arthur with a Demon Cat and with a giant of St. Michael's Mount or as does Gawain with a Green Knight who survives decapitation; he has a carpenter's chest of tools and he struggles against commonplace nature. This chest was "much more valuable than a shiploading of gold would have been at that time." The world of romance contains splendid castles and enchanted forests, but Crusoe's world contains not much more than a plot of ground, some animals and vegetables, and Friday. "I fancied I could make all but the wheel [of a wheelbarrow Crusoe needed], but that I had no notion of, neither did I know how to go about it; besides, I had no possible way to make the iron gudgeons for the spindle or axis of the wheel to run in, so I gave it over." The book, in short, emphasizes not the strange, but (given the initial situation) the usual, the commonsensical, the probable. The world of *Robinson Crusoe* is hardly different from the world we meet in the beginning of almost any novel:

> We were in study hall when the headmaster walked in, followed by a new boy not wearing a school uniform, and by a janitor carrying a large desk. Those who were sleeping awoke, and we all stood up as though interrupting our work.
>
> Gustave Flaubert, Madame Bovary

> My father's family name being Pirrip, and my Christian name Philip, my infant tongue could make of both names nothing longer or more explicit than Pip. So I called myself Pip, and came to be called Pip.
>
> I give Pirrip as my father's family name, on the authority of his tombstone and my sister — Mrs. Joe Gargery, who married the blacksmith.
>
> Charles Dickens, Great Expectations

> In beginning the life story of my hero, Alexey Fyodorovich Karamazov, I find myself in somewhat of a quandary. Namely, although I call Alexey Fyodorovich my hero, I myself know that he is by no means a great man, and hence I foresee such unavoidable questions as these: "What is so remarkable about your Alexey Fyodorovich, that you have chosen him as your hero? What has he accomplished? What is he known for, and by whom? Why should I, the reader, spend time learning the facts of his life?"
>
> Fyodor Dostoyevsky, The Brothers Karamazov

> If you really want to hear about it, the first thing you'll probably want to know is where I was born, and what my lousy childhood was like, and how my parents were occupied and all before they had me, and all that David Copperfield kind of crap, but I don't feel like going into it, if you want to know the truth.
>
> J. D. Salinger, The Catcher in the Rye

> It was June, 1933, one week after Commencement, when Kay Leiland Strong, Vassar '33, the first of her class to run around the table at the Class Day dinner, was married to Harald Petersen, Reed '27, in the chapel of St. George's Church, P.E., Karl F. Reiland, Rector. Outside, on Stuyvesant Square, the trees were in full leaf, and the wedding guests arriving

by twos and threes in taxis heard the voices of children playing
round the statue of Peter Stuyvesant in the park.

Mary McCarthy, *The Group*

Sleepy boys in a school room; the brother of the wife of a
blacksmith named Joe Gargery; a hero who "is by no means a
great man"; a boy who in boy's language seems reluctant to talk
of his "lousy childhood"; a young woman who ran around the
table at the Class Day dinner. In all these passages, and in the
openings of most other novels, we are confronted with current
biography, and, indeed, a fair number of important novels — for
example, D. H. Lawrence's *Sons and Lovers,* James Joyce's *A Portrait
of the Artist as a Young Man,* Jack Kerouac's *On the Road* — are
highly autobiographical.* In contrast to these beginnings, look at
the beginning of one of Chaucer's great romances:

Whilom,° as olde stories tellen us,	*once*
There was a duc that highte° Theseus;	*was named*
Of Atthenes he was lord and governour,	
And in his tyme swich° a conquerour,	*such*
That gretter was ther noon under the sonne.	

"Whilom." "Olde stories." "Gretter was ther noon under the
sonne." We are in a timeless past, in which unusual people dwell.
But the novel is almost always set in the present or very recent
past, and it deals with ordinary people. It so often deals with
ordinary people, and presents them, apparently, in so ordinary a
fashion that we sometimes wonder what is the point of it. Although
the romance is often "escape" literature, it usually is didactic,
holding up to us images of noble and ignoble behavior, revealing
the rewards of courage and the power of love. In the preface to
The Marble Faun, for instance, Hawthorne says he "proposed to
himself to merely write a fanciful story, evolving a thoughtful
moral, and did not propose attempting a portraiture of Italian

---

* Recently even the veil of fiction has been removed, and a new form, the "nonfiction
novel" has developed. The term apparently was coined by Truman Capote to
describe *In Cold Blood,* his account of a multiple murder committed in Kansas in
1959. The details are all true, but the book is written with a novelist's sense of
irony and of symbolic details; in short, it is history written by a novelist — but
this form is not to be confused with the "historical novel," which by its usual
emphasis on plot and on the exotic is a kind of romance. Other examples of the
nonfiction novel: Norman Mailer's *The Armies of the Night,* describing the anti-
Vietnam war march of 1967 and subsequent related events, in which Mailer writes
of himself in the third person, and *The Executioner's Song,* which Mailer calls his
"true life novel" about Gary Gilmore, the convicted murderer who refused an
appeal and insisted on having his death penalty carried out by a firing squad.

manners and character." But portraiture is what the novelist gives us. Intent on revealing the world of real men and women going about their daily work and play, he does not simplify his characters into representatives of vices and virtues as does the romancer who wishes to evolve a thoughtful moral, but gives abundant detail — some of it apparently irrelevant. The innumerable details add up to a long book, although there need not be many physical happenings. The novel tells a story, of course, but the story is not only about what people overtly do but also about what they think (i.e., their mental doings) and about the society in which they are immersed and by which they are in part shaped. In the much-quoted preface to *Pierre and Jean,* Maupassant says:

> The skill of the novelist's plan will not reside in emotional effects, in attractive writing, in a striking beginning or a moving dénouement, but in the artful building up of solid details from which the essential meaning of the work will emerge.

As we read a novel we feel we are seeing not the "higher reality" or the "inner reality" so often mentioned by students of the arts, but the real reality.*

The short story, too, is detailed, but commonly it reveals only a single character at a moment of crisis, whereas the novel commonly traces the development of an individual, a group of people, a world. The novelist, of course, has an attitude toward his world; he is not compiling an almanac but telling an invented story, making a work of art, offering not merely a representation of reality but a response to it, and he therefore selects and shapes his material. One way of selecting and shaping the material is through the chosen point of view: we do not get everything in nineteenth-century England, but only everything that Pip remembers or chooses to set down about his experiences, and what he sets down is colored by his personality. "I remember Mr. Hubble as a tough high-shouldered stooping old man, of a saw-dusty fragrance,

---

* It should be mentioned that in the 1950s the *nouveau roman* or "new novel" developed, in reaction to the novels of the sort we have been talking about. Writers of the new novel (such as Alain Robbe-Grillet, Nathalie Sarraute, and Claude Simon) argue that the traditional novel is utterly false, for it presents characters (whereas people are not psychologically consistent creatures, but a complex series of appearances), plots (whereas plots do not exist in nature), cause and effect (a naive assumption), and it assumes that there is a connection between people and the objects of the world they move in (another naive assumption). The new novel, instead of presenting a story of coherent characters acting in a context, offers a sort of dream-like series of perceptions; the identities of the perceivers and the chronology are usually unclear, and, of course, the story has no conclusion.

with his legs extraordinarily wide apart: so that in my short days I always saw some miles of open country between them when I met him coming up the lane." In any case, the coherence in a novel seems inclusive rather than exclusive. The novelist usually conveys the sense that he, as distinct from his characters, is — in the words of Christopher Isherwood's *The Berlin Stories* — "a camera with its shutter open, quite passive, recording not thinking. Recording the man shaving at the windows opposite and the woman in the kimono washing her hair. Some day, all of this will have to be developed, carefully fixed, printed."

It is not merely that the novel gives us details. *Gulliver's Travels* has plenty of details about people six inches tall and people sixty feet tall, and about a flying island and rational horses. But these things are recognized as fanciful inventions, though they do turn our mind toward the real world. *Gulliver* is a satire that holds up to us a picture of a fantastic world by which, paradoxically, we come to see the real world a little more clearly. The diminutive stature of the Lilliputians is an amusing and potent metaphor for the littleness of man, the flying island for abstract thinkers who have lost touch with reality, and so on. But the novelist who wants to show us the littleness of man invents not Lilliputians but a world of normal-sized people who do little things and have little thoughts.

Having spent so much time saying that the novel is not the epic or romance or fable, we must mention that a work may hover on the borderlines of these forms. Insofar as *Moby Dick* narrates with abundant realistic detail the experiences of a whaler ("This book," Dorothy Parker has said, "taught me more about whales than I ever wanted to know"), it is a novel; but in its evocation of mystery — Queequeg, the prophecies, Ishmael's miraculous rescue from the sea filled with sharks who "glided by as if with padlocks on their mouths" — it is a romance with strong symbolic implications.

The point is that although a reader of a long piece of prose fiction can complain that he did not get what he paid for, he should find out what he did get, rather than damn it for not being what it isn't. Bishop Butler's famous remark is relevant to literary criticism: "Everything is what it is and not another thing."

Poetry

10
Lyric Poetry

For the ancient Greeks, a **lyric** was a song accompanied by a lyre. It was short, and it usually expressed a single emotion, such as joy or sorrow. The word is now used more broadly, referring to a poem that, neither narrative (telling a story) nor strictly dramatic (performed by actors), is an emotional or reflective soliloquy. Still, it is rarely very far from a singing voice. James Joyce saw the lyric as the "verbal vesture of an instant of emotion, a rhythmical cry such as ages ago cheered on the man who pulled at the oar." Such lyrics, too, were sung more recently than "ages ago." Here is a song that American slaves sang when rowing heavy loads.

Anonymous
Michael Row the Boat Ashore

Michael row the boat ashore, Hallelujah!
Michael's boat's a freedom boat, Hallelujah!
Sister, help to trim the sail, Hallelujah!
Jordan stream is wide and deep, Hallelujah!
Freedom stands on the other side, Hallelujah!

We might pause for a moment to comment on why people sing at work. There are at least three reasons: (1) work done rhythmically goes more efficiently; (2) the songs relieve the boredom of the work; and (3) the songs — whether narrative or lyrical — provide something of an outlet for the workers' frustrations.

Speaking roughly, we can say that whereas a narrative (whether in prose or poetry) is set in the past, telling what happened, a lyric is set in the present, catching a speaker in a moment of expression. But lyric can, of course, glance backward or forward, as in this folk song, usually called "Careless Love."

Anonymous

Careless Love

Love, O love, O careless love,
You see what careless love can do.
When I wore my apron low,
Couldn't keep you from my do,°   *door*
    Fare you well, fare you well.
Now I wear my apron high,
Scarce see you passin' by,
    Fare you well, fare you well.

Notice, too, that a lyric, like a narrative, can have a sort of plot: "Michael" moves toward the idea of freedom, and "Careless Love" implies a story of desertion, but again, the emphasis is on a present state of mind.

Lyrics are sometimes differentiated among themselves. For example, if a lyric is melancholy or mournfully contemplative, especially if it laments a death, it may be called an **elegy** (though before Gray's famous "Elegy" the word often denoted a personal poem written in pairs of lines, on whatever theme). If a lyric is rather long, elaborate, and on a lofty theme such as immortality or a hero's victory, it may be called an **ode** or a **hymn**. Greek odes were choral pieces of praise in elaborate stanzas, but in Rome, Horace (65–8 B.C.) applied the word to quieter pieces, usually in stanzas of four lines, celebrating love, patriotism, or duty. Distinctions among lyrics are often vague, and one person's ode may be another's elegy. Still, when writers use one of these words in their titles, they are inviting the reader to recall the tradition in which they are working. Of the poet's link to tradition T. S. Eliot said:

No poet, no artist of any art, has his complete meaning alone.
His significance, his appreciation is the appreciation of his

relation to the dead poets and artists. You cannot value him alone; you must set him, for contrast and comparison, among the dead.

Although the lyric is often ostensibly addressed to someone (the "you" in "Careless Love"), the reader usually feels that the speaker is really talking to himself or herself. In "Careless Love," the speaker need not be in the presence of her man; rather, her heart is overflowing (the reader senses) and she pretends to address him. A comment by John Stuart Mill on poetry is especially true of the lyric:

> Eloquence is *heard,* poetry is *over*heard. Eloquence supposes an audience; the peculiarity of poetry appears to us to lie in the poet's utter unconsciousness of a listener. Poetry is feeling confessing itself to itself, in moments of solitude.

This is especially true, of course, in work-songs such as "Michael Row the Boat Ashore," where there is no audience: the singers sing for themselves, participating rather than performing. As one prisoner in Texas said: "They really be singing about the way they feel inside. Since they can't say it to nobody, they sing a song about it." The sense of "feeling confessing itself to itself, in moments of solitude" or of "singing about the way they feel inside" is strong and clear in this short cowboy song.

Anonymous

The Colorado Trail

Eyes like the morning star,
Cheeks like a rose,
Laura was a pretty girl,
God Almighty knows.

Weep all ye little rains,
Wail winds wail,
All along, along, along
The Colorado trail.

Here is another anonymous poem, this one probably written in the early sixteenth century.

Anonymous

Western Wind

Western wind, when wilt thou blow,
The small rain down can rain?
Christ, if my love were in my arms,
And I in my bed again!

QUESTIONS

1. In "Western Wind," what do you think is the tone of the speaker's voice in the first two lines? Angry? Impatient? Supplicating? Be as precise as possible. What is the tone in the next two lines?
2. In England, the west wind, warmed by the Gulf Stream, rises in the spring. What associations link the wind and rain of lines 1 and 2 with lines 3 and 4?
3. Ought we to have been told why the lovers are separated? Explain.

The next poem, written by an unmarried proper New England lady of the nineteenth century, is strongly erotic.

Emily Dickinson (*American. 1830–1886*)

Wild nights, wild nights!

Wild nights, wild nights!
Were I with thee,
Wild nights should be
Our luxury.

Futile the winds
To a heart in port,
Done with the compass,
Done with the chart.

Rowing in Eden —
Ah, the sea!
Might I but moor
To-night in thee.

QUESTIONS

1. Probably "wild nights" refers chiefly to a storm outside of
   the lovers' room, but it can of course also describe their love.
   "Luxury" (from the Latin *luxuria,* which meant "excess,"
   or "extravagance") in line 4 probably retains some of the
   meaning that it first had when it entered into English, "lust"
   or sensual enjoyment. What does the second stanza say about
   the nature of their love? How does the third stanza modify
   the idea?
2. What makes this lyric lyrical?
3. Do you think that the poem is sentimental? Explain.

Langston Hughes (American. 1902–1967)

Evenin' Air Blues

Folks, I come up North
Cause they told me de North was fine.
I come up North
Cause they told me de North was fine.
Been up here six months —   5
I'm about to lose my mind.

This mornin' for breakfast
I chawed de mornin' air.
This mornin' for breakfast
Chawed de mornin' air.   10
But this evenin' for supper,
I got evenin' air to spare.

Believe I'll do a little dancin'
Just to drive my blues away —
A little dancin'   15
To drive my blues away,
Cause when I'm dancin'
De blues forgets to stay.

But if you was to ask me
How de blues they come to be,   *20*
Says if you was to ask me
How de blues they come to be —
You wouldn't need to ask me:
Just look at me and see!

QUESTION

In what ways (subject, language) does this poem resemble
blues you may have heard? Does it differ in any ways?

John Lennon (*English. 1940–1980*)
Paul McCartney (*English. b. 1942*)

Eleanor Rigby

Ah, look at all the lonely people!
Ah, look at all the lonely people!

Eleanor Rigby
Picks up the rice in the church where a wedding has been,
Lives in a dream.   *5*
Waits at the window
Wearing the face that she keeps in a jar by the door.
Who is it for?

All the lonely people,
Where do they all come from?   *10*
All the lonely people,
Where do they all belong?

Father McKenzie,
Writing the words of a sermon that no one will hear,
No one comes near.   *15*

Look at him working,
Darning his socks in the night when there's nobody there.
What does he care?

All the lonely people,
Where do they all come from?   *20*
All the lonely people,
Where do they all belong?

Ah, look at all the lonely people!
Ah, look at all the lonely people!

Eleanor Rigby   *25*
Died in the church and was buried along with her name,
Nobody came.
Father McKenzie,
Wiping the dirt from his hands as he walks from the grave,
No one was saved.   *30*

All the lonely people,
Where do they all come from?
All the lonely people,
Where do they all belong?

Ah, look at all the lonely people!   *35*
Ah, look at all the lonely people!

QUESTION

Is the poem chiefly about Eleanor Rigby? What is Father
McKenzie doing in the poem?

Julia Ward Howe (*American. 1819–1910*)

Battle Hymn of the Republic

Mine eyes have seen the glory of the coming of the Lord:
He is trampling out the vintage where the grapes of wrath are
      stored;
He hath loosed the fateful lightning of his terrible swift sword;
      His truth is marching on.   *4*

Chorus
      Glory! glory! Hallelujah!
      Glory! glory! Hallelujah!
      Glory! glory! Hallelujah!
            His truth is marching on!   *8*

I have seen him in the watch-fires of a hundred circling camps;
They have builded him an altar in the evening dews and damps;
I can read his righteous sentence by the dim and flaring lamps:
      His day is marching on.   *12*

I have read a fiery gospel, writ in burnished rows of steel:
"As ye deal with my contemners, so with you my grace shall
    deal;
Let the Hero, born of woman, crush the serpent with his heel,
    Since God is marching on."   **16**

He has sounded forth the trumpet that shall never call retreat;
He is sifting out the hearts of men before his judgment-seat;
Oh, be swift, my soul, to answer him! be jubilant, my feet!
Our God is marching on.   **20**

In the beauty of the lilies Christ was born across the sea,
With a glory in his bosom that transfigures you and me:
As he died to make men holy, let us die to make men free,
    While God is marching on.   **24**

QUESTION

This poem of the Civil War, written to the tune of "John
Brown's Body," draws some of its militant imagery from
the Bible, especially from Revelation 19: 11–15. Do the lines
on Christ seem incongruous here?

Wilfred Owen (English. 1893–1918)

Anthem for Doomed Youth

What passing-bells for these who die as cattle?
Only the monstrous anger of the guns.
Only the stuttering rifles' rapid rattle
Can patter out their hasty orisons.
No mockeries for them from prayers or bells,   *5*
Nor any voice of mourning save the choirs —
The shrill, demented choirs of wailing shells;
And bugles calling for them from sad shires.

What candles may be held to speed° them all?   *aid*
Not in the hands of boys, but in their eyes   *10*
Shall shine the holy glimmers of good-byes.
The pallor of girls' brows shall be their pall;
Their flowers the tenderness of patient minds,
And each slow dusk a drawing-down of blinds.

QUESTIONS

1. Exactly what is an anthem? What are some of the words or phrases in this poem that might be found in a traditional anthem? What are some of the words or phrases that you would not expect in an anthem?
2. How would you characterize the speaker's state of mind? (Your response probably will require more than one word.)

Walt Whitman (*American. 1819–1892*)

A Noiseless Patient Spider

A noiseless patient spider,
I mark'd where on a little promontory it stood isolated,
Mark'd how to explore the vacant vast surrounding,
It launch'd forth filament, filament, filament, out of itself,
Ever unreeling them, ever tirelessly speeding them.   *5*

And you O my soul where you stand,
Surrounded, detached, in measureless oceans of space,
Ceaselessly musing, venturing, throwing, seeking the spheres to
      connect them,
Till the bridge you will need be form'd, till the ductile anchor
      hold,
Till the gossamer thread you fling catch somewhere,
      O my soul.   *10*

QUESTIONS

1. How are the suggestions in "launch'd" (line 4) and "unreeling" (line 5) continued in the second stanza?
2. How are the varying lengths of lines 1, 4, and 8 relevant to their ideas?
3. The second stanza is not a complete sentence. Why? The poem is unrhymed. What effect does the near-rhyme (hold: soul) in the last two lines have on you?

Robert Frost (American. 1874–1963)

Stopping by Woods on a Snowy Evening

Whose woods these are I think I know.
His house is in the village though;
He will not see me stopping here
To watch his woods fill up with snow.   *4*

My little horse must think it queer
To stop without a farmhouse near
Between the woods and frozen lake
The darkest evening of the year.   *8*

He gives his harness bells a shake
To ask if there is some mistake.
The only other sound's the sweep
Of easy wind and downy flake.   *12*

The woods are lovely, dark and deep.
But I have promises to keep,
And miles to go before I sleep,
And miles to go before I sleep.   *16*

QUESTIONS

1. Line 5 originally read: "The steaming horses think it queer."
   Line 7 read: "Between a forest and a lake." Which version
   do you prefer? Why?
2. The rhyming words in the first stanza can be indicated by
   aaba; the second stanza picks up the *b* rhyme: *bbcb.* Indicate
   the rhymes for the third stanza. For the fourth. Why is it
   appropriate that the rhyme scheme differs in the fourth stanza?
3. Hearing that the poem had been interpreted as a "death
   poem," Frost said, "I never intended that, but I did have
   the feeling it was loaded with ulteriority." What "ulteriority"
   is implicit? How is the time of day and year significant? How
   does the horse's attitude make a contrast with the man's?

John Keats (*English. 1795–1821*)

Ode on a Grecian Urn

I

Thou still unravished bride of quietness,
    Thou foster-child of silence and slow time,
Sylvan historian, who canst thus express
    A flowery tale more sweetly than our rhyme:
What leaf-fringed legend haunts about thy shape   *5*
    Of deities or mortals, or of both,
        In Tempe or the dales of Arcady?
    What men or gods are these? What maidens loth?
What mad pursuit? What struggle to escape?
        What pipes and timbrels? What wild ecstasy?   *10*

II

Heard melodies are sweet, but those unheard
    Are sweeter; therefore, ye soft pipes, play on;
Not to the sensual° ear, but, more endeared,   *sensuous*
    Pipe to the spirit ditties of no tone:
Fair youth, beneath the trees, thou canst not leave   *15*
    Thy song, nor ever can those trees be bare;
        Bold Lover, never, never canst thou kiss,
Though winning near the goal — yet, do not grieve;
        She cannot fade, though thou hast not thy bliss,
    For ever wilt thou love, and she be fair!   *20*

III

Ah, happy, happy boughs! that cannot shed
    Your leaves, nor ever bid the Spring adieu;
And, happy melodist, unwearied,
    For ever piping songs for ever new;
More happy love! more happy, happy love!   *25*
    For ever warm and still to be enjoyed,
        For ever panting, and for ever young;
All breathing human passion far above,
    That leaves a heart high-sorrowful and cloyed,
        A burning forehead, and a parching tongue.   *30*

IV

Who are these coming to the sacrifice?
    To what green altar, O mysterious priest,

Lead'st thou that heifer lowing at the skies,
    And all her silken flanks with garlands drest?
What little town by river or sea shore,   35
        Or mountain-built with peaceful citadel,
            Is emptied of this folk, this pious morn?
And, little town, thy streets for evermore
        Will silent be; and not a soul to tell
            Why thou art desolate can e'er return.   40

       V

O Attic shape! Fair attitude! with brede°   design
    Of marble men and maidens overwrought,
With forest branches and the trodden weed;
        Thou, silent form, dost tease us out of thought
As doth eternity: Cold Pastoral!   45
When old age shall this generation waste,
        Thou shalt remain, in midst of other woe
        Than ours, a friend to man, to whom thou say'st,
"Beauty is truth, truth beauty," — that is all
        Ye know on earth, and all ye need to know.   50

    QUESTIONS

    1. If you do not know the meaning of "sylvan," check a dic-
       tionary. Why does Keats call the urn a "sylvan" historian
       (line 3)? As the poem continues, what evidence is there that
       the urn cannot "express" (line 3) a tale so sweetly as the
       speaker said?
    2. What do you make of lines 11–14?
    3. What do you think the urn may stand for in the first three
       stanzas? In the third stanza is the speaker caught up in the
       urn's world or is he sharply aware of his own?
    4. Do you take "tease us out of thought" (line 44) to mean
       "draw us into a realm of imaginative experience superior to
       that of reason" or to mean "draw us into futile and frustrating
       questions"? Or both? Or neither? What suggestions do you
       find in "Cold Pastoral' (line 45)?
    5. Do lines 49–50 perhaps mean that imagination, stimulated
       by the urn, achieves a realm richer than the daily world? Or
       perhaps that art, the highest earthly wisdom, suggests there
       is a realm wherein earthly troubles are resolved?

11

The Speaking Tone of Voice

> Everything written is as good as it is dramatic. . . . [A poem is] heard as sung or spoken by a person in a scene — in character, in a setting. By whom, where and when is the question. By the dreamer of a better world out in a storm in Autumn; by a lover under a window at night.
>
> Robert Frost, Preface, *A Way Out*

If we fall into the habit of saying "Whitman says, 'A noiseless patient spider,/ I mark'd' " or "Keats says, 'Heard melodies are sweet, but those unheard are sweeter,' " we neglect the important truth in Frost's comment: a poem is written by an author, but it is spoken by an invented speaker. The author counterfeits the speech of a person in a particular situation. The anonymous author of "Western Wind" (page 412) invents the speech of an unhappy lover who longs for the spring; Robert Frost in "Stopping by Woods" (page 418) invents the speech of a person who, sitting in a horse-drawn sleigh, is surveying woods that are "lovely, dark and deep."

The speaker's voice, of course, often has the ring of the author's own voice, and to make a distinction between speaker and author may at times seem perverse. Robert Burns, for example, sometimes lets us know that the poem is spoken by "Rob"; he may address his wife by name; beneath the title "To a Mouse" he writes, "On Turning Up Her Nest with the Plow, November, 1785," and beneath the title "To a Mountain Daisy" he writes, "On Turning One Down with the Plow in April, 1786." Still, even in these allegedly autobiographical poems, it may be convenient to distinguish between author and speaker; the speaker is Burns the lover, or Burns the meditative man, or Burns the compassionate man, not simply Robert Burns the poet. Here are two poems by Burns; in the first the lover speaks, in the second we hear a different speaker. (If you read the poems aloud, the meanings of many of the Scot's words will become clear. Thus, in line 5, "wad" is "would." And if you read the poems aloud, you will get a strong sense of the speakers.)

Robert Burns (*Scottish. 1759–1796*)

Mary Morison

O Mary, at thy window be,
 It is the wished, the trysted hour!
Those smiles and glances let me see,
 That make the miser's treasure poor: **4**
How blithely wad I bide the stour,°   *endure the struggle*
 A weary slave frae sun to sun,
Could I the rich reward secure,
 The lovely Mary Morison.   **8**

Yestreen when to the trembling string
 The dance gaed° through the lighted ha',   *went*
To thee my fancy took its wing,
 · I sat, but neither heard nor saw: **12**
Though this was fair, and that was braw,°   *handsome*
 And yon the toast of a' the town,
I sighed, and said amang them a',
 "Ye are na Mary Morison."   **16**

O Mary, canst thou wreck his peace,
 Wha for thy sake wad gladly die?
Or canst thou break that heart of his,
 Whase only faut° is loving thee?   *fault* **20**
If love for love thou wilt na gie,°   *give*
 At least be pity to me shown!
A thought ungentle canna be
 The thought o' Mary Morison.   **24**

Robert Burns (Scottish. *1759–1796*)

John Anderson My Jo

John Anderson my jo,° John,   *sweetheart*
    When we were first acquent,
Your locks were like the raven,
    Your bonnie brow was brent;°   *smooth*   4
But now your brow is beld, John,
    Your locks are like the snaw,
But blessings on your frosty pow,°   *head*
    John Anderson my jo!   8

John Anderson my jo, John,
    We clamb the hill thegither,
And monie a cantie° day, John   *happy*
    We've had wi' ane anither: 12
Now we maun° totter down, John,   *must*
    And hand in hand we'll go,
And sleep thegither at the foot,
    John Anderson my jo!   16

QUESTIONS

1. In the first poem, do we imagine the speaker as really addressing Mary Morison?
2. In "Mary Morison," how convincing are the assertions of the first stanza (that her smiles and glances are more valuable than great wealth; that he would willingly be a "weary slave" if only he could win her)? Does the third stanza somehow sound truer, more convincing? If so, why? The poem is excellent throughout, but many readers find the second stanza the best of the three. Do you?
3. In "John Anderson My Jo," the speaker cannot be identified with Burns, but do we feel that there is in the poem anything of the particular accent of an old lady? Why?

Although all poems are "dramatic" in Frost's sense of being uttered by a speaker in a situation, and although most short poems are monologues, the term **dramatic monologue** is reserved for those poems in which a single character — not the poet — is speaking at a critical moment to a person or persons whose presence we strongly feel. The most famous example is Robert Browning's "My Last Duchess."

Robert Browning (*English. 1812–1889*)

My Last Duchess

FERRARA°   *town in Italy*

That's my last Duchess painted on the wall,
Looking as if she were alive. I call
That piece a wonder, now; Frà Pandolf's° hands   *a fictitious*
Worked busily a day, and there she stands.   *painter*
Will't please you sit and look at her? I said   5
"Frà Pandolf" by design, for never read
Strangers like you that pictured countenance,
The depth and passion of its earnest glance,
But to myself they turned (since none puts by
The curtain I have drawn for you, but I)   10
And seemed as they would ask me, if they durst,
How such a glance came there; so, not the first
Are you to turn and ask thus. Sir, 'twas not
Her husband's presence only, called that spot
Of joy into the Duchess' cheek; perhaps   15
Frà Pandolf chanced to say "Her mantle laps
Over my Lady's wrist too much," or, "Paint
Must never hope to reproduce the faint
Half-flush that dies along her throat." Such stuff
Was courtesy, she thought, and cause enough   20
For calling up that spot of joy. She had
A heart — how shall I say? — too soon made glad,
Too easily impressed; she liked whate'er
She looked on, and her looks went everywhere.
Sir, 'twas all one! My favor at her breast,   25
The dropping of the daylight in the west,
The bough of cherries some officious fool
Broke in the orchard for her, the white mule
She rode with round the terrace — all and each
Would draw from her alike the approving speech,   30
Or blush, at least. She thanked men — good! but thanked
Somehow — I know not how — as if she ranked
My gift of a nine-hundred-years-old name
With anybody's gift. Who'd stoop to blame
This sort of trifling? Even had you skill   35
In speech — (which I have not) — to make your will
Quite clear to such an one, and say, "Just this
Or that in you disgusts me; here you miss,
Or there exceed the mark" — and if she let

Herself be lessoned so, nor plainly set 40
Her wits to yours, forsooth, and made excuse,
— E'en then would be some stooping; and I choose
Never to stoop. Oh, Sir, she smiled, no doubt,
Whene'er I passed her; but who passed without
Much the same smile? This grew; I gave commands; 45
Then all smiles stopped together. There she stands
As if alive. Will't please you rise? We'll meet
The company below, then. I repeat,
The Count your master's known munificence
Is ample warrant that no just pretense 50
Of mine for dowry will be disallowed;
Though his fair daughter's self, as I avowed
At starting, is my object. Nay, we'll go
Together down, Sir. Notice Neptune, though,
Taming a sea-horse, thought a rarity, 55
Which Claus of Innsbruck° cast in bronze for me! *a fictitious sculptor*

QUESTIONS

1. Who is speaking to whom? On what occasion?
2. What words or lines do you think especially convey the speaker's arrogance? What is your attitude toward the speaker? Loathing? Fascination? Respect? Explain.
3. The time and place are Renaissance Italy; how do they affect your attitude toward the duke? What would be the effect if the poem were set in the twentieth century?
4. Why does this poem sound more like talk and less like song than Burns's "John Anderson"?
5. Years after writing this poem, Browning explained that the duke's "commands" (line 45) were "that she should be put to death, or he might have had her shut up in a convent." Do you think the poem should have been more explicit? Does Browning's later uncertainty indicate that the poem is badly thought out? Suppose we did not have Browning's comment on line 45. Do you think the line then could mean only that he commanded her to stop smiling and that she obeyed? Explain.

DICTION

From the whole of language, one consciously or unconsciously selects certain words and grammatical constructions; this selection constitutes one's **diction**. It is partly by the diction that we come to know the speaker of a poem. "Amang" and "frae sun to sun" tell us that the speaker of "Mary Morison" is a Scot. In "My Last Duchess" such words as "countenance," "munificence," and "disallowed" — none of which is conceivable in Burns's poem — help us form our impression of the duke. Of course, some words are used in both poems: "I said," "and," "smile[s]," "glance[s]," etc. The fact remains, however, that although a large part of language is shared by all speakers, certain parts of language are used only by certain speakers.

Like some words, some grammatical constructions are used only by certain kinds of speakers. Consider these two passages:

> In Adam's fall
> We sinned all.
>   Anonymous, *The New England Primer*

> Of Man's first disobedience, and the fruit
> Of that forbidden tree whose mortal taste
> Brought death into the World, and all our woe,
> With loss of Eden, till one greater Man
> Restore us, and regain the blissful seat,
> Sing, Heavenly Muse, that, on the secret top
> Of Oreb, or of Sinai, didst inspire
> That shepherd who first taught the chosen seed
> In the beginning how the heavens and earth
> Rose out of Chaos. . . .
>   Milton, *Paradise Lost*

There is an enormous difference in the diction of these two passages. Milton, speaking as an inspired poet, appropriately uses words and grammatical constructions somewhat removed from common life. Hence, while the anonymous author of the primer speaks directly of "Adam's fall," Milton speaks allusively of the fall, calling it "Man's first disobedience." Milton's sentence is nothing that any Englishman ever said in conversation; its genitive beginning, its length (the sentence continues for six lines beyond the quoted passage), and its postponement of the main verb until the sixth line mark it as the utterance of a poet working in the tradition of Latin poetry. The primer's statement, by its choice of words as well as by its brevity, suggests a far less sophisticated speaker.

TONE

Speakers have attitudes toward themselves, their subjects, and their audiences, and (consciously or unconsciously) they choose their words, pitch, and modulation accordingly; all these add up to the **tone**. In written literature, tone must be detected without the aid of the ear; the reader must understand by the selection and sequence of words the way in which they are meant to be heard (that is, playfully, angrily, confidentially, sarcastically, etc.). The reader must catch what Frost calls "the speaking tone of voice somehow entangled in the words and fastened to the page of the ear of the imagination."*

Robert Herrick (English. 1591–1674)

To the Virgins, to Make Much of Time

Gather ye rosebuds while ye may,
    Old Time is still a-flying;
And this same flower that smiles today,
    Tomorrow will be dying.   *4*

The glorious lamp of heaven, the sun,
    The higher he's a-getting,
The sooner will his race be run,
    And nearer he's to setting.   *8*

That age is best which is the first,
    When youth and blood are warmer;
But being spent, the worse, and worst
    Times still succeed the former.   *12*

Then be not coy, but use your time;
    And while ye may, go marry:
For having lost but once your prime,
    You may for ever tarry.   *16*

Carpe diem (Latin: "seize the day") is the theme. But if we want to get the full force of the poem, we must understand who is talking to whom. Look, for example, at "Old Time" in line 2. Time is "old," of course, in the sense of having been around a

---

* This discussion concentrates on the speaker's tone. But one can also talk of the author's tone, that is, of the author's attitude toward the invented speaker. The speaker's tone might, for example, be angry, but the author's tone (as detected by the reader) might be humorous. For further comment on the author's tone, see page 85.

long while, but doesn't "old" in this context suggest also that the speaker regards Time with easy familiarity, almost affection? We visit the old school, and our friend is old George. Time is destructive, yes, and the speaker urges the young maidens to make the most of their spring, but the speaker is neither bitter nor importunate; rather, he seems to be the wise old man, the counselor, the man who has made his peace with Time and is giving advice to the young. Time moves rapidly in the poem (the rosebud of line 1 is already a flower in line 3), but the speaker is unhurried; in line 5 he has leisure to explain that the glorious lamp of heaven is the sun.

In "To the Virgins," the pauses, indicated by punctuation at the ends of the lines (except in line 11, where we tumble without stopping from "worse" to "Times"), slow the reader down. But even if there is no punctuation at the end of a line of poetry, the reader probably pauses slightly or gives the final word an additional bit of emphasis. Similarly, the space between stanzas slows a reader down, increasing the emphasis on the last word of one stanza and the first word of the next.

Thomas Hardy (*English. 1840–1928*)

The Man He Killed

"Had he and I but met
By some old ancient inn,
We should have sat us down to wet
Right many a nipperkin°!   *cup*

"But ranged as infantry,   5
And staring face to face,
I shot at him as he at me,
And killed him in his place.

"I shot him dead because —
Because he was my foe,   10
Just so: my foe of course he was;
That's clear enough; although

"He thought he'd 'list, perhaps,
Off-hand like — just as I —
Was out of work — had sold his traps° — *personal belongings*   15
No other reason why.

"Yes; quaint and curious war is!
You shoot a fellow down
You'd treat if met where any bar is,
Or help to half-a-crown."   20

QUESTIONS

1. What do we learn about the speaker's life before he enlisted in the infantry? How does his diction characterize him?
2. What is the effect of the series of monosyllables in lines 7 and 8?
3. Consider the punctuation of the third and fourth stanzas. Why are the heavy, frequent pauses appropriate? What question is the speaker trying to answer?
4. In the last stanza what attitudes toward war does the speaker express? What, from the evidence of this poem, would you infer Hardy's attitude toward war to be?

Michael Drayton (*English. 1563–1631*)

Since There's No Help

Since there's no help, come let us kiss and part;
Nay, I have done, you get no more of me,
And I am glad, yea glad with all my heart
That thus so cleanly I myself can free;
Shake hands for ever, cancel all our vows,   5
And when we meet at any time again,
Be it not seen in either of our brows
That we one jot of former love retain.
Now at the last gasp of Love's latest breath,
When, his pulse failing, Passion speechless lies,   10
When Faith is kneeling by his bed of death,
And Innocence is closing up his eyes,
        Now if thou wouldst, when all have given him over,
        From death to life thou mightst him yet recover.

QUESTIONS

1. What do you think is the tone of lines 1–8? What words especially establish this tone? What do you think is the tone of lines 9–14?
2. What is the significance of the shift from "you" (line 2) to "thou" (line 13)?

Elizabeth Bishop (*American. 1911–1979*)

Filling Station

Oh, but it is dirty!
— this little filling station,
oil-soaked, oil-permeated
to a disturbing, over-all
black translucency.   5
Be careful with that match!

Father wears a dirty,
oil-soaked monkey suit
that cuts him under the arms,
and several quick and saucy   10
and greasy sons assist him
(it's a family filling station),
all quite thoroughly dirty.

Do they live in the station?
It has a cement porch   15
behind the pumps, and on it
a set of crushed and grease-
impregnated wickerwork;
on the wicker sofa
a dirty dog, quite comfy.   20

Some comic books provide
the only note of color —
of certain color. They lie
upon a big dim doily
draping a taboret   25
(part of the set), beside
a big hirsute begonia.

Why the extraneous plant?
Why the taboret?
Why, oh why, the doily? 30
(Embroidered in daisy stitch
with marguerites, I think,
and heavy with gray crochet.)

Somebody embroidered the doily.
Somebody waters the plant, 35
or oils it, maybe. Somebody
arranges the rows of cans
so that they softly say:
ESSO° — SO — SO — SO   *a brand of gasoline, now Exxon*
to high-strung automobiles. 40
Somebody loves us all.

QUESTIONS

1. Elizabeth Bishop, though a woman, might have chosen to invent a male speaker. But she didn't. What words or phrases in "Filling Station" convince you that the speaker is a woman?
2. Taking into account only the first 14 lines, how would you characterize the speaker?
3. Would you agree that in the third stanza a reader begins to feel more sympathetic toward the speaker? Why? Because the speaker seems to be somewhat more sympathetic toward the family and the gas station? What do you make of "comfy" in line 20? Is it the speaker's word? Or is the speaker using a word that might be used by the owners of the gas station?
4. In lines 21–30, what evidence suggests that the speaker feels that her taste is superior to the taste of the family? Do you think that she changes her tone later? A little, a lot, or not at all?

Robert Frost (*American. 1874–1963*)

Mending Wall

Something there is that doesn't love a wall,
That sends the frozen-ground-swell under it,
And spills the upper boulders in the sun;
And makes gaps even two can pass abreast.

The work of hunters is another thing: 5
I have come after them and made repair
Where they have left not one stone on a stone,
But they would have the rabbit out of hiding,
To please the yelping dogs. The gaps I mean,
No one has seen them made or heard them made,   10
But at spring-mending time we find them there.
I let my neighbor know beyond the hill;
And on a day we meet to walk the line
And set the wall between us once again.
We keep the wall between us as we go.   15
To each the boulders that have fallen to each.
And some are loaves and some so nearly balls
We have to use a spell to make them balance:
"Stay where you are until our backs are turned!"
We wear our fingers rough with handling them.   20
Oh, just another kind of outdoor game,
One on a side. It comes to little more:
There where it is we do not need the wall:
He is all pine and I am apple orchard.
My apple trees will never get across   25
And eat the cones under his pines, I tell him.
He only says, "Good fences make good neighbors."
Spring is the mischief in me, and I wonder
If I could put a notion in his head:
"*Why* do they make good neighbors? Isn't it   30
Where there are cows? But here there are no cows.
Before I built a wall I'd ask to know
What I was walling in or walling out,
And to whom I was like to give offense.
Something there is that doesn't love a wall,   35
That wants it down." I could say "Elves" to him,
But it's not elves exactly, and I'd rather
He said it for himself. I see him there
Bringing a stone grasped firmly by the top
In each hand, like an old-stone savage armed.   40
He moves in darkness as it seems to me,
Not of woods only and the shade of trees.
He will not go behind his father's saying,
And he likes having thought of it so well
He says again, "Good fences make good neighbors."   45

QUESTIONS

1. How does the speech of the speaker's neighbor characterize
   him?

2. Specify some passages that allow one to say that "Mending Wall" is conversational or colloquial in tone. Consider also lines 41–42: "He moves in darkness as it seems to me,/ Not of woods only and the shade of trees." Would you characterize these lines as colloquial or lyrical or both? Why?

3. Is it reasonable to assume that the two views about the wall have political and ethical implications? Explain.

Gerard Manley Hopkins (English. 1844–1889)

Spring and Fall: To a Young Child

Márgarét, are you gríeving
Over Goldengrove unleaving?
Léaves, líke the things of man, you
With your fresh thoughts care for, can you?
Áh! ás the heart grows older   5
It will come to such sights colder
By and by, nor spare a sigh
Though worlds of wanwood leafmeal lie;
And yet you will weep and know why.
Now no matter, child, the name: 10
Sórrow's spríngs áre the same.
Nor mouth had, no nor mind, expressed
What heart heard of, ghost° guessed: *spirit*
It ís the blight man was born for,
It ís Margaret you mourn for.   15

QUESTIONS

1. About how old do you think the speaker is? What is his tone? What connection can you make between the title and the speaker and Margaret? What meanings do you think may be in "Fall"?

2. What is meant by Margaret's "fresh thoughts" (line 4)? Paraphrase lines 3–4 and lines 12–13.

3. "Wanwood" and "leafmeal" are words coined by Hopkins. What do they suggest to you?

4. How can you explain the apparent contradiction that Margaret weeps for herself (line 15) after the speaker has said that she weeps for "Goldengrove unleaving" (line 2)?

Ted Hughes (English. b. 1930)

Hawk Roosting

I sit in the top of the wood, my eyes closed.
Inaction, no falsifying dream
Between my hooked head and hooked feet:
Or in sleep rehearse perfect kills and eat.   *4*

The convenience of the high trees!
The air's buoyancy and the sun's ray
Are of advantage to me;
And the earth's face upward for my inspection.   *8*

My feet are locked upon the rough bark.
It took the whole of Creation
To produce my foot, my each feather:
Now I hold Creation in my foot   *12*

Or fly up, and revolve it all slowly —
I kill where I please because it is all mine.
There is no sophistry in my body:
My manners are tearing off heads —   *16*

The allotment of death.
For the one path of my flight is direct
Through the bones of the living.
No arguments assert my right: *20*

The sun is behind me.
Nothing has changed since I began.
My eye has permitted no change.
I am going to keep things like this.   *24*

QUESTIONS

1. Many of the sentences are short — only one line long. What is the effect of these short sentences, especially in the last stanza, where each of the four lines is a separate sentence?
2. Hawks cannot speak. Do you think this poem therefore is nonsense?

THE VOICE OF THE SATIRIST

The writer of **satire,** in one way or another, ridicules an aspect or several aspects of human behavior, seeking to arouse in the reader some degree of amused contempt for the object. However urbane in tone, the satirist is always critical. By cleverly holding up foibles or vices for the world's derision, satire (Alexander Pope claimed) "heals with morals what it hurts with wit." The laughter of comedy is an end in itself; the laughter of satire is a weapon against the world: "The intellectual dagger," Frank O'Connor called satire, "opposing the real dagger." Jonathan Swift, of whom O'Connor is speaking, insisted that his satires were not malice but medicine:

> His satire points at no defect
> But what all mortals may correct. . . .
> He spared a hump or crooked nose,
> Whose owners set not up for beaux.

But Swift, although he claimed that satire is therapeutic, also saw its futility: "Satire is a sort of glass wherein beholders do generally discover everybody's face but their own."

Sometimes the satirist speaks out directly as defender of public morals, abusively but wittily chopping off heads. Byron, for example, wrote:

> Prepare for rhyme — I'll publish, right or wrong:
> Fools are my theme, let Satire be my song.

But sometimes the satirist chooses to invent a speaker far removed from himself or herself, just as Browning chose to invent a Renaissance duke. The satirist may, for example, invent a callous brigadier-general or a pompous judge who unconsciously annihilates himself. Consider this satirical poem by E. E. Cummings.

E. E. Cummings (American. 1894–1963)

next to of course god america i

"next to of course god america i
love you land of the pilgrims' and so forth oh
say can you see by the dawn's early my
country 'tis of centuries come and go   *4*

and are no more what of it we should worry
in every language even deafanddumb
thy sons acclaim your glorious name by gorry
by jingo by gee by gosh by gum   8
why talk of beauty what could be more beauti-
ful than these heroic happy dead
who rushed like lions to the roaring slaughter
they did not stop to think they died instead   12
then shall the voice of liberty be mute?"

He spoke. And drank rapidly a glass of water

Cummings might have written, in the voice of a solid citizen or
a good poet, a direct attack on chauvinistic windbags; instead, he
chose to invent a windbag whose rhetoric punctures itself. Yet
the last line tells that we are really hearing someone who is recounting
what the windbag said; that is, the speaker of all the lines but the
last is a sort of combination of the chauvinist *and* the satiric observer
of the chauvinist. (When Cummings himself recited these lines
there was mockery in his voice.) Only in the final line of the poem
does the author seem to speak entirely on his own, and even here
he adopts a matter-of-fact pose that is far more potent than **invective**
(direct abuse) would be. Yet the last line is not totally free of
explicit hostility. It might, for example, have run, "He spoke.
And poured slowly a glass of water." Why does this version lack
the punch of Cummings's? And what do you think is implied by
the absence of a final period in line 14?

John Updike (*American. b. 1932*)

Youth's Progress

> *Dick Schneider of Wisconsin . . . was elected "Greek God"*
> *for an interfraternity ball.*   — *Life*

When I was born, my mother taped my ears
So they lay flat. When I had aged ten years,
My teeth were firmly braced and much improved.
Two years went by; my tonsils were removed.   4

At fourteen, I began to comb my hair
A fancy way. Though nothing much was there,
I shaved my upper lip — next year, my chin.
At seventeen, the freckles left my skin.   8

Just turned nineteen, a nicely molded lad,
I said goodbye to Sis and Mother; Dad
Drove me to Wisconsin and set me loose.
At twenty-one, I was elected Zeus.   12

QUESTIONS

1. Suppose the first two lines ran thus:

   > To keep them flat, my mother taped my ears;
   > And then, at last, when I had aged ten years. . . .

   How does this revision destroy the special tone of voice in
   the original two lines? (Notice that in the revision there is
   a heavy pause at the end of the first line.) Why, in the second
   line of the revision, is "at last" false to the "tone" or "voice"
   in the rest of the poem?
2. What do you think is the speaker's attitude toward himself?
   What is the author's attitude toward the speaker?

Marge Piercy (American. b. 1936)

Barbie Doll

This girlchild was born as usual   *free verse*
and presented dolls that did pee-pee
and miniature GE stoves and irons
and wee lipsticks the color of cherry candy.
Then in the magic of puberty, a classmate said: 5
You have a great big nose and fat legs.

She was healthy, tested intelligent,
possessed strong arms and back,
abundant sexual drive and manual dexterity.
She went to and fro apologizing.   10
Everyone saw a fat nose on thick legs.

She was advised to play coy,
exhorted to come on hearty,
exercise, diet, smile and wheedle.   *15*
Her good nature wore out
like a fan belt.
So she cut off her nose and her legs
and offered them up.

In the casket displayed on satin she lay
with the undertaker's cosmetics painted on,   *20*
a turned-up putty nose,
dressed in a pink and white nightie.
Doesn't she look pretty? everyone said.
Consummation at last.
To every woman a happy ending.   *25*

QUESTIONS

1. Why is the poem called "Barbie Doll"
2. What voice do you hear in lines 1–4? Line 6 is, we are told,
   the voice of "a classmate." How do these voices differ? What
   voice do you hear in the first three lines of the second stanza?
3. Explain in your own words what Piercy is saying about
   women in this poem. Does her view seem to you fair, slightly
   exaggerated, or greatly exaggerated?

Marge Piercy (*American. b. 1936*)

What's That Smell in the Kitchen?

All over America women are burning dinners.
It's lambchops in Peoria; it's haddock
in Providence; it's steak in Chicago;
tofu delight in Big Sur; red
rice and beans in Dallas.   *5*
All over America women are burning
food they're supposed to bring with calico
smile on platters glittering like wax.
Anger sputters in her brainpan, confined
but spewing out missiles of hot fat.   *10*

Carbonized despair presses like a clinker
from a barbecue against the back of her eyes.
If she wants to grill anything, it's
her husband spitted over a slow fire.
If she wants to serve him anything   *15*
it's a dead rat with a bomb in its belly
ticking like the heart of an insomniac.
Her life is cooked and digested,
nothing but leftovers in Tupperware.
Look, she says, once I was roast duck   *20*
on your platter with parsley but now I am Spam.
Burning dinner is not incompetence but war.

QUESTIONS

1. Suppose a friend told you that she didn't understand lines
   20–21. How would you paraphrase the lines?
2. Who speaks the title?
3. If a poem begins, "All over America women are . . . ," what
   words might a reader reasonably expect next?
4. Do you take the poem to be chiefly comic? Superficially but
   essentially comic but a work with a serious purpose? Or
   what?

Phyllis McGinley (*American. 1905–1977*)

A Garland of Precepts

Though a seeker since my birth,
Here is all I've learned on earth,
This is the gist of what I know:
Give advice and buy a foe.
Random truths are all I find   *5*
Stuck like burs about my mind.
Salve a blister. Burn a letter.
Do not wash a cashmere sweater.
Tell a tale but seldom twice.
Give a stone before advice.   *10*

Pressed for rules and verities,
All I recollect are these:
Feed a cold to starve a fever.
Argue with no true believer.
Think-too-long is never-act.   *15*
Scratch a myth and find a fact.
Stitch in time saves twenty stitches.
Give the rich, to please them, riches.
Give to love your hearth and hall.
But do not give advice at all.   *20*

QUESTIONS

1. How would you characterize the tone of the first line? Of the entire poem?
2. Which "precept" does McGinley give the greatest emphasis to? What is the effect of lumping this precept with "Do not wash a cashmere sweater"? With "Salve a blister"?
3. We put this poem in the section on satire. If indeed there is an object of satire here, what (or who) is it?

12

Figurative Language: Simile, Metaphor, Personification, Apostrophe

Hippolyta. 'Tis strange, my Theseus, that these lovers speak of.
Theseus. More strange than true. I never may believe
    These antique fables, nor these fairy toys.
    Lovers and madmen have such seething brains,
    Such shaping fantasies, that apprehend
    More than cool reason ever comprehends.
    The lunatic, the lover, and the poet,
    Are of imagination all compact.
    One sees more devils than vast hell can hold,
    That is the madman. The lover, all as frantic,
    Sees Helen's beauty in a brow of Egypt.
    The poet's eye, in a fine frenzy rolling,
    Doth glance from heaven to earth, from earth to heaven;
    And as imagination bodies forth
    The forms of things unknown, the poet's pen
    Turns them to shapes, and gives to airy nothing
    A local habitation and a name.

       Shakespeare, *A Midsummer Night's Dream,* V.i. 1-17

Theseus was neither the first nor the last to suggest that poets, like lunatics and lovers, freely employ their imagination. Terms such as "poetic license" and "poetic justice" imply that poets are free to depict a never-never land. One has only to leaf through any anthology of poetry to encounter numerous statements that are, from a logical point of view, lunacies. Here are a few:

> Look like th' innocent flower,
> But be the serpent under 't.
>
> — Shakespeare

> Each outcry from the hunted hare
> A fiber from the brain does tear.
>
> — William Blake

> Every thread of summer is at last unwoven.
>
> — Wallace Stevens

On a literal level, such assertions are nonsense (so, too, is Theseus's notion that reason is cool). But of course they are not to be taken literally; rather, they employ **figures of speech** — departures from logical usage that are aimed at gaining special effects. Consider the lunacies that Robert Burns heaps up here.

Robert Burns (*Scottish. 1759–1796*)

A Red, Red Rose

> O, my luve is like a red, red rose,
>   That's newly sprung in June.
> O, my luve is like the melodie,
>   That's sweetly played in tune.   *4*
>
> As fair art thou, my bonnie lass,
>   So deep in luve am I,
> And I will luve thee still, my dear,
>   Till a'° the seas gang° dry.   *all; go*   *8*
>
> Till a' the seas gang dry, my dear,
>   And the rocks melt wi' the sun!
> And I will luve thee still, my dear,
>   While the sands o' life shall run.   *12*
>
> And fare thee weel, my only luve,
>   And fare thee weel awhile!
> And I will come again, my luve,
>   Though it were ten thousand mile!   *16*

To the charge that these lines are lunacies or untruths, at least two replies can be made. First, it might be said that the speaker is not really making assertions about a girl; he is saying he feels a certain way. His words, it can be argued, are not assertions about external reality but expressions of his state of mind, just as a tune one whistles asserts nothing about external reality but expresses the whistler's state of mind. In this view, the nonlogical language of poetry (like a groan of pain or an exclamation of joy) is an expression of emotion; its further aim, if it has one, is to induce in the hearer an emotion. Second, and more to the point here, it can be said that nonlogical language does indeed make assertions about external reality, and even gives the reader an insight into this reality that logical language cannot. The opening comparison in Burns's poem ("my luve is like a red, red rose") brings before our eyes the lady's beauty in a way that the reasonable assertion "She is beautiful" does not. By comparing the woman to a rose, the poet invites us to see the woman through a special sort of lens: she is fragrant; her lips (and perhaps her cheeks) are like a rose in texture and color; she will not keep her beauty long. Also, "my love is like a red, red rose" says something different from "like a red, red beet," or "a red, red cabbage."

The poet, then, has not only communicated a state of mind but also has discovered, through the lens of imagination, some things (both in the beloved and in the lover's own feelings) that interest us. The discovery is not world-shaking; it is less important than the discovery of America or the discovery that the meek are blessed, but it *is* a discovery and it leaves the reader with the feeling, "Yes, that's right. I hadn't quite thought of it that way, but that's right." A poem, Robert Frost said, "assumes direction with the first line laid down, . . . runs a course of lucky events, and ends in a clarification of life — not necessarily a great clarification, such as sects and cults are founded on, but in a momentary stay against confusion." What is clarified? In another paragraph Frost gives an answer: "For me the initial delight is in the surprise of remembering something I didn't know I knew." John Keats made a similar statement: "Poetry . . . should strike the Reader as a wording of his own highest thoughts, and appear almost a Remembrance."

Some figures of speech are, in effect, riddling ways of speech. To call fishermen "farmers of the sea" — a metaphor — is a sort of veiled description of fishermen, bringing out, when it is properly understood, certain aspects of a fisherman's activities. And a riddle, after all, is a veiled description — though intentionally obscure or deceptive — calling attention to characteristics, especially similarities,

not usually noticed. ("Riddle," like "read," is from Old English
redan, "to guess," "to interpret," and thus its solution provides
knowledge.) "Two sisters upstairs, often looking but never seeing
each other" is (after the riddle is explained) a way of calling attention
to the curious fact that the eye, the instrument of vision, never
sees its mate.

In the next poem the connection between riddles and metaphors
is easily seen.

Sylvia Plath (American. 1932–1963)

Metaphors

I'm a riddle in nine syllables,
An elephant, a ponderous house,
A melon strolling on two tendrils.
O red fruit, ivory, fine timbers!
This loaf's big with its yeasty rising.
Money's new-minted in this fat purse.
I'm a means, a stage, a cow in calf.
I've eaten a bag of green apples,
Boarded the train there's no getting off.

The riddling speaker says that she is, among other things, "A
melon strolling on two tendrils," and "a cow in calf." What is
she?

SIMILE

In a **simile,** items from different classes are explicitly compared
by a connective such as "like," "as," or "than" or by a verb such
as "appears" or "seems." (If the objects compared are from the
same class, e.g., "New York is like London," no simile is present.)

Sometimes I feel like a motherless child.
— Anonymous

It is a beauteous evening, calm and free.
The holy time is quiet as a Nun,
Breathless with adoration.

— Wordsworth

How sharper than a serpent's tooth it is
To have a thankless child.

— Shakespeare

Seems he a dove? His feathers are but borrowed.

— Shakespeare

The following two lines constitute an entire poem.

Robert Herrick (*English. 1591–1674*)

Her Legs

Fain would I kiss my Julia's dainty leg,
Which is as white and hairless as an egg.

METAPHOR

A **metaphor** asserts the identity, without a connective such as "like" or a verb such as "appears," of terms that are literally incompatible.

She is the rose, the glory of the day.

— Spenser

O western orb sailing the heaven.

— Whitman

Notice how in the second example only one of the terms ("orb") is stated; the other ("ship") is implied in "sailing."

John Keats (*English. 1795–1821*)

On First Looking into Chapman's Homer

Much have I traveled in the realms of gold,
And many goodly states and kingdoms seen;
Round many western islands have I been
Which bards in fealty to Apollo hold.   *4*
Oft of one wide expanse have I been told
That deep-browed Homer ruled as his demesne;
Yet did I never breathe its pure serene
Till I heard Chapman speak out loud and bold: *8*
Then felt I like some watcher of the skies
When a new planet swims into his ken;
Or like stout Cortez when with eagle eyes
He stared at the Pacific — and all his men   *12*
Looked at each other with a wild surmise —
Silent, upon a peak in Darien.

QUESTIONS

1. In line 1, what do you think "realms of gold" stands for? Chapman was an Elizabethan; how does this fact add relevance to the metaphor in the first line?
2. Does line 9 introduce a totally new idea, or can you somehow connect it to the opening metaphor?

Langston Hughes (*American. 1902–1967*)

Harlem

What happens to a dream deferred?

Does it dry up
like a raisin in the sun?
Or fester like a sore —
and then run?   *5*

Does it stink like rotten meat?
Or crust and sugar over —
like a syrupy sweet?

Maybe it just sags
like a heavy load.   *10*

Or does it explode?

QUESTION

One might keep the first line where it is and then rearrange
the other stanzas — for instance, putting lines 2–8 after 9–
11. Which version (Hughes's or the one just mentioned) do
you prefer? Why?

Amy Clampitt (American. b. 1924)

The Cormorant in His Element

That bony potbellied arrow, wing-pumping along
implacably, with a ramrod's rigid adherence,
airborne, to the horizontal, discloses talents
one would never have guessed at. Plummeting

waterward, big black feet splayed for a landing   *5*
gear, slim head turning and turning, vermilion-
strapped, this way and that, with a lightning glance
over the shoulder, the cormorant astounding-

ly, in one sleek involuted arabesque, a vertical
turn on a dime, goes into that inimitable   *10*
vanishing-and-emerging-from-under-the-briny-

deep act which, unlike the works of Homo Houdini,
is performed for reasons having nothing at all
to do with ego, guilt, ambition, or even money.

QUESTIONS

1. Why would one "never have guessed" that a cormorant in action has hidden talents?
2. If you do not know who Houdini was, check a dictionary or an encyclopedia. What is the point of comparison between the cormorant and Houdini? What does Clampitt mean by "Homo Houdini"?
3. Which, if any, of Clampitt's figures of speech seem to you to be especially effective?

Two types of metaphor deserve special mention. In **metonymy,** something is named that replaces something closely related to it; "City Hall," for example, sometimes is used to stand for municipal authority. In the following passage James Shirley names certain objects, using them to replace social classes to which they are related:

> Scepter and crown must tumble down
> And in the dust be equal made
> With the poor crooked scythe and spade.

In **synecdoche,** the whole is replaced by the part, or the part by the whole. For example, "bread" in "Give us this day our daily bread" replaces the whole class of edibles. Similarly, an automobile can be "wheels," and workers are "hands." Robert Frost was fond of calling himself "a Synecdochist" because he believed that it is the nature of poetry to "have intimations of something more than itself. It almost always comes under the head of synecdoche, a part, a hem of the garment for the whole garment."

PERSONIFICATION

The attribution of human feelings or characteristics to abstractions or to inanimate objects is called **personification.**

> But Time did beckon to the flowers, and they
> By noon most cunningly did steal away.
> — Herbert

Herbert attributes a human gesture to Time and shrewdness to flowers. Of all figures, personification most surely gives to airy nothings a local habitation and a name:

There's Wrath who has learnt every trick of guerrilla warfare,
The shamming dead, the night-raid, the feinted retreat.
— Auden

Hope, thou bold taster of delight.
— Crashaw

Emily Dickinson (American. 1830–1886)

Apparently with no surprise

Apparently with no surprise
To any happy Flower
The Frost beheads it at its play —
In accidental power —
The blonde Assassin passes on —   5
The Sun proceeds unmoved
To measure off another Day
For an Approving God.

QUESTIONS

1. What personifications do you find here?
2. In line 5, how does "blonde" strike you? Try substituting another word — perhaps "quick" or "blind" or "harsh" — and evaluate the difference.

APOSTROPHE

Crashaw's personification, "Hope, thou bold taster of delight," is also an example of the figure called **apostrophe,** an address to a person or thing not literally listening. Wordsworth begins a sonnet by apostrophizing John Milton:

Milton, thou shouldst be living at this hour,

And Shelley begins an ode by apostrophizing a skylark:

Hail to thee, blithe Spirit!

The following poem is largely built on apostrophe.

Edmund Waller (English. 1606–1687)

Song

Go, lovely rose,
Tell her that wastes her time and me,
   That now she knows,
When I resemble her to thee,
   How sweet and fair she seems to be.   *5*

Tell her that's young,
And shuns to have her graces spied,
   That hadst thou sprung
In deserts where no men abide,
   Thou must have uncommended died.   *10*

Small is the worth
Of beauty from the light retired:
   Bid her come forth,
Suffer her self to be desired,
   And not blush so to be admired.   *15*

Then die, that she
The common fate of all things rare
   May read in thee,
How small a part of time they share,
   That are so wondrous sweet and fair.   *20*

What conclusions, then, can we draw about **figurative language?** First, figurative language, with its literally incompatible terms, forces the reader to attend to the **connotations** (suggestions, associations) rather than to the **denotations** (dictionary definitions) of one of the terms. Second, although figurative language is said to differ from ordinary discourse, it is found in ordinary discourse as well as in literature. "It rained cats and dogs," "War is hell," "Don't be a pig," and other tired figures are part of our daily utterances. But through repeated use, these (and most of the figures we use) have lost whatever impact they once had and are only a shade removed from expressions which, though once figurative, have become literal: the *eye* of a needle, a *branch* office, the *face* of a clock. Third, good figurative language is usually (a) concrete, (b) condensed, and (c) interesting.

    The concreteness lends precision and vividness; when Keats writes that he felt "like some watcher of the skies/ When a new planet swims into his ken," he more sharply characterizes his feelings than if he had said, "I felt excited." His simile isolates for us a precise kind of excitement, and the metaphoric "swims" vividly brings up the oceanic aspect of the sky. The second of these three qualities, condensation, can be seen by attempting to paraphrase some of the figures. A paraphrase or rewording will commonly use more words than the original and will have less impact — as the gradual coming of night usually has less impact on us than a sudden darkening of the sky or as a prolonged push has less impact than a sudden blow. The third quality, interest, largely depends on the previous two: the successful figure often makes us open our eyes wider and take notice. Keats's "deep-browed Homer" arouses our interest in Homer as "thoughtful Homer" or "meditative Homer" does not. Similarly, when W. B. Yeats says (page 541):

> An aged man is but a paltry thing,
> A tattered coat upon a stick, unless
> Soul clap its hands and sing, and louder sing
> For every tatter in its mortal dress,

the metaphoric identification of an old man with a scarecrow jolts us out of all our usual unthinking attitudes about old men as kind, happy folk content to have passed from youth to senior citizenship.

Finally, two points must be made: first, though figurative language is common in poetry, it is not essential; and second, a poem that seems to contain no figures may in fact be one extended figure. Let us take the first point first. The anonymous ballad "Edward" (page 511) contains no figures, yet surely it is a poem and no one would say that the addition of figures would make it a better poem. Here is another poem that employs no figures, the epigraph to Robert Frost's *Collected Poems*.

Robert Frost (*American. 1874–1963*)

The Pasture

I'm going out to clean the pasture spring;
I'll only stop to rake the leaves away
(And wait to watch the water clear, I may):
I shan't be gone long. — You come too.

I'm going out to fetch the little calf
That's standing by the mother. It's so young
It totters when she licks it with her tongue.
I shan't be gone long. — You come too.

Everything here can be taken literally; someone might have said
this to someone else, and there is not a word in it that is illogical.
Yet surely it is a poem. Now for the second point, that an entire
poem may be an extended figure. By placing "The Pasture" at
the opening of his *Collected Poems,* Frost allows us to read it as a
figure; the invitation to accompany the speaker on a trip to the
pasture can easily be read as an invitation to accompany the poet
on a trip to the poet's world — his poems. But even in isolation
the poem as a whole is more than the sum of its parts. The clearing
of the water, the calf solicitously tended by its mother and by the
speaker, somehow join, and somehow are related to the speaker's
solicitous care for the "you" whom he addresses, and we feel that
the poem is not only about what the speaker plans to do, but
about the loving care that enhances life.

Here is another short poem. Does it contain any figures of
speech?

William Carlos Williams (American. 1883–1963)

The Red Wheelbarrow

so much depends
upon

a red wheel
barrow

glazed with rain
water

beside the white
chickens.

The following poems rely heavily on figures of speech.

Alfred, Lord Tennyson (*English. 1809–1892*)

The Eagle

Fragment

He clasps the crag with crooked hands;
Close to the sun in lonely lands,
Ringed with the azure world, he stands.
The wrinkled sea beneath him crawls:
He watches from his mountain walls,
And like a thunderbolt he falls.

QUESTIONS

1. What figure is used in line 1? In line 4? In line 6? Can it be argued that the figures give us a sense of the eagle that is not to be found in a literal description?
2. In line 2 we get overstatement, or hyperbole, for the eagle is not really close to the sun. Suppose instead of "close to the sun" Tennyson had written "Waiting on high"? Do you think the poem would be improved or worsened?

Christina Rossetti (*English. 1830–1894*)

Uphill

Does the road wind uphill all the way?
   Yes, to the very end.
Will the day's journey take the whole long day?
   From morn to night, my friend.   *4*

But is there for the night a resting-place?
   A roof for when the slow dark hours begin.
May not the darkness hide it from my face?
   You cannot miss that inn.   *8*

Shall I meet other wayfarers at night?
   Those who have gone before.
Then must I knock, or call when just in sight?
   They will not keep you standing at that door.   *12*

Shall I find comfort, travel-sore and weak?
   Of labor you shall find the sum.
Will there be beds for me and all who seek?
   Yea, beds for all who come.   *16*

QUESTIONS

1. Suppose that someone told you this poem is about a person preparing to go on a hike. The person is supposedly making inquiries about the road and the possible hotel arrangements. What would you reply?
2. Who is the questioner? A woman? A man? All human beings collectively? Can one say that in "Uphill" the questioner and the answerer are the same person?
3. Are the answers unambiguously comforting? Or can it, for instance, be argued that the "roof" is (perhaps among other things) the lid of a coffin — hence the questioner will certainly not be kept "standing at the door"? If the poem can be read along these lines, is it chilling rather than comforting?

Emily Dickinson (*American. 1830–1886*)

Because I could not stop for Death

Because I could not stop for Death —
He kindly stopped for me —
The Carriage held but just Ourselves —
And Immortality.   *4*

We slowly drove — He knew no haste
And I had put away
My labor and my leisure too,
For His Civility —   *8*

We passed the School, where Children strove
At Recess — in the Ring —
We passed the Fields of Gazing Grain —
We passed the Setting Sun —   12

Or rather — He passed Us —
The Dews drew quivering and chill —
For only Gossamer, my Gown —
My Tippet — only Tulle —   16

We paused before a House that seemed
A Swelling of the Ground —
The Roof was scarcely visible —
The Cornice — in the Ground —   20

Since then — 'tis Centuries — and yet
Feels shorter than the Day
I first surmised the Horses' Heads
Were toward Eternity —   24

QUESTIONS

1. Characterize death as it appears in lines 1–8.
2. What is the significance of the details and their arrangement
   in the third stanza? Why "strove" rather than "played" (line
   9)? What meanings do you think "Ring" (line 10) has? Do
   you think "Gazing Grain" is better than "Golden Grain"?
3. The "House" in the fifth stanza is a sort of riddle. What is
   the answer? Does this stanza introduce an aspect of death
   not present — or present only very faintly — in the rest of
   the poem? Explain.

Randall Jarrell (*American. 1914–1965*)

The Death of the Ball Turret Gunner

From my mother's sleep I fell into the State,
And I hunched in its belly till my wet fur froze.
Six miles from earth, loosed from its dream of life,
I woke to black flak and the nightmare fighters.
When I died they washed me out of the turret with a hose.

Jarrell has furnished an explanatory note: "A ball turret was a plexiglass sphere set into the belly of a B-17 or B-24, and inhabited by two .50 caliber machine-guns and one man, a short small man. When this gunner tracked with his machine-guns a fighter attacking his bomber from below, he revolved with the turret; hunched upside-down in his little sphere, he looked like the fetus in the womb. The fighters which attacked him were armed with cannon firing explosive shells. The hose was a steam hose."

QUESTIONS

1. What is implied in the first line? In "I woke to . . . nightmare"? Taking account of the title, do you think "wet fur" is literal or metaphoric or both? Do you find the simplicity of the last line anti-climactic? How does it continue the metaphor of birth?
2. Why do you think Jarrell ended each line with punctuation?

Seamus Heaney (Irish. b. 1939)

Digging

Between my finger and my thumb
The squat pen rests; snug as a gun.

Under my window, a clean rasping sound
When the spade sinks into gravelly ground:
My father, digging. I look down   5

Till his straining rump among the flowerbeds
Bends low, comes up twenty years away
Stooping in rhythm through potato drills
Where he was digging.

The coarse boot nestled on the lug, the shaft   10
Against the inside knee was levered firmly.
He rooted out tall tops, buried the bright edge deep
To scatter new potatoes that we picked
Loving their cool hardness in our hands.

By God, the old man could handle a spade.   *15*
Just like his old man.

My grandfather cut more turf in a day
Than any other man on Toner's bog.
Once I carried him milk in a bottle
Corked sloppily with paper. He straightened up   *20*
To drink it, then fell to right away

Nicking and slicing neatly, heaving sods
Over his shoulder, going down and down
For the good turf. Digging.

The cold smell of potato mould, the squelch and slap   *25*
Of soggy peat, the curt cuts of an edge
Through living roots awaken in my head.
But I've no spade to follow men like them.

Between my finger and my thumb
The squat pen rests.   *30*
I'll dig with it.

QUESTIONS

1. The poem ends with the speaker saying that he will "dig" with his pen. Given all the preceding lines, what will he dig?
2. The first lines compare the pen with a gun. What implications are suggested by this comparison?

13

Figurative Language: Imagery and Symbolism

When we read "rose" we may more or less call to mind a picture of a rose, or perhaps we are reminded of the odor or texture of a rose. Whatever in a poem appeals to any of our senses (including sensations of heat and pressure as well as of sight, smell, taste, touch, and sound) is an **image.** In short, images are the sensory content of a work, whether literal or figurative. Waller's rose (page 450) is an image that happens to be compared in the first stanza to the woman ("I resemble her to thee"); later in the poem this image comes to stand for "all things rare." Yet we never forget that the rose is a rose, and that the poem is chiefly a revelation of the poet's attitude toward his beloved.

When a poet says "My rose" and he or she is speaking about a rose, we have no figure of speech — though we still have an image. If, however, "My rose" is a shortened form of "My beloved is a rose," some would say that the poet is using a metaphor, but others would say that because the first term is omitted ("My beloved is"), the rose is a **symbol.** A poem about the transience of a rose might, for example, compel the reader to feel that the transience of female beauty is the larger theme even though it is never explicitly stated.

Some symbols are **conventional symbols,** which people have agreed to accept as standing for something other than themselves: a poem about the cross would probably be about Christianity.

Similarly, the rose has long been a symbol for love. In Virginia Woolf's novel *Mrs. Dalloway,* the husband communicates his love by proffering this conventional symbol: "He was holding out flowers — roses, red and white roses. (But he could not bring himself to say he loved her; not in so many words.)" Objects that are not conventional symbols, however, also may give rise to rich, multiple, indefinable associations. (Nonconventional symbolism is evident in Faulkner's "The Bear," page 67, a highly symbolic story in which the wilderness, the bear, the compass, the dog, and other things acquire a significance far beyond anything that tradition has attributed to them.) The following poem uses the traditional symbol of the rose, but uses it in a nontraditional way.

William Blake (*English. 1757–1827*)

The Sick Rose

O Rose, thou art sick.
The invisible worm
That flies in the night
In the howling storm

Has found out thy bed
Of crimson joy,
And his dark secret love
Does thy life destroy.

One might perhaps argue that the worm is "invisible" (line 2) merely because it is hidden within the rose, but an "invisible worm / That flies in the night" is more than a long, slender, soft-bodied creeping animal; and a rose that has, or is, a "bed/ Of crimson joy" is more than a gardener's rose.

Blake's worm and rose suggest things beyond themselves — a stranger, more vibrant world than the world we are usually aware of. Many readers find themselves half-thinking, for example, that the worm is male, the rose female, and that the poem is about the violation of virginity. Or that the poem is about the destruction of beauty: woman's beauty, rooted in joy, is destroyed by a power that feeds on her. But these interpretations are not fully satisfying: the poem presents a worm and a rose, and yet it is not merely about a worm and a rose. These objects resonate, stimulating our thoughts toward something else, but the something else is elusive, whereas it is not elusive in Burns's "A Red, Red Rose" or in Waller's "Go, lovely rose."

A **symbol,** then, is an image so loaded with significance that it is not simply literal, and it does not simply stand for something else; it is both itself *and* something else that it richly suggests, a kind of manifestation of something too complex or too elusive to be otherwise revealed. Blake's poem is about a blighted rose and at the same time about much more. In a symbol, as Thomas Carlyle wrote, "the Infinite is made to blend with the Finite, to stand visible, and as it were, attainable there."* Probably it is not fanciful to say that the American slaves who sang "Joshua fought the battle of Jericho,/ And the walls came tumbling down" were singing both about an ancient occurrence *and* about a new embodiment of the ancient, the imminent collapse of slavery in the nineteenth century. Not one or the other, but both: the present partook of the past, and the past partook of the present.

D. H. Lawrence (English. 1885–1930)

Snake

A snake came to my water-trough
On a hot, hot day, and I in pajamas for the heat,
To drink there.

In the deep, strange-scented shade of the great dark carob-tree
I came down the steps with my pitcher   5
And must wait, must stand and wait, for there he was at the
    trough before me.

---

* Isabel C. Hungerland defines a symbol somewhat differently. She says:

> A man may remind me of my father, a kitchen bowl of a certain recipe; neither, according to my proposal, is *ipso facto* a symbol.
> What is lacking? . . . It is the transference of trains of thought and the accompanying attitude and feelings (which may work mainly in one or in both directions) from one object to another. If I began to think and feel about a man, in certain respects, as I did about my father, and to treat him as I treated my father, then he becomes a father symbol for me. Analogously, in fictional contexts, when we transfer trains of thought and the related attitudes and feelings from one object to another, a symbol is established.

Poetic Discourse (Berkeley, Cal., 1958), p. 138

He reached down from a fissure in the earth-wall in the gloom
And trailed his yellow-brown slackness soft-bellied down, over
      the edge of the stone trough
And rested his throat upon the stone bottom,
And where the water had dripped from the tap,
      in a small clearness,   *10*
He sipped with his straight mouth,
Softly drank through his straight gums, into his slack long body,
Silently.

Someone was before me at my water-trough,
And I, like a second comer, waiting.   *15*

He lifted his head from his drinking, as cattle do,
And looked at me vaguely, as drinking cattle do,
And flickered his two-forked tongue from his lips,
      and mused a moment,
And stooped and drank a little more,
Being earth-brown, earth-golden from the
      burning bowels of the earth   *20*
On the day of Sicilian July, with Etna smoking.

The voice of my education said to me
He must be killed,
For in Sicily the black, black snakes are innocent,
      the gold are venomous.

And voices in me said, If you were a man   *25*
You would take a stick and break him now, and finish him off.

But must I confess how I liked him,
How glad I was he had come like a guest in quiet,
      to drink at my water-trough
And depart peaceful, pacified, and thankless,
Into the burning bowels of this earth?   *30*

Was it cowardice, that I dared not kill him?
Was it perversity, that I longed to talk to him?
Was it humility, to feel so honored?
I felt so honored.

And yet those voices: *35*
If you were not afraid, you would kill him!

And truly I was afraid, I was most afraid,
But even só, honored still more
That he should seek my hospitality
From out the dark door of the secret earth.   *40*

He drank enough
And lifted his head, dreamily, as one who has drunken,
And flickered his tongue like a forked night on the air, so black,
Seeming to lick his lips,
And looked around like a god, unseeing, into the air,   45
And slowly turned his head,
And slowly, very slowly, as if thrice adream,
Proceeded to draw his slow length curving round
And climb again the broken bank of my wall-face.

And as he put his head into that dreadful hole,   50
And as he slowly drew up, snake-easing his shoulders,
        and entered farther,
A sort of horror, a sort of protest against his withdrawing
        into that horrid black hole,
Deliberately going into the blackness, and slowly
        drawing himself after,
Overcame me now his back was turned.

I looked round, I put down my pitcher,   55
I picked up a clumsy log
And threw it at the water-trough with a clatter.

I think it did not hit him,
But suddenly that part of him that was left behind
        convulsed in undignified haste,
Writhed like lightning, and was gone   60
Into the black hole, the earth-lipped fissure in the wall-front,
At which, in the intense still noon, I stared with fascination.

And immediately I regretted it.
I thought how paltry, how vulgar, what a mean act!
I despised myself and the voices of my accursed
        human education.   65
And I thought of the albatross,
And I wished he would come back, my snake.

For he seemed to me again like a king,
Like a king in exile, uncrowned in the underworld,
Now due to be crowned again.   70

And so, I missed my chance with one of the lords
Of life.
And I have something to expiate:
A pettiness.

QUESTIONS

1. In line 6 and later Lawrence calls the snake "he"; in line 14, "someone," thus elevating the snake. What other figures are used to give the snake dignity? How does Lawrence diminish himself?
2. What do you think Lawrence means by "The voice of my education" (line 22)? It explicitly speaks in lines 23–26. Where else in the poem do you hear this voice? What might you call the opposing voice?

When Coleridge published "Kubla Khan" in 1816, he prefaced it with this explanatory note:

> The following fragment is here published at the request of a poet of great and deserved celebrity, and, as far as the author's own opinions are concerned, rather as a psychological curiosity, than on the ground of any supposed *poetic* merits.
>
> In the summer of the year 1797, the author, then in ill health, had retired to a lonely farmhouse between Porlock and Linton, on the Exmoor confines of Somerset and Devonshire. In consequence of a slight indisposition, an anodyne had been prescribed, from the effects of which he fell asleep in his chair at the moment that he was reading the following sentence, or words of the same substance, in *Purchas's Pilgrimage:* "Here the Khan Kubla commanded a palace to be built, and a stately garden thereunto. And thus ten miles of fertile ground were inclosed with a wall." The author continued for about three hours in a profound sleep, at least of the external senses, during which time he has the most vivid confidence that he could not have composed less than from two to three hundred lines; if that indeed can be called composition in which all the images rose up before him as *things,* with a parallel production of the correspondent expressions, without any sensation or consciousness of effort. On awaking he appeared to himself to have a distinct recollection of the whole, and taking his pen, ink, and paper, instantly and eagerly wrote down the lines that are here preserved. At this moment he was unfortunately called out by a person on business from Porlock, and detained by him above an hour, and on his return to his room, found, to his no small surprise and mortification, that though he still retained some vague and dim recollection of the general purport of the vision, yet, with the exception of some eight or ten scattered lines and images, all the rest had passed away like the images on the surface of a stream into which a stone has been cast, but, alas! without the after restoration of the latter!

> Then all the charm
> Is broken — all that phantom world so fair
> Vanishes, and a thousand circlets spread,
> And each misshape[s] the other. Stay awhile,
> Poor youth! who scarcely dar'st lift up thine eyes —
> The stream will soon renew its smoothness, soon
> The visions will return! And lo, he stays,
> And soon the fragments dim of lovely forms
> Come trembling back, unite, and now once more
> The pool becomes a mirror.
>
> — Coleridge, *The Picture; or, the Lover's Resolution,*
> lines 91–100

Yet from the still surviving recollections in his mind, the author has frequently purposed to finish for himself what had been originally, as it were, given to him. Σαμερον αδιον ασω [today I shall sing more sweetly]: But the tomorrow is yet to come.

Samuel Taylor Coleridge *(English. 1772–1834)*

Kubla Khan

Or, A Vision in a Dream. A Fragment.

In Xanadu did Kubla Khan
A stately pleasure-dome decree:
Where Alph, the sacred river, ran
Through caverns measureless to man
    Down to a sunless sea.   5
So twice five miles of fertile ground
With walls and towers were girdled round:
And here were gardens bright with sinuous rills,
Where blossomed many an incense-bearing tree;
And here were forests ancient as the hills,   10
Enfolding sunny spots of greenery.

But oh! that deep romantic chasm which slanted
Down the green hill athwart a cedarn cover!
A savage place! as holy and enchanted
As e'er beneath a waning moon was haunted   15
By woman wailing for her demon-lover!
And from this chasm, with ceaseless turmoil seething,

As if this earth in fast thick pants were breathing
A mighty fountain momently was forced;
Amid whose swift half-intermitted burst   20
Huge fragments vaulted like rebounding hail,
Or chaffy grain beneath the thresher's flail:
And 'mid these dancing rocks at once and ever
It flung up momently the sacred river.
Five miles meandering with a mazy motion   25
Through wood and dale the sacred river ran,
Then reached the caverns measureless to man,
And sank in tumult to a lifeless ocean:
And 'mid this tumult Kubla heard from far
Ancestral voices prophesying war!   30
     The shadow of the dome of pleasure
     Floated midway on the waves;
     Where was heard the mingled measure
     From the fountain and the caves.
It was a miracle of rare device,   35
A sunny pleasure-dome with caves of ice!
     A damsel with a dulcimer
     In a vision once I saw:
     It was an Abyssinian maid,
     And on her dulcimer she played,   40
     Singing of Mount Abora.
     Could I revive within me
     Her symphony and song,
     To such a deep delight 'twould win me,
That with music loud and long,   45
I would build that dome in air,
That sunny dome! those caves of ice!
And all who heard should see them there,
And all should cry, Beware! Beware!
His flashing eyes, his floating hair!   50
Weave a circle round him thrice,
And close your eyes with holy dread,
For he on honey-dew hath fed,
And drunk the milk of Paradise.

QUESTIONS

1. Coleridge changed the "palace" of his source into a "dome" (line 2). What do you think are the relevant associations of "dome"?

2. What pairs of contrasts (e.g., underground river, fountain) do you find? What do you think they contribute to the poem?
3. If Coleridge had not said that the poem is a fragment, might you take it as a complete poem, the first thirty-six lines describing the creative imagination, and the remainder lamenting the loss of poetic power?

Adrienne Rich (*American. b. 1929*)

Diving into the Wreck

First having read the book of myths,
and loaded the camera,
and checked the edge of the knife-blade,
I put on
the body-armor of black rubber   5
the absurd flippers
the grave and awkward mask.
I am having to do this
not like Cousteau* with his
assiduous team   10
aboard the sun-flooded schooner
but here alone.

There is a ladder.
The ladder is always there
hanging innocently   15
close to the side of the schooner.
We know what it is for,
we who have used it.
Otherwise
it's a piece of maritime floss   20
some sundry equipment.

I go down.
Rung after rung and still
the oxygen immerses me
the blue light   25
the clear atoms

* Jacques Cousteau (b. 1910)   French underwater explorer

of our human air.
I go down.
My flippers cripple me,
I crawl like an insect down the ladder   30
and there is no one
to tell me when the ocean
will begin.

First the air is blue and then
it is bluer and then green and then   35
black I am blacking out and yet
my mask is powerful
it pumps my blood with power
the sea is another story
the sea is not a question of power   40
I have to learn alone
to turn my body without force
in the deep element.

And now: it is easy to forget
what I came for   45
among so many who have always
lived here
swaying their crenellated fans
between the reefs
and besides   50
you breathe differently down here.

I came to explore the wreck.
The words are purposes.
The words are maps.
I came to see the damage that was done   55
and the treasures that prevail.
I stroke the beam of my lamp
slowly along the flank
of something more permanent
than fish or weed   60

the thing I came for:
the wreck and not the story of the wreck
the thing itself and not the myth
the drowned face always staring
toward the sun   65
the evidence of damage

worn by salt and sway into this threadbare beauty
the ribs of the disaster
curving their assertion
among the tentative haunters.   *70*

This is the place.
And I am here, the mermaid whose dark hair
streams black, the merman in his armored body
We circle silently
about the wreck   *75*
we dive into the hold.
I am she: I am he

whose drowned face sleeps with open eyes
whose breasts still bear the stress
whose silver, copper, vermeil cargo lies   *80*
obscurely inside barrels
half-wedged and left to rot
we are the half-destroyed instruments
that once held to a course
the water-eaten log   *85*
the fouled compass

We are, I am, you are
by cowardice or courage
the one who find our way
back to this scene   *90*
carrying a knife, a camera
a book of myths
in which
our names do not appear.

QUESTIONS

1. Do you think the "wreck" can be defined fairly precisely?
   In any case, what do you think the wreck is?
2. In lines 62–63 the speaker says that she came to explore "the
   wreck and not the story of the wreck / the thing itself and
   not the myth." Lines 1 and 92 speak of a "book of myths."
   What sort of "myths" do you think the poet is talking about?
3. In line 72 the speaker is a mermaid; in line 73, a merman;
   in lines 74 and 76, "we"; and in line 77, "I am she: I am
   he." What do you make of this?

Wallace Stevens (*American. 1879–1955*)

Anecdote of the Jar

I placed a jar in Tennessee,
And round it was, upon a hill.
It made the slovenly wilderness
Surround that hill.   *4*

The wilderness rose up to it,
And sprawled around, no longer wild.
The jar was round upon the ground
And tall and of a port in air.   *8*

It took dominion everywhere.
The jar was gray and bare.
It did not give of bird or bush,
Like nothing else in Tennessee.   *12*

Stevens, asked for an interpretation of another poem, said (in *The Explicator,* November 1948): "Things that have their origin in the imagination or in the emotions (poems) . . . very often take on a form that is ambiguous or uncertain. It is not possible to attach a single, rational meaning to such things without destroying the imaginative or emotional ambiguity or uncertainty that is inherent in them and that is why poets do not like to explain. That the meanings given by others are sometimes meanings not intended by the poet or that were never present in his mind does not impair them as meanings."

QUESTIONS

1. What is the meaning of line 8? Check "port" in a dictionary.
2. Do you think the poem suggests that the jar organizes slovenly nature, or that the jar impoverishes abundant nature? Or both, or neither? What do you think of the view that the jar is a symbol of the imagination, or of the arts, or of material progress?

Wallace Stevens (American. 1879–1955)

The Emperor of Ice-Cream

Call the roller of big cigars,
The muscular one, and bid him whip
In kitchen cups concupiscent curds.
Let the wenches dawdle in such dress
As they are used to wear, and let the boys   5
Bring flowers in last month's newspapers.
Let be be finale of seem.
The only emperor is the emperor of ice-cream.

Take from the dresser of deal,°   *fir or pine wood*
Lacking the three glass knobs, that sheet   10
On which she embroidered fantails once
And spread it so as to cover her face.
If her horny feet protrude, they come
To show how cold she is, and dumb.
Let the lamp affix its beam.   15
The only emperor is the emperor of ice-cream.

QUESTION

What associations does the word "emperor" have for you?
The word "ice-cream"? What, then, do you make of "the
emperor of ice-cream"? The poem describes the preparations
for a wake, and in line 15 ("Let the lamp affix its beam")
it insists on facing the reality of death. In this context, then,
what do you make of the last line of each stanza?

Wallace Stevens (American. 1879–1955)

The Snow Man

One must have a mind of winter
To regard the frost and the boughs
Of the pine-trees crusted with snow;

And have been cold a long time
To behold the junipers shagged with ice,   *5*
The spruces rough in the distant glitter

Of the January sun; and not to think
Of any misery in the sound of the wind,
In the sound of a few leaves,

Which is the sound of the land   *10*
Full of the same wind
That is blowing in the same bare place

For the listener, who listens in the snow,
And, nothing himself, beholds
Nothing that is not there and the nothing that is.   *15*

QUESTIONS

1. What do you think is meant by "a mind of winter" (line 1)?
2. Do you think the title of the poem is good? Helpful? Is the snow man a figure made out of snow — literally a snowman — or is it a metaphor for the observer? Or both? Or what?

14

Irony and Paradox

There is a kind of discourse which, though nonliteral, need not use similes, metaphors, apostrophes, personification, or symbols. Without using these figures, speakers may say things that are not to be taken literally. They may, in short, employ **irony.** In Greek comedy, the *eiron* was the sly underdog who, by dissembling inferiority, outwitted his opponent. As Aristotle put it, irony (employed by the *eiron*) is a "pretense tending toward the underside" of truth. Later, Cicero somewhat altered the meaning of the word: he defined it as saying one thing and meaning another, and he held that Socrates, who feigned ignorance and let his opponents entrap themselves in their own arguments, was the ironist par excellence.

In **verbal irony,** as the term is now used, what is stated is in some degree negated by what is suggested. A classic example is Lady Macbeth's order to get ready for King Duncan's visit: "He that's coming / Must be provided for." The words seem to say that she and Macbeth must busy themselves with household preparations so that the king may be received in appropriate style, but this suggestion of hospitality is undercut by an opposite meaning: preparations must be made for the murder of the king. Two other examples of verbal irony are Melville's comment,

> What like a bullet can undeceive!

and the lover's assertion (in Marvell's "To His Coy Mistress") that

> The grave's a fine and private place,
> But none, I think, do there embrace.

Under Marvell's cautious words we detect a wryness; the **understatement** masks yet reveals a deep-felt awareness of mortality and the barrenness of the grave. The self-mockery in this understatement proclaims modesty, but suggests assurance. The speaker here, like most ironists is both playful and serious at once. Irony packs a great deal into a few words.* What we call irony here, it should be mentioned, is often called **sarcasm,** but a distinction can be made: sarcasm is notably contemptuous and crude or heavy-handed ("You're a great guy, a real friend," said to a friend who won't lend you ten dollars), and this is only one kind of irony, and a kind almost never found in literature.

Overstatement (hyperbole) as well as understatement is ironic when it contains a contradictory suggestion:

> For Brutus is an honorable man;
> So are they all, all honorable men.

The sense of contradiction that is inherent in verbal irony is also inherent in a paradox. **Paradox** has several meanings for philosophers, but we need only be concerned with its meaning of an apparent contradiction. In Gerard Manley Hopkins's "Spring and Fall" (page 433), there is an apparent contradiction in the assertions that Margaret is weeping for the woods (line 2) and for herself (line 15), but the contradiction is not real: both the woods and Margaret are parts of the nature blighted by Adam's sin. Other paradoxes are

> The child is father of the man;
>
> — Wordsworth

and (on the soldiers who died to preserve the British Empire)

> The saviors come not home tonight;
> Themselves they could not save;
>
> — Housman

and

> One short sleep past, we wake eternally,
> And Death shall be no more; Death, thou shalt die.
>
> — Donne

Donne's lines are a reminder that paradox is not only an instrument of the poet. Christianity embodies several paradoxes: God became man; through the death on the cross, man can obtain eternal life; man does not live fully until he dies.

---

* A word of caution: We have been talking about verbal irony, not **irony of situation.** Like ironic words, ironic situations have in them an element of contrast. A clown whose heart is breaking must make his audience laugh; an author's worst book is her only financial success; a fool solves a problem that vexes the wise.

Some critics have put a high premium on ironic and paradoxical poetry. Briefly, the argument runs that great poetry recognizes the complexity of experience, and that irony and paradox are ways of doing justice to this complexity. I. A. Richards uses "irony" to denote "The bringing in of the opposite, the complementary impulses," and suggests (in *The Principles of Literary Criticism*) that irony in this sense is a characteristic of poetry of "the highest order." It is dubious that all poets must always bring in the opposite, but it is certain that much poetry is ironic and paradoxical.

John Hall Wheelock (*American. 1886–1978*)

Earth

"A planet doesn't explode of itself," said drily
The Martian astronomer, gazing off into the air —
"That they were able to do it is proof that highly
Intelligent beings must have been living there."

QUESTIONS

1. What is the "it" (line 3) that has been done?
2. How do you think the Martian astronomer would characterize himself or herself? How do you think the author would characterize the astronomer?

Percy Bysshe Shelley (*English. 1792–1822*)

Ozymandias

I met a traveler from an antique land
Who said: Two vast and trunkless legs of stone
Stand in the desert . . . Near them, on the sand,
Half sunk, a shattered visage lies, whose frown,   *4*
And wrinkled lip, and sneer of cold command,
Tell that its sculptor well those passions read
Which yet survive, stamped on these lifeless things,
The hand that mocked them, and the heart that fed: *8*

And on the pedestal these words appear:
"My name is Ozymandias, king of kings:
Look on my works, ye Mighty, and despair!"
Nothing beside remains. Round the decay   *12*
Of that colossal wreck, boundless and bare
The lone and level sands stretch far away.

Lines 4–8 are somewhat obscure, but the gist is that the passions
— still evident in the "shattered visage" — survive the sculptor's
hand that "mocked" — that is, (1) copied, (2) derided — them,
and the passions also survive the king's heart that had nourished
them.

QUESTION

There is, of course, a sort of irony of plot here: Ozymandias
believed that he created enduring works, but his intentions
came to nothing. However, another sort of irony is also
present: How are his words, in a way he did not intend,
true?

William Shakespeare (*English. 1564–1616*)
Sonnet 146

Poor soul, the center of my sinful earth,
My sinful earth these rebel pow'rs that thee array,
Why dost thou pine within and suffer dearth,
Painting thy outward walls so costly gay?   *4*
Why so large cost,° having so short a lease,   *expense*
Dost thou upon thy fading mansion spend?
Shall worms, inheritors of this excess,
Eat up thy charge? Is this thy body's end?   *8*
Then, soul, live thou upon thy servant's loss,
And let that pine to aggravate thy store;
Buy terms divine° in selling hours of dross; *buy ages of immortality*
Within be fed, without be rich no more.   *12*
    So shalt thou feed on Death, that feeds on men,
    And death once dead, there's no more dying then.

QUESTIONS

1. In line 2, "My sinful earth" is doubtless a printer's error, an unintentional repetition of the last word of the first line. Among suggested emendations are "Thrall to," "Fooled by," "Rebuke these," "Leagued with," "Feeding." Which do you prefer? Why?
2. How would you characterize the tone of the first two lines? Where in the poem does the thought take its chief turn? What do you think is the tone of the couplet?
3. What does "array" (line 2) mean?
4. Explain the paradox in lines 13–14.
5. In a poem on the relation between body and soul, do you find battle imagery surprising? Commercial imagery (lines 5–12)? What other imagery is in the poem? Do you think the sonnet is a dull sermon?

Stevie Smith (*English. 1902–1971*)

Not Waving but Drowning

Nobody heard him, the dead man,
But still he lay moaning:
I was much further out than you thought
And not waving but drowning.   *4*

Poor chap, he always loved larking
And now he's dead
It must have been too cold for him his heart gave way,
They said.   *8*

Oh, no no no, it was too cold always
(Still the dead one lay moaning)
I was much too far out all my life
And not waving but drowning.   *12*

QUESTIONS

1. What sort of man did the friends of the dead man think he was? What sort of man do you think he was?
2. The first line, "Nobody heard him, the dead man," is of

course literally true. Dead men do not speak. In what other ways is it true?

John Crowe Ransom (American. 1888–1974)

Bells for John Whiteside's Daughter

There was such speed in her little body,
And such lightness in her footfall,
It is no wonder her brown study
Astonishes us all.   4

Her wars were bruited in our high window.
We looked among orchard trees and beyond
Where she took arms against her shadow,
Or harried unto the pond   8

The lazy geese, like a snow cloud
Dripping their snow on the green grass,
Tricking and stopping, sleepy and proud,
Who cried in goose, Alas,   12

For the tireless heart within the little
Lady with rod that made them rise
From their noon apple-dreams and scuttle
Goose-fashion under the skies!   16

But now go the bells, and we are ready,
In one house we are sternly stopped
To say we are vexed at her brown study,
Lying so primly propped.   20

QUESTIONS

1. What is the usual meaning of "a brown study" in line 3? For what is it an understatement here? What do you think the poet is referring to when he speaks of "her wars" (line 5)? What are the literal and figurative suggestions of "took arms against her shadow" in line 7?
2. Why is "tireless heart" (line 13) ironic?
3. In line 17 the speaker says "we are ready." Ready for what? Do you think he is ready?

Andrew Marvell (*English. 1621–1678*)

To His Coy Mistress

Had we but world enough, and time,
This coyness, lady, were no crime.
We would sit down, and think which way
To walk, and pass our long love's day.
Thou by the Indian Ganges' side   *5*
Should'st rubies find: I by the tide
Of Humber would complain.° I would   *write love poems*
Love you ten years before the Flood,
And you should, if you please, refuse
Till the conversion of the Jews.   *10*
My vegetable° love should grow   *i.e., unconsciously growing*
Vaster than empires, and more slow.
An hundred years should go to praise
Thine eyes, and on thy forehead gaze:
Two hundred to adore each breast: *15*
But thirty thousand to the rest.
An age at least to every part,
And the last age should show your heart.
For, lady, you deserve this state,
Nor would I love at lower rate.   *20*
      But at my back I always hear
Time's winged chariot hurrying near;
And yonder all before us lie
Deserts of vast eternity.
Thy beauty shall no more be found,   *25*
Nor in thy marble vault shall sound
My echoing song; then worms shall try
That long preserved virginity,
And your quaint honor turn to dust,
And into ashes all my lust.   *30*
The grave's a fine and private place,
But none, I think, do there embrace.
      Now therefore, while the youthful hue
Sits on thy skin like morning dew,
And while thy willing soul transpires   *35*
At every pore with instant fires,
Now let us sport us while we may;
And now, like am'rous birds of prey,
Rather at once our time devour,
Than languish in his slow-chapt° power,   *slowly devouring*   *40*

Let us roll all our strength, and all
Our sweetness, up into one ball;
And tear our pleasures with rough strife
Thorough° the iron gates of life.   *through*
Thus, though we cannot make our sun   *45*
Stand still, yet we will make him run.

QUESTIONS

1. Do you find the assertions in lines 1–20 so inflated that you detect behind them a playfully ironic tone? Explain. Why does the speaker say, in line 8, that he would love "ten years before the Flood," rather than merely "since the Flood"?
2. Explain lines 21–24. Why is time behind the speaker, and eternity in front of him? Is this "eternity" the same as the period discussed in lines 1–20? What do you make of the change in the speaker's tone after line 20.
3. Do you agree with the comment on pages 472–473 about the understatement in lines 31–32? What more can you say about these lines, in context?
4. Why "am'rous birds of prey" (line 38) rather than the conventional doves? Is the idea of preying continued in the poem?
5. Try to explain the last two lines, and characterize the speaker's tone. Do you find these lines anticlimactic?
6. The poem is organized in the form of an argument. Trace the steps.

John Donne (English. 1572–1631)

The Flea

Mark but this flea, and mark in this
How little that which thou deny'st me is;
It sucked me first, and now sucks thee,
And in this flea our two bloods mingled be;
Thou know'st that this cannot be said   *5*
A sin, nor shame, nor loss of maidenhead;
    Yet this enjoys before it woo,
    And pampered swells with one blood made of two,
    And this, alas, is more than we would do.

Oh stay, three lives in one flea spare,   *10*
Where we almost, yea, more than married are.
This flea is you and I, and this
Our marriage bed and marriage temple is;
Though parents grudge, and you, we are met
And cloistered in these living walls of jet.   *15*
    Though use° make you apt to kill me,   *custom*
    Let not to that, self-murder added be,
    And sacrilege, three sins in killing three.

Cruel and sudden, hast thou since
Purpled thy nail in blood of innocence?   *20*
Wherein could this flea guilty be,
Except in that drop which it sucked from thee?
Yet thou triumph'st and say'st that thou
Find'st not thyself, nor me the weaker now.
    'Tis true. Then learn how false fears be: *25*
    Just so much honor, when thou yield'st to me,
    Will waste, as this flea's death took life from thee.

QUESTIONS

1. What is hyperbolic about line 10? Why does the speaker
   overstate the matter in the second stanza? How does the
   overstatement serve to diminish the subject?
2. What has the lady done between the second and third stanzas?
   In line 25 the speaker says that the lady's view is "true."
   Has he changed his mind during the course of the poem, or
   has he been leading up to this point?

John Donne (*English. 1572–1631*)

Holy Sonnet XIV

Batter my heart, three-personed God; for you
As yet but knock, breathe, shine, and seek to mend;
That I may rise and stand, o'erthrow me, and bend
Your force, to break, blow, burn, and make me new.   *4*
I, like an usurped town, to another due,
Labor to admit you, but oh, to no end,
Reason, your viceroy in me, me should defend,
But is captived, and proves weak or untrue.   *8*

Yet dearly I love you, and would be loved fain,
But am betrothed unto your enemy:
Divorce me, untie, or break that knot again,
Take me to you, imprison me, for I   *12*
Except you enthrall me, never shall be free,
Nor ever chaste, except you ravish me.

QUESTIONS

1. Explain the paradoxes in lines 1, 3, 13, and 14. Explain the double meanings of "enthrall" (line 13) and "ravish" (line 14).
2. In lines 1–4, what is God implicitly compared to (considering especially lines 2 and 4)? How does this comparison lead into the comparison that dominates lines 5–8? What words in lines 9–12 are especially related to the earlier lines?
3. What do you think is gained by piling up verbs in lines 2–4?
4. Do you find sexual references irreverent in a religious poem? Donne, incidentally, was an Anglican priest.

A. E. Housman (*English. 1859–1936*)

Shropshire Lad #27

"Is my team ploughing,
      That I was used to drive
And hear the harness jingle
      When I was man alive?"   *4*

Ay, the horses trample,
      The harness jingles now;
No change though you lie under
      The land you used to plough.   *8*

"Is football playing
      Along the river shore,
With lads to chase the leather,
      Now I stand up no more?"   *12*

Ay, the ball is flying,
      The lads play heart and soul;
The goal stands up, the keeper
      Stands up to keep the goal.   *16*

"Is my girl happy,
    That I thought hard to leave,
And has she tired of weeping
    As she lies down at eve?"   20

Ay, she lies down lightly,
    She lies not down to weep:
Your girl is well contented.
    Be still, my lad, and sleep.   24

"Is my friend hearty,
    Now I am thin and pine,
And has he found to sleep in
    A better bed than mine?"   28

Yes, lad, I lie easy,
    I lie as lads would choose;
I cheer a dead man's sweetheart,
    Never ask me whose.   32

QUESTIONS

1. Characterize the speaker of the first, third, fifth, and seventh stanzas. Who is the speaker in the other stanzas?
2. How does the answer in the sixth stanza differ significantly from the answer in the second and fourth stanzas? How do you account for the difference?
3. If you have read any of the ballads in Chapter 16, and especially "Edward," list some of the characteristics in "Is My Team Ploughing" that show Housman's use of ballads.

Langston Hughes (American. 1902–1967)

Dream Boogie

Good morning, daddy!
Ain't you heard
The boogie-woogie rumble
Of a dream deferred?

Listen closely: 5
You'll hear their feet
Beating out and beating out a —

You think
It's a happy beat?

Listen to it closely: 10
Ain't you heard
something underneath
like a —

What did I say?

Sure,   15
I'm happy!
Take it away!

Hey, pop!
Re-bop!
Mop!   20

Y-e-a-h!

What don't bug
them white kids
sure bugs me:
We knows everybody   25
ain't free!

Some of these young ones is cert'ly bad —
One batted a hard ball right through my window
and my gold fish et the glass.

What's written down   30
for white folks
ain't for us a-tall:
"Liberty And Justice —
Huh — For All."

Oop-pop-a-da!   35
Skee! Daddle-de-do!
Be-bop!

Salt'peanuts!

De-dop!

QUESTIONS

1. What is boogie, or boogie-woogie?
2. Why did many whites assume that boogie was "a happy beat" (line 9)? In fact, what was boogie chiefly an expression of?
3. Why does Hughes in lines 32–34 quote part of the Pledge of Allegiance?

Langston Hughes (*American. 1902–1967*)

Theme for English B

The instructor said,

> Go home and write
> a page tonight.
> And let that page come out of you —
> Then, it will be true.   5

I wonder if it's that simple?
I am twenty-two, colored, born in Winston-Salem.*
I went to school there, then Durham, then here
to this college on the hill above Harlem.
I am the only colored student in my class.   10
The steps from the hill lead down into Harlem,
through a park, then I cross St. Nicholas,
Eighth Avenue, Seventh, and I come to the Y,
the Harlem Branch Y, where I take the elevator
up to my room, sit down, and write this page: 15

It's not easy to know what is true for you or me
at twenty-two, my age. But I guess I'm what
I feel and see and hear, Harlem, I hear you:
hear you, hear me — we two — you, me, talk on this page.
(I hear New York, too.) Me — who?   20

---

* Winston-Salem and Durham (line 8) are in North Carolina; the places later named are in New York; in line 24, Bessie Smith (1898?–1937) was a black singer of blues.

Well, I like to eat, sleep, drink, and be in love.
I like to work, read, learn and understand life.
I like a pipe for a Christmas present,
or records — Bessie, bop, or Bach.
I guess being colored doesn't make me *not* like   25
the same things other folks like who are other races.
So will my page be colored that I write?

Being me, it will not be white.
But it will be
a part of you, instructor.   30
You are white —
yet a part of me, as I am a part of you.
That's American.
Sometimes perhaps you don't want to be a part of me.
Nor do I often want to be a part of you.   35
But we are, that's true!
As I learn from you,
I guess you learn from me —
although you're older — and white —
and somewhat more free.   40

This is my page for English B.

QUESTIONS

1. On your first reading of the poem did the instructor's lines (2–5) sound sensible and convincing to you? On a second reading, how do they sound?
2. How much sense does it make for the speaker to say that his essay will be "a part of you, instructor," and "You are white — / yet a part of me, as I am a part of you" (lines 30–32)?
3. Do you think lines 37–40 are meant to be spoken with conscious verbal irony?
4. There are two voices or speakers in the poem — the instructor and the student. Which of the two strikes you as the more thoughtful?

15
Rhythm

Ezra Pound (*American. 1885–1973*)

An Immorality

Sing we for love and idleness,
Naught else is worth the having.

Though I have been in many a land,
There is naught else in living.

And I would rather have my sweet,
Though rose-leaves die of grieving,

Than do high deeds in Hungary
To pass all men's believing.

A good poem. To begin with, it sings; as Pound said, "Poetry withers and dries out when it leaves music, or at least imagined music, too far behind it. Poets who are not interested in music are, or become, bad poets." Hymns and ballads, it must be remembered, are songs, and other poetry, too, is sung, especially by children. Children reciting a counting-out rhyme, or singing on their way home from school, are enjoying poetry:

> Pease-porridge hot,
>> Pease-porridge cold,
> Pease-porridge in the pot
>> Nine days old.

Nothing very important is being said, but for generations children have enjoyed the music of these lines, and adults, too, have recalled them with pleasure — though few people know what pease-porridge is.

The "music" — the catchiness of certain sounds — should not be underestimated. Here are lines chanted by the witches in *Macbeth:*

> Double, double, toil and trouble;
> Fire burn and cauldron bubble.

This is rather far from words that mean approximately the same thing: "Twice, twice, work and care; / Fire ignite, and pot boil." The difference is more in the sounds than in the instructions. What is lost in the paraphrase is the magic, the incantation, which resides in elaborate repetitions of sounds and stresses.

Rhythm (most simply, in English poetry, stresses at regular intervals) has a power of its own. A good march, said John Philip Sousa (the composer of "Stars and Stripes Forever") should make even someone with a wooden leg "step out." A highly pronounced rhythm is common in such forms of poetry as charms, college yells, and lullabies; all of them (like the witches' speech) are aimed at inducing a special effect magically. It is not surprising that *carmen,* the Latin word for poem or song, is also the Latin word for charm, and the word from which "charm" is derived.

> Rain, rain, go away;
> Come again another day.
>
> Block that kick! Block that kick! Block that kick!
>
> Rock-a-bye baby, on the tree top,
> When the wind blows, the cradle will rock.

In much poetry rhythm is only half-heard, but its omnipresence is suggested by the fact that when poetry is printed it is customary to begin each line with a capital letter. Prose (from Latin *prorsus,* "forward," "straight on") keeps running across the paper until the righthand margin is reached, and then, merely because the paper has given out, the writer or printer starts again at the left, with a small letter. But verse (Latin *versus,* "a turning") often ends well short of the righthand margin, and the next line begins at the left — usually with a capital — not because paper has run out but because the rhythmic pattern begins again. Lines of poetry are continually reminding us that they have a pattern.

Before turning to some other highly rhythmic pieces, a word of caution: a mechanical, unvarying rhythm may be good to put the baby to sleep, but it can be deadly to readers who wish to keep awake. Poets vary their rhythm according to their purpose; a poet ought not to be so regular that he or she is (in W. H. Auden's words) an "accentual pest." In competent hands, rhythm contributes to meaning; it says something. The rhythm in the lines from *Macbeth,* for example, helps suggest the strong binding power of magic. Again Ezra Pound has a relevant comment: "Rhythm *must* have meaning. It can't be merely a careless dash off, with no grip and no real hold to the words and sense, a tumty tum tumty tum tum ta." Some examples will be useful.

Consider this description of Hell from *Paradise Lost* (the heavier stresses are marked by ´):

> Rócks, cáves, laḱes, féns, bógs, déns, aňd shádes ŏf deáth.

Such a succession of stresses is highly unusual. Elsewhere in the poem Milton chiefly uses iambic feet — alternating unstressed and stressed syllables — but here he immediately follows one heavy stress with another, thereby helping to communicate the "meaning" — the impressive monotony of Hell. As a second example, consider the function of the rhythm in two lines by Alexander Pope:

> Whĕn Ájăx striv́es sŏme róck's vást wéight tŏ thrów,
>
> Thĕ líne tóo lábŏrs, aňd thĕ wórds móve slów.

The heavier stresses (again, marked by ´) do not merely alternate with the lighter ones (marked ˘); rather, the great weight of the rock is suggested by three consecutive stressed words, "rock's vast weight," and the great effort involved in moving it is suggested by another three consecutive stresses, "line too labors," and by yet another three, "words move slow." Note, also, the abundant pauses within the lines. In the first line, unless one's speech is slovenly, one must pause at least slightly after "Ajax," "strives," "rock's," "vast," "weight," and "throw." The grating sounds in "Ajax" and "rocks" do their work, too, and so do the explosive *t*'s. When Pope wishes to suggest lightness, he reverses his procedure and he groups unstressed syllables:

> Not so, when swift Camilla scours the plain,
>
> Fliés o'ĕr th'ŭnbéndĭng córn, aňd skíms ălŏng thĕ máin.

This last line has twelve syllables and is thus longer than the line about Ajax, but the addition of "along" helps to communicate lightness and swiftness because in this line (it can be argued) neither syllable of "along" is strongly stressed. If "along" is omitted, the line still makes grammatical sense and becomes more "regular," but it also becomes less imitative of lightness.

The very regularity of a line may be meaningful too. Shakespeare begins a sonnet thus:

> Whĕn Í dŏ coúnt thĕ clóck thăt télls thĕ tiḿe.

This line about a mechanism runs with appropriate regularity. (It is worth noting, too, that "*c*ount the *c*lock" and "*t*ells the *t*ime" emphasize the regularity by the repetition of sounds and syntax.) But notice what Shakespeare does in the middle of the next line:

> Aňd sée thĕ bráve dáy súnk iň hídeŏus níght.

What has he done? And what is the effect?

Here is another poem that refers to a clock. In England, until capital punishment was abolished, executions regularly took place at 8:00 A.M.

A. E. Housman (*English. 1859–1936*)

Eight O'Clock

He stood, and heard the steeple
  Sprinkle the quarters on the morning town.
One, two, three, four, to market-place and people
  It tossed them down.

Strapped, noosed, nighing his hour,
  He stood and counted them and cursed his luck;
And then the clock collected in the tower
  Its strength, and struck.

The chief (but not unvarying) pattern is iambic, that is, the odd syllables are less emphatic than the even ones, as in

> Hĕ stóod, aňd héard thĕ stéeple

Try to mark the syllables, stressed and unstressed, in the rest of the poem. Be guided by your ear, not by a mechanical principle, and don't worry too much about difficult or uncertain parts; different readers may reasonably come up with different results.

QUESTIONS

1. Where do you find two or more consecutive stresses? What explanations (related to meaning) can be offered?
2. What do you think is the effect of the short line at the end of each stanza? And what significance can you attach to the fact that these lines (unlike the first and third lines in each stanza) end with a stress?

Following are some poems in which the strongly felt pulsations are highly important.

William Carlos Williams (American. 1883–1963)

The Dance

In Breughel's great picture, The Kermess,
the dancers go round, they go round and
around, the squeal and the blare and the
tweedle of bagpipes, a bugle and fiddles
tipping their bellies (round as the thick-   5
sided glasses whose wash they impound)
their hips and their bellies off balance
to turn them. Kicking and rolling about
the Fair Grounds, swinging their butts, those
shanks must be sound to bear up under such   10
rollicking measures, prance as they dance
in Breughel's great picture, The Kermess.

QUESTIONS

1. Read the poem aloud several times, and decide where the heavy stresses fall. Mark the heavily stressed syllables (´), the lightly stressed ones (ˆ), and the unstressed ones (ˇ). Are all the lines identical? What effect is thus gained, especially when read aloud? What does the parenthetical statement (lines 5–6) do to the rhythm? Does a final syllable often receive a heavy stress here? Are there noticeable pauses at the ends of the lines? What is the consequence? Are the dancers waltzing?
2. What syllables rhyme or are repeated (e.g., "round" in lines

2 and 5, and "-pound" in line 6; "-ing" in lines 5, 8, 9, and 11)? What effect do they have?

3. What do you think the absence at the beginning of each line of the customary capital contributes to the meaning? Why is the last line the same as the first?

Theodore Roethke (*American. 1908–1963*)

My Papa's Waltz

The whiskey on your breath
Could make a small boy dizzy;
But I hung on like death:
Such waltzing was not easy.   *4*

We romped until the pans
Slid from the kitchen shelf;
My mother's countenance
Could not unfrown itself.   *8*

The hand that held my wrist
Was battered on one knuckle;
At every step you missed
My right ear scraped a buckle.   *12*

You beat time on my head
With a palm caked hard by dirt,
Then waltzed me off to bed
Still clinging to your shirt.   *16*

QUESTIONS

1. Is the rhythm more regular than in Williams' "The Dance"? Do the syntactical pauses vary much from stanza to stanza? Be specific. Would you say that the rhythm suggests lightness? Why?
2. Does the rhythm parallel or ironically contrast with the episode described? Was the dance a graceful waltz? Explain.
3. What would you say is the function of the stresses in lines 13–14?

Gwendolyn Brooks (*American. b. 1915*)

We Real Cool

The Pool Players.
Seven at the Golden Shovel.

We real cool. We
Left school. We

Lurk late. We
Strike straight. We   4

Sing sin. We
Thin gin. We

Jazz June. We
Die soon.   8

QUESTION

The stanzas could, of course, have been written thus:

> We real cool.
> We left school.
>
> We lurk late.
> We strike straight.

And so forth. Why do you think Brooks wrote them, or printed them, the way she did?

Dylan Thomas (*Welsh. 1914–1953*)

Do not go gentle into that good night

Do not go gentle into that good night,
Old age should burn and rave at close of day;
Rage, rage against the dying of the light.

Though wise men at their end know dark is right,
Because their words had forked no lightning they   5
Do not go gentle into that good night.

Good men, the last wave by, crying how bright
Their frail deeds might have danced in a green bay,
Rage, rage against the dying of the light.

Wild men who caught and sang the sun in flight,   10
And learn, too late, they grieved it on its way,
Do not go gentle into that good night.

Grave men, near death, who see with blinding sight
Blind eyes could blaze like meteors and be gay,
Rage, rage against the dying of the light.   15

And you, my father, there on the sad height,
Curse, bless, me now with your fierce tears, I pray.
Do not go gentle into that good night.
Rage, rage against the dying of the light.

This poem is written in an elaborate French form, the **villanelle,**
that is, five tercets (stanzas of three lines each, the first and third
lines rhyming) and a final quatrain (stanza of four lines, the first,
third, and fourth lines all rhyming with the first and third lines
of the tercets, and the second line rhyming with the middle lines
of the tercets). Moreover, the first line of the poem is the last line
of the second and fourth tercets; the third line of the poem is the
last line of the third and fifth tercets, and these two lines reappear
yet again as a pair of rhyming lines at the end of the poem.

QUESTION

The intricate form of the villanelle might seem too fussy for
a serious poem about dying. Do you find it too fussy? Or
does the form here somehow succeed?

16

Some Principles of Versification

Robert Francis (*American. 1901–1987*)

The Pitcher

His art is eccentricity, his aim
How not to hit the mark he seems to aim at,

His passion how to avoid the obvious,
His technique how to vary the avoidance.   *4*

The others throw to be comprehended. He
Throws to be a moment misunderstood.

Yet not too much. Not errant, arrant, wild,
But every seeming aberration willed.   *8*

Not to, yet still, still to communicate
Making the batter understand too late.

If you read this poem aloud, pausing appropriately where the
punctuation tells you to, you will hear the poet trying to represent
something of the pitcher's "eccentricity." ("Eccentric," by the
way, literally means "off center.") A pitcher tries to deceive a

batter, perhaps by throwing a ball that will unexpectedly curve over the plate; the poet playfully deceives the reader, for instance, with unexpected pauses. In line 5, for example, he puts a heavy pause (indicated by a period) not at the end of the line, but just *before* the end. Note, too, that some lines contain no pauses, but the next-to-last line contains two within it (indicated by commas) and no pause at the end of it, making us as uneasy as the batter. And what significance can be attached to the fact that only the last two lines really rhyme ("communicate: late"), whereas other lines are, so to speak, inconclusive: "aim: aim at," "wild: willed"?

The technical vocabulary of **prosody** (the study of the principles of verse structure, including meter, rhyme and other sound effects, and stanzaic patterns) is large. An understanding of these terms will not turn anyone into a poet, but it will enable one to discuss some aspects of poetry more efficiently. A knowledge of them, like a knowledge of most other technical terms (e.g., "misplaced modifier," "woofer," "automatic transmission"), allows for quick and accurate communication. The following are the chief terms of prosody.

Most English poetry has a pattern of **stressed (accented)** sounds, and this pattern is the **meter** (from the Greek word for "measure"). Although in Old English poetry (poetry written in England before the Norman-French Conquest in 1066) a line may have any number of unstressed syllables in addition to four stressed syllables, most poetry written in England since the Conquest not only has a fixed number of stresses in a line, but also has a fixed number of unstressed syllables before or after each stressed one. (One really ought not to talk of "unstressed" or "unaccented" syllables, since to utter a syllable — however lightly — is to give it some stress. It is really a matter of *relative* stress, but the fact is that "unstressed" or "unaccented" are parts of the established terminology of versification.)

In a line of poetry, the **foot** is the basic unit of measurement. On rare occasions it is a single stressed syllable, but generally a foot consists of two or three syllables, one of which is stressed. (Stress is indicated by ´; lack of stress by ˇ.) The repetition of feet, then, produces a pattern of stresses throughout the poem.

Two cautions:

1. A poem will seldom contain only one kind of foot throughout; significant variations usually occur, but one kind of foot is dominant.

2. In reading a poem one pays attention to the sense as well as to the metrical pattern. By paying attention to the sense, one

often finds that the stress falls on a word that according to the metrical pattern would be unstressed. Or a word that according to the pattern would be stressed may be seen to be unstressed. Furthermore, by reading for sense, one finds that not all stresses are equally heavy; some are almost as light as unstressed syllables, and sometimes there is a **hovering stress;** that is, the stress is equally distributed over two adjacent syllables. To repeat: one reads for sense, allowing the syntax to help indicate the stresses.

The most common feet in English poetry are:

iamb (adjective: **iambic**): one unstressed syllable followed by one stressed syllable. The iamb, said to be the most common pattern in English speech, is surely the most common in English poetry. It is called a **rising meter,** the foot rising toward the stress. The following example has five iambic feet:

> Ĭ sáw | thĕ ský | dĕscénd | iňg bláck | aňd whíte.
>
> — Robert Lowell

trochee (trochaic): one stressed syllable followed by one unstressed; a **falling meter,** the foot falling away from the stress:

> Lét hĕr | liv́e tŏ | eárn hĕr | dínnĕrs.
>
> — J. M. Synge

anapest (anapestic): two unstressed syllables followed by one stressed; a rising meter:

> Thĕre aře mán | ў whŏ sáy | thăt ă dóg | hăs hĭs dáy.
>
> — Dylan Thomas

dactyl (dactylic): one stressed syllable followed by two unstressed; a falling meter. This trisyllabic foot, like the anapest, is common in light verse, or verse suggesting joy, but its use is not limited to such material. Thomas Hood's sentimental "The Bridge of Sighs" begins:

> Táke hĕr ŭp | téndĕrlў.

spondee (spondaic): two stressed syllables; most often used as a substitute for an iamb or trochee; it neither rises nor falls.

> Smárt lád, | tŏ slíp | bĕtiḿes | ăwáy.
>
> — A. E. Housman

Because the **pyrrhic foot** (two unstressed syllables) lacks a stress, it is often not considered a legitimate foot in English.

A metrical line consists of one or more feet and is named for the number of feet in it. The following names are used:

monometer:	one foot	**pentameter:**	five feet
dimeter:	two feet	**hexameter:**	six feet
trimeter:	three feet	**heptameter:**	seven feet
tetrameter:	four feet	**octameter:**	eight feet

A line is scanned for the kind and number of feet in it, and the **scansion** tells you if it is, say, anapestic trimeter (three anapests):

Ăs Ĭ cáme | ťo thĕ edǵe | ŏf thĕ wóods.

— Frost

Another example, this time iambic pentameter:

Sińce bráss, | nŏr stóne, | nŏr eárth, | nŏr boúnd | lĕss séa.

— Shakespeare

In prosody, as in the rest of life, male chauvinism has left its mark: a line ending with a stress has a **masculine ending** or **strong ending;** a line ending with an unstressed syllable has a **feminine ending** or **weak ending.** The lines above by Synge and Hood have feminine endings; those by Lowell, Thomas, Housman, Frost, and Shakespeare have masculine endings.

The **caesura** (usually indicated by the symbol //) is a slight pause within the line. It need not be indicated by punctuation, and it does not affect the metrical count:

Awake, my St. John! // leave all meaner things
To low ambition, // and the pride of kings.
Let us // (since Life can little more supply
Than just to look about us // and to die)
Expatiate free // o'er all this scene of Man;
A mighty maze! // but not without a plan;
A wild, // where weeds and flowers promiscuous shoot;
Or garden, // tempting with forbidden fruit.

— Pope

The varying position of the caesura helps to give Pope's lines an informality that plays against the formality of the pairs of rhyming lines.

An **end-stopped line** concludes with a distinct syntactical pause, but a **run-on line** has its sense carried over into the next line without syntactical pause. (The running-on of a line is called **enjambment.**) In the following passage, only the first is a run-on line:

Yet if we look more closely we shall find
Most have the seeds of judgment in their mind:
Nature affords at least a glimmering light;
The lines, though touched but faintly, are drawn right.

— Pope

Meter produces **rhythm,** recurrences at equal intervals, but rhythm (from a Greek word meaning "flow") is usually applied to larger units than feet. Often it depends most obviously on pauses.

Thus, a poem with run-on lines will have a different rhythm from a poem with end-stopped lines, even though both are in the same meter. And prose, though it is unmetrical, can thus have rhythm, too. In addition to being affected by syntactical pauses, rhythm is affected by pauses due to consonant clusters and the length of words. Polysyllabic words establish a different rhythm from monosyllabic words, even in metrically identical lines.

One can say, then, that rhythm is altered by shifts in meter, syntax, and the ease of pronunciation. But even with no such shift, even if a line is repeated verbatim, a reader may sense a change in rhythm. The rhythm of the final line of a poem may well differ from that of the line before, even though in all other respects the lines are identical, as in Frost's "Stopping by Woods" (page 418), which concludes by repeating "And miles to go before I sleep." One may simply sense that this final line ought to be spoken, say, more slowly.

Though rhythm is basic to poetry, **rhyme** is not. Rhyme is the repetition of the identical or similar stressed sound or sounds. It is, presumably, pleasant in itself; it suggests order; and it also may be related to meaning, for it brings two words sharply together, often implying a relationship, as in the overworked rhymes "moon" and "June," "love" and "dove." **Perfect** or **exact rhymes** occur when differing consonant sounds are followed by identical stressed vowel sounds, and the following sounds, if any, are identical (foe: toe; meet: fleet; buffer: rougher). Notice that perfect rhyme involves identity of sound, not of spelling. "Fix" and "sticks," like "buffer" and "rougher," are perfect rhymes.

In **half-rhyme** (or **slant rhyme, approximate rhyme, near-rhyme, off-rhyme**), only the final consonant sounds of the rhyming words are identical; the stressed vowel sounds as well as the initial consonant sounds, if any, differ (soul: oil; mirth: forth; trolley: bully). **Eye rhyme** is not really rhyme; it merely looks like rhyme (cough: bough: rough). The final syllables in **masculine rhyme** are stressed and, after their differing initial consonant sounds, are identical in sound (stark: mark; support: retort). In **feminine rhyme** (or **double rhyme**), stressed rhyming syllables are followed by identical unstressed syllables (revival: arrival; flatter: batter). **Triple rhyme** is a kind of feminine rhyme in which identical stressed vowel sounds are followed by two identical unstressed syllables (machinery: scenery; tenderly: slenderly). **End rhyme** (or **terminal rhyme**) has the rhyming word at the end of the line. **Internal rhyme** has at least one of the rhyming words within the line (as in Wilde's "Each narrow *cell* in which we *dwell*").

Alliteration is sometimes defined as the repetition of initial sounds ("*All* the *aw*ful *au*guries" or "*B*ring me my *b*ow of *b*urning gold"), sometimes as the prominent repetition of a consonant ("a*f*ter life's *f*it*f*ul *f*ever"). In **assonance** identical vowel sounds in words in proximity are preceded and followed by differing consonant sounds. Whereas "tide" and "hide" are rhymes, "tide" and "mine" are assonantal. (The Irish poet Austin Clarke nicely said of assonance that it "takes the clapper from the bell of rhyme.") **Consonance** is the repetition of a pattern of identical consonant sounds and differing vowel sounds in words in proximity (fail: feel; rough: roof; pitter: patter). Sometimes consonance is more loosely defined merely as the repetition of a consonant (fai*l*: pee*l*). The following poem makes witty use of assonance and consonance.

George Starbuck (American. b. 1931)

Fable for Blackboard

Here is the grackle, people.
Here is the fox, folks.
The grackle sits in the bracken. The fox hopes.

Here are the fronds, friends,
that cover the fox.
The fronds get in a frenzy. The grackle looks.

Here are the ticks, tykes,
that live in the leaves, loves.
The fox is confounded,
and God is above.

Onomatopoeia is said to occur when the sound of a word echoes or suggests the meaning of a word. "Hiss," "gulp," and "buzz" are onomatopoetic. In Emily Dickinson's "A narrow Fellow in the Grass" — a poem about a snake — the words "His notice sudden is —" probably evoke a snake's hissing. But there is a mistaken tendency to see onomatopoeia everywhere, for example, in "thunder," "beauty," and "horror." Many words sometimes thought to be onomatopoetic are not clearly imitative of the thing they denote; they merely contain some sounds which — when we know what the word means — seem to have some resemblance to the thing they denote. Tennyson's lines from "Come down, O maid" are usually cited as an example of onomatopoeia:

> The moan of doves in immemorial elms
> And murmuring of innumerable bees.

But John Crowe Ransom has pointed out that if many of the sounds of "murmuring of innumerable bees" are reproduced in a line of different meaning — "murdering of innumerable beeves" — the suggestiveness is lost.

Lines of poetry are commonly arranged in a rhythmical unit called a **stanza** (from an Italian word meaning a "room" or "stopping-place"). Usually all the stanzas in a poem have the same rhyme pattern. A stanza is sometimes called a **verse,** though "verse" may also mean a single line of poetry. (In discussing stanzas, rhymes are indicated by identical letters. Thus, *abab* indicates that the first and third lines rhyme with each other, while the second and fourth lines are linked by a different rhyme. An unrhymed line is denoted by *x*.) The following stanzaic forms are common in English poetry:

couplet: stanza of two lines, usually (but not necessarily) with end rhymes. Seamus Heaney describes the couplet as "that little pile-driver among the meters, banging, knocking, butting, beating time." "Couplet" is also used for a pair of rhyming lines. The **octosyllabic couplet** is iambic or trochaic tetrameter:

> Had we but world enough, and time,
> This coyness, lady, were no crime.
>
> — Marvell

heroic couplet: a rhyming couplet of iambic pentameter, often "closed," that is, containing a complete thought, with a fairly heavy pause at the end of the first line and a still heavier one at the end of the second. Commonly, there is a parallel or an antithesis within a line, or between the two lines. It is called heroic because in England, especially in the eighteenth century, it was much used for heroic (epic) poems.

> Some foreign writers, some our own despise;
> The ancients only, or the moderns, prize.
>
> — Pope

triplet (or **tercet**): a three-line stanza, usually with one rhyme.

> Whenas in silks my Julia goes
> Then, then (methinks) how sweetly flows
> That liquefaction of her clothes.
>
> — Herrick

One kind of tercet is **terza rima,** rhyming *aba bcb cdc,* and so forth.

quatrain: a four-line stanza, rhymed or unrhymed. The **heroic** (or **elegiac**) **quatrain** is iambic pentameter, rhyming *abab.* The **ballad stanza** is a quatrain alternating iambic tetrameter with iambic trimeter lines, usually rhyming *abxb.* Sometimes it is followed by a **refrain,** a line or lines repeated several times.

sonnet: a fourteen-line poem. The rhyme scheme of the **Petrarchan** (or **Italian**) **sonnet** is organized into an **octave** (the first eight lines) and a **sestet** (the last six). It usually rhymes *abbaabba cdecde,* but the sestet often has variations. In Petrarch's sonnets and in those of many of his imitators, there is a "turn" with the beginning of the ninth line; for example, a generalization in the octave may be illustrated by a particularization in the sestet. But, whether from indifference or inability, this nice disposition of parts is not always observed by English writers, and it is dangerous to generalize about the perfection of the Italian structure as a lyric vehicle. The **Shakespearean** (or **English**) **sonnet** has the fourteen lines of the Petrarchan, but organizes them into three quatrains (four lines each) and a couplet (pair of lines): *abab cdcd efef gg.* The couplet has frequently caused trouble: sometimes it seems a needless appendage, often it seems too snappy a close; less often it seems just right.

Why poets choose to imprison themselves in fourteen tightly rhymed lines is something of a mystery. Tradition has a great deal to do with it: the form, having been handled successfully by major poets, stands as a challenge. In writing a sonnet a poet gains a little of the authority of Petrarch, Shakespeare, Milton, Wordsworth, and other masters who showed that the sonnet is not merely a trick. A second reason perhaps resides in the very tightness of the rhymes, which can help as well as hinder. Many poets have felt, along with Richard Wilbur (in *Mid-Century American Poets,* ed. John Ciardi), that the need for a rhyme has suggested

. . . arbitrary connections of which the mind may take advantage if it likes. For example, if one has to rhyme with *tide,* a great number of rhyme-words at once come to mind (ride, bide, shied, confide, Akenside, etc.). Most of these, in combination with *tide,* will probably suggest nothing apropos, but one of them may reveal precisely what one wanted to say. If none of them does, *tide* must be dispensed with. Rhyme, austerely used, may be a stimulus to discovery and a stretcher of the attention.

A good deal of English poetry is unrhymed, much of it in **blank verse,** that is, unrhymed iambic pentameter. Introduced into English poetry by Surrey in the middle of the sixteenth century, late in the century it became the standard medium (especially in the hands of Marlowe and Shakespeare) of English drama. In the seventeenth century, Milton used it for *Paradise Lost,* and it has continued to be used in both dramatic and nondramatic literature. For an example see the passage from Shakespeare on page 441. A passage of blank verse that has a rhetorical unity is sometimes called a **verse paragraph.**

The second kind of unrhymed poetry fairly common in English, especially in the twentieth century, is **free verse** (or **vers libre**): rhythmical lines varying in length, adhering to no fixed metrical pattern and usually unrhymed. Such poetry may seem formless; Robert Frost, who strongly preferred rhyme, said that he would not consider writing free verse any more than he would consider playing tennis without a net. But free verse does have a form or pattern, often largely based on repetition and parallel grammatical structure. Whitman's "A Noiseless Patient Spider" (page 417) is an example; Arnold's "Dover Beach" (page 532) is another example, though less typical because it uses rhyme. Thoroughly typical is Whitman's "When I Heard the Learn'd Astronomer."

Walt Whitman (*American. 1819–1892*)

When I Heard the Learn'd Astronomer

When I heard the learn'd astronomer,
When the proofs, the figures, were ranged in columns before me,
When I was shown the charts and diagrams, to add, divide, and
    measure them,

When I sitting heard the astronomer where he lectured with much
    applause in the lecture-room,
How soon unaccountable I became tired and sick,
Till rising and gliding out I wander'd off by myself,
In the mystical moist night-air, and from time to time,
Look'd up in perfect silence at the stars.

What can be said about the rhythmic structure of this poem?
Rhymes are absent, and the lines vary greatly in the number of
syllables, ranging from nine (the first line) to twenty-three (the
fourth line), but when we read the poem we sense a rhythmic
structure. The first four lines obviously hang together, each beginning with "When"; indeed, three of these four lines begin
"When I." We may notice, too, that each of these four lines has
more syllables than its predecessor (the numbers are nine, fourteen,
eighteen, and twenty-three); this increase in length, like the initial
repetition, is a kind of pattern. But then, with the fifth line, which
speaks of fatigue and surfeit, there is a shrinkage to fourteen syllables,
offering an enormous relief from the previous swollen line with
its twenty-three syllables. The second half of the poem — the
pattern established by "When" in the first four lines is dropped,
and in effect we get a new stanza, also of four lines — does not
relentlessly diminish the number of syllables in each succeeding
line, but it *almost* does so: fourteen, fourteen, thirteen, ten.

    The second half of the poem thus has a pattern too, and this
pattern is more or less the reverse of the first half of the poem.
We may notice too that the last line (in which the poet, now
released from the oppressive lecture hall, is in communion with
nature) is very close to an iambic pentameter line; that is, the poem
concludes with a metrical form said to be the most natural in
English. The effect of naturalness or ease in this final line, moreover,
is increased by the absence of repetitions (e.g., not only of "When
I," but even of such syntactic repetitions as "charts and diagrams,"
"tired and sick," "rising and gliding") that characterize most of
the previous lines. But of course this final effect of naturalness is
part of a carefully constructed pattern in which rhythmic structure
is part of meaning. Though at first glance free verse may appear
unrestrained, as T. S. Eliot (a practitioner) said, "No *vers* is *libre*
for the man who wants to do a good job" — or for the woman
who wants to do a good job.

17

Summing Up: Reading Poetry Responsively

Responses may be stimulated in part by first reading the poem aloud and then considering the following questions.

SPEAKER

1. Who is the speaker? (Consider age, sex, personality, frame of mind.)
2. Do you think the speaker is fully aware of what he or she is saying, or does the speaker reveal himself or herself unconsciously? In short, what are the speaker's values and personality? What is your attitude toward this speaker?

AUDIENCE

3. To whom is the speaker speaking? What is the situation (including time and place)?

STRUCTURE

4. Does the poem proceed in a straightforward way, or at some points does the speaker reverse course, altering his or her

tone or perception? If there is a shift, what do you make of it?

5. Does the poem proceed by sections? If so, what are these sections — stanzas, for instance? — and how does each section (characterized, perhaps, by a certain tone of voice) grow out of what precedes it?

CENTER OF INTEREST

6. Is the interest chiefly in character or in meditation — that is, is the poem chiefly psychological or chiefly philosophical?

DICTION

7. Do certain words have rich and relevant associations that relate to other words to help to define the speaker and the theme, or both?

8. What is the role of figurative language, if any? Does it help to define the speaker or the theme?

9. What do you think is to be taken symbolically, and what literally?

SOUND EFFECTS, METRICS

10. What is the role of sound effects, including repetitions of sound and of entire words, and shifts in versification?

11. If there are off-rhymes, what do you make of them?

12. If there are unexpected stresses or pauses, what functions do they serve?

FORM

13. What is the effect on you of the form — say, quatrains (stanzas of four lines) or blank verse (unrhymed lines of ten syllables)? If the sense overflows the form, running without pause from (for example) one quatrain into the next, what effect does it have on you?

18
A Collection of Poems

A NOTE ON FOLK BALLADS

Folk ballads, or **popular ballads,** are anonymous stories told in song. They acquired their distinctive flavor by being passed down orally from generation to generation, each singer consciously or unconsciously modifying his or her inheritance. Most ballad singers probably were composers only by accident; they intended to transmit what they had heard, but their memories were sometimes faulty and their imaginations active. The modifications effected by oral transmission generally give a ballad three noticeable qualities:

1. It is impersonal; even if there is an "I" who sings the tale, this "I" is usually characterless.

2. The ballad — like other oral literature such as the nursery rhyme or the counting-out rhyme ("one potato, two potato") — is filled with repetition, sometimes of lines, sometimes of words. Consider, for example, "Go saddle me the black, the black, / Go saddle me the brown," or "O wha is this has done this deid, / This ill deid don to me?" Sometimes, in fact, the story is told by repeating lines with only a few significant variations. This **incremental repetition** (repetition with slight variations advancing the narrative) is the heart of "Edward." Furthermore, **stock epithets** are repeated from ballad to ballad: "true love," "milk-white steed," "golden hair." Oddly, these clichés do not bore us, but by their impersonality often lend a simplicity that effectively contrasts with the violence of the tale.

3. Because the ballads are transmitted orally, residing in the memory rather than on the printed page, weak stanzas have often been dropped, leaving a series of sharp scenes, frequently with dialogue:

> The king sits in Dumferling toune,
> Drinking the blude-reid wine:

> "O whar will I get guid sailor,
> To sail this schip of mine?"

Because ballads were sung rather than printed, and because singers made alterations, there is no one version of a ballad that is the "correct" one. The versions printed here have become such favorites that they are almost regarded as definitive, but the reader should consult a collection of ballads to get some idea of the wide variety.

Popular ballads have been much imitated by professional poets, especially since the late eighteenth century. Two such **literary ballads** are Keats's "La Belle Dame sans Merci" (page 526), and Coleridge's "The Rime of the Ancient Mariner." In a literary ballad the story is often infused with multiple meanings, with insistent symbolic implications. Ambiguity is often found in the popular ballad also, but it is of a rather different sort. Whether it is due to the loss of stanzas or to the creator's unconcern with some elements of the narrative, the ambiguity of the popular ballad commonly lies in the narrative itself rather than in the significance of the narrative.

Here are six popular ballads:

Anonymous

Sir Patrick Spence

The king sits in Dumferling toune,
    Drinking the blude-reid wine:
"O whar will I get guid sailor,
    To sail this schip of mine?"   4

Up and spak an eldern knicht,
    Sat at the kings richt kne:
"Sir Patrick Spence is the best sailor,
    That sails upon the se."   8

The king has written a braid° letter,   *broad, open*
    And signed it wi' his hand,
And sent it to Sir Patrick Spence,
    Was walking on the sand.   12

The first line that Sir Patrick red,
    A loud lauch° lauched he;   *laugh*
The next line that Sir Patrick red,
    The teir blinded his ee.   16

"O wha is this has done this deid,
    This ill deid don to me,
To send me out this time o' the yeir,
    To sail upon the se?   20

"Mak hast, mak hast, my mirry men all,
    Our guid schip sails the morne":
"O say na sae, my master deir,
    For I feir a deadlie storme.   24

"Late late yestreen I saw the new moone,
    Wi' the auld moone in hir arme,
And I feir, I feir, my deir master,
    That we will cum to harme."   28

O our Scots nobles wer richt laith°   *loath*
    To weet their cork-heild schoone;°   *cork-heeled shoes*
Bot lang owre° a' the play wer playd,   *ere*
    Thair hats they swam aboone.°   *above*   32

O lang, lang may their ladies sit,
    Wi' thair fans into their hand,
Or eir° they se Sir Patrick Spence   *ere*
    Cum sailing to the land.   36

O lang, lang may the ladies stand,
    Wi' thair gold kems in their hair,
Waiting for their ain deir lords,
    For they'll se thame na mair.   40

Have owre,° have owre to Aberdour, *half over*
It's fiftie fadom deip,
And thair lies guid Sir Patrick Spence,
Wi' the Scots lords at his feit.

Anonymous

The Three Ravens

* Alternate guitar chords transposing the tune into a key easier to play on a guitar are given in parentheses.

There were three ravens sat on a tree,
    Downe a downe, hay down, hay downe
There were three ravens sat on a tree,
    With a downe
There were three ravens sat on a tree,   5
They were as blacke as they might be,
    With a downe derrie, derrie, derrie, downe, downe.

The one of them said to his mate,
"Where shall we our breakfast take?"

"Down in yonder greene field,   10
There lies a knight slain under his shield.

"His hounds they lie downe at his feete,
So well they can their master keepe.

"His haukes they flie so eagerly,
There's no fowle dare him come nie."   15

Downe there comes a fallow° doe,*   *brown*
As great with yong as she might goe.

She lift up his bloudy hed,
And kist his wounds that were so red.

She got him up upon her backe,   20
And carried him to earthen lake.°   *pit*

She buried him before the prime,°   *about nine* A.M.
She was dead herselfe ere even-song time.

God send every gentleman
Such haukes, such hounds, and such a leman.°   *sweetheart* 25

Anonymous

The Twa Corbies

As I was walking all alane,
I heard twa corbies° making a mane;°   *two ravens; lament*

---

* The "doe" (line 16), often taken as a suggestive description of the knight's beloved, is probably a vestige of the folk belief that an animal may be an enchanted human being.

The tane° unto the t' other say,　　　　　　　　　　*one*
"Where sall we gang° and dine to-day?"　　　*shall we go*　4

"In behint yon auld fail dyke,°　　　　　　　*old turf wall*
I wot° there lies a new-slain knight;　　　　　　　　*know*
And naebody kens° that he lies there,　　　　　　*knows*
But his hawk, his hound, and lady fair.　　　　　　8

"His hound is to the hunting gane,
His hawk, to fetch the wild-fowl hame,
His lady's ta'en another mate,
So we may mak our dinner sweet.　　　　　　　　12

"Ye'll sit on his white hause-bane,°　　　　　*neck bone*
And I'll pike out his bonny blue een.°　　　　　　*eyes*
Wi' ae° lock o' his gowden° hair　　　*with one; golden*
We'll theek° our nest when it grows bare.　*thatch*　16

"Mony a one for him makes mane,
But nane sall ken whare he is gane;
O'er his white banes, when they are bare,
The wind sall blaw for evermair."　　　　　　　　20

Anonymous

Edward

"Why dois your brand° sae° drap wi' bluid,　　*sword; so*
　　　Edward, Edward?
Why dois your brand sae drap wi' bluid?
　　　And why sae sad gang° yee, O?"　　　　*go*　4
"O, I hae killed my hauke sae guid,
　　　Mither, mither,
O, I hae killed my hauke sae guid,
　　　And I had nae mair bot hee, O."　　　　　　8

"Your haukis bluid was nevir sae reid,
　　　Edward, Edward,
Your haukis bluid was nevir sae reid,
　　　My deir son I tell thee, O."　　　　　　　12
"O, I hae killed my reid-roan steid,
　　　Mither, mither,

O, I hae killed my reid-roan steid,
    That erst° was sae fair and frie,° O."   *once; spirited* **16**

"Your steid was auld, and ye hae gat mair,
    Edward, Edward,
Your steid was auld, and ye hae gat mair,
    Sum other dule° ye drie,° O."   *grief; suffer* **20**
"O, I hae killed my fadir deir,
    Mither, mither,
O, I hae killed my fadir, deir,
    Alas, and wae is mee, O!"   **24**

"And whatten penance wul ye drie for that,
    Edward, Edward?
And whatten penance wul ye drie for that?
    My deir son, now tell me, O."   **28**
"Ile set my feit in yonder boat,
    Mither, mither,
Ile set my feit in yonder boat,
    And Ile fare ovir the sea, O."   **32**

"And what wul ye doe wi' your towirs and your ha',° *hall*
    Edward, Edward,
And what wul ye doe wi' your towirs and your ha',
    That were sae fair to see, O?"   **36**
"Ile let thame stand tul they doun fa',°   *fall*
    Mither, mither,
Ile let thame stand tul they doun fa',
    For here nevir mair maun° I bee, O."   *must* **40**

"And what wul ye leive to your bairns° and your wife, *children*
    Edward, Edward?
And what wul ye leive to your bairns and your wife,
    When ye gang ovir the sea, O?"   **44**
"The warldis° room, late° them beg thrae° life, *world's; let; through*
    Mither, mither,
The warldis room, late them beg thrae life,
    For thame nevir mair wul I see, O."   **48**

"And what wul ye leive to your ain mither deir,
    Edward, Edward?
And what wul ye leive to your ain mither deir?
    My deir son, now tell me, O."   **52**
"The curse of hell frae me sall ye beir,
    Mither, mither,
The curse of hell frae me sall ye beir,
    Sic° counseils ye gave to me, O."   *such* **56**

Anonymous

The Demon Lover

"O where have you been, my long, long love, This
long sev-en year and mair?" "O I'm come to seek my
for - mer vows ye— gran-ted— me— be - fore."

"O where have you been, my long, long love,
        This long seven years and mair?"
"O I'm come to seek my former vows
        Ye granted me before."   **4**

"O hold your tongue of your former vows,
        For they will breed sad strife;
O hold your tongue of your former vows,
        For I am become a wife."   **8**

He turned him right and round about,
        And the tear blinded his ee:
"I wad never hae trodden on Irish ground,
        If it had not been for thee.   **12**

"I might hae had a king's daughter,
        Far, far beyond the sea;
I might have had a king's daughter,
        Had it not been for love o thee."   **16**

"If ye might have had a king's daughter,
        Yer sel ye had to blame;
Ye might have taken the king's daughter,
        For ye kend° that I was nane.   *knew*   **20**

"If I was to leave my husband dear,
  And my two babes also,
O what have you to take me to,
  If with you I should go?"   24

"I hae seven ships upon the sea —
  The eighth brought me to land —
With four-and-twenty bold mariners,
  And music on every hand."   28

She has taken up her two little babes,
  Kissed them baith cheek and chin:
"O fair ye weel, my ain two babes,
  For I'll never see you again."   32

She set her foot upon the ship,
  No mariners could she behold;
But the sails were o the taffetie,
  And the masts o the beaten gold.   36

They had not sailed a league, a league,
  A league but barely three,
When dismal grew his countenance,
  And drumlie° grew his ee.   *gloomy*   40

They had not sailed a league, a league,
  A league but barely three,
Until she espied his cloven foot,
  And she wept right bitterlie.   44

"O hold your tongue of your weeping," says he,
  "Of your weeping now let me be;
I will show you how the lilies grow
  On the banks of Italy."   48

"O what hills are yon, yon pleasant hills,
  That the sun shines sweetly on?"
"O yon are the hills of heaven," he said,
  "Where you will never win."°   *gain, get to*   52

"O whaten mountain is yon," she said,
  "All so dreary wi frost and snow?"
"O yon is the mountain of hell," he cried,
  "Where you and I will go."   56

He strack the tap-mast wi his hand,
  The fore-mast wi his knee,
And he brake that gallant ship in twain,
  And sank her in the sea.   60

Anonymous

John Henry*

John Henry was a very small boy,
Sitting on his mammy's knee;
He picked up a hammer and a little piece of steel,
Saying, "A hammer'll be the death of me, O Lord,
A hammer'll be the death of me."   5

John Henry went up on the mountain
And he came down on the side.
The mountain was so tall and John Henry was so small
That he laid down his hammer and he cried, "O Lord,"
He laid down his hammer and he cried.   10

John Henry was a man just six feet in height,
Nearly two feet and a half across the breast.
He'd take a nine-pound hammer and hammer all day long
And never get tired and want to rest, O Lord,
And never get tired and want to rest.   15

John Henry was a steel-driving man, O Lord,
He drove all over the world.
He come to Big Bend Tunnel on the C. & O. Road
Where he beat the steam drill down, O Lord,
Where he beat the steam drill down.   20

John Henry said to the captain,
"Captain, you go to town,
Bring me back a twelve-pound hammer
And I'll beat that steam drill down, O Lord,
And I'll beat that steam drill down."   25

They placed John Henry on the right-hand side,
The steam drill on the left;
He said, "Before I let that steam drill beat me down
I'll die with my hammer in my hand, O Lord,
And send my soul to rest."   30

The white folks all got scared,
Thought Big Bend was a-fallin' in;

* John Henry, a black steel driver from West Virginia, worked on the Chesapeake
and Ohio's Big Bend Tunnel around 1870. The steel driver hammered a drill (held
by his assistant, the "shaker") into rocks so that explosives could then be poured
in. In the 1870s, mechanical steel drills were introduced, displacing the steel driver.

John Henry hollered out with a very loud shout,
"It's my hammer a-fallin' in the wind, O Lord,
It's my hammer a-fallin' in the wind."   *35*

John Henry said to his shaker,
"Shaker, you better pray,
For if I miss that little piece of steel
Tomorrow'll be your buryin' day, O Lord,
Tomorrow'll be your buryin' day."   *40*

The man that invented that steam drill
He thought he was mighty fine.
John Henry sunk the steel fourteen feet
While the steam drill only made nine, O Lord,
While the steam drill only made nine.   *45*

John Henry said to his loving little wife,
"I'm sick and want to go to bed.
Fix me a place to lay down, Child;
There's a roarin' in my head, O Lord,
There's a roarin' in my head."   *50*

Sir Thomas Wyatt (English. 1503–1542)

They Flee from Me

They flee from me that sometime did me seek
With naked foot stalking in my chamber.
I have seen them gentle, tame, and meek
That now are wild and do not remember
That sometime they put themselves in danger   *5*
To take bread at my hand; and now they range
Busily seeking with a continual change.

Thankèd be Fortune, it hath been otherwise
Twenty times better; but once in special,
In thin array after a pleasant guise,   *10*
When her loose gown from her shoulders did fall,
And she me caught in her arms long and small°;   *narrow*
And therewithall sweetly did me kiss,
And softly said, "Dear heart, how like you this?"

It was no dream; I lay broad waking.   *15*
But all is turned thorough my gentleness
Into a strange fashion of forsaking;
And I have leave to go of her goodness,
And she also to use newfangleness.
But since that I so kindely° am served,   *naturally, kindly (ironic)*   *20*
I fain would know what she hath deserved.

Robert Herrick (*English. 1591–1674*)

Upon Julia's Clothes

Whenas in silks my Julia goes,
Then, then, methinks, how sweetly flows
That liquefaction of her clothes.

Next, when I cast mine eyes, and see
That brave vibration, each way free,
O,how that glittering taketh me!

Robert Herrick (*English. 1591–1674*)

Delight in Disorder

A sweet disorder in the dress
Kindles in clothes a wantonness.
A lawn° about the shoulders thrown   *a scarf*
Into a fine distraction;   *4*
An erring lace, which here and there
Enthralls the crimson stomacher,°   *an ornamental cloth*
A cuff neglectful, and thereby
Ribbons to flow confusedly;   *8*
A winning wave, deserving note,
In the tempestuous petticoat;
A careless shoestring, in whose tie
I see a wild civility;   *12*
Do more bewitch me than when art
Is too precise in every part.

William Shakespeare (English. 1564–1616)

Sonnet 29

When, in disgrace with Fortune and men's eyes,
I all alone beweep my outcast state,
And trouble deaf heaven with my bootless° cries,   *useless*
And look upon myself and curse my fate,   *4*
Wishing me like to one more rich in hope,
Featured like him, like him° with friends possessed,   *like a second*
Desiring this man's art, and that man's scope,   *man, like a third man*
With what I most enjoy contented least;   *8*
Yet in these thoughts myself almost despising,
Haply° I think on thee, and then my state,   *perchance*
Like to the lark at break of day arising
From sullen earth, sings hymns at heaven's gate;   *12*
  For thy sweet love rememb'red such wealth brings,
  That then I scorn to change my state with kings.

William Shakespeare (English. 1564–1616)

Sonnet 73

That time of year thou mayst in me behold
When yellow leaves, or none, or few, do hang
Upon those boughs which shake against the cold,
Bare ruined choirs* where late the sweet birds sang.   *4*
In me thou see'st the twilight of such day
As after sunset fadeth in the west,
Which by-and-by black night doth take away,
Death's second self that seals up all in rest.   *8*
In me thou see'st the glowing of such fire
That on the ashes of his youth doth lie,
As the deathbed whereon it must expire,
Consumed with that which it was nourished by.   *12*
  This thou perceiv'st, which makes thy love more strong,
  To love that well which thou must leave ere long.

* The part of the church where services were sung.

William Shakespeare (English. 1564–1616)

Sonnet 116

Let me not to the marriage of true minds
Admit impediments; love is not love
Which alters when it alteration finds,
Or bends with the remover to remove.   **4**
O, no, it is an ever-fixèd mark°   *guide to mariners*
That looks on tempests and is never shaken;
It is the star° to every wand'ring bark,   *the North Star*
Whose worth's unknown, although his height be taken.   **8**
Love's not Time's fool,° though rosy lips and cheeks   *plaything*
Within his bending sickle's compass° come;   *range*
Love alters not with his° brief hours and weeks   *Time's*
But bears° it out even to the edge of doom.°   *endures;* **12**
   If this be error and upon me proved,   *Judgment Day*
   I never writ, nor no man ever loved.

John Donne (English. 1572–1631)

A Valediction: Forbidding Mourning

As virtuous men pass mildly away;
   And whisper to their souls, to go,
Whilst some of their sad friends do say,
   "The breath goes now," and some say, "No":   **4**

So let us melt, and make no noise.
   No tear-floods, nor sigh-tempests move.
'Twere profanation of our joys
   To tell the laity our love.   **8**

Moving of the earth° brings harms and fears,   *an earthquake*
   Men reckon what it did and meant;
But trepidation of the spheres,
   Though greater far, is innocent.*   **12**

---

* But the movement of the heavenly spheres (in Ptolemaic astronomy), though
far greater, is harmless.

Dull sublunary° lovers' love   *under the moon, i.e., earthly*
    (Whose soul is sense) cannot admit
Absence, because it doth remove
    Those things which elemented it.   *16*

But we, by a love so much refined
    That our selves know not what it is,
Inter-assuréd of the mind,
    Care less, eyes, lips, and hands to miss.   *20*

Our two souls therefore, which are one,
    Though I must go, endure not yet
A breach, but an expansion,
    Like gold to airy thinness beat.   *24*

If they be two, they are two so
    As stiff twin compasses° are two: *i.e., a carpenter's compass*
Thy soul, the fixed foot, makes no show
    To move, but doth, if the other do.   *28*

And though it in the center sit,
    Yet when the other far doth roam,
It leans, and hearkens after it,
    And grows erect, as that comes home.   *32*

Such wilt thou be to me, who must
    Like the other foot, obliquely run:
Thy firmness makes my circle just,
    And makes me end where I begun.   *36*

John Milton (*English. 1608–1674*)

When I consider how my light is spent

When I consider how my light is spent
    Ere half my days, in this dark world and wide,
    And that one talent which is death to hide*
    Lodged with me useless, though my soul more bent   *4*

---

* There is a pun here, relating Milton's literary talent to Christ's "Parable of the Talents" (Matthew 25: 14 ff.), in which a servant is rebuked for not putting his talent (a unit of money) to use. Note also line 4, where "useless" includes a pun on "use," i.e., usury, interest.

To serve therewith my Maker, and present
    My true account, lest he returning chide;
    "Doth God exact day-labor, light denied?"
    I fondly° ask; but Patience to prevent°   *foolishly; forestall* **8**
That murmur, soon replies, "God doth not need
    Either man's work or his own gifts; who best
    Bear his mild yoke, they serve him best. His state
Is kingly. Thousands at his bidding speed   **12**
    And post o'er land and ocean without rest:
    They also serve who only stand and wait."

Thomas Gray (English. 1716–1771)

Ode on the Death of a Favorite Cat Drowned in a Tub of Gold-Fishes

'Twas on a lofty vase's side,
Where China's gayest art had dyed
    The azure flowers that blow;
Demurest of the tabby kind,
The pensive Selima, reclined,   *5*
    Gazed on the lake below.

Her conscious tail her joy declared;
The fair round face, the snowy beard,
    The velvet of her paws,
Her coat, that with the tortoise vies,   *10*
Her ears of jet, and emerald eyes,
    She saw; and purred applause.

Still had she gazed; but 'midst the tide
Two angel forms were seen to glide,
    The genii° of the stream: *guardian spirits* *15*
Their scaly armor's Tyrian hue°   *reddish*
Through richest purple to the view
    Betrayed a golden gleam.

The hapless nymph with wonder saw:
A whisker first and then a claw,   *20*
    With many an ardent wish,
She stretched in vain to reach the prize.

What female heart can gold despise?
　　What cat's averse to fish?

Presumptuous maid! with looks intent   *25*
Again she stretched, again she bent,
　　Nor knew the gulf between.
(Malignant Fate sat by and smiled)
The slippery verge her feet beguiled,
　　She tumbled headlong in.   *30*

Eight times emerging from the flood
She mewed to every watery god,
　　Some speedy aid to send.
No dolphin* came, no Nereid° stirred;   *a sea nymph*
Nor cruel Tom, nor Susan heard;   *35*
　　A favorite has no friend!

From hence, ye beauties, undeceived,
Know, one false step is ne'er retrieved,
　　And be with caution bold.
Not all that tempts your wandering eyes   *40*
And heedless hearts, is lawful prize;
　　Nor all that glisters, gold.

William Blake (*English. 1757–1827*)

The Lamb

　　Little Lamb, who made thee?
　　Dost thou know who made thee?
Gave thee life, and bid thee feed
By the stream and o'er the mead;
Gave thee clothing of delight,   *5*
Softest clothing, wooly, bright;
Gave thee such a tender voice,
Making all the vales rejoice?
　　Little Lamb, who made thee?
　　Dost thou know who made thee?   *10*

---

* Legend held that Arion, a Greek musician, was saved by a dolphin.

> Little Lamb, I'll tell thee,
> Little Lamb, I'll tell thee:
> He is calléd by thy name,
> For he calls himself a Lamb.
> He is meek, and he is mild; 15
> He became a little child.
> I a child, and thou a lamb,
> We are calléd by his name.
> > Little Lamb, God bless thee!
> > Little Lamb, God bless thee! 20

William Blake (English. 1757–1827)

The Tyger

Tyger! Tyger! burning bright
In the forests of the night,
What immortal hand or eye
Could frame thy fearful symmetry? 4

In what distant deeps or skies
Burnt the fire of thine eyes?
On what wings dare he aspire?
What the hand dare seize the fire? 8

And what shoulder, and what art,
Could twist the sinews of thy heart?
And, when thy heart began to beat,
What dread hand? and what dread feet? 12

What the hammer? what the chain?
In what furnace was thy brain?
What the anvil? what dread grasp
Dare its deadly terrors clasp? 16

When the stars threw down their spears,
And watered heaven with their tears,
Did he smile his work to see?
Did he who made the lamb make thee? 20

Tyger! Tyger! burning bright
In the forests of the night,
What immortal hand or eye,
Dare frame thy fearful symmetry? 24

William Blake (English. 1757–1827)

London

I wander through each chartered street,
Near where the chartered Thames does flow,
And mark in every face I meet
Marks of weakness, marks of woe.   *4*

In every cry of every man,
In every Infant's cry of fear,
In every voice, in every ban,
The mind-forged manacles I hear.   *8*

How the Chimney-sweeper's cry
Every black'ning Church appalls;
And the hapless Soldier's sigh
Runs in blood down Palace walls.   *12*

But most through midnight streets I hear
How the youthful Harlot's curse
Blasts the new-born Infant's tear,
And blights with plagues the Marriage hearse.   *16*

William Blake (English. 1757–1827)

The Echoing Green

The Sun does arise,
And make happy the skies;
The merry bells ring
To welcome the Spring;   *4*
The skylark and thrush,
The birds of the bush,
Sing louder around
To the bells' cheerful sound,   *8*
While our sports shall be seen
On the Echoing Green.

Old John, with white hair,
Does laugh away care,   *12*

Sitting under the oak,
Among the old folk.
They laugh at our play,
And soon they all say: *16*
"Such, such were the joys
When we all, girls and boys,
In our youth time were seen
On the Echoing Green."   *20*

Till the little ones, weary,
No more can be merry;
The sun does descend,
And our sports have an end.   *24*
Round the laps of their mothers
Many sisters and brothers,
Like birds in their nest,
Are ready for rest,   *28*
And sport no more seen
On the darkening Green.

William Wordsworth (English. 1770–1850)

The World Is Too Much with Us

The world is too much with us; late and soon,
Getting and spending, we lay waste our powers;
Little we see in Nature that is ours;
We have given our hearts away, a sordid boon!°   *gift* *4*
This Sea that bares her bosom to the moon,
The winds that will be howling at all hours,
And are up-gathered now like sleeping flowers,
For this, for everything, we are out of tune;   *8*
It moves us not. — Great God! I'd rather be
A Pagan suckled in a creed outworn;
So might I, standing on this pleasant lea,
Have glimpses that would make me less forlorn;   *12*
Have sight of Proteus* rising from the sea;
Or hear old Triton blow his wreathéd horn.

* Proteus and Triton are sea gods.

William Wordsworth (English. 1770–1850)

I Wandered Lonely as a Cloud

I wandered lonely as a cloud
That floats on high o'er vales and hills,
When all at once I saw a crowd,
A host, of golden daffodils,
Beside the lake, beneath the trees,   5
Fluttering and dancing in the breeze.

Continuous as the stars that shine
And twinkle on the milky way,
They stretched in never-ending line
Along the margin of a bay;   10
Ten thousand saw I at a glance,
Tossing their heads in sprightly dance.

The waves beside them danced, but they
Outdid the sparkling waves in glee;
A poet could not but be gay,   15
In such a jocund company;
I gazed — and gazed — but little thought
What wealth the show to me had brought:

For oft, when on my couch I lie
In vacant or in pensive mood,   20
They flash upon that inward eye
Which is the bliss of solitude;
And then my heart with pleasure fills,
And dances with the daffodils.

John Keats (English. 1795–1821)

La Belle Dame sans Merci

O what can ail thee, knight-at-arms,
    Alone and palely loitering?
The sedge has withered from the lake,
    And no birds sing.   4

O what can ail thee, knight-at-arms,
    So haggard and so woe-begone?
The squirrel's granary is full,
    And the harvest's done.   *8*

I see a lily on thy brow,
    With anguish moist and fever dew,
And on thy cheeks a fading rose
    Fast withereth too.   *12*

"I met a lady in the meads,
    Full beautiful — a faery's child,
Her hair was long, her foot was light,
    And her eyes were wild.   *16*

"I made a garland for her head,
    And bracelets too, and fragrant zone;°   *belt of flowers*
She looked at me as she did love,
    And made sweet moan.   *20*

"I set her on my pacing steed,
    And nothing else saw all day long,
For sidelong would she bend and sing
    A faery's song.   *24*

"She found me roots of relish sweet,
    And honey wild, and manna dew,
And sure in language strange she said
    'I love thee true.'   *28*

"She took me to her elfin grot,
    And there she wept and sighed full sore,
And there I shut her wild wild eyes
    With kisses four.   *32*

"And there she lullèd me asleep,
    And there I dreamed — Ah! woe betide!
The latest dream I ever dreamt
    On the cold hill side.   *36*

"I saw pale kings and princes too,
    Pale warriors, death-pale were they all;
They cried, 'La Belle Dame sans Merci°   *the beautiful pitiless lady*
    Thee hath in thrall!'   *40*

"I saw their starved lips in the gloam
    With horrid warning gapèd wide,
And I awoke, and found me here,
    On the cold hill's side.   *44*

"And this is why I sojourn here,
    Alone and palely loitering,
Though the sedge is withered from the lake,
    And no birds sing."   **48**

John Keats (*English. 1795–1821*)

To Autumn

I

Season of mists and mellow fruitfulness,
    Close bosom-friend of the maturing sun;
Conspiring with him how to load and bless
    With fruit the vines that round the thatch-eaves run;
To bend with apples the mossed cottage-trees,   **5**
    And fill all fruit with ripeness to the core;
        To swell the gourd, and plump the hazel shells
With a sweet kernel; to set budding more,
    And still more, later flowers for the bees,
    Until they think warm days will never cease,   **10**
        For summer has o'er-brimmed their clammy cells.

II

Who hath not seen thee oft amid thy store?
    Sometimes whoever seeks abroad may find
Thee sitting careless on a granary floor,
    Thy hair soft-lifted by the winnowing wind;   **15**
Or on a half-reaped furrow sound asleep,
    Drowsed with the fume of poppies, while thy hook
        Spares the next swath and all its twinèd flowers:
And sometime like a gleaner thou dost keep
    Steady thy laden head across a brook;   **20**
    Or by a cider-press, with patient look,
        Thou watchest the last oozings hours by hours.

III

Where are the songs of Spring? Ay, where are they?
    Think not of them, thou hast thy music too, —
While barred clouds bloom the soft-dying day,   **25**
    And touch the stubble-plains with rosy hue;

Then in a wailful choir the small gnats mourn
   Among the river sallows, borne aloft
      Or sinking as the light wind lives or dies;
And full-grown lambs loud bleat from hilly bourn;   *30*
   Hedge-crickets sing; and now with treble soft
   The red-breast whistles from a garden-croft;
      And gathering swallows twitter in the skies.

Alfred, Lord Tennyson (English. 1809–1892)

Ulysses

It little profits that an idle king,
By this still hearth, among these barren crags,
Matched with an aged wife, I mete and dole
Unequal laws unto a savage race,
That hoard, and sleep, and feed, and know not me.   *5*
I cannot rest from travel; I will drink
Life to the lees. All times I have enjoyed
Greatly, have suffered greatly, both with those
That loved me, and alone; on shore, and when
Thro' scudding drifts the rainy Hyades   *10*
Vext the dim sea. I am become a name;
For always roaming with a hungry heart
Much have I seen and known, — cities of men
And manners, climates, councils, governments,
Myself not least, but honored of them all, —   *15*
And drunk delight of battle with my peers,
Far on the ringing plains of windy Troy.
I am a part of all that I have met;
Yet all experience is an arch wherethro'
Gleams that untravelled world whose margin fades   *20*
For ever and for ever when I move.
How dull it is to pause, to make an end,
To rust unburnished, not to shine in use!
As tho' to breathe were life! Life piled on life
Were all too little, and of one to me   *25*
Little remains; but every hour is saved
From that eternal silence, something more,
A bringer of new things; and vile it were

For some three suns to store and hoard myself,
And this gray spirit yearning in desire   30
To follow knowledge like a sinking star,
Beyond the utmost bound of human thought.

    This is my son, mine own Telemachus,
To whom I leave the scepter and the isle, —
Well-loved of me, discerning to fulfill   35
This labor, by slow prudence to make mild
A rugged people, and thro' soft degrees
Subdue them to the useful and the good.
Most blameless is he, centered in the sphere
Of common duties, decent not to fail   40
In offices of tenderness, and pay
Meet adoration to my household gods,
When I am gone. He works his work, I mine.

    There lies the port; the vessel puffs her sail;
There gloom the dark, broad seas. My mariners,   45
Souls that have toiled, and wrought, and thought with me, —
That ever with a frolic welcome took
The thunder and the sunshine, and opposed
Free hearts, free foreheads, — you and I are old;
Old age hath yet his honor and his toil.   50
Death closes all; but something ere the end,
Some work of noble note, may yet be done,
Not unbecoming men that strove with Gods.
The lights begin to twinkle from the rocks;
The long day wanes; the slow moon climbs; the deep   55
Moans round with many voices. Come, my friends.
'Tis not too late to seek a newer world.
Push off, and sitting well in order smite
The sounding furrows; for my purpose holds
To sail beyond the sunset, and the baths   60
Of all the western stars, until I die.
It may be that the gulfs will wash us down;
It may be we shall touch the Happy Isles,
And see the great Achilles, whom we knew.
Tho' much is taken, much abides; and tho'   65
We are not now that strength which in old days
Moved earth and heaven, that which we are, we are.
One equal temper of heroic hearts,
Made weak by time and fate, but strong in will
To strive, to seek, to find, and not to yield.   70

Robert Browning (*English. 1812–1889*)

Porphyria's Lover

The rain set early in tonight,
    The sullen wind was soon awake,
It tore the elm-tops down for spite,
    And did its worst to vex the lake:
I listened with heart fit to break.   *5*
When glided in Porphyria; straight
    She shut the cold out and the storm,
And kneeled and made the cheerless grate
    Blaze up, and all the cottage warm;
Which done, she rose, and from her form   *10*
Withdrew the dripping cloak and shawl,
    And laid her soiled gloves by, untied
Her hat and let the damp hair fall,
    And, last, she sat down by my side
And called me. When no voice replied,   *15*
She put my arm about her waist,
    And made her smooth white shoulder bare
And all her yellow hair displaced,
    And stooping, made my cheek lie there,
And spread, o'er all, her yellow hair,   *20*
Murmuring how she loved me — she
    Too weak, for all her heart's endeavor,
To set its struggling passion free
    From pride, and vainer ties dissever,
And give herself to me forever.   *25*
But passion sometimes would prevail,
    Nor could tonight's gay feast restrain
A sudden thought of one so pale
    For love of her, and all in vain:
So, she was come through wind and rain.   *30*
Be sure I looked up at her eyes
    Happy and proud; at last I knew
Porphyria worshipped me; surprise
    Made my heart swell, and still it grew
While I debated what to do.   *35*
That moment she was mine, mine, fair,
    Perfectly pure and good: I found
A thing to do, and all her hair
    In one long yellow string I wound

Three times her little throat around,   40
And strangled her. No pain felt she;
    I am quite sure she felt no pain.
As a shut bud that holds a bee,
    I warily oped her lids: again
Laughed the blue eyes without a stain.   45
And I untightened next the tress
    About her neck; her cheek once more
Blushed bright beneath my burning kiss:
    I propped her head up as before,
Only, this time my shoulder bore   50
Her head, which droops upon it still:
    The smiling rosy little head,
So glad it has its utmost will,
    That all it scorned at once is fled,
And I, its love, am gained instead!   55
Porphyria's love: she guessed not how
    Her darling one wish would be heard.
And thus we sit together now,
    And all night long we have not stirred,
And yet God has not said a word!   60

Matthew Arnold (*English. 1822–1888*)

Dover Beach

The sea is calm to-night.
The tide is full, the moon lies fair
Upon the straits; — on the French coast the light
Gleams and is gone; the cliffs of England stand,
Glimmering and vast, out in the tranquil bay.   5
Come to the window, sweet is the night-air!
Only, from the long line of spray
Where the sea meets the moon-blanch'd land,
Listen! you hear the grating roar
Of pebbles which the waves draw back, and fling,   10
At their return, up the high strand,
Begin, and cease, and then again begin,
With tremulous cadence slow, and bring
The eternal note of sadness in.

Sophocles long ago 15
Heard it on the Ægean, and it brought
Into his mind the turbid ebb and flow
Of human misery; we
Find also in the sound a thought,
Hearing it by this distant northern sea. 20

The Sea of Faith
Was once, too, at the full, and round earth's shore
Lay like the folds of a bright girdle furl'd.
But now I only hear
Its melancholy, long, withdrawing roar, 25
Retreating, to the breath
Of the night-wind, down the vast edges drear
And naked shingles° of the world. *pebbled beaches*

Ah, love, let us be true
To one another! for the world, which seems
To lie before us like a land of dreams, 30
So various, so beautiful, so new,
Hath really neither joy, nor love, nor light,
Nor certitude, nor peace, nor help for pain;
And we are here as on a darkling plain 35
Swept with confused alarms of struggle and flight,
Where ignorant armies clash by night.

Emily Dickinson (*American. 1830–1886*)

A narrow Fellow in the Grass

A narrow Fellow in the Grass
Occasionally rides —
You may have met Him — did you not
His notice sudden is — 4

The Grass divides as with a Comb —
A spotted shaft is seen —
And then it closes at your feet
And opens further on — 8

He likes a Boggy Acre
A Floor too cool for Corn —
Yet when a Boy, and Barefoot —
I more than once at Noon   *12*
Have passed, I thought, a Whip lash
Unbraiding in the Sun
When stopping to secure it
It wrinkled, and was gone —   *16*

Several of Nature's People
I know, and they know me —
I feel for them a transport
Of cordiality —   *20*

But never met this Fellow
Attended, or alone
Without a tighter breathing
And Zero at the Bone —   *24*

Emily Dickinson (*American. 1830–1886*)

I heard a Fly buzz — when I died

I heard a Fly buzz — when I died —
The Stillness in the Room
Was like the Stillness in the Air —
Between the Heaves of Storm —   *4*

The Eyes around — had wrung them dry —
And Breaths were gathering firm
For the last Onset — when the King
Be witnessed — in the Room —   *8*

I willed my Keepsakes — Signed away
What portion of me be
Assignable — and then it was
There interposed a Fly —   *12*

With Blue — uncertain stumbling Buzz —
Between the light — and me —
And then the Windows failed — and then
I could not see to see —   *16*

Emily Dickinson (*American. 1830–1886*)

The Soul selects her own Society

The Soul selects her own Society —
Then — shuts the Door —
To her divine Majority —
Present no more —   4

Unmoved — she notes the Chariots — pausing —
At her low Gate —
Unmoved — an Emperor be kneeling
Upon her Mat —   8

I've known her — from an ample nation —
Choose One —
Then — close the Valves* of her attention —
Like Stone —   12

Thomas Hardy (*English. 1840–1928*)

Ah, Are You Digging on My Grave?

"Ah, are you digging on my grave,
      My loved one? — planting rue?"
— "No: yesterday he went to wed
One of the brightest wealth has bred.
'It cannot hurt her now,' he said,   5
      'That I should not be true.' "

"Then who is digging on my grave?
      My nearest dearest kin?"
— "Ah, no: they sit and think, 'What use!
What good will planting flowers produce?   10
No tendance of her mound can loose
      Her spirit from Death's gin.' "

* The two halves of a hinged door, such as is now found on telephone booths.
Possibly also an allusion to a bivalve, such as an oyster or a clam, having a shell
consisting of two hinged parts.

"But some one digs upon my grave?
    My enemy? — prodding sly?"
— "Nay: When she heard you had passed the Gate   15
That shuts on all flesh soon or late,
She thought you no more worth her hate,
    And cares not where you lie."

"Then, who is digging on my grave?
    Say — since I have not guessed!"   20
— "O it is I, my mistress dear,
Your little dog, who still lives near,
And much I hope my movements here
    Have not disturbed your rest?"

"Ah, yes! *You* dig upon my grave . . .   25
    Why flashed it not on me
That one true heart was left behind!
What feeling do we ever find
To equal among human kind
    A dog's fidelity!"   30

"Mistress, I dug upon your grave
    To bury a bone, in case
I should be hungry near this spot
When passing on my daily trot.
I am sorry, but I quite forgot   35
    It was your resting-place."

Thomas Hardy (*English. 1840–1928*)

The Convergence of the Twain
Lines on the Loss of the Titanic

I

In a solitude of the sea
Deep from human vanity,
And the Pride of Life that planned her, stilly couches she.

II

Steel chambers, late the pyres
    Of her salamandrine fires,   5
Cold currents thrid,° and turn to rhythmic tidal lyres.   *thread*

III

Over the mirrors meant
To glass the opulent
The sea-worm crawls — grotesque, slimed, dumb, indifferent.

IV

Jewels in joy designed   *10*
To ravish the sensuous mind
Lie lightless, all their sparkles bleared and black and blind.

V

Dim moon-eyed fishes near
Gaze at the gilded gear
And query: "What does this vaingloriousness down here?"   *15*

VI

Well: while was fashioning
This creature of cleaving wing,
The Immanent Will that stirs and urges everything

VII

Prepared a sinister mate
For her — so gaily great —   *20*
A Shape of Ice, for the time far and dissociate.

VIII

And as the smart ship grew
In stature, grace, and hue,
In shadowy silent distance grew the Iceberg too.

IX

Alien they seemed to be: *25*
No mortal eye could see
The intimate welding of their later history,

X

Or sign that they were bent
By paths coincident
On being anon twin halves of one august event,   *30*

XI

Till the Spinner of the Years
Said "Now!" And each one hears,
And consummation comes, and jars two hemispheres.

Gerard Manley Hopkins (*English. 1844–1889*)

God's Grandeur

The world is charged with the grandeur of God.
    It will flame out, like shining from shook foil;
    It gathers to a greatness, like the ooze of oil
Crushed. Why do men then now not reck his rod?   *4*
Generations have trod, have trod, have trod;
    And all is seared with trade; bleared, smeared with toil;
    And wears man's smudge and shares man's smell: the soil
Is bare now, nor can foot feel, being shod.   *8*

And for all this, nature is never spent;
    There lives the dearest freshness deep down things;
And though the last lights off the black West went
    Oh, morning, at the brown brink eastward, springs —   *12*
Because the Holy Ghost over the bent
    World broods with warm breast and with ah! bright wings.

Gerard Manley Hopkins (*English. 1844–1889*)

The Windhover*

To Christ Our Lord

I caught this morning morning's minion,° king-   *favorite*
    dom of daylight's dauphin, dapple-dawn-drawn Falcon, in
        his riding
    Of the rolling level underneath him steady air, and striding
High there, how he rung upon the rein† of a wimpling° *rippling*
        wing   *4*
In his ecstacy! then off, off forth on swing,
    As a skate's heel sweeps smooth on a bow-bend; the hurl
        and gliding
    Rebuffed the big wind. My heart in hiding
Stirred for a bird, — the achieve of, the mastery of the thing! *8*

---

* A small falcon.
† Hopkins is using a term from horsemanship in which the horse circles around
his trainer at the end of a long rein.

Brute beauty and valor and act, oh, air, pride, plume, here
    Buckle! AND the fire that breaks from thee then, a billion
Times told lovelier, more dangerous, O my chevalier!°   *champion*

    No wonder of it: shéer plód makes plough down sillion* *12*
Shine, and blue-bleak embers, ah my dear,
    Fall, gall themselves, and gash gold-vermilion.

A. E. Housman (*English. 1859–1936*)

Shropshire Lad #19
(To an Athlete Dying Young)

The time you won your town the race
We chaired you through the market-place;
Man and boy stood cheering by,
And home we brought you shoulder-high.   *4*

Today, the road all runners come,
Shoulder-high we bring you home,
And set you at your threshold down,
Townsman of a stiller town.   *8*

Smart lad, to slip betimes away
From fields where glory does not stay
And early though the laurel grows
It withers quicker than the rose.   *12*

Eyes the shady night has shut
Cannot see the record cut,
And silence sounds no worse than cheers
After earth has stopped the ears: *16*

Now you will not swell the rout
Of lads that wore their honors out,
Runners whom renown outran
And the name died before the man.   *20*

So set, before its echoes fade,
The fleet foot on the sill of shade,
And hold to the low lintel° up   *beam over a doorway*
The still-defended challenge-cup.   *24*

* The ridge between two furrows.

And round that early-laureled head
Will flock to gaze the strengthless dead,
And find unwithered on its curls
The garland briefer than a girl's.   *28*

William Butler Yeats (Irish. *1865–1939*)

Leda and the Swan*

A sudden blow: the great wings beating still
Above the staggering girl, her thighs caressed
By the dark webs, her nape caught in his bill,
He holds her helpless breast upon his breast.   *4*

How can those terrified vague fingers push
The feathered glory from her loosening thighs?
And how can body, laid in that white rush,
But feel the strange heart beating where it lies?   *8*

A shudder in the loins engenders there
The broken wall, the burning roof and tower
And Agamemnon dead.
                              Being so caught up,
So mastered by the brute blood of the air,   *12*
Did she put on his knowledge with his power
Before the indifferent beak could let her drop?

William Butler Yeats (Irish. *1865–1939*)

The Second Coming

Turning and turning in the widening gyre°   *circular or spiral motion*
The falcon cannot hear the falconer;

* According to Greek mythology, Zeus fell in love with Leda, disguised himself
as a swan, and raped her. Among the offspring of this union were Helen and
Clytemnestra. Paris abducted Helen, causing the Greeks to raze Troy; Clytemnestra,
wife of Agamemnon, murdered her husband on his triumphant return to Greece.

Things fall apart; the center cannot hold;
Mere anarchy is loosed upon the world,
The blood-dimmed tide is loosed, and everywhere   5
The ceremony of innocence is drowned;
The best lack all conviction, while the worst
Are full of passionate intensity.

Surely some revelation is at hand;
Surely the Second Coming is at hand;   10
The Second Coming! Hardly are those words out
When a vast image out of *Spiritus Mundi°*   *Soul of the Universe*
Troubles my sight: somewhere in the sands of the desert
A shape with lion body and the head of a man,
A gaze blank and pitiless as the sun,   15
Is moving its slow thighs, while all about it
Reel shadows of the indignant desert birds.
The darkness drops again; but now I know
That twenty centuries of stony sleep
Were vexed to nightmare by a rocking cradle,   20
And what rough beast, its hour come round at last,
Slouches towards Bethlehem to be born?

William Butler Yeats (*Irish. 1865–1939*)

Sailing to Byzantium*

I

That is no country for old men. The young
In one another's arms, birds in the trees
— Those dying generations — at their song,
The salmon-falls, the mackerel-crowded seas,   4
Fish, flesh, or fowl, commend all summer long
Whatever is begotten, born, and dies.
Caught in that sensual music all neglect
Monuments of unaging intellect.   8

---

* The modern Istanbul. Byzantium was the the chief city of the Roman Empire
in the east and the capital of Eastern Christianity.

II

An aged man is but a paltry thing,
A tattered coat upon a stick, unless
Soul clap its hands and sing, and louder sing
For every tatter in its mortal dress,   *12*
Nor is there singing school but studying
Monuments of its own magnificence;
And therefore I have sailed the seas and come
To the holy city of Byzantium.   *16*

III

O sages standing in God's holy fire
As in the gold mosaic of a wall,
Come from the holy fire, perne° in a gyre,   *whirl down*
And be the singing-masters of my soul.   *20*
Consume my heart away; sick with desire
And fastened to a dying animal
It knows not what it is; and gather me
Into the artifice of eternity.   *24*

IV

Once out of nature I shall never take
My bodily form from any natural thing,
But such a form as Grecian goldsmiths make
Of hammered gold and gold enameling   *28*
To keep a drowsy Emperor awake;
Or set upon a golden bough to sing
To lords and ladies of Byzantium
Of what is past, or passing, or to come.   *32*

William Butler Yeats (*Irish. 1865–1939*)

An Irish Airman Foresees His Death*

I know that I shall meet my fate
Somewhere among the clouds above;
Those that I fight I do not hate,
Those that I guard I do not love;

* The airman, Major Robert Gregory, was the son of Yeats's old friend Lady
Augusta Gregory and the father of Anne Gregory. His plane was shot down by
Germans in 1918 while he was fighting on the English side.

My country is Kiltartan Cross,* 5
My countrymen Kiltartan's poor,
No likely end could bring them loss
Or leave them happier than before.
Nor law, nor duty bade me fight,
Nor public men, nor cheering crowds, 10
A lonely impulse of delight
Drove to this tumult in the clouds;
I balanced all, brought all to mind,
The years to come seemed waste of breath,
A waste of breath the years behind 15
In balance with this life, this death.

William Butler Yeats *(Irish. 1865–1939)*

For Anne Gregory †

"Never shall a young man,
Thrown into despair
By those great honey-coloured
Ramparts at your ear
Love you for yourself alone 5
And not your yellow hair."

"But I can get a hair-dye
And set such colour there,
Brown, or black, or carrot,
That young men in despair 10
May love me for myself alone
And not my yellow hair."

"I heard an old religious man
But yesternight declare
That he had found a text to prove 15
That only God, my dear,
Could love you for yourself alone
And not your yellow hair."

* Kiltartan Cross is the crossroads in Kiltartan, an Irish village near the Gregory estate in western Ireland.

† Yeats was sixty-five when he wrote this poem for Anne Gregory, the nineteen-year-old granddaughter of Lady Augusta Gregory, a woman whom Yeats had admired. Anne Gregory's father was Major Rober Gregory, the subject of the previous poem by Yeats.

Edwin Arlington Robinson (*American. 1869–1935*)

Mr. Flood's Party

Old Eben Flood, climbing alone one night
Over the hill between the town below
And the forsaken upland hermitage
That held as much as he should ever know   4
On earth again of home, paused warily.
The road was his with not a native near;
And Eben, having leisure, said aloud;
For no man else in Tilbury Town to hear: 8

"Well, Mr. Flood, we have the harvest moon
Again, and we may not have many more;
The bird is on the wing, the poet says,
And you and I have said it here before.   12
Drink to the bird." He raised up to the light
The jug that he had gone so far to fill,
And answered huskily: "Well, Mr. Flood,
Since you propose it, I believe I will."   16

Alone, as if enduring to the end
A valiant armor of scarred hopes outworn,
He stood there in the middle of the road
Like Roland's ghost winding a silent horn.   20
Below him, in the town among the trees,
Where friends of other days had honored him,
A phantom salutation of the dead
Rang thinly till old Eben's eyes were dim.   24

Then, as a mother lays her sleeping child
Down tenderly, fearing it may awake,
He set the jug down slowly at his feet
With trembling care, knowing that most things break; 28
And only when assured that on firm earth
It stood, as the uncertain lives of men
Assuredly did not, he paced away,
And with his hand extended paused again: 32

"Well, Mr. Flood, we have not met like this
In a long time; and many a change has come
To both of us, I fear, since last it was
We had a drop together. Welcome home!"   36
Convivially returning with himself,

Again he raised the jug up to the light;
And with an acquiescent quaver said:
"Well, Mr. Flood, if you insist, I might.   40

"Only a very little, Mr. Flood —
For auld lang syne. No more, sir; that will do."
So, for the time, apparently it did,
And Eben evidently thought so too;   44
For soon amid the silver loneliness
Of night he lifted up his voice and sang,
Secure, with only two moons listening,
Until the whole harmonious landscape rang —   48

"For auld lang syne." The weary throat gave out,
The last word wavered; and the song being done,
He raised again the jug regretfully
And shook his head, and was again alone.   52
There was not much that was ahead of him,
And there was nothing in the town below —
Where strangers would have shut the many doors
That many friends had opened long ago.   56

Walter de la Mare (*English. 1873–1956*)

The Listeners

"Is there anybody there?" said the Traveler,
        Knocking on the moonlit door;
And his horse in the silence champed the grasses
        Of the forest's ferny floor.
And a bird flew up out of the turret,   5
        Above the Traveler's head:

And he smote upon the door again a second time;
        "Is there anybody there?" he said.
But no one descended to the Traveler;
        No head from the leaf-fringed sill   10
Leaned over and looked into his gray eyes,
        Where he stood perplexed and still.
But only a host of phantom listeners
        That dwelt in the lone house then

Stood listening in the quiet of the moonlight   *15*
    To that voice from the world of men:
Stood thronging the faint moonbeams on the dark stair
    That goes down to the empty hall,
Hearkening in an air stirred and shaken
    By the lonely Traveler's call.   *20*

And he felt in his heart their strangeness,
    Their stillness answering his cry,
While his horse moved, cropping the dark turf,
    'Neath the starred and leafy sky;
For he suddenly smote on the door, even   *25*
    Louder, and lifted his head: —
"Tell them I came, and no one answered,
    That I kept my word," he said.
Never the least stir made the listeners,
    Though every word he spake   *30*
Fell echoing through the shadowiness of the still house
    From the one man left awake:
Aye, they heard his foot upon the stirrup,
    And the sound of iron on stone,
And how the silence surged softly backward,   *35*
    When the plunging hoofs were gone.

Robert Frost (*American. 1874–1963*)

Design

I found a dimpled spider, fat and white,
On a white heal-all,° holding up a moth   *a flower, normally blue*
Like a white piece of rigid satin cloth —
Assorted characters of death and blight   *4*
Mixed ready to begin the morning right,
Like the ingredients of a witches' broth —
A snow-drop spider, a flower like froth,
And dead wings carried like a paper kite.   *8*

What had that flower to do with being white,
The wayside blue and innocent heal-all?
What brought the kindred spider to that height,
Then steered the white moth thither in the night?   *12*
What but design of darkness to appall? —
If design govern in a thing so small.

Robert Frost (*American. 1874–1963*)

The Road Not Taken

Two roads diverged in a yellow wood, *A*
And sorry I could not travel both *B*
And be one traveler, long I stood *A*
And looked down one as far as I could *A*
To where it bent in the undergrowth; *B*   *5*

Then took the other, as just as fair, *C*
And having perhaps the better claim, *D*
Because it was grassy and wanted wear; *C*
Though as for that the passing there *C*
Had worn them really about the same, *D*   *10*

And both that morning equally lay
In leaves no step had trodden black.
Oh, I kept the first for another day!
Yet knowing how way leads on to way,
I doubted if I should ever come back.   *15*

I shall be telling this with a sigh
Somewhere ages and ages hence:
Two roads diverged in a wood, and I —
I took the one less traveled by,
And that has made all the difference.   *20*

Robert Frost (*American. 1874–1963*)

The Oven Bird

There is a singer everyone has heard,
Loud, a mid-summer and a mid-wood bird,
Who makes the solid tree trunks sound again.
He says that leaves are old and that for flowers
Mid-summer is to spring as one to ten.   *5*
He says the early petal-fall is past
When pear and cherry bloom went down in showers
On sunny days a moment overcast;
And comes that other fall we name the fall.
He says the highway dust is over all.   *10*

The bird would cease and be as other birds
But that he knows in singing not to sing.
The question that he frames in all but words
Is what to make of a diminished thing.

William Carlos Williams (*American. 1883–1963*)

Spring and All

By the road to the contagious hospital
under the surge of the blue
mottled clouds driven from the
northeast — a cold wind. Beyond, the
waste of broad, muddy fields   5
brown with dried weeds, standing and fallen

patches of standing water
the scattering of tall trees

All along the road the reddish
purplish, forked, upstanding, twiggy   10
stuff of bushes and small trees
with dead, brown leaves under them
leafless vines —

Lifeless in appearance, sluggish
dazed spring approaches —   15

They enter the new world naked,
cold, uncertain of all
save that they enter. All about them
the cold, familiar wind —

Now the grass, tomorrow   20
the stiff curl of wildcarrot leaf
One by one objects are defined —
It quickens: clarity, outline of leaf

But now the stark dignity of
entrance — Still, the profound change   25
has come upon them: rooted, they
grip down and begin to awaken

William Carlos Williams (American. 1883–1963)

A Sort of a Song

Let the snake wait under
his weed
and the writing
be of words, slow and quick, sharp
to strike, quiet to wait,   5
sleepless.

— through metaphor to reconcile
the people and the stones.
Compose. (No ideas
but in things) Invent!   10
Saxifrage is my flower that splits
the rocks.

Marianne Moore (American. 1887–1972)

Poetry*

I, too, dislike it: there are things that are important beyond all
                                                this fiddle.
        Reading it, however, with a perfect contempt for it, one
                                                discovers in
        it after all, a place for the genuine.
                Hands that can grasp, eyes
                that can dilate, hair that can rise   5
                    if it must, these things are important not because a

---

* In a note to this poem, Moore says that the quotation in lines 17–18 is derived
from *The Diaries of Leo Tolstoy;* the quotation in lines 21–22, from W. B. Yeats's
Ideas of Good and Evil.
        A comment in *Predilections,* her volume of literary essays, affords some
insight into her style: "My own fondness for the unaccepted rhyme derives, I
think, from an instinctive effort to ensure naturalness. Even elate and fearsome
rightness like Shakespeare's is only preserved from the offense of being 'poetic'
by his well-nested effects of helpless naturalness."

high-sounding interpretation can be put upon them but because
they are
useful. When they become so derivative as to become
unintelligible,
the same thing may be said for all of us, that we
do not admire what   *10*
we cannot understand: the bat
holding on upside down or in quest of something to
eat, elephants pushing, a wild horse taking a roll, a tireless
wolf under
a tree, the immovable critic twitching his skin like a horse
that feels a flea, the base-
ball fan, the statistician —   *15*
nor is it valid
to discriminate against "business documents and

school-books"; all these phenomena are important. One must
make a distinction
however: when dragged into prominence by half poets, the
result is not poetry,
nor till the poets among us can be   *20*
"literalists of
the imagination" — above
insolence and triviality and can present

for inspection, "imaginary gardens with real toads in them"
shall we have
it. In the meantime, if you demand on the one hand,   *25*
the raw material of poetry in
all its rawness and
that which is on the other hand
genuine, you are interested in poetry.

T. S. Eliot (*American/English. 1888–1965*)

The Love Song of J. Alfred Prufrock

S'io credesse che mia risposta fosse
A persona che mai tornasse al mondo,
Questa fiamma staria senza più scosse.
Ma perciocchè giammai di questo fondo
Non torno vivo alcun, s' i' odo il vero,
*Senza tema d'infamia ti rispondo.**

Let us go then, you and I,
When the evening is spread out against the sky
Like a patient etherised upon a table;
Let us go, through certain half-deserted streets,
The muttering retreats   5
Of restless nights in one-night cheap hotels
And sawdust restaurants with oyster-shells:
Streets that follow like a tedious argument
Of insidious intent
To lead you to an overwhelming question . . .   10
Oh, do not ask, "What is it?"
Let us go and make our visit.

In the room the women come and go
Talking of Michelangelo.

The yellow fog that rubs its back upon the window-panes,   15
The yellow smoke that rubs its muzzle on the window-panes,
Licked its tongue into the corners of the evening,
Lingered upon the pools that stand in drains,
Let fall upon its back the soot that falls from chimneys,

---

* In Dante's *Inferno* XXVII:61–66, a damned soul who had sought absolution before committing a crime addresses Dante, thinking that his words will never reach the earth: "If I believed that my answer were to a person who could ever return to the world, this flame would no longer quiver. But because no one ever returned from this depth, if what I hear is true, without fear of infamy, I answer you."

    Explanations of allusions in the poem may be helpful. "Works and days" (line 29) is the title of a poem on farm life by Hesiod (eighth century B.C.); "dying fall" (line 52) echoes *Twelfth Night* I.i.4; lines 81–83 allude to John the Baptist (see Matthew 14:1–11); line 92 echoes lines 41–42 of Marvell's "To His Coy Mistress" (see page 478); for "Lazarus" (line 94) see Luke 16 and John 11; lines 112–117 allude to Polonius and perhaps to other figures in *Hamlet;* "full of high sentence" (line 117) comes from Chaucer's description of the Clerk of Oxford in the *Canterbury Tales.*

Slipped by the terrace, made a sudden leap,   *20*
And seeing that it was a soft October night,
Curled once about the house, and fell asleep.

And indeed there will be time
For the yellow smoke that slides along the street,
Rubbing its back upon the window-panes;   *25*
There will be time, there will be time
To prepare a face to meet the faces that you meet;
There will be time to murder and create,
And time for all the works and days of hands
That lift and drop a question on your plate;   *30*
Time for you and time for me,
And time yet for a hundred indecisions,
And for a hundred visions and revisions,
Before the taking of a toast and tea.

In the room the women come and go   *35*
Talking of Michelangelo
And indeed there will be time
To wonder, "Do I dare?" and, "Do I dare?"
Time to turn back and descend the stair,
With a bald spot in the middle of my hair —   *40*
[They will say: "How his hair is growing thin!"]
My morning coat, my collar mounting firmly to the chin,
My necktie rich and modest, but asserted by a simple pin —
[They will say: "But how his arms and legs are thin!"]
Do I dare   *45*
Disturb the universe?
In a minute there is time
For decisions and revisions which a minute will reverse.

For I have known them all already, known them all: —
Have known the evenings, mornings, afternoons,   *50*
I have measured out my life with coffee spoons;
I know the voices dying with a dying fall
Beneath the music from a farther room.
            So how should I presume?

And I have known the eyes already, known them all —   *55*
The eyes that fix you in a formulated phrase,
And when I am formulated, sprawling on a pin,
When I am pinned and wriggling on the wall,
Then how should I begin
To spit out all the butt-ends of my days and ways?   *60*
            And how should I presume?

And I have known the arms already, known them all —
Arms that are braceleted and white and bare
[But in the lamplight, downed with light brown hair!]
Is it perfume from a dress   65
That makes me so digress?
Arms that lie along a table, or wrap about a shawl.
     And should I then presume?
     And how should I begin?

           . . . . .

Shall I say, I have gone at dusk through narrow streets   70
And watched the smoke that rises from the pipes
Of lonely men in shirt-sleeves, leaning out of windows? . . .

I should have been a pair of ragged claws
Scuttling across the floors of silent seas.

           . . . . .

And the afternoon, the evening, sleeps so peacefully!   75
Smoothed by long fingers,
Asleep . . . tired . . . or it malingers,
Stretched on the floor, here beside you and me.
Should I, after tea and cakes and ices,
Have the strength to force the moment to its crisis?   80
But though I have wept and fasted, wept and prayed,
Though I have seen my head [grown slightly bald]
     brought in upon a platter,
I am no prophet — and here's no great matter;
I have seen the moment of my greatness flicker,
And I have seen the eternal Footman hold my coat, and
     snicker,   85
And in short, I was afraid.

And would it have been worth it, after all,
After the cups, the marmalade, the tea,
Among the porcelain, among some talk of you and me,
Would it have been worth while,   90
To have bitten off the matter with a smile,
To have squeezed the universe into a ball
To roll it toward some overwhelming question,
To say: "I am Lazarus, come from the dead,
Come back to tell you all, I shall tell you all" —   95
If one, settling a pillow by her head,
     Should say: "That is not what I meant at all.
     That is not it, at all."

And would it have been worth it, after all,
Would it have been worth while,   100
After the sunsets and the dooryards and the sprinkled streets,
After the novels, after the teacups, after the skirts
    that trail along the floor —
And this, and so much more? —
It is impossible to say just what I mean!
But as if a magic lantern threw the nerves in patterns
    on a screen: 105
Would it have been worth while
If one, settling a pillow or throwing off a shawl,
And turning toward the window, should say:
    "That is not it at all,
    That is not what I meant, at all."   110

        . . . . .

No! I am not Prince Hamlet, nor was meant to be;
Am an attendant lord, one that will do
To swell a progress, start a scene or two,
Advise the prince; no doubt, an easy tool,
Deferential, glad to be of use,   115
Politic, cautious, and meticulous;
Full of high sentence, but a bit obtuse;
At times, indeed, almost ridiculous —
Almost, at times, the Fool.

I grow old . . . I grow old . . .   120
I shall wear the bottoms of my trousers rolled.

Shall I part my hair behind? Do I dare to eat a peach?
I shall wear white flannel trousers, and walk upon the beach.
I have heard the mermaids singing, each to each.

I do not think that they will sing to me.   125

I have seen them riding seaward on the waves
Combing the white hair of the waves blown back
When the wind blows the water white and black.

We have lingered in the chambers of the sea
By sea-girls wreathed with seaweed red and brown   130
Till human voices wake us, and we drown.

John Crowe Ransom *(American. 1888–1974)*

Piazza Piece

— I am a gentleman in a dustcoat trying
To make you hear. Your ears are soft and small
And listen to an old man not at all,
They want the young men's whispering and sighing.   *4*
But see the roses on your trellis dying
And hear the spectral singing of the moon;
For I must have my lovely lady soon,
I am a gentleman in a dustcoat trying.   *8*

— I am a lady young in beauty waiting
Until my truelove comes, and then we kiss.
But what gray man among the vines is this
Whose words are dry and faint as in a dream?   *12*
Back from my trellis, Sir, before I scream!
I am a lady young in beauty waiting.

Archibald MacLeish *(American. 1892–1982)*

Ars Poetica

A poem should be palpable and mute
As a globed fruit,

Dumb
As old medallions to the thumb,   *4*

Silent as the sleeve-worn stone
Of casement ledges where the moss has grown —

A poem should be wordless
As the flight of birds.   *8*

A poem should be motionless in time
As the moon climbs,

Leaving, as the moon releases
Twig by twig the night-entangled trees,   *12*

Leaving, as the moon behind the winter leaves,
Memory by memory the mind —

A poem should be motionless in time
As the moon climbs.   *16*

A poem should be equal to:
Not true.

For all the history of grief
An empty doorway and a maple leaf.   *20*

For love
The leaning grasses and two lights above the sea —

A poem should not mean
But be.   *24*

Wilfred Owen (*English. 1893–1918*)

Dulce et Decorum Est*

Bent double, like old beggars under sacks,
Knock-kneed, coughing like hags, we cursed through sludge,
Till on the haunting flares we turned our backs
And towards our distant rest began to trudge.
Men marched asleep. Many had lost their boots   *5*
But limped on, blood-shod. All went lame; all blind;
Drunk with fatigue; deaf even to the hoots
Of tired, outstripped Five-Nines° that dropped behind.   *shells con-
                                                          taining poison gas*

Gas! Gas! Quick, boys! — An ecstasy of fumbling,
Fitting the clumsy helmets just in time;   *10*
But someone still was yelling out and stumbling
And flound'ring like a man in fire or lime . . .

Dim, through the misty panes and thick green light,
As under a green sea, I saw him drowning.
In all my dreams, before my helpless sight,   *15*
He plunges at me, guttering, choking, drowning.

If in some smothering dreams you too could pace
Behind the wagon that we flung him in,

* From the Latin poet Horace's *Odes* (III:2.13): *Dulce et decorum est pro patria mori*
— "It is sweet and honorable to die for your country."

And watch the white eyes writhing in his face,
His hanging face, like a devil's sick of sin;   *20*
If you could hear, at every jolt, the blood
Come gargling from the froth-corrupted lungs,
Obscene as cancer, bitter as the cud
Of vile, incurable sores on innocent tongues, —
My friend,* you would not tell with such high zest   *25*
To children ardent for some desperate glory,
The old Lie: Dulce et decorum est
Pro patria mori.

E. E. Cummings (American. 1894–1962)

in Just-

in Just-
spring   when the world is mud-
luscious the little
lame balloonman   *4*

whistles   far   and wee

and eddieandbill come
running from marbles and
piracies and it's   *8*
spring

when the world is puddle-wonderful

the queer
old balloonman whistles   *12*
far   and   wee
and bettyandisbel come dancing

from hop-scotch and jump-rope and

it's   *16*
spring
and
     the

* Early drafts of the poem are dedicated to Jessie Pope, author of children's books and conventional patriotic verse.

20

goat-footed

balloonMan   whistles
far
and
wee   *24*

W. H. Auden *(English/American. 1907–1973)*

Lay Your Sleeping Head, My Love

Lay your sleeping head, my love,
Human on my faithless arm;
Time and fevers burn away
Individual beauty from

Thoughtful children, and the grave   *5*
Proves the child ephemeral:
But in my arms till break of day
Let the living creature lie,
Mortal, guilty, but to me
The entirely beautiful.   *10*

Soul and body have no bounds:
To lovers as they lie upon
Her tolerant enchanted slope
In their ordinary swoon,
Grave the vision Venus sends   *15*
Of supernatural sympathy,
Universal love and hope;
While an abstract insight wakes
Among the glaciers and the rocks
The hermit's sensual ecstasy.   *20*

Certainty, fidelity
On the stroke of midnight pass
Like vibrations of a bell,
And fashionable madmen raise
Their pedantic boring cry: *25*
Every farthing of the cost,
All the dreaded cards foretell,
Shall be paid, but from this night

Not a whisper, not a thought,
Not a kiss nor look be lost.   *30*

Beauty, midnight, vision dies:
Let the winds of dawn that blow
Softly round your dreaming head
Such a day of sweetness show
Eye and knocking heart may bless,   *35*
Find the mortal world enough;
Noons of dryness see you fed
By the involuntary powers,
Nights of insult let you pass
Watched by every human love.   *40*

W. H. Auden (English/American. 1907–1973)

Musée des Beaux Arts

About suffering they were never wrong,
The Old Masters: how well they understood
Its human position; how it takes place
While someone else is eating or opening a window
        or just walking dully along;
How, when the aged are reverently, passionately waiting   *5*
For the miraculous birth, there always must be
Children who did not specially want it to happen, skating
On a pond at the edge of the wood:
They never forgot
That even the dreadful martyrdom must run its course   *10*
Anyhow in a corner, some untidy spot
Where the dogs go on with their doggy life and the torturer's
        horse
Scratches its innocent behind on a tree.

In Brueghel's *Icarus,* for instance: how everything turns away
Quite leisurely from the disaster; the ploughman may   *15*
Have heard the splash, the forsaken cry,
But for him it was not an important failure; the sun shone
As it had to on the white legs disappearing into the green
Water; and the expensive delicate ship that must have seen
Something amazing, a boy falling out of the sky,   *20*
Had somewhere to get to and sailed calmly on.

W. H. Auden (*English/American. 1907–1973*)

The Unknown Citizen

(*To JS/07/M/378*
This Marble Monument
Is Erected by the State)

He was found by the Bureau of Statistics to be
One against whom there was no official complaint,
And all the reports on his conduct agree
That, in the modern sense of an old-fashioned word, he was a
saint,
For in everything he did he served the Greater Community.   *5*
Except for the War till the day he retired
He worked in a factory and never got fired,
But satisfied his employers, Fudge Motors Inc.
Yet he wasn't a scab or odd in his views,
For his Union reports that he paid his dues,   *10*
(Our report on his Union shows it was sound)
And our Social Psychology workers found
That he was popular with his mates and liked a drink.
The Press are convinced that he bought a paper every day
And that his reactions to advertisements were normal
        in every way.   *15*
Policies taken out in his name prove that he was fully insured,
And his Health-card shows he was once in hospital
        but left it cured.
Both Producers Research and High-Grade Living declare
He was fully sensible to the advantages of the Installment Plan
And had everything necessary to the Modern Man,   *20*
A phonograph, radio, a car and a frigidaire.
Our researchers into Public Opinion are content
That he held the proper opinions for the time of year;
When there was peace, he was for peace; when there
        was war, he went.
He was married and added five children
        to the population,   *25*
Which our Eugenist says was the right number
        for a parent of his generation,
And our teachers report that he never interfered
        with their education.
Was he free? Was he happy? The question is absurd:
Had anything been wrong, we should certainly have heard.

Elizabeth Bishop (*American. 1911–1979*)

The Fish

I caught a tremendous fish
and held him beside the boat
half out of water, with my hook
fast in a corner of his mouth.
He didn't fight.   5
He hadn't fought at all.
He hung a grunting weight,
battered and venerable
and homely. Here and there
his brown skin hung in strips   10
like ancient wall-paper,
and its pattern of darker brown
was like wall-paper:
shapes like full-blown roses
stained and lost through age.   15
He was speckled with barnacles,
fine rosettes of lime,
and infested
with tiny white sea-lice,
and underneath two or three   20
rags of green weed hung down.
While his gills were breathing in
the terrible oxygen
— the frightening gills,
fresh and crisp with blood,   25
that can cut so badly —
I thought of the coarse white flesh
packed in like feathers,
the big bones and the little bones,
the dramatic reds and blacks   30
of his shiny entrails,
and the pink swim-bladder
like a big peony.
I looked into his eyes
which were far larger than mine   35
but shallower, and yellowed,
the irises backed and packed
with tarnished tinfoil
seen through the lenses
of old scratched isinglass.   40

They shifted a little, but not
to return my stare.
— It was more like the tipping
of an object toward the light.
I admired his sullen face,   45
the mechanism of his jaw,
and then I saw
that from his lower lip
— if you could call it a lip —
grim, wet, and weapon-like,   50
hung five old pieces of fish-line,
or four and a wire leader
with the swivel still attached,
with all their five big hooks
grown firmly in his mouth.   55
A green line, frayed at the end
where he broke it, two heavier lines,
and a fine black thread
still crimped from the strain and snap
when it broke and he got away.   60
Like medals with their ribbons
frayed and wavering,
a five-haired beard of wisdom
trailing from his aching jaw.
I stared and stared   65
and victory filled up
the little rented boat,
from the pool of bilge
where oil had spread a rainbow
around the rusted engine   70
to the bailer rusted orange,
the sun-cracked thwarts,
the oarlocks on their strings,
the gunnels — until everything
was rainbow, rainbow, rainbow!   75
And I let the fish go.

Elizabeth Bishop *(American. 1911–1979)*

Poem

About the size of an old-style dollar bill,
American or Canadian,
mostly the same whites, gray greens, and steel grays
— this little painting (a sketch for a larger one?)
has never earned any money in its life.   5
Useless and free, it has spent seventy years
as a minor family relic
handed along collaterally to owners
who looked at it sometimes, or didn't bother to.

It must be Nova Scotia; only there   10
does one see gabled wooden houses
painted that awful shade of brown.
The other houses, the bits that show, are white.
Elm trees, low hills, a thin church steeple
— that gray-blue wisp — or is it? In the foreground   15
a water meadow with some tiny cows,
two brushstrokes each, but confidently cows;
two minuscule white geese in the blue water,
back-to-back, feeding, and a slanting stick.
Up closer, a wild iris, white and yellow,   20
fresh-squiggled from the tube.
The air is fresh and cold; cold early spring
clear as gray glass; a half inch of blue sky
below the steel-gray storm clouds.
(They were the artist's specialty.)   25
A specklike bird is flying to the left.
Or is it a flyspeck looking like a bird?

Heavens, I recognize the place, I know it!
It's behind — I can almost remember the farmer's name.
His barn backed on that meadow. There it is,   30
titanium white, one dab. The hint of steeple,
filaments of brush-hairs, barely there,
must be the Presbyterian church.
Would that be Miss Gillespie's house?
Those particular geese and cows   35
are naturally before my time.

A sketch done in an hour, "in one breath,"
once taken from a trunk and handed over.
Would you like this? I'll probably never
have room to hang these things again.   40
Your Uncle George, no, mine, my Uncle George,
he'd be your great-uncle, left them all with Mother
when he went back to England.
You know, he was quite famous, an R.A.° . . .   *a member of the Royal*
                                                          Academy

I never knew him. We both knew this place,   45
apparently, this literal small backwater,
looked at it long enough to memorize it,
our years apart. How strange. And it's still loved,
or its memory is (it must have changed a lot).
Our visions coincided — "visions" is   50
too serious a word — our looks, two looks:
art "copying from life" and life itself,
life and the memory of it so compressed
they've turned into each other. Which is which?
Life and the memory of it cramped,   55
dim, on a piece of Bristol board,
dim, but how live, how touching in detail
— the little that we get for free,
the little of our earthly trust. Not much.
About the size of our abidance   60
along with theirs: the munching cows,
the iris, crisp and shivering, the water
still standing from spring freshets,
the yet-to-be-dismantled elms, the geese.

Robert Hayden (*American. 1913–1980*)

Those Winter Sundays

Sundays too my father got up early
and put his clothes on in the blueblack cold,
then with cracked hands that ached
from labor in the weekday weather made
banked fires blaze. No one ever thanked him.   5

I'd wake and hear the cold splintering, breaking.
When the rooms were warm, he'd call,
and slowly I would rise and dress,
fearing the chronic angers of that house,

Speaking indifferently to him,   *10*
who had driven out the cold
and polished my good shoes as well.
What did I know, what did I know
of love's austere and lonely offices?

Henry Reed (English. b. 1914)

Naming of Parts

To-day we have naming of parts. Yesterday,
We had daily cleaning. And to-morrow morning,
We shall have what to do after firing. But to-day,
To-day we have naming of parts. Japonica°   *Japanese quince*
Glistens like coral in all of the neighboring gardens,   *5*
        And to-day we have naming of parts.

This is the lower sling swivel. And this
Is the upper sling swivel, whose use you will see,
When you are given your slings. And this is the piling swivel,
Which in your case you have not got. The branches   *10*
Hold in the gardens their silent, eloquent gestures,
        Which in our case we have not got.

This is the safety-catch, which is always released
With an easy flick of the thumb. And please do not let me
See anyone using his finger. You can do it quite easy   *15*
If you have any strength in your thumb. The blossoms
Are fragile and motionless, never letting anyone see
        Any of them using their finger.

And this you can see is the bolt. The purpose of this
Is to open the breech, as you see. We can slide it   *20*
Rapidly backwards and forwards: we call this
Easing the spring. And rapidly backwards and forwards
The early bees are assaulting and fumbling the flowers:
        They call it easing the Spring.

They call it easing the Spring: it is perfectly easy   *25*
If you have any strength in your thumb: like the bolt,
And the breech, and the cocking-piece, and the point of balance,
Which in our case we have not got; and the almond-blossom
Silent in all of the gardens and the bees going backwards and
    forwards,
      For to-day we have naming of parts.   *30*

Dylan Thomas (Welsh. 1914–1953)

Fern Hill

Now as I was young and easy under the apple boughs
About the lilting house and happy as the grass was green,
    The night above the dingle starry,
      Time let me hail and climb
    Golden in the heydays of his eyes,   *5*
And honored among wagons I was prince of the apple towns
And once below a time I lordly had the trees and leaves
      Trail with daisies and barley
    Down the rivers of the windfall light.

And as I was green and carefree, famous among the barns   *10*
About the happy yard and singing as the farm was home,
    In the sun that is young once only,
      Time let me play and be
    Golden in the mercy of his means,
And green and golden I was huntsman and herdsman,
    the calves   *15*
Sang to my horn, the foxes on the hills barked clear and cold,
      And the sabbath rang slowly
    In the pebbles of the holy streams.

All the sun long it was running, it was lovely, the hay
Fields high as the house, the tunes from the chimneys,
      it was air   *20*
    And playing, lovely and watery
      And fire green as grass.
    And nightly under the simple stars
As I rode to sleep the owls were bearing the farm away,
All the moon long I heard, blessed among stables, the night-
    jars   *25*
    Flying with the ricks, and the horses
      Flashing into the dark.

And then to awake, and the farm, like a wanderer white
With the dew, come back, the cock on his shoulder: it was all
    Shining, it was Adam and maiden,   30
        The sky gathered again
    And the sun grew round that very day.
So it must have been after the birth of the simple light
In the first, spinning place, the spellbound horses walking warm
    Out of the whinnying green stable   35
        On to the fields of praise.

And honored among foxes and pheasants by the gay house
Under the new made clouds and happy as the heart was long,
    In the sun born over and over,
        I ran my heedless ways,   40
    My wishes raced through the house high hay
And nothing I cared, at my sky blue trades, that time allows
In all his tuneful turning so few and such morning songs
    Before the children green and golden
        Follow him out of grace,   45

Nothing I cared, in the lamb white days, that time would take me
Up to the swallow thronged loft by the shadow of my hand,
    In the moon that is always rising,
        Nor that riding to sleep
    I should hear him fly with the high fields   50
And wake to the farm forever fled from the childless land.
Oh as I was young and easy in the mercy of his means,
        Time held me green and dying
    Though I sang in my chains like the sea.

Randall Jarrell (American. 1914–1965)

The Woman at the Washington Zoo

The saris go by me from the embassies.

Cloth from the moon. Cloth from another planet.
They look back at the leopard like the leopard.

And I. . . .
        this print of mine, that has kept its color
Alive through so many cleanings; this dull null   5

Navy I wear to work, and wear from work, and so
To my bed, so to my grave, with no
Complaints, no comment: neither from my chief,
The Deputy Chief Assistant, nor his chief —
Only I complain. . . . this serviceable   *10*
Body that no sunlight dyes, no hand suffuses
But, dome-shadowed, withering among columns,
Wavy beneath fountains — small, far-off, shining
In the eyes of animals, these beings trapped
As I am trapped but not, themselves, the trap,   *15*
Aging, but without knowledge of their age,
Kept safe here, knowing not of death, for death —
Oh, bars of my own body, open, open!

The world goes by my cage and never sees me.
And there come not to me, as come to these,   *20*
The wild beasts, sparrows pecking the llamas' grain,
Pigeons settling on the bears' bread, buzzards
Tearing the meat the flies have clouded. . . .
                                           Vulture,
When you come for the white rat that the foxes left,
Take off the red helmet of your head, the black   *25*
Wings that have shadowed me, and step to me as man:
The wild brother at whose feet the white wolves fawn,
To whose hand of power the great lioness
Stalks, purring. . . .
                         You know what I was,
You see what I am: change me, change me!   *30*

Robert Lowell (*American. 1917–1977*)

Skunk Hour

For Elizabeth Bishop

Nautilus Island's hermit
heiress still lives through winters in her Spartan cottage;
her sheep still graze above the sea.
Her son's a bishop. Her farmer
is first selectman in our village;   *5*
she's in her dotage.

Thirsting for
the hierarchic privacy
of Queen Victoria's century,
she buys up all   *10*
the eyesores facing her shore,
and lets them fall.

The season's ill —
we've lost our summer millionaire,
who seemed to leap from an L. L. Bean   *15*
catalogue. His nine-knot yawl
was auctioned off to lobstermen.
A red fox stain covers Blue Hill.

And now our fairy
decorator brightens his stop for fall;   *20*
his fishnet's filled with orange cork,
orange, his cobbler's bench and awl;
there is no money in his work,
he'd rather marry.

One dark night,   *25*
my Tudor Ford climbed the hill's skull;
I watched for love-cars. Lights turned down,
they lay together, hull to hull,
where the graveyard shelves on the town. . . .
My mind's not right.   *30*

A car radio bleats,
"Love, O careless Love. . . ." I hear
my ill-spirit sob in each blood cell,
as if my hand were at its throat. . . .
I myself am hell;   *35*
nobody's here —

only skunks, that search
in the moonlight for a bite to eat.
They march on their soles up Main Street:
white stripes, moonstruck eyes' red fire   *40*
under the chalk-dry and spar spire
of the Trinitarian Church.

I stand on top
of our back steps and breathe the rich air —
a mother skunk with her column of kittens swills the garbage
          pail.   45
She jabs her wedge-head in a cup
of sour cream, drops her ostrich tail,
and will not scare.

Lawrence Ferlinghetti (American. b. 1919)

Constantly risking absurdity

      Constantly risking absurdity
                  and death
        whenever he performs
               above the heads
                  of his audience 5
   the poet like an acrobat
         climbs on rime
            to a high wire of his own making
and balancing on eyebeams
              above a sea of faces   10
       paces his way
             to the other side of day
    performing *entrechats°*   *a leap in ballet*
             and sleight-of-foot tricks
and other high theatrics   15
        and all without mistaking
   any thing
       for what it may not be

   For he's the super realist
          who must perforce perceive   20
     taut truth
        before the taking of each stance or step

 in his supposed advance
         toward that still higher perch
where Beauty stands and waits   25
        with gravity
           to start her death-defying leap

And he
        a little charleychaplin man
                            who may or may not catch   *30*
            her fair eternal form
                        spreadeagled in the empty air
                of existence

Richard Wilbur (*American. b. 1921*)

Love Calls Us to the Things of This World

        The eyes open to a cry of pulleys,
And spirited from sleep, the astounded soul
Hangs for a moment bodiless and simple
As false dawn.
            Outside the open window
The morning air is all awash with angels.   *5*

        Some are in bed-sheets, some are in blouses,
Some are in smocks: but truly there they are.
Now they are rising together in calm swells
Of halcyon feeling, filling whatever they wear
With the deep joy of their impersonal breathing;   *10*

        Now they are flying in place, conveying
The terrible speed of their omnipresence, moving
And staying like white water; and now of a sudden
They swoon down into so rapt a quiet
That nobody seems to be there.   *15*
                    The soul shrinks

        From all that it is about to remember,
From the punctual rape of every blessèd day,
And cries,
            "Oh, let there be nothing on earth but laundry,
Nothing but rosy hands in the rising steam
And clear dances done in the sight of heaven."   *20*

        Yet, as the sun acknowledges
With a warm look the world's hunks and colors,
The soul descends once more in bitter love
To accept the waking body, saying now
In a changed voice as the man yawns and rises,   *25*

"Bring them down from their ruddy gallows;
Let there be clean linen for the backs of thieves;
Let lovers go fresh and sweet to be undone,
And the heaviest nuns walk in a pure floating
Of dark habits,
                    keeping their difficult balance."   *30*

Anthony Hecht (American. b. 1922)

The Dover Bitch

A Criticism of Life

For Andrews Wanning

So there stood Matthew Arnold and this girl
With the cliffs of England crumbling away behind them,
And he said to her, "Try to be true to me,
And I'll do the same for you, for things are bad
All over, etc., etc."   *5*
Well now, I knew this girl. It's true she had read
Sophocles in a fairly good translation
And caught that bitter allusion to the sea,
But all the time he was talking she had in mind
The notion of what his whiskers would feel like   *10*
On the back of her neck. She told me later on
That after a while she got to looking out
At the lights across the channel, and really felt sad,
Thinking of all the wine and enormous beds
And blandishments in French and the perfumes.   *15*
And then she got really angry. To have been brought
All the way down from London, and then be addressed
As sort of a mournful cosmic last resort
Is really tough on a girl, and she was pretty.
Anyway, she watched him pace the room   *20*
And finger his watch-chain and seem to sweat a bit,
And then she said one or two unprintable things.
But you mustn't judge her by that. What I mean to say is,
She's really all right. I still see her once in a while
And she always treats me right.

We have a drink 25
And I give her a good time, and perhaps it's a year
Before I see her again, but there she is,
Running to fat, but dependable as they come,
And sometimes I bring her a bottle of *Nuit d'Amour.*

Allen Ginsberg (American. b. 1926)

A Supermarket in California

What thoughts I have of you tonight, Walt Whitman, for I walked down the sidestreets under the trees with a headache self-conscious looking at the full moon.

In my hungry fatigue, and shopping for images, I went into the neon fruit supermarket, dreaming of your enumerations!

What peaches and what penumbras! Whole families shopping at night! Aisles full of husbands! Wives in the avocados, babies in the tomatoes! — and you, Garcia Lorca,* what were you doing down by the watermelons?

I saw you, Walt Whitman, childless, lonely old grubber, poking among the meats in the refrigerator and eyeing the grocery boys.

I heard you asking questions of each: Who killed the pork chops? What price bananas? Are you my Angel? 5

I wandered in and out of the brilliant stacks of cans following you, and followed in my imagination by the store detective.

We strode down the open corridors together in our solitary fancy tasting artichokes, possessing every frozen delicacy, and never passing the cashier.

Where are we going, Walt Whitman? The doors close in an hour. Which way does your beard point tonight?

(I touch your book and dream of our odyssey in the supermarket and feel absurd.)

Will we walk all night through solitary streets? The trees add shade to shade, lights out in the houses, we'll both be lonely. 10

Will we stroll dreaming of the lost America of love past blue automobiles in driveways, home to our silent cottage?

---

* *Federico Garcia Lorca (1899–1936), Spanish poet*

Ah, dear father, graybeard, lonely old courage-teacher, what America did you have when Charon quit poling his ferry and you got out on a smoking bank and stood watching the boat disappear on the black water of Lethe?

Frank O'Hara (*American. 1926–1966*)

Ave Maria

Mothers of America
       let your kids go to the movies!
get them out of the house so they won't know what you're up
    to
it's true that fresh air is good for the body
        but what about the soul   *5*
that grows in darkness, embossed by silvery images
and when you grow old as grow old you must
         they won't hate you
they won't criticise you they won't know
       they'll be in some glamorous country *10*
they first saw on a Saturday afternoon or playing hookey
they may even be grateful to you
       for their first sexual experience
which only cost you a quarter
       and didn't upset the peaceful home *15*
they will know where candy bars come from
       and gratuitious bags of popcorn
as gratuitous as leaving the movie before it's over
with a pleasant stranger whose apartment is in the
         Heaven on Earth Bldg *20*
near the Williamsburg Bridge
     oh mothers you will have made the little tykes
so happy because if nobody does pick them up in the movies
they won't know the difference
      and if somebody does it'll be sheer gravy *25*
and they'll have been truly entertained either way
instead of hanging around the yard
       or up in their room
         hating you

prematurely since you won't have done anything horribly
mean yet *30*
except keeping them from the darker joys
it's unforgivable the latter
so don't blame me if you won't take this advice
and the family breaks up
and your children grow old and blind in front of a TV set   *35*
seeing
movies you wouldn't let them see when they were young

Adrienne Rich (*American. b. 1929*)

Living in Sin

She had thought the studio would keep itself,
no dust upon the furniture of love.
Half heresy, to wish the taps less vocal,
the panes relieved of grime. A plate of pears,
a piano with a Persian shawl, a cat   *5*
stalking the picturesque amusing mouse
had risen at his urging.
Not that at five each separate stair would writhe
under the milkman's tramp; that morning light
so coldly would delineate the scraps   *10*
of last night's cheese and three sepulchral bottles;
that on the kitchen shelf among the saucers
a pair of beetle-eyes would fix her own —
envoy from some black village in the mouldings . . .
Meanwhile, he, with a yawn,   *15*
sounded a dozen notes upon the keyboard,
declared it out of tune, shrugged at the mirror,
rubbed at his beard, went out for cigarettes;
while she, jeered by the minor demons,
pulled back the sheets and made the bed and found   *20*
a towel to dust the table-top,
and let the coffee-pot boil over on the stove.
By evening she was back in love again,
though not so wholly but throughout the night
she woke sometimes to feel the daylight coming   *25*
like a relentless milkman up the stairs.

Linda Pastan (*American. b. 1932*)

Marks

My husband gives me an A
for last night's supper,
an incomplete for my ironing,
a B plus in bed.   *4*
My son says I am average,
an average mother, but if
I put my mind to it
I could improve.   *8*
My daughter believes
in Pass/Fail and tells me
I pass. Wait 'til they learn
I'm dropping out.   *12*

Sylvia Plath (*American. 1932–1963*)

Mushrooms

Overnight, very
Whitely, discreetly,
Very quietly

Our toes, our noses
Take hold on the loam,   *5*
Acquire the air.

Nobody sees us,
Stops us, betrays us;
The small grains make room.

Soft fists insist on   *10*
Heaving the needles,
The leafy bedding,

Even the paving.
Our hammers, our rams,
Earless and eyeless,   *15*

Perfectly voiceless,
Widen the crannies,
Shoulder through holes. We

Diet on water,
On crumbs of shadow, 20
Bland-mannered, asking

Little or nothing.
So many of us!
So many of us!

We are shelves, we are 25
Tables, we are meek,
We are edible,

Nudgers and shovers
In spite of ourselves.
Our kind multiplies: 30

We shall by morning
Inherit the earth.
Our foot's in the door.

Sylvia Plath (*American. 1932–1963*)

Daddy

You do not do, you do not do
Any more, black shoe
In which I have lived like a foot
For thirty years, poor and white,
Barely daring to breathe or Achoo. 5

Daddy, I have had to kill you.
You died before I had time —
Marble-heavy, a bag full of God,
Ghastly statue with one gray toe
Big as a Frisco seal 10

And a head in the freakish Atlantic
Where it pours bean green over blue
In the waters off beautiful Nauset.
I used to pray to recover you.
Ach, du. 15

In the German tongue, in the Polish town
Scraped flat by the roller
Of wars, wars, wars.
But the name of the town is common.
My Polack friend   *20*

Says there are a dozen or two.
So I never could tell where you
Put your foot, your root,
I never could talk to you.
The tongue stuck in my jaw.   *25*

It stuck in a barb wire snare.
Ich, ich, ich, ich,
I could hardly speak.
I thought every German was you.
And the language obscene   *30*

An engine, an engine
Chuffing me off like a Jew.
A Jew to Dachau, Auschwitz, Belsen.
I began to talk like a Jew.
I think I may well be a Jew.   *35*

The snows of the Tyrol, the clear beer of Vienna
Are not very pure or true.
With my gypsy ancestress and my weird luck
And my Taroc pack and my Taroc pack
I may be a bit of a Jew.   *40*

I have always been scared of *you,*
With your Luftwaffe, your gobbledygoo.
And your neat moustache
And your Aryan eye, bright blue,
Panzer-man, panzer-man, O You —   *45*

Not God but a swastika
So black no sky could squeak through.
Every woman adores a Fascist,
The boot in the face, the brute
Brute heart of a brute like you.   *50*

You stand at the blackboard, daddy,
In the picture I have of you,
A cleft in your chin instead of your foot
But no less a devil for that, no not
Any less the black man who   *55*

Bit my pretty red heart in two.
I was ten when they buried you.
At twenty I tried to die
And get back, back, back to you.
I thought even the bones would do.   60

But they pulled me out of the sack,
And they stuck me together with glue,
And then I knew what to do.
I made a model of you,
A man in black with a Meinkampf look   65

And a love of the rack and the screw.
And I said I do, I do.
So daddy, I'm finally through.
The black telephone's off at the root,
The voices just can't worm through.   70

If I've killed one man, I've killed two —
The vampire who said he was you
And drank my blood for a year,
Seven years, if you want to know.
Daddy, you can lie back now.   75

There's a stake in your fat black heart
And the villagers never liked you.
They are dancing and stamping on you.
They always *knew* it was you.
Daddy, daddy, you bastard, I'm through.   80

Lucille Clifton (*American. b. 1936*)

in the inner city

in the inner city
or
like we call it
home
we think a lot about uptown   5
and the silent nights
and the houses straight as
dead men

and the pastel lights
and we hang on to our no place   *10*
happy to be alive
and in the inner city
or
like we call it
home   *15*

Seamus Heaney (Irish. b. 1939)

The Haw Lantern

The wintry haw° is burning out of season,   *hawthorn bush*
crab of the thorn, a small light for small people,
wanting no more from them but that they keep
the wick of self-respect from dying out,   *4*
not having to blind them with illumination.

But sometimes when your breath plumes in the frost
it takes the roaming shape of Diogenes*
with his lantern, seeking one just man;   *8*
so you end up scrutinized from behind the haw
he holds up at eye-level on its twig,
and you flinch before its bonded pith and stone,
its blood-prick that you wish would test and clear you,   *12*
its pecked-at ripeness that scans you, then moves on.

Don L. Lee (American. b. 1942)

But He Was Cool
or: he even stopped for green lights

super-cool
ultrablack
a tan / purple
had a beautiful shade.

* Diogenes (412?–323? B.C.) was a Greek philosopher noted for his asceticism.

he had a double-natural   5
that wd put the sisters to shame.
his dashikis were tailor made
& his beads were imported sea shells
        (from some blk/country i never heard of)
he was triple-hip.   10

his tikis were hand carved
out of ivory
& came express from the motherland.
he would greet u in swahili
& say good-by in yoruba.   15

woooooooooooo-jim he bes so cool & ill tel li gent
        cool-cool is so cool he was un-cooled by other niggers' cool
        cool-cool ultracool was bop-cool/ice box cool so cool cold
                cool
        his wine didn't have to be cooled, him was air conditioned
                cool
        cool-cool/real cool made me cool — now ain't that cool 20
        cool-cool so cool him nick-named refrigerator.

cool-cool so cool
he didn't know,
after detroit, newark, chicago &c.,
we had to hip   25
        cool-cool / super-cool / real cool
        that
to be black
is   30
to be
very-hot.

Nikki Giovanni (American. b. 1943)

Master Charge Blues

its wednesday night baby
and i'm all alone
wednesday night baby
and i'm all alone
sitting with myself   5
waiting for the telephone

wanted you baby
but you said you had to go
wanted you yeah
but you said you had to go   10
called your best friend
but he can't come 'cross no more

did you ever go to bed
at the end of a busy day
look over and see the smooth   15
where your hump usta lay
feminine odor and no reason why
i said feminine odor and no reason why
asked the lord to help me
he shook his head "not i"   20

but i'm a modern woman baby
ain't gonna let this get me down
i'm a modern woman
ain't gonna let this get me down
gonna take my master charge   25
and get everything in town

Craig Raine (English. b. 1945)

A Martian Sends a Postcard Home

Caxtons* are mechanical birds with many wings
and some are treasured for their markings —

they cause the eyes to melt
or the body to shriek without pain.

I have never seen one fly, but   5
sometimes they perch on the hand.

Mist is when the sky is tired of flight
and rests its soft machine on ground:

---

* William Caxton (c.1422–1491) was the first English printer of books.

then the world is dim and bookish
like engravings under tissue paper.   *10*

Rain is when the earth is television.
It has the property of making colours darker.

Model T* is a room with the lock inside —
a key is turned to free the world

for movement, so quick there is a film   *15*
to watch for anything missed.

But time is tied to the wrist
or kept in a box, ticking with impatience.

In homes, a haunted apparatus sleeps,
that snores when you pick it up.   *20*

If the ghost cries, they carry it
to their lips and soothe it to sleep

with sounds. And yet, they wake it up
deliberately, by tickling with a finger.

Only the young are allowed to suffer   *25*
openly. Adults go to a punishment room

with water but nothing to eat.
They lock the door and suffer the noises

alone. No one is exempt
and everyone's pain has a different smell.   *30*

At night, when all the colours die,
they hide in pairs

and read about themselves —
in colour, with their eyelids shut.

* A Ford automobile made between 1908 and 1928.

Rita Dove (American. b. 1952)

Geometry

I prove a theorem and the house expands:
the windows jerk free to hover near the ceiling,
the ceiling floats away with a sigh.

As the walls clear themselves of everything
but transparency, the scent of carnations   5
leaves with them. I am out in the open

and above the windows have hinged into butterflies,
sunlight glinting where they've intersected.
They are going to some point true and unproven.

Rita Dove (American. b. 1952)

The Fish in the Stone

The fish in the stone
would like to fall
back into the sea.

He is weary   4
of analysis, the small
predictable truths.

He is weary of waiting
in the open,
his profile stamped   8
by a white light.

In the ocean the silence
moves and moves   12

and so much is unnecessary!
Patient, he drifts
until the moment comes
to cast his   16
skeletal blossom.

The fish in the stone
knows to fail is
to do the living
a favor.

He knows why the ant
engineers a gangster's
funeral, garish
and perfectly amber.
He knows why the scientist
in secret delight
strokes the fern's
voluptuous braille.

Drama

19

Some Elements of Drama

The earlier parts of this book have dealt with narrative, both in prose and in verse, and with what can roughly be called song or lyric. A third literary type (to use a traditional system of classification) is drama, consisting of plays written for the theater.* In a play, the author has receded from his creation; the words are communicated by actors who impersonate the characters. Of course both story and song have their dramatic aspects. In narratives, the authors usually include **dialogue** (conversation), in which the characters are heard directly rather than through the voice of the narrator, and the narrators themselves may be invented characters. Similarly, the author of a lyric poem invents a speaker and a situation. The distinguishing characteristic of a play, then, is not invented speakers or dialogue, but impersonation by actors.

Below is a brief play, a tenth-century imitation (that is, representation or re-creation) of the New Testament narrative of the discovery that the crucified Christ had risen from the tomb. This play, known as *Quem Quaeritis* (Latin: "Whom do you seek?") is commonly considered the earliest extant European play after the end of the Roman drama. Three priests represent the three Marys who visited the tomb. They go to a place representing the tomb and find an angel (a fourth priest, dressed in white, holding a palm branch) who, by displaying a cloth in which the cross had

---

* **Drama,** unfortunately, has acquired too many meanings. It can denote (as above) the whole body of work written for the theater, or a single play, or a serious but untragic play, or (as in "Life is full of drama") events that contain conflict, tension, surprise.

previously been wrapped, shows that Christ has risen. The bits of dialogue (based closely on Matthew 28:1–7 and Mark 16:1–8) had developed in the ninth century, but the tenth-century Latin account by Ethelwold, Bishop of Winchester, gives us the stage directions for the play. What follows is a translation of Ethelwold,* run together with a translation of the play.

Anonymous

Quem Quaeritis

While the third lesson is being chanted, let four brethren vest themselves. Let one of these, vested in an alb, enter as though to take part in the service, and let him approach the sepulcher without attracting attention and sit there quietly with a palm in his hand. While the third respond is chanted, let the remaining three follow, and let them all, vested in copes, bearing in their hands thuribles with incense, and stepping delicately as those who seek something, approach the sepulcher. These things are done in imitation of the angel sitting in the monument, and the women with spices coming to anoint the body of Jesus. When therefore he who sits there beholds the three approach him like folk lost and seeking something, let him begin in a dulcet voice of medium pitch to sing:

> Whom do you seek in the sepulcher, O followers of Christ?

And when he has sung it to the end, let the three reply in unison:

> Jesus of Nazareth who was crucified, O celestial one!

So he:

> He is not here, He has risen as He foretold.
> Go, announce that He is risen from the dead.

At the word of this bidding let those three turn to the choir and say:

> Alleluia! The Lord is risen today,
> The strong lion, Christ the Son of God! Unto God give
> thanks, eia!

* The translation is by E. K. Chambers, The Medieval Stage (Oxford, 1903), II, 14–15.

This said, let the one, still sitting there and as if recalling them, say the anthem:

> Come, and see the place where the Lord was laid,
> Alleluia! Alleluia!

And saying this, let him rise, and lift the veil, and show them the place bare of the cross, but only the cloths laid there in which the cross was wrapped:

> Go quickly, and tell the disciples that the Lord is risen.
> Alleluia! Alleluia!

And when they have seen this, let them set down the thuribles which they bear in that same sepulcher, and take the cloth, and hold it up in the face of the clergy, and as if to demonstrate that the Lord has risen and is no longer wrapped therein, let them sing the anthem:

> The Lord is risen from the sepulcher,
> Who for us was hanged on the cross, alleluia!

and lay the cloth upon the altar. When the anthem is done, let the prior, sharing in their gladness at the triumph of our King, in that, having vanquished death, He rose again, begin the hymn *Te Deum laudamus.* And this begun, all the bells chime out together.

All the elements of a play are here: an action (i.e., not the gestures but a story, a happening, the movement from doubt to joyful certainty) imitated by impersonators (priests). Notice, too, that the impersonation is aided by **scenery** ("the place bare of the cross"), **properties** (the angel's palm branch), **costumes** (copes and an alb), and **gestures** ("stepping delicately as those who seek something"). Even **sound effects** are used: "All the bells chime out together."

Before looking at a longer and more complex play, a few words should be said about **plot.** Although plot is sometimes equated with the gist of the narrative — the story — it is sometimes reserved to denote the writer's *arrangement* of the happenings in the story. Thus, all plays about the assassination of Julius Caesar have pretty much the same story, but by beginning with a scene of workmen enjoying a holiday (and thereby introducing the motif of the fickleness of the mob), Shakespeare's play has a plot different from a play that omits such a scene.

Handbooks on the drama often suggest that a plot (arrangement of happenings) should have a **rising action,** a **climax,** and a

falling action. This sort of plot can be diagramed as a pyramid, the tension rising through complications, or **crises,** to a climax, at which point the fate of the **protagonist** (chief character) is firmly established; the climax is the apex, and the tension allegedly slackens as we witness the **dénouement** (unknotting). Shakespeare sometimes used a pyramidal structure, placing his climax neatly in the middle of what seems to us to be the third of five acts.*
Roughly the first half of *Julius Caesar* shows Brutus rising, reaching his height in III.i with the death of Caesar; but later in this scene he gives Marc Antony permission to speak at Caesar's funeral and thus he sets in motion his own fall, which occupies the second half of the play. In *Macbeth,* the protagonist attains his height in III.i ("Thou hast it now: King"), but he soon perceives that he is going downhill:

> I am in blood
> Stepped in so far, that, should I wade no more,
> Returning were as tedious as go o'er.

In *Hamlet,* the protagonist proves to his own satisfaction Claudius's guilt (by the play within the play) in III.ii, but almost immediately he begins to worsen his position by failing to kill Claudius when he is an easy target (III.iii) and by contaminating himself with the murder of Polonius (III.iv).

Of course, no law demands such a structure, and a hunt for the pyramid usually causes the hunter to overlook all the crises but the middle one. William Butler Yeats once suggestively diagramed a good plot not as a pyramid but as a line moving diagonally upward, punctuated by several crises. Perhaps it is sufficient to say that a good plot has its moments of tension, but the location of these will vary with the play. They are the product of **conflict,** but not all conflict produces tension; there is conflict but little tension in a ball game when the score is 10–0 and the visiting

---

* An **act** is a main division in a drama or opera. Act divisions probably stem from Roman theory and derive ultimately from the Greek practice of separating episodes in a play by choral interludes, but Greek (and probably Roman) plays were performed without interruption, for the choral interludes were part of the plays themselves. Elizabethan plays, too, may have been performed without breaks; the division of Elizabethan plays into five acts is usually the work of editors rather than of authors. Frequently an act division today (commonly indicated by lowering the curtain and turning up the houselights) denotes change in locale and lapse of time. A **scene** is a smaller unit, either (1) a division with no change of locale or abrupt shift of time, or (2) a division consisting of an actor or group of actors on the stage; according to the second definition, the departure or entrance of an actor changes the composition of the group and thus introduces a new scene. (In an entirely different sense, the scene is the locale where a work is set.)

pitcher comes to bat in the ninth inning with two out and none on base.

Regardless of how a plot is diagramed, the **exposition** is that part that tells the audience what it has to know about the past, the **antecedent action.** When the three Marys say they are seeking Jesus, "who was crucified," they are offering exposition. In later plays, the two gossiping servants who tell each other that after a year away in Paris the young master is coming home tomorrow with a new wife are giving the audience the exposition. The Elizabethans and the Greeks sometimes tossed out all pretense at dialogue and began with a **prologue,** like the one spoken by the Chorus at the outset of *Romeo and Juliet:*

> Two households, both alike in dignity
> > In fair Verona, where we lay our scene,
> From ancient grudge break to new mutiny,
> > Where civil blood makes civil hands unclean.
> From forth the fatal loins of these two foes
> > A pair of star-crossed lovers take their life. . . .

And in Tennessee Williams's *The Glass Menagerie,* Tom's first speech is a sort of prologue. However, the exposition also may extend far into the play, being given in dribs and drabs. Occasionally the **soliloquy** (speech of a character alone on the stage, revealing his thoughts) or the **aside** (speech in the presence of others but unheard by them) is used to do the job of putting the audience in possession of the essential facts. The soliloquy and the aside, of course, are not limited to exposition; they are used to reveal the private thoughts of characters who, like people in real life, do not always tell others what their inner thoughts are. The soliloquy is especially used for meditation, where we might say the character is interacting not with another character but with himself or herself.

Exposition has been discussed as though it consists simply of informing the audience about events; but exposition can do much more: it can give us an understanding of the characters who themselves are talking about other characters; it can evoke a mood; and it can generate tension. Thus, although Shakespeare packs a good deal of necessary information into Horatio's speech in I.i.80–107, the scene is equally important for its creation of an atmosphere of uncertainty, of the supernatural, of loyalty to young Hamlet, and of many other things. When we summarize the opening act of a play and treat it as "mere exposition," we are probably losing what is in fact dramatic in it.

Because a play is not simply words but words spoken with accompanying gestures by performers who are usually costumed and in a particular setting, it may be argued that to read a play (rather than to see and hear it) is to falsify it. Drama is not literature, some people hold, but theater. However, there are replies: a play can be literature as well as theater, and the reader of a play can perhaps enact in the theater of his mind a more effective play than the one put on by imperfect actors ("The best in this kind are but shadows," Shakespeare's Duke Theseus says) in front of an audience that coughs and whispers. This mental enactment is aided by abundant stage direction in many contemporary plays. In Eugene O'Neill's *Desire Under the Elms,* about four hundred words (describing the set and the gestures of some of the characters) precede the first speech. This speech consists of two words, "God! Purty!" and it is followed by two hundred words of further description. O'Neill informs the reader that the elms over the house have "a sinister maternity," that Eben, twenty-five years old, "finds himself trapped but inwardly unsubdued," that Simeon is thirty-nine, that Peter is thirty-seven, and so forth. (In the theater, not every actor can communicate by his words, gestures, and makeup that he is twenty-five or thirty-nine or thirty-seven.) Bernard Shaw sometimes outdid O'Neill in writing for the reader: many of his plays have enormous prefaces, and some (such as *Candida*) have unactable stage directions: "They embrace. But they do not know the secret in the poet's heart." Furthermore, the author's dialogue rarely reaches the stage intact; in addition to interpreting, directors cut and reshape scenes, so that it is often accurate to say we get Gielgud's or Olivier's rather than Shakespeare's *Hamlet.*

20
Tragedy

Aristotle defined "tragedy" as a dramatization of a serious happening — not necessarily one ending with the death of the protagonist — and his definition remains among the best. But many plays have been written since Aristotle defined tragedy. When we think of Shakespeare's tragedies, we cannot resist narrowing Aristotle's definition by adding something like "showing a struggle that rends the protagonist's whole being"; and when we think of the "problem plays" of the last hundred years — the serious treatments of such sociological problems as alcoholism and race prejudice — we cannot resist excluding some of them by adding to the definition something about the need for universal appeal. The question remains: Is there a single quality present in all works that we call tragedy and absent from works not called tragedy? If there is, no one has yet pointed it out to general satisfaction. But this failure does not mean that there is no such classification as "tragedy." We sense that tragedies resemble each other as members of the same family resemble each other: two children have the mother's coloring and eyes, a third child has the mother's coloring but the father's eyes, a fourth child has the mother's eyes but the father's coloring.

The next few pages will examine three comments on tragedy, none of which is entirely acceptable, but each of which seems to have some degree of truth, and each of which can help us detect resemblances and differences among tragedies. The first comment is by Cyril Tourneur, a tragic dramatist of the early seventeenth century:

> When the bad bleed, then is the tragedy good.

We think of Macbeth ("usurper," "butcher"). Macbeth, of course, is much more than a usurper and butcher, but it is undeniable that he is an offender against the moral order. Whatever the merits of Tourneur's statement, however, if we think of *Romeo and Juliet*

(to consider only one play), we realize its inadequacy. Tourneur
so stresses the guilt of the protagonist that his or her suffering
becomes mere retributive justice. But we cannot plausibly say, for
example, that Romeo and Juliet deserved to die because they married
without their parents' consent; it is much too simple to call them
"bad." Romeo and Juliet are young, in love, nobler in spirit than
their parents. Tourneur's view is probably derived ultimately from
an influential passage in Aristotle's *Poetics* in which Aristotle speaks
of **hamartia,** sometimes literally translated as "missing the target,"
sometimes as "vice" or "flaw" or "weakness," but perhaps best
translated as "mistake." Aristotle seems to imply that the hero is
undone because of some mistake he or she commits, but this
mistake need not be the result of a moral fault; it may be simply
a miscalculation — for example, failure to foresee the consequences
of a deed. Brutus makes a strategic mistake when he lets Marc
Antony speak at Caesar's funeral, but we can hardly call it a vice.
Because Aristotle's *hamartia* includes mistakes of this sort, the
common translation "tragic flaw" is erroneous. In many Greek
tragedies the hero's *hamartia* is **hybris** (or **hubris**), usually translated
as "overweening pride." The hero forgets that he or she is fallible,
acts as though he or she has the power and wisdom of the gods,
and is later humbled for this arrogance. But one can argue that
this self-assertiveness is not a vice but a virtue, not a weakness
but a strength; if the hero is destroyed for self-assertion, he or she
is nevertheless greater than the surrounding people, just as the
person who tries to stem a lynch mob is greater than the mob,
although that person also may be lynched for his or her virtue.
Or a hero may be undone by a high-mindedness that makes him
or her vulnerable. Hamlet is vulnerable because he is, as his enemy
says, "most generous and free from all contriving"; because Hamlet
is high-minded, he will not suspect that the proposed fencing
match is a murderous plot.

Next, here is a statement more or less the reverse of Tourneur's,
by a Soviet critic, L. I. Timofeev:

> Tragedy in Soviet literature arouses a feeling of pride for the
> man who has accomplished a great deed for the people's hap-
> piness; it calls for continued struggle against the things which
> brought about the hero's death.

The distortions in Soviet criticism are often amusing: Hamlet is
sometimes seen as an incipient Communist, undone by the decadent
aristocracy; or Romeo and Juliet as young people of the future,
undone by bourgeois parents. Recent Soviet drama so consistently

shows the triumph of the worker that Western visitors to Russia have commented on the absence of contemporary tragic plays. Still, there is much in the idea that the tragic hero accomplishes "a great deed" and perhaps we do resent "the things which brought about the hero's death." The stubbornness of the Montagues and Capulets, the fury of the mob that turns against Brutus, the crimes of Claudius in *Hamlet* — all these would seem in some measure to call for our indignation.

The third comment is by Arthur Miller:

> If it is true to say that in essence the tragic hero is intent upon claiming his whole due as a personality, and if this struggle must be total and without reservation, then it automatically demonstrates the indestructible will of man to achieve his humanity. . . . It is curious, although edifying, that the plays we revere, century after century, are the tragedies. In them, and in them alone, lies the belief — optimistic, if you will — in the perfectibility of man.

There is much in Miller's suggestions that the tragic hero makes a large and total claim and that the audience often senses triumph rather than despair in tragedies. We often feel that we have witnessed human greatness — that the hero, despite profound suffering, has lived according to his or her ideals. We may feel that we have achieved new insight into human greatness. But the perfectibility of man? Do we feel that *Julius Caesar* or *Macbeth* or *Hamlet* have to do with human perfectibility? Don't these plays suggest rather that man, whatever his nobility, has within him the seeds of his own destruction? Without overstressing the guilt of the protagonists, don't we feel that in part the plays dramatize the *im*perfectibility of man? In much tragedy, after all, the destruction comes from within, not from without:

> In tragic life, God wot,
> No villain need be! Passions spin the plot:
> We are betrayed by what is false within.
> — George Meredith

What we are talking about is **tragic irony,** the contrast between what is believed to be so and what is so, or between expectations and accomplishments.* Several examples from *Macbeth* illustrate something of the range of tragic irony within a single play. In the

---

* Tragic irony is sometimes called **dramatic irony** or **Sophoclean irony.** The terms are often applied to speeches or actions that the audience understands in a sense fuller than or different from the sense in which the dramatic characters understand them.

first act, King Duncan bestows on Macbeth the title of Thane of Cawdor. By his kindness Duncan seals his own doom, for Macbeth, having achieved this rank, will next want to achieve a higher one. In the third act, Macbeth, knowing that Banquo will soon be murdered, hypocritically urges Banquo to "fail not our feast." But Macbeth's hollow request is ironically fulfilled: the ghost of Banquo terrorizes Macbeth during the feast. The most pervasive irony of all, of course, is that Macbeth aims at happiness when he kills Duncan and takes the throne, but he wins only sorrow.

Aristotle's discussion of **peripeteia (reversal)** and **anagnorisis (recognition)** may be a way of getting at this sort of irony. He may simply have meant a reversal of fortune (for example, good luck ceases) and a recognition of who is who (for example, the pauper is really the prince), but more likely he meant profounder things. One can say that the reversal in *Macbeth* lies in the sorrow that Macbeth's increased power brings; the recognition comes when he realizes the consequences of his deeds:

> I have lived long enough: my way of life
> Is fall'n into the sere, the yellow leaf;
> And that which should accompany old age,
> As honor, love, obedience, troops of friends,
> I must not look to have; but, in their stead,
> Curses, not loud but deep, mouth-honor, breath
> Which the poor heart would fain deny, and dare not.

That a person's deeds often undo him or her, that a person aiming at his or her good can produce ruin, was not, of course, a discovery of the tragic dramatists. The archetype is the story of Adam and Eve: these two aimed at becoming like God, and as a consequence, they brought upon themselves corruption, death, the loss of their earthly paradise. The Bible is filled with stories of tragic irony. A brief quotation from Ecclesiastes (10:8–9) can stand as an epitome of these stories:

> He that diggeth a pit shall fall into it; and whoso breaketh
> an hedge, a serpent shall bite him.
> Whoso removeth stones shall be hurt therewith; and he
> that cleaveth wood shall be endangered thereby.

"He that cleaveth wood shall be endangered thereby." Activity involves danger. To be inactive is, often, to be ignoble, but to be active is necessarily to imperil oneself. Perhaps we can attempt a summary of tragic man: he acts, and he suffers, usually as a consequence of his action. The question is not of his action's being particularly bad (Tourneur's view) or particularly good (Timofeev's view); the action is often both good and bad, a sign of man's courage and also of his arrogance, a sign of man's greatness and also of his limitations.

Finally, a brief consideration of the pleasure of tragedy: Why do we enjoy plays about suffering? Aristotle has some obscure comments on **catharsis (purgation)** that are often interpreted as saying that tragedy arouses in us both pity and fear and then purges us of these emotions. The idea, perhaps, is that just as we can harmlessly discharge our aggressive impulses by witnessing a prize fight or by shouting at an umpire, so we can harmlessly discharge our impulses to pity and to fear by witnessing the dramatization of a person's destruction. The theater in this view is an outlet for emotions that elsewhere would be harmful. But, it must be repeated, Aristotle's comments on catharsis are obscure; perhaps, too, they are wrong. Most later theories on the pleasure of tragedy are footnotes to Aristotle's words on catharsis. Some say that our pleasure is sadistic (we enjoy the sight of suffering); some, that our pleasure is masochistic (we enjoy lacerating ourselves); some, that it lies in sympathy (we enjoy extending pity and benevolence to the wretched); some, that it lies in self-congratulation (we are reminded, when we see suffering, of our own good fortune); some, that we take pleasure in tragedy because the tragic hero acts out our secret desires, and we rejoice in his or her aggression, expiating our guilt in his or her suffering; and so on.

But this is all rather uncertain psychology, and it mostly neglects the distinction between real suffering and dramatized suffering. In the latter, surely, part of the pleasure is in the contemplation of an aesthetic object, an object that is unified and complete. The chaos of real life seems, for a few moments in drama, to be ordered: the protagonist's action, his or her subsequent suffering, and the total cosmos seem somehow related. Tragedy has no use for the passerby who is killed by a falling brick. The events (the person's walk, the brick's fall) have no meaningful relation. But suppose a person chooses to climb a mountain, and in making the ascent sets in motion an avalanche that destroys that person. Here we find (however simple the illustration) something closer to tragedy. We do not say that people should avoid mountains, or that mountain-climbers deserve to die by avalanches. But we feel that the event is unified, as the accidental conjunction of brick and passerby is not. Tragedy thus presents some sort of ordered action; tragic drama itself is orderly. As we see or read it, we feel it cannot be otherwise; word begets word, deed begets deed, and every moment is exquisitely appropriate. Whatever the relevance of sadism, masochism, sympathy, and the rest, the pleasure of tragedy surely comes in part from the artistic shaping of the material.

A NOTE ON GREEK TRAGEDY

Little or nothing is known for certain of the origin of Greek tragedy. The most common hypothesis holds that it developed from improvised speeches during choral dances honoring Dionysus, a Greek nature god associated with spring, fertility, and wine. Thespis (who perhaps never existed) is said to have introduced an actor into these choral performances in the sixth century B.C. Aeschylus (525–456 B.C.), Greece's first great writer of tragedies, added the second actor, and Sophocles (496?–406 B.C.) added the third actor and fixed the size of the chorus at fifteen. (Because the chorus leader often functioned as an additional actor, and because the actors sometimes doubled in their parts, a Greek tragedy could have more characters than might at first be thought.)

All the extant great Greek tragedy is of the fifth century B.C. It was performed at religious festivals in the winter and early spring, in large outdoor amphitheaters built on hillsides. Some of these theaters were enormous; the one at Epidaurus held about fifteen thousand people. The audience sat in tiers, looking down on the **orchestra** (a dancing place), with the acting area behind it and the **skene** (the scene building) yet farther back. The scene building served as dressing room, background (suggesting a palace or temple), and place for occasional entrances and exits. Furthermore, this building helped to provide good acoustics, for speech travels well if there is a solid barrier behind the speaker and a hard, smooth surface in front of him, and if the audience sits in tiers. The wall of the scene building provided the barrier; the orchestra provided the surface in front of the actors; and the seats on the hillside fulfilled the third requirement. Moreover, the acoustics were some-what improved by slightly elevating the actors above the orchestra, but it is not known exactly when this platform was first constructed in front of the scene building.

A tragedy commonly begins with a **prologos** (prologue), during which the exposition is given. Next comes the **párodos,** the chorus's ode of entrance, sung while the chorus marches into the theater through the side aisles and onto the orchestra. The **epeisodion** (episode) is the ensuing scene; it is followed by a **stasimon** (choral song, ode). Usually there are four or five *epeisodia,* alternating with *stasima.* Each of these choral odes has a **strophe** (lines presumably sung while the chorus dances in one direction) and an **antistrophe** (lines presumably sung while the chorus retraces its steps). Sometimes a third part, an **epode,** concludes an ode. (In addition to odes that are *stasima,* there can be odes within episodes; the fourth episode of *Antigone* contains an ode complete

Fig. 18-1. *Greek Theatre of Epidaurus on the Peloponnesus east of Nauplia. (Photograph: Frederick Ayer, Photo Researchers, Inc.)*

with *epode*.) After the last part of the last ode comes the **exodos,** the epilogue or final scene.

The actors (all male) wore masks, and they seem to have chanted much of the play. Perhaps the total result of combining speech with music and dancing was a sort of music-drama roughly akin to opera with some spoken dialogue, such as Mozart's *Magic Flute*.

Sophocles *(c. 495–406* B.C.*)*

Antigone

Translated into English verse by H. D. F. Kitto

List of Characters

Antigone, daughter of Oedipus and Iocasta
Ismene, her sister
Creon, King of Thebes, brother of Iocasta
Haemon, his son
A Guard
Teiresias, a Seer
*Messenger or messengers**
Eurydice, wife to Creon
Chorus of Theban nobles

Scene.

Thebes, before the royal palace. Antigone and Ismene are the last members of a royal line which stretched back, through Oedipus and Laius, to Cadmus who had founded the city by sowing the Dragon's teeth from which sprang its warrior-race.

Enter, from the palace, Antigone and Ismene

---

* There is not the slightest indication in the text whether the messenger who brings the news of Eurydice's death is a man or a woman. Presumably Sophocles used the same man who had brought the news from the cavern, but it is a matter of complete indifference. [Kitto.]

Antigone. Ismene, my own sister, dear Ismene,
How many miseries our father caused!
And is there one of them that does not fall
On us while yet we live? Unhappiness,
Calamity, disgrace, dishonor — which
Of these have you and I not known? And now
Again: there is the order which they say
Brave Creon has proclaimed to all the city.
You understand? or do you not yet know
What outrage threatens one of those we love?   10
Ismene. Of them, Antigone, I have not heard
Good news or bad — nothing, since we two sisters
Were robbed of our two brothers on one day
When each destroyed the other. During the night
The enemy has fled: so much I know,
But nothing more, either for grief or joy.
Antigone. I knew it; therefore I have brought you here,
Outside the doors, to tell you secretly.
Ismene. What is it? Some dark shadow is upon you.
Antigone. Our brothers' burial. — Creon has ordained   20
Honor for one, dishonor for the other.
Eteocles, they say, has been entombed
With every solemn rite and ceremony
To do him honor in the world below;
But as for Polyneices, Creon has ordered
That none shall bury him or mourn for him;
He must be left to lie unwept, unburied,
For hungry birds of prey to swoop and feast
On his poor body. So he has decreed,
Our noble Creon, to all the citizens: 30
To you, to me. To me! And he is coming
To make it public here, that no one may
Be left in ignorance; nor does he hold it
Of little moment: he who disobeys
In any detail shall be put to death
By public stoning in the streets of Thebes.
So it is now for you to show if you
Are worthy, or unworthy, of your birth.
Ismene. O my poor sister! If it has to come to this
What can I do, either to help or hinder?   40
Antigone. Will you join hands with me and share my task?
Ismene. What dangerous enterprise have you in mind?
Antigone. Will you join me in taking up the body?
Ismene. What? Would you bury him, against the law?

Antigone. No one shall say *I* failed him! I will bury
  My brother — and yours too, if you will not.
Ismene. You reckless girl! When Creon has forbidden?
Antigone. He has no right to keep me from my own!
Ismene. Think of our father, dear Antigone,
  And how we saw him die, hated and scorned,   *50*
  When his own hands had blinded his own eyes
  Because of sins which he himself disclosed;
  And how his mother-wife, two names in one,
  Knotted a rope, and so destroyed herself.
  And, last of all, upon a single day
  Our brothers fought each other to the death
  And shed upon the ground the blood that joined them.
  Now you and I are left, alone; and think:
  If we defy the King's prerogative
  And break the law, our death will be more shameful   *60*
  Even than theirs. Remember too that we
  Are women, not made to fight with men. Since they
  Who rule us now are stronger far than we,
  In this and worse than this we must obey them.
  Therefore, beseeching pardon from the dead,
  Since what I do is done on hard compulsion,
  I yield to those who have authority;
  For useless meddling has no sense at all.
Antigone. I will not urge you. Even if you should wish
  To give your help I would not take it now.   *70*
  Your choice is made. But I shall bury him.
  And if I have to die for this pure crime,
  I am content, for I shall rest beside him;
  His love will answer mine. I have to please
  The dead far longer than I need to please
  The living; with them, I have to dwell for ever.
  But you, if so you choose, you may dishonor
  The sacred laws that Heaven holds in honor.
Ismene. I do them no dishonor, but to act
  Against the city's will I am too weak.   *80*
Antigone. Make that your pretext! I will go and heap
  The earth upon the brother whom I love.
Ismene. You reckless girl! I tremble for your life.
Antigone. Look to yourself and do not fear for me.
Ismene. At least let no one hear of it, but keep
  Your purpose secret, and so too will I.
Antigone. Go and denounce me! I shall hate you more
  If you keep silent and do not proclaim it.

Ismene. Your heart is hot upon a wintry work!
Antigone. I know I please whom most I ought to please.   *90*
Ismene. But can you do it? It is impossible!
Antigone. When I can do no more, then I will stop.
Ismene. But why attempt a hopeless task at all?
Antigone. O stop, or I shall hate you! He will hate
    You too, for ever, justly. Let me be,
    Me and my folly! I will face the danger
    That so dismays you, for it cannot be
    So dreadful as to die a coward's death.
Ismene. Then go and do it, if you must. It is
    Blind folly — but those who love you love you dearly.   *100*

                                           Exit separately.

FIRST ODE

Strophe 1

Chorus. Welcome, light of the Sun, the fairest
(Glyconics°) Sun that ever has dawned upon
    Thebes, the city of seven gates!
    At last thou art arisen, great
    Orb of shining day, pouring
    Light across the gleaming water of Dirkê.
    Thou hast turned into headlong flight,
    Galloping faster and faster, the foe who
    Bearing a snow-white shield in full
    Panoply came from Argos.   *110*

(Anapests°) He had come to destroy us, in Polyneices'
    Fierce quarrel. *He* brought them against our land;
    And like some eagle screaming his rage
    From the sky he descended upon us,
    With his armor about him, shining like snow,
        With spear upon spear,
    And with plumes that swayed on their helmets.

---

[102] *glyconics* metrical feet consisting of a spondee (two long syllables), a dactyl (two short syllables followed by one long syllable), and an amphimacer, or cretic (one long syllable followed by one short syllable followed by one long syllable) [111] *anapests* metrical feet consisting of two short syllables followed by one long syllable

Antistrophe 1

(Glyconics) Close he hovered above our houses,
    Circling around our seven gates, with
    Spears that thirsted to drink our blood.   *120*
    He's gone! gone before ever his jaws
    Snapped on our flesh, before he sated
    Himself with our blood, before his blazing fire-brand
    Seized with its fire our city's towers.
    Terrible clangor of arms repelled him,
    Driving him back, for hard it is to
    Strive with the sons of a Dragon.

(Anapests) For the arrogant boast of an impious man
    Zeus hateth exceedingly. So, when he saw
    This army advancing in swollen flood   *130*
    In the pride of its gilded equipment,
    He struck them down from the rampart's edge
        With a fiery bolt
    In the midst of their shout of "Triumph!"

Strophe 2

(More strongly marked rhythm) Heavily down to the earth did he
                fall, and lie there,
    He who with torch in his hand and possessed with frenzy
        Breathed forth bitterest hate
        Like some fierce tempestuous wind.
           So it fared then with him;
    And of the rest, each met his own terrible doom,   *140*
    Given by the great War-god, our deliverer.

(Anapests) Seven foemen appointed to our seven gates
    Each fell to a Theban, and Argive arms
    Shall grace our Theban temple of Zeus:
    Save two, those two of unnatural hate,
    Two sons of one mother, two sons of one King;
    They strove for the crown, and shared with the sword
    Their estate, each slain by his brother.

Antistrophe 2

    Yet do we see in our midst, and acclaim with gladness,
    Victory, glorious Victory, smiling, welcome.   *150*

Now, since danger is past,
Thoughts of war shall pass from our minds.
Come! let all thank the gods,
Dancing before temple and shrine all through the night,
Following Thee, Theban Dionysus.
Chorus-leader. But here comes Creon, the new king of Thebes,
In these new fortunes that the gods have given us.
What purpose is he furthering, that he
Has called this gathering of his Counsellors?

    Enter Creon, attended.

Creon. My lords: for what concerns the state, the gods   *160*
Who tossed it on the angry surge of strife
Have righted it again; and therefore you
By royal edict I have summoned here,
Chosen from all our number. I know well
How you revered the throne of Laius;
And then, when Oedipus maintained our state,
And when he perished, round his sons you rallied,
Still firm and steadfast in your loyalty.
Since they have fallen by a double doom
Upon a single day, two brothers each   *170*
Killing the other with polluted sword,
I now possess the throne and royal power
By right of nearest kinship with the dead.
    There is no art that teaches us to know
The temper, mind or spirit of any man
Until he has been proved by government
And lawgiving. A man who rules a state
And will not ever steer the wisest course,
But is afraid, and says not what he thinks,
That man is worthless; and if any holds   *180*
A friend of more account than his own city,
I scorn him; for if I should see destruction
Threatening the safety of my citizens,
I would not hold my peace, nor would I count
That man my friend who was my country's foe,
Zeus be my witness. For be sure of this:
It is the city that protects us all;
She bears us through the storm; only when she
Rides safe and sound can we make loyal friends.
    This I believe, and thus will I maintain   *190*
Our city's greatness. — Now, conformably,

Of Oedipus' two sons I have proclaimed
This edict: he who in his country's cause
Fought gloriously and so laid down his life,
Shall be entombed and graced with every rite
That men can pay to those who die with honor;
But for his brother, him called Polyneices,
Who came from exile to lay waste his land,
To burn the temples of his native gods,
To drink his kindred blood, and to enslave   *200*
The rest, I have proclaimed to Thebes that none
Shall give him funeral honors or lament him,
But leave him there unburied, to be devoured
By dogs and birds, mangled most hideously.
Such is my will; never shall I allow
The villian to win more honor than the upright;
But any who show love to this our city
In life and death alike shall win my praise.
Chorus-leader. Such is your will, my lord; so you requite
Our city's champion and our city's foe.   *210*
You, being sovereign, make what laws you will
Both for the dead and those of us who live.
Creon. See then that you defend the law now made.
Chorus-leader. No, lay that burden on some younger men.
Creon. I have appointed guards to watch the body.
Chorus-leader. What further charge, then, do you lay on us?
Creon. Not to connive at those that disobey me.
Chorus-leader. None are so foolish as to long for death.
Creon. Death is indeed the price, but love of gain
Has often lured a man to his destruction.   *220*

   Enter a Guard.

Guard. My lord: I cannot say that I am come
All out of breath with running. More than once
I stopped and thought and turned round in my path
And started to go back. My mind had much
To say to me. One time it said "You fool!
Why do you go to certain punishment?"
Another time "What? Standing still, you wretch?
You'll smart for it, if Creon comes to hear
From someone else." And so I went along
Debating with myself, not swift nor sure.   *230*
This way, a short road soon becomes a long one.

At last this was the verdict: I must come
And tell you. It may be worse than nothing; still,
I'll tell you. I can suffer nothing more
Than what is in my fate. There is my comfort!
Creon. And what is this that makes you so despondent?
Guard. First for myself: I did not see it done,
  I do not know who did it. Plainly then,
  I cannot rightly come to any harm.
Creon. You are a cautious fellow, building up   *240*
  This barricade. You bring unpleasant news?
Guard. I do, and peril makes a man pause long.
Creon. O, won't you tell your story and be gone?
Guard. Then, here it is. The body: someone has
  Just buried it, and gone away. He sprinkled
  Dry dust on it, with all the sacred rites.
Creon. What? Buried it? What man has so defied me?
Guard. How can I tell? There was no mark of pickaxe,
  No sign of digging; the earth was hard and dry
  And undisturbed; no waggon had been there;   *250*
  He who had done it left no trace at all.
  So, when the first day-watchman showed it to us,
  We were appalled. We could not see the body;
  It was not buried but it was thinly covered
  With dust, as if by someone who had sought
  To avoid a curse. Although we looked, we saw
  No sign that any dog or bird had come
  And torn the body. Angry accusations
  Flew up between us; each man blamed another,
  And in the end it would have come to blows,   *260*
  For there was none to stop it. Each single man
  Seemed guilty, yet proclaimed his ignorance
  And could not be convicted. We were all
  Ready to take hot iron in our hands,
  To walk through fire, to swear by all the gods
  We had not done it, nor had secret knowledge
  Of any man who did it or contrived it.
  We could not find a clue. Then one man spoke:
  It made us hang our heads in terror, yet
  No one could answer him, nor could we see   *270*
  Much profit for ourselves if we should do it.
  He said "We must report this thing to Creon;
  We dare not hide it"; and his word prevailed.
  I am the unlucky man who drew the prize

When we cast lots, and therefore I am come
Unwilling and, for certain, most unwelcome:
Nobody loves the bringer of bad news.
Chorus-leader. My lord, the thought has risen in my mind:
    Do we not see in this the hand of God?
Creon. Silence! or you will anger me. You are   280
    An old man: must you be a fool as well?
    Intolerable, that you suppose the gods
    Should have a single thought for this dead body.
    What? should they honor him with burial
    As one who served them well, when he had come
    To burn their pillared temples, to destroy
    Their treasuries, to devastate their land
    And overturn its laws? Or have you noticed
    The gods prefer the vile? No, from the first
    There was a muttering against my edict,   290
    Wagging of heads in secret, restiveness
    And discontent with my authority.
    I know that some of these perverted others
    And bribed them to this act. Of all vile things
    Current on earth, none is so vile as money.
    For money opens wide the city-gates
    To ravishers, it drives the citizens
    To exile, it perverts the honest mind
    To shamefulness, it teaches men to practice
    All forms of wickedness and impiety.   300
    These criminals who sold themselves for money
    Have bought with it their certain punishment;
    For, as I reverence the throne of Zeus,
    I tell you plainly, and confirm it with
    My oath: unless you find, and bring before me,
    The very author of this burial-rite
    Mere death shall not suffice; you shall be hanged
    Alive, until you have disclosed the crime,
    That for the future you may ply your trade
    More cleverly, and learn not every pocket   310
    Is safely to be picked. Ill-gotten gains
    More often lead to ruin than to safety.
Guard. May I reply? Or must I turn and go?
Creon. Now, as before, your very voice offends me.
Guard. Is it your ears that feel it, or your mind?
Creon. Why must you probe the seat of our displeasure?
Guard. The rebel hurts your mind; I but your ears.
Creon. No more of this! You are a babbling fool!

Guard. If so, I cannot be the one who did it.
Creon. Yes, but you did — selling your life for money!   *320*
Guard. It's bad, to judge at random, and judge wrong!
Creon. You judge my judgment as you will — but bring
    The man who did it, or you shall proclaim
    What punishment is earned by crooked dealings.
Guard. God grant he may be found! But whether he
    Be found or not — for this must lie with chance —
    You will not see me coming *here* again.
    Alive beyond my hope and expectation,
    I thank the gods who have delivered me.

                          Exit separately Creon and Guard.

SECOND ODE

Strophe 1

Chorus. Wonders are many, yet of all   *330*
(*Glyconics*) Things is Man the most wonderful.
        He can sail on the stormy sea
        Though the tempest rage, and the loud
        Waves roar around, as he makes his
        Path amid the towering surge.

(*Dactyls°*) Earth inexhaustible, ageless, he wearies, as
    Backwards and forwards, from season to season, his
    Ox-team drives along the ploughshare.

Antistrophe 1

He can entrap the cheerful birds,   *340*
Setting a snare, and all the wild
Beasts of the earth he has learned to catch, and

Fish that teem in the deep sea, with
Nets knotted of stout cords; of
Such inventiveness is man.

---

[336] **dactyls** metrical feet consisting of two short syllables followed by one long
syllable

Through his inventions he becomes lord
Even of the beasts of the mountain: the long-haired
Horse he subdues to the yoke on his neck, and the
Hill-bred bull, of strength untiring.

Strophe 2

And speech he has learned, and thought   *350*
So swift, and the temper of mind
To dwell within cities, and not to lie bare
Amid the keen, biting frosts
Or cower beneath pelting rain;
Full of resource against all that comes to him
Is Man. Against Death alone
He is left with no defence.
But painful sickness he can cure
    By his own skill.

Antistrophe 2

Surpassing belief, the device and   *360*
Cunning that Man has attained,
And it bringeth him now to evil, now to good.
If he observe Law, and tread
The righteous path God ordained,
Honored is he; dishonored, the man whose reckless heart
Shall make him join hands with sin:
May I not think like him,
Nor may such an impious man
    Dwell in my house.

Enter Guard, with Antigone.

Chorus-leader. What evil spirit is abroad? I know   *370*
    Her well: Antigone. But how can I
    Believe it? Why, O you unlucky daughter
    Of an unlucky father, what is this?
    Can it be you, so mad and so defiant,
    So disobedient to a King's decree?
Guard. Here is the one who did the deed, this girl;
    We caught her burying him. — but where is Creon?
Chorus-leader. He comes, just as you need him, from the palace.

Enter Creon, attended.

Creon. How? What occasion makes my coming timely?
Guard. Sir, against nothing should a man take oath,   380
    For second thoughts belie him. Under your threats
    That lashed me like a hailstorm, I'd have said
    I would not quickly have come here again;
    But joy that comes beyond our dearest hope
    Surpasses all in magnitude. So I
    Return, though I had sworn I never would,
    Bringing this girl detected in the act
    Of honoring the body. This time no lot
    Was cast; the windfall is my very own.
    And so, my lord, do as you please: take her   390
    Yourself, examine her, cross-question her.
    I claim the right of free and final quittance.
Creon. Why do you bring this girl? Where was she taken?
Guard. In burying the body. That is all.
Creon. You know what you are saying? Do you mean it?
Guard. I saw her giving burial to the corpse
    You had forbidden. Is that plain and clear?
Creon. How did you see and take her so red-handed?
Guard. It was like this. When we had reached the place,
    Those dreadful threats of yours upon our heads,   400
    We swept aside each grain of dust that hid
    The clammy body, leaving it quite bare,
    And sat down on a hill, to the windward side
    That so we might avoid the smell if it.
    We kept sharp look-out; each man roundly cursed
    His neighbor, if he should neglect his duty.
    So the time passed, until the blazing sun
    Reached his mid-course and burned us with his heat.
    Then, suddenly, a whirlwind came from heaven
    And raised a storm of dust, which blotted out   410
    The earth and sky; the air was filled with sand
    And leaves ripped from the trees. We closed our eyes
    And bore this visitation as we could.
    At last it ended; then we saw the girl.
    She raised a bitter cry, as will a bird
    Returning to its nest and finding it
    Despoiled, a cradle empty of its young.
    So, when she saw the body bare, she raised
    A cry of anguish mixed with imprecations
    Laid upon those who did it; then at once   420
    Brought handfuls of dry dust, and raised aloft
    A shapely vase of bronze, and three times poured

The funeral libation for the dead.
We rushed upon her swiftly, seized our prey,
And charged her both with this offense and that.
She faced us calmly; she did not disown
The double crime. How glad I was! — and yet
How sorry too; it is a painful thing
To bring a friend to ruin. Still, for me,
My own escape comes before everything.   430
Creon. You there, who keep your eyes fixed on the ground,
    Do you admit this, or do you deny it?
Antigone. No, I do not deny it. I admit it.
Creon (to Guard). Then you may go; go where you like. You
                                                          have
    Been fully cleared of that grave accusation.

                                                Exit Guard.

You: tell me briefly — I want no long speech:
    Did you not know that this had been forbidden?
Antigone. Of course I knew. There was a proclamation.
Creon. And so you dared to disobey the law?
Antigone. It was not Zeus who published this decree,   440
    Nor have the Powers who rule among the dead
    Imposed such laws as this upon mankind;
    Nor could I think that a decree of yours —
    A man — could override the laws of Heaven
    Unwritten and unchanging. Not of today
    Or yesterday is their authority;
    They are eternal; no man saw their birth.
    Was I to stand before the gods' tribunal
    For disobeying *them,* because I feared
    A man? I knew that I should have to die,   450
    Even without your edict; if I die
    Before my time, why then, I count it gain;
    To one who lives as I do, ringed about
    With countless miseries, why, death is welcome.
    For me to meet this doom is little grief;
    But when my mother's son lay dead, had I
    Neglected him and left him there unburied,
    That would have caused me grief; this causes none.
    And if you think it folly, then perhaps
    I am accused of folly by the fool.   460
Chorus-leader. The daughter shows her father's temper — fierce,
    Defiant; she will not yield to any storm.

Creon. But it is those that are most obstinate
   Suffer the greatest fall; the hardest iron,
   Most fiercely tempered in the fire, that is
   Most often snapped and splintered. I have seen
   The wildest horses tamed, and only by
   The tiny bit. There is no room for pride
   In one who is a slave! This girl already
   Had fully learned the art of insolence   *470*
   When she transgressed the laws that I established;
   And now to that she adds a second outrage —
   To boast of what she did, and laugh at us.
   Now she would be the man, not I, if she
   Defeated me and did not pay for it.
   But though she be my niece, or closer still
   Than all our family, she shall not escape
   The direst penalty; no, nor shall her sister:
   I judge her guilty too; she played her part
   In burying the body. Summon her.   *480*
   Just now I saw her raving and distracted
   Within the palace. So it often is:
   Those who plan crime in secret are betrayed
   Despite themselves; they show it in their faces.
   But this is worst of all: to be convicted
   And then to glorify the crime as virtue.

                         Exit some guards.

Antigone. Would you do more than simply take and kill me?
Creon. I will have nothing more, and nothing less.
Antigone. Then why delay? To me no word of yours
   Is pleasing — God forbid it should be so! —   *490*
   And everything in me displeases you.
   Yet what could I have done to win renown
   More glorious than giving burial
   To my own brother? These men too would say it,
   Except that terror cows them into silence.
   A king has many a privilege: the greatest,
   That he can say and do all that he will.
Creon. You are the only one in Thebes to think it!
Antigone. These think as I do — but they dare not speak.
Creon. Have you no shame, not to conform with others?   *500*
Antigone. To reverence a brother is no shame.
Creon. Was he no brother, he who died for Thebes?
Antigone. One mother and one father gave them birth.

Creon. Honoring the traitor, you dishonor *him.*
Antigone. He will not bear this testimony, in death.
Creon. Yes! if the traitor fare the same as he.
Antigone. It was a brother, not a slave who died!
Creon. He died attacking Thebes; the other saved us.
Antigone. Even so, the god of Death demands these rites.
Creon. The good demand more honor than the wicked.   510
Antigone. Who knows? In death they may be reconciled.
Creon. Death does not make an enemy a friend!
Antigone. Even so, I give both love, not share their hatred.
Creon. Down then to Hell! Love there, if love you must.
   While I am living, no woman shall have rule.

    Enter guards, with Ismene.

Chorus-leader. See where Ismene leaves the palace-gate,
   In tears shed for her sister. On her brow
   A cloud of grief has blotted out her sun,
   And breaks in rain upon her comeliness.
Creon. You, lurking like a serpent in my house,   520
   Drinking my life-blood unawares; nor did
   I know that I was cherishing two fiends,
   Subverters of my throne: come, tell me this:
   Do you confess you shared this burial,
   Or will you swear you had no knowledge of it?
Ismene. I did it too, if she allows my claim;
   I share the burden of this heavy charge.
Antigone. No! Justice will not suffer that; for you
   Refused, and I gave you no part in it.
Ismene. But in your stormy voyage I am glad   530
   To share the danger, traveling at your side.
Antigone. Whose was the deed the god of Death knows well;
   I love not those who love in words alone.
Ismene. My sister, do not scorn me, nor refuse
   That I may die with you, honoring the dead.
Antigone. You shall not die with me, nor claim as yours
   What you rejected. My death will be enough.
Ismene. What life is left to me if I lose you?
Antigone. Ask Creon! It was Creon that you cared for.
Ismene. O why taunt me, when it does not help you?   540
Antigone. If I do taunt you, it is to my pain.
Ismene. Can I not help you, even at this late hour?
Antigone. Save your own life. I grudge not your escape.
Ismene. Alas! Can I not join you in your fate?

Antigone. You cannot: you chose life, and I chose death.
Ismene. But not without the warning that I gave you!
Antigone. Some thought *you* wise; the dead commended me.
Ismene. But my offense has been as great as yours.
Antigone. Be comforted; you live, but I have given
   My life already, in service of the dead.   550
Creon. Of these two girls, one has been driven frantic,
   The other has been frantic since her birth.
Ismene. Not so, my lord; but when disaster comes
   The reason that one has can not stand firm.
Creon. Yours did not, when you chose to partner crime!
Ismene. But what is life to me, without my sister?
Creon. Say not "my sister": sister you have none.
Ismene. But she is Haemon's bride — and can you kill her?
Creon. Is she the only woman he can bed with?
Ismene. The only one so joined in love with him.   560
Creon. I hate a son to have an evil wife.
Antigone. O my dear Haemon! How your father wrongs you!
Creon. I hear too much of you and of your marriage.
Ismene. He is your son; how can you take her from him?
Creon. It is not I, but Death, that stops this wedding.
Chorus-leader. It is determined, then, that she must die?
Creon. For you, and me, determined. (*To the guards*) Take
                                         them in
   At once; no more delay. Henceforward let
   Them stay at home, like women, not roam abroad.
   Even the bold, you know, will seek escape   570
   When they see death at last standing beside them.

     Exit Antigone and Ismene into the palace, guarded. Creon remains.

THIRD ODE

Strophe 1

Chorus. Thrice happy are they who have never known disaster!
   Once a house is shaken of Heaven, disaster
   Never leaves it, from generation to generation.
     'Tis even as the swelling sea,
      When the roaring wind from Thrace
   Drives blustering over the water and makes it black:
     It bears up from below

A thick, dark cloud of mud,
And groaning cliffs repel the smack of wind and angry   *580*
                                                    breakers.

Antistrophe 1

I see, in the house of our kings, how ancient sorrows
    Rise again; disaster is linked with disaster.
    Woe again must each generation inherit. Some god
    Besets them, nor will give release.
    On the last of royal blood
There gleamed a shimmering light in the house of Oedipus.
    But Death comes once again
    With blood-stained axe, and hews
The sapling down; and Frenzy lends her aid, and vengeful
                                                    Madness.

Strophe 2

Thy power, Zeus, is almighty! No   *590*
    Mortal insolence can oppose Thee!
Sleep, which conquers all else, cannot overcome Thee,
    Nor can the never-wearied
    Years, but throughout
    Time Thou art strong and ageless,
        In thy own Olympus
    Ruling in radiant splendor.
    For today, and in all past time,
    And through all time to come,
    This is the law: that in Man's   *600*
Life every success brings with it some disaster.

Antistrophe 2

Hope springs high, and to many a man
    Hope brings comfort and consolation;
Yet she is to some nothing but fond illusion:
    Swiftly they come to ruin,
    As when a man
    Treads unawares on hot fire.
        For it was a wise man
    First made that ancient saying:
    To the man whom God will ruin   *610*
    One day shall evil seem

Good, in his twisted judgment
He comes in a short time to fell disaster.
Chorus-leader. See, here comes Haemon, last-born of your children,
　Grieving, it may be, for Antigone.
Creon. Soon we shall know, better than seers can tell us.

　　Enter Haemon.

My son:
You have not come in rage against your father
Because your bride must die? Or are you still
My loyal son, whatever I may do?　　　　　　　　　620
Haemon. Father, I am your son; may your wise judgment
Rule me, and may I always follow it.
No marriage shall be thought a greater prize
For me to win than your good government.
Creon. So may you ever be resolved, my son,
In all things to be guided by your father.
It is for this men pray that they may have
Obedient children, that they may requite
Their father's enemy with enmity
And honor whom their father loves to honor.　　　630
One who begets unprofitable children
Makes trouble for himself, and gives his foes
Nothing but laughter. Therefore do not let
Your pleasure in a woman overcome
Your judgment, knowing this, that if you have
An evil wife to share your house, you'll find
Cold comfort in your bed. What other wound
Can cut so deep as treachery at home?
So, think this girl your enemy; spit on her
And let her find her husband down in Hell!　　　640
She is the only one that I have found
In all the city disobedient.
I will not make myself a liar. I
Have caught her; I will kill her. Let her sing
Her hymns to Sacred Kinship! If I breed
Rebellion in the house, then it is certain
There'll be no lack of rebels out of doors.
No man can rule a city uprightly
Who is not just in ruling his own household.
Never will I approve of one who breaks　　　650
And violates the law, or would dictate
To those who rule. Lawful authority

Must be obeyed in all things, great or small,
Just and unjust alike; and such a man
Would win my confidence both in command
And as a subject; standing at my side
In the storm of battle he would hold his ground,
Not leave me unprotected. But there is
No greater curse than disobedience.
This brings destruction on a city, this   660
Drives men from hearth and home, this brings about
A sudden panic in the battle-front.
Where all goes well, obedience is the cause.
So we must vindicate the law; we must not be
Defeated by a woman. Better far
Be overthrown, if need be, by a man
Than to be called the victim of a woman.

Chorus-leader. Unless the years have stolen away our wits,
    All you say is said most prudently.

Haemon. Father, it is the gods who give us wisdom;   670
    No gift of theirs more precious. I cannot say
    That you are wrong, nor would I ever learn
    That impudence, although perhaps another
    Might fairly say it. But it falls to me,
    Being your son, to note what others say,
    Or do, or censure in you, for your glance
    Intimidates the common citizen;
    He will not say, before your face, what might
    Displease you; I can listen freely, how
    The city mourns this girl. "No other woman,"   680
    So they are saying, "so undeservedly
    Has been condemned for such a glorious deed.
    When her own brother had been slain in battle
    She would not let his body lie unburied
    To be devoured by dogs or birds of prey.
    Is not this worthy of a crown of gold?" —
    Such is the muttering that spreads everywhere.
        Father, no greater treasure can I have
    Than your prosperity; no son can find
    A greater prize than his own father's fame,   690
    No father than his son's. Therefore let not
    This single thought possess you: only what
    You say is right, and nothing else. The man
    Who thinks that he alone is wise, that he
    Is best in speech or counsel, such a man
    Brought to the proof is found but emptiness.

There's no disgrace, even if one is wise,
In learning more, and knowing when to yield.
See how the trees that grow beside a torrent
Preserve their branches, if they bend; the others,   **700**
Those that resist, are torn out, root and branch.
So too the captain of a ship; let him
Refuse to shorten sail, despite the storm —
He'll end his voyage bottom uppermost.
No, let your anger cool, and be persuaded.
If one who is still young can speak with sense,
Then I would say that he does best who has
Most understanding; second best, the man
Who profits from the wisdom of another.

Chorus-leader. My lord, he has not spoken foolishly;   **710**
    You each can learn some wisdom from the other.

Creon. What? men of our age go to school again
    And take a lesson from a very boy?

Haemon. If it is worth the taking. I am young,
    But think what should be done, not of my age.

Creon. What should be done! To honor disobedience!

Haemon. I would not have you honor criminals.

Creon. And is this girl then not a criminal?

Haemon. The city with a single voice denies it.

Creon. Must I give orders then by their permission?   **720**

Haemon. If youth is folly, this is childishness.

Creon. Am I to rule for them, not for myself?

Haemon. That is not government, but tyranny.

Creon. The king is lord and master of his city.

Haemon. Then you had better rule a desert island!

Creon. This man, it seems, is the ally of the woman.

Haemon. If you're the woman, yes! I fight for you.

Creon. Villain! Do you oppose your father's will?

Haemon. Only because you are opposing Justice.

Creon. When I regard my own prerogative?   **730**

Haemon. Opposing God's, you disregard your own.

Creon. Scoundrel, so to surrender to a woman!

Haemon. But not to anything that brings me shame.

Creon. Your every word is in defence of her.

Haemon. And me, and you — and of the gods below.

Creon. You shall not marry her this side the grave!

Haemon. So, she must die — and will not die alone.

Creon. What? Threaten me? Are you so insolent?

Haemon. It is no threat, if I reply to folly.

Creon. The fool would teach me sense! You'll pay for it.   **740**

Haemon. I'd call you mad, if you were not my father.
Creon. I'll hear no chatter from a woman's plaything.
Haemon. Would you have all the talk, and hear no answer?
Creon. So?
   I swear to God, you shall not bandy words
   With me and not repent it! Bring her out,
   That loathsome creature! I will have her killed
   At once, before her bridegroom's very eyes.
Haemon. How can you think it? I will not see that,
   Nor shall you ever see my face again.   750
   Those friends of yours who can must tolerate
   Your raging madness; I will not endure it.

> *Exit Haemon.*

Chorus-leader. How angrily he went, my lord! The young,
   When they are greatly hurt, grow desperate.
Creon. Then let his pride and folly do their worst!
   He shall not save these women from their doom.
Chorus-leader. Is it your purpose then to kill them both?
Creon. Not her who had no part in it. — I thank you.
Chorus-leader. And for the other: how is she to die?
Creon. I'll find a cave in some deserted spot,   760
   And there I will imprison her alive
   With so much food — no more — as will avert
   Pollution and a curse upon the city.
   There let her pray to Death, the only god
   Whom she reveres, to rescue her from death,
   Or learn at last, though it be late, that it
   Is wanton folly to respect the dead.

> *Creon remains on the stage.*

FOURTH ODE

Strophe

Chorus. Invincible, implacable Love, O
   Love, that makes havoc of all wealth;
   That peacefully keeps his night-watch   770
   On tender cheek of a maiden:
   The Sea is no barrier, nor

Mountainous waste to Love's flight; for
No one can escape Love's domination,
Man, no, nor immortal god. Love's
Prey is possessed by madness.

Antistrophe

By Love, the mind even of the just
  Is bent awry; he becomes unjust.
  So here: it is Love that stirred up
  This quarrel of son with father.   *780*
  The kindling light of Love in the soft
  Eye of a bride conquers, for
  Love sits on his throne, one of the great Powers;
  Nought else can prevail against
  Invincible Aphrodite.

*Enter Antigone, under guard. (From this point up to the end of
the fifth ode everything is sung, except the two speeches in blank
verse.)*

Chorus. I too, when I see this sight, cannot stay
(Anapests) Within bounds; I cannot keep back my tears
  Which rise like a flood. For behold, they bring
  Antigone here, on the journey that all
  Must make, to the silence of Hades.   *790*

COMMOS

Strophe 1

Antigone. Behold me, O lords of my native city!
(Glyconics) Now do I make my last journey;
    Now do I see the last
  Sun that ever I shall behold.
  Never another! Death, that lulls
  All to sleep, takes me while I live
  Down to the grim shore of Acheron.
    No wedding day can be
  Mine, no hymn will be raised to honor
  Marriage of mine; for I   *800*
Go to espouse the bridegroom, Death.

Chorus. Yet a glorious death, and rich in fame
(Anapests) Is yours; you go to the silent tomb
  Not smitten with wasting sickness, nor
  Repaying a debt to the sharp-edged sword;
  But alone among mortals you go to the home
  Of the dead while yet you are living.

Antistrophe 1

Antigone. They tell of how cruelly she did perish,
(Glyconics) Niobe, Queen in Thebes;
  For, as ivy grows on a tree,   *810*
  Strangling it, so she slowly turned to
  Stone on a Phrygian mountain-top.
  Now the rain-storms wear her away —
    So does the story run — and
  Snow clings to her always:
  Tears fall from her weeping eyes for
  Ever and ever. Like to hers, the
  Cruel death that now awaits me.
Chorus. But she was a goddess, and born of the gods;
(Anapests) We are but mortals, of mortals born.   *820*
  For a mortal to share in the doom of a god,
  That brings her renown while yet she lives,
  And a glory that long will outlive her.

Strophe 2

Antigone. Alas, they laugh! O by the gods of Thebes, my
(more passionate rhythm)   native city,
  Mock me, if you must, when I am gone, not to my face!
  O Thebes my city, O you lordly men of Thebes!
  O water of Dirkê's stream! Holy soil where our chariots run!
  You, you do I call upon; you, you shall testify
  How all unwept of friends, by what harsh decree,
  They send me to the cavern that shall be my everlasting
                             grave.   *830*
  Ah, cruel doom! to be banished from earth, nor welcomed
  Among the dead, set apart, for ever!
Chorus. Too bold, too reckless, you affronted
(more spirited) Justice. Now that awful power
  Takes terrible vengeance, O my child.
  For some old sin you make atonement.

Antistrophe 2

Antigone. My father's sin! There is the source of all my anguish.
    Harsh fate that befell my father! Harsh fate that has held
    Fast in its grip the whole renowned race of Labdacus!
    O the blind madness of my father's and my mother's
                                        marriage!   *840*
    O cursed union of a son with his own mother!
    From such as those I draw my own unhappy life;
    And now I go to dwell with them, unwedded and accursed.
    O brother, through an evil marriage you were slain; and I
    Live — but your dead hand destroys me.
Chorus. Such loyalty is a holy thing.
      Yet none that holds authority
      Can brook disobedience, O my child.
    Your self-willed pride has been your ruin.

Epode

Antigone. Unwept, unwedded and unbefriended,   *850*
    Alone, pitilessly used,
    Now they drag me to death.
    Never again, O thou Sun in the heavens,
    May I look on thy holy radiance!
    Such is my fate, and no one laments it;
    No friend is here to mourn me.
Creon. Enough of this! If tears and lamentations
    Could stave off death they would go on for ever.
    Take her away at once, and wall her up
    Inside a cavern, as I have commanded,   *860*
    And leave her there, alone, in solitude.
    Her home shall be her tomb; there she may live
    Or die, as she may choose: my hands are clean;
    But she shall live no more among the living.
Antigone. O grave, my bridal-chamber, everlasting
    Prison within a rock: now I must go
    To join my own, those many who have died
    And whom Persephone has welcomed home;
    And now to me, the last of all, so young,
    Death comes, so cruelly. And yet I go   *870*
    In the sure hope that you will welcome me,
    Father, and you, my mother; you, my brother.
    For when you died it was my hands that washed
    And dressed you, laid you in your graves, and poured

The last libations. Now, because to you,
Polyneices, I have given burial,
To me they give a recompense like this!
Yet what I did, the wise will all approve.
For had I lost a son, or lost a husband,
Never would I have ventured such an act   *880*
Against the city's will. And wherefore so?
My husband dead, I might have found another;
Another son from him, if I had lost
A son. But since my mother and my father
Have both gone to the grave, there can be none
Henceforth that I can ever call my brother.
It was for this I paid you such an honor,
Dear Polyneices, and in Creon's eyes
Thus wantonly and gravely have offended.
So with rude hands he drags me to my death.   *890*
No chanted wedding-hymn, no bridal-joy,
No tender care of children can be mine;
But like an outcast, and without a friend,
They take me to the cavernous home of death.
What ordinance of the gods have I transgressed?
Why should I look to Heaven any more
For help, or seek an ally among men?
If this is what the gods approve, why then,
When I am dead I shall discern my fault;
If theirs the sin, may they endure a doom   *900*
No worse than mine, so wantonly inflicted!
Chorus. Still from the same quarter the same wild winds
(Anapests) Blow fiercely, and shake her stubborn soul.
Creon. And therefore, for this, these men shall have cause,
(Anapests) Bitter cause, to lament their tardiness.
Chorus. I fear these words bring us closer yet
               To the verge of death.
Creon. I have nothing to say, no comfort to give:
   The sentence is passed, and the end is here.
Antigone. O city of Thebes where my fathers dwelt,   *910*
    O gods of our race,
  Now at last their hands are upon me!
  You princes of Thebes, O look upon me,
  The last that remain of a line of kings!
  How savagely impious men use me,
  For keeping a law that is holy.

             Exit Antigone, under guard. Creon remains.

FIFTH ODE

Strophe 1

Chorus. There was one in days of old who was imprisoned
(slow three-time) In a chamber like a grave, within a tower:
    Fair Danaë, who in darkness was held, and never saw the
                                              pure daylight.
    Yet she too, O my child, was of an ancient line,   *920*
    Entrusted with divine seed that had come in shower of gold.
    Mysterious, overmastering, is the power of Fate.
(faster three-time) From this, nor wealth nor force of arms
        Nor strong encircling city-walls
        Nor storm-tossed ship can give deliverance.

Antistrophe 1

    Close bondage was ordained by Dionysus
    For one who in a frenzy had denied
    His godhead: in a cavern Lycurgus, for his sin, was imprisoned.
    In such wise did his madness bear a bitter fruit,
    Which withered in a dungeon. So he learned it was a god *930*
    He had ventured in his blindness to revile and taunt.
        The sacred dances he had tried
        To quell, and end the Bacchic rite,
        Offending all the tuneful Muses.

Strophe 2

(Fairly fast, becoming faster; three- and four-time mixed) There is
                a town by the rocks where a sea meets another sea,
    Two black rocks by the Bosphorus, near the Thracian coast,
    Salmŷdessus; and there a wife had been spurned,
        Held close in bitter constraint.*
        Then upon both her children
    A blinding wound fell from her cruel rival: *940*
    With shuttle in hand she smote the open eyes with sharp
    And blood-stained point, and brought to Phineus'
    Two sons a darkness that cried for vengeance.

---

* These two verses are a paraphrase rather than a translation. It seemed better to give the audience something which it could follow rather than the mythological reference in the Greek, which it certainly would not. [Kitto.]

Antistrophe 2

In bitter grief and despair they bewailed their unhappy lot,
Children born to a mother whose marriage proved accursed.
Yet she came of a race of ancient kings,
    Her sire the offspring of gods.
    Reared in a distant country,
    Among her fierce, northern father's tempests,
She went, a Boread, swift as horses, over the lofty   *950*
Mountains. Yet not even she was
Safe against the long-lived Fates, my daughter.

    Enter Teiresias, led by a boy.

Teiresias. My lords, I share my journey with this boy
    Whose eyes must see for both; for so the blind
    Must move abroad, with one to guide their steps.
Creon. Why, what is this? Why are *you* here, Teiresias?
Teiresias. I will explain; you will do well to listen.
Creon. Have I not always followed your good counsel?
Teiresias. You have; therefore we have been guided well.
Creon. I have had much experience of your wisdom.   *960*
Teiresias. Then think: once more you tread the razor's edge.
Creon. You make me tremble! What is it you mean?
Teiresias. What divination has revealed to me,
    That I will tell you. To my ancient seat
    Of augury I went, where all the birds
    Foregather. There I sat, and heard a clamor
    Strange and unnatural — birds screaming in rage.
    I knew that they were tearing at each other
    With murderous claws: the beating of their wings
    Meant nothing less than that: and I was frightened.   *970*
    I made a blazing fire upon the altar
    And offered sacrifice: it would not burn;
    The melting fat oozed out upon the embers
    And smoked and bubbled; high into the air
    The bladder spirted gall, and from the bones
    The fatty meat slid off and left them bare.
    Such omens, baffling, indistinct, I learned
    From him who guides me, as I am guide to others.
    Sickness has come upon us, and the cause
    Is you: our altars and our scared hearths   *980*
    Are all polluted by the dogs and birds
    That have been gorging on the fallen body

Of Polyneices. Therefore heaven will not
Accept from us our prayers, no fire will burn
Our offerings, nor will birds give out clear sounds,
For they are glutted with the blood of men.
Be warned, my son. No man alive is free
From error, but the wise and prudent man
When he has fallen into evil courses
Does not persist, but tries to find amendment.   *990*
It is the stubborn man who is the fool.
Yield to the dead, forbear to strike the fallen;
To slay the slain, is that a deed of valor?
Your good is what I seek; and that instruction
Is best that comes from wisdom, and brings profit.
Creon. Sir, all of you, like bowmen at a target,
Let fly your shafts at me. Now they have turned
Even diviners on me! By that tribe
I am bought and sold and stowed away on board.
Go, make your profits, drive your trade   *1000*
In Lydian silver or in Indian gold,
But him you shall not bury in a tomb,
No, not though Zeus' own eagles eat the corpse
And bear the carrion to their master's throne:
Not even so, for fear of that defilement,
Will I permit his burial — for well I know
That mortal man can not defile the gods.
But, old Teiresias, even the cleverest men
Fall shamefully when for a little money
They use fair words to mask their villainy.   *1010*
Teiresias. Does any man reflect, does any know . . .
Creon. Know *what?* Why do you preach at me like this?
Teiresias. How much the greatest blessing is good counsel?
Creon. As much, I think, as folly is his plague.
Teiresias. Yet with this plague you are yourself infected.
Creon. I will not bandy words with any prophet.
Teiresias. And yet you say my prophecies are dishonest!
Creon. Prophets have always been too fond of gold.
Teiresias. And tyrants, of the shameful use of power.
Creon. You know it is your King of whom you speak?   *1020*
Teiresias. King of the land I saved from mortal danger.
Creon. A clever prophet — but an evil one.
Teiresias. You'll rouse me to awaken my dark secret.
Creon. Awaken it, but do not speak for money.
Teiresias. And do you think that I am come to *that?*
Creon. You shall not buy and sell *my* policy.

Teiresias. Then I will tell you this: you will not live
    Through many circuits of the racing sun
    Before you give a child of your own body
    To make amends for murder, death for death;   *1030*
    Because you have thrust down within the earth
    One who should walk upon it, and have lodged
    A living soul dishonorably in a tomb;
    And impiously have kept upon the earth
    Unburied and unblest one who belongs
    Neither to you nor to the upper gods
    But to the gods below, who are despoiled
    By you. Therefore the gods arouse against you
    Their sure avengers; they lie in your path
    Even now to trap you and to make you pay   *1040*
    Their price. — Now think: do I say *this* for money?
    Not many hours will pass before your house
    Rings loud with lamentation, men and women.
    Hatred for you is moving in those cities
    Whose mangled sons had funeral-rites from dogs
    Or from some bird of prey, whose wings have carried
    The taint of dead men's flesh to their own homes,
    Polluting hearth and altar.
    These are the arrows that I launch at you,
    Because you anger me. I shall not miss   *1050*
    My aim, and you shall not escape their smart.
    Boy, lead me home again, that he may vent
    His rage upon some younger man, and learn
    To moderate his violent tongue, and find
    More understanding than he has today.

                                  Exit Teiresias.

Chorus-leader. And so, my lord, he leaves us, with a threat
    Of doom. I have lived long, but I am sure
    Of this: no single prophecy that he
    Has made to Thebes has gone without fulfilment.
Creon. I know it too, and I am terrified.   *1060*
    To yield is very hard, but to resist
    And meet disaster, that is harder still.
Chorus-leader. Creon, this is no time for wrong decison.
Creon. What shall I do? Advise me; I will listen.
Chorus-leader. Release Antigone from her rock-hewn dungeon,
    And lay the unburied body in a tomb.
Creon. Is this your counsel? You would have me yield?

Chorus-leader. I would, and quickly. The destroying hand
  Of Heaven is quick to punish human error.
Creon. How hard it is! And yet one cannot fight   *1070*
  Against Necessity. — I will give way.
Chorus-leader. Go then and do it; leave it not to others.
Creon. Just as I am I go. — You men-at-arms,
  You here, and those within: away at once
  Up to the hill, and take your implements.
  Now that my resolution is reversed
  I who imprisoned her will set her free. —
    I fear it may be wisest to observe
  Throughout one's life the laws that are established.

Exit Creon.

SIXTH ODE

Strophe 1

Chorus. Thou Spirit whose names are many, Dionysus,   *1080*
  Born to Zeus the loud-thunderer,
  Joy of thy Theban mother-nymph,
  Lover of famous Italy:
  King art thou in the crowded shrine
  Where Demeter has her abode, O
  Bacchus! Here is thy mother's home,
  Here is thine, by the smooth Is-
  mênus' flood, here where the savage
  Dragon's teeth had offspring.

Antistrophe 1

Thou art seen by the nymphs amid the smoky torchlight, *1090*
  Where, upon Parnassus' height,
  They hold revels to honor Thee
  Close to the spring of Castaly.
  Thou art come from the ivy-clad
  Slopes of Asian hills, and vineyards
  Hanging thick with clustering grapes.
  Mystic voices chant: "O
  Bacchus! O Bacchus!" in
  The roads and ways of Thebê.

Strophe 2

Here is thy chosen home,   *1100*
In Thebes above all lands,
With thy mother, bride of Zeus.
Wherefore, since a pollution holds
All our people fast in its grip,
O come with swift healing across the wall of high Parnassus,
Or over the rough Eurîpus.

Antistrophe 2

Stars that move, breathing flame,
Honor Thee as they dance;
Voices cry to Thee in the night.
Son begotten of Zeus, appear!   *1110*
Come, Lord, with thy company,
Thy own nymphs, who with wild, nightlong dances praise
                                                   Thee,
Bountiful Dionysus!

Enter a messenger.

Messenger. You noblemen of Thebes, how insecure
Is human fortune! Chance will overthrow
The great, and raise the lowly; nothing's firm,
Either for confidence or for despair;
No one can prophesy what lies in store.
An hour ago, how much I envied Creon!
He had saved Thebes, we had accorded him   *1120*
The sovereign power; he ruled our land
Supported by a noble prince, his son.
Now all is lost, and he who forfeits joy
Forfeits his life; he is a breathing corpse.
Heap treasures in your palace, if you will,
And wear the pomp of royalty; but if
You have no happiness, I would not give
A straw for all of it, compared with joy.
Chorus-leader. What is this weight of heavy news you bring?
Messenger. Death! — and the blood-guilt rests upon the
                                          living. *1130*
Chorus-leader. Death? Who is dead? And who has killed him?
                                          Tell me.
Messenger. Haemon is dead, and by no stranger's hand.

Chorus-leader. But by his father's? Or was it his own?
Messenger. His own — inflamed with anger at his father.
Chorus-leader. Yours was no idle prophecy, Teiresias!
Messenger. That is my news. What next, remains with you.
Chorus-leader. But look! There is his wife, Eurydice;
    She is coming from the palace. Has she heard
    About her son, or is she here by chance?

    Enter Eurydice.

Eurydice. You citizens of Thebes, I overheard   *1140*
    When I was standing at the gates, for I
    Had come to make an offering at the shrine
    Of Pallas, and my hand was on the bar
    That holds the gate, to draw it; then there fell
    Upon my ears a voice that spoke of death.
    My terror took away my strength; I fell
    Into my servants' arms and swooned away.
    But tell it me once more; I can endure
    To listen; I am no stranger to bad news.
Messenger. Dear lady, I was there, and I will tell   *1150*
    The truth; I will not keep it back from you.
    Why should I gloze it over? You would hear
    From someone else, and I should seem a liar.
    The truth is always best.
                                I went with Creon
    Up to the hill where Polyneices' body
    Still lay, unpitied, torn by animals.
    We gave it holy washing, and we prayed
    To Hecate and Pluto that they would
    Restrain their anger and be merciful.
    And then we cut some branches, and we burned   *1160*
    What little had been left, and built a mound
    Over his ashes of his native soil.
    Then, to the cavern, to the home of death,
    The bridal-chamber with its bed of stone.
    One of us heard a cry of lamentation
    From that unhallowed place; he went to Creon
    And told him. On the wind, as he came near,
    Cries of despair were borne. He groaned aloud
    In anguish: "O, and are my fears come true?
    Of all the journeys I have made, am I   *1170*
    To find this one the most calamitous?
    It is my son's voice greets me. Hurry, men;

Run to the place, and when you reach the tomb
Creep in between the gaping stones and see
If it be Haemon there, or if the gods
Are cheating me." Upon this desperate order
We ran and looked. Within the furthest chamber
We saw her hanging, dead; strips from her dress
Had served her for a rope. Haemon we saw
Embracing her dead body and lamenting   *1180*
His loss, his father's deed, and her destruction.
When Creon saw him he cried out in anguish,
Went in, and called to him: "My son! my son!
O why? What have you done? What brought you here?
What is this madness? O come out, my son,
Come, I implore you!" Haemon glared at him
With anger in his eyes, spat in his face,
Said nothing, drew his double-hilted sword,
But missed his aim as Creon leapt aside.
Then in remorse he leaned upon the blade   *1190*
And drove it half its length into his body.
While yet the life was in him he embraced
The girl with failing arms, and breathing hard
Poured out his life-blood on to her white face.
So side by side they lie, and both are dead.
Not in this world but in the world below
He wins his bride, and shows to all mankind
That folly is the worst of human evils.

Exit Eurydice.

Chorus-leader. What can we think of this? The Queen is gone
  Without one word of good or evil omen.   *1200*
Messenger. What can it mean? But yet we may sustain
  The hope that she would not display her grief
  In public, but will rouse the sad lament
  For Haemon's death among her serving-women
  Inside the palace. She has true discretion,
  And she would never do what is unseemly.
Chorus-leader. I cannot say, but wild lament would be
  Less ominous than this unnatural silence.
Messenger. It *is* unnatural; there may be danger.
  I'll follow her; it may be she is hiding   *1210*
  Some secret purpose in her passionate heart.

Exit Messenger, into the palace.

Chorus. Look, Creon draws near, and the burden he bears
(Anapests) Gives witness to his misdeeds; the cause
                Lies only in his blind error.

      *Enter Creon and the guards, with the body of Haemon.**

Strophe 1

Creon. Alas!
    The wrongs I have done by ill-counseling!
      Cruel and fraught with death.
      You behold, men of Thebes,
    The slayer, the slain; a father, a son.
    My own stubborn ways have borne bitter fruit.   *1220*
    My son! Dead, my son! So soon torn from me,
      So young, so young!
    The fault only mine, not yours, O my son.
Chorus-leader. Too late, too late you see the path of wisdom.
Creon. Alas!
    A bitter lesson I have learned! The god
    Coming with all his weight has borne down on me,
      And smitten me with all his cruelty;
    My joy overturned, trampled beneath his feet.
    What suffering besets the whole race of men!   *1230*

      Enter Messenger, from the palace.

Messenger. My master, when you came you brought a burden
    Of sorrow with you; now, within your house,
    A second store of misery confronts you.
Creon. Another sorrow come to crown my sorrow?
Messenger. The Queen, true mother of her son, is dead;
    In grief she drove a blade into her heart.

Antistrophe 1

Creon. Alas!
    Thou grim hand of death, greedy and unappeased,
      Why so implacable?

---

* From this point up to the final utterance of the chorus the dialogue is in strictly strophic form. Creon's lines, except those rendered in blank verse, are sung; they are in the strongly marked dochmiac rhythm. [Kitto.]

Voice of doom, you who bring   *1240*
Such dire news of grief, O, can it be true?
What have you said, my son? O, you have slain the slain!
Tell me, can it be true? Is death crowning death?
    My wife! my wife!
My son dead, and now my wife taken too!

Eurydice's body is discovered.

Chorus-leader. But raise your eyes: there is her lifeless body.
Creon. Alas!
    Here is a sorrow that redoubles sorrow.
    Where will it end? What else can Fate hold in store?
    While yet I clasp my dead son in my arms   *1250*
    Before me there lies another struck by death.
    Alas cruel doom! the mother's and the son's.
Messenger. She took a sharp-edged knife, stood by the altar,
    And made lament for Megareus who was killed
    Of old, and next for Haemon. Then at last,
    Invoking evil upon you, the slayer
    Of both her sons, she closed her eyes in death.

Strophe 2

Creon. A curse, a thing of terror! O, is there none
    Will unsheathe a sword to end all my woes
    With one deadly thrust? My grief crushes me.   *1260*
Messenger. She cursed you for the guilt of Haemon's death
    And of the other son who died before.
Creon. What did she do? How did she end her life?
Messenger. She heard my bitter story; then she put
    A dagger to her heart and drove it home.
Creon. The guilt falls on me alone; none but I
    Have slain her; no other shares in the sin.
    'Twas I dealt the blow. This is the truth, my friends.
    Away, take me away, far from the sight of men!
    My life now is death. Lead me away from here.   *1270*
Chorus-leader. That would be well, if anything is well.
    Briefest is best when such disaster comes.

Antistrophe 2

Creon. O come, best of all the days I can see,
    The last day of all, the day that brings death.

O come quickly! Come, thou night with no dawn!
Chorus-leader. That's for the future; here and now are duties
    That fall on those to whom they are allotted.
Creon. I prayed for death; I wish for nothing else.
Chorus-leader. Then pray no more; from suffering that has been
    Decreed no man will ever find escape.   *1280*
Creon. Lead me away, a rash, a misguided man,
    Whose blindness has killed a wife and a son.
    O where can I look? What strength can I find?
    On me has fallen a doom greater than I can bear.

          Exit Creon and guards into the palace.

Chorus. Of happiness, far the greatest part
(Anapests) Is wisdon, and reverence towards the gods.
    Proud words of the arrogant man, in the end,
    Meet punishment, great as his pride was great,
    Till at last he is schooled in wisdom.

QUESTIONS

1. Would you use masks for some (or all) of the characters? If so, masks that fully cover the face, Greek-style, or some sort of half-masks?

2. How would you costume the players? Would you dress them as the Greeks might have? Why? (One argument sometimes used by those who hold that modern productions of Greek drama should use classical costumes is that Greek drama *ought* to be remote and ritualistic. Evaluate this view.) What sort of modern dress might be effective?

3. If you were directing a college production of *Antigone,* how large a chorus would you use? (Sophocles is said to have used a chorus of fifteen.) Would you have the chorus recite (or chant) the choral passages in unison, or would you assign lines to single speakers?

4. If you have read *Oedipus the King,* compare and contrast the Creon of *Antigone* with the Creon of *Oedipus.*

5. Although Sophocles called his play *Antigone,* many critics say that Creon is the real tragic hero, pointing out that Antigone is absent from the last third of the play. Evaluate this view.

6. In some Greek tragedies, fate plays a great role in bringing about the downfall of the tragic hero. Although there are references to the curse on the House of Oedipus in *Antigone,*

do you feel that Antigone goes to her death as a result of the workings of fate? Do you feel that fate is responsibe for Creon's fall? Are both Antigone and Creon the creators of their own tragedy?

7. Are the words *hamartia* and *hybris* (page 596) relevant to Antigone? To Creon?

8. Why does Creon, contrary to the chorus's advice (lines 1065–1066), bury the body of Polyneices before he releases Antigone? Does his action show a zeal for piety as short-sighted as his earlier zeal for law? Is his action plausible, in view of the facts that Teiresias has dwelt on the wrong done to Polyneices and that Antigone has ritual food to sustain her? Or are we not to worry about Creon's motive?

9. A "foil" is a character who, by contrast, sets off or helps define another character. To what extent is Ismene a foil to Antigone? Is she entirely without courage?

10. What function does Eurydice serve? How deeply do we feel about her fate?

21
Comedy

Though etymology is not always helpful (after all, is it really illuminating to say that "tragedy" may come from a Greek word meaning "goat song"?), the etymology of "comedy" helps to reveal comedy's fundamental nature. **Comedy** (Greek: *komoidia*) is a revel-song; ancient Greek comedies are descended from fertility rituals, and they dramatize the joy of renewal, the joy of triumphing over obstacles, the joy of being (in a sense) reborn. The movement of tragedy, speaking roughly, is from prosperity to disaster; the movement of comedy is from some sort of minor disaster to prosperity.

To say, however, that comedy dramatizes the triumph over obstacles is to describe it as though it were melodrama, a play in which, after hairbreadth adventures, good prevails over evil, often in the form of the hero's unlikely last-minute rescue of the fair Belinda from the clutches of the villain. What distinguishes comedy from melodrama is the pervasive high spirits of comedy. The joyous ending in comedy — usually a marriage — is in the spirit of what has gone before; the entire play, not only the end, is a celebration of fecundity.

The threats in the world of comedy are not taken very seriously; the parental tyranny that helps make *Romeo and Juliet* and *Antigone* tragedies is, in comedy, laughable throughout. Parents may fret, fume, and lock doors, but in doing so they make themselves ridiculous, for love will find a way. Villains may threaten, but the audience never takes the threats seriously.

In the first act of *As You Like It,* Rosalind, at the mercy of a cruel uncle who has driven her father from his own dukedom, says: "O, how full of briers is this working-day world." The immediate reply is, "They are but burrs, cousin, thrown upon thee in holiday foolery." And this spirit of holiday foolery dominates the whole play and culminates in marriage, the symbol of life renewing itself. In the last act of a comedy things work out — as from the start we knew they would; whereas *Antigone* concludes with Creon looking at the corpses of his wife, son, and intended daughter-in-law, a comedy usually concludes with preparation for a marriage.

These marriages and renewals of society, so usual at the end of comedy, are most improbable, but they do not therefore weaken the comedy. The stuff of comedy is, in part, improbability. In *A Midsummer Night's Dream,* Puck speaks for the spectator when he says:

> And those things do best please me
> That befall preposterously.

In tragedy, probability is important; in comedy, the improbable is often desirable, for at least three reasons. First, comedy seeks to include as much as possible, to reveal the rich abundance of life. The motto of comedy (and the implication in the weddings with which it usually concludes) is the more the merrier. Second, the improbable is the surprising; surprise often evokes laughter, and laughter surely has a central place in comedy. Third, by getting his or her characters into improbable situations, the dramatist can show off the absurdity of their behavior — a point that needs amplification.

Comedy often shows the absurdity of ideals. The miser, the puritan, the health-faddist, and so on, are people of ideals, but their ideals are suffocating. The miser, for example, treats everything in terms of money; the miser's ideal causes him or her to renounce much of the abundance and joy of life. He or she is in love, but is unwilling to support a spouse; or he or she has a headache, but will not be so extravagant as to take an aspirin tablet. If a thief accosts the miser with "Your money or your life," the miser will prefer to give up his or her life — and that is what in fact he or she has been doing all the while. Now, by putting this miser in a series of improbable situations, the dramatist can continue to demonstrate entertainingly the miser's absurdity.*

---

* A character who is dominated by a single trait — avarice, jealousy, timidity, and so forth — is sometimes called a **humor character.** Medieval and Renaissance psychology held that a man's personality depended on the mixture of four liquids (humors): blood (Latin: *sanguis*), choler, phlegm, and bile. An overabundance of one fluid produced a dominant trait, and even today "sanguine," "choleric," "phlegmatic," and "bilious" describe personalities.

Not all comedy, of course, depends on humor characters placed in situations that exhibit their absurdity. **High comedy** is largely verbal, depending on witty language; **farce,** at the other extreme, is dependent on inherently ludicrous situations, for example, a hobo is mistaken for a millionaire. Situation comedy, then, may use humor characters, but it need not do so.

The comic protagonist's tenacious hold on his or her ideals is not very far from that of the tragic protagonist. In general, however, tragedy suggests the nobility of ideals; the tragic hero's ideals undo him or her, and they may be ideals about which we have serious reservations, but still we admire the nobility of these ideals. Romeo and Juliet will not put off their love for each other; Antigone will not yield to Creon, and Creon holds almost impossibly long to his stern position. But the comic protagonist who is always trying to keep his or her hands clean is funny; we laugh at this refusal to touch dirt with the rest of us, this refusal to enjoy the abundance life has to offer. The comic protagonist who is always talking about his or her beloved is funny; we laugh at his or her failure to see that the world is filled with people more attractive than the one who obsesses him or her.

In short, the ideals for which the tragic protagonist loses the world seem important to us and gain, in large measure, our sympathy, but the ideals for which the comic protagonist loses the world seem trivial compared with the rich variety that life has to offer, and we laugh at their absurdity. The tragic figure makes a claim on our sympathy. The absurd comic figure continually sets up obstacles to our sympathetic interest; we feel detached from, superior to, and amused by him or her. Something along these lines is behind William Butler Yeats's insistence that character is always present in comedy but not in tragedy. Though Yeats is eccentric in his notion that individual character is obliterated in tragedy, he interestingly gets at one of the important elements in comedy:

> When the tragic reverie is at its height . . . [we do not say,] "How well that man is realized. I should know him were I to meet him in the street," for it is always ourselves that we see upon the [tragic] stage. . . . Tragedy must always be a drowning and breaking of the dikes that separate man from man, and . . . it is upon these dikes comedy keeps house.

Most comic plays can roughly be sorted into one of two types: romantic comedy and satiric comedy. Romantic comedy presents an ideal world, a golden world, a world more delightful than our own; if there are difficulties in it, they are not briers but "burrs . . . thrown . . . in holiday foolery." It is the world of most of Shakespeare's comedies, a world of Illyria, of the Forest of Arden, of Belmont. The chief figures are young lovers; the course of their love is not smooth, but the outcome is never in doubt and the course is the more fun for being bumpy. Occasionally in this golden world there is a villain, but if so, the villain is a great bungler who never really does any harm; the world seems to be guided by a benevolent providence who prevents villains from seriously harming even themselves. In these plays, the world belongs to golden lads and lasses. When we laugh, we laugh not so much *at* them as *with* them.

If romantic comedy shows us a world with more attractive people than we find in our own, satiric comedy shows us a world with less attractive people. The satiric world seems dominated by morally inferior people — the decrepit wooer, the jealous spouse, the demanding parent. These unengaging figures go through their paces, revealing again and again their absurdity. The audience laughs at (rather than with) such figures, and writers justify this kind of comedy by claiming to reform society: antisocial members of the audience will see their grotesque images on the stage and will reform themselves when they leave the theater. But it is hard to believe that this theory is rooted in fact. Jonathan Swift (as we mentioned earlier) was probably right when he said, "Satire is a sort of glass wherein beholders do generally discover everybody's face but their own."

Near the conclusion of a satiric comedy, the obstructing characters are dismissed, often perfunctorily, allowing for a happy ending — commonly the marriage of figures less colorful than the obstructionist. And so all-encompassing are the festivities at the end that even obstructionists are invited to join in the wedding feast. If they refuse to join, we may find them — yet again — laughable rather than sympathetic, though admittedly one may also feel lingering regret that this somewhat shabby world of ours cannot live up to the exalted (even if rigid and rather crazy) standards of the outsider who refuses to go along with the way of the world.

Anton Chekhov (*Russian. 1860–1904*)

The Brute*
A Joke in One Act

English Version by Eric Bentley

List of Characters

Mrs. Popov, widow and landowner, small, with dimpled cheeks.
Mr. Grigory S. Smirnov, gentleman farmer, middle-aged.
Luka, Mrs. Popov's footman, an old man.
Gardener
Coachman
Hired Men

Scene.

The drawing room of a country house. Mrs. Popov, *in deep mourning, is staring hard at a photograph.* Luka *is with her.*

Luka. It's not right, ma'am, you're killing yourself. The cook has gone off with the maid to pick berries. The cat's having a high old time in the yard catching birds. Every living thing is happy. But you stay moping here in the house like it was a convent, taking no pleasure in nothing. I mean it, ma'am! It must be a full year since you set foot out of doors.

Mrs. Popov. I must never set foot out of doors again, Luka. Never! I have nothing to set foot out of doors *for.* My life is done. *He* is in his grave. I have buried myself alive in this house. We are *both* in our graves.

Luka. You're off again, ma'am. I just won't listen to you no more. Mr. Popov is dead, but what can we do about that? It's God's doing. God's will be done. You've cried over him, you've done your share of mourning, haven't you? There's a limit to everything. You can't go on weeping and wailing forever. My old lady died, for that matter, and I wept and wailed over her a whole month long. Well, that was it. I couldn't weep and wail all my life, she just wasn't worth it. (*He sighs.*) As for the neighbors, you've forgotten all about them, ma'am. You don't visit them and you don't let them visit you. You and I are like a pair of spiders — excuse the expression, ma'am — here we are in this house like a pair of spiders, we never see the light of day. And it isn't like there was no nice people around either. The whole county's swarming with 'em. There's a regiment quartered at Riblov, and the officers are so good-looking! The girls can't take their eyes off them — There's a ball at the camp every Friday — The military band plays most every day of the week — What do you say, ma'am? You're young, you're pretty, you could enjoy youself! Ten years from now you may want to strut and show your feathers to the officers, and it'll be too late.

Mrs. Popov (firmly). You must never bring this subject up again, Luka. Since Popov died, life has been an empty dream to me, you know that. *You* may think I am alive. Poor ignorant Luka! You are wrong. I am dead. I'm in my grave. Never more shall I see the light of day, never strip from my body this . . . raiment of death! Are you listening, Luka? Let his ghost learn how I love him! Yes, *I* know, and *you* know, he was often unfair to me, he was cruel to me, and he was unfaithful to me. What of it? *I* shall be faithful to *him,* that's all. I will show him how *I* can love. Hereafter, in a better world than this, he will welcome me back, the same loyal girl I always was —

Luka. Instead of carrying on this way, ma'am, you should go out in the garden and take a bit of a walk, ma'am. Or why not harness Toby and take a drive? Call on a couple of the neighbours, ma'am?

Mrs. Popov (breaking down). Oh, Luka!

Luka. Yes, ma'am? What have I said, ma'am? Oh dear!

Mrs. Popov. Toby! You said Toby! He adored that horse. When he drove me out to the Korchagins and the Vlasovs, it was always with Toby! He was a wonderful driver, do you remember, Luka? So graceful! So strong! I can see him now, pulling at those reins with all his might and main! Toby! Luka, tell them to give Toby an extra portion of oats today.

Luka. Yes, ma'am.

A bell rings.

Mrs. Popov. Who is that? Tell them I'm not at home.

Luka. Very good, ma'am. (*Exit.*)

Mrs. Popov (gazing again at the photograph). You shall see, my Popov, how a wife can love and forgive. Till death do us part. Longer than that. Till death re-unite us forever! (*Suddenly a titter breaks through her tears.*) Aren't you ashamed of yourself, Popov? Here's your little wife, being good, being faithful, so faithful she's locked up here waiting for her own funeral, while you — doesn't it make you ashamed, you naughty boy? You were terrible, you know. You were unfaithful, and you made those awful scenes about it, you stormed out and left me alone for weeks —

Enter Luka.

Luka (upset). There's someone asking for you, ma'am. Says he must —

Mrs. Popov. I suppose you told him that since my husband's death I see no one?

Luka. Yes, ma'am. I did, ma'am. But he wouldn't listen, ma'am. He says it's urgent.

Mrs. Popov (shrilly). I see no one!!

Luka. He won't take no for an answer, ma'am. He just curses and swears and comes in anyway. He's a perfect monster, ma'am. He's in the dining room right now.

Mrs. Popov. In the dining room, is he? I'll give him his come uppance. Bring him in here this minute.

Exit Luka.

(*Suddenly sad again.*) Why do they do this to me? Why? Insulting my grief, intruding on my solitude? (*She sighs.*) I'm afraid I'll have to enter a convent. I will, I *must* enter a convent!

Enter Mr. Smirnov and Luka.

Smirnov (to Luka). Dolt! Idiot! You talk too much! *(Seeing Mrs. Popov. With dignity.)* May I have the honor of introducing myself, madam? Gregory S. Smirnov, landowner and lieutenant of artillery, retired. Forgive me, madam, if I disturb your peace and quiet, but my business is both urgent and weighty.

Mrs. Popov (declining to offer him her hand). What is it you wish, sir?

Smirnov. At the time of his death, your late husband — with whom I had the honor to be acquainted, ma'am — was in my debt to the tune of twelve hundred rubles. I have two notes to prove it. Tomorrow, ma'am, I must pay the interest on a bank loan. I have therefore no alternative, ma'am, but to ask you to pay me the money today.

Mrs. Popov. Twelve hundred rubles? But what did my husband owe it to you for?

Smirnov. He used to buy his oats from me, madam.

Mrs. Popov (to Luka, with a sigh). Remember what I said, Luka: tell them to give Toby an extra portion of oats today!

Exit Luka.

My dear Mr. — what was the name again?

Smirnov. Smirnov, ma'am.

Mrs. Popov. My dear Mr. Smirnov, if Mr. Popov owed you money, you shall be paid — to the last ruble, to the last kopeck. But today — you must excuse me, Mr. — what was it?

Smirnov. Smirnov, ma'am.

Mrs. Popov. Today, Mr. Smirnov, I have no ready cash in the house. *(Smirnov starts to speak.)* Tomorrow, Mr. Smirnov, no, the day after tomorrow, all will be well. My steward will be back from town. I shall see that he pays what is owing. Today, no. In any case, today is exactly seven months from Mr. Popov's death. On such a day you will understand that I am in no mood to think of money.

Smirnov. Madam, if you don't pay up now, you can carry me out feet foremost. They'll seize my estate.

Mrs. Popov. You can have your money. *(He starts to thank her.)* Tomorrow. *(He again starts to speak.)* That is: the day after tomorrow.

Smirnov. I don't need the money the day after tomorrow. I need it today.

Mrs. Popov. I'm sorry, Mr. —

Smirnov (shouting). Smirnov!

Mrs. Popov (sweetly). Yes, of course. But you can't have it today.

Smirnov. But I can't wait for it any longer!

Mrs. Popov. Be sensible, Mr. Smirnov. How can I pay you if I don't have it?

Smirnov. You don't have it?

Mrs. Popov. I don't have it.

Smirnov. Sure?

Mrs. Popov. Positive.

Smirnov. Very well. I'll make a note to that effect. (*Shrugging.*) And then they want me to keep cool. I meet the tax commissioner on the street, and he says, "Why are you always in such a bad humor, Smirnov?" Bad humor! How can I help it, in God's name? I need money, I need it desperately. Take yesterday: I leave home at the crack of dawn, I call on all my debtors. Not a one of them pays up. Footsore and weary, I creep at midnight into some little dive, and try to snatch a few winks of sleep on the floor by the vodka barrel. Then today, I come here, fifty miles from home, saying to myself, "At last, at last, I can be sure of something," and you're not in the mood! You give me a mood! Christ, how can I help getting all worked up?

Mrs. Popov. I thought I'd made it clear, Mr. Smirnov, that you'll get your money the minute my steward is back from town?

Smirnov. What the hell do I care about your steward? Pardon the expression, ma'am. But it was you I came to see.

Mrs. Popov. What language! What a tone to take to a lady! I refuse to hear another word. (*Quickly, exit.*)

Smirnov. Not in the mood, huh? 'Exactly seven months since Popov's death,' huh? How about me? (*Shouting after her.*) Is there this interest to pay, or isn't there? I'm asking you a question: is there this interest to pay, or isn't there? So your husband died, and you're not in the mood, and your steward's gone off some place, and so forth and so on, but what can *I* do about all that, huh? What do *you* think I should do? Take a running jump and shove my head through the wall? Take off in a balloon? You don't know my *other* debtors. I call on Gruzdeff. Not at home. I look for Yaroshevitch. He's hiding out. I find Kooritsin. He kicks up a row, and I have to throw him through the window. I work my way right down the list. Not a kopeck. Then I come to you, and God damn it to hell, if you'll pardon the expression, you're not in the mood! (*Quietly, as he realizes he's talking to air.*) I've spoiled them all, that's what, I've let them play me for a sucker. Well, I'll show them. I'll show this one. I'll stay right here till she pays up. Ugh! *(He shudders with rage.)* I'm in a rage! I'm in a positively towering rage! Every nerve in my body is trembling at forty to the dozen! I can't breathe, I feel ill, I think I'm going to faint, hey, you there!

Enter Luka.

Luka. Yes, sir? Is there anything you wish, sir?
Smirnov. Water! Water! No, make it vodka.

Exit Luka.

Consider the logic of it. A fellow creature is desperately in need of cash, so desperately in need that he has to seriously contemplate hanging himself, and this woman, this mere chit of a girl, won't pay up, and why not? Because, forsooth, she isn't in the mood! Oh, the logic of women! Come to that, I never have liked them, I could do without the whole sex. Talk to a woman? I'd rather sit on a barrel of dynamite, the very thought gives me gooseflesh. Women! Creatures of poetry and romance! Just to see one in the distance gets me mad. My legs start twitching with rage. I feel like yelling for help.

Enter Luka, handing Smirnov a glass of water.

Luka. Mrs. Popov is indisposed, sir. She is seeing no one.
Smirnov. Get out.

Exit Luka.

Indisposed, is she? Seeing no one, huh? Well, she can see me or not, but I'll be here, I'll be right here till she pays up. If you're sick for a week, I'll be here for a week. If you're sick for a year, I'll be here for a year. You won't get around *me* with your widow's weeds and your schoolgirl dimples. I know all about dimples. *(Shouting through the window.)* Semyon, let the horses out of those shafts, we're not leaving, we're staying, and tell them to give the horses some oats, yes, oats, you fool, what do you think? *(Walking away from the window.)* What a mess, what an unholy mess! I didn't sleep last night, the heat is terrific today, not a damn one of 'em has paid up, and here's this — this skirt in mourning that's not in the mood! My head aches, where's that — *(He drinks from the glass.)* Water, ugh! You there!

Enter Luka.

Luka. Yes, sir. You wish for something, sir?
Smirnov. Where's that confounded vodka I asked for?

Exit Luka.

(Smirnov sits and looks himself over.) Oof! A fine figure of a man *I* am! Unwashed, uncombed, unshaven, straw on my vest, dust all over me. The little woman must've taken me for a highwayman. *(Yawns.)* I suppose it wouldn't be considered polite to barge into a drawing room in this state, but who cares? I'm not a visitor, I'm a creditor — most unwelcome of guests, second only to Death.

Enter Luka.

Luka (handing him the vodka). If I may say so, sir, you take too many liberties, sir.
Smirnov. What?!
Luka. Oh, nothing, sir, nothing.
Smirnov. Who in hell do you think you're talking to? Shut your mouth!
Luka (aside). There's an evil spirit abroad. The Devil must have sent him. Oh! *(Exit Luka.)*
Smirnov. What a rage I'm in! I'll grind the whole world to powder. Oh, I feel ill again. You there!

Enter Mrs. Popov.

Mrs. Popov (looking at the floor). In the solitude of my rural retreat, Mr. Smirnov, I've long since grown unaccustomed to the sound of the human voice. Above all, I cannot bear shouting. I must beg you not to break the silence.
Smirnov. Very well. Pay me my money and I'll go.
Mrs. Popov. I told you before, and I tell you again, Mr. Smirnov. I have no cash, you'll have to wait till the day after tomorrow. Can I express myself more plainly?
Smirnov. And *I* told *you* before, and *I* tell *you* again, that I need the money today, that the day after tomorrow is too late,

and that if you don't pay, and pay now, I'll have to hang myself in the morning!

Mrs. Popov. But I have no cash. This is quite a puzzle.

Smirnov. You won't pay, huh?

Mrs. Popov. I *can't* pay, Mr. Smirnov.

Smirnov. In that case, I'm going to sit here and wait. *(Sits down.)* You'll pay up the day after tomorrow? Very good. Till the day after tomorrow, here I sit. *(Pause. He jumps up.)* Now look, do I have to pay that interest tomorrow, or don't I? Or do you think I'm joking?

Mrs. Popov. I must ask you not to raise your voice, Mr. Smirnov. This is not a stable.

Smirnov. Who said it was? Do I have to pay the interest tomorrow or not?

Mrs. Popov. Mr. Smirnov, do you know how to behave in the presence of a lady?

Smirnov. No, madam, I do not know how to behave in the presence of a lady.

Mrs. Popov. Just what I thought. I look at you, and I say: ugh! I hear you talk, and I say to myself: "That man doesn't know how to talk to a lady."

Smirnov. You'd like me to come simpering to you in French, I suppose. *"Enchanté, madame! Merci beaucoup* for not paying zee money, *madame! Pardonnez-moi* if I 'ave disturbed you, *madame!* How *charmante* you look in mourning, *madame!"*

Mrs. Popov. Now you're being silly, Mr. Smirnov.

Smirnov (mimicking). "Now you're being silly, Mr. Smirnov." "You don't know how to talk to a lady, Mr. Smirnov." Look here, Mrs. Popov, I've known more women than you've known pussy cats. I've fought three duels on their account. I've jilted twelve, and been jilted by nine others. Oh, yes, Mrs. Popov, I've played the fool in my time, whispered sweet nothings, bowed and scraped and endeavored to please. Don't tell me I don't know what it is to love, to pine away with longing, to have the blues, to melt like butter, to be weak as water. I was full of tender emotion. I was carried away with passion. I squandered half my fortune on the sex. I chattered about women's emancipation. But there's an end to everything, dear madam. Burning eyes, dark eyelashes, ripe, red lips, dimpled cheeks, heaving bosoms, soft whisperings, the moon above; the lake below — I don't give a rap for that sort of nonsense any more, Mrs. Popov. I've found out about women. Present company excepted, they're liars. Their behavior is mere play acting; their conversation is sheer gossip. Yes, dear lady, women, young or old, are false, petty, vain, cruel, malicious, unreasonable. As for intelligence, any sparrow could give them points. Appearances, I admit, can be deceptive. In appearance, a woman may be all poetry and romance, goddess and angel, muslin and fluff. To look at her exterior is to be transported to heaven. But I have looked at her interior, Mrs. Popov, and what did I find there — in her very soul? A crocodile. *(He has gripped the back of the chair so firmly that it snaps.)* And, what is more revolting, a crocodile with an illusion, a crocodile that imagines tender sentiments are its own special province, a crocodile that thinks itself queen of the realm of love! Whereas, in sober fact, dear madam, if a woman can love anything except a lapdog you can hang me by the feet on that nail. For a man, love is suffering, love is sacrifice. A woman just swishes her train around and tightens her grip on your nose. Now, you're a woman, aren't you, Mrs. Popov? You must be an expert on some of this. Tell me, quite frankly, did you ever know a woman to be — faithful, for instance? Or even sincere? Only old hags, huh? Though some women are old hags from birth. But as for the others? You're right: a faithful woman is a freak of nature — like a cat with horns.

Mrs. Popov. Who *is* faithful, then? Who *have* you cast for the faithful lover? Not man?

Smirnov. Right first time, Mrs. Popov: man.

Mrs. Popov (going off into a peal of bitter laughter). Man! Man is faithful! that's a new one! *(Fiercely.)* What right do you have to say this, Mr. Smirnov? Men faithful? Let me tell you something. Of all the men I have ever known my late husband Popov was the best. I loved him, and there are women who know how to love, Mr. Smirnov. I gave him my youth, my happiness, my life, my fortune. I worshipped the ground he trod on — and what happened? The best of men was unfaithful to me, Mr. Smirnov. Not once in a while. All the time. After he died, I found his desk drawer full of love letters. While he was alive, he was always going away for the week-end. He squandered my money. He made love to other women before my very eyes. But, in spite of all, Mr. Smirnov, *I* was faithful. Unto death. And beyond. I am *still* faithful, Mr. Smirnov! Buried alive in this house, I shall wear mourning till the day I, too, am called to my eternal rest.

Smirnov (laughing scornfully). Expect me to believe that? As if I couldn't see through all this hocus-pocus. Buried alive! Till you're called to your eternal rest! Till when? Till some little poet — or some little subaltern with his first moustache — comes riding by and asks: "Can that be the house of the mysterious Tamara who for love of her late husband has buried herself alive, vowing to see no man?" Ha!

Mrs. Popov (flaring up). How dare you? How dare you insinuate — ?

Smirnov. You may have buried yourself alive, Mrs. Popov, but you haven't forgotten to powder your nose.

Mrs. Popov (incoherent). How dare you? How — ?

Smirnov. Who's raising his voice now? Just because I call a spade a spade. Because I shoot straight from the shoulder. Well, don't shout at me, I'm not your steward.

Mrs. Popov. I'm not shouting, you're shouting! Oh, leave me alone!

Smirnov. Pay me the money, and I will.

Mrs. Popov. You'll get no money out of me!

Smirnov. Oh, so that's it!

Mrs. Popov. Not a ruble, nót a kopeck. Get out! Leave me alone!

Smirnov. Not being your husband, I must ask you not to make scenes with me. *(He sits.)* I don't like scenes.

Mrs. Popov (choking with rage). You're sitting down?

Smirnov. Correct, I'm sitting down.

Mrs. Popov. I asked you to leave!

Smirnov. Then give me the money. *(Aside.)* Oh, what a rage I'm in, what a rage!

Mrs. Popov. The impudence of the man! I won't talk to you a moment longer. Get out. *(Pause.)* Are you going?

Smirnov. No.

Mrs. Popov. No?!

Smirnov. No.

Mrs. Popov. On your head be it. Luka!

Enter Luka.

Show the gentleman out, Luka.

Luka (approaching). I'm afraid, sir, I'll have to ask you, um, to leave, sir, now, um —

Smirnov (jumping up). Shut your mouth, you old idiot! Who do you think you're talking to? I'll make mincemeat of you.

Luka (clutching his heart). Mercy on us! Holy saints above! *(He falls into an armchair.)* I'm taken sick! I can't breathe!!

Mrs. Popov. Then where's Dasha? Dasha! Dasha! Come here at once! *(She rings.)*

Luka. They gone picking berries, ma'am, I'm alone here — Water, water, I'm taken sick!

Mrs. Popov (to Smirnov). Get out, you!

Smirnov. Can't you even be polite with me, Mrs. Popov?

Mrs. Popov (clenching her fists and stamping her feet). With you? You're a wild animal, you were never house-broken!

Smirnov. What? What did you say?

Mrs. Popov. I said you were a wild animal, you were never house-broken.

Smirnov (advancing upon her). And what right do you have to talk to me like that?

Mrs. Popov. Like what?

Smirnov. You have insulted me, madam.

Mrs. Popov. What of it? Do you think I'm scared of you?

Smirnov. So you think you can get away with it because you're a woman. A creature of poetry and romance, huh? Well, it doesn't go down with me. I hereby challenge you to a duel.

Luka. Mercy on us! Holy saints alive! Water!

Smirnov. I propose we shoot it out.

Mrs. Popov. Trying to scare me again? Just because you have big fists and a voice like a bull? You're a brute.

Smirnov. No one insults Grigory S. Smirnov with impunity! And I don't care if you *are* a female.

Mrs. Popov (trying to outshout him). Brute, brute, brute!

Smirnov. The sexes are equal, are they? Fine: then it's just prejudice to expect men alone to pay for insults. I hereby challenge —

Mrs. Popov (screaming). All right! You want to shoot it out? All right! Let's shoot it out!

Smirnov. And let it be here and now!

Mrs. Popov. Here and now! All right! I'll have Popov's pistols here in one minute! *(Walks away, then turns.)* Putting one of Popov's bullets through your silly head will be a pleasure! Au revoir. *(Exit.)*

Smirnov. I'll bring her down like a duck, a sitting duck. I'm not one of your little poets, I'm no little subaltern with his first moustache. No, sir, there's no weaker sex where I'm concerned!

Luka. Sir! Master! *(He goes down on his knees.)* Take pity on a poor old man, and do me a favor: go away. It was bad enough before, you nearly scared me to death. But a duel — !

Smirnov (ignoring him). A duel! That's equality of the sexes for you! That's women's emancipation! Just as a matter of principle

I'll bring her down like a duck. But what a woman! "Putting one of Popov's bullets through your silly head . . ." Her cheeks were flushed, her eyes were gleaming! And, by God, she's accepted the challenge! I never knew a woman like this before!

Luka. Sir! Master! Please go away! I'll always pray for you!

Smirnov (again ignoring him). What a woman! Phew!! *She's* no sour puss, *she's* no cry baby. She's fire and brimstone. She's a human cannon ball. What a shame I have to kill her!

Luka (weeping). Please, kind sir, please, go away!

Smirnov (as before). I like her, isn't that funny? With those dimples and all? I like her. I'm even prepared to consider letting her off that debt. And where's my rage? It's gone. I never knew a woman like this before.

Enter Mrs. Popov with pistols.

Mrs. Popov (boldly). Pistols, Mr. Smirnov! *(Matter of fact.)* But before we start, you'd better show me how it's done, I'm not too familiar with these things. In fact I never gave a pistol a second look.

Luka. Lord, have mercy on us, I must go hunt up the gardener and the coachman. Why has this catastrophe fallen upon us, O Lord? *(Exit.)*

Smirnov (examining the pistols). Well, it's like this. There are several makes: one is the Mortimer, with capsules, especially constructed for dueling. What you have here are Smith and Wesson triple-action revolvers, with extractor, first-rate job, worth ninety rubles at the very least. You hold it this way. *(Aside.)* My God, what eyes she has! They're setting me on fire.

Mrs. Popov. This way?

Smirnov. Yes, that's right. You cock the trigger, take aim like this, head up, arm out like this. Then you just press with this finger here, and it's all over. The main thing is, keep cool, take slow aim, and don't let your arm jump.

Mrs. Popov. I see. And if it's inconvenient to do the job here, we can go out in the garden.

Smirnov. Very good. Of course, I should warn you: I'll be firing in the air.

Mrs. Popov. What? This is the end. Why?

Smirnov. Oh, well — because — for private reasons.

Mrs. Popov. Scared, huh? *(She laughs heartily.)* Now don't you try to get out of it, Mr. Smirnov. My blood is up. I won't be happy till I've drilled a hole through that skull of yours. Follow me. What's the matter? Scared?

Smirnov. That's right. I'm scared.

Mrs. Popov. Oh, come on, what's the matter with you?

Smirnov. Well, um, Mrs. Popov, I, um, I like you.

Mrs. Popov (laughing bitterly). Good God! He likes me, does he? The gall of the man. *(Showing him the door.)* You may leave, Mr. Smirnov.

Smirnov (quietly puts the gun down, takes his hat, and walks to the door. Then he stops and the pair look at each other without a word. Then, approaching gingerly). Listen, Mrs. Popov. Are you still mad at me? I'm in the devil of a temper myself, of course. But then, you see — what I mean is — it's this way — the fact is — *(Roaring.)* Well, is it my fault, damn it, if I like you? *(Clutches the back of a chair. It breaks.)* Christ, what fragile furniture you have here. I like you. Know what I mean? I could fall in love with you.

Mrs. Popov. I hate you. Get out!

Smirnov. What a woman! I never saw anything like it. Oh, I'm lost, I'm done for, I'm a mouse in a trap.

Mrs. Popov. Leave this house, or I shoot!

Smirnov. Shoot away! What bliss to die of a shot that was fired by that little velvet hand! To die gazing into those enchanting eyes. I'm out of my mind. I know: you must decide at once. Think for one second, then decide. Because if I leave now, I'll never be back. Decide! I'm a pretty decent chap. Landed gentleman, I should say. Ten thousand a year. Good stable. Throw a kopeck up in the air, and I'll put a bullet through it. Will you marry me?

Mrs. Popov (indignant, brandishing the gun). We'll shoot it out! Get going! Take your pistol!

Smirnov. I'm out of my mind. I don't understand anything any more. *(Shouting.)* You there! That vodka!

Mrs. Popov. No excuses! No delays! We'll shoot it out!

Smirnov. I'm out of my mind. I'm falling in love. I *have* fallen in love. *(He takes her hand vigorously; she squeals.)* I love you. *(He goes down on his knees.)* I love you as I've never loved before. I jilted twelve, and was jilted by nine others. But I didn't love a one of them as I love you. I'm full of tender emotion. I'm melting like butter. I'm weak as water. I'm on my knees like a fool, and I offer you my hand. It's a shame, it's a disgrace. I haven't been in love in five years. I took a vow against it. And now, all of a sudden, to be swept off my feet, it's a scandal. I offer you my hand, dear lady. Will you or won't you? You won't? Then don't! *(He rises and walks toward the door.)*

Mrs. Popov. I didn't say anything.

Smirnov (stopping). What?

Mrs. Popov. Oh, nothing, you can go. Well, no, just a minute. No, you can go. Go! I detest you! But, just a moment. Oh, if you knew how furious I feel! *(Throws the gun on the table.)* My fingers have gone to sleep holding that horrid thing. *(She is tearing her handkerchief to shreds.)* And what are you standing around for? Get out of here!

Smirnov. Goodbye.

Mrs. Popov. Go, go, go! *(Shouting.)* Where are you going? Wait a minute! No, no, it's all right, just go. I'm fighting mad. Don't come near me, don't come near me!

Smirnov (who is coming near her). I'm pretty disgusted with myself — falling in love like a kid, going down on my knees like some moongazing whippersnapper, the very thought gives me gooseflesh. *(Rudely.)* I love you. But it doesn't make sense. Tomorrow, I have to pay that interest, and we've already started mowing. *(He puts his arm about her waist.)* I shall never forgive myself for this.

Mrs. Popov. Take your hands off me, I hate you! Let's shoot it out!

A long kiss. Enter Luka with an axe, the Gardener with a rake, the coachman with a pitchfork, hired men with sticks.)

Luka (seeing the kiss). Mercy on us! Holy saints above!

Mrs. Popov (dropping her eyes). Luka, tell them in the stable that Toby is *not* to have any oats today.

QUESTIONS

1. What do you think of Luka's first two speeches? Are they reasonable? By the end of the play, how large a role is reason seen to have in life?
2. What do you think of Mrs. Popov's first two speeches? Are they reasonable? In the second of these two speeches, what ideal is she upholding? Do we regard her here as noble — or silly, or both?
3. What impression do you form of the late Mr. Popov?
4. Judging from the early speeches, exactly what are Mrs. Popov's motives for remaining faithful to the late Popov?
5. Why, just after the opening speeches, does Mrs. Popov tell

Luka to give Toby extra oats? Why, at the end of the play, does she tell Luka to give Toby no oats?

6. On page 648 Smirnov says, "Women! Creatures of poetry and romance!" Given what we see of Mrs. Popov up to this point, does she fit Smirnov's description? He then goes on to say, "Just to see one in the distance gets me mad. My legs start twitching with rage. I feel like yelling for help." Why do you think he feels like yelling for help? Is he, perhaps, also a creature of romance?

7. In a long speech on page 650 Smirnov says that he used to be full of "tender emotion" and was "carried away with passion," but he doesn't "give a rap for that sort of nonsense any more." Can it be argued that Smirnov, no less than Mrs. Popov, is imprisoned by a constricting code, a code that interferes with life?

8. When Smirnov explains to Mrs. Popov how a pistol should be held, what actions do you think might accompany the dialogue?

9. Are the sudden changes in the two chief characters believable? If not, does it matter?

22
Summing Up: Reading Drama Responsively

PLOT

1. Are certain happenings or situations recurrent? If so, what significance do you attach to them?
2. If there is a subplot, does it seem to you to be related to the main plot? In what ways?
3. What is the function of a particular scene?
4. Why do certain scenes occur when and where they do? Do any scenes strike you as irrelevant?
5. Are certain scenes so strongly foreshadowed that you anticipated them? If so, did the happenings in these scenes merely fulfill your expectations, or did they also surprise you?

CHARACTER

6. What sort of person is So-and-So? (Of course, a dramatic character is not likely to be thoroughly realistic in the sense of being a copy of someone we might know, but is the character coherent, perhaps representative of some human type?)
7. How is the character defined? (Consider what the character says and does, and what others say about him or her and

do to him or her. Also consider other characters who more or less resemble the character in question, because the similarities — and the differences — may be significant.)

8. What do you make of the minor characters? Are they merely necessary to the plot, or are they foils to other characters?

9. Are certain words or images repeated, so that they take on special importance?

10. If a character is tragic, does the tragedy seem to you to proceed from a moral flaw, from an intellectual error, from the malice of others, from sheer chance, or from some combination of these?

11. If a character is comic, do you laugh *with* or *at* the character?

12. Do you think that the characters are adequately motivated?

13. Is a given character so meditative that you feel he or she is engaged less in a dialogue with others than in a dialogue with the self? If so, do you feel that this character is in large degree a spokesperson for the author, commenting not only on the world of the play but also on the outside world?

NONVERBAL LANGUAGE

14. If the playwright does not provide full stage directions, try to imagine, for at least one scene, what gestures and tones might accompany each speech.

15. What do you make of the setting? Do changes of scene strike you as symbolic?

16. Do certain objects — perhaps a fireplace, a window, or a lamp — strike you (because they are sufficiently emphasized) as symbolic?

23
Nine Plays for Further Study

Sophocles (*c. 495–406 B.C.*)

Oedipus the King*

Translated into English verse by H. D. F. Kitto

List of Characters

Oedipus, King of Thebes
Priest of Zeus
Creon, brother of Iocasta
Teiresias, a Seer
Iocasta, Queen of Thebes
A Corinthian Shepherd
A Theban Shepherd
A Messenger
Chorus of Theban citizens
Priests, Attendants, etc.

* From *Sophocles: Three Tragedies. Antigone, Oedipus the King, Electra,* translated by H. D. F. Kitto. Copyright © 1962 by Oxford University Press. Reprinted by permission.

Scene.

Thebes, before the royal palace.

Oedipus. My children, latest brood of ancient Cadmus,
What purpose brings you here, a multitude
Bearing the boughs that mark the suppliant?
Why is our air so full of frankincense,
So full of hymns and prayers and lamentations?   *5*
This, children, was no matter to entrust
To others: therefore I myself am come
Whose fame is known to all — I, Oedipus.
— You, Sir, are pointed out by length of years
To be the spokesman: tell me, what is in   *10*
Your hearts? What fear? What sorrow? Count on all
That I can do, for I am not so hard
As not to pity such a supplication.
Priest. Great King of Thebes, and sovereign Oedipus,
Look on us, who now stand before the altars —   *15*
Some young, still weak of wing; some bowed with age —
The priests, as I, of Zeus; and these, the best
Of our young men; and in the market-place,
And by Athena's temples and the shrine
Of fiery divination, there is kneeling,   *20*
Each with his suppliant branch, the rest of Thebes.
The city, as you see yourself, is now
Storm-tossed, and can no longer raise its head
Above the waves and angry surge of death.
The fruitful blossoms of the land are barren,   *25*
The herds upon our pastures, and our wives
In childbirth, barren. Last, and worst of all,
The withering god of fever swoops on us
To empty Cadmus' city and enrich
Dark Hades with our groans and lamentations   *30*
No god we count you, that we bring our prayers,
I and these children, to your palace-door,
But wise above all other men to read
Life's riddles, and the hidden ways of Heaven;
For it was you who came and set us free   *35*
From the blood-tribute that the cruel Sphinx
Had laid upon our city; without our aid
Or our instruction, but, as we believe,
With god as ally, you gave us back our life.
So now, most dear, most mighty Oedipus,   *40*

We all entreat you on our bended knees,
Come to our rescue, whether from the gods
Or from some man you can find means to save.
For I have noted, *that* man's counsel is
Of best effect, who has been tried in action.   *45*
Come, noble Oedipus! Come, save our city.
Be well advised; for that past service given
This city calls you Savior; of your kingship
Let not the record be that first we rose
From ruin, then to ruin fell again.   *50*
No, save our city, let it stand secure.
You brought us gladness and deliverance
Before; now do no less. You rule this land;
Better to rule it full of living men
Than rule a desert; citadel or ship   *55*
Without its company of men is nothing.
Oedipus. My children, what you long for, that I know
Indeed, and pity you. I know how cruelly
You suffer; yet, though sick, not one of you
Suffers a sickness half as great as mine.   *60*
Yours is a single pain; each man of you
Feels but his own. My heart is heavy with
The city's pain, my own, and yours together.
You come to me not as to one asleep
And needing to be wakened; many a tear   *65*
I have been shedding, every path of thought
Have I been pacing; and what remedy,
What single hope my anxious thought has found
That I have tried. Creon, Menoeceus' son,
My own wife's brother, I have sent to Delphi   *70*
To ask in Phoebus' house what act of mine,
What word of mine, may bring deliverance.
Now, as I count the days, it troubles me
What he is doing; his absence is prolonged
Beyond the proper time. But when he comes   *75*
Then write me down a villain, if I do
Not each particular that the god discloses.
Priest. You give us hope. — And here is more, for they
Are signaling that Creon has returned.
Oedipus. O Lord Apollo, even as Creon smiles,   *80*
Smile now on us, and let it be deliverance!
Priest. The news is good; or he would not be wearing
That ample wreath of richly-berried laurel.
Oedipus. We soon shall know; my voice will reach so far:

Creon my lord, my kinsman, what response 85
Do you bring with you from the god of Delphi?

Enter Creon.

Creon. Good news! Our sufferings, if they are guided right,
Can even yet turn to a happy issue.
Oedipus. This only leaves my fear and confidence
In equal balance: what did Phoebus say? 90
Creon. Is it your wish to hear it now, in public,
Or in the palace? I am at your service.
Oedipus. Let them all hear! Their sufferings distress
Me more than if my own life were at stake.
Creon. Then I will tell you what Apollo said — 95
And it was very clear. There is pollution
Here in our midst, long-standing. This must we
Expel, nor let it grow past remedy.
Oedipus. What has defiled us? and how are we to purge it?
Creon. By banishing or killing one who murdered, 100
And so called down this pestilence upon us.
Oedipus. Who is the man whose death the god denounces?
Creon. Before the city passed into your care,
My lord, we had a king called Laius.
Oedipus. So I have often heard. — I never saw him. 105
Creon. His death, Apollo clearly charges us,
We must avenge upon his murderers.
Oedipus. Where are they now? And where shall we disclose
The unseen traces of that ancient crime?
Creon. The god said, Here. — A man who hunts with care 110
May often find what other men will miss.
Oedipus. Where was he murdered? In the palace here?
Or in the country? Or was he abroad?
Creon. He made a journey to consult the god,
He said — and never came back home again. 115
Oedipus. But was there no report? no fellow traveler
Whose knowledge might have helped you in your search?
Creon. All died, except one terror-stricken man,
And he could tell us nothing — next to nothing.
Oedipus. And what was that? One thing might lead to much, 120
If only we could find one ray of light.
Creon. He said they met with brigands — not with one,
But a whole company; they killed Laius.
Oedipus. A brigand would not *dare* — unless perhaps
Conspirators in Thebes had bribed the man. 125

Creon. There *was* conjecture; but disaster came
    And we were leaderless, without our king.
Oedipus. Disaster? With a king cut down like that
    You did not seek the cause? Where was the hindrance?
Creon. The Sphinx. *Her* riddle pressed us harder still;   *130*
    For Laius — out of sight was out of mind.
Oedipus. I will begin again; *I'*ll find the truth.
    The dead man's cause has found a true defender
    In Phoebus, and in you. And I will join you
    In seeking vengeance on behalf of Thebes   *135*
    And Phoebus too; indeed, I must: if I
    Remove this taint, it is not for a stranger,
    But for myself: the man who murdered him
    Might make the same attempt on me; and so,
    Avenging him, I shall protect myself. —   *140*
    Now you, my sons, without delay, arise,
    Take up your suppliant branches. — Someone, go
    And call the people here, for I will do
    What can be done; and either, by the grace
    Of God we shall be saved — or we shall fall.   *145*
Priest. My children, we will go; the King has promised
    All that we came to ask. — O Phoebus, thou
    Hast given us an answer: give us too
    Protection! grant remission of the plague!

                         Exit Creon, Priests,
                           etc. Oedipus remains.
  Enter the Chorus representing the citizens of Thebes.

Strophe 1

Chorus. Sweet is the voice of the god, that   *150*
    [*mainly dactyls:*°*⁴₄]†   sounds in the

* The degree sign (°) indicates a footnote, which is keyed to the text by line
number. Text references are printed in **boldface italic** type; the annotation follows
in roman type.
† Taking a hint from the French translators for the Budé series I have here and
there added to the lyrical portions a quasi-musical indication of tempo or mood,
on no authority except that of common sense. These may at least serve to remind
the reader, if he needs reminding, that the lyrics were not recited; they were a
fusion of intense poetry, music, and dancing. Of the music we know nothing; of
the dance we can at least infer that its range extended from grave processional
movements to the expression of great excitement, whether of joy or despair.
[Kitto.]

¹⁵¹ **dactyls** lines consisting of feet composed of two short syllables followed by
one long syllable

Golden shrine of Delphi.
What message has it sent to Thebes? My trembling
Heart is torn with anguish.
Thou god of Healing, Phoebus Apollo,   *155*
How do I fear! What hast thou in mind
To bring upon us now? what is to be fulfilled
From days of old?
Tell me this, O Voice divine,
Thou child of golden Hope.

Antistrophe 1

First on the Daughter of Zeus I call for
Help, divine Athene;   *160*
And Artemis, whose throne is all the earth, whose
Shrine is in our city;
Apollo too, who shoots from afar:
Trinity of Powers, come to our defence!   *165*
If ever in the past, when ruin threatened us,
You stayed its course
And turned aside the flood of Death,
O then, protect us now!

Strophe 2

[*Agitated:* $\frac{3}{8}$] Past counting are the woes we suffer;   *170*
Affliction bears on all the city, and
Nowhere is any defence against destruction.
The holy soil can bring no increase,
Our women suffer and cry in childbirth
But do not bring forth living children.   *175*
The souls of those who perish, one by one,
Unceasingly, swift as raging fire,
Rise and take their flight to the dark realms of the dead.

Antistrophe 2

Past counting, those of us who perish:
They lie upon the ground, unpitied,   *180*
Unburied, infecting the air with deadly pollution.
Young wives, and grey-haired mothers with them,
From every quarter approach the altars
And cry aloud in supplication.
The prayer for healing, the loud wail of lament,   *185*

Together are heard in dissonance:
O thou golden Daughter of Zeus, grant thy aid!

Strophe 3

[*Mainly iambic°:* $\frac{3}{8}$] The fierce god of War has laid aside
His spear; but yet his terrible cry
Rings in our ears; he spreads death and destruction.   *190*
Ye gods, drive him back to his distant home!
For what the light of day has spared,
That the darkness of night destroys.
Zeus our father! All power is thine:
The lightning-flash is thine: hurl upon him   *195*
Thy thunderbolt, and quell this god of War!

Antistrophe 3

We pray, Lord Apollo: draw thy bow
In our defense. Thy quiver is full of
Arrows unerring: shoot! slay the destroyer!
And thou, radiant Artemis, lend thy aid!   *200*
Thou whose hair is bound in gold,
Bacchus, lord of the sacred dance,
Theban Bacchus! Come, show thyself!
Display thy blazing torch; drive from our midst
The savage god, abhorred by other gods!
Oedipus. Would you have answer to these prayers? Then hear *205*
My words; give heed; your help may bring
Deliverance, and the end of all our troubles.
Here do I stand before you all, a stranger
Both to the deed and to the story. — What
Could I have done alone, without a clue?   *210*
But I was yet a foreigner; it was later
That I became a Theban among Thebans.
So now do I proclaim to all the city:
If any Theban knows by what man's hand
He perished, Laius, son of Labdacus,   *215*
Him I command to tell me all he can;
And if he is afraid, let him annul
Himself the charge he fears; no punishment
Shall fall on him, save only to depart

---

[188] *iambic*   a metrical foot consisting of one short syllable followed by one long
syllable

Unharmed from Thebes. Further, if any knows   *220*
The slayer to be a stranger from abroad,
Let him speak out; I will reward him, and
Besides, he will have all my gratitude.
But if you still keep silent, if any man
Fearing for self or friend shall disobey me,   *225*
This will I do — and listen to my words:
Whoever he may be, I do forbid
All in this realm, of which I am the King
And high authority, to shelter in their houses
Or speak to him, or let him be their partner   *230*
In prayers or sacrifices to the gods, or give
Him lustral water; I command you all
To drive him from your doors; for he it is
That brings this plague upon us, as the god
Of Delphi has but now declared to me. —   *235*
So stern an ally do I make myself
Both of the god and of our murdered king. —
And for the man that slew him, whether he
Slew him alone, or with a band of helpers,
I lay this curse upon him, that the wretch   *240*
In wretchedness and misery may live.
And more; if with my knowledge he be found
To share my hearth and home, then upon me
Descend that doom that I invoke on him.
This charge I lay upon you, to observe   *245*
All my commands: to aid myself, the god,
And this our land, so spurned of Heaven, so ravaged.
For such a taint we should not leave unpurged —
The death of such a man, and he your king —
Even if Heaven had not commanded us,   *250*
But we should search it out. Now, since 'tis I
That wear the crown that he had worn before me,
And have his Queen to wife, and common children
Were born to us, but that his own did perish,
And sudden death has carried him away —   *255*
Because of this, I will defend his cause
As if it were my father's; nothing I
Will leave undone to find the man who killed
The son of Labdacus, and offspring of
Polydorus, Cadmus, and of old Agênor.   *260*
On those that disobey, this is my curse:
May never field of theirs give increase, nor
Their wives have children; may our present plagues,

And worse, be ever theirs, for their destruction.
But for the others, all with whom my words   *265*
Find favor, this I pray: Justice and all
The gods be ever at your side to help you.
Chorus-leader. Your curse constrains me; therefore will I speak.
    I did not kill him, neither can I tell
    Who did. It is for Phoebus, since he laid   *270*
    The task upon us, to declare the man.
Oedipus. True; but to force the gods against their will —
    That is a thing beyond all human power.
Chorus-leader. All I could say is but a second best.
Oedipus. Though it were third best, do not hold it back.   *275*
Chorus-leader. I know of none that reads Apollo's mind
    So surely as the lord Teiresias;
    Consulting him you best might learn the truth.
Oedipus. Not even this have I neglected: Creon
    Advised me, and already I have sent   *280*
    Two messengers. — Strange he has not come.
Chorus-leader. There's nothing else but old and idle gossip.
Oedipus. And what was that? I clutch at any straw.
Chorus-leader. They said that he was killed by travelers.
Oedipus. So I have heard; but no one knows a witness.   *285*
Chorus-leader. But if he is not proof against *all* fear
    He'll not keep silent when he hears your curse.
Oedipus. And will they fear a curse, who dared to kill?
Chorus-leader. Here is the one to find him, for at last
    They bring the prophet here. He is inspired,   *290*
    The only man whose heart is filled with truth.

    Enter Teiresias, led by a boy.

Oedipus. Teiresias, by your art you read the signs
    And secrets of the earth and of the sky;
    Therefore you now, although you cannot see,
    The plague that is besetting us; from this
    No other man but you, my lord, can save us.   *295*
    Phoebus has said — you may have heard already —
    In answer to our question, that this plague
    Will never cease unless we can discover
    What men they were who murdered Laius.   *300*
    And punish them with death or banishment.
    Therefore give freely all that you have learned
    From birds or other form of divination;
    Save us; save me, the city, and yourself,

From the pollution that his bloodshed causes.   *305*
No finer task, than to give all one has
In helping others; we are in your hands.
Teiresias. Ah! what a burden knowledge is, when knowledge
Can be of no avail! I knew this well,
And yet forgot, or I should not have come.   *310*
Oedipus. Why, what is this? Why are you so despondent?
Teiresias. Let me go home! It will be best for you,
And best for me, if you will let me go.
Oedipus. But to withhold your knowledge! This is wrong,
Disloyal to the city of your birth.   *315*
Teiresias. I know that what you say will lead you on
To ruin; therefore, lest the same befall me too . . .
Oedipus. No, by the gods! Say all you know, for we
Go down upon our knees, your suppliants.
Teiresias. Because *you* do *not* know! I never shall   *320*
Reveal my burden — I will not say *yours*.
Oedipus. You know, and will not tell us? Do you wish
To ruin Thebes and to destroy us all?
Teiresias. My pain, and yours, will not be caused by me.
Why these vain questions? — for I will not speak.   *325*
Oedipus. You villain! — for you would provoke a stone
To anger: you'll not speak, but show yourself
So hard of heart and so inflexible?
Teiresias. You heap the blame on me; but what is yours
You do not know — therefore *I* am the villain!   *330*
Oedipus. And who would not be angry, finding that
You treat our people with such cold disdain?
Teiresias. The truth will come to light, without *my* help.
Oedipus. If it is bound to come, you ought to speak it.
Teiresias. I'll say no more, and you, if so you choose,   *335*
May rage and bluster on without restraint.
Oedipus. Restraint? Then I'll show none! I'll tell you all
That I can see in you: I do believe
This crime was planned and carried out by you,
All but the killing; and were you not blind   *340*
I'd say your hand alone had done the murder.
Teiresias. So? Then I tell you this: submit yourself
To that decree that you have made; from now
Address no word to these men nor to me:
You are the man whose crimes pollute our city.   *345*
Oedipus. What, does your impudence extend thus far?
And do you hope that it will go scot-free?
Teiresias. It will. I have a champion — the truth.

Oedipus. Who taught you that? For it was not your art.
Teiresias. No; you! You made me speak, against my will.   *350*
Oedipus. Speak what? Say it again, and say it clearly.
Teiresias. Was I not clear? Or are you tempting me?
Oedipus. Not clear enough for me. Say it again.
Teiresias. You are yourself the murderer you seek.
Oedipus. You'll not affront me twice and go unpunished!   *355*
Teiresias. Then shall I give you still more cause for rage?
Oedipus. Say what you will; you'll say it to no purpose.
Teiresias. I know, *you* do not know, the hideous life
    Of shame you lead with those most near to you.
Oedipus. You'll pay most dearly for this insolence!   *360*
Teiresias. No, not if Truth is strong, and can prevail.
Oedipus. It is — except in you; for you are blind
    In eyes and ears and brains and everything.
Teiresias. You'll not forget these insults that you throw
    At me, when all men throw the same at you.   *365*
Oedipus. You live in darkness; you can do no harm
    To me or any man who has his eyes.
Teiresias. No; *I* am not to bring you down, because
    Apollo is enough; he'll see to it.
Oedipus. Creon, or you? Which of you made this plot?   *370*
Teiresias. Creon's no enemy of yours; you are your own.
Oedipus. O Wealth! O Royalty! whose commanding art
    Outstrips all other arts in life's contentions!
    How great a store of envy lies upon you,
    If for this scepter, that the city gave   *375*
    Freely to me, unasked — if now my friend,
    The trusty Creon, burns to drive me hence
    And steal it from me! So he has suborned
    This crafty schemer here, this mountebank,
    Whose purse alone has eyes, whose art is blind. —   *380*
    Come, prophet, show your title! When the Sphinx
    Chanted her music here, why did not *you*
    Speak out and save the city? Yet such a question
    Was one for augury, not for mother wit.
    You were no prophet then; your birds, your voice   *385*
    From Heaven, were dumb. But I, who came by chance,
    I, knowing nothing, put the Sphinx to flight,
    Thanks to my wit — no thanks to divination!
    And now you try to drive me out; you hope
    When Creon's king to bask in Creon's favor.   *390*
    You'll expiate the curse? Aye, and repent it,

Both you and your accomplice. But that you
Seem old, I'd teach you what you gain by treason!
Chorus-leader. My lord, he spoke in anger; so I think,
Did you. What help in angry speeches? Come,   395
This is the task, how we can best discharge
The duty that the god has laid on us.
Teiresias. King though you are, I claim the privilege
Of equal answer. No, I have the right;
I am no slave of yours — I serve Apollo,   400
And therefore am not listed Creon's man.
Listen — since you have taunted me with blindness!
You have your sight, and yet you cannot see
Where, nor with whom, you live, nor in what horror.
Your parents — do you know them? or that you   405
Are enemy to your kin, alive or dead?
And that a father's and a mother's curse
Shall join to drive you headlong out of Thebes
And change the light that now you see to darkness?
Your cries of agony, where will they not reach?   410
Where on Cithaeron will they not re-echo?
Where you have learned what meant the marriage-song
Which bore you to an evil haven here
After so fair a voyage? And you are blind
To other horrors, which shall make you one   415
With your own children. Therefore, heap your scorn
On Creon and on me, for no man living
Will meet a doom more terrible than yours.
Oedipus. What? Am I to suffer words like this from him?
Ruin, damnation seize you! Off at once   420
Out of our sight! Go! Get you whence you came!
Teiresias. Had you not called me, I should not be here.
Oedipus. And had I known that you would talk such folly,
I'd not have called you to a house of mine.
Teiresias. To you I seem a fool, but to your parents,   425
To those who did beget you, I was wise.
Oedipus. Stop! Who were they? Who were my parents? Tell me!
Teiresias. This day will show your birth and your destruction.
Oedipus. You are too fond of dark obscurities.
Teiresias. But do you not excel in reading riddles?   430
Oedipus. I scorn your taunts; my skill has brought me glory.
Teiresias. And this success brought you to ruin too.
Oedipus. I am content, if so I saved this city.
Teiresias. Then I will leave you. Come, boy, take my hand.

Oedipus. Yes, let him take it. You are nothing but   *435*
  Vexation here. Begone, and give me peace!
Teiresias. When I have had my say. No frown of yours
  Shall frighten *me*; you cannot injure me.
  Here is my message: that man whom you seek
  With threats and proclamations for the death   *440*
  Of Laius, he is living here; he's thought
  To be a foreigner, but shall be found
  Theban by birth — and little joy will this
  Bring *him*; when, with his eyesight turned to blindness,
  His wealth to beggary, on foreign soil   *445*
  With staff in hand he'll tap his way along,
  His children with him; and he will be known
  Himself to be their father and their brother,
  The husband of the mother who gave him birth,
  Supplanter of his father, and his slayer.   *450*
  — There! Go, and think on this; and if you find
  That I'm deceived, say then — and not before —
  That I am ignorant in divination.

      Exeunt severally Teiresias and Oedipus.

Strophe 1

Chorus. The voice of god rang out in the holy cavern,
  Denouncing one who has killed a King — the crime of
    crimes.   *455*
    Who is the man? Let him begone in
    Headlong flight, swift as a horse!
  [*Anapests°*] For the terrible god, like a warrior armed,
  Stands ready to strike with a lightning-flash:
    The Furies who punish crime, and never fail,   *460*
    Are hot in their pursuit.

Antistrophe 1

  The snow is white on the cliffs of high Parnassus.
  It has flashed a message: Let every Theban join the hunt!
    Lurking in caves among the mountains,
    Deep in the woods — where is the man?   *465*
  [*Anapests*] In wearisome flight, unresting, alone,

---

[458] *anapests* metrical feet consisting of two short syllables followed by one long
syllable

An outlaw, he shuns Apollo's shrine;
But ever the living menace of the god
Hovers around his head.

Strophe 2

[*Choriambics°*] Strange, disturbing, what the wise   470
Prophet has said. What can he mean?
Neither can I believe, nor can I disbelieve;
I do not know what to say.
I look here, and there; nothing can I find —
No strife, either now or in the past,   475
Between the kings of Thebes and Corinth.
A hand unknown struck down the King;
Though I would learn who it was dealt the blow,
That *he* is guilty whom all revere —
How can I believe this with no proof?   480

Antistrophe 2

Zeus, Apollo — they have knowledge;
They understand the ways of life.
Prophets are men, like me; that they can understand
More than is revealed to me —
Of that, I can find nowhere certain proof,   485
Though one man is wise, another foolish.
Until the charge is manifest
I will not credit his accusers.
I saw myself how the Sphinx challenged him:
He proved his wisdom; he saved our city;   490
Therefore how can I now condemn him?

Enter Creon.

Creon. They tell me, Sirs, that Oedipus the King
Has made against me such an accusation
That I will not endure. For if he thinks
That in this present trouble I have done   495
Or said a single thing to do him harm,
Then let me die, and not drag out my days
With such a name as that. For it is not

---

⁴⁷⁰ **choriambics** metrical feet consisting of a trochee (a long syllable followed by
a short syllable) and an iamb (a short syllable followed by a long syllable)

One injury this accusation does me;
It touches my whole life, if you, my friends,   *500*
And all the city are to call me traitor.
Chorus-leader. The accusation may perhaps have come
From heat of temper, not from sober judgment.
Creon. What was it made him think contrivances
Of mine suborned the seer to tell his lies?   *505*
Chorus-leader. Those were his words; I do not know his reasons.
Creon. Was he in earnest, master of himself,
When he attacked me with this accusation?
Chorus-leader. I do not closely scan what kings are doing. —
But here he comes in person from the palace.   *510*

Enter Oedipus.

Oedipus. What, *you?* You dare come here? How can you find
The impudence to show yourself before
My house, when you are clearly proven
To have sought my life and tried to steal my crown?
Why, do you think me then a coward, or   *515*
A fool, that you should try to lay this plot?
Or that I should not see what you were scheming,
And so fall unresisting, blindly, to you?
But you were mad, so to attempt the throne,
Poor and unaided; this is not encompassed   *520*
Without the strong support of friends and money!
Creon. This you must do: now you have had your say
Hear my reply; then yourself shall judge.
Oedipus. A ready tongue! But I am bad at listening —
To you. For I have found how much you hate me.   *525*
Creon. One thing: first listen to what I have to say.
Oedipus. One thing: do not pretend you're not a villain.
Creon. If you believe it is a thing worth having,
Insensate stubbornness, then you are wrong.
Oedipus. If you believe that one can harm a kinsman   *530*
Without retaliation, you are wrong.
Creon. With this I have no quarrel; but explain
What injury you say that I have done you.
Oedipus. Did you advise, or did you not, that I
Should send a man for that most reverend prophet?   *535*
Creon. I did, and I am still of that advice.
Oedipus. How long a time is it since Laius . . .
Creon. Since Laius did *what?* How can I say?
Oedipus. Was seen no more, but met a violent death?

Creon. It would be many years now past and gone. *540*
Oedipus. And had this prophet learned his art already?
Creon. Yes, his repute was great — as it is now.
Oedipus. Did he make any mention then of me?
Creon. He never spoke of you within my hearing.
Oedipus. Touching the murder: did you make no search? *545*
Creon. No search? Of course we did; but we found nothing.
Oedipus. And why did this wise prophet not speak *then*?
Creon. Who knows? Where I know nothing I say nothing.
Oedipus. This much you know — and you'll do well to answer:
Creon. What is it? If I know, I'll tell you freely. *550*
Oedipus. That if he had not joined with you, he'd not
    Have said that I was Laius' murderer.
Creon. If he said this, I did not know. — But I
    May rightly question you, as you have me.
Oedipus. Ask what you will. You'll never prove *I* killed him. *555*
Creon. Why then: are you not married to my sister?
Oedipus. I am indeed; it cannot be denied.
Creon. You share with her the sovereignty of Thebes?
Oedipus. She need but ask, and anything is hers.
Creon. And am I not myself conjoined with you? *560*
Oedipus. You are; not rebel therefore, but a traitor!
Creon. Not so, if you will reason with yourself;
    As I with you. This first: would any man,
    To gain no increase of authority,
    Choose kingship, with its fears and sleepless nights? *565*
    Not I. What I desire, what every man
    Desires, if he has wisdom, is to take
    The substance, not the show, of royalty.
    For now, through you, I have both power and ease,
    But were I king, I'd be oppressed with cares. *570*
    Not so: while I have ample sovereignty
    And rule in peace, why should I want the crown?
    I am not yet so mad as to give up
    All that which brings me honor and advantage.
    Now, every man greets me, and I greet him; *575*
    Those who have need of you make much of me,
    Since I can make or mar them. Why should I
    Surrender this to load myself with that?
    A man of sense was never yet a traitor;
    I have no taste for that, nor could I force *580*
    Myself to aid another's treachery.
      But you can test me: go to Delphi; ask
    If I reported rightly what was said.

And further: if you find that I had dealings
With that diviner, you may take and kill me   *585*
Not with your single vote, but yours and mine,
But not on bare suspicion, unsupported.
How wrong it is, to use a random judgment
And think the false man true, the true man false!
To spurn a loyal friend, that is no better   *590*
Than to destroy the life to which we cling.
This you will learn in time, for Time alone
Reveals the upright man; a single day
Suffices to unmask the treacherous.

Chorus-leader. My lord, he speaks with caution, to avoid   *595*
  Grave error. Hasty judgment is not sure.
Oedipus. But when an enemy is quick to plot
  And strike, I must be quick in answer too,
  If I am slow, and wait, then I shall find
  That he has gained his end, and I am lost.   *600*
Creon. What do you wish? To drive me into exile?
Oedipus. No, more than exile: I will have your life.*
Creon. <When will it cease, this monstrous rage of yours?>
Oedipus. When your example shows what comes of envy.
Creon. Must you be stubborn? Cannot you believe me?   *605*
Oedipus. <You speak to me as if I were a fool!>
Creon. Because I know you're wrong.
Oedipus. Right, for myself!
Creon. It is not right for me!
Oedipus. But you're a traitor.   *610*
Creon. What if your charge is false?
Oedipus. I have to govern.
Creon. Not govern badly!
Oedipus. Listen to him, Thebes!
Creon. You're not the city! I am Theban too.   *615*
Chorus-leader. My lords, no more! Here comes the Queen, and not

---

* The next two verses, as they stand in the mss., are impossible. Editors are agreed
on this, though no single remedy has found general acceptance. The mss. attribute
v.624 [Oedipus' next speech] to Creon, and v. 625 [Creon's next speech] to Oedipus.
I can make no real sense of this: the only φθόνος, "envy," that is in question is
the envy of his royal power that Oedipus is attributing to Creon; and the words
υπειξων, "yield," "not to be stubborn," and πιστευσων, "believe," must surely
be used by Creon of Oedipus, not by Oedipus of Creon. Since a translator who
hopes to be acted must give the actors something to say, preferably good sense,
and cannot fob them off with a row of dots, I have reconstructed the passage by
guesswork, putting my guesses within brackets. I have assumed that two verses
were lost, one after v. 623 and one after v. 625, and that the wrong attribution
of vv. 624 and 625 followed almost inevitably. [Kitto.]

Too soon, to join you. With her help, you must
Compose the bitter strife that now divides you.

Enter Iocasta.

Iocasta. You frantic men! What has aroused this wild
    Dispute? Have you no shame, when such a plague   *620*
    Afflicts us, to indulge in private quarrels?
    Creon, go home, I pray. You, Oedipus,
    Come in; do not make much of what is nothing.
Creon. My sister: Oedipus, your husband here,
    Has thought it right to punish me with one   *625*
    Of two most awful dooms: exile, or death.
Oedipus. I have: I have convicted him, Iocasta,
    Of plotting secretly against my life.
Creon. If I am guilty in a single point
    Of such a crime, then may I die accursed.   *630*
Iocasta. O, by the gods, believe him, Oedipus!
    Respect the oath that he has sworn, and have
    Regard for me, and for these citizens.

[*In what follows, the parts given to the chorus are sung, the rest,
    presumably, spoken. The rhythm of the music and dance is
    either dochmiac°, 5-time, or a combination of 3- and 5-time.*]

Strophe

Chorus. My lord, I pray, give consent.
    Yield to us; ponder well.   *635*
Oedipus. What is it you would have me yield?
Chorus. Respect a man ripe in years,
    Bound by this mighty oath he has sworn.
Oedipus. Your wish is clear?
Chorus. It is.   *640*
Oedipus. Then tell it me.
Chorus. Not to repel, and drive out of our midst a friend,
    Scorning a solemn curse, for uncertain cause.
Oedipus. I tell you this: your prayer will mean for me
    My banishment from Thebes, or else my death.   *645*
Chorus. No, no! by the Sun, the chief of gods,
    Ruin and desolation and all evil come upon me
    If I harbor thoughts such as these!

° *dochmiac* usually, but not necessarily, a metrical foot consisting of three long
and two short syllables

No; our land racked with plague breaks my heart.
Do not now deal a new wound on Thebes to crown
    the old!   *650*
Oedipus. Then let him be, though I must die twice over,
  Or be dishonored, spurned and driven out.
  It's your entreaty, and not his, that moves
  My pity; he shall have my lasting hatred.
Creon. You yield ungenerously; but when your wrath   *655*
  Has cooled, how it will prick you! Natures such
  As yours give most vexation to themselves.
Oedipus. O, let me be! Get from my sight.
Creon. I go,
  Misjudged by you — but these will judge me
    better [*indicating Chorus*].   *660*
                              Exit Creon.

Antistrophe

Chorus. My lady, why now delay?
  Let the King go in with you.
Iocasta. When you have told me what has passed.
Chorus. Suspicion came. — Random words, undeserved,
  Will provoke men to wrath.   *665*
Iocasta. It was from both?
Chorus. It was.
Iocasta. And what was said?
Chorus. It is enough for me, more than enough, when I
  Think of our ills, that this should rest where it lies.   *670*
Oedipus. You and your wise advice, blunting my wrath.
  Frustrated me — and it has come to this!
Chorus. This, O my King, I said, and say again:
    I should be mad, distraught,
    I should be a fool, and worse,   *675*
    If I sought to drive you away.
    Thebes was near sinking; you brought her safe
  Through the storm. Now again we pray that you may save
    us.
Iocasta. In Heaven's name, my lord, I too must know
  What was the reason for this blazing anger.   *680*
Oedipus. There's none to whom I more defer; and so,
  I'll tell you: Creon and his vile plot against me.
Iocasta. What has he done, that you are so incensed?
Oedipus. He says that I am Laius' murderer.
Iocasta. From his own knowledge? Or has someone told him? *685*

Oedipus. No; that suspicion should not fall upon
    Himself, he used a tool — a crafty prophet.
Iocasta. Why, have no fear of *that*. Listen to me,
    And you will learn that the prophetic art
    Touches our human fortunes not at all.   *690*
    I soon can give you proof. — An oracle
    Once came to Laius — from the god himself
    I do not say, but from his ministers:
    His fate it was, that should he have a son
    By me, that son would take his father's life.   *695*
    But he was killed — or so they said — by strangers.
    By brigands, at a place where three ways meet.
    As for the child, it was not three days old
    When Laius fastened both its feet together
    And had it cast over a precipice.   *700*
    Therefore Apollo failed; for neither did
    His son kill Laius, nor did Laius meet
    The awful end he feared, killed by his son.
        So much for what prophetic voices uttered.
    Have no regard for them. The god will bring   *705*
    To light himself whatever thing he chooses.
Oedipus. Iocasta, terror seizes me, and shakes
    My very soul, at one thing you have said.
Iocasta. Why so? What have I said to frighten you?
Oedipus. I think I heard you say that Laius   *710*
    Was murdered at a place where three ways meet?
Iocasta. So it was said — indeed, they say it still.
Oedipus. Where is the place where this encounter happened?
Iocasta. They call the country Phokis, and a road
    From Delphi joins a road from Daulia.   *715*
Oedipus. Since that was done, how many years have passed?
Iocasta. It was proclaimed in Thebes a little time
    Before the city offered you the crown.
Oedipus. O Zeus, what fate hast thou ordained for me?
Iocasta. What is the fear that so oppresses you?   *720*
Oedipus. One moment yet: tell me of Laius.
    What age was he? and what was his appearance?
Iocasta. A tall man, and his hair was touched with white;
    In figure he was not unlike yourself.
Oedipus. O God! Did I, then, in my ignorance,   *725*
    Proclaim that awful curse against myself?
Iocasta. What are you saying? How you frighten me!
Oedipus. I greatly fear that prophet was not blind.
    But yet one question; that will show me more.

Iocasta. For all my fear, I'll tell you what I can.   730
Oedipus. Was he alone, or did he have with him
    A royal bodyguard of men-at-arms?
Iocasta. The company in all were five; the King
    Rode in a carriage, and there was a Herald.
Oedipus. Ah God! How clear the picture is! . . . But who,   735
    Iocasta, brought report of this to Thebes?
Iocasta. A slave, the only man that was not killed.
Oedipus. And is he round about the palace now?
Iocasta. No, he is not. When he returned, and saw
    You ruling in the place of the dead King,   740
    He begged me, on his bended knees, to send him
    Into the hills as shepherd, out of sight,
    As far as could be from the city here.
    I sent him, for he was a loyal slave;
    He well deserved this favor — and much more.   745
Oedipus. Could he be brought back here — at once — to see me?
Iocasta. He could; but why do you desire his coming?
Oedipus. I fear I have already said, Iocasta,
    More than enough; and therefore I will see him.
Iocasta. Then he shall come. But, as your wife, I ask you,   750
    What is the terror that possesses you?
Oedipus. And you shall know it, since my fears have grown
    So great; for who is more to me than you,
    That I should speak to *him* at such a moment?
        My father, then, was Polybus of Corinth;   755
    My mother, Meropê. My station there
    Was high as any man's — until a thing
    Befell me that was strange indeed, though not
    Deserving of the thought I gave to it.
    A man said at a banquet — he was full   760
    Of wine — that I was not my father's son.
    It angered me; but I restrained myself
    That day. The next I went and questioned both
    My parents. They were much incensed with him.
    Who had let fall the insult. So, from them,   765
    I had assurance. Yet the slander spread
    And always chafed me. Therefore secretly,
    My mother and my father unaware,
    I went to Delphi. Phoebus would return
    No answer to my question, but declared   770
    A thing most horrible: he foretold that I
    Should mate with my own mother, and beget

A brood that men would shudder to behold,
And that I was to be the murderer
Of my own father,
                Therefore, back to Corinth   *775*
I never went — the stars alone have told me
Where Corinth lies — that I might never see
Cruel fulfillment of that oracle.
So journeying, I came to that same spot
Where, as you say, this King was killed. And now,   *780*
This is the truth, Iocasta: when I reached
The place where three ways meet, I met a herald,
And in a carriage drawn by colts was such
A man as you describe. By violence
The herald and the older man attempted   *785*
To push me off the road, I, in my rage,
Struck at the driver, who was hustling me.
The old man, when he saw me level with him,
Taking a double-goad, aimed at my head
A murderous blow. He paid for that, full measure.   *790*
Swiftly I hit him with my staff; he rolled
Out of his carriage, flat upon his back.
I killed them all. — But if, between this stranger
And Laius there was any bond of kinship,
Who could be in more desperate plight than I?   *795*
Who more accursèd in the eyes of Heaven?
For neither citizen nor stranger may
Receive me in his house, nor speak to me,
But he must bar the door. And it was none
But I invoked this curse on my own head!   *800*
And I pollute the bed of him I slew
With my own hands! Say, am I vile? Am I
Not all impure? Seeing I must be exiled,
And even in my exile must not go
And see my parents, nor set foot upon   *805*
My native land; or, if I do, I must
Marry my mother, and kill Polybus
My father, who engendered me and reared me.
If one should say it was a cruel god
Brought this upon me, would he not speak right?   *810*
No, no, you holy powers above! Let me
Not see that day! but rather let me pass
Beyond the sight of men, before I see
The stain of such pollution come upon me!

Chorus-leader. My lord, this frightens me. But you must
        hope,   *815*
    Until we hear the tale from him that saw it.
Oedipus. That is the only hope that's left to me;
    We must await the coming of the shepherd.
Iocasta. What do you hope from him, when he is here?
Oedipus. I'll tell you: if his story shall be found   *820*
    The same as yours, then I am free of guilt.
Iocasta. But what have *I* said of especial note?
Oedipus. You said that he reported it was brigands
    Who killed the king. If he still speaks of "men,"
    It was not I; a single man, and "men,"   *825*
    Are not the same. but if he says it was
    A traveler journeying alone, why then,
    The burden of the guilt must fall on me.
Iocasta. But that *is* what he said, I do assure you!
    He cannot take it back again! Not I   *830*
    Alone, but the whole city heard him say it!
    But even if he should revoke the tale
    He told before, not even so, my lord,
    Will he establish that the King was slain
    According to the prophecy. For that was clear: *835*
    His son, and mine, should slay him. — He, poor thing,
    Was killed himself, and never killed his father.
    Therefore, so far as divination goes,
    Or prophecy, I'll take no notice of it.
Oedipus. And that is wise. — But send a man to bring   *840*
    The shepherd; I would not have that neglected.
Iocasta. I'll send at once. — But come with me; for I
    Would not do anything that could displease you.

                         Exeunt Oedipus and Iocasta.

Strophe 1

Chorus. I pray that I may pass my life
[*in a steady rhythm*] In reverent holiness of word and deed.   *845*
    For there are laws enthroned above;
    Heaven created them,
    Olympus was their father,
    And mortal men had no part in their birth;
    Nor ever shall their power pass from sight   *850*
    In dull forgetfulness;
    A god moves in them; he grows not old.

Antistrophe 1

Pride makes the tyrant — pride of wealth
And power, too great for wisdom and restraint;
For Pride will climb the topmost height;   *855*
Then is the man cast down
To uttermost destruction.
There he finds no escape, no resource.
But high contention for the city's good
May the gods preserve.   *860*
For me — may the gods be my defense!

Strophe 2

If there is one who walks in pride
Of word or deed, and has no fear of Justice,
No reverence for holy shrines —
May utter ruin fall on him!   *865*
So may his ill-starred pride be given its reward.
Those who seek dishonorable advantage
And lay violent hands on holy things
And do not shun impiety —
Who among these will secure himself from the wrath of
    God?   *870*
If deeds like these are honored,
Why should I join in the sacred dance?

Antistrophe 2

No longer shall Apollo's shrine,
The holy center of the Earth, receive my worship;
No, nor his seat at Abae, nor   *875*
The temple of Olympian Zeus,
If what the god foretold does not come to pass.
Mighty Zeus — if so I should address Thee —
O great Ruler of all things, look on this!
Now are thy oracles falling into contempt, and men   *880*
Deny Apollo's power.
Worship of the gods is passing away.

Enter Iocasta, attended by a girl carrying a wreath and incense.

Iocasta. My lords of Thebes, I have bethought myself
    To approach the altars of the gods, and lay

These wreaths on them, and burn this frankincense.   *885*
For every kind of terror has laid hold
On Oedipus; his judgment is distracted.
He will not read the future by the past
But yields himself to any who speaks fear.
Since then no words of mine suffice to calm him   *890*
I turn to Thee Apollo — Thou art nearest —
Thy suppliant, with these votive offerings.
Grant us deliverance and peace, for now
Fear is on all, when we see Oedipus,
The helmsman of the ship, so terrified.   *895*

*A reverent silence, while Iocasta lays the wreath at the altar and
sets fire to the incense. The wreath will remain and the incense
smoke during the rest of the play. Enter a Shepherd from Corinth.*

Corinthian. Might I inquire of you where I may find
   The royal palace of King Oedipus?
   Or, better, where himself is to be found?
Chorus-leader. There is the palace; himself, Sir, is within,
   But here his wife and mother of his children.   *900*
Corinthian. Ever may happiness attend on her,
   And hers, the wedded wife of such a man.
Iocasta. May you enjoy the same; your gentle words
   Deserve no less. — Now, Sir, declare your purpose;
   With what request, what message have you come?   *905*
Corinthian. With good news for your husband and his house.
Iocasta. What news is this? And who has sent you here?
Corinthian. I come from Corinth, and the news I bring
   Will give you joy, though joy be crossed with grief.
Iocasta. What is this, with its two-fold influence?   *910*
Corinthian. The common talk in Corinth is that they
   Will call on Oedipus to be their king.
Iocasta. What? Does old Polybus no longer reign?
Corinthian. Not now, for Death has laid him in his grave.
Iocasta. Go quickly to your master, girl; give him   *915*
   The news. — You oracles, where are you now?
   This is the man whom Oedipus so long
   Has shunned, fearing to kill him; now he's dead,
   And killed by Fortune, not by Oedipus.

Enter Oedipus, very nervous.

Oedipus. My dear Iocasta, tell me, my dear wife,   *920*
   Why have you sent to fetch me from the palace?

Iocasta. Listen to *him,* and as you hear, reflect
    What has become of all those oracles.
Oedipus. Who is this man? — What has he to tell me?
Iocasta. He is from Corinth, and he brings you news   *925*
    About your father. Polybus is dead.
Oedipus. What say you, sir? Tell me the news yourself.
Corinthian. If you would have me first report on this,
    I tell you; death has carried him away.
Oedipus. By treachery? Or did sickness come to him?   *930*
Corinthian. A small mischance will lay an old man low.
Oedipus. Poor Polybus! He died, then, of a sickness?
Corinthian. That, and the measure of his many years.
Oedipus. Ah me! Why then, Iocasta, should a man
    Regard the Pythian house of oracles,   *935*
    Or screaming birds, on whose authority
    I was to slay my father? But he is dead;
    The earth has covered him; and here am I,
    My sword undrawn — unless perchance *my* loss
    Has killed him; so might I be called his slayer.   *940*
    But for those oracles about my father,
    Those he has taken with him to the grave
    Wherein he lies, and they are come to nothing.
Iocasta. Did I not say long since it would be so?
Oedipus. You did; but I was led astray by fear.   *945*
Iocasta. So none of this deserves another thought.
Oedipus. Yet how can I not fear my mother's bed?
Iocasta. Why should we fear, seeing that man is ruled
    By chance, and there is room for no clear forethought?
    No; live at random, live as best one can.   *950*
    So do not fear this marriage with your mother;
    Many a man has suffered this before —
    But only in his dreams. Whoever thinks
    The least of this, he lives most comfortably.
Oedipus. Your every word I do accept, if she   *955*
    That bore me did not live; but as she does —
    Despite your wisdom, how can I but tremble?
Iocasta. Yet there is comfort in your father's death.
Oedipus. Great comfort, but still fear of her who lives.
Corinthian. And who is this who makes you so afraid?   *960*
Oedipus. Meropê, my man, the wife of Polybus.
Corinthian. And what in *her* gives cause of fear in *you?*
Oedipus. There was an awful warning from the gods.
Corinthian. Can it be told, or must it be kept secret?
Oedipus. No secret. Once Apollo said that I   *965*

Was doomed to lie with my own mother, and
Defile my own hands with my father's blood.
Wherefore has Corinth been, these many years,
My home no more. My fortunes have been fair. —
But it is good to see a parent's face.   *970*
Corinthian. It was for fear of *this* you fled the city?
Oedipus. This, and the shedding of my father's blood.
Corinthian. Why then, my lord, since I am come in friendship,
  I'll rid you here and now of that misgiving.
Oedipus. Be sure, your recompense would be in keeping.   *975*
Corinthian. It was the chief cause of my coming here
  That your return might bring me some advantage.
Oedipus. Back to my parents I will never go.
Corinthian. My son, it is clear, you know not what you
  do. . . .
Oedipus. Not know? What is this? Tell me what you mean. *980*
Corinthian. If for this reason you avoid your home.
Oedipus. Fearing Apollo's oracle may come true.
Corinthian. And you incur pollution from your parents?
Oedipus. That is the thought that makes me live in terror.
Corinthian. I tell you then, this fear of yours is idle. *985*
Oedipus. How? Am I not their child, and they my parents?
Corinthian. Because there's none of Polybus in you.
Oedipus. How can you say so? Was he not my father?
Corinthian. I am your father just as much as he!
Oedipus. A stranger equal to the father? How?   *990*
Corinthian. Neither did he beget you, nor did I.
Oedipus. Then for what reason did he call me son?
Corinthian. He had you as a gift — from my own hands.
Oedipus. And showed such love to me? Me, not his own?
Corinthian. Yes, his own childlessness so worked on him. *995*
Oedipus. You, when you gave me: had you bought, or found me?
Corinthian. I found you in the woods upon Cithaeron.
Oedipus. Why were you traveling in that neighborhood?
Corinthian. I tended flocks of sheep upon the mountain.
Oedipus. You were a shepherd, then, wandering for hire? *1000*
Corinthian. I was, my son; but that day, your preserver.
Oedipus. How so? What ailed me when you took me up?
Corinthian. For that, your ankles might give evidence.
Oedipus. Alas! Why speak of this, my life-long trouble?
Corinthian. I loosed the fetters clamped upon your feet. *1005*
Oedipus. A pretty gift to carry from the cradle!
Corinthian. It was for this they named you Oedipus.
Oedipus. Who did, my father or my mother? Tell me.

Corinthian. I cannot; he knows more, from whom I had
    you.
Oedipus. It was another, not yourself, that found me?   *1010*
Corinthian. Yes, you were given me by another shepherd.
Oedipus. Who? Do you know him? Can you name the man?
Corinthian. They said that he belonged to Laius.
Oedipus. What — him who once was ruler here in Thebes?
Corinthian. Yes, he it was for whom this man was shepherd. *1015*
Oedipus. And is he still alive, that I can see him?
Corinthian (turning to the Chorus). You that are native here would
    know that best.
Oedipus. Has any man of you now present here
    Acquaintance with this shepherd, him he speaks of?
    Has any seen him, here, or in the fields?   *1020*
    Speak; on this moment hangs discovery.
Chorus-leader. It is, I think, the man that you have sent for,
    The slave now in the country. But who should know
    The truth of this more than Iocasta here?
Oedipus. The man he speaks of: do you think, Iocasta,   *1025*
    He is the one I have already summoned?
Iocasta. What matters who he is? Pay no regard. —
    The tale is idle; it is best forgotten.
Oedipus. It cannot be that I should have this clue
    And then not find the secret of my birth.   *1030*
Iocasta. In God's name stop, if you have any thought
    For your own life! My ruin is enough.
Oedipus. Be not dismayed; nothing can prove you base.
    Not though I find my mother thrice a slave.
Iocasta. O, I beseech you, do not! Seek no more!   *1035*
Oedipus. You cannot move me. I *will* know the truth.
Iocasta. I know that what I say is for the best.
Oedipus. This "best" of yours! I have no patience with it.
Iocasta. O may you never learn what man you are!
Oedipus. Go, someone, bring the herdsman here to me,   *1040*
    And leave her to enjoy her pride of birth.
Iocasta. O man of doom! For by no other name
    Can I address you now or evermore.

                        Exit Iocasta.

Chorus-leader. The Queen has fled, my lord, as if before
    Some driving storm of grief. I fear that from   *1045*
    Her silence may break forth some great disaster.
Oedipus. Break forth what will! My birth, however humble,
    I am resolved to find. But she, perhaps,
    Is proud, as women will be; is ashamed

Of my low birth. But I do rate myself   *1050*
The child of Fortune, giver of all good,
And I shall not be put to shame, for I
Am born of Her; the Years who are my kinsmen
Distinguished my estate, now high, now low;
So born, I could not make me someone else   *1055*
And not do all to find my parentage.

Strophe 1

Chorus. If I have power of prophecy,
 [*animated rhythm*] If I have judgement wise and sure, Cithaeron
 (I swear by Olympus),
 Thou shalt be honored when the moon   *1060*
 Next is full, as mother and foster-nurse
 And birth-place of Oedipus, with festival and dancing,
 For thou hast given great blessings to our King.
 To Thee, Apollo, now we raise our cry:
 O grant our prayer find favor in thy sight!   *1065*

Antistrophe

 Who is thy mother, O my son?
 Is she an ageless nymph among the mountains,
 That bore thee to Pan?
 Or did Apollo father thee?
 For dear to him are the pastures in the hills.   *1070*
 Or Hermes, who ruleth from the summit of Kyllene?
 Or Dionysus on the mountain-tops,
 Did he receive thee from thy mother's arms,
 A nymph who follows him on Helicon?
Oedipus. If I, who never yet have met the man,   *1075*
 May risk conjecture, I think I see the herdsman
 Whom we have long been seeking. In his age
 He well accords; and more, I recognize
 Those who are with him as of my own household.
 But as for knowing, you will have advantage   *1080*
 Of me, if you have seen the man before.
Chorus-leader. 'Tis he, for certain — one of Laius' men,
 One of the shepherds whom he trusted most.

Enter the Theban Shepherd.

Oedipus. You first I ask, you who have come from Corinth:
 Is that the man you mean?   *1085*

Corinthian. That very man.

Oedipus. Come here, my man; look at me; answer me
  My questions. Were you ever Laius' man?

Theban. I was; his slave — born in the house, not bought.

Oedipus. What was your charge, or what your way of life? *1090*

Theban. Tending the sheep, the most part of my life.

Oedipus. And to what regions did you most resort?

Theban. Now it was Cithaeron, now the country round.

Oedipus. And was this man of your acquaintance there?

Theban. In what employment? Which is the man you mean? *1095*

Oedipus. Him yonder. Had you any dealings with him?

Theban. Not such that I can quickly call to mind.

Corinthian. No wonder, Sir, but though he has forgotten
  I can remind him. I am very sure,
  He knows the time when, round about Cithaeron, *1100*
  He with a double flock, and I with one,
  We spent together three whole summer seasons,
  From spring until the rising of Arcturus.
  Then, with the coming on of winter, I
  Drove my flocks home, he his, to Laius' folds. *1105*
  Is this the truth? or am I telling lies?

Theban. It is true, although it happened long ago.

Corinthian. Then tell me: do you recollect a baby
  You gave me once to bring up for my own?

Theban. Why this? Why are you asking me this question? *1110*

Corinthian. My friend, *here* is the man who was that baby!

Theban. O, devil take you! Cannot you keep silent?

Oedipus. Here, Sir! This man needs no reproof from you.
  Your tongue needs chastisement much more than his.

Theban. O best of masters, how am I offending? *1115*

Oedipus. Not telling of the child of whom he speaks.

Theban. He? He knows nothing. He is wasting time.

Oedipus. (*threatening*). If you'll not speak from pleasure, speak from
  pain.

Theban. No, no, I pray! Not torture an old man!

Oedipus. Here, someone quickly! Twist this fellow's arms! *1120*

Theban. Why, wretched man? What would you know besides?

Oedipus. That child: you gave it him, the one he speaks of?

Theban. I did. Ah God, would I have died instead!

Oedipus. And die you shall, unless you speak the truth.

Theban. And if I do, then death is still more certain. *1125*

Oedipus. This man, I think, is trying to delay me.

Theban. Not I! I said I gave the child — just now.

Oedipus. And got it — where? Your own? or someone else's?

Theban. No, not my own. Someone had given it me.

Oedipus. Who? Which of these our citizens? From what
    house?   *1130*
Theban. No, I implore you, master! Do not ask!
Oedipus. You die if I must question you again.
Theban. Then, 'twas a child of one in Laius' house.
Oedipus. You mean a slave? Or someone of his kin?
Theban. God! I am on the verge of saying it.   *1135*
Oedipus. And I of hearing it, but hear I must.
Theban. His own, or so they said. But she within
    Could tell you best — your wife — the truth of it.
Oedipus. What, did she give you it?
Theban. She did, my lord.   *1140*
Oedipus. With what intention?
Theban. That I should destroy it.
Oedipus. Her own? — How could she?
Theban. Frightened by oracles.
Oedipus. What oracles?   *1145*
Theban. That it would kill its parents.
Oedipus. Why did you let it go to this man here?
Theban. I pitied it, my lord. I thought to send
    The child abroad, whence this man came. And he
    Saved it, for utter doom. For if you are   *1150*
    The man he says, then you were born for ruin.
Oedipus. Ah God! Ah God! This is the truth, at last!
    O Sun, let me behold thee this once more,
    I who am proved accursed in my conception,
    And in my marriage, and in him I slew.   *1155*
           Exeunt severally Oedipus, Corinthian, Theban.

Strophe 1

Chorus. Alas! you generations of men!
    [*glyconics°*] Even while you live you are next to nothing!
    Has any man won for himself
    More than the shadow of happiness,
    A shadow that swiftly fades away?   *1160*
    Oedipus, now as I look on you,
    See your ruin, how can I say that
    Mortal man can be happy?

[1157] *glyconics* metrical feet consisting of a spondee (two long syllables), a dactyl
(two short syllables followed by one long syllable), and an amphimacer, or cretic
(one long syllable, followed by one short syllable, followed by one long syllable)

Antistrophe 1

For who won greater prosperity?
Sovereignty and wealth beyond all desiring?   *1165*
The crooked-clawed, riddling Sphinx,
Maiden and bird, you overcame;
You stood like a tower of strength to Thebes.
So you received our crown, received the
Highest honors that we could give —   *1170*
King in our mighty city.

Strophe 2

Who more wretched, more afflicted now,
With cruel misery, with fell disaster,
Your life in dust and ashes?
        O noble Oedipus!   *1175*
        How could it be? to come again
A bridegroom of her who gave you birth!
How could such a monstrous thing
Endure so long, unknown?

Antistrophe 2

Time sees all, and Time, in your despite,   *1180*
Disclosed and punished your unnatural marriage —
A child, and then a husband.
        O son of Laius,
        Would I had never looked on you!
I mourn you as one who mourns the dead.   *1185*
First you gave me back my life,
And now, that life is death.

Enter, from the palace, a Messenger.

Messenger. My Lords, most honored citizens of Thebes,
        What deeds am I to tell of, you to see!
        What heavy grief to bear, if still remains   *1190*
        Your native loyalty to our line of kings.
        For not the Ister, no, nor Phasis' flood.
        Could purify this house, such things it hides,
        Such others will it soon display to all,
        Evils self-sought. Of all our sufferings   *1195*
        Those hurt the most that we ourselves inflict.

Chorus-leader. Sorrow enough — too much — in what was known
    Already. What new sorrow do you bring?
Messenger. Quickest for me to say and you to hear:
    It is the Queen, Iocasta — she is dead.   *1200*
Chorus-leader. Iocasta, dead? But how? What was the cause?
Messenger. By her own hand. Of what has passed, the worst
    Cannot be yours: that was, to see it.
    But you shall hear, so far as memory serves,
    The cruel story. — In her agony   *1205*
    She ran across the courtyard, snatching at
    Her hair with both her hands. She made her way
    Straight to her chamber; she barred fast the doors
    And called on Laius, these long years dead,
    Remembering their by-gone procreation.   *1210*
    "Through this did you meet death yourself, and leave
    To me, the mother, child-bearing accursed
    To my own child." She cried aloud upon
    The bed where she had borne a double brood.
    Husband from husband, children from a child.   *1215*
    And thereupon she died, I know not how;
    For, groaning, Oedipus burst in, and we,
    For watching him, saw not *her* agony
    And how it ended. He, ranging through the palace,
    Came up to each man calling for a sword,   *1220*
    Calling for her whom he had called his wife,
    Asking where was she who had borne them all,
    Himself and his own children. So he raved.
    And then some deity showed him the way,
    For it was none of us that stood around;   *1225*
    He cried aloud, as if to someone who
    Was leading him; he leapt upon the doors,
    Burst from their sockets the yielding bars, and fell
    Into the room; and there, hanged by the neck,
    We saw his wife, held in a swinging cord.   *1230*
    He, when he saw it, groaned in misery
    And loosed her body from the rope. When now
    She lay upon the ground, awful to see
    Was that which followed: from her dress he tore
    The golden brooches that she had been wearing,   *1235*
    Raised them, and with their points struck his own eyes,
    Crying aloud that they should never see
    What he had suffered and what he had done,
    But in the dark henceforth they should behold
    Those whom they ought not; nor should recognize   *1240*

Those whom he longed to see. To such refrain
He smote his eyeballs with the pins, not once,
Nor twice; and as he smote them, blood ran down
His face, not dripping slowly, but there fell
Showers of black rain and blood-red hail together.   *1245*
Not on his head alone, but on them both,
Husband and wife, this common storm has broken.
Their ancient happiness of early days
Was happiness indeed; but now, today,
Death, ruin, lamentation, shame — of all   *1250*
The ills there are, not one is wanting here.
Chorus-leader. Now is there intermission in his agony?
Messenger. He shouts for someone to unbar the gates,
And to display to Thebes the parricide,
His mother's — no, I cannot speak the words;   *1255*
For, by the doom he uttered, he will cast
Himself beyond our borders, not remain
To be a curse at home. But he needs strength,
And one to guide him; for these wounds are greater
Than he can bear — as you shall see; for look!   *1260*
They draw the bolts. A sight you will behold
To move the pity even of an enemy.

The doors open. Oedipus slowly advances.
Chorus: O horrible, dreadful sight. More dreadful far

These verses sung or chanted in a slow march-time.

Than any I have yet seen. What cruel frenzy
Came over you? What spirit with superhuman leap   *1265*
Came to assist your grim destiny?
Ah, most unhappy man!
But no! I cannot bear even to look at you,
Though there is much that I would ask and see and hear.
But I shudder at the very sight of you.   *1270*
Oedipus (sings in the dochmiac rhythm). Alas! alas! and woe for my
      misery!
Where are my steps taking me?
My random voice is lost in the air.
O God! how hast thou crushed me!
Chorus-leader (spoken). Too terribly for us to hear or see.   *1275*
Oedipus (sings). O cloud of darkness abominable,
My enemy unspeakable,
In cruel onset insuperable.

Alas! alas! Assailed at once by pain
Of pin-points and of memory of crimes.   *1280*
Chorus-leader. In such tormenting pains you well may cry
   A double grief and feel a double woe.
Oedipus (sings). Ah, my friend!
   Still at my side? Still steadfast?
   Still can you endure me?   *1285*
   Still care for me, a blind man?
   (Speaks.) For it is you, my friend; I know 'tis you;
   Though all is darkness, yet I know your voice.
Chorus-leader. O, to destroy your sight! How could you
   bring
   Yourself to do it? What god incited you?   *1290*
Oedipus (sings). It was Apollo, friends, Apollo.
   He decreed that I should suffer what I suffer;
   But the hand that struck, alas! was my own,
   And not another's.
   For why should I have sight,   *1295*
   When sight of nothing could give me pleasure?
Chorus. It was even as you say.
Oedipus. What have I left, my friends, to see,
   To cherish, whom to speak with, or
   To listen to, with joy?   *1300*
   Lead me away at once, far from Thebes;
   Lead me away, my friends!
   I have destroyed; I am accursed, and, what is more,
   Hateful to Heaven, as no other.
Chorus-leader (speaks). Unhappy your intention, and unhappy *1305*
   Your fate. O would that I had never known you!
Oedipus (sings). Curses on him, whoever he was,
   Who took the savage fetters from my feet,
      Snatched me from death, and saved me.
      No thanks I owe him,   *1310*
      For had I died that day
   Less ruin had I brought on me and mine.
Chorus. That wish is my wish too.
Oedipus. I had not then come and slain my father.
      Nor then would men have called me   *1315*
      Husband of her that bore me.
   Now am I God's enemy, child of the guilty,
   And she that bore me has borne too my children;
   And if there is evil surpassing evil,
      That has come to Oedipus.   *1320*

Chorus-leader. How can I say that you have counseled well?
    Far better to be dead than to be blind.
Oedipus. That what is done was not done for the best
    Seek not to teach me: counsel me no more.
    I know not how I could have gone to Hades   *1325*
    And with these eyes have looked upon my father
    Or on my mother; such things have I done
    To them, death is no worthy punishment.
    Or could I look for pleasure in the sight
    Of my own children, born as they were born?   *1330*
    Never! No pleasure there, for eyes of mine,
    Nor in this city, nor its battlements
    Nor sacred images. From these — ah, miserable! —
    I, the most nobly born of any Theban
    Am banned for ever by my own decree   *1335*
    That the defiler should be driven forth,
    The man accursed of Heaven and Laius' house.
    Was I to find such taint in me, and then
    With level eyes to look *them* in the face?
    Nay more: if for my ears I could have built   *1340*
    Some dam to stay the flood of sound, that I
    Might lose both sight and hearing, and seal up
    My wretched body — that I would have done.
    How good to dwell beyond the reach of pain!
       Cithaeron! Why did you accept me? Why   *1345*
    Did you not take and kill me? Never then
    Should I have come to dwell among the Thebans.
       O Polybus! Corinth! and that ancient home
    I thought my father's — what a thing you nurtured!
    How fair, how foul beneath! For I am found   *1350*
    Foul in myself and in my parentage.
       O you three ways, that in a hidden glen
    Do meet: you narrow branching roads within
    The forest — you, through my own hands, did drink
    My father's blood, that was my own. — Ah! do you   *1355*
    Remember what you saw me do? And what
    I did again in Thebes? You marriages!
    You did beget me: then, having begotten,
    Bore the same crop again, and brought to light
    Commingled blood of fathers, brothers, sons,   *1360*
    Brides, mothers, wives; all that there can be
    Among the human kind most horrible!
       But that which it is foul to do, it is

Not fair to speak of. Quick as you can, I beg,
Banish me, hide me, slay me! Throw me forth   1365
Into the sea, where I may sink from view.
I pray you, deign to touch one so afflicted,
And do not fear: there is no man alive
Can bear this load of evil but myself.
Chorus-leader. To listen to your prayers, Creon is here,   1370
For act or guidance opportune; for he,
In your defection, is our champion.

Enter Creon.

Oedipus. Alas! alas! How can I speak to him?
What word of credit find? In all my commerce
With him aforetime I am proven false.   1375
Creon. No exultation, Oedipus, and no reproach
Of injuries inflicted brings me here;
But if the face of men moves not your shame,
Then reverence show to that all-nurturing fire,
The holy Sun, that he be not polluted   1380
By such accursèd sight, which neither Earth
Nor rain from Heaven nor sunlight can endure.
    Take him within, and quickly: it is right
His kinsmen only should behold and hear
Evils that chiefly on his kinsmen fall.   1385
Oedipus. In Heaven's name — since you cheat my expectation,
So noble towards my baseness — grant me this:
It is for you I ask it, not myself.
Creon. What is this supplication that you make?
Oedipus. Drive me at once beyond your bounds, where I   1390
Shall be alone, and no one speak to me.
Creon. I would have done it; but I first desired
To ask the God what he would have me do.
Oedipus. No, his command was given in full, to slay
Me, the polluter and the parricide.   1395
Creon. Those were his words; but in our present need
It would be wise to ask what we should do.
Oedipus. You will inquire for such a wretch as I?
Creon. I will; for now *you* may believe the god.
Oedipus. Yes; and on you I lay this charge and duty: 1400
Give burial, as you will, to her who lies
Within — for she is yours, and this is proper;
And, while I live, let not my father's city
Endure to have me as a citizen.
My home must be the mountains— on Cithaeron,   1405

Which, while they lived, my parents chose to be
My tomb: they wished to slay me; now they shall.
For this I know: sickness can never kill me,
Nor any other evil; I was not saved
That day from death, except for some strange doom.   1410
My fate must take the course it will. — Now, for my sons,
Be not concerned for them: they can, being men,
Fend for themselves, wherever they may be:
But my unhappy daughters, my two girls,
Whose chairs were always set beside my own   1415
At table — they who shared in every dish
That was prepared for me — oh Creon! these
Do I commend to you. And grant me this:
To take them in my arms, and weep for them.
My lord! most noble Creon! could I now   1420
But hold them in my arms, then I should think
I had them as I had when I could see them.
Ah! what is this?
Ah Heaven! do I not hear my dear ones, sobbing?
Has Creon, in his pity, sent to me   1425
My darling children? Has he? Is it true?

Creon. It is; they have been always your delight;
    So, knowing this, I had them brought to you.

Oedipus. Then Heaven reward you, and for this kind service
    Protect you better than it protected me!   1430
    Where are you, children? Where? O come to me!
    Come, let me clasp you with a brother's arms,
    These hands, which helped your father's eyes, once bright,
    To look upon you as they see you now —
    Your father who, not seeing, nor inquiring.   1435
    Gave you for mother her who bore himself.
    See you I cannot; but I weep for you,
    For the unhappiness that must be yours,
    And for the bitter life that you must lead.
    What gathering of the citizens, what festivals,   1440
    Will you have part in? Your high celebrations
    Will be to go back home, and sit in tears.
    And when the time for marriage comes, what man
    Will stake upon the ruin and the shame
    That *I* am to my parents and to you?   1445
    Nothing is wanting there: your father slew
    His father, married her who gave him birth,
    And then, from that same source whence he himself
    Had sprung, got you. — With these things they will taunt

> you;
> And who will take you then in marriage? — Nobody; *1450*
> But you must waste, unwedded and unfruitful.
>   Ah, Creon! Since they have no parent now
> But you — for both of us who gave them life
> Have perished — suffer them not to be cast out
> Homeless and beggars; for they are your kin.   *1455*
> Have pity on them, for they are so young,
> So desolate, except for you alone.
> Say "Yes," good Creon! Let your hand confirm it.
> And now, my children, for my exhortation
> You are too young; but you can pray that I   *1460*
> May live henceforward — where I should; and you
> More happily than the father who begot you.

Creon. Now make an end of tears, and go within.
Oedipus. Then I must go — against my will.
Creon. There is a time for everything.   *1465*
Oedipus. You know what I would have you do?
Creon. If you will tell me, I shall know.
Oedipus. Send me away, away from Thebes.
Creon. The God, not I, must grant you this.
Oedipus. The gods hate no man more than me!   *1470*
Creon. Then what you ask they soon will give.
Oedipus. You promise this?
Creon. Ah no! When I
>   Am ignorant, I do not speak.
Oedipus. Then lead me in; I say no more.   *1475*
Creon. Release the children then, and come.
Oedipus. What? Take these children from me? No!
Creon. Seek not to have your way in all things:
>   Where you had your way before,
>   Your mastery broke before the end.   *1480*

[*There was no doubt a short concluding utterance from the Chorus.
What stands in the mss. appears to be spurious.*]*

---

* Few other scholars share Professor Kitto's suspicion that the concluding lines in
the manuscript are spurious. The passage is translated thus by J. T. Sheppard:

> *Chorus.* Look, ye who dwell in Thebes. This man was Oedipus.
> That mighty King, who knew the riddle's mystery,
> Whom all the city envied, Fortune's favorite.
> Behold, in the event, the storm of his calamities,
> And, being mortal, think on that last day of death,
> Which all must see, and speak of no man's happiness
> Till, without sorrow, he hath passed the goal of life.

QUESTIONS

1. On the basis of lines 1–149, characterize Oedipus. What additional traits are revealed in lines 205–491?
2. Is it fair to say that Oedipus is morally guilty? Does he argue that he is morally innocent because he did not intend to do immoral deeds? Can it be said that he is guilty of *hybris* but that *hybris* (see page 596) has nothing to do with his fall?
3. Oedipus says that he blinds himself in order not to look upon people he should not. What further reasons can be given? Why does he not (like his mother) commit suicide?
4. How fair is it to say that the play shows the contemptibleness of human efforts to act intelligently?
5. How fair is it to say that in *Oedipus* the gods are evil?
6. Are the choral odes lyrical interludes that serve to separate the scenes, or do they advance the dramatic action?
7. Matthew Arnold said that Sophocles saw life steadily and saw it whole. But in this play is Sophocles facing the facts of life, or, on the contrary, is he avoiding life as it usually is and presenting a series of unnatural and outrageous coincidences?
8. Can you describe your emotions at the end of the play? Do they include pity for Oedipus? Pity for all human beings, including yourself? Fear that you might be punished for some unintended transgression? Awe, engendered by a perception of the interrelatedness of things? Relief that the story is only a story? Exhilaration?

A NOTE ON THE ELIZABETHAN THEATER

Shakespeare's theater was wooden, round, or polygonal (the Chorus in *Henry V* calls it a "wooden O"). About eight hundred spectators could stand in the yard in front of — and perhaps along the two sides of — the stage that jutted from the rear wall, and another fifteen hundred or so spectators could sit in the three roofed galleries that ringed the stage. That portion of the galleries that was above the rear of the stage was sometimes used by actors. Entry to the stage was normally gained by doors at the rear, but some use was made of a curtained alcove — or perhaps a booth — between the doors, which allowed characters to be "discovered" (revealed) as in the modern proscenium theater, which normally employs a curtain. A performance was probably uninterrupted by intermissions or by long pauses for the changing of scenery; a group of characters leaves the stage, another enters, and if the locale has changed, the new characters somehow tell us. (Modern editors customarily add indications of locales to help a reader, but it should be understood that the action of the Elizabethan stage was continuous.)

A NOTE ON THE TEXT OF *HAMLET*

Shakespeare's *Hamlet* comes to us in three versions. The first, known as the First Quarto (Q1), was published in 1603. It is an illegitimate garbled version, perhaps derived from the memory of the actor who played Marcellus (this part is conspicuously more accurate than the rest of the play) in a short version of the play. The second printed version (Q2), which appeared in 1604, is almost twice as long as Q1; all in all, it is the best text we have, doubtless published (as Q1 was not) with the permission of Shakespeare's theatrical company. The third printed version, in the First Folio (the collected edition of Shakespeare's plays, published in 1623), is also legitimate, but it seems to be an acting version, for it lacks some two hundred lines of Q2. On the other hand, the Folio text includes some ninety lines not found in Q2. Because Q2 is the longest version, giving us more of the play as Shakespeare conceived it than either of the other texts, it serves as the basic version for this text. Unfortunately, the printers of it often worked carelessly: words and phrases are omitted, there are plain misreadings of what must have been in Shakespeare's manuscript, and speeches are

Johannes de Witt, a Continental visitor to London, made a drawing of the Swan
Theatre in about the year 1596. The original drawing is lost; this is Arend van
Buchel's copy of it.

sometimes wrongly assigned. It was therefore necessary to turn to the First Folio for many readings. It has been found useful, also, to divide the play into acts and scenes; these divisions, not found in Q2 (and only a few are found in the Folio), are purely editorial additions, and they are therefore enclosed in square brackets.

William Shakespeare *(English. 1564–1616)*

The Tragedy of Hamlet
Prince of Denmark

[List of Characters

Claudius, King of Denmark
Hamlet, son to the late, and nephew to the present, King
Polonius, Lord Chamberlain
Horatio, friend to Hamlet
Laertes, son to Polonius
Voltemand
Cornelius
Rosencrantz } courtiers
Guildenstern
Osric
A Gentleman
A Priest
Marcellus } officers
Barnardo
Francisco, a soldier
Reynaldo, servant to Polonius
Players
Two Clowns, gravediggers
Fortinbras, Prince of Norway
A Norwegian Captain
English Ambassadors
Gertrude, Queen of Denmark, mother to Hamlet
Ophelia, daughter to Polonius
Ghost of Hamlet's father
Lords, Ladies, Officers, Soldiers, Sailors, Messengers, Attendants

Scene. *Elsinore]*

[ACT I
Scene I. *A guard platform of the castle.]*

Enter Barnardo and Francisco, two sentinels.

Barnardo. Who's there?

Francisco. Nay, answer me. Stand and unfold°* yourself.
Barnardo. Long live the King!°
Francisco. Barnardo?
Barnardo. He.   5
Francisco. You come most carefully upon your hour.
Barnardo. 'Tis now struck twelve. Get thee to bed, Francisco.
Francisco. For this relief much thanks. 'Tis bitter cold,
    And I am sick at heart.
Barnardo. Have you had quiet guard?
Francisco.   Not a mouse stirring.   10
Barnardo. Well, good night.
    If you do meet Horatio and Marcellus,
    The rivals° of my watch, bid them make haste.

    Enter Horatio and Marcellus.

Francisco. I think I hear them. Stand, ho! Who is there?
Horatio. Friends to this ground.
Marcellus.   And liegemen to the Dane.°   15
Francisco. Give you° good night.
Marcellus.   O, farewell, honest soldier.
    Who hath relieved you?
Francisco.   Barnardo hath my place.
    Give you good night.
                              Exit Francisco.
Marcellus.   Holla, Barnardo!
Barnardo.   Say —
    What, is Horatio there?
Horatio.   A piece of him.
Barnardo. Welcome, Horatio. Welcome, good Marcellus.   20
Marcellus. What, has this thing appeared again tonight?
Barnardo. I have seen nothing.
Marcellus. Horatio says 'tis but our fantasy,
    And will not let belief take hold of him
    Touching this dreaded sight twice seen of us;   25
    Therefore I have entreated him along
    With us to watch the minutes of this night,
    That, if again this apparition come,
    He may approve° our eyes and speak to it.
Horatio. Tush, tush, 'twill not appear.

---

* The degree sign (°) indicates a footnote, which is keyed to the text by line numbers. Text references are printed in **boldface italic** type; the annotation follows in roman type. The notes are Edward Hubler's for the Signet edition of *Hamlet*. I.i. **²unfold** disclose **³Long live the King** (perhaps a password, perhaps a greeting) **¹³rivals** partners **¹⁵liegemen to the Dane** loyal subjects to the King of Denmark **¹⁶Give you** God give you **²⁹approve** confirm

Barnardo.   Sit down awhile,   *30*
    And let us once again assail your ears,
    That are so fortified against our story,
    What we have two nights seen.
Horatio.   Well, sit we down,
    And let us hear Barnardo speak of this.
Barnardo. Last night of all,   *35*
    When yond same star that's westward from the pole°
    Had made his course t' illume that part of heaven
    Where now it burns, Marcellus and myself,
    The bell then beating one —

    Enter Ghost.

Marcellus. Peace, break thee off. Look where it comes again.   *40*
Barnardo. In the same figure like the king that's dead.
Marcellus. Thou art a scholar; speak to it, Horatio.
Barnardo. Looks 'a not like the king? Mark it, Horatio.
Horatio. Most like: it harrows me with fear and wonder.
Barnardo. It would be spoke to.
Marcellus.   Speak to it, Horatio.   *45*
Horatio. What art thou that usurp'st this time of night,
    Together with that fair and warlike form
    In which the majesty of buried Denmark°
    Did sometimes march? By heaven I charge thee, speak.
Marcellus. It is offended.
Barnardo.   See, it stalks away.   *50*
Horatio. Stay! Speak, speak. I charge thee, speak.
                          Exit Ghost.
Marcellus. 'Tis gone and will not answer.
Barnardo. How now, Horatio? You tremble and look pale.
    Is not this something more than fantasy?
    What think you on't?   *55*
Horatio. Before my God, I might not this believe
    Without the sensible and true avouch°
    Of mine own eyes.
Marcellus.   Is it not like the King?
Horatio. As thou art to thyself.
    Such was the very armor he had on   *60*
    When he the ambitious Norway° combated:
    So frowned he once, when, in an angry parle,°
    He smote the sledded Polacks° on the ice.

---

[36]*pole* polestar   [48]***buried Denmark*** the buried King of Denmark   [57]***sensible and
true avouch*** sensory and true proof   [61]***Norway*** King of Norway   [62]***parle*** parley
[63]***sledded Polacks*** Poles in sledges

'Tis strange.

Marcellus. Thus twice before, and jump° at this dead hour,   65
     With martial stalk hath he gone by our watch.

Horatio. In what particular thought to work I know not;
     But, in the gross and scope° of my opinion,
     This bodes some strange eruption to our state.

Marcellus. Good now, sit down, and tell me he that knows,   70
     Why this same strict and most observant watch
     So nightly toils the subject° of the land,
     And why such daily cast of brazen cannon
     And foreign mart° for implements of war,
     Why such impress° of shipwrights, whose sore task   75
     Does not divide the Sunday from the week,
     What might be toward° that this sweaty haste
     Doth make the night joint-laborer with the day?
     Who is't that can inform me?

Horatio.   That can I.
     At least the whisper goes so: our last king,   80
     Whose image even but now appeared to us,
     Was, as you know, by Fortinbras of Norway,
     Thereto pricked on by a most emulate pride,
     Dared to the combat; in which our valiant Hamlet
     (For so this side of our known world esteemed him)   85
     Did slay this Fortinbras, who, by a sealed compact
     Well ratified by law and heraldry,°
     Did forfeit, with his life, all those his lands
     Which he stood seized° of, to the conqueror;
     Against the which a moiety competent°   90
     Was gagèd° by our King, which had returned
     To the inheritance of Fortinbras,
     Had he been vanquisher, as, by the same comart°
     And carriage of the article designed,°
     His fell to Hamlet. Now, sir, young Fortinbras,   95
     Of unimprovèd° mettle hot and full,
     Hath in the skirts° of Norway here and there
     Sharked up° a list of lawless resolutes,°

---

[65]*jump* just   [68]*gross and scope* general drift   [72]*toils the subject* makes the subjects toil   [74]*mart* trading   [75]*impress* forced service   [77]*toward* in preparation   [87]*law and heraldry* heraldic law (governing the combat)   [89]*seized* possessed   [90]*moiety competent* equal portion   [91]*gagèd* engaged, pledged   [93]*comart* agreement   [94]*carriage of the article designed* import of the agreement drawn up   [96]*unimprovèd* untried   [97]*skirts* borders   [98]*Sharked up* collected indiscriminately (as a shark gulps its prey)   [98]*resolutes* desperadoes

For food and diet, to some enterprise
That hath a stomach in't;° which is no other,   *100*
As it doth well appear unto our state,
But to recover of us by strong hand
And terms compulsatory, those foresaid lands
So by his father lost; and this, I take it,
Is the main motive of our preparations,   *105*
The source of this our watch, and the chief head°
Of this posthaste and romage° in the land.
Barnardo. I think it be no other but e'en so;
    Well may it sort° that this portentous figure
    Comes armèd through our watch so like the King   *110*
    That was and is the question of these wars.
Horatio. A mote it is to trouble the mind's eye:
    In the most high and palmy state of Rome,
    A little ere the mightiest Julius fell,
    The graves stood tenantless, and the sheeted dead   *115*
    Did squeak and gibber in the Roman streets;°
    As stars with trains of fire and dews of blood,
    Disasters° in the sun; and the moist star,°
    Upon whose influence Neptune's empire stands,
    Was sick almost to doomsday with eclipse.   *120*
    And even the like precurse° of feared events,
    As harbingers° preceding still° the fates
    And prologue to the omen° coming on,
    Have heaven and earth together demonstrated
    Unto our climatures° and countrymen.   *125*

Enter Ghost.

But soft, behold, lo where it comes again!
I'll cross it,° though it blast me. — Stay, illusion.

It spreads his° arms.

If thou hast any sound or use of voice,
Speak to me.

---

[100]*hath   a   stomach   in't* i.e., requires courage [106]*head* fountainhead,
origin [107]*romage* bustle [109]*sort* befit [116]*Did squeak . . . Roman streets* (the
break in the sense which follows this line suggests that a line has dropped
out) [118]*Disasters* threatening signs [118]*moist star* moon [121]*precurse* precursor,
foreshadowing [122]*harbingers* forerunners [122]*still* always [123]*omen* calamity
[125]*climatures* regions [127]*cross it* (1) cross its path, confront it, (2) make the sign
of the cross in front of it [127] s.d. *his* i.e., its, the ghost's (though possibly what
is meant is that Horatio spreads his own arms, making a cross of himself)

If there be any good thing to be done 130
That may to thee do ease and grace to me,
Speak to me.
If thou art privy to thy country's fate,
Which happily° foreknowing may avoid,
O, speak! 135
Or if thou hast uphoarded in thy life
Extorted° treasure in the womb of earth,
For which, they say, you spirits oft walk in death,

The cock crows.

Speak of it. Stay and speak. Stop it, Marcellus.
Marcellus. Shall I strike at it with my partisan°? 140
Horatio. Do, if it will not stand.
Barnardo.   'Tis here.
Horatio.   'Tis here.
Marcellus. 'Tis gone.

Exit Ghost.

We do it wrong, being so majestical,
To offer it the show of violence,
For it is as the air, invulnerable, 145
And our vain blows malicious mockery.
Barnardo. It was about to speak when the cock crew.
Horatio. And then it started, like a guilty thing
Upon a fearful summons. I have heard,
The cock, that is the trumpet to the morn, 150
Doth with his lofty and shrill-sounding throat
Awake the god of day, and at his warning,
Whether in sea or fire, in earth or air,
Th' extravagant and erring° spirit hies
To his confine; and of the truth herein 155
This present object made probation.°
Marcellus. It faded on the crowing of the cock.
Some say that ever 'gainst° that season comes
Wherein our Savior's birth is celebrated,
This bird of dawning singeth all night long, 160
And then, they say, no spirit dare stir abroad,
The nights are wholesome, then no planets strike,°
No fairy takes,° nor witch hath power to charm:
So hallowed and so gracious is that time.

---

¹³⁴*happily* haply, perhaps ¹³⁷*Extorted* ill-won ¹⁴⁰*partisan* pike (a long-handled weapon) ¹⁵⁴*extravagant* **and** *erring* out of bounds and wandering ¹⁵⁶*probation* proof ¹⁵⁸*'gainst* just before ¹⁶²*strike* exert an evil influence ¹⁶³*takes* bewitches

Horatio. So have I heard and do in part believe it.   *165*
    But look, the morn in russet mantle clad
    Walks o'er the dew of yon high eastward hill.
    Break we our watch up, and by my advice
    Let us impart what we have seen tonight
    Unto young Hamlet, for upon my life   *170*
    This spirit, dumb to us, will speak to him.
    Do you consent we shall acquaint him with it,
    As needful in our loves, fitting our duty?
Marcellus. Let's do 't, I pray, and I this morning know
    Where we shall find him most convenient.   *175*
                                    Exeunt.

    [Scene II. *The castle.*]

    Flourish.° Enter Claudius, King of Denmark, Gertrude the Queen,
    Councilors, Polonius and his son Laertes, Hamlet, cum aliis° [in-
    cluding Voltemand and Cornelius].

King. Though yet of Hamlet our dear brother's death
    The memory be green, and that it us befitted
    To bear our hearts in grief, and our whole kingdom
    To be contracted in one brow of woe,
    Yet so far hath discretion fought with nature   *5*
    That we with wisest sorrow think on him
    Together with remembrance of ourselves.
    Therefore our sometime sister,° now our Queen,
    Th' imperial jointress° to this warlike state,
    Have we, as 'twere, with a defeated joy,   *10*
    With an auspicious° and a dropping eye,
    With mirth in funeral, and with dirge in marriage,
    In equal scale weighing delight and dole,
    Taken to wife. Nor have we herein barred
    Your better wisdoms, which have freely gone   *15*
    With this affair along. For all, our thanks.
    Now follows that you know young Fortinbras,
    Holding a weak supposal of our worth,
    Or thinking by our late dear brother's death
    Our state to be disjoint and out of frame,°   *20*
    Colleaguèd with this dream of his advantage,°

I.ii. ˢ·ᵈ·*Flourish* fanfare of trumpets ˢ·ᵈ·*cum aliis* with others (Latin) ⁸*our sometime*
sister my (the royal "we") former sister-in-law ⁹*jointress* joint tenant,
partner ¹¹*auspicious* joyful ²⁰*frame* order ²¹*advantage* superiority

He hath not failed to pester us with message,
Importing the surrender of those lands
Lost by his father, with all bands of law,
To our most valiant brother. So much for him.   *25*
Now for ourself and for this time of meeting.
Thus much the business is: we have here writ
To Norway, uncle of young Fortinbras —
Who, impotent and bedrid, scarcely hears
Of this his nephew's purpose — to suppress   *30*
His further gait° herein, in that the levies,
The lists, and full proportions° are all made
Out of his subject;° and we here dispatch
You, good Cornelius, and you, Voltemand,
For bearers of this greeting to old Norway,   *35*
Giving to you no further personal power
To business with the King, more than the scope
Of these delated articles° allow.
Farewell, and let your haste commend your duty.

Cornelius, Voltemand. In that, and all things, will we show our
          duty.   *40*

King. We doubt it nothing. Heartily farewell.

                              Exit Voltemand and Cornelius.
And now, Laertes, what's the news with you?
You told us of some suit. What is't, Laertes?
You cannot speak of reason to the Dane
And lose your voice.° What wouldst thou beg, Laertes,   *45*
That shall not be my offer, not thy asking?
The head is not more native° to the heart,
The hand more instrumental to the mouth,
Than is the throne of Denmark to thy father.
What wouldst thou have, Laertes?

Laertes.   My dread lord,   *50*
Your leave and favor to return to France,
From whence though willingly I came to Denmark
To show my duty in your coronation,
Yet now I must confess, that duty done,
My thoughts and wishes bend again toward France   *55*
And bow them to your gracious leave and pardon.

King. Have you your father's leave? What says Polonius?

Polonius. He hath, my lord, wrung from me my slow leave

---

[31]*gait*   proceeding   [32]***proportions***   supplies for war   [33]***Out of his subject***   i.e.,
out of old Norway's subjects and realm   [38]***delated articles***   detailed documents   [45]*lose*
your voice   waste your breath   [47]***native***   related

By laborsome petition, and at last
Upon his will I sealed my hard consent.°   *60*
I do beseech you give him leave to go.
King. Take thy fair hour, Laertes. Time be thine,
And thy best graces spend it at thy will.
But now, my cousin° Hamlet, and my son —
Hamlet [*aside*]. A little more than kin, and less than kind!°   *65*
King. How is it that the clouds still hang on you?
Hamlet. Not so, my lord. I am too much in the sun.°
Queen. Good Hamlet, cast thy nighted color off,
And let thine eye look like a friend on Denmark.
Do not forever with thy vailèd° lids   *70*
Seek for thy noble father in the dust.
Thou know'st 'tis common; all that lives must die,
Passing through nature to eternity.
Hamlet. Ay, madam, it is common.°
Queen.   If it be,
Why seems it so particular with thee?   *75*
Hamlet. Seems, madam? Nay, it is. I know not "seems."
'Tis not alone my inky cloak, good mother,
Nor customary suits of solemn black,
Nor windy suspiration° of forced breath,
No, nor the fruitful river in the eye,   *80*
Nor the dejected havior of the visage,
Together with all forms, moods, shapes of grief,
That can denote me truly. These indeed seem,
For they are actions that a man might play,
But I have that within which passes show;   *85*
These but the trappings and the suits of woe.
King. 'Tis sweet and commendable in your nature, Hamlet,
To give these mourning duties to your father,
But you must know your father lost a father,
That father lost, lost his, and the survivor bound   *90*
In filial obligation for some term
To do obsequious° sorrow. But to persever
In obstinate condolement° is a course

---

⁶⁰*Upon   his . . .   hard   consent* to his desire I gave my reluctant
consent ⁶⁴*cousin* kinsman ⁶⁵*kind* (pun on the meanings "kindly" and "natural";
though doubly related — *more than kin* — Hamlet asserts that he neither resembles
Claudius in nature nor feels kindly toward him) ⁶⁷*sun* sunshine of royal favor
(with a pun on "son") ⁷⁰*vailèd* lowered ⁷⁴*common* (1) universal, (2)
vulgar ⁷⁹*windy suspiration* heavy sighing ⁹²*obsequious* suitable to obsequies
(funerals) ⁹³*condolement* mourning

Of impious stubbornness. 'Tis unmanly grief.
It shows a will most incorrect to heaven,   *95*
A heart unfortified, a mind impatient,
An understanding simple and unschooled.
For what we know must be and is as common
As any the most vulgar° thing to sense,
Why should we in our peevish opposition   *100*
Take it to heart? Fie, 'tis a fault to heaven,
A fault against the dead, a fault to nature,
To reason most absurd, whose common theme
Is death of fathers, and who still hath cried,
From the first corse° till he that died today,   *105*
"This must be so." We pray you throw to earth
This unprevailing° woe, and think of us
As of a father, for let the world take note
You are the most immediate to our throne,
And with no less nobility of love   *110*
Than that which dearest father bears his son
Do I impart toward you. For your intent
In going back to school in Wittenberg,
It is most retrograde° to our desire,
And we beseech you, bend you° to remain   *115*
Here in the cheer and comfort of our eye,
Our chiefest courtier, cousin, and our son.
Queen. Let not thy mother lose her prayers, Hamlet.
I pray thee stay with us, go not to Wittenberg.
Hamlet. I shall in all my best obey you, madam.   *120*
King. Why, 'tis a loving and a fair reply.
Be as ourself in Denmark. Madam, come.
This gentle and unforced accord of Hamlet
Sits smiling to my heart, in grace whereof
No jocund health that Denmark drinks today,   *125*
But the great cannon to the clouds shall tell,
And the King's rouse° the heaven shall bruit° again,
Respeaking earthly thunder. Come away.

                                    Flourish. Exit all but Hamlet.
Hamlet. O that this too too sullied° flesh would melt,
Thaw, and resolve itself into a dew,   *130*

---

⁹⁹*vulgar* common   ¹⁰⁵*corse* corpse   ¹⁰⁷*unprevailing* unavailing   ¹¹⁴*retrograde*
contrary   ¹¹⁵*bend you* incline   ¹²⁷*rouse* deep drink   ¹²⁷*bruit* announce noisily
¹²⁹*sullied* (Q2 has *sallied,* here modernized to *sullied,* which makes sense and is
therefore given; but the Folio reading, *solid,* which fits better with *melt,* is quite
possibly correct)

Or that the Everlasting had not fixed
His canon° 'gainst self-slaughter. O God, God,
How weary, stale, flat, and unprofitable
Seem to me all the uses of this world!
Fie on't, ah, fie, 'tis an unweeded garden   *135*
That grows to seed. Things rank and gross in nature
Possess it merely.° That it should come to this:
But two months dead, nay, not so much, not two,
So excellent a king, that was to this
Hyperion° to a satyr, so loving to my mother   *140*
That he might not beteem° the winds of heaven
Visit her face too roughly. Heaven and earth,
Must I remember? Why, she would hang on him
As if increase of appetite had grown
By what it fed on; and yet within a month —   *145*
Let me not think on't; frailty, thy name is woman —
A little month, or ere those shoes were old
With which she followed my poor father's body
Like Niobe,° all tears, why she, even she —
O God, a beast that wants discourse of reason°   *150*
Would have mourned longer — married with my uncle,
My father's brother, but no more like my father
Than I to Hercules. Within a month,
Ere yet the salt of most unrighteous tears
Had left the flushing° in her gallèd eyes,   *155*
She married. O, most wicked speed, to post°
With such dexterity to incestuous° sheets!
It is not, nor it cannot come to good.
But break my heart, for I must hold my tongue.

Enter Horatio, Marcellus, and Barnardo.

Horatio. Hail to your lordship!
Hamlet.   I am glad to see you well.   *160*
  Horatio — or I do forget myself.
Horatio. The same, my lord, and your poor servant ever.
Hamlet. Sir, my good friend, I'll change° that name with you.
  And what make you from Wittenberg, Horatio?

---

¹³²*canon* law ¹³⁷*merely* entirely ¹⁴⁰*Hyperion* the sun god, a model of
beauty ¹⁴¹*beteem* allow ¹⁴⁹*Niobe* (a mother who wept profusely at the death
of her children) ¹⁵⁰*wants discourse of reason* lacks reasoning power ¹⁵⁵*left the
flushing* stopped reddening ¹⁵⁶*post* hasten ¹⁵⁷*incestuous* (canon law considered
marriage with a deceased brother's widow to be incestuous) ¹⁶³*change* exchange

Marcellus?   *165*
Marcellus. My good lord!
Hamlet. I am very glad to see you. [*To Barnardo.*] Good even, sir.
   But what, in faith, make you from Wittenberg?
Horatio. A truant disposition, good my lord.
Hamlet. I would not hear your enemy say so,   *170*
   Nor shall you do my ear that violence
   To make it truster° of your own report
   Against yourself. I know you are no truant.
   But what is your affair in Elsinore?
   We'll teach you to drink deep ere you depart.   *175*
Horatio. My lord, I came to see your father's funeral.
Hamlet. I prithee do not mock me, fellow student.
   I think it was to see my mother's wedding.
Horatio. Indeed, my lord, it followed hard upon.
Hamlet. Thrift, thrift, Horatio. The funeral baked meats   *180*
   Did coldly furnish forth the marriage tables.
   Would I had met my dearest° foe in heaven
   Or ever I had seen that day, Horatio!
   My father, methinks I see my father.
Horatio. Where, my lord?
Hamlet.   In my mind's eye, Horatio.   *185*
Horatio. I saw him once. 'A° was a goodly king.
Hamlet. 'A was a man, take him for all in all,
   I shall not look upon his like again.
Horatio. My lord, I think I saw him yesternight.
Hamlet. Saw? Who?   *190*
Horatio. My lord, the King your father.
Hamlet.   The King my father?
Horatio. Season your admiration° for a while
   With an attent ear till I may deliver
   Upon the witness of these gentlemen
   This marvel to you.
Hamlet.   For God's love let me hear!   *195*
Horatio. Two nights together had these gentlemen,
   Marcellus and Barnardo, on their watch
   In the dead waste and middle of the night
   Been thus encountered. A figure like your father,
   Armèd at point exactly, cap-a-pe,°   *200*
   Appears before them, and with solemn march

---

¹⁷²*truster*   believer   ¹⁸²*dearest*   most intensely felt   ¹⁸⁶*'A*   he   ¹⁹²*Season your ad-*
miration   control your wonder   ²⁰⁰*cap-a-pe*   head to foot

Goes slow and stately by them. Thrice he walked
By their oppressed and fear-surprisèd eyes,
Within his truncheon's length,° whilst they, distilled°
Almost to jelly with the act° of fear,   *205*
Stand dumb and speak not to him. This to me
In dreadful° secrecy impart they did,
And I with them the third night kept the watch,
Where, as they had delivered, both in time,
Form of the thing, each word made true and good,   *210*
The apparition comes. I knew your father.
These hands are not more like.

Hamlet.   But where was this?
Marcellus. My lord, upon the platform where we watched.
Hamlet. Did you not speak to it?
Horatio.   My lord, I did;
But answer made it none. Yet once methought   *215*
It lifted up it° head and did address
Itself to motion like as it would speak:
But even then the morning cock crew loud,
And at the sound it shrunk in haste away
And vanished from our sight.

Hamlet.   'Tis very strange.   *220*
Horatio. As I do live, my honored lord, 'tis true,
And we did think it writ down in our duty
To let you know of it.
Hamlet. Indeed, indeed, sirs, but this troubles me.
Hold you the watch tonight?

All.   We do, my lord.   *225*
Hamlet. Armed, say you?
All. Armed, my lord.
Hamlet. From top to toe?
All.   My lord, from head to foot.
Hamlet. Then saw you not his face.
Horatio. O, yes, my lord. He wore his beaver° up.   *230*
Hamlet. What, looked he frowningly?
Horatio. A countenance more in sorrow than in anger.
Hamlet. Pale or red?
Horatio. Nay, very pale.
Hamlet.   And fixed his eyes upon you?
Horatio. Most constantly.

---

[204]*truncheon's length*   space of a short staff   [204]*distilled*   reduced   [205]*act*   action
[207]*dreadful*   terrified   [216]*it*   its   [230]*beaver*   visor, face guard

Hamlet.   I would I had been there.   *235*
Horatio. It would have much amazed you.
Hamlet. Very like, very like. Stayed it long?
Horatio. While one with moderate haste might tell° a hundred.
Both. Longer, longer.
Horatio. Not when I saw't.
Hamlet.   His beard was grizzled,° no?   *240*
Horatio. It was as I have seen it in his life,
     A sable silvered.°
Hamlet.   I will watch tonight.
     Perchance 'twill walk again.
Horatio.   I warr'nt it will.
Hamlet. If it assume my noble father's person,
     I'll speak to it though hell itself should gape   *245*
     And bid me hold my peace. I pray you all,
     If you have hitherto concealed this sight,
     Let it be tenable° in your silence still,
     And whatsomever else shall hap tonight,
     Give it an understanding but no tongue;   *250*
     I will requite your loves. So fare you well.
     Upon the platform 'twixt eleven and twelve
     I'll visit you.
All.   Our duty to your honor.
Hamlet. Your loves, as mine to you. Farewell.
                         Exeunt [all but Hamlet].
     My father's spirit — in arms? All is not well.   *255*
     I doubt° some foul play. Would the night were come!
     Till then sit still, my soul. Foul deeds will rise,
     Though all the earth o'erwhelm them, to men's eyes.
                                   Exit.

[Scene III. *A room.*]

Enter Laertes and Ophelia, his sister.

Laertes. My necessaries are embarked. Farewell.
     And, sister, as the winds give benefit
     And convoy° is assistant, do not sleep,
     But let me hear from you.
Ophelia.   Do you doubt that?
Laertes. For Hamlet, and the trifling of his favor,   *5*
     Hold it a fashion and a toy° in blood,

---

²³⁸*tell* count   ²⁴⁰*grizzled* gray   ²⁴²*sable silvered* black mingled with white   ²⁴⁸*tenable* held   ²⁵⁶*doubt* suspect   I.iii.   ³*convoy* conveyance   ⁶*toy* idle fancy

A violet in the youth of primy° nature,
Forward,° not permanent, sweet, not lasting,
The perfume and suppliance° of a minute,
No more.

Ophelia.   No more but so?

Laertes.   Think it no more.   **10**
For nature crescent° does not grow alone
In thews° and bulk, but as this temple° waxes,
The inward service of the mind and soul
Grows wide withal. Perhaps he loves you now,
And now no soil nor cautel° doth besmirch   **15**
The virtue of his will; but you must fear,
His greatness weighed,° his will is not his own.
For he himself is subject to his birth.
He may not, as unvalued° persons do,
Carve for himself; for on his choice depends   **20**
The safety and health of this whole state;
And therefore must his choice be circumscribed
Unto the voice and yielding of that body
Whereof he is the head. Then if he says he loves you,
It fits your wisdom so far to believe it   **25**
As he in his particular act and place
May give his saying deed, which is no further
Than the main voice of Denmark goes withal.
Then weigh what loss your honor may sustain
If with too credent° ear you list his songs,   **30**
Or lose your heart, or your chaste treasure open
To his unmastered importunity.
Fear it, Ophelia, fear it, my dear sister,
And keep you in the rear of your affection,
Out of the shot and danger of desire.   **35**
The chariest maid is prodigal enough
If she unmask her beauty to the moon.
Virtue itself scapes not calumnious strokes.
The canker° galls the infants of the spring
Too oft before their buttons° be disclosed,   **40**
And in the morn and liquid dew of youth
Contagious blastments are most imminent.
Be wary then; best safety lies in fear;

---

⁷*primy* springlike   ⁸*Forward* premature   ⁹*suppliance* diversion
¹¹*crescent* growing ¹²*thews* muscles and sinews ¹²*temple* i.e., the
body ¹⁵*cautel* deceit ¹⁷*greatness weighed* high rank considered ¹⁹*unvalued* of
low rank ³⁰*credent* credulous ³⁹*canker* cankerworm ⁴⁰*buttons* buds

Youth to itself rebels, though none else near.

Ophelia. I shall the effect of this good lesson keep   *45*
    As watchman to my heart, but, good my brother,
    Do not, as some ungracious° pastors do,
    Show me the steep and thorny way to heaven,
    Whiles, like a puffed and reckless libertine,
    Himself the primrose path of dalliance treads   *50*
    And recks not his own rede.°

    Enter Polonius.

Laertes.   O, fear me not.
    I stay too long. But here my father comes.
    A double blessing is a double grace;
    Occasion smiles upon a second leave.

Polonius. Yet here, Laertes? Aboard, aboard, for shame!   *55*
    The wind sits in the shoulder of your sail,
    And you are stayed for. There — my blessing with thee,
    And these few precepts in thy memory
    Look thou character.° Give thy thoughts no tongue,
    Nor any unproportioned° thought his act.   *60*
    Be thou familiar, but by no means vulgar.
    Those friends thou hast, and their adoption tried,
    Grapple them unto thy soul with hoops of steel,
    But do not dull thy palm with entertainment
    Of each new-hatched, unfledged courage.° Beware   *65*
    Of entrance to a quarrel; but being in,
    Bear't that th' opposèd may beware of thee.
    Give every man thine ear, but few thy voice;
    Take each man's censure,° but reserve thy judgment.
    Costly thy habits as thy purse can buy,   *70*
    But not expressed in fancy; rich, not gaudy,
    For the apparel oft proclaims the man,
    And they in France of the best rank and station
    Are of a most select and generous, chief in that.°
    Neither a borrower nor a lender be,   *75*
    For loan oft loses both itself and friend,
    And borrowing dulleth edge of husbandry.°
    This above all, to thine own self be true,

47ungracious lacking grace **51recks not his own rede** does not heed his own
advice **59character** inscribe **60unproportioned** unbalanced **65courage** gallant
youth **69censure** opinion **74Are of . . . in that** show their fine taste and their
gentlemanly instincts more in that than in any other point of manners
(Kittredge) **77husbandry** thrift

And it must follow, as the night the day,
Thou canst not then be false to any man.   *80*
Farewell. My blessing season this° in thee!
Laertes. Most humbly do I take my leave, my lord.
Polonius. The time invites you. Go, your servants tend.°
Laertes. Farewell, Ophelia, and remember well
    What I have said to you.
Ophelia.   'Tis in my memory locked,   *85*
And you yourself shall keep the key of it.
Laertes. Farewell.

                                                    Exit Laertes.

Polonius. What is't, Ophelia, he hath said to you?
Ophelia. So please you, something touching the Lord Hamlet.
Polonius. Marry,° well bethought.   *90*
    'Tis told me he hath very oft of late
    Given private time to you, and you yourself
    Have of your audience been most free and bounteous.
    If it be so — as so 'tis put on me,
    And that in way of caution — I must tell you   *95*
    You do not understand yourself so clearly
    As it behooves my daughter and your honor.
    What is between you? Give me up the truth.
Ophelia. He hath, my lord, of late made many tenders°
    Of his affection to me.   *100*
Polonius. Affection pooh! You speak like a green girl,
    Unsifted° in such perilous circumstance.
    Do you believe his tenders, as you call them?
Ophelia. I do not know, my lord, what I should think.
Polonius. Marry, I will teach you. Think yourself a baby   *105*
    That you have ta'en these tenders for true pay
    Which are not sterling. Tender yourself more dearly,
    Or (not to crack the wind of the poor phrase)
    Tend'ring it thus you'll tender me a fool.°
Ophelia. My lord, he hath importuned me with love   *110*
    In honorable fashion.
Polonius. Ay, fashion you may call it. Go to, go to.
Ophelia. And hath given countenance to his speech, my lord,
    With almost all the holy vows of heaven.

---

[81]*season this* make fruitful this (advice) [83]*tend* attend [90]*Marry* (a light oath, from "By the Virgin Mary") [99]*tenders* offers (in line 103 it has the same meaning, but in line 106 Polonius speaks of "tenders" in the sense of counters or chips; in line 109 "Tend'ring" means "holding," and "tender" means "give," "present") [102]*Unsifted* untried [109]*tender me a fool* (1) present me with a fool, (2) present me with a baby

Polonius. Ay, springes to catch woodcocks.° I do know,   *115*
   When the blood burns, how prodigal the soul
   Lends the tongue vows. These blazes, daughter,
   Giving more light than heat, extinct in both,
   Even in their promise, as it is a-making,
   You must not take for fire. From this time   *120*
   Be something scanter of your maiden presence.
   Set your entreatments° at a higher rate
   Than a command to parley. For Lord Hamlet,
   Believe so much in him that he is young,
   And with a larger tether may he walk   *125*
   Than may be given you. In few, Ophelia,
   Do not believe his vows, for they are brokers,°
   Not of that dye° which their investments° show,
   But mere implorators° of unholy suits,
   Breathing like sanctified and pious bonds,°   *130*
   The better to beguile. This is for all:
   I would not, in plain terms, from this time forth
   Have you so slander° any moment leisure
   As to give words or talk with the Lord Hamlet.
   Look to't, I charge you. Come your ways.   *135*
Ophelia. I shall obey, my lord.

                                      Exeunt.

   [Scene IV. *A guard platform.*]

    Enter Hamlet, Horatio, and Marcellus.

Hamlet. The air bites shrewdly;° it is very cold.
Horatio. It is a nipping and an eager° air.
Hamlet. What hour now?
Horatio.   I think it lacks of twelve.
Marcellus. No, it is struck.
Horatio. Indeed? I heard it not. It then draws near the season   *5*
   Wherein the spirit held his wont to walk.

    A flourish of trumpets, and two pieces go off.

   What does this mean, my lord?
Hamlet. The King doth wake° tonight and takes his rouse,°

---

[115]*springes   to   catch   woodcocks* snares   to   catch   stupid   birds
[122]*entreatments* interviews   [127]*brokers* procurers   [128]*dye* i.e., kind   [128]*invest-*
ments garments [129]*implorators* solicitors [130]*bonds* pledges [133]*slander* disgrace I.iv.
[1]*shrewdly* bitterly [2]*eager* sharp [8]*wake* hold a revel by night [8]*takes his*
rouse carouses

Keeps wassail, and the swagg'ring upspring° reels,
And as he drains his draughts of Rhenish° down   10
The kettledrum and trumpet thus bray out
The triumph of his pledge.°

Horatio.   Is it a custom?

Hamlet. Ay, marry, is't,
But to my mind, though I am native here
And to the manner born, it is a custom   15
More honored in the breach than the observance.
This heavy-headed revel east and west
Makes us traduced and taxed of° other nations.
They clepe° us drunkards and with swinish phrase
Soil our addition,° and indeed it takes   20
From our achievements, though performed at height,
The pith and marrow of our attribute.°
So oft it chances in particular men
That for some vicious mole° of nature in them,
As in their birth, wherein they are not guilty,   25
(Since nature cannot choose his origin)
By the o'ergrowth of some complexion,°
Oft breaking down the pales° and forts of reason,
Or by some habit that too much o'erleavens°
The form of plausive° manners, that (these men,   30
Carrying, I say, the stamp of one defect,
Being nature's livery, or fortune's star°)
Their virtues else, be they as pure as grace,
As infinite as man may undergo,
Shall in the general censure° take corruption   35
From that particular fault. The dram of evil
Doth all the noble substance of a doubt,
To his own scandal.°

Enter Ghost.

Horatio.   Look, my lord, it comes.

°*upspring* (a dance)   [10]*Rhenish* Rhine wine   [12]*The triumph of his pledge*   the
achievement (of drinking a wine cup in one draught) of his toast   [18]*taxed of* blamed
by   [19]*clepe* call   [20]*addition* reputation (literally, "title of honor")   [22]*attribute*
reputation   [24]*mole* blemish   [27]*complexion* natural disposition   [28]*pales* enclosures
[129]*o'erleavens* mixes with, corrupts   [30]*plausive* pleasing   [32]*nature's livery, or for-*
tune's star nature's equipment (i.e., "innate"), or a person's destiny determined
by the stars   [35]*general censure* popular judgment   [36-38]*The dram . . . own scan-*
dal (though the drift is clear, there is no agreement as to the exact meaning of
these lines)

Hamlet. Angels and ministers of grace defend us!
    Be thou a spirit of health° or goblin damned,   **40**
    Bring with thee airs from heaven or blasts from hell,
    Be thy intents wicked or charitable,
    Thou com'st in such a questionable° shape
    That I will speak to thee. I'll call thee Hamlet,
    King, father, royal Dane. O, answer me!   **45**
    Let me not burst in ignorance, but tell
    Why thy canonized° bones, hearsèd in death,
    Have burst their cerements,° why the sepulcher
    Wherein we saw thee quietly interred
    Hath oped his ponderous and marble jaws   **50**
    To cast thee up again. What may this mean
    That thou, dead corse, again in complete steel,
    Revisits thus the glimpses of the moon,
    Making night hideous, and we fools of nature
    So horridly to shake our disposition°   **55**
    With thoughts beyond the reaches of our souls?
    Say, why is this? Wherefore? What should we do?

    Ghost beckons Hamlet.

Horatio. It beckons you to go away with it,
    As if it some impartment° did desire
    To you alone.
Marcellus.   Look with what courteous action   **60**
    It waves you to a more removèd ground.
    But do not go with it.
Horatio.   No, by no means.
Hamlet. It will not speak. Then I will follow it.
Horatio. Do not, my lord.
Hamlet.   Why, what should be the fear?
    I do not set my life at a pin's fee,   **65**
    And for my soul, what can it do to that,
    Being a thing immortal as itself?
    It waves me forth again. I'll follow it.
Horatio. What if it tempt you toward the flood, my lord,
    Or to the dreadful summit of the cliff   **70**
    That beetles° o'er his base into the sea,
    And there assume some other horrible form,

---

⁴⁰*spirit of health* good spirit ⁴³*questionable* (1) capable of discourse, (2) dubious ⁴⁷*canonized* buried according to the canon or ordinance of the church ⁴⁸*cerements* waxed linen shroud ⁵⁵*shake our disposition* disturb us ⁵⁹*impartment* communication ⁷¹*beetles* juts out

Which might deprive your sovereignty of reason°
And draw you into madness? Think of it.
The very place puts toys° of desperation,   *75*
Without more motive, into every brain
That looks so many fathoms to the sea
And hears it roar beneath.
Hamlet.   It waves me still.
   Go on; I'll follow thee.
Marcellus. You shall not go, my lord.
Hamlet.   Hold off your hands.   *80*
Horatio. Be ruled. You shall not go.
Hamlet.   My fate cries out
And makes each petty artere° in this body
As hardy as the Nemean lion's nerve.°
Still am I called! Unhand me, gentlemen.
By heaven, I'll make a ghost of him that lets° me!   *85*
I say, away! Go on. I'll follow thee.
              Exit Ghost, and Hamlet.
Horatio. He waxes desperate with imagination.
Marcellus. Let's follow.'Tis not fit thus to obey him.
Horatio. Have after! To what issue will this come?
Marcellus. Something is rotten in the state of Denmark.   *90*
Horatio. Heaven will direct it.
Marcellus.   Nay, let's follow him.
                    Exeunt.

[Scene V. *The battlements.*]

   Enter Ghost and Hamlet.

Hamlet. Whither wilt thou lead me? Speak; I'll go no further.
Ghost. Mark me.
Hamlet.   I will.
Ghost.   My hour is almost come,
When I to sulf'rous and tormenting flames
Must render up myself.
Hamlet.   Alas, poor ghost.
Ghost. Pity me not, but lend thy serious hearing   *5*
To what I shall unfold.
Hamlet.   Speak. I am bound to hear.
Ghost. So art thou to revenge, when thou shalt hear.

---

[73]*deprive   your   sovereignty   of   reason*   destroy   the   sovereignty   of   your
reason   [75]*toys*   whims, fancies   [82]*artere*   artery   [83]*Nemean lion's nerve*   sinews
of the mythical lion slain by Hercules   [85]*lets*   hinders

Hamlet. What?
Ghost. I am thy father's spirit,
    Doomed for a certain term to walk the night,   *10*
    And for the day confined to fast in fires,
    Till the foul crimes° done in my days of nature
    Are burnt and purged away. But that I am forbid
    To tell the secrets of my prison house,
    I could a tale unfold whose lightest word   *15*
    Would harrow up thy soul, freeze thy young blood,
    Make thy two eyes like stars start from their spheres,°
    Thy knotted and combinèd locks to part,
    And each particular hair to stand an end
    Like quills upon the fearful porpentine.°   *20*
    But this eternal blazon° must not be
    To ears of flesh and blood. List, list, O, list!
    If thou didst ever thy dear father love —
Hamlet. O God!
Ghost. Revenge his foul and most unnatural murder.   *25*
Hamlet. Murder?
Ghost. Murder most foul, as in the best it is,
    But this most foul, strange, and unnatural.
Hamlet. Haste me to know't, that I, with wings as swift
    As meditation° or the thoughts of love,   *30*
    May sweep to my revenge.
Ghost.   I find thee apt,
    And duller shouldst thou be than the fat weed
    That roots itself in ease on Lethe wharf,°
    Wouldst thou not stir in this. Now, Hamlet, hear.
    'Tis given out that, sleeping in my orchard,   *35*
    A serpent stung me. So the whole ear of Denmark
    Is by a forgèd process° of my death
    Rankly abused. But know, thou noble youth,
    The serpent that did sting thy father's life
    Now wears his crown.
Hamlet.   O my prophetic soul!   *40*
    My uncle?
Ghost. Ay, that incestuous, that adulterate° beast,
    With witchcraft of his wits, with traitorous gifts—

I.v. [12]*crimes* sins [17]*spheres* (in Ptolemaic astronomy, each planet was fixed in a hollow transparent shell concentric with the earth) [20]*fearful porpentine* timid porcupine [21]*eternal blazon* revelation of eternity [30]*meditation* thought [33]*Lethe wharf* bank of the river of forgetfulness in Hades [37]*forgèd process* false account [42]*adulterate* adulterous

O wicked wit and gifts, that have the power
So to seduce! — won to his shameful lust   45
The will of my most seeming-virtuous queen.
O Hamlet, what a falling-off was there,
From me, whose love was of that dignity
That it went hand in hand even with the vow
I made to her in marriage, and to decline   50
Upon a wretch whose natural gifts were poor
To those of mine.
But virtue, as it never will be moved,
Though lewdness° court it in a shape of heaven,
So lust, though to a radiant angel linked,   55
Will sate itself in a celestial bed
And prey on garbage.
But soft, methinks I scent the morning air;
Brief let me be. Sleeping within my orchard,
My custom always of the afternoon,   60
Upon my secure° hour thy uncle stole
With juice of cursed hebona° in a vial,
And in the porches of my ears did pour
The leperous distillment, whose effect
Holds such an enmity with blood of man   65
That swift as quicksilver it courses through
The natural gates and alleys of the body,
And with a sudden vigor it doth posset°
And curd, like eager° droppings into milk,
The thin and wholesome blood. So did it mine,   70
And a most instant tetter° barked about
Most lazarlike° with vile and loathsome crust
All my smooth body.
Thus was I, sleeping, by a brother's hand
Of life, of crown, of queen at once dispatched,   75
Cut off even in the blossoms of my sin,
Unhouseled, disappointed, unaneled,°
No reck'ning made, but sent to my account
With all my imperfections on my head.
O, horrible! O, horrible! Most horrible!   80
If thou hast nature in thee, bear it not.

---

[54]*lewdness* lust [61]*secure*   unsuspecting [62]*hebona* a   poisonous   plant
[68]*posset* curdle [69]*eager* acid [71]*tetter* scab [72]*lazarlike* leperlike [77]**Unhouseled,
disappointed, unaneled**   without the sacrament of communion, unabsolved, without
extreme unction

Let not the royal bed of Denmark be
A couch for luxury° and damnèd incest.
But howsomever thou pursues this act,
Taint not thy mind, nor let thy soul contrive   *85*
Against thy mother aught. Leave her to heaven
And to those thorns that in her bosom lodge
To prick and sting her. Fare thee well at once.
The glowworm shows the matin° to be near
And 'gins to pale his uneffectual fire.   *90*
Adieu, adieu, adieu. Remember me.

                                          Exit.

Hamlet. O all you host of heaven! O earth! What else?
And shall I couple hell? O fie! Hold, hold, my heart,
And you, my sinews, grow not instant old,
But bear me stiffly up. Remember thee?   *95*
Ay, thou poor ghost, whiles memory holds a seat
In this distracted globe.° Remember thee?
Yea, from the table° of my memory
I'll wipe away all trivial fond° records,
All saws° of books, all forms, all pressures° past   *100*
That youth and observation copied there,
And thy commandment all alone shall live
Within the book and volume of my brain,
Unmixed with baser matter. Yes, by heaven!
O most pernicious woman!   *105*
O villain, villain, smiling, damnèd villain!
My tables — meet it is I set it down
That one may smile, and smile, and be a villain.
At least I am sure it may be so in Denmark. [*Writes.*]
So, uncle, there you are. Now to my word: *110*
It is "Adieu, adieu, remember me."
I have sworn't.
Horatio and Marcellus (within). My lord, my lord!

    Enter Horatio and Marcellus.

Marcellus.   Lord Hamlet!
Horatio.   Heavens secure him!
Hamlet. So be it!
Marcellus. Illo, ho, ho,° my lord!   *115*
Hamlet. Hillo, ho, ho, boy! Come, bird, come.

°³*luxury* lust ⁸⁹*matin* morning ⁹⁷*globe* i.e.,   his   head ⁹⁸*table* tablet,
notebook ⁹⁹*fond* foolish ¹⁰⁰*saws* maxims ¹⁰⁰*pressures* impressions ¹¹⁵*Illo,*
ho, ho (falconer's call to his hawk)

Marcellus. How is't, my noble lord?
Horatio.   What news, my lord?
Hamlet. O, wonderful!
Horatio. Good my lord, tell it.
Hamlet.   No, you will reveal it.
Horatio. Not I, my lord, by heaven.
Marcellus.   Nor I, my lord.   120
Hamlet. How say you then? Would heart of man once think it?
     But you'll be secret?
Both.   Ay, by heaven, my lord.
Hamlet. There's never a villain dwelling in all Denmark
     But he's an arrant knave.
Horatio. There needs no ghost, my lord, come from the grave   125
     To tell us this.
Hamlet.   Why, right, you are in the right;
     And so, without more circumstance° at all,
     I hold it fit that we shake hands and part:
     You, as your business and desire shall point you,
     For every man hath business and desire   130
     Such as it is, and for my own poor part,
     Look you, I'll go pray.
Horatio. These are but wild and whirling words, my lord.
Hamlet. I am sorry they offend you, heartily;
     Yes, faith, heartily.
Horatio.   There's no offense, my lord.   135
Hamlet. Yes, by Saint Patrick, but there is, Horatio,
     And much offense too. Touching this vision here,
     It is an honest ghost,° that let me tell you.
     For your desire to know what is between us,
     O'ermaster't as you may. And now, good friends,   140
     As you are friends, scholars, and soldiers,
     Give me one poor request.
Horatio. What is't, my lord? We will.
Hamlet. Never make known what you have seen tonight.
Both. My lord, we will not.
Hamlet.   Nay, but swear't.
Horatio.   In faith,   145
     My lord, not I.
Marcellus.   Nor I, my lord — in faith.
Hamlet. Upon my sword.
Marcellus.   We have sworn, my lord, already.

---

[127]*circumstance*   details   [138]*honest ghost*   i.e., not a demon in his father's shape

Hamlet. Indeed, upon my sword, indeed.

   Ghost cries under the stage.

Ghost. Swear.
Hamlet. Ha, ha, boy, say'st thou so? Art thou there,
    truepenny?°   *150*
    Come on. You hear this fellow in the cellarage.
    Consent to swear.
Horatio.   Propose the oath, my lord.
Hamlet. Never to speak of this that you have seen.
    Swear by my sword.
Ghost [beneath]. Swear.   *155*
Hamlet. Hic et ubique?° Then we'll shift our ground;
    Come hither, gentlemen,
    And lay your hands again upon my sword.
    Swear by my sword
    Never to speak of this that you have heard.   *160*
Ghost [beneath]. Swear by his sword.
Hamlet. Well said, old mole! Canst work i' th' earth so fast?
    A worthy pioner!° Once more remove, good friends.
Horatio. O day and night, but this is wondrous strange!
Hamlet. And therefore as a stranger give it welcome.   *165*
    There are more things in heaven and earth, Horatio,
    Than are dreamt of in your philosophy.
    But come:
    Here as before, never, so help you mercy,
    How strange or odd some'er I bear myself   *170*
    (As I perchance hereafter shall think meet
    To put an antic disposition° on),
    That you, at such times seeing me, never shall
    With arms encumb'red° thus, or this headshake,
    Or by pronouncing of some doubtful phrase,   *175*
    As "Well, well, we know," or "We could, an if we would,"
    Or "If we list to speak," or "There be, an if they might,"
    Or such ambiguous giving out, to note
    That you know aught of me — this do swear,
    So grace and mercy at your most need help you.   *180*
Ghost [beneath]. Swear.

   [*They swear.*]

Hamlet. Rest, rest, perturbèd spirit. So, gentlemen,

[150]*truepenny* honest fellow   [156]*Hic et ubique* here and everywhere (Latin)
[163]*pioner* digger of mines   [172]*antic disposition* fantastic behavior   [174]*encumb'red*
folded

With all my love I do commend me° to you,
And what so poor a man as Hamlet is
May do t' express his love and friending to you,   *185*
God willing, shall not lack. Let us go in together,
And still your fingers on your lips, I pray.
The time is out of joint. O cursèd spite,
That ever I was born to set it right!
Nay, come, let's go together.   *190*
                                                   Exeunt.

[ACT II

Scene I. *A room.*]

Enter old Polonius, with his man Reynaldo.

Polonius. Give him this money and these notes, Reynaldo.
Reynaldo. I will, my lord.
Polonius. You shall do marvell's° wisely, good Reynaldo,
Before you visit him, to make inquire
Of his behavior.
Reynaldo.   My lord, I did intend it.   *5*
Polonius. Marry, well said, very well said. Look you sir,
Inquire me first what Danskers° are in Paris,
And how, and who, what means, and where they keep,°
What company, at what expense; and finding
By this encompassment° and drift of question   *10*
That they do know my son, come you more nearer
Than your particular demands° will touch it.
Take you as 'twere some distant knowledge of him,
As thus, "I know his father and his friends,
And in part him." Do you mark this, Reynaldo?   *15*
Reynaldo. Ay, very well, my lord.
Polonius. "And in part him, but," you may say, "not well,
But if't be he I mean, he's very wild,
Addicted so and so." And there put on him
What forgeries° you please; marry, none so rank   *20*
As may dishonor him — take heed of that —
But, sir, such wanton, wild, and usual slips
As are companions noted and most known
To youth and liberty.

---

[183]*commend me* entrust myself   II.i. [3]*marvell's* marvelous(ly)   [7]*Danskers* Danes
[8]*keep* dwell [10]*encompassment* circling [12]*demands* questions [20]*forgeries* inventions

Reynaldo. As gaming, my lord.
Polonius. Ay, or drinking, fencing, swearing, quarreling,   *25*
    Drabbing.° You may go so far.
Reynaldo. My lord, that would dishonor him.
Polonius. Faith, no, as you may season it in the charge.
    You must not put another scandal on him,
    That he is open to incontinency.°   *30*
    That's not my meaning. But breathe his faults so quaintly°
    That they may seem the taints of liberty,
    The flash and outbreak of a fiery mind,
    A savageness in unreclaimèd blood,
    Of general assault.°
Reynaldo. But, my good lord —   *35*
Polonius. Wherefore should you do this?
Reynaldo. Ay, my lord,
    I would know that.
Polonius. Marry, sir, here's my drift,
    And I believe it is a fetch of warrant.°
    You laying these slight sullies on my son
    As 'twere a thing a little soiled i' th' working,   *40*
    Mark you,
    Your party in converse, him you would sound,
    Having ever seen in the prenominate crimes°
    The youth you breathe of guilty, be assured
    He closes with you in this consequence:°   *45*
    "Good sir," or so, or "friend," or "gentleman" —
    According to the phrase or the addition°
    Of man and country —
Reynaldo. Very good, my lord.
Polonius. And then, sir, does 'a° this — 'a does —
    What was I about to say? By the mass, I was about   *50*
    to say something! Where did I leave?
Reynaldo. At "closes in the consequence," at "friend or so," and
    "gentlemen."
Polonius. At "closes in the consequence" — Ay, marry!
    He closes thus: "I know the gentleman;   *55*
    I saw him yesterday, or t'other day,
    Or then, or then, with such or such, and, as you say,
    There was 'a gaming, there o'ertook in's rouse,

---

[26]*Drabbing* wenching [30]*incontinency* habitual licentiousness [31]*quaintly* ingeniously, delicately [35]*Of general assault* common to all men [38]*fetch of warrant* justifiable device [43]*Having . . . crimes* if he has ever seen in the aforementioned crimes [45]*He closes . . . this consequence* he falls in with you in this conclusion [47]*addition* title [49]*'a* he

There falling out at tennis"; or perchance,
"I saw him enter such a house of sale," 60
Videlicet,° a brothel, or so forth.
See you now —
Your bait of falsehood take this carp of truth,
And thus do we of wisdom and of reach,°
With windlasses° and with assays of bias,° 65
By indirections find directions out.
So, by my former lecture and advice,
Shall you my son. You have me, have you not?
Reynaldo. My lord, I have.
Polonius.   God bye ye, fare ye well.
Reynaldo. Good my lord.
Polonius. Observe his inclination in yourself.° 70
Reynaldo. I shall, my lord.
Polonius. And let him ply his music.
Reynaldo.   Well, my lord.
Polonius. Farewell.

                                    Exit Reynaldo.

    Enter Ophelia.

                How now, Ophelia, what's the matter?
Ophelia. O my lord, my lord, I have been so affrighted! 75
Polonius. With what, i' th' name of God?
Ophelia. My lord, as I was sewing in my closet,°
    Lord Hamlet, with his doublet all unbraced,°
    No hat upon his head, his stockings fouled,
    Ungartered, and down-gyvèd° to his ankle, 80
    Pale as his shirt, his knees knocking each other,
    And with a look so piteous in purport,°
    As if he had been loosèd out of hell
    To speak of horrors — he comes before me.
Polonius. Mad for thy love?
Ophelia.   My lord, I do not know, 85
    But truly I do fear it.
Polonius.   What said he?
Ophelia. He took me by the wrist and held me hard;
    Then goes he to the length of all his arm,

---

⁶¹*Videlicet* namely ⁶⁴*reach* far-reaching awareness(?) ⁶⁵*windlasses* circuitous
courses ⁶⁵*assays of bias* indirect attempts (metaphor from bowling; "bias" =
curved course) ⁷¹*in yourself* for yourself ⁷⁷*closet* private room ⁷⁸*doublet all
unbraced* jacket entirely unlaced ⁸⁰*down-gyvèd* hanging down like
fetters ⁸²*purport* expression

And with his other hand thus o'er his brow
He falls to such perusal of my face   *90*
As 'a would draw it. Long stayed he so.
At last, a little shaking of mine arm,
And thrice his head thus waving up and down,
He raised a sigh so piteous and profound
As it did seem to shatter all his bulk   *95*
And end his being. That done, he lets me go,
And, with his head over his shoulder turned,
He seemed to find his way without his eyes,
For out o' doors he went without their helps,
And to the last bended their light on me.   *100*
Polonius. Come, go with me. I will go seek the King.
This is the very ecstasy° of love,
Whose violent property fordoes° itself
And leads the will to desperate undertakings
As oft as any passions under heaven   *105*
That does afflict our natures. I am sorry.
What, have you given him any hard words of late?
Ophelia. No, my good lord; but as you did command,
I did repel his letters and denied
His access to me.
Polonius.   That hath made him mad.   *110*
I am sorry that with better heed and judgment
I had not quoted° him. I feared he did but trifle
And meant to wrack thee; but beshrew my jealousy.°
By heaven, it is as proper° to our age
To cast beyond ourselves° in our opinions   *115*
As it is common for the younger sort
To lack discretion. Come, go we to the King.
This must be known, which, being kept close, might move
More grief to hide than hate to utter love.°
Come.   *120*
                                                    Exeunt.

[**Scene II.** *The castle.*]

Flourish. Enter King and Queen, Rosencrantz, and Guildenstern
[*with others*].

---

¹⁰²*ecstasy* madness ¹⁰³*property fordoes* quality destroys ¹¹²*quoted* noted
¹¹³*beshrew my jealousy* curse on my suspicions ¹¹⁴*proper* natural ¹¹⁵*To cast
beyond ourselves* to be overcalculating ¹¹⁷⁻¹¹⁹*Come, go . . . utter love* (the general
meaning is that while telling the King of Hamlet's love may anger the King, more
grief would come from keeping it secret)

King. Welcome, dear Rosencrantz and Guildenstern.
　　　Moreover that° we much did long to see you,
　　　The need we have to use you did provoke
　　　Our hasty sending. Something have you heard
　　　Of Hamlet's transformation: so call it,   5
　　　Sith° nor th' exterior nor the inward man
　　　Resembles that it was. What it should be,
　　　More than his father's death, that thus hath put him
　　　So much from th' understanding of himself,
　　　I cannot dream of. I entreat you both   10
　　　That, being of so° young days brought up with him,
　　　And sith so neighbored to his youth and havior,°
　　　That you vouchsafe your rest° here in our court
　　　Some little time, so by your companies
　　　To draw him on to pleasures, and to gather   15
　　　So much as from occasion you may glean,
　　　Whether aught to us unknown afflicts him thus,
　　　That opened° lies within our remedy.
Queen. Good gentlemen, he hath much talked of you,
　　　And sure I am, two men there is not living   20
　　　To whom he more adheres. If it will please you
　　　To show us so much gentry° and good will
　　　As to expend your time with us awhile
　　　For the supply and profit of our hope,
　　　Your visitation shall receive such thanks   25
　　　As fits a king's remembrance.
Rosencrantz.　　　　　　　　　　　　Both your Majesties
　　　Might, by the sovereign power you have of us,
　　　Put your dread pleasures more into command
　　　Than to entreaty.
Guildenstern.　　　　　　But we both obey,
　　　And here give up ourselves in the full bent°   30
　　　To lay our service freely at your feet,
　　　To be commanded.
King. Thanks, Rosencrantz and gentle Guildenstern.
Queen. Thanks, Guildenstern and gentle Rosencrantz.
　　　And I beseech you instantly to visit   35
　　　My too much changèd son. Go, some of you,
　　　And bring these gentlemen where Hamlet is.

II.ii. **²*Moreover that*** beside the fact that **⁶*Sith*** since **¹¹*of so*** from such **¹²*youth and havior*** behavior in his youth **¹³*vouchsafe your rest*** consent to remain **¹⁸*opened*** revealed **²²*gentry*** courtesy **³⁰*in the full bent*** entirely (the figure is of a bow bent to its capacity)

Guildenstern. Heavens make our presence and our practices
    Pleasant and helpful to him!
Queen.   Ay, amen!
                     Exit Rosencrantz and Guildenstern
                               [with some Attendants].

    Enter Polonius.

Polonius. Th' ambassadors from Norway, my good lord,   **40**
    Are joyfully returned.
King. Thou still° hast been the father of good news.
Polonius. Have I, my lord? Assure you, my good liege,
    I hold my duty, as I hold my soul,
    Both to my God and to my gracious king;   **45**
    And I do think, or else this brain of mine
    Hunts not the trail of policy so sure°
    As it hath used to do, that I have found
    The very cause of Hamlet's lunacy.
King. O, speak of that! That do I long to hear.   **50**
Polonius. Give first admittance to th' ambassadors.
    My news shall be the fruit to that great feast.
King. Thyself do grace to them and bring them in.
                            [Exit Polonius.]
    He tells me, my dear Gertrude, he hath found
    The head and source of all your son's distemper.   **55**
Queen. I doubt° it is no other but the main,°
    His father's death and our o'erhasty marriage.
King. Well, we shall sift him.

    Enter Polonius, Voltemand, and Cornelius.

                      Welcome, my good friends.
    Say, Voltemand, what from our brother Norway?
Voltemand. Most fair return of greetings and desires.   **60**
    Upon our first,° he sent out to suppress
    His nephew's levies, which to him appeared
    To be a preparation 'gainst the Polack;
    But better looked into, he truly found
    It was against your Highness, whereat grieved,   **65**
    That so his sickness, age, and impotence
    Was falsely borne in hand,° sends out arrests
    On Fortinbras; which he, in brief, obeys,

42*still* always   **47***Hunts not . . . so sure* does not follow clues of political doings with such sureness   **56***doubt* suspect   **56***main* principal point   **61***first* first
audience   **67***borne in hand* deceived

Receives rebuke from Norway, and in fine,°
Makes vow before his uncle never more   *70*
To give th' assay° of arms against your Majesty.
Whereon old Norway, overcome with joy,
Gives him threescore thousand crowns in annual fee
And his commission to employ those soldiers,
So levied as before, against the Polack,   *75*
With an entreaty, herein further shown, [*gives a paper*]
That it might please you to give quiet pass
Through your dominions for this enterprise,
On such regards of safety and allowance°
As therein are set down.

King.   It likes us well;   *80*
And at our more considered time° we'll read,
Answer, and think upon this business.
Meantime, we thank you for your well-took labor.
Go to your rest; at night we'll feast together.
Most welcome home!

Exit Ambassadors.

Polonius.   This business is well ended.   *85*
My liege and madam, to expostulate°
What majesty should be, what duty is,
Why day is day, night night, and time is time,
Were nothing but to waste night, day, and time.
Therefore, since brevity is the soul of wit,°   *90*
And tediousness the limbs and outward flourishes,
I will be brief. Your noble son is mad.
Mad call I it, for, to define true madness,
What is't but to be nothing else but mad?
But let that go.

Queen.   More matter, with less art.   *95*
Polonius. Madam, I swear I use no art at all.
That he's mad, 'tis true: 'tis true 'tis pity,
And pity 'tis 'tis true — a foolish figure.°
But farewell it, for I will use no art.
Mad let us grant him then; and now remains   *100*
That we find out the cause of this effect,
Or rather say, the cause of this defect,
For this effect defective comes by cause.

---

[69]*in fine* finally [71]*assay* trial [79]*regards of safety and allowance* i.e., conditions [81]*considered time* time proper for considering [86]*expostulate* discuss [90]*wit* wisdom, understanding [98]*figure* figure of rhetoric

Thus it remains, and the remainder thus.
Perpend.°   *105*
I have a daughter: have, while she is mine,
Who in her duty and obedience, mark,
Hath given me this. Now gather, and surmise.

[Reads] the letter.

> "To the celestial, and my soul's idol, the most
> beautified Ophelia" —   *110*

That's an ill phrase, a vile phrase; "beautified" is a vile
phrase. But you shall hear. Thus:

> "In her excellent white bosom, these, &c."

Queen. Came this from Hamlet to her?
Polonius. Good madam, stay awhile. I will be faithful.   *115*

> "Doubt thou the stars are fire,
>   Doubt that the sun doth move;
> Doubt° truth to be a liar,
>   But never doubt I love.

> O dear Ophelia, I am ill at these numbers.° I have   *120*
> not art to reckon my groans; but that I love thee
> best, O most best, believe it. Adieu.

>   Thine evermore, most dear lady,
>   whilst this machine° is to him, HAMLET."

This in obedience hath my daughter shown me,   *125*
And more above° hath his solicitings,
As they fell out by time, by means, and place,
All given to mine ear.
King.   But how hath she
Received his love?
Polonius.   What do you think of me?
King. As of a man faithful and honorable.   *130*
Polonius. I would fain prove so. But what might you think,
When I had seen this hot love on the wing
(As I perceived it, I must tell you that,
Before my daughter told me), what might you,

°105**Perpend** consider carefully °118**Doubt** suspect °120**ill at these numbers** unskilled
in verses °124**machine** complex device (here, his body) °126**more above** in addition

Or my dear Majesty your Queen here, think,   *135*
If I had played the desk or table book,°
Or given my heart a winking,° mute and dumb,
Or looked upon this love with idle sight?
What might you think? No, I went round to work
And my young mistress thus I did bespeak: *140*
"Lord Hamlet is a prince, out of thy star.°
This must not be." And then I prescripts gave her,
That she should lock herself from his resort,
Admit no messengers, receive no tokens.
Which done, she took the fruits of my advice,   *145*
And he, repellèd, a short tale to make,
Fell into a sadness, then into a fast,
Thence to a watch,° thence into a weakness,
Thence to a lightness,° and, by this declension,
Into the madness wherein now he raves,   *150*
And all we mourn for.

King.   Do you think 'tis this?

Queen. It may be, very like.

Polonius. Hath there been such a time, I would fain know that,
That I have positively said "'Tis so,"
When it proved otherwise?

King.   Not that I know.   *155*

Polonius [*pointing to his head and shoulder*]. Take this from this,
    if this be otherwise.
    If circumstances lead me, I will find
    Where truth is hid, though it were hid indeed
    Within the center.°

King.   How may we try it further?

Polonius. You know sometimes he walks four hours together   *160*
    Here in the lobby.

Queen.   So he does indeed.

Polonius. At such a time I'll loose my daughter to him.
    Be you and I behind an arras° then.
    Mark the encounter. If he love her not,
    And be not from his reason fall'n thereon,   *165*
    Let me be no assistant for a state
    But keep a farm and carters.

---

[136]*played the desk or table book* i.e., been a passive recipient of
secrets [137]*winking* closing of the eyes [141]*star* sphere [148]*watch* wakefulness
[149]*lightness* mental derangement [159]*center* center of the earth [163]*arras* tapestry
hanging in front of a wall

King.   We will try it.

    Enter Hamlet reading on a book.

Queen. But look where sadly the poor wretch comes reading.
Polonius. Away, I do beseech you both, away.
                                 Exit King and Queen.
I'll board him presently.° O, give me leave.   170
How does my good Lord Hamlet?
Hamlet. Well, God-a-mercy.
Polonius. Do you know me, my lord?
Hamlet. Excellent well. You are a fishmonger.°
Polonius. Not I, my lord.   175
Hamlet. Then I would you were so honest a man.
Polonius. Honest, my lord?
Hamlet. Ay, sir. To be honest, as this world goes, is to be one
    man picked out of ten thousand.
Polonius. That's very true, my lord.   180
Hamlet. For if the sun breed maggots in a dead dog, being
    a good kissing carrion° — Have you a daughter?
Polonius. I have, my lord.
Hamlet. Let her not walk i' th' sun. Conception° is a blessing,
    but as your daughter may conceive, friend, look to't.   185
Polonius [*aside*]. How say you by that? Still harping on my
    daughter. Yet he knew me not at first. 'A said I was
    a fishmonger. 'A is far gone, far gone. And truly in
    my youth I suffered much extremity for love, very
    near this. I'll speak to him again. — What do you read,   190
    my lord?
Hamlet. Words, words, words.
Polonius. What is the matter,° my lord?
Hamlet. Between who?
Polonius. I mean the matter that you read, my lord.   195
Hamlet. Slanders, sir; for the satirical rogue says here that
    old men have gray beards, that their faces are wrinkled,
    their eyes purging thick amber and plumtree gum, and
    that they have a plentiful lack of wit, together with
    most weak hams. All which, sir, though I most pow-   200
    erfully and potently believe, yet I hold it not honesty°

---

[170]**board him presently** accost him at once [174]**fishmonger** dealer in fish (slang for a procurer) [182]**a good kissing carrion** (perhaps the meaning is "a good piece of flesh to kiss," but many editors emend "good" to "god," taking the word to refer to the sun) [184]**Conception** (1) understanding, (2) becoming pregnant [193]**matter** (Polonius means "subject matter," but Hamlet pretends to take the word in the sense of "quarrel") [201]**honesty** decency

to have it thus set down; for you yourself, sir, should
be old as I am if, like a crab, you could go backward.

Polonius [*aside*]. Though this be madness, yet there is method
in't. Will you walk out of the air, my lord?   *205*

Hamlet. Into my grave.

Polonius. Indeed, that's out of the air. [*Aside.*] How pregnant°
sometimes his replies are! A happiness° that often madness
hits on, which reason and sanity could not so pros-
perously be delivered of. I will leave him and suddenly   *210*
contrive the means of meeting between him and my
daughter. — My lord, I will take my leave of you.

Hamlet. You cannot take from me anything that I will more
willingly part withal — except my life, except my life,
except my life.   *215*

    Enter Guildenstern and Rosencrantz.

Polonius. Fare you well, my lord.

Hamlet. These tedious old fools!

Polonius. You go to seek the Lord Hamlet? There he is.

Rosencrantz [*to Polonius*]. God save you, sir! [*Exit Polonius.*]

Guildenstern. My honored lord!   *220*

Rosencrantz. My most dear lord!

Hamlet. My excellent good friends! How dost thou, Guildenstern? Ah, Rosencrantz! Good lads, how do you
both?

Rosencrantz. As the indifferent° children of the earth.   *225*

Guildenstern. Happy in that we are not overhappy. On Fortune's
cap we are not the very button.

Hamlet. Nor the soles of her shoe?

Rosencrantz. Neither, my lord.

Hamlet. Then you live about her waist, or in the middle of   *230*
her favors?

Guildenstern. Faith, her privates° we.

Hamlet. In the secret parts of Fortune? O, most true! She is
a strumpet. What news?

Rosencrantz. None, my lord, but that the world's grown   *235*
honest.

Hamlet. Then is doomsday near. But your news is not true.
Let me question more in particular. What have you,
my good friends, deserved at the hands of Fortune that
she sends you to prison hither?   *240*

---

[207]*pregnant* meaningful   [208]*happiness* apt turn of phrase   [225]*indifferent* ordinary
[232]*privates* ordinary men (with a pun on "private parts")

Guildenstern. Prison, my lord?

Hamlet. Denmark's a prison.

Rosencrantz. Then is the world one.

Hamlet. A goodly one, in which there are many confines,
    wards,° and dungeons, Denmark being one o' th' worst.   245

Rosencrantz. We think not so, my lord.

Hamlet. Why, then 'tis none to you, for there is nothing
    either good or bad but thinking makes it so. To me it
    is a prison.

Rosencrantz. Why then your ambition makes it one. 'Tis too   250
    narrow for your mind.

Hamlet. O God, I could be bounded in a nutshell and count
    myself a king of infinite space, were it not that I have
    bad dreams.

Guildenstern. Which dreams indeed are ambition, for the very   255
    substance of the ambitious is merely the shadow of a
    dream.

Hamlet. A dream itself is but a shadow.

Rosencrantz. Truly, and I hold ambition of so airy and light
    a quality that it is but a shadow's shadow.   260

Hamlet. Then are our beggars bodies, and our monarchs and
    outstretched heroes the beggars' shadows.° Shall we to
    th' court? For, by my fay,° I cannot reason.

Both. We'll wait upon you.

Hamlet. No such matter. I will not sort you with the rest of   265
    my servants, for, to speak to you like an honest man,
    I am most dreadfully attended. But in the beaten way
    of friendship, what make you at Elsinore?

Rosencrantz. To visit you, my lord; no other occasion.

Hamlet. Beggar that I am, I am even poor in thanks, but I   270
    thank you; and sure, dear friends, my thanks are too
    dear a half penny.° Were you not sent for? Is it your
    own inclining? Is it a free visitation? Come, come, deal
    justly with me. Come, come; nay, speak.

Guildenstern. What should we say, my lord?   275

Hamlet. Why anything — but to th' purpose. You were sent
    for, and there is a kind of confession in your looks,
    which your modesties have not craft enough to color.
    I know the good King and Queen have sent for you.

---

²⁴⁵*wards*   cells   ²⁶¹⁻²⁶²*Then are . . . beggars' shadows*   i.e., by your logic, beggars
(lacking   ambition)   are   substantial,   and   great   men   are   elongated
shadows   ²⁶³*fay*   faith   ²⁷¹⁻²⁷²*too dear a halfpenny*   i.e., not worth a halfpenny

Rosencrantz. To what end, my lord?   *280*

Hamlet. That you must teach me. But let me conjure you
   by the rights of our fellowship, by the consonancy of
   our youth, by the obligation of our ever preserved love,
   and by what more dear a better proposer can charge
   you withal, be even and direct with me, whether you   *285*
   were sent for or no.

Rosencrantz [*aside to Guildenstern*]. What say you?

Hamlet [*aside*]. Nay then, I have an eye of you. — If you
   love me, hold not off.

Guildenstern. My lord, we were sent for.   *290*

Hamlet. I will tell you why; so shall my anticipation prevent
   your discovery,° and your secrecy to the King and
   Queen molt no feather. I have of late, but wherefore
   I know not, lost all my mirth, forgone all custom of
   exercises; and indeed, it goes so heavily with my dis-   *295*
   position that this goodly frame, the earth, seems to me
   a sterile promontory; this most excellent canopy, the
   air, look you, this brave o'erhanging firmament, this
   majestical roof fretted° with golden fire: why, it appeareth
   nothing to me but a foul and pestilent congregation of   *300*
   vapors. What a piece of work is a man, how noble in
   reason, how infinite in faculties, in form and moving
   how express° and admirable, in action how like an
   angel, in apprehension how like a god: the beauty of   *305*
   the world, the paragon of animals; and yet to me, what
   is this quintessence of dust? Man delights not me; nor
   woman neither, though by your smiling you seem to
   say so.

Rosencrantz. My lord, there was no such stuff in my thoughts.

Hamlet. Why did ye laugh then, when I said "Man delights   *310*
   not me"?

Rosencrantz. To think, my lord, if you delight not in man,
   what lenten° entertainment the players shall receive from
   you. We coted° them on the way, and hither are they
   coming to offer you service.   *315*

Hamlet. He that plays the king shall be welcome; his Majesty
   shall have tribute of me; the adventurous knight shall
   use his foil and target;° the lover shall not sigh gratis;
   the humorous man° shall end his part in peace; the

---

²⁹¹⁻²⁹²*prevent   your   discovery* forestall   your   disclosure   ²⁹⁹*fretted*
adorned   ³⁰³*express* exact   ³¹³*lenten* leager   ³¹⁴*coted* overtook   ³¹⁸*target* shield
³¹⁹*humorous man*   i.e., eccentric man (among stock characters in dramas were men
dominated by a "humor" or odd trait)

clown shall make those laugh whose lungs are tickle o' *320*
th' sere;° and the lady shall say her mind freely, or° the
blank verse shall halt° for't. What players are they?

Rosencrantz. Even those you were wont to take such delight
in, the tragedians of the city.

Hamlet. How chances it they travel? Their residence, both in *325*
reputation and profit, was better both ways.

Rosencrantz. I think their inhibition° comes by the means of
the innovation.°

Hamlet. Do they hold the same estimation they did when I
was in the city? Are they so followed? *330*

Rosencrantz. No indeed, are they not.

Hamlet. How comes it? Do they grow rusty?

Rosencrantz. Nay, their endeavor keeps in the wonted pace,
but there is, sir, an eyrie° of children, little eyases, that
cry out on the top of question° and are most tyrannically° *335*
clapped for't. These are now the fashion, and so berattle
the common stages° (so they call them) that many wearing rapiers are afraid of goosequills° and dare scarce
come thither.

Hamlet. What, are they children? Who maintains 'em? How *340*
are they escoted?° Will they pursue the quality° no longer
than they can sing? Will they not say afterwards, if they
should grow themselves to common players (as it is
most like, if their means are no better), their writers
do them wrong to make them exclaim against their *345*
own succession?°

Rosencrantz. Faith, there has been much to-do on both sides,
and the nation holds it no sin to tarre° them to con-
troversy. There was, for a while, no money bid for
argument° unless the poet and the player went to cuffs *350*
in the question.

Hamlet. Is't possible?

---

³²⁰⁻³²¹**tickle o' th' sere** on hair trigger ("sere" = part of the gunlock) ³²¹**or** else
³²²**halt** limp ³²⁷**inhibition** hindrance ³²⁸**innovation** (probably an allusion to the
companies of child actors that had become popular and were offering serious
competition to the adult actors) ³³⁴**eyrie** nest ³³⁴⁻³³⁵**eyases, that . . . of question**
unfledged hawks that cry shrilly above others in matter of debate ³³⁵**tyrannically**
violently ³³⁶⁻³³⁷**berattle the common stages** cry down the public theaters (with
the adult acting companies) ³³⁸**goosequills** pens (of satirists who ridicule the public
theaters and their audiences) ³⁴¹**escoted** financially supported ³⁴¹**quality** profession
of acting ³⁴⁶**succession** future ³⁴⁸**tarre** incite ³⁵⁰**argument** plot of a play

Guildenstern. O, there has been much throwing about of brains.

Hamlet. Do the boys carry it away?   *355*

Rosencrantz. Ay, that they do, my lord — Hercules and his load° too.

Hamlet. It is not very strange, for my uncle is King of Denmark, and those that would make mouths at him while my father lived give twenty, forty, fifty, a hundred ducats   *360* apiece for his picture in little. 'Sblood,° there is something in this more than natural, if philosophy could find it out.

> *A flourish.*

Guildenstern. There are the players.

Hamlet. Gentlemen, you are welcome to Elsinore. Your hands,   *365* come then. Th' appurtenance of welcome is fashion and ceremony. Let me comply° with you in this garb,° lest my extent° to the players (which I tell you must show fairly outwards) should more appear like entertainment than yours. You are welcome. But my uncle-father and   *370* aunt-mother are deceived.

Guildenstern. In what, my dear lord?

Hamlet. I am but mad north-northwest:° when the wind is southerly I know a hawk from a handsaw.°

> *Enter Polonius.*

Polonius. Well be with you, gentlemen.   *375*

Hamlet. Hark you, Guildenstern, and you too; at each ear a hearer. That great baby you see there is not yet out of his swaddling clouts.

Rosencrantz. Happily° he is the second time come to them, for they say an old man is twice a child.   *380*

Hamlet. I will prophesy he comes to tell me of the players. Mark it. — You say right, sir; a Monday morning, 'twas then indeed.

Polonius. My lord, I have news to tell you.

356-357 ***Hercules and his load*** i.e., the whole world (with a reference to the Globe Theatre, which had a sign that represented Hercules bearing the globe)   **361** ***'Sblood*** by God's blood   **367** ***comply*** be courteous   **367** ***garb*** outward show   **368** ***extent*** behavior   **373** ***north-northwest*** i.e., on one point of the compass only   **374** ***hawk from a handsaw*** ("hawk" can refer not only to a bird but to a kind of pickax; "handsaw" — a carpenter's tool — may involve a similar pun on "hernshaw," a heron)   **379** ***Happily*** perhaps

Hamlet. My lord, I have news to tell you. When Roscius° 385
was an actor in Rome —
Polonius. The actors are come hither, my lord.
Hamlet. Buzz, buzz.°
Polonius. Upon my honor —
Hamlet. Then came each actor on his ass — 390
Polonius. The best actors in the world, either for tragedy,
comedy, history, pastoral, pastoral-comical, historical-
pastoral, tragical-historical, tragical-comical-historical-
pastoral; scene individable,° or poem unlimited.° Seneca°
cannot be too heavy, nor Plautus° too light. For the 395
law of writ and the liberty,° these are the only men.
Hamlet. O Jeptha, judge of Israel,° what a treasure hadst thou!
Polonius. What a treasure had he, my lord?
Hamlet. Why,

> "One fair daughter, and no more, 400
>   The which he lovèd passing well."

Polonius [aside]. Still on my daughter.
Hamlet. Am I not i' th' right, old Jeptha?
Polonius. If you call me Jeptha, my lord, I have a daughter
that I love passing well. 405
Hamlet. Nay, that follows not.
Polonius. What follows then, my lord?
Hamlet. Why,

> "As by lot, God wot,"

and then, you know, 410

> "It came to pass, as most like it was."

The first row of the pious chanson° will show you
more, for look where my abridgment° comes.

Enter the Players.

---

[385]*Roscius* (a famous Roman comic actor) [388]*Buzz, buzz* (an interjection, perhaps
indicating that the news is old) [394]*scene individable* plays observing the unities
of time, place, and action [394]*poem unlimited* plays not restricted by the tenets
of criticism [394]*Seneca* (Roman tragic dramatist) [395]*Plautus* (Roman comic
dramatist) [395-396]*For the law of writ and the liberty* (perhaps "for sticking to the
text and for improvising"; perhaps "for classical plays and for modern loosely
written plays") [397]*Jeptha, judge of Israel* (the title of a ballad on the Hebrew
judge who sacrificed his daughter; see Judges 11) [412]*row of the pious chanson* stanza
of the scriptural song [413]*abridgment* (1) i.e., entertainers, who abridge the time,
(2) interrupters

You are welcome, masters, welcome, all. I am glad to
see thee well. Welcome, good friends. O, old friend,   *415*
why, thy face is valanced° since I saw thee last. Com'st
thou to beard me in Denmark? What, my young lady°
and mistress? By'r Lady, your ladyship is nearer to
heaven than when I saw you last by the altitude of a
chopine.° Pray God your voice, like a piece of uncurrent   *420*
gold, be not cracked within the ring.° — Masters, you
are all welcome. We'll e'en to't like French falconers,
fly at anything we see. We'll have a speech straight.
Come, give us a taste of your quality. Come, a passionate
speech.   *425*

Player. What speech, my good lord?

Hamlet. I heard thee speak me a speech once, but it was never
acted, or if it was, not above once, for the play, I
remember, pleased not the million; 'twas caviary to the
general,° but it was (as I received it, and others, whose   *430*
judgments in such matters cried in the top of° mine)
an excellent play, well digested in the scenes, set down
with as much modesty as cunning.° I remember one
said there were no sallets° in the lines to make the matter
savory; nor no matter in the phrase that might indict   *435*
the author of affectation, but called it an honest method,
as wholesome as sweet, and by very much more handsome than fine.° One speech in't I chiefly loved. 'Twas
Aeneas' tale to Dido, and thereabout of it especially
when he speaks of Priam's slaughter. If it live in your   *440*
memory, begin at this line — let me see, let me see:

> "The rugged Pyrrhus, like th' Hyrcanian beast° — "

'Tis not so; it begins with Pyrrhus:

> "The rugged Pyrrhus, he whose sable° arms,
> Black as his purpose, did the night resemble   *445*
> When he lay couchèd in th' ominous horse,°
> Hath now this dread and black complexion smeared

416valanced fringed (with a beard) **417young lady** i.e., boy for female
roles **420chopine** thick-soled shoe **420-421like a piece . . . the ring** (a coin was
unfit for legal tender if a crack extended from the edge through the ring enclosing
the monarch's head. Hamlet, punning on "ring," refers to the change of voice
that the boy actor will undergo) **429-430caviary to the general** i.e., too choice for
the multitude **431in the top of** overtopping **433modesty as a cunning** restraint
as art **434sallets** salads, spicy jests **437-438more handsome than fine** well-pro-
portioned rather than ornamented **442Hyrcanian beast** i.e., tiger (Hyrcania was
in Asia) **444sable** black **446ominous horse** i.e., wooden horse at the siege of
Troy

With heraldry more dismal.° Head to foot
Now is he total gules, horridly tricked°
With blood of fathers, mothers, daughters, sons,   450
Baked and impasted° with the parching streets,
That lend a tyrannous and a damnèd light
To their lord's murder. Roasted in wrath and fire,
And thus o'ersizèd° with coagulate gore,
With eyes like carbuncles, the hellish Pyrrhus   455
Old grandsire Priam seeks."

So, proceed you.

Polonius. Fore God, my lord, well spoken, with good accent
and good discretion.

Player.   "Anon he finds him,   460
Striking too short at Greeks. His antique sword,
Rebellious to his arm, lies where it falls,
Repugnant to command.° Unequal matched,
Pyrrhus at Priam drives, in rage strikes wide,
But with the whiff and wind of his fell sword   465
Th' unnervèd father falls. Then senseless Ilium,°
Seeming to feel this blow, with flaming top
Stoops to his base,° and with a hideous crash
Takes prisoner Pyrrhus' ear. For lo, his sword,
Which was declining on the milky head   470
Of reverend Priam, seemed i' th' air to stick.
So as a painted tyrant° Pyrrhus stood,
And like a neutral to his will and matter°
Did nothing.
But as we often see, against° some storm,   475
A silence in the heavens, the rack° stand still,
The bold winds speechless, and the orb below
As hush as death, anon the dreadful thunder
Doth rend the region, so after Pyrrhus' pause,
A rousèd vengeance sets him new awork,   480
And never did the Cyclops' hammers fall
On Mars's armor, forged for proof eterne,°
With less remorse than Pyrrhus' bleeding sword
Now falls on Priam.

---

[448]*dismal* ill-omened [449]*total gules, horridly tricked* all red, horridly
adorned [451]*impasted* encrusted [454]*o'ersizèd* smeared over [463]*Repugnant to
command* disobedient [466]*senseless Ilium* insensate Troy [468]*Stoops to his base*
collapses ("his" = its) [472]*painted tyrant* tyrant in a picture
[473]*matter* task [475]*against* just before [476]*rack* clouds [482]*proof eterne* eternal
endurance

Out, out, thou strumpet Fortune! All you gods,   485
In general synod° take away her power,
Break all the spokes and fellies° from her wheel,
And bowl the round nave° down the hill of heaven,
As low as to the fiends."

Polonius. This is too long.   490

Hamlet. It shall to the barber's, with your beard. — Prithee
say on. He's for a jig or a tale of bawdry, or he sleeps.
Say on; come to Hecuba.

Player. "But who (ah woe!) had seen the mobled° queen — "

Hamlet. "The mobled queen"?   495
Polonius. That's good. "Mobled queen" is good.

Player.   "Run barefoot up and down, threat'ning the flames
With bisson rheum;° a clout° upon that head
Where late the diadem stood, and for a robe,
About her lank and all o'erteemèd° loins,   500
A blanket in the alarm of fear caught up —
Who this had seen, with tongue in venom steeped
'Gainst Fortune's state would treason have pronounced.
But if the gods themselves did see her then,
When she saw Pyrrhus make malicious sport   505
In mincing with his sword her husband's limbs,
The instant burst of clamor that she made
(Unless things mortal move them not at all)
Would have made milch° the burning eyes of
         heaven
And passion in the gods."   510

Polonius. Look, whe'r° he has not turned his color, and has
tears in's eyes. Prithee no more.

Hamlet. 'Tis well. I'll have thee speak out the rest of this
soon. Good my lord, will you see the players well
bestowed?° Do you hear? Let them be well used, for   515
they are the abstract and brief chronicles of the time.
After your death you were better have a bad epitaph
than their ill report while you live.

Polonius. My lord, I will use them according to their desert.

Hamlet. God's bodkin,° man, much better! Use every man   520

---

[486]*synod* council [487]*fellies* rims [488]*nave* hub [494]*mobled* muffled [498]*bisson*
rheum blinding tears [498]*clout* rag [500]*o'erteemèd* exhausted with child-
bearing [509]*milch* moist (literally, "milk-giving") [511]*whe'r* whether [515]*bestowed*
housed [520]*God's bodkin* by God's little body

after his desert, and who shall scape whipping? Use
them after your own honor and dignity. The less they
deserve, the more merit is in your bounty. Take them
in.

Polonius. Come, sirs.   525

Hamlet. Follow him, friends. We'll hear a play tomorrow.
[*Aside to Player.*] Dost thou hear me, old friend? Can
you play *The Murder of Gonzago?*

Player. Ay, my lord.

Hamlet. We'll ha't tomorrow night. You could for a need   530
study a speech of some dozen or sixteen lines which
I would set down and insert in't, could you not?

Player. Ay, my lord.

Hamlet. Very well. Follow that lord, and look you mock
him not. My good friends, I'll leave you till night. You   535
are welcome to Elsinore.

                                            Exit Polonius and Players.

Rosencrantz. Good my lord.

                                    Exeunt [Rosencrantz and Guildenstern].

Hamlet. Ay, so, God bye to you. — Now I am alone.
    O, what a rogue and peasant slave am I!
    Is it not monstrous that this player here,   540
    But in a fiction, in a dream of passion,°
    Could force his soul so to his own conceit°
    That from her working all his visage wanned,
    Tears in his eyes, distraction in his aspect,
    A broken voice, and his whole function° suiting   545
    With forms° to his conceit? And all for nothing!
    For Hecuba!
    What's Hecuba to him, or he to Hecuba,
    That he should weep for her? What would he do
    Had he the motive and the cue for passion   550
    That I have? He would drown the stage with tears
    And cleave the general ear with horrid speech,
    Make mad the guilty and appall the free,°
    Confound the ignorant, and amaze indeed
    The very faculties of eyes and ears.   555
    Yet I,
    A dull and muddy-mettled° rascal, peak
    Like John-a-dreams,° unpregnant of° my cause,

---

⁵⁴¹*dream of passion* imaginary emotion   ⁵⁴²*conceit* imagination   ⁵⁴⁵*function*
action   ⁵⁴⁶*forms* bodily expressions   ⁵⁵³*appall the free* terrify (make pale?) the
guiltless   ⁵⁵⁷*muddy-mettled* weak-spirited   ⁵⁵⁷⁻⁵⁵⁸*peak/Like John-a-dreams* mope
like a dreamer   ⁵⁵⁸*unpregnant of* unquickened by

And can say nothing. No, not for a king,
Upon whose property and most dear life   *560*
A damned defeat was made. Am I a coward?
Who calls me villain? Breaks my pate across?
Plucks off my beard and blows it in my face?
Tweaks me by the nose? Gives me the lie i' th' throat
As deep as to the lungs? Who does me this?   *565*
Ha, 'swounds,° I should take it, for it cannot be
But I am pigeon-livered° and lack gall
To make oppression bitter, or ere this
I should ha' fatted all the region kites°
With this slave's offal. Bloody, bawdy villain!   *570*
Remorseless, treacherous, lecherous, kindless° villain!
O, vengeance!
Why, what an ass am I! This is most brave,°
That I, the son of a dear father murdered,
Prompted to my revenge by heaven and hell,   *575*
Must, like a whore, unpack my heart with words
And fall a-cursing like a very drab,°
A stallion!° Fie upon't, foh! About,° my brains.
Hum —
I have heard that guilty creatures sitting at a play   *580*
Have by the very cunning of the scene
Been struck so to the soul that presently°
They have proclaimed their malefactions.
For murder, though it have no tongue, will speak
With most miraculous organ. I'll have these players   *585*
Play something like the murder of my father
Before mine uncle. I'll observe his looks,
I'll tent° him to the quick. If 'a do blench,°
I know my course. The spirit that I have seen
May be a devil, and the devil hath power   *590*
T' assume a pleasing shape, yea, and perhaps
Out of my weakness and my melancholy,
As he is very potent with such spirits,
Abuses me to damn me. I'll have grounds

---

566 *'swounds* by God's wounds **567** *pigeon-livered* gentle as a dove **569** *region kites* kites (scavenger birds) of the sky **571** *kindless* unnatural **573** *brave* fine **577** *drab* prostitute **578** *stallion* male prostitute (perhaps one should adopt the Folio reading, "scullion" = kitchen wench) **578** *About* to work **582** *presently* immediately **588** *tent* probe **588** *blench* flinch

More relative° than this. The play's the thing   595
Wherein I'll catch the conscience of the King.

Exit.

[ACT III

Scene I. *The castle.*]

Enter King, Queen, Polonius, Ophelia, Rosencrantz, Guildenstern, Lords.

King. And can you by no drift of conference°
Get from him why he puts on this confusion,
Grating so harshly all his days of quiet
With turbulent and dangerous lunacy?
Rosencrantz. He does confess he feels himself distracted,   5
But from what cause 'a will by no means speak.
Guildenstern. Nor do we find him forward to be sounded,°
But with a crafty madness keeps aloof
When we would bring him on to some confession
Of his true state.
Queen.   Did he receive you well?   10
Rosencrantz. Most like a gentleman.
Guildenstern. But with much forcing of his disposition.°
Rosencrantz. Niggard of question,° but of our demands
Most free in his reply.
Queen.   Did you assay° him
To any pastime?   15
Rosencrantz. Madam, it so fell out that certain players
We o'erraught° on the way; of these we told him,
And there did seem in him a kind of joy
To hear of it. They are here about the court,
And, as I think, they have already order   20
This night to play before him.
Polonius.   'Tis most true,
And he beseeched me to entreat your Majesties
To hear and see the matter.
King. With all my heart, and it doth much content me
To hear him so inclined.   25

°⁵⁹⁵*relative* (probably "pertinent," but possibly "able to be related plausibly")
III.i ¹*drift of conference* management of conversation ⁷*forward to be sounded*
willing to be questioned ¹²*forcing of his disposition* effort ¹³*Niggard of ques-*
tion uninclined to talk ¹⁴*assay* tempt ¹⁷*o'erraught* overtook

                    Good gentlemen, give him a further edge
                    And drive his purpose into these delights.
Rosencrantz. We shall, my lord.
                                        Exit Rosencrantz and Guildenstern.
King.   Sweet Gertrude, leave us too,
                    For we have closely° sent for Hamlet hither,
                    That he, as 'twere by accident, may here   30
                    Affront° Ophelia.
                    Her father and myself (lawful espials°)
                    Will so bestow ourselves that, seeing unseen,
                    We may of their encounter frankly judge
                    And gather by him, as he is behaved,   35
                    If't be th' affliction of his love or no
                    That thus he suffers for.
Queen.   I shall obey you.
                    And for your part, Ophelia, I do wish
                    That your good beauties be the happy cause
                    Of Hamlet's wildness. So shall I hope your virtues   40
                    Will bring him to his wonted way again,
                    To both your honors.
Ophelia.   Madam, I wish it may.
                                                    [*Exit Queen.*]
Polonius. Ophelia, walk you here. — Gracious, so please you,
                    We will bestow ourselves. [*To Ophelia.*] Read on this book,
                    That show of such an exercise may color°   45
                    Your loneliness. We are oft to blame in this,
                    'Tis too much proved, that with devotion's visage
                    And pious action we do sugar o'er
                    The devil himself.
King [*aside*].   O, 'tis too true.
                    How smart a lash that speech doth give my conscience! 50
                    The harlot's cheek, beautied with plast'ring art,
                    Is not more ugly to the thing that helps it
                    Than is my deed to my most painted word.
                    O heavy burden!
Polonius. I hear him coming. Let's withdraw, my lord.   55
                                        [*Exit King and Polonius.*]
                    Enter Hamlet.

Hamlet. To be, or not to be: that is the question:

---

²⁹***closely***   secretly   ³¹***Affront***   meet face to face   ³²***espials***   spies   ⁴⁵***exercise may***
color   act of devotion may give a plausible hue to (the book is one of devotion)

Whether 'tis nobler in the mind to suffer
The slings and arrows of outrageous fortune,
Or to take arms against a sea of troubles,
And by opposing end them. To die, to sleep —   60
No more — and by a sleep to say we end
The heartache, and the thousand natural shocks
That flesh is heir to! 'Tis a consummation
Devoutly to be wished. To die, to sleep —
To sleep — perchance to dream: ay, there's the rub,°   65
For in that sleep of death what dreams may come
When we have shuffled off this mortal coil,°
Must give us pause. There's the respect°
That makes calamity of so long life:°
For who would bear the whips and scorns of time,   70
Th' oppressor's wrong, the proud man's contumely,
The pangs of despised love, the law's delay,
The insolence of office, and the spurns
That patient merit of th' unworthy takes,
When he himself might his quietus° make   75
With a bare bodkin?° Who would fardels° bear,
To grunt and sweat under a weary life,
But that the dread of something after death
The undiscovered country, from whose bourn°
No traveler returns, puzzles the will,   80
And makes us rather bear those ills we have,
Than fly to others that we know not of?
Thus conscience° does make cowards of us all,
And thus the native hue of resolution
Is sicklied o'er with the pale cast° of thought,   85
And enterprises of great pitch° and moment,
With this regard° their currents turn awry,
And lose the name of action. — Soft you now,
The fair Ophelia! — Nymph, in thy orisons°
Be all my sins remembered.

Ophelia.   Good my lord,   90
How does your honor for this many a day?

---

[65]*rub*   impediment (obstruction to a bowler's ball)   [67]*coil*   (1) turmoil, (2) a ring of rope (here the flesh encircling the soul)   [68]*respect*   consideration   [69]*makes calamity of so long life*   (1) makes calamity so long-lived, (2) makes living so long a calamity   [75]*quietus*   full   discharge   (a   legal   term)   [76]*bodkin*   dagger   [76]*fardels*   burdens   [79]*bourn*   region   [83]*conscience*   self-consciousness, introspection   [85]*cast*   color   [86]*pitch*   height (a term from falconry)   [87]*regard*   consideration   [89]*orisons*   prayers

Hamlet. I humbly thank you; well, well, well.

Ophelia. My lord, I have remembrances of yours
      That I have longèd long to redeliver.
      I pray you now, receive them.

Hamlet.   No, not I,   *95*
      I never gave you aught.

Ophelia. My honored lord, you know right well you did,
      And with them words of so sweet breath composed
      As made these things more rich. Their perfume lost,
      Take these again, for to the noble mind   *100*
      Rich gifts wax poor when givers prove unkind.
      There, my lord.

Hamlet. Ha, ha! Are you honest?°

Ophelia. My lord?

Hamlet. Are you fair?   *105*

Ophelia. What means your lordship?

Hamlet. That if you be honest and fair, your honesty should
      admit no discourse to your beauty.°

Ophelia. Could beauty, my lord, have better commerce than
      with honesty?   *110*

Hamlet. Ay, truly; for the power of beauty will sooner trans-
      form honesty from what it is to a bawd° than the force
      of honesty can translate beauty into his likeness. This
      was sometime a paradox, but now the time gives it
      proof. I did love you once.   *115*

Ophelia. Indeed, my lord, you made me believe so.

Hamlet. You should not have believed me, for virtue cannot
      so inoculate° our old stock but we shall relish of it.° I
      loved you not.

Ophelia. I was the more deceived.   *120*

Hamlet. Get thee to a nunnery. Why wouldst thou be a
      breeder of sinners? I am myself indifferent honest,° but
      yet I could accuse me of such things that it were better
      my mother had not borne me: I am very proud, re-
      vengeful, ambitious, with more offenses at my beck°   *125*
      than I have thoughts to put them in, imagination to
      give them shape, or time to act them in. What should
      such fellows as I do crawling between earth and heaven?

---

[103]*Are you honest*   (1) are you modest, (2) are you chaste, (3) have you integrity
[107-108]*your honesty . . . to your beauty*   your modesty should permit no approach
to your beauty   [112]*bawd* procurer   [118]*inoculate* graft   [118]*relish of it* smack of
it (our old sinful nature)   [122]*indifferent honest* moderately virtuous   [125]*beck* call

We are arrant knaves all; believe none of us. Go thy
ways to a nunnery. Where's your father?   *130*
Ophelia. At home, my lord.
Hamlet. Let the doors be shut upon him, that he may play
the fool nowhere but in's own house. Farewell.
Ophelia. O help him, you sweet heavens!
Hamlet. If thou dost marry, I'll give thee this plague for thy   *135*
dowry: be thou as chaste as ice, as pure as snow, thou
shalt not escape calumny. Get thee to a nunnery. Go,
farewell. Or if thou wilt needs marry, marry a fool,
for wise men know well enough what monsters° you
make of them. To a nunnery, go, and quickly too.
Farewell.   *140*
Ophelia. Heavenly powers, restore him!
Hamlet. I have heard of your paintings, well enough. God
hath given you one face, and you make yourselves
another. You jig and amble, and you lisp; you nickname
God's creatures and make your wantonness your ig-   *145*
norance.° Go to, I'll no more on't; it hath made me
mad. I say we will have no moe° marriage. Those that
are married already — all but one — shall live. The
rest shall keep as they are. To a nunnery, go.

                                                         Exit.
Ophelia. O what a noble mind is here o'erthrown!   *150*
The courtier's, soldier's, scholar's, eye, tongue, sword,
Th' expectancy and rose° of the fair state,
The glass of fashion, and the mold of form,°
Th' observed of all observers, quite, quite down!
And I, of ladies most deject and wretched,   *155*
That sucked the honey of his musicked vows,
Now see that noble and most sovereign reason
Like sweet bells jangled, out of time and harsh,
That unmatched form and feature of blown° youth
Blasted with ecstasy.° O, woe is me   *160*
T' have seen what I have seen, see what I see!

Enter King and Polonius.

King. Love? His affections° do not that way tend,
Nor what he spake, though it lacked form a little,

---

[138]*monsters* horned beasts, cuckolds   [145]*make your wantonness your ignorance*
excuse your wanton speech by pretending ignorance   [147]*moe* more   [152]*expectancy
and rose* i.e., fair hope   [153]*The glass . . . of form* the mirror of fashion, and
the pattern of excellent behavior   [159]*blown* blooming   [160]*ecstasy* madness [162]*affections*
inclinations

Was not like madness. There's something in his soul
O'er which his melancholy sits on brood,   *165*
And I do doubt° the hatch and the disclose
Will be some danger; which for to prevent,
I have in quick determination
Thus set it down: he shall with speed to England
For the demand of our neglected tribute.   *170*
Haply the seas, and countries different,
With variable objects, shall expel
This something-settled° matter in his heart,
Whereon his brains still beating puts him thus
From fashion of himself. What think you on't?   *175*
Polonius. It shall do well. But yet do I believe
The origin and commencement of his grief
Sprung from neglected love. How now, Ophelia?
You need not tell us what Lord Hamlet said;
We heard it all. My lord, do as you please,   *180*
But if you hold it fit, after the play,
Let his queen mother all alone entreat him
To show his grief. Let her be round° with him,
And I'll be placed, so please you, in the ear
Of all their conference. If she find him not,°   *185*
To England send him, or confine him where
Your wisdom best shall think.
King.   It shall be so.
Madness in great ones must not unwatched go.

                                              Exeunt.

[**Scene II.** *The castle.*]

Enter Hamlet and three of the Players.

Hamlet. Speak the speech, I pray you, as I pronounced it to
you, trippingly on the tongue. But if you mouth it, as
many of our players do, I had as lief the town crier
spoke my lines. Nor do not saw the air too much with
your hand, thus, but use all gently, for in the very   *5*
torrent, tempest, and (as I may say) whirlwind of your
passion, you must acquire and beget a temperance that
may give it smoothness. O, it offends me to the soul
to hear a robustious periwig-pated° fellow tear a passion

---

¹⁶⁶**doubt** fear   ¹⁷³**something-settled** somewhat settled   ¹⁸³**round** blunt   ¹⁸⁵**find him
not** does not find him out   III.ii.   ⁹**robustious periwig-pated** boisterous wig-
headed

to tatters, to very rags, to split the ears of the ground- 10
lings,° who for the most part are capable of° nothing
but inexplicable dumb shows° and noise. I would have
such a fellow whipped for o'erdoing Termagant. It out-
herods Herod.° Pray you avoid it.

Player. I warrant your honor. 15

Hamlet. Be not too tame neither, but let your own discretion
be your tutor. Suit the action to the word, the word
to the action, with this special observance, that you
o'erstep not the modesty of nature. For anything so
o'erdone is from° the purpose of playing, whose end, 20
both at the first and now, was and is, to hold, as 'twere,
the mirror up to nature; to show virtue her own feature,
scorn her own image, and the very age and body of
the time his form and pressure.° Now, this overdone,
or come tardy off, though it makes the unskillful laugh, 25
cannot but make the judicious grieve, the censure of
the which one must in your allowance o'erweigh a
whole theater of others. O, there be players that I have
seen play, and heard others praise, and that highly (not
to speak it profanely), that neither having th' accent of 30
Christians, nor the gait of Christian, pagan, nor man,
have so strutted and bellowed that I have thought some
of Nature's journeymen° had made men, and not made
them well, they imitated humanity so abominably.

Player. I hope we have reformed that indifferently° with us, 35
sir.

Hamlet. O, reform it altogether! And let those that play your
clowns speak no more than is set down for them, for
there be of them that will themselves laugh, to set on
some quantity of barren spectators to laugh too, though 40
in the meantime some necessary question of the play
be then to be considered. That's villainous and shows
a most pitiful ambition in the fool that uses it. Go make
you ready.

                                        Exit Players.

Enter Polonius, Guildenstern, and Rosencrantz.

10-11groundlings those who stood in the pit of the theater (the poorest and presumably
most ignorant of the audience) **11are capable of** are able to understand **12dumb
shows** (it had been the fashion for actors to preface plays or parts of plays with
silent mime) **13-14Termagant . . . Herod** (boisterous characters in the old mystery
plays) **20from** contrary to **24pressure** image, impress **33journeymen** workers
not yet masters of their craft **35indifferently** tolerably

How now, my lord? Will the King hear this piece of   45
work?

Polonius. And the Queen too, and that presently.

Hamlet. Bid the players make haste.

>   *Exit Polonius.*

Will you two help to hasten them?

Rosencrantz. Ay, my lord.   50

>   *Exeunt they two.*

Hamlet. What, ho, Horatio!

> *Enter Horatio.*

Horatio. Here, sweet lord, at your service.

Hamlet. Horatio, thou art e'en as just a man
   As e'er my conversation coped withal.°

Horatio. O, my dear lord —

Hamlet.   Nay, do not think I flatter.   55
   For what advancement° may I hope from thee,
   That no revenue hast but thy good spirits
   To feed and clothe thee? Why should the poor be flattered?
   No, let the candied° tongue lick absurd pomp,
   And crook the pregnant° hinges of the knee   60
   Where thrift° may follow fawning. Dost thou hear?
   Since my dear soul was mistress of her choice
   And could of men distinguish her election,
   S' hath sealed thee° for herself, for thou hast been
   As one, in suff'ring all, that suffers nothing,   65
   A man that Fortune's buffets and rewards
   Hast ta'en with equal thanks; and blest are those
   Whose blood° and judgment are so well commeddled°
   That they are not a pipe for Fortune's finger
   To sound what stop she please. Give me that man   70
   That is not passion's slave, and I will wear him
   In my heart's core, ay, in my heart of heart,
   As I do thee. Something too much of this —
   There is a play tonight before the King.
   One scene of it comes near the circumstance   75
   Which I have told thee, of my father's death.
   I prithee, when thou seest that act afoot,
   Even with the very comment° of thy soul

---

[54] ***coped   withal*** met   with   [56] ***advancement*** promotion   [59] ***candied*** sugared, flattering   [60] ***pregnant*** (1) pliant, (2) full of promise of good fortune   [61] ***thrift*** profit   [64] ***S' hath sealed thee*** she (the soul) has set a mark on you   [68] ***blood*** passion   [68] ***commeddled*** blended   [78] ***very comment*** deepest wisdom

Observe my uncle. If his occulted° guilt
Do not itself unkennel in one speech,   *80*
It is a damnèd ghost that we have seen,
And my imaginations are as foul
As Vulcan's stithy.° Give him heedful note,
For I mine eyes will rivet to his face,
And after we will both our judgments join   *85*
In censure of his seeming.°
Horatio.   Well, my lord.
If 'a steal aught the whilst this play is playing,
And scape detecting, I will pay the theft.

Enter Trumpets and Kettledrums, King, Queen, Polonius, Ophelia,
Rosencrantz, Guildenstern, and other Lords attendant with his
Guard carrying torches. Danish March. Sound a Flourish.

Hamlet. They are coming to the play: I must be idle;°
Get you a place.   *90*
King. How fares our cousin Hamlet?
Hamlet. Excellent, i' faith, of the chameleon's dish;° I eat the
air, promise-crammed; you cannot feed capons so.
King. I have nothing with this answer, Hamlet; these words
are not mine.   *95*
Hamlet. No, nor mine now. [*To Polonius.*] My lord, you
played once i' th' university, you say?
Polonius. That did I, my lord, and was accounted a good actor.
Hamlet. What did you enact?
Polonius. I did enact Julius Caesar. I was killed i' th' Capitol; *100*
Brutus killed me.
Hamlet. It was a brute part of him to kill so capital a calf
there. Be the players ready?
Rosencrantz. Ay, my lord. They stay upon your patience.
Queen. Come hither, my dear Hamlet, sit by me.   *105*
Hamlet. No, good mother. Here's metal more attractive.°
Polonius [*to the king*]. O ho! Do you mark that?
Hamlet. Lady, shall I lie in your lap?

[*He lies at Ophelia's feet.*]

Ophelia. No, my lord.
Hamlet. I mean, my head upon your lap?   *110*

---

[79]*occulted* hidden [83]*stithy* forge, smithy [86]*censure of his seeming* judgment
on his looks [89]*be idle* play the fool [92]*the chameleon's dish* air (on which cha-
meleons were thought to live) [106]*attractive* magnetic

Ophelia. Ay, my lord.

Hamlet. Do you think I meant country matters?°

Ophelia. I think nothing, my lord.

Hamlet. That's a fair thought to lie between maids' legs.

Ophelia. What is, my lord?   115

Hamlet. Nothing.

Ophelia. You are merry, my lord.

Hamlet. Who, I?

Ophelia. Ay, my lord.

Hamlet. O God, your only jig-maker!° What should a man   120
    do but be merry? For look you how cheerfully my
    mother looks, and my father died within's two hours.

Ophelia. Nay, 'tis twice two months, my lord.

Hamlet. So long? Nay then, let the devil wear black, for I'll
    have a suit of sables.° O heavens! Die two months ago,   125
    and not forgotten yet? Then there's hope a great man's
    memory may outlive his life half a year. But, by'r Lady,
    'a must build churches then, or else shall 'a suffer not
    thinking on, with the hobbyhorse,° whose epitaph is
    "For O, for O, the hobbyhorse is forgot!"   130

The trumpets sound. Dumb show follows:

*Enter a King and a Queen very lovingly, the Queen embracing
him, and he her. She kneels; and makes show of protestation unto
him. He takes her up, and declines his head upon her neck. He
lies him down upon a bank of flowers. She, seeing him asleep,
leaves him. Anon come in another man: takes off his crown, kisses
it, pours poison in the sleeper's ears, and leaves him. The Queen
returns, finds the King dead, makes passionate action. The poisoner,
with some three or four, come in again, seem to condole with her.
The dead body is carried away. The poisoner woos the Queen with
gifts; she seems harsh awhile, but in the end accepts love.*

                                                                                             Exeunt.

Ophelia. What means this, my lord?

Hamlet. Marry, this is miching mallecho;° it means mischief.

Ophelia. Belike this show imports the argument° of the play.

Enter Prologue.

---

[112]***country matters*** rustic doings (with a pun on the vulgar word for the pud-
endum) [120]***jig-maker*** composer of songs and dances (often a Fool, who performed
them) [125]***sables*** (pun on "black" and "luxurious furs") [129]***hobbyhorse*** mock
horse worn by a performer in the morris dance [132]***miching mallecho*** sneaking
mischief [133]***argument*** plot

Hamlet. We shall know by this fellow. The players cannot   *135*
    keep counsel; they'll tell all.
Ophelia. Will 'a tell us what this show meant?
Hamlet. Ay, or any show that you will show him. Be not
    you ashamed to show, he'll not shame to tell you what
    it means.
Ophelia. You are naught,° you are naught; I'll mark the play.   *140*
Prologue. For us, and for our tragedy,
    Here stooping to your clemency,
    We beg your hearing patiently.

                                                                          [Exit.]

Hamlet. Is this a prologue, or the posy of a ring?°
Ophelia. 'Tis brief, my lord.   *145*
Hamlet. As woman's love.

    Enter [two Players as] King and Queen.

Player King. Full thirty times hath Phoebus' cart° gone round
    Neptune's salt wash° and Tellus'° orbèd ground,
    And thirty dozen moons with borrowed sheen
    About the world have times twelve thirties been,   *150*
    Since love our hearts, and Hymen did our hands,
    Unite commutual in most sacred bands.
Player Queen. So many journeys may the sun and moon
    Make us again count o'er ere love be done!
    But woe is me, you are so sick of late,   *155*
    So far from cheer and from your former state,
    That I distrust° you. Yet, though I distrust,
    Discomfort you, my lord, it nothing must.
    For women fear too much, even as they love,
    And women's fear and love hold quantity,   *160*
    In neither aught, or in extremity.°
    Now what my love is, proof° hath made you know,
    And as my love is sized, my fear is so.
    Where love is great, the littlest doubts are fear;
    Where little fears grow great, great love grows there.   *165*
Player King. Faith, I must leave thee, love, and shortly too;
    My operant° powers their functions leave to do:
    And thou shalt live in this fair world behind,

---

¹⁴⁰*naught* wicked, improper ¹⁴⁴*posy of a ring* motto inscribed in a
ring ¹⁴⁷*Phoebus' cart* the sun's chariot ¹⁴⁸*Neptune's salt wash* the sea
¹⁴⁸*Tellus* Roman goddess of the earth ¹⁵⁷*distrust* am anxious about ¹⁶⁰⁻¹⁶¹*And
women's . . . in extremity* (perhaps the idea is that women's anxiety is great or
little in proportion to their love. The previous line, unrhymed, may be a false
start that Shakespeare neglected to delete) ¹⁶²*proof* experience ¹⁶⁷*operant* active

Honored, beloved, and haply one as kind
For husband shalt thou —
Player Queen.   O, confound the rest!   *170*
Such love must needs be treason in my breast.
In second husband let me be accurst!
None wed the second but who killed the first.
Hamlet [*aside*]. That's wormwood.°
Player Queen. The instances° that second marriage move°   *175*
Are base respects of thrift,° but none of love.
A second time I kill my husband dead
When second husband kisses me in bed.
Player King. I do believe you think what now you speak,
But what we do determine oft we break.   *180*
Purpose is but the slave to memory,
Of violent birth, but poor validity,°
Which now like fruit unripe sticks on the tree,
But fall unshaken when they mellow be.
Most necessary 'tis that we forget   *185*
To pay ourselves what to ourselves is debt.
What to ourselves in passion we propose,
The passion ending, doth the purpose lose.
The violence of either grief or joy
Their own enactures° with themselves destroy: *190*
Where joy most revels, grief doth most lament;
Grief joys, joy grieves, on slender accident.
This world is not for aye, nor 'tis not strange
That even our loves should with our fortunes change,
For 'tis a question left us yet to prove,   *195*
Whether love lead fortune, or else fortune love.
The great man down, you mark his favorite flies;
The poor advanced makes friends of enemies;
And hitherto doth love on fortune tend,
For who not needs shall never lack a friend;   *200*
And who in want a hollow friend doth try,
Directly seasons him° his enemy.
But, orderly to end where I begun,
Our wills and fates do so contrary run
That our devices still are overthrown;   *205*
Our thoughts are ours, their ends none of our own.
So think thou wilt no second husband wed,

---

[174]*wormwood* a bitter herb [175]*instances* motives [175]*move* induce [176]*respects
of thrift* considerations of profit [182]*validity* strength [190]*enactures* acts
[202]*seasons him* ripens him into

But die thy thoughts when thy first lord is dead.
Player Queen. Nor earth to give me food, nor heaven light,
Sport and repose lock from me day and night,   *210*
To desperation turn my trust and hope,
An anchor's° cheer in prison be my scope,
Each opposite that blanks° the face of joy
Meet what I would have well, and it destroy:
Both here and hence pursue me lasting strife,   *215*
If, once a widow, ever I be wife!
Hamlet. If she should break it now!
Player King. 'Tis deeply sworn. Sweet, leave me here awhile;
My spirits grow dull, and fain I would beguile
The tedious day with sleep.
Player Queen.   Sleep rock thy brain,   *220*

[*He*] *sleeps.*

And never come mischance between us twain!

                                                                Exit.

Hamlet. Madam, how like you this play?
Queen. The lady doth protest too much, methinks.
Hamlet. O, but she'll keep her word.
King. Have you heard the argument?° Is there no offense in't?   *225*
Hamlet. No, no, they do but jest, poison in jest; no offense
    i' th' world.
King. What do you call the play?
Hamlet. *The Mousetrap.* Marry, how? Tropically.° This play
    is the image of a murder done in Vienna: Gonzago is   *230*
    the Duke's name; his wife, Baptista. You shall see anon.
    'Tis a knavish piece of work, but what of that? Your
    Majesty, and we that have free° souls, it touches us
    not. Let the galled jade winch;° our withers are unwrung.

Enter Lucianus.

This is one Lucianus, nephew to the King.   *235*
Ophelia. You are as good as a chorus, my lord.
Hamlet. I could interpret° between you and your love, if I
    could see the puppets dallying.
Ophelia. You are keen,° my lord, you are keen.

---

²¹²*anchor's* anchorite's, hermit's ²¹³*opposite that blanks* adverse thing that
blanches ²²⁵*argument* plot ²²⁹*Tropically* figuratively (with a pun on
"trap") ²³³*free* innocent ²³⁴*galled jade winch* chafed horse wince
²³⁷*interpret* (like a showman explaining the action of puppets) ²³⁹*keen* (1) sharp,
(2) sexually aroused

Hamlet. It would cost you a groaning to take off mine edge.   *240*
Ophelia. Still better, and worse.
Hamlet. So you mistake° your husbands. — Begin, murderer.
  Leave thy damnable faces and begin. Come, the croaking
  raven doth bellow for revenge.
Lucianus. Thoughts black, hands apt, drugs fit, and time agreeing,   *245*
  Confederate season,° else no creature seeing,
  Thou mixture rank, of midnight weeds collected,
  With Hecate's ban° thrice blasted, thrice infected,
  Thy natural magic and dire property°
  On wholesome life usurps immediately.   *250*

  Pours the poison in his ears.

Hamlet. 'A poisons him i' th' garden for his estate. His name's
  Gonzago. The story is extant, and written in very choice
  Italian. You shall see anon how the murderer gets the
  love of Gonzago's wife.
Ophelia. The King rises.   *255*
Hamlet. What, frighted with false fire?°
Queen. How fares my lord?
Polonius. Give o'er the play.
King. Give me some light. Away!
Polonius. Lights, lights, lights!   *260*
                                Exit all but Hamlet and Horatio.
Hamlet.   Why, let the strucken deer go weep,
                The hart ungallèd play:
            For some must watch, while some must sleep;
                Thus runs the world away.
        Would not this, sir, and a forest of feathers° — if the   *265*
  rest of my fortunes turn Turk° with me — with two
  Provincial roses° on my razed° shoes, get me a fellowship
  in a cry° of players?
Horatio. Half a share.
Hamlet. A whole one, I.   *270*

        For thou dost know, O Damon dear,
            This realm dismantled was

---

²⁴²*mistake* err in taking ²⁴⁶*Confederate season* the opportunity allied with
me ²⁴⁸*Hecate's ban* the curse of the goddess of sorcery ²⁴⁹*property*
nature ²⁵⁶*false fire* blank discharge of firearms ²⁶⁵*feathers* (plumes were sometimes part of a costume) ²⁶⁶*turn Turk* i.e., go bad, treat me badly ²⁶⁷*Provincial*
roses rosettes like the roses of Provence(?) ²⁶⁷*razed* ornamented with
slashes ²⁶⁸*cry* pack, company

　　　　　Of Jove himself; and now reigns here
　　　　　　　A very, very — pajock.°
Horatio. You might have rhymed.°　　　　　　　　　　275
Hamlet. O good Horatio, I'll take the ghost's word for a
　　thousand pound. Didst perceive?
Horatio. Very well, my lord.
Hamlet. Upon the talk of poisoning?
Horatio. I did very well note him.　　　　　　　　　280
Hamlet. Ah ha! Come, some music! Come, the recorders!°

　　　　　For if the King like not the comedy,
　　　　　Why then, belike he likes it not, perdy.°

　　Come, some music!

　　Enter Rosencrantz and Guildenstern.

Guildenstern. Good my lord, vouchsafe me a word with you.　　285
Hamlet. Sir, a whole history.
Guildenstern. The King, sir —
Hamlet. Ay, sir, what of him?
Guildenstern. Is in his retirement marvelous distemp'red.
Hamlet. With drink, sir?　　　　　　　　　　　　290
Guildenstern. No, my lord, with choler.°
Hamlet. Your wisdom should show itself more richer to signify
　　this to the doctor, for me to put him to his purgation
　　would perhaps plunge him into more choler.
Guildenstern. Good my lord, put your discourse into some　　295
　　frame,° and start not so wildly from my affair.
Hamlet. I am tame, sir; pronounce.
Guildenstern. The Queen, your mother, in most great affliction
　　of spirit hath sent me to you.
Hamlet. You are welcome.　　　　　　　　　　　300
Guildenstern. Nay, good my lord, this courtesy is not of the
　　right breed. If it shall please you to make me a whole-
　　some answer, I will do your mother's commandment:
　　if not, your pardon and my return shall be the end of
　　my business.　　　　　　　　　　　　　　305
Hamlet. Sir, I cannot.
Rosencrantz. What, my lord?

---

[274]*pajock* peacock　[275]*You might have rhymed* i.e., rhymed "was" with
"ass"　[281]*recorders* flutelike instruments　[283]*perdy* by God (French: *par
dieu*)　[291]*choler* anger (but Hamlet pretends to take the word in its sense of "bil-
iousness")　[296]*frame* order, control

Hamlet. Make you a wholesome° answer; my wit's diseased.
But, sir, such answer as I can make, you shall command,
or rather, as you say, my mother. Therefore no more,   *310*
but to the matter. My mother, you say —
Rosencrantz. Then thus she says: your behavior hath struck
her into amazement and admiration.°
Hamlet. O wonderful son, that can so stonish a mother! But
is there no sequel at the heels of this mother's admiration?   *315*
Impart.
Rosencrantz. She desires to speak with you in her closet ere
you go to bed.
Hamlet. We shall obey, were she ten times our mother. Have
you any further trade with us?   *320*
Rosencrantz. My lord, you once did love me.
Hamlet. And do still, by these pickers and stealers.°
Rosencrantz. Good my lord, what is your cause of distemper?
You do surely bar the door upon your own liberty, if
you deny your griefs to your friend.   *325*
Hamlet. Sir, I lack advancement.°
Rosencrantz. How can that be, when you have the voice of
the King himself for your succession in Denmark?

Enter the Players with recorders.

Hamlet. Ay, sir, but "while the grass grows" — the proverb°
is something musty. O, the recorders. Let me see one.   *330*
To withdraw° with you — why do you go about to
recover the wind° of me as if you would drive me into
a toil?°
Guildenstern. O my lord, if my duty be too bold, my love
is too unmannerly.°   *335*
Hamlet. I do not well understand that. Will you play upon
this pipe?
Guildenstern. My lord, I cannot.
Hamlet. I pray you.
Guildenstern. Believe me, I cannot.   *340*

---

[308]*wholesome* sane [313]*admiration* wonder [322]*pickers and stealers* i.e., hands
(with reference to the prayer; "Keep my hands from picking and steal-
ing") [326]*advancement* promotion [329]*proverb* ("While the grass groweth, the
horse starveth") [331]*withdraw* speak in private [332]*recover the wind* get on the
windward side (as in hunting) [333]*toil* snare [334-335]*if my duty . . . too unmannerly* i.e., if these questions seem rude, it is because my love for you leads me
beyond good manners

Hamlet. I do beseech you.

Guildenstern. I know no touch of it, my lord.

Hamlet. It is as easy as lying. Govern these ventages° with
your fingers and thumb, give it breath with your mouth,
and it will discourse most eloquent music. Look you,   *345*
these are the stops.

Guildenstern. But these cannot I command to any utt'rance
of harmony; I have not the skill.

Hamlet. Why, look you now, how unworthy a thing you
make of me! You would play upon me; you would   *350*
seem to know my stops; you would pluck out the heart
of my mystery; you would sound me from my lowest
note to the top of my compass;° and there is much
music, excellent voice, in this little organ,° yet cannot
you make it speak. 'Sblood, do you think I am easier   *355*
to be played on than a pipe? Call me what instrument
you will, though you can fret° me, you cannot play
upon me.

Enter Polonius.

God bless you, sir!

Polonius. My lord, the Queen would speak with you, and   *360*
presently.

Hamlet. Do you see yonder cloud that's almost in shape of
a camel?

Polonius. By th' mass and 'tis, like a camel indeed.

Hamlet. Methinks it is like a weasel.   *365*

Polonius. It is backed like a weasel.

Hamlet. Or like a whale.

Polonius. Very like a whale.

Hamlet. Then I will come to my mother by and by. [*Aside.*]
They fool me to the top of my bent.° — I will come   *370*
by and by.°

Polonius. I will say so.

Exit.

Hamlet. "By and by" is easily said. Leave me, friends.

[*Exit all but Hamlet.*]
'Tis now the very witching time of night,
When churchyards yawn, and hell itself breathes out   *375*
Contagion to this world. Now could I drink hot blood

---

³⁴³*ventages* vents, stops on a recorder   ³⁵³*compass* range of voice   ³⁵⁴*organ* i.e.,
the recorder   ³⁵⁷*fret* vex (with a pun alluding to the frets, or ridges, that guide
the fingering on some instruments)   ³⁷⁰*They fool . . . my bent* they compel me
to play the fool to the limit of my capacity   ³⁷¹*by and by* very soon

And do such bitter business as the day
Would quake to look on. Soft, now to my mother.
O heart, lose not thy nature; let not ever
The soul of Nero° enter this firm bosom.   380
Let me be cruel, not unnatural;
I will speak daggers to her, but use none.
My tongue and soul in this be hypocrites:
How in my words somever she be shent,°
To give them seals° never, my soul, consent!   385
                                                         Exit.

[Scene III. *The castle.*]

Enter King, Rosencrantz, and Guildenstern.

King. I like him not, nor stands it safe with us
    To let his madness range. Therefore prepare you.
    I your commission will forthwith dispatch,
    And he to England shall along with you.
    The terms° of our estate may not endure   5
    Hazard so near's° as doth hourly grow
    Out of his brows.
Guildenstern.   We will ourselves provide.
    Most holy and religious fear it is
    To keep those many many bodies safe
    That live and feed upon your Majesty.   10
Rosencrantz. The single and peculiar° life is bound
    With all the strength and armor of the mind
    To keep itself from noyance,° but much more
    That spirit upon whose weal depends and rests
    The lives of many. The cess of majesty°   15
    Dies not alone, but like a gulf° doth draw
    What's near it with it; or it is a massy wheel
    Fixed on the summit of the highest mount,
    To whose huge spokes ten thousand lesser things
    Are mortised and adjoined, which when it falls,   20
    Each small annexment, petty consequence,
    Attends° the boist'rous ruin. Never alone
    Did the King sigh, but with a general groan.

---

[380]*Nero* (Roman emperor who had his mother murdered)
[384]*shent* rebuked [385]*give them seals* confirm them with deeds III.iii.
[5]*terms* conditions [6]*near's* near us [11]*peculiar* individual, private [13]*noyance*
injury [15]*cess of majesty* cessation (death) of a king [16]*gulf* whirlpool
[22]*Attends* waits on, participates in

King. Arm° you, I pray you, to this speedy voyage,
    For we will fetters put about this fear,   25
    Which now goes too free-footed.
Rosencrantz.   We will haste us.
                                            Exit Gentlemen.
    Enter Polonius.

Polonius. My lord, he's going to his mother's closet.°
    Behind the arras I'll convey myself
    To hear the process.° I'll warrant she'll tax him home,°
    And, as you said, and wisely was it said,   30
    'Tis meet that some more audience than a mother,
    Since nature makes them partial, should o'erhear
    The speech of vantage.° Fare you well, my liege.
    I'll call upon you ere you go to bed
    And tell you what I know.
King.   Thanks, dear my lord.   35
                                         Exit [Polonius].
    O, my offense is rank, it smells to heaven;
    It hath the primal eldest curse° upon't,
    A brother's murder. Pray can I not,
    Though inclination be as sharp as will.
    My stronger guilt defeats my strong intent,   40
    And like a man to double business bound
    I stand in pause where I shall first begin,
    And both neglect. What if this cursèd hand
    Were thicker than itself with brother's blood,
    Is there not rain enough in the sweet heavens   45
    To wash it white as snow? Whereto serves mercy
    But to confront° the visage of offense?
    And what's in prayer but this twofold force,
    To be forestallèd ere we come to fall,
    Or pardoned being down? Then I'll look up.   50
    My fault is past. But, O, what form of prayer
    Can serve my turn? "Forgive me my foul murder"?
    That cannot be, since I am still possessed
    Of those effects° for which I did the murder,
    My crown, mine own ambition, and my queen.   55
    May one be pardoned and retain th' offense?
    In the corrupted currents of this world

---

[24]**Arm**   prepare   [27]**closet** private room   [29]**process** proceedings   [29]**tax him home**
censure him sharply   [33]**of vantage**   from an advantageous place   [37]**primal eldest
curse** (curse of Cain, who killed Abel)   [47]**confront** oppose   [54]**effects**   things gained

Offense's gilded hand may shove by justice,
And oft 'tis seen the wicked prize itself
Buys out the law. But 'tis not so above.   *60*
There is no shuffling;° there the action lies
In his true nature, and we ourselves compelled,
Even to the teeth and forehead of our faults,
To give in evidence. What then? What rests?°
Try what repentance can. What can it not?   *65*
Yet what can it when one cannot repent?
O wretched state! O bosom black as death!
O limèd° soul, that struggling to be free
Art more engaged!° Help, angels! Make assay.°
Bow, stubborn knees, and, heart with strings of steel,   *70*
Be soft as sinews of the newborn babe.
All may be well. [*He kneels.*]

> *Enter Hamlet.*

Hamlet. Now might I do it pat, now 'a is a-praying,
And now I'll do't. And so 'a goes to heaven,
And so am I revenged. That would be scanned.°   *75*
A villain kills my father, and for that
I, his sole son, do this same villain send
To heaven.
Why, this is hire and salary, not revenge.
'A took my father grossly, full of bread,°   *80*
With all his crimes broad blown,° as flush° as May;
And how his audit° stands, who knows save heaven?
But in our circumstance and course of thought,
'Tis heavy with him; and am I then revenged,
To take him in the purging of his soul,   *85*
When he is fit and seasoned for his passage?
No.
Up, sword, and know thou a more horrid hent.°
When he is drunk asleep, or in his rage,
Or in th' incestuous pleasure of his bed,   *90*
At game a-swearing, or about some act
That has no relish° of salvation in't —
Then trip him, that his heels may kick at heaven,
And that his soul may be as damned and black

---

⁶¹*shuffling* trickery ⁶⁴*rests* remains ⁶⁸*limèd* caught (as with birdlime, a sticky substance spread on boughs to snare birds) ⁶⁹*engaged* ensnared ⁶⁹*assay* an attempt ⁷⁵*would be scanned* ought to be looked into ⁸⁰*bread* i.e., worldly gratification ⁸¹*crimes broad blown* sins in full bloom ⁸¹*flush* vigorous ⁸²*audit* account ⁸⁸*hent* grasp (here, occasion for seizing) ⁹²*relish* flavor

As hell, whereto it goes. My mother stays. 95
This physic° but prolongs thy sickly days.

Exit.

King [*rises*]. My words fly up, my thoughts remain below.
Words without thoughts never to heaven go.

Exit.

[**Scene IV.** *The Queen's closet.*]

Enter [*Queen*] *Gertrude and Polonius.*

Polonius. 'A will come straight. Look you lay home° to him.
Tell him his pranks have been too broad° to bear with,
And that your Grace hath screened and stood between
Much heat and him. I'll silence me even here.
Pray you be round with him. 5
Hamlet (within). Mother, Mother, Mother!
Queen. I'll warrant you; fear me not. Withdraw; I hear him
coming.

[*Polonius hides behind the arras.*]

Enter Hamlet.

Hamlet. Now, Mother, what's the matter?
Queen. Hamlet, thou hast thy father much offended. 10
Hamlet. Mother, you have my father much offended.
Queen. Come, come, you answer with an idle° tongue.
Hamlet. Go, go, you question with a wicked tongue.
Queen. Why, how now, Hamlet?
Hamlet.　　　　　　　　　What's the matter now?
Queen. Have you forgot me?
Hamlet.　　　　　　　　No, by the rood,° not so! 15
You are the Queen, your husband's brother's wife,
And, would it were not so, you are my mother.
Queen. Nay, then I'll set those to you that can speak.
Hamlet. Come, come, and sit you down. You shall not budge.
You go not till I set you up a glass° 20
Where you may see the inmost part of you!
Queen. What wilt thou do? Thou wilt not murder me?
Help, ho!
Polonius [*behind*]. What, ho! Help!
Hamlet [*draws*]. How now? A rat? Dead for a ducat, dead! 25

---

⁹⁶physic (Claudius' purgation by prayer, as Hamlet thinks in line 85)　III.iv. **¹lay home** thrust (rebuke) him sharply　**²broad** unrestrained　**¹²idle** foolish　**¹⁵rood** cross　**²⁰glass** mirror

[*Makes a pass through the arras and*] *kills Polonius.*

Polonius [*behind*]. O, I am slain!
Queen.   O me, what hast thou done?
Hamlet. Nay, I know not. Is it the King?
Queen. O, what a rash and bloody deed is this!
Hamlet. A bloody deed — almost as bad, good Mother,
    As kill a king, and marry with his brother.   30
Queen. As kill a king?
Hamlet.   Ay, lady, it was my word.

    [*Lifts up the arras and sees Polonius.*]

    Thou wretched, rash, intruding fool, farewell!
    I took thee for thy better. Take thy fortune.
    Thou find'st to be too busy is some danger. —
    Leave wringing of your hands. Peace, sit you down   35
    And let me wring your heart, for so I shall
    If it be made of penetrable stuff,
    If damnèd custom have not brazed° it so
    That it be proof° and bulwark against sense.°
Queen. What have I done that thou dar'st wag thy tongue   40
    In noise so rude against me?
Hamlet.   Such an act
    That blurs the grace and blush of modesty,
    Calls virtue hypocrite, takes off the rose
    From the fair forehead of an innocent love,
    And sets a blister° there, makes marriage vows   45
    As false as dicers' oaths. O, such a deed
    As from the body of contraction° plucks
    The very soul, and sweet religion makes
    A rhapsody° of words! Heaven's face does glow
    O'er this solidity and compound mass   50
    With heated visage, as against the doom
    Is thoughtsick at the act.°
Queen.   Ay me, what act,
    That roars so loud and thunders in the index?°
Hamlet. Look here upon this picture, and on this,
    The counterfeit presentment° of two brothers.   55

---

[38]**brazed** hardened like brass [39]**proof** armor [39]**sense** feeling [45]**sets a blister**
brands (as a harlot) [47]**contraction** marriage contract [49]**rhapsody** senseless string
[49-52]**Heaven's face . . . the act** i.e., the face of heaven blushes over this earth
(compounded of four elements), the face hot, as if Judgment Day were near, and
it is thoughtsick at the act [53]**index** prologue [55]**counterfeit presentment** represented
image

See what a grace was seated on this brow:
Hyperion's curls, the front° of Jove himself,
An eye like Mars, to threaten and command,
A station° like the herald Mercury
New lighted on a heaven-kissing hill —   *60*
A combination and a form indeed
Where every god did seem to set his seal
To give the world assurance of a man.
This was your husband. Look you now what follows.
Here is your husband, like a mildewed ear   *65*
Blasting his wholesome brother. Have you eyes?
Could you on this fair mountain leave to feed,
And batten° on this moor? Ha! Have you eyes?
You cannot call it love, for at your age
The heyday° in the blood is tame, it's humble,   *70*
And waits upon the judgment, and what judgment
Would step from this to this? Sense° sure you have,
Else could you not have motion, but sure that sense
Is apoplexed,° for madness would not err,
Nor sense to ecstasy° was ne'er so thralled   *75*
But it reserved some quantity of choice
To serve in such a difference. What devil wast
That thus hath cozened you at hoodman-blind?°
Eyes without feeling, feeling without sight,
Ears without hands or eyes, smelling sans° all,   *80*
Or but a sickly part of one true sense
Could not so mope.°
O shame, where is thy blush? Rebellious hell,
If thou canst mutine in a matron's bones,
To flaming youth let virtue be as wax   *85*
And melt in her own fire. Proclaim no shame
When the compulsive ardor° gives the charge,
Since frost itself as actively doth burn,
And reason panders will.°

Queen.   O Hamlet, speak no more.
Thou turn'st mine eyes into my very soul,   *90*
And there I see such black and grainèd° spots
As will not leave their tinct.°

---

⁵⁷*front* forehead ⁵⁹*station* bearing ⁶⁸*batten* feed gluttonously ⁷⁰*heyday* excitement ⁷²*Sense* feeling ⁷⁴*apoplexed* paralyzed ⁷⁵*ecstasy* madness ⁷⁸*cozened you at hoodman-blind* cheated you at blindman's buff ⁸⁰*sans* without ⁸²*mope* be stupid ⁸⁷*compulsive ardor* compelling passion ⁸⁹*reason panders will* reason acts as a procurer for desire ⁹¹*grainèd* dyed in grain (fast dyed) ⁹²*tinct* color

Hamlet.   Nay, but to live
In the rank sweat of an enseamèd° bed,
Stewed in corruption, honeying and making love
Over the nasty sty —
Queen.   O, speak to me no more.   95
These words like daggers enter in my ears.
No more, sweet Hamlet.
Hamlet.   A murderer and a villain,
A slave that is not twentieth part the tithe°
Of your precedent lord, a vice° of kings,
A cutpurse of the empire and the rule,   100
That from a shelf the precious diadem stole
And put it in his pocket —
Queen.   No more.

Enter Ghost.

Hamlet. A king of shreds and patches —
Save me and hover o'er me with your wings,
You heavenly guards! What would your gracious figure?   105
Queen. Alas, he's mad.
Hamlet. Do you not come your tardy son to chide,
That, lapsed in time and passion, lets go by
Th' important acting of your dread command?
O, say!   110
Ghost. Do not forget. This visitation
Is but to whet thy almost blunted purpose.
But look, amazement on thy mother sits.
O, step between her and her fighting soul!
Conceit° in weakest bodies strongest works.   115
Speak to her, Hamlet.
Hamlet.   How is it with you, lady?
Queen. Alas, how is't with you,
That you do bend your eye on vacancy,
And with th' incorporal° air do hold discourse?
Forth at your eyes your spirits wildly peep,   120
And as the sleeping soldiers in th' alarm
Your bedded hair° like life in excrements°
Start up and stand an end.° O gentle son,
Upon the heat and flame of thy distemper

---

⁹³*enseamèd* (perhaps "soaked in grease," i.e., sweaty; perhaps "much wrinkled") ⁹⁸*tithe* tenth part ⁹⁹*vice* (like the Vice, a fool and mischiefmaker in the old morality plays) ¹¹⁵*Conceit* imagination ¹¹⁹*incorporal* bodiless ¹²²*bedded hair* hairs laid flat ¹²²*excrements* outgrowths (here, the hair) ¹²³*an end* on end

Sprinkle cool patience. Whereon do you look?   *125*
Hamlet. On him, on him! Look you, how pale he glares!
His form and cause conjoined, preaching to stones,
Would make them capable.° — Do not look upon me,
Lest with this piteous action you convert
My stern effects.° Then what I have to do   *130*
Will want true color; tears perchance for blood.
Queen. To whom do you speak this?
Hamlet.   Do you see nothing there?
Queen. Nothing at all; yet all that is I see.
Hamlet. Nor did you nothing hear?
Queen.   No, nothing but ourselves.
Hamlet. Why, look you there! Look how it steals away!   *135*
My father, in his habit° as he lived!
Look where he goes even now at the portal!

                                               Exit Ghost.

Queen. This is the very coinage of your brain.
This bodiless creation ecstasy
Is very cunning in.
Hamlet.   Ecstasy?   *140*
My pulse as yours doth temperately keep time
And makes as healthful music. It is not madness
That I have uttered. Bring me to the test,
And I the matter will reword, which madness
Would gambol° from. Mother, for love of grace,   *145*
Lay not that flattering unction° to your soul,
That not your trespass but my madness speaks.
It will but skin and film the ulcerous place
Whiles rank corruption, mining° all within,
Infects unseen. Confess yourself to heaven,   *150*
Repent what's past, avoid what is to come,
And do not spread the compost° on the weeds
To make them ranker. Forgive me this my virtue.
For in the fatness of these pursy° times
Virtue itself of vice must pardon beg,   *155*
Yea, curb° and woo for leave to do him good.
Queen. O Hamlet, thou hast cleft my heart in twain.
Hamlet. O, throw away the worser part of it,

---

¹²⁸*capable* receptive ¹²⁹⁻¹³⁰*convert/My stern effects* divert my stern
deeds ¹³⁶*habit* garment (Q1, though a "bad" quarto, is probably correct in saying
that at line 102 the ghost enters "in his nightgown," i.e., dressing
gown) ¹⁴⁵*gambol* start away ¹⁴⁶*unction* ointment ¹⁴⁹*mining* undermining
¹⁵²*compost* fertilizing substance ¹⁵⁴*pursy* bloated ¹⁵⁶*curb* bow low

And live the purer with the other half.
Good night — but go not to my uncle's bed.   *160*
Assume a virtue, if you have it not.
That monster custom, who all sense doth eat,
Of habits devil, is angel yet in this,
That to the use° of actions fair and good
He likewise gives a frock or livery°   *165*
That aptly is put on. Refrain tonight,
And that shall lend a kind of easiness
To the next abstinence; the next more easy;
For use almost can change the stamp of nature,
And either° the devil, or throw him out   *170*
With wondrous potency. Once more, good night,
And when you are desirous to be blest,
I'll blessing beg of you. — For this same lord,
I do repent; but heaven hath pleased it so,
To punish me with this, and this with me,   *175*
That I must be their° scourge and minister.
I will bestow° him and will answer well
The death I gave him. So again, good night.
I must be cruel only to be kind.
Thus bad begins, and worse remains behind.   *180*
One word more, good lady.
Queen.   What shall I do?
Hamlet. Not this, by no means, that I bid you do:
Let the bloat King tempt you again to bed,
Pinch wanton on your cheek, call you his mouse,
And let him, for a pair of reechy° kisses,   *185*
Or paddling in your neck with his damned fingers,
Make you to ravel° all this matter out,
That I essentially am not in madness,
But mad in craft. 'Twere good you let him know,
For who that's but a queen, fair, sober, wise,   *190*
Would from a paddock,° from a bat, a gib,°
Such dear concernings hide? Who would do so?
No, in despite of sense and secrecy,
Unpeg the basket on the house's top,
Let the birds fly, and like the famous ape,   *195*

---

¹⁶⁴*use* practice   ¹⁶⁵*livery* characteristic garment (punning on "habits" in line
163)   ¹⁷⁰*either* (probably a word is missing after "either"; among suggestions are
"master," "curb," and "house"; but possibly "either" is a verb meaning "make
easier")   ¹⁷⁶*their* i.e., the heavens'   ¹⁷⁷*bestow* stow, lodge   ¹⁸⁵*reechy* foul (literally "smoky")   ¹⁸⁷*ravel* unravel, reveal   ¹⁹¹*paddock* toad   ¹⁹¹*gib* tomcat

To try conclusions,° in the basket creep
And break your own neck down.

Queen. Be thou assured, if words be made of breath,
And breath of life, I have no life to breathe
What thou hast said to me.   *200*

Hamlet. I must to England; you know that?

Queen.   Alack,
I had forgot. 'Tis so concluded on.

Hamlet. There's letters sealed, and my two school-fellows,
Whom I will trust as I will adders fanged,
They bear the mandate;° they must sweep my way   *205*
And marshal me to knavery. Let it work;
For 'tis the sport to have the enginer
Hoist with his own petar,° and 't shall go hard
But I will delve one yard below their mines
And blow them at the moon. O,'tis most sweet   *210*
When in one line two crafts° directly meet.
This man shall set me packing:
I'll lug the guts into the neighbor room.
Mother, good night. Indeed, this counselor
Is now most still, most secret, and most grave,   *215*
Who was in life a foolish prating knave.
Come, sir, to draw toward an end with you.
Good night, Mother.
                      [*Exit the Queen. Then*] *exit Hamlet,*
                               tugging in Polonius.

[**ACT IV**

Scene I. *The castle.*]

Enter King and Queen, with Rosencrantz and Guildenstern.

King. There's matter in these sighs. These profound heaves
You must translate; 'tis fit we understand them.
Where is your son?

Queen. Bestow this place on us a little while.
                [*Exeunt Rosencrantz and Guildenstern.*]
Ah, mine own lord, what have I seen tonight!   *5*

King. What, Gertrude? How does Hamlet?

---

[196]*To try conclusions* to make experiments   [205]*mandate* command   [208]*petar* bomb
[211]*crafts* (1) boats, (2) acts of guile, crafty schemes

Queen. Mad as the sea and wind when both contend
    Which is the mightier. In his lawless fit,
    Behind the arras hearing something stir,
    Whips out his rapier, cries, "A rat, a rat!"   *10*
    And in this brainish apprehension° kills
    The unseen good old man.
King.   O heavy deed!
    It had been so with us, had we been there.
    His liberty is full of threats to all,
    To you yourself, to us, to every one.   *15*
    Alas, how shall this bloody deed be answered?
    It will be laid to us, whose providence°
    Should have kept short, restrained, and out of haunt°
    This mad young man. But so much was our love
    We would not understand what was most fit,   *20*
    But, like the owner of a foul disease,
    To keep it from divulging, let it feed
    Even on the pith of life. Where is he gone?
Queen. To draw apart the body he hath killed;
    O'er whom his very madness, like some ore   *25*
    Among a mineral° of metals base,
    Shows itself pure. 'A weeps for what is done.
King. O Gertrude, come away!
    The sun no sooner shall the mountains touch
    But we will ship him hence, and this vile deed   *30*
    We must with all our majesty and skill
    Both countenance and excuse. Ho, Guildenstern!

Enter Rosencrantz and Guildenstern.

    Friends both, go join you with some further aid:
    Hamlet in madness hath Polonius slain,
    And from his mother's closet hath he dragged him.   *35*
    Go seek him out; speak fair, and bring the body
    Into the chapel. I pray you haste in this.
                [*Exit Rosencrantz and Guildenstern.*]
    Come, Gertrude, we'll call up our wisest friends
    And let them know both what we mean to do
    And what's untimely done . . .°   *40*
    Whose whisper o'er the world's diameter,

IV.i. [11]*brainish apprehension* mad imagination [17]*providence* foresight [18]*out of haunt* away from association with others [25-26]*ore/Among a mineral* vein of gold in a mine [40]*done . . .* (evidently something has dropped out of the text. Cappell's conjecture, "So, haply slander," is usually printed)

As level as the cannon to his blank°
Transports his poisoned shot, may miss our name
And hit the woundless° air. O, come away!
My soul is full of discord and dismay.   *45*

                          Exeunt.

[Scene II. *The castle.*]

Enter Hamlet.

Hamlet. Safely stowed.
Gentlemen (within). Hamlet! Lord Hamlet!
Hamlet. But soft, what noise? Who calls on Hamlet?
     O, here they come.

Enter Rosencrantz and Guildenstern.

Rosencrantz. What have you done, my lord, with the dead
            body?   *5*
Hamlet. Compounded it with dust, whereto 'tis kin.
Rosencrantz. Tell us where 'tis, that we may take it thence
     And bear it to the chapel.
Hamlet. Do not believe it.
Rosencrantz. Believe what?   *10*
Hamlet. That I can keep your counsel and not mine own.
     Besides, to be demanded of° a sponge, what replication°
     should be made by the son of a king?
Rosencrantz. Take you me for a sponge, my lord?
Hamlet. Ay, sir, that soaks up the King's countenance,° his   *15*
     rewards, his authorities. But such officers do the King
     best service in the end. He keeps them, like an ape, in
     the corner of his jaw, first mouthed, to be last swallowed.
     When he needs what you have gleaned, it is but squeezing
     you and, sponge, you shall be dry again.   *20*
Rosencrantz. I understand you not, my lord.
Hamlet. I am glad of it: a knavish speech sleeps in a foolish ear.
Rosencrantz. My lord, you must tell us where the body is
     and go with us to the King.
Hamlet. The body is with the King, but the King is not with   *25*
     the body.° The King is a thing —

---

⁴²*blank*   white center of a target   ⁴⁴*woundless*   invulnerable   IV.ii.   ¹²*demanded
of*   questioned by   ¹²*replication*   reply   ¹⁵*countenance*   favor   ²⁵⁻²⁶*The body . . .
body*   i.e., the body of authority is with Claudius, but spiritually he is not the
true king

Guildenstern. A thing, my lord?
Hamlet. Of nothing. Bring me to him. Hide fox, and all after.°

                                                               Exeunt.

      [Scene III. *The castle.*]

      Enter King, and two or three.

King. I have sent to seek him and to find the body:
    How dangerous is it that this man goes loose!
    Yet must not we put the strong law on him:
    He's loved of the distracted° multitude,
    Who like not in their judgment, but their eyes,   5
    And where 'tis so, th' offender's scourge is weighed,
    But never the offense. To bear° all smooth and even,
    This sudden sending him away must seem
    Deliberate pause.° Diseases desperate grown
    By desperate appliance are relieved,   10
    Or not at all.

      Enter Rosencrantz, [*Guildenstern,*] *and all the rest.*

                    How now? What hath befall'n?
Rosencrantz. Where the dead body is bestowed, my lord,
    We cannot get from him.
King.   But where is he?
Rosencrantz. Without, my lord; guarded, to know your pleasure.
King. Bring him before us.
Rosencrantz.   Ho! Bring in the lord.   15

      They enter.

King. Now, Hamlet, where's Polonius?
Hamlet. At supper.
King. At supper? Where?
Hamlet. Not where he eats, but where 'a is eaten. A certain
    convocation of politic° worms are e'en at him. Your   20
    worm is your only emperor for diet. We fat all creatures
    else to fat us, and we fat ourselves for maggots. Your
    fat king and your lean beggar is but variable service°
    — two dishes, but to one table. That's the end.

---

[28]***Hide fox, and all after*** (a cry in a game such as hide-and-seek; Hamlet runs
from the stage) IV.iii. [4]***distracted*** bewildered, senseless [7]***bear*** carry
out [9]***pause*** planning [20]***politic*** statesmanlike, shrewd [23]***variable service*** different courses

King. Alas, alas!   *25*

Hamlet. A man may fish with the worm that hath eat of a
    king, and eat of the fish that hath fed of that worm.

King. What dost thou mean by this?

Hamlet. Nothing but to show you how a king may go a
    progress° through the guts of a beggar.   *30*

King. Where is Polonius?

Hamlet. In heaven. Send thither to see. If your messenger
    find him not there, seek him i' th' other place yourself.
    But if indeed you find him not within this month, you
    shall nose him as you go up the stairs into the lobby.   *35*

King [*to Attendants*]. Go seek him there.

Hamlet. 'A will stay till you come.

                                [*Exit Attendants.*]

King. Hamlet, this deed, for thine especial safety,
    Which we do tender° as we dearly grieve
    For that which thou hast done, must send thee hence   *40*
    With fiery quickness. Therefore prepare thyself.
    The bark is ready and the wind at help,
    Th' associates tend,° and everything is bent
    For England.

Hamlet.   For England?

King.   Ay, Hamlet.

Hamlet.   Good.

King. So is it, if thou knew'st our purposes.   *45*

Hamlet. I see a cherub° that sees them. But come, for England!
    Farewell, dear Mother.

King. Thy loving father, Hamlet.

Hamlet. My mother — father and mother is man and wife,
    man and wife is one flesh, and so, my mother. Come,   *50*
    for England!

                                          Exit.

King. Follow him at foot;° tempt him with speed abroad.
    Delay it not; I'll have him hence tonight.
    Away! For everything is sealed and done
    That else leans° on th' affair. Pray you make haste.   *55*

                             [*Exit all but the King.*]

    And, England, if my love thou hold'st at aught —
    As my great power thereof may give thee sense,
    Since yet thy cicatrice° looks raw and red
    After the Danish sword, and thy free awe°

---

[30]*progress* royal journey   [39]*tender* hold dear   [43]*tend* wait   [46]*cherub* angel of
knowledge   [52]*at foot* closely   [55]*leans* depends   [58]*cicatrice* scar   [59]*free awe*
uncompelled submission

Pays homage to us — thou mayst not coldly set 60
Our sovereign process,° which imports at full
By letters congruing to that effect
The present° death of Hamlet. Do it, England,
For like the hectic° in my blood he rages,
And thou must cure me. Till I know 'tis done, 65
How'er my haps,° my joys were ne'er begun.

Exit.

[**Scene IV.** *A plain in Denmark.*]

Enter Fortinbras with his Army over the stage.

Fortinbras. Go, Captain, from me greet the Danish king.
Tell him that by his license Fortinbras
Craves the conveyance of° a promised march
Over his kingdom. You know the rendezvous.
If that his Majesty would aught with us, 5
We shall express our duty in his eye;°
And let him know so.
Captain.   I will do't, my lord.
Fortinbras. Go softly° on.

[*Exit all but the Captain.*]

Enter Hamlet, Rosencrantz, &c.

Hamlet. Good sir, whose powers° are these?
Captain. They are of Norway, sir. 10
Hamlet. How purposed, sir, I pray you?
Captain. Against some part of Poland.
Hamlet. Who commands them, sir?
Captain. The nephew to old Norway, Fortinbras.
Hamlet. Goes it against the main° of Poland, sir, 15
Or for some frontier?
Captain. Truly to speak, and with no addition,°
We go to gain a little patch of ground
That hath in it no profit but the name.
To pay five ducats, five, I would not farm it, 20
Nor will it yield to Norway or the Pole
A ranker° rate, should it be sold in fee.°
Hamlet. Why, then the Polack never will defend it.

---

⁶⁰⁻⁶¹*coldly   set/Our   sovereign   process* regard   slightly   our   royal
command ⁶³*present* instant ⁶⁴*hectic* fever ⁶⁶*haps* chances, fortunes IV.iv.
³*conveyance of* escort for ⁶*in his eye* before his eyes (i.e., in his presence) ⁸*softly* slowly ⁹*powers* forces ¹⁵*main* main   part ¹⁷*with   no
addition* plainly ²²*ranker* higher ²²*in fee* outright

Captain. Yes, it is already garrisoned.
Hamlet. Two thousand souls and twenty thousand ducats   25
    Will not debate° the question of this straw.
    This is th' imposthume° of much wealth and peace,
    That inward breaks, and shows no cause without
    Why the man dies. I humbly thank you, sir.
Captain. God bye you, sir.
                                              [*Exit.*]
Rosencrantz.   Will't please you go, my lord?   30
Hamlet. I'll be with you straight. Go a little before.
                           [*Exit all but Hamlet.*]
    How all occasions do inform against me
    And spur my dull revenge! What is a man,
    If his chief good and market° of his time
    Be but to sleep and feed? A beast, no more.   35
    Sure he that made us with such large discourse,°
    Looking before and after, gave us not
    That capability and godlike reason
    To fust° in us unused. Now, whether it be
    Bestial oblivion,° or some craven scruple   40
    Of thinking too precisely on th' event° —
    A thought which, quartered, hath but one part wisdom
    And ever three parts coward — I do not know
    Why yet I live to say, "This thing's to do,"
    Sith I have cause, and will, and strength, and means   45
    To do't. Examples gross° as earth exhort me.
    Witness this army of such mass and charge,°
    Led by a delicate and tender prince,
    Whose spirit, with divine ambition puffed,
    Makes mouths at the invisible event,°   50
    Exposing what is mortal and unsure
    To all that fortune, death, and danger dare,
    Even for an eggshell. Rightly to be great
    Is not° to stir without great argument,°
    But greatly° to find quarrel in a straw   55
    When honor's at the stake. How stand I then,
    That have a father killed, a mother stained,
    Excitements° of my reason and my blood,

---

[26]*debate* settle [27]*imposthume* abscess, ulcer [34]*market* profit [36]*discourse* understanding [39]*fust* grow moldy [40]*oblivion* forgetfulness [41]*event* outcome [46]*gross* large, obvious [47]*charge* expense [50]*Makes mouths at the invisible event* makes scornful faces (is contemptuous of) the unseen outcome [54]*not* (the sense seems to require "not not") [54]*argument* reason [55]*greatly* i.e., nobly [58]*Excitements* incentives

And let all sleep, while to my shame I see
The imminent death of twenty thousand men   60
That for a fantasy and trick of fame°
Go to their graves like beds, fight for a plot
Whereon the numbers cannot try the cause,
Which is not tomb enough and continent°
To hide the slain? O, from this time forth,   65
My thoughts be bloody, or be nothing worth!

                                                    Exit.

[**Scene V.** *The castle.*]

    Enter Horatio, [Queen] Gertrude, and a Gentleman.

Queen. I will not speak with her.
Gentleman. She is importunate, indeed distract.
    Her mood will needs be pitied.
Queen.   What would she have?
Gentleman. She speaks much of her father, says she hears
    There's tricks i' th' world, and hems, and beats her heart,   5
    Spurns enviously at straws,° speaks things in doubt°
    That carry but half sense. Her speech is nothing,
    Yet the unshapèd use of it doth move
    The hearers to collection;° they yawn° at it,
    And botch the words up fit to their own thoughts,   10
    Which, as her winks and nods and gestures yield them,
    Indeed would make one think there might be thought,
    Though nothing sure, yet much unhappily.
Horatio. 'Twere good she were spoken with, for she may strew
    Dangerous conjectures in ill-breeding minds.   15
Queen. Let her come in.

                                           [*Exit Gentleman.*]

    [*Aside.*] To my sick soul (as sin's true nature is)
    Each toy seems prologue to some great amiss;°
    So full of artless jealousy° is guilt
    It spills° itself in fearing to be spilt.   20

    Enter Ophelia [distracted].

---

[61]*fantasy and trick of fame* illusion and trifle of reputation   [64]*continent* receptacle, container IV.v. [6]*Spurns enviously at straws* objects spitefully to insignificant matters [6]*in doubt* uncertainly [8–9]*Yet the . . . to collection* i.e., yet the formless manner of it moves her listeners to gather up some sort of meaning [9]*yawn* gape (?) [18]*amiss* misfortune [19]*artless jealousy* crude suspicion [20]*spills* destroys

Ophelia. Where is the beauteous majesty of Denmark?
Queen. How now, Ophelia?
Ophelia. (*She sings.*)

> How should I your truelove know
> From another one?
> By his cockle hat° and staff   *25*
> And his sandal shoon.°

Queen. Alas, sweet lady, what imports this song?
Ophelia. Say you? Nay, pray you mark.

> He is dead and gone, lady,   (*Song.*)
> He is dead and gone;   *30*
> At his head a grass-green turf,
> At his heels a stone.

> O, ho!

Queen. Nay, but Ophelia —
Ophelia. Pray you mark. [*Sings.*]   *35*

> White his shroud as the mountain snow —

Enter King.

Queen. Alas, look here, my lord.
Ophelia.

> Larded° all with sweet flowers   (*Song.*)
> Which bewept to the grave did not go
> With truelove showers.   *40*

King. How do you, pretty lady?
Ophelia. Well, God dild° you! They say the owl was a baker's
    daughter.° Lord, we know what we are, but know not
    what we may be. God be at your table!
King. Conceit° upon her father.   *45*
Ophelia. Pray let's have no words of this, but when they ask
    you what it means, say you this:

> Tomorrow is Saint Valentine's day.°   (*Song.*)
> All in the morning betime,

---

²⁵*cockle hat* (a cockleshell on the hat was the sign of a pilgrim who had journeyed
to shrines overseas. The association of lovers and pilgrims was a common
one.) ²⁶*shoon* shoes ³⁸*Larded* decorated ⁴²*dild* yield, i.e., reward ^{42–43}*baker's
daughter* (an allusion to a tale of a baker's daughter who begrudged bread to
Christ and was turned into an owl) ⁴⁵*Conceit* brooding ⁴⁸*Saint Valentine's
day* Feb. 14 (the notion was that a bachelor would become the truelove of the
first girl he saw on this day)

And I a maid at your window,   *50*
  To be your Valentine.

Then up he rose and donned his clothes
  And dupped° the chamber door,
Let in the maid, that out a maid
  Never departed more.   *55*

King. Pretty Ophelia.
Ophelia. Indeed, la, without an oath, I'll make an end on't:

[*Sings.*]

By Gis° and by Saint Charity,
  Alack, and fie for shame!
Young men will do't if they come to't,   *60*
  By Cock,° they are to blame.
Quoth she, "Before you tumbled me,
  You promised me to wed."

He answers:

"So would I 'a' done, by yonder sun,   *65*
  An thou hadst not come to my bed."

King. How long hath she been thus?
Ophelia. I hope all will be well. We must be patient, but I
  cannot choose but weep to think they would lay him
  i' th' cold ground. My brother shall know of it; and   *70*
  so I thank you for your good counsel. Come, my coach!
  Good night, ladies, good night. Sweet ladies, good
  night, good night.
                                                        Exit.

King. Follow her close; give her good watch, I pray you.
                                          [*Exit Horatio.*]
O, this is the poison of deep grief; it springs   *75*
All from her father's death — and now behold!
O Gertrude, Gertrude,
When sorrows come, they come not single spies,
But in battalions; first, her father slain;
Next, your son gone, and he most violent author   *80*
Of his own just remove; the people muddied,°
Thick and unwholesome in their thoughts and whispers
For good Polonius' death, and we have done but greenly°
In huggermugger° to inter him; poor Ophelia

---

⁵³*dupped* opened (did up)   ⁵⁸*Gis* (contraction of "Jesus")   ⁶¹*Cock* (1) God, (2)
phallus   ⁸¹*muddied* muddled   ⁸³*greenly* foolishly   ⁸⁴*huggermugger* secret haste

Divided from herself and her fair judgment,   *85*
Without the which we are pictures or mere beasts;
Last, and as much containing as all these,
Her brother is in secret come from France,
Feeds on his wonder,° keeps himself in clouds,
And wants not buzzers° to infect his ear   *90*
With pestilent speeches of his father's death,
Wherein necessity, of matter beggared,°
Will nothing stick° our person to arraign
In ear and ear. O my dear Gertrude, this,
Like to a murd'ring piece,° in many places   *95*
Gives me superfluous death.   *A noise within.*

Enter a Messenger.

Queen.   Alack, what noise is this?
King. Attend, where are my Switzers?° Let them guard the door.
  What is the matter?
Messenger.   Save yourself, my lord.
  The ocean, overpeering of his list,°
  Eats not the flats with more impiteous haste   *100*
  Than young Laertes, in a riotous head,°
  O'erbears your officers. The rabble call him lord,
  And, as the world were now but to begin,
  Antiquity forgot, custom not known,
  The ratifiers and props of every word,   *105*
  They cry, "Choose we! Laertes shall be king!"
  Caps, hands, and tongues applaud it to the clouds,
  "Laertes shall be king! Laertes king!"
                                      A noise within.
Queen. How cheerfully on the false trail they cry!
  O, this is counter,° you false Danish dogs!   *110*

Enter Laertes with others.

King. The doors are broke.
Laertes. Where is this king? — Sirs, stand you all without.
All. No, let's come in.
Laertes.   I pray you give me leave.
All. We will, we will.
Laertes. I thank you. Keep the door.   *[Exit his Followers.]*

---

[89]*wonder* suspicion [90]*wants not buzzers* does not lack talebearers [92]*of matter beggared* unprovided with facts [93]*Will nothing stick* will not hesitate [95]*murd'ring piece* (a cannon that shot a kind of shrapnel) [97]*Switzers* Swiss guards [99]*list* shore [101]*in a riotous head* with a rebellious force [110]*counter* (a hound runs counter when he follows the scent backward from the prey)

                                    O thou vile King,   *115*
    Give me my father.
Queen.   Calmly, good Laertes.
Laertes. That drop of blood that's calm proclaims me bastard,
    Cries cuckold° to my father, brands the harlot
    Even here between the chaste unsmirchèd brow
    Of my true mother.
King.   What is the cause, Laertes,   *120*
    That thy rebellion looks so giantlike?
    Let him go, Gertrude. Do not fear° our person.
    There's such divinity doth hedge a king
    That treason can but peep to° what it would,
    Acts little of his will. Tell me, Laertes,   *125*
    Why thou art thus incensed. Let him go, Gertrude.
    Speak, man.
Laertes. Where is my father?
King.   Dead.
Queen.   But not by him.
King. Let him demand his fill.
Laertes. How came he dead? I'll not be juggled with.   *130*
    To hell allegiance, vows to the blackest devil,
    Conscience and grace to the profoundest pit!
    I dare damnation. To this point I stand,
    That both the worlds I give to negligence,°
    Let come what comes, only I'll be revenged   *135*
    Most throughly for my father.
King.   Who shall stay you?
Laertes. My will, not all the world's.
    And for my means, I'll husband them° so well
    They shall go far with little.
King.   Good Laertes,
    If you desire to know the certainty   *140*
    Of your dear father, is't writ in your revenge
    That swoopstake° you will draw both friend and foe,
    Winner and loser?
Laertes. None but his enemies.
King.   Will you know them then?
Laertes. To his good friends thus wide I'll ope my arms   *145*
    And like the kind life-rend'ring pelican°

---

[118]*cuckold*   man whose wife is unfaithful   [122]*fear*   fear for   [124]*peep to*   i.e., look
at from a distance   [134]*That both . . . to negligence*   i.e., I care not what may
happen (to me) in this world or the next   [138]*husband them*   use them economically
[142]*swoopstake*   in a clean sweep   [146]*pelican*   (thought to feed its young with its
own blood)

Repast° them with my blood.

King.   Why, now you speak
Like a good child and a true gentleman.
That I am guiltless of your father's death,
And am most sensibly° in grief for it,   *150*
It shall as level to your judgment 'pear
As day does to your eye.

                         A noise within: "Let her come in."

Laertes. How now? What noise is that?

   Enter Ophelia.

O heat, dry up my brains; tears seven times salt
Burn out the sense and virtue° of mine eye!   *155*
By heaven, thy madness shall be paid with weight
Till our scale turn the beam.° O rose of May,
Dear maid, kind sister, sweet Ophelia!
O heavens, is't possible a young maid's wits
Should be as mortal as an old man's life?   *160*
Nature is fine° in love, and where 'tis fine,
It sends some precious instance° of itself
After the thing it loves.

Ophelia.

      They bore him barefaced on the bier   *(Song.)*
         Hey non nony, nony, hey nony   *165*
      And in his grave rained many a tear —

Fare you well, my dove!

Laertes. Hadst thou thy wits, and didst persuade revenge,
It could not move thus.

Ophelia. You must sing "A-down a-down, and you call him   *170*
a-down-a." O, how the wheel° becomes it! It is the
false steward, that stole his master's daughter.

Laertes. This nothing's more than matter°.

Ophelia. There's rosemary, that's for remembrance. Pray
you, love, remember. And there is pansies, that's for   *175*
thoughts.

Laertes. A document° in madness, thoughts and remembrance
fitted.

---

[147]*Repast* feed   [150]*sensibly* acutely   [155]*virtue* power   [157]*turn the beam* weigh
down the bar (of the balance)   [161]*fine* refined, delicate   [162]*instance* sample   [171]*wheel*
(of uncertain meaning, but probably a turn or dance of Ophelia's, rather than
Fortune's wheel)   [173]*This nothing's more than matter* this nonsense has more
meaning than matters of consequence   [177]*document* lesson

Ophelia. There's fennel° for you, and columbines. There's
          rue for you, and here's some for me. We may call it   **180**
          herb of grace o' Sundays. O, you must wear your rue
          with a difference. There's a daisy. I would give you
          some violets, but they withered all when my father
          died. They say 'a made a good end.

                                                    [*Sings.*]

               For bonny sweet Robin is all my joy.   **185**

Laertes. Thought and affliction, passion, hell itself,
          She turns to favor° and to prettiness.
Ophelia.

               And will 'a not come again?   (*Song.*)
               And will 'a not come again?
                    No, no, he is dead,   **190**
                    Go to thy deathbed,
               He never will come again.

               His beard was as white as snow,
               All flaxen was his poll.°
                    He is gone, he is gone,   **195**
                    And we cast away moan.
               God 'a' mercy on his soul!

          And of all Christian souls, I pray God. God bye you.

                                                    [*Exit.*]

Laertes. Do you see this, O God?
King. Laertes, I must commune with your grief,   **200**
          Or you deny me right. Go but apart,
          Make choice of whom your wisest friends you will,
          And they shall hear and judge 'twixt you and me.
          If by direct or by collateral° hand
          They find us touched,° we will our kingdom give,   **205**
          Our crown, our life, and all that we call ours,
          To you in satisfaction; but if not,
          Be you content to lend your patience to us,
          And we shall jointly labor with your soul
          To give it due content.

---

[179] *fennel* (the distribution of flowers in the ensuing lines has symbolic meaning,
but the meaning is disputed. Perhaps "fennel", flattery; "columbines", cuckoldry;
"rue", sorrow for Ophelia and repentance for the Queen; "daisy", dissembling;
"violets", faithfulness. For other interpretations, see J. W. Lever in *Review of
English Studies,* New Series 3 [1952], pp. 123–129)   [187] *favor* charm, beauty   [194] *All
flaxen was his poll* white as flax was his head   [204] *collateral* indirect
[205] *touched* implicated

Laertes.   Let this be so.   210
His means of death, his obscure funeral —
No trophy, sword, nor hatchment° o'er his bones,
No noble rite nor formal ostentation° —
Cry to be heard, as 'twere from heaven to earth,
That I must call't in question.
King.   So you shall;   215
And where th' offense is, let the great ax fall.
I pray you go with me.

                                        Exeunt.

[**Scene VI.** *The castle.*]

Enter Horatio and others.

Horatio. What are they that would speak with me?
Gentleman. Seafaring men, sir. They say they have letters for
    you.
Horatio. Let them come in.

                            [*Exit Attendant.*]
I do not know from what part of the world   5
I should be greeted, if not from Lord Hamlet.

Enter Sailors.

Sailor. God bless you, sir.
Horatio. Let Him bless thee too.
Sailor. 'A shall, sir, an't please Him. There's a letter for you,
    sir — it came from th' ambassador that was bound for   10
    England — if your name be Horatio, as I am let to
    know it is.
Horatio [*reads the letter*].
    "Horatio, when thou shalt have overlooked° this, give
    these fellows some means to the King. They have letters
    for him. Ere we were two days old at sea, a pirate of   15
    very warlike appointment° gave us chase. Finding our-
    selves too slow of sail, we put on a compelled valor,
    and in the grapple I boarded them. On the instant they
    got clear of our ship; so I alone became their prisoner.
    They have dealt with me like thieves of mercy, but   20
    they knew what they did: I am to do a good turn for
    them. Let the King have the letters I have sent, and

---

²¹²***hatchment***   tablet bearing the coat of arms of the dead   ²¹³***ostentation***   ceremony
IV.vi ¹³***overlooked***   surveyed   ¹⁶***appointment***   equipment

repair thou to me with as much speed as thou wouldest
fly death. I have words to speak in thine ear will make
thee dumb; yet are they much too light for the bore°   *25*
of the matter. These good fellows will bring thee where
I am. Rosencrantz and Guildenstern hold their course
for England. Of them I have much to tell thee. Farewell.
He that thou knowest thine, HAMLET.''

Come, I will give you way for these your letters,   *30*
And do 't the speedier that you may direct me
To him from whom you brought them.   *Exeunt.*

[Scene VII. *The castle.*]

Enter King and Laertes.

King. Now must your conscience my acquittance seal,
    And you must put me in your heart for friend,
    Sith you have heard, and with a knowing ear,
    That he which hath your noble father slain
    Pursued my life.
Laertes.   It well appears. But tell me   *5*
    Why you proceeded not against these feats
    So criminal and so capital° in nature,
    As by your safety, greatness, wisdom, all things else,
    You mainly° were stirred up.
King.   O, for two special reasons,
    Which may to you perhaps seem much unsinewed,°   *10*
    But yet to me they're strong. The Queen his mother
    Lives almost by his looks, and for myself —
    My virtue or my plague, be it either which —
    She is so conjunctive° to my life and soul,
    That, as the star moves not but in his sphere,   *15*
    I could not but by her. The other motive
    Why to a public count° I might not go
    Is the great love the general gender° bear him,
    Who, dipping all his faults in their affection,
    Would, like the spring that turneth wood to stone,°   *20*
    Convert his gyves° to graces; so that my arrows,
    Too slightly timbered° for so loud a wind,

---

[25]**bore** caliber (here, "importance") IV.vii.   [7]**capital** deserving death
[9]**mainly** powerfully   [10]**unsinewed** weak   [14]**conjunctive** closely united   [17]**count**
reckoning   [18]**general gender** common people   [20]**spring that turneth wood to stone**
(a spring in Shakespeare's county was so charged with lime that it would petrify
wood placed in it)   [21]**gyves** fetters   [22]**timbered** shafted

Would have reverted to my bow again,
And not where I had aimed them.

Laertes. And so have I a noble father lost,   *25*
A sister driven into desp'rate terms,°
Whose worth, if praises may go back again,°
Stood challenger on mount of all the age
For her perfections. But my revenge will come.

King. Break not your sleeps for that. You must not think   *30*
That we are made of stuff so flat and dull
That we can let our beard be shook with danger,
And think it pastime. You shortly shall hear more.
I loved your father, and we love ourself,
And that, I hope, will teach you to imagine —   *35*

Enter a Messenger with letters.

How now? What news?

Messenger.   Letters, my lord, from Hamlet:
These to your Majesty; this to the Queen.

King. From Hamlet? Who brought them?

Messenger. Sailors, my lord, they say; I saw them not.
They were given me by Claudio; he received them   *40*
Of him that brought them.

King.   Laertes, you shall hear them. —
Leave us. [*Reads.*]

                                        Exit Messenger.

"High and mighty, you shall know I am set naked° on
your kingdom. Tomorrow shall I beg leave to see your
kingly eyes; when I shall (first asking your pardon   *45*
thereunto) recount the occasion of my sudden and more
strange return.

                                        HAMLET."

What should this mean? Are all the rest come back?
Or is it some abuse,° and no such thing?   *50*

Laertes. Know you the hand?

King.   'Tis Hamlet's character.° "Naked"!
.   And in a postscript here, he says "alone."
Can you devise° me?

Laertes. I am lost in it, my lord. But let him come.
It warms the very sickness in my heart   *55*
That I shall live and tell him to his teeth,
"Thus did'st thou."

---

[26]*terms* conditions [27]*go back again* revert to what is past [43]*naked*
destitute [50]*abuse* deception [51]*character* handwriting [53]*devise* advise

King.   If it be so, Laertes
    (As how should it be so? How otherwise?),
    Will you be ruled by me?
Laertes.   Ay, my lord,
    So you will not o'errule me to a peace.   *60*
King. To thine own peace. If he be now returned,
    As checking at° his voyage, and that he means
    No more to undertake it, I will work him
    To an exploit now ripe in my device,
    Under the which he shall not choose but fall;   *65*
    And for his death no wind of blame shall breathe,
    But even his mother shall uncharge the practice°
    And call it accident.
Laertes.   My lord, I will be ruled;
    The rather if you could devise it so
    That I might be the organ.
King.   It falls right.   *70*
    You have been talked of since your travel much,
    And that in Hamlet's hearing, for a quality
    Wherein they say you shine. Your sum of parts
    Did not together pluck such envy from him
    As did that one, and that, in my regard,   *75*
    Of the unworthiest siege.°
Laertes.   What part is that, my lord?
King. A very riband in the cap of youth,
    Yet needful too, for youth no less becomes
    The light and careless livery that it wears
    Than settled age his sables and his weeds,°   *80*
    Importing health and graveness. Two months since
    Here was a gentleman of Normandy.
    I have seen myself, and served against, the French,
    And they can° well on horseback, but this gallant
    Had witchcraft in't. He grew unto his seat,   *85*
    And to such wondrous doing brought his horse
    As had he been incorpsed and deminatured
    With the brave beast. So far he topped my thought
    That I, in forgery° of shapes and tricks,
    Come short of what he did.
Laertes.   A Norman was't?   *90*
King. A Norman.

---

[62]**checking at**   turning away from (a term in falconry)   [67]**uncharge the practice**   not
charge the device with treachery   [76]**seige**   rank   [80]**sables and his weeds**   i.e., sober
attire   [84]**can**   do   [89]**forgery**   invention

Laertes. Upon my life, Lamord.

King. The very same.

Laertes. I know him well. He is the brooch° indeed
And gem of all the nation.

King. He made confession° of you,   95
And gave you such a masterly report,
For art and exercise in your defense,
And for your rapier most especial,
That he cried out 'twould be a sight indeed
If one could match you. The scrimers° of their nation   100
He swore had neither motion, guard, nor eye,
If you opposed them. Sir, this report of his
Did Hamlet so envenom with his envy
That he could nothing do but wish and beg
Your sudden coming o'er to play with you.   105
Now, out of this —

Laertes. What out of this, my lord?

King. Laertes, was your father dear to you?
Or are you like the painting of a sorrow,
A face without a heart?

Laertes. Why ask you this?

King. Not that I think you did not love your father,   110
But that I know love is begun by time,
And that I see, in passages of proof.°
Time qualifies° the spark and fire of it.
There lives within the very flame of love
A kind of wick or snuff° that will abate it,   115
And nothing is at a like goodness still,°
For goodness, growing to a plurisy,°
Dies in his own too-much. That we would do
We should do when we would, for this "would" changes,
And hath abatements and delays as many   120
As there are tongues, are hands, are accidents,
And then this "should" is like a spendthrift sigh,°
That hurts by easing. But to the quick° of th' ulcer —
Hamlet comes back; what would you undertake
To show yourself in deed your father's son   125
More than in words?

---

⁹³*brooch* ornament ⁹⁵*confession* report ¹⁰⁰*scrimers* fencers ¹¹²*passages of proof* proved cases ¹¹³*qualifies* diminishes ¹¹⁵*snuff* residue of burnt wick (which dims the light) ¹¹⁶*still* always ¹¹⁷*plurisy* fullness, excess ¹²²*spendthrift sigh* (sighing provides ease, but because it was thought to thin the blood and so shorten life it was spendthrift) ¹²³*quick* sensitive flesh

Laertes.   To cut his throat i' th' church!

King. No place indeed should murder sanctuarize;°
Revenge should have no bounds. But, good Laertes,
Will you do this? Keep close within your chamber.
Hamlet returned shall know you are come home.   130
We'll put on those° shall praise your excellence
And set a double varnish on the fame
The Frenchman gave you, bring you in fine° together
And wager on your heads. He, being remiss,
Most generous, and free from all contriving,   135
Will not peruse the foils, so that with ease,
Or with a little shuffling, you may choose
A sword unbated,° and, in a pass of practice,°
Requite him for your father.

Laertes.   I will do't,
And for that purpose I'll anoint my sword.   140
I bought an unction of a mountebank,°
So mortal that, but dip a knife in it,
Where it draws blood, no cataplasm° so rare,
Collected from all simples° that have virtue°
Under the moon, can save the thing from death   145
That is but scratched withal. I'll touch my point
With this contagion, that, if I gall him slightly,
It may be death.

King.   Let's further think of this,
Weigh what convenience both of time and means
May fit us to our shape.° If this should fail,   150
And that our drift look through° our bad performance,
'Twere better not assayed. Therefore this project
Should have a back or second, that might hold
If this did blast in proof.° Soft, let me see.
We'll make a solemn wager on your cunnings —   155
I ha't!
When in your motion you are hot and dry —
As make your bouts more violent to that end —
And that he calls for drink, I'll have prepared him
A chalice for the nonce,° whereon but sipping,   160

---

¹²⁷*sanctuarize* protect ¹³¹*We'll put on those* we'll incite persons who ¹³³*in fine* finally ¹³⁸*unbated* not blunted ¹³⁸*pass of practice* treacherous thrust ¹⁴¹*mountebank* quack ¹⁴³*cataplasm* poultice ¹⁴⁴*simples* medicinal herbs ¹⁴⁴*virtue* power (to heal) ¹⁵⁰*shape* role ¹⁵¹*drift look through* purpose show through ¹⁵⁴*blast in proof* burst (fail) in performance ¹⁶⁰*nonce* occasion

If he by chance escape your venomed stuck,°
Our purpose may hold there. — But stay, what noise?

Enter Queen.

Queen. One woe doth tread upon another's heel.
    So fast they follow. Your sister's drowned, Laertes.
Laertes. Drowned! O, where?   165
Queen. There is a willow grows askant° the brook,
    That shows his hoar° leaves in the glassy stream:
    Therewith° fantastic garlands did she make
    Of crowflowers, nettles, daisies, and long purples,
    That liberal° shepherds give a grosser name,   170
    But our cold maids do dead men's fingers call them.
    There on the pendent boughs her crownet° weeds
    Clamb'ring to hang, an envious sliver° broke,
    When down her weedy trophies and herself
    Fell in the weeping brook. Her clothes spread wide,   175
    And mermaidlike awhile they bore her up,
    Which time she chanted snatches of old lauds,°
    As one incapable° of her own distress,
    Or like a creature native and indued°
    Unto that element. But long it could not be   180
    Till that her garments, heavy with their drink,
    Pulled the poor wretch from her melodious lay
    To muddy death.
Laertes.   Alas, then she is drowned?
Queen. Drowned, drowned.
Laertes. Too much of water hast thou, poor Ophelia,   185
    And therefore I forbid my tears; but yet
    It is our trick;° nature her custom holds,
    Let shame say what it will: when these are gone,
    The woman° will be out. Adieu, my lord.
    I have a speech o' fire, that fain would blaze,   190
    But that this folly drowns it.
                                    Exit.

King.   Let's follow, Gertrude.
    How much I had to do to calm his rage!
    Now fear I this will give it start again;
    Therefore let's follow.
                                  Exeunt.

---

[161]*stuck* thrust   [166]*askant* aslant   [167]*hoar* silver-gray   [168]*therewith* i.e., with willow twigs   [170]*liberal* free-spoken, coarse-mouthed   [172]*crownet* coronet   [173]*envious sliver* malicious branch   [177]*lauds* hymns   [178]*incapable* unaware   [179]*indued* in harmony with   [187]*trick* trait, way   [189]*woman* i.e., womanly part of me

[ACT V.

Scene I. *A churchyard.*]

Enter two Clowns.°

Clown. Is she to be buried in Christian burial when she willfully
  seeks her own salvation?

Other. I tell thee she is. Therefore make her grave straight.°
  The crowner° hath sate on her, and finds it Christian
  burial.   5

Clown. How can that be, unless she drowned herself in her
  own defense?

Other. Why, 'tis found so.

Clown. It must be *se offendendo;*° it cannot be else. For here
  lies the point: if I drown myself wittingly, it argues an   10
  act, and an act hath three branches — it is to act, to
  do, to perform. Argal,° she drowned herself wittingly.

Other. Nay, but hear you, Goodman Delver.

Clown. Give me leave. Here lies the water — good. Here
  stands the man — good. If the man go to this water   15
  and drown himself, it is, will he nill he,° he goes; mark
  you that. But if the water come to him and drown
  him, he drowns not himself. Argal, he that is not guilty
  of his own death, shortens not his own life.

Other. But is this law?   20

Clown. Ay marry, is't — crowner's quest° law.

Other. Will you ha' the truth on't? If this had not been a
  gentlewoman, she should have been buried out o'
  Christian burial.

Clown. Why, there thou say'st. And the more pity that great   25
  folk should have count'nance° in this world to drown
  or hang themselves more than their even-Christen.°
  Come, my spade. There is no ancient gentlemen but
  gard'ners, ditchers, and gravemakers. They hold up°
  Adam's profession.   30

Other. Was he a gentleman?

Clown. 'A was the first that ever bore arms.°

Other. Why, he had none.

V.i. **s.d.** *Clowns* rustics ³*straight* straightway ⁴*crowner* coroner ⁹*se offendendo* (blunder for *se defendendo,* a legal term meaning "in self-de-
fense") ¹²*Argal* (blunder for Latin *ergo,* "therefore") ¹⁶*will he nill he* will he
or will he not (whether he will or will not) ²¹*quest* inquest
²⁶*count'nance* privilege ²⁷*even-Christen* fellow Christian ²⁹*hold up* keep up
³²*bore arms* had a coat of arms (the sign of a gentleman)

Clown. What, art a heathen? How dost thou understand the
Scripture? The Scripture says Adam digged. Could he dig   35
without arms? I'll put another question to thee. If thou
answerest me not to the purpose, confess thyself —

Other. Go to.

Clown. What is he that builds stronger than either the mason,
the shipwright, or the carpenter?   40

Other. The gallowsmaker, for that frame outlives a thousand
tenants.

Clown. I like thy wit well, in good faith. The gallows does
well. But how does it well? It does well to those that
do ill. Now thou dost ill to say the gallows is built   45
stronger than the church. Argal, the gallows may do
well to thee. To't again, come.

Other. Who builds stronger than a mason, a shipwright, or
a carpenter?

Clown. Ay, tell me that, and unyoke.°   50

Other. Marry, now I can tell.

Clown. To't.

Other. Mass,° I cannot tell.

Enter Hamlet and Horatio afar off.

Clown. Cudgel thy brains no more about it, for your dull
ass will not mend his pace with beating. And when   55
you are asked this question next, say "a gravemaker."
The houses he makes lasts till doomsday. Go, get thee
in, and fetch me a stoup° of liquor.

[*Exit Other Clown.*]

In youth when I did love, did love   [*Song.*]
Methought it was very sweet   60
To contract — O — the time for — a — my behove,°
O, methought there — a — was nothing —
a — meet.

Hamlet. Has this fellow no feeling of his business? 'A sings
in gravemaking.

Horatio. Custom hath made it in him a property of easiness.°   65

Hamlet. 'Tis e'en so. The hand of little employment hath the
daintier sense.°

---

⁵⁰*unyoke* i.e., stop work for the day ⁵³*Mass* by the mass ⁵⁸*stoup*
tankard ⁶¹*behove* advantage ⁶⁵*in him a property of easiness* easy for him
⁶⁶⁻⁶⁷*hath the daintier sense* is more sensitive (because it is not calloused)

Clown.

> But age with his stealing steps   (*Song.*)
>> Hath clawed me in his clutch,
> And hath shipped me into the land,   *70*
>> As if I had never been such.

[*Throws up a skull.*]

Hamlet. That skull had a tongue in it, and could sing once.
How the knave jowls° it to the ground, as if 'twere
Cain's jawbone, that did the first murder! This might
be the pate of a politician, which this ass now o'erreaches,°   *75*
one that would circumvent God, might it not?
Horatio. It might, my lord.
Hamlet. Or of a courtier, which could say "Good morrow,
sweet lord! How dost thou, sweet lord?" This might
be my Lord Such-a-one, that praised my Lord Such-   *80*
a-one's horse when 'a went to beg it, might it not?
Horatio. Ay, my lord.
Hamlet. Why, e'en so, and now my Lady Worm's, chapless,°
and knocked about the mazzard° with a sexton's spade.
Here's fine revolution, an we had the trick to see't. Did   *85*
these bones cost no more the breeding but to play at
loggets° with them? Mine ache to think on't.
Clown.

> A pickax and a spade, a spade,   (*Song.*)
>> For and a shrouding sheet;
> O, a pit of clay for to be made   *90*
>> For such a guest is meet.

[*Throws up another skull.*]

Hamlet. There's another. Why may not that be the skull of
a lawyer? Where be his quiddities° now, his quillities,°
his cases, his tenures,° and his tricks? Why does he suffer
this mad knave now to knock him about the sconce°   *95*
with a dirty shovel, and will not tell him of his action
of battery? Hum! This fellow might be in's time a great
buyer of land, with his statutes, his recognizances, his
fines,° his double vouchers, his recoveries. Is this the

°73*jowls* hurls   °75*o'erreaches* (1) reaches over, (2) has the advantage
over   °83*chapless* lacking the lower jaw   °84*mazzard* head   °87*loggets* (a game in
which small pieces of wood were thrown at an object)   °93*quiddities* subtle arguments
(from Latin *quidditas*, "whatness")   °93*quillities* fine distinctions   °94*tenures* legal
means of holding land   °95*sconce* head   °98-99*his statutes, his recognizances, his
fines* his documents giving a creditor control of a debtor's land, his bonds of
surety, his documents changing an entailed estate into fee simple (unrestricted
ownership)

fine° of his fines, and the recovery of his recoveries, to　*100*
have his fine pate full of fine dirt? Will his vouchers
vouch him no more of his purchases, and double ones
too, than the length and breadth of a pair of indentures?°
The very conveyances° of his lands will scarcely lie in
this box, and must th' inheritor himself have no more,　*105*
ha?

Horatio. Not a jot more, my lord.

Hamlet. Is not parchment made of sheepskins?

Horatio. Ay, my lord, and of calveskins too.

Hamlet. They are sheep and calves which seek out assurance°　*110*
in that. I will speak to this fellow. Whose grave's this,
sirrah?

Clown. Mine, sir. [*Sings.*]

　　O, pit of clay for to be made
　　　For such a guest is meet.　　　　　　　　　　*115*

Hamlet. I think it be thine indeed, for thou liest in't.

Clown. You lie out on't, sir, and therefore 'tis not yours.
For my part, I do not lie in't, yet it is mine.

Hamlet. Thou dost lie in't, to be in't and say it is thine. 'Tis
for the dead, not for the quick;° therefore thou liest.　*120*

Clown. 'Tis a quick lie, sir; 'twill away again from me to you.

Hamlet. What man dost thou dig it for?

Clown. For no man, sir.

Hamlet. What woman then?

Clown. For none neither.　　　　　　　　　　　　　*125*

Hamlet. Who is to be buried in't?

Clown. One that was a woman, sir; but, rest her soul, she's
dead.

Hamlet. How absolute° the knave is! We must speak by the
card,° or equivocation° will undo us. By the Lord,　*130*
Horatio, this three years I have took note of it, the age
is grown so picked° that the toe of the peasant comes
so near the heel of the courtier he galls his kibe.° How
long hast thou been a gravemaker?

Clown. Of all the days i' th' year, I came to't that day that　*135*
our last king Hamlet overcame Fortinbras.

Hamlet. How long is that since?

---

¹⁰⁰*fine* end　¹⁰³*indentures* contracts　¹⁰⁴*conveyances* legal documents for the
transference of land　¹¹⁰*assurance* safety　¹²⁰*quick* living　¹²⁹*absolute* positive,
decided　¹²⁹⁻¹³⁰*by the card* by the compass card, i.e., exactly　¹³⁰*equivo-
cation* ambiguity　¹³²*picked* refined　¹³³*kibe* sore on the back of the heel

Clown. Cannot you tell that? Every fool can tell that. It was
that very day that young Hamlet was born — he that
is mad, and sent into England.   *140*

Hamlet. Ay, marry, why was he sent into England?

Clown. Why, because 'a was mad. 'A shall recover his wits
there; or, if 'a do not, 'tis no great matter there.

Hamlet. Why?

Clown. 'Twill not be seen in him there. There the men are   *145*
as mad as he.

Hamlet. How came he mad?

Clown. Very strangely, they say.

Hamlet. How strangely?

Clown. Faith, e'en with losing his wits.   *150*

Hamlet. Upon what ground?

Clown. Why, here in Denmark. I have been sexton here, man
and boy, thirty years.

Hamlet. How long will a man lie i' th' earth ere he rot?

Clown. Faith, if 'a be not rotten before 'a die (as we have   *155*
many pocky corses° nowadays that will scarce hold the
laying in), 'a will last you some eight year or nine year.
A tanner will last you nine year.

Hamlet. Why he, more than another?

Clown. Why, sir, his hide is so tanned with his trade that 'a   *160*
will keep out water a great while, and your water is a
sore decayer of your whoreson dead body. Here's a skull
now hath lien you i' th' earth three and twenty years.

Hamlet. Whose was it?

Clown. A whoreson mad fellow's it was. Whose do you think   *165*
it was?

Hamlet. Nay, I know not.

Clown. A pestilence on him for a mad rogue! 'A poured a
flagon of Rhenish on my head once. This same skull,
sir, was, sir, Yorick's skull, the King's jester.   *170*

Hamlet. This?

Clown. E'en that.

Hamlet. Let me see. [*Takes the skull.*] Alas, poor Yorick! I
knew him, Horatio, a fellow of infinite jest, of most
excellent fancy. He hath borne me on his back a thousand   *175*
times. And now how abhorred in my imagination it
is! My gorge rises at it. Here hung those lips that I
have kissed I know not how oft. Where be your gibes

---

[156]***pocky corses*** bodies of persons who had been infected with the pox (syphilis)

now? Your gambols, your songs, your flashes of mer-
riment that were wont to set the table on a roar? Not　　**180**
one now to mock your own grinning? Quite chapfall'n?°
Now get you to my lady's chamber, and tell her, let
her paint an inch thick, to this favor° she must come.
Make her laugh at that. Prithee, Horatio, tell me one
thing.　　**185**

Horatio. What's that, my lord?

Hamlet. Dost thou think Alexander looked o' this fashion i'
th' earth?

Horatio. E'en so.

Hamlet. And smelt so? Pah! [*Puts down the skull.*]　　**190**

Horatio. E'en so, my lord.

Hamlet. To what base uses we may return, Horatio! Why
may not imagination trace the noble dust of Alexander
till a' find it stopping a bunghole?

Horatio. 'Twere to consider too curiously,° to consider so.　　**195**

Hamlet. No, faith, not a jot, but to follow him thither with
modesty enough,° and likelihood to lead it; as thus:
Alexander died, Alexander was buried, Alexander re-
turneth to dust; the dust is earth; of earth we make
loam; and why of that loam whereto he was converted　　**200**
might they not stop a beer barrel?
Imperious Caesar, dead and turned to clay,
Might stop a hole to keep the wind away.
O, that that earth which kept the world in awe
Should patch a wall t' expel the winter's flaw!°　　**205**
But soft, but soft awhile! Here comes the King.

*Enter King, Queen, Laertes, and a coffin, with Lords attendant
[and a Doctor of Divinity].*

The Queen, the courtiers. Who is this they follow?
And with such maimèd° rites? This doth betoken
The corse they follow did with desp'rate hand
Fordo it° own life. 'Twas of some estate.°　　**210**
Couch° we awhile, and mark.

　　　　　　　　　　　[*Retires with Horatio.*]

Laertes. What ceremony else?

Hamlet. 　　　　　　　　That is Laertes,
A very noble youth. Mark.

---

[181]*chapfall'n* (1) down in the mouth, (2) jawless　[183]*favor* facial appearance
[195]*curiously* minutely　[196-197]*with modesty enough* without exaggeration
[205]*flaw* gust　[208]*maimèd* incomplete　[210]*Fordo it* destroy its　[210]*estate* high
rank　[211]*Couch* hide

Laertes. What ceremony else?

Doctor. Her obsequies have been as far enlarged   215
　　　As we have warranty. Her death was doubtful,°
　　　And, but that great command o'ersways the order,
　　　She should in ground unsanctified been lodged
　　　Till the last trumpet. For charitable prayers,
　　　Shards,° flints, and pebbles should be thrown on her.   220
　　　Yet here she is allowed her virgin crants,°
　　　Her maiden strewments,° and the bringing home
　　　Of bell and burial.

Laertes. Must there no more be done?

Doctor.   No more be done.
　　　We should profane the service of the dead   225
　　　To sing a requiem and such rest to her
　　　As to peace-parted souls.

Laertes.   Lay her i' th' earth,
　　　And from her fair and unpolluted flesh
　　　May violets spring! I tell thee, churlish priest,
　　　A minist'ring angel shall my sister be   230
　　　When thou liest howling!

Hamlet.   What, the fair Ophelia?

Queen. Sweets to the sweet! Farewell. [*Scatters flowers.*]
　　　I hoped thou shouldst have been my Hamlet's wife.
　　　I thought thy bride bed to have decked, sweet maid,
　　　And not have strewed thy grave.

Laertes.   O, treble woe   235
　　　Fall ten times treble on that cursèd head
　　　Whose wicked deed thy most ingenious sense°
　　　Deprived thee of! Hold off the earth awhile,
　　　Till I have caught her once more in mine arms.

　　　Leaps in the grave.

　　　Now pile your dust upon the quick and dead   240
　　　Till of this flat a mountain you have made
　　　T'o'ertop old Pelion° or the skyish head
　　　Of blue Olympus.

Hamlet [*coming forward*]. What is he whose grief
　　　Bears such an emphasis, whose phrase of sorrow   245
　　　Conjures the wand'ring stars,° and makes them stand

---

[216] ***doubtful*** suspicious   [220] ***Shards*** broken pieces of pottery   [221] ***crants*** garlands
[222] ***strewments*** i.e., of flowers   [237] ***most ingenious sense*** finely endowed mind
[242] ***Pelion*** (according to classical legend, giants in their fight with the gods sought to reach heaven by piling Mount Pelion and Mount Ossa on Mount Olympus)
[246] ***wand'ring stars*** planets

Like wonder-wounded hearers? This is I,
Hamlet the Dane.

Laertes.   The devil take thy soul!

[*Grapples with him.*]°

Hamlet. Thou pray'st not well.
I prithee take thy fingers from my throat,   250
For, though I am not splenitive° and rash,
Yet have I in me something dangerous,
Which let thy wisdom fear. Hold off thy hand.

King. Pluck them asunder.

Queen.   Hamlet, Hamlet!

All. Gentlemen!

Horatio.   Good my lord, be quiet.   255

Attendants part them.

Hamlet. Why, I will fight with him upon this theme
Until my eyelids will no longer wag.

Queen. O my son, what theme?

Hamlet. I loved Ophelia. Forty thousand brothers
Could not with all their quantity of love   260
Make up my sum. What wilt thou do for her?

King. O, he is mad, Laertes.

Queen. For love of God forbear him.

Hamlet. 'Swounds, show me what thou't do.
Woo't weep? Woo't fight? Woo't fast? Woo't tear
thyself?   265
Woo't drink up eisel?° Eat a crocodile?
I'll do't. Dost thou come here to whine?
To outface me with leaping in her grave?
Be buried quick with her, and so will I.
And if thou prate of mountains, let them throw   270
Millions of acres on us, till our ground,
Singeing his pate against the burning zone,°
Make Ossa like a wart! Nay, an thou'lt mouth,
I'll rant as well as thou.

Queen.   This is mere madness;
And thus a while the fit will work on him.   275

---

²⁴⁸ ˢ·ᵈ· *Grapples with him* (Q1, a bad quarto, presumably reporting a version that toured, has a previous direction saying "Hamlet leaps in after Laertes." Possibly he does so, somewhat hysterically. But such a direction — absent from the two good texts, Q2 and F — makes Hamlet the aggressor, somewhat contradicting his next speech. Perhaps Laertes leaps out of the grave to attack Hamlet) ²⁵¹*splenitive* fiery (the spleen was thought to be the seat of anger) ²⁶⁶*eisel* vinegar ²⁷²*burning zone* sun's orbit

Anon, as patient as the female dove
When that her golden couplets are disclosed,°
His silence will sit drooping.
Hamlet.   Hear you, sir.
What is the reason that you use me thus?
I loved you ever. But it is no matter.   *280*
Let Hercules himself do what he may,
The cat will mew, and dog will have his day.
King. I pray thee, good Horatio, wait upon him.
                        Exit Hamlet and Horatio.
[*To Laertes.*] Strengthen your patience in our last night's
    speech.
We'll put the matter to the present push.°   *285*
Good Gertrude, set some watch over your son.
This grave shall have a living° monument.
An hour of quiet shortly shall we see;
Till then in patience our proceeding be.
                                        Exeunt.

[**Scene II.** *The castle.*]

Enter Hamlet and Horatio.

Hamlet. So much for this, sir; now shall you see the other.
    You do remember all the circumstance?
Horatio. Remember it, my lord!
Hamlet. Sir, in my heart there was a kind of fighting
    That would not let me sleep. Methought I lay   *5*
    Worse than the mutines in the bilboes.° Rashly
    (And praised be rashness for it) let us know,
    Our indiscretion sometime serves us well
    When our deep plots do pall,° and that should learn us
    There's a divinity that shapes our ends,   *10*
    Rough-hew them how we will.
Horatio.   That is most certain.
Hamlet. Up from my cabin,
    My sea gown scarfed about me, in the dark
    Groped I to find out them, had my desire,
    Fingered° their packet, and in fine° withdrew   *15*

---

²⁷⁷*golden couplets are disclosed* (the dove lays two eggs, and the newly hatched
["disclosed"] young are covered with golden down)   ²⁸⁵*present push* immediate
test   ²⁸⁷*living* lasting (with perhaps also a reference to the plot against Hamlet's
life) V.ii.   ⁶*mutines   in   the   bilboes* mutineers   in   fetters ⁹*pall* fail
¹⁵*Fingered* stole   ¹⁵*in fine* finally

To mine own room again, making so bold,
My fears forgetting manners, to unseal
Their grand commission; where I found, Horatio —
Ah, royal knavery! — an exact command,
Larded° with many several sorts of reasons,   *20*
Importing Denmark's health, and England's too,
With, ho, such bugs and goblins in my life,°
That on the supervise,° no leisure bated,°
No, not to stay the grinding of the ax,
My head should be struck off.

Horatio.   Is't possible?   *25*

Hamlet. Here's the commission; read it at more leisure.
But wilt thou hear now how I did proceed?

Horatio. I beseech you.

Hamlet. Being thus benetted round with villains,
Or° I could make a prologue to my brains,   *30*
They had begun the play. I sat me down,
Devised a new commission, wrote it fair.
I once did hold it, as our statists° do,
A baseness to write fair,° and labored much
How to forget that learning, but, sir, now   *35*
It did me yeoman's service. Wilt thou know
Th' effect° of what I wrote?

Horatio.   Ay, good my lord.

Hamlet. An earnest conjuration from the King,
As England was his faithful tributary,
As love between them like the palm might flourish,   *40*
As peace should still her wheaten garland wear
And stand a comma° 'tween their amities,
And many suchlike as's of great charge,°
That on the view and knowing of these contents,
Without debatement further, more or less,   *45*
He should those bearers put to sudden death,
Not shriving° time allowed.

Horatio.   How was this sealed?

Hamlet. Why, even in that was heaven ordinant.°
I had my father's signet in my purse,
Which was the model° of that Danish seal,   *50*

---

²⁰*Larded* enriched ²²*such bugs and goblins in my life* such bugbears and imagined
terrors if I were allowed to live ²³*supervise* reading ²³*leisure bated* delay allowed
³⁰*Or* ere ³³*statists* statesmen ³⁴*fair* clearly ³⁷*effect* purport ⁴²*comma* link ⁴³*great
charge* (1) serious exhortation, (2) heavy burden (punning on "as's" and "asses")
⁴⁷*shriving* absolution ⁴⁸*ordinant* ruling ⁵⁰*model* counterpart

Folded the writ up in the form of th' other,
Subscribed it, gave't th' impression, placed it safely,
The changeling never known. Now, the next day
Was our sea fight, and what to this was sequent
Thou knowest already.   55
Horatio. So Guildenstern and Rosencrantz go to't.
Hamlet. Why, man, they did make love to this employment.
   They are not near my conscience; their defeat
   Does by their own insinuation° grow.
   'Tis dangerous when the baser nature comes   60
   Between the pass° and fell° incensèd points
   Of mighty opposites.
Horatio.   Why, what a king is this!
Hamlet. Does it not, think thee, stand me now upon° —
   He that hath killed my king, and whored my mother,
   Popped in between th' election° and my hopes,   65
   Thrown out his angle° for my proper life,°
   And with such coz'nage° — is't not perfect conscience
   To quit° him with this arm? And is't not to be damned
   To let this canker of our nature come
   In further evil?   70
Horatio. It must be shortly known to him from England
   What is the issue of the business there.
Hamlet. It will be short; the interim's mine,
   And a man's life's no more than to say "one."
   But I am very sorry, good Horatio,   75
   That to Laertes I forgot myself,
   For by the image of my cause I see
   The portraiture of his. I'll court his favors.
   But sure the bravery° of his grief did put me
   Into a tow'ring passion.
Horatio.   Peace, who comes here?   80

   Enter young Osric, a courtier.

Osric. Your lordship is right welcome back to Denmark.
Hamlet. I humbly thank you, sir. [*Aside to Horatio.*] Dost
   know this waterfly?
Horatio [*aside to Hamlet*]. No, my good lord.
Hamlet [*aside to Horatio*]. Thy state is the more gracious, for   85

°**insinuation** meddling °**pass** thrust °**fell** cruel °**stand me now upon**
become incumbent upon me °**election** (the Danish monarchy was elec-
tive) °**angle** fishing line °**my proper life** my own life °**coz'nage** trickery
°**quit** pay back °**bravery** bravado

'tis a vice to know him. He hath much land, and fertile.
Let a beast be lord of beasts, and his crib shall stand
at the king's mess.° 'Tis a chough,° but, as I say, spacious°
in the possession of dirt.

Osric. Sweet lord, if your lordship were at leisure, I should   *90*
impart a thing to you from his Majesty.

Hamlet. I will receive it, sir, with all diligence of spirit. Put
your bonnet to his right use. 'Tis for the head.

Osric. I thank your lordship, it is very hot.

Hamlet. No, believe me, 'tis very cold; the wind is northerly.   *95*

Osric. It is indifferent cold, my lord, indeed.

Hamlet. But yet methinks it is very sultry and hot for my
complexion.°

Osric. Exceedingly, my lord; it is very sultry, as 'twere — I
cannot tell how. But, my lord, his Majesty bade me   *100*
signify to you that 'a has laid a great wager on your
head. Sir, this is the matter —

Hamlet. I beseech you remember.

[*Hamlet moves him to put on his hat.*]

Osric. Nay, good my lord; for my ease, in good faith. Sir,
here is newly come to court Laertes — believe me, an   *105*
absolute gentleman, full of most excellent differences,°
of very soft society and great showing. Indeed, to speak
feelingly° of him, he is the card° or calendar of gentry;
for you shall find in him the continent° of what part a
gentleman would see.   *110*

Hamlet. Sir, his definement° suffers no perdition° in you,
though, I know, to divide him inventorially would
dozy° th' arithmetic of memory, and yet but yaw neither
in respect of his quick sail.° But, in the verity of ex-
tolment, I take him to be a soul of great article,° and   *115*
his infusion° of such dearth and rareness as, to make
true diction° of him, his semblable° is his mirror, and
who else would trace him, his umbrage,° nothing more.

---

⁸⁸*mess* table ⁸⁸*chough* jackdaw (here chatterer) ⁸⁸*spacious* well off
⁹⁸*complexion* temperament ¹⁰⁶*differences* distinguishing characteristics ¹⁰⁸*feelingly*
justly ¹⁰⁸*card* chart ¹⁰⁹*continent* summary ¹¹¹*definement* description ¹¹¹*perdition*
loss ¹¹³*dozy* dizzy ¹¹³⁻¹¹⁴*and yet . . . quick sail* i.e., and yet only stagger despite
all ("yaw neither") in trying to overtake his virtues ¹¹⁵*article* (literally, "item,"
but here perhaps "traits" or "importance") ¹¹⁶*infusion* essential quality ¹¹⁷*diction*
description ¹¹⁷*semblable* likeness ¹¹⁸*umbrage* shadow

Osric. Your lordship speaks most infallibly of him.

Hamlet. The concernancy,° sir? Why do we wrap the gentleman   120
in our more rawer breath?

Osric. Sir?

Horatio. Is't not possible to understand in another tongue?
You will to't,° sir, really.

Hamlet. What imports the nomination of this gentleman?   125

Osric. Of Laertes?

Horatio [*aside to Hamlet*]. His purse is empty already. All's
golden words are spent.

Hamlet. Of him, sir.

Osric. I know you are not ignorant —   130

Hamlet. I would you did, sir; yet, in faith, if you did, it
would not much approve° me. Well, sir?

Osric. You are not ignorant of what excellence Laertes is —

Hamlet. I dare not confess that, lest I should compare with
him in excellence; but to know a man well were to   135
know himself.

Osric. I mean, sir, for his weapon; but in the imputation°
laid on him by them, in his meed° he's unfellowed.

Hamlet. What's his weapon?

Osric. Rapier and dagger.   140

Hamlet. That's two of his weapons — but well.

Osric. The King, sir, hath wagered with him six Barbary
horses, against the which he has impawned,° as I take
it, six French rapiers and poniards, with their assigns,°
as girdle, hangers,° and so. Three of the carriages,° in   145
faith, are very dear to fancy, very responsive° to the
hilts, most delicate carriages, and of very liberal conceit.°

Hamlet. What call you the carriages?

Horatio [*aside to Hamlet*]. I knew you must be edified by the
margent° ere you had done.   150

Osric. The carriages, sir, are the hangers.

Hamlet. The phrase would be more germane to the matter
if we could carry a cannon by our sides. I would it
might be hangers till then. But on! Six Barbary horses
against six French swords, their assigns, and three liberal-   155
conceited carriages — that's the French bet against the
Danish. Why is this all impawned, as you call it?

---

¹²⁰*concernancy* meaning ¹²⁴*will to't* will get there ¹³²*approve* commend
¹³⁷*imputation* reputation ¹³⁸*meed* merit ¹⁴³*impawned* wagered ¹⁴⁴*assigns* accompaniments ¹⁴⁵*hangers* straps hanging the sword to the belt ¹⁴⁵*carriages* (an
affected word for hangers) ¹⁴⁶*responsive* corresponding ¹⁴⁷*liberal conceit* elaborate
design ¹⁵⁰*margent* i.e., marginal (explanatory comment)

Osric. The King, sir, hath laid, sir, that in a dozen passes
between yourself and him he shall not exceed you three
hits; he hath laid on twelve for nine, and it would come   *160*
to immediate trial if your lordship would vouchsafe the
answer.

Hamlet. How if I answer no?

Osric. I mean, my lord, the opposition of your person in trial.

Hamlet. Sir, I will walk here in the hall. If it please his   *165*
Majesty, it is the breathing time of day with me.° Let
the foils be brought, the gentleman willing, and the
King hold his purpose, I will win for him an I can; if
not, I will gain nothing but my shame and the odd
hits.   *170*

Osric. Shall I deliver you e'en so?

Hamlet. To this effect, sir, after what flourish your nature will.

Osric. I commend my duty to your lordship.

Hamlet. Yours, yours.

[*Exit Osric.*]

He does well to commend it himself; there are no tongues   *175*
else for's turn.

Horatio. This lapwing° runs away with the shell on his head.

Hamlet. 'A did comply, sir, with his dug° before 'a sucked
it. Thus has he, and many more of the same breed that
I know the drossy age dotes on, only got the tune of   *180*
the time and, out of an habit of encounter,° a kind of
yeasty° collection, which carries them through and
through the most fanned and winnowed opinions; and
do but blow them to their trial, the bubbles are out.°

Enter a Lord.

Lord. My lord, his Majesty commended him to you by young   *185*
Osric, who brings back to him that you attend him in
the hall. He sends to know if your pleasure hold to
play with Laertes, or that you will take longer time.

Hamlet. I am constant to my purposes; they follow the King's
pleasure. If his fitness speaks, mine is ready; now or   *190*
whensoever, provided I be so able as now.

Lord. The King and Queen and all are coming down.

---

[166]***breathing time of day with me*** time when I take exercise   [177]***lapwing*** (the
new-hatched lapwing was thought to run around with half its shell on its head)   [178]***'A
did comply, sir, with his dug*** he was ceremoniously polite to his mother's
breast   [181]***out of an habit of encounter*** out of his own superficial way of meeting
and conversing with people   [182]***yeasty*** frothy   [184]***the bubbles are out*** i.e., they
are blown away (the reference is to the "yeasty collection")

Hamlet. In happy time.

Lord. The Queen desires you to use some gentle entertainment°
to Laertes before you fall to play.   *195*

Hamlet. She well instructs me.

[*Exit Lord.*]

Horatio. You will lose this wager, my lord.

Hamlet. I do not think so. Since he went into France I have
been in continual practice. I shall win at the odds. But
thou wouldst not think how ill all's here about my   *200*
heart. But it is no matter.

Horatio. Nay, good my lord —

Hamlet. It is but foolery, but it is such a kind of gain-giving°
as would perhaps trouble a woman.

Horatio. If your mind dislike anything, obey it. I will forestall   *205*
their repair hither and say you are not fit.

Hamlet. Not a whit, we defy augury. There is special providence
in the fall of a sparrow.° If it be now, 'tis not to come;
if it be not to come, it will be now; if it be not now,
yet it will come. The readiness is all. Since no man of   *210*
aught he leaves knows, what is't to leave betimes?° Let
be.

A table prepared. [*Enter*] *Trumpets, Drums, and Officers with
cushions; King, Queen,* [*Osric,*] *and all the State,* [*with*] *foils,
daggers,* [*and stoups of wine borne in*]; *and Laertes.*

King. Come, Hamlet, come, and take this hand from me.

[*The King puts Laertes' hand into Hamlet's.*]

Hamlet. Give me your pardon, sir. I have done you wrong,
But pardon't, as you are a gentleman.   *215*
This presence° knows, and you must needs have heard,
How I am punished with a sore distraction.
What I have done
That might your nature, honor, and exception°
Roughly awake, I here proclaim was madness.   *220*
Was't Hamlet wronged Laertes? Never Hamlet.
If Hamlet from himself be ta'en away,
And when he's not himself does wrong Laertes,
Then Hamlet does it not, Hamlet denies it.
Who does it then? His madness. If't be so,   *225*

---

¹⁹⁴*to use some gentle entertainment* to be courteous ²⁰³*gain-giving*
misgiving ²⁰⁸*the fall of a sparrow* (cf. Matthew 10:29 "Are not two sparrows
sold for a farthing? and one of them shall not fall on the ground without your
Father") ²¹¹*betimes* early ²¹⁶*presence* royal assembly ²¹⁹*exception* disapproval

Hamlet is of the faction° that is wronged;
His madness is poor Hamlet's enemy.
Sir, in this audience,
Let my disclaiming from a purposed evil
Free me so far in your most generous thoughts   230
That I have shot my arrow o'er the house
And hurt my brother.

Laertes.   I am satisfied in nature,
Whose motive in this case should stir me most
To my revenge. But in my terms of honor
I stand aloof, and will no reconcilement   235
Till by some elder masters of known honor
I have a voice and precedent° of peace
To keep my name ungored. But till that time
I do receive your offered love like love,
And will not wrong it.

Hamlet.   I embrace it freely,   240
And will this brother's wager frankly play.
Give us the foils. Come on.

Laertes.   Come, one for me.

Hamlet. I'll be your foil,° Laertes. In mine ignorance
Your skill shall, like a star i' th' darkest night,
Stick fiery off° indeed.

Laertes.   You mock me, sir.   245

Hamlet. No, by this hand.

King. Give them the foils, young Osric. Cousin Hamlet,
You know the wager?

Hamlet.   Very well, my lord.
Your grace has laid the odds o' th' weaker side.

King. I do not fear it, I have seen you both;   250
But since he is bettered,° we have therefore odds.

Laertes. This is too heavy; let me see another.

Hamlet. This likes me well. These foils have all a length?

Prepare to play.

Osric. Ay, my good lord.

King. Set me the stoups of wine upon that table.   255
If Hamlet give the first or second hit,
Or quit° in answer of the third exchange,

---

²²⁶*faction* party, side   ²³⁷*voice and precedent* authoritative opinion justified by
precedent   ²⁴³*foil* (1) blunt sword, (2) background (of metallic leaf) for a
jewel   ²⁴⁵*Stick fiery off* stand out brilliantly   ²⁵¹*bettered* has improved (in
France)   ²⁵⁷*quit* repay, hit back

Let all the battlements their ordnance fire.
The King shall drink to Hamlet's better breath,
And in the cup an union° shall he throw   *260*
Richer than that which four successive kings
In Denmark's crown have worn. Give me the cups,
And let the kettle° to the trumpet speak,
The trumpet to the cannoneer without,
The cannons to the heavens, the heaven to earth,   *265*
"Now the King drinks to Hamlet." Come, begin.

Trumpets the while.

And you, the judges, bear a wary eye.
Hamlet. Come on, sir.
Laertes.   Come, my lord!

They play.

Hamlet.   One!
Laertes.   No.
Hamlet.   Judgment?
Osric. A hit, a very palpable hit.

Drum, trumpets, and shot. Flourish; a piece goes off.

Laertes.   Well, again.
King. Stay, give me drink. Hamlet, this pearl is thine.   *270*
 Here's to thy health. Give him the cup.
Hamlet. I'll play this bout first; set it by awhile.
 Come.

[*They play.*]

           Another hit. What say you?
Laertes. A touch, a touch; I do confess't.
King. Our son shall win.
Queen.   He's fat,° and scant of breath.   *275*
 Here, Hamlet, take my napkin, rub thy brows.
 The Queen carouses to thy fortune, Hamlet.
Hamlet. Good madam!
King.   Gertrude, do not drink.
Queen. I will, my lord; I pray you pardon me. [*Drinks.*]
King [*aside*]. It is the poisoned cup; it is too late.   *280*
Hamlet. I dare not drink yet, madam — by and by.
Queen. Come, let me wipe thy face.

---

[260]**union** pearl   [263]**kettle** kettledrum   [275]**fat** (1) sweaty, (2) out of training

Laertes. My lord, I'll hit him now.
King.   I do not think't.
Laertes [*aside*]. And yet it is almost against my conscience.
Hamlet. Come for the third, Laertes. You do but dally.   *285*
    I pray you pass with your best violence;
    I am sure you make a wanton° of me.

    [*They*] *play.*

Laertes. Say you so? Come on.
Osric. Nothing neither way.
Laertes. Have at you now!

    In scuffling they change rapiers, [*and both are wounded.*]

King.   Part them. They are incensed.   *290*
Hamlet. Nay, come — again!
    [*The Queen fails.*]
Osric.   Look to the Queen there, ho!
Horatio. They bleed on both sides. How is it, my lord?
Osric. How is't, Laertes?
Laertes. Why, as a woodcock to mine own springe,° Osric.
    I am justly killed with mine own treachery.   *295*
Hamlet. How does the Queen?
King.   She sounds° to see them bleed.
Queen. No, no, the drink, the drink! O my dear Hamlet!
    The drink, the drink! I am poisoned.

                                            [*Dies.*]

Hamlet. O villainy! Ho! Let the door be locked.
    Treachery! Seek it out.   *300*

    [*Laertes falls.*]

Laertes. It is here, Hamlet. Hamlet, thou art slain;
    No med'cine in the world can do thee good.
    In thee there is not half an hour's life.
    The treacherous instrument is in thy hand,
    Unbated and envenomed. The foul practice°   *305*
    Hath turned itself on me. Lo, here I lie,
    Never to rise again. Thy mother's poisoned.
    I can no more. The King, the King's to blame.
Hamlet. The point envenomed too?
    Then, venom, to thy work.   *310*
                                        Hurts the King.
All. Treason! Treason!

---

²⁸⁷*wanton*   spoiled child   ²⁹⁴*springe*   snare   ²⁹⁶*sounds*   swoons   ³⁰⁵*practice*   deception

King. O, yet defend me, friends. I am but hurt.
Hamlet. Here, thou incestuous, murd'rous, damnèd Dane,
    Drink off this potion. Is thy union here?
    Follow my mother.

                               King dies.

Laertes.   He is justly served.   315
    It is a poison tempered° by himself.
    Exchange forgiveness with me, noble Hamlet.
    Mine and my father's death come not upon thee,
    Nor thine on me!

                                    Dies.

Hamlet. Heaven make thee free of it! I follow thee. 320
    I am dead, Horatio. Wretched Queen, adieu!
    You that look pale and tremble at this chance,
    That are but mutes° or audience to this act,
    Had I but time (as this fell sergeant,° Death,
    Is strict in his arrest) O, I could tell you —   325
    But let it be. Horatio, I am dead;
    Thou livest; report me and my cause aright
    To the unsatisfied.°
Horatio.   Never believe it.
    I am more an antique Roman° than a Dane.
    Here's yet some liquor left.
Hamlet.   As th' art a man,   330
    Give me the cup. Let go. By heaven, I'll ha't!
    O God, Horatio, what a wounded name,
    Things standing thus unknown, shall live behind me!
    If thou didst ever hold me in thy heart,
    Absent thee from felicity° awhile,   335
    And in this harsh world draw thy breath in pain,
    To tell my story.

                    A march afar off. [*Exit Osric.*]
    What warlike noise is this?

    Enter Osric.

Osric. Young Fortinbras, with conquest come from Poland,
    To th' ambassadors of England gives
    This warlike volley.
Hamlet.   O, I die, Horatio!   340
    The potent poison quite o'ercrows° my spirit.
    I cannot live to hear the news from England,

---

[316]*tempered*   mixed   [323]*mutes*   performers who have no words to speak   [324]*fell sergeant*   dread   sheriff's   officer   [328]*unsatisfied*   uniformed   [329]*antique Roman*   (with reference to the old Roman fashion of suicide)   [335]*felicity*   i.e., the felicity of death   [341]*o'ercrows*   overpowers (as a triumphant cock crows over its weak opponent)

But I do prophesy th' election lights
On Fortinbras. He has my dying voice.
So tell him, with th' occurrents,° more and less,   *345*
Which have solicited° — the rest is silence.

                                                        Dies.

Horatio. Now cracks a noble heart. Good night, sweet Prince,
And flights of angels sing thee to thy rest.

                                            [*March within.*]

Why does the drum come hither?

*Enter Fortinbras, with the Ambassadors with Drum, Colors, and
Attendants.*

Fortinbras. Where is this sight?
Horatio.   What is it you would see?   *350*
If aught of woe or wonder, cease your search.
Fortinbras. This quarry° cries on havoc.° O proud Death,
What feast is toward° in thine eternal cell
That thou so many princes at a shot
So bloodily hast struck?
Ambassador.   The sight is dismal;   *355*
And our affairs from England come too late.
The ears are senseless that should give us hearing
To tell him his commandment is fulfilled,
That Rosencrantz and Guildenstern are dead.
Where should we have our thanks?
Horatio.   Not from his° mouth,   *360*
Had it th' ability of life to thank you.
He never gave commandment for their death.
But since, so jump° upon this bloody question,
You from the Polack wars, and you from England,
Are here arrived, give order that these bodies   *365*
High on a stage° be placèd to the view,
And let me speak to th' yet unknowing world
How these things came about. So shall you hear
Of carnal, bloody, and unnatural acts,
Of accidental judgments, casual° slaughters,   *370*
Of deaths put on by cunning and forced cause,
And, in this upshot, purposes mistook
Fall'n on th' inventors' heads. All this can I
Truly deliver.

---

[345]***occurrents*** occurrences   [346]***solicited*** incited   [352]***quarry*** heap of slain bodies
[352]***cries on havoc*** proclaims general slaughter   [353]***toward*** in preparation   [360]***his***
(Claudius')   [363]***jump*** precisely   [366]***stage*** platform   [370]***casual*** not humanly planned,
chance

Fortinbras.   Let us haste to hear it,
          And call the noblest to the audience.   375
          For me, with sorrow I embrace my fortune.
          I have some rights of memory° in this kingdom,
          Which now to claim my vantage doth invite me.
Horatio. Of that I shall have also cause to speak,
          And from his mouth whose voice will draw on° more. 380
          But let this same be presently performed,
          Even while men's minds are wild, lest more mischance
          On° plots and errors happen.
Fortinbras.   Let four captains
          Bear Hamlet like a soldier to the stage,
          For he was likely, had he been put on,°   385
          To have proved most royal; and for his passage°
          The soldiers' music and the rite of war
          Speak loudly for him.
          Take up the bodies. Such a sight as this
          Becomes the field,° but here shows much amiss.   390
          Go, bid the soldiers shoot.

                              Exeunt marching;
              after the which a peal of ordnance are shot off.

                         Finis

QUESTIONS

Act I

1. The first scene (like many other scenes in this play) is full
   of expressions of uncertainty. What are some of these uncertainties? The Ghost first appears at I.i.39. Does his appearance surprise us, or have we been prepared for it? Or
   is there both preparation and surprise? How do the last four
   speeches of I.i help to introduce a note of hope?
2. Does the King's opening speech in I.ii reveal him to be an
   accomplished public speaker — or are lines 10–14 offensive?
   In his second speech (lines 41–50), what is the effect of
   naming Laertes four times? Claudius sometimes uses the
   royal pronouns (we, our), sometimes the more intimate "I"
   and "my." Study his use of these in lines 1–4 and in 106–
   117. What is he getting at?
3. Hamlet's first soliloquy (I.ii.129–159) reveals that not simply

---

[377] **rights of memory** remembered claims   [380] **voice will draw on** vote will
influence   [383] **On** on top of   [385] **put on** advanced (to the throne)
[386] **passage** death   [390] **field** battlefield

his father's death distresses him. Be as specific as possible about the causes of Hamlet's anguish here. What traits does Hamlet reveal in his conversation with Horatio (I.ii.160–254)?

4. What do you make of Polonius's advice to Laertes (I.iii.59–80)? Is it sound? Sound advice, but here uttered by a fool? Ignoble advice? How would one follow the advice of line 78: "to thine own self be true"? In his words to Ophelia in I.iii.101–135, what does he reveal about himself?

5. Can I.iv.17–38 reasonably be taken as a speech on "the tragic flaw"? Or is the passage a much more limited discussion, a comment simply on Danish drinking habits?

6. How in this scene (and in I.i) does Shakespeare suggest that the Ghost may be an evil spirit? Do such suggestions dominate?

7. The Ghost, claiming to be in a state of purgation (in I.v), seeks revenge. Does its uncharitable request convince us that the Ghost must really be an evil spirit trying to trap Hamlet into doing a damnable murder? Or do we accept the call to revenge as valid?

8. Hamlet is convinced in I.v.95–104 that the Ghost has told the truth, indeed, told the only important truth. But do we detect in 105–112 a hint of a tone suggesting that Hamlet delights in hating villainy? If so, can it be said that later this delight grows, and that in some scenes (e.g., III.iii) we feel that Hamlet has almost become a diabolic revenger?

9. Scenes fairly often end with a couplet (pair of rhyming lines). What is the effect of adding an *un*rhymed line to the couplet, at the end of I.v?

Act II

1. Characterize Polonius on the basis of II.i.1–74.

2. In light of what we have seen of Hamlet, is Ophelia's report of his strange behavior when he visits her understandable?

3. Why does II.ii.33–34 seem almost comic? How do these lines help us to form a view about Rosencrantz and Guildenstern?

4. In lines 85–98 Polonius uses wordplay. Does it suggest that he is witty, or foolish? Hamlet too uses wordplay (e.g., II.ii.193), but the effect differs. How?

5. Is "the hellish Pyrrhus" (II.ii.455) Hamlet's version of Claudius? Or is he Hamlet, who soon will be responsible for the deaths of Polonius, Rosencrantz and Guildenstern, Claudius, Gertrude, Ophelia, and Laertes?

6. Is the Player's speech (II.ii.460–510) a huffing speech? If so, why? To distinguish it from the poetry of the play itself? To characterize the bloody deeds that Hamlet cannot descend to?

7. In II.ii.556–578 Hamlet rebukes himself for not acting. Why has he not acted? Because he is a coward (line 556)? Because he has a conscience? Because no action can restore his father and his mother's purity? Because he doubts the Ghost?

Act III

1. What do you make of Hamlet's assertion to Ophelia: "I loved you not" (III.i.118–119)? Of his characterization of himself as full of "offenses" (III.i.125)? Why is Hamlet so harsh to Ophelia?

2. Hamlet praises Horatio as a man who "is not passion's slave" (III.ii.71). But is such a man a hero? Will he avenge a wronged father? Can we reasonably apply the Player King's comments on passion (III.ii.187–192) and fate (III.ii.204–206) to the play of *Hamlet* itself?

3. In III.iii.11–23 Rosencrantz is speaking about Claudius, but to what degree do his words apply to Hamlet's father?

4. In III.iii.36–72 Claudius's conscience afflicts him. But is he repentant?

5. Is Hamlet other than abhorrent in III.iii.74–96? Do we want him to kill Claudius at this moment, when Claudius (presumably with his back to Hamlet) is praying?

6. The Ghost speaks of Hamlet's "almost blunted purpose" (III.iv.112). Is the accusation fair?

7. How would you characterize the Hamlet who speaks in III.iv. 203–217?

Act IV

1. Is Gertrude protecting Hamlet when she says he is mad (IV.i.7), or does she believe that he is mad? If she believes he is mad, does it follow that she no longer feels ashamed and guilty?

2. Why should Hamlet hide Polonius's body (in IV.ii)? Is he feigning madness? Is he on the edge of madness?

3. How can we explain Hamlet's willingness to go to England (IV.iii.44)?

4. Judging from IV.v, what has driven Ophelia mad? Is Laertes heroic, or somewhat foolish? Consider also the way Claudius treats him in IV.vii.

Act V

1. What would be lost if the Gravediggers in V.i were omitted?
2. To what extent do we judge Hamlet severely for sending Rosencrantz and Guildenstern to their deaths, as he reports in V.ii? On the whole do we think of Hamlet as an intriguer? What other intrigues has he engendered? How successful were they?
3. Does V.ii.207–212 show a paralysis of the will, or a wise recognition that more is needed than mere human scheming?
4. Does V.ii.290 suggest that Laertes takes advantage of a momentary pause and unfairly stabs Hamlet? Is the exchange of weapons accidental, or does Hamlet (as in Olivier's film version), realizing that he has been betrayed, deliberately get possession of Laertes's deadly weapon?
5. Fortinbras is often cut from the play. How much is lost by the cut?
6. Fortinbras gives Hamlet a soldier's funeral. Is this ridiculous? Can it fairly be said that, in a sense, Hamlet has been at war?

General Questions

1. Hamlet in V.ii.10–11 speaks of a "divinity that shapes our ends." To what extent does "divinity" (or Fate or mysterious Chance) play a role in the happenings?
2. How do Laertes, Fortinbras, and Horatio help to define Hamlet for us?
3. T. S. Eliot says (in "Shakespeare and the Stoicism of Seneca") that Hamlet, having made a mess, "dies fairly well pleased with himself." Evaluate.

William Shakespeare (English. 1564–1616)

The Tragedy of Macbeth*

[Dramatis Personae

Duncan, King of Scotland

Malcolm
Donalbain } his sons

Macbeth
Banquo
Macduff
Lennox
Ross } noblemen of Scotland
Menteith
Angus
Caithness

Fleance, son to Banquo

Siward, Earl of Northumberland, general of the English forces

Young Siward, his son

Seyton, an officer attending on Macbeth

Son to Macduff

An English doctor

A Scottish doctor

A porter

An old man

Three murderers

Lady Macbeth

Lady Macduff

A gentlewoman, attending on Lady Macbeth

Hecate

Witches

Apparitions

Lords, officers, soldiers, attendants, and messengers

Scene: *Scotland; England]*

---

*This text of *Macbeth* is based on the First Folio edition of Shakespeare's plays (1623). Material enclosed in square brackets has been added by the editor of the present edition.

ACT I

Scene I. [*An open place.*]

Thunder and lightning. Enter Three Witches.

First Witch. When shall we three meet again?
  In thunder, lightning, or in rain?
Second Witch. When the hurlyburly's done,
  When the battle's lost and won.
Third Witch. That will be ere the set of sun.   5
First Witch. Where the place?
Second Witch.   Upon the hearth.
Third Witch. There to meet with Macbeth.
First Witch. I come, Graymalkin.°*
Second Witch. Paddock° calls.
Third Witch.   Anon!°
All. Fair is foul, and foul is fair.   10
  Hover through the fog and filthy air.

                                 Exeunt.

Scene II. [*A camp.*]

Alarum within.° Enter King [Duncan], Malcolm. Donalbain, Lennox, with Attendants, meeting a bleeding Captain.

King. What bloody man is that? He can report,
  As seemeth by his plight, of the revolt
  The newest state.
Malcolm.   This is the sergeant°
  Who like a good and hardy soldier fought
  'Gainst my captivity. Hail, brave friend!   5
  Say to the king the knowledge of the broil°
  As thou didst leave it.
Captain.   Doubtful it stood,
  As two spent swimmers that do cling together
  And choke their art.° The merciless Macdonwald —
  Worthy to be a rebel for to that   10

---

* The degree sign (°) indicates a footnote, which is keyed to the text by line number. Text references are printed in **boldface italic** type; the annotation follows in roman type.
I.i. [8] **Graymalkin** (the witch's attendant spirit, a gray cat) [9] **Paddock** toad [9] **Anon** at once   I.ii [s.d.] **Alarum within** trumpet call offstage [3] **sergeant** i.e., officer (he is called, perhaps with no inconsistency in Shakespeare's day, a captain in the s.d. and speech prefixes. **Sergeant** is trisyllabic) [6] **broil** quarrel [9] **choke their art** hamper each other's doings

The multiplying villainies of nature
Do swarm upon him — from the Western Isles°
Of kerns and gallowglasses° is supplied;
And Fortune, on his damnèd quarrel° smiling,
Showed like a rebel's whore:° but all's too weak: *15*
For brave Macbeth — well he deserves that name —
Disdaining Fortune, with his brandished steel,
Which smoked with bloody execution,
Like valor's minion° carved out his passage
Till he faced the slave;   *20*
Which nev'r shook hands, nor bade farewell to him,
Till he unseamed him from the nave to th' chops,°
And fixed his head upon our battlements.

King. O valiant cousin! Worthy gentleman!

Captain. As whence the sun 'gins his reflection°   *25*
Shipwracking storms and direful thunders break,
So from that spring whence comfort seemed to come
Discomfort swells. Mark, King of Scotland, mark:
No sooner justice had, with valor armed,
Compelled these skipping kerns to trust their heels   *30*
But the Norweyan lord, surveying vantage,°
With furbished arms and new supplies of men,
Began a fresh assault.

King.   Dismayed not this
Our captains, Macbeth and Banquo?

Captain.   Yes;
As sparrows eagles, or the hare the lion.   *35*
If I say sooth,° I must report they were
As cannons overcharged with double cracks;°
So they doubly redoubled strokes upon the foe.
Except° they meant to bathe in reeking wounds,
Or memorize another Golgotha,°   *40*
I cannot tell —
But I am faint; my gashes cry for help.

King. So well thy words become thee as thy wounds;
They smack of honor both. Go get him surgeons.

                                         [*Exit Captain, attended.*]

---

[12] ***Western Isles*** Hebrides   [13] ***Of kerns and gallowglasses***   with lightly armed Irish
foot soldiers and heavily armed ones   [14] ***damnèd quarrel*** accursed cause   [15] ***Showed
like a rebel's whore***   i.e., falsely appeared to favor Macdonwald   [19] ***minion*** (trisyllabic) favorite   [22] ***nave to th' chops*** navel to the jaws   [25] ***reflection***   (four
syllables; the ending — *ion* here and often elsewhere in the play — is disyllabic)
[31] ***surveying vantage*** seeing an opportunity   [36] ***sooth*** truth   [37] ***cracks*** explosives
[39] ***Except*** unless   [40] ***memorize another Golgotha***   make the place as memorable
as Golgotha, "the place of the skull"

Enter Ross and Angus.

Who comes here?
Malcolm.   The worthy Thane° of Ross.   *45*
Lennox. What a haste looks through his eyes! So should he look
   That seems to° speak things strange.
Ross.   God save the king!
King. Whence cam'st thou, worthy Thane?
Ross.   From Fife, great King;
   Where the Norweyan banners flout the sky
   And fan our people cold.   *50*
   Norway° himself, with terrible numbers,
   Assisted by that most disloyal traitor
   The Thane of Cawdor, began a dismal° conflict;
   Till that Bellona's bridegroom, lapped in proof,°
   Confronted him with self-comparisons,°   *55*
   Point against point, rebellious arm 'gainst arm,
   Curbing his lavish° spirit: and, to conclude,
   The victory fell on us.
King.   Great happiness!
Ross.   That now
   Sweno, the Norways' king, craves composition;°
   Nor would we deign him burial of his men   *60*
   Till he disbursèd, at Saint Colme's Inch,°
   Ten thousand dollars° to our general use.
King. No more that Thane of Cawdor shall deceive
   Our bosom interest:° go pronounce his present° death,
   And with his former title greet Macbeth.   *65*
Ross. I'll see it done.
King. What he hath lost, noble Macbeth hath won.
                                            Exeunt.

Scene III.   [*A heath.*]

Thunder. Enter the Three Witches.

First Witch. Where hast thou been, sister?
Second Witch. Killing swine.

---

[45] **Thane** (a Scottish title of nobility)   [47] **seems to** seems about to   [51] **Norway**
the King of Norway   [53] **dismal** threatening   [54] **Bellona's . . . proof** the mate of
the goddess of war, clan in tested (proved) armor   [55] **self-comparisons** counter-
movements   [57] **lavish** insolent   [59] **composition** terms of peace   [61] **Inch** island
[62] **dollars** (Spanish and Dutch currency)   [64] **Our bosom interest** my (plural of
royalty) heart's trust   [64] **present** immediate

Third Witch. Sister, where thou?
First Witch. A sailor's wife had chestnuts in her lap,
    And mounched, and mounched, and mounched.
        "Give me," quoth I.   5
        "Aroint thee,° witch!" the rump-fed ronyon° cries.
    Her husband's to Aleppo gone, master o' th' Tiger:
    But in a sieve I'll thither sail,
    And, like a rat without a tail,
    I'll do, I'll do, and I'll do.   10
Second Witch. I'll give thee a wind.
First Witch. Th' art kind.
Third Witch. And I another.
First Witch. I myself have all the other;
    And the very ports they blow,°   15
    All the quarters that they know
    I' th' shipman's card.°
    I'll drain him dry as hay:
    Sleep shall neither night nor day
    Hang upon his penthouse lid;°   20
    He shall live a man forbid:°
    Weary sev'nights nine times nine
    Shall he dwindle, peak,° and pine:
    Though his bark cannot be lost,
    Yet it shall be tempest-tossed.   25
    Look what I have.
Second Witch. Show me, show me.
First Witch. Here I have a pilot's thumb,
    Wracked as homeward he did come.

    Drum within.

Third Witch. A drum, a drum!   30
    Macbeth doth come.
All. The weïrd° sisters, hand in hand,
    Posters° of the sea and land,
    Thus do go about, about:
    Thrice to thine, and thrice to mine,   35
    And thrice again, to make up nine.
    Peace! The charm's wound up.

I.iii. ⁶ *Aroint thee* begone ⁶ *rump-fed ronyon* fat-rumped scabby creature ¹⁵ *ports they blow* harbors to which the winds blow (?) ¹⁷ *card* compass card ²⁰ *penthouse lid* eyelid (the figure is of a lean-to) ²¹ *forbid* cursed ²³ *peak* waste away ³² *weïrd* destiny-serving (?) ³³ *Posters* swift travelers

Enter Macbeth and Banquo.

Macbeth. So foul and fair a day I have not seen.
Banquo. How far is 't called to Forres? What are these
    So withered, and so wild in their attire,   *40*
    That look not like th' inhabitants o' th' earth,
    And yet are on 't? Live you, or are you aught
    That man may question?° You seem to understand me,
    By each at once her choppy° finger laying
    Upon her skinny lips. You should be women,   *45*
    And yet your beards forbid me to interpret
    That you are so.
Macbeth.   Speak, if you can: what are you?
First Witch. All hail, Macbeth! Hail to thee, Thane of Glamis!
Second Witch. All hail, Macbeth! Hail to thee, Thane of Cawdor!
Third Witch. All hail, Macbeth, that shalt be King hereafter! *50*
Banquo. Good sir, why do you start, and seem to fear
    Things that do sound so fair? I' th' name of truth,
    Are ye fantastical,° or that indeed
    Which outwardly ye show? My noble partner
    You greet with present grace° and great prediction   *55*
    Of noble having° and of royal hope,
    That he seems rapt withal:° to me you speak not.
    If you can look into the seeds of time,
    And say which grain will grow and which will not,
    Speak then to me, who neither beg nor fear   *60*
    Your favors nor your hate.
First Witch. Hail!
Second Witch. Hail!
Third Witch. Hail!
First Witch. Lesser than Macbeth, and greater.   *65*
Second Witch. Not so happy,° yet much happier.
Third Witch. Thou shalt get° kings, though thou be none.
    So all hail, Macbeth and Banquo!
First Witch. Banquo and Macbeth, all hail!
Macbeth. Stay, you imperfect° speakers, tell me more: *70*
    By Sinel's° death I know I am Thane of Glamis;
    But how of Cawdor? The Thane of Cawdor lives,
    A prosperous gentleman; and to be King
    Stands not within the prospect of belief,

---

[43] **question** talk to [44] **choppy** chapped [53] **fantastical** imaginary [55] **grace** honor
[56] **having** possession [57] **rapt withal** entranced by it [66] **happy** fortunate [66] **get**
beget [70] **imperfect** incomplete [71] **Sinel** (Macbeth's father)

No more than to be Cawdor. Say from whence   75
You owe° this strange intelligence?° Or why
Upon this blasted heath you stop our way
With such prophetic greeting? Speak, I charge you.

                                          Witches vanish.
Banquo. The earth hath bubbles as the water has,
And these are of them. Whither are they vanished?   80
Macbeth. Into the air, and what seemed corporal° melted
As breath into the wind. Would they had stayed!
Banquo. Were such things here as we do speak about?
Or have we eaten on the insane° root
That takes the reason prisoner?   85
Macbeth. Your children shall be kings.
Banquo.   You shall be King.
Macbeth. And Thane of Cawdor too. Went it not so?
Banquo. To th' selfsame tune and words. Who's here?

    Enter Ross and Angus.

Ross. The King hath happily received, Macbeth,
The news of thy success; and when he reads°   90
Thy personal venture in the rebels' fight,
His wonders and his praises do contend
Which should be thine or his.° Silenced with that,
In viewing o'er the rest o' th' selfsame day,
He finds thee in the stout Norweyan ranks,   95
Nothing afeard of what thyself didst make,
Strange images of death. As thick as tale
Came post with post,° and every one did bear
Thy praises in his kingdom's great defense,
And poured them down before him.
Angus.   We are sent   100
To give thee, from our royal master, thanks;
Only to herald thee into his sight,
Not pay thee.
Ross. And for an earnest° of a greater honor,
He bade me, from him, call thee Thane of Cawdor;   105
In which addition,° hail, most worthy Thane!
For it is thine.

---

[76] **owe** own, have [76] **intelligence** information [81] **corporal** corporeal [84] **insane** insanity-producing [90] **reads** considers [92–93] **His wonders . . . his** i.e., Duncan's speechless admiration, appropriate to him, contends with his desire to praise you (?) [97–98] **As thick . . . post** as fast as could be counted came messenger after messenger [104] **earnest** pledge [106] **addition** title

Banquo.   What, can the devil speak true?
Macbeth. The Thane of Cawdor lives: why do you dress me
    In borrowed robes?
Angus.   Who was the thane lives yet,
    But under heavy judgment bears that life   *110*
    Which he deserves to lose. Whether he was combined°
    With those of Norway, or did line° the rebel
    With hidden help and vantage,° or that with both
    He labored in his country's wrack,° I know not;
    But treasons capital, confessed and proved,   *115*
    Have overthrown him.
Macbeth.   [*Aside*] Glamis, and Thane of Cawdor:
    The greatest is behind.° [*To Ross and Angus*] Thanks for your
        pains.
    [*Aside to Banquo*] Do you not hope your children shall be
        kings,
    When those that gave the Thane of Cawdor to me
    Promised no less to them?
Banquo. [*Aside to Macbeth*] That, trusted home,°   *120*
    Might yet enkindle you unto the crown,
    Besides the Thane of Cawdor. But 'tis strange:
    And oftentimes, to win us to our harm,
    The instruments of darkness tell us truths,
    Win us with honest trifles, to betray's   *125*
    In deepest consequence.°
    Cousins,° a word, I pray you.
Macbeth.   [*Aside*] Two truths are told,
    As happy prologues to the swelling° act
    Of the imperial theme. — I thank you, gentlemen. —
    [*Aside*] This supernatural soliciting°   *130*
    Cannot be ill, cannot be good. If ill,
    Why hath it given me earnest of success,
    Commencing in a truth? I am Thane of Cawdor:
    If good, why do I yield to that suggestion
    Whose horrid image doth unfix my hair   *135*
    And make my seated° heart knock at my ribs,
    Against the use of nature?° Present fears
    Are less than horrible imaginings.

---

¹¹¹ *combined* allied ¹¹² *line* support ¹¹³ *vantage* opportunity ¹¹⁴ *wrack* ruin
¹¹⁷ *behind* i.e., to follow ¹²⁰ *home* all the way ¹²⁶ *In deepest consequence* in
the most significant sequel ¹²⁷ *Cousins* i.e., fellow noblemen ¹²⁸ *swelling* stately
¹³⁰ *soliciting* inviting ¹³⁶ *seated* fixed ¹³⁷ *Against the use of nature* contrary
to my natural way

My thought, whose murder yet is but fantastical,°
Shakes so my single° state of man that function   *140*
Is smothered in surmise, and nothing is
But what is not.
Banquo.   Look, how our partner's rapt.
Macbeth. [*Aside*] If chance will have me King, why, chance may
    crown me,
  Without my stir.
Banquo.   New honors come upon him,
  Like our strange° garments, cleave not to their mold   *145*
  But with the aid of use.
Macbeth.   [*Aside*] Come what come may,
  Time and the hour runs through the roughest day.
Banquo. Worthy Macbeth, we stay upon your leisure.°
Macbeth. Give me your favor.° My dull brain was wrought
  With things forgotten. Kind gentlemen, your pains   *150*
  Are registered where every day I turn
  The leaf to read them. Let us toward the King.
  [*Aside to Banquo*] Think upon what hath chanced, and at
    more time,
  The interim having weighed it,° let us speak
  Our free hearts° each to other.
Banquo.   Very gladly.   *155*
Macbeth. Till then, enough. Come, friends.

                                Exeunt.

Scene IV. [*Forres. The palace.*]

Flourish.° Enter King [*Duncan*], *Lennox, Malcolm, Donalbain,
and Attendants.*

King. Is execution done on Cawdor? Are not
  Those in commission° yet returned?
Malcolm.   My liege,
  They are not yet come back. But I have spoke
  With one that saw him die, who did report
  That very frankly he confessed his treasons,   *5*
  Implored your Highness' pardon and set forth

---

[139] *fantastical* imaginary [140] *single* unaided, weak (or "entire"?) [145] *strange* new
[148] *stay upon your leisure* await your convenience [149] *favor* pardon [154] *The
interim having weighed it* i.e., when we have had time to think [155] *Our free
hearts* our minds freely I.iv.[s.d.] *Flourish* fanfare [2] *in commission* i.e., commissioned to oversee the execution

A deep repentance: nothing in his life
Became him like the leaving it. He died
As one that had been studied° in his death,
To throw away the dearest thing he owed°   10
As 'twere a careless° trifle.
King.   There's no art
To find the mind's construction in the face:
He was a gentleman on whom I built
An absolute trust.

Enter Macbeth, Banquo, Ross, and Angus.

                    O worthiest cousin!
The sin of my ingratitude even now   15
Was heavy on me: thou art so far before,
That swiftest wing of recompense is slow
To overtake thee. Would thou hadst less deserved,
That the proportion° both of thanks and payment
Might have been mine! Only I have left to say,   20
More is thy due than more than all can pay.
Macbeth. The service and the loyalty I owe,
In doing it, pays itself.° Your Highness' part
Is to receive our duties: and our duties
Are to your throne and state children and servants;   25
Which do but what they should, by doing every thing
Safe toward° your love and honor.
King.   Welcome hither.
I have begun to plant thee, and will labor
To make thee full of growing. Noble Banquo,
That hast no less deserved, nor must be known   30
No less to have done so, let me enfold thee
And hold thee to my heart.
Banquo.   There if I grow,
The harvest is your own.
King.   My plenteous joys,
Wanton° in fullness, seek to hide themselves
In drops of sorrow. Sons, kinsmen, thanes,   35
And you whose places are the nearest, know,
We will establish our estate° upon
Our eldest, Malcolm, whom we name hereafter
The Prince of Cumberland: which honor must

---

⁹ *studied* rehearsed ¹⁰ *owed* owned ¹¹ *careless* uncared-for ¹⁹ *proportion* preponderance ²³ *pays itself* is its own reward ²⁷ *Safe toward* safeguarding (?) ³⁴ *Wanton* unrestrained ³⁷ *establish our estate* settle the succession

Not unaccompanied invest him only,   *40*
But signs of nobleness, like stars, shall shine
On all deservers. From hence to Inverness,
And bind us further to you.
Macbeth. The rest is labor, which is not used for you.°
I'll be myself the harbinger, and make joyful   *45*
The hearing of my wife with your approach;
So, humbly take my leave.
King.   My worthy Cawdor!
Macbeth. [*Aside*] The Prince of Cumberland! That is a step
On which I must fall down, or else o'erleap,
For in my way it lies. Stars, hide your fires;   *50*
Let not light see my black and deep desires:
The eye wink at the hand;° yet let that be
Which the eye fears, when it is done, to see.
                                                        Exit.
King. True, worthy Banquo; he is full so valiant,
And in his commendations° I am fed;   *55*
It is a banquet to me. Let's after him,
Whose care is gone before to bid us welcome.
It is a peerless kinsman.   *Flourish. Exeunt.*

Scene V. [*Inverness. Macbeth's castle.*]

Enter Macbeth's wife, alone, with a letter.

Lady Macbeth. [*Reads*] "They met me in the day of success;
and I have learned by the perfect'st report they have
more in them than mortal knowledge. When I burned
in desire to question them further, they made themselves
air, into which they vanished. Whiles I stood rapt in   *5*
the wonder of it, came missives° from the King, who
all-hailed me 'Thane of Cawdor'; by which title, before,
these weïrd sisters saluted me, and referred me to the
coming on of time, with 'Hail, King that shalt be!' This
have I thought good to deliver thee,° my dearest partner   *10*
of greatness, that thou mightst not lose the dues of
rejoicing, by being ignorant of what greatness is promised
thee. Lay it to thy heart, and farewell."

---

44 *The rest . . . you* i.e., repose is laborious when not employed for you   **52 *wink at the hand*** i.e., be blind to the hand's deed   **55 *his commendations*** commendations of him   I.v.   **6 *missives*** messengers   **10 *deliver thee*** report to you

Glamis thou art, and Cawdor, and shalt be
What thou art promised. Yet do I fear thy nature;   15
It is too full o' th' milk of human kindness°
To catch the nearest way. Thou wouldst be great,
Art not without ambition, but without
The illness° should attend it. What thou wouldst highly,
That wouldst thou holily; wouldst not play false,   20
And yet wouldst wrongly win. Thou'dst have, great
    Glamis,
That which cries "Thus thou must do" if thou have
    it;
And that which rather thou dost fear to do
Than wishest should be undone. Hie thee higher,
That I may pour my spirits in thine ear,   25
And chastise with the valor of my tongue
All that impedes thee from the golden round°
Which fate and metaphysical° aid doth seem
To have thee crowned withal. °

Enter Messenger.

                    What is your tidings?
Messenger. The King comes here tonight.
Lady Macbeth.   Thou'rt mad to say it!   30
Is not thy master with him, who, were 't so,
Would have informed for preparation?
Messenger. So please you, it is true. Our thane is coming.
One of my fellows had the speed of him,°
Who, almost dead for breath, had scarcely more   35
Than would make up his message.
Lady Macbeth.   Give him tending;
He brings great news.   *Exit Messenger.*
                    The raven himself is hoarse
That croaks the fatal entrance of Duncan
Under my battlements. Come, you spirits
That tend on mortal° thoughts, unsex me here,   40
And fill me, from the crown to the toe, top-full
Of direst cruelty! Make thick my blood,
Stop up th' access and passage to remorse,°
That no compunctious visitings of nature°
Shake my fell° purpose, nor keep peace between   45
Th' effect° and it! Come to my woman's breasts,

---

[16] *milk of human kindness* i.e., gentle quality of human nature   [19] *illness* wickedness
[27] *round* crown   [28] *metaphysical* supernatural   [29] *withal* with   [34] *had the speed
of him* outdistanced him   [40] *mortal* deadly   [43] *remorse* compassion
[44] *compunctious visitings of nature* natural feelings of compassion

And take my milk for° gall, you murd'ring ministers,°
Wherever in your sightless° substances
You wait on° nature's mischief! Come, thick night,
And pall° thee in the dunnest° smoke of hell,   *50*
That my keen knife see not the wound it makes,
Nor heaven peep through the blanket of the dark,
To cry, "Hold, hold!"

Enter Macbeth.

                              Great Glamis! Worthy Cawdor!
Greater than both, by the all-hail hereafter!°
Thy letters have transported me beyond   *55*
This ignorant° present, and I feel now
The future in the instant.°
Macbeth.   My dearest love,
Duncan comes here tonight.
Lady Macbeth.   And when goes hence?
Macbeth. Tomorrow, as he purposes.
Lady Macbeth.   O, never
Shall sun that morrow see!   *60*
Your face, my Thane, is as a book where men
May read strange matters. To beguile the time,°
Look like the time; bear welcome in your eye,
Your hand, your tongue: look like th' innocent flower,
But be the serpent under 't. He that's coming   *65*
Must be provided for: and you shall put
This night's great business into my dispatch;°
Which shall to all our nights and days to come
Give solely sovereign sway and masterdom.
Macbeth. We will speak further.
Lady Macbeth.   Only look up clear.°   *70*
To alter favor ever is to fear.°
Leave all the rest to me.   *Exeunt.*

Scene VI. [*Before Macbeth's castle.*]

Hautboys° and torches. Enter King [Duncan], Malcolm. Donalbain,
Banquo, Lennox, Macduff, Ross, Angus, and Attendants.

---

⁴⁵ *fell* savage ⁴⁶ *effect* fulfillment ⁴⁷ *for* in exchange for ⁴⁷ *ministers* agents
⁴⁸ *sightless* invisible ⁴⁹ *wait on* assist ⁵⁰ *pall* enshroud ⁵⁰ *dunnest* darkest
⁵⁴ *all-hail hereafter* the third all-hail (?) the all-hail of the future(?) ⁵⁶ *ignorant*
unknowing ⁵⁷ *instant* present ⁶² *To beguile the time* i.e., to deceive people of
the day ⁶⁷ *dispatch* management ⁷⁰ *look up clear* appear undisturbed ⁷¹ *To*
alter . . . fear to show a disturbed face is dangerous I.v. ˢ·ᵈ· *Hautboys* oboes

King. This castle hath a pleasant seat;° the air
    Nimbly and sweetly recommends itself
    Unto our gentle° senses.
Banquo.   This guest of summer,
    The temple-haunting martlet,° does approve°
    By his loved mansionry° that the heaven's breath   5
    Smells wooingly here. No jutty,° frieze,
    Buttress, nor coign of vantage,° but this bird
    Hath made his pendent bed and procreant° cradle.
    Where they most breed and haunt,° I have observed
    The air is delicate.

Enter Lady [Macbeth].

King.   See, see, our honored hostess!   10
    The love that follows us sometime is our trouble,
    Which still we thank as love.° Herein I teach you
    How you shall bid God 'ield° for us for your pains
    And thank us for your trouble.
Lady Macbeth.   All our service
    In every point twice done, and then done double,   15
    Were poor and single business° to contend
    Against those honors deep and broad wherewith
    Your Majesty loads our house: for those of old,
    And the late dignities heaped up to them,
    We rest your hermits.°
King.   Where's the Thane of Cawdor?   20
    We coursed° him at the heels, and had a purpose
    To be his purveyor:° but he rides well,
    And his great love, sharp as his spur, hath holp° him
    To his home before us. Fair and noble hostess,
    We are your guest tonight.
Lady Macbeth.   Your servants ever   25
    Have theirs, themselves, and what is theirs, in compt,°
    To make their audit at your Highness' pleasure,
    Still° to return to your own.
King.   Give me your hand.

---

[1] **seat** site   [3] **gentle** soothed   [4] **temple-haunting martlet** martin (swift) nesting
in churches   [4] **approve** prove   [5] **mansionry** nests   [6] **jutty** projection   [7] **coign
of vantage** advantageous corner   [8] **procreant** breeding   [9] **haunt** visit   [11-12] **The
love . . . love** the love offered me sometimes inconveniences me, but still I value
it as love   [13] **'ield** reward   [16] **single business** feeble service   [20] **your hermits**
dependents bound to pray for you   [21] **coursed** pursued   [22] **purveyor** advance-
supply officer   [23] **holp** helped   [26] **Have theirs . . . compt** have their dependents,
themselves, and their possessions in trust   [28] **Still** always

Conduct me to mine host: we love him highly,
And shall continue our graces towards him.   *30*
By your leave, hostess.   *Exeunt.*

Scene VII. [*Macbeth's castle.*]

*Hautboys. Torches. Enter a Sewer,° and diverse Servants with
dishes and service over the stage. Then enter Macbeth.*

Macbeth. If it were done° when 'tis done, then 'twere well
  It were done quickly. If th' assassination
  Could trammel up° the consequence, and catch,
  With his surcease,° success;° that but this blow
  Might be the be-all and the end-all — here,   *5*
  But here, upon this bank and shoal of time,
  We'd jump° the life to come. But in these cases
  We still° have judgment here; that we but teach
  Bloody instructions, which, being taught, return
  To plague th' inventor: this even-handed° justice   *10*
  Commends° th' ingredients of our poisoned chalice
  To our own lips. He's here in double trust:
  First, as I am his kinsman and his subject,
  Strong both against the deed; then, as his host,
  Who should against his murderer shut the door,   *15*
  Not bear the knife myself. Besides, this Duncan
  Hath borne his faculties° so meek, hath been
  So clear° in his great office, that his virtues
  Will plead like angels trumpet-tongued against
  The deep damnation of his taking-off;   *20*
  And pity, like a naked newborn babe,
  Striding° the blast, or heaven's cherubin horsed
  Upon the sightless couriers° of the air,
  Shall blow the horrid deed in every eye,
  That° tears shall drown the wind. I have no spur   *25*
  To prick the sides of my intent, but only
  Vaulting ambition, which o'erleaps itself
  And falls on th' other —

Enter Lady [Macbeth].

I.vii. ˢ·ᵈ· **Sewer** chief butler [1] **done** over and done with [3] **trammel up** catch
in a net [4] **his surcease** Duncan's death (?) the consequence's cessation (?) [4] **success**
what follows [7] **jump** risk [8] **still** always [10] **even-handed** impartial [11] **Commends**
offers [17] **faculties** powers [18] **clear** spotless [22] **Striding** bestriding [23] **sightless**
couriers invisible coursers (i.e., the winds) [25] **That** so that

How now! What news?

Lady Macbeth. He has almost supped. Why have you left the chamber?

Macbeth. Hath he asked for me?

Lady Macbeth.   Know you not he has?   30

Macbeth. We will proceed no further in this business:

He hath honored me of late, and I have bought°
Golden opinions from all sorts of people,
Which would be worn now in their newest gloss,
Not cast aside so soon.

Lady Macbeth.   Was the hope drunk   35
Wherein you dressed yourself? Hath it slept since?
And wakes it now, to look so green° and pale
At what it did so freely? From this time
Such I account thy love. Art thou afeard
To be the same in thine own act and valor   40
As thou art in desire? Wouldst thou have that
Which thou esteem'st the ornament of life,
And live a coward in thine own esteem,
Letting "I dare not" wait upon° "I would,"
Like the poor cat° i' th' adage?

Macbeth.   Prithee, peace!   45
I dare do all that may become a man;
Who dares do more is none.

Lady Macbeth.   What beast was 't then
That made you break° this enterprise to me?
When you durst do it, then you were a man;
And to be more than what you were, you would   50
Be so much more the man. Nor time nor place
Did then adhere,° and yet you would make both.
They have made themselves, and that their° fitness now
Does unmake you. I have given suck, and know
How tender 'tis to love the babe that milks me: 55
I would, while it was smiling in my face,
Have plucked my nipple from his boneless gums,
And dashed the brains out, had I so sworn as you
Have done to this.

Macbeth. If we should fail?

Lady Macbeth.   We fail?
But° screw your courage to the sticking-place,°   60
And we'll not fail. When Duncan is asleep —

---

³² **bought** acquired ³⁷ **green** sickly ⁴⁴ **wait upon** follow ⁴⁵ **cat** (who wants fish but fears to wet its paws) ⁴⁸ **break** broach ⁵² **adhere** suit ⁵³ **that their** their very ⁶⁰ **But** only ⁶⁰ **sticking place** notch (holding the bowstring of a taut crossbow)

Whereto the rather shall his day's hard journey
Soundly invite him — his two chamberlains
Will I with wine and wassail° so convince,°
That memory, the warder° of the brain,   *65*
Shall be a fume, and the receipt of reason
A limbec only:° when in swinish sleep
Their drenchèd natures lies° as in a death,
What cannot you and I perform upon
Th' unguarded Duncan, what not put upon   *70*
His spongy° officers, who shall bear the guilt
Of our great quell?°
Macbeth.   Bring forth men-children only;
For thy undaunted mettle° should compose
Nothing but males. Will it not be received,
When we have marked with blood those sleepy two   *75*
Of his own chamber, and used their very daggers,
That they have done 't?
Lady Macbeth.   Who dares receive it other,°
As we shall make our griefs and clamor roar
Upon his death?
Macbeth.   I am settled, and bend up
Each corporal agent to this terrible feat.   *80*
Away, and mock the time° with fairest show:
False face must hide what the false heart doth know.

                                              Exeunt.

ACT II

Scene I. [*Inverness. Court of Macbeth's castle.*]

Enter Banquo, and Fleance, with a torch before him.

Banquo. How goes the night, boy?
Fleance. The moon is down; I have not heard the clock.
Banquo. And she goes down at twelve.
Fleance.   I take't, 'tis later, sir.
Banquo. Hold, take my sword. There's husbandry° in heaven.

---

[64] **wassail** carousing [64] **convince** overpower [65] **warder** guard [66-67] **receipt . . .
only** i.e., the receptacle ("receipt"), which should collect the distillate of thought
— reason — will be a mere vessel ("limbeck") of distilled liquids [68] **lies** lie
[71] **spongy** sodden [72] **quell** killing [73] **mettle** substance [77] **other** otherwise
[81] **mock the time** beguile the world II.i. [4] **husbandry** frugality

Their candles are all out. Take thee that too.   *5*
A heavy summons° lies like lead upon me,
And yet I would not sleep. Merciful powers,
Restrain in me the cursèd thoughts that nature
Gives way to in repose!

Enter Macbeth, and a Servant with a torch.

                            Give me my sword!
Who's there?   *10*
Macbeth. A friend.
Banquo. What, sir, not yet at rest? The King's a-bed:
     He hath been in unusual pleasure, and
     Sent forth great largess to your offices:°
     This diamond he greets your wife withal,   *15*
     By the name of most kind hostess; and shut up°
     In measureless content.
Macbeth.   Being unprepared,
     Our will became the servant to defect,°
     Which else should free have wrought.
Banquo.   All's well.
     I dreamt last night of the three weïrd sisters: *20*
     To you they have showed some truth.
Macbeth.   I think not of them.
     Yet, when we can entreat an hour to serve,
     We would spend it in some words upon that business,
     If you would grant the time.
Banquo.   At your kind'st leisure.
Macbeth. If you shall cleave to my consent, when 'tis,° *25*
     It shall make honor for you.
Banquo.   So° I lose none
     In seeking to augment it, but still keep
     My bosom franchised° and allegiance clear,°
     I shall be counseled.
Macbeth.   Good repose the while!
Banquo. Thanks, sir. The like to you!
                         Exit Banquo [with Fleance].   *30*
Macbeth. Go bid thy mistress, when my drink is ready,

---

⁶ *summons* call (to sleep)   ¹⁴ *largess to your offices* gifts to your servant's quarters
¹⁶ *shut up* concluded   ¹⁸ *Our . . . defect* our good will was hampered by our
deficient preparations   ²⁵ *cleave . . . 'tis* join my cause, when the time comes
²⁶ *So* provided that   ²⁸ *franchised* free (from guilt)   ²⁸ *clear* spotless

She strike upon the bell. Get thee to bed.

Exit [*Servant*].

Is this a dagger which I see before me,
The handle toward my hand? Come, let me clutch thee.
I have thee not, and yet I see thee still.   *35*
Art thou not, fatal vision, sensible°
To feeling as to sight, or art thou but
A dagger of the mind, a false creation,
Proceeding from the heat-oppressèd brain?
I see thee yet, in form as palpable   *40*
As this which now I draw.
Thou marshal'st me the way that I was going;
And such an instrument I was to use.
Mine eyes are made the fools o' th' other senses,
Or else worth all the rest. I see thee still;   *45*
And on thy blade and dudgeon° gouts° of blood,
Which was not so before. There's no such thing.
It is the bloody business which informs°
Thus to mine eyes. Now o'er the one half-world
Nature seems dead, and wicked dreams abuse°   *50*
The curtained sleep; witchcraft celebrates
Pale Hecate's offerings;° and withered murder,
Alarumed° by his sentinel, the wolf,
Whose howl's his watch, thus with his stealthy pace,
With Tarquin's° ravishing strides, towards his design   *55*
Moves like a ghost. Thou sure and firm-set earth,
Hear not my steps, which way they walk, for fear
Thy very stones prate of my whereabout,
And take the present horror from the time,
Which now suits with it.° Whiles I threat, he lives: *60*
Words to the heat of deeds too cold breath lives.

A bell rings.

I go, and it is done: the bell invites me.
Hear it not, Duncan, for it is a knell
That summons thee to heaven, or to hell.

Exit.

---

[36] ***sensible*** perceptible   [46] ***dudgeon*** wooden hilt   [46] ***gouts*** large drops   [48] ***informs*** gives shape (?)   [50] ***abuse*** deceive   [52] ***Hecate's offerings*** offerings to Hecate (goddess of sorcery)   [53] ***Alarumed*** called to action   [55] ***Tarquin*** (Roman tyrant who ravished Lucrece)   [59–60] ***take . . . it*** remove (by noise) the horrible silence attendant on this moment and suitable to it (?)

Scene II. [*Macbeth's Castle.*]

Enter Lady [*Macbeth*].

Lady Macbeth. That which hath made them drunk hath made me
    bold;
  What hath quenched them hath given me fire. Hark! Peace!
  It was the owl that shrieked, the fatal bellman,
  Which gives the stern'st good-night.° He is about it.
  The doors are open, and the surfeited grooms   5
  Do mock their charge with snores. I have drugged
    their possets,°
  That death and nature° do contend about them,
  Whether they live or die.
Macbeth.   [*Within*] Who's there? What, ho?
Lady Macbeth. Alack, I am afraid they have awaked
  And 'tis not done! Th' attempt and not the deed   10
  Confounds° us. Hark! I laid their daggers ready;
  He could not miss 'em. Had he not resembled
  My father as he slept, I had done't.

Enter Macbeth.

                        My husband!

Macbeth. I have done the deed. Didst thou not hear a noise?
Lady Macbeth. I heard the owl scream and the crickets cry.   15
  Did not you speak?
Macbeth.   When?
Lady Macbeth.   Now.
Macbeth.   As I descended?
Lady Macbeth. Ay.
Macbeth. Hark!
  Who lies i' th' second chamber?
Lady Macbeth.   Donalbain.
Macbeth. This is a sorry° sight.   20
Lady Macbeth. A foolish thought, to say a sorry sight.
Macbeth. There's one did laugh in 's sleep, and one cried "Murder!"
  That they did wake each other. I stood and heard them.
  But they did say their prayers, and addressed them
  Again to sleep.

II.ii [3-4] ***bellman . . . good-night*** i.e., the owl's call, portending death, is like the
town crier's call to a condemned man [6] ***possets*** (bedtime drinks) [7] ***nature*** natural
vitality [11] ***Confounds*** ruins [20] ***sorry*** miserable

Lady Macbeth. There are two lodged together.   25
Macbeth. One cried "God bless us!" and "Amen" the other,
    As they had seen me with these hangman's° hands:
    List'ning their fear, I could not say "Amen,"
    When they did say "God bless us!"
Lady Macbeth.   Consider it not so deeply.
Macbeth. But wherefore could not I pronounce "Amen"?   30
    I had most need of blessing, and "Amen"
    Stuck in my throat.
Lady Macbeth.   These deeds must not be thought
    After these ways; so, it will make us mad.
Macbeth. Methought I heard a voice cry "Sleep no more!
    Macbeth does murder sleep" — the innocent sleep,   35
    Sleep that knits up the raveled sleave° of care,
    The death of each day's life, sore labor's bath,
    Balm of hurt minds, great nature's second course,°
    Chief nourisher in life's feast —
Lady Macbeth.   What do you mean?
Macbeth. Still it cried "Sleep no more!" to all the house: 40
    "Glamis hath murdered sleep, and therefore Cawdor
    Shall sleep no more: Macbeth shall sleep no more."
Lady Macbeth. Who was it that thus cried? Why, worthy Thane,
    You do unbend° your noble strength, to think
    So brainsickly of things. Go get some water,   45
    And wash this filthy witness° from your hand.
    Why did you bring these daggers from the place?
    They must lie there: go carry them, and smear
    The sleepy grooms with blood.
Macbeth.   I'll go no more.
    I am afraid to think what I have done;   50
    Look on 't again I dare not.
Lady Macbeth.   Infirm of purpose!
    Give me the daggers. The sleeping and the dead
    Are but as pictures. 'Tis the eye of childhood
    That fears a painted° devil. If he do bleed,
    I'll gild° the faces of the grooms withal,   55
    For it must seem their guilt.
                     Exit. Knock within.

---

[27] **hangman's** executioner's (i.e., bloody)   [36] **knits up the raveled sleave** straightens
out the tangled skein   [38] **second course** i.e., sleep (the less substantial first course
is food)   [44] **unbend** relax   [46] **witness** evidence   [54] **painted** depicted   [55] **gild** paint

Macbeth.   Whence is that knocking?
How is 't with me, when every noise appalls me?
What hands are here? Ha! They pluck out mine eyes!
Will all great Neptune's ocean wash this blood
Clean from my hand? No; this my hand will rather   60
The multitudinous seas incarnadine,°
Making the green one red.°

Enter Lady [Macbeth].

Lady Macbeth. My hands are of your color, but I shame
To wear a heart so white. (*Knock.*) I hear a knocking
At the south entry. Retire we to our chamber.   65
A little water clears us of this deed:
How easy is it then! Your constancy
Hath left you unattended.° (*Knock.*) Hark! more knocking.
Get on your nightgown,° lest occasion call us
And show us to be watchers.° Be not lost   70
So poorly° in your thoughts.
Macbeth. To know my deed, 'twere best not know myself. (*Knock.*)
Wake Duncan with thy knocking! I would thou couldst!

                                              Exeunt.

Scene III. [*Macbeth's Castle.*]

Enter a Porter. Knocking within.

Porter. Here's a knocking indeed! If a man were porter of
hell gate, he should have old° turning the key. (*Knock.*)
Knock, knock, knock! Who's there, i' th' name of Beel-
zebub? Here's a farmer that hanged himself on th' expectation of plenty.° Come in time! Have napkins enow°   5
about you; here you'll sweat for 't. (*Knock.*) Knock,
knock! Who's there, in th' other devil's name? Faith,
here's an equivocator,° that could swear in both the
scales against either scale; who committed treason enough

---

⁶¹ *incarnadine* redden   ⁶² *the green one red*   (perhaps "the green one" means "the
ocean," but perhaps "one" here means "totally," "uniformly")   ⁶⁷⁻⁶⁸ *Your . . .
unattended*   your firmness has deserted you   ⁶⁹ *nightgown*   dressing-gown
⁷⁰ *watchers* i.e., up late   ⁷¹ *poorly* weakly   II.iii.   ² *should have old*   would certainly
have plenty of   ⁴⁻⁵ *farmer . . . plenty*   (the farmer hoarded so he could later
sell high, but when it looked as though there would be a crop surplus he hanged
himself)   ⁵ *enow*   enough   ⁸ *equivocator*   i.e., Jesuit (who allegedly employed
deceptive speech to further God's ends)

for God's sake, yet could not equivocate to heaven. O,   *10*
come in, equivocator. (*Knock.*) Knock, knock, knock!
Who's there? Faith, here's an English tailor come hither
for stealing out of a French hose:° come in, tailor. Here
you may roast your goose.° (*Knock.*) Knock, knock;
never at quiet! What are you? But this place is too cold   *15*
for hell. I'll devil porter it no further. I had thought
to have let in some of all professions that go the primrose
way to th' everlasting bonfire. (*Knock.*) Anon, anon!
[*Opens an entrance.*] I pray you, remember the porter.

Enter Macduff and Lennox.

Macduff. Was it so late, friend, ere you went to bed,   *20*
   That you do lie so late?
Porter. Faith, sir, we were carousing till the second cock:°
   and drink, sir, is a great provoker of three things.
Macduff. What three things does drink especially provoke?
Porter. Marry, sir, nose-painting, sleep, and urine. Lechery,   *25*
   sir, it provokes and unprovokes; it provokes the desire,
   but it takes away the performance: therefore much drink
   may be said to be an equivocator with lechery: it makes
   him and it mars him; it sets him on and it takes him
   off; it persuades him and disheartens him; makes him   *30*
   stand to and not stand to; in conclusion, equivocates
   him in a sleep, and giving him the lie, leaves
   him.
Macduff. I believe drink gave thee the lie° last night.
Porter. That it did, sir, i' the very throat on me: but I re-   *35*
   quited him for his lie, and, I think, being too strong
   for him, though he took up my legs sometime, yet I
   make a shift to cast° him.
Macduff. Is thy master stirring?

Enter Macbeth.

   Our knocking has awaked him; here he comes.   *40*
Lennox. Good morrow, noble sir.
Macbeth.   Good morrow, both.
Macduff. Is the king stirring, worthy Thane?
Macbeth.   Not yet.

---

[13] **French hose** tight-fitting hose   [14] **goose** pressing iron   [22] **second cock** (about
3 A.M.)   [34] **gave thee the lie** called you a liar (with a pun on "stretched you out")
[38] **cast** (with a pun on "cast," meaning "vomit")

Macduff. He did command me to call timely° on him:
    I have almost slipped° the hour.
Macbeth.   I'll bring you to him.
Macduff. I know this is a joyful trouble to you;   **45**
    But yet 'tis one.
Macbeth. The labor we delight in physics pain.°
    This is the door.
Macduff.   I'll make so bold to call,
    For 'tis my limited service.°
                                Exit Macduff.
Lennox. Goes the king hence today?
Macbeth.   He does: he did appoint so. **50**
Lennox. The night has been unruly. Where we lay,
    Our chimneys were blown down, and, as they say,
    Lamentings heard i' th' air, strange screams of death,
    And prophesying with accents terrible
    Of dire combustion° and confused events   **55**
    New hatched to th' woeful time: the obscure bird°
    Clamored the livelong night. Some say, the earth
    Was feverous and did shake.
Macbeth.   'Twas a rough night.
Lennox. My young remembrance cannot parallel
    A fellow to it.   **60**

    Enter Macduff.

Macduff. O horror, horror, horror! Tongue nor heart
    Cannot conceive nor name thee.
Macbeth and Lennox.   What's the matter?
Macduff. Confusion° now hath made his masterpiece.
    Most sacrilegious murder hath broke ope
    The Lord's anointed temple, and stole thence   **65**
    The life o' th' building.
Macbeth.   What is 't you say? The life?
Lennox. Mean you his Majesty?
Macduff. Approach the chamber, and destroy your sight
    With a new Gorgon:° do not bid me speak;
    See, and then speak yourselves. Awake, awake!   **70**
                      Exeunt Macbeth and Lennox.

---

[43] *timely* early   [44] *slipped* let slip   [47] *The labor . . . pain* labor that gives us pleasure cures discomfort   [49] *limited service* appointed duty   [55] *combustion* tumult [56] *obscure bird* bird of darkness, i.e., the owl   [63] *Confusion* destruction   [69] *Gorgon* (creature capable of turning beholders to stone)

Ring the alarum bell. Murder and Treason!
Banquo and Donalbain! Malcolm! Awake!
Shake off this downy sleep, death's counterfeit,°
And look on death itself! Up, up, and see
The great doom's image!° Malcolm! Banquo!   *75*
As from your graves rise up, and walk like sprites,°
To countenance° this horror. Ring the bell.

Bell rings. Enter Lady [Macbeth].

Lady Macbeth. What's the business,
    That such a hideous trumpet calls to parley
    The sleepers of the house? Speak, speak!
Macduff.   O gentle lady,   *80*
    'Tis not for you to hear what I can speak:
    The repetition,° in a woman's ear,
    Would murder as it fell.

Enter Banquo.

                     O Banquo, Banquo!
    Our royal master's murdered.
Lady Macbeth.   Woe, alas!
    What, in our house?
Banquo.   Too cruel anywhere.   *85*
    Dear Duff, I prithee, contradict thyself,
    And say it is not so.

Enter Macbeth, Lennox, and Ross.

Macbeth. Had I but died an hour before this chance,
    I had lived a blessèd time; for from this instant
    There's nothing serious in mortality:°   *90*
    All is but toys.° Renown and grace is dead,
    The wine of life is drawn, and the mere lees°
    Is left this vault° to brag of.

Enter Malcolm and Donalbain.

Donalbain. What is amiss?
Macbeth.   You are, and do not know 't.

---

[73] **counterfeit** imitation   [75] **great doom's image** likeness of Judgment Day   [76] **sprites**
spirits   [77] **countenance** be in keeping with   [82] **repetition** report   [90] **serious in
mortality** worthwhile in mortal life   [91] **toys** trifles   [92] **lees** dregs   [93] **vault** (1)
wine vault (2) earth, with the sky as roof (?)

The spring, the head, the fountain of your blood   95
Is stopped; the very source of it is stopped.
Macduff. Your royal father's murdered.
Malcolm.   O, by whom?
Lennox. Those of his chamber, as it seemed, had done 't:
Their hands and faces were all badged° with blood;
So were their daggers, which unwiped we found   100
Upon their pillows. They stared, and were
    distracted.
No man's life was to be trusted with them.
Macbeth. O, yet I do repent me of my fury,
That I did kill them.
Macduff.   Wherefore did you so?
Macbeth. Who can be wise, amazed,° temp'rate and furious,   105
Loyal and neutral, in a moment? No man.
The expedition° of my violent love
Outrun the pauser, reason. Here lay Duncan,
His silver skin laced with his golden blood,
And his gashed stabs looked like a breach in nature   110
For ruin's wasteful entrance: there, the murderers,
Steeped in the colors of their trade, their daggers
Unmannerly breeched with gore.° Who could refrain,°
That had a heart to love, and in that heart
Courage to make 's love known?
Lady Macbeth.   Help me hence, ho!   115
Macduff. Look to° the lady.
Malcolm. [*Aside to Donalbain*] Why do we hold our tongues,
That most may claim this argument for ours?°
Donalbain. [*Aside to Malcolm*] What should be spoken here,
Where our fate, hid in an auger-hole,°   120
May rush, and seize us? Let's away:
Our tears are not yet brewed.
Malcolm. [*Aside to Donalbain*] Nor our strong sorrow
Upon the foot of motion.°
Banquo.   Look to the lady.

                              [*Lady Macbeth is carried out.*]

---

⁹⁹ **badged** marked ¹⁰⁵ **amazed** bewildered ¹⁰⁷ **expedition** haste ¹¹³ **Unmannerly
breeched with gore** covered with unseemly breeches of blood ¹¹³ **refrain** check
oneself ¹¹⁶ **Look to** look after ¹¹⁸ **That most . . . ours?** who are the most concerned
with this topic ¹²⁰ **auger-hole** i.e., unsuspected place ¹²²⁻¹²⁴ **Our tears . . . motion**
i.e., we have not yet had time for tears nor to express our sorrows in action (?)

And when we have our naked frailties hid,°   *125*
That suffer in exposure, let us meet
And question° this most bloody piece of work,
To know it further. Fears and scruples° shake us.
In the great hand of God I stand, and thence
Against the undivulged pretense° I fight   *130*
Of treasonous malice.
Macduff.   And so do I.
All.   So all.
Macbeth. Let's briefly° put on manly readiness,
And meet i' th' hall together.
All.   Well contented.

            Exeunt [all but Malcolm and Donalbain].

Malcolm. What will you do? Let's not consort with them.
To show an unfelt sorrow is an office°   *135*
Which the false man does easy. I'll to England.
Donalbain. To Ireland, I; our separated fortune
Shall keep us both the safer. Where we are
There's daggers in men's smiles; the near in blood,
The nearer bloody.
Malcolm.   This murderous shaft that's shot   *140*
Hath not yet lighted, and our safest way
Is to avoid the aim. Therefore to horse;
And let us not be dainty of° leave-taking,
But shift away. There's warrant° in that theft
Which steals itself° when there's no mercy left.   *145*
                 Exeunt.

Scene IV. [*Outside Macbeth's castle.*]

Enter Ross with an Old Man.

Old Man. Threescore and ten I can remember well:
Within the volume of which time I have seen
Hours dreadful and things strange, but this sore° night
Hath trifled former knowings.°

°*naked frailties hid* poor bodies clothed °*question* discuss °*scruples* suspicions °*undivulged pretense* hidden purpose °*briefly* quickly °*office* function °*dainty of* fussy about °*warrant* justification °*steals itself* steals oneself away II.iv. ³ *sore* grievous ⁴ *trifled former knowings* made trifles of former experiences

Ross. Ha, good father,
Thou seest the heavens, as troubled with man's act,   5
Threatens his bloody stage. By th' clock 'tis day,
And yet dark night strangles the traveling lamp:°
Is 't night's predominance,° or the day's shame,
That darkness does the face of earth entomb,
When living light should kiss it?
Old Man.   'Tis unnatural,   10
Even like the deed that's done. On Tuesday last
A falcon, tow'ring in her pride of place,°
Was by a mousing° owl hawked at and killed.
Ross. And Duncan's horses — a thing most strange and
     certain —
Beauteous and swift, the minions° of their race,   15
Turned wild in nature, broke their stalls, flung out,°
Contending 'gainst obedience, as they would make
War with mankind.
Old Man.   'Tis said they eat° each other.
Ross. They did so, to th' amazement of mine eyes,
That looked upon 't.

Enter Macduff.

     Here comes the good Macduff. 20
How goes the world, sir, now?
Macduff.   Why, see you not?
Ross. Is 't known who did this more than bloody deed?
Macduff. Those that Macbeth hath slain.
Ross.   Alas, the day!
What good could they pretend?°
Macduff.   They were suborned:°
Malcolm and Donalbain, the king's two sons,   25
Are stol'n away and fled, which puts upon them
Suspicion of the deed.
Ross.   'Gainst nature still.
Thriftless° ambition, that will ravin up°
Thine own life's means! Then 'tis most like
The sovereignty will fall upon Macbeth.   30
Macduff. He is already named,° and gone to Scone
To be invested.°

---

[7] *traveling lamp* i.e., the sun   [8] *predominance* astrological supremacy
[12] *tow'ring . . . place* soaring at her summit   [13] *mousing* i.e., normally mouse-eating   [15] *minions* darlings   [16] *flung out* lunged wildly   [18] *eat* ate   [24] *pretend* hope for   [24] *suborned* bribed   [28] *Thriftless* wasteful   [28] *ravin up* greedily devour
[31] *named* elected   [32] *invested* installed as king

Ross.   Where is Duncan's body?
Macduff. Carried to Colmekill,
    The sacred storehouse of his predecessors
    And guardian of their bones.
Ross.   Will you to Scone?   35
Macduff. No, cousin, I'll to fife.
Ross.   Well, I will thither.
Macduff. Well, may you see things well done there.
        Adieu,
    Lest our old robes sit easier than our new!
Ross. Farewell, father.
Old Man. God's benison° go with you, and with those   40
    That would make good of bad, and friends of foes!

                                        Exeunt omnes.

ACT III

Scene I. [*Forres. The palace.*]

Enter Banquo.

Banquo. Thou hast it now: King, Cawdor, Glamis, all,
    As the weïrd women promised, and I fear
    Thou play'dst most foully for 't. Yet it was said
    It should not stand° in thy posterity,
    But that myself should be the root and father   5
    Of many kings. If there come truth from them —
    As upon thee, Macbeth, their speeches shine —
    Why, by the verities on thee made good,
    May they not be my oracles as well
    And set me up in hope? But hush, no more!   10

    Sennet° sounded. Enter Macbeth as King, Lady [Macbeth], Lennox,
        Ross, Lords, and Attendants

Macbeth. Here's our chief guest.
Lady Macbeth.   If he had been forgotten,
    It had been as a gap in our great feast,
    And all-thing° unbecoming.
Macbeth. Tonight we hold a solemn° supper, sir,
    And I'll request your presence.

_____

[40] **benison** blessing III.i [4] **stand** continue s.d. **Sennet** trumpet call [13] **all-thing**
altogether [14] **solemn** ceremonious

Banquo.   Let your Highness   15
  Command upon me, to the which my duties
  Are with a most indissoluble tie
  For ever knit.
Macbeth. Ride you this afternoon?
Banquo.   Ay, my good lord.
Macbeth. We should have else desired your good advice   20
  (Which still° hath been both grave and prosperous°)
  In this day's council; but we'll take tomorrow.
  Is 't far your ride?
Banquo. As far, my lord, as will fill up the time
  'Twixt this and supper. Go not my horse the better,°   25
  I must become a borrower of the night
  For a dark hour or twain.
Macbeth.   Fail not our feast.
Banquo. My lord, I will not.
Macbeth. We hear our bloody cousins are bestowed°
  In England and in Ireland, not confessing   30
  Their cruel parricide, filling their hearers
  With strange invention.° But of that tomorrow,
  When therewithal we shall have cause of state
  Craving us jointly.° Hie you to horse. Adieu,
  Till you return at night. Goes Fleance with you?   35
Banquo. Ay, my good lord: our time does call upon 's.
Macbeth. I wish your horses swift and sure of foot,
  And so I do commend you to their backs.
  Farewell.   *Exit Banquo.*
  Let every man be master of his time   40
  Till seven at night. To make society
  The sweeter welcome, we will keep ourself
  Till supper-time alone. While° then, God be with you!

              Exeunt Lords [and all but Macbeth and a Servant].

  Sirrah,° a word with you: attend° those men
  Our pleasure?   45
Attendant. They are, my lord, without° the palace gate.
Macbeth. Bring them before us.   *Exit Servant.*
  To be thus is nothing, but° to be safely thus —

---

[21] *still* always   [21] *grave and prosperous* weighty and profitable   [25] *Go . . . better*
unless my horse goes better than I expect   [29] *are bestowed* have taken refuge
[32] *invention* lies   [33–34] *cause . . . jointly* matters of state demanding our joint
attention   [43] *While* until   [44] *Sirrah* (common address to an inferior)   [44] *attend*
await   [46] *without* outside   [48] *but* unless

Our fears in° Banquo stick deep,
And in his royalty of nature reigns that   *50*
Which would° be feared. 'Tis much he dares;
And, to° that dauntless temper° of his mind,
He hath a wisdom that doth guide his valor
To act in safety. There is none but he
Whose being I do fear: and under him   *55*
My genius is rebuked,° as it is said
Mark Antony's was by Cæsar. He chid the sisters,
When first they put the name of King upon me,
And bade them speak to him; then prophetlike
They hailed him father to a line of kings.   *60*
Upon my head they placed a fruitless crown
And put a barren scepter in my gripe,°
Thence to be wrenched with an unlineal hand,
No son of mine succeeding. If 't be so,
For Banquo's issue have I filed° my mind;   *65*
For them the gracious Duncan have I murdered;
Put rancors° in the vessel of my peace
Only for them, and mine eternal jewel°
Given to the common enemy of man,°
To make them kings, the seeds of Banquo kings!   *70*
Rather than so, come, fate, into the list,°
And champion me to th' utterance!° Who's there?

Enter Servant and Two Murderers.

Now go to the door, and stay there till we call.
                                              Exit Servant.
Was it not yesterday we spoke together?
Murderers. It was, so please your Highness.
Macbeth.   Well then, now   *75*
Have you considered of my speeches? Know
That it was he in the times past, which held you
So under fortune,° which you thought had been
Our innocent self: this I made good to you
In our last conference; passed in probation° with you,   *80*
How you were born in hand,° how crossed;° the instruments,°

---

[49] *in* about   [51] *would* must   [52] *to* added to   [52] *temper* quality   [56] *genius is
rebuked* guardian spirit is cowed   [62] *gripe* grasp   [65] *filed* defiled   [67] *rancors*
bitter enmities   [68] *eternal jewel* i.e., soul   [69] *common enemy of man* i.e., the
Devil   [71] *list* lists   [72] *champion me to th' utterance* fight against me to the death
[77-78] *held . . . fortune* kept you from good fortune (?)   [80] *passed in probation*
reviewed the proofs   [81] *borne in hand* deceived   [81] *crossed* thwarted   [81] *instruments*
tools

Who wrought with them, and all things else that might
To half a soul° and to a notion° crazed
Say "Thus did Banquo."
First Murderer.   You made it known to us.
Macbeth. I did so; and went further, which is now   *85*
    Our point of second meeting. Do you find
    Your patience so predominant in your nature,
    That you can let this go? Are you so gospeled,°
    To pray for this good man and for his issue,
    Whose heavy hand hath bowed you to the grave   *90*
    And beggared yours for ever?
First Murderer.   We are men, my liege.
Macbeth. Ay, in the catalogue ye go for° men;
    As hounds and greyhounds, mongrels, spaniels, curs,
    Shoughs, water-rugs° and demi-wolves, are clept°
    All by the name of dogs: the valued file°   *95*
    Distinguishes the swift, the slow, the subtle,
    The housekeeper,° the hunter, every one
    According to the gift which bounteous nature
    Hath in him closed,° whereby he does receive
    Particular addition, from the bill°   *100*
    That writes them all alike: and so of men.
    Now if you have a station in the file,
    Not i' th' worst rank of manhood, say 't,
    And I will put that business in your bosoms
    Whose execution takes your enemy off,   *105*
    Grapples you to the heart and love of us,
    Who wear our health but sickly in his life,°
    Which in his death were perfect.
Second Murderer.   I am one, my liege,
    Whom the vile blows and buffets of the world
    Hath so incensed that I am reckless what   *110*
    I do to spite the world.
First Murderer.   And I another
    So weary with disasters, tugged with fortune,
    That I would set° my life on any chance,
    To mend it or be rid on 't.
Macbeth.   Both of you
    Know Banquo was your enemy.

---

[83] *half a soul* a halfwit [83] *notion* mind [88] *gospeled* i.e., made meek by the gospel [92] *go for* pass as [94] *Shoughs, water-rugs* shaggy dogs, long-haired water dogs [94] *clept* called [95] *valued file* classification by valuable traits [97] *housekeeper* watchdog [99] *closed* enclosed [100] *Particular addition, from the bill* special distinction in opposition to the list [107] *wear . . . life* have only imperfect health while he lives [113] *set* risk

Both Murderers.   True, my lord.   *115*
Macbeth. So is he mine, and in such bloody distance°
    That every minute of his being thrusts
    Against my near'st of life:° and though I could
    With barefaced power sweep him from my sight
    And bid my will avouch° it, yet I must not,   *120*
    For° certain friends that are both his and mine,
    Whose loves I may not drop, but wail his fall°
    Who I myself struck down: and thence it is
    That I to your assistance do make love,
    Masking the business from the common eye   *125*
    For sundry weighty reasons.
Second Murderer.   We shall, my lord,
    Perform what you command us.
First Murderer.   Though our lives ——
Macbeth. Your spirits shine through you. Within this hour at most
    I will advise you where to plant yourselves,
    Acquaint you with the perfect spy° o' th' time,   *130*
    The moment on 't;° for 't must be done tonight,
    And something° from the palace; always thought°
    That I require a clearness:° and with him —
    To leave no rubs° nor botches in the work —
    Fleance his son, that keeps him company,   *135*
    Whose absence is no less material to me
    Than is his father's, must embrace the fate
    Of that dark hour. Resolve yourselves apart:°
    I'll come to you anon.
Murderers.   We are resolved, my lord.
Macbeth. I'll call upon you straight.° Abide within.   *140*
    It is concluded: Banquo, thy soul's flight,
    If it find heaven, must find it out tonight.   *Exeunt.*

Scene II. [*The palace.*]

Enter Macbeth's Lady and a Servant.

Lady Macbeth. Is Banquo gone from court?
Servant. Ay, madam, but returns again tonight.

---

[116] *distance* quarrel   [118] *near'st of life* most vital spot   [120] *avouch* justify   [121] *For* because of   [122] *wail his fall* bewail his death   [130] *perfect spy* exact information (?) ("spy" literally means "observation"; apparently Macbeth already has the Third Murderer in mind)   [131] *on 't* of it   [132] *something* some distance   [132] *thought* remembered   [133] *clearness* freedom from suspicion   [134] *rubs* flaws   [138] *Resolve yourselves apart* decide by yourself   [140] *straight* immediately

Lady Macbeth. Say to the King, I would attend his leisure
    For a few words.
Servant.   Madam, I will.   *Exit.*
Lady Macbeth.   Nought's had, all's spent,
    Where our desire is got without content: 5
    'Tis safer to be that which we destroy
    Than by destruction dwell in doubtful joy.

Enter Macbeth.

    How now, my lord! Why do you keep alone,
    Of sorriest° fancies your companions making,
    Using those thoughts which should indeed have died   10
    With them they think on? Things without° all remedy
    Should be without regard: what's done is done.
Macbeth. We have scorched° the snake, not killed it:
    She'll close° and be herself, whilst our poor malice°
    Remains in danger of her former tooth.   15
    But let the frame of things disjoint,° both the worlds° suffer,
    Ere we will eat our meal in fear, and sleep
    In the affliction of these terrrible dreams
    That shake us nightly: better be with the dead,
    Whom we, to gain our peace, have sent to peace,   20
    Than on the torture° of the mind to lie
    In restless ecstasy.° Duncan is in his grave;
    After life's fitful fever he sleeps well.
    Treason has done his° worst: nor steel, nor poison,
    Malice domestic,° foreign levy, nothing,   25
    Can touch him further.
Lady Macbeth.   Come on.
    Gentle my lord, sleek° o'er your rugged° looks;
    Be bright and jovial among your guests tonight.
Macbeth. So shall I, love; and so, I pray, be you:
    Let your remembrance apply to Banquo;°   30
    Present him eminence,° both with eye and tongue:
    Unsafe the while, that we must lave°
    Our honors in these flattering streams

II.ii.   ⁹ *sorriest* most despicable   ¹¹ *without* beyond   ¹³ *scorched* slashed, scored
¹⁴ *close* heal   ¹⁴ *poor malice* feeble enmity   ¹⁶ *frame of things disjoint* universe
collapse   ¹⁶ *both the worlds* heaven and earth (?)   ²¹ *torture* i.e., rack   ²² *ecstasy*
frenzy   ²⁴ *his* its   ²⁵ *Malice domestic* civil war   ²⁷ *sleek* smooth   ²⁷ *rugged*
furrowed   ³⁰ *Let . . . Banquo* focus your thoughts on Banquo   ³¹ *Present him*
eminence honor him   ³² *unsafe . . . lave* i.e., you and I are unsafe because we
must dip

And make our faces vizards° to our hearts,
Disguising what they are.
Lady Macbeth.   You must leave this.   35
Macbeth. O, full of scorpions is my mind, dear wife!
Thous know'st that Banquo, and his Fleance, lives.
Lady Macbeth. But in them nature's copy's° not eterne.
Macbeth. There's comfort yet; they are assailable.
Then be thou jocund. Ere the bat hath flown   40
His cloistered flight, ere to black Hecate's summons
The shard-borne° beetle with his drowsy hums
Hath rung night's yawning peal, there shall be done
A deed of dreadful note.
Lady Macbeth.   What's to be done?
Macbeth. Be innocent of the knowledge, dearest chuck,°   45
Till thou applaud the deed. Come, seeling° night,
Scarf up° the tender eye of pitiful day,
And with thy bloody and invisible hand
Cancel and tear to pieces that great bond°
Which keeps me pale! Light thickens, and the crow   50
Makes wing to th' rooky° wood.
Good things of day begin to droop and drowse,
Whiles night's black agents to their preys do rouse.
Thou marvel'st at my words: but hold thee still;
Things bad begun make strong themselves by ill: 55
So, prithee, go with me.   *Exeunt.*

Scene III. [*Near the palace.*]

Enter Three Murderers.

First Murderer. But who did bid thee join with us?
Third Murderer.   Macbeth.
Second Murderer. He needs not our mistrust; since he delivers
Our offices and what we have to do
To the direction just.°
First Murderer.   Then stand with us.

---

[34] *vizards* masks [38] *nature's copy* nature's lease (?) imitation (i.e., a son) made
by nature (?) [42] *shard-borne* borne on scaly wings (?) dung-bred (?) [45] *chuck*
chick (a term of endearment) [46] *seeling* eye-closing [47] *Scarf up* blindfold [49] *bond*
i.e., between Banquo and fate (?) Banquo's lease on life (?) Macbeth's link to
humanity (?) [51] *rooky* full of rooks III.iii. [2-4] *He needs . . . just* we need not
mistrust him (i.e., the Third Murderer) since he describes our duties according to
our exact directions

The west yet glimmers with some streaks of day.   5
Now spurs the lated° traveler apace
To gain the timely inn, and near approaches
The subject of our watch.
Third Murderer. Hark! I hear horses.
Banquo. (Within) Give us a light there, ho!
Second Murderer.   Then 'tis he. The rest
That are within the note of expectation°   10
Already are i' th' court.
First Murderer. His horses go about.
Third Murderer. Almost a mile: but he does usually —
So all men do — from hence to th' palace gate
Make it their walk.

Enter Banquo and Fleance, with a torch.

Second Murderer. A light, a light!
Third Murderer.   'Tis he.
First Murderer.   Stand to 't.   15
Banquo. It will be rain tonight.
First Murderer.   Let it come down.

        [*They set upon Banquo.*]

Banquo. O, treachery! Fly, good Fleance, fly, fly, fly!
                                [*Exit Fleance.*]
        Thou mayst revenge. O slave! [*Dies.*]
Third Murderer. Who did strike out the light?
First Murderer.   Was 't not the way?°
Third Murderer. There's but one down; the son is fled.   20
Second Murderer. We have lost best half of our affair.
First Murderer. Well, let's away and say how much is done
                                        Exeunt.

Scene IV. [*The palace.*]

Banquet prepared. Enter Macbeth, Lady [Macbeth], Ross, Lennox,
Lords, and Attendants.

Macbeth. You know your own degrees;° sit down:
        At first and last, the hearty welcome.
Lords. Thanks to your Majesty.
Macbeth. Ourself will mingle with society°
        And play the humble host.   5

---

⁶ *lated* belated   ¹⁰ *within the note of expectation*   on the list of expected guests
¹⁹ *way*   i.e., thing to do   III.iv.   ¹ *degrees*   ranks   ⁴ *society*   the company

Our hostess keeps her state,° but in best time
We will require° her welcome.
Lady Macbeth. Pronounce it for me, sir, to all our friends,
For my heart speaks they are welcome.

Enter First Murderer.

Macbeth. See, they encounter° thee with their hearts' thanks.   *10*
Both sides are even: here I'll sit i' th' midst:
Be large in mirth; anon we'll drink a measure°
The table round. [*Goes to Murderer*] There's blood upon thy
face.
Murderer. 'Tis Banquo's then.
Macbeth. 'Tis better thee without than he within.°   *15*
Is he dispatched?
Murderer. My lord, his throat is cut; that I did for him.
Macbeth. Thou art the best o' th' cutthroats.
Yet he's good that did the like for Fleance;
If thou didst it, thou art the nonpareil.   *20*
Murderer. Most royal sir, Fleance is 'scaped.
Macbeth. [*Aside*] Then comes my fit again: I had else been perfect,
Whole as the marble, founded° as the rock,
As broad and general as the casing° air:
But now I am cabined, cribbed,° confined, bound in   *25*
To saucy° doubts and fears. — But Banquo's safe?
Murderer. Ay, my good lord: safe in a ditch he bides,
With twenty trenchèd° gashes on his head,
The least a death to nature.
Macbeth.   Thanks for that.
[*Aside*] There the grown serpent lies; the worm°
that's fled   *30*
Hath nature that in time will venom breed,
No teeth for th' present. Get thee gone. Tomorrow
We'll hear ourselves° again.   *Exit Murderer.*
Lady Macbeth.   My royal lord,
You do not give the cheer.° The feast is sold
That is not often vouched, while 'tis a-making,   *35*
'Tis given with welcome. To feed were best at home;°

---

⁶ *keeps her state* remains seated in her chair of state   ⁷ *require* request   ¹⁰ *encounter* meet   ¹² *measure* goblet   ¹⁵ *thee without than he within* outside you than inside him   ²³ *founded* firmly based   ²⁴ *broad . . . casing* unconfined as the surrounding   ²⁵ *cribbed* penned up   ²⁶ *saucy* insolent   ²⁸ *trenchèd* trenchlike   ³⁰ *worm* serpent   ³³ *hear ourselves* talk it over   ³⁴ *the cheer* a sense of cordiality   ³⁴⁻³⁶ *The feast . . . home* i.e., the feast seems sold (not given) during which the host fails to welcome the guests. Mere eating is best done at home

From thence, the sauce to meat° is ceremony;
Meeting were bare without it.

Enter the Ghost of Banquo, and sits in Macbeth's place.

Macbeth.   Sweet remembrancer!°
Now good digestion wait on appetite,
And health on both!
Lennox.   May 't please your Highness sit.   *40*
Macbeth. Here had we now our country's honor roofed,°
Were the graced person of our Banquo present —
Who may I rather challenge for unkindness
Than pity for mischance!°
Ross.   His absence, sir,
Lays blame upon his promise. Please 't your Highness   *45*
To grace us with your royal company?
Macbeth. The table's full.
Lennox.   Here is a place reserved, sir.
Macbeth. Where?
Lennox. Here, my good lord. What is 't that moves your Highness?
Macbeth. Which of you have done this?
Lords.   What, my good lord?   *50*
Macbeth. Thou canst not say I did it. Never shake
Thy gory locks at me.
Ross. Gentlemen, rise, his Highness is not well.
Lady Macbeth. Sit, worthy friends. My lord is often thus,
And hath been from his youth. Pray you, keep seat.   *55*
The fit is momentary; upon a thought°
He will again be well. If much you note him,
You shall offend him and extend his passion.°
Feed, and regard him not. — Are you a man?
Macbeth. Ay, and a bold one, that dare look on that   *60*
Which might appall the devil.
Lady Macbeth.   O proper stuff!
This is the very painting of your fear.
This is the air-drawn dagger which, you said,
Led you to Duncan. O, these flaws° and starts,
Impostors to° true fear, would well become   *65*
A woman's story at a winter's fire,

---

[37] *meat* food   [38] *remembrancer* reminder   [41] *our country's honor roofed* our nobility under one roof   [43–44] *Who . . . mischance* whom I hope I may reprove because he is unkind rather than pity because he has encountered an accident   [56] *upon a thought* as quick as thought   [58] *extend his passion* lengthen his fit   [64] *flaws* gusts, outbursts   [65] *to* compared with

Authorized° by her grandam. Shame itself!
Why do you make such faces? When all's done,
You look but on a stool.
Macbeth.   Prithee, see there!
    Behold! Look! Lo! How say you?   *70*
    Why, what care I? If thou canst nod, speak too.
    If charnel houses° and our graves must send
    Those that we bury back, our monuments
    Shall be the maws of kites.°   [*Exit Ghost.*]
Lady Macbeth.   What, quite unmanned in folly?
Macbeth. If I stand here, I saw him.
Lady Macbeth.   Fie, for shame!   *75*
Macbeth. Blood hath been shed ere now, i' th' olden time,
    Ere humane statute purged the gentle weal;°
    Ay, and since, too, murders have been performed
    Too terrible for the ear. The times has been
    That, when the brains were out, the man would die,   *80*
    And there an end; but now they rise again,
    With twenty mortal murders on their crowns,°
    And push us from our stools. This is more strange
    Than such a murder is.
Lady Macbeth.   My worthy lord,
    Your noble friends do lack you.
Macbeth.   I do forget.   *85*
    Do not muse at me, my most worthy friends;
    I have a strange infirmity, which is nothing
    To those that know me. Come, love and health to all!
    Then I'll sit down. Give me some wine, fill full.

    Enter Ghost.

    I drink to th' general joy o' th' whole table,   *90*
    And to our dear friend Banquo, whom we miss;
    Would he were here! To all and him we thirst,°
    And all to all.°
Lords.   Our duties, and the pledge.
Macbeth. Avaunt! and quit my sight! Let the earth hide thee!
    Thy bones are marrowless, thy blood is cold;   *95*

---

[67] **Authorized** vouched for   [72] **charnel houses** vaults containing bones   [73–74] **our . . . kites** our tombs shall be the bellies of rapacious birds   [77] **purged the gentle weal** i.e., cleansed the state and made it gentle   [82] **mortal murders on their crowns** deadly wounds on their heads   [92] **thirst** desire to drink   [93] **all to all** everything to everybody (?) let everybody drink to everybody (?)

Thous hast no speculation° in those eyes
Which thou dost glare with.
Lady Macbeth.   Think of this, good peers,
But as a thing of custom; 'tis no other.
Only it spoils the pleasure of the time.
Macbeth. What man dare, I dare.   **100**
Approach thou like the rugged Russian bear,
The armed rhinoceros, or th' Hyrcan° tiger;
Take any shape but that, and my firm nerves°
Shall never tremble. Or be alive again,
And dare me to the desert° with thy sword.   **105**
If trembling I inhabit then, protest me
The baby of a girl.° Hence, horrible shadow!
Unreal mock'ry, hence!   [*Exit Ghost.*]
                    Why, so: being gone,
I am a man again. Pray you, sit still.
Lady Macbeth. You have displaced the mirth, broke the
                    good meeting.   **110**
With most admired° disorder.
Macbeth.   Can such things be,
And overcome us° like a summer's cloud,
Without our special wonder? You make me strange
Even to the disposition that I owe,°
When now I think you can behold such sights,   **115**
And keep the natural ruby of your cheeks,
When mine is blanched with fear.
Ross.   What sights, my lord?
Lady Macbeth. I pray you, speak not: he grows worse and worse;
Question enrages him: at once, good night.
Stand not upon the order of your going,°   **120**
But go at once.
Lennox. Good night; and better health
Attend his Majesty!
Lady Macbeth.   A kind good night to all!
                                        Exit Lords.
Macbeth. It will have blood, they say: blood will have blood.
Stones have been known to move and trees to speak;
Augures and understood relations° have   **125**

---

⁹⁶ *speculation* sight   ¹⁰² *Hyrcan* of Hyrcania (near the Caspian Sea)   ¹⁰³ *nerves*
sinews   ¹⁰⁵ *the desert* a lonely place   ¹⁰⁶⁻¹⁰⁷ *If . . . girl* if then I tremble, proclaim
me a baby girl   ¹¹¹ *admired* amazing   ¹¹² *overcome us* come over us   ¹¹³⁻¹¹⁴ *You
. . . owe* i.e., you make me wonder what my nature is   ¹²⁰ *Stand . . . going* do
not insist on departing in your order of rank   ¹²⁵ *Augures and understood relations*
auguries and comprehended reports

By maggot-pies and choughs and rooks brought forth°
The secret'st man of blood. What is the night?°
Lady Macbeth. Almost at odds° with morning, which is which.
Macbeth. How say'st thou, that Macduff denies his person
   At our great bidding?
Lady Macbeth.   Did you send to him, sir?   130
Macbeth. I hear it by the way,° but I will send:
   There's not a one of them but in his house
   I keep a servant fee'd.° I will tomorrow,
   And betimes° I will, to the weïrd sisters:
   More shall they speak, for now I am bent° to know   135
   By the worst means the worst. For mine own good
   All causes° shall give way. I am in blood
   Stepped in so far that, should I wade no more,
   Returning were as tedious as go o'er.
   Strange things I have in head that will to hand,   140
   Which must be acted ere they may be scanned.°
Lady Macbeth. You lack the season of all natures,° sleep.
Macbeth. Come, we'll to sleep. My strange and self-abuse°
   Is the initiate fear that wants hard use.°
   We are yet but young in deed.   *Exeunt.* 145

Scene V. [*A Witches' haunt.*]

Thunder. Enter the Three Witches, meeting Hecate.

First Witch. Why, how now, Hecate! you look angerly.
Hecate. Have I not reason, beldams° as you are,
   Saucy and overbold? How did you dare
   To trade and traffic with Macbeth
   In riddles and affairs of death;   5
   And I, the mistress of your charms,
   The close contriver° of all harms,
   Was never called to bear my part,
   Or show the glory of our art?
   And, which is worse, all you have done   10
   Hath been but for a wayward son,

---

¹²⁶ *By . . . forth* by magpies, choughs, and rooks (telltale birds) revealed   ¹²⁷ *What is the night* what time of night is it   ¹²⁸ *at odds* striving   ¹³¹ *by the way* incidentally   ¹³³ *fee'd* i.e., paid to spy   ¹³⁴ *betimes* quickly   ¹³⁵ *bent* determined   ¹³⁷ *causes* considerations   ¹⁴¹ *may be scanned* can be examined   ¹⁴² *season of all natures* seasoning (preservative) of all living creatures   ¹⁴³ *My strange and self-abuse* my strange delusion   ¹⁴⁴ *initiate . . . use* beginner's fear that lacks hardening practice   III.v.   ² *beldams* hags   ⁷ *close contriver* secret inventor

Spiteful and wrathful; who, as others do,
Loves for his own ends, not for you.
But make amends now: get you gone,
And at the pit of Acheron° 15
Meet me i' th' morning: thither he
Will come to know his destiny.
Your vessels and your spells provide,
Your charms and everything beside.
I am for th' air; this night I'll spend 20
Unto a dismal and a fatal end:
Great business must be wrought ere noon.
Upon the corner of the moon
There hangs a vap'rous drop profound;°
I'll catch it ere it come to ground: 25
And that distilled by magic sleights°
Shall raise such artificial sprites°
As by the strength of their illusion
Shall draw him on to his confusion.°
He shall spurn fate, scorn death, and bear 30
His hopes 'bove wisdom, grace, and fear:
And you all know security°
Is mortals' chiefest enemy.

Music and a song.

Hark! I am called; my little spirit, see,
Sits in a foggy cloud and stays for me. [*Exit.*] 35

Sing within, "Come away, come away," *&c.*

First Witch. Come, let's make haste; she'll soon be back again.
                                                    Exeunt.

Scene VI. [*The palace.*]

Enter Lennox and another Lord.

Lennox. My former speeches have but hit your thoughts,°
Which can interpret farther, Only I say
Things have been strangely borne.° The gracious Duncan
Was pitied of Macbeth: marry, he was dead.

---

[15] **Acheron** (river of Hades) [24] **profound** heavy [26] **sleights** arts [27] **artificial sprites** spirits created by magic arts (?) artful (cunning) spirits (?) [29] **confusion** ruin [32] **security** overconfidence III.vi [1] **My . . . thoughts** i.e., my recent words have only coincided with what you have in your mind [3] **borne** managed

And the right-valiant Banquo walked too late;   5
Whom, you may say, if 't please you, Fleance killed,
For Fleance fled. Men must not walk too late.
Who cannot want the thought,° how monstrous
It was for Malcolm and for Donalbain
To kill their gracious father? Damnèd fact!°   10
How it did grieve Macbeth! Did he not straight,
In pious rage, the two delinquents tear,
That were the slaves of drink and thralls° of sleep?
Was not that nobly done? Ay, and wisely too;
For 'twould have angered any heart alive   15
To hear the men deny 't. So that I say
He has borne° all things well: and I do think
That, had he Duncan's sons under his key —
As, an 't° please heaven, he shall not — they should find
What 'twere to kill a father. So should Fleance.   20
But, peace! for from broad words,° and 'cause he failed
His presence at the tyrant's feast, I hear,
Macduff lives in disgrace. Sir, can you tell
Where he bestows himself?

Lord.   The son of Duncan,
From whom this tyrant holds the due of birth,°   25
Lives in the English court, and is received
Of the most pious Edward° with such grace
That the malevolence of fortune nothing
Takes from his high respect.° Thither Macduff
Is gone to pray the holy King, upon his aid°   30
To wake Northumberland° and warlike Siward;
That by the help of these, with Him above
To ratify the work, we may again
Give to our tables meat, sleep to our nights,
Free from our feasts and banquets bloody knives,   35
Do faithful homage and receive free° honors:
All which we pine for now. And this report
Hath so exasperate the King that he
Prepares for some attempt of war.

Lennox.   Sent he to Macduff?

---

[8] *cannot want the thought* can fail to think   [10] *fact* evil deed   [13] *thralls* slaves
[17] *borne* managed   [19] *an 't* if it   [21] *for from broad words* because of frank talk
[25] *due of birth* birthright   [27] *Edward* Edward the Confessor (reigned 1042–1066)
[28–29] *nothing . . . respect* does not diminish the high respect in which he is held
[30] *upon his aid* to aid him (Malcolm)   [31] *To wake Northumberland* i.e., to arouse
the people in an English county near Scotland   [36] *free* freely granted

Lord. He did: and with an absolute "Sir, not I," 40
 The cloudy° messenger turns me his back,
 And hums, as who should say "You'll rue the time
 That clogs° me with this answer."
Lennox. And that well might
 Advise him to a caution, t'hold what distance
 His wisdom can provide. Some holy angel 45
 Fly to the court of England and unfold
 His message ere he come, that a swift blessing
 May soon return to this our suffering country
 Under a hand accursed!
Lord. I'll send my prayers with him.
 Exeunt.

ACT IV

Scene I. [*A Witches' haunt.*]

Thunder. Enter the Three Witches.

First Witch. Thrice the brinded° cat hath mewed.
Second Witch. Thrice and once the hedge-pig° whined.
Third Witch. Harpier° cries. 'Tis time, 'tis time.
First Witch. Round about the caldron go:
 In the poisoned entrails throw. 5
 Toad, that under cold stone
 Days and nights has thirty-one
 Swelt'red venom sleeping got,°
 Boil thou first i' th' charmèd pot.
All. Double, double, toil and trouble; 10
 Fire burn and caldron bubble.
Second Witch. Fillet° of a fenny° snake,
 In the caldron boil and bake;
 Eye of newt and toe of frog,
 Wool of bat and tongue of dog, 15
 Adder's fork° and blindworm's° sting,
 Lizard's leg and howlet's° wing,
 For a charm of pow'rful trouble,
 Like a hell-broth boil and bubble.

---

[41] *cloudy* disturbed [43] *clogs* burdens IV.i. [1] *brinded* brindled [2] *hedge-pig*
hedgehog [3] *Harpier* (an attendant spirit, like Graymalkin and Paddock in I.i)
[8] *Swelt'red venom sleeping got* venom sweated out while sleeping [12] *Fillet* slice
[12] *fenny* from a swamp [16] *fork* forked tongue [16] *blindworm* (a legless lizard)
[17] *howlet* owlet

All. Double, double, toil and trouble;   *20*
    Fire burn and caldron bubble.
Third Witch. Scale of dragon, tooth of wolf,
    Witch's mummy,° maw and gulf°
    Of the ravined° salt-sea shark,
    Root of hemlock digged i' th' dark,   *25*
    Liver of blaspheming Jew,
    Gall of goat, and slips of yew
    Slivered in the moon's eclipse,
    Nose of Turk and Tartar's lips,
    Finger of birth-strangled babe   *30*
    Ditch-delivered by a drab,°
    Make the gruel thick and slab:°
    Add thereto a tiger's chaudron,°
    For th' ingredience of our caldron.
All. Double, double, toil and trouble;   *35*
    Fire burn and caldron bubble.
Second Witch. Cool it with a baboon's blood,
    Then the charm is firm and good.

    Enter Hecate and the other Three Witches.

Hecate. O, well done! I commend your pains;
    And every one shall share i' th' gains: *40*
    And now about the caldron sing,
    Like elves and fairies in a ring,
    Enchanting all that you put in.

    Music and a song: "Black Spirits," &c.
        [*Exeunt Hecate and the other Three Witches.*]

Second Witch. By the pricking of my thumbs,
    Something wicked this way comes: *45*
    Open, locks,
    Whoever knocks!

    Enter Macbeth.

Macbeth. How now, you secret, black, and midnight hags!
    What is 't you do?
All.   A deed without a name.
Macbeth. I conjure you, by that which you profess,   *50*
    Howe'er you come to know it, answer me:

---

[23] **Witch's mummy** mummified flesh of a witch   [23.] **maw and gulf** stomach and gullet   [24] **ravined** ravenous   [31] **ditch-delivered by a drab** born in a ditch of a harlot   [32] **slab** viscous   [33] **chaudron** entrails

Though you untie the winds and let them fight
Against the churches; though the yesty° waves
Confound° and swallow navigation up;
Though bladed corn be lodged° and trees blown down;　55
Though castles topple on their warders' heads;
Though palaces and pyramids do slope°
Their heads to their foundations; though the treasure
Of nature's germens° tumble all together,
Even till destruction sicken,° answer me　　　　　60
To what I ask you.

First Witch.　　　　　　Speak.
Second Witch.　　　　　　　　Demand.
Third Witch.　　　　　　　　　　We'll answer.
First Witch. Say, if th' hadst rather hear it from our mouths,
Or from our masters?
Macbeth.　　　　　Call 'em, let me see 'em.
First Witch. Pour in sow's blood, that hath eaten
Her nine farrow;° grease that's sweaten°　　　　65
From the murderer's gibbet throw
Into the flame.
All.　　　　　Come, high or low,
Thyself and office° deftly show!

Thunder. First Apparition: an Armed Head.

Macbeth. Tell me, thou unknown power —
First Witch.　　　　　　　　He knows thy thought:
Hear his speech, but say thou nought.　　　　　70
First Apparition. Macbeth! Macbeth! Macbeth! Beware Macduff!
Beware the Thane of Fife. Dismiss me: enough.
　　　　　　　　　　　　　He descends.
Macbeth. Whate'er thou art, for thy good caution thanks:
Thou hast harped° my fear aright. But one word more —
First Witch. He will not be commanded. Here's another,　75
More potent than the first.

Thunder. Second Apparition: a Bloody Child.

Second Apparition. Macbeth! Macbeth! Macbeth!
Macbeth. Had I three ears, I'd hear thee.
Second Apparition. Be bloody, bold, and resolute!

---

[53] **yesty** foamy　[54] **Confound** destroy　[55] **bladed corn be lodged** grain in the ear
be beaten down　[57] **slope** bend　[59] **nature's germens** seeds of all life　[60] **sicken**
i.e., sicken at its own work　[65] **farrow** young pigs　[65] **sweaten** sweated　[68] **office**
function　[74] **harped** hit upon, struck the note of

Laugh to scorn
The pow'r of man, for none of woman born   *80*
Shall harm Macbeth.

Descends.

Macbeth. Then live, Macduff: what need I fear of thee?
But yet I'll make assurance double sure,
And take a bond of fate.° Thou shalt not live;
That I may tell pale-hearted fear it lies,   *85*
And sleep in spite of thunder.

Thunder. Third Apparition: A Child Crowned, with a tree in
his hand.

What is this,
That rises like the issue° of a king,
And wears upon his baby-brow the round
And top of sovereignty?°

All.   Listen, but speak not to 't.

Third Apparition. Be lion-mettled, proud, and take no care   *90*
Who chafes, who frets, or where conspirers are:
Macbeth shall never vanquished be until
Great Birnam Wood to high Dunsinane Hill
Shall come against him.   *Descends.*

Macbeth.   That will never be.
Who can impress° the forest, bid the tree   *95*
Unfix his earth-bound root? Sweet bodements,° good!
Rebellious dead,° rise never, till the Wood
Of Birnam rise, and our high-placed Macbeth
Shall live the lease of nature,° pay his breath
To time and mortal custom.° Yet my heart   *100*
Throbs to know one thing. Tell me, if your art
Can tell so much: shall Banquo's issue ever
Reign in this kingdom?

All.   Seek to know no more.

Macbeth. I will be satisfied.° Deny me this,
And an eternal curse fall on you! Let me know.   *105*
Why sinks that caldron? And what noise° is this?

Hautboys.

---

⁸⁴ *take a bond of fate* get a guarantee from fate (i.e., he will kill Macduff and
thus will compel fate to keep its word) ⁸⁷ *issue* offspring ⁸⁸⁻⁸⁹ *round/And top*
of sovereignty i.e., crown ⁹⁵ *impress* conscript ⁹⁶ *bodements* prophecies
⁹⁷ *Rebellious dead* (perhaps a reference to Banquo; but perhaps a misprint for
"rebellion's head") ⁹⁹ *lease of nature* natural lifespan ¹⁰⁰ *mortal custom* natural
death ¹⁰⁴ *satisfied* i.e., fully informed ¹⁰⁶ *noise* music

First Witch. Show!
Second Witch. Show!
Third Witch. Show!
All. Show his eyes, and grieve his heart;   110
    Come like shadows, so depart!

> *A show of eight Kings and Banquo, last [King] with a glass° in*
> *his hand.*

Macbeth. Thou art too like the spirit of Banquo. Down!
    Thy crown does sear mine eyelids. And thy hair,
    Thou other gold-bound brow, is like the first.
    A third is like the former. Filthy hags!   115
    Why do you show me this? A fourth! Start,° eyes!
    What, will the line stretch out to th' crack of doom?°
    Another yet! A seventh! I'll see no more.
    And yet the eighth appears, who bears a glass
    Which shows me many more; and some I see   120
    That twofold balls and treble scepters° carry:
    Horrible sight! Now I see 'tis true;
    For the blood-boltered° Banquo smiles upon me,
    And points at them for his. What, is this so?
First Witch. Ay, sir, all this is so. But why   125
    Stands Macbeth thus amazedly?
    Come sisters, cheer we up his sprites,°
    And show the best of our delights:
    I'll charm the air to give a sound,
    While you perform your antic round,°   130
    That this great king may kindly say
    Our duties did his welcome pay.

> *Music. The Witches dance, and vanish.*

Macbeth. Where are they? Gone? Let this pernicious hour
    Stand aye accursèd in the calendar!
    Come in, without there!

> *Enter Lennox.*

Lennox.

                 What's your Grace's will?   135

---

s.d. *glass* mirror 116 *Start* i.e., from the sockets 117 *crack of doom* blast (of a trumpet?) at doomsday 121 *twofold balls and treble scepters* (coronation emblems) 123 *Blood-boltered* matted with blood 127 *sprites* spirits 130 *Antic round* grotesque circular dance

Macbeth. Saw you the weïrd sisters?
Lennox.   No, my lord.
Macbeth. Came they not by you?
Lennox.   No indeed, my lord.
Macbeth. Infected be the air whereon they ride,
   And damned all those that trust them! I did hear
   The galloping of horse.° Who was 't came by?   *140*
Lennox. 'Tis two or three, my lord, that brings you word
   Macduff is fled to England.
Macbeth.   Fled to England?
Lennox. Ay, my good lord.
Macbeth. [*Aside*] Time, thou anticipat'st° my dread exploits
   The flighty purpose never is o'ertook   *145*
   Unless the deed go with it.° From this moment
   The very firstlings of my heart° shall be
   The firstlings of my hand. And even now,
   To crown my thought with acts, be it thought and done:
   The castle of Macduff I will surprise;°   *150*
   Seize upon Fife; give to th' edge o' th' sword
   His wife, his babes, and all unfortunate souls
   That trace him in his line.° No boasting like a fool;
   This deed I'll do before this purpose cool:
   But no more sights! — Where are those gentlemen?
   Come, bring me where they are.   *Exeunt.*

Scene II. [*Macduff's castle.*]

Enter Macduff's wife, her Son, and Ross.

Lady Macduff. What had he done, to make him fly the land?
Ross. You must have patience, madam.
Lady Macduff.   He had none:
   His flight was madness. When our actions do not,
   Our fears do make us traitors.
Ross.   You know not
   Whether it was his wisdom or his fear.   *5*
Lady Macduff. Wisdom! To leave his wife, to leave his babes,
   His mansion and his titles,° in a place
   From whence himself does fly? He loves us not;

---

¹⁴⁰ **horse** horses (or "horsemen")   ¹⁴⁴ **anticipat'st** foretold   ¹⁴⁵⁻¹⁴⁶ **The flighty . . . it** the fleeting plan is never fulfilled unless an action accompanies it   ¹⁴⁷ **firstlings of my heart** i.e., first thoughts, impulses   ¹⁵⁰ **surprise** attack suddenly   ¹⁵³ **trace him in his line** are of his lineage   IV.ii. ⁷ **titles** possessions

He wants the natural touch:° for the poor wren,
The most diminutive of birds, will fight,   *10*
Her young ones in her nest, against the owl.
All is the fear and nothing is the love;
As little is the wisdom, where the flight
So runs against all reason.
Ross.   My dearest coz,°
I pray you, school° yourself. But, for your husband,   *15*
He is noble, wise, judicious, and best knows
The fits o' th' season.° I dare not speak much further:
But cruel are the times, when we are traitors
And do not know ourselves; when we hold rumor
From what we fear,° yet know not what we fear,   *20*
But float upon a wild and violent sea
Each way and move. I take my leave of you.
Shall not be long but I'll be here again.
Things at the worst will cease,° or else climb upward
To what they were before. My pretty cousin,   *25*
Blessing upon you!
Lady Macduff. Fathered he is, and yet he's fatherless.
Ross. I am so much a fool, should I stay longer,
It would be my disgrace° and your discomfort.
I take my leave at once.   *Exit Ross.*
Lady Macduff.   Sirrah,° your father's dead: *30*
And what will you do now? How will you live?
Son. As birds do, mother.
Lady Macduff.   What, with worms and flies?
Son. With what I get, I mean; and so do they.
Lady Macduff. Poor bird! thou'dst never fear the net nor lime,°
The pitfall nor the gin.°   *35*
Son. Why should I, mother? Poor birds they are not set for.
My father is not dead, for all your saying.
Lady Macduff. Yes, he is dead: how wilt thou do for a father?
Son. Nay, how will you do for a husband?
Lady Macduff. Why, I can buy me twenty at any market.   *40*
Son. Then you'll buy 'em to sell° again.
Lady Macduff. Thou speak'st with all thy wit, and yet, i' faith,
With wit enough for thee.°

---

⁹ *wants the natural touch* i.e., lacks natural affection for his wife and children
¹⁴ *coz* cousin   ¹⁵ *school* control   ¹⁷ *fits o' th' season* disorders of the time
¹⁹⁻²⁰ *hold rumor/From what we fear* believe rumors because we fear   ²⁴ *cease*
i.e., cease worsening   ²⁹ *It would be my disgrace* i.e., I would weep   ³⁰ *Sirrah*
(here an affectionate address to a child)   ³⁴ *lime* bird-lime (smeared on branches
to catch birds)   ³⁵ *gin* trap   ⁴¹ *sell* betray   ⁴³ *for thee* i.e., for a child

Son. Was my father a traitor, mother?

Lady Macduff. Ay, that he was.   45

Son. What is a traitor?

Lady Macduff. Why, one that swears and lies.°

Son. And be all traitors that do so?

Lady Macduff. Every one that does so is a traitor, and must be
hanged.   50

Son. And must they all be hanged that swear and lie?

Lady Macduff. Every one.

Son. Who must hang them?

Lady Macduff. Why, the honest men.

Son. Then the liars and swearers are fools; for there are liars   55
and swearers enow° to beat the honest men and hang
up them.

Lady Macduff. Now, God help thee, poor monkey! But how
wilt thou do for a father?

Son. If he were dead, you'd weep for him. If you would   60
not, it were a good sign that I should quickly have a
new father.

Lady Macduff. Poor prattler, how thou talk'st!

Enter a Messenger.

Messenger. Bless you, fair dame! I am not to you known,
Though in your state of honor I am perfect.°   65
I doubt° some danger does approach you nearly:
If you will take a homely° man's advice,
Be not found here; hence, with your little ones.
To fright you thus, methinks I am too savage;
To do worse to you were fell° cruelty,   70
Which is too nigh your person. Heaven preserve you!
I dare abide no longer.   *Exit Messenger.*

Lady Macduff.   Whither should I fly?
I have done no harm. But I remember now
I am in this earthly world, where to do harm
Is often laudable, to do good sometime   75
Accounted dangerous folly. Why then, alas,
Do I put up that womanly defense,
To say I have done no harm — What are these faces?

Enter Murderers.

---

⁴⁷ *swears and lies* i.e., takes an oath and breaks it   ⁵⁶ *enow* enough   ⁶⁵ *in . . .
perfect* I am fully informed of your honorable rank   ⁶⁶ *doubt* fear   ⁶⁷ *homely*
plain   ⁷⁰ *fell* fierce

Murderer. Where is your husband?

Lady Macduff. I hope, in no place so unsanctified   80
  Where such as thou mayst find him.

Murderer.   He's a traitor.

Son. Thou li'st, thou shag-eared° villain!

Murderer.   What, you egg!

  [*Stabbing him.*]

  Young fry° of treachery!

Son.   He has killed me mother:
  Run away, I pray you!

  [*Dies.*]

                  Exit [*Lady Macduff*], *crying "Murder!"* [*followed by
                                     Murderers*].

Scene III. [*England. Before the King's palace.*]

Enter Malcolm and Macduff.

Malcolm. Let us seek out some desolate shade, and there
  Weep our sad bosoms empty.

Macduff.   Let us rather
  Hold fast the mortal° sword, and like good men
  Bestride our down-fall'n birthdom.° Each new morn
  New widows howl, new orphans cry, new sorrows   5
  Strike heaven on the face, that° it resounds
  As if it felt with Scotland and yelled out
  Like syllable of dolor.°

Malcolm.   What I believe, I'll wail;
  What know, believe; and what I can redress,
  As I shall find the time to friend,° I will.   10
  What you have spoke, it may be so perchance.
  This tyrant, whose sole° name blisters our tongues,
  Was once thought honest:° you have loved him well;
  He hath not touched you yet. I am young; but something
  You may deserve of him through me;° and wisdom°   15
  To offer up a weak, poor, innocent lamb
  T' appease an angry god.

---

⁸² *shag-eared* hairy-eared (?), with shaggy hair hanging over the ears (?)   ⁸³ *fry*
spawn IV.iii. ³ *mortal* deadly ⁴ *Bestride our down-fall'n birthdom* protectively
stand over our native land ⁶ *that* so that ⁸ *Like syllable of dolor* similar sound
of grief ¹⁰ *to friend* friendly, propitious ¹² *sole* very ¹³ *honest* good ¹⁵ *deserve
of him through me* i.e., earn by betraying me to Macbeth ¹⁵ *wisdom* it may
be wise

Macduff. I am not treacherous.
Malcolm.   But Macbeth is.
    A good and virtuous nature may recoil
    In° an imperial charge. But I shall crave your pardon;   20
    That which you are, my thoughts cannot transpose:°
    Angels are bright still, though the brightest° fell:
    Though all things foul would wear° the brows of grace,
    Yet grace must still look so.°
Macduff.   I have lost my hopes.
Malcolm. Perchance even there where I did find my doubts.   25
    Why in that rawness° left you wife and child,
    Those precious motives, those strong knots of love,
    Without leave-taking? I pray you,
    Let not my jealousies° be your dishonors,
    But mine own safeties. You may be rightly just°   30
    Whatever I shall think.
Macduff.   Bleed, bleed, poor country:
    Great tyranny, lay thou thy basis° sure,
    For goodness dare not check° thee: wear thou thy wrongs;
    The title is affeered.° Fare thee well, lord:
    I would not be the villain that thou think'st   35
    For the whole space that's in the tyrant's grasp
    And the rich East to boot.
Malcolm.   Be not offended:
    I speak not as in absolute fear of you.
    I think our country sinks beneath the yoke;
    It weeps, it bleeds, and each new day a gash   40
    Is added to her wounds. I think withal°
    There would be hands uplifted in my right;°
    And here from gracious England° have I offer
    Of goodly thousands: but, for° all this,
    When I shall tread upon the tyrant's head,   45
    Or wear it on my sword, yet my poor country
    Shall have more vices than it had before,
    More suffer, and more sundry ways than ever,
    By him that shall succeed.
Macduff.   What should he be?
Malcolm. It is myself I mean, in whom I know   50

[19-20] *recoil/In*   give way under   [21] *transpose* transform   [22] *the brightest*   i.e.,
Lucifer   [23] *would wear*   desire to wear   [24] *so*   i.e., like itself   [26] *rawness* unprotected
condition   [29] *jealousies*   suspicions   [30] *rightly just*   perfectly honorable   [32] *basis*
foundation   [33] *check*   restrain   [34] *affeered*   legally confirmed   [41] *withal*   moreover
[42] *in my right*   on behalf of my claim   [43] *England*   i.e., the King of England
[44] *for*   despite

All the particulars° of vice so grafted°
That, when they shall be opened,° black Macbeth
Will seem as pure as snow, and the poor state
Esteem him as a lamb, being compared
With my confineless harms.°

Macduff.   Not in the legions   *55*
Of horrid hell can come a devil more damned
In evils to top Macbeth.

Malcolm.   I grant him bloody,
Luxurious,° avaricious, false, deceitful,
Sudden,° malicious, smacking of every sin
That has a name: but there's no bottom, none,   *60*
In my voluptuousness:° your wives, your daughters,
Your matrons and your maids, could not fill up
The cistern of my lust, and my desire
All continent° impediments would o'erbear,
That did oppose my will. Better Macbeth   *65*
Than such an one to reign.

Macduff.   Boundless intemperance
In nature° is a tyranny; it hath been
Th' untimely emptying of the happy throne,
And fall of many kings. But fear not yet
To take upon you what is yours: you may   *70*
Convey° your pleasures in a spacious plenty,
And yet seem cold, the time° you may so hoodwink.
We have willing dames enough. There cannot be
That vulture in you, to devour so many
As will to greatness dedicate themselves,   *75*
Finding it so inclined.

Malcolm.   With this there grows
In my most ill-composed affection° such
A stanchless° avarice that, were I King,
I should cut off the nobles for their lands,
Desire his jewels and this other's house: *80*
And my more-having would be as a sauce
To make me hunger more, that I should forge
Quarrels unjust against the good and loyal,
Destroying them for wealth.

---

[51] *particulars* special kinds [51] *grafted* engrafted [52] *opened* in bloom, i.e., revealed
[55] *confineless harms* unbounded evils [58] *Luxurious* lecherous [59] *Sudden* violent
[61] *voluptuousness* lust [64] *continent* restraining [67] *In nature* in man's nature
[71] *Convey* secretly manage [72] *time* age, i.e., people [77] *ill-composed affection*
evilly compounded character [78] *stanchless* never-ending

Macduff.   This avarice
   Sticks deeper, grows with more pernicious root   85
   Than summer-seeming° lust, and it hath been
   The sword of our slain kings.° Yet do not fear.
   Scotland hath foisons to fill up your will
   Of your mere own.° All these are portable,°
   With other graces weighed.   90
Malcolm. But I have none: the king-becoming graces,
   As justice, verity, temp'rance, stableness,
   Bounty, perseverance, mercy, lowliness,
   Devotion, patience, courage, fortitude,
   I have no relish of° them, but abound   95
   In the division of each several crime,°
   Acting it many ways. Nay, had I pow'r, I should
   Pour the sweet milk of concord into hell,
   Uproar° the universal peace, confound
   All unity on earth.
Macduff.   O Scotland, Scotland!   100
Malcolm. If such a one be fit to govern, speak:
   I am as I have spoken.
Macduff.   Fit to govern!
   No, not to live. O nation miserable!
   With an untitled tyrant bloody-sceptered,
   When shalt thou see thy wholesome days again,   105
   Since that the truest issue of thy throne
   By his own interdiction° stands accursed,
   And does blaspheme his breed?° Thy royal father
   Was a most sainted king: the queen that bore thee,
   Oft'ner upon her knees than on her feet,   110
   Died° every day she lived. Fare thee well!
   These evils thou repeat'st upon thyself
   Hath banished me from Scotland. O my breast,
   Thy hope ends here!
Malcolm.   Macduff, this noble passion,
   Child of integrity, hath from my soul   115
   Wiped the black scruples,° reconciled my thoughts

---

[86] **summer-seeming** befitting summer, i.e., youthful (?) transitory (?) [87] **sword of our slain kings** i.e., the cause of death to our kings [88–89] **foisons . . . own** enough abundance of your own to satisfy your covetousness [89] **portable** bearable [95] **relish of** taste for (?) trace of (?) [96] **division of each several crime** variations of each kind of crime [99] **Uproar** put into a tumult [107] **interdiction** curse, exclusion [108] **breed** ancestry [111] **Died** i.e., prepared for heaven [116] **scruples** suspicions

To thy good truth and honor. Devilish Macbeth
By many of these trains° hath sought to win me
Into his power; and modest wisdom° plucks me
From over-credulous haste: but God above   *120*
Deal between thee and me! For even now
I put myself to° thy direction, and
Unspeak mine own detraction; here abjure
The taints and blames I laid upon myself,
For° strangers to my nature. I am yet   *125*
Unknown to woman, never was forsworn,
Scarcely have coveted what was mine own,
At no time broke my faith, would not betray
The devil to his fellow, and delight
No less in truth than life. My first false speaking *130*
Was this upon myself. What I am truly,
Is thine and my poor country's to command:
Whither indeed, before thy here-approach,
Old Siward, with ten thousand warlike men,
Already at a point,° was setting forth.   *135*
Now we'll together, and the chance of goodness
Be like our warranted quarrel!° Why are you silent?
Macduff. Such welcome and unwelcome things at once
'Tis hard to reconcile.

Enter a Doctor.

Malcolm. Well, more anon. Comes the king forth, I pray
    you?   *140*
Doctor. Ay, sir. There are a crew of wretched souls
That stay° his cure: their malady convinces
The great assay of art;° but at his touch,
Such sanctity hath heaven given his hand,
They presently amend.°   *145*
Malcolm.   I thank you, doctor.
                                   Exit [*Doctor*].

Macduff. What's the disease he means?
Malcolm.   'Tis called the evil:°

---

[118] *trains* plots [119] *modest wisdom* i.e., prudence [122] *to* under [125] *For* as
[135] *at a point* prepared [136-137] *the chance . . . quarrel* i.e., may our chance of
success equal the justice of our cause [142] *stay* await [142-143] *convinces/The great
assay of art* i.e., defies the efforts of medical science [145] *presently amend* immediately recover [146] *evil* (scrofula, called "the king's evil" because it could
allegedly be cured by the king's touch)

A most miraculous work in this good King,
Which often since my here-remain in England
I have seen him do. How he solicits heaven,
Himself best knows: but strangely-visited° people,   *150*
All swoll'n and ulcerous, pitiful to the eye,
The mere° despair of surgery, he cures,
Hanging a golden stamp° about their necks,
Put on with holy prayers: and 'tis spoken,
To the succeeding royalty he leaves   *155*
The healing benediction. With this strange virtue°
He hath a heavenly gift of prophecy,
And sundry blessings hang about his throne
That speak° him full of grace.

    Enter Ross.

Macduff.   See, who comes here?
Malcolm. My countryman; but yet I know him not.   *160*
Macduff. My ever gentle° cousin, welcome hither.
Malcolm. I know him now: good God, betimes° remove
    The means that makes us strangers!
Ross.   Sir, amen.
Macduff. Stands Scotland where it did?
Ross.   Alas, poor country!
    Almost afraid to know itself! It cannot   *165*
    Be called our mother but our grave, where nothing°
    But who knows nothing is once seen to smile;
    Where sighs and groans, and shrieks that rent the air,
    Are made, not marked;° where violent sorrow seems
    A modern ecstasy.° The dead man's knell   *170*
    Is there scarce asked for who, and good men's lives
    Expire before the flowers in their caps,
    Dying or ere they sicken.
Macduff.   O, relation
    Too nice,° and yet too true!
Malcolm.   What's the newest grief?
Ross. That of an hour's age doth hiss the speaker;°   *175*
    Each minute teems° a new one.
Macduff.   How does my wife?

---

[150] **strangely-visited** oddly afflicted [152] **mere** utter [153] **stamp** coin [156] **virtue** power [159] **speak** proclaim [161] **gentle** noble [162] **betimes** quickly [166] **nothing** no one [169] **marked** noticed [170] **modern ecstasy** i.e., ordinary emotion [173–174] **relation/Too nice** tale too accurate [175] **That . . . speaker** i.e., the report of the grief of an hour ago is hissed as stale news [176] **teems** gives birth to

Ross. Why, well.
Macduff.   And all my children?
Ross.   Well too.
Macduff. The tyrant has not battered at their peace?
Ross. No; they were well at peace when I did leave 'em.
Macduff. Be not a niggard of your speech: how goes 't?   180
Ross. When I came hither to transport the tidings,
    Which I have heavily° borne, there ran a rumor
    Of many worthy fellows that were out;°
    Which was to my belief witnessed° the rather,
    For that I saw the tyrant's power° afoot.   185
    Now is the time of help. Your eye in Scotland
    Would create soldiers, make our women fight,
    To doff their dire distresses.
Malcolm.   Be 't their comfort
    We are coming thither. Gracious England hath
    Lent us good Siward and ten thousand men;   190
    An older and a better soldier none
    That Christendom gives out.°
Ross.   Would I could answer
    This comfort with the like! But I have words
    That would° be howled out in the desert air,
    Where hearing should not latch° them.
Macduff.   What concern they?   195
    The general cause or is it a fee-grief
    Due to some single breast?°
Ross.   No mind that's honest
    But in it shares some woe, though the main part
    Pertains to you alone.
Macduff.   If it be mine.
    Keep it not from me, quickly let me have it.   200
Ross. Let not your ears despise my tongue for ever,
    Which shall possess them with the heaviest sound
    That ever yet they heard.
Macduff.   Humh! I guess at it.
Ross. Your castle is surprised;° your wife and babes
    Savagely slaughtered. To relate the manner,   205
    Were, on the quarry° of these murdered deer,
    To add the death of you.
Malcolm.   Merciful heaven!

---

[182] **heavily** sadly   [183] **out** i.e., up in arms   [184] **witnessed** attested   [185] **power** army   [192] **gives out** reports   [194] **would** should   [195] **latch** catch   [196–197] **fee-grief/Due to some single breast** i.e., a personal grief belonging to an individual   [204] **surprised** suddenly attacked   [206] **quarry** heap of slaughtered game

What, man! Ne'er pull your hat upon your brows;
Give sorrow words. The grief that does not speak
Whispers the o'er-fraught heart,° and bids it break.   *210*
Macduff. My children too?
Ross.   Wife, children, servants, all
That could be found.
Macduff.   And I must be from thence!
My wife killed too?
Ross.   I have said.
Malcolm.   Be comforted.
Let's make us med'cines of our great revenge,
To cure this deadly grief.   *215*
Macduff. He has no children. All my pretty ones?
Did you say all? O hell-kite!° All?
What, all my pretty chickens and their dam
At one fell swoop?
Malcolm. Dispute° it like a man.
Macduff.   I shall do so;   *220*
But I must also feel it as a man.
I cannot but remember such things were,
That were most precious to me. Did heaven look on,
And would not take their part? Sinful Macduff,
They were all struck for thee! Naught° that I am,   *225*
Not for their own demerits but for mine
Fell slaughter on their souls. Heaven rest them now!
Malcolm. Be this the whetstone of your sword. Let grief
Convert to anger; blunt not the heart, enrage it.
Macduff. O, I could play the woman with mine eyes,   *230*
And braggart with my tongue! But, gentle heavens,
Cut short all intermission;° front to front°
Bring thou this fiend of Scotland and myself;
Within my sword's length set him. If he 'scape,
Heaven forgive him too!
Malcolm.   This time goes manly.   *235*
Come, go we to the King. Our power is ready;
Our lack is nothing but our leave.° Macbeth
Is ripe for shaking, and the pow'rs above
Put on their instruments.° Receive what cheer you may.
The night is long that never finds the day.   *Exeunt.*   *240*

---

210 ***Whispers the o'er-fraught heart*** whispers to the overburdened heart   **217** ***hell-kite*** hellish bird of prey   **220** ***Dispute*** counter   **225** ***Naught*** wicked   **232** ***intermission*** interval   **232** ***front to front*** forehead to forehead, i.e., face to face   **237** ***Our lack is nothing but our leave*** i.e., we need only to take our leave   **239** ***Put on their instruments*** arm themselves (?) urge us, their agents, onward (?)

ACT V

Scene I. [*Dunsinane. In the castle.*]

Enter a Doctor of Physic and a Waiting-Gentlewoman.

Doctor. I have two nights watched with you, but can perceive no truth in your report. When was it she last walked?

Gentlewoman. Since his Majesty went into the field, I have seen her rise from her bed, throw her nightgown 5
upon her, unlock her closet,° take forth paper, fold it, write upon 't, read it, afterwards seal it, and again return to bed; yet all this while in a most fast sleep.

Doctor. A great perturbation in nature, to receive at once the benefit of sleep and do the effects of watching!° In 10
this slumb'ry agitation, besides her walking and other actual performances,° what, at any time, have you heard her say?

Gentlewoman. That, sir, which I will not report after her.

Doctor. You may to me, and 'tis most meet° you should. 15

Gentlewoman. Neither to you nor anyone, having no witness to confirm my speech.

Enter Lady [*Macbeth*], *with a taper.*

Lo you, here she comes! This is her very guise,° and, upon my life, fast asleep! Observe her; stand close.°

Doctor. How came she by that light? 20

Gentlewoman. Why, it stood by her. She has light by her continually. 'Tis her command.

Doctor. You see, her eyes are open.

Gentlewoman. Ay, but their sense° are shut.

Doctor. What is it she does now? Look, how she rubs her 25
hands.

Gentlewoman. It is an accustomed action with her, to seem thus washing her hands: I have known her continue in this a quarter of an hour.

V.i. **⁶ closet** chest **¹⁰ effects of watching** deeds of one awake **¹² actual performance** deeds **¹⁵ meet** suitable **¹⁸ guise** custom **¹⁹ close** hidden **²⁴ sense** i.e., powers of sight

Lady Macbeth. Yet here's a spot.   *30*

Doctor. Hark! she speaks. I will set down what comes from
   her, to satisfy° my remembrance the more strongly.

Lady Macbeth. Out, damned spot! Out, I say! One: two: why,
   then 'tis time to do 't. Hell is murky. Fie, my lord,
   fie! A soldier, and afeard? What need we fear who   *35*
   knows it, when none can call our pow'r to accompt?°
   Yet who would have thought the old man to have
   had so much blood in him?

Doctor. Do you mark that?

Lady Macbeth. The Thane of Fife had a wife. Where is she   *40*
   now? What, will these hands ne'er be clean? No more
   o' that, my lord, no more o' that! You mar all with
   this starting.

Doctor. Go to°, go to! You have known what you should
   not.

Gentlewoman. She has spoke what she should not, I am   *45*
   sure of that. Heaven knows what she has known.

Lady Macbeth. Here's the smell of the blood still. All the
   perfumes of Arabia will not sweeten this little hand.
   Oh, Oh, Oh!

Doctor. What a sigh is there! The heart is sorely charged.°   *50*

Gentlewoman. I would not have such a heart in my bosom
   for the dignity° of the whole body.

Doctor. Well, well, well —

Gentlewoman. Pray God it be, sir.

Doctor. This disease is beyond my practice.° Yet I have known   *55*
   those which have walked in their sleep who have
   died holily in their beds.

Lady Macbeth. Wash your hands; put on your nightgown;
   look not so pale! I tell you yet again, Banquo's buried.
   He cannot come out on 's° grave.   *60*

Doctor. Even so?

Lady Macbeth. To bed, to bed! There's knocking at the gate.
   Come, come, come, come, give me your hand! What's
   done cannot be undone. To bed, to bed, to bed!

                          Exit Lady [Macbeth].

Doctor. Will she go now to bed?   *65*

Gentlewoman. Directly.

---

[32] **satisfy** confirm   [36] **to accompt** into account   [44] **Go to** (an exclamation)
[50] **charged** burdened   [52] **dignity** worth, rank   [55] **practice** professional skill
[60] **on 's** of his

Doctor. Foul whisp'rings are abroad. Unnatural deeds
    Do breed unnatural troubles. Infected minds
    To their deaf pillows will discharge their secrets.
    More needs she the divine than the physician.   *70*
    God, God forgive us all! Look after her;
    Remove from her the means of all annoyance,°
    And still° keep eyes upon her. So good night.
    My mind she has mated° and amazed my sight:
    I think, but dare not speak.
Gentlewoman.   Good night, good doctor.   *75*
                                  Exeunt.

Scene II. [*The country near Dunsinane.*]

*Drum and colors. Enter Menteith, Caithness, Angus, Lennox,
Soldiers.*

Menteith. The English pow'r° is near, led on by Malcolm,
    His uncle Siward and the good Macduff.
    Revenges burn in them; for their dear° causes
    Would to the bleeding and the grim alarm
    Excite the mortified man.°
Angus.   Near Birnam Wood   *5*
    Shall we well meet them; that way are they coming.
Caithness. Who knows if Donalbain be with his brother?
Lennox. For certain, sir, he is not. I have a file°
    Of all the gentry: there is Siward's son,
    And many unrough° youths that even now   *10*
    Protest° their first of manhood.
Menteith.   What does the tyrant?
Caithness. Great Dunsinane he strongly fortifies.
    Some say he's mad; others, that lesser hate him,
    Do call it valiant fury: but, for certain,
    He cannot buckle his distempered° cause   *15*
    Within the belt of rule.°
Angus.   Now does he feel
    His secret murders sticking on his hands;
    Now minutely revolts upbraid° his faith-breach.
    Those he commands move only in command,

---

[72] *annoyance* injury [73] *still* continuously [74] *mated* baffled V.ii. [1] *pow'r* army
[3] *dear* heartfelt [4–5] *Would . . . man* i.e., would incite a dead man (or "a paralyzed
man") to join the bloody and grim call to battle [8] *file* list [10] *unrough* i.e.,
beardless [11] *Protest* assert [15] *distempered* swollen by dropsy [16] *rule* self-
control [18] *minutely revolts upbraid* rebellions every minute rebuke

Nothing in love. Now does he feel his title   20
Hang loose about him, like a giant's robe
Upon a dwarfish thief.
Menteith.   Who then shall blame
His pestered° senses to recoil and start,
When all that is within him does condemn
Itself for being there?
Caithness.   Well, march we on,   25
To give obedience where 'tis truly owed.
Meet we the med'cine° of the sickly weal,°
And with him pour we, in our country's purge,
Each drop of us.°
Lennox.   Or so much as it needs
To dew° the sovereign° flower and drown the weeds.   30
Make we our march towards Birnam.

                              Exeunt, marching.

Scene III. [*Dunsinane. In the castle.*]

Enter Macbeth, Doctor, and Attendants.

Macbeth. Bring me no more reports; let them fly all!
Till Birnam Wood remove to Dunsinane
I cannot taint° with fear. What's the boy Malcolm?
Was he not born of woman? The spirits that know
All mortal consequences° have pronounced me thus: 5
"Fear not, Macbeth; no man that's born of woman
Shall e'er have power upon thee." Then fly, false thanes,
And mingle with the English epicures.
The mind I sway° by and the heart I bear
Shall never sag with doubt nor shake with fear.   10

Enter Servant.

The devil damn thee black, thou cream-faced loon!°
Where got'st thou that goose look?
Servant. There is ten thousand —
Macbeth.   Geese, villain?
Servant.   Soldiers, sir.
Macbeth. Go prick thy face and over-red° thy fear,

---

²³ **pestered** tormented ²⁷ **med'cine** i.e., Malcolm ²⁷ **weal** commonwealth ²⁹ **Each drop of us** i.e., every last drop of our blood (?) ³⁰ **dew** bedew, water (and thus make grow) ³⁰ **sovereign** (1) royal (2) remedial V.iii. ³ **taint** become infected ⁵ **mortal consequences** future human events ⁹ **sway** move ¹¹ **loon** fool ¹⁴ **over-red** cover with red

Thou lily-livered boy. What soldiers, patch?° 15
Death of° thy soul! Those linen° cheeks of thine
Are counselors to fear. What soldiers, whey-face?
Servant. The English force, so please you.
Macbeth. Take thy face hence. [*Exit Servant.*]
                  Seyton! — I am sick at heart,
When I behold — Seyton, I say! — This push° 20
Will cheer me ever, or disseat° me now.
I have lived long enough. My way of life
Is fall'n into the sear,° the yellow leaf,
And that which should accompany old age,
As honor, love, obedience, troops of friends, 25
I must not look to have; but, in their stead,
Curses not loud but deep, mouth-honor, breath,
Which the poor heart would fain deny, and dare not.
Seyton!

    Enter Seyton.

Seyton. What's your gracious pleasure?
Macbeth.   What news more? 30
Seyton. All is confirmed, my lord, which was reported.
Macbeth. I'll fight, till from my bones my flesh be hacked.
    Give me my armor.
Seyton.   'Tis not needed yet.
Macbeth. I'll put it on.
    Send out moe° horses, skirr° the country round. 35
    Hang those that talk of fear. Give me mine armor.
    How does your patient, doctor?
Doctor.   Not so sick, my lord,
As she is troubled with thick-coming fancies
That keep her from her rest.
Macbeth.   Cure her of that.
Canst thou not minister to a mind diseased, 40
Pluck from the memory a rooted sorrow,
Raze out° the written troubles of the brain,
And with some sweet oblivious° antidote
Cleanse the stuffed bosom of that perilous stuff
Which weighs upon the heart?
Doctor.   Therein the patient 45
Must minister to himself.

---

¹⁵ *patch* fool ¹⁶ *of* upon ¹⁶ *linen* i.e., pale ²⁰ *push* effort ²¹ *disseat* i.e.,
unthrone (with wordplay on "cheer," pronounced "chair") ²³ *sear* withered
³⁵ *moe* more ³⁵ *skirr* scour ⁴² *Raze out* erase ⁴³ *oblivious* causing forgetfulness

Macbeth. Throw physic° to the dogs, I'll none of it.
    Come, put mine armor on. Give me my staff.
    Seyton, send out. — Doctor, the thanes fly from me. —
    Come, sir, dispatch.° If thou couldst, doctor, cast   50
    The water° of my land, find her disease
    And purge it to a sound and pristine health,
    I would applaud thee to the very echo,
    That should applaud again. — Pull 't off, I say. —
    What rhubarb, senna, or what purgative drug,   55
    Would scour these English hence? Hear'st thou of them?
Doctor. Ay, my good lord; your royal preparation
    Makes us hear something.
Macbeth.   Bring it° after me.
    I will not be afraid of death and bane°
    Till Birnam Forest come to Dunsinane.   60
Doctor. [*Aside*] Were I from Dunsinane away and clear,
    Profit again should hardly draw me here.   *Exeunt.*

Scene IV. [*Country near Birnam Wood.*]

Drum and colors. Enter Malcolm, Siward, Macduff, Siward's Son,
Menteith, Caithness, Angus, and Soldiers, marching.

Malcolm. Cousins, I hope the days are near at hand
    That chambers will be safe.°
Menteith.   We doubt it nothing.°
Siward. What wood is this before us?
Menteith.   The Wood of Birnam.
Malcolm. Let every soldier hew him down a bough
    And bear 't before him. Thereby shall we shadow   5
    The numbers of our host, and make discovery°
    Err in report of us.
Soldiers.   It shall be done.
Siward. We learn no other but° the confident tyrant
    Keeps still in Dunsinane, and will endure°
    Our setting down before 't.
Malcolm.   'Tis his main hope,   10
    For where there is advantage to be given°
    Both more and less° have given him the revolt,

---

[47] *physic* medical science   [50] *dispatch* hurry   [50–51] *cast/The water* analyze the urine   [58] *it* i.e., the armor   [59] *bane* destruction   V.iv. [2] *That chambers will be safe* i.e., that a man will be safe in his bedroom   [2] *nothing* not at all   [6] *discovery* reconnaisance   [8] *No other but* nothing but that   [9] *endure* allow   [11] *advantage to be given* afforded an opportunity   [12] *more and less* high and low

And none serve with him but constrainèd things
Whose hearts are absent too.
Macduff.   Let our just censures
Attend the true event,° and put we on   *15*
Industrious soldiership.
Siward.   The time approaches,
That will with due decision make us know
What we shall say we have and what we owe.°
Thoughts speculative their unsure hopes relate,
But certain issue strokes must arbitrate:°   *20*
Towards which advance the war.°

                                        Exeunt, marching.

Scene V. [*Dunsinane. Within the castle.*]

Enter Macbeth, Seyton, and Soldiers, with drum and colors.

Macbeth. Hang out our banners on the outward walls.
The cry is still "They come!" Our castle's strength
Will laugh a siege to scorn. Here let them lie
Till famine and the ague° eat them up.
Were they not forced° with those that should be ours,   *5*
We might have met them dareful,° beard to beard,
And beat them backward home.

A cry within of women.

                                        What is that noise?
Seyton. It is the cry of women, my good lord.   [*Exit.*]
Macbeth. I have almost forgot the taste of fears:
The time has been, my senses would have cooled   *10*
To hear a night-shriek, and my fell° of hair
Would at a dismal treatise° rouse and stir
As life were in 't. I have supped full with horrors.
Direness, familiar to my slaughterous thoughts,
Cannot once start° me.

[*Enter Seyton.*]

                                        Wherefore was that cry?   *15*
Seyton. The Queen, my lord, is dead.

---

¹⁴⁻¹⁵ *just censures/Attend the true event* true judgment await the actual outcome
¹⁸ *owe* own (the contrast is between "what we shall say we have" and "what we
shall really have") ²⁰ *certain issue strokes must arbitrate* the definite outcome
must be decided by battle ²¹ *war* army V.v. ⁴ *ague* fever ⁵ *forced* reinforced
⁶ *met them dareful* i.e., met them in the battlefield boldly ¹¹ *fell* pelt ¹² *treatise*
story ¹⁵ *start* startle

Macbeth. She should° have died hereafter;
    There would have been a time for such a word.°
    Tomorrow, and tomorrow, and tomorrow
    Creeps in this petty pace from day to day,   *20*
    To the last syllable of recorded time;
    And all our yesterdays have lighted fools
    The way to dusty death. Out, out, brief candle!
    Life's but a walking shadow, a poor player
    That struts and frets his hour upon the stage   *25*
    And then is heard no more. It is a tale
    Told by an idiot, full of sound and fury
    Signifying nothing.

    Enter a Messenger.

    Thou com'st to use thy tongue; thy story quickly!
Messenger. Gracious my lord,   *30*
    I should report that which I say I saw,
    But know not how to do 't.
Macbeth.   Well, say, sir.
Messenger. As I did stand my watch upon the hill,
    I looked toward Birnam, and anon, methought,
    The wood began to move.
Macbeth.   Liar and slave!   *35*
Messenger. Let me endure your wrath, if 't be not so.
    Within this three mile may you see it coming;
    I say a moving grove.
Macbeth.   If thou speak'st false,
    Upon the next tree shalt thou hang alive,
    Till famine cling° thee. If thy speech be sooth,°   *40*
    I care not if thou dost for me as much.
    I pull in resolution,° and begin
    To doubt° th' equivocation of the fiend
    That lies like truth: "Fear not, till Birnam Wood
    Do come to Dunsinane!" And now a wood   *45*
    Comes toward Dunsinane. Arm, arm, and out!
    If this which he avouches° does appear,
    There is nor flying hence nor tarrying here.
    I 'gin to be aweary of the sun,
    And wish th' estate° o' th' world were now undone.   *50*
    Ring the alarum bell! Blow wind, come wrack!
    At least we'll die with harness° on our back.

                                  Exeunt.

---

[17] *should* inevitably would (?)   [18] *word* message   [40] *cling* wither   [40] *sooth* truth
[42] *pull in resolution* restrain confidence   [43] *doubt* suspect   [47] *avouches* asserts
[50] *th' estate* the orderly condition   [52] *harness* armor

Scene VI. [*Dunsinane. Before the castle.*]

Drum and colors. Enter Malcolm, Siward, Macduff, and their army, with boughs.

Malcolm. Now near enough. Your leavy° screens throw down,
And show like those you are. You, worthy uncle,
Shall, with my cousin, your right noble son,
Lead our first battle.° Worthy Macduff and we°
Shall take upon 's what else remains to do,   5
According to our order.°
Siward.   Fare you well.
Do we° but find the tyrant's power° tonight,
Let us be beaten, if we cannot fight.
Macduff. Make all our trumpets speak; give them all breath,
Those clamorous harbingers of blood and death.   10
                              Exeunt. Alarums continued.

Scene VII. [*Another part of the field.*]

Enter Macbeth.

Macbeth. They have tied me to a stake; I cannot fly,
But bearlike I must fight the course.° What's he
That was not born of woman? Such a one
Am I to fear, or none.

Enter Young Siward.

Young Siward. What is thy name?
Macbeth.   Thou'lt be afraid to hear it.   5
Young Siward. No; though thou call'st thyself a hotter name
Than any is in hell.
Macbeth.   My name's Macbeth.
Young Siward. The devil himself could not pronounce a title
More hateful to mine ear.
Macbeth.   No, nor more fearful.
Young Siward. Thou liest, abhorrèd tyrant; with my sword   10
I'll prove the lie thou speak'st.

Fight, and Young Siward slain.

Macbeth.   Thou wast born of woman.

V.vi. ¹ **leavy** leafy ⁴ **battle** battalion ⁴ **we** (Malcolm uses the royal "we")
⁶ **order** plan ⁷ **Do we** if we do ⁷ **power** forces V.vii. ² **course** bout, round
(he has in mind an attack of dogs or men upon a bear chained to a stake)

But swords I smile at, weapons laugh to scorn,
Brandished by man that's of a woman born.

Exit.

Alarums. Enter Macduff.

Macduff. That way the noise is. Tyrant, show thy face!
    If thou be'st slain and with no stroke of mine,   15
    My wife and children's ghosts will haunt me still.
    I cannot strike at wretched kerns,° whose arms
    Are hired to bear their staves.° Either thou, Macbeth,
    Or else my sword, with an unbattered edge,
    I sheathe again undeeded.° There thou shouldst be;   20
    By this great clatter, one of greatest note
    Seems bruited.° Let me find him, Fortune!
    And more I beg not.   *Exit. Alarums.*

Enter Malcolm and Siward.

Siward. This way, my lord. The castle's gently rend'red:°
    The tyrant's people on both sides do fight;   25
    The noble thanes do bravely in the war;
    The day almost itself professes° yours,
    And little is to do.
Malcolm.   We have met with foes
    That strike beside us.°
Siward.   Enter, sir, the castle.

Exeunt. Alarum.

Scene VIII. [*Another part of the field.*]

Enter Macbeth.

Macbeth. Why should I play the Roman fool, and die
    On mine own sword? Whiles I see lives,° the gashes
    Do better upon them.

Enter Macduff.

Macduff.   Turn, hell-hound, turn!
Macbeth. Of all men else I have avoided thee.

---

[17] **kerns** foot soldiers (contemptuous)   [18] **staves** spears   [20] **undeeded** i.e., having done nothing   [22] **bruited** reported   [24] **gently rend'red** surrendered without a struggle   [27] **itself professes** declares itself   [29] **beside us** i.e., deliberately miss us (?) as our comrades (?)   V.viii.   [2] **Whiles I see lives** so long as I see living men

But get thee back! My soul is too much charged°   5
With blood of thine already.
Macduff.   I have no words:
My voice is in my sword, thou bloodier villain
Than terms can give thee out!°

Fight. Alarum.

Macbeth.   Thou losest labor:
As easy mayst thou the intrenchant° air
With thy keen sword impress° as make me bleed: 10
Let fall thy blade on vulnerable crests;
I bear a charmèd life, which must not yield
To one of woman born.
Macduff.   Despair° thy charm,
And let the angel° whom thou still hast served
Tell thee, Macduff was from his mother's womb   15
Untimely ripped.
Macbeth. Accursèd be that tongue that tells me so,
For it hath cowed my better part of man!°
And be these juggling fiends no more believed,
That palter° with us in a double sense;   20
That keep the word of promise to our ear,
And break it to our hope. I'll not fight with thee.
Macduff. Then yield thee, coward,
And live to be the show and gaze o' th' time:°
We'll have thee, as our rarer monsters° are,   25
Painted upon a pole,° and underwrit,
"Here may you see the tyrant."
Macbeth.   I will not yield,
To kiss the ground before young Malcolm's feet,
And to be baited° with the rabble's curse.
Though Birnam Wood be come to Dunsinane,   30
And thou opposed, being of no woman born,
Yet I will try the last. Before my body
I throw my warlike shield. Lay on, Macduff;
And damned be him that first cries "Hold, enough!"
                     Exeunt, fighting. Alarums.

---

[5] **charged** burdened   [8] **terms can give thee out** words can describe you   [9] **intrenchant** incapable of being cut   [10] **impress** make an impression on   [13] **Despair** despair of   [14] **angel** i.e., fallen angel, fiend   [18] **better part of man** manly spirit   [20] **palter** equivocate   [24] **gaze o' th' time** spectacle of the age   [25] **monsters** freaks   [26] **Painted upon a pole** i.e., pictured on a banner set by a showman's booth   [29] **baited** assailed (like a bear by dogs)

[Re-]enter fighting, and Macbeth slain. [Exit Macduff, with Mac-
beth.] Retreat and flourish.° Enter, with drum and colors,
Malcolm, Siward, Ross, Thanes, and Soldiers.

Malcolm. I would the friends we miss were safe arrived.   35
Siward. Some must go off;° and yet, by these I see,
    So great a day as this is cheaply bought.
Malcolm. Macduff is missing, and your noble son.
Ross. Your son, my lord, has paid a soldier's debt:
    He only lived but till he was a man;   40
    The which no sooner had his prowess confirmed
    In the unshrinking station° where he fought,
    But like a man he died.
Siward.   Then he is dead?
Ross. Ay, and brought off the field. Your cause of sorrow
    Must not be measured by his worth, for then   45
    It hath no end.
Siward.   Had he his hurts before?
Ross. Ay, on the front.
Siward.   Why then, God's soldier be he!
    Had I as many sons as I have hairs,
    I would not wish them to a fairer death:
    And so his knell is knolled.
Malcolm.   He's worth more sorrow,   50
    And that I'll spend for him.
Siward.   He's worth no more:
    They say he parted well and paid his score:°
    And so God be with him! Here comes newer comfort.

Enter Macduff, with Macbeth's head.

Macduff. Hail, King! for so thou art: behold, where stands
    Th' usurper's cursèd head. The time is free.°   55
    I see thee compassed° with thy kingdom's pearl,
    That speak my salutation in their minds,
    Whose voices I desire aloud with mine:
    Hail, King of Scotland!
All.   Hail, King of Scotland!

Flourish.

---

s.d. *Retreat and flourish* trumpet call to withdraw, and fanfare   **36** *go off* die
(theatrical metaphor)   **42** *unshrinking station* i.e., place at which he stood firmly
52 *parted well and paid his score* departed well and settled his account   **55** *The
time is free* the world is liberated   **56** *compassed* surrounded

Malcolm. We shall not spend a large expense of time   *60*
    Before we reckon with your several loves,°
    And make us even with you. My thanes and kinsmen,
    Henceforth be earls, the first that ever Scotland
    In such an honor named. What's more to do,
    Which would be planted newly with the time° —   *65*
    As calling home our exiled friends abroad
    That fled the snares of watchful tyranny,
    Producing forth the cruel ministers°
    Of this dead butcher and his fiendlike queen,
    Who, as 'tis thought, by self and violent° hands   *70*
    Took off her life — this, and what needful else
    That calls upon us,° by the grace of Grace
    We will perform in measure, time, and place:°
    So thanks to all at once and to each one,
    Whom we invite to see us crowned at Scone.   *75*
                     Flourish. Exeunt Omnes.

            FINIS

QUESTIONS

Act I

1. In I.i we hear Macbeth's name, but nothing is said about his character. Is it fair, however, to say that since the Witches name him, a spectator or reader responds by assuming that Macbeth is evil?

2. What is your response to Macbeth, on the basis of what the Captain says about him in I.ii.34–40?

3. Banquo, not Macbeth, is the first to speak to the Witches (I.iii.39), but they do not reply to him. Judging from his comment, each Witch puts a finger on her lips — presumably a gesture of silence. But when Macbeth addresses the Witches they reply to Macbeth. What do you make out of their initial refusal to speak to Banquo? (Recall, too, that the Witches did not mention Banquo in I.i.)

4. Banquo in I.iii.51 asks why Macbeth startles and seems to fear good news. What explanations can you offer? Why does Macbeth seem "rapt" (I.iii.57)? Is Banquo also "rapt"? How do you know?

---

[61] *reckon with your several loves* reward the devotion of each of you   [64–65] *What's more . . . time* i.e., what else must be done which should be newly established in this age   [68] *ministers* agents   [70] *self and violent* her own violent   [72] *calls upon us* demands my attention   [73] *in measure, time, and place* fittingly, at the appropriate time and place

5. Macbeth and Banquo both receive prophecies in I.iii. Do their responses differentiate the two men? A little? A lot? By the end of this scene, how would you characterize each of the two?

6. What impression do you form of Duncan in I.iv?

7. I.vii is set against an introductory background of a banquet (music, torches, servants), but since only Macbeth and Lady Macbeth speak, the locale could be their bedroom or any other private place. Why do you think Shakespeare chose to set the dialogue against a banquet?

8. Judging from I.vii.46–52, what is Macbeth's idea of manhood, and what is Lady Macbeth's idea of manhood?

Act II

1. In II.i.7–9 Banquo speaks of the "cursèd thoughts" that enter into one's dreams. What do you imagine his thoughts are? Judging from this scene as a whole, how would you compare Banquo with Macbeth? (What do you think Macbeth is getting at in II.i.25–26, and what is Banquo communicating in II.i.26–29?)

2. The knocking at II.ii.56, which startles Macbeth, presumably also startles the reader or spectator. Would you go so far as to say that although Macbeth's villainy is evident to you, you hope he will *not* (at least for a while) be detected?

3. On the basis of II.ii, what is your impression of Lady Macbeth?

4. The business of the drunken porter in II.iii is often said to provide comic relief, i.e., to relax (momentarily) a tension that has become almost unbearable. Does it have this effect on you?

Act III

1. What is your response to Macbeth's speech in III.i.47–72? Is he repentent? If not, what state of mind is he in?

2. In III.i.75–114 Macbeth goes to some pains to assure the murderers that Banquo is their enemy. Since the murderers make it clear in III.i.108–114 that they need no persuasion to kill Banquo, why do you suppose Macbeth bothers to try to convince them that Banquo is blameworthy?

3. In III.ii.8 Lady Macbeth asks Macbeth, "Why do you keep alone?" In III.ii.44 she asks him, "What's to be done?" but Macbeth refuses to share with her his plan to kill Banquo and Fleance. Why do you think he has not been sharing his thoughts with the woman who in I.0.11 was his "dearest partner in greatness"?

4. Seeing the ghost of Banquo, Macbeth says (III.iv.51–52), "Thou canst not say I did it. Never shake / Thy gory locks at me." Exactly what do you suppose he means? Do you think he believes what he says? What is your response to him when you hear him say this?

Act IV

1. In IV.i.150–154 Macbeth plans the murder of Macduff's wife. How does his state of mind here compare with his state of mind when he planned to murder Duncan? When he planned to murder Banquo?
2. The words in a play are not, of course, just words; they are revelations of states of mind. Try, in particular, to enter into the minds of Macduff, Ross, and Malcolm in IV.iii.164–240, where Ross tells Macduff of the murder of Lady Macduff and the children. How, for instance — with what tone — do you think lines 170–173 (Ross on the general condition of Scotland) should be spoken? Line 179 (Ross reporting that Macduff's family is "at peace")? Lines 208–210 (Malcolm urging Macduff to speak)? Lines 216–227 (Macduff and Malcolm)? In line 216, what do you think Macduff is thinking when he says, "He has no children"?

Act V

1. What is your response toward Lady Macbeth in the sleep-walking scene (V.i). Does the scene evoke the Aristotelian emotions (see page 599) of pity and terror?
2. In V.ii.13–14 Caithness says that some people describe Macbeth's behavior as "mad," others as "valiant fury." How would you describe the Macbeth whom you see in the rest of this scene? If you were directing actors in V.iii.30–62, what gestures would you want them to use?
3. What do you think Macbeth's state of mind is at V.v.9–15 after "A cry within of women"?
4. In V.vii.1–2 Macbeth says, "They have tied me to a stake; I cannot fly / But bearlike I must fight the course." Who are "they," and are "they" responsible for Macbeth's plight? Or is Macbeth?
5. What do you make of V.viii.4–9? Do you hear a note of remorse in it? Or fear of retribution? Or what?
6. How would you characterize Macbeth as he speaks his final speech (V.viii.27–34)?
7. In V.viii.69 Malcolm speaks of "this dead butcher and his fiendlike queen." How satisfactory do you find this as a characterization of Macbeth and Lady Macbeth?

Henrik Ibsen (*Norwegian. 1828–1906*)

A Doll's House

Translated by Otto Reinert

List of Characters

Torvald Helmer, a lawyer
Nora, his wife
Dr. Rank
Mrs. Linde
Krogstad
The Helmers' three small children
Anne-Marie, the children's nurse
A housemaid
A porter

Scene. *The Helmers' living room*

ACT I

A pleasant, tastefully but not expensively furnished, living room. A door on the rear wall, right, leads to the front hall, another door, left, to Helmer's study. Between the two doors a piano. A third door in the middle of the left wall; further front a window. Near the window a round table with easy chairs and a small couch. Towards the rear of the right wall a fourth door; further front a tile stove with a rocking chair and a couple of arm chairs in front of it. Between the stove and the side door a small table. Copperplate etchings on the walls. A whatnot with porcelain figurines and other small objects. A small bookcase with deluxe editions. A rug on the floor; fire in the stove. Winter day.

The doorbell rings, then the sound of the front door opening. Nora, dressed for outdoors, enters, humming cheerfully. She carries several packages, which she puts down on the table, right. She leaves the door to the front hall open; there a Porter is seen holding a Christmas tree and a basket. He gives them to the Maid, who has let them in.

Nora. Be sure to hide the Christmas tree, Helene. The children mustn't see it before tonight when we've trimmed it. (*Opens her purse; to the Porter.*) How much?

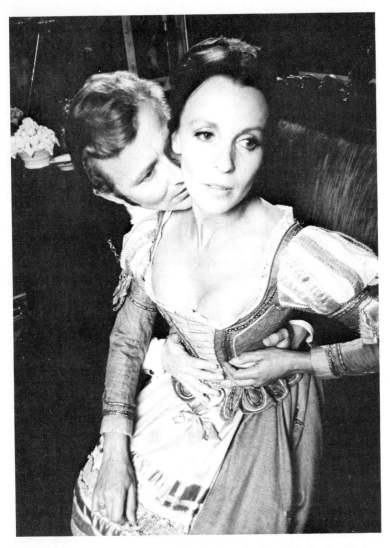

Claire Bloom starred as Nora in the 1971 production of A Doll's House.
Photograph © by Martha Swope. Used by permission.

Porter. Fifty øre.

Nora. Here's a crown. No, keep the change. (*The Porter thanks her, leaves. Nora closes the door. She keeps laughing quietly to herself as she takes off her coat, etc. She takes a bag of macaroons from her pocket and eats a couple. She walks cautiously over to the door to the study and listens.*) Yes, he's home. (*Resumes her humming, walks over to the table, right.*)

Helmer (*in his study*). Is that my little lark twittering out there?

Nora (*opening some of the packages*). That's right.

Helmer. My squirrel bustling about?

Nora. Yes.

Helmer. When did squirrel come home?

Nora. Just now. (*Puts the bag of macaroons back in her pocket, wipes her mouth.*) Come out here, Torvald. I want to show you what I've bought.

Helmer. I'm busy! (*After a little while he opens the door and looks in, pen in hand.*) Bought, eh? All that? So little wastrel has been throwing money around again?

Nora. Oh but Torvald, this Christmas we can be a little extravagant, can't we? It's the first Christmas we don't have to scrimp.

Helmer. I don't know about that. We certainly don't have money to waste.

Nora. Yes, Torvald, we do. A little, anyway. Just a tiny little bit? Now that you're going to get that big salary and make lots and lots of money.

Helmer. Starting at New Year's, yes. But payday isn't till the end of the quarter.

Nora. That doesn't matter. We can always borrow.

Helmer. Nora! (*Goes over to her and playfully pulls her ear.*) There you go being irresponsible again. Suppose I borrowed a thousand crowns today and you spent it all for Christmas and on New Year's Eve a tile hit me in the head and laid me out cold.

Nora (*putting her hand over his mouth*). I won't have you say such horrid things.

Helmer. But suppose it happened. Then what?

Nora. If it did, I wouldn't care whether we owed money or not.

Helmer. But what about the people I had borrowed from?

Nora. Who cares about them! They are strangers.

Helmer. Nora, Nora, you are a woman. No, really! You know how I feel about that. No debts! A home in debt isn't a free home, and if it isn't free it isn't beautiful. We've managed nicely so far, you and I, and that's the way we'll go on. It won't be for much longer.

Nora (*walks over toward the stove*). All right, Torvald. Whatever you say.

Helmer (*follows her*). Come, come, my little songbird mustn't droop her wings. What's this? Can't have a pouty squirrel in the house, you know. (*Takes out his wallet.*) Nora, what do you think I have here?

Nora (*turns around quickly*). Money!

Helmer. Here. (*Gives her some bills.*) Don't you think I know Christmas is expensive?

Nora (*counting*). Ten — twenty — thirty — forty. Thank you, thank you, Torvald. This helps a lot.

Helmer. I certainly hope so.

Nora. It does, it does. But I want to show you what I got. It was cheap, too. Look. New clothes for Ivar. And a sword. And a horse and trumpet for Bob. And a doll and a little bed for Emmy. It isn't any good, but it wouldn't last, anyway. And here's some dress material and scarves for the maids. I feel bad about old Anne-Marie, though. She really should be getting much more.

Helmer. And what's in here?

Nora (*cries*). Not till tonight!

Helmer. I see. But now what does my little prodigal have in mind for herself?

Nora. Oh, nothing. I really don't care.

Helmer. Of course you do. Tell me what you'd like. Within reason.

Nora. Oh, I don't know. Really, I don't. The only thing —

Helmer. Well?

Nora (*fiddling with his buttons, without looking at him*). If you really want to give me something, you might — you could —

Helmer. All right, let's have it.

Nora (*quickly*). Some money, Torvald. Just as much as you think you can spare. Then I'll buy myself something one of these days.

Helmer. No, really Nora —

Nora. Oh yes, please, Torvald. Please? I'll wrap the money in pretty gold paper and hang it on the tree. Won't that be nice?

Helmer. What's the name for little birds that are always spending money?

Nora. Wastrels, I know. But please let's do it my way, Torvald. Then I'll have time to decide what I need most. Now that's sensible, isn't it?

Helmer (*smiling*). Oh, very sensible. That is, if you really bought yourself something you could use. But it all disappears in

the household expenses or you buy things you don't need.
And then you come back to me for more.

Nora. Oh, but Torvald —

Helmer. That's the truth, dear little Nora, and you know it. (*Puts
his arm around her.*) My wastrel is a little sweetheart, but she
does go through an awful lot of money awfully fast. You've
no idea how expensive it is for a man to keep a wastrel.

Nora. That's not fair, Torvald. I really save all I can.

Helmer (*laughs*). Oh, I believe that. All you can. Meaning, exactly
nothing!

Nora (*hums, smiles mysteriously*). You don't know all the things we
songbirds and squirrels need money for, Torvald.

Helmer. You know, you're funny. Just like your father. You're
always looking for ways to get money, but as soon as you
do it runs through your fingers and you can never say what
you spent it for. Well, I guess I'll just have to take you the
way you are. It's in your blood. Yes, that sort of thing is
hereditary, Nora.

Nora. In that case, I wish I had inherited many of Daddy's qualities.

Helmer. And I don't want you any different from just what you
are — my own sweet little songbird. Hey! — I think I just
noticed something. Aren't you looking — what's the word?
— a little — sly — ?

Nora. I am?

Helmer. You definitely are. Look at me.

Nora (*looks at him*). Well?

Helmer (*wagging a finger*). Little sweet-tooth hasn't by any chance
been on a rampage today, has she?

Nora. Of course not. Whatever makes you think that?

Helmer. A little detour by the pastryshop maybe?

Nora. No, I assure you, Torvald —

Helmer. Nibbled a little jam?

Nora. Certainly not!

Helmer. Munched a macaroon or two?

Nora. No, really, Torvald, I honestly —

Helmer. All right. Of course I was only joking.

Nora (*walks toward the table, right*). You know I wouldn't do anything
to displease you.

Helmer. I know. And I have your promise. (*Over to her.*) All right,
keep your little Christmas secrets to yourself, Nora darling.
They'll all come out tonight, I suppose, when we light the
tree.

Nora. Did you remember to invite Rank?

Helmer. No, but there's no need to. He knows he'll have dinner with us. Anyway, I'll see him later this morning. I'll ask him then. I did order some good wine. Oh Nora, you've no idea how much I'm looking forward to tonight!

Nora. Me too. And the children, Torvald! They'll have such a good time!

Helmer. You know, it *is* nice to have a good, safe job and a comfortable income. Feels good just thinking about it. Don't you agree?

Nora. Oh, it's wonderful!

Helmer. Remember last Christmas? For three whole weeks you shut yourself up every evening till long after midnight, making ornaments for the Christmas tree and I don't know what else. Some big surprise for all of us, anyway. I'll be damned if I've ever been so bored in my whole life!

Nora. I wasn't bored at all.

Helmer (smiling). But you've got to admit you didn't have much to show for it in the end.

Nora. Oh, don't tease me again about that! Could I help it that the cat got in and tore up everything?

Helmer. Of course you couldn't, my poor little Nora. You just wanted to please the rest of us, and that's the important thing. But I am glad the hard times are behind us. Aren't you?

Nora. Oh yes. I think it's just wonderful.

Helmer. This year I won't be bored and lonely. And you won't have to strain your dear eyes and your delicate little hands —

Nora (claps her hands). No I won't, will I, Torvald? Oh, how wonderful, how lovely, to hear you say that! (*Puts her arm under his.*) Let me tell you how I think we should arrange things, Torvald. Soon as Christmas is over — (*The doorbell rings.*) Someone's at the door. (*Straightens things up a bit.*) A caller, I suppose. Bother!

Helmer. Remember, I'm not home for visitors.

The Maid (in the door to the front hall). Ma'am, there's a lady here —

Nora. All right. Ask her to come in.

The Maid (to Helmer). And the Doctor just arrived.

Helmer. Is he in the study?

The Maid. Yes, sir.

Helmer exits into his study. The Maid shows Mrs. Linde in and closes the door behind her as she leaves. Mrs. Linde is in travel dress.

Mrs. Linde (timid and a little hesitant). Good morning, Nora.

Nora (uncertainly). Good morning.

Mrs. Linde. I don't believe you know who I am.

Nora. No — I'm not sure — Though I know I should — Of course! Kristine! It's you!

Mrs. Linde. Yes, it's me.

Nora. And I didn't even recognize you! I had no idea! (*In a lower voice.*) You've changed, Kristine.

Mrs. Linde. I'm sure I have. It's been nine or ten long years.

Nora. Has it really been that long? Yes, you're right. I've been so happy these last eight years. And now you're here. Such a long trip in the middle of winter. How brave!

Mrs. Linde. I got in on the steamer this morning.

Nora. To have some fun over the holidays, of course. That's lovely. For we *are* going to have fun. But take off your coat! You aren't cold, are you? (*Helps her.*) There, now! Let's sit down here by the fire and just relax and talk. No, you sit there. I want the rocking chair. (*Takes her hands.*) And now you've got your old face back. It was just for a minute, right at first — Though you are a little more pale, Kristine. And maybe a little thinner.

Mrs. Linde. And much, much older, Nora.

Nora. Maybe a little older. Just a teeny-weeny bit, not much. (*Interrupts herself, serious.*) Oh, but how thoughtless of me, chatting away like this! Sweet, good Kristine, can you forgive me?

Mrs. Linde. Forgive you what, Nora?

Nora (*in a low voice*). You poor dear, you lost your husband, didn't you?

Mrs. Linde. Three years ago, yes.

Nora. I know. I saw it in the paper. Oh please believe me, Kristine. I really meant to write you, but I never got around to it. Something was always coming up.

Mrs. Linde. Of course, Nora. I understand.

Nora. No, that wasn't very nice of me. You poor thing, all you must have been through. And he didn't leave you much, either, did he?

Mrs. Linde. No.

Nora. And no children?

Mrs. Linde. No.

Nora. Nothing at all, in other words?

Mrs. Linde. Not so much as a sense of loss — a grief to live on —

Nora (*incredulous*). But Kristine, how can that *be*?

Mrs. Linde (*with a sad smile, strokes Nora's hair*). That's the way it sometimes is, Nora.

Nora. All alone. How awful for you. I have three darling children.

You can't see them right now, though; they're out with their
nurse. But now you must tell me everything —

Mrs. Linde. No, no; I'd rather listen to you.

Nora. No, you begin. Today I won't be selfish. Today I'll think
only of you. Except there's one thing I've just got to tell
you first. Something marvelous that's happened to us just
these last few days. You haven't heard, have you?

Mrs. Linde. No; tell me.

Nora. Just think. My husband's been made manager of the Mutual
Bank.

Mrs. Linde. Your husband — ! Oh, I'm so glad!

Nora. Yes, isn't that great? You see, private law practice is so
uncertain, especially when you won't have anything to do
with cases that aren't — you know — quite nice. And of
course Torvald won't do that, and I quite agree with him.
Oh, you've no idea how delighted we are! He takes over at
New Year's, and he'll be getting a big salary and all sorts
of extras. From now on we'll be able to live in quite a
different way — exactly as we like. Oh, Kristine! I feel so
carefree and happy! It's lovely to have lots and lots of money
and not have to worry about a thing! Don't you agree?

Mrs. Linde. It would be nice to have enough, at any rate.

Nora. No, I don't mean just enough. I mean lots and lots!

Mrs. Linde (smiles). Nora, Nora, when are you going to be sensible?
In school you spent a great deal of money.

Nora (quietly laughing). Yes, and Torvald says I still do. (*Raises her
finger at Mrs. Linde.*) But "Nora, Nora" isn't so crazy as you
all think. Believe me, we've had nothing to be extravagant
with. We've both had to work.

Mrs. Linde. You too?

Nora. Yes. Oh, it's been little things mostly — sewing, crocheting,
embroidery — that sort of thing. (*Casually.*) And other things
too. You know, of course, that Torvald left government
service when we got married? There was no chance of promotion in his department, and of course he had to make
more money than he had been making. So for the first few
years he worked altogether too hard. He had to take jobs
on the side and work night and day. It turned out to be too
much for him. He became seriously ill. The doctors told
him he needed to go south.

Mrs. Linde. That's right; you spent a year in Italy, didn't you?

Nora. Yes, we did. But you won't believe how hard it was to get
away. Ivar had just been born. But of course we had to go.
Oh, it was a wonderful trip. And it saved Torvald's life.
But it took a lot of money, Kristine.

Mrs. Linde. I'm sure it did.

Nora. Twelve hundred specie dollars. Four thousand eight hundred crowns. That's a lot of money.

Mrs. Linde. Yes. So it's lucky you have it when something like that happens.

Nora. Well, actually we got the money from Daddy.

Mrs. Linde. I see. That was about the time your father died, I believe.

Nora. Yes, just about then. And I couldn't even go and take care of him. I was expecting little Ivar any day. And I had poor Torvald to look after, desperately sick and all. My dear, good Daddy! I never saw him again, Kristine. That's the saddest thing that's happened to me since I got married.

Mrs. Linde. I know you were very fond of him. But then you went to Italy?

Nora. Yes, for now we had the money, and the doctors urged us to go. So we left about a month later.

Mrs. Linde. And when you came back your husband was well again?

Nora. Healthy as a horse!

Mrs. Linde. But — the doctor?

Nora. What do you mean?

Mrs. Linde. I thought the maid said it was the doctor, that gentleman who came the same time I did.

Nora. Oh, that's Dr. Rank. He doesn't come as a doctor. He's our closest friend. He looks in at least once every day. No, Torvald hasn't been sick once since then. And the children are strong and healthy, too, and so am I. (*Jumps up and claps her hands.*) Oh God, Kristine! Isn't it wonderful to be alive and happy! Isn't it just lovely! — But now I'm being mean again, talking only about myself and my things. (*Sits down on a footstool close to Mrs. Linde and puts her arms on her lap.*) Please, don't be angry with me! Tell me, is it really true that you didn't care for your husband? Then why did you marry him?

Mrs. Linde. Mother was still alive then, but she was bedridden and helpless. And I had my two younger brothers to look after. I didn't think I had the right to turn him down.

Nora. No, I suppose not. So he had money then?

Mrs. Linde. He was quite well off, I think. But it was an uncertain business, Nora. When he died, the whole thing collapsed and there was nothing left.

Nora. And then — ?

Mrs. Linde. Well, I had to manage as best I could. With a little store and a little school and anything else I could think of.

The last three years have been one long work day for me,
Nora, without any rest. But now it's over. My poor mother
doesn't need me any more. She passed away. And the boys
are on their own too. They've both got jobs and support
themselves.

Nora. What a relief for you —

Mrs. Linde. No, not relief. Just a great emptiness. Nobody to live
for any more. (*Gets up, restlessly.*) That's why I couldn't
stand it any longer in that little hole. Here in town it has
to be easier to find something to keep me busy and occupy
my thoughts. With a little luck I should be able to find a
permanent job, something in an office —

Nora. Oh but Kristine, that's exhausting work, and you look worn
out already. It would be much better for you to go to a
resort.

Mrs. Linde (*walks over to the window*). I don't have a Daddy who
can give me the money, Nora.

Nora (*getting up*). Oh, don't be angry with me.

Mrs. Linde (*over to her*). Dear Nora, don't *you* be angry with *me.*
That's the worst thing about my kind of situation: you become
so bitter. You've nobody to work for, and yet you have to
look out for yourself, somehow. You've got to keep on
living, and so you become selfish. Do you know — when
you told me about your husband's new position I was delighted
not so much for your sake as for my own.

Nora. Why was that? Oh, I see. You think maybe Torvald can
give you a job?

Mrs. Linde. That's what I had in mind.

Nora. And he will too, Kristine. Just leave it to me. I'll be ever
so subtle about it. I'll think of something nice to tell him,
something he'll like. Oh I so much want to help you.

Mrs. Linde. That's very good of you, Nora — making an effort
like that for me. Especially since you've known so little
trouble and hardship in your own life.

Nora. I — ? — have known so little — ?

Mrs. Linde (*smiling*). Oh well, a little sewing or whatever it was.
You're still a child, Nora.

Nora (*with a toss of her head, walks away*). You shouldn't sound so
superior.

Mrs. Linde. I shouldn't?

Nora. You're just like all the others. None of you think I'm good
for anything really serious.

Mrs. Linde. Well, now —

Nora. That I've never been through anything difficult.

Mrs. Linde. But Nora! You just told me all your troubles!

Nora. That's nothing. (*Lowers her voice.*) I haven't told you about *it.*

Mrs. Linde. It? What's that? What do you mean?

Nora. You patronize me, Kristine, and that's not fair. You're proud that you worked so long and so hard for your mother.

Mrs. Linde. I don't think I patronize anyone. But it *is* true that I'm both proud and happy that I could make mother's last years comparatively easy.

Nora. And you're proud of all you did for your brothers.

Mrs. Linde. I think I have the right to be.

Nora. And so do I. But now I want to tell you something, Kristine. I have something to be proud and happy about too.

Mrs. Linde. I don't doubt that for a moment. But what exactly do you mean?

Nora. Not so loud! Torvald mustn't hear — not for anything in the world. Nobody must know about this, Kristine. Nobody but you.

Mrs. Linde. But what is it?

Nora. Come here. (*Pulls her down on the couch beside her.*) You see, I *do* have something to be proud and happy about. I've saved Torvald's life.

Mrs. Linde. Saved — ? How do you mean — "saved"?

Nora. I told you about our trip to Italy. Torvald would have died if he hadn't gone.

Mrs. Linde. I understand that. And so your father gave you the money you needed.

Nora (*smiles*). Yes, that's what Torvald and all the others think. But —

Mrs. Linde. But what?

Nora. Daddy didn't give us a penny. *I* raised that money.

Mrs. Linde. *You* did? That whole big amount?

Nora. Twelve hundred specie dollars. Four thousand eight hundred crowns. *Now* what do you say?

Mrs. Linde. But Nora, how could you? Did you win in the state lottery?

Nora (*contemptuously*). State lottery! (*Snorts.*) What is so great about that?

Mrs. Linde. Where did it come from then?

Nora (*humming and smiling, enjoying her secret*). Hmmm. Tra-la-la-la-la!

Mrs. Linde. You certainly couldn't have borrowed it.

Nora. Oh? And why not?

Mrs. Linde. A wife can't borrow money without her husband's consent.

Nora (*with a toss of her head*). Oh, I don't know — take a wife
    with a little bit of a head for business — a wife who knows
    how to manage things —
Mrs. Linde. But Nora, I don't understand at all —
Nora. You don't have to. I didn't say I borrowed the money, did
    I? I could have gotten it some other way. (*Leans back.*) An
    admirer may have given it to me. When you're as tolerably
    goodlooking as I am —
Mrs. Linde. Oh, you're crazy.
Nora. I think you're dying from curiosity, Kristine.
Mrs. Linde. I'm beginning to think you've done something very
    foolish, Nora.
Nora (*sits up*). Is it foolish to save your husband's life?
Mrs. Linde. I say it's foolish to act behind his back.
Nora. But don't you see: he couldn't be told! You're missing the
    whole point, Kristine. We couldn't even let him know how
    seriously ill he was. The doctors came to *me* and told me
    his life was in danger, that nothing could save him but a
    stay in the south. Don't you think I tried to work on him?
    I told him how lovely it would be if I could go abroad like
    other young wives. I cried and begged. I said he'd better
    remember what condition I was in, that he had to be nice
    to me and do what I wanted. I even hinted he could borrow
    the money. But that almost made him angry with me. He
    told me I was being irresponsible and that it was his duty
    as my husband not to give in to my moods and whims —
    I think that's what he called it. All right, I said to myself,
    you've got to be saved somehow, and so I found a way —
Mrs. Linde. And your husband never learned from your father that
    the money didn't come from him?
Nora. Never. Daddy died that same week. I thought of telling
    him all about it and ask him not to say anything. But since
    he was so sick — It turned out I didn't have to —
Mrs. Linde. And you've never told your husband?
Nora. Of course not! Good heavens, how could I? He, with his
    strict principles! Besides, you know how men are. Torvald
    would find it embarrassing and humiliating to learn that he
    owed me anything. It would upset our whole relationship.
    Our happy, beautiful home would no longer be what it is.
Mrs. Linde. Aren't you ever going to tell him?
Nora (*reflectively, half smiling*). Yes — one day, maybe. Many,
    many years from now, when I'm no longer young and pretty.
    Don't laugh! I mean when Torvald no longer feels about me
    the way he does now, when he no longer thinks it's fun

when I dance for him and put on costumes and recite for
him. Then it will be good to have something in reserve —
(*Interrupts herself*) Oh, I'm just being silly! That day will
never come. — Well, now, Kristine, what do you think of
my great secret? Don't you think I'm good for something
too? — By the way, you wouldn't believe all the worry I've
had because of it. It's been very hard to meet my obligations
on schedule. You see, in business there's something called
quarterly interest and something called installments on the
principal, and those are terribly hard to come up with. I've
had to save a little here and a little there, whenever I could.
I couldn't use much of the housekeeping money, for Torvald
has to eat well. And I couldn't use what I got for clothes
for the children. They have to look nice, and I didn't think
it would be right to spend less than I got — the sweet little
things!

Mrs. Linde. Poor Nora! So you had to take it from your own
allowance?

Nora. Yes, of course. After all, it was my affair. Every time
Torvald gave me money for a new dress and things like
that, I never used more than half of it. I always bought the
cheapest, simplest things for myself. Thank God, everything
looks good on me, so Torvald never noticed. But it was
hard many times, Kristine, for it's fun to have pretty clothes.
Don't you think?

Mrs. Linde. Certainly.

Nora. Anyway, I had other ways of making money too. Last
winter I was lucky enough to get some copying work. So
I locked the door and sat up writing every night till quite
late. God! I often got so tired — ! But it was great fun, too,
working and making money. It was almost like being a man.

Mrs. Linde. But how much have you been able to pay off this
way?

Nora. I couldn't tell you exactly. You see, it's very difficult to
keep track of business like that. All I know is I have been
paying off as much as I've been able to scrape together.
Many times I just didn't know what to do. (*Smiles.*) Then
I used to imagine a rich old gentleman had fallen in love
with me —

Mrs. Linde. What! What old gentleman?

Nora. Phooey! And now he was dead and they were reading his
will, and there it said in big letters, "All my money is to
be paid in cash immediately to the charming Mrs. Nora
Helmer."

Mrs. Linde. But dearest Nora — who was this old gentleman?

Nora. For heaven's sake, Kristine, don't you see! There was no old gentleman. He was just somebody I made up when I couldn't think of any way to raise the money. But never mind him. The old bore can be anyone he likes to for all I care. I have no use for him or his last will, for now I don't have a single worry in the world. (*Jumps up.*) Dear God, what a lovely thought that is! To be able to play and have fun with the children, to have everything nice and pretty in the house, just the way Torvald likes it! Not a care! And soon spring will be here, and the air will be blue and high. Maybe we can travel again. Maybe I'll see the ocean again! Oh, yes, yes! — it's wonderful to be alive and happy!

The doorbell rings.

Mrs. Linde (getting up). There's the doorbell. Maybe I better be going.

Nora. No, please stay. I'm sure it's just someone for Torvald —

The Maid (in the hall door). Excuse me, ma'am. There's a gentleman here who'd like to see Mr. Helmer.

Nora. You mean the bank manager.

The Maid. Sorry, ma'am; the bank manager. But I didn't know — since the Doctor is with him —

Nora. Who is the gentleman?

Krogstad (appearing in the door). It's just me, Mrs. Helmer.

Mrs. Linde starts, looks, turns away toward the window.

Nora (takes a step toward him, tense, in a low voice). You? What do you want? What do you want with my husband?

Krogstad. Bank business — in a way. I have a small job in the Mutual, and I understand your husband is going to be our new manager —

Nora. So it's just —

Krogstad. Just routine business, ma'am. Nothing else.

Nora. All right. In that case, why don't you go through the door to the office.

Dismisses him casually as she closes the door. Walks over to the stove and tends the fire.

Mrs. Linde. Nora — who was that man?

Nora. His name's Krogstad. He's a lawyer.

Mrs. Linde. So it *was* him.

Nora. Do you know him?

Mrs. Linde. I used to — many years ago. For a while he clerked in our part of the country.

Nora. Right. He did.

Mrs. Linde. He has changed a great deal.

Nora. I believe he had a very unhappy marriage.

Mrs. Linde. And now he's a widower, isn't he?

Nora. With many children. There now; it's burning nicely again. (*Closes the stove and moves the rocking chair a little to the side.*)

Mrs. Linde. They say he's into all sorts of business.

Nora. Really? Maybe so. I wouldn't know. But let's not think about business. It's such a bore.

Dr. Rank (*appears in the door to Helmer's study*). No, I don't want to be in the way. I'd rather talk to your wife a bit. (*Closes the door and notices Mrs. Linde.*) Oh, I beg your pardon. I believe I'm in the way here too.

Nora. No, not at all. (*Introduces them.*) Dr. Rank. Mrs. Linde.

Rank. Aha. A name often heard in this house. I believe I passed you on the stairs coming up.

Mrs. Linde. Yes. I'm afraid I climb stairs very slowly. They aren't good for me.

Rank. I see. A slight case of inner decay, perhaps?

Mrs. Linde. Overwork, rather.

Rank. Oh, is that all? And now you've come to town to relax at all the parties?

Mrs. Linde. I have come to look for a job.

Rank. A proven cure for overwork, I take it?

Mrs. Linde. One has to live, Doctor.

Rank. Yes, that seems to be the common opinion.

Nora. Come on, Dr. Rank — you want to live just as much as the rest of us.

Rank. Of course I do. Miserable as I am, I prefer to go on being tortured as long as possible. All my patients feel the same way. And that's true of the moral invalids too. Helmer is talking with a specimen right this minute.

Mrs. Linde (*in a low voice*). Ah!

Nora. What do you mean?

Rank. Oh, this lawyer, Krogstad. You don't know him. The roots of his character are decayed. But even he began by saying something about having *to live* — as if it were a matter of the highest importance.

Nora. Oh? What did he want with Torvald?

Rank. I don't really know. All I heard was something about the bank.

Nora. I didn't know that Krog — that this Krogstad had anything to do with the Mutual Bank.

Rank. Yes, he seems to have some kind of job there. (*To Mrs. Linde.*) I don't know if you are familiar in your part of the country with the kind of person who is always running around trying to sniff out cases of moral decrepitude and as soon as he finds one puts the individual under observation in some excellent position or other. All the healthy ones are left out in the cold.

Mrs. Linde. I should think it's the sick who need looking after the most.

Rank (*shrugs his shoulders*). There we are. That's the attitude that turns society into a hospital.

Nora, absorbed in her own thoughts, suddenly starts giggling and clapping her hands.

Rank. What's so funny about that? Do you even know what society is?

Nora. What do I care about your stupid society! I laughed at something entirely different — something terribly amusing. Tell me, Dr. Rank — all the employees in the Mutual Bank, from now on they'll all be dependent on Torvald, right?

Rank. Is that what you find so enormously amusing?

Nora (*smiles and hums*). That's my business, that's my business! (*Walks around.*) Yes, I do think it's fun that we — that Torvald is going to have so much influence on so many people's lives. (*Brings out the bag of macaroons.*) Have a macaroon, Dr. Rank.

Rank. Well, well — macaroons. I thought they were banned around here.

Nora. Yes, but these were some that Kristine gave me.

Mrs. Linde. What! I?

Nora. That's all right. Don't look so scared. You couldn't know that Torvald won't let me have them. He's afraid they'll ruin my teeth. But who cares! Just once in a while — ! Right, Dr. Rank? Have one! (*Puts a macaroon into his mouth.*) You too, Kristine. And one for me. A very small one. Or at most two. (*Walks around again.*) Yes, I really feel very, very happy. Now there's just one thing I'm dying to do.

Rank. Oh? And what's that?

Nora. Something I'm dying to say so Torvald could hear.

Rank. And why can't you?

Nora. I don't dare to, for it's not nice.

Mrs. Linde. Not nice?

Rank. In that case, I guess you'd better not. But surely to the two of us — ? What is it you'd like to say for Helmer to hear?
Nora. I want to say, "Goddammit!"
Rank. Are you out of your mind!
Mrs. Linde. For heaven's sake, Nora!
Rank. Say it. Here he comes.
Nora (*hiding the macaroons*). Shhh!

Helmer enters from his study, carrying his hat and overcoat.

Nora (*going to him*). Well, dear, did you get rid of him?
Helmer. Yes, he just left.
Nora. Torvald, I want you to meet Kristine. She's just come to town.
Helmer. Kristine — ? I'm sorry; I don't think —
Nora. Mrs. Linde, Torvald dear. Mrs. Kristine Linde.
Helmer. Ah, yes. A childhood friend of my wife's, I suppose.
Mrs. Linde. Yes, we've known each other for a long time.
Nora. Just think; she has come all this way just to see you.
Helmer. I'm not sure I understand —
Mrs. Linde. Well, not really —
Nora. You see, Kristine is an absolutely fantastic secretary, and she would so much like to work for a competent executive and learn more than she knows already —
Helmer. Very sensible, I'm sure, Mrs. Linde.
Nora. So when she heard about your appointment — they got a wire about it — she came here as fast as she could. How about it, Torvald? Couldn't you do something for Kristine? For my sake. Please?
Helmer. Quite possibly. I take it you're a widow, Mrs. Linde?
Mrs. Linde. Yes.
Helmer. And you've had office experience?
Mrs. Linde. Some — yes.
Helmer. In that case I think it's quite likely that I'll be able to find you a position.
Nora (*claps her hands*). I knew it! I knew it!
Helmer. You've arrived at a most opportune time, Mrs. Linde.
Mrs. Linde. Oh, how can I ever thank you —
Helmer. Not at all, not at all. (*Puts his coat on.*) But today you'll have to excuse me —
Rank. Wait a minute; I'll come with you. (*Gets his fur coat from the front hall, warms it by the stove.*)
Nora. Don't be long, Torvald.
Helmer. An hour or so; no more.
Nora. Are you leaving, too, Kristine?

Mrs. Linde (putting on her things). Yes, I'd better go and find a place to stay.

Helmer. Good. Then we'll be going the same way.

Nora (helping her). I'm sorry this place is so small, but I don't think we very well could —

Mrs. Linde. Of course! Don't be silly, Nora. Goodbye, and thank you for everything.

Nora. Goodbye. We'll see you soon. You'll be back this evening, of course. And you too, Dr. Rank; right? If you feel well enough? Of course you will. Just wrap yourself up.

> *General small talk as all exit into the hall. Children's voices are heard on the stairs.*

Nora. There they are! There they are! (*She runs and opens the door. The nurse Anne-Marie enters with the children.*)

Nora. Come in! Come in! (*Bends over and kisses them.*) Oh, you sweet, sweet darlings! Look at them, Kristine! Aren't they beautiful?

Rank. No standing around in the draft!

Helmer. Come along, Mrs. Linde. This place isn't fit for anyone but mothers right now.

> *Dr. Rank, Helmer, and Mrs. Linde go down the stairs. The Nurse enters the living room with the children. Nora follows, closing the door behind her.*

Nora. My, how nice you all look! Such red cheeks! Like apples and roses. (*The children all talk at the same time.*) You've had so much fun? I bet you have. Oh, isn't that nice! You pulled both Emmy and Bob on your sleigh? Both at the same time? That's very good, Ivar. Oh, let me hold her for a minute, Anne-Marie. My sweet little doll baby! (*Takes the smallest of the children from the Nurse and dances with her.*) Yes, yes, of course; Mama'll dance with you too, Bob. What? You threw snowballs? Oh, I wish I'd been there! No, no; I want to take their clothes off, Anne-Marie. Please let me; I think it's so much fun. You go on in. You look frozen. There's hot coffee on the stove.

> *The Nurse exits into the room to the left. Nora takes the children's wraps off and throws them all around. They all keep telling her things at the same time.*

Nora. Oh, really? A big dog ran after you? But it didn't bite you. Of course not. Dogs don't bite sweet little doll babies. Don't peek at the packages, Ivar! What's in them? Wouldn't you

like to know! No, no; that's something terrible! Play? You
want to play? What do you want to play? Okay, let's play
hide-and-seek. Bob hides first. You want *me* to? All right.
I'll go first.

*Laughing and shouting, Nora and the children play in the living
room and in the adjacent room, right. Finally, Nora hides herself
under the table; the children rush in, look for her, can't find her.
They hear her low giggle, run to the table, lift the rug that covers
it, see her. General hilarity. She crawls out, pretends to scare them.
New delight. In the meantime there has been a knock on the door
between the living room and the front hall, but nobody has noticed.
Now the door is opened halfway; Krogstad appears. He waits a
little. The playing goes on.*

Krogstad. Pardon me, Mrs. Helmer —
Nora (with a muted cry turns around, jumps up). Ah! What do you
    want?
Krogstad. I'm sorry. The front door was open. Somebody must
    have forgotten to close it —
Nora (standing up). My husband isn't here, Mr. Krogstad.
Krogstad. I know.
Nora. So what do you want?
Krogstad. I'd like a word with you.
Nora. With — ? *(To the children in a low voice.)* Go in to Anne-
    Marie. What? No, the strange man won't do anything bad
    to Mama. When he's gone we'll play some more.

She takes the children into the room to the left and closes the door.

Nora (tense, troubled). You want to speak with me?
Krogstad. Yes I do.
Nora. Today — ? It isn't the first of the month yet.
Krogstad. No, it's Christmas Eve. It's up to you what kind of
    holiday you'll have.
Nora. What do you want? I can't possibly —
Krogstad. Let's not talk about that just yet. There's something else.
    You do have a few minutes, don't you?
Nora. Yes. Yes, of course. That is —
Krogstad. Good. I was sitting in Olsen's restaurant when I saw
    your husband go by.
Nora. Yes — ?
Krogstad. — with a lady.
Nora. What of it?
Krogstad. May I be so free as to ask: wasn't that lady Mrs. Linde?
Nora. Yes.

Krogstad. Just arrived in town?

Nora. Yes, today.

Krogstad. She's a good friend of yours, I understand?

Nora. Yes, she is. But I fail to see —

Krogstad. I used to know her myself.

Nora. I know that.

Krogstad. So you know about that. I thought as much. In that case, let me ask you a simple question. Is Mrs. Linde going to be employed in the bank?

Nora. What makes you think you have the right to cross-examine me like this, Mr. Krogstad — you, one of my husband's employees? But since you ask, I'll tell you. Yes, Mrs. Linde is going to be working in the bank. And it was I who recommended her, Mr. Krogstad. Now you know.

Krogstad. So I was right.

Nora (walks up and down). After all, one does have a little influence, you know. Just because you're a woman, it doesn't mean that — Really, Mr. Krogstad, people in a subordinate position should be careful not to offend someone who — oh well —

Krogstad. — has influence?

Nora. Exactly.

Krogstad (changing his tone). Mrs. Helmer, I must ask you to be good enough to use your influence on my behalf.

Nora. What do you mean?

Krogstad. I want you to make sure that I am going to keep my subordinate position in the bank.

Nora. I don't understand. Who is going to take your position away from you?

Krogstad. There's no point in playing ignorant with me, Mrs. Helmer. I can very well appreciate that your friend would find it unpleasant to run into me. So now I know who I can thank for my dismissal.

Nora. But I assure you —

Krogstad. Never mind. Just want to say you still have time. I advise you to use your influence to prevent it.

Nora. But Mr. Krogstad, I don't have any influence — none at all.

Krogstad. No? I thought you just said —

Nora. Of course I didn't mean it that way. I! Whatever makes you think that I have any influence of that kind on my husband?

Krogstad. I went to law school with your husband. I have no reason to think that the bank manager is less susceptible than other husbands.

Nora. If you're going to insult my husband, I'll ask you to leave.

Krogstad. You're brave, Mrs. Helmer.

Nora. I'm not afraid of you any more. After New Year's I'll be out of this thing with you.

Krogstad (more controlled). Listen, Mrs. Helmer. If necessary, I'll fight as for my life to keep my little job in the bank.

Nora. So it seems.

Krogstad. It isn't just the money; that's really the smallest part of it. There is something else — Well, I guess I might as well tell you. It's like this. I'm sure you know, like everybody else, that some years ago I committed — an impropriety.

Nora. I believe I've heard it mentioned.

Krogstad. The case never came to court, but from that moment all doors were closed to me. So I took up the kind of business you know about. I had to do something, and I think I can say about myself that I have not been among the worst. But now I want to get out of all that. My sons are growing up. For their sake I must get back as much of my good name as I can. This job in the bank was like the first rung on the ladder. And now your husband wants to kick me down and leave me back in the mud again.

Nora. But I swear to you, Mr. Krogstad; it's not at all in my power to help you.

Krogstad. That's because you don't want to. But I have the means to force you.

Nora. You don't mean you're going to tell my husband I owe you money?

Krogstad. And if I did?

Nora. That would be a mean thing to do. (*Almost crying.*) That secret, which is my joy and my pride — for him to learn about it in such a coarse and ugly manner — to learn it from you — ! It would be terribly unpleasant for me.

Krogstad. Just unpleasant?

Nora (heatedly). But go ahead! Do it! It will be worse for you than for me. When my husband realizes what a bad person you are, you'll be sure to lose your job.

Krogstad. I asked you if it was just domestic unpleasantness you were afraid of?

Nora. When my husband finds out, of course he'll pay off the loan, and then we won't have anything more to do with you.

Krogstad (stepping closer). Listen, Mrs. Helmer — either you have a very bad memory, or you don't know much about business. I think I had better straighten you out on a few things.

Nora. What do you mean?

Krogstad. When your husband was ill, you came to me to borrow twelve hundred dollars.

Nora. I knew nobody else.

Krogstad. I promised to get you the money —

Nora. And you did.

Krogstad. I promised to get you the money on certain conditions. At the time you were so anxious about your husband's health and so set on getting him away that I doubt very much that you paid much attention to the details of our transaction. That's why I remind you of them now. Anyway, I promised to get you the money if you would sign an I.O.U., which I drafted.

Nora. And which I signed.

Krogstad. Good. But below your signature I added a few lines, making your father security for the loan. Your father was supposed to put his signature to those lines.

Nora. Supposed to — ? He did.

Krogstad. I had left the date blank. That is, your father was to date his own signature. You recall that, don't you, Mrs. Helmer?

Nora. I guess so —

Krogstad. I gave the note to you. You were to mail it to your father. Am I correct?

Nora. Yes.

Krogstad. And of course you did so right away, for no more than five or six days later you brought the paper back to me, signed by your father. Then I paid you the money.

Nora. Well? And haven't I been keeping up with the payments?

Krogstad. Fairly well, yes. But to get back to what we were talking about — those were difficult days for you, weren't they, Mrs. Helmer?

Nora. Yes, they were.

Krogstad. Your father was quite ill, I believe.

Nora. He was dying.

Krogstad. And died shortly afterwards?

Nora. That's right.

Krogstad. Tell me, Mrs. Helmer; do you happen to remember the date of your father's death? I mean the exact day of the month?

Nora. Daddy died on September 29.

Krogstad. Quite correct. I have ascertained that fact. That's why there is something peculiar about this (*takes out a piece of paper*), which I can't account for.

Nora. Peculiar? How? I don't understand —

Krogstad. It seems very peculiar, Mrs. Helmer, that your father signed this promissory note three days after his death.

Nora. How so? I don't see what —

Krogstad. Your father died on September 29. Now look. He has dated his signature October 2. Isn't that odd?

Nora remains silent.

Krogstad. Can you explain it?

Nora is still silent.

Krogstad. I also find it striking that the date and the month and the year are not in your father's handwriting but in a hand I think I recognize. Well, that might be explained. Your father may have forgotten to date his signature and somebody else may have done it here, guessing at the date before he had learned of your father's death. That's all right. It's only the signature itself that matters. And that is genuine, isn't it, Mrs. Helmer? Your father did put his name to this note?

Nora (after a brief silence tosses her head back and looks defiantly at him). No, he didn't. *I* wrote Daddy's name.

Krogstad. Mrs. Helmer — do you realize what a dangerous admission you just made?

Nora. Why? You'll get your money soon.

Krogstad. Let me ask you something. Why didn't you mail this note to your father?

Nora. Because it was impossible. Daddy was sick — you know that. If I had asked him to sign it, I would have had to tell him what the money was for. But I couldn't tell him, as sick as he was, that my husband's life was in danger. That was impossible. Surely you can see that.

Krogstad. Then it would have been better for you if you had given up your trip abroad.

Nora. No, that was impossible! That trip was to save my husband's life. I couldn't give it up.

Krogstad. But didn't you realize that what you did amounted to fraud against me?

Nora. I couldn't let that make any difference. I didn't care about you at all. I hated the way you made all those difficulties for me, even though you knew the danger my husband was in. I thought you were cold and unfeeling.

Krogstad. Mrs. Helmer, obviously you have no clear idea of what you have done. Let me tell you that what I did that time was no more and no worse. And it ruined my name and reputation.

Nora. You! Are you trying to tell me that you did something brave once in order to save your wife's life?

Krogstad. The law doesn't ask about motives.

Nora. Then it's a bad law.

Krogstad. Bad or not — if I produce this note in court you'll be judged according to the law.

Nora. I refuse to believe you. A daughter shouldn't have the right to spare her dying old father worry and anxiety? A wife shouldn't have the right to save her husband's life? I don't know the laws very well, but I'm sure that somewhere they make allowance for cases like that. And you, a lawyer, don't know that? I think you must be a bad lawyer, Mr. Krogstad.

Krogstad. That may be. But business — the kind of business you and I have with one another — don't you think I know something about that? Very well. Do what you like. But let me tell you this: if I'm going to be kicked out again, you'll keep me company. (*He bows and exits through the front hall.*)

Nora (*pauses thoughtfully; then, with a defiant toss of her head*). Oh, nonsense! Trying to scare me like that! I'm not all that silly. (*Starts picking up the children's clothes; soon stops.*) But — ? No! That's impossible! I did it for love!

The Children (*in the door to the left*). Mama, the strange man just left. We saw him.

Nora. Yes, yes; I know. But don't tell anybody about the strange man. Do you hear? Not even Daddy.

The Children. We won't. But now you'll play with us again, won't you, Mama?

Nora. No, not right now.

The Children. But Mama — you promised.

Nora. I know, but I can't just now. Go to your own room. I've so much to do. Be nice now, my little darlings. Do as I say. (*She nudges them gently into the other room and closes the door. She sits down on the couch, picks up a piece of embroidery, makes a few stitches, then stops.*) No! (*Throws the embroidery down, goes to the hall door and calls out.*) Helene! Bring the Christmas tree in here, please! (*Goes to the table, left, opens the drawer, halts.*) No — that's impossible!

The Maid (*with the Christmas tree*). Where do you want it, ma'am?

Nora. There. The middle of the floor.

The Maid. You want anything else?

Nora. No, thanks. I have everything I need. (*The Maid goes out. Nora starts trimming the tree.*) I want candles — and flowers — That awful man! Oh, nonsense! There's nothing wrong.

This will be a lovely tree. I'll do everything you want me to, Torvald. I'll sing for you — dance for you —

Helmer, a bundle of papers under his arm, enters from outside.

Nora. Ah — you're back already?

Helmer. Yes. Has anybody been here?

Nora. Here? No.

Helmer. That's funny. I saw Krogstad leaving just now.

Nora. Oh? Oh yes, that's right. Krogstad was here for just a moment.

Helmer. I can tell from your face that he came to ask you to put in a word for him.

Nora. Yes.

Helmer. And it was supposed to be your own idea, wasn't it? You were not to tell me he'd been here. He asked you that too, didn't he?

Nora. Yes, Torvald, but —

Helmer. Nora, Nora, how could you! Talk to a man like that and make him promises! And lying to me about it afterwards — !

Nora. Lying — ?

Helmer. Didn't you say nobody had been here? (*Shakes his finger at her.*) My little songbird must never do that again. Songbirds are supposed to have clean beaks to chirp with — no false notes. (*Puts his arm around her waist.*) Isn't that so? Of course it is. (*Lets her go.*) And that's enough about that. (*Sits down in front of the fireplace.*) Ah, it's nice and warm in here. (*Begins to leaf through his papers.*)

Nora (*busy with the tree; after a brief pause*). Torvald.

Helmer. Yes.

Nora. I'm looking forward so much to the Stenborgs' costume party day after tomorrow.

Helmer. And I can't wait to find out what you're going to surprise me with.

Nora. Oh, that silly idea!

Helmer. Oh?

Nora. I can't think of anything. It all seems so foolish and pointless.

Helmer. Ah, my little Nora admits that?

Nora (*behind his chair, her arms on the back of the chair*). Are you very busy, Torvald?

Helmer. Well —

Nora. What are all those papers?

Helmer. Bank business.

Nora. Already?

Helmer. I've asked the board to give me the authority to make certain changes in organization and personnel. That's what I'll be doing over the holidays. I want it all settled before New Year's.

Nora. So that's why this poor Krogstad —

Helmer. Hm.

Nora (*leisurely playing with the hair on his neck*). If you weren't so busy, Torvald, I'd ask you for a great big favor.

Helmer. Let's hear it, anyway.

Nora. I don't know anyone with better taste than you, and I want so much to look nice at the party. Couldn't you sort of take charge of me, Torvald, and decide what I'll wear — Help me with my costume?

Helmer. Aha! Little Lady Obstinate is looking for someone to rescue her?

Nora. Yes, Torvald. I won't get anywhere without your help.

Helmer. All right. I'll think about it. We'll come up with something.

Nora. Oh, you *are* nice! (*Goes back to the Christmas tree. A pause.*) Those red flowers look so pretty. — Tell me, was it really all that bad what this Krogstad fellow did?

Helmer. He forged signatures. Do you have any idea what that means?

Nora. Couldn't it have been because he felt he had to?

Helmer. Yes, or like so many others he may simply have been thoughtless. I'm not so heartless as to condemn a man absolutely because of a single imprudent act.

Nora. Of course not, Torvald!

Helmer. People like him can redeem themselves morally by openly confessing their crime and taking their punishment.

Nora. Punishment?

Helmer. But that was not the way Krogstad chose. He got out of it with tricks and evasions. That's what has corrupted him.

Nora. So you think that if — ?

Helmer. Can't you imagine how a guilty person like that has to lie and fake and dissemble wherever he goes — putting on a mask before everybody he's close to, even his own wife and children. It's this thing with the children that's the worst part of it, Nora.

Nora. Why is that?

Helmer. Because when a man lives inside such a circle of stinking lies he brings infection into his own home and contaminates his whole family. With every breath of air his children inhale the germs of something ugly.

Nora (moving closer behind him). Are you so sure of that?

Helmer. Of course I am. I have seen enough examples of that in my work. Nearly all young criminals have had mothers who lied.

Nora. Why mothers — particularly?

Helmer. Most often mothers. But of course fathers tend to have the same influence. Every lawyer knows that. And yet, for years this Krogstad has been poisoning his own children in an atmosphere of lies and deceit. That's why I call him a lost soul morally. *(Reaches out for her hands.)* And that's why my sweet little Nora must promise me never to take his side again. Let's shake on that. — What? What's this? Give me your hand. There! Now that's settled. I assure you, I would find it impossible to work in the same room with that man. I feel literally sick when I'm around people like that.

Nora (withdraws her hand and goes to the other side of the Christmas tree). It's so hot in here. And I have so much to do.

Helmer (gets up and collects his papers). Yes, and I really should try to get some of this reading done before dinner. I must think about your costume too. And maybe just possibly I'll have something to wrap in gilt paper and hang on the Christmas tree. *(Puts his hand on her head.)* Oh my adorable little songbird! *(Enters his study and closes the door.)*

Nora (after a pause, in a low voice). It's all a lot of nonsense. It's not that way at all. It's impossible. It has to be impossible.

The Nurse (in the door, left). The little ones are asking ever so nicely if they can't come in and be with their mamma.

Nora. No, no, no! Don't let them in here! You stay with them, Anne-Marie.

The Nurse. If you say so, ma'am. *(Closes the door.)*

Nora (pale with terror). Corrupt my little children — ! Poison my home — ? *(Brief pause; she lifts her head.)* That's not true. Never. Never in a million years.

ACT II

The same room. The Christmas tree is in the corner by the piano, stripped shabby-looking, with burnt-down candles. Nora's outside clothes are on the couch. Nora is alone. She walks around restlessly. She stops by the couch and picks up her coat.

Nora (drops the coat again). There's somebody now! *(Goes to the door, listens.)* No. Nobody. Of course not — not on Christmas.

And not tomorrow either° — But perhaps — (*Opens the door and looks.*) No, nothing in the mailbox. All empty. (*Comes forward.*) How silly I am! Of course he isn't serious. Nothing like that could happen. After all, I have three small children.

The Nurse enters from the room, left, carrying a big carton.

The Nurse. Well, at last I found it — the box with your costume.

Nora. Thanks. Just put it on the table.

Nurse (*does so*). But it's all a big mess, I'm afraid.

Nora. Oh, I wish I could tear the whole thing to little pieces!

Nurse. Heavens! It's not as bad as all that. It can be fixed all right. All it takes is a little patience.

Nora. I'll go over and get Mrs. Linde to help me.

Nurse. Going out again? In this awful weather? You'll catch a cold.

Nora. That might not be such a bad thing. How are the children?

Nurse. The poor little dears are playing with their presents, but —

Nora. Do they keep asking for me?

Nurse. Well, you know, they're used to being with their mamma.

Nora. I know. But Anne-Marie, from now on I can't be with them as much as before.

Nurse. Oh well. Little children get used to everything.

Nora. You think so? Do you think they'll forget their mamma if I were gone altogether?

Nurse. Goodness me — gone altogether?

Nora. Listen, Anne-Marie — something I've wondered about. How could you bring yourself to leave your child with strangers?

Nurse. But I had to, if I were to nurse you.

Nora. Yes, but how could you *want* to?

Nurse. When I could get such a nice place? When something like that happens to a poor young girl, she'd better be grateful for whatever she gets. For *he* didn't do a thing for me — the louse!

Nora. But your daughter has forgotten all about you, hasn't she?

Nurse. Oh no! Not at all! She wrote to me both when she was confirmed and when she got married.

Nora (*putting her arms around her neck*). You dear old thing — you were a good mother to me when I was little.

Nurse. Poor little Nora had no one else, you know.

Nora. And if my little ones didn't, I know you'd — oh, I'm being silly! (*Opens the carton.*) Go in to them, please. I really should — Tomorrow you'll see how pretty I'll be.

And not tomorrow either In Norway both December 25 and 26 are legal holidays.

Nurse. I know. There won't be anybody at that party half as pretty as you, ma'am. (*Goes out, left.*)

Nora (*begins to take clothes out of the carton; in a moment she throws it all down*). If only I dared to go out. If only I knew nobody would come. That nothing would happen while I was gone. — How silly! Nobody'll come. Just don't think about it. Brush the muff. Beautiful gloves. Beautiful gloves. Forget it. Forget it. One, two, three, four, five, six — (*Cries out.*) There they are! (*Moves toward the door, stops irresolutely.*)

Mrs. Linde enters from the hall. She has already taken off her coat.

Nora. Oh, it's you, Kristine. There's no one else out there, is there? I'm so glad you're here.

Mrs. Linde. They told me you'd asked for me.

Nora. I just happened to walk by. I need your help with something — badly. Let's sit here on the couch. Look. Torvald and I are going to a costume party tomorrow night — at Consul Stenborg's upstairs — and Torvald wants me to go as a Neapolitan fisher girl and dance the tarantella. I learned it when we were on Capri.

Mrs. Linde. Well, well! So you'll be putting on a whole show?

Nora. Yes. Torvald thinks I should. Look, here's the costume. Torvald had it made for me while we were there. But it's all so torn and everything. I just don't know —

Mrs. Linde. Oh, that can be fixed. It's not that much. The trimmings have come loose in a few places. Do you have needle and thread? Ah, here we are. All set.

Nora. I really appreciate it, Kristine.

Mrs. Linde (*sewing*). So you'll be in disguise tomorrow night, eh? You know — I may come by for just a moment, just to look at you. — Oh dear. I haven't even thanked you for the nice evening last night.

Nora (*gets up, moves around*). Oh, I don't know. I don't think last night was as nice as it usually is. — You should have come to town a little earlier, Kristine. — Yes, Torvald knows how to make it nice and pretty around here.

Mrs. Linde. You too, I should think. After all, you're your father's daughter. By the way, is Dr. Rank always as depressed as he was last night?

Nora. No, last night was unusual. He's a very sick man, you know — very sick. Poor Rank, his spine is rotting away. Tuberculosis, I think. You see, his father was a nasty old man

with mistresses and all that sort of thing. Rank has been
sickly ever since he was a little boy.

Mrs. Linde (dropping her sewing to her lap). But dearest Nora, where
have you learned about things like that?

Nora (still walking about). Oh, you know — with three children
you sometimes get to talk with — other wives. Some of
them know quite a bit about medicine. So you pick up a
few things.

Mrs. Linde (resumes her sewing; after a brief pause). Does Dr. Rank
come here every day?

Nora. Every single day. He's Torvald's oldest and best friend, after
all. And my friend too, for that matter. He's part of the
family, almost.

Mrs. Linde. But tell me, is he quite sincere? I mean, isn't he the
kind of man who likes to say nice things to people?

Nora. No, not at all. Rather the opposite, in fact. What makes
you say that?

Mrs. Linde. When you introduced us yesterday, he told me he'd
often heard my name mentioned in this house. But later on
it was quite obvious that your husband really had no idea
who I was. So how could Dr. Rank — ?

Nora. You're right, Kristine, but I can explain that. You see,
Torvald loves me so very much that he wants me all to
himself. That's what he says. When we were first married
he got almost jealous when I as much as mentioned anybody
from back home that I was fond of. So of course I soon
stopped doing that. But with Dr. Rank I often talk about
home. You see, he likes to listen to me.

Mrs. Linde. Look here, Nora. In many ways you're still a child.
After all, I'm quite a bit older than you and have had more
experience. I want to give you a piece of advice. I think you
should get out of this thing with Dr. Rank.

Nora. Get out of what thing?

Mrs. Linde. Several things in fact, if you want my opinion. Yesterday
you said something about a rich admirer who was going to
give you money —

Nora. One who doesn't exist, unfortunately. What of it?

Mrs. Linde. Does Dr. Rank have money?

Nora. Yes, he does.

Mrs. Linde. And no dependents?

Nora. No. But — ?

Mrs. Linde. And he comes here every day?

Nora. Yes, I told you that already.

Mrs. Linde. But how can that sensitive man be so tactless?

Nora. I haven't the slightest idea what you're talking about.

Mrs. Linde. Don't play games with me, Nora. Don't you think I know who you borrowed the twelve hundred dollars from?

Nora. Are you out of your mind! The very idea — ! A friend of both of us who sees us every day — ! What a dreadfully — uncomfortable position that would be!

Mrs. Linde. So it really isn't Dr. Rank?

Nora. Most certainly not! I would never have dreamed of asking him — not for a moment. Anyway, he didn't have any money then. He inherited it afterwards.

Mrs. Linde. Well, I still think it may have been lucky for you, Nora dear.

Nora. The idea! It would never have occurred to me to ask Dr. Rank — Though I'm sure that if I *did* ask him —

Mrs. Linde. But of course you wouldn't.

Nora. Of course not. I can't imagine that that would ever be necessary. But I am quite sure that if I told Dr. Rank —

Mrs. Linde. Behind your husband's back?

Nora. I must get out of — this other thing. That's also behind his back. I must get out of it.

Mrs. Linde. That's what I told you yesterday. But —

Nora (*walking up and down*). A man manages these things so much better than a woman —

Mrs. Linde. One's husband, yes.

Nora. Silly, silly! (*Stops.*) When you've paid off all you owe, you get your I.O.U. back; right?

Mrs. Linde. Yes, of course.

Nora. And you can tear it into a hundred thousand little pieces and burn it — that dirty, filthy, paper!

Mrs. Linde (*looks hard at her, puts down her sewing, rises slowly*). Nora — you're hiding something from me.

Nora. Can you tell?

Mrs. Linde. Something's happened to you, Nora, since yesterday morning. What is it?

Nora (*going to her*). Kristine! (*Listens.*) Shhh. Torvald just came back. Listen. Why don't you go in to the children for a while. Torvald can't stand having sewing around. Get Anne-Marie to help you.

Mrs. Linde (*gathers some of the sewing things together*). All right, but I'm not leaving here till you and I have talked.

She goes out left, just as Helmer enters from the front hall.

Nora (*towards him*). I have been waiting and waiting for you, Torvald.

Helmer. Was that the dressmaker?

Nora. No, it was Kristine. She's helping me with my costume.
Oh Torvald, just wait till you see how nice I'll look!

Helmer. I told you. Pretty good idea I had, wasn't it?

Nora. Lovely! And wasn't it nice of me to go along with it?

Helmer (*his hand under her chin*). Nice? To do what your husband
tells you? All right, you little rascal; I know you didn't mean
it that way. But don't let me interrupt you. I suppose you
want to try it on.

Nora. And you'll be working?

Helmer. Yes. (*Shows her a pile of papers.*) Look. I've been down to
the bank. (*Is about to enter his study.*)

Nora. Torvald.

Helmer (*halts*). Yes?

Nora. What if your little squirrel asked you ever so nicely —

Helmer. For what?

Nora. Would you do it?

Helmer. Depends on what it is.

Nora. Squirrel would run around and do all sorts of fun tricks if
you'd be nice and agreeable.

Helmer. All right. What is it?

Nora. Lark would chirp and twitter in all the rooms, up and
down —

Helmer. So what? Lark does that anyway.

Nora. I'll be your elfmaid and dance for you in the moonlight,
Torvald.

Helmer. Nora, don't tell me it's the same thing you mentioned
this morning?

Nora (*closer to him*). Yes, Torvald. I beg you!

Helmer. You really have the nerve to bring that up again?

Nora. Yes. You've just got to do as I say. You *must* let Krogstad
keep his job.

Helmer. My dear Nora. It's his job I intend to give to Mrs. Linde.

Nora. I know. And that's ever so nice of you. But can't you just
fire somebody else?

Helmer. This is incredible! You just don't give up, do you? Because
you make some foolish promise, *I* am supposed to — !

Nora. That's not the reason, Torvald. It's for your own sake. That
man writes for the worst newspapers. You've said so yourself.
There's no telling what he may do to you. I'm scared to
death of him.

Helmer. Ah, I understand. You're afraid because of what happened
before.

Nora. What do you mean?

Helmer. You're thinking of your father, of course.

Nora. Yes. Yes, you're right. Remember the awful things they wrote about Daddy in the newspapers. I really think they might have forced him to resign if the ministry hadn't sent you to look into the charges and if you hadn't been so helpful and understanding.

Helmer. My dear little Nora, there is a world of difference between your father and me. Your father's official conduct was not above reproach. Mine is, and I intend for it to remain that way as long as I hold my position.

Nora. Oh, but you don't know what vicious people like that may think of. Oh, Torvald! Now all of us could be so happy together here in our own home, peaceful and carefree. Such a good life, Torvald, for you and me and the children! That's why I implore you —

Helmer. And it's exactly because you plead for him that you make it impossible for me to keep him. It's already common knowledge in the bank that I intend to let Krogstad go. If it gets out that the new manager has changed his mind because of his wife —

Nora. Yes? What then?

Helmer. No, of course, that wouldn't matter at all as long as little Mrs. Pighead here got her way! Do you want me to make myself look ridiculous before my whole staff — make people think I can be swayed by just anybody — by outsiders? Believe me, I would soon enough find out what the consequences would be! Besides, there's another thing that makes it absolutely impossible for Krogstad to stay on in the bank now that I'm in charge.

Nora. What's that?

Helmer. I suppose in a pinch I could overlook his moral shortcomings —

Nora. Yes, you could; couldn't you, Torvald?

Helmer. And I understand he's quite a good worker, too. But we've known each other for a long time. It's one of those imprudent relationships you get into when you're young that embarrass you for the rest of your life. I guess I might as well be frank with you: he and I are on a first name basis. And that tactless fellow never hides the fact even when other people are around. Rather, he seems to think it entitles him to be familiar with me. Every chance he gets he comes out with his damn "Torvald, Torvald." I'm telling you, I find it most awkward. He would make my position in the bank intolerable.

Nora. You don't really mean any of this, Torvald.

Helmer. Oh? I don't? And why not?

Nora. No, for it's all so petty.

Helmer. What! Petty? You think I'm being petty!

Nora. No, I *don't* think you are petty, Torvald dear. That's exactly why I —

Helmer. Never mind. You think my reasons are petty, so it follows that I must be petty too. Petty! Indeed! By God, I'll put an end to this right now! (*Opens the door to the front hall and calls out.*) Helene!

Nora. What are you doing?

Helmer (*searching among his papers*). Making a decision. (*The Maid enters.*) Here. Take this letter. Go out with it right away. Find somebody to deliver it. But quick. The address is on the envelope. Wait. Here's money.

The Maid. Very good, sir. (*She takes the letter and goes out.*)

Helmer (*collecting his papers*). There now, little Mrs. Obstinate!

Nora (*breathless*). Torvald — what was that letter?

Helmer. Krogstad's dismissal.

Nora. Call it back, Torvald! There's still time! Oh Torvald, please — call it back! For my sake, for your own sake, for the sake of the children! Listen to me, Torvald! Do it! You don't know what you're doing to all of us!

Helmer. Too late.

Nora. Yes. Too late.

Helmer. Dear Nora, I forgive you this fear you're in, although it really is an insult to me. Yes, it is! It's an insult to think that I am scared of a shabby scrivener's revenge. But I forgive you, for it's such a beautiful proof how much you love me. (*Takes her in his arms.*) And that's the way it should be, my sweet darling. Whatever happens, you'll see that when things get really rough I have both strength and courage. You'll find out that I am man enough to shoulder the whole burden.

Nora (*terrified*). What do you mean by that?

Helmer. All of it, I tell you —

Nora (*composed*). You'll never have to do that.

Helmer. Good. Then we'll share the burden, Nora — like husband and wife, the way it ought to be. (*Caresses her.*) Now are you satisfied? There, there, there. Not that look in your eyes — like a frightened dove. It's all your own foolish imagination. — Why don't you practice the tarantella — and your tambourine, too. I'll be in the inner office and close both doors, so I won't hear you. You can make as much noise as you like. (*Turning in the doorway.*) And when Rank comes, tell him where to find me. (*He nods to her, enters his study carrying his papers, and closes the door.*)

Nora (*transfixed by terror, whispers*). He would do it. He'll do it. He'll do it in spite of the whole world. — No, this mustn't happen. Anything rather than that! There must be a way — ! (*The doorbell rings.*) Dr. Rank! Anything rather than that! Anything — anything at all!

She passes her hand over her face, pulls herself together, and opens the door to the hall. Dr. Rank is out there, hanging up his coat. Darkness begins to fall during the following scene.

Nora. Hello there, Dr. Rank. I recognized your ringing. Don't go in to Torvald yet. I think he's busy.

Rank. And you?

Nora (*as he enters and she closes the door behind him*). You know I always have time for you.

Rank. Thanks. I'll make use of that as long as I can.

Nora. What do you mean by that — As long as you can?

Rank. Does that frighten you?

Nora. Well, it's a funny expression. As if something was going to happen.

Rank. Something is going to happen that I've long been expecting. But I admit I hadn't thought it would come quite so soon.

Nora (*seizes his arm*). What is it you've found out? Dr. Rank — tell me!

Rank (*sits down by the stove*). I'm going downhill fast. There's nothing to do about that.

Nora (*with audible relief*). So it's *you* —

Rank. Who else? No point in lying to myself. I'm in worse shape than any of my other patients, Mrs. Helmer. These last few days I've been conducting an audit on my inner condition. Bankrupt. Chances are that within a month I'll be rotting up in the cemetery.

Nora. Shame on you! Talking that horrid way!

Rank. The thing itself is horrid — damn horrid. The worst of it, though, is all that other horror that comes first. There is only one more test I need to make. After that I'll have a pretty good idea when I'll start coming apart. There is something I want to say to you. Helmer's refined nature can't stand anything hideous. I don't want him in my sick room.

Nora. Oh, but Dr. Rank —

Rank. I don't want him there. Under no circumstance. I'll close my door to him. As soon as I have full certainty that the worst is about to begin I'll give you my card with a black cross on it. Then you'll know the last horror of destruction has started.

Nora. Today you're really quite impossible. And I had hoped you'd be in a particularly good mood.

Rank. With death on my hands? Paying for someone else's sins? Is there justice in that? And yet there isn't a single family that isn't ruled by that same law of ruthless retribution, in one way or another.

Nora (*puts her hands over her ears*). Poppycock! Be fun! Be fun!

Rank. Well, yes. You may just as well laugh at the whole thing. My poor, innocent spine is suffering for my father's frolics as a young lieutenant.

Nora (*over by the table, left*). Right. He was addicted to asparagus and goose liver paté, wasn't he?

Rank. And truffles.

Nora. Of course. Truffles. And oysters too, I think.

Rank. And oysters. Obviously.

Nora. And all the port and champagne that go with it. It's really too bad that goodies like that ruin your backbone.

Rank. Particularly an unfortunate backbone that never enjoyed any of it.

Nora. Ah yes, that's the saddest part of it all.

Rank (*looks searchingly at her*). Hm —

Nora (*after a brief pause*). Why did you smile just then?

Rank. No, it was you that laughed.

Nora. No, it was you that smiled, Dr. Rank!

Rank (*gets up*). You're more of a mischief-maker than I thought.

Nora. I feel in the mood for mischief today.

Rank. So it seems.

Nora (*with both her hands on his shoulders*). Dear, dear Dr. Rank, don't you go and die and leave Torvald and me.

Rank. Oh, you won't miss me for very long. Those who go away are soon forgotten.

Nora (*with an anxious look*). Do you believe that?

Rank. You'll make new friends, and then —

Nora. Who'll make new friends?

Rank. Both you and Helmer, once I'm gone. You yourself seem to have made a good start already. What was this Mrs. Linde doing here last night? .

Nora. Aha — Don't tell me you're jealous of poor Kristine?

Rank. Yes, I am. She'll be my successor in this house. As soon as I have made my excuses, that woman is likely to —

Nora. Shh — not so loud. She's in there.

Rank. Today too? There you are!

Nora. She's mending my costume. My God, you really *are* unreasonable. (*Sits down on the couch.*) Now be nice, Dr. Rank. Tomorrow you'll see how beautifully I'll dance, and then you are to pretend I'm dancing just for you — and for Torvald too, of course. (*Takes several items out of the carton.*) Sit down, Dr. Rank; I want to show you something.

Rank (sitting down). What?

Nora. Look.

Rank. Silk stockings.

Nora. Flesh-colored. Aren't they lovely? Now it's getting dark in here, but tomorrow — No, no. You only get to see the foot. Oh well, you might as well see all of it.

Rank. Hmm.

Nora. Why do you look so critical? Don't you think they'll fit?

Rank. That's something I can't possibly have a reasoned opinion about.

Nora (looks at him for a moment). Shame on you. (*Slaps his ear lightly with the stocking.*) That's what you get. (*Puts the things back in the carton.*)

Rank. And what other treasures are you going to show me?

Nora. Nothing at all, because you're naughty. (*She hums a little and rummages in the carton.*)

Rank (after a brief silence). When I sit here like this, talking confidently with you, I can't imagine — I can't possibly imagine what would have become of me if I hadn't had you and Helmer.

Nora (smiles). Well, yes — I do believe you like being with us.

Rank (in a lower voice, lost in thought). And then to have to go away from it all —

Nora. Nonsense. You are not going anywhere.

Rank (as before). — and not to leave behind as much as a poor little token of gratitude, hardly a brief memory of someone missed, nothing but a vacant place that anyone can fill.

Nora. And what if I were to ask you — ? No —

Rank. Ask me what?

Nora. For a great proof of your friendship —

Rank. Yes, yes — ?

Nora. No, I mean — for an enormous favor —

Rank. Would you really for once make me as happy as all that?

Nora. But you don't even know what it is.

Rank. Well, then; tell me.

Nora. Oh, but I can't, Dr. Rank. It's altogether too much to ask — It's advice and help and a favor —

Rank. So much the better. I can't even begin to guess what it is you have in mind. So for heaven's sake tell me! Don't you trust me?

Nora. Yes, I trust you more than anyone else I know. You are my best and most faithful friend. I know that. So I will tell you. All right, Dr. Rank. There is something you can help me prevent. You know how much Torvald loves me — beyond all words. Never for a moment would he hesitate to give his life for me.

Rank (leaning over to her). Nora — do you really think he's the only one — ?

Nora (with a slight start). Who — ?

Rank. — would gladly give his life for you.

Nora (heavily). I see.

Rank. I have sworn an oath to myself to tell you before I go. I'll never find a better occasion. — All right, Nora; now you know. And now you also know that you can confide in me more than in anyone else.

Nora (gets up; in a calm, steady voice). Let me get by.

Rank (makes room for her but remains seated). Nora —

Nora (in the door to the front hall). Helene, bring the lamp in here, please. (*Walks over to the stove.*) Oh, dear Dr. Rank. That really wasn't very nice of you.

Rank (gets up). That I have loved you as much as anybody — was that not nice?

Nora. No, not that. But that you told me. There was no need for that.

Rank. What do you mean? Have you known — ?

The Maid enters with the lamp, puts it on the table, and goes out.

Rank. Nora — Mrs. Helmer — I'm asking you: did you know?

Nora. Oh, how can I tell what I knew and didn't know! I really can't say — But that you could be so awkward, Dr. Rank! Just when everything was so comfortable.

Rank. Well, anyway, now you know that I'm at your service with my life and soul. And now you must speak.

Nora (looks at him). After what just happened?

Rank. I beg of you — let me know what it is.

Nora. There is nothing I can tell you now.

Rank. Yes, yes. You mustn't punish me this way. Please let me do for you whatever anyone *can* do.

Nora. Now there is nothing you can do. Besides, I don't think I really need any help, anyway. It's probably just my imagination. Of course that's all it is. I'm sure of it! (*Sits down*

in the rocking chair, looks at him, smiles.) Well, well, well, Dr.
Rank! What a fine gentleman you turned out to be! Aren't
you ashamed of yourself, now that we have light?

Rank. No, not really. But perhaps I ought to leave — and not
come back?

Nora. Don't be silly; of course not! You'll come here exactly as
you have been doing. You know perfectly well that Torvald
can't do without you.

Rank. Yes, but what about you?

Nora. Oh, I always think it's perfectly delightful when you come.

Rank. That's the very thing that misled me. You are a riddle to
me. It has often seemed to me that you'd just as soon be
with me as with Helmer.

Nora. Well, you see, there are people you love, and then there are
other people you'd almost rather be with.

Rank. Yes, there is something in that.

Nora. When I lived at home with Daddy, of course I loved him
most. But I always thought it was so much fun to sneak off
down to the maids' room, for they never gave me good
advice and they always talked about such fun things.

Rank. Aha! So it's *their* place I have taken.

Nora (*jumps up and goes over to him*). Oh dear, kind Dr. Rank,
you know very well I didn't mean it that way. Can't you
see that with Torvald it is the way it used to be with Daddy?

The Maid enters from the front hall.

The Maid. Ma'am! (*Whispers to her and gives her a caller's card.*)

Nora (*glances at the card*). Ah! (*Puts it in her pocket.*)

Rank. Anything wrong?

Nora. No, no; not at all. It's nothing — just my new costume —

Rank. But your costume is lying right there!

Nora. Oh yes, that one. But this is another one. I ordered it.
Torvald mustn't know —

Rank. Aha. So that's the great secret.

Nora. That's it. Why don't you go in to him, please. He's in the
inner office. And keep him there for a while —

Rank. Don't worry. He won't get away. (*Enters Helmer's study.*)

Nora (*to The Maid*). You say he's waiting in the kitchen?

The Maid. Yes. He came up the back stairs.

Nora. But didn't you tell him there was somebody with me?

The Maid. Yes, but he wouldn't listen.

Nora. He won't leave?

The Maid. No, not till he's had a word with you, ma'am.

Nora. All right. But try not to make any noise. And, Helene —

don't tell anyone he's here. It's supposed to be a surprise for
my husband.

The Maid. I understand, ma'am — (*She leaves.*)

Nora. The terrible is happening. It's happening, after all. No, no,
no. It can't happen. It won't happen. (*She bolts the study door.*)

*The Maid opens the front hall door for Krogstad and closes the
door behind him. He wears a fur coat for traveling, boots, and a
fur hat.*

Nora (*toward him*). Keep your voice down. My husband's home.

Krogstad. That's all right.

Nora. What do you want?

Krogstad. To find out something.

Nora. Be quick, then. What is it?

Krogstad. I expect you know I've been fired.

Nora. I couldn't prevent it, Mr. Krogstad. I fought for you as
long and as hard as I could, but it didn't do any good.

Krogstad. Your husband doesn't love you any more than that? He
knows what I can do to you, and yet he runs the risk —

Nora. Surely you didn't think I'd tell him?

Krogstad. No, I really didn't. It wouldn't be like Torvald Helmer
to show that kind of guts —

Nora. Mr. Krogstad, I insist that you show respect for my husband.

Krogstad. By all means. All due respect. But since you're so anxious
to keep this a secret, may I assume that you are a little better
informed than yesterday about exactly what you have done?

Nora. Better than *you* could ever teach me.

Krogstad. Of course. Such a bad lawyer as I am —

Nora. What do you want of me?

Krogstad. I just wanted to find out how you are, Mrs. Helmer.
I've been thinking about you all day. You see, even a bill
collector, a pen pusher, a — anyway, someone like me —
even he has a little of what they call a heart.

Nora. Then show it. Think of my little children.

Krogstad. Have you and your husband thought of mine? Never
mind. All I want to tell you is that you don't need to take
this business too seriously. I have no intention of bringing
charges right away.

Nora. Oh no, you wouldn't; would you? I knew you wouldn't.

Krogstad. The whole thing can be settled quite amiably. Nobody
else needs to know anything. It will be between the three
of us.

Nora. My husband must never find out about this.

Krogstad. How are you going to prevent that? Maybe you can pay
  me the balance on the loan?

Nora. No, not right now.

Krogstad. Or do you have a way of raising the money one of these
  next few days?

Nora. None I intend to make use of.

Krogstad. It wouldn't do you any good, anyway. Even if you had
  the cash in your hand right this minute, I wouldn't give you
  your note back. It wouldn't make any difference *how* much
  money you offered me.

Nora. Then you'll have to tell me what you plan to use the note
  for.

Krogstad. Just keep it; that's all. Have it on hand, so to speak. I
  won't say a word to anybody else. So if you've been thinking
  about doing something desperate —

Nora. I have.

Krogstad. — like leaving house and home —

Nora. I have!

Krogstad. — or even something worse —

Nora. How did you know?

Krogstad. — then: don't.

Nora. How did you know I was thinking of *that?*

Krogstad. Most of us do, right at first. I did, too, but when it
  came down to it I didn't have the courage —

Nora (*tonelessly*). Nor do I.

Krogstad (*relieved*). See what I mean? I thought so. You don't either.

Nora. I don't. I don't.

Krogstad. Besides, it would be very silly of you. Once that first
  domestic blow-up is behind you — . Here in my pocket is
  a letter for your husband.

Nora. Telling him everything?

Krogstad. As delicately as possible.

Nora (*quickly*). He mustn't get that letter. Tear it up. I'll get you
  the money somehow.

Krogstad. Excuse me, Mrs. Helmer. I thought I just told you —

Nora. I'm not talking about the money I owe you. Just let me
  know how much money you want from my husband, and
  I'll get it for you.

Krogstad. I want no money from your husband.

Nora. Then, what *do* you want?

Krogstad. I'll tell you, Mrs. Helmer. I want to rehabilitate myself;
  I want to get up in the world; and your husband is going
  to help me. For a year and a half I haven't done anything

disreputable. All that time I have been struggling with the most miserable circumstances. I was content to work my way up step by step. Now I've been kicked out, and I'm no longer satisfied just getting my old job back. I want more than that; I want to get to the top. I'm being quite serious. I want the bank to take me back but in a higher position. I want your husband to create a new job for me —

Nora. He'll never do that!

Krogstad. He will. I know him. He won't dare not to. And once I'm back inside and he and I are working together, you'll see! Within a year I'll be the manager's right hand. It will be Nils Krogstad and not Torvald Helmer who'll be running the Mutual Bank!

Nora. You'll never see that happen!

Krogstad. Are you thinking of — ?

Nora. Now I *do* have the courage.

Krogstad. You can't scare me. A fine, spoiled lady like you —

Nora. You'll see, you'll see!

Krogstad. Under the ice, perhaps? Down into that cold, black water? Then spring comes, and you float up again — hideous, can't be identified, hair all gone —

Nora. You don't frighten me.

Krogstad. Nor you me. One doesn't do that sort of thing, Mrs. Helmer. Besides, what good would it do? He'd still be in my power.

Nora. Afterwards? When I'm no longer — ?

Krogstad. Aren't you forgetting that your reputation would be in my hands?

Nora stares at him, speechless.

Krogstad. All right; now I've told you what to expect. So don't do anything foolish. When Helmer gets my letter I expect to hear from him. And don't you forget that it's your husband himself who forces me to use such means again. That I'll never forgive him. Goodbye, Mrs. Helmer. (*Goes out through the hall.*)

Nora (at the door, opens it a little, listens). He's going. And no letter. Of course not! That would be impossible! (*Opens the door more.*) What's he doing? He's still there. Doesn't go down. Having second thoughts — ? Will he — ?

The sound of a letter dropping into the mailbox. Then Krogstad's steps are heard going down the stairs, gradually dying away.

Nora (with a muted cry runs forward to the table by the couch; brief pause). In the mailbox. (*Tiptoes back to the door to the front hall.*) There it is. Torvald, Torvald — now we're lost!

Mrs. Linde (*enters from the left, carrying Nora's Capri costume*). There now. I think it's all fixed. Why don't we try it on you —

Nora (*in a low, hoarse voice*). Kristine, come here.

Mrs. Linde. What's wrong with you? You look quite beside yourself.

Nora. Come over here. Do you see that letter? There, look — through the glass in the mailbox.

Mrs. Linde. Yes, yes; I see it.

Nora. That letter is from Krogstad.

Mrs. Linde. Nora — it was Krogstad who lent you the money!

Nora. Yes, and now Torvald will find out about it.

Mrs. Linde. Oh believe me, Nora. That's the best thing for both of you.

Nora. There's more to it than you know. I forged a signature —

Mrs. Linde. Oh my God — !

Nora. I just want to tell you this, Kristine, that you must be my witness.

Mrs. Linde. Witness? How? Witness to what?

Nora. If I lose my mind — and that could very well happen —

Mrs. Linde. Nora!

Nora. — or if something were to happen to me — something that made it impossible for me to be here —

Mrs. Linde. Nora, Nora! You're not yourself!

Nora. — and if someone were to take all the blame, assume the whole responsibility — Do you understand — ?

Mrs. Linde. Yes, yes; but how can you think — !

Nora. — then you are to witness that that's not so, Kristine. I am not beside myself. I am perfectly rational, and what I'm telling you is that nobody else has known about this. I've done it all by myself, the whole thing. Just remember that.

Mrs. Linde. I will. But I don't understand any of it.

Nora. Oh, how could you! For it's the wonderful that's about to happen.

Mrs. Linde. The wonderful?

Nora. Yes, the wonderful. But it's so terrible, Kristine. It mustn't happen for anything in the whole world!

Mrs. Linde. I'm going over to talk to Krogstad right now.

Nora. No, don't. Don't go to him. He'll do something bad to you.

Mrs. Linde. There was a time when he would have done anything for me.

Nora. He!

Mrs. Linde. Where does he live?

Nora. Oh, I don't know — Yes, wait a minute — (*Reaches into her pocket.*) here's his card — But the letter, the letter —

Helmer (*in his study, knocks on the door*). Nora!

Nora (*cries out in fear*). Oh, what is it? What do you want?

Helmer. That's all right. Nothing to be scared about. We're not coming in. For one thing, you've bolted the door, you know. Are you modeling your costume?

Nora. Yes, yes; I am. I'm going to be so pretty, Torvald.

Mrs. Linde (*having looked at the card*). He lives just around the corner.

Nora. Yes, but it's no use. Nothing can save us now. The letter is in the mailbox.

Mrs. Linde. And your husband has the key?

Nora. Yes. He always keeps it with him.

Mrs. Linde. Krogstad must ask for his letter back, unread. He's got to think up some pretext or other —

Nora. But this is just the time of day when Torvald —

Mrs. Linde. Delay him. Go in to him. I'll be back as soon as I can. (*She hurries out through the hall door.*)

Nora (*walks over to Helmer's door, opens it, and peeks in*). Torvald!

Helmer (*still offstage*). Well, well! So now one's allowed in one's own living room again. Come on, Rank. Now we'll see — (*In the doorway.*) But what's this?

Nora. What, Torvald dear?

Helmer. Rank prepared me for a splendid metamorphosis.

Rank (*in the doorway*). That's how I understood it. Evidently I was mistaken.

Nora. Nobody gets to admire me in my costume before tomorrow.

Helmer. But, dearest Nora — you look all done in. Have you been practicing too hard?

Nora. No, I haven't practiced at all.

Helmer. But you'll have to, you know.

Nora. I know it, Torvald. I simply must. But I can't do a thing unless you help me. I have forgotten everything.

Helmer. Oh it will all come back. We'll work on it.

Nora. Oh yes, please, Torvald. You just have to help me. Promise? I am so nervous. That big party — . You mustn't do anything else tonight. Not a bit of business. Don't even touch a pen. Will you promise, Torvald?

Helmer. I promise. Tonight I'll be entirely at your service — you helpless little thing. — Just a moment, though. First I want to — (*Goes to the door to the front hall.*)

Nora. What are you doing out there?

Helmer. Just looking to see if there's any mail.
Nora. No, no! Don't, Torvald!
Helmer. Why not?
Nora. Torvald, I beg you. There is no mail.
Helmer. Let me just look, anyway. (*Is about to go out.*)

> *Nora by the piano, plays the first bars of the tarantella dance.*

Helmer (halts at the door). Aha!
Nora. I won't be able to dance tomorrow if I don't get to practice with you.
Helmer (goes to her). Are you really all that scared, Nora dear?
Nora. Yes, so terribly scared. Let's try it right now. There's still time before we eat. Oh please, sit down and play for me, Torvald. Teach me, coach me, the way you always do.
Helmer. Of course I will, my darling, if that's what you want. (*Sits down at the piano.*)

> *Nora takes the tambourine out of the carton, as well as a long, many-colored shawl. She quickly drapes the shawl around herself, then leaps into the middle of the floor.*

Nora. Play for me! I want to dance!

> *Helmer plays and Nora dances. Dr. Rank stands by the piano behind Helmer and watches.*

Helmer (playing). Slow down, slow down!
Nora. Can't!
Helmer. Not so violent, Nora!
Nora. It has to be this way.
Helmer (stops playing). No, no. This won't do at all.
Nora (laughing, swinging her tambourine). What did I tell you?
Rank. Why don't you let me play?
Helmer (getting up). Good idea. Then I can direct her better.

> *Rank sits down at the piano and starts playing. Nora dances more and more wildly. Helmer stands over by the stove, repeatedly correcting her. She doesn't seem to hear. Her hair comes loose and falls down over her shoulders. She doesn't notice but keeps on dancing. Mrs. Linde enters.*

Mrs. Linde (stops by the door, dumbfounded). Ah — !
Nora (dancing). We're having such fun, Kristine!
Helmer. My dearest Nora, you're dancing as if it were a matter of life and death!
Nora. It is! It is!

Helmer. Rank, stop. This is sheer madness. Stop it, I say!

Rank stops playing; Nora suddenly stops dancing.

Helmer (*goes over to her*). If I hadn't seen it I wouldn't have believed it. You've forgotten every single thing I ever taught you.

Nora (*tosses away the tambourine*). See? I told you.

Helmer. Well! You certainly need coaching.

Nora. Didn't I tell you I did? Now you've seen for yourself. I'll need your help till the very minute we're leaving for the party. Will you promise, Torvald?

Helmer. You can count on it.

Nora. You're not to think of anything except me — not tonight and not tomorrow. You're not to read any letters — not to look in the mailbox —

Helmer. Ah, I see. You're still afraid of that man.

Nora. Yes — yes, that too.

Helmer. Nora, I can tell from looking at you. There's a letter from him out there.

Nora. I don't know. I think so. But you're not to read it now. I don't want anything ugly to come between us before it's all over.

Rank (*to Helmer in a low voice*). Better not argue with her.

Helmer (*throws his arm around her*). The child shall have her way. But tomorrow night, when you've done your dance —

Nora. Then you'll be free.

The Maid (*in the door, right*). Dinner can be served any time, ma'am.

Nora. We want champagne, Helene.

The Maid. Very good, ma'am. (*Goes out.*)

Helmer. Aha! Having a party, eh?

Nora. Champagne from now till sunrise! (*Calls out.*) And some macaroons, Helene. Lots! — just this once.

Helmer (*taking her hands*). There, there — I don't like this wild — frenzy — Be my own sweet little lark again, the way you always are.

Nora. Oh, I will. But you go on in. You too, Dr. Rank. Kristine, please help me put up my hair.

Rank (*in a low voice to Helmer as they go out*). You don't think she is — you know — expecting — ?

Helmer. Oh no. Nothing like that. It's just this childish fear I was telling you about. (*They go out, right.*)

Nora. Well?

Mrs. Linde. Left town.

Nora. I saw it in your face.

Mrs. Linde. He'll be back tomorrow night. I left him a note.

Nora. You shouldn't have. I don't want you to try to stop anything. You see, it's a kind of ecstasy, too, this waiting for the wonderful.

Mrs. Linde. But what is it you're waiting *for?*

Nora. You wouldn't understand. Why don't you go in to the others. I'll be there in a minute.

Mrs. Linde enters the dining room, right.

Nora (stands still for a little while, as if collecting herself; she looks at her watch). Five o'clock. Seven hours till midnight. Twenty-four more hours till next midnight. Then the tarantella is over. Twenty-four plus seven — thirty-one more hours to live.

Helmer (in the door, right). What's happening to my little lark?

Nora (to him, with open arms). Here's your lark!

ACT III

The same room. The table by the couch and the chairs around it have been moved to the middle of the floor. A lighted lamp is on the table. The door to the front hall is open. Dance music is heard from upstairs.

Mrs. Linde is seated by the table, idly leafing through the pages of a book. She tries to read but seems unable to concentrate. Once or twice she turns her head in the direction of the door, anxiously listening.

Mrs. Linde (looks at her watch). Not yet. It's almost too late. If only he hasn't — (*Listens again.*) Ah! There he is. (*She goes to the hall and opens the front door carefully. Quiet footsteps on the stairs. She whispers.*) Come in. There's nobody here.

Krogstad (in the door). I found your note when I got home. What's this all about?

Mrs. Linde. I've got to talk to you.

Krogstad. Oh? And it has to be here?

Mrs. Linde. It couldn't be at my place. My room doesn't have a separate entrance. Come in. We're all alone. The maid is asleep and the Helmers are at a party upstairs.

Krogstad (entering). Really? The Helmers are dancing tonight, are they?

Mrs. Linde. And why not?

Krogstad. You're right. Why not, indeed.

Mrs. Linde. All right, Krogstad. Let's talk, you and I.

Krogstad. I didn't know we had anything to talk about.

Mrs. Linde. We have much to talk about.

Krogstad. I didn't think so.

Mrs. Linde. No, because you've never really understood me.

Krogstad. What was there to understand? What happened was perfectly commonplace. A heartless woman jilts a man when she gets a more attractive offer.

Mrs. Linde. Do you think I'm all that heartless? And do you think it was easy for me to break with you?

Krogstad. No?

Mrs. Linde. You really thought it was?

Krogstad. If it wasn't, why did you write the way you did that time?

Mrs. Linde. What else could I do? If I had to make a break, I also had the duty to destroy whatever feelings you had for me.

Krogstad (clenching his hands). So that's the way it was. And you did — *that* — just for money!

Mrs. Linde. Don't forget I had a helpless mother and two small brothers. We couldn't wait for you, Krogstad. You know yourself how uncertain your prospects were then.

Krogstad. All right. But you still didn't have the right to throw me over for somebody else.

Mrs. Linde. I don't know. I have asked myself that question many times. Did I have that right?

Krogstad (in a lower voice). When I lost you I lost my footing. Look at me now. A shipwrecked man on a raft.

Mrs. Linde. Rescue may be near.

Krogstad. It *was* near. Then you came between.

Mrs. Linde. I didn't know that, Krogstad. Only today did I find out it's your job I'm taking over in the bank.

Krogstad. I believe you when you say so. But now that you *do* know, aren't you going to step aside?

Mrs. Linde. No, for it wouldn't do you any good.

Krogstad. Whether it would or not — *I* would do it.

Mrs. Linde. I have learned common sense. Life and hard necessity have taught me that.

Krogstad. And life has taught me not to believe in pretty speeches.

Mrs. Linde. Then life has taught you a very sensible thing. But you do believe in actions, don't you?

Krogstad. How do you mean?

Mrs. Linde. You referred to yourself just now as a shipwrecked man.

Krogstad. It seems to me I had every reason to do so.

Mrs. Linde. And I am a shipwrecked woman. No one to grieve for, no one to care for.

Krogstad. You made your choice.

Mrs. Linde. I had no other choice that time.

Krogstad. Let's say you didn't. What then?

Mrs. Linde. Krogstad, how would it be if we two shipwrecked people got together?

Krogstad. What's this!

Mrs. Linde. Two on one wreck are better off than each on his own.

Krogstad. Kristine!

Mrs. Linde. Why do you think I came to town?

Krogstad. Surely not because of me?

Mrs. Linde. If I'm going to live at all I must work. All my life, for as long as I can remember, I have worked. That's been my one and only pleasure. But now that I'm all alone in the world I feel nothing but this terrible emptiness and desolation. There is no joy in working just for yourself. Krogstad — give me someone and something to work for.

Krogstad. I don't believe this. Only hysterical females go in for that kind of high-minded self-sacrifice.

Mrs. Linde. Did you ever know me to be hysterical?

Krogstad. You really could do this? Listen — do you know about my past? All of it?

Mrs. Linde. Yes, I do.

Krogstad. Do you also know what people think of me around here?

Mrs. Linde. A little while ago you sounded as if you thought that together with me you might have become a different person.

Krogstad. I'm sure of it.

Mrs. Linde. Couldn't that still be?

Krogstad. Kristine — do you know what you are doing? Yes, I see you do. And you think you have the courage?

Mrs. Linde. I need someone to be a mother to, and your children need a mother. You and I need one another. Nils, I believe in you — in the real you. Together with you I dare to do anything.

Krogstad (seizes her hands). Thanks, thanks, Kristine — now I know I'll raise myself in the eyes of others. — Ah, but I forget — !

Mrs. Linde (listening). Shh! — There's the tarantella. You must go; hurry!

Krogstad. Why? What is it?

Mrs. Linde. Do you hear what they're playing up there? When that dance is over they'll be down.

Krogstad. All right. I'm leaving. The whole thing is pointless, anyway. Of course you don't know what I'm doing to the Helmers.

Mrs. Linde. Yes, Krogstad; I do know.

Krogstad. Still, you're brave enough — ?

Mrs. Linde. I very well understand to what extremes despair can drive a man like you.

Krogstad. If only it could be undone!

Mrs. Linde. It could, for your letter is still out there in the mailbox.

Krogstad. Are you sure?

Mrs. Linde. Quite sure. But —

Krogstad (looks searchingly at her). Maybe I'm beginning to understand. You want to save your friend at any cost. Be honest with me. That's it, isn't it?

Mrs. Linde. Krogstad, you may sell yourself once for somebody else's sake, but you don't do it twice.

Krogstad. I'll demand my letter back.

Mrs. Linde. No, no.

Krogstad. Yes, of course. I'll wait here till Helmer comes down. Then I'll ask him for my letter. I'll tell him it's just about my dismissal — that he shouldn't read it.

Mrs. Linde. No, Krogstad. You are not to ask for that letter back.

Krogstad. But tell me — wasn't that the real reason you wanted to meet me here?

Mrs. Linde. At first it was, because I was so frightened. But that was yesterday. Since then I have seen the most incredible things going on in this house. Helmer must learn the whole truth. This miserable secret must come out in the open; those two must come to a full understanding. They simply can't continue with all this concealment and evasion.

Krogstad. All right; if you want to take that chance. But there is one thing I *can* do, and I'll do that right now.

Mrs. Linde (listening). But hurry! Go! The dance is over. We aren't safe another minute.

Krogstad. I'll be waiting for you downstairs.

Mrs. Linde. Yes, do. You must see me home.

Krogstad. I've never been so happy in my whole life. (*He leaves through the front door. The door between the living room and the front hall remains open.*)

Mrs. Linde (straightens up the room a little and gets her things ready). What a change! Oh yes! — what a change! People to work for — to live for — a home to bring happiness to. I can't wait to get to work — ! If only they'd come soon — (*Listens.*)

Ah, there they are. Get my coat on — (*Puts on her coat and hat.*)

Helmer's and Nora's voices are heard outside. A key is turned in the lock, and Helmer almost forces Nora into the hall. She is dressed in her Italian costume, with a big black shawl over her shoulders. He is in evening dress under an open black domino.

Nora (*in the door, still resisting*). No, no, no! I don't want to! I want to go back upstairs. I don't want to leave so early.

Helmer. But dearest Nora —

Nora. Oh please, Torvald — please! I'm asking you as nicely as I can — just another hour!

Helmer. Not another minute, sweet. You know we agreed. There now. Get inside. You'll catch a cold out here. (*She still resists, but he guides her gently into the room.*)

Mrs. Linde. Good evening.

Nora. Kristine!

Helmer. Ah, Mrs. Linde. Still here?

Mrs. Linde. I know. I really should apologize, but I so much wanted to see Nora in her costume.

Nora. You've been waiting up for me?

Mrs. Linde. Yes, unfortunately I didn't get here in time. You were already upstairs, but I just didn't feel like leaving till I had seen you.

Helmer (*removing Nora's shawl*). Yes, do take a good look at her, Mrs. Linde. I think I may say she's worth looking at. Isn't she lovely?

Mrs. Linde. She certainly is —

Helmer. Isn't she a miracle of loveliness, though? That was the general opinion at the party, too. But dreadfully obstinate — that she is, the sweet little thing. What can we do about that? Will you believe it — I practically had to use force to get her away.

Nora. Oh Torvald, you're going to be sorry you didn't give me even half an hour more.

Helmer. See what I mean, Mrs. Linde? She dances the tarantella — she is a tremendous success — quite deservedly so, though perhaps her performance was a little too natural — I mean, more than could be reconciled with the rules of art. But all right! The point is: she's a success, a tremendous success. So should I let her stay after that? Spoil the effect? Of course not. So I take my lovely little Capri girl — I might say, my capricious little Capri girl — under my arm — a quick turn around the room — a graceful bow in all directions, and — as they say in the novels — the beautiful apparition is gone. A finale should always be done for effect, Mrs. Linde, but there doesn't seem to be any way of getting that into Nora's head. Poooh — ! It's hot in here. (*Throws his cloak down on a chair and opens the door to his room.*) Why, it's dark in here! Of course. Excuse me — (*Goes inside and lights a couple of candles.*)

Nora (*in a hurried, breathless whisper*). Well?

Mrs. Linde (*in a low voice*). I have talked to him.

Nora. And — ?

Mrs. Linde. Nora — you've got to tell your husband everything.

Nora (*no expression in her voice*). I knew it.

Mrs. Linde. You have nothing to fear from Krogstad. But you must speak.

Nora. I'll say nothing.

Mrs. Linde. Then the letter will.

Nora. Thank you, Kristine. Now I know what I have to do. Shh!

Helmer (*returning*). Well, Mrs. Linde, have you looked your fill?

Mrs. Linde. Yes. And now I'll say goodnight.

Helmer. So soon? Is that your knitting?

Mrs. Linde (*takes it*). Yes, thank you. I almost forgot.

Helmer. So you knit, do you?

Mrs. Linde. Oh yes.

Helmer. You know — you ought to take up embroidery instead.

Mrs. Linde. Oh? Why?

Helmer. Because it's so much more beautiful. Look. You hold the embroidery so — in your left hand. Then with your right you move the needle — like this — in an easy, elongated arc — you see?

Mrs. Linde. Maybe you're right —

Helmer. Knitting, on the other hand, can never be anything but ugly. Look here: arms pressed close to the sides — the needles going up and down — there's something Chinese about it somehow — . That really was an excellent champagne they served us tonight.

Mrs. Linde. Well, goodnight, Nora. And don't be obstinate any more.

Helmer. Well said, Mrs. Linde!

Mrs. Linde. Goodnight, sir.

Helmer (*sees her to the front door*). Goodnight, goodnight. I hope you'll get home all right? I'd be very glad to — but of course you don't have far to walk, do you? Goodnight, goodnight. (*She leaves. He closes the door behind her and returns to the living*

room.) There! At last we got rid of her. She really is an
incredible bore, that woman.

Nora. Aren't you very tired, Torvald?

Helmer. No, not in the least.

Nora. Not sleepy either?

Helmer. Not at all. Quite the opposite. I feel enormously — animated.
How about you? Yes, you do look tired and sleepy.

Nora. Yes, I am very tired. Soon I'll be asleep.

Helmer. What did I tell you? I was right, wasn't I? Good thing I
didn't let you stay any longer.

Nora. Everything you do is right.

Helmer (kissing her forehead). Now my little lark is talking like a
human being. But did you notice what splendid spirits Rank
was in tonight?

Nora. Was he? I didn't notice. I didn't get to talk with him.

Helmer. Nor did I — hardly. But I haven't seen him in such a
good mood for a long time. (*Looks at her, comes closer to her.*)
Ah! It does feel good to be back in our own home again,
to be quite alone with you — my young, lovely, ravishing
woman!

Nora. Don't look at me like that, Torvald!

Helmer. Am I not to look at my most precious possession? All
that loveliness that is mine, nobody's but mine, all of it
mine.

Nora (walks to the other side of the table). I won't have you talk to
me like that tonight.

Helmer (follows her). The tarantella is still in your blood. I can tell.
That only makes you all the more alluring. Listen! The guests
are beginning to leave. (*Softly.*) Nora — soon the whole
house will be quiet.

Nora. Yes, I hope so.

Helmer. Yes, don't you, my darling? Do you know — when I'm
at a party with you, like tonight — do you know why I
hardly ever talk to you, why I keep away from you, only
look at you once in a while — a few stolen glances — do
you know why I do that? It's because I pretend that you are
my secret love, my young, secret bride-to-be, and nobody
has the slightest suspicion that there is anything between us.

Nora. Yes, I know. All your thoughts are with me.

Helmer. Then when we're leaving and I lay your shawl around
your delicate young shoulders — around that wonderful curve
of your neck — then I imagine you're my young bride, that
we're coming away from the wedding, that I am taking you
to my home for the first time — that I am alone with you

for the first time — quite alone with you, you young, trembling beauty! I have desired you all evening — there hasn't been a longing in me that hasn't been for you. When you were dancing the tarantella, chasing, inviting — my blood was on fire; I couldn't stand it any longer — that's why I brought you down so early —

Nora. Leave me now, Torvald. Please! I don't want all this.

Helmer. What do you mean? You're only playing your little teasing bird game with me; aren't you, Nora? Don't want to? I'm your husband, aren't I?

There is a knock on the front door.

Nora (with a start). Did you hear that — ?

Helmer (on his way to the hall). Who is it?

Rank (outside). It's me. May I come in for a moment?

Helmer (in a low voice, annoyed). Oh, what does he want now? (*Aloud.*) Just a minute. (*Opens the door.*) Well! How good of you not to pass by our door.

Rank. I thought I heard your voice, so I felt like saying hello. (*Looks around.*) Ah yes — this dear, familiar room. What a cozy, comfortable place you have here, you two.

Helmer. Looked to me as if you were quite comfortable upstairs too.

Rank. I certainly was. Why not? Why not enjoy all you can in this world? As much as you can for as long as you can, anyway. Excellent wine.

Helmer. The champagne, particularly.

Rank. You noticed that too? Incredible how much I managed to put away.

Nora. Torvald drank a lot of champagne tonight, too.

Rank. Did he?

Nora. Yes, he did, and then he's always so much fun afterwards.

Rank. Well, why not have some fun in the evening after a well spent day?

Helmer. Well spent? I'm afraid I can't claim that.

Rank (slapping him lightly on the shoulder). But you see, I can!

Nora. Dr. Rank, I believe you must have been conducting a scientific test today.

Rank. Exactly.

Helmer. What do you know — little Nora talking about scientific tests!

Nora. May I congratulate you on the result?

Rank. You may indeed.

Nora. It was a good one?

Rank. The best possible for both doctor and patient — certainty.

Nora (a quick query). Certainty?

Rank. Absolute certainty. So why shouldn't I have myself an enjoyable evening afterwards?

Nora. I quite agree with you, Dr. Rank. You should.

Helmer. And so do I. If only you don't pay for it tomorrow.

Rank. Oh well — you get nothing for nothing in this world.

Nora. Dr. Rank — you are fond of costume parties, aren't you?

Rank. Yes, particularly when there is a reasonable number of amusing disguises.

Nora. Listen — what are the two of us going to be the next time?

Helmer. You frivolous little thing! Already thinking about the next party!

Rank. You and I? That's easy. You'll be Fortune's Child.

Helmer. Yes, but what is a fitting costume for that?

Rank. Let your wife appear just the way she always is.

Helmer. Beautiful. Very good indeed. But how about yourself? Don't you know what you'll go as?

Rank. Yes, my friend. I know precisely what I'll be.

Helmer. Yes?

Rank. At the next masquerade I'll be invisible.

Helmer. That's a funny idea.

Rank. There's a certain big, black hat — you've heard about the hat that makes you invisible, haven't you? You put that on, and nobody can see you.

Helmer (suppressing a smile). I guess that's right.

Rank. But I'm forgetting what I came for. Helmer, give me a cigar — one of your dark Havanas.

Helmer. With the greatest pleasure. (*Offers him his case.*)

Rank (takes one and cuts off the tip). Thanks.

Nora (striking a match). Let me give you a light.

Rank. Thanks. (*She holds the match; he lights his cigar.*) And now goodbye!

Helmer. Goodbye, goodbye, my friend.

Nora. Sleep well, Dr. Rank.

Rank. I thank you.

Nora. Wish me the same.

Rank. You? Well, if you really want me to — . Sleep well. And thanks for the light. (*He nods to both of them and goes out.*)

Helmer (in a low voice). He had had quite a bit to drink.

Nora (absently). Maybe so.

Helmer takes out his keys and goes out into the hall.

Nora. Torvald — what are you doing out there?

Helmer. Got to empty the mailbox. It is quite full. There wouldn't
be room for the newspapers in the morning —

Nora. Are you going to work tonight?

Helmer. You know very well I won't. — Say! What's this? Somebody's been at the lock.

Nora. The lock — ?

Helmer. Yes. Why, I wonder. I hate to think that any of the
maids — . Here's a broken hairpin. It's one of yours, Nora.

Nora (quickly). Then it must be one of the children.

Helmer. You better make damn sure they stop that. Hm, hm. —
There! I got it open, finally. (*Gathers up the mail, calls out to
the kitchen.*) Helene? — Oh Helene — turn out the light here
in the hall, will you? (*He comes back into the living room and
closes the door.*) Look how it's been piling up. (*Shows her the
bundle of letters. Starts leafing through it.*) What's this?

Nora (by the window). The letter! Oh no, no, Torvald!

Helmer. Two calling cards — from Rank.

Nora. From Dr. Rank?

Helmer (looking at them). "Doctor medicinae Rank." They were
on top. He must have put them there when he left just now.

Nora. Anything written on them?

Helmer. A black cross above the name. Look. What a macabre
idea. Like announcing his own death.

Nora. That's what it is.

Helmer. Hm? You know about this? Has he said anything to you?

Nora. That card means he has said goodbye to us. He'll lock himself
up to die.

Helmer. My poor friend. I knew of course he wouldn't be with
me very long. But so soon — . And hiding himself away
like a wounded animal —

Nora. When it has to be, it's better it happens without words.
Don't you think so, Torvald?

Helmer (walking up and down). He'd grown so close to us. I find
it hard to think of him as gone. With his suffering and
loneliness he was like a clouded background for our happy
sunshine. Well, it may be better this way. For him, at any
rate. (*Stops.*) And perhaps for us, too, Nora. For now we
have nobody but each other. (*Embraces her.*) Oh you — my
beloved wife! I feel I just can't hold you close enough. Do
you know, Nora — many times I have wished some great
danger threatened you, so I could risk my life and blood
and everything — everything, for your sake.

Nora (frees herself and says in a strong and firm voice). I think you
should go and read your letters now, Torvald.

Helmer. No, no — not tonight. I want to be with you, my darling.

Nora. With the thought of your dying friend — ?

Helmer. You are right. This has shaken both of us. Something not
beautiful has come between us. Thoughts of death and dissolution. We must try to get over it — out of it. Till then
— we'll each go to our own room.

Nora (her arms around his neck). Torvald — goodnight! Goodnight!

Helmer (kisses her forehead). Goodnight, my little songbird. Sleep
well, Nora. Now I'll read my letters. (*He goes into his room,
carrying the mail. Closes the door.*)

*Nora (her eyes desperate, her hands groping, finds Helmer's domino and
throws it around her; she whispers, quickly, brokenly, hoarsely).*
Never see him again. Never. Never. Never. (*Puts her shawl
over her head.*) And never see the children again, either. Never;
never. — The black, icy water — fathomless — this — ! If
only it was all over. — Now he has it. Now he's reading
it. No, no; not yet. Torvald — goodbye — you — the
children —

*She is about to hurry through the hall, when Helmer flings open
the door to his room and stands there with an open letter in his
hand.*

Helmer. Nora!

Nora (cries out). Ah — !

Helmer. What is it? You know what's in this letter?

Nora. Yes, I do! Let me go! Let me out!

Helmer (holds her back). Where do you think you're going?

Nora (trying to tear herself loose from him). I won't let you save me,
Torvald!

Helmer (tumbles back). True! Is it true what he writes? Oh my God!
No, no — this can't possibly be true.

Nora. It is true. I have loved you more than anything else in the
whole world.

Helmer. Oh, don't give me any silly excuses.

Nora (taking a step towards him). Torvald —

Helmer. You wretch! What have you done!

Nora. Let me go. You are not to sacrifice yourself for me. You
are not to take the blame.

Helmer. No more playacting. (*Locks the door to the front hall.*) You'll
stay here and answer me. Do you understand what you have
done? Answer me! Do you understand?

Nora (gazes steadily at him with an increasingly frozen expression).
Yes. Now I'm beginning to understand.

Helmer (walking up and down). What a dreadful awakening. All these years — all these eight years — she, my pride and my joy — a hypocrite, a liar — oh worse! worse! — a criminal! Oh, the bottomless ugliness in all this! Damn! Damn! Damn!

Nora, silent, keeps gazing at him.

Helmer (*stops in front of her*). I ought to have guessed that something like this would happen. I should have expected it. All your father's loose principles — Silence! You have inherited every one of your father's loose principles. No religion, no morals, no sense of duty — . Now I am being punished for my leniency with him. I did it for your sake, and this is how you pay me back.

Nora. Yes. This is how.

Helmer. You have ruined all my happiness. My whole future — that's what you have destroyed. Oh, it's terrible to think about. I am at the mercy of an unscrupulous man. He can do with me whatever he likes, demand anything of me, command me and dispose of me just as he pleases — I dare not say a word! To go down so miserably, to be destroyed — all because of an irresponsible woman!

Nora. When I am gone from the world, you'll be free.

Helmer. No noble gestures, please. Your father was always full of such phrases too. What good would it do me if you were gone from the world, as you put it? Not the slightest good at all. He could still make the whole thing public, and if he did I wouldn't be surprised if people thought I'd put you up to it. They might even think it was my idea — that it was I who urged you to do it! And for all this I have you to thank — you, whom I've borne on my hands through all the years of our marriage. *Now* do you understand what you've done to me?

Nora (*with cold calm*). Yes.

Helmer. I just can't get it into my head that this is happening; it's all so incredible. But we have to come to terms with it somehow. Take your shawl off. Take it off, I say! I have to satisfy him one way or another. The whole affair must be kept quiet at whatever cost. — And as far as you and I are concerned, nothing must seem to have changed. I'm talking about appearances, of course. You'll go on living here; that goes without saying. But I won't let you bring up the children; I dare not trust you with them. — Oh! Having to say this to one I have loved so much, and whom I still — ! But all that is past. It's not a question of happiness

any more but of hanging on to what can be salvaged —
pieces, appearances — (*The doorbell rings.*)

Helmer (*jumps.*) What's that? So late. Is the worst — ? Has
he — ! Hide, Nora! Say you're sick.

Nora doesn't move. Helmer opens the door to the hall.

The Maid (*half dressed, out in the hall*). A letter for your wife, sir.

Helmer. Give it to me. (*Takes the letter and closes the door.*) Yes, it's
from him. But I won't let you have it. I'll read it myself.

Nora. Yes — you read it.

Helmer (*by the lamp*). I hardly dare. Perhaps we're lost, both you
and I. No; I've got to know. (*Tears the letter open, glances
through it, looks at an enclosure; a cry of joy.*) Nora!

Nora looks at him with a question in her eyes.

Helmer. Nora! — No, I must read it again. — Yes, yes; it is so!
I'm saved! Nora, I'm saved!

Nora. And I?

Helmer. You too, of course; we're both saved, both you and I.
Look! He's returning your note. He writes that he's sorry,
he regrets, a happy turn in his life — oh, it doesn't matter
what he writes. We're saved, Nora! Nobody can do anything
to you now. Oh Nora, Nora — . No, I want to get rid of
this disgusting thing first. Let me see — (*Looks at the signature.*)
No, I don't want to see it. I don't want it to be more than
a bad dream, the whole thing. (*Tears up the note and both
letters, throws the pieces in the stove, and watches them burn.*)
There! Now it's gone. — He wrote that ever since Christmas
Eve — . Good God, Nora, these must have been three
terrible days for you.

Nora. I have fought a hard fight these last three days.

Helmer. And been in agony and seen no other way out than — .
No, we won't think of all that ugliness. We'll just rejoice
and tell ourselves it's over, it's all over! Oh, listen to me,
Nora. You don't seem to understand. It's over. What *is* it?
Why do you look like that — that frozen expression on your
face? Oh my poor little Nora, don't you think I know what
it is? You can't make yourself believe that I have forgiven
you. But I have, Nora; I swear to you, I have forgiven you
for everything. Of course I know that what you did was
for love of me.

Nora. That is true.

Helmer. You have loved me the way a wife ought to love her husband. You just didn't have the wisdom to judge the means. But do you think I love you any less because you don't know how to act on your own? Of course not. Just lean on me. I'll advise you; I'll guide you. I wouldn't be a man if I didn't find you twice as attractive because of your womanly helplessness. You mustn't pay any attention to the hard words I said to you right at first. It was just that first shock when I thought everything was collapsing all around me. I have forgiven you, Nora. I swear to you — I really have forgiven you.

Nora. I thank you for your forgiveness. (*She goes out through the door, right.*)

Helmer. No, stay — (*Looks into the room she entered.*) What are you doing in there?

Nora (*within*). Getting out of my costume.

Helmer (*by the open door*). Good, good. Try to calm down and compose yourself, my poor little frightened songbird. Rest safely; I have broad wings to cover you with. (*Walks around near the door.*) What a nice and cozy home we have, Nora. Here's shelter for you. Here I'll keep you safe like a hunted dove I have rescued from the hawk's talons. Believe me: I'll know how to quiet your beating heart. It will happen by and by, Nora; you'll see. Why, tomorrow you'll look at all this in quite a different light. And soon everything will be just the way it was before. I won't need to keep reassuring you that I have forgiven you; you'll feel it yourself. Did you really think I could have abandoned you, or even reproached you? Oh, you don't know a real man's heart, Nora. There is something unspeakably sweet and satisfactory for a man to know deep in himself that he has forgiven his wife — forgiven her in all the fullness of his honest heart. You see, that way she becomes his very own all over again — in a double sense, you might say. He has, so to speak, given her a second birth; it is as if she had become his wife and his child, both. From now on that's what you'll be to me, you lost and helpless creature. Don't worry about a thing, Nora. Only be frank with me, and I'll be your will and your conscience. — What's this? You're not in bed? You've changed your dress — !

Nora (*in an everyday dress*). Yes, Torvald. I have changed my dress.

Helmer. But why — now — this late?

Nora. I'm not going to sleep tonight.

Helmer. But my dear Nora —

Nora (*looks at her watch*). It isn't all that late. Sit down here with me, Torvald. You and I have much to talk about. (*Sits down at the table.*)

Helmer. Nora — what is this all about? That rigid face —

Nora. Sit down. This will take a while. I have much to say to you.

Helmer (*sits down, facing her across the table*). You worry me, Nora. I don't understand you.

Nora. No, that's just it. You don't understand me. And I have never understood you — not till tonight. No, don't interrupt me. Just listen to what I have to say. — This is a settling of accounts, Torvald.

Helmer. What do you mean by that?

Nora (*after a brief silence*). Doesn't one thing strike you, now that we are sitting together like this?

Helmer. What would that be?

Nora. We have been married for eight years. Doesn't it occur to you that this is the first time that you and I, husband and wife, are having a serious talk?

Helmer. Well — serious — . What do you mean by that?

Nora. For eight whole years — longer, in fact — ever since we first met, we have never talked seriously to each other about a single serious thing.

Helmer. You mean I should forever have been telling you about worries you couldn't have helped me with anyway?

Nora. I am not talking about worries. I'm saying we have never tried seriously to get to the bottom of anything together.

Helmer. But dearest Nora, I hardly think that would have been something *you* —

Nora. That's the whole point. You have never understood me. Great wrong has been done to me, Torvald. First by Daddy and then by you.

Helmer. What! By us two? We who have loved you more deeply than anyone else?

Nora (*shakes her head*). You never loved me — neither Daddy nor you. You only thought it was fun to be in love with me.

Helmer. But, Nora — what an expression to use!

Nora. That's the way it has been, Torvald. When I was home with Daddy, he told me all his opinions, and so they became my opinions too. If I disagreed with him I kept it to myself, for he wouldn't have liked that. He called me his little doll baby, and he played with me the way I played with my dolls. Then I came to your house —

Helmer. What a way to talk about our marriage!

Nora (*imperturbably*). I mean that I passed from Daddy's hands into yours. You arranged everything according to your taste, and so I came to share it — or I pretended to; I'm not sure which. I think it was a little of both, now one and now the other. When I look back on it now, it seems to me I've been living here like a pauper — just a hand-to-mouth kind of existence. I have earned my keep by doing tricks for you, Torvald. But that's the way you wanted it. You have great sins against me to answer for, Daddy and you. It's your fault that nothing has become of me.

Helmer. Nora, you're being both unreasonable and ungrateful. Haven't you been happy here?

Nora. No, never. I thought I was, but I wasn't.

Helmer. Not — not happy!

Nora. No; just having fun. And you have always been very good to me. But our home has never been more than a playroom. I have been your doll wife here, just the way I used to be Daddy's doll child. And the children have been my dolls. I thought it was fun when you played with me, just as they thought it was fun when I played with them. That's been our marriage, Torvald.

Helmer. There is something in what you are saying — exaggerated and hysterical though it is. But from now on things will be different. Playtime is over; it's time for growing up.

Nora. Whose growing up — mine or the children's?

Helmer. Both yours and the children's, Nora darling.

Nora. Oh Torvald, you're not the man to bring me up to be the right kind of wife for you.

Helmer. How can you say that?

Nora. And I — ? What qualifications do I have for bringing up the children?

Helmer. Nora!

Nora. You said so yourself a minute ago — that you didn't dare to trust me with them.

Helmer. In the first flush of anger, yes. Surely, you're not going to count that.

Nora. But you were quite right. I am *not* qualified. Something else has to come first. Somehow I have to grow up myself. And you are not the man to help me do that. That's a job I have to do by myself. And that's why I'm leaving you.

Helmer (*jumps up*). What did you say!

Nora. I have to be by myself if I am to find out about myself and about all the other things too. So I can't stay here with you any longer.

Helmer. Nora, Nora!

Nora. I'm leaving now. I'm sure Kristine will put me up for tonight.

Helmer. You're out of your mind! I won't let you! I forbid you!

Nora. You can't forbid me anything any more; it won't do any good. I'm taking my own things with me. I won't accept anything from you, either now or later.

Helmer. But this is madness!

Nora. Tomorrow I'm going home — I mean back to my old hometown. It will be easier for me to find some kind of job there.

Helmer. Oh, you blind, inexperienced creature — !

Nora. I must see to it that I get experience, Torvald.

Helmer. Leaving your home, your husband, your children! Not a thought of what people will say!

Nora. I can't worry about that. All I know is that I have to leave.

Helmer. Oh, this is shocking! Betraying your most sacred duties like this!

Nora. And what do you consider my most sacred duties?

Helmer. Do I need to tell you that? They are your duties to your husband and your children.

Nora. I have other duties equally sacred.

Helmer. You do not. What duties would they be?

Nora. My duties to myself.

Helmer. You are a wife and a mother before you are anything else.

Nora. I don't believe that any more. I believe I am first of all a human being, just as much as you — or at any rate that I must try to become one. Oh, I know very well that most people agree with you, Torvald, and that it says something like that in all the books. But what people say and what the books say is no longer enough for me. I have to think about these things myself and see if I can't find the answers.

Helmer. You mean to tell me you don't know what your proper place in your own home is? Don't you have a reliable guide in such matters? Don't you have religion?

Nora. Oh but Torvald — I don't really know what religion is.

Helmer. What are you saying!

Nora. All I know is what the Reverend Hansen told me when he prepared me for confirmation. He said that religion was *this* and it was *that.* When I get by myself, away from here, I'll have to look into that, too. I have to decide if what the Reverend Hansen said was right, or anyway if it is right for *me.*

Helmer. Oh, this is unheard of in a young woman! If religion can't
    guide you, let me appeal to your conscience. For surely you
    have moral feelings? Or — answer me — maybe you don't?
Nora. Well, you see, Torvald, I don't really know what to say. I
    just don't know. I am confused about these things. All I
    know is that my ideas are quite different from yours. I have
    just found out that the laws are different from what I thought
    they were, but in no way can I get it into my head that
    those laws are right. A woman shouldn't have the right to
    spare her dying old father or save her husband's life! I just
    can't believe that.
Helmer. You speak like a child. You don't understand the society
    you live in.
Nora. No, I don't. But I want to find out about it. I have to make
    up my mind who is right, society or I.
Helmer. You are sick, Nora; you have a fever. I really don't think
    you are in your right mind.
Nora. I have never felt so clearheaded and sure of myself as I do
    tonight.
Helmer. And clearheaded and sure of yourself you're leaving your
    husband and children?
Nora. Yes.
Helmer. Then there is only one possible explanation.
Nora. What?
Helmer. You don't love me any more.
Nora. No, that's just it.
Helmer. Nora! Can you say that?
Nora. I am sorry, Torvald, for you have always been so good to
    me. But I can't help it. I don't love you any more.
Helmer (*with forced composure*). And this too is a clear and sure
    conviction?
Nora. Completely clear and sure. That's why I don't want to stay
    here any more.
Helmer. And are you ready to explain to me how I came to forfeit
    your love?
Nora. Certainly I am. It was tonight, when the wonderful didn't
    happen. That was when I realized you were not the man I
    thought you were.
Helmer. You have to explain. I don't understand.
Nora. I have waited patiently for eight years, for I wasn't such a
    fool that I thought the wonderful is something that happens
    any old day. Then this — thing — came crashing in on me,
    and then there wasn't a doubt in my mind that now — now
    comes the wonderful. When Krogstad's letter was in that

mailbox, never for a moment did it even occur to me that you would submit to his conditions. I was so absolutely certain that you would say to him: make the whole thing public — tell everybody. And when that had happened —

Helmer. Yes, then what? When I had surrendered my own wife to shame and disgrace — !

Nora. When that had happened, I was absolutely certain that you would stand up and take the blame and say, "I'm the guilty one."

Helmer. Nora!

Nora. You mean I never would have accepted such a sacrifice from you? Of course not. But what would my protests have counted against yours? *That* was the wonderful I was waiting for in hope and terror. And to prevent that I was going to kill myself.

Helmer. I'd gladly work nights and days for you, Nora — endure sorrow and want for your sake. But nobody sacrifices his *honor* for his love.

Nora. A hundred thousand women have done so.

Helmer. Oh, you think and talk like a silly child.

Nora. All right. But you don't think and talk like the man I can live with. When you had gotten over your fright — not because of what threatened *me* but because of the risk to *you* — and the whole danger was past, then you acted as if nothing at all had happened. Once again I was your little songbird, your doll, just as before, only now you had to handle her even more carefully, because she was so frail and weak. (*Rises.*) Torvald — that moment I realized that I had been living here for eight years with a stranger and had borne him three children — Oh, I can't stand thinking about it! I feel like tearing myself to pieces!

Helmer (*heavily*). I see it, I see it. An abyss has opened up between us. — Oh but Nora — surely it can be filled?

Nora. The way I am now I am no wife for you.

Helmer. I have it in me to change.

Nora. Perhaps — if your doll is taken from you.

Helmer. To part — to part from you! No, no, Nora! I can't grasp that thought!

Nora (*goes out, right*). All the more reason why it has to be. (*She returns with her outdoor clothes and a small bag, which she sets down on the chair by the table.*)

Helmer. Nora, Nora! Not now! Wait till tomorrow.

Nora (*putting on her coat*). I can't spend the night in a stranger's rooms.

Helmer. But couldn't we live here together like brother and
  sister — ?
Nora (*tying on her hat*). You know very well that wouldn't last
  long — . (*Wraps her shawl around her.*) Goodbye, Torvald. I
  don't want to see the children. I know I leave them in better
  hands than mine. The way I am now I can't be anything to
  them.
Helmer. But some day, Nora — some day?
Nora. How can I tell? I have no idea what's going to become of
  me.
Helmer. But you're still my wife, both as you are now and as you
  will be.
Nora. Listen, Torvald — when a wife leaves her husband's house,
  the way I am doing now, I have heard he has no more legal
  responsibilities for her. At any rate, I now release you from
  all responsibility. You are not to feel yourself obliged to me
  for anything, and I have no obligations to you. There has
  to be full freedom on both sides. Here is your ring back.
  Now give me mine.
Helmer. Even this?
Nora. Even this.
Helmer. Here it is.
Nora. There. So now it's over. I'm putting the keys here. The
  maids know everything about the house — better than I.
  Tomorrow, after I'm gone, Kristine will come over and pack
  my things from home. I want them sent after me.
Helmer. Over! It's all over! Nora, will you never think of me?
Nora. I'm sure I'll often think of you and the children and this
  house.
Helmer. May I write to you, Nora?
Nora. No — never. I won't have that.
Helmer. But send you things — ? You must let me.
Nora. Nothing, nothing.
Helmer. — help you, when you need help —
Nora. I told you, no; I won't have it. I'll accept nothing from
  strangers.
Helmer. Nora — can I never again be more to you than a stranger?
Nora (*picks up her bag*). Oh Torvald — then the most wonderful
  of all would have to happen —
Helmer. Tell me what that would be — !
Nora. For that to happen, both you and I would have to change
  so that — Oh Torvald; I no longer believe in the wonderful.
Helmer. But I *will* believe. Tell me! Change, so that — ?

Nora. So that our living together would become a true marriage.
    Goodbye. (*She goes out through the hall.*)
Helmer (*sinks down on a chair near the door and covers his face with
    his hands*). Nora! Nora! (*Looks around him and gets up.*) All
    empty. She's gone. (*With sudden hope.*) The most wonderful
    — ?!

From downstairs comes the sound of a heavy door slamming shut.

QUESTIONS

1. Near the beginning of the play, how does Mrs. Linde's
   presence help to define Nora's character? How does Nora's
   response to Krogstad's entrance tell us something about Nora?
2. What does Dr. Rank contribute to the play? If he were
   eliminated, what would be lost?
3. Ibsen very reluctantly acceded to a request for an alternate
   ending for a German production. In the new ending Helmer
   forces Nora to look at their sleeping children and reminds
   her that "tomorrow, when they wake up and call for their
   mother, they will be — motherless." Nora "struggles with
   herself" and concludes by saying, "Oh, this is a sin against
   myself, but I cannot leave them." In view of the fact that
   the last act several times seems to be moving toward a "happy
   ending" (e.g., Krogstad promises to recall his letter), what
   is wrong with this alternate ending?
4. Can it be argued that although at the end Nora goes out to
   achieve self-realization, her abandonment of her children —
   especially to Torvald's loathsome conventional morality —
   is a crime? (By the way, exactly why does Nora leave the
   children? She seems to imply, in some passages, that because
   she forged a signature she is unfit to bring them up. But do
   you agree with her?)
5. Michael Meyer, in his splendid biography *Henrik Ibsen,* says
   that the play is not so much about women's rights as about
   "the need of every individual to find out the kind of person
   he or she really is, and to strive to become that person."
   What evidence can you offer to support this interpretation?
6. In *The Quintessence of Ibsenism* Bernard Shaw says that Ibsen,
   reacting against a common theatrical preference for strange
   situations, "saw that . . . the more familiar the situation, the
   more interesting the play. Shakespear had put ourselves on
   the stage but not our situations. Our uncles seldom murder

our fathers and . . . marry our mothers. . . . Ibsen . . . gives
us not only ourselves, but ourselves in our own situations.
The things that happen to his stage figures are things that
happen to us. One consequence is that his plays are much
more important to us than Shakespear's. Another is that they
are capable both of hurting us cruelly and of filling us with
excited hopes of escape from idealistic tyrannies, and with
visions of intenser life in the future." How much of this do
you believe?

Tennessee Williams *(American. 1914–1983)*

The Glass Menagerie

Nobody, not even the rain, has such small hands.
                                        — *E. E. Cummings*

List of Characters

Amanda Wingfield, the mother. A little woman of great but
confused vitality clinging frantically to another time and place.
Her characterization must be carefully created, not copied
from type. She is not paranoiac, but her life is paranoia.
There is much to admire in Amanda, and as much to love
and pity as there is to laugh at. Certainly she has endurance
and a kind of heroism, and though her foolishness makes
her unwittingly cruel at times, there is tenderness in her
slight person.

Laura Wingfield, her daughter. Amanda, having failed to establish contact with reality, continues to live vitally in her
illusions, but Laura's situation is even graver. A childhood
illness has left her crippled, one leg slightly shorter than the
other, and held in a brace. This defect need not be more
than suggested on the stage. Stemming from this, Laura's
separation increases till she is like a piece of her own glass
collection, too exquisitely fragile to move from the shelf.

Tom Wingfield, her son. And the narrator of the play. A poet
with a job in a warehouse. His nature is not remorseless,
but to escape from a trap he has to act without pity.

Jim O'Connor, the gentleman caller. A nice, ordinary, young
man.

This is a scene from the opening production of The Glass Menagerie *at The Playhouse in New York on March 31, 1945, starring Lorette Taylor, Julie Hayden, Eddie Dowling, and Anthony Ross. Reproduced by courtesy of the New York Public Library, The Billy Rose Theater Collection.*

Scene. *An alley in St. Louis.*

Part I.   *Preparation for a Gentleman Caller.*
Part II.   *The Gentleman Calls.*

Time. *Now and the Past.*

SCENE I

The Wingfeld apartment is in the rear of the building, one of those vast hive-like conglomerations of cellular living-units that flower as warty growths in overcrowded urban centers of lower middle-class population and are symptomatic of the impulse of this largest and fundamentally enslaved section of American society to avoid fluidity and differentiation and to exist and function as one interfused mass of automatism.

The apartment faces an alley and is entered by a fire-escape, a structure whose name is a touch of accidental poetic truth, for all of these huge buildings are always burning with the slow and implacable fires of human desperation. The fire-escape is included in the set — that is, the landing of it and steps descending from it.

The scene is memory and is therefore nonrealistic. Memory takes a lot of poetic license. It omits some details; others are exaggerated, according to the emotional value of the articles it touches, for memory is seated predominantly in the heart. The interior is therefore rather dim and poetic.

At the rise of the curtain, the audience is faced with the dark, grim rear wall of the Wingfeld tenement. This building, which runs parallel to the footlights, is flanked on both sides by dark, narrow alleys which run into murky canyons of tangled clotheslines, garbage cans and the sinister latticework of neighboring fire-escapes. It is up and down these side alleys that exterior entrances and exits are made, during the play. At the end of Tom's opening commentary, the dark tenement wall slowly reveals (by means of a transparency) the interior of the ground floor Wingfield apartment.

Downstage is the living room, which also serves as a sleeping room for Laura, the sofa unfolding to make her bed. Upstage, center, and divided by a wide arch or second proscenium with transparent faded portieres (or second curtain), is the dining room. In an old-fashioned what-not in the living room are seen scores of transparent glass animals. A blown-up photograph of the father hangs on the wall of the living room, facing the audience, to the left of the archway. It is the face of a very handsome young man in a doughboy's First World War cap. He is gallantly smiling, ineluctably smiling, as if to say, "I will be smiling forever."

The audience hears and sees the opening scene in the dining room through both the transparent fourth wall of the building and the transparent gauze portieres of the dining-room arch. It is during this revealing scene that the fourth wall slowly ascends, out of sight.

This transparent exterior wall is not brought down again until the very end of the play, during Tom's final speech.

The narrator is an undisguised convention of the play. He takes whatever license with dramatic convention as is convenient to his purposes.

Tom enters dressed as a merchant sailor from alley, stage left, and strolls across the front of the stage to the fire-escape. There he stops and lights a cigarette. He addresses the audience.

Tom. Yes, I have tricks in my pocket, I have things up my sleeve. But I am the opposite of a stage magician. He gives you illusion that has the appearance of truth. I give you truth in the pleasant disguise of illusion. To begin with, I turn back time. I reverse it to that quaint period, the thirties, when the huge middle class of America was matriculating in a school for the blind. Their eyes had failed them, or they had failed their eyes, and so they were having their fingers pressed forcibly down on the fiery Braille alphabet of a dissolving economy. In Spain there was revolution. Here there was only shouting and confusion. In Spain there was Guernica. Here there were disturbances of labor, sometimes pretty violent, in otherwise peaceful cities such as Chicago, Cleveland, Saint Louis. . . . This is the social background of the play.

(Music.)

The play is memory. Being a memory play, it is dimly lighted, it is sentimental, it is not realistic. In memory everything seems to happen to music. That explains the fiddle in the wings. I am the narrator of the play, and also a character in it. The other characters are my mother, Amanda, my sister, Laura, and a gentleman caller who appears in the final scenes. He is the most realistic character in the play, being an emissary from a world of reality that we were somehow set apart from. But since I have a poet's weakness for symbols, I am using this character also as a symbol; he is the long delayed but always expected something that we live for. There is a fifth character in the play who doesn't appear except in this larger-than-life photograph over the mantel. This is our father who left us a long time ago. He was a telephone man who fell in love with long distances; he gave up his job with the telephone company and skipped the light fantastic out of town. . . . The last we heard of him was a picture post-card from Mazatlan, on the Pacific coast of Mexico, containing a message of two words — "Hello — Goodbye!" and no address. I think the rest of the play will explain itself. . . .

Amanda's voice becomes audible through the portieres.

(Legend on Screen: "Où Sont les Neiges?")

He divides the portieres and enters the upstage area.

Amanda and Laura are seated at a drop-leaf table. Eating is indicated by gestures without food or utensils. Amanda faces the audience. Tom and Laura are seated in profile.

The interior has lit up softly and through the scrim we see Amanda and Laura seated at the table in the upstage area.

Amanda (calling). Tom?
Tom. Yes, Mother.
Amanda. We can't say grace until you come to the table!
Tom. Coming, Mother. (*He bows slightly and withdraws, reappearing a few moments later in his place at the table.*)
Amanda (to her son). Honey, don't *push* with your *fingers.* If you have to push with something, the thing to push with is a crust of bread. And chew — chew! Animals have sections in their stomachs which enable them to digest food without mastication, but human beings are supposed to chew their food before they swallow it down. Eat food leisurely, son, and really enjoy it. A well-cooked meal has lots of delicate flavors that have to be held in the mouth for appreciation. So chew your food and give your salivary glands a chance to function!

Tom deliberately lays his imaginary fork down and pushes his chair back from the table.

Tom. I haven't enjoyed one bite of this dinner because of your constant directions on how to eat it. It's you that makes me rush through meals with your hawk-like attention to every bite I take. Sickening — spoils my appetite — all this discussion of animals' secretion — salivary glands — mastication!

Amanda (lightly). Temperament like a Metropolitan star! (*He rises and crosses downstage.*) You're not excused from the table.

Tom. I am getting a cigarette.

Amanda. You smoke too much.

Laura rises.

Laura. I'll bring in the blanc mange.

He remains standing with his cigarette by the portieres during the following.

Amanda (rising). No, sister, no, sister — you be the lady this time and I'll be the darky.

Laura. I'm already up.

Amanda. Resume your seat, little sister — I want you to stay fresh and pretty — for gentlemen callers!

Laura. I'm not expecting any gentlemen callers.

Amanda (crossing out to kitchenette. Airily). Sometimes they come when they are least expected! Why, I remember one Sunday afternoon in Blue Mountain — (*Enters kitchenette.*)

Tom. I know what's coming!

Laura. Yes. But let her tell it.

Tom. Again?

Laura. She loves to tell it.

Amanda returns with bowl of dessert.

Amanda. One Sunday afternoon in Blue Mountain — your mother received — *seventeen!* — gentlemen callers! Why, sometimes there weren't chairs enough to accommodate them all. We had to send the nigger over to bring in folding chairs from the parish house.

Tom (remaining at portieres). How did you entertain those gentlemen callers?

Amanda. I understood the art of conversation!

Tom. I bet you could talk.

Amanda. Girls in those days *knew* how to talk, I can tell you.

Tom. Yes?

(*Image: Amanda as a Girl on a Porch Greeting Callers.*)

Amanda. They knew how to entertain their gentlemen callers. It wasn't enough for a girl to be possessed of a pretty face and a graceful figure — although I wasn't slighted in either respect. She also needed to have a nimble wit and a tongue to meet all occasions.

Tom. What did you talk about?

Amanda. Things of importance going on in the world! Never anything coarse or common or vulgar. (*She addresses Tom as though he were seated in the vacant chair at the table though he remains by portieres. He plays this scene as though he held the book.*) My callers were gentlemen — all! Among my callers were some of the most prominent young planters of the Mississippi Delta — planters and sons of planters!

Tom motions for music and a spot of light on Amanda.

Her eyes lift, her face glows, her voice becomes rich and elegiac.

(*Screen Legend: "Où Sont les Neiges?"*)

There was young Champ Laughlin who later became vice-president of the Delta Planters Bank. Hadley Stevenson who was drowned in Moon Lake and left his widow one hundred and fifty thousand in Government bonds. There were the Cutrere brothers, Wesley and Bates. Bates was one of my bright particular beaux! He got in a quarrel with that wild Wainright boy. They shot it out on the floor of Moon Lake Casino. Bates was shot through the stomach. Died in the ambulance on his way to Memphis. His widow was also well-provided for, came into eight or ten thousand acres, that's all. She married him on the rebound — never loved her — carried my picture on him the night he died! And there was that boy that every girl in the Delta had set her cap for! That beautiful, brilliant young Fitzhugh boy from Green County!

Tom. What did he leave his widow?

Amanda. He never married! Gracious, you talk as though all of my old admirers had turned up their toes to the daisies!

Tom. Isn't this the first you mentioned that still survives?

Amanda. That Fitzhugh boy went North and made a fortune — came to be known as the Wolf of Wall Street! He had the Midas touch, whatever he touched turned to gold! And I could have been Mrs. Duncan J. Fitzhugh, mind you! But — I picked your *father!*

Laura (*rising*). Mother, let me clear the table.

Amanda. No dear, you go in front and study your typewriter chart. Or practice your shorthand a little. Stay fresh and pretty! — It's almost time for our gentlemen callers to start arriving. (*She flounces girlishly toward the kitchenette.*) How many do you suppose we're going to entertain this afternoon?

Tom throws down the paper and jumps up with a groan.

Laura (alone in the dining room). I don't believe we're going to receive any, Mother.

Amanda (reappearing, airily). What? No one — not one? You must be joking! (*Laura nervously echoes her laugh. She slips in a fugitive manner through the half-open portieres and draws them gently behind her. A shaft of very clear light is thrown on her face against the faded tapestry of the curtains.*) (*Music: "The Glass Menagerie" Under Faintly.*) (*Lightly.*) Not one gentleman caller? It can't be true! There must be a flood, there must have been a tornado!

Laura. It isn't a flood, it's not a tornado, Mother. I'm just not popular like you were in Blue Mountain. . . . (*Tom utters another groan. Laura glances at him with a faint, apologetic smile. Her voice catching a little.*) Mother's afraid I'm going to be an old maid.

(*The Scene Dims Out with "Glass Menagerie" Music.*)

SCENE II

"Laura, Haven't You Ever Liked Some Boy?"

On the dark stage the screen is lighted with the image of blue roses. Gradually Laura's figure becomes apparent and the screen goes out. The music subsides.

Laura is seated in the delicate ivory chair at the small clawfoot table.

She wears a dress of soft violet material for a kimono — her hair tied back from her forehead with a ribbon.

She is washing and polishing her collection of glass.

Amanda appears on the fire-escape steps. At the sound of her ascent, Laura catches her breath, thrusts the bowl of ornaments away and seats herself stiffly before the diagram of the typewriter keyboard as though it held her spellbound. Something has happened to Amanda. It is written in her face as she climbs to the landing: a look that is grim and hopeless and a little absurd.

She has on one of those cheap or imitation velvety-looking cloth coats with imitation fur collar. Her hat is five or six years old, one of those dreadful cloche hats that were worn in the late twenties, and she is clasping an enormous black patent-leather pocketbook with nickel clasp and initials. This is her full-dress outfit, the one she usually wears to the D.A.R.

Before entering she looks through the door.

She purses her lips, opens her eyes wide, rolls them upward and shakes her head.

Then she slowly lets herself in the door. Seeing her mother's expression Laura touches her lips with a nervous gesture.

Laura. Hello, Mother, I was — (*She makes a nervous gesture toward the chart on the wall. Amanda leans against the shut door and stares at Laura with a martyred look.*)

Amanda. Deception? Deception? (*She slowly removes her hat and gloves, continuing the swift suffering stare. She lets the hat and gloves fall on the floor — a bit of acting.*)

Laura (*shakily*). How was the D.A.R. meeting? (*Amanda slowly opens her purse and removes a dainty white handkerchief which she shakes out delicately and delicately touches to her lips and nostrils.*) Didn't you go to the D.A.R. meeting, Mother?

Amanda (*faintly, almost inaudibly*). — No. — No. (*Then more forcibly.*) I did not have the strength — to go to the D.A.R. In fact, I did not have the courage! I wanted to find a hole in the ground and hide myself in it forever! (*She crosses slowly to the wall and removes the diagram of the typewriter keyboard. She holds it in front of her for a second, staring at it sweetly and sorrowfully — then bites her lips and tears it in two pieces.*)

Laura (*faintly*). Why did you do that, Mother? (*Amanda repeats the same procedure with the chart of the Gregg Alphabet.*) Why are you —

Amanda. Why? Why? How old are you, Laura?

Laura. Mother, you know my age.

Amanda. I thought that you were an adult; it seems that I was mistaken. (*She crosses slowly to the sofa and sinks down and stares at Laura.*)

Laura. Please don't stare at me, Mother.

Amanda closes her eyes and lowers her head. Count ten.

Amanda. What are we going to do, what is going to become of us, what is the future?

Count ten.

Laura. Has something happened, Mother? (*Amanda draws a long breath and takes out the handkerchief again. Dabbing process.*) Mother, has — something happened?

Amanda. I'll be all right in a minute. I'm just bewildered — (*count
   five*) — by life. . . .
Laura. Mother, I wish that you would tell me what's happened.
Amanda. As you know, I was supposed to be inducted into my
   office at the D.A.R. this afternoon. (*Image: A Swarm of
   Typewriters.*) But I stopped off at Rubicam's Business College
   to speak to your teachers about your having a cold and ask
   them what progress they thought you were making down
   there.
Laura. Oh. . . .
Amanda. I went to the typing instructor and introduced myself as
   your mother. She didn't know who you were. Wingfield,
   she said. We don't have any such student enrolled at the
   school! I assured her she did, that you had been going to
   classes since early in January. "I wonder," she said, "if you
   could be talking about that terribly shy little girl who dropped
   out of school after only a few days' attendance?" "No," I
   said, "Laura, my daughter, has been going to school every
   day for the past six weeks!" "Excuse me," she said. She
   took the attendance book out and there was your name,
   unmistakably printed, and all the dates you were absent until
   they decided that you had dropped out of school. I still said,
   "No, there must have been some mistake! There must have
   been some mix-up in the records!" And she said, "No — I
   remember her perfectly now. Her hand shook so that she
   couldn't hit the right keys! The first time we gave a speed-
   test, she broke down completely — was sick at the stomach
   and almost had to be carried into the wash-room! After that
   morning she never showed up any more. We phoned the
   house but never got any answer" — while I was working
   at Famous and Barr, I suppose, demonstrating those — Oh!
   I felt so weak I could barely keep on my feet. I had to sit
   down while they got me a glass of water! Fifty dollars'
   tuition, all of our plans — my hopes and ambitions for you
   — just gone up the spout, just gone up the spout like that.
   (*Laura draws a long breath and gets awkwardly to her feet. She
   crosses to the victrola and winds it up.*) What are you doing?
Laura. Oh! (*She releases the handle and returns to her seat.*)
Amanda. Laura, where have you been going when you've gone
   out pretending that you were going to business college?
Laura. I've just been going out walking.
Amanda. That's not true.
Laura. It is. I just went walking.

Amanda. Walking? Walking? In winter? Deliberately courting pneumonia in that light coat? Where did you walk to, Laura?

Laura. It was the lesser of two evils, Mother. *(Image: Winter Scene in Park.)* I couldn't go back up. I — threw up — on the floor!

Amanda. From half past seven till after five every day you mean to tell me you walked around in the park, because you wanted to make me think that you were still going to Rubicam's Business College?

Laura. It wasn't as bad as it sounds. I went inside places to get warmed up.

Amanda. Inside where?

Laura. I went in the art museum and the bird-houses at the Zoo. I visited the penguins every day! Sometimes I did without lunch and went to the movies. Lately I've been spending most of my afternoons in the Jewel-box, that big glass house where they raise the tropical flowers.

Amanda. You did all this to deceive me, just for the deception? *(Laura looks down.)* Why?

Laura. Mother, when you're disappointed, you get that awful suffering look on your face, like the picture of Jesus' mother in the museum!

Amanda. Hush!

Laura. I couldn't face it.

Pause. A whisper of strings.

(Legend: "The Crust of Humility.")

Amanda (hopelessly fingering the huge pocketbook). So what are we going to do the rest of our lives? Stay home and watch the parades go by? Amuse ourselves with the glass menagerie, darling? Eternally play those worn-out phonograph records your father left as a painful reminder of him? We won't have a business career — we've given that up because it gave us nervous indigestion! *(Laughs wearily.)* What is there left but dependency all our lives? I know so well what becomes of unmarried women who aren't prepared to occupy a position. I've seen such pitiful cases in the South — barely tolerated spinsters living upon the grudging patronage of sister's husband or brother's wife! — stuck away in some little mousetrap of a room — encouraged by one in-law to visit another — little birdlike women without any nest — eating the crust of humility all their life! Is that the future that we've mapped out for ourselves? I swear it's the only alternative I can think of! It isn't a very pleasant alternative, is it? Of course — some girls *do marry.* (*Laura twists her hands nervously.*) Haven't you ever liked some boy?

Laura. Yes. I liked one once. (*Rises.*) I came across his picture a while ago.

Amanda (*with some interest*). He gave you his picture?

Laura. No, it's in the year-book.

Amanda (*disappointed*). Oh — a high-school boy.

(Screen Image: Jim as a High-School Hero Bearing a Silver Cup.)

Laura. Yes. His name was Jim. (*Laura lifts the heavy annual from the clawfoot table.*) Here he is in *The Pirates of Penzance.*

Amanda (*absently*). The what?

Laura. The operetta the senior class put on. He had a wonderful voice and we sat across the aisle from each other Mondays, Wednesdays and Fridays in the Aud. Here he is with the silver cup for debating! See his grin?

Amanda (*absently*). He must have had a jolly disposition.

Laura. He used to call me — Blue Roses.

(Image: Blue Roses.)

Amanda. Why did he call you such a name as that?

Laura. When I had that attack of pleurosis — he asked me what was the matter when I came back. I said pleurosis — he thought that I said Blue Roses! So that's what he always called me after that. Whenever he saw me, he'd holler, "Hello, Blue Roses!" I didn't care for the girl that he went out with. Emily Meisenbach. Emily was the best-dressed girl at Soldan. She never struck me, though, as being sincere. . . . It says in the Personal Section — they're engaged. That's — six years ago! They must be married by now.

Amanda. Girls that aren't cut out for business careers usually wind up married to some nice man. (*Gets up with a spark of revival.*) Sister, that's what you'll do!

Laura utters a startled, doubtful laugh. She reaches quickly for a piece of glass.

Laura. But, Mother —

Amanda. Yes? (*Crossing to photograph.*)

Laura (*in a tone of frightened apology*). I'm — crippled!

(Image: Screen.)

Amanda. Nonsense! Laura, I've told you never, never to use that word. Why, you're not crippled, you just have a little defect — hardly noticeable, even! When people have some slight disadvantage like that, they cultivate other things to make up for it — develop charm — and vivacity — and — *charm!* That's all you have to do! (*She turns again to the photograph.*) One thing your father had *plenty of* — was *charm!*

Tom motions to the fiddle in the wings.

(The Scene Fades out with Music.)

SCENE III

(Legend on the Screen: "After the Fiasco — ")

Tom speaks from the fire-escape landing.

Tom. After the fiasco at Rubicam's Business College, the idea of getting a gentleman caller for Laura began to play a more important part in Mother's calculations. It became an obsession. Like some archetype of the universal unconscious, the image of the gentleman caller haunted our small apartment. . . . *(Image: Young Man at Door with Flowers.)* An evening at home rarely passed without some allusion to this image, this specter, this hope. . . . Even when he wasn't mentioned, his presence hung in Mother's preoccupied look and in my sister's frightened, apologetic manner — hung like a sentence passed upon the Wingfields! Mother was a woman of action as well as words. She began to take logical steps in the planned direction. Late that winter and in the early spring — realizing that extra money would be needed to properly feather the nest and plume the bird — she conducted a vigorous campaign on the telephone, roping in subscribers to one of those magazines for matrons called *The Home-maker's Companion,* the type of journal that features the serialized sublimations of ladies of letters who think in terms of delicate cuplike breasts, slim, tapering waists, rich, creamy thighs, eyes like wood-smoke in autumn, fingers that soothe and caress like strains of music, bodies as powerful as Etruscan sculpture.

(Screen Image: Glamor Magazine Cover.)

Amanda enters with phone on long extension cord. She is spotted in the dim stage.

Amanda. Ida Scott? This is Amanda Wingfield! We *missed* you at the D.A.R. last Monday! I said to myself: She's probably suffering with that sinus condition! How is that sinus condition? Horrors! Heaven have mercy! — You're a Christian martyr, yes, that's what you are, a Christian martyr! Well, I just now happened to notice that your subscription to the *Companion's* about to expire! Yes, it expires with the next issue, honey! — just when that wonderful new serial by Bessie Mae Hopper is getting off to such an exciting start. Oh, honey, it's something that you can't miss! You remember how *Gone With the Wind* took everybody by storm? You simply couldn't go out if you hadn't read it. All everybody *talked* was Scarlett O'Hara. Well, this is a book that critics already compare to *Gone With the Wind*. It's the *Gone With the Wind* of the post-World War generation! — What? — Burning? — Oh, honey, don't let them burn, go take a look in the oven and I'll hold the wire! Heavens — I think she's hung up!

(Dim Out.)

(Legend on Screen: "You Think I'm in Love with Continental Shoemakers?")

Before the stage is lighted, the violent voices of Tom and Amanda are heard. They are quarreling behind the portieres. In front of them stands Laura with clenched hands and panicky expression.

A clear pool of light on her figure throughout this scene.

Tom. What in Christ's name am I —
Amanda (*shrilly*). Don't you use that —
Tom. Supposed to do!
Amanda. Expression! Not in my —
Tom. Ohhh!
Amanda. Presence! Have you gone out of your senses?
Tom. I have, that's true, *driven* out!
Amanda. What is the matter with you, you — big — big — IDIOT!
Tom. Look — I've got *no thing,* no single thing —
Amanda. Lower your voice!
Tom. In my life here that I can call my OWN! Everything is —
Amanda. Stop that shouting!

Tom. Yesterday you confiscated my books! You had the nerve to —

Amanda. I took that horrible novel back to the library — yes! That hideous book by that insane Mr. Lawrence. (*Tom laughs wildly.*) I cannot control the output of diseased minds or people who cater to them — (*Tom laughs still more wildly.*) BUT I WON'T ALLOW SUCH FILTH BROUGHT INTO MY HOUSE! No, no, no, no, no!

Tom. House, house! Who pays rent on it, who makes a slave of himself to —

Amanda (*fairly screeching*). Don't you DARE to —

Tom. No, no, I musn't say things! *I've* got to just —

Amanda. Let me tell you —

Tom. I don't want to hear any more! (*He tears the portieres open. The upstage area is lit with a turgid smoky red glow.*)

Amanda's hair is in metal curlers and she wears a very old bathrobe, much too large for her slight figure, a relic of the faithless Mr. Wingfield.

An upright typewriter and a wild disarray of manuscripts are on the drop-leaf table. The quarrel was probably precipitated by Amanda's interruption of his creative labor. A chair lying overthrown on the floor.

Their gesticulating shadows are cast on the ceiling by the fiery glow.

Amanda. You *will* hear more, you —

Tom. No, I won't hear more, I'm going out!

Amanda. You come right back in —

Tom. Out, out out! Because I'm —

Amanda. Come back here, Tom Wingfield! I'm not through talking to you!

Tom. Oh, go —

Laura (*desperately*). Tom!

Amanda. You're going to listen, and no more insolence from you! I'm at the end of my patience! (*He comes back toward her.*)

Tom. What do you think I'm at? Aren't I supposed to have any patience to reach the end of, Mother? I know, I know. It seems unimportant to you, what I'm *doing* — what I *want* to do — having a little *difference* between them! You don't think that —

Amanda. I think you've been doing things that you're ashamed of. That's why you act like this. I don't believe that you go every night to the movies. Nobody goes to the movies night

after night. Nobody in their right minds goes to the movies
as often as you pretend to. People don't go to the movies
at nearly midnight, and movies don't let out at two A.M.
Come in stumbling. Muttering to yourself like a maniac!
You get three hours' sleep and then go to work. Oh, I can
picture the way you're doing down there. Moping, doping,
because you're in no condition.

Tom (*wildly*). No, I'm in no condition!

Amanda. What right have you got to jeopardize your job? Jeopardize
the security of us all? How do you think we'd manage if
you were —

Tom. Listen! You think I'm crazy *about* the *warehouse*? (*He bends
fiercely toward her slight figure.*) You think I'm in love with
the Continental Shoemakers? You think I want to spend
fifty-five *years* down there in that — *celotex interior!* with —
fluorescent — tubes! Look! I'd rather somebody picked up a
crowbar and battered out my brains — than go back mornings!
I *go!* Every time you come in yelling that God damn *"Rise
and Shine!" "Rise and Shine!"* I say to myself "How *lucky
dead* people are!" But I get up. I *go!* For sixty-five dollars a
month I give up all that I dream of doing and being *ever!*
And you say self — *self's* all I ever think of. Why, listen,
if self is what I thought of, Mother, I'd be where he is —
GONE! (*Pointing to father's picture.*) As far as the system of
transportation reaches! (*He starts past her. She grabs his arm.*)
Don't grab at me, Mother!

Amanda. Where are you going?

Tom. I'm going to the *movies!*

Amanda. I don't believe that lie!

Tom (*crouching toward her, overtowering her tiny figure. She backs away,
gasping*). I'm going to opium dens! Yes, opium dens, dens
of vice and criminals' hang-outs, Mother. I've joined the
Hogan gang, I'm a hired assassin, I carry a tommy-gun in
a violin case! I run a string of cat-houses in the Valley! They
call me Killer, Killer Wingfield, I'm leading a double-life, a
simple, honest warehouse worker by day, by night a dynamic
czar of the *underworld, Mother.* I go to gambling casinos, I
spin away fortunes on the roulette table! I wear a patch over
one eye and a false mustache, sometimes I put on green
whiskers. On those occasions they call me — *El Diablo!* Oh,
I could tell you things to make you sleepless! My enemies
plan to dynamite this place. They're going to blow us all
sky-high some night! I'll be glad, very happy, and so will
you! You'll go up, up on a broomstick, over Blue Mountain

with seventeen gentlemen callers! You ugly — babbling old
— witch. . . . (*He goes through a series of violent, clumsy movements,
seizing his overcoat, lunging to the door, pulling it fiercely open.
The women watch him, aghast. His arm catches in the sleeve of
the coat as he struggles to pull it on. For a moment he is pinioned
by the bulky garment. With an outraged groan he tears the coat
off again, splitting the shoulders of it, and hurls it across the room.
It strikes against the shelf of Laura's glass collection, there is a
tinkle of shattering glass. Laura cries out as if wounded.*)

(*Music Legend: "The Glass Menagerie."*)

Laura (*shrilly*). My glass! — menagerie. . . . (*She covers her face and
turns away.*)

> But Amanda is still stunned and stupefied by the "ugly witch" so
> that she barely notices this occurrence. Now she recovers her speech.

Amanda (*in an awful voice*). I won't speak to you — until you
apologize! (*She crosses through portieres and draws them together
behind her. Tom is left with Laura. Laura clings weakly to the
mantel with her face averted. Tom stares at her stupidly for a
moment. Then he crosses to shelf. Drops awkwardly to his knees
to collect the fallen glass, glancing at Laura as if he would speak
but couldn't.*)

"*The Glass Menagerie*" steals in as

(*The Scene Dims Out.*)

SCENE IV

The interior is dark. Faint light in the alley.

*A deep-voiced bell in a church is tolling the hour of five as the
scene commences.*

*Tom appears at the top of the alley. After each solemn boom of
the bell in the tower, he shakes a little noise-maker or rattle as if
to express the tiny spasm of man in contrast to the sustained power
and dignity of the Almighty. This and the unsteadiness of his
advance make it evident that he has been drinking.*

*As he climbs the few steps to the fire-escape landing light steals
up inside. Laura appears in night-dress, observing Tom's empty
bed in the front room.*

Tom fishes in his pockets for the door-key, removing a motley assortment of articles in the search, including a perfect shower of movie-ticket stubs and an empty bottle. At last he finds the key, but just as he is about to insert it, it slips from his fingers. He strikes a match and crouches below the door.

Tom (*bitterly*). One crack — and it falls through!

Laura opens the door.

Laura. Tom! Tom, what are you doing?

Tom. Looking for a door-key.

Laura. Where have you been all this time?

Tom. I have been to the movies.

Laura. All this time at the movies?

Tom. There was a very long program. There was a Garbo picture and a Mickey Mouse and a travelogue and a newsreel and a preview of coming attractions. And there was an organ solo and a collection for the milk-fund — simultaneously — which ended up in a terrible fight between a fat lady and an usher!

Laura (*innocently*). Did you have to stay through everything?

Tom. Of course! And, oh, I forgot! There was a big stage show! The headliner on this stage show was Malvolio the Magician. He performed wonderful tricks, many of them, such as pouring water back and forth between pitchers. First it turned to wine and then it turned to beer and then it turned to whiskey. I know it was whiskey it finally turned into because he needed somebody to come up out of the audience to help him, and I came up — both shows! It was Kentucky Straight Bourbon. A very generous fellow, he gave souvenirs. (*He pulls from his back pocket a shimmering rainbow-colored scarf.*) He gave me this. This is his magic scarf. You can have it, Laura. You wave it over a canary cage and you get a bowl of gold-fish. You wave it over the gold-fish bowl and they fly away canaries. . . . But the wonderfullest trick of all was the coffin trick. We nailed him into a coffin and he got out of the coffin without removing one nail. (*He has come inside.*) There is a trick that would come in handy for me — get me out of this 2 by 4 situation! (*Flops onto bed and starts removing shoes.*)

Laura. Tom — Shhh!

Tom. What you shushing me for?

Laura. You'll wake up Mother.

Tom. Goody, goody! Pay 'er back for all those "Rise an' Shines."

(*Lies down, groaning.*) You know it don't take much intelligence to get yourself into a nailed-up coffin, Laura. But who in hell ever got himself out of one without removing one nail?

As if in answer, the father's grinning photograph lights up.

(*Scene Dims Out.*)

Immediately following: The church bell is heard striking six. At the sixth stroke the alarm clock goes off in Amanda's room, and after a few moments we hear her calling: "Rise and Shine! Rise and Shine! Laura, go tell your brother to rise and shine!"

Tom (*sitting up slowly*). I'll rise — but I won't shine.

The light increases.

Amanda. Laura, tell your brother his coffee is ready.

Laura slips into front room.

Laura. Tom! it's nearly seven. Don't make Mother nervous. (*He stares at her stupidly. Beseechingly.*) Tom, speak to Mother this morning. Make up with her, apologize, speak to her!
Tom. She won't to me. It's her that started not speaking.
Laura. If you just say you're sorry she'll start speaking.
Tom. Her not speaking — is that such a tragedy?
Laura. Please — please!
Amanda (*calling from kitchenette*). Laura, are you going to do what I asked you to do, or do I have to get dressed and go out myself?
Laura. Going, going — soon as I get on my coat! (*She pulls on a shapeless felt hat with nervous, jerky movement, pleadingly glancing at Tom. Rushes awkwardly for coat. The coat is one of Amanda's, inaccurately made-over, the sleeves too short for Laura.*) Butter and what else?
Amanda (*entering upstage*). Just butter. Tell them to charge it.
Laura. Mother, they make such faces when I do that.
Amanda. Sticks and stones may break my bones, but the expression on Mr. Garfinkel's face won't harm us! Tell your brother his coffee is getting cold.
Laura (*at door*). Do what I asked you, will you, will you, Tom?

He looks sullenly away.

Amanda. Laura, go now or just don't go at all!
Laura (*rushing out*). Going — going! (*A second later she cries out.*

*Tom springs up and crosses to the door. Amanda rushes anxiously
in. Tom opens the door.)*

Tom. Laura?

Laura. I'm all right. I slipped, but I'm all right.

Amanda (peering anxiously after her). If anyone breaks a leg on those
fire-escape steps, the landlord ought to be sued for every
cent he possesses! *(She shuts door. Remembers she isn't speaking
and returns to other room.)*

*As Tom enters listlessly for his coffee, she turns her back to him
and stands rigidly facing the window on the gloomy gray vault of
the areaway. Its light on her face with its aged but childish features
is cruelly sharp, satirical as a Daumier print.*

(Music Under: "Ave Maria.")

*Tom glances sheepishly but sullenly at her averted figure and slumps
at the table. The coffee is scalding hot; he sips it and gasps and
spits it back in the cup. At his gasp, Amanda catches her breath
and half turns. Then catches herself and turns back to window.*

*Tom blows on his coffee, glancing sidewise at his mother. She
clears her throat. Tom clears his. He starts to rise. Sinks back
down again, scratches his head, clears his throat again. Amanda
coughs. Tom raises his cup in both hands to blow on it, his eyes
staring over the rim of it at his mother for several moments. Then
he slowly sets the cup down and awkwardly and hesitantly rises
from the chair.*

Tom (hoarsely). Mother. I — I apologize. Mother. *(Amanda draws
a quick, shuddering breath. Her face works grotesquely. She breaks
into childlike tears.)* I'm sorry for what I said, for everything
that I said, I didn't mean it.

Amanda (sobbingly). My devotion has made me a witch and so I
make myself hateful to my children!

Tom. No, you *don't.*

Amanda. I worry so much, don't sleep, it makes me nervous!

Tom (gently). I understand that.

Amanda. I've had to put up a solitary battle all these years. But
you're my right-hand bower! Don't fall down, don't fail!

Tom (gently). I try, Mother.

Amanda (with great enthusiasm). Try and you will SUCCEED! *(The
notion makes her breathless.)* Why, you — you're just *full* of
natural endowments! Both of my children — they're *unusual*
children! Don't you think I know it? I'm so — *proud!* Happy

and — feel I've — so much to be thankful for but — Promise me one thing, son!

Tom. What, Mother?

Amanda. Promise, son, you'll — never be a drunkard!

Tom (turns to her grinning). I will never be a drunkard, Mother.

Amanda. That's what frightened me so, that you'd be drinking! Eat a bowl of Purina!

Tom. Just coffee, Mother.

Amanda. Shredded wheat biscuit?

Tom. No. No, Mother, just coffee.

Amanda. You can't put in a day's work on an empty stomach. You've got ten minutes — don't gulp! Drinking too-hot liquids makes cancer of the stomach. . . . Put cream in.

Tom. No, thank you.

Amanda. To cool it.

Tom. No! No, thank you, I want it black.

Amanda. I know, but it's not good for you. We have to do all that we can to build ourselves up. In these trying times we live in, all that we have to cling to is — each other. . . . That's why it's so important to — Tom, I — I sent out your sister so I could discuss something with you. If you hadn't spoken I would have spoken to you. *(Sits down.)*

Tom (gently). What is it, Mother, that you want to discuss?

Amanda. Laura!

Tom puts his cup down slowly.

(Legend on Screen: "Laura.")

(Music: "The Glass Menagerie.")

Tom. — Oh. — Laura . . .

Amanda (touching his sleeve). You know how Laura is. So quiet but — still water runs deep! She notices things and I think she — broods about them. *(Tom looks up.)* A few days ago I came in and she was crying.

Tom. What about?

Amanda. You.

Tom. Me?

Amanda. She has an idea that you're not happy here.

Tom. What gave her that idea?

Amanda. What gives her any idea? However, you do act strangely. I — I'm not criticizing, understand *that!* I know your ambitions do not lie in the warehouse, that like everybody in the whole wide world — you've had to — make sacrifices, but — Tom — Tom — life's not easy, it calls for — Spartan endurance! There's so many things in my heart that I cannot describe to you! I've never told you but I — *loved* your father. . . .

Tom (*gently*). I know that, Mother.

Amanda. And you — when I see you taking after his ways! Staying out late — and — well, you *had* been drinking the night you were in that — terrifying condition! Laura says that you hate the apartment and that you go out nights to get away from it! Is that true, Tom?

Tom. No. You say there's so much in your heart that you can't describe to me. That's true of me, too. There's so much in my heart that I can't describe to *you!* So let's respect each other's —

Amanda. But, why — *why,* Tom — are you always so *restless?* Where do you go to, nights?

Tom. I — go to the movies.

Amanda. Why do you go to the movies so much, Tom?

Tom. I go to the movies because — I like adventure. Adventure is something I don't have much of at work, so I go to the movies.

Amanda. But, Tom, you go to the movies *entirely too much!*

Tom. I like a lot of adventure.

Amanda looks baffled, then hurt. As the familiar inquisition resumes he becomes hard and impatient again. Amanda slips back into her querulous attitude toward him.

(Image on Screen: Sailing Vessel with Jolly Roger.)

Amanda. Most young men find adventure in their careers.

Tom. Then most young men are not employed in a warehouse.

Amanda. The world is full of young men employed in warehouses and offices and factories.

Tom. Do all of them find adventure in their careers?

Amanda. They do or they do without it! Not everybody has a craze for adventure.

Tom. Man is by instinct a lover, a hunter, a fighter, and none of those instincts are given much play at the warehouse!

Amanda. Man is by instinct! Don't quote instinct to me! Instinct is something that people have got away from! It belongs to animals! Christian adults don't want it!

Tom. What do Christian adults want, then, Mother?

Amanda. Superior things! Things of the mind and the spirit! Only

animals have to satisfy instincts! Surely your aims are somewhat
higher than theirs! Than monkeys — pigs —

Tom. I reckon they're not.

Amanda. You're joking. However, that isn't what I wanted to
discuss.

Tom (*rising*). I haven't much time.

Amanda (*pushing his shoulders*). Sit down.

Tom. You want me to punch in red at the warehouse, Mother?

Amanda. You have five minutes. I want to talk about Laura.

(Legend: "Plans and Provisions.")

Tom. All right! What about Laura?

Amanda. We have to be making plans and provisions for her. She's
older than you, two years, and nothing has happened. She
just drifts along doing nothing. It frightens me terribly how
she just drifts along.

Tom. I guess she's the type that people call home girls.

Amanda. There's no such type, and if there is, it's a pity! That is
unless the home is hers, with a husband!

Tom. What?

Amanda. Oh, I can see the handwriting on the wall as plain as I
see the nose in front of my face! It's terrifying! More and
more you remind me of your father! He was out all hours
without explanation — Then *left! Goodbye!* And me with the
bag to hold. I saw that letter you got from the Merchant
Marine. I know what you're dreaming of. I'm not standing
here blindfolded. Very well, then. Then *do* it! But not till
there's somebody to take your place.

Tom. What do you mean?

Amanda. I mean that as soon as Laura has got somebody to take
care of her, married, a home of her own, independent —
why, then you'll be free to go wherever you please, on land,
on sea, whichever way the wind blows! But until that time
you've got to look out for your sister. I don't say me because
I'm old and don't matter! I say for your sister because she's
young and dependent. I put her in business college — a
dismal failure! Frightened her so it made her sick to her
stomach. I took her over to the Young People's League at
the church. Another fiasco. She spoke to nobody, nobody
spoke to her. Now all she does is fool with those pieces of
glass and play those worn-out records. What kind of a life
is that for a girl to lead!

Tom. What can I do about it?

Amanda. Overcome selfishness! Self, self, self is all that you ever think of! (*Tom springs up and crosses to get his coat. It is ugly and bulky. He pulls on a cap with earmuffs.*) Where is your muffler? Put your wool muffler on! (*He snatches it angrily from the closet and tosses it around his neck and pulls both ends tight.*) Tom! I haven't said what I had in mind to ask you.

Tom. I'm too late to —

Amanda (*catching his arms — very importunately. Then shyly*). Down at the warehouse, aren't there some — nice young men?

Tom. No!

Amanda. There *must* be — *some.*

Tom. Mother —

> *Gesture.*

Amanda. Find out one that's clean-living — doesn't drink and — ask him out for sister!

Tom. What?

Amanda. For *sister!* To *meet!* Get *acquainted!*

Tom (*stamping to door*). Oh, my *go-osh!*

Amanda. Will you? (*He opens door. Imploringly.*) Will you? (*He starts down.*) Will you? *Will* you, dear?

Tom (*calling back*). YES!

Amanda closes the door hesitantly and with a troubled but faintly hopeful expression.

(Screen Image: Glamor Magazine Cover.)

Spot Amanda at phone.

Amanda. Ella Cartwright? This is Amanda Wingfield! How are you, honey? How is that kidney condition? (*Count five.*) Horrors! (*Count five.*) You're a Christian martyr, yes, honey, that's what you are, a Christian martyr! Well, I just happened to notice in my little red book that your subscription to the *Companion* has just run out! I knew that you wouldn't want to miss out on the wonderful serial starting in this new issue. It's by Bessie Mae Hopper, the first thing she's written since *Honeymoon for Three.* Wasn't that a strange and interesting story? Well, this one is even lovelier, I believe. It has a sophisticated society background. It's all about the horsey set on Long Island!

(Fade Out.)

SCENE V

(Legend on Screen: "Annunciation.") Fade with music.

It is early dusk of a spring evening. Supper has just been finished in the Wingfield apartment. Amanda and Laura in light colored dresses are removing dishes from the table, in the upstage area, which is shadowy, their movements formalized almost as a dance or ritual, their moving forms as pale and silent as moths.

Tom, in white shirt and trousers, rises from the table and crosses toward the fire-escape.

Amanda (as he passes her). Son, will you do me a favor?

Tom. What?

Amanda. Comb your hair! You look so pretty when your hair is combed! (*Tom slouches on sofa with evening paper. Enormous caption "Franco Triumphs."*) There is only one respect in which I would like you to emulate your father.

Tom. What respect is that?

Amanda. The care he always took of his appearance. He never allowed himself to look untidy. (*He throws down the paper and crosses to fire-escape.*) Where are you going?

Tom. I'm going out to smoke.

Amanda. You smoke too much. A pack a day at fifteen cents a pack. How much would that amount to in a month? Thirty times fifteen is how much, Tom? Figure it out and you will be astounded at what you could save. Enough to give you a night-school course in accounting at Washington U! Just think what a wonderful thing that would be for you, son!

Tom is unmoved by the thought.

Tom. I'd rather smoke. (*He steps out on landing, letting the screen door slam.*)

Amanda (sharply). I know! That's the tragedy of it. . . . (*Alone, she turns to look at her husband's picture.*)

(Dance Music: "All the World Is Waiting for the Sunrise!")

Tom (to the audience). Across the alley from us was the Paradise Dance Hall. On evenings in spring the windows and doors were open and the music came outdoors. Sometimes the lights were turned out except for a large glass sphere that hung from the ceiling. It would turn slowly about and filter the dusk with delicate rainbow colors. Then the orchestra played a waltz or a tango, something that had a slow and sensuous rhythm. Couples would come outside, to the relative privacy of the alley. You could see them kissing behind ash-pits and telephone poles. This was the compensation for lives that passed like mine, without any change or adventure. Adventure and change were imminent in this year. They were waiting around the corner for all these kids. Suspended in the mist over Berchtesgaden, caught in the folds of Chamberlain's umbrella — In Spain there was Guernica! But here there was only hot swing music and liquor, dance halls, bars, and movies, and sex that hung in the gloom like a chandelier and flooded the world with brief, deceptive rainbows. . . . All the world was waiting for bombardments!

Amanda turns from the picture and comes outside.

Amanda (*sighing*). A fire-escape landing's a poor excuse for a porch. (*She spreads a newspaper on a step and sits down, gracefully and demurely as if she were settling into a swing on a Mississippi veranda.*) What are you looking at?

Tom. The moon.

Amanda. Is there a moon this evening?

Tom. It's rising over Garfinkel's Delicatessen.

Amanda. So it is! A little silver slipper of a moon. Have you made a wish on it yet?

Tom. Um-hum.

Amanda. What did you wish for?

Tom. That's a secret.

Amanda. A secret, huh? Well, I won't tell mine either. I will be just as mysterious as you.

Tom. I bet I can guess what yours is.

Amanda. Is my head so transparent?

Tom. You're not a sphinx.

Amanda. No, I don't have secrets. I'll tell you what I wished for on the moon. Success and happiness for my precious children! I wish for that whenever there's a moon, and when there isn't a moon, I wish for it, too.

Tom. I thought perhaps you wished for a gentleman caller.

Amanda. Why do you say that?

Tom. Don't you remember asking me to fetch one?

Amanda. I remember suggesting that it would be nice for your sister if you brought home some nice young man from the warehouse. I think I've made that suggestion more than once.

Tom. Yes, you have made it repeatedly.

Amanda. Well?

Tom. We are going to have one.

Amanda. What?

Tom. A gentleman caller!

(The Annunciation Is Celebrated with Music.)

Amanda rises.

(Image on Screen: Caller with Bouquet.)

Amanda. You mean you have asked some nice young man to come over?

Tom. Yep. I've asked him to dinner.

Amanda. You really did?

Tom. I did!

Amanda. You did, and did he — *accept?*

Tom. He did!

Amanda. Well, well — well, well! That's — lovely!

Tom. I thought that you would be pleased.

Amanda. It's definite, then?

Tom. Very definite.

Amanda. Soon?

Tom. Very soon.

Amanda. For heaven's sake, stop putting on and tell me some things, will you?

Tom. What things do you want me to tell you?

Amanda. Naturally I would like to know when he's *coming!*

Tom. He's coming tomorrow.

Amanda. Tomorrow?

Tom. Yep. Tomorrow.

Amanda. But, Tom!

Tom. Yes, Mother?

Amanda. Tomorrow gives me no time!

Tom. Time for what?

Amanda. Preparations! Why didn't you phone me at once, as soon as you asked him, the minute that he accepted? Then, don't you see, I could have been getting ready!

Tom. You don't have to make any fuss.

Amanda. Oh, Tom, Tom, Tom, of course I have to make a fuss! I want things nice, not sloppy! Not thrown together. I'll certainly have to do some fast thinking, won't I?

Tom. I don't see why you have to think at all.

Amanda. You just don't know. We can't have a gentleman caller in a pig-sty! All my wedding silver has to be polished, the monogrammed table linen ought to be laundered! The windows have to be washed and fresh curtains put up. And how about clothes? We have to *wear* something, don't we?

Tom. Mother, this boy is no one to make a fuss over!

Amanda. Do you realize he's the first young man we've introduced to your sister? It's terrible, dreadful, disgraceful that poor little sister has never received a single gentleman caller! Tom, come inside! (*She opens the screen door.*)

Tom. What for?

Amanda. I want to ask you some things.

Tom. If you're going to make such a fuss, I'll call it off, I'll tell him not to come.

Amanda. You certainly won't do anything of the kind. Nothing offends people worse than broken engagements. It simply means I'll have to work like a Turk! We won't be brilliant, but we'll pass inspection. Come on inside. (*Tom follows, groaning.*) Sit down.

Tom. Any particular place you would like me to sit?

Amanda. Thank heavens I've got that new sofa! I'm also making payments on a floor lamp I'll have sent out! And put the chintz covers on, they'll brighten things up! Of course I'd hoped to have these walls re-papered. . . . What is the young man's name?

Tom. His name is O'Connor.

Amanda. That, of course, means fish — tomorrow is Friday! I'll have that salmon loaf — with Durkee's dressing! What does he do? He works at the warehouse?

Tom. Of course! How else would I —

Amanda. Tom, he — doesn't drink?

Tom. Why do you ask me that?

Amanda. Your father *did!*

Tom. Don't get started on that!

Amanda. He *does* drink, then?

Tom. Not that I know of!

Amanda. Make sure, be certain! The last thing I want for my daughter's a boy who drinks!

Tom. Aren't you being a little premature? Mr. O'Connor has not yet appeared on the scene!

Amanda. But will tomorrow. To meet your sister, and what do I know about his character? Nothing! Old maids are better off than wives of drunkards!

Tom. Oh, my God!

Amanda. Be still!

Tom (*leaning forward to whisper*). Lots of fellows meet girls whom they don't marry!

Amanda. Oh, talk sensibly, Tom — and don't be sarcastic! (*She has gotten a hairbrush.*)

Tom. What are you doing?

Amanda. I'm brushing that cow-lick down! What is this young man's position at the warehouse?

Tom (*submitting grimly to the brush and the interrogation*). This young man's position is that of a shipping clerk, Mother.

Amanda. Sounds to me like a fairly responsible job, the sort of a job *you* would be in if you just had more *get-up.* What is his salary? Have you got any idea?

Tom. I would judge it to be approximately eighty-five dollars a month.

Amanda. Well — not princely, but —

Tom. Twenty more than I make.

Amanda. Yes, how well I know! But for a family man, eighty-five dollars a month is not much more than you can just get by on. . . .

Tom. Yes, but Mr. O'Connor is not a family man.

Amanda. He might be, mightn't he? Some time in the future?

Tom. I see. Plans and provisions.

Amanda. You are the only young man that I know of who ignores the fact that the future becomes the present, the present the past, and the past turns into everlasting regret if you don't plan for it!

Tom. I will think that over and see what I can make of it.

Amanda. Don't be supercilious with your mother! Tell me some more about this — what do you call him?

Tom. James D. O'Connor. The D. is for Delaney.

Amanda. Irish on *both* sides! *Gracious!* And doesn't drink?

Tom. Shall I call him up and ask him right this minute?

Amanda. The only way to find out about those things is to make discreet inquiries at the proper moment. When I was a girl in Blue Mountain and it was suspected that a young man drank, the girl whose attentions he had been receiving, if any girl *was,* would sometimes speak to the minister of his church, or rather her father would if her father was living, and sort of feel him out on the young man's character. That is the way such things are discreetly handled to keep a young woman from making a tragic mistake!

Tom. Then how did you happen to make a tragic mistake?

Amanda. That innocent look of your father's had everyone fooled! He *smiled* — the world was *enchanted!* No girl can do worse

than put herself at the mercy of a handsome appearance! I
hope that Mr. O'Connor is not too good-looking.

Tom. No, he's not too good-looking. He's covered with freckles
and hasn't too much of a nose.

Amanda. He's not right-down homely, though?

Tom. Not right-down homely. Just medium homely, I'd say.

Amanda. Character's what to look for in a man.

Tom. That's what I've always said, Mother.

Amanda. You've never said anything of the kind and I suspect you
would never give it a thought.

Tom. Don't be suspicious of me.

Amanda. At least I hope he's the type that's up and coming.

Tom. I think he really goes in for self-improvement.

Amanda. What reason have you to think so?

Tom. He goes to night school.

Amanda (beaming). Splendid! What does he do, I mean study?

Tom. Radio engineering and public speaking!

Amanda. Then he has visions of being advanced in the world! Any
young man who studies public speaking is aiming to have
an executive job some day! And radio engineering? A thing
for the future! Both of these facts are very illuminating.
Those are the sort of things that a mother should know
concerning any young man who comes to call on her daughter.
Seriously or — not.

Tom. One little warning. He doesn't know about Laura. I didn't
let on that we had dark ulterior motives. I just said, why
don't you come have dinner with us? He said okay and that
was the whole conversation.

Amanda. I bet it was! You're eloquent as an oyster. However, he'll
know about Laura when he gets here. When he sees how
lovely and sweet and pretty she is, he'll thank his lucky stars
he was asked to dinner.

Tom. Mother, you mustn't expect too much of Laura.

Amanda. What do you mean?

Tom. Laura seems all those things to you and me because she's
ours and we love her. We don't even notice she's crippled
any more.

Amanda. Don't say crippled! You know that I never allow that
word to be used!

Tom. But face facts, Mother. She is and — that's not all —

Amanda. What do you mean "not all"?

Tom. Laura is very different from other girls.

Amanda. I think the difference is all to her advantage.

Tom. Not quite all — in the eyes of others — strangers — she's

terribly shy and lives in a world of her own and those things make her seem a little peculiar to people outside the house.
Amanda. Don't say peculiar.
Tom. Face the facts. She is.

(The Dance-Hall Music Changes to a Tango that Has a Minor and Somewhat Ominous Tone.)

Amanda. In what way is she peculiar — may I ask?
Tom (gently). She lives in a world of her own — a world of — little glass ornaments, Mother. . . . *(Gets up. Amanda remains holding brush, looking at him, troubled.)* She plays old phonograph records and — that's about all — *(He glances at himself in the mirror and crosses to door.)*
Amanda (sharply). Where are you going?
Tom. I'm going to the movies. *(Out screen door.)*
Amanda. Not to the movies, every night to the movies! *(Follows quickly to screen door.)* I don't believe you always go to the movies! *(He is gone. Amanda looks worriedly after him for a moment. Then vitality and optimism return and she turns from the door. Crossing to portieres.)* Laura! Laura! *(Laura answers from kitchenette.)*
Laura. Yes, Mother.
Amanda. Let those dishes go and come in front! *(Laura appears with dish towel. Gaily.)* Laura, come here and make a wish on the moon!
Laura (entering). Moon — moon?
Amanda. A little silver slipper of a moon. Look over your left shoulder, Laura, and make a wish! *(Laura looks faintly puzzled as if called out of sleep. Amanda seizes her shoulders and turns her at angle by the door.)* Now! Now, darling, *wish!*
Laura. What shall I wish for, Mother?
Amanda (her voice trembling and her eyes suddenly filling with tears). Happiness! Good Fortune!

The violin rises and the stage dims out.

SCENE VI

(Image: High School Hero.)

Tom. And so the following evening I brought Jim home to dinner. I had known Jim slightly in high school. In high school Jim was a hero. He had tremendous Irish good nature and vitality with the scrubbed and polished look of white chinaware. He seemed to move in a continual spotlight. He was a star in basketball, captain of the debating club, president of the senior class and the glee club and he sang the male lead in the annual light operas. He was always running or bounding, never just walking. He seemed always at the point of defeating the law of gravity. He was shooting with such velocity through his adolescence that you would logically expect him to arrive at nothing short of the White House by the time he was thirty. But Jim apparently ran into more interference after his graduation from Soldan. His speed had definitely slowed. Six years after he left high school he was holding a job that wasn't much better than mine.

(Image: Clerk.)

He was the only one at the warehouse with whom I was on friendly terms. I was valuable to him as someone who could remember his former glory, who had seen him win basketball games and the silver cup in debating. He knew of my secret practice of retiring to a cabinet of the washroom to work on poems when business was slack in the warehouse. He called me Shakespeare. And while the other boys in the warehouse regarded me with suspicious hostility, Jim took a humorous attitude toward me. Gradually his attitude affected the others, their hostility wore off and they also began to smile at me as people smile at an oddly fashioned dog who trots across their path at some distance.

I knew that Jim and Laura had known each other at Soldan, and I had heard Laura speak admiringly of his voice. I didn't know if Jim remembered her or not. In high school Laura had been as unobtrusive as Jim had been astonishing. If he did remember Laura, it was not as my sister, for when I asked him to dinner, he grinned and said, "You know, Shakespeare, I never thought of you as having folks!"

He was about to discover that I did. . . .

(Light up Stage.)

(Legend on Screen: "The Accent of a Coming Foot.")

Friday evening. It is about five o'clock of a late spring evening which comes "scattering poems in the sky."

A delicate lemony light is in the Wingfield apartment.

Amanda has worked like a Turk in preparation for the gentleman caller. The results are astonishing. The new floor lamp with its rose-silk shade is in place, a colored paper lantern conceals the broken light fixture in the ceiling, new billowing white curtains are at the windows, chintz covers are on chairs and sofa, a pair of new sofa pillows make their initial appearance.

Open boxes and tissue paper are scattered on the floor.

Laura stands in the middle with lifted arms while Amanda crouches before her, adjusting the hem of the new dress, devout and ritualistic. The dress is colored and designed by memory. The arrangement of Laura's hair is changed; it is softer and more becoming. A fragile, unearthly prettiness has come out in Laura: she is like a piece of translucent glass touched by light, given a momentary radiance, not actual, not lasting.

Amanda (*impatiently*). Why are you trembling?
Laura. Mother, you've made me so nervous!
Amanda. How have I made you nervous?
Laura. By all this fuss! You make it seem so important!
Amanda. I don't understand you, Laura. You couldn't be satisfied with just sitting home, and yet whenever I try to arrange something for you, you seem to resist it. (*She gets up.*) Now take a look at yourself. No, wait! Wait just a moment — I have an idea!
Laura. What is it now?

Amanda produces two powder puffs which she wraps in handkerchiefs and stuffs in Laura's bosom.

Laura. Mother, what are you doing?
Amanda. They call them "Gay Deceivers"!
Laura. I won't wear them!
Amanda. You will!
Laura. Why should I?
Amanda. Because, to be painfully honest, your chest is flat.
Laura. You make it seem like we were setting a trap.
Amanda. All pretty girls are a trap, a pretty trap, and men expect them to be. *(Legend: "A Pretty Trap.")* Now look at yourself, young lady. This is the prettiest you will ever be! I've got to fix myself now! You're going to be surprised by your mother's appearance! (*She crosses through portieres, humming gaily.*)

Laura moves slowly to the long mirror and stares solemnly at herself.

A wind blows the white curtains inward in a slow, graceful motion and with a faint, sorrowful sighing.

Amanda (*off stage*). It isn't dark enough yet. (*She turns slowly before the mirror with a troubled look.*)

(*Legend on Screen: "This Is My Sister: Celebrate Her with Strings!" Music.*)

Amanda (*laughing, off*). I'm going to show you something. I'm going to make a spectacular appearance!

Laura. What is it, Mother?

Amanda. Possess your soul in patience — you will see! Something I've resurrected from that old trunk! Styles haven't changed so terribly much after all. . . . (*She parts the portieres.*) Now just look at your mother! (*She wears a girlish frock of yellowed voile with a blue silk sash. She carries a bunch of jonquils — the legend of her youth is nearly revived. Feverishly.*) This is the dress in which I led the cotillion. Won the cakewalk twice at Sunset Hill, wore one spring to the Governor's ball in Jackson! See how I sashayed around the ballroom, Laura? (*She raises her skirt and does a mincing step around the room.*) I wore it on Sundays for my gentlemen callers! I had it on the day I met your father — I had malaria fever all that spring. The change of climate from East Tennessee to the Delta — weakened resistance — I had a little temperature all the time — not enough to be serious — just enough to make me restless and giddy! Invitations poured in — parties all over the Delta! — "Stay in bed," said Mother, "you have fever!" — but I just wouldn't. — I took quinine but kept on going, going! — Evenings, dances! — Afternoons, long, long rides! Picnics — lovely! — So lovely, that country in May. — All lacy with dogwood, literally flooded with jonquils! — That was the spring I had the craze for jonquils. Jonquils became an absolute obsession. Mother said, "Honey, there's no more room for jonquils." And still I kept bringing in more jonquils. Whenever, wherever I saw them, I'd say, "Stop! Stop! I see jonquils!" I made the young men help me gather the jonquils! It was a joke, Amanda and her jonquils! Finally there were no more vases to hold them, every available space was filled with jonquils. No vases to hold them? All right, I'll hold them myself! And then I — (*She stops in front of the picture.*) (*Music.*) met your father! Malaria fever and jonquils and then — this — boy. . . . (*She switches on the rose-colored lamp.*) I hope they get here before it starts to rain. (*She crosses upstage and places the jonquils in bowl on table.*) I gave your brother a little extra change so he and Mr. O'Connor could take the service car home.

Laura (*with altered look*). What did you say his name was?

Amanda. O'Connor.

Laura. What is his first name?

Amanda. I don't remember. Oh, yes, I do. It was — Jim!

Laura sways slightly and catches hold of a chair.

(*Legend on Screen: "Not Jim!"*)

Laura (*faintly*). Not — Jim!

Amanda. Yes, that was it, it was Jim! I've never known a Jim that wasn't nice!

(*Music: Ominous.*)

Laura. Are you sure his name is Jim O'Connor?

Amanda. Yes. Why?

Laura. Is he the one that Tom used to know in high school?

Amanda. He didn't say so. I think he just got to know him at the warehouse.

Laura. There was a Jim O'Connor we both knew in high school — (*Then, with effort.*) If that is the one that Tom is bringing to dinner — you'll have to excuse me, I won't come to the table.

Amanda. What sort of nonsense is this?

Laura. You asked me once if I'd ever liked a boy. Don't you remember I showed you this boy's picture?

Amanda. You mean the boy you showed me in the year book?

Laura. Yes, that boy.

Amanda. Laura, Laura, were you in love with that boy?

Laura. I don't know, Mother. All I know is I couldn't sit at the table if it was him!

Amanda. It won't be him! It isn't the least bit likely. But whether it is or not, you will come to the table. You will not be excused.

Laura. I'll have to be, Mother.

Amanda. I don't intend to humor your silliness, Laura. I've had too much from you and your brother, both! So just sit down and compose yourself till they come. Tom has forgotten his key so you'll have to let them in, when they arrive.

Laura (panicky). Oh, Mother — *you* answer the door!
Amanda (lightly). I'll be in the kitchen — busy!
Laura. Oh, Mother, please answer the door, don't make me do
    it!
Amanda (crossing into kitchenette). I've got to fix the dressing for
    the salmon. Fuss, fuss — silliness! — over a gentleman caller!

> *Door swings shut. Laura is left alone.*

(Legend: "Terror!")

> *She utters a low moan and turns off the lamp — sits stiffly on the
> edge of the sofa, knotting her fingers together.*

(Legend on Screen: "The Opening of a Door!")

> *Tom and Jim appear on the fire-escape steps and climb to landing.
> Hearing their approach, Laura rises with a panicky gesture. She
> retreats to the portieres.*
>
> *The doorbell. Laura catches her breath and touches her throat. Low
> drums.*

Amanda (calling). Laura, sweetheart! The door!

> *Laura stares at it without moving.*

Jim. I think we just beat the rain.
Tom. Uh-huh. *(He rings again, nervously. Jim whistles and fishes for
    a cigarette.)*
Amanda (very, very gaily). Laura, that is your brother and Mr.
    O'Connor! Will you let them in, darling?

> *Laura crosses toward kitchenette door.*

Laura (breathlessly). Mother — you go to the door!

> *Amanda steps out of kitchenette and stares furiously at Laura. She
> points imperiously at the door.*

Laura. Please, please!
Amanda (in a fierce whisper). What is the matter with you, you silly
    thing?
Laura (desperately). Please, you answer it, *please!*
Amanda. I told you I wasn't going to humor you, Laura. Why
    have you chosen this moment to lose your mind?
Laura. Please, please, please, you go!
Amanda. You'll have to go to the door because I can't!

Laura (despairingly). I can't either!
Amanda. Why?
Laura. I'm *sick!*
Amanda. I'm sick, too — of your nonsense! Why can't you and
your brother be normal people? Fantastic whims and behavior!
(*Tom gives a long ring.*) Preposterous goings on! Can you
give me one reason — (*Calls out lyrically.*) COMING! JUST ONE
SECOND! — why should you be afraid to open a door? Now
you answer it, Laura!
Laura. Oh, oh, oh . . . (*She returns through the portieres. Darts to
the victrola and winds it frantically and turns it on.*)
Amanda. Laura Wingfield, you march right to that door!
Laura. Yes — yes, Mother!

> *A faraway, scratchy rendition of "Dardanella" softens the air and
> gives her strength to move through it. She slips to the door and
> draws it cautiously open.*

> *Tom enters with the caller, Jim O'Connor.*

Tom. Laura, this is Jim. Jim, this is my sister, Laura.
Jim (stepping inside). I didn't know that Shakespeare had a sister!
Laura (retreating stiff and trembling from the door). How — how do
you do?
Jim (heartily extending his hand). Okay!

> *Laura touches it hesitantly with hers.*

Jim. Your hand's *cold*, Laura!
Laura. Yes, well — I've been playing the victrola. . . .
Jim. Must have been playing classical music on it! You ought to
play a little hot swing music to warm you up!
Laura. Excuse me — I haven't finished playing the victrola. . . .

> *She turns awkwardly and hurries into the front room. She pauses
> a second by the victrola. Then catches her breath and darts through
> the portieres like a frightened deer.*

Jim (grinning). What was the matter?
Tom. Oh — with Laura? Laura is — terribly shy.
Jim. Shy, huh? It's unusual to meet a shy girl nowadays. I don't
believe you ever mentioned you had a sister.
Tom. Well, now you know. I have one. Here is the *Post Dispatch.*
You want a piece of it?
Jim. Uh-huh.
Tom. What piece? The comics?
Jim. Sports! (*Glances at it.*) Ole Dizzy Dean is on his bad behavior.

Tom (disinterest). Yeah? (*Lights cigarette and crosses back to fire-escape door.*)

Jim. Where are *you* going?

Tom. I'm going out on the terrace.

Jim (goes after him). You know, Shakespeare — I'm going to sell you a bill of goods!

Tom. What goods?

Jim. A course I'm taking.

Tom. Huh?

Jim. In public speaking! You and me, we're not the warehouse type.

Tom. Thanks — that's good news. But what has public speaking got to do with it?

Jim. It fits you for — executive positions!

Tom. Awww.

Jim. I tell you it's done a helluva lot for me.

(Image: Executive at Desk.)

Tom. In what respect?

Jim. In every! Ask yourself what is the difference between you an' me and men in the office down front? Brains? — No! — Ability? — No! Then what? Just one little thing —

Tom. What is that one little thing?

Jim. Primarily it amounts to — social poise! Being able to square up to people and hold your own on any social level!

Amanda (off stage). Tom?

Tom. Yes, Mother?

Amanda. Is that you and Mr. O'Connor?

Tom. Yes, Mother.

Amanda. Well, you just make yourselves comfortable in there.

Tom. Yes, Mother.

Amanda. Ask Mr. O'Connor if he would like to wash his hands.

Jim. Aw — no — no — thank you — I took care of that at the warehouse. Tom —

Tom. Yes?

Jim. Mr. Mendoza was speaking to me about you.

Tom. Favorably?

Jim. What do you think?

Tom. Well —

Jim. You're going to be out of a job if you don't wake up.

Tom. I am waking up —

Jim. You show no signs.

Tom. The signs are interior.

(Image on Screen: The Sailing Vessel with Jolly Roger Again.)

Tom. I'm planning to change. (*He leans over the rail speaking with quiet exhilaration. The incandescent marquees and signs of the first-run movie houses light his face from across the alley. He looks like a voyager.*) I'm right at the point of committing myself to a future that doesn't include the warehouse and Mr. Mendoza or even a night-school course in public speaking.

Jim. What are you gassing about?

Tom. I'm tired of the movies.

Jim. Movies!

Tom. Yes, movies! Look at them — (*A wave toward the marvels of Grand Avenue.*) All of those glamorous people — having adventures — hogging it all, gobbling the whole thing up! You know what happens? People go to the *movies* instead of *moving!* Hollywood characters are supposed to have all the adventures for everybody in America, while everybody in America sits in a dark room and watches them have them! Yes, until there's a war. That's when adventure becomes available to the masses! *Everyone's* dish, not only Gable's! Then the people in the dark room come out of the dark room to have some adventures themselves — Goody, goody — It's our turn now, to go to the South Sea Island — to make a safari — to be exotic, far-off — But I'm not patient. I don't want to wait till then. I'm tired of the *movies* and I am *about* to *move!*

Jim (*incredulously*). Move?

Tom. Yes.

Jim. When?

Tom. Soon!

Jim. Where? Where?

(Theme Three: Music Seems to Answer the Question, while Tom Thinks it Over. He Searches among his Pockets.)

Tom. I'm starting to boil inside. I know I seem dreamy, but inside — well, I'm boiling! Whenever I pick up a shoe, I shudder a little thinking how short life is and what I am doing! — Whatever that means. I know it doesn't mean shoes — except as something to wear on a traveler's feet! (*Finds paper.*) Look —

Jim. What?

Tom. I'm a member.

Jim (*reading*). The Union of Merchant Seamen.

Tom. I paid my dues this month, instead of the light bill.

Jim. You will regret it when they turn the lights off.

Tom. I won't be here.

Jim. How about your mother?

Tom. I'm like my father. The bastard son of a bastard! See how
he grins? And he's been absent going on sixteen years!

Jim. You're just talking, you drip. How does your mother feel
about it?

Tom. Shhh — Here comes Mother! Mother is not acquainted with
my plans!

Amanda (*enters portieres*). Where are you all?

Tom. On the terrace, Mother.

> *They start inside. She advances to them. Tom is distinctly shocked
> at her appearance. Even Jim blinks a little. He is making his first
> contact with girlish Southern vivacity and in spite of the night-
> school course in public speaking is somewhat thrown off the beam
> by the unexpected outlay of social charm.*
>
> *Certain responses are attempted by Jim but are swept aside by
> Amanda's gay laughter and chatter. Tom is embarrassed but after
> the first shock Jim reacts very warmly. Grins and chuckles, is
> altogether won over.*

(Image: Amanda as a Girl.)

Amanda (*coyly smiling, shaking her girlish ringlets*). Well, well, well,
so this is Mr. O'Connor. Introductions entirely unnecessary.
I've heard so much about you from my boy. I finally said
to him, Tom — good gracious! — why don't you bring this
paragon to supper? I'd like to meet this nice young man at
the warehouse! — Instead of just hearing him sing your
praises so much! I don't know why my son is so standoffish — that's not Southern behavior! Let's sit down and
— I think we could stand a little more air in here! Tom,
leave the door open. I felt a nice fresh breeze a moment ago.
Where has it gone? Mmm, so warm already! And not quite
summer, even. We're going to burn up when summer really
gets started. However, we're having — we're having a very
light supper. I think light things are better fo' this time of
year. The same as light clothes are. Light clothes an' light
food are what warm weather calls fo'. You know our blood
gets so thick during th' winter — it takes a while fo' us to
adjust ou'selves! — when the season changes . . . It's come
so quick this year. I wasn't prepared. All of a sudden —

heavens! Already summer! — I ran to the trunk an' pulled out this light dress — Terribly old! Historical almost! But feels so good — so good an' co-ol, y'know. . . .

Tom. Mother —

Amanda. Yes, honey?

Tom. How about — supper?

Amanda. Honey, you go ask Sister if supper is ready! You know that Sister is in full charge of supper! Tell her you hungry boys are waiting for it. (*To Jim.*) Have you met Laura?

Jim. She —

Amanda. Let you in? Oh, good, you've met already! It's rare for a girl as sweet an' pretty as Laura to be domestic! But Laura is, thank heavens, not only pretty but also very domestic. I'm not at all. I never was a bit. I never could make a thing but angel-food cake. Well, in the South we had so many servants. Gone, gone, gone. All vestiges of gracious living! Gone completely! I wasn't prepared for what the future brought me. All of my gentlemen callers were sons of planters and so of course I assumed that I would be married to one and raise my family on a large piece of land with plenty of servants. But man proposes — and woman accepts the proposal! — To vary that old, old saying a little bit — I married no planter! I married a man who worked for the telephone company! — that gallantly smiling gentleman over there! (*Points to the picture.*) A telephone man who — fell in love with long distance! — Now he travels and I don't even know where! — But what am I going on for about my — tribulations! Tell me yours — I hope you don't have any! Tom?

Tom (*returning*). Yes, Mother?

Amanda. Is supper nearly ready?

Tom. It looks to me like supper is on the table.

Amanda. Let me look — (*She rises prettily and looks through portieres.*) Oh, lovely — But where is Sister?

Tom. Laura is not feeling well and she says that she thinks she'd better not come to the table.

Amanda. What? — Nonsense! — Laura? Oh, Laura!

Laura (*off stage, faintly*). Yes, Mother.

Amanda. You really must come to the table. We won't be seated until you come to the table! Come in, Mr. O'Connor. You sit over there and I'll — Laura? Laura Wingfield! You're keeping us waiting, honey! We can't say grace until you come to the table!

The back door is pushed weakly open and Laura comes in. She

*is obviously quite faint, her lips trembling, her eyes wide and
staring. She moves unsteadily toward the table.*

(Legend: "Terror!")

*Outside a summer storm is coming abruptly. The white curtains
billow inward at the windows and there is a sorowful murmur and
deep blue dusk.*

*Laura suddenly stumbles — She catches at a chair with a faint
moan.*

Tom. Laura!

Amanda. Laura! (*There is a clap of thunder.*) (*Legend: "Ah!"*) (*Despairingly.*) Why, Laura, you *are* sick, darling! Tom, help
your sister into the living room, dear! Sit in the living room,
Laura — rest on the sofa. Well! (*To the gentleman caller.*)
Standing over the hot stove made her ill! — I told her that
it was just too warm this evening, but — (*Tom comes back
in. Laura is on the sofa.*) Is Laura all right now?

Tom. Yes.

Amanda. What *is* that? Rain? A nice cool rain has come up! (*She
gives the gentleman caller a frightened look.*) I think we may —
have grace — now . . . (*Tom looks at her stupidly.*) Tom,
honey — you say grace!

Tom. Oh . . . "For these and all thy mercies — " (*They bow their
heads, Amanda stealing a nervous glance at Jim. In the living
room Laura, stretched on the sofa, clenches her hand to her lips,
to hold back a shuddering sob.*) God's Holy Name be praised —

(The Scene Dims Out.)

SCENE VII

A Souvenir

*Half an hour later. Dinner is just being finished in the upstage
area which is concealed by the drawn portieres.*

*As the curtain rises Laura is still huddled upon the sofa, her feet
drawn under her, her head resting on a pale blue pillow, her eyes
wide and mysteriously watchful. The new floor lamp with its shade
of rose-colored silk gives a soft, becoming light to her face, bringing
out the fragile, unearthly prettiness which usually escapes attention.
There is a steady murmur of rain, but it is slackening and stops*

soon after the scene begins; the air outside becomes pale and luminous as the moon breaks out.

A moment after the curtain rises, the lights in both rooms flicker and go out.

Jim. Hey, there, Mr. Light Bulb!

Amanda laughs nervously.

(Legend: "Suspension of a Public Service.")

Amanda. Where was Moses when the lights went out? Ha-ha. Do you know the answer to that one, Mr. O'Connor?

Jim. No, Ma'am, what's the answer?

Amanda. In the dark! *(Jim laughs appreciatively.)* Everybody sit still. I'll light the candles. Isn't it lucky we have them on the table? Where's a match? Which of you gentlemen can provide a match?

Jim. Here.

Amanda. Thank you, sir.

Jim. Not at all, Ma'am!

Amanda. I guess the fuse has burnt out. Mr. O'Connor, can you tell a burnt-out fuse? I know I can't and Tom is a total loss when it comes to mechanics. *(Sound: Getting Up: Voices Recede a Little to Kitchenette.)* Oh, be careful you don't bump into something. We don't want our gentleman caller to break his neck. Now wouldn't that be a fine howdy-do?

Jim. Ha-ha! Where is the fuse-box?

Amanda. Right here next to the stove. Can you see anything?

Jim. Just a minute.

Amanda. Isn't electricity a mysterious thing? Wasn't it Benjamin Franklin who tied a key to a kite? We live in such a mysterious universe, don't we? Some people say that science clears up all the mysteries for us. In my opinion it only creates more! Have you found it yet?

Jim. No, Ma'am. All these fuses look okay to me.

Amanda. Tom!

Tom. Yes, Mother?

Amanda. That light bill I gave you several days ago. The one I told you we got the notices about?

Tom. Oh. — Yeah.

(Legend: "Ha!")

Amanda. You didn't neglect to pay it by any chance?

Tom. Why, I —

Amanda. Didn't! I might have known it!

Jim. Shakespeare probably wrote a poem on that light bill, Mrs. Wingfield.

Amanda. I might have known better than to trust him with it! There's such a high price for negligence in this world!

Jim. Maybe the poem will win a ten-dollar prize.

Amanda. We'll just have to spend the remainder of the evening in the nineteenth century, before Mr. Edison made the Mazda lamp!

Jim. Candlelight is my favorite kind of light.

Amanda. That shows you're romantic! But that's no excuse for Tom. Well, we got through dinner. Very considerate of them to let us get through dinner before they plunged us into everlasting darkness, wasn't it, Mr. O'Connor?

Jim. Ha-ha!

Amanda. Tom, as a penalty for your carelessness you can help me with the dishes.

Jim. Let me give you a hand.

Amanda. Indeed you will not!

Jim. I ought to be good for something.

Amanda. Good for something? (*Her tone is rhapsodic.*) *You?* Why, Mr. O'Connor, nobody, *nobody's* given me this much entertainment in years — as you have!

Jim. Aw, now, Mrs. Wingfield!

Amanda. I'm not exaggerating, not one bit! But Sister is all by her lonesome. You go keep her company in the parlor! I'll give you this lovely old candelabrum that used to be on the altar at the church of the Heavenly Rest. It was melted a little out of shape when the church burnt down. Lightning struck it one spring. Gypsy Jones was holding a revival at the time and he intimated that the church was destroyed because the Episcopalians gave card parties.

Jim. Ha-ha.

Amanda. And how about coaxing Sister to drink a little wine? I think it would be good for her! Can you carry both at once?

Jim. Sure. I'm Superman!

Amanda. Now, Thomas, get into this apron!

The door of kitchenette swings closed on Amanda's gay laughter; the flickering light approaches the portieres.

Laura sits up nervously as he enters. Her speech at first is low and breathless from the almost intolerable strain of being alone with a stranger.

(Legend: "I Don't Suppose You Remember Me at All!")

*In her first speeches in this scene, before Jim's warmth overcomes
her paralyzing shyness, Laura's voice is thin and breathless as
though she has run up a steep flight of stairs.*

*Jim's attitude is gently humorous. In playing this scene it should
be stressed that while the incident is apparently unimportant, it is
to Laura the climax of her secret life.*

Jim. Hello, there, Laura.
Laura (faintly). Hello. *(She clears her throat.)*
Jim. How are you feeling now? Better?
Laura. Yes. Yes, thank you.
Jim. This is for you. A little dandelion wine. *(He extends it toward
her with extravagant gallantry.)*
Laura. Thank you.
Jim. Drink it — but don't get drunk! *(He laughs heartily. Laura
takes the glass uncertainly; laughs shyly.)* Where shall I set the
candles?
Laura. Oh — oh, anywhere . . .
Jim. How about here on the floor? Any objections?
Laura. No.
Jim. I'll spread a newspaper under to catch the drippings. I like
to sit on the floor. Mind if I do?
Laura. Oh, no.
Jim. Give me a pillow?
Laura. What?
Jim. A pillow!
Laura. Oh . . . *(Hands him one quickly.)*
Jim. How about you? Don't you like to sit on the floor?
Laura. Oh — yes.
Jim. Why don't you, then?
Laura. I — will.
Jim. Take a pillow! *(Laura does. Sits on the other side of the candelabrum.
Jim crosses his legs and smiles engagingly at her.)* I can't hardly
see you sitting way over there.
Laura. I can — see you.
Jim. I know, but that's not fair, I'm in the limelight. *(Laura moves
her pillow closer.)* Good! Now I can see you! Comfortable?
Laura. Yes.
Jim. So am I. Comfortable as a cow. Will you have some gum?
Laura. No, thank you.
Jim. I think that I will indulge, with your permission. *(Musingly
unwraps it and holds it up.)* Think of the fortune made by the

guy that invented the first piece of chewing gum. Amazing, huh? The Wrigley Building is one of the sights of Chicago. — I saw it summer before last when I went up to the Century of Progress. Did you take in the Century of Progress?

Laura. No, I didn't.

Jim. Well, it was quite a wonderful exposition. What impressed me most was the Hall of Science. Gives you an idea of what the future will be in America, even more wonderful than the present time is! (*Pause. Smiling at her.*) Your brother tells me you're shy. Is that right, Laura?

Laura. I — don't know.

Jim. I judge you to be an old-fashioned type of girl. Well, I think that's a pretty good type to be. Hope you don't think I'm being too personal — do you?

Laura (*hastily, out of embarrassment*). I believe I *will* take a piece of gum, if you — don't mind. (*Clearing her throat.*) Mr. O'-Connor, have you — kept up with your singing?

Jim. Singing? Me?

Laura. Yes. I remember what a beautiful voice you had.

Jim. When did you hear me sing?

(*Voice Offstage in the Pause.*)

Voice (*offstage*).
　　O blow, ye winds, heigh-ho,
　　A-roving I will go!
　　I'm off to my love
　　With a boxing glove —
　　Ten thousand miles away!

Jim. You say you've heard me sing?

Laura. Oh, yes! Yes, very often . . . I — don't suppose you remember me — at all?

Jim (*smiling doubtfully*). You know I have an idea I've seen you before. I had that idea soon as you opened the door. It seemed almost like I was about to remember your name. But the name that I started to call you — wasn't a name! And so I stopped myself before I said it.

Laura. Wasn't it — Blue Roses?

Jim (*springs up, grinning*). Blue Roses! My gosh, yes — Blue Roses! That's what I had on my tongue when you opened the door! Isn't it funny what tricks your memory plays? I didn't connect you with the high school somehow or other. But that's where it was; it was high school. I didn't even know you were Shakespeare's sister! Gosh, I'm sorry.

Laura. I didn't expect you to. You — barely knew me!

Jim. But we did have a speaking acquaintance, huh?

Laura. Yes, we — spoke to each other.

Jim. When did you recognize me?

Laura. Oh, right away!

Jim. Soon as I came in the door?

Laura. When I heard your name I thought it was probably you. I knew that Tom used to know you a little in high school. So when you came in the door — Well, then I was — sure.

Jim. Why didn't you *say* something, then?

Laura (breathlessly). I didn't know what to say, I was — too surprised!

Jim. For goodness' sakes! You know, this sure is funny!

Laura. Yes! Yes, isn't it, though. . .

Jim. Didn't we have a class in something together?

Laura. Yes, we did.

Jim. What class was that?

Laura. It was — singing — Chorus!

Jim. Aw!

Laura. I sat across the aisle from you in the Aud.

Jim. Aw.

Laura. Mondays, Wednesdays and Fridays.

Jim. Now I remember — you always came in late.

Laura. Yes, it was so hard for me, getting upstairs. I had that brace on my leg — it clumped so loud!

Jim. I never heard any clumping.

Laura (wincing at the recollection). To me it sounded like — thunder!

Jim. Well, well, well. I never even noticed.

Laura. And everybody was seated before I came in. I had to walk in front of all those people. My seat was in the back row. I had to go clumping all the way up the aisle with everyone watching!

Jim. You shouldn't have been self-conscious.

Laura. I know, but I was. It was always such a relief when the singing started.

Jim. Aw, yes, I've placed you now! I used to call you Blue Roses. How was it that I got started calling you that?

Laura. I was out of school a little while with pleurosis. When I came back you asked me what was the matter. I said I had pleurosis — you thought I said Blue Roses. That's what you always called me after that!

Jim. I hope you didn't mind.

Laura. Oh, no — I liked it. You see, I wasn't acquainted with many — people. . . .

Jim. As I remember you sort of stuck by yourself.

Laura. I — I — never had much luck at — making friends.

Jim. I don't see why you wouldn't.

Laura. Well, I — started out badly.

Jim. You mean being —

Laura. Yes, it sort of — stood between me —

Jim. You shouldn't have let it!

Laura. I know, but it did, and —

Jim. You were shy with people!

Laura. I tried not to be but never could —

Jim. Overcome it?

Laura. No, I — I never could!

Jim. I guess being shy is something you have to work out of kind of gradually.

Laura (sorrowfully). Yes — I guess it —

Jim. Takes time!

Laura. Yes —

Jim. People are not so dreadful when you know them. That's what you have to remember! And everybody has problems, not just you, but practically everybody has got some problems. You think of yourself as having the only problems, as being the only one who is disappointed. But just look around you and you will see lots of people as disappointed as you are. For instance, I hoped when I was going to high school that I would be further along at this time, six years later, than I am now — You remember that wonderful write-up I had in *The Torch?*

Laura. Yes! (*She rises and crosses to table.*)

Jim. It said I was bound to succeed in anything I went into! (*Laura returns with the annual.*) Holy Jeez! *The Torch!* (*He accepts it reverently. They smile across it with mutual wonder. Laura crouches beside him and they begin to turn through it. Laura's shyness is dissolving in his warmth.*)

Laura. Here you are in *Pirates of Penzance!*

Jim (wistfully). I sang the baritone lead in that operetta.

Laura (rapidly). So — *beautifully!*

Jim (protesting). Aw —

Laura. Yes, yes — beautifully — beautifully!

Jim. You heard me?

Laura. All three times!

Jim. No!

Laura. Yes!

Jim. All three performances?

Laura (looking down). Yes.

Jim. Why?

Laura. I — wanted to ask you to — autograph my program.

Jim. Why didn't you ask me to?

Laura. You were always surrounded by your own friends so much that I never had a chance to.

Jim. You should have just —

Laura. Well, I — thought you might think I was —

Jim. Thought I might think you was — what?

Laura. Oh —

Jim (*with reflective relish*). I was beleaguered by females in those days.

Laura. You were terribly popular!

Jim. Yeah —

Laura. You had such a — friendly way —

Jim. I was spoiled in high school.

Laura. Everybody — liked you!

Jim. Including you?

Laura. I — yes, I — I did, too — (*She gently closes the book in her lap.*)

Jim. Well, well, well! — Give me that program, Laura. (*She hands it to him. He signs it with a flourish.*) There you are — better late than never!

Laura. Oh, I — what a — surprise!

Jim. My signature isn't worth very much right now. But some day — maybe — it will increase in value! Being disappointed is one thing and being discouraged is something else. I am disappointed but I'm not discouraged. I'm twenty-three years old. How old are you?

Laura. I'll be twenty-four in June.

Jim. That's not old age!

Laura. No, but —

Jim. You finished high school?

Laura (*with difficulty*). I didn't go back.

Jim. You mean you dropped out?

Laura. I made bad grades in my final examinations. (*She rises and replaces the book and the program. Her voice strained.*) How is — Emily Meisenbach getting along?

Jim. Oh, that kraut-head!

Laura. Why do you call her that?

Jim. That's what she was.

Laura. You're not still — going with her?

Jim. I never see her.

Laura. It said in the Personal Section that you were — engaged!

Jim. I know, but I wasn't impressed by that — propaganda!

Laura. It wasn't — the truth?

Jim. Only in Emily's optimistic opinion!
Laura. Oh —

(Legend: "What Have You Done since High School?")

> *Jim lights a cigarette and leans indolently back on his elbows smiling at Laura with a warmth and charm which light her inwardly with altar candles. She remains by the table and turns in her hands a piece of glass to cover her tumult.*

Jim (after several reflective puffs on a cigarette). What have you done since high school? (*She seems not to hear him.*) Huh? (*Laura looks up.*) I said what have you done since high school, Laura?
Laura. Nothing much.
Jim. You must have been doing something these six long years.
Laura. Yes.
Jim. Well, then, such as what?
Laura. I took a business course at business college —
Jim. How did that work out?
Laura. Well, not very — well — I had to drop out, it gave me — indigestion —

> *Jim laughs gently.*

Jim. What are you doing now?
Laura. I don't do anything — much. Oh, please don't think I sit around doing nothing! My glass collection takes up a good deal of my time. Glass is something you have to take good care of.
Jim. What did you say — about glass?
Laura. Collection I said — I have one — (*She clears her throat and turns away again, acutely shy.*)
Jim (abruptly). You know what I judge to be the trouble with you? Inferiority complex! Know what that is? That's what they call it when someone low-rates himself! I understand it because I had it, too. Although my case was not so aggravated as yours seems to be. I had it until I took up public speaking, developed my voice, and learned that I had an aptitude for science. Before that time I never thought of myself as being outstanding in any way whatsoever! Now I've never made a regular study of it, but I have a friend who says I can analyze people better than doctors that make a profession of it. I don't claim that to be necessarily true, but I can sure guess a person's psychology, Laura! (*Takes out his gum.*) Excuse me, Laura. I always take it out when the flavor is gone. I'll

use this scrap of paper to wrap it in. I know how it is to get it stuck on a shoe. Yep — that's what I judge to be your principal trouble. A lack of confidence in yourself as a person. You don't have the proper amount of faith in yourself. I'm basing that fact on a number of your remarks and also on certain observations I've made. For instance that clumping you thought was so awful in high school. You say that you even dreaded to walk into class. You see what you did? You dropped out of school, you gave up an education because of a clump, which as far as I know was practically non-existent! A little physical defect is what you have. Hardly noticeable even! Magnified thousands of times by imagination! You know what my strong advice to you is? Think of yourself as *superior* in some way!

Laura. In what way would I think?

Jim. Why, man alive, Laura! Just look about you a little. What do you see? A world full of common people! All of 'em born and all of 'em going to die! Which of them has one-tenth of your good points! Or mine! Or anyone else's, as far as that goes — Gosh! Everybody excels in some one thing. Some in many! (*Unconsciously glances at himself in the mirror.*) All you've got to do is discover in *what!* Take me, for instance. (*He adjusts his tie at the mirror.*) My interest happens to lie in electrodynamics. I'm taking a course in radio engineering at night school, Laura, on top of a fairly responsible job at the warehouse. I'm taking that course and studying public speaking.

Laura. Ohhhh.

Jim. Because I believe in the future of television! (*Turning back to her.*) I wish to be ready to go up right along with it. Therefore I'm planning to get in on the ground floor. In fact, I've already made the right connections and all that remains is for the industry itself to get under way! Full steam — (*His eyes are starry.*) *Knowledge* — Zzzzzp! *Money* — Zzzzzzp! — *Power!* That's the cycle democracy is built on! (*His attitude is convincingly dynamic. Laura stares at him, even her shyness eclipsed in her absolute wonder. He suddenly grins.*) I guess you think I think a lot of myself!

Laura. No — o-o-o, I —

Jim. Now how about you? Isn't there something you take more interest in than anything else?

Laura. Well, I do — as I said — have my — glass collection —

A peal of girlish laughter from the kitchen.

Jim. I'm not right sure I know what you're talking about. What kind of glass is it?

Laura. Little articles of it, they're ornaments mostly! Most of them are little animals made out of glass, the tiniest little animals in the world. Mother calls them a glass menagerie! Here's an example of one, if you'd like to see it! This one is one of the oldest. It's nearly thirteen. (*He stretches out his hand.*) (*Music: "The Glass Menagerie."*) Oh, be careful — if you breathe, it breaks!

Jim. I'd better not take it. I'm pretty clumsy with things.

Laura. Go on, I trust you with him! (*Places it in his palm.*) There now — you're holding him gently! Hold him over the light, he loves the light! You see how the light shines through him?

Jim. It sure does shine!

Laura. I shouldn't be partial, but he is my favorite one.

Jim. What kind of a thing is this one supposed to be?

Laura. Haven't you noticed the single horn on his forehead?

Jim. A unicorn, huh?

Laura. Mmm-hmmm!

Jim. Unicorns, aren't they extinct in the modern world?

Laura. I know!

Jim. Poor little fellow, he must feel sort of lonesome.

Laura (*smiling*). Well, if he does he doesn't complain about it. He stays on a shelf with some horses that don't have horns and all of them seem to get along nicely together.

Jim. How do you know?

Laura (*lightly*). I haven't heard any arguments among them!

Jim (*grinning*). No arguments, huh? Well, that's a pretty good sign! Where shall I set him?

Laura. Put him on the table. They all like a change of scenery once in a while!

Jim (*stretching*). Well, well, well, well — Look how big my shadow is when I stretch!

Laura. Oh, oh, yes — it stretches across the ceiling!

Jim (*crossing to door*). I think it's stopped raining. (*Opens fire-escape door.*) Where does the music come from?

Laura. From the Paradise Dance Hall across the alley.

Jim. How about cutting the rug a little, Miss Wingfield?

Laura. Oh, I —

Jim. Or is your program filled up? Let me have a look at it. (*Grasps imaginary card.*) Why, every dance is taken! I'll just have to scratch some out. (*Waltz Music: "La Golondrina."*) Ahhh, a waltz! (*He executes some sweeping turns by himself then holds his arms toward Laura.*)

Laura (*breathlessly*). I — can't dance!

Jim. There you go, that inferiority stuff!

Laura. I've never danced in my life!

Jim. Come on, try!

Laura. Oh, but I'd step on you!

Jim. I'm not made out of glass.

Laura. How — how — how do we start?

Jim. Just leave it to me. You hold your arms out a little.

Laura. Like this?

Jim. A little bit higher. Right. Now don't tighten up, that's the main thing about it — relax.

Laura (*laughing breathlessly*). It's hard not to.

Jim. Okay.

Laura. I'm afraid you can't budge me.

Jim. What do you bet I can't? (*He swings her into motion.*)

Laura. Goodness, yes, you can!

Jim. Let yourself go, now, Laura, just let yourself go.

Laura. I'm —

Jim. Come on!

Laura. Trying!

Jim. Not so stiff — Easy does it!

Laura. I know but I'm —

Jim. Loosen th' backbone! There now, that's a lot better.

Laura. Am I?

Jim. Lots, lots better! (*He moves her about the room in a clumsy waltz.*)

Laura. Oh, my!

Jim. Ha-ha!

Laura. Goodness, yes you can!

Jim. Ha-ha-ha! (*They suddenly bump into the table. Jim stops.*) What did we hit on?

Laura. Table.

Jim. Did something fall off it? I think —

Laura. Yes.

Jim. I hope that it wasn't the little glass horse with the horn!

Laura. Yes.

Jim. Aw, aw, aw. Is it broken?

Laura. Now it is just like all the other horses.

Jim. It's lost its —

Laura. Horn! It doesn't matter. Maybe it's a blessing in disguise.

Jim. You'll never forgive me. I bet that that was your favorite piece of glass.

Laura. I don't have favorites much. It's no tragedy, Freckles. Glass breaks so easily. No matter how careful you are. The traffic jars the shelves and things fall off them.

Jim. Still I'm awfully sorry that I was the cause.

Laura (smiling). I'll just imagine he had an operation. The horn was removed to make him feel less — freakish! (*They both laugh.*) Now he will feel more at home with the other horses, the ones that don't have horns. . .

Jim. Ha-ha, that's very funny! (*Suddenly serious.*) I'm glad to see that you have a sense of humor. You know — you're — well — very different! Surprisingly different from anyone else I know! (*His voice becomes soft and hesitant with a genuine feeling.*) Do you mind me telling you that? (*Laura is abashed beyond speech.*) You make me feel sort of — I don't know how to put it! I'm usually pretty good at expressing things, but — This is something that I don't know how to say! (*Laura touches her throat and clears it — turns the broken unicorn in her hands.*) (*Even softer.*) Has anyone ever told you that you were pretty? (*Pause: Music.*) (*Laura looks up slowly, with wonder, and shakes her head.*) Well, you are! In a very different way from anyone else. And all the nicer because of the difference, too. (*His voice becomes low and husky. Laura turns away, nearly faint with the novelty of her emotions.*) I wish that you were my sister. I'd teach you to have some confidence in yourself. The different people are not like other people, but being different is nothing to be ashamed of. Because other people are not such wonderful people. They're one hundred times one thousand. You're one times one! They walk all over the earth. You just stay here. They're common as — weeds, but — you — well, you're — *Blue Roses!*

(*Image on Screen: Blue Roses.*)

(*Music Changes.*)

Laura. But blue is wrong for — roses. . .

Jim. It's right for you — You're — pretty!

Laura. In what respect am I pretty?

Jim. In all respects — believe me! Your eyes — your hair — are pretty! Your hands are pretty! (*He catches hold of her hand.*) You think I'm making this up because I'm invited to dinner and have to be nice. Oh, I could do that! I could put on an act for you, Laura, and say lots of things without being very sincere. But this time I am. I'm talking to you sincerely. I happened to notice you had this inferiority complex that keeps you from feeling comfortable with people. Somebody needs to build your confidence up and make you proud instead of shy and turning away and — blushing — Somebody ought to — ought to — *kiss* you, Laura! (*His hand slips slowly up her arm to her shoulder.*) (*Music Swells Tumultuously.*) (*He suddenly turns her about and kisses her on the lips. When he releases her Laura sinks on the sofa with a bright, dazed look. Jim backs away and fishes in his pocket for a cigarette.*) (*Legend on Screen: "Souvenir."*) Stumble-john! (*He lights the cigarette, avoiding her look. There is a peal of girlish laughter from Amanda in the kitchen. Laura slowly raises and opens her hand. It still contains the little broken glass animal. She looks at it with a tender, bewildered expression.*) Stumble-john! I shouldn't have done that — That was way off the beam. You don't smoke, do you? (*She looks up, smiling, not hearing the question. He sits beside her a little gingerly. She looks at him speechlessly — waiting. He coughs decorously and moves a little farther aside as he considers the situation and senses her feelings, dimly, with perturbation. Gently.*) Would you — care for a — mint? (*She doesn't seem to hear him but her look grows brighter even.*) Peppermint — Life Saver? My pocket's a regular drug store — wherever I go . . . (*He pops a mint in his mouth. Then gulps and decides to make a clean breast of it. He speaks slowly and gingerly.*) Laura, you know, if I had a sister like you, I'd do the same thing as Tom. I'd bring out fellows — introduce her to them. The right type of boys of a type to — appreciate her. Only — well — he made a mistake about me. Maybe I've got no call to be saying this. That may not have been the idea in having me over. But what if it was? There's nothing wrong about that. The only trouble is that in my case — I'm not in a situation to — do the right thing. I can't take down your number and say I'll phone. I can't call up next week and — ask for a date. I thought I had better explain the situation in case you misunderstood it and — hurt your feelings. . . . (*Pause. Slowly, very slowly, Laura's look changes, her eyes returning slowly from his to the ornament in her palm.*)

Amanda utters another gay laugh in the kitchen.

Laura (*faintly*). You — won't — call again?
Jim. No, Laura, I can't. (*He rises from the sofa.*) As I was just explaining, I've — got strings on me, Laura, I've — been going steady! I go out all the time with a girl named Betty. She's a home-girl like you, and Catholic, and Irish, and in a great many ways we — get along fine. I met her last

summer on a moonlight boat trip up the river to Alton, on the *Majestic*. Well — right away from the start it was — love! *(Legend: Love!) (Laura sways slightly forward and grips the arm of the sofa. He fails to notice, now enrapt in his own comfortable being.)* Being in love has made a new man of me! *(Leaning stiffly forward, clutching the arm of the sofa, Laura struggles visibly with her storm. But Jim is oblivious, she is a long way off.)* The power of love is really pretty tremendous! Love is something that — changes the whole world, Laura! *(The storm abates a little and Laura leans back. He notices her again.)* It happened that Betty's aunt took sick, she got a wire and had to go to Centralia. So Tom — when he asked me to dinner — I naturally just accepted the invitation, not knowing that you — that he — that I — *(He stops awkwardly.)* Huh — I'm a stumble-john! *(He flops back on the sofa. The holy candles in the altar of Laura's face have been snuffed out! There is a look of almost infinite desolation. Jim glances at her uneasily.)* I wish that you would — say something. *(She bites her lip which was trembling and then bravely smiles. She opens her hand again on the broken glass ornament. Then she gently takes his hand and raises it level with her own. She carefully places the unicorn in the palm of his hand, then pushes his fingers closed upon it.)* What are you — doing that for? You want me to have him? — Laura? *(She nods.)* What for?

Laura. A — souvenir . . .

She rises unsteadily and crouches beside the victrola to wind it up.

(Legend on Screen: "Things Have a Way of Turning Out So Badly.")

(Or Image: "Gentleman Caller Waving Good-Bye! — Gaily.")

At this moment Amanda rushes brightly back in the front room. She bears a pitcher of fruit punch in an old-fashioned cut-glass pitcher and a plate of macaroons. The plate has a gold border and poppies painted on it.

Amanda. Well, well, well! Isn't the air delightful after the shower? I've made you children a little liquid refreshment. *(Turns gaily to the gentleman caller.)* Jim, do you know that song about lemonade?

"Lemonade, lemonade
Made in the shade and stirred with a spade —
Good enough for any old maid!"

Jim (uneasily). Ha-ha! No — I never heard it.

Amanda. Why, Laura! You look so serious!

Jim. We were having a serious conversation.

Amanda. Good! Now you're better acquainted!

Jim (uncertainly). Ha-ha! Yes.

Amanda. You modern young people are much more serious-minded than my generation. I was so gay as a girl!

Jim. You haven't changed, Mrs. Wingfield.

Amanda. Tonight I'm rejuvenated! The gaiety of the occasion, Mr. O'Connor! (*She tosses her head with a peal of laughter. Spills lemonade.*) Oooo! I'm baptizing myself!

Jim. Here — let me —

Amanda (setting the pitcher down). There now. I discovered we had some maraschino cherries. I dumped them in, juice and all!

Jim. You shouldn't have gone to that trouble, Mrs. Wingfield.

Amanda. Trouble, trouble? Why it was loads of fun! Didn't you hear me cutting up in the kitchen? I bet your ears were burning! I told Tom how outdone with him I was for keeping you to himself so long a time! He should have brought you over much, much sooner! Well, now that you've found your way, I want you to be a very frequent caller! Not just occasional but all the time. Oh, we're going to have a lot of gay times together! I see them coming! Mmm, just breathe that air! So fresh, and the moon's so pretty! I'll skip back out — I know where my place is when young folks are having a — serious conversation!

Jim. Oh, don't go out, Mrs. Wingfield. The fact of the matter is I've got to be going.

Amanda. Going, now? You're joking! Why, it's only the shank of the evening, Mr. O'Connor!

Jim. Well, you know how it is.

Amanda. You mean you're a young workingman and have to keep workingmen's hours. We'll let you off early tonight. But only on the condition that next time you stay later. What's the best night for you? Isn't Saturday night the best night for you workingmen?

Jim. I have a couple of time-clocks to punch, Mrs. Wingfield. One at morning, another one at night!

Amanda. My, but you *are* ambitious! You work at night, too?

Jim. No, Ma'am, not work but — Betty! (*He crosses deliberately to pick up his hat. The band at the Paradise Dance Hall goes into a tender waltz.*)

Amanda. Betty? Betty? Who's — Betty! (*There is an ominous cracking sound in the sky.*)

Jim. Oh, just a girl. The girl I go steady with! (*He smiles charmingly. The sky falls.*)

(*Legend: "The Sky Falls."*)

Amanda (*a long-drawn exhalation*). Ohhhh . . . Is it a serious romance, Mr. O'Connor?

Jim. We're going to be married the second Sunday in June.

Amanda. Ohhhh — how nice! Tom didn't mention that you were engaged to be married.

Jim. The cat's not out of the bag at the warehouse yet. You know how they are. They call you Romeo and stuff like that. (*He stops at the oval mirror to put on his hat. He carefully shapes the brim and the crown to give a discreetly dashing effect.*) It's been a wonderful evening, Mrs. Wingfield. I guess this is what they mean by Southern hospitality.

Amanda. It really wasn't anything at all.

Jim. I hope it don't seem like I'm rushing off. But I promised Betty I'd pick her up at the Wabash depot, an' by the time I get my jalopy down there her train'll be in. Some women are pretty upset if you keep 'em waiting.

Amanda. Yes, I know — The tyranny of women! (*Extends her hand.*) Goodbye, Mr. O'Connor. I wish you luck — and happiness — and success! All three of them, and so does Laura! — Don't you, Laura?

Laura. Yes!

Jim (*taking her hand*). Goodbye, Laura. I'm certainly going to treasure that souvenir. And don't you forget the good advice I gave you. (*Raises his voice to a cheery shout.*) So long, Shakespeare! Thanks again, ladies — Good night!

He grins and ducks jauntily out.

Still bravely grimacing, Amanda closes the door on the gentleman caller. Then she turns back to the room with a puzzled expression. She and Laura don't dare to face each other. Laura crouches beside the victrola to wind it.

Amanda (*faintly*). Things have a way of turning out so badly. I don't believe that I would play the victrola. Well, well — well — Our gentleman caller was engaged to be married! Tom!

Tom (*from back*). Yes, Mother?

Amanda. Come in here a minute. I want to tell you something awfully funny.

Tom (*enters with macaroon and a glass of the lemonade*). Has the gentleman caller gotten away already?

Amanda. The gentleman caller has made an early departure. What a wonderful joke you played on us!

Tom. How do you mean?

Amanda. You didn't mention that he was engaged to be married.

Tom. Jim? Engaged?

Amanda. That's what he just informed us.

Tom. I'll be jiggered! I didn't know about that.

Amanda. That seems very peculiar.

Tom. What's peculiar about it?

Amanda. Didn't you call him your best friend down at the warehouse?

Tom. He is, but how did I know?

Amanda. It seems extremely peculiar that you wouldn't know your best friend was going to be married!

Tom. The warehouse is where I work, not where I know things about people!

Amanda. You don't know things anywhere! You live in a dream; you manufacture illusions! (*He crosses to door.*) Where are you going?

Tom. I'm going to the movies.

Amanda. That's right, now that you've had us make such fools of ourselves. The effort, the preparations, all the expense! The new floor lamp, the rug, the clothes for Laura! All for what? To entertain some other girl's fiancé! Go to the movies, go! Don't think about us, a mother deserted, an unmarried sister who's crippled and has no job! Don't let anything interfere with your selfish pleasure! Just go, go, go — to the movies!

Tom. All right, I will! The more you shout about my selfishness to me the quicker I'll go, and I won't go to the movies!

Amanda. Go, then! Then go to the moon — you selfish dreamer!

Tom smashes his glass on the floor. He plunges out on the fire-escape, slamming the door. Laura screams — cut by door.

Dance-hall music up. Tom goes to the rail and grips it desperately, lifting his face in the chill white moonlight penetrating the narrow abyss of the alley.

(*Legend on Screen: "And So Good-Bye . . ."*)

Tom's closing speech is timed with the interior pantomime. The interior scene is played as though viewed through sound-proof glass. Amanda appears to be making a comforting speech to Laura who is huddled upon the sofa. Now that we cannot hear the mother's speech, her silliness is gone and she has dignity and tragic beauty. Laura's dark hair hides her face until at the end of the speech she lifts it to smile at her mother. Amanda's gestures are slow and graceful, almost dancelike, as she comforts the daughter. At the end of her speech she glances a moment at the father's picture — then withdraws through the portieres. At close of Tom's speech, Laura blows out the candles, ending the play.

Tom. I didn't go to the moon, I went much further — for time is the longest distance between two places — Not long after that I was fired for writing a poem on the lid of a shoe-box. I left Saint Louis. I descended the steps of this fire-escape for a last time and followed, from then on, in my father's footsteps, attempting to find in motion what was lost in space — I traveled around a great deal. The cities swept about me like dead leaves, leaves that were brightly colored but torn away from the branches. I would have stopped, but I was pursued by something. It always came upon me unawares, taking me altogether by surprise. Perhaps it was a familiar bit of music. Perhaps it was only a piece of transparent glass — Perhaps I am walking along a street at night, in some strange city, before I have found companions. I pass the lighted window of a shop where perfume is sold. The window is filled with pieces of colored glass, tiny transparent bottles in delicate colors, like bits of a shattered rainbow. Then all at once my sister touches my shoulder. I turn around and look into her eyes . . . Oh, Laura, Laura, I tried to leave you behind me, but I am more faithful than I intended to be! I reach for a cigarette, I cross the street, I run into the movies or a bar, I buy a drink, I speak to the nearest stranger — anything that can blow your candles out! (*Laura bends over the candles.*) — for nowadays the world is lit by lightning! Blow out your candles, Laura — and so goodbye . . .

She blows the candles out.

(The Scene Dissolves.)

PRODUCTION NOTES

Being a "memory play," *The Glass Menagerie* can be presented with unusual freedom of convention. Because of its considerably delicate or tenuous material, atmospheric touches and subtleties of direction play a particularly important part. Expressionism and all other unconventional techniques in drama have only one valid aim, and that is a closer approach to truth. When a play employs unconventional techniques, it is not, or certainly shouldn't be, trying to escape its responsibility of dealing with reality, or interpreting experience, but is actually or should be attempting to find a closer approach, a more penetrating and vivid expression of things as they are. The straight realistic play with its genuine frigidaire and authentic ice cubes, its characters that speak exactly as its audience speaks, corresponds to the academic landscape and has the same virtue of a photographic likeness. Everyone should know nowadays the unimportance of the photographic in art: that truth, life, or reality is an organic thing which the poetic imagination can represent or suggest, in essence, only through transformation, through changing into other forms than those which were merely present in appearance.

These remarks are not meant as comments only on this particular play. They have to do with a conception of a new, plastic theater which must take the place of the exhausted theater of realistic conventions if the theater is to resume vitality as a part of our culture.

The Screen Device

There is *only one important difference between the original and acting version of the play* and that is the *omission* in the latter of the device which I tentatively included in my *original* script. This device was the use of a screen on which were projected magic-lantern slides bearing images or titles. I do not regret the omission of this device from the . . . Broadway production. The extraordinary power of Miss Taylor's performance made it suitable to have the utmost simplicity in the physical production. But I think it may be interesting to some readers to see how this device was conceived. So I am putting it into the published manuscript. These images and legends, projected from behind, were cast on a section of wall between the front-room and dining-room areas, which should be indistinguishable from the rest when not in use.

The purpose of this will probably be apparent. It is to give accent to certain values in each scene. Each scene contains a particular point (or several) which is structurally the most important. In an episodic play, such as this, the basic structure or narrative line may be obscured from the audience; the effect may seem fragmentary rather than architectural. This may not be the fault of the play so much as a lack of attention in the audience. The legend or image upon the screen will strengthen the effect of what is merely allusion in the writing and allow the primary point to be made more simply and lightly than if the entire responsibility were on the spoken lines. Aside from this structural value, I think the screen will have a definite emotional appeal, less definable but just as important. An imaginative producer or director may invent many other uses for this device than those indicated in the present script. In fact the possibilities of the device seem much larger to me than the instance of this play can possibly utilize.

The Music

Another extra-literary accent in this play is provided by the use of music. A single recurring tune, "The Glass Menagerie," is used to give emotional emphasis to suitable passages. This tune is like circus music, not when you are on the grounds or in the immediate vicinity of the parade, but when you are at some distance and very likely thinking of something else. It seems under those circumstances to continue almost interminably and it weaves in and out of your preoccupied consciousness; then it is the lightest, most delicate music in the world and perhaps the saddest. It expresses the surface vivacity of life with the underlying strain of immutable and inexpressible sorrow. When you look at a piece of delicately spun glass you think of two things: how beautiful it is and how easily it can be broken. Both of those ideas should be woven into the recurring tune, which dips in and out of the play as if it were carried on a wind that changes. It serves as a thread of connection and allusion between the narrator with his separate point in time and space and the subject of his story. Between each episode it returns as reference to the emotion, nostalgia, which is the first condition of the play. It is primarily Laura's music and therefore comes out most clearly when the play focuses upon her and the lovely fragility of glass which is her image.

The Lighting

The lighting in the play is not realistic. In keeping with the atmosphere of memory, the stage is dim. Shafts of light are focused on selected areas or actors, sometimes in contradistinction to what is the apparent center. For instance, in the quarrel scene between Tom and Amanda, in which Laura has no active part, the clearest pool of light is on her figure. This is also true of the supper scene. The light upon Laura should be distinct from the others, having a peculiar pristine clarity such as light used in early religious portraits of female saints or madonnas. A certain correspondence to light in religious paintings, such as El Greco's, where the figures are radiant in atmosphere that is relatively dusky, could be effectively used throughout the play. (It will also permit a more effective use of the screen.) A free, imaginative use of light can be of enormous value in giving a mobile, plastic quality to plays of a more or less static nature.

QUESTIONS

1. When produced in New York, the magic-lantern slides were omitted. Is the device an extraneous gimmick? Might it even interfere with the play, by oversimplifying and thus in a way belittling the actions?
2. What does the victrola offer to Laura? Why is the typewriter a better symbol (for the purposes of the play) than, say, a piano? After all, Laura could have been taking piano lessons. Explain the symbolism of the unicorn, and the loss of its horn. What is Laura saying to Jim in the gesture of giving him the unicorn?
3. Laura escapes to her glass menagerie. To what do Amanda and Tom escape? How complete is Tom's escape at the end of the play?
4. What is meant at the end when Laura blows out the candles? Is she blowing out illusions? Or life? Or both?
5. Did Williams make a slip in having Amanda say Laura is "crippled" on page 1020?
6. There is an implication that had Jim not been going steady he might have rescued Laura, but Jim also seems to represent (for example, in his lines about money and power) the corrupt outside world that no longer values humanity. Is this a slip on Williams's part, or is it an interesting complexity?
7. On pages 1020–1021 Williams says, in a stage direction, "Now that we cannot hear the mother's speech, her silliness is gone and she has dignity and tragic beauty." Is Williams simply dragging in the word "tragic" because of its prestige, or is it legitimate? "Tragedy" is often distinguished from "pathos": in the tragic, the suffering is experienced by persons

who act and are in some measure responsible for their suffering; in the pathetic, the suffering is experienced by the passive and the innocent. For example, in discussing Aeschylus's *The Suppliants* (in *Greek Tragedy*), H. D. F. Kitto says: "The Suppliants are not only pathetic, as the victims of outrage, but also tragic, as the victims of their own misconceptions." Given this distinction, to what extent are Amanda and Laura tragic? Pathetic?

Arthur Miller (*American. b. 1915*)

Death of a Salesman
Certain Private Conversations
in Two Acts and a Requiem

List of Characters

Willy Loman
Linda
Biff
Happy
Bernard
The Woman
Charley
Uncle Ben
Howard Wagner
Jenny
Stanley
Miss Forsythe
Letta

Scene. *The action takes place in Willy Loman's house and yard and in various places he visits in the New York and Boston of today.*

ACT I

Scene: *A melody is heard, played upon a flute. It is small and fine, telling of grass and trees and the horizon. The curtain rises.*

Top: *Lee J. Cobb starred as Willy Loman in the 1949 original Broadway production of* Death of a Salesman. *Photograph reproduced courtesy of the Theatre Arts Library, Harry Ransom Humanities Research Center, The University of Texas at Austin. Bottom: Dustin Hoffman, as Willy Loman, and John Malkovich, as Biff, face each other in this scene from the 1984 production. Photograph by Inge Morath; reproduced by permission of Magnum Photos, Inc.*

Before us is the Salesman's house. We are aware of towering, angular shapes behind it, surrounding it on all sides. Only the blue light of the sky falls upon the house and forestage; the surrounding area shows an angry glow of orange. As more light appears, we see a solid vault of apartment houses around the small, fragile-seeming home. An air of the dream clings to the place, a dream rising out of reality. The kitchen at center seems actual enough, for there is a kitchen table with three chairs, and a refrigerator. But no other fixtures are seen. At the back of the kitchen there is a draped entrance, which leads to the living room. To the right of the kitchen, on a level raised two feet, is a bedroom furnished only with a brass bedstead and a straight chair. On a shelf over the bed a silver athletic trophy stands. A window opens onto the apartment house at the side.

Behind the kitchen, on a level raised six and a half feet, is the boys' bedroom, at present barely visible. Two beds are dimly seen, and at the back of the room a dormer window. (This bedroom is above the unseen living room.) At the left a stairway curves up to it from the kitchen.

The entire setting is wholly or, in some places, partially transparent. The roof-line of the house is one-dimensional; under and over it we see the apartment buildings. Before the house lies an apron, curving beyond the forestage into the orchestra. This forward area serves as the back yard as well as the locale of all Willy's imaginings and of his city scenes. Whenever the action is in the present the actors observe the imaginary wall-lines, entering the house only through its door at the left. But in the scenes of the past these boundaries are broken, and characters enter or leave a room by stepping "through" a wall onto the forestage.

From the right, Willy Loman, the Salesman, enters, carrying two large sample cases. The flute plays on. He hears but is not aware of it. He is past sixty years of age, dressed quietly. Even as he crosses the stage to the doorway of the house, his exhaustion is apparent. He unlocks the door, comes into the kitchen, and thankfully lets his burden down, feeling the soreness of his palms. A word-sigh escapes his lips — it might be "Oh, boy, oh, boy." He closes the door, then carries his cases out into the living room, through the draped kitchen doorway.

Linda, his wife, has stirred in her bed at the right. She gets out and puts on a robe, listening. Most often jovial, she has developed an iron repression of her exceptions to Willy's behavior — she more than loves him, she admires him, as though his mercurial *nature, his temper, his massive dreams and little cruelties, served her only as sharp reminders of the turbulent longings within him, longings which she shares but lacks the temperament to utter and follow to their end.*

Linda (*hearing Willy outside the bedroom, calls with some trepidation*). Willy!

Willy. It's all right. I came back.

Linda. Why? What happened? (*Slight pause.*) Did something happen, Willy?

Willy. No, nothing happened.

Linda. You didn't smash the car, did you?

Willy (*with casual irritation*). I said nothing happened. Didn't you hear me?

Linda. Don't you feel well?

Willy. I'm tired to the death. (*The flute has faded away. He sits on the bed beside her, a little numb.*) I couldn't make it. I just couldn't make it, Linda.

Linda (*very carefully, delicately*). Where were you all day? You look terrible.

Willy. I got as far as a little above Yonkers. I stopped for a cup of coffee. Maybe it was the coffee.

Linda. What?

Willy (*after a pause*). I suddenly couldn't drive any more. The car kept going off onto the shoulder, y'know?

Linda (*helpfully*). Oh. Maybe it was the steering again. I don't think Angelo knows the Studebaker.

Willy. No, it's me, it's me. Suddenly I realize I'm goin' sixty miles an hour and I don't remember the last five minutes. I'm — I can't seem to — keep my mind to it.

Linda. Maybe it's your glasses. You never went for your new glasses.

Willy. No, I see everything. I came back ten miles an hour. It took me nearly four hours from Yonkers.

Linda (*resigned*). Well, you'll just have to take a rest, Willy, you can't continue this way.

Willy. I just got back from Florida.

Linda. But you didn't rest your mind. Your mind is overactive, and the mind is what counts, dear.

Willy. I'll start out in the morning. Maybe I'll feel better in the morning. (*She is taking off his shoes.*) These goddam arch supports are killing me.

Linda. Take an aspirin. Should I get you an aspirin? It'll soothe you.

Willy (*with wonder*). I was driving along, you understand? And I was fine. I was even observing the scenery. You can imagine, me looking at scenery, on the road every week of my life. But it's so beautiful up there, Linda, the trees are so thick, and the sun is warm. I opened the windshield and just let the warm air bathe over me. And then all of a sudden I'm goin' off the road! I'm tellin' ya, I absolutely forgot I was driving. If I'd've gone the other way over the white line I might've killed somebody. So I went on again — and five minutes later I'm dreamin' again, and I nearly . . . (*He presses two fingers against his eyes.*) I have such thoughts, I have such strange thoughts.

Linda. Willy, dear. Talk to them again. There's no reason why you can't work in New York.

Willy. They don't need me in New York. I'm the New England man. I'm vital in New England.

Linda. But you're sixty years old. They can't expect you to keep traveling every week.

Willy. I'll have to send a wire to Portland. I'm supposed to see Brown and Morrison tomorrow morning at ten o'clock to show the line. Goddammit, I could sell them! (*He starts putting on his jacket.*)

Linda (*taking the jacket from him*). Why don't you go down to the place tomorrow and tell Howard you've simply got to work in New York? You're too accommodating, dear.

Willy. If old man Wagner was alive I'd a been in charge of New York now! That man was a prince, he was a masterful man. But that boy of his, that Howard, he don't appreciate. When I went north the first time, the Wagner Company didn't know where New England was!

Linda. Why don't you tell those things to Howard, dear?

Willy (*encouraged*). I will, I definitely will. Is there any cheese?

Linda. I'll make you a sandwich.

Willy. No, go to sleep. I'll take some milk. I'll be up right away. The boys in?

Linda. They're sleeping. Happy took Biff on a date tonight.

Willy (*interested*). That so?

Linda. It was so nice to see them shaving together, one behind the other, in the bathroom. And going out together. You notice? The whole house smells of shaving lotion.

Willy. Figure it out. Work a lifetime to pay off a house. You finally own it, and there's nobody to live in it.

Linda. Well, dear, life is a casting off. It's always that way.

Willy. No, no, some people — some people accomplish something. Did Biff say anything after I went this morning?

Linda. You shouldn't have criticized him, Willy, especially after he just got off the train. You mustn't lose your temper with him.

Willy. When the hell did I lose my temper? I simply asked him if he was making any money. Is that a criticism?

Linda. But, dear, how could he make any money?

Willy (*worried and angered*). There's such an undercurrent in him. He became a moody man. Did he apologize when I left this morning?

Linda. He was crestfallen, Willy. You know how he admires you. I think if he finds himself, then you'll both be happier and not fight any more.

Willy. How can he find himself on a farm? Is that a life? A farm hand? In the beginning, when he was young, I thought, well, a young man, it's good for him to tramp around, take a lot of different jobs. But it's more than ten years now and he has yet to make thirty-five dollars a week!

Linda. He's finding himself, Willy.

Willy. Not finding yourself at the age of thirty-four is a disgrace!

Linda. Shh!

Willy. The trouble is he's lazy, goddammit!

Linda. Willy, please!

Willy. Biff is a lazy bum!

Linda. They're sleeping. Get something to eat. Go on down.

Willy. Why did he come home? I would like to know what brought him home.

Linda. I don't know. I think he's still lost, Willy. I think he's very lost.

Willy. Biff Loman is lost. In the greatest country in the world a young man with such — personal attractiveness, gets lost. And such a hard worker. There's one thing about Biff — he's not lazy.

Linda. Never.

Willy (*with pity and resolve*). I'll see him in the morning; I'll have a nice talk with him. I'll get him a job selling. He could be big in no time. My God! Remember how they used to follow him around in high school? When he smiled at one of them their faces lit up. When he walked down the street . . . (*He loses himself in reminiscences.*)

Linda (*trying to bring him out of it*). Willy, dear, I got a new kind of American-type cheese today. It's whipped.

Willy. Why do you get American when I like Swiss?

Linda. I just thought you'd like a change . . .

Willy. I don't want a change! I want Swiss cheese. Why am I always being contradicted?

Linda (with a covering laugh). I thought it would be a surprise.

Willy. Why don't you open a window in here, for God's sake?

Linda (with infinite patience). They're all open, dear.

Willy. The way they boxed us in here. Bricks and windows, windows and bricks.

Linda. We should've bought the land next door.

Willy. The street is lined with cars. There's not a breath of fresh air in the neighborhood. The grass don't grow any more, you can't raise a carrot in the back yard. They should've had a law against apartment houses. Remember those two beautiful elm trees out there? When I and Biff hung the swing between them?

Linda. Yeah, like being a million miles from the city.

Willy. They should've arrested the builder for cutting those down. They massacred the neighborhood. (*Lost.*) More and more I think of those days, Linda. This time of year it was lilac and wisteria. And then the peonies would come out, and the daffodils. What fragrance in this room!

Linda. Well, after all, people had to move somewhere.

Willy. No, there's more people now.

Linda. I don't think there's more people. I think . . .

Willy. There's more people! That's what's ruining this country! Population is getting out of control. The competition is maddening! Smell the stink from that apartment house! And another one on the other side . . . How can they whip cheese?

On Willy's last line, Biff and Happy raise themselves up in their beds, listening.

Linda. Go down, try it. And be quiet.

Willy (turning to Linda, guiltily). You're not worried about me, are you, sweetheart?

Biff. What's the matter?

Happy. Listen!

Linda. You've got too much on the ball to worry about.

Willy. You're my foundation and my support, Linda.

Linda. Just try to relax, dear. You make mountains out of molehills.

Willy. I won't fight with him any more. If he wants to go back to Texas, let him go.

Linda. He'll find his way.

Willy. Sure. Certain men just don't get started till later in life.

Like Thomas Edison, I think. Or B. F. Goodrich. One of them was deaf. (*He starts for the bedroom doorway.*) I'll put my money on Biff.

Linda. And Willy — if it's warm Sunday we'll drive in the country. And we'll open the windshield, and take lunch.

Willy. No, the windshields don't open on the new cars.

Linda. But you opened it today.

Willy. Me? I didn't. (*He stops.*) Now isn't that peculiar! Isn't that a remarkable . . . (*He breaks off in amazement and fright as the flute is heard distantly.*)

Linda. What, darling?

Willy. That is the most remarkable thing.

Linda. What, dear?

Willy. I was thinking of the Chevvy. (*Slight pause.*) Nineteen twenty-eight . . . when I had that red Chevvy . . . (*Breaks off.*) That funny? I coulda sworn I was driving that Chevvy today.

Linda. Well, that's nothing. Something must've reminded you.

Willy. Remarkable. Ts. Remember those days? The way Biff used to simonize that car? The dealer refused to believe there was eighty thousand miles on it. (*He shakes his head.*) Heh! (*To Linda.*) Close your eyes, I'll be right up. (*He walks out of the bedroom.*)

Happy (*to Biff*). Jesus, maybe he smashed up the car again!

Linda (*calling after Willy*). Be careful on the stairs, dear! The cheese is on the middle shelf. (*She turns, goes over to the bed, takes his jacket, and goes out of the bedroom.*)

Light has risen on the boys' room. Unseen, Willy is heard talking to himself, "Eighty thousand miles," and a little laugh. Biff gets out of bed, comes downstage a bit, and stands attentively. Biff is two years older than his brother Happy, well built, but in these days bears a worn air and seems less self-assured. He has succeeded less, and his dreams are stronger and less acceptable than Happy's. Happy is tall, powerfully made. Sexuality is like a visible color on him, or a scent that many women have discovered. He, like his brother, is lost, but in a different way, for he has never allowed himself to turn his face toward defeat and is thus more confused and hard-skinned, although seemingly more content.

Happy (*getting out of bed*). He's going to get his license taken away if he keeps that up. I'm getting nervous about him, y'know, Biff?

Biff. His eyes are going.

Happy. No, I've driven with him. He sees all right. He just doesn't keep his mind on it. I drove into the city with him last week.

He stops at a green light and then it turns red and he goes.
(*He laughs.*)

Biff. Maybe he's color-blind.

Happy. Pop? Why he's got the finest eye for color in the business.
You know that.

Biff (*sitting down on his bed*). I'm going to sleep.

Happy. You're not still sour on Dad, are you, Biff?

Biff. He's all right, I guess.

Willy (*underneath them, in the living room*). Yes, sir, eighty thousand
miles — eighty-two thousand!

Biff. You smoking?

Happy (*holding out a pack of cigarettes*). Want one?

Biff (*taking a cigarette*). I can never sleep when I smell it.

Willy. What a simonizing job, heh!

Happy (*with deep sentiment*). Funny, Biff, y'know? Us sleeping in
here again? The old beds. (*He pats his bed affectionately.*) All
the talk that went across those two beds, huh? Our whole
lives.

Biff. Yeah. Lotta dreams and plans.

Happy (*with a deep and masculine laugh*). About five hundred women
would like to know what was said in this room. (*They share
a soft laugh.*)

Biff. Remember that big Betsy something — what the hell was
her name — over on Bushwick Avenue?

Happy (*combing his hair*). With the collie dog!

Biff. That's the one. I got you in there, remember?

Happy. Yeah, that was my first time — I think. Boy, there was
a pig. (*They laugh, almost crudely.*) You taught me everything
I know about women. Don't forget that.

Biff. I bet you forgot how bashful you used to be. Especially with
girls.

Happy. Oh, I still am, Biff.

Biff. Oh, go on.

Happy. I just control it, that's all. I think I got less bashful and
you got more so. What happened, Biff? Where's the old
humor, the old confidence? (*He shakes Biff's knee. Biff gets
up and moves restlessly about the room.*) What's the matter?

Biff. Why does Dad mock me all the time?

Happy. He's not mocking you, he . . .

Biff. Everything I say there's a twist of mockery on his face. I
can't get near him.

Happy. He just wants you to make good, that's all. I wanted to
talk to you about Dad for a long time, Biff. Something's
— happening to him. He — talks to himself.

Biff. I noticed that this morning. But he always mumbled.

Happy. But not so noticeable. It got so embarrassing I sent him to Florida. And you know something? Most of the time he's talking to you.

Biff. What's he say about me?

Happy. I can't make it out.

Biff. What's he say about me?

Happy. I think the fact that you're not settled, that you're still kind of up in the air . . .

Biff. There's one or two other things depressing him, Happy.

Happy. What do you mean?

Biff. Never mind. Just don't lay it all to me.

Happy. But I think if you just got started — I mean — is there any future for you out there?

Biff. I tell ya, Hap, I don't know what the future is. I don't know — what I'm supposed to want.

Happy. What do you mean?

Biff. Well, I spent six or seven years after high school trying to work myself up. Shipping clerk, salesman, business of one kind or another. And it's a measly manner of existence. To get on that subway on the hot mornings in summer. To devote your whole life to keeping stock, or making phone calls, or selling or buying. To suffer fifty weeks of the year for the sake of a two-week vacation, when all you really desire is to be outdoors, with your shirt off. And always to have to get ahead of the next fella. And still — that's how you build a future.

Happy. Well, you really enjoy it on a farm? Are you content out there?

Biff (with rising agitation). Hap, I've had twenty or thirty different kinds of jobs since I left home before the war, and it always turns out the same. I just realized it lately. In Nebraska when I herded cattle, and the Dakotas, and Arizona, and now in Texas. It's why I came home now, I guess, because I realized it. This farm I work on, it's spring there now, see? And they've got about fifteen new colts. There's nothing more inspiring or — beautiful than the sight of a mare and a new colt. And it's cool there now, see? Texas is cool now, and it's spring. And whenever spring comes to where I am, I suddenly get the feeling, my God, I'm not gettin' anywhere! What the hell am I doing, playing around with horses, twenty-eight dollars a week! I'm thirty-four years old, I oughta be makin' my future. That's when I come running home. And now, I get here, and I don't know what to do with myself.

(*After a pause.*) I've always made a point of not wasting my life, and everytime I come back here I know that all I've done is to waste my life.

Happy. You're a poet, you know that, Biff? You're a — you're an idealist!

Biff. No, I'm mixed up very bad. Maybe I oughta get married. Maybe I oughta get stuck into something. Maybe that's my trouble. I'm like a boy. I'm not married, I'm not in business, I just — I'm like a boy. Are you content, Hap? You're a success, aren't you? Are you content?

Happy. Hell, no!

Biff. Why? You're making money, aren't you?

Happy (*moving about with energy, expressiveness*). All I can do now is wait for the merchandise manager to die. And suppose I get to be merchandise manager? He's a good friend of mine, and he just built a terrific estate on Long Island. And he lived there about two months and sold it, and now he's building another one. He can't enjoy it once it's finished. And I know that's just what I would do. I don't know what the hell I'm workin' for. Sometimes I sit in my apartment — all alone. And I think of the rent I'm paying. And it's crazy. But then, it's what I always wanted. My own apartment, a car, and plenty of women. And still, goddammit, I'm lonely.

Biff (*with enthusiasm*). Listen, why don't you come out West with me?

Happy. You and I, heh?

Biff. Sure, maybe we could buy a ranch. Raise cattle, use our muscles. Men built like we are should be working out in the open.

Happy (*avidly*). The Loman Brothers, heh?

Biff (*with vast affection*). Sure, we'd be known all over the counties!

Happy (*enthralled*). That's what I dream about, Biff. Sometimes I want to just rip my clothes off in the middle of the store and outbox that goddam merchandise manager. I mean I can outbox, outrun, and outlift anybody in that store, and I have to take orders from those common, petty sons-of-bitches till I can't stand it any more.

Biff. I'm tellin' you, kid, if you were with me I'd be happy out there.

Happy (*enthused*). See, Biff, everybody around me is so false that I'm constantly lowering my ideals . . .

Biff. Baby, together we'd stand up for one another, we'd have someone to trust.

Happy. If I were around you . . .

Biff. Hap, the trouble is we weren't brought up to grub for money. I don't know how to do it.

Happy. Neither can I!

Biff. Then let's go!

Happy. The only thing is — what can you make out there?

Biff. But look at your friend. Builds an estate and then hasn't the peace of mind to live in it.

Happy. Yeah, but when he walks into the store the waves part in front of him. That's fifty-two thousand dollars a year coming through the revolving door, and I got more in my pinky finger than he's got in his head.

Biff. Yeah, but you just said . . .

Happy. I gotta show some of those pompous, self-important executives over there that Hap Loman can make the grade. I want to walk into the store the way he walks in. Then I'll go with you, Biff. We'll be together yet, I swear. But take those two we had tonight. Now weren't they gorgeous creatures?

Biff. Yeah, yeah, most gorgeous I've had in years.

Happy. I get that any time I want, Biff. Whenever I feel disgusted. The only trouble is, it gets like bowling or something. I just keep knockin' them over and it doesn't mean anything. You still run around a lot?

Biff. Naa. I'd like to find a girl — steady, somebody with substance.

Happy. That's what I long for.

Biff. Go on! You'd never come home.

Happy. I would! Somebody with character, with resistance! Like Mom, y'know? You're gonna call me a bastard when I tell you this. That girl Charlotte I was with tonight is engaged to be married in five weeks. (*He tries on his new hat.*)

Biff. No kiddin'!

Happy. Sure, the guy's in line for the vice-presidency of the store. I don't know what gets into me, maybe I just have an over-developed sense of competition or something, but I went and ruined her, and furthermore I can't get rid of her. And he's the third executive I've done that to. Isn't that a crummy characteristic? And to top it all, I go to their weddings! (*Indignantly, but laughing.*) Like I'm not supposed to take bribes. Manufacturers offer me a hundred-dollar bill now and then to throw an order their way. You know how honest I am, but it's like this girl, see. I hate myself for it. Because I don't want the girl, and, still, I take it and — I love it!

Biff. Let's go to sleep.

Happy. I guess we didn't settle anything, heh?

Biff. I just got one idea that I think I'm going to try.

Happy. What's that?

Biff. Remember Bill Oliver?

Happy. Sure, Oliver is very big now. You want to work for him again?

Biff. No, but when I quit he said something to me. He put his arm on my shoulder, and he said, "Biff, if you ever need anything, come to me."

Happy. I remember that. That sounds good.

Biff. I think I'll go to see him. If I could get ten thousand or even seven or eight thousand dollars I could buy a beautiful ranch.

Happy. I bet he'd back you. 'Cause he thought highly of you, Biff. I mean, they all do. You're well liked, Biff. That's why I say to come back here, and we both have the apartment. And I'm tellin' you, Biff, any babe you want . . .

Biff. No, with a ranch I could do the work I like and still be something. I just wonder though. I wonder if Oliver still thinks I stole that carton of basketballs.

Happy. Oh, he probably forgot that long ago. It's almost ten years. You're too sensitive. Anyway, he didn't really fire you.

Biff. Well, I think he was going to. I think that's why I quit. I was never sure whether he knew or not. I know he thought the world of me, though. I was the only one he'd let lock up the place.

Willy (below). You gonna wash the engine, Biff?

Happy. Shh!

Biff looks at Happy, who is gazing down, listening. Willy is mumbling in the parlor.

Happy. You hear that?

They listen. Willy laughs warmly.

Biff (growing angry). Doesn't he know Mom can hear that?

Willy. Don't get your sweater dirty, Biff!

A look of pain crosses Biff's face.

Happy. Isn't that terrible? Don't leave again, will you? You'll find a job here. You gotta stick around. I don't know what to do about him, it's getting embarrassing.

Willy. What a simonizing job!

Biff. Mom's hearing that!

Willy. No kiddin', Biff, you got a date? Wonderful!

Happy. Go on to sleep. But talk to him in the morning, will you?

Biff (reluctantly getting into bed). With her in the house. Brother!

Happy (getting into bed). I wish you'd have a good talk with him.

The light on their room begins to fade.

Biff (to himself in bed). That selfish, stupid . . .

Happy. Sh . . . Sleep, Biff.

Their light is out. Well before they have finished speaking, Willy's form is dimly seen below in the darkened kitchen. He opens the refrigerator, searches in there, and takes out a bottle of milk. The apartment houses are fading out, and the entire house and surroundings become covered with leaves. Music insinuates itself as the leaves appear.

Willy. Just wanna be careful with those girls, Biff, that's all. Don't make any promises. No promises of any kind. Because a girl, y'know, they always believe what you tell 'em, and you're very young, Biff, you're too young to be talking seriously to girls.

Light rises on the kitchen. Willy, talking, shuts the refrigerator door and comes downstage to the kitchen table. He pours milk into a glass. He is totally immersed in himself, smiling faintly.

Willy. Too young entirely, Biff. You want to watch your schooling first. Then when you're all set, there'll be plenty of girls for a boy like you. (*He smiles broadly at a kitchen chair.*) That so? The girls pay for you? (*He laughs.*) Boy, you must really be makin' a hit.

Willy is gradually addressing — physically — a point offstage, speaking through the wall of the kitchen, and his voice has been rising in volume to that of a normal conversation.

Willy. I been wondering why you polish the car so careful. Ha! Don't leave the hubcaps, boys. Get the chamois to the hubcaps. Happy, use newspaper on the windows, it's the easiest thing. Show him how to do it, Biff! You see, Happy? Pad it up, use it like a pad. That's it, that's it, good work. You're doin' all right, Hap. (*He pauses, then nods in approbation for a few seconds, then looks upward.*) Biff, first thing we gotta do when we get time is clip that big branch over the house. Afraid it's gonna fall in a storm and hit the roof. Tell you what. We get a rope and sling her around, and then we climb up there with a couple of saws and take her down. Soon as you finish the car, boys, I wanna see ya. I got a surprise for you, boys.

Biff (*offstage*). Whatta ya got, Dad?

Willy. No, you finish first. Never leave a job till you're finished — remember that. (*Looking toward the "big trees."*) Biff, up in Albany I saw a beautiful hammock. I think I'll buy it next trip, and we'll hang it right between those two elms. Wouldn't that be something? Just swingin' there under those branches. Boy, that would be . . .

Young Biff and Young Happy appear from the direction Willy was addressing. Happy carries rags and a pail of water. Biff, wearing a sweater with a block "S," carries a football.

Biff (*pointing in the direction of the car offstage*). How's that, Pop, professional?

Willy. Terrific. Terrific job, boys. Good work, Biff.

Happy. Where's the surprise, Pop?

Willy. In the back seat of the car.

Happy. Boy! (*He runs off.*)

Biff. What is it, Dad? Tell me, what'd you buy?

Willy (*laughing, cuffs him*). Never mind, something I want you to have.

Biff (*turns and starts off*). What is it, Hap?

Happy (*offstage*). It's a punching bag!

Biff. Oh, Pop!

Willy. It's got Gene Tunney's signature on it!

Happy runs onstage with a punching bag.

Biff. Gee, how'd you know we wanted a punching bag?

Willy. Well, it's the finest thing for the timing.

Happy (*lies down on his back and pedals with his feet*). I'm losing weight, you notice, Pop?

Willy (*to Happy*). Jumping rope is good too.

Biff. Did you see the new football I got?

Willy (*examining the ball*). Where'd you get a new ball?

Biff. The coach told me to practice my passing.

Willy. That so? And he gave you the ball, heh?

Biff. Well, I borrowed it from the locker room. (*He laughs confidentially.*)

Willy (*laughing with him at the theft*). I want you to return that.

Happy. I told you he wouldn't like it!

Biff (*angrily*). Well, I'm bringing it back!

Willy (*stopping the incipient argument, to Happy*). Sure, he's gotta practice with a regulation ball, doesn't he? (*To Biff.*) Coach'll probably congratulate you on your initiative!

Biff. Oh, he keeps congratulating my initiative all the time, Pop.

Willy. That's because he likes you. If somebody else took that ball there'd be an uproar. So what's the report, boys, what's the report?

Biff. Where'd you go this time, Dad? Gee we were lonesome for you.

Willy (*pleased, puts an arm around each boy and they come down to the apron*). Lonesome, heh?

Biff. Missed you every minute.

Willy. Don't say? Tell you a secret, boys. Don't breathe it to a soul. Someday I'll have my own business, and I'll never have to leave home any more.

Happy. Like Uncle Charley, heh?

Willy. Bigger than Uncle Charley! Because Charley is not — liked. He's liked, but he's not — well liked.

Biff. Where'd you go this time, Dad?

Willy. Well, I got on the road, and I went north to Providence. Met the Mayor.

Biff. The Mayor of Providence!

Willy. He was sitting in the hotel lobby.

Biff. What'd he say?

Willy. He said, "Morning!" And I said, "You got a fine city here, Mayor." And then he had coffee with me. And then I went to Waterbury. Waterbury is a fine city. Big clock city, the famous Waterbury clock. Sold a nice bill there. And then Boston — Boston is the cradle of the Revolution. A fine city. And a couple of other towns in Mass., and on to Portland and Bangor and straight home!

Biff. Gee, I'd love to go with you sometime, Dad.

Willy. Soon as summer comes.

Happy. Promise?

Willy. You and Hap and I, and I'll show you all the towns. America is full of beautiful towns and fine, upstanding people. And they know me, boys, they know me up and down New England. The finest people. And when I bring you fellas up, there'll be open sesame for all of us, 'cause one thing, boys: I have friends. I can park my car in any street in New England, and the cops protect it like their own. This summer, heh?

Biff and Happy (*together*). Yeah! You bet!

Willy. We'll take our bathing suits.

Happy. We'll carry your bags, Pop!

Willy. Oh, won't that be something! Me comin' into the Boston stores with you boys carryin' my bags. What a sensation!

Biff is prancing around, practicing passing the ball.

Willy. You nervous, Biff, about the game?

Biff. Not if you're gonna be there.

Willy. What do they say about you in school, now that they made you captain?

Happy. There's a crowd of girls behind him everytime the classes change.

Biff (taking Willy's hand). This Saturday, Pop, this Saturday — just for you, I'm going to break through for a touchdown.

Happy. You're supposed to pass.

Biff. I'm takin' one play for Pop. You watch me, Pop, and when I take off my helmet, that means I'm breakin' out. Then you watch me crash through that line!

Willy (kisses Biff). Oh, wait'll I tell this in Boston!

Bernard enters in knickers. He is younger than Biff, earnest and loyal, a worried boy.

Bernard. Biff, where are you? You're supposed to study with me today.

Willy. Hey, looka Bernard. What're you lookin' so anemic about, Bernard?

Bernard. He's gotta study, Uncle Willy. He's got Regents next week.

Happy (tauntingly, spinning Bernard around). Let's box, Bernard!

Bernard. Biff! *(He gets away from Happy.)* Listen, Biff, I heard Mr. Birnbaum say that if you don't start studyin' math he's gonna flunk you, and you won't graduate. I heard him!

Willy. You better study with him, Biff. Go ahead now.

Bernard. I heard him!

Biff. Oh, Pop, you didn't see my sneakers! *(He holds up a foot for Willy to look at.)*

Willy. Hey, that's a beautiful job of printing!

Bernard (wiping his glasses). Just because he printed University of Virginia on his sneakers doesn't mean they've got to graduate him, Uncle Willy!

Willy (angrily). What're you talking about? With scholarships to three universities they're gonna flunk him?

Bernard. But I heard Mr. Birnbaum say . . .

Willy. Don't be a pest, Bernard! *(To his boys.)* What an anemic!

Bernard. Okay, I'm waiting for you in my house, Biff.

Bernard goes off. The Lomans laugh.

Willy. Bernard is not well liked, is he?

Biff. He's liked, but he's not well liked.

Happy. That's right, Pop.

Willy. That's just what I mean. Bernard can get the best marks
in school, y'understand, but when he gets out in the business
world, y'understand, you are going to be five times ahead
of him. That's why I thank Almighty God you're both built
like Adonises. Because the man who makes an appearance
in the business world, the man who creates personal interest,
is the man who gets ahead. Be liked and you will never
want. You take me, for instance. I never have to wait in
line to see a buyer. "Willy Loman is here!" That's all they
have to know, and I go right through.

Biff. Did you knock them dead, Pop?

Willy. Knocked 'em cold in Providence, slaughtered 'em in Boston.

Happy (*on his back, pedaling again*). I'm losing weight, you notice,
Pop?

*Linda enters as of old, a ribbon in her hair, carrying a basket of
washing.*

Linda (*with youthful energy*). Hello, dear!

Willy. Sweetheart!

Linda. How'd the Chevvy run?

Willy. Chevrolet, Linda, is the greatest car ever built. (*To the boys.*)
Since when do you let your mother carry wash up the stairs?

Biff. Grab hold there, boy!

Happy. Where to, Mom?

Linda. Hang them up on the line. And you better go down to
your friends, Biff. The cellar is full of boys. They don't
know what to do with themselves.

Biff. Ah, when Pop comes home they can wait!

Willy (*laughs appreciatively*). You better go down and tell them
what to do, Biff.

Biff. I think I'll have them sweep out the furnace room.

Willy. Good work, Biff.

Biff (*goes through wall-line of kitchen to doorway at back and calls
down*). Fellas! Everybody sweep out the furnace room! I'll
be right down!

Voices. All right! Okay, Biff.

Biff. George and Sam and Frank, come out back! We're hangin' up the wash! Come on, Hap, on the double! (*He and Happy carry out the basket.*)

Linda. The way they obey him!

Willy. Well, that's training, the training. I'm tellin' you, I was sellin' thousands and thousands, but I had to come home.

Linda. Oh, the whole block'll be at that game. Did you sell anything?

Willy. I did five hundred gross in Providence and seven hundred gross in Boston.

Linda. No! Wait a minute, I've got a pencil. (*She pulls pencil and paper out of her apron pocket.*) That makes your commission . . . Two hundred — my God! Two hundred and twelve dollars!

Willy. Well, I didn't figure it yet, but . . .

Linda. How much did you do?

Willy. Well, I — I did — about a hundred and eighty gross in Providence. Well, no — it came to — roughly two hundred gross on the whole trip.

Linda (*without hesitation*). Two hundred gross. That's . . . (*She figures.*)

Willy. The trouble was that three of the stores were half-closed for inventory in Boston. Otherwise I woulda broke records.

Linda. Well, it makes seventy dollars and some pennies. That's very good.

Willy. What do we owe?

Linda. Well, on the first there's sixteen dollars on the refrigerator . . .

Willy. Why sixteen?

Linda. Well, the fan belt broke, so it was a dollar eighty.

Willy. But it's brand new.

Linda. Well, the man said that's the way it is. Till they work themselves in, y'know.

They move through the wall-line into the kitchen.

Willy. I hope we didn't get stuck on that machine.

Linda. They got the biggest ads of any of them!

Willy. I know, it's a fine machine. What else?

Linda. Well, there's nine-sixty for the washing machine. And for the vacuum cleaner there's three and a half due on the fifteenth. Then the roof, you got twenty-one dollars remaining.

Willy. It don't leak, does it?

Linda. No, they did a wonderful job. Then you owe Frank for the carburetor.

Willy. I'm not going to pay that man! That goddam Chevrolet, they ought to prohibit the manufacture of that car!

Linda. Well, you owe him three and a half. And odds and ends, comes to around a hundred and twenty dollars by the fifteenth.

Willy. A hundred and twenty dollars! My God, if business don't pick up I don't know what I'm gonna do!

Linda. Well, next week you'll do better.

Willy. Oh, I'll knock 'em dead next week. I'll go to Hartford. I'm very well liked in Hartford. You know, the trouble is, Linda, people don't seem to take to me.

They move onto the forestage.

Linda. Oh, don't be foolish.

Willy. I know it when I walk in. They seem to laugh at me.

Linda. Why? Why would they laugh at you? Don't talk that way, Willy.

Willy moves to the edge of the stage. Linda goes into the kitchen and starts to darn stockings.

Willy. I don't know the reason for it, but they just pass me by. I'm not noticed.

Linda. But you're doing wonderful, dear. You're making seventy to a hundred dollars a week.

Willy. But I gotta be at it ten, twelve hours a day. Other men — I don't know — they do it easier. I don't know why — I can't stop myself — I talk too much. A man oughta come in with a few words. One thing about Charley. He's a man of few words, and they respect him.

Linda. You don't talk too much, you're just lively.

Willy (*smiling*). Well, I figure, what the hell, life is short, a couple of jokes. (*To himself.*) I joke too much! (*The smile goes.*)

Linda. Why? You're . . .

Willy. I'm fat. I'm very — foolish to look at, Linda. I didn't tell you, but Christmas time I happened to be calling on F. H. Stewarts, and a salesman I know, as I was going in to see the buyer I heard him say something about — walrus. And I — I cracked him right across the face. I won't take that. I simply will not take that. But they do laugh at me. I know that.

Linda. Darling . . .

Willy. I gotta overcome it. I know I gotta overcome it. I'm not dressing to advantage, maybe.

Linda. Willy, darling, you're the handsomest man in the world . . .

Willy. Oh, no, Linda.

Linda. To me you are. (*Slight pause.*) The handsomest.

> *From the darkness is heard the laughter of a woman. Willy doesn't turn to it, but it continues through Linda's lines.*

Linda. And the boys, Willy. Few men are idolized by their children the way you are.

> *Music is heard as behind a scrim, to the left of the house; The Woman, dimly seen, is dressing.*

Willy (*with great feeling*). You're the best there is, Linda, you're a pal, you know that? On the road — on the road I want to grab you sometimes and just kiss the life outa you.

> *The laughter is loud now, and he moves into a brightening area at the left, where The Woman has come from behind the scrim and is standing, putting on her hat, looking into a "mirror" and laughing.*

Willy. 'Cause I get so lonely — especially when business is bad and there's nobody to talk to. I get the feeling that I'll never sell anything again, that I won't make a living for you, or a business, a business for the boys. (*He talks through The Woman's subsiding laughter; The Woman primps at the "mirror."*) There's so much I want to make for . . .

The Woman. Me? You didn't make me, Willy. I picked you.

Willy (*pleased*). You picked me?

The Woman (*who is quite proper-looking, Willy's age*). I did. I've been sitting at that desk watching all the salesmen go by, day in, day out. But you've got such a sense of humor, and we do have such a good time together, don't we?

Willy. Sure, sure. (*He takes her in his arms.*) Why do you have to go now?

The Woman. It's two o'clock . . .

Willy. No, come on in! (*He pulls her.*)

The Woman. . . . . my sisters'll be scandalized. When'll you be back?

Willy. Oh, two weeks about. Will you come up again?

The Woman. Sure thing. You do make me laugh. It's good for me. (*She squeezes his arm, kisses him.*) And I think you're a wonderful man.

Willy. You picked me, heh?

The Woman. Sure. Because you're so sweet. And such a kidder.

Willy. Well, I'll see you next time I'm in Boston.

The Woman. I'll put you right through to the buyers.

Willy (*slapping her bottom*). Right. Well, bottoms up!

The Woman (*slaps him gently and laughs*). You just kill me, Willy. (*He suddenly grabs her and kisses her roughly.*) You kill me.

And thanks for the stockings. I love a lot of stockings. Well, good night.

Willy. Good night. And keep your pores open!

The Woman. Oh, Willy!

The Woman bursts out laughing, and Linda's laughter blends in. The Woman disappears into the dark. Now the area at the kitchen table brightens. Linda is sitting where she was at the kitchen table, but now is mending a pair of her silk stockings.

Linda. You are, Willy. The handsomest man. You've got no reason to feel that . . .

Willy (coming out of The Woman's dimming area and going over to Linda). I'll make it all up to you, Linda, I'll . . .

Linda. There's nothing to make up, dear. You're doing fine, better than . . .

Willy (noticing her mending). What's that?

Linda. Just mending my stockings. They're so expensive . . .

Willy (angrily, taking them from her). I won't have you mending stockings in this house! Now throw them out!

Linda puts the stockings in her pocket.

Bernard (entering on the run). Where is he? If he doesn't study!

Willy (moving to the forestage, with great agitation). You'll give him the answers!

Bernard. I do, but I can't on a Regents! That's a state exam! They're liable to arrest me!

Willy. Where is he? I'll whip him, I'll whip him!

Linda. And he'd better give back that football, Willy, it's not nice.

Willy. Biff! Where is he? Why is he taking everything?

Linda. He's too rough with the girls, Willy. All the mothers are afraid of him!

Willy. I'll whip him!

Bernard. He's driving the car without a license!

The Woman's laugh is heard.

Willy. Shut up!

Linda. All the mothers . . .

Willy. Shut up!

Bernard (backing quietly away and out). Mr. Birnbaum says he's stuck up.

Willy. Get outa here!

Bernard. If he doesn't buckle down he'll flunk math! (*He goes off.*)

Linda. He's right, Willy, you've gotta . . .

Willy (exploding at her). There's nothing the matter with him! You

want him to be a worm like Bernard? He's got spirit, personality . . .

*As he speaks, Linda, almost in tears, exits into the living room.
Willy is alone in the kitchen, wilting and staring. The leaves are
gone. It is night again, and the apartment houses look down from
behind.*

Willy. Loaded with it. Loaded! What is he stealing? He's giving
it back, isn't he? Why is he stealing? What did I tell him? I
never in my life told him anything but decent things.

*Happy in pajamas has come down the stairs; Willy suddenly becomes
aware of Happy's presence.*

Happy. Let's go now, come on.
Willy (*sitting down at the kitchen table*). Huh! Why did she have to
wax the floors herself? Everytime she waxes the floors she
keels over. She knows that!
Happy. Shh! Take it easy. What brought you back tonight?
Willy. I got an awful scare. Nearly hit a kid in Yonkers. God!
Why didn't I go to Alaska with my brother Ben that time!
Ben! That man was a genius, that man was success incarnate!
What a mistake! He begged me to go.
Happy. Well, there's no use in . . .
Willy. You guys! There was a man started with the clothes on his
back and ended up with diamond mines!
Happy. Boy, someday I'd like to know how he did it.
Willy. What's the mystery? The man knew what he wanted and
went out and got it! Walked into a jungle, and comes out,
the age of twenty-one, and he's rich! The world is an oyster,
but you don't crack it open on a mattress!
Happy. Pop, I told you I'm gonna retire you for life.
Willy. You'll retire me for life on seventy goddam dollars a week?
And your women and your car and your apartment, and
you'll retire me for life! Christ's sake, I couldn't get past
Yonkers today! Where are you guys, where are you? The
woods are burning! I can't drive a car!

*Charley has appeared in the doorway. He is a large man, slow
of speech, laconic, immovable. In all he says, despite what he says,
there is pity, and, now, trepidation. He has a robe over pajamas,
slippers on his feet. He enters the kitchen.*

Charley. Everything all right?
Happy. Yeah, Charley, everything's . . .
Willy. What's the matter?

Charley. I heard some noise. I thought something happened. Can't
we do something about the walls? You sneeze in here, and
in my house hats blow off.

Happy. Let's go to bed, Dad. Come on.

Charley signals to Happy to go.

Willy. You go ahead, I'm not tired at the moment.

Happy (to Willy). Take it easy, huh? (*He exits.*)

Willy. What're you doin' up?

Charley (sitting down at the kitchen table opposite Willy). Couldn't
sleep good. I had a heartburn.

Willy. Well, you don't know how to eat.

Charley. I eat with my mouth.

Willy. No, you're ignorant. You gotta know about vitamins and
things like that.

Charley. Come on, let's shoot. Tire you out a little.

Willy (hesitantly). All right. You got cards?

Charley (taking a deck from his pocket). Yeah, I got them. Someplace.
What is it with those vitamins?

Willy (dealing). They build up your bones. Chemistry.

Charley. Yeah, but there's no bones in a heartburn.

Willy. What are you talkin' about? Do you know the first thing
about it?

Charley. Don't get insulted.

Willy. Don't talk about something you don't know anything about.

They are playing. Pause.

Charley. What're you doin' home?

Willy. A little trouble with the car.

Charley. Oh. (*Pause.*) I'd like to take a trip to California.

Willy. Don't say.

Charley. You want a job?

Willy. I got a job, I told you that. (*After a slight pause.*) What the
hell are you offering me a job for?

Charley. Don't get insulted.

Willy. Don't insult me.

Charley. I don't see no sense in it. You don't have to go on this
way.

Willy. I got a good job. (*Slight pause.*) What do you keep comin'
in here for?

Charley. You want me to go?

Willy (after a pause, withering). I can't understand it. He's going
back to Texas again. What the hell is that?

Charley. Let him go.

Willy. I got nothin' to give him, Charley, I'm clean, I'm clean.

Charley. He won't starve. None a them starve. Forget about him.

Willy. Then what have I got to remember?

Charley. You take it too hard. To hell with it. When a deposit bottle is broken you don't get your nickel back.

Willy. That's easy enough for you to say.

Charley. That ain't easy for me to say.

Willy. Did you see the ceiling I put up in the living room?

Charley. Yeah, that's a piece of work. To put up a ceiling is a mystery to me. How do you do it?

Willy. What's the difference?

Charley. Well, talk about it.

Willy. You gonna put up a ceiling?

Charley. How could I put up a ceiling?

Willy. Then what the hell are you bothering me for?

Charley. You're insulted again.

Willy. A man who can't handle tools is not a man. You're disgusting.

Charley. Don't call me disgusting, Willy.

> *Uncle Ben, carrying a valise and an umbrella, enters the forestage from around the right corner of the house. He is a stolid man, in his sixties, with a mustache and an authoritative air. He is utterly certain of his destiny, and there is an aura of far places about him. He enters exactly as Willy speaks.*

Willy. I'm getting awfully tired, Ben.

> *Ben's music is heard. Ben looks around at everything.*

Charley. Good, keep playing; you'll sleep better. Did you call me Ben?

> *Ben looks at his watch.*

Willy. That's funny. For a second there you reminded me of my brother Ben.

Ben. I only have a few minutes. (*He strolls, inspecting the place. Willy and Charley continue playing.*)

Charley. You never heard from him again, heh? Since that time?

Willy. Didn't Linda tell you? Couple of weeks ago we got a letter from his wife in Africa. He died.

Charley. That so.

Ben (*chuckling*). So this is Brooklyn, eh?

Charley. Maybe you're in for some of his money.

Willy. Naa, he had seven sons. There's just one opportunity I had with that man . . .

Ben. I must make a train, William. There are several properties
I'm looking at in Alaska.

Willy. Sure, sure! If I'd gone with him to Alaska that time, everything would've been totally different.

Charley. Go on, you'd froze to death up there.

Willy. What're you talking about?

Ben. Opportunity is tremendous in Alaska, William. Surprised
you're not up there.

Willy. Sure, tremendous.

Charley. Heh?

Willy. There was the only man I ever met who knew the answers.

Charley. Who?

Ben. How are you all?

Willy (*taking a pot, smiling*). Fine, fine.

Charley. Pretty sharp tonight.

Ben. Is Mother living with you?

Willy. No, she died a long time ago.

Charley. Who?

Ben. That's too bad. Fine specimen of a lady, Mother.

Willy (*to Charley*). Heh?

Ben. I'd hoped to see the old girl.

Charley. Who died?

Ben. Heard anything from Father, have you?

Willy (*unnerved*). What do you mean, who died?

Charley (*taking a pot*). What're you talkin' about?

Ben (*looking at his watch*). William, it's half-past eight!

Willy (*as though to dispel his confusion he angrily stops Charley's
hand*). That's my build!

Charley. I put the ace . . .

Willy. If you don't know how to play the game I'm not gonna
throw my money away on you!

Charley (*rising*). It was my ace, for God's sake!

Willy. I'm through, I'm through!

Ben. When did Mother die?

Willy. Long ago. Since the beginning you never knew how to
play cards.

Charley (*picks up the cards and goes to the door*). All right! Next time
I'll bring a deck with five aces.

Willy. I don't play that kind of game!

Charley (*turning to him*). You ought to be ashamed of yourself!

Willy. Yeah?

Charley. Yeah! (*He goes out.*)

Willy (*slamming the door after him*). Ignoramus!

Ben (as Willy comes toward him through the wall-line of the kitchen). So you're William.

Willy (shaking Ben's hand). Ben! I've been waiting for you so long! What's the answer? How did you do it?

Ben. Oh, there's a story in that.

Linda enters the forestage, as of old, carrying the wash basket.

Linda. Is this Ben?

Ben (gallantly). How do you do, my dear.

Linda. Where've you been all these years? Willy's always wondered why you . . .

Willy (pulling Ben away from her impatiently). Where is Dad? Didn't you follow him? How did you get started?

Ben. Well, I don't know how much you remember.

Willy. Well, I was just a baby, of course, only three or four years old . . .

Ben. Three years and eleven months.

Willy. What a memory, Ben!

Ben. I have many enterprises, William, and I have never kept books.

Willy. I remember I was sitting under the wagon in — was it Nebraska?

Ben. It was South Dakota, and I gave you a bunch of wild flowers.

Willy. I remember you walking away down some open road.

Ben (laughing). I was going to find Father in Alaska.

Willy. Where is he?

Ben. At that age I had a very faulty view of geography, William. I discovered after a few days that I was heading due south, so instead of Alaska, I ended up in Africa.

Linda. Africa!

Willy. The Gold Coast!

Ben. Principally diamond mines.

Linda. Diamond mines!

Ben. Yes, my dear. But I've only a few minutes . . .

Willy. No! Boys! Boys! (*Young Biff and Happy appear.*) Listen to this. This is your Uncle Ben, a great man! Tell my boys, Ben!

Ben. Why, boys, when I was seventeen I walked into the jungle, and when I was twenty-one I walked out. (*He laughs.*) And by God I was rich.

Willy (to the boys). You see what I been talking about? The greatest things can happen!

Ben (glancing at his watch). I have an appointment in Ketchikan Tuesday week.

Willy. No, Ben! Please tell about Dad. I want my boys to hear. I want them to know the kind of stock they spring from. All I remember is a man with a big beard, and I was in Mamma's lap, sitting around a fire, and some kind of high music.

Ben. His flute. He played the flute.

Willy. Sure, the flute, that's right!

New music is heard, a high, rollicking tune.

Ben. Father was a very great and a very wild-hearted man. We would start in Boston, and he'd toss the whole family into the wagon, and then he'd drive the team right across the country; through Ohio, and Indiana, Michigan, Illinois, and all the Western states. And we'd stop in the towns and sell the flutes that he'd made on the way. Great inventor, Father. With one gadget he made more in a week than a man like you could make in a lifetime.

Willy. That's just the way I'm bringing them up, Ben — rugged, well liked, all-around.

Ben. Yeah? (*To Biff.*) Hit that, boy — hard as you can. (*He pounds his stomach.*)

Biff. Oh, no, sir!

Ben (*taking boxing stance*). Come on, get to me! (*He laughs.*)

Willy. Go to it. Biff! Go ahead, show him!

Biff. Okay! (*He cocks his fists and starts in.*)

Linda (*to Willy*). Why must he fight, dear?

Ben (*sparring with Biff*). Good boy! Good boy!

Willy. How's that, Ben, heh?

Happy. Give him the left, Biff!

Linda. Why are you fighting?

Ben. Good boy! (*Suddenly comes in, trips Biff, and stands over him, the point of his umbrella poised over Biff's eye.*)

Linda. Look out, Biff!

Biff. Gee!

Ben (*patting Biff's knee*). Never fight fair with a stranger, boy. You'll never get out of the jungle that way. (*Taking Linda's hand and bowing.*) It was an honor and a pleasure to meet you, Linda.

Linda (*withdrawing her hand coldly, frightened*). Have a nice — trip.

Ben (*to Willy*). And good luck with your — what do you do?

Willy. Selling.

Ben. Yes. Well . . . (*He raises his hand in farewell to all.*)

Willy. No, Ben, I don't want you to think . . . (*He takes Ben's arm to show him.*) It's Brooklyn, I know, but we hunt too.

Ben. Really, now.

Willy. Oh, sure, there's snakes and rabbits and — that's why I moved out here. Why, Biff can fell any one of these trees in no time! Boys! Go right over to where they're building the apartment house and get some sand. We're gonna rebuild the entire front stoop right now! Watch this, Ben!

Biff. Yes, sir! On the double, Hap!

Happy (as he and Biff run off). I lost weight, Pop, you notice?

Charley enters in knickers, even before the boys are gone.

Charley. Listen, if they steal any more from that building the watchman'll put the cops on them!

Linda (to Willy). Don't let Biff . . .

Ben laughs lustily.

Willy. You shoulda seen the lumber they brought home last week. At least a dozen six-by-tens worth all kinds a money.

Charley. Listen, if that watchman . . .

Willy. I gave them hell, understand. But I got a couple of fearless characters there.

Charley. Willy, the jails are full of fearless characters.

Ben (clapping Willy on the back, with a laugh at Charley). And the stock exchange, friend!

Willy (joining in Ben's laughter). Where are the rest of your pants?

Charley. My wife bought them.

Willy. Now all you need is a golf club and you can go upstairs and go to sleep. (*To Ben.*) Great athlete! Between him and his son Bernard they can't hammer a nail!

Bernard (rushing in). The watchman's chasing Biff!

Willy (angrily). Shut up! He's not stealing anything!

Linda (alarmed, hurrying off left). Where is he? Biff, dear! (*She exits.*)

Willy (moving toward the left, away from Ben). There's nothing wrong. What's the matter with you?

Ben. Nervy boy. Good!

Willy (laughing). Oh, nerves of iron, that Biff!

Charley. Don't know what it is. My New England man comes back and he's bleedin', they murdered him up there.

Willy. It's contacts, Charley, I got important contacts!

Charley (sarcastically). Glad to hear it, Willy. Come in later, we'll shoot a little casino. I'll take some of your Portland money. (*He laughs at Willy and exits.*)

Willy (turning to Ben). Business is bad, it's murderous. But not for me, of course.

Ben. I'll stop by on my way back to Africa.

Willy (*longingly*). Can't you stay a few days? You're just what I
need, Ben, because I — I have a fine position here, but I —
well, Dad left when I was such a baby and I never had a
chance to talk to him and I still feel — kind of temporary
about myself.

Ben. I'll be late for my train.

They are at opposite ends of the stage.

Willy. Ben, my boys — can't we talk? They'd go into the jaws
of hell for me, see, but I . . .

Ben. William, you're being first-rate with your boys. Outstanding,
manly chaps!

Willy (*hanging on to his words*). Oh, Ben, that's good to hear! Because sometimes I'm afraid that I'm not teaching them the
right kind of — Ben, how should I teach them?

Ben (*giving great weight to each word, and with a certain vicious audacity*).
William, when I walked into the jungle, I was seventeen.
When I walked out I was twenty-one. And, by God, I was
rich! (*He goes off into darkness around the right corner of the house.*)

Willy . . . . was rich! That's just the spirit I want to imbue them
with! To walk into a jungle! I was right! I was right! I was
right!

Ben is gone, but Willy is still speaking to him as Linda, in
nightgown and robe, enters the kitchen, glances around for Willy,
then goes to the door of the house, looks out and sees him. Comes
down to his left. He looks at her.

Linda. Willy, dear? Willy?

Willy. I was right!

Linda. Did you have some cheese? (*He can't answer.*) It's very late,
darling. Come to bed, heh?

Willy (*looking straight up*). Gotta break your neck to see a star in
this yard.

Linda. You coming in?

Willy. Whatever happened to that diamond watch fob? Remember?
When Ben came from Africa that time? Didn't he give me
a watch fob with a diamond in it?

Linda. You pawned it, dear. Twelve, thirteen years ago. For Biff's
radio correspondence course.

Willy. Gee, that was a beautiful thing. I'll take a walk.

Linda. But you're in your slippers.

Willy (*starting to go around the house at the left*). I was right! I was!
(*Half to Linda, as he goes, shaking his head.*) What a man! There
was a man worth talking to. I was right!

Linda (calling after Willy). But in your slippers, Willy!

> *Willy is almost gone when Biff, in his pajamas, comes down the stairs and enters the kitchen.*

Biff. What is he doing out there?

Linda. Sh!

Biff. God Almighty, Mom, how long has he been doing this?

Linda. Don't, he'll hear you.

Biff. What the hell is the matter with him?

Linda. It'll pass by morning.

Biff. Shouldn't we do anything?

Linda. Oh, my dear, you should do a lot of things, but there's nothing to do, so go to sleep.

> *Happy comes down the stair and sits on the steps.*

Happy. I never heard him so loud, Mom.

Linda. Well, come around more often; you'll hear him. (*She sits down at the table and mends the lining of Willy's jacket.*)

Biff. Why didn't you ever write me about this, Mom?

Linda. How would I write to you? For over three months you had no address.

Biff. I was on the move. But you know I thought of you all the time. You know that, don't you, pal?

Linda. I know, dear, I know. But he likes to have a letter. Just to know that there's still a possibility for better things.

Biff. He's not like this all the time, is he?

Linda. It's when you come home he's always the worst.

Biff. When I come home?

Linda. When you write you're coming, he's all smiles, and talks about the future, and — he's just wonderful. And then the closer you seem to come, the more shaky he gets, and then, by the time you get here, he's arguing, and he seems angry at you. I think it's just that maybe he can't bring himself to — to open up to you. Why are you so hateful to each other? Why is that?

Biff (evasively). I'm not hateful, Mom.

Linda. But you no sooner come in the door than you're fighting!

Biff. I don't know why. I mean to change. I'm tryin', Mom, you understand?

Linda. Are you home to stay now?

Biff. I don't know. I want to look around, see what's doin'.

Linda. Biff, you can't look around all your life, can you?

Biff. I just can't take hold, Mom. I can't take hold of some kind of a life.

Linda. Biff, a man is not a bird, to come and go with the spring time.

Biff. Your hair . . . (*He touches her hair.*) Your hair got so gray.

Linda. Oh, it's been gray since you were in high school. I just stopped dyeing it, that's all.

Biff. Dye it again, will ya? I don't want my pal looking old. (*He smiles.*)

Linda. You're such a boy! You think you can go away for a year and . . . You've got to get it into your head now that one day you'll knock on this door and there'll be strange people here . . .

Biff. What are you talking about? You're not even sixty, Mom.

Linda. But what about your father?

Biff (*lamely*). Well, I meant him too.

Happy. He admires Pop.

Linda. Biff, dear, if you don't have any feeling for him, then you can't have any feeling for me.

Biff. Sure I can, Mom.

Linda. No. You can't just come to see me, because I love him. (*With a threat, but only a threat, of tears.*) He's the dearest man in the world to me, and I won't have anyone making him feel unwanted and low and blue. You've got to make up your mind now, darling, there's no leeway any more. Either he's your father and you pay him that respect, or else you're not to come here. I know he's not easy to get along with — nobody knows that better than me — but . . .

Willy (*from the left, with a laugh*). Hey, hey, Biffo!

Biff (*starting to go out after Willy*). What the hell is the matter with him? (*Happy stops him.*)

Linda. Don't — don't go near him!

Biff. Stop making excuses for him! He always, always wiped the floor with you. Never had an ounce of respect for you.

Happy. He's always had respect for . . .

Biff. What the hell do you know about it?

Happy (*surlily*). Just don't call him crazy!

Biff. He's got no character — Charley wouldn't do this. Not in his own house — spewing out that vomit from his mind.

Happy. Charley never had to cope with what he's got to.

Biff. People are worse off than Willy Loman. Believe me, I've seen them!

Linda. Then make Charley your father, Biff. You can't do that, can you? I don't say he's a great man. Willy Loman never made a lot of money. His name was never in the paper. He's not the finest character that ever lived. But he's a human being, and a terrible thing is happening to him. So attention must be paid. He's not to be allowed to fall into his grave like an old dog. Attention, attention must be finally paid to such a person. You called him crazy . . .

Biff. I didn't mean . . .

Linda. No, a lot of people think he's lost his — balance. But you don't have to be very smart to know what his trouble is. The man is exhausted.

Happy. Sure!

Linda. A small man can be just as exhausted as a great man. He works for a company thirty-six years this March, opens up unheard-of territories to their trademark, and now in his old age they take his salary away.

Happy (*indignantly*). I didn't know that, Mom.

Linda. You never asked, my dear! Now that you get your spending money someplace else you don't trouble your mind with him.

Happy. But I gave you money last . . .

Linda. Christmas time, fifty dollars! To fix the hot water it cost ninety-seven fifty! For five weeks he's been on straight commission, like a beginner, an unknown!

Biff. Those ungrateful bastards!

Linda. Are they any worse than his sons? When he brought them business, when he was young, they were glad to see him. But now his old friends, the old buyers that loved him so and always found some order to hand him in a pinch — they're all dead, retired. He used to be able to make six, seven calls a day in Boston. Now he takes his valises out of the car and puts them back and takes them out again and he's exhausted. Instead of walking he talks now. He drives seven hundred miles, and when he gets there no one knows him any more, no one welcomes him. And what goes through a man's mind, driving seven hundred miles home without having earned a cent? Why shouldn't he talk to himself? Why? When he has to go to Charley and borrow fifty dollars a week and pretend to me that it's his pay? How long can that go on? How long? You see what I'm sitting here and waiting for? And you tell me he has no character? The man who never worked a day but for your benefit? When does he get the medal for that? Is this his reward — to turn around at the age of sixty-three and find his sons, who he loved better than his life, one a philandering bum . . .

Happy. Mom!

Linda. That's all you are, my baby! (*To Biff.*) And you! What happened to the love you had for him? You were such pals! How you used to talk to him on the phone every night! How lonely he was till he could come home to you!

Biff. All right, Mom. I'll live here in my room, and I'll get a job. I'll keep away from him, that's all.

Linda. No, Biff. You can't stay here and fight all the time.

Biff. He threw me out of this house, remember that.

Linda. Why did he do that? I never knew why.

Biff. Because I know he's a fake and he doesn't like anybody around who knows!

Linda. Why a fake? In what way? What do you mean?

Biff. Just don't lay it all at my feet. It's between me and him — that's all I have to say. I'll chip in from now on. He'll settle for half my paycheck. He'll be all right. I'm going to bed. (*He starts for the stairs.*)

Linda. He won't be all right.

Biff (*turning on the stairs, furiously*). I hate this city and I'll stay here. Now what do you want?

Linda. He's dying, Biff.

Happy turns quickly to her, shocked.

Biff (*after a pause*). Why is he dying?

Linda. He's been trying to kill himself.

Biff (*with great horror*). How?

Linda. I live from day to day.

Biff. What're you talking about?

Linda. Remember I wrote you that he smashed up the car again? In February?

Biff. Well?

Linda. The insurance inspector came. He said that they have evidence. That all these accidents in the last year — weren't — weren't — accidents.

Happy. How can they tell that? That's a lie.

⎧ *Linda.* It seems there's a woman . . . (*She takes a breath as:*)
⎨ *Biff* (*sharply but contained*). What woman?
⎩ *Linda* (*simultaneously*). . . . and this woman . . .

Linda. What?

Biff. Nothing. Go ahead.

Linda. What did you say?

Biff. Nothing. I just said what woman?

Happy. What about her?

Linda. Well, it seems she was walking down the road and saw his car. She says that he wasn't driving fast at all, and that he didn't skid. She says he came to that little bridge, and then deliberately smashed into the railing, and it was only the shallowness of the water that saved him.

Biff. Oh, no, he probably just fell asleep again.

Linda. I don't think he fell asleep.

Biff. Why not?

Linda. Last month . . . (*With great difficulty.*) Oh, boys, it's so hard to say a thing like this! He's just a big stupid man to you, but I tell you there's more good in him than in many other people. (*She chokes, wipes her eyes.*) I was looking for a fuse. The lights blew out, and I went down the cellar. And behind the fuse box — it happened to fall out — was a length of rubber pipe — just short.

Happy. No kidding!

Linda. There's a little attachment on the end of it. I knew right away. And sure enough, on the bottom of the water heater there's a new little nipple on the gas pipe.

Happy (*angrily*). That — jerk.

Biff. Did you have it taken off?

Linda. I'm — I'm ashamed to. How can I mention it to him? Every day I go down and take away that little rubber pipe. But, when he comes home, I put it back where it was. How can I insult him that way? I don't know what to do. I live from day to day, boys. I tell you, I know every thought in his mind. It sounds so old-fashioned and silly, but I tell you he put his whole life into you and you've turned your backs on him. (*She is bent over in the chair, weeping, her face in her hands.*) Biff, I swear to God! Biff, his life is in your hands!

Happy (*to Biff*). How do you like that damned fool!

Biff (*kissing her*). All right, pal, all right. It's all settled now. I've been remiss. I know that, Mom. But now I'll stay, and I swear to you, I'll apply myself. (*Kneeling in front of her, in a fever of self-reproach.*) It's just — you see, Mom, I don't fit in business. Not that I won't try. I'll try, and I'll make good.

Happy. Sure you will. The trouble with you in business was you never tried to please people.

Biff. I know, I . . .

Happy. Like when you worked for Harrison's. Bob Harrison said you were tops, and then you go and do some damn fool thing like whistling whole songs in the elevator like a comedian.

Biff (*against Happy*). So what? I like to whistle sometimes.

Happy. You don't raise a guy to a responsible job who whistles in the elevator!

Linda. Well, don't argue about it now.

Happy. Like when you'd go off and swim in the middle of the day instead of taking the line around.

Biff (*his resentment rising*). Well, don't you run off? You take off sometimes, don't you? On a nice summer day?

Happy. Yeah, but I cover myself!

Linda. Boys!

Happy. If I'm going to take a fade the boss can call any number where I'm supposed to be and they'll swear to him that I just left. I'll tell you something that I hate to say, Biff, but in the business world some of them think you're crazy.

Biff (*angered*). Screw the business world!

Happy. All right, screw it! Great, but cover yourself!

Linda. Hap, Hap!

Biff. I don't care what they think! They've laughed at Dad for years, and you know why? Because we don't belong in this nuthouse of a city! We should be mixing cement on some open plain or — or carpenters. A carpenter is allowed to whistle!

Willy walks in from the entrance of the house, at left.

Willy. Even your grandfather was better than a carpenter. (*Pause. They watch him.*) You never grew up. Bernard does not whistle in the elevator, I assure you.

Biff (*as though to laugh Willy out of it*). Yeah, but you do, Pop.

Willy. I never in my life whistled in an elevator! And who in the business world thinks I'm crazy?

Biff. I didn't mean it like that, Pop. Now don't make a whole thing out of it, will ya?

Willy. Go back to the West! Be a carpenter, a cowboy, enjoy your-self!

Linda. Willy, he was just saying . . .

Willy. I heard what he said!

Happy (*trying to quiet Willy*). Hey, Pop, come on now . . .

Willy (*continuing over Happy's line*). They laugh at me, heh? Go to Filene's, go to the Hub, go to Slattery's, Boston. Call out the name Willy Loman and see what happens! Big shot!

Biff. All right, Pop.

Willy. Big!

Biff. All right!

Willy. Why do you always insult me?

Biff. I didn't say a word. (*To Linda.*) Did I say a word?

Linda. He didn't say anything, Willy.

Willy (*going to the doorway of the living room*). All right, good night, good night.

Linda. Willy, dear, he just decided . . .

Willy (to Biff). If you get tired hanging around tomorrow, paint the ceiling I put up in the living room.

Biff. I'm leaving early tomorrow.

Happy. He's going to see Bill Oliver, Pop.

Willy (interestedly). Oliver? For what?

Biff (with reserve, but trying, trying). He always said he'd stake me. I'd like to go into business, so maybe I can take him up on it.

Linda. Isn't that wonderful?

Willy. Don't interrupt. What's wonderful about it? There's fifty men in the City of New York who'd stake him. *(To Biff.)* Sporting goods?

Biff. I guess so. I know something about it and . . .

Willy. He knows something about it! You know sporting goods better than Spalding, for God's sake! How much is he giving you?

Biff. I don't know, I didn't even see him yet, but . . .

Willy. Then what're you talkin' about?

Biff (getting angry). Well, all I said was I'm gonna see him, that's all!

Willy (turning away). Ah, you're counting your chickens again.

Biff (starting left for the stairs). Oh, Jesus, I'm going to sleep!

Willy (calling after him). Don't curse in this house!

Biff (turning). Since when did you get so clean?

Happy (trying to stop them). Wait a . . .

Willy. Don't use that language to me! I won't have it!

Happy (grabbing Biff, shouts). Wait a minute! I got an idea. I got a feasible idea. Come here, Biff, let's talk this over now, let's talk some sense here. When I was down in Florida last time, I thought of a great idea to sell sporting goods. It just came back to me. You and I, Biff — we have a line, the Loman Line. We train a couple of weeks, and put on a couple of exhibitions, see?

Willy. That's an idea!

Happy. Wait! We form two basketball teams, see? Two water-polo teams. We play each other. It's a million dollars' worth of publicity. Two brothers, see? The Loman Brothers. Displays in the Royal Palms — all the hotels. And banners over the ring and the basketball court: "Loman Brothers." Baby, we could sell sporting goods!

Willy. That is a one-million-dollar idea!

Linda. Marvelous!

Biff. I'm in great shape as far as that's concerned.

Happy. And the beauty of it is, Biff, it wouldn't be like a business. We'd be out playin' ball again.

Biff (enthused). Yeah, that's . . .

Willy. Million-dollar . . .

Happy. And you wouldn't get fed up with it, Biff. It'd be the family again. There'd be the old honor, and comradeship, and if you wanted to go off for a swim or somethin' — well, you'd do it! Without some smart cooky gettin' up ahead of you!

Willy. Lick the world! You guys together could absolutely lick the civilized world.

Biff. I'll see Oliver tomorrow. Hap, if we could work that out . . .

Linda. Maybe things are beginning to . . .

Willy (wildly enthused, to Linda). Stop interrupting! *(To Biff.)* But don't wear sport jacket and slacks when you see Oliver.

Biff. No, I'll . . .

Willy. A business suit, and talk as little as possible, and don't crack any jokes.

Biff. He did like me. Always liked me.

Linda. He loved you!

Willy (to Linda). Will you stop! *(To Biff.)* Walk in very serious. You are not applying for a boy's job. Money is to pass. Be quiet, fine, and serious. Everybody likes a kidder, but nobody lends him money.

Happy. I'll try to get some myself, Biff. I'm sure I can.

Willy. I see great things for you kids, I think your troubles are over. But remember, start big and you'll end big. Ask for fifteen. How much you gonna ask for?

Biff. Gee, I don't know . . .

Willy. And don't say "Gee." "Gee" is a boy's word. A man walking in for fifteen thousand dollars does not say "Gee!"

Biff. Ten, I think, would be top though.

Willy. Don't be so modest. You always started too low. Walk in with a big laugh. Don't look worried. Start off with a couple of your good stories to lighten things up. It's not what you say, it's how you say it — because personality always wins the day.

Linda. Oliver always thought the highest of him . . .

Willy. Will you let me talk?

Biff. Don't yell at her, Pop, will ya?

Willy (angrily). I was talking, wasn't I?

Biff. I don't like you yelling at her all the time, and I'm tellin' you, that's all.

Willy. What're you, takin' over this house?

Linda. Willy . . .

Willy (turning to her). Don't take his side all the time, goddammit!

Biff (furiously). Stop yelling at her!

Willy (suddenly pulling on his cheek, beaten down, guilt ridden). Give my best to Bill Oliver — he may remember me. (*He exits through the living room doorway.*)

Linda (her voice subdued). What'd you have to start that for? (*Biff turns away.*) You see how sweet he was as soon as you talked hopefully? (*She goes over to Biff.*) Come up and say good night to him. Don't let him go to bed that way.

Happy. Come on, Biff, let's buck him up.

Linda. Please, dear. Just say good night. It takes so little to make him happy. Come. (*She goes through the living room doorway, calling upstairs from within the living room.*) Your pajamas are hanging in the bathroom, Willy!

Happy (looking toward where Linda went out). What a woman! They broke the mold when they made her. You know that, Biff?

Biff. He's off salary. My God, working on commission!

Happy. Well, let's face it: he's no hot-shot selling man. Except that sometimes, you have to admit, he's a sweet personality.

Biff (deciding). Lend me ten bucks, will ya? I want to buy some new ties.

Happy. I'll take you to a place I know. Beautiful stuff. Wear one of my striped shirts tomorrow.

Biff. She got gray. Mom got awful old. Gee, I'm gonna go in to Oliver tomorrow and knock him for a . . .

Happy. Come on up. Tell that to Dad. Let's give him a whirl. Come on.

Biff (steamed up). You know, with ten thousand bucks, boy!

Happy (as they go into the living room). That's the talk, Biff, that's the first time I've heard the old confidence out of you! (*From within the living room, fading off*) You're gonna live with me, kid, and any babe you want just say the word . . . (*The last lines are hardly heard. They are mounting the stairs to their parents' bedroom.*)

Linda (entering her bedroom and addressing Willy, who is in the bathroom. She is straightening the bed for him). Can you do anything about the shower? It drips.

Willy (from the bathroom). All of a sudden everything falls to pieces. Goddam plumbing, oughta be sued, those people. I hardly finished putting it in and the thing . . . (*His words rumble off.*)

Linda. I'm just wondering if Oliver will remember him. You think he might?

Willy (coming out of the bathroom in his pajamas). Remember him?

What's the matter with you, you crazy? If he'd've stayed with Oliver he'd be on top by now! Wait'll Oliver gets a look at him. You don't know the average caliber any more. The average young man today — (*he is getting into bed*) — is got a caliber of zero. Greatest thing in the world for him was to bum around.

Biff and Happy enter the bedroom. Slight pause.

Willy (*stops short, looking at Biff*). Glad to hear it, boy.

Happy. He wanted to say good night to you, sport.

Willy (*to Biff*). Yeah. Knock him dead, boy. What'd you want to tell me?

Biff. Just take it easy, Pop. Good night. (*He turns to go.*)

Willy (*unable to resist*). And if anything falls off the desk while you're talking to him — like a package or something — don't you pick it up. They have office boys for that.

Linda. I'll make a big breakfast . . .

Willy. Will you let me finish? (*To Biff.*) Tell him you were in the business in the West. Not farm work.

Biff. All right, Dad.

Linda. I think everything . . .

Willy (*going right through her speech*). And don't undersell yourself. No less than fifteen thousand dollars.

Biff (*unable to bear him*). Okay. Good night, Mom. (*He starts moving.*)

Willy. Because you got a greatness in you, Biff, remember that. You got all kinds of greatness . . . (*He lies back, exhausted. Biff walks out.*)

Linda (*calling after Biff*). Sleep well, darling!

Happy. I'm gonna get married, Mom. I wanted to tell you.

Linda. Go to sleep, dear.

Happy (*going*). I just wanted to tell you.

Willy. Keep up the good work. (*Happy exits.*) God . . . remember that Ebbets Field game? The championship of the city?

Linda. Just rest. Should I sing to you?

Willy. Yeah. Sing to me. (*Linda hums a soft lullaby.*) When that team came out — he was the tallest, remember?

Linda. Oh, yes. And in gold.

Biff enters the darkened kitchen, takes a cigarette, and leaves the house. He comes downstage into a golden pool of light. He smokes, staring at the night.

Willy. Like a young god. Hercules — something like that. And the sun, the sun all around him. Remember how he waved to me? Right up from the field, with the representatives of three colleges standing by? And the buyers I brought, and the cheers when he came out — Loman, Loman, Loman! God Almighty, he'll be great yet. A star like that, magnificent, can never really fade away!

The light on Willy is fading. The gas heater begins to glow through the kitchen wall, near the stairs, a blue flame beneath red coils.

Linda (*timidly*). Willy dear, what has he got against you?
Willy. I'm so tired. Don't talk any more.

Biff slowly returns to the kitchen. He stops, stares toward the heater.

Linda. Will you ask Howard to let you work in New York?
Willy. First thing in the morning. Everything'll be all right.

Biff reaches behind the heater and draws out a length of rubber tubing. He is horrified and turns his head toward Willy's room, still dimly lit, from which the strains of Linda's desperate but monotonous humming rise.

Willy (*staring through the window into the moonlight*). Gee, look at the moon moving between the buildings!

Biff wraps the tubing around his hand and quickly goes up the stairs.

ACT II

Scene: *Music is heard, gay and bright. The curtain rises as the music fades away. Willy, in shirt sleeves, is sitting at the kitchen table, sipping coffee, his hat in his lap. Linda is filling his cup when she can.*

Willy. Wonderful coffee. Meal in itself.
Linda. Can I make you some eggs?
Willy. No. Take a breath.
Linda. You look so rested, dear.
Willy. I slept like a dead one. First time in months. Imagine, sleeping till ten on a Tuesday morning. Boys left nice and early, heh?
Linda. They were out of here by eight o'clock.
Willy. Good work!
Linda. It was so thrilling to see them leaving together. I can't get over the shaving lotion in this house!
Willy (*smiling*). Mmm . . .
Linda. Biff was very changed this morning. His whole attitude

seemed to be hopeful. He couldn't wait to get downtown to see Oliver.

Willy. He's heading for a change. There's no question, there simply are certain men that take longer to get — solidified. How did he dress?

Linda. His blue suit. He's so handsome in that suit. He could be a — anything in that suit!

Willy gets up from the table. Linda holds his jacket for him.

Willy. There's no question, no question at all. Gee, on the way home tonight I'd like to buy some seeds.

Linda (laughing). That'd be wonderful. But not enough sun gets back there. Nothing'll grow any more.

Willy. You wait, kid, before it's all over we're gonna get a little place out in the country, and I'll raise some vegetables, a couple of chickens . . .

Linda. You'll do it yet, dear.

Willy walks out of his jacket. Linda follows him.

Willy. And they'll get married, and come for a weekend. I'd build a little guest house. 'Cause I got so many fine tools, all I'd need would be a little lumber and some peace of mind.

Linda (joyfully). I sewed the lining . . .

Willy. I could build two guest houses, so they'd both come. Did he decide how much he's going to ask Oliver for?

Linda (getting him into the jacket). He didn't mention it, but I imagine ten or fifteen thousand. You going to talk to Howard today?

Willy. Yeah. I'll put it to him straight and simple. He'll just have to take me off the road.

Linda. And Willy, don't forget to ask for a little advance, because we've got the insurance premium. It's the grace period now.

Willy. That's a hundred . . . ?

Linda. A hundred and eight, sixty-eight. Because we're a little short again.

Willy. Why are we short?

Linda. Well, you had the motor job on the car . . .

Willy. That goddam Studebaker!

Linda. And you got one more payment on the refrigerator . . .

Willy. But it just broke again!

Linda. Well, it's old, dear.

Willy. I told you we should've bought a well-advertised machine. Charley bought a General Electric and it's twenty years old and it's still good, that son-of-a-bitch.

Linda. But, Willy . . .

Willy. Whoever heard of a Hastings refrigerator? Once in my life I would like to own something outright before it's broken! I'm always in a race with the junkyard! I just finished paying for the car and it's on its last legs. The refrigerator consumes belts like a goddamn maniac. They time those things. They time them so when you finally paid for them, they're used up.

Linda (buttoning up his jacket as he unbuttons it). All told, about two hundred dollars would carry us, dear. But that includes the last payment on the mortgage. After this payment, Willy, the house belongs to us.

Willy. It's twenty-five years!

Linda. Biff was nine years old when we bought it.

Willy. Well, that's a great thing. To weather a twenty-five year mortgage is . . .

Linda. It's an accomplishment.

Willy. All the cement, the lumber, the reconstruction I put in this house! There ain't a crack to be found in it any more.

Linda. Well, it served its purpose.

Willy. What purpose? Some stranger'll come along, move in, and that's that. If only Biff would take this house, and raise a family . . . (*He starts to go.*) Good-by, I'm late.

Linda (suddenly remembering). Oh, I forgot! You're supposed to meet them for dinner.

Willy. Me?

Linda. At Frank's Chop House on Forty-eighth near Sixth Avenue.

Willy. Is that so! How about you?

Linda. No, just the three of you. They're gonna blow you to a big meal!

Willy. Don't say! Who thought of that?

Linda. Biff came to me this morning, Willy, and he said, "Tell Dad, we want to blow him to a big meal." Be there six o'clock. You and your two boys are going to have dinner.

Willy. Gee whiz! That's really somethin'. I'm gonna knock Howard for a loop, kid. I'll get an advance, and I'll come home with a New York job. Goddammit, now I'm gonna do it!

Linda. Oh, that's the spirit, Willy!

Willy. I will never get behind a wheel the rest of my life!

Linda. It's changing, Willy, I can feel it changing!

Willy. Beyond a question. G'by, I'm late. (*He starts to go again.*)

Linda (calling after him as she runs to the kitchen table for a handkerchief). You got your glasses?

Willy (feels for them, then comes back in). Yeah, yeah, got my glasses.

Linda (giving him the handkerchief). And a handkerchief.

Willy. Yeah, handkerchief.
Linda. And your saccharine?
Willy. Yeah, my saccharine.
Linda. Be careful on the subway stairs.

She kisses him, and a silk stocking is seen hanging from her hand. Willy notices it.

Willy. Will you stop mending stockings? At least while I'm in the house. It gets me nervous. I can't tell you. Please.

Linda hides the stocking in her hand as she follows Willy across the forestage in front of the house.

Linda. Remember, Frank's Chop House.
Willy (passing the apron). Maybe beets would grow out there.
Linda (laughing). But you tried so many times.
Willy. Yeah. Well, don't work hard today. (*He disappears around the right corner of the house.*)
Linda. Be careful!

As Willy vanishes, Linda waves to him. Suddenly the phone rings. She runs across the stage and into the kitchen and lifts it.

Linda. Hello? Oh, Biff! I'm so glad you called, I just . . . Yes, sure, I just told him. Yes, he'll be there for dinner at six o'clock, I didn't forget. Listen, I was just dying to tell you. You know that little rubber pipe I told you about? That he connected to the gas heater? I finally decided to go down the cellar this morning and take it away and destroy it. But it's gone! Imagine? He took it away himself, it isn't there! (*She listens.*) When? Oh, then you took it. Oh — nothing, it's just that I'd hoped he'd taken it away himself. Oh, I'm not worried, darling, because this morning he left in such high spirits, it was like the old days! I'm not afraid any more. Did Mr. Oliver see you? . . . Well, you wait there then. And make a nice impression on him, darling. Just don't perspire too much before you see him. And have a nice time with Dad. He may have big news too! . . . That's right, a New York job. And be sweet to him tonight, dear. Be loving to him. Because he's only a little boat looking for a harbor. (*She is trembling with sorrow and joy.*) Oh, that's wonderful, Biff, you'll save his life. Thanks, darling. Just put your arm around him when he comes into the restaurant. Give him a smile. That's the boy . . . Good-by, dear. . . . You got your comb? . . . That's fine. Good-by, Biff dear.

In the middle of her speech, Howard Wagner, thirty-six, wheels in a small typewriter table on which is a wire-recording machine and proceeds to plug it in. This is on the left forestage. Light slowly fades on Linda as it rises on Howard. Howard is intent on threading the machine and only glances over his shoulder as Willy appears.

Willy. Pst! Pst!

Howard. Hello, Willy, come in.

Willy. Like to have a little talk with you, Howard.

Howard. Sorry to keep you waiting. I'll be with you in a minute.

Willy. What's that, Howard?

Howard. Didn't you ever see one of these? Wire recorder.

Willy. Oh. Can we talk a minute?

Howard. Records things. Just got delivery yesterday. Been driving me crazy, the most terrific machine I ever saw in my life. I was up all night with it.

Willy. What do you do with it?

Howard. I bought it for dictation, but you can do anything with it. Listen to this. I had it home last night. Listen to what I picked up. The first one is my daughter. Get this. (*He flicks the switch and "Roll out the Barrel" is heard being whistled.*) Listen to that kid whistle.

Willy. That is lifelike, isn't it?

Howard. Seven years old. Get that tone.

Willy. Ts, ts. Like to ask a little favor if you . . .

The whistling breaks off, and the voice of Howard's daughter is heard.

His Daughter. "Now you, Daddy."

Howard. She's crazy for me! (*Again the same song is whistled.*) That's me! Ha! (*He winks.*)

Willy. You're very good!

The whistling breaks off again. The machine runs silent for a moment.

Howard. Sh! Get this now, this is my son.

His Son. "The capital of Alabama is Montgomery; the capital of Arizona is Phoenix; the capital of Arkansas is Little Rock; the capital of California is Sacramento . . ." (*and on, and on.*)

Howard (*holding up five fingers*). Five years old, Willy!

Willy. He'll make an announcer some day!

His Son (*continuing*). "The capital . . ."

Howard. Get that — alphabetical order! (*The machine breaks off suddenly.*) Wait a minute. The maid kicked the plug out.

Willy. It certainly is a . . .

Howard. Sh, for God's sake!

His Son. "It's nine o'clock, Bulova watch time. So I have to go to sleep."

Willy. That really is . . .

Howard. Wait a minute! The next is my wife.

They wait.

Howard's Voice. "Go on, say something." (*Pause.*) "Well, you gonna talk?"

His Wife. "I can't think of anything."

Howard's Voice. "Well, talk — it's turning."

His Wife (*shyly, beaten*). "Hello." (*Silence.*) "Oh, Howard, I can't talk into this . . ."

Howard (*snapping the machine off*). That was my wife.

Willy. That is a wonderful machine. Can we . . .

Howard. I tell you, Willy, I'm gonna take my camera, and my bandsaw, and all my hobbies, and out they go. This is the most fascinating relaxation I ever found.

Willy. I think I'll get one myself.

Howard. Sure, they're only a hundred and a half. You can't do without it. Supposing you wanna hear Jack Benny, see? But you can't be at home at that hour. So you tell the maid to turn the radio on when Jack Benny comes on, and this automatically goes on with the radio . . .

Willy. And when you come home you . . .

Howard. You can come home twelve o'clock, one o'clock, any time you like, and you get yourself a Coke and sit yourself down, throw the switch, and there's Jack Benny's program in the middle of the night!

Willy. I'm definitely going to get one. Because lots of times I'm on the road, and I think to myself, what I must be missing on the radio!

Howard. Don't you have a radio in the car?

Willy. Well, yeah, but who ever thinks of turning it on?

Howard. Say, aren't you supposed to be in Boston?

Willy. That's what I want to talk to you about, Howard. You got a minute? (*He draws a chair in from the wing.*)

Howard. What happened? What're you doing here?

Willy. Well . . .

Howard. You didn't crack up again, did you?

Willy. Oh, no. No . . .

Howard. Geez, you had me worried there for a minute. What's the trouble?

Willy. Well, tell you the truth, Howard. I've come to the decision that I'd rather not travel any more.

Howard. Not travel! Well, what'll you do?

Willy. Remember, Christmas time, when you had the party here? You said you'd try to think of some spot for me here in town.

Howard. With us?

Willy. Well, sure.

Howard. Oh, yeah, yeah. I remember. Well, I couldn't think of anything for you, Willy.

Willy. I tell ya, Howard. The kids are all grown up, y'know. I don't need much any more. If I could take home — well, sixty-five dollars a week, I could swing it.

Howard. Yeah, but Willy, see I . . .

Willy. I tell ya why, Howard. Speaking frankly and between the two of us, y'know — I'm just a little tired.

Howard. Oh, I could understand that, Willy. But you're a road man, Willy, and we do a road business. We've only got a half-dozen salesmen on the floor here.

Willy. God knows, Howard. I never asked a favor of any man. But I was with the firm when your father used to carry you in here in his arms.

Howard. I know that, Willy, but . . .

Willy. Your father came to me the day you were born and asked me what I thought of the name Howard, may he rest in peace.

Howard. I appreciate that, Willy, but there just is no spot here for you. If I had a spot I'd slam you right in, but I just don't have a single solitary spot.

He looks for his lighter. Willy has picked it up and gives it to him. Pause.

Willy (*with increasing anger*). Howard, all I need to set my table is fifty dollars a week.

Howard. But where am I going to put you, kid?

Willy. Look, it isn't a question of whether I can sell merchandise, is it?

Howard. No, but it's business, kid, and everybody's gotta pull his own weight.

Willy (*desperately*). Just let me tell you a story, Howard . . .

Howard. 'Cause you gotta admit, business is business.

Willy (*angrily*). Business is definitely business, but just listen for a minute. You don't understand this. When I was a boy — eighteen, nineteen — I was already on the road. And there was a question in my mind as to whether selling had a future for me. Because in those days I had a yearning to go to Alaska. See, there were three gold strikes in one month in

Alaska, and I felt like going out. Just for the ride, you might
say.

Howard (*barely interested*). Don't say.

Willy. Oh, yeah, my father lived many years in Alaska. He was
an adventurous man. We've got quite a little streak of self-
reliance in our family. I thought I'd go out with my older
brother and try to locate him, and maybe settle in the North
with the old man. And I was almost decided to go, when
I met a salesman in the Parker House. His name was Dave
Singleman. And he was eighty-four years old, and he'd
drummed merchandise in thirty-one states. And old Dave,
he'd go up to his room, y'understand, put on his green velvet
slippers — I'll never forget — and pick up his phone and
call the buyers, and without ever leaving his room, at the
age of eighty-four, he made his living. And when I saw that,
I realized that selling was the greatest career a man could
want. 'Cause what could be more satisfying than to be able
to go, at the age of eighty-four, into twenty or thirty different
cities, and pick up a phone, and be remembered and loved
and helped by so many different people? Do you know?
when he died — and by the way he died the death of a
salesman, in his green velvet slippers in the smoker of the
New York, New Haven and Hartford, going into Boston
— when he died, hundreds of salesmen and buyers were at
his funeral. Things were sad on a lotta trains for months
after that. (*He stands up. Howard has not looked at him.*) In
those days there was personality in it, Howard. There was
respect, and comradeship, and gratitude in it. Today, it's all
cut and dried, and there's no chance for bringing friendship
to bear — or personality. You see what I mean? They don't
know me any more.

Howard (*moving away, to the right*). That's just the thing, Willy.

Willy. If I had forty dollars a week — that's all I'd need. Forty
dollars, Howard.

Howard. Kid, I can't take blood from a stone, I . . .

Willy (*desperation is on him now*). Howard, the year Al Smith was
nominated, your father came to me and . . .

Howard (*starting to go off*). I've got to see some people, kid.

Willy (*stopping him*). I'm talking about your father! There were
promises made across this desk! You mustn't tell me you've
got people to see — I put thirty-four years into this firm,
Howard, and now I can't pay my insurance! You can't eat
the orange and throw the peel away — a man is not a piece
of fruit! (*After a pause.*) Now pay attention. Your father —

in 1928 I had a big year. I averaged a hundred and seventy dollars a week in commissions.

Howard (impatiently). Now, Willy, you never averaged . . .

Willy (banging his hand on the desk). I averaged a hundred and seventy dollars a week in the year of 1928! And your father came to me — or rather, I was in the office here — it was right over this desk — and he put his hand on my shoulder . . .

Howard (getting up). You'll have to excuse me, Willy, I gotta see some people. Pull yourself together. (*Going out.*) I'll be back in a little while.

On Howard's exit, the light on his chair grows very bright and strange.

Willy. Pull myself together! What the hell did I say to him? My God, I was yelling at him! How could I? (*Willy breaks off, staring at the light, which occupies the chair, animating it. He approaches this chair, standing across the desk from it.*) Frank, Frank, don't you remember what you told me that time? How you put your hand on my shoulder, and Frank . . . (*He leans on the desk and as he speaks the dead man's name he accidentally switches on the recorder, and instantly*)

Howard's Son. ". . . of New York is Albany. The capital of Ohio is Cincinnati, the capital of Rhode Island is . . ." (*The recitation continues.*)

Willy (leaping away with fright, shouting). Ha! Howard! Howard! Howard!

Howard (rushing in). What happened?

Willy (pointing at the machine, which continues nasally, childishly, with the capital cities). Shut it off! Shut it off!

Howard (pulling the plug out). Look, Willy . . .

Willy (pressing his hands to his eyes). I gotta get myself some coffee. I'll get some coffee . . .

Willy starts to walk out. Howard stops him.

Howard (rolling up the cord). Willy, look . . .

Willy. I'll go to Boston.

Howard. Willy, you can't go to Boston for us.

Willy. Why can't I go?

Howard. I don't want you to represent us. I've been meaning to tell you for a long time now.

Willy. Howard, are you firing me?

Howard. I think you need a good long rest, Willy.

Willy. Howard . . .

Howard. And when you feel better, come back, and we'll see if we can work something out.

Willy. But I gotta earn money, Howard. I'm in no position to . . .

Howard. Where are your sons? Why don't your sons give you a hand?

Willy. They're working on a very big deal.

Howard. This is no time for false pride, Willy. You go to your sons and you tell them that you're tired. You've got two great boys, haven't you?

Willy. Oh, no question, no question, but in the meantime . . .

Howard. Then that's that, heh?

Willy. All right, I'll go to Boston tomorrow.

Howard. No, no.

Willy. I can't throw myself on my sons. I'm not a cripple!

Howard. Look, kid, I'm busy this morning.

Willy (grasping Howard's arm). Howard, you've got to let me go to Boston!

Howard (hard, keeping himself under control). I've got a line of people to see this morning. Sit down, take five minutes, and pull yourself together, and then go home, will ya? I need the office, Willy. (*He starts to go, turns, remembering the recorder, starts to push off the table holding the recorder.*) Oh, yeah. Whenever you can this week, stop by and drop off the samples. You'll feel better, Willy, and then come back and we'll talk. Pull yourself together, kid, there's people outside.

Howard exits, pushing the table off left. Willy stares into space, exhausted. Now the music is heard — Ben's music — first distantly, then closer, closer. As Willy speaks, Ben enters from the right. He carries valise and umbrella.

Willy. Oh, Ben, how did you do it? What is the answer? Did you wind up the Alaska deal already?

Ben. Doesn't take much time if you know what you're doing. Just a short business trip. Boarding ship in an hour. Wanted to say good-by.

Willy. Ben, I've got to talk to you.

Ben (glancing at his watch). Haven't the time, William.

Willy (crossing the apron to Ben). Ben, nothing's working out. I don't know what to do.

Ben. Now, look here, William. I've bought timberland in Alaska and I need a man to look after things for me.

Willy. God, timberland! Me and my boys in those grand outdoors!

Ben. You've a new continent at your doorstep, William. Get out of these cities, they're full of talk and time payments and courts of law. Screw on your fists and you can fight for a fortune up there.

Willy. Yes, yes! Linda, Linda!

Linda enters as of old, with the wash.

Linda. Oh, you're back?

Ben. I haven't much time.

Willy. No, wait! Linda, he's got a proposition for me in Alaska.

Linda. But you've got . . . (*To Ben.*) He's got a beautiful job here.

Willy. But in Alaska, kid, I could . . .

Linda. You're doing well enough, Willy!

Ben (*to Linda*). Enough for what, my dear?

Linda (*frightened of Ben and angry at him*). Don't say those things to him! Enough to be happy right here, right now. (*To Willy, while Ben laughs.*) Why must everybody conquer the world? You're well liked, and the boys love you, and someday — (*To Ben*) — why, old man Wagner told him just the other day that if he keeps it up he'll be a member of the firm, didn't he, Willy?

Willy. Sure, sure. I am building something with this firm, Ben, and if a man is building something he must be on the right track, mustn't he?

Ben. What are you building? Lay your hand on it. Where is it?

Willy (*hesitantly*). That's true, Linda, there's nothing.

Linda. Why? (*To Ben.*) There's a man eighty-four years old . . .

Willy. That's right, Ben, that's right. When I look at that man I say, what is there to worry about?

Ben. Bah!

Willy. It's true, Ben. All he has to do is go into any city, pick up the phone, and he's making his living and you know why?

Ben (*picking up his valise*). I've got to go.

Willy (*holding Ben back*). Look at this boy!

Biff, in his high school sweater, enters carrying suitcase. Happy carries Biff's shoulder guards, gold helmet, and football pants.

Willy. Without a penny to his name, three great universities are begging for him, and from there the sky's the limit, because it's not what you do, Ben. It's who you know and the smile on your face! It's contacts, Ben, contacts! The whole wealth of Alaska passes over the lunch table at the Commodore Hotel, and that's the wonder, the wonder of this country, that a man can end with diamonds here on the basis of being liked! (*He turns to Biff.*) And that's why when you get out on that field today it's important. Because thousands of people will be rooting for you and loving you. (*To Ben, who has again begun to leave.*) And Ben! when he walks into a business office his name will sound out like a bell and all the doors will open to him! I've seen it, Ben, I've seen it a thousand times! You can't feel it with your hand like timber, but it's there!

Ben. Good-by, William.

Willy. Ben, am I right? Don't you think I'm right? I value your advice.

Ben. There's a new continent at your doorstep, William. You could walk out rich. Rich! (*He is gone.*)

Willy. We'll do it here, Ben! You hear me? We're gonna do it here!

Young Bernard rushes in. The gay music of the Boys is heard.

Bernard. Oh, gee, I was afraid you left already!

Willy. Why? What time is it?

Bernard. It's half-past one!

Willy. Well, come on, everybody! Ebbets Field next stop! Where's the pennants? (*He rushes through the wall-line of the kitchen and out into the living room.*)

Linda (to Biff). Did you pack fresh underwear?

Biff (who has been limbering up). I want to go!

Bernard. Biff, I'm carrying your helmet, ain't I?

Happy. No, I'm carrying the helmet.

Bernard. Oh, Biff, you promised me.

Happy. I'm carrying the helmet.

Bernard. How am I going to get in the locker room?

Linda. Let him carry the shoulder guards. (*She puts her coat and hat on in the kitchen.*)

Bernard. Can I, Biff? 'Cause I told everybody I'm going to be in the locker room.

Happy. In Ebbets Field it's the clubhouse.

Bernard. I meant the clubhouse. Biff!

Happy. Biff!

Biff (grandly, after a slight pause). Let him carry the shoulder guards.

Happy (as he gives Bernard the shoulder guards). Stay close to us now.

Willy rushes in with the pennants.

Willy (handing them out). Everybody wave when Biff comes out on the field. (*Happy and Bernard run off.*) You set now, boy?

The music has died away.

Biff. Ready to go, Pop. Every muscle is ready.

Willy (at the edge of the apron). You realize what this means?

Biff. That's right, Pop.

Willy (*feeling Biff's muscles*). You're comin' home this afternoon captain of the All-Scholastic Championship Team of the City of New York.

Biff. I got it, Pop. And remember, pal, when I take off my helmet, that touchdown is for you.

Willy. Let's go! (*He is starting out, with his arm around Biff, when Charley enters, as of old, in knickers.*) I got no room for you, Charley.

Charley. Room? For what?

Willy. In the car.

Charley. You goin' for a ride? I wanted to shoot some casino.

Willy (*furiously*). Casino! (*Incredulously.*) Don't you realize what today is?

Linda. Oh, he knows, Willy. He's just kidding you.

Willy. That's nothing to kid about!

Charley. No, Linda, what's goin' on?

Linda. He's playing in Ebbets Field.

Charley. Baseball in this weather?

Willy. Don't talk to him. Come on, come on! (*He is pushing them out.*)

Charley. Wait a minute, didn't you hear the news?

Willy. What?

Charley. Don't you listen to the radio? Ebbets Field just blew up.

Willy. You go to hell! (*Charley laughs. Pushing them out.*) Come on, come on! We're late.

Charley (*as they go*). Knock a homer, Biff, knock a homer!

Willy (*the last to leave, turning to Charley*). I don't think that was funny, Charley. This is the greatest day of his life.

Charley. Willy, when are you going to grow up?

Willy. Yeah, heh? When this game is over, Charley, you'll be laughing out of the other side of your face. They'll be calling him another Red Grange. Twenty-five thousand a year.

Charley (*kidding*). Is that so?

Willy. Yeah, that's so.

Charley. Well, then, I'm sorry, Willy. But tell me something.

Willy. What?

Charley. Who is Red Grange?

Willy. Put up your hands. Goddam you, put up your hands!

> *Charley, chuckling, shakes his head and walks away, around the left corner of the stage. Willy follows him. The music rises to a mocking frenzy.*

Willy. Who the hell do you think you are, better than everybody else? You don't know everything, you big, ignorant, stupid . . . Put up your hands!

Light rises, on the right side of the forestage, on a small table in the reception room of Charley's office. Traffic sounds are heard. Bernard, now mature, sits whistling to himself. A pair of tennis rackets and an overnight bag are on the floor beside him.

Willy (*offstage*). What are you walking away for? Don't walk away! If you're going to say something say it to my face! I know you laugh at me behind my back. You'll laugh out of the other side of your goddam face after this game. Touchdown! Touchdown! Eighty thousand people! Touchdown! Right between the goal posts.

Bernard is a quiet, earnest, but self-assured young man. Willy's voice is coming from right upstage now. Bernard lowers his feet off the table and listens. Jenny, his father's secretary, enters.

Jenny (*distressed*). Say, Bernard, will you go out in the hall?
Bernard. What is that noise? Who is it?
Jenny. Mr. Loman. He just got off the elevator.
Bernard (*getting up*). Who's he arguing with?
Jenny. Nobody. There's nobody with him. I can't deal with him any more, and your father gets all upset every time he comes. I've got a lot of typing to do, and your father's waiting to sign it. Will you see him?
Willy (*entering*). Touchdown! Touch — (*He sees Jenny.*) Jenny, Jenny, good to see you. How're ya? Workin'? Or still honest?
Jenny. Fine. How've you been feeling?
Willy. Not much any more, Jenny. Ha, ha! (*He is surprised to see the rackets.*)
Bernard. Hello, Uncle Willy.
Willy (*almost shocked*). Bernard! Well, look who's here! (*He comes quickly, guiltily, to Bernard and warmly shakes his hand.*)
Bernard. How are you? Good to see you.
Willy. What are you doing here?
Bernard. Oh, just stopped by to see Pop. Get off my feet till my train leaves. I'm going to Washington in a few minutes.
Willy. Is he in?
Bernard. Yes, he's in his office with the accountant. Sit down.
Willy (*sitting down*). What're you going to do in Washington?
Bernard. Oh, just a case I've got there, Willy.
Willy. That so? (*Indicating the rackets.*) You going to play tennis there?

Bernard. I'm staying with a friend who's got a court.

Willy. Don't say. His own tennis court. Must be fine people, I bet.

Bernard. They are, very nice. Dad tells me Biff's in town.

Willy (with a big smile). Yeah, Biff's in. Working on a very big deal, Bernard.

Bernard. What's Biff doing?

Willy. Well, he's been doing very big things in the West. But he decided to establish himself here. Very big. We're having dinner. Did I hear your wife had a boy?

Bernard. That's right. Our second.

Willy. Two boys! What do you know!

Bernard. What kind of a deal has Biff got?

Willy. Well, Bill Oliver — very big sporting-goods man — he wants Biff very badly. Called him in from the West. Long distance, carte blanche, special deliveries. Your friends have their own private tennis court?

Bernard. You still with the old firm, Willy?

Willy (after a pause). I'm — I'm overjoyed to see how you made the grade, Bernard, overjoyed. It's an encouraging thing to see a young man really — really . . . Looks very good for Biff — very. . . (*He breaks off, then.*) Bernard . . . (*He is so full of emotion, he breaks off again.*)

Bernard. What is it, Willy?

Willy (small and alone). What — what's the secret?

Bernard. What secret?

Willy. How — how did you? Why didn't he ever catch on?

Bernard. I wouldn't know that, Willy.

Willy (confidentially, desperately). You were his friend, his boyhood friend. There's something I don't understand about it. His life ended after that Ebbets Field game. From the age of seventeen nothing good ever happened to him.

Bernard. He never trained himself for anything.

Willy. But he did, he did. After high school he took so many correspondence courses. Radio mechanics; television; God knows what, and never made the slightest mark.

Bernard (taking off his glasses). Willy, do you want to talk candidly?

Willy (rising, faces Bernard). I regard you as a very brilliant man, Bernard. I value your advice.

Bernard. Oh, the hell with the advice, Willy. I couldn't advise you. There's just one thing I've always wanted to ask you. When he was supposed to graduate, and the math teacher flunked him . . .

Willy. Oh, that son-of-a-bitch ruined his life.

Bernard. Yeah, but, Willy, all he had to do was go to summer school and make up that subject.

Willy. That's right, that's right.

Bernard. Did you tell him not to go to summer school?

Willy. Me? I begged him to go. I ordered him to go!

Bernard. Then why wouldn't he go?

Willy. Why? Why! Bernard, that question has been trailing me like a ghost for the last fifteen years. He flunked the subject, and laid down and died like a hammer hit him!

Bernard. Take it easy, kid.

Willy. Let me talk to you — I got nobody to talk to. Bernard, Bernard, was it my fault? Y'see? It keeps going around in my mind, maybe I did something to him. I got nothing to give him.

Bernard. Don't take it so hard.

Willy. Why did he lay down? What is the story there? You were his friend!

Bernard. Willy, I remember, it was June, and our grades came out. And he'd flunked math.

Willy. That son-of-a-bitch!

Bernard. No, it wasn't right then. Biff just got very angry, I remember, and he was ready to enroll in summer school.

Willy (surprised). He was?

Bernard. He wasn't beaten by it at all. But then, Willy, he disappeared from the block for almost a month. And I got the idea that he'd gone up to New England to see you. Did he have a talk with you then?

Willy stares in silence.

Bernard. Willy?

Willy (with a strong edge of resentment in his voice). Yeah, he came to Boston. What about it?

Bernard. Well, just that when he came back — I'll never forget this, it always mystifies me. Because I'd thought so well of Biff, even though he'd always taken advantage of me. I loved him, Willy, y'know? And he came back after that month and took his sneakers — remember those sneakers with "University of Virginia" printed on them? He was so proud of those, wore them every day. And he took them down in the cellar, and burned them up in the furnace. We had a fist fight. It lasted at least half an hour. Just the two of us, punching each other down the cellar, and crying right through it. I've often thought of how strange it was that I knew he'd given up his life. What happened in Boston, Willy?

Willy looks at him as at an intruder.

Bernard. I just bring it up because you asked me.

Willy (angrily). Nothing. What do you mean, "What happened?" What's that got to do with anything?

Bernard. Well, don't get sore.

Willy. What are you trying to do, blame it on me? If a boy lays down is that my fault?

Bernard. Now, Willy, don't get . . .

Willy. Well, don't — don't talk to me that way! What does that mean, "What happened?"

Charley enters. He is in his vest, and he carries a bottle of bourbon.

Charley. Hey, you're going to miss that train. (*He waves the bottle.*)

Bernard. Yeah, I'm going. (*He takes the bottle.*) Thanks, Pop. (*He picks up his rackets and bag.*) Good-by, Willy, and don't worry about it. You know, "If at first you don't succeed . . ."

Willy. Yes, I believe in that.

Bernard. But sometimes, Willy, it's better for a man just to walk away.

Willy. Walk away?

Bernard. That's right.

Willy. But if you can't walk away?

Bernard (after a slight pause). I guess that's when it's tough. (*Extending his hand.*) Good-by, Willy.

Willy (shaking Bernard's hand). Good-by, boy.

Charley (an arm on Bernard's shoulder). How do you like this kid? Gonna argue a case in front of the Supreme Court.

Bernard (protesting). Pop!

Willy (genuinely shocked, pained, and happy). No! The Supreme Court!

Bernard. I gotta run. 'By, Dad!

Charley. Knock 'em dead, Bernard!

Bernard goes off.

Willy (as Charley takes out his wallet). The Supreme Court! And he didn't even mention it!

Charley (counting out money on the desk). He don't have to — he's gonna do it.

Willy. And you never told him what to do, did you? You never took any interest in him.

Charley. My salvation is that I never took any interest in anything. There's some money — fifty dollars. I got an accountant inside.

Willy. Charley, look . . . (*With difficulty.*) I got my insurance to
    pay. If you can manage it — I need a hundred and ten dollars.

    Charley doesn't reply for a moment; merely stops moving.

Willy. I'd draw it from my bank but Linda would know, and
    I . . .
Charley. Sit down, Willy.
Willy (*moving toward the chair*). I'm keeping an account of every-
    thing, remember. I'll pay every penny back. (*He sits.*)
Charley. Now listen to me, Willy.
Willy. I want you to know I appreciate . . .
Charley (*sitting down on the table*). Willy, what're you doin'? What
    the hell is going on in your head?
Willy. Why? I'm simply . . .
Charley. I offered you a job. You make fifty dollars a week. And
    I won't send you on the road.
Willy. I've got a job.
Charley. Without pay? What kind of a job is a job without pay?
    (*He rises.*) Now, look, kid, enough is enough. I'm no genius
    but I know when I'm being insulted.
Willy. Insulted!
Charley. Why don't you want to work for me?
Willy. What's the matter with you? I've got a job.
Charley. Then what're you walkin' in here every week for?
Willy (*getting up*). Well, if you don't want me to walk in here . . .
Charley. I'm offering you a job.
Willy. I don't want your goddam job!
Charley. When the hell are you going to grow up?
Willy (*furiously*). You big ignoramus, if you say that to me again
    I'll rap you one! I don't care how big you are! (*He's ready
    to fight.*)

    Pause.

Charley (*kindly, going to him*). How much do you need, Willy?
Willy. Charley, I'm strapped. I'm strapped. I don't know what to
    do. I was just fired.
Charley. Howard fired you?
Willy. That snotnose. Imagine that? I named him. I named him
    Howard.
Charley. Willy, when're you gonna realize that them things don't
    mean anything? You named him Howard, but you can't sell
    that. The only thing you got in this world is what you can
    sell. And the funny thing is that you're a salesman, and you
    don't know that.

Willy. I've always tried to think otherwise, I guess. I always felt
that if a man was impressive, and well liked, that nothing . . .

Charley. Why must everybody like you? Who liked J.P. Morgan?
Was he impressive? In a Turkish bath he'd look like a butcher.
But with his pockets on he was very well liked. Now listen,
Willy, I know you don't like me, and nobody can say I'm
in love with you, but I'll give you a job because — just for
the hell of it, put it that way. Now what do you say?

Willy. I — I just can't work for you, Charley.

Charley. What're you, jealous of me?

Willy. I can't work for you, that's all, don't ask me why.

Charley (angered, takes out more bills). You been jealous of me all
your life, you dammed fool! Here, pay your insurance. (*He
puts the money in Willy's hand.*)

Willy. I'm keeping strict accounts.

Charley. I've got some work to do. Take care of yourself. And
pay your insurance.

Willy (moving to the right). Funny, y'know? After all the highways,
and the trains, and the appointments, and the years, you end
up worth more dead than alive.

Charley. Willy, nobody's worth nothin' dead. (*After a slight pause.*)
Did you hear what I said?

Willy stands still, dreaming.

Charley. Willy!

Willy. Apologize to Bernard for me when you see him. I didn't
mean to argue with him. He's a fine boy. They're all fine
boys, and they'll end up big — all of them. Someday they'll
all play tennis together. Wish me luck, Charley. He saw Bill
Oliver today.

Charley. Good luck.

Willy (on the verge of tears). Charley, you're the only friend I got.
Isn't that a remarkable thing? (*He goes out.*)

Charley. Jesus!

*Charley stares after him a moment and follows. All light blacks
out. Suddenly raucous music is heard, and a red glow rises behind
the screen at right. Stanley, a young waiter, appears, carrying a
table, followed by Happy, who is carrying two chairs.*

Stanley (putting the table down). That's all right, Mr. Loman, I can
handle it myself. (*He turns and takes the chairs from Happy and
places them at the table.*)

Happy (*glancing around*). Oh, this is better.

Stanley. Sure, in the front there you're in the middle of all kinds of noise. Whenever you got a party, Mr. Loman, you just tell me and I'll put you back here. Y'know, there's a lotta people they don't like it private, because when they go out they like to see a lotta action around them because they're sick and tired to stay in the house by theirself. But I know you, you ain't from Hackensack. You know what I mean?

Happy (*sitting down*). So how's it coming, Stanley?

Stanley. Ah, it's a dog life. I only wish during the war they'd a took me in the Army. I coulda been dead by now.

Happy. My brother's back, Stanley.

Stanley. Oh, he come back, heh? From the Far West.

Happy. Yeah, big cattle man, my brother, so treat him right. And my father's coming too.

Stanley. Oh, your father too!

Happy. You got a couple of nice lobsters?

Stanley. Hundred per cent, big.

Happy. I want them with the claws.

Stanley. Don't worry, I don't give you no mice. (*Happy laughs.*) How about some wine? It'll put a head on the meal.

Happy. No. You remember, Stanley, that recipe I brought you from overseas? With the champagne in it?

Stanley. Oh, yeah, sure. I still got it tacked up yet in the kitchen. But that'll have to cost a buck apiece anyways.

Happy. That's all right.

Stanley. What'd you, hit a number or somethin'?

Happy. No, it's a little celebration. My brother is — I think he pulled off a big deal today. I think we're going into business together.

Stanley. Great! That's the best for you. Because a family business, you know what I mean? — that's the best.

Happy. That's what I think.

Stanley. 'Cause what's the difference? Somebody steals? It's in the family. Know what I mean? (*Sotto voce.*) Like this bartender here. The boss is goin' crazy what kinda leak he's got in the cash register. You put it in but it don't come out.

Happy (*raising his head*). Sh!

Stanley. What?

Happy. You notice I wasn't lookin' right or left, was I?

Stanley. No.

Happy. And my eyes are closed.

Stanley. So what's the . . . ?

Happy. Strudel's comin'.

Stanley (catching on, looks around). Ah, no, there's no . . .

> *He breaks off as a furred, lavishly dressed Girl enters and sits at the next table. Both follow her with their eyes.*

Stanley. Geez, how'd ya know?

Happy. I got radar or something. (*Staring directly at her profile.*) Oooooooo . . . Stanley.

Stanley. I think that's for you, Mr. Loman.

Happy. Look at that mouth. Oh, God. And the binoculars.

Stanley. Geez, you got a life, Mr. Loman.

Happy. Wait on her.

Stanley (going to the Girl's table). Would you like a menu, ma'am?

Girl. I'm expecting someone, but I'd like a . . .

Happy. Why don't you bring her — excuse me, miss, do you mind? I sell champagne, and I'd like you to try my brand. Bring her a champagne, Stanley.

Girl. That's awfully nice of you.

Happy. Don't mention it. It's all company money. (*He laughs.*)

Girl. That's a charming product to be selling, isn't it?

Happy. Oh, gets to be like everything else. Selling is selling, y'know.

Girl. I suppose.

Happy. You don't happen to sell, do you?

Girl. No, I don't sell.

Happy. Would you object to a compliment from a stranger? You ought to be on a magazine cover.

Girl (looking at him a little archly). I have been.

> *Stanley comes in with a glass of champagne.*

Happy. What'd I say before, Stanley? You see? She's a cover girl.

Stanley. Oh, I could see, I could see.

Happy (to the Girl). What magazine?

Girl. Oh, a lot of them. (*She takes the drink.*) Thank you.

Happy. You know what they say in France, don't you? "Champagne is the drink of the complexion" — Hya, Biff!

> *Biff has entered and sits with Happy.*

Biff. Hello, kid. Sorry I'm late.

Happy. I just got here. Uh, Miss . . . ?

Girl. Forsythe.

Happy. Miss Forsythe, this is my brother.

Biff. Is Dad here?

Happy. His name is Biff. You might've heard of him. Great football player.

Girl. Really? What team?

Happy. Are you familiar with football?

Girl. No, I'm afraid I'm not.

Happy. Biff is quarterback with the New York Giants.

Girl. Well, that is nice, isn't it? (*She drinks.*)

Happy. Good health.

Girl. I'm happy to meet you.

Happy. That's my name. Hap. It's really Harold, but at West Point
they called me Happy.

Girl (*now really impressed*). Oh, I see. How do you do? (*She turns
her profile.*)

Biff. Isn't Dad coming?

Happy. You want her?

Biff. Oh, I could never make that.

Happy. I remember the time that idea would never come into your
head. Where's the old confidence, Biff?

Biff. I just saw Oliver . . .

Happy. Wait a minute. I've got to see that old confidence again.
Do you want her? She's on call.

Biff. Oh, no. (*He turns to look at the Girl.*)

Happy. I'm telling you. Watch this. (*Turning to the Girl.*) Honey?
(*She turns to him.*) Are you busy?

Girl. Well, I am . . . but I could make a phone call.

Happy. Do that, will you, honey? And see if you can get a friend.
We'll be here for a while. Biff is one of the greatest football
players in the country.

Girl (*standing up*). Well, I'm certainly happy to meet you.

Happy. Come back soon.

Girl. I'll try.

Happy. Don't try, honey, try hard.

> The Girl exits. Stanley follows, shaking his head in bewildered
> admiration.

Happy. Isn't that a shame now? A beautiful girl like that? That's
why I can't get married. There's not a good woman in a
thousand. New York is loaded with them, kid!

Biff. Hap, look . . .

Happy. I told you she was on call!

Biff (*strangely unnerved*). Cut it out, will ya? I want to say something
to you.

Happy. Did you see Oliver?

Biff. I saw him all right. Now look, I want to tell Dad a couple
of things and I want you to help me.

Happy. What? Is he going to back you?

Biff. Are you crazy? You're out of your goddam head, you know that?

Happy. Why? What happened?

Biff (breathlessly). I did a terrible thing today, Hap. It's been the strangest day I ever went through. I'm all numb, I swear.

Happy. You mean he wouldn't see you?

Biff. Well, I waited six hours for him, see? All day. Kept sending my name in. Even tried to date his secretary so she'd get me to him, but no soap.

Happy. Because you're not showin' the old confidence, Biff. He remembered you, didn't he?

Biff (stopping Happy with a gesture). Finally, about five o'clock, he comes out. Didn't remember who I was or anything. I felt like such an idiot, Hap.

Happy. Did you tell him my Florida idea?

Biff. He walked away. I saw him for one minute. I got so mad I could've torn the walls down! How the hell did I ever get the idea I was a salesman there? I even believed myself that I'd been a salesman for him! And then he gave me one look and — I realized what a ridiculous lie my whole life has been! We've been talking in a dream for fifteen years. I was a shipping clerk.

Happy. What'd you do?

Biff (with great tension and wonder). Well, he left, see. And the secretary went out. I was all alone in the waiting room. I don't know what came over me, Hap. The next thing I know I'm in his office — paneled walls, everything. I can't explain it. I — Hap, I took his fountain pen.

Happy. Geez, did he catch you?

Biff. I ran out. I ran down all eleven flights. I ran and ran and ran.

Happy. That was an awful dumb — what'd you do that for?

Biff (agonized). I don't know, I just — wanted to take something, I don't know. You gotta help me, Hap. I'm gonna tell Pop.

Happy. You crazy? What for?

Biff. Hap, he's got to understand that I'm not the man somebody lends that kind of money to. He thinks I've been spiting him all these years and it's eating him up.

Happy. That's just it. You tell him something nice.

Biff. I can't.

Happy. Say you got a lunch date with Oliver tomorrow.

Biff. So what do I do tomorrow?

Happy. You leave the house tomorrow and come back at night and say Oliver is thinking it over. And he thinks it over for a couple of weeks, and gradually it fades away and nobody's the worse.

Biff. But it'll go on forever!

Happy. Dad is never so happy as when he's looking forward to something!

Willy enters.

Happy. Hello, scout!

Willy. Gee, I haven't been here in years!

Stanley has followed Willy in and sets a chair for him. Stanley starts off but Happy stops him.

Happy. Stanley!

Stanley stands by, waiting for an order.

Biff (going to Willy with guilt, as to an invalid). Sit down, Pop. You want a drink?

Willy. Sure, I don't mind.

Biff. Let's get a load on.

Willy. You look worried.

Biff. N-no. (*To Stanley.*) Scotch all around. Make it doubles.

Stanley. Doubles, right. (*He goes.*)

Willy. You had a couple already, didn't you?

Biff. Just a couple, yeah.

Willy. Well, what happened, boy? (*Nodding affirmatively, with a smile.*) Everything go all right?

Biff (takes a breath, then reaches out and grasps Willy's hand). Pal . . . (*He is smiling bravely, and Willy is smiling too.*) I had an experience today.

Happy. Terrific, Pop.

Willy. That so? What happened?

Biff (high, slightly alcoholic, above the earth). I'm going to tell you everything from first to last. It's been a strange day. (*Silence. He looks around, composes himself as best he can, but his breath keeps breaking the rhythm of his voice.*) I had to wait quite a while for him, and . . .

Willy. Oliver?

Biff. Yeah, Oliver. All day, as a matter of cold fact. And a lot of — instances — facts, Pop, facts about my life came back to me. Who was it, Pop? Who ever said I was a salesman with Oliver?

Willy. Well, you were.

Biff. No, Dad, I was a shipping clerk.

Willy. But you were practically . . .

Biff (with determination). Dad, I don't know who said it first, but I was never a salesman for Bill Oliver.

Willy. What're you talking about?

Biff. Let's hold on to the facts tonight, Pop. We're not going to get anywhere bullin' around. I was a shipping clerk.

Willy (angrily). All right, now listen to me . . .

Biff. Why don't you let me finish?

Willy. I'm not interested in stories about the past or any crap of that kind because the woods are burning, boys, you understand? There's a big blaze going on all around. I was fired today.

Biff (shocked). How could you be?

Willy. I was fired, and I'm looking for a little good news to tell your mother, because the woman has waited and the woman has suffered. The gist of it is that I haven't got a story left in my head, Biff. So don't give me a lecture about facts and aspects. I am not interested. Now what've you got to say to me?

Stanley enters with three drinks. They wait until he leaves.

Willy. Did you see Oliver?

Biff. Jesus, Dad!

Willy. You mean you didn't go up there?

Happy. Sure he went up there.

Biff. I did. I — saw him. How could they fire you?

Willy (on the edge of his chair). What kind of a welcome did he give you?

Biff. He won't even let you work on commission?

Willy. I'm out! (*Driving.*) So tell me, he gave you a warm welcome?

Happy. Sure, Pop, sure!

Biff (driven). Well, it was kind of . . .

Willy. I was wondering if he'd remember you. (*To Happy.*) Imagine, man doesn't see him for ten, twelve years and gives him that kind of a welcome!

Happy. Damn right!

Biff (trying to return to the offensive). Pop, look . . .

Willy. You know why he remembered you, don't you? Because you impressed him in those days.

Biff. Let's talk quietly and get this down to the facts, huh?

Willy (as though Biff had been interrupting). Well, what happened? It's great news, Biff. Did he take you into his office or'd you talk in the waiting room?

Biff. Well, he came in, see, and . . .

Willy (*with a big smile*). What'd he say? Betcha he threw his arm around you.

Biff. Well, he kinda . . .

Willy. He's a fine man. (*To Happy.*) Very hard man to see, y'know.

Happy (*agreeing*). Oh, I know.

Willy (*to Biff*). Is that where you had the drinks?

Biff. Yeah, he gave me a couple of — no, no!

Happy (*cutting in*). He told him my Florida idea.

Willy. Don't interrupt. (*To Biff.*) How'd he react to the Florida idea?

Biff. Dad, will you give me a minute to explain?

Willy. I've been waiting for you to explain since I sat down here! What happened? He took you into his office and what?

Biff. Well — I talked. And — and he listened, see.

Willy. Famous for the way he listens, y'know. What was his answer?

Biff. His answer was — (*He breaks off, suddenly angry.*) Dad, you're not letting me tell you what I want to tell you!

Willy (*accusing, angered*). You didn't see him, did you?

Biff. I did see him!

Willy. What'd you insult him or something? You insulted him, didn't you?

Biff. Listen, will you let me out of it, will you just let me out of it!

Happy. What the hell!

Willy. Tell me what happened!

Biff (*to Happy*). I can't talk to him!

A single trumpet note jars the ear. The light of green leaves stains the house, which holds the air of night and a dream. Young Bernard enters and knocks on the door of the house.

Young Bernard (*frantically*). Mrs. Loman, Mrs. Loman!

Happy. Tell him what happened!

Biff (*to Happy*). Shut up and leave me alone!

Willy. No, no! You had to go and flunk math!

Biff. What math? What're you talking about?

Young Bernard. Mrs. Loman, Mrs. Loman!

Linda appears in the house, as of old.

Willy (*wildly*). Math, math, math!

Biff. Take it easy, Pop!

Young Bernard. Mrs. Loman!

Willy (*furiously*). If you hadn't flunked you'd've been set by now!

Biff. Now, look, I'm gonna tell you what happened, and you're going to listen to me.

Young Bernard. Mrs. Loman!

Biff. I waited six hours . . .

Happy. What the hell are you saying?

Biff. I kept sending in my name but he wouldn't see me. So finally he . . . (*He continues unheard as light fades low on the restaurant.*)

Young Bernard. Biff flunked math!

Linda. No!

Young Bernard. Birnbaum flunked him! They won't graduate him!

Linda. But they have to. He's gotta go to the university. Where is he? Biff! Biff!

Young Bernard. No, he left. He went to Grand Central.

Linda. Grand — You mean he went to Boston!

Young Bernard. Is Uncle Willy in Boston?

Linda. Oh, maybe Willy can talk to the teacher. Oh, the poor, poor boy!

> *Light on house area snaps out.*

Biff (*at the table, now audible, holding up a gold fountain pen*) . . . so I'm washed up with Oliver, you understand? Are you listening to me?

Willy (*at a loss*). Yeah, sure. If you hadn't flunked . . .

Biff. Flunked what? What're you talking about?

Willy. Don't blame everything on me! I didn't flunk math — you did! What pen?

Happy. That was awful dumb, Biff, a pen like that is worth —

Willy (*seeing the pen for the first time*). You took Oliver's pen?

Biff (*weakening*). Dad, I just explained it to you.

Willy. You stole Bill Oliver's fountain pen!

Biff. I didn't exactly steal it! That's just what I've been explaining to you!

Happy. He had it in his hand and just then Oliver walked in, so he got nervous and stuck it in his pocket!

Willy. My God, Biff!

Biff. I never intended to do it, Dad!

Operator's Voice. Standish Arms, good evening!

Willy (*shouting*). I'm not in my room!

Biff (*frightened*). Dad, what's the matter? (*He and Happy stand up.*)

Operator. Ringing Mr. Loman for you!

Willy. I'm not there, stop it!

Biff (*horrified, gets down on one knee before Willy*). Dad, I'll make good, I'll make good. (*Willy tries to get to his feet. Biff holds him down.*) Sit down now.

Willy. No, you're no good, you're no good for anything.

Biff. I am, Dad, I'll find something else, you understand? Now don't worry about anything. (*He holds up Willy's face.*) Talk to me, Dad.

Operator. Mr. Loman does not answer. Shall I page him?

Willy (*attempting to stand, as though to rush and silence the Operator*). No, no, no!

Happy. He'll strike something, Pop.

Willy. No, no . . .

Biff (*desperately, standing over Willy*). Pop, listen! Listen to me! I'm telling you something good. Oliver talked to his partner about the Florida idea. You listening? He — he talked to his partner, and he came to me . . . I'm going to be all right, you hear? Dad, listen to me, he said it was just a question of the amount!

Willy. Then you . . . got it?

Happy. He's gonna be terrific, Pop!

Willy (*trying to stand*). Then you got it, haven't you? You got it! You got it!

Biff (*agonized, holds Willy down*). No, no. Look, Pop. I'm supposed to have lunch with them tomorrow. I'm just telling you this so you'll know that I can still make an impression, Pop. And I'll make good somewhere, but I can't go tomorrow, see?

Willy. Why not? You simply . . .

Biff. But the pen, Pop!

Willy. You give it to him and tell him it was an oversight!

Happy. Sure, have lunch tomorrow!

Biff. I can't say that . . .

Willy. You were doing a crossword puzzle and accidentally used his pen!

Biff. Listen, kid, I took those balls years ago, now I walk in with his fountain pen? That clinches it, don't you see? I can't face him like that! I'll try elsewhere.

Page's Voice. Paging Mr. Loman!

Willy. Don't you want to be anything?

Biff. Pop, how can I go back?

Willy. You don't want to be anything, is that what's behind it?

Biff (*now angry at Willy for not crediting his sympathy*). Don't take it that way! You think it was easy walking into that office after what I'd done to him? A team of horses couldn't have dragged me back to Bill Oliver!

Willy. Then why'd you go?

Biff. Why did I go? Why did I go! Look at you! Look at what's become of you!

    Off left, The Woman laughs.

Willy. Biff, you're going to go to that lunch tomorrow, or . . .
Biff. I can't go. I've got no appointment!
Happy. Biff, for . . . !
Willy. Are you spiting me?
Biff. Don't take it that way! Goddammit!
Willy (strikes Biff and falters away from the table). You rotten little louse! Are you spiting me?
The Woman. Someone's at the door, Willy!
Biff. I'm no good, can't you see what I am?
Happy (separating them). Hey, you're in a restaurant! Now cut it out, both of you! *(The girls enter.)* Hello, girls, sit down.

    The Woman laughs, off left.

Miss Forsythe. I guess we might as well. This is Letta.
The Woman. Willy, are you going to wake up?
Biff (ignoring Willy). How're ya, miss, sit down. What do you drink?
Miss Forsythe. Letta might not be able to stay long.
Letta. I gotta get up very early tomorrow. I got jury duty. I'm so excited! Were you fellows ever on a jury?
Biff. No, but I been in front of them! *(The girls laugh.)* This is my father.
Letta. Isn't he cute? Sit down with us, Pop.
Happy. Sit him down, Biff!
Biff (going to him). Come on, slugger, drink us under the table. To hell with it! Come on, sit down, pal.

    On Biff's last insistence, Willy is about to sit.

The Woman (now urgently). Willy, are you going to answer the door!

    The Woman's call pulls Willy back. He starts right, befuddled.

Biff. Hey, where are you going?
Willy. Open the door.
Biff. The door?
Willy. The washroom . . . the door . . . where's the door?
Biff (leading Willy to the left). Just go straight down.

    Willy moves left.

The Woman. Willy, Willy, are you going to get up, get up, get up, get up?

Willy exits left.

Letta. I think it's sweet you bring your daddy along.

Miss Forsythe. Oh, he isn't really your father!

Biff (*at left, turning to her resentfully*). Miss Forsythe, you've just seen a prince walk by. A fine, troubled prince. A hard-working, unappreciated prince. A pal, you understand? A good companion. Always for his boys.

Letta. That's so sweet.

Happy. Well, girls, what's the program? We're wasting time. Come on, Biff. Gather round. Where would you like to go?

Biff. Why don't you do something for him?

Happy. Me!

Biff. Don't you give a damn for him, Hap?

Happy. What're you talking about? I'm the one who . . .

Biff. I sense it, you don't give a good goddam about him. (*He takes the rolled-up hose from his pocket and puts it on the table in front of Happy.*) Look what I found in the cellar, for Christ's sake. How can you bear to let it go on?

Happy. Me? Who goes away? Who runs off and . . .

Biff. Yeah, but he doesn't mean anything to you. You could help him — I can't! Don't you understand what I'm talking about? He's going to kill himself, don't you know that?

Happy. Don't I know it! Me!

Biff. Hap, help him! Jesus . . . help him . . . Help me, help me, I can't bear to look at his face! (*Ready to weep, he hurries out, up right.*)

Happy (*starting after him*). Where are you going?

Miss Forsythe. What's he so mad about?

Happy. Come on, girls, we'll catch up with him.

Miss Forsythe (*as Happy pushes her out*). Say, I don't like that temper of his!

Happy. He's just a little overstrung, he'll be all right!

Willy (*off left, as The Woman laughs*). Don't answer! Don't answer!

Letta. Don't you want to tell your father . . .

Happy. No, that's not my father. He's just a guy. Come on, we'll catch Biff, and, honey, we're going to paint this town! Stanley, where's the check! Hey, Stanley!

They exit. Stanley looks toward left.

Stanley (*calling to Happy indignantly*). Mr. Loman! Mr. Loman!

Stanley picks up a chair and follows them off. Knocking is heard off left. The Woman enters, laughing. Willy follows her. She is in a black slip; he is buttoning his shirt. Raw, sensuous music accompanies their speech:

Willy. Will you stop laughing? Will you stop?

The Woman. Aren't you going to answer the door? He'll wake the whole hotel.

Willy. I'm not expecting anybody.

The Woman. Whyn't you have another drink, honey, and stop being so damn self-centered?

Willy. I'm so lonely.

The Woman. You know you ruined me, Willy? From now on, whenever you come to the office, I'll see that you go right through to the buyers. No waiting at my desk anymore, Willy. You ruined me.

Willy. That's nice of you to say that.

The Woman. Gee, you are self-centered! Why so sad? You are the saddest, self-centeredest soul I ever did see-saw. (*She laughs. He kisses her.*) Come on inside, drummer boy. It's silly to be dressing in the middle of the night. (*As knocking is heard.*) Aren't you going to answer the door?

Willy. They're knocking on the wrong door.

The Woman. But I felt the knocking. And he heard us talking in here. Maybe the hotel's on fire!

Willy (*his terror rising*). It's a mistake.

The Woman. Then tell him to go away!

Willy. There's nobody there.

The Woman. It's getting on my nerves, Willy. There's somebody standing out there and it's getting on my nerves!

Willy (*pushing her away from him*). All right, stay in the bathroom here, and don't come out. I think there's a law in Massachusetts about it, so don't come out. It may be that new room clerk. He looked very mean. So don't come out. It's a mistake, there's no fire.

The knocking is heard again. He takes a few steps away from her, and she vanishes into the wing. The light follows him, and now he is facing Young Biff, who carries a suitcase. Biff steps toward him. The music is gone.

Biff. Why didn't you answer?

Willy. Biff! What are you doing in Boston?

Biff. Why didn't you answer? I've been knocking for five minutes, I called you on the phone . . .

Willy. I just heard you. I was in the bathroom and had the door
  shut. Did anything happen home?
Biff. Dad — I let you down.
Willy. What do you mean?
Biff. Dad . . .
Willy. Biffo, what's this about? (*Putting his arm around Biff.*) Come
  on, let's go downstairs and get you a malted.
Biff. Dad, I flunked math.
Willy. Not for the term?
Biff. The term. I haven't got enough credits to graduate.
Willy. You mean to say Bernard wouldn't give you the answers?
Biff. He did, he tried, but I only got a sixty-one.
Willy. And they wouldn't give you four points?
Biff. Birnbaum refused absolutely. I begged him, Pop, but he
  won't give me those points. You gotta talk to him before
  they close the school. Because if he saw the kind of man
  you are, and you just talked to him in your way, I'm sure
  he'd come through for me. The class came right before
  practice, see, and I didn't go enough. Would you talk to
  him? He'd like you, Pop. You know the way you could
  talk.
Willy. You're on. We'll drive right back.
Biff. Oh, Dad, good work! I'm sure he'll change it for you!
Willy. Go downstairs and tell the clerk I'm checkin' out. Go right
  down.
Biff. Yes, sir! See, the reason he hates me, Pop — one day he was
  late for class so I got up at the blackboard and imitated him.
  I crossed my eyes and talked with a lithp.
Willy (*laughing*). You did? The kids like it?
Biff. They nearly died laughing!
Willy. Yeah? What'd you do?
Biff. The thquare root of thixty twee is . . . (*Willy bursts out
  laughing; Biff joins.*) And in the middle of it he walked in!

  Willy laughs and The Woman joins in offstage.

Willy (*without hesitation*). Hurry downstairs and . . .
Biff. Somebody in there?
Willy. No, that was next door.

  The Woman laughs offstage.

Biff. Somebody got in your bathroom!
Willy. No, it's the next room, there's a party . . .
The Woman (*enters, laughing; she lisps this*). Can I come in? There's
  something in the bathtub, Willy, and it's moving!

Willy looks at Biff, who is staring open-mouthed and horrified at The Woman.

Willy. Ah — you better go back to your room. They must be finished painting by now. They're painting her room so I let her take a shower here. Go back, go back . . . (*He pushes her.*)

The Woman (*resisting*). But I've got to get dressed, Willy, I can't . . .

Willy. Get out of here! Go back, go back . . . (*Suddenly striving for the ordinary.*) This is Miss Francis, Biff, she's a buyer. They're painting her room. Go back, Miss Francis, go back . . .

The Woman. But my clothes, I can't go out naked in the hall!

Willy (*pushing her offstage*). Get outa here! Go back, go back!

Biff slowly sits down on his suitcase as the argument continues offstage.

The Woman. Where's my stockings? You promised me stockings, Willy!

Willy. I have no stockings here!

The Woman. You had two boxes of size nine sheers for me, and I want them!

Willy. Here, for God's sake, will you get outa here!

The Woman (*enters holding a box of stockings*). I just hope there's nobody in the hall. That's all I hope. (*To Biff.*) Are you football or baseball?

Biff. Football.

The Woman (*angry, humiliated*). That's me too. G'night. (*She snatches her clothes from Willy, and walks out.*)

Willy (*after a pause*). Well, better get going. I want to get to the school first thing in the morning. Get my suits out of the closet. I'll get my valise. (*Biff doesn't move.*) What's the matter! (*Biff remains motionless, tears falling.*) She's a buyer. Buys for J. H. Simmons. She lives down the hall — they're painting. You don't imagine — (*He breaks off. After a pause.*) Now listen, pal, she's just a buyer. She sees merchandise in her room and they have to keep it looking just so . . . (*Pause. Assuming command.*) All right, get my suits. (*Biff doesn't move.*) Now stop crying and do as I say. I gave you an order. Biff, I gave you an order! Is that what you do when I give you an order? How dare you cry! (*Putting his arm around Biff.*) Now look, Biff, when you grow up you'll understand about these things. You mustn't — you mustn't overemphasize a thing like this. I'll see Birnbaum first thing in the morning.

Biff. Never mind.

Willy (*getting down beside Biff*). Never mind! He's going to give you those points. I'll see to it.

Biff. He wouldn't listen to you.

Willy. He certainly will listen to me. You need those points for the U. of Virginia.

Biff. I'm not going there.

Willy. Heh? If I can't get him to change that mark you'll make it up in summer school. You've got all summer to . . .

Biff (*his weeping breaking from him*). Dad . . .

Willy (*infected by it*). Oh, my boy . . .

Biff. Dad . . .

Willy. She's nothing to me, Biff. I was lonely, I was terribly lonely.

Biff. You — you gave her Mama's stockings! (*His tears break through and he rises to go.*)

Willy (*grabbing for Biff*). I gave you an order!

Biff. Don't touch me, you — liar!

Willy. Apologize for that!

Biff. You fake! You phony little fake! You fake! (*Overcome, he turns quickly and weeping fully goes out with his suitcase. Willy is left on the floor on his knees.*)

Willy. I gave you an order! Biff, come back here or I'll beat you! Come back here! I'll whip you!

> *Stanley comes quickly in from the right and stands in front of Willy.*

Willy (*shouts at Stanley*). I gave you an order . . .

Stanley. Hey, let's pick it up, pick it up, Mr. Loman. (*He helps Willy to his feet.*) Your boys left with the chippies. They said they'll see you home.

> *A second waiter watches some distance away.*

Willy. But we were supposed to have dinner together.

> *Music is heard, Willy's theme.*

Stanley. Can you make it?

Willy. I'll — sure, I can make it. (*Suddenly concerned about his clothes.*) Do I — I look all right?

Stanley. Sure, you look all right. (*He flicks a speck off Willy's lapel.*)

Willy. Here — here's a dollar.

Stanley. Oh, your son paid me. It's all right.

Willy (*putting it in Stanley's hand*). No, take it. You're a good boy.

Stanley. Oh, no, you don't have to . . .

Willy. Here — here's some more, I don't need it any more. (*After*

a slight pause.) Tell me — is there a seed store in the neighborhood?
Stanley. Seeds? You mean like to plant?

As Willy turns, Stanley slips the money back into his jacket pocket.

Willy. Yes. Carrots, peas . . .
Stanley. Well, there's hardware stores on Sixth Avenue, but it may
be too late now.
Willy (*anxiously*). Oh, I'd better hurry. I've got to get some seeds.
(*He starts off to the right.*) I've got to get some seeds, right
away. Nothing's planted. I don't have a thing in the ground.

*Willy hurries out as the light goes down. Stanley moves over to
the right after him, watches him off. The other waiter has been
staring at Willy.*

Stanley (*to the waiter*). Well, whatta you looking at?

*The waiter picks up the chairs and moves off right. Stanley takes
the table and follows him. The light fades on this area. There is
a long pause, the sound of the flute coming over. The light gradually
rises on the kitchen, which is empty. Happy appears at the door
of the house, followed by Biff. Happy is carrying a large bunch
of long-stemmed roses. He enters the kitchen, looks around for
Linda. Not seeing her, he turns to Biff, who is just outside the
house door, and makes a gesture with his hands, indicating "Not
here, I guess." He looks into the living room and freezes. Inside,
Linda, unseen, is seated, Willy's coat on her lap. She rises ominously
and quietly and moves toward Happy, who backs up into the
kitchen, afraid.*

Happy. Hey, what're you doing up? (*Linda says nothing but moves
toward him implacably.*) Where's Pop? (*He keeps backing to the
right, and now Linda is in full view in the doorway to the living
room.*) Is he sleeping?
Linda. Where were you?
Happy (*trying to laugh it off*). We met two girls, Mom, very fine
types. Here, we brought you some flowers. (*Offering them
to her.*) Put them in your room, Ma.

*She knocks them to the floor at Biff's feet. He has now come inside
and closed the door behind him. She stares at Biff, silent.*

Happy. Now what'd you do that for? Mom, I want you to have
some flowers . . .
Linda (*cutting Happy off, violently to Biff*). Don't you care whether
he lives or dies?

Happy (going to the stairs). Come upstairs, Biff.

Biff (with a flare of disgust, to Happy). Go away from me! (*To Linda.*) What do you mean, lives or dies? Nobody's dying around here, pal.

Linda. Get out of my sight! Get out of here!

Biff. I wanna see the boss.

Linda. You're not going near him!

Biff. Where is he? (*He moves into the living room and Linda follows.*)

Linda (shouting after Biff). You invite him for dinner. He looks forward to it all day — (*Biff appears in his parents' bedroom, looks around, and exits*) — and then you desert him there. There's no stranger you'd do that to!

Happy. Why? He had a swell time with us. Listen, when I — (*Linda comes back into the kitchen*) — desert him I hope I don't outlive the day!

Linda. Get out of here!

Happy. Now look, Mom . . .

Linda. Did you have to go to women tonight? You and your lousy rotten whores!

> *Biff re-enters the kitchen.*

Happy. Mom, all we did was follow Biff around trying to cheer him up! (*To Biff.*) Boy, what a night you gave me!

Linda. Get out of here, both of you, and don't come back! I don't want you tormenting him any more. Go on now, get your things together! (*To Biff.*) You can sleep in his apartment. (*She starts to pick up the flowers and stops herself.*) Pick up this stuff, I'm not your maid any more. Pick it up, you bum, you!

> *Happy turns his back to her in refusal. Biff slowly moves over and gets down on his knees, picking up the flowers.*

Linda. You're a pair of animals! Not one, not another living soul would have had the cruelty to walk out on that man in a restaurant!

Biff (not looking at her). Is that what he said?

Linda. He didn't have to say anything. He was so humiliated he nearly limped when he came in.

Happy. But, Mom, he had a great time with us . . .

Biff (cutting him off violently). Shut up!

> *Without another word, Happy goes upstairs.*

Linda. You! You didn't even go in to see if he was all right!

Biff (still on the floor in front of Linda, the flowers in his hand; with self-loathing). No. Didn't. Didn't do a damned thing. How do you like that, heh? Left him babbling in a toilet.

Linda. You louse. You . . .

Biff. Now you hit it on the nose! (*He gets up, throws the flowers in the wastebasket.*) The scum of the earth, and you're looking at him!

Linda. Get out of here!

Biff. I gotta talk to the boss, Mom. Where is he?

Linda. You're not going near him. Get out of this house!

Biff (with absolute assurance, determination). No. We're gonna have an abrupt conversation, him and me.

Linda. You're not talking to him.

Hammering is heard from outside the house, off right. Biff turns toward the noise.

Linda (*suddenly pleading*). Will you please leave him alone?

Biff. What's he doing out there?

Linda. He's planting the garden!

Biff (quietly). Now? Oh, my God!

Biff moves outside, Linda following. The light dies down on them and comes up on the center of the apron as Willy walks into it. He is carrying a flashlight, a hoe, and a handful of seed packets. He raps the top of the hoe sharply to fix it firmly, and then moves to the left, measuring off the distance with his foot. He holds the flashlight to look at the seed packets, reading off the instructions. He is in the blue of night.

Willy. Carrots . . . quarter-inch apart. Rows . . . one-foot rows. (*He measures it off.*) One foot. (*He puts down a package and measures off.*) Beets. (*He puts down another package and measures again.*) Lettuce. (*He reads the package, puts it down.*) One foot — (*He breaks off as Ben appears at the right and moves slowly down to him.*) What a proposition, ts, ts. Terrific, terrific. 'Cause she's suffered, Ben, the woman has suffered. You understand me? A man can't go out the way he came in, Ben, a man has got to add up to something. You can't, you can't — (*Ben moves toward him as though to interrupt.*) You gotta consider now. Don't answer so quick. Remember, it's a guaranteed twenty-thousand-dollar proposition. Now look, Ben, I want you to go through the ins and outs of this thing with me. I've got nobody to talk to, Ben, and the woman has suffered, you hear me?

Ben (*standing still, considering*). What's the proposition?

Willy. It's twenty thousand dollars on the barrelhead. Guaranteed, gilt-edged, you understand?

Ben. You don't want to make a fool of yourself. They might not honor the policy.

Willy. How can they dare refuse? Didn't I work like a coolie to meet every premium on the nose? And now they don't pay off? Impossible!

Ben. It's called a cowardly thing, William.

Willy. Why? Does it take more guts to stand here the rest of my life ringing up a zero?

Ben (*yielding*). That's a point, William. (*He moves, thinking, turns.*) And twenty thousand — that *is* something one can feel with the hand, it is there.

Willy (*now assured, with rising power*). Oh, Ben, that's the whole beauty of it! I see it like a diamond, shining in the dark, hard and rough, that I can pick up and touch in my hand. Not like — like an appointment! This would not be another damned-fool appointment, Ben, and it changes all the aspects. Because he thinks I'm nothing, see, and so he spites me. But the funeral . . . (*Straightening up.*) Ben, that funeral will be massive! They'll come from Maine, Massachusetts, Vermont, New Hampshire! All the old-timers with the strange license plates — that boy will be thunderstruck, Ben, because he never realized — I am known! Rhode Island, New York, New Jersey — I am known, Ben, and he'll see it with his eyes once and for all. He'll see what I am, Ben! He's in for a shock, that boy!

Ben (*coming down to the edge of the garden*). He'll call you a coward.

Willy (*suddenly fearful*). No, that would be terrible.

Ben. Yes. And a damned fool.

Willy. No, no, he mustn't, I won't have that! (*He is broken and desperate.*)

Ben. He'll hate you, William.

The gay music of the Boys is heard.

Willy. Oh, Ben, how do we get back to all the great times? Used to be so full of light, and comradeship, the sleigh-riding in winter, and the ruddiness on his cheeks. And always some kind of good news coming up, always something nice coming up ahead. And never even let me carry the valises in the house, and simonizing, simonizing that little red car! Why, why can't I give him something and not have him hate me?

Ben. Let me think about it. (*He glances at his watch.*) I still have a little time. Remarkable proposition, but you've got to be sure you're not making a fool of yourself.

Ben drifts off upstage and goes out of sight. Biff comes down from the left.

Willy (*suddenly conscious of Biff, turns and looks up at him, then begins picking up the packages of seeds in confusion.*) Where the hell is that seed? (*Indignantly.*) You can't see nothing out here! They boxed in the whole goddam neighborhood!

Biff. There are people all around here. Don't you realize that?

Willy. I'm busy. Don't bother me.

Biff (*taking the hoe from Willy*). I'm saying good-by to you, Pop. (*Willy looks at him, silent, unable to move.*) I'm not coming back any more.

Willy. You're not going to see Oliver tomorrow?

Biff. I've got no appointment, Dad.

Willy. He put his arm around you, and you've got no appointment?

Biff. Pop, get this now, will you? Everytime I've left it's been a fight that sent me out of here. Today I realized something about myself and I tried to explain it to you and I — I think I'm just not smart enough to make any sense out of it for you. To hell with whose fault it is or anything like that. (*He takes Willy's arm.*) Let's just wrap it up, heh? Come on in, we'll tell Mom. (*He gently tries to pull Willy to left.*)

Willy (*frozen, immobile, with guilt in his voice*). No, I don't want to see her.

Biff. Come on! (*He pulls again, and Willy tries to pull away.*)

Willy (*highly nervous*). No, no, I don't want to see her.

Biff (*tries to look into Willy's face, as if to find the answer there*). Why don't you want to see her?

Willy (*more harshly now*). Don't bother me, will you?

Biff. What do you mean, you don't want to see her? You don't want them calling you yellow, do you? This isn't your fault; it's me, I'm a bum. Now come inside! (*Willy strains to get away.*) Did you hear what I said to you?

Willy pulls away and quickly goes by himself into the house. Biff follows.

Linda (*to Willy*). Did you plant, dear?

Biff (*at the door, to Linda*). All right, we had it out. I'm going and I'm not writing any more.

Linda (*going to Willy in the kitchen*). I think that's the best way, dear. 'Cause there's no use drawing it out, you'll just never get along.

Willy doesn't respond.

Biff. People ask where I am and what I'm doing, you don't know, and you don't care. That way it'll be off your mind and you can start brightening up again. All right? That clears it, doesn't it? (*Willy is silent, and Biff goes to him.*) You gonna wish me luck, scout? (*He extends his hand.*) What do you say?

Linda. Shake his hand, Willy.

Willy (*turning to her, seething with hurt*). There's no necessity to mention the pen at all, y'know.

Biff (*gently*). I've got no appointment, Dad.

Willy (*erupting fiercely*). He put his arm around . . . ?

Biff. Dad, you're never going to see what I am, so what's the use of arguing? If I strike oil I'll send you a check. Meantime forget I'm alive.

Willy (*to Linda*). Spite, see?

Biff. Shake hands, Dad.

Willy. Not my hand.

Biff. I was hoping not to go this way.

Willy. Well, this is the way you're going. Good-by.

> *Biff looks at him a moment, then turns sharply and goes to the stairs.*

Willy (*stops him with*). May you rot in hell if you leave this house!

Biff (*turning*). Exactly what is it that you want from me?

Willy. I want you to know, on the train, in the mountains, in the valleys, wherever you go, that you cut down your life for spite!

Biff. No, no.

Willy. Spite, spite, is the word of your undoing! And when you're down and out, remember what did it. When you're rotting somewhere beside the railroad tracks, remember, and don't you dare blame it on me!

Biff. I'm not blaming it on you!

Willy. I won't take the rap for this, you hear?

> *Happy comes down the stairs and stands on the bottom step, watching.*

Biff. That's just what I'm telling you!

Willy (*sinking into a chair at a table, with full accusation*). You're trying to put a knife in me — don't think I don't know what you're doing!

Biff. All right, phony! Then let's lay it on the line. (*He whips the rubber tube out of his pocket and puts it on the table.*)

Happy. You crazy . . .

Linda. Biff! (*She moves to grab the hose, but Biff holds it down with his hand.*)

Biff. Leave it there! Don't move it!

Willy (*not looking at it*). What is that?

Biff. You know goddam well what that is.

Willy (*caged, wanting to escape*). I never saw that.

Biff. You saw it. The mice didn't bring it into the cellar! What is this supposed to do, make a hero out of you? This supposed to make me sorry for you?

Willy. Never heard of it.

Biff. There'll be no pity for you, you hear it? No pity!

Willy (*to Linda*). You hear the spite!

Biff. No, you're going to hear the truth — what you are and what I am!

Linda. Stop it!

Willy. Spite!

Happy (*coming down toward Biff*). You cut it now!

Biff (*to Happy*). The man don't know who we are! The man is gonna know! (*To Willy.*) We never told the truth for ten minutes in this house!

Happy. We always told the truth!

Biff (*turning on him*). You big blow, are you the assistant buyer? You're one of the two assistants to the assistant, aren't you?

Happy. Well, I'm practically . . .

Biff. You're practically full of it! We all are! and I'm through with it. (*To Willy.*) Now hear this, Willy, this is me.

Willy. I know you!

Biff. You know why I had no address for three months? I stole a suit in Kansas City and I was in jail. (*To Linda, who is sobbing.*) Stop crying. I'm through with it.

Linda turns away from them, her hands covering her face.

Willy. I suppose that's my fault!

Biff. I stole myself out of every good job since high school!

Willy. And whose fault is that?

Biff. And I never got anywhere because you blew me so full of hot air I could never stand taking orders from anybody! That's whose fault it is!

Willy. I hear that!

Linda. Don't, Biff!

Biff. It's goddam time you heard that! I had to be boss big shot in two weeks, and I'm through with it!

Willy. Then hang yourself! For spite, hang yourself!

Biff. No! Nobody's hanging himself, Willy! I ran down eleven flights with a pen in my hand today. And suddenly I stopped, you hear me? And in the middle of that office building, do you hear this? I stopped in the middle of that building and I saw — the sky. I saw the things that I love in this world. The work and the food and time to sit and smoke. And I looked at the pen and said to myself, what the hell am I grabbing this for? Why am I trying to become what I don't want to be? What am I doing in an office, making a contemptuous, begging fool of myself, when all I want is out there, waiting for me the minute I say I know who I am! Why can't I say that, Willy? (*He tries to make Willy face him, but Willy pulls away and moves to the left.*)

Willy (*with hatred, threateningly*). The door of your life is wide open!

Biff. Pop! I'm a dime a dozen, and so are you!

Willy (*turning on him now in an uncontrolled outburst*). I am not a dime a dozen! I am Willy Loman, and you are Biff Loman!

Biff starts for Willy, but is blocked by Happy. In his fury, Biff seems on the verge of attacking his father.

Biff. I am not a leader of men, Willy, and neither are you. You were never anything but a hard-working drummer who landed in the ash can like all the rest of them! I'm one dollar an hour, Willy! I tried seven states and couldn't raise it. A buck an hour! Do you gather my meaning? I'm not bringing home any prizes any more, and you're going to stop waiting for me to bring them home!

Willy (*directly to Biff*). You vengeful, spiteful mutt!

Biff breaks from Happy. Willy, in fright, starts up the stairs. Biff grabs him.

Biff (*at the peak of his fury*). Pop, I'm nothing! I'm nothing, Pop. Can't you understand that? There's no spite in it any more. I'm just what I am, that's all.

Biff's fury has spent itself and he breaks down, sobbing, holding on to Willy, who dumbly fumbles for Biff's face.

Willy (*astonished*). What're you doing? What're you doing? (*To Linda.*) Why is he crying?

Biff (*crying, broken*). Will you let me go, for Christ's sake? Will you take that phony dream and burn it before something happens? (*Struggling to contain himself he pulls away and moves to the stairs.*) I'll go in the morning. Put him — put him to bed. (*Exhausted, Biff moves up the stairs to his room.*)

Willy (after a long pause, astonished, elevated). Isn't that — isn't that remarkable? Biff — he likes me!

Linda. He loves you, Willy!

Happy (deeply moved). Always did, Pop.

Willy. Oh, Biff! (*Staring wildly.*) He cried! Cried to me. (*He is choking with his love, and now cries out his promise.*) That boy — that boy is going to be magnificent!

Ben appears in the light just outside the kitchen.

Ben. Yes, outstanding, with twenty thousand behind him.

Linda (sensing the racing of his mind, fearfully, carefully). Now come to bed, Willy. It's all settled now.

Willy (finding it difficult not to rush out of the house). Yes, we'll sleep. Come on. Go to sleep, Hap.

Ben. And it does take a great kind of a man to crack the jungle.

In accents of dread, Ben's idyllic music starts up.

Happy (his arm around Linda). I'm getting married, Pop, don't forget it. I'm changing everything. I'm gonna run that department before the year is up. You'll see, Mom. (*He kisses her.*)

Ben. The jungle is dark but full of diamonds, Willy.

Willy turns, moves, listening to Ben.

Linda. Be good. You're both good boys, just act that way, that's all.

Happy. 'Night, Pop. (*He goes upstairs.*)

Linda (to Willy). Come, dear.

Ben (with greater force). One must go in to fetch a diamond out.

Willy (to Linda, as he moves slowly along the edge of kitchen, toward the door). I just want to get settled down, Linda. Let me sit alone for a little.

Linda (almost uttering her fear). I want you upstairs.

Willy (taking her in his arms). In a few minutes, Linda. I couldn't sleep right now. Go on, you look awful tired. (*He kisses her.*)

Ben. Not like an appointment at all. A diamond is rough and hard to the touch.

Willy. Go on now. I'll be right up.

Linda. I think this is the only way, Willy.

Willy. Sure, it's the best thing.

Ben. Best thing!

Willy. The only way. Everything is gonna be — go on, kid, get to bed. You look so tired.

Linda. Come right up.

Willy. Two minutes.

> *Linda goes into the living room, then reappears in her bedroom. Willy moves just outside the kitchen door.*

Willy. Loves me. (*Wonderingly.*) Always loved me. Isn't that a remarkable thing? Ben, he'll worship me for it!

Ben (*with promise*). It's dark there, but full of diamonds.

Willy. Can you imagine that magnificence with twenty thousand dollars in his pocket?

Linda (*calling from her room*). Willy! Come up!

Willy (*calling into the kitchen*). Yes! yes. Coming! It's very smart, you realize that, don't you, sweetheart? Even Ben sees it. I gotta go, baby. 'By! 'By! (*Going over to Ben, almost dancing.*) Imagine? When the mail comes he'll be ahead of Bernard again!

Ben. A perfect proposition all around.

Willy. Did you see how he cried to me? Oh, if I could kiss him, Ben!

Ben. Time, William, time!

Willy. Oh, Ben, I always knew one way or another we were gonna make it, Biff and I!

Ben (*looking at his watch*). The boat. We'll be late. (*He moves slowly off into the darkness.*)

Willy (*elegiacally, turning to the house*). Now when you kick off, boy, I want a seventy-yard boot, and get right down the field under the ball, and when you hit, hit low and hit hard, because it's important, boy. (*He swings around and faces the audience.*) There's all kinds of important people in the stands, and the first thing you know . . . (*Suddenly realizing he is alone.*) Ben! Ben, where do I . . . ? (*He makes a sudden movement of search.*) Ben, how do I . . . ?

Linda (*calling*). Willy, you coming up?

Willy (*uttering a gasp of fear, whirling about as if to quiet her*). Sh! (*He turns around as if to find his way; sounds, faces, voices, seem to be swarming in upon him and he flicks at them, crying.*) Sh! Sh! (*Suddenly music, faint and high, stops him. It rises in intensity, almost to an unbearable scream. He goes up and down on his toes, and rushes off around the house.*) Shhh!

Linda. Willy?

> *There is no answer. Linda waits. Biff gets up off his bed. He is still in his clothes. Happy sits up. Biff stands listening.*

Linda (*with real fear*). Willy, answer me! Willy!

> *There is the sound of a car starting and moving away at full speed.*

Linda. No!

Biff (*rushing down the stairs*). Pop!

> *As the car speeds off the music crashes down in a frenzy of sound, which becomes the soft pulsation of a single cello string. Biff slowly returns to his bedroom. He and Happy gravely don their jackets. Linda slowly walks out of her room. The music has developed into a dead march. The leaves of day are appearing over everything. Charley and Bernard, somberly dressed, appear and knock on the kitchen door. Biff and Happy slowly descend the stairs to the kitchen as Charley and Bernard enter. All stop a moment when Linda, in clothes of mourning, bearing a little bunch of roses, comes through the draped doorway into the kitchen. She goes to Charley and takes his arm. Now all move toward the audience, through the wall-line of the kitchen. At the limit of the apron, Linda lays down the flowers, kneels, and sits back on her heels. All stare down at the grave.*

REQUIEM

Charley. It's getting dark, Linda.

> *Linda doesn't react. She stares at the grave.*

Biff. How about it, Mom? Better get some rest, heh? They'll be closing the gate soon.

> *Linda makes no move. Pause.*

Happy (*deeply angered*). He had no right to do that. There was no necessity for it. We would've helped him.

Charley (*grunting*). Hmmm.

Biff. Come along, Mom.

Linda. Why didn't anybody come?

Charley. It was a very nice funeral.

Linda. But where are all the people he knew? Maybe they blame him.

Charley. Naa. It's a rough world, Linda. They wouldn't blame him.

Linda. I can't understand it. At this time especially. First time in thirty-five years we were just about free and clear. He only needed a little salary. He was even finished with the dentist.

Charley. No man only needs a little salary.

Linda. I can't understand it.

Biff. There were a lot of nice days. When he'd come home from a trip; or on Sundays, making the stoop; finishing the cellar; putting on the new porch; when he built the extra bathroom; and put up the garage. You know something, Charley, there's more of him in that front stoop than in all the sales he ever made.

Charley. Yeah. He was a happy man with a batch of cement.

Linda. He was so wonderful with his hands.

Biff. He had the wrong dreams. All, all, wrong.

Happy (almost ready to fight Biff). Don't say that!

Biff. He never knew who he was.

Charley (stopping Happy's movement and reply; to Biff). Nobody dast blame this man. You don't understand: Willy was a salesman. And for a salesman, there is no rock bottom to the life. He don't put a bolt to a nut, he don't tell you the law or give you medicine. He's a man way out there in the blue, riding on a smile and a shoeshine. And when they start not smiling back — that's an earthquake. And then you get yourself a couple of spots on your hat, and you're finished. Nobody dast blame this man. A salesman is got to dream, boy. It comes with the territory.

Biff. Charley, the man didn't know who he was.

Happy (infuriated). Don't say that!

Biff. Why don't you come with me, Happy?

Happy. I'm not licked that easily. I'm staying right in this city, and I'm gonna beat this racket! (*He looks at Biff, his chin set.*) The Loman Brothers!

Biff. I know who I am, kid.

Happy. All right, boy. I'm gonna show you and everybody else that Willy Loman did not die in vain. He had a good dream. It's the only dream you can have — to come out number-one man. He fought it out here, and this is where I'm gonna win it for him.

Biff (with a hopeless glance at Happy, bends toward his mother). Let's go, Mom.

Linda. I'll be with you in a minute. Go on, Charley. (*He hesitates.*) I want to, just for a minute. I never had a chance to say good-by.

> *Charley moves away, followed by Happy. Biff remains a slight distance up and left of Linda. She sits there, summoning herself. The flute begins, not far away, playing behind her speech.*

Linda. Forgive me, dear. I can't cry. I don't know what it is, but I can't cry. I don't understand it. Why did you ever do that?

Help me, Willy, I can't cry. It seems to me that you're just on another trip. I keep expecting you. Willy, dear, I can't cry. Why did you do it? I search and search and I search, and I can't understand it, Willy. I made the last payment on the house today. Today, dear. And there'll be nobody home. (*A sob rises in her throat.*) We're free and clear. (*Sobbing mournfully, released.*) We're free. (*Biff comes slowly toward her.*) We're free . . . We're free . . .

Biff lifts her to her feet and moves out up right with her in his arms. Linda sobs quietly. Bernard and Charley come together and follow them, followed by Happy. Only the music of the flute is left on the darkening stage as over the house the hard towers of the apartment buildings rise into sharp focus, and the curtain falls.

QUESTIONS

1. Miller said in the *New York Times* (February 27, 1949, Sec. II, p. 1) that tragedy shows man's struggle to secure "his sense of personal dignity," and that "his destruction in the attempt posits a wrong or an evil in his environment." Does this make sense when applied to some earlier tragedy (for example, *Oedipus Rex* or *Hamlet*), and does it apply convincingly to *Death of a Salesman*? Is this the tragedy of an individual's own making? Or is society at fault for corrupting and exploiting Willy? Or both?
2. Is Willy pathetic rather than tragic? If pathetic, does this imply that the play is less worthy than if he is tragic?
3. Do you feel that Miller is straining too hard to turn a play about a little man into a big, impressive play? For example, do the musical themes, the unrealistic setting, the appearances of Ben, and the speech at the grave seem out of keeping in a play about the death of a salesman?
4. We don't know what Willy sells, and we don't know whether or not the insurance will be paid after his death. Do you consider these uncertainties to be faults in the play?
5. Is Howard a villain?
6. Characterize Linda.

The 1962 Cherry Lane Theater production of The Sandbox *starred John C. Becher and Jane Hoffman.* © *1962 Alix Jeffry/Harvard Theatre Collection.*

Edward Albee (American. b. 1928)

The Sandbox

A Brief Play, in Memory of My Grandmother (1876–1959)

Music by William Flanagan

List of Characters

The Young Man, 25, a good-looking, well-built boy in a bathing suit.
Mommy, 55, a well-dressed, imposing woman.
Daddy, 60, a small man; gray, thin.
Grandma, 86, a tiny, wizened woman with bright eyes.
The Musician, no particular age, but young would be nice.

Note: When, in the course of the play, Mommy and Daddy call each other by these names, there should be no suggestion of regionalism. These names are of empty affection and point up the presenility and vacuity of their characters.

Scene. *A bare stage, with only the following: Near the footlights, far stage-right, two simple chairs set side by side, facing the audience; near the footlights, far stage-left, a chair facing stage-right with a music stand before it; farther back, and stage-center, slightly elevated and raked, a large child's sandbox with a toy pail and shovel; the background is the sky, which alters from brightest day to deepest night.*

At the beginning, it is brightest day; the Young Man is alone on stage, to the rear of the sandbox, and to one side. He is doing calesthenics; he does calesthenics until quite at the very end of the play. These calesthenics, employing the arms only, should suggest the beating and fluttering of wings. The Young Man is, after all, the Angel of Death.

Mommy and Daddy enter from stage-left, Mommy first.

Mommy (motioning to Daddy). Well, here we are; this is the beach.
Daddy (whining). I'm cold.
Mommy (dismissing him with a little laugh). Don't be silly; it's as

warm as toast. Look at that nice young man over there: *he*
doesn't think it's cold. (*Waves to the Young Man.*) Hello.
Young Man (*with an endearing smile*). Hi!
Mommy (*looking about*). This will do perfectly . . . don't you think
so, Daddy? There's sand there . . . and the water beyond.
What do you think, Daddy?
Daddy (*vaguely*). Whatever you say, Mommy.
Mommy (*with the same little laugh*). Well, of course . . . whatever
I say. Then, it's settled, is it?
Daddy (*shrugs*). She's *your* mother, not mine.
Mommy. I know she's my mother. What do you take me for? (*A
pause.*) All right, now; let's get on with it. (*She shouts into
the wings, stage-left.*) You! Out there! You can come in now.

*The Musician enters, seats himself in the chair, stage-left, places
music on the music stand, is ready to play. Mommy nods approvingly.*

Mommy. Very nice; very nice. Are you ready, Daddy? Let's go
get Grandma.
Daddy. Whatever you say, Mommy.
Mommy (*leading the way out, stage-left*). Of course, whatever I say.
(*To the Musician.*) You can begin now.

*The Musician begins playing; Mommy and Daddy exit; the Musician,
all the while playing, nods to the Young Man.*

Young Man (*with the same endearing smile*). Hi!

*After a moment, Mommy and Daddy re-enter, carrying Grandma.
She is borne in by their hands under her armpits; she is quite rigid;
her legs are drawn up; her feet do not touch the ground; the
expression on her ancient face is that of puzzlement and fear.*

Daddy. Where do we put her?
Mommy (*the same little laugh*). Wherever I say, of course. Let me
see . . . well . . . all right, over there . . . in the sandbox.
(*Pause.*) Well, what are you waiting for, Daddy? . . . The
sandbox!

*Together they carry Grandma over to the sandbox and more or
less dump her in.*

Grandma (*righting herself to a sitting position, her voice a cross between
a baby's laugh and cry*). Ahhhhhh! Graaaaa!
Daddy (*dusting himself*). What do we do now?
Mommy (*to the Musician*). You can stop now.

The Musician stops.

(*Back to Daddy.*) What do you mean, what do we do now? We
go over there and sit down, of course. (*To the Young Man.*)
Hello there.

Young Man (*again smiling*). Hi!

> *Mommy and Daddy move to the chairs, stage-right, and sit down.*
> *A pause.*

Grandma (*same as before*). Ahhhhhh! Ah-haaaaaa! Graaaaaa!

Daddy. Do you think . . . do you think she's . . . comfortable?

Mommy (*impatiently*). How would I know?

Daddy (*pause*). What do we do now?

Mommy (*as if remembering*). We . . . wait. We . . . sit here . . . and
we wait . . . that's what we do.

Daddy (*after a pause*). Shall we talk to each other?

Mommy (*with that little laugh; picking something off her dress*). Well,
you can talk, if you want to . . . if you can think of anything
to *say* . . . if you can think of anything *new*.

Daddy (*thinks*). No . . . I suppose not.

Mommy (*with a triumphant laugh*). Of course not!

Grandma (*banging the toy shovel against the pail*). Haaaaaa! Ah-haaaaaa!

Mommy (*out over the audience*). Be quiet, Grandma . . . just be
quiet, and wait.

> *Grandma throws a shovelful of sand at Mommy.*

Mommy (*still out over the audience*). She's throwing sand at me! You
stop that, Grandma; you stop throwing sand at Mommy!
(*To Daddy.*) She's throwing sand at me.

> *Daddy looks around at Grandma, who screams at him.*

Grandma. GRAAAAAA!

Mommy. Don't look at her. Just . . . sit here . . . be very still . . .
and wait. (*To the Musician.*) You . . . uh . . . you go ahead
and do whatever it is you do.

> *The Musician plays.*

> *Mommy and Daddy are fixed, staring out beyond the audience.*
> *Grandma looks at them, looks at the Musician, looks at the sandbox,*
> *throws down the shovel.*

Grandma. Ah-haaaaaa! Graaaaaa! (*Looks for reaction; gets none. Now*
. . . *directly to the audience.*) Honestly! What a way to treat
an old woman! Drag her out of the house . . . stick her in
a car . . . bring her out here from the city . . . dump her
in a pile of sand . . . and leave her here to set. I'm eighty-
six years old! I was married when I was seventeen. To a

farmer. He died when I was thirty. (*To the Musician.*) Will
you stop that, please?

The Musician stops playing.

I'm a feeble old woman . . . how do you expect anybody
to hear me over that peep! peep! peep! (*To herself.*) There's
no respect around here. (*To the Young Man.*) There's no
respect around here!

Young Man (*same smile*). Hi!

Grandma (*after a pause, a mild double-take, continues, to the audience*).
My husband died when I was thrity (*indicates Mommy*), and
I had to raise that big cow over there all by my lonesome.
You can imagine what *that was like*. Lordy! (*To the Young
Man.*) Where'd they get *you*?

Young Man. Oh . . . I've been around for a while.

Grandma. I'll bet you have! Heh, heh, heh. Will you look at you!

Young Man (*flexing his muscles*). Isn't that something? (*Continues
his calesthenics.*)

Grandma. Boy, oh boy; I'll say. Pretty good.

Young Man (*sweetly*). I'll say.

Grandma. Where ya from?

Young Man. Southern California.

Grandma (*nodding*). Figgers; figgers. What's your name, honey?

Young Man. I don't know. . . .

Grandma (*to the audience*). Bright, too!

Young Man. I mean . . . I mean, they haven't given me one yet
. . . the studio . . .

Grandma (*giving him the once-over*). You don't say . . . you don't
say. Well . . . uh, I've got to talk some more . . . don't you
go 'way.

Young Man. Oh, no.

Grandma (*turning her attention back to the audience*). Fine; fine. (*Then,
once more, back to the Young Man.*) You're . . . you're an
actor, hunh?

Young Man (*beaming*). Yes. I am.

Grandma (*to the audience again; shrugs*). I'm smart that way. *Anyhow*,
I had to raise . . . *that* over there all by my lonesome; and
what's next to her there . . . that's what she married. Rich?
I tell you . . . money, money, money. They took me off
the *farm* . . . which was real decent of them . . . and they
moved me into the big town house with *them* . . . fixed a
nice place for me under the stove . . . gave me an army
blanket . . . and my own dish . . . my very own dish! So,
what have I got to complain about? Nothing, of course. I'm

not complaining. (*She looks up at the sky, shouts to someone off stage.*) Shouldn't it be getting dark now, dear?

The lights dim; night comes on. The Musician begins to play; it becomes deepest night. There are spots on all the players, including the Young Man, who is, of course, continuing his calisthenics.

Daddy (*stirring*). It's nighttime.
Mommy. Shhhh. Be still . . . wait.
Daddy (*whining*). It's so hot.
Mommy. Shhhhhh. Be still . . . wait.
Grandma (*to herself*). That's better. Night. (*To the Musician.*)
Honey, do you play all through this part?

The Musician nods.

Well, keep it nice and soft; that's a good boy.

The Musician nods again; plays softly.

That's nice.

There is an off-stage rumble.

Daddy (*starting*). What was that?
Mommy (*beginning to weep*). It was nothing.
Daddy. It was . . . it was . . . thunder . . . or a wave breaking . . . or something.
Mommy (*whispering, through her tears*). It was an off-stage rumble . . . and you know what *that* means. . . .
Daddy. I forget. . . .
Mommy (*barely able to talk*). It means the time has come for poor Grandma . . . and I can't bear it!
Daddy (*vacantly*). I . . . I suppose you've got to be brave.
Grandma (*mocking*). That's right, kid; be brave. You'll bear up; you'll get over it.

Another off-stage rumble . . . louder.

Mommy. Ohhhhhhhhhh . . . poor Grandma . . . poor Grandma.
. . .
Grandma (*to Mommy*). I'm fine! I'm all right! It hasn't happened yet!

A violent off-stage rumble. All the lights go out, save the spot on the Young Man; the Musician stops playing.

Mommy. Ohhhhhhhhhh. . . . Ohhhhhhhhhh. . . .

Silence.

Grandma. Don't put the lights up yet . . . I'm not ready; I'm not quite ready. (*Silence.*) All right, dear . . . I'm about done.

The lights come up again, to brightest day; the Musician begins to play. Grandma is discovered, still in the sandbox, lying on her side, propped up on an elbow, half covered, busily shoveling sand over herself.

Grandma (muttering). I don't know how I'm supposed to do anything with this goddam toy shovel. . . .

Daddy. Mommy! It's daylight!

Mommy (brightly). So it is! Well! Our long night is over. We must put away our tears, take off our mourning . . . and face the future. It's our duty.

Grandma (still shoveling; mimicking). . . . take off our mourning . . . face the future. . . . Lordy!

Mommy and Daddy rise, stretch. Mommy waves to the Young Man.

Young Man (with that smile). Hi!

Grandma plays dead. (!) Mommy and Daddy go over to look at her; she is a little more than half buried in the sand; the toy shovel is in her hands, which are crossed on her breast.

Mommy (before the sandbox; shaking her head). Lovely! It's . . . it's hard to be sad . . . she looks . . . so happy. (*With pride and conviction.*) It pays to do things well. (*To the Musician.*) All right, you can stop now, if you want to. I mean, stay around for a swim, or something; it's all right with us. (*She sighs heavily.*) Well, Daddy . . . off we go.

Daddy. Brave Mommy!

Mommy. Brave Daddy!

They exit, stage-left.

Grandma (after they leave; lying quite still). It pays to do things well. . . . Boy, oh boy! (*She tries to sit up.*) . . . well, kids . . . (*But she finds she can't.*) . . . I . . . I can't get up. I . . . can't move. . . .

The Young Man stops his calisthenics, nods to the Musician, walks over to Grandma, kneels down by the sandbox.

Grandma. I . . . can't move. . . .

Young Man. Shhhhh . . . be very still. . . .

Grandma. I . . . I can't move. . . .

Young Man. Uh . . . ma'am; I . . . I have a line here.

Grandma. Oh, I'm sorry, sweetie; you go right ahead.

Young Man. I am . . . uh . . .

Grandma. Take your time, dear.

Young Man (prepares; delivers the line like a real amateur). I am the Angel of Death. I am . . . uh . . . I am come for you.

Grandma. What . . . wha . . . *(Then, with resignation.)* . . . ohhhh . . . ohhhh, I see.

The Young Man bends over, kisses Grandma gently on the forehead.

Grandma (her eyes closed, her hands folded on her breast again, the shovel between her hands, a sweet smile on her face). Well . . . that was very nice, dear. . . .

Young Man (still kneeling). Shhhhhh . . . be still. . . .

Grandma. What I meant was . . . you did that very well, dear. . . .

Young Man (blushing). . . . oh . . .

Grandma. No; I mean it. You've got that . . . you've got a quality.

Young Man (with his endearing smile). Oh . . . thank you; thank you very much . . . ma'am.

Grandma (slowly; softly — as the Young Man puts his hands on top of Grandma's). You're . . . you're welcome . . . dear.

Tableau. The Musician continues to play as the curtain slowly comes down.

CURTAIN

QUESTIONS

1. In a sentence characterize Mommy, and in another sentence characterize Daddy.
2. Of the four characters in the play, which do you find the most sympathetic?
3. In a longer play, *The American Dream,* Albee uses the same four characters that he uses in *The Sandbox.* Of *The American Dream* he wrote:

   The play is . . . a condemnation of complacency, cruelty, emasculation and vacuity; it is a stand against the fiction that everything in this slipping land of ours is peachy-keen.

   To what extent does this statement help you to understand (and to enjoy) *The Sandbox?*
4. In the *New York Times Magazine,* February 25, 1962, Albee protested against the view that his plays, and others of the

so-called Theater of the Absurd, are depressing. He includes a quotation from Martin Esslin's book, *The Theatre of the Absurd:*

Ultimately . . . The Theatre of the Absurd does not reflect despair or a return to dark irrational forces but expresses modern man's endeavor to come to terms with the world in which he lives. It attempts to make him face up to the human condition as it really is, to free him from illusions that are bound to cause constant maladjustment and disappointment. . . . For the dignity of man lies in his ability to face reality in all its senselessness; to accept it freely, without fear, without illusions — and to laugh at it.

In what ways is this statement helpful? In what ways is it not helpful? Explain.

Clare Boothe Luce (*American. 1903–1987*)

Slam the Door Softly

The scene is the Thaw Walds' cheerfully furnished middle-class living room in New York's suburbia. There are a front door and hall, a door to the kitchen area, and a staircase to the bedroom floor. Two easy chairs and two low hassocks with toys on them, grouped around a television, indicate a family of four. Drinks are on a bar cart at one end of a comfortable sofa, and an end table at the other. There are slightly more than the average number of bookshelves. The lamps are on, but as we don't hear the children, we know it is the Parents' Hour.

As the curtain rises, Thaw Wald, a good-looking fellow, about 35, is sitting in one of the easy chairs, smoking and watching TV. His back is to the sofa and staircase, so he does not see his wife coming down the stairs. Nora Wald is a rather pretty woman of about 32. She is carrying a suitcase, handbag, and an armful of books.

Thaw switches channels, and lands in the middle of a panel show. During the TV dialogue that follows Nora somewhat furtively deposits her suitcase in the hall, takes her coat out of the hall closet, and comes back to the sofa carrying coat, purse, and books. She lays her coat on the sofa, and the books on the end table. The books are full of little paper slips — bookmarkers. All of the above

*actions are unobserved by Thaw. We cannot see the TV screen,
but we hear the voices of four women, all talking excitedly at once.*

Thaw (to the screen and the world in general). God, these Liberation
gals! Still at it.

Male Moderator's Voice (full of paternal patience wearing a bit thin).
Ladies! Lay-deez! Can't we switch now from the question
of the sex-typing of jobs to what the Women's Liberation
Movement thinks about —

Older Woman's Voice. May I finish! In the Soviet Union 83 percent
of the dentists, 75 percent of the doctors and 37 percent of
the lawyers are women. In Poland and Denmark —

Moderator. I think you have already amply made your point, Mrs.
Epstein — anything men can do, women can do better!

Young Woman's Voice (angrily). That was *not* her point — and you
know it! What she said was, there are very few professional
jobs men are doing that women couldn't do, if only —

Thaw. Well, for God's sake then, shaddup, and go do 'em —

Black Woman's Voice. What she's been saying, what we've all been
saying, and you men just don't want to hear us, is — things
are the same for women as they are for us black people. We
try to get up, you just sit down on us, like a big elephant
sits down on a bunch of poor little mice.

Moderator. Well, sometimes moderators have to play the elephant,
and sit down on one subject in order to develop another.
As I was about to say, ladies, there *is one thing* a woman
can do, no man can do — *(in his best holy-night-all-is-bright
voice)* give birth to a child.

Young Woman's Voice. So what else is new?

Thaw. One gets you ten, she's a Lesbo —

Moderator (forcefully). And *that* brings us to marriage! Now, if *I*
may be permitted to get in just *one* statistic, edgewise: two
thirds of all adult American females are married women.
And now! *(At last he's got them where he wants them.)* What
is the Women's Lib view of Woman's No. 1 job — Occupation
Housewife?

Thaw. Ha! That's the one none of 'em can handle —

Young Woman's Voice (loud and clear). Marriage, as an institution,
is as thoroughly corrupt as prostitution. It is, in fact, legalized
and romanticized prostitution. A woman who marries is
selling her sexual services and domestic services for permanent
bed and board —

Black Woman's Voice. There's no human being a man can buy
anymore — except a woman —

Thaw (snapping off the TV). Crrr-ap! Boy, what a bunch of battle-
   axes! *(He goes back to studying his TV listings.)*
Nora (raising her voice). Thaw! I'd like to say something about what
   they just said about marriage —
Thaw (in a warning voice). Uh-uh, Nora! We both agreed months
   ago, you'd lay off the feminist bit, if I'd lay off watching
   Saturday football —
Nora. And do something with the children. . . . But Thaw, there's
   something maybe, I ought to try to tell you myself —

> *Thaw is not listening. Nora makes a "what's the use" gesture,*
> *then opens her purse, takes out three envelopes, carefully inserts*
> *two of them under the covers of the top two books.*

Thaw. Like to hear Senators Smithers, Smethers and Smothers on
   "How Fast Can We Get Out of Vietnam?"
Nora (cool mockery). That bunch of pot-bellied, bald-headed old
   goats! Not one of them could get a woman — well, yes,
   maybe for two dollars.
Thaw. You don't look at Senators, Nora. You listen to them.
Nora (nodding). Women are only to look at. Men are to listen to.
   Got it.

> *Thaw snaps off the TV. He is now neither looking at her nor*
> *listening to her, as he methodically turns pages of the magazine*
> *he has picked up.*

Thaw. Finished reading to the kids?
Nora. I haven't been reading to the children. I've been reading to
   myself — and talking to myself — for a long time now.
Thaw. That's good. *(She passes him, carrying the third envelope, and*
   goes into kitchen.)
Thaw (unenthusiastically). Want some help with the dishes?
Nora's Voice. I'm not doing the dishes.
Thaw (enthusiastically). Say, Nora, this is quite an ad we've got
   in *LIFE* for Stove Mountain Life Insurance.
Nora's Voice. Yes, I saw it. Great. *(She comes back and goes to sofa.)*
Thaw. It's the kind of ad that grabs you. This sad-faced, nice-
   looking woman of 50, sitting on a bench with a lot of dis-
   couraged old biddies, in an employment agency. Great caption
   — *(reading)*
Nora and Thaw (together). "Could this happen to *your* wife?"
Nora. I'll let you know the answer very shortly. *(A pause.)* You
   really don't hear me anymore, do you? *(He really doesn't.*
   She buttons herself into her coat, pulls on her gloves.) Well, there
   are enough groceries for a week. All the telephone numbers

you'll need and menus for the children are in the envelope on the spindle. A girl will come in to take care of them after school — until your mother gets here.

Thaw. Uh-huh. . . .

Nora (looks around sadly). Well, goodby dear little doll house. Goodby dear husband. You've had the best ten years of my life.

She goes to the staircase, blows two deep kisses upstairs, just as Thaw glances up briefly at her, but returns automatically to his magazine. Nora picks up suitcase, opens the door, goes out, closing it quietly.

Thaw (like a man suddenly snapping out of a hypnotic trance). Nora? Nora? NOR-RA! *(He is out of the door in two seconds.)*

Thaw's and Nora's Voices. Nora, where're you going? — I'll miss my train — I don't understand — it's all in my letter — let me go! — You come back —

They return. He is pulling her by the arm. He yanks the suitcase away from her, drops it in the hall.

Nora. Ouch! You're hurting me!

Thaw. Now what is this all about? *(He shoves her into the room, then stands between her and door.)* Why the hell . . . What're you sneaking out of the house . . . What's that suitcase for?

Nora. I wasn't sneaking. I told you. But you weren't listening.

Thaw. I was listening . . . it just didn't register. You said you were reading to yourself. Then you started yakking about the kids and the groceries and the doll house mother sent . . . *(flabbergasted.)* Goodby?! What the hell do you mean, *goodby?!*

Nora. Just that. I'm leaving you. *(Pointing to books.)* My letter will explain everything —

Thaw. Have you blown your mind?

Nora. Thaw, I've got to scoot, or I'll miss the eight-o-nine.

Thaw. You'll miss it. *(He backs her to the sofa, pushes her onto it, goes and slams the door and strides back.)* Now, my girl, explain all this.

Nora. That's easy. Muscle. The heavier musculature of the male is a secondary sexual characteristic. Although that's not certain. It could be just the result of selective breeding. In primitive times, of course, the heavier musculature of the male was necessary to protect the pregnant female and the immobile young —

Thaw (his anger evaporates). Nora, are you sick?

Nora. But what's just happened now shows that nothing has changed

— I mean, fundamentally changed — in centuries, in the relations between the sexes. *You* still Tarzan, *me* still Jane.

Thaw (sits on sofa beside her, feels her head). I've noticed you've been . . . well . . . acting funny lately. . . .

Nora. Funny?

Thaw. Like there was something on your mind. . . . Tell me, what's wrong, sweetheart? Where does it hurt?

Nora. It hurts *(taps head)* here. Isn't that where thinking hurts *you?* No. You're used to it. I was, too, when I was at Wellesley. But I sort of stopped when I left. It's really hard to think of anything else when you're having babies.

Thaw. Nora, isn't it about time for your period?

Nora. But if God had wanted us to think just with our wombs, why did He give us a brain? No matter what men say, Thaw, the female brain is not a vestigial organ, like a vermiform appendix.

Thaw. Nora . . .

Nora. Thaw, I can just about make my train. I'll leave the car and keys in the usual place at the station. Now, I have a very important appointment in the morning. *(She starts to rise.)*

Thaw. Appointment? *(Grabs her shoulders.)* Nora, look at me! You weren't sneaking out of the house to . . . get an abortion?

Nora. When a man can't explain a woman's actions, the first thing he thinks about is the condition of her uterus. Thaw, if you were leaving me and I didn't know why, would I ask, first thing, if you were having prostrate trouble?

Thaw. Don't try to throw me off the track, sweetie! Now, if you want another baby . . .

Nora. Thaw, don't you remember, we both agreed about the overpopulation problem —

Thaw. To hell with the overpopulation problem. Let Nixon solve that. Nora, I can swing another baby —

Nora. Maybe you can. I can't. For me there are no more splendid, new truths to be learned from scanning the contents of babies' diapers. Thaw, I *am* pregnant. But not in a feminine way. In the way only men are supposed to get pregnant.

Thaw. Men, pregnant?

Nora (nodding). With ideas. Pregnancies there *(taps his head)* are masculine. And a very superior form of labor. Pregnancies here *(taps her tummy)* are feminine — a very inferior form of labor. That's an example of male linguistic chauvinism. Mary Ellmann is *great* on that. You'll enjoy her *Thinking about Women.* . . .

Thaw (going to telephone near bookshelf). I'm getting the doctor.

(Nora makes a dash for the door, he drops the phone.) Oh, no you don't!

He reaches for her as she passes, misses. Grabs her ponytail and hauls her back by it, and shoves her into the easy chair.

Nora. Brother, Millett sure had you taped.

Thaw. Milly *who? (A new thought comes to him.)* Has one of your goddamgossipyfemale friends been trying to break up our marriage? *(He suddenly checks his conscience. It is not altogether pure.)* What did she tell you? That she saw me having lunch, uh, dinner, with some girl?

Nora *(nodding to herself).* Right on the button!

Thaw. Now, Nora, I can explain about that girl —

Nora. You don't have to. Let's face it. Monogamy is not natural to the male —

Thaw. You know I'm not in love with anybody but you —

Nora. It's not natural to the female, either. Making women think it is is man's most successful form of brainwashing —

Thaw. Nora, I swear, that girl means nothing to me —

Nora. And you probably mean nothing to her. So whose skin is off whose nose?

Thaw *(relieved, but puzzled).* Well, uh, I'm glad you feel that way about — uh — things.

Nora. Oh, it's not the way I *feel.* It's the way things really are. What with the general collapse of the mores, and now the Pill, women are becoming as promiscuous as men. It figures. We're educated from birth to think of ourselves just as man-traps. Of course, in my mother's day, good women thought of themselves as private man-traps. Only bad women were public man-traps. Now we've all gone public. *(Looks at watch.)* I'll have to take the eight-forty.

She gets out of her coat, lays it, ready to slip into, on back of sofa.

Thaw *(a gathering suspicion).* Nora, are you trying to tell me . . . that *you* —

Nora. Of course, a lot of it, today, is the fault of the advertising industry. Making women think they're failures in life if they don't make like sex-pots around the clock. We're even supposed to wear false eyelashes when we're vacuuming. Betty Friedan's great on that. She says many lonely suburban housewives, unable to identify their real problem, think more sex is the answer. So they sleep with the milkman, or the delivery boy. If I felt like sleeping with anybody like that,

I'd pick the plumber. When you need *him,* boy you *need* him!

Thaw (the unpleasant thought he has been wrestling with has now jelled). Nora . . . are you . . . trying to tell me you are leaving me — for someone else?

Nora. Why, Thaw Wald! How could you even *think* such a thing? *(To herself.)* Now, how naïve can I be? What else do men think about, in connection with women, *but sex?* He is saying to himself, she's not having her period, she's not pregnant, she's not jealous: it's *got* to be another man.

Thaw. Stop muttering to yourself, and answer my question.

Nora. I forgot what it was. Oh, yes. *No.*

Thaw. No what?

Nora. No, I'm not in love with anybody else. I was a virgin when I married you. And intacta. And that wasn't par for the course — even at Wellesley. And I've never slept with anybody else, partly because I never wanted to. And partly because, I suppose, of our family's Presbyterian hangup. So, now that all the vital statistics are out of the way, I'll just drive around until —

Begins to slip her arms into coat. He grabs coat, throws it on easy chair.

Thaw. You're not leaving until you tell me *why.*

Nora. But it's all in my letter. *(Points.)* The fat one sticking out of Simone de Beauvoir's *Second Sex* —

Thaw. If you have a bill of particulars against me, I want it — straight. From you.

Nora. Oh, darling, I have no bill of particulars. By all the standards of our present-day society, you are a very good husband. And, mark me, you'll be president of Stove Mountain Life Insurance Company before you're 50. The point is, what will I be when I'm 50 —

Thaw. You'll be my wife, if I have anything to say. Okay. So you're not leaving me because I'm a bad husband, or because my financial future is dim.

Nora. No. Oh, Thaw, you just wouldn't understand.

Thaw (patiently). I might, if you would try, for just one minute, to talk logically —

Nora. Thaw, women aren't trained to talk logically. Men don't like women who talk logically. They find them unfeminine — aggressive —

Thaw. Dammit, Nora, will you talk sense . . .

Nora. But Boy! does a man get sore when a woman won't talk

logically when *he* wants her to, and *(snaps fingers)* like that!
And *that* isn't illogical? What women men are! Now, if you
will step aside —

Thaw (grabbing her and shaking her). You're going to tell me why
you're walking out on me, if I have to *sock* you!

Nora. Thaw, eyeball to eyeball, *I am leaving you* — and not for a
man. For reasons of my own I just don't think you *can*
understand. And if you mean to stop me, you'll have to beat
me to a pulp. But I'm black and blue already.

Thaw (seizes her tenderly in his arms, kisses her). Nora, sweetheart!
You know I couldn't really hurt you. *(Kisses, kisses.)* Ba-
aaby, what do you say we call it a night? *(Scoops her up in
his arms.)* You can tell me *all* about it in bed . . .

Nora. The classical male one-two. Sock 'em and screw 'em.

Thaw (dumping her on sofa). Well, it's been known to work on a
lot of occasions. Something tells me this isn't one of them.
(Pours a drink.)

Nora. I guess I need one, too. *(He mixes them.)* Thaw?

Thaw. Yes.

Nora. I couldn't help being a *little* pleased when you made like a
caveman. It shows you really do value my sexual services.

Thaw. Jee-zus!

Nora. Well, it can't be my domestic services — you don't realize,
yet, what they're worth. *(Drinks.)* Thaw, you do have a
problem with me. But you can't solve it with force. And *I*
do have a problem. But I can't solve it with sex.

Thaw. Could you, would you, *try* to tell me what my-you-our
problem is?

Nora. Friedan's *Feminine Mystique* is very good on The Problem.
I've marked all the relevant passages. And I've personalized
them in my letter —

*He goes to book. Yanks out letter, starts to tear it up. Nora groans.
He changes his mind, and stuffs it in his pocket.*

Thaw. Look, Nora, there's one thing I've always said about you.
For a woman, you're pretty damn honest. Don't you think
you owe it to me to level and give me a chance to defend
myself?

Nora. The trouble is, *you* would have to listen to *me*. And that's
hard for you. I *understand why*. Not listening to women is
a habit that's been passed on from father to son for generations.
You could almost say, tuning out on women is another
secondary sexual male characteristic.

Thaw. So our problem is that *I* don't listen?

Nora. Thaw, you always go on talking, no matter how hard I'm interrupting.

Thaw. Okay. You have the floor.

Nora. Well, let's begin where this started tonight. When you oppressed me, and treated me as an inferior —

Thaw. I oppressed . . . *(Hesitates.)* Lay on, MacDuff.

Nora. You honestly don't think that yanking me around by my hair and threatening to sock me are not the oppressive gestures of a superior male toward an inferior female?

Thaw. For Chrissake, Nora, a man isn't going to let the woman he loves leave him, if he can stop her!

Nora. Exactly. Domination of the insubordinate female is an almost instinctive male reflex. *In extremis,* Thaw, it is *rape.* Now, would I like it if you should say you were going to leave me? No. But could I drag you back —

Thaw. You'd just have to crook your little finger.

Nora. Flattery will get you nowhere this evening. So, where was I?

Thaw. I am a born rapist.

Nora. Wasn't that what you had in mind when you tried to adjourn this to our bedroom? But that's just your primitive side. There's your civilized side too. You are a patriarchal *pater familias.*

Thaw. What am I now?

Nora. Thaw, you do realize we all live in a patriarchy, where men govern women by playing sexual politics?

Thaw. Look, you're not still sore because I talked you into voting for Nixon? *(She gives him a withering look.)* Okay. So we all live in a patriarchy . . .

Nora. Our little family, the Walds, are just one nuclear patriarchal unit among the millions in our patriarchal male-dominated civilization, which is worldwide. It's all in that book —

Thaw. Look Nora, I promise I'll read the damn book — but . . .

Nora. So who's interrupting? Well, Thaw, all history shows that the hand that cradles the *rock* has ruled the world, *not* the hand that rocks the cradle! Do you know what brutal things men have done to women? Bought and sold them like cattle. Bound their feet at birth to deform them — so they couldn't run away — like in China. Made widows throw themselves on the funeral pyres of their husbands, like in India. Cut off their clitorises, so they could be bred but not enjoy sex. Thaw, did you know that the clitoris is the only sexual organ, in either sex, solely designed by nature for sexual pleasure?

Thaw. That fascinating fact, up to now, has escaped me.

Nora. Yes, it's a pity. Well . . . men who committed adultery were almost never punished. But women were always brutally punished. Why, in many countries unfaithful wives were *stoned* to death —

Thaw. This is America, 1970, Nora. And here, when wives are unfaithful, *husbands* get stoned. *(Drinks.)* Mind if *I* do?

Nora. Be your guest. Oh, there's no doubt that relations between the sexes have been greatly ameliorated . . .

Thaw. Now, about *our* relations, Nora. You're not holding it against *me* that men, the dirty bastards, have done a lot of foul things to women in the past?

Nora (indignant). What do you mean, in the *past?*

Thaw (determined to be patient). Past, present, future — what has what other men have done to other women got to do with us?

Nora. Quite a lot. We *are* a male and a female —

Thaw. That's the supposition I've always gone on. But Nora, we are a *particular* male and a *particular* female: Thaw Wald and his wife, Nora —

Nora. Yes. That's why it's so shattering when you find out you are such a typical husband and —

Thaw (a new effort to take command). Nora, how many men do you know who are still in love with their wives after ten years?

Nora. Not many. And, Thaw, listen, maybe the reason is —

Thaw. So you agree that's not typical? Okay. Now, do I ever grumble about paying the bills? So that's not typical. I liked my mother-in-law, even when she was alive. And God knows that's not typical. And don't I do every damn thing I can to keep *my* mother off your back? And that's not typical. I'm even thoughtful about the little things. You said so yourself, remember, when I bought you that black see-through nightgown for Mother's Day. That I went out and chose myself. And which *you* never wear.

Nora. I had to return it. It was too small. and do you know what the saleswoman said? She said, "Men who buy their wives things in this department are in love with them. But why do they all seem to think they are married to midgets?" That's it, Thaw, that's *it!* Men "think little" — like "thinking thin" — even about women they love. They don't think at all about women they don't love or want to sleep with. Now, I can't help it if you think of me as a midget. But don't you see, I've got to stop thinking of myself as one. Thaw, *listen* . . .

Thaw. Why the devil should *you* think of yourself as a midget? *I* think you're a great woman. A *real* woman! Why, you're the dearest, sweetest, most understanding little wife — most of the time — a man ever had. And the most intelligent and wonderful little mother! Dammit, those kids are the smartest, best-behaved, most self-reliant little kids . . .

Nora. Oh, I've been pretty good at Occupation Housewife, if I do say so myself. But Thaw, *listen.* Can't you even imagine that there might be something *more* a woman needs and wants —

Thaw. My God. Nora, what more can a woman want than a nice home, fine children and a husband who adores her?

Nora (discouraged). You sound like old Dr. Freud, in person.

Thaw. I sound like Freud? I wish I were. Then I'd know why you're so uptight.

Nora. Oh, no you wouldn't. Know what Freud wrote in his diary, when he was 77? "What do women want? My God, what do they want?" Fifty years this giant brain spends analyzing women. And he still can't find out what they want. So this makes him the world's greatest expert on feminine psychology? *(She starts to look at her watch.)* To think I bought him, in college.

Thaw. You've got plenty of time. You were saying about Freud — *(He lights a cigarette, hands it to her, determined to stick with it to the end.)*

Nora. History is full of ironies! Freud was the foremost exponent of the theory of the natural inferiority of women. You know, "Anatomy is destiny"?

Thaw. I was in the School of Business, remember?

Nora. Well, old Freud died in 1939. He didn't live to see what happened when Hitler adopted his theory that "anatomy is destiny." Six millions of his own people went to the gas chambers. One reason, Hitler said, that the Jews were *naturally* inferior was because they were effeminate people, with a slave mentality. He said they were full of those vices which men always identify with women — when they're feeling hostile: You know, sneakiness and deception, scheming and wheedling, whining and pushiness, oh, and materialism, sensuousness and sexuality. Thaw, what's *your* favorite feminine vice?

Thaw. At this moment, feminine monologues.

Nora. I didn't think you'd have the nerve to say sneakiness. I saw you sneak a look at your watch, and egg me on to talk about Freud, hoping I'll miss my train. I won't.

Thaw. So nothing I've said — what little I've had a chance to say
. . . *(she shakes her head)* — you still intend to divorce me?

Nora. Oh, I never said I was divorcing you. I'm deserting you.
So you can divorce me.

Thaw. You do realize, Nora, that if a wife deserts her husband
he doesn't have to pay her alimony?

Nora. I don't want alimony. But I do want severance pay. *(Points
to books.)* There's my bill, rendered for 10 years of domestic
services — the thing sticking in *Woman's Place,* by Cynthia
Fuchs Epstein. I figured it at the going agency rates for a
full-time cook, cleaning woman, handyman, laundress,
seamstress, and part-time gardener and chauffeur. I've worked
an average ten-hour day. So I've charged for overtime. Of
course, you've paid my rent, taxes, clothing, medical expenses
and food. So I've deducted those. Even though as a housewife,
I've had no fringe benefits. Just the same, the bill . . . well,
I'm afraid you're going to be staggered. I was. It comes to
over $53,000. I'd like to be paid in 10 installments.

Thaw (he is staggered). Mathematics isn't really your bag, Nora.

Nora. I did it on that little calculating machine you gave me at
Christmas. If you think it's not really fair, I'll be glad to
negotiate. And, please notice, I haven't charged anything for
sleeping with you!

Thaw. Wow! *(He is really punch drunk.)*

Nora. I'm not a prostitute. And *this* is what I wanted to say about
the Lib girls. They're right about women who marry *just*
for money. But they're wrong about women who marry
for love. It's love makes all the difference —

Thaw (dispirited). Well, *vive la différence.*

Nora. And, of course, I haven't charged anything for being a nurse.
I've adored taking care of the children, especially when they
were babies. I'm going to miss them — *awfully.*

Thaw (on his feet, with outrage). You're deserting the children, too?
My God, Nora, what kind of woman *are* you? You're going
to leave those poor little kids alone in this house —

Nora. You're here. And I told you, your mother is coming. I
wired her that her son needed her. She'll be happy again —
and be needed again — for the first time in years —

Thaw (this is a real blow). My *mother!* Oh, migod, you *can't,* Nora.
You know how she — *swarms* over me! She thinks I'm still
12 years old . . . *(His head is now in his hands.)* You know
she drives me out of my cotton-picking mind.

Nora. Yes. But you never said so before.

Thaw. I love my mother. She's been a good mother, and wife.

But Nora, she's a *very* limited woman! Yak, yak — food, shopping, the kids . . .

Nora. Thaw, the children love this house, and I don't want to take them out of school. And I can't give them another home. Women, you know, can't borrow money to buy a house. Besides, legally this house and everything in it, except mother's few things, are yours. All the worldly goods with which thou didst me endow seem to be in that suitcase.

Thaw. Nora, you know damn well that all my life insurance is in your name. If I died tomorrow — and I may blow my brains out tonight — everything would go to you and the kids.

Nora. Widowhood is one of the few fringe benefits of marriage. But, today, all the money I have is what I've saved in the past year out of my clothes allowance — $260.33. But I hope you will give me my severance pay —

Thaw. And if I don't — you know legally I don't have to — how do you propose to support yourself?

Nora. Well, if I can't get a job right away — sell my engagement ring. That's why they say diamonds are a gal's best friend. What else do jobless women *have* they can turn into ready cash — except their bodies?

Thaw. What kind of job do you figure on getting?

Nora. Well, I do have a master's in English. So I'm going to try for a spot in *TIME* Research. That's the intellectual harem kept by the Time Inc. editors. The starting pay is good.

Thaw. How do you know that?

Nora. From your own research assistant, Molly Peapack. We're both Wellesley, you know. She's a friend of the chief researcher at *TIME*, Marylois Vega. Also, Molly says, computer programming is a field that may open to women —

Thaw (indignant). You told Peapack you were leaving me? Before you even told *me*? How do you like *that* for treating a mate like an inferior!

Nora. Thaw, I've told you at least three times a week for the last year that with the kids both in school, I'd like to get a job. You always laughed at me. You said I was too old to be a Playboy Bunny, and that the only job an inexperienced woman my age could get would be as a saleswoman —

Thaw. Okay. Where are you going to live? That 200 won't go far —

Nora. Peapack's offered to let me stay with her until I find something.

Thaw. I'm going to have a word with Miss Molly Peapack tomorrow. She's been too damned aggressive lately, anyway —

Nora. She's going to have a word with you, too. She's leaving.

Thaw. Peapack is leaving? Leaving *me*?

Nora. When you got her from Prudential, you promised her, remember, you'd recommend her for promotion to office manager. So, last week you took on a man. A new man. Now she's got a job offer where she's sure she's got a 40–60 chance for advancement to management. *(Pause.)* So you've lost your home wife and your office wife.

Thaw. Jesus! And *this* is a male-dominated world?

Nora. Well, I've got five minutes —

Thaw. You've still not told me *why*.

Nora. Oh, Thaw darling! You poor — *man*. I have told you why: I'm leaving because I want a job. I want to do some share, however small, of the world's work, and be paid for it. Isn't the work you do in the world — and the salary you get — what makes you respect yourself, and other men respect you? Women have begun to want respect themselves a little, too —

Thaw. You mean, the real reason you are leaving is that you want a *paying* job?

Nora. Yes.

Thaw. God, Nora, why didn't you say that in the beginning. All right, go get a job, if it's that important to you. But that doesn't mean you have to leave me and the kids.

Nora. I'm afraid it does. Otherwise, I'd have to do two jobs. Out there. And here.

Thaw. Look, Nora, I heard some of the Lib gals say there are millions of working wives and mothers who are doing two jobs. Housework can't be all that rough —

Nora. Scrubbing floors, walls. Cleaning pots, pans, windows, ovens. Messes — dog messes, toilet messes, children's messes. Garbage. Laundry. Shopping for pounds of stuff. Loading them into the car, out of the car — *(A pause.)* Not all of it hard. But all of it routine. All of it *boring*.

Thaw. Listen, Nora, what say, you work, I work. And we split the housework? How's that for a deal?

Nora. It's a deal you are not quite free to make, Thaw. You sometimes *can't* get home until very late. And you have to travel a lot, you know. Oh, it might work for a little while. But not for long. After 10 years, you still won't empty an ashtray, or pick up after yourself in the bathroom. No. I don't have the physical or moral strength to swing two jobs. So I've got to choose the one, before it's too late, that's most important for me — oh, not for me just now, but for when *I'm* 50 —

Thaw. When you're 50, Nora, if you don't leave me, you'll be the wife of the president of Stove Mountain Life Insurance Company. Sharing my wealth, sharing whatever status I have in the community. And with servants of your own. Now you listen to *me*, Nora. It's a man's world, out there. It's a man's world where there are a lot of women working. I see them every day. What are most of them really doing? Marking time, and looking, always looking, for a man who will offer them a woman's world . . . the world you have here. Marriage is still the best deal that the world has to offer women. And most women know it. It's always been like that. And it's going to be like that for a long, long time.

Nora. Just now I feel that the best deal I, Nora Wald, can hope to get out of life is to learn to esteem myself as a person . . . to stop feeling that every day a little bit more of my mind — and heart — is being washed down the drain with the soapsuds. . . . Thaw — listen. If I don't stop shrinking, I'll end up secretly hating you, and trying to cut you — and *your* son — down to my size. The way your poor, dear mother does you and your father. And you'll become like your father, the typical henpecked husband. Thinking of his old wife as the Ball and Chain. You know he has a mistress? *(Thaw knows.)* A smart gal who owns her own shop . . . who doesn't bore him.

Thaw. Well, Nora . . . *(Pours drinks.)* One for the road?

Nora. Right. For the road.

Thaw. Nora . . . I'll wait. But I don't know how long —

Nora. I've thought of that, too . . . that you might remarry . . . that girl, maybe, who means nothing —

Thaw. Goddammit, a man needs a woman of his own —

Nora (nodding). I know. A sleep-in, sleep-with body servant of his very own. Well, that's your problem. Just now, I have to wrestle with mine. *(Goes to door, picks up suitcase.)* I'm not bursting with self-confidence, Thaw. I do love you. And I also need . . . a man. So I'm not slamming the door. I'm closing it . . . very . . . softly.

Exits. Curtain falls.

QUESTIONS

1. Based on the little that we hear of the televison program at the start of the play, characterize the moderator of the program.
2. What dramatic purposes do you think are served by including the bit about the television program?

3. Very early in the dialogue Thaw warns Nora: "Uh-uh, Nora! We both agreed months ago, you'd lay off the feminist bit if I lay off watching Saturday football." What does this tell us about Thaw? And about Nora? Do you think they made a fair bargain? (Notice also the first line that Nora speaks after Thaw's line.)

4. What are the implications of the ad by Stove Mountain Life Insurance? Why does Thaw think it is "quite an ad"? What do you think of it?

5. Trace the course of Thaw's methods in his attempts to keep Nora from leaving.

6. How much do you think Thaw has learned by the end of the play?

7. In some ways the play — though certainly serious — is a comedy. What, if anything, do you find funny in it?

8. If you have read Ibsen's *A Doll's House,* compare the treatment of sex in the two plays.

Marsha Norman (American. b. 1947)

'night, Mother

List of Characters

Jessie Cates, in her late thirties or early forties, is pale and vaguely unsteady physically. It is only in the last year that Jessie has gained control of her mind and body, and tonight she is determined to hold on to that control. She wears pants and a long black sweater with deep pockets, which contain scraps of paper, and there may be a pencil behind her ear or a pen clipped to one of the pockets of the sweater.

As a rule, Jessie doesn't feel much like talking. Other people have rarely found her quirky sense of humor amusing. She has a peaceful energy on this night, a sense of purpose, but is clearly aware of the time passing moment by moment. Oddly enough, Jessie has never been as communicative or as enjoyable as she is on this evening, but we must know she has not always been this way. There is a familiarity between these two women that comes from having lived together for a long time. There is a shorthand to the talk and a sense of routine comfort in the way they relate to each other physically. Naturally, there are also routine aggravations.

Kathy Bates, as Jessie, and Anne Pitoniak, as Mama, are shown here in the Pulitzer Prize–winning, original production of 'night, Mother, which opened during the 1982–1983 season at the American Repertory Theatre in Cambridge, Massachusetts. Photograph courtesy of the American Repertory Theatre.

Thelma Cates, "Mama," *is Jessie's mother, in her late fifties or early sixties. She has begun to feel her age and so takes it easy when she can, or when it serves her purpose to let someone help her. But she speaks quickly and enjoys talking. She believes that things* are *what she says they are. Her sturdiness is more a mental quality than a physical one, finally. She is chatty and nosy, and this is* her *house.*

The play takes place in a relatively new house built way out on a country road, with a living room and connecting kitchen, and a center hall that leads off to the bedrooms. A pull cord in the hall ceiling releases a ladder which leads to the attic. One of these bedrooms opens directly onto the hall, and its entry should be visible to everyone in the audience. It should be, in fact, the focal point of the entire set, and the lighting should make it disappear completely at times and draw the entire set into it at others. It is a point of both threat and promise. It is an ordinary door that opens onto absolute nothingness. That door is the point of all the action, and the utmost care should be given to its design and construction.

The living room is cluttered with magazines and needlework catalogues, ashtrays and candy dishes. Examples of Mama's needlework are everywhere — pillows, afghans, and quilts, doilies and rugs, and they are quite nice examples. The house is more comfortable than messy, but there is quite a lot to keep in place here. It is more personal than charming. It is not quaint. Under no circumstances should the set and its dressing make a judgment about the intelligence or taste of Jessie and Mama. It should simply indicate that they are very specific real people who happen to live in a particular part of the country. Heavy accents, which would further distance the audience from Jessie and Mama, are also wrong.

The time is the present, with the action beginning about 8:15. Clocks onstage in the kitchen and on a table in the living room should run throughout the performance and be visible to the audience.

There will be no intermission.

Mama stretches to reach the cupcakes in a cabinet in the kitchen. She can't see them, but she can feel around for them, and she's eager to have one, so she's working pretty hard at it. This may be the most serious exercise Mama ever gets. She finds a cupcake, the coconut-covered, raspberry-and-marshmallow-filled kind known as a snowball, but sees that there's one missing from the package. She calls to Jessie, who is apparently somewhere else in the house.

Mama (*unwrapping the cupcake*). Jessie, it's the last snowball, sugar.

Put it on the list, O.K.? And we're out of Hershey bars, and where's that peanut brittle? I think maybe Dawson's been in it again. I ought to put a big mirror on the refrigerator door. That'll keep him out of my treats, won't it? You hear me, honey? (*Then more to herself.*) I hate it when the coconut falls off. Why does the coconut fall off?

Jessie enters from her bedroom, carrying a stack of newspapers.

Jessie. We got any old towels?

Mama. There you are!

Jessie (*holding a towel that was on the stack of newspapers*). Towels you don't want anymore. (*Picking up Mama's snowball wrapper.*) How about this swimming towel Loretta gave us? Beach towel, that's the name of it. You want it? (*Mama shakes her head no.*)

Mama. What have you been doing in there?

Jessie. And a big piece of plastic like a rubber sheet or something. Garbage bags would do if there's enough.

Mama. Don't go making a big mess, Jessie. It's eight o'clock already.

Jessie. Maybe an old blanket or towels we got in a soap box sometime?

Mama. I said don't make a mess. Your hair is black enough, hon.

Jessie (*continuing to search the kitchen cabinets, finding two or three more towels to add to her stack*). It's not for my hair, Mama. What about some old pillows anywhere, or a foam cushion out of a yard chair would be real good.

Mama. You haven't forgot what night it is, have you? (*Holding up her fingernails.*) They're all chipped, see? I've been waiting all week, Jess. It's Saturday night, sugar.

Jessie. I know. I got it on the schedule.

Mama (*crossing to the living room*). You want me to wash 'em now or are you making your mess first? (*Looking at the snowball.*) We're out of these. Did I say that already?

Jessie. There's more coming tomorrow. I ordered you a whole case.

Mama (*checking the* TV Guide). A whole case will go stale, Jessie.

Jessie. They can go in the freezer till you're ready for them. Where's Daddy's gun?

Mama. In the attic.

Jessie. Where in the attic? I looked your whole nap and couldn't find it anywhere.

Mama. One of his shoeboxes, I think.

Jessie. Full of shoes. I looked already.

Mama. Well, you didn't look good enough, then. There's that box from the ones he wore to the hospital. When he died, they told me I could have them back, but I never did like those shoes.

Jessie (pulling them out of her pocket). I found the bullets. They were in an old milk can.

Mama (as Jessie starts for the hall). Dawson took the shotgun, didn't he? Hand me that basket, hon.

Jessie (getting the basket for her). Dawson better not've taken that pistol.

Mama (stopping her again). Now my glasses, please. (*Jessie returns to get the glasses.*) I told him to take those rubber boots, too, but he said they were for fishing. I told him to take up fishing.

Jessie reaches for the cleaning spray, and cleans Mama's glasses for her.

Jessie. He's just too lazy to climb up there, Mama. Or maybe he's just being smart. That floor's not very steady.

Mama (getting out a piece of knitting). It's not a floor at all, hon, it's a board now and then. Measure this for me. I need six inches.

Jessie (as she measures). Dawson could probably use some of those clothes up there. Somebody should have them. You ought to call the Salvation Army before the whole thing falls in on .you. Six inches exactly.

Mama. It's plenty safe! As long as you don't go up there.

Jessie (turning to go again). I'm careful.

Mama. What do you want the gun for, Jess?

Jessie (not returning this time. Opening the ladder in the hall). Protection. (*She steadies the ladder as Mama talks.*)

Mama. You take the TV way too serious, hon. I've never seen a criminal in my life. This is way too far to come for what's out here to steal. Never seen a one.

Jessie (taking her first step up). Except for Ricky.

Mama. Ricky is mixed up. That's not a crime.

Jessie. Get your hands washed. I'll be right back. And get 'em real dry. You dry your hands till I get back or it's no go, all right?

Mama. I thought Dawson told you not to go up those stairs.

Jessie (going up). He did.

Mama. I don't like the idea of a gun, Jess.

Jessie (calling down from the attic). Which shoebox, do you remember?

Mama. Black.

Jessie. The box was black?

Mama. The shoes were black.

Jessie. That doesn't help much, Mother.

Mama. I'm not trying to help, sugar. (*No answer.*) We don't have anything anybody'd want, Jessie. I mean, I don't even want what we got, Jessie.

Jessie. Neither do I. Wash your hands. (*Mama gets up and crosses to stand under the ladder.*)

Mama. You come down from there before you have a fit. I can't come up and get you, you know.

Jessie. I know.

Mama. We'll just hand it over to them when they come, how's that? Whatever they want, the criminals.

Jessie. That's a good idea, Mama.

Mama. Ricky will grow out of this and be a real fine boy, Jess. But I have to tell you, I wouldn't want Ricky to know we had a gun in the house.

Jessie. Here it is. I found it.

Mama. It's just something Ricky's going through. Maybe he's in with some bad people. He just needs some time, sugar. He'll get back in school or get a job or one day you'll get a call and he'll say he's sorry for all the trouble he's caused and invite you out for supper someplace dress-up.

Jessie (*coming back down the steps*). Don't worry. It's not for him, it's for me.

Mama. I didn't think you would shoot your own boy, Jessie. I know you've felt like it, well, we've all felt like shooting somebody, but we don't do it. I just don't think we need . . .

Jessie (*interrupting*). Your hands aren't washed. Do you want a manicure or not?

Mama. Yes, I do, but . . .

Jessie (*crossing to the chair*). Then wash your hands and don't talk to me any more about Ricky. Those two rings he took were the last valuable things *I* had, so now he's started in on other people, door to door. I hope they put him away sometime. I'd turn him in myself if I knew where he was.

Mama. You don't mean that.

Jessie. Every word. Wash your hands and that's the last time I'm telling you.

Jessie sits down with the gun and starts cleaning it, pushing the cylinder out, checking to see that the chambers and barrel are empty, then putting some oil on a small patch of cloth and pushing it through the barrel with the push rod that was in the box. Mama

*goes to the kitchen and washes her hands, as instructed, trying not
to show her concern about the gun.*

Mama. I shoulda got you to bring down that milk can. Agnes
　　Fletcher sold hers to somebody with a flea market for forty
　　dollars apiece.
Jessie. I'll go back and get it in a minute. There's a wagon wheel
　　up there, too. There's even a churn. I'll get it all if you want.
Mama (*coming over, now, taking over now*). What are you doing?
Jessie. The barrel has to be clean, Mama. Old powder, dust gets
　　in it . . .
Mama. What for?
Jessie. I told you.
Mama (*reaching for the gun*). And I told you, we don't get criminals
　　out here.
Jessie (*quickly pulling it to her*). And I told you . . . (*Then trying to
　　be calm.*) The gun is for me.
Mama. Well, you can have it if you want. When I die, you'll get
　　it all, anyway.
Jessie. I'm going to kill myself, Mama.
Mama (*returning to the sofa*). Very funny. Very funny.
Jessie. I am.
Mama. You are not! Don't even say such a thing, Jessie.
Jessie. How would you know if I didn't say it? You want it to be
　　a surprise? You're lying there in your bed or maybe you're
　　just brushing your teeth and you hear this . . . noise down
　　the hall?
Mama. Kill yourself.
Jessie. Shoot myself. In a couple of hours.
Mama. It must be time for your medicine.
Jessie. Took it already.
Mama. What's the matter with you?
Jessie. Not a thing. Feel fine.
Mama. You feel fine. You're just going to kill yourself.
Jessie. Waited until I felt good enough, in fact.
Mama. Don't make jokes, Jessie. I'm too old for jokes.
Jessie. It's not a joke, Mama.

Mama watches for a moment in silence.

Mama. That gun's no good, you know. He broke it right before
　　he died. He dropped it in the mud one day.
Jessie. Seems O.K. (*She spins the chamber, cocks the pistol, and pulls
　　the trigger. The gun is not yet loaded, so all we hear is the click,*

but it will definitely work. It's also obvious that Jessie knows her way around a gun. Mama cannot speak.) I had Cecil's all ready in there, just in case I couldn't find this one, but I'd rather use Daddy's.

Mama. Those bullets are at least fifteen years old.

Jessie (*pulling out another box*). These are from last week.

Mama. Where did you get those?

Jessie. Feed store Dawson told me about.

Mama. Dawson!

Jessie. I told him I was worried about prowlers. He said he thought it was a good idea. He told me what kind to ask for.

Mama. If he had any idea . . .

Jessie. He took it as a compliment. He thought I might be taking an interest in things. He got through telling me all about the bullets and then he said we ought to talk like this more often.

Mama. And where was I while this was going on?

Jessie. On the phone with Agnes. About the milk can, I guess. Anyway, I asked Dawson if he thought they'd send me some bullets and he said he'd just call for me, because he knew they'd send them if he told them to. And he was absolutely right. Here they are.

Mama. How could he do that?

Jessie. Just trying to help, Mama.

Mama. And then I told you where the gun was.

Jessie (*smiling, enjoying this joke*). See? Everybody's doing what they can.

Mama. You told me it was for protection!

Jessie. It *is!* I'm still doing your nails, though. Want to try that new Chinaberry color?

Mama. Well, I'm calling Dawson right now. We'll just see what he has to say about this little stunt.

Jessie. Dawson doesn't have any more to do with this.

Mama. He's your brother.

Jessie. And that's all.

Mama (*stands up, moves toward the phone*). Dawson will put a stop to this. Yes he will. He'll take the gun away.

Jessie. If you call him, I'll just have to do it before he gets here. Soon as you hang up the phone, I'll just walk in the bedroom and lock the door. Dawson will get here just in time to help you clean up. Go ahead, call him. Then call the police. Then call the funeral home. Then call Loretta and see if *she'll* do your nails.

Mama. You will not! This is crazy talk, Jessie!

> *Mama goes directly to the telephone and starts to dial, but Jessie is fast, coming up behind her and taking the receiver out of her hand, putting it back down.*

Jessie (firm and quiet). I said no. This is private. Dawson is not invited.

Mama. Just me.

Jessie. I don't want anybody else over here. Just you and me. If Dawson comes over, it'll make me feel stupid for not doing it ten years ago.

Mama. I think we better call the doctor. Or how about the ambulance. You like that one driver, I know. What's his name, Timmy? Get you somebody to talk to.

Jessie (going back to her chair). I'm through talking, Mama. You're it. No more.

Mama. We're just going to sit around like every other night in the world and then you're going to kill yourself? *(Jessie doesn't answer.)* You'll miss. *(Again there is no response.)* You'll just wind up a vegetable. How would you like that? Shoot your ear off? You know what the doctor said about getting excited. You'll cock the pistol and have a fit.

Jessie. I think I can kill myself, Mama.

Mama. You're not going to kill yourself, Jessie. You're not even upset! *(Jessie smiles, or laughs quietly, and Mama tries a different approach.)* People don't really kill themselves, Jessie. No, mam, doesn't make sense, unless you're retarded or deranged, and you're as normal as they come, Jessie, for the most part. We're all *afraid* to die.

Jessie. I'm not, Mama. I'm cold all the time, anyway.

Mama. That's ridiculous.

Jessie. It's exactly what I want. It's dark and quiet.

Mama. So is the back yard, Jessie! Close your eyes. Stuff cotton in your ears. Take a nap! It's quiet in your room. I'll leave the TV off all night.

Jessie. So quiet I don't know it's quiet. So nobody can get me.

Mama. You don't know what dead is like. It might not be quiet at all. What if it's like an alarm clock and you can't wake up so you can't shut it off. Ever.

Jessie. Dead is everybody and everything I ever knew, gone. Dead is dead quiet.

Mama. It's a sin. You'll go to hell.

Jessie. Uh-huh.

Mama. You will!

Jessie. Jesus was a suicide, if you ask me.

Mama. You'll go to hell just for saying that. Jessie!

Jessie (*with genuine surprise*). I didn't know I thought that.

Mama. Jessie!

> *Jessie doesn't answer. She puts the now-loaded gun back in the box and crosses to the kitchen. But Mama is afraid she's headed for the bedroom.*

Mama (*in a panic*). You can't use my towels! They're my towels. I've had them for a long time. I like my towels.

Jessie. I asked you if you wanted that swimming towel and you said you didn't.

Mama. And you can't use your father's gun, either. It's mine now, too. And you can't do it in my house.

Jessie. Oh, come on.

Mama. No. You can't do it. I won't let you. The house is in my name.

Jessie. I have to go in the bedroom and lock the door behind me so they won't arrest you for killing me. They'll probably test your hands for gunpowder, anyway, but you'll pass.

Mama. Not in my house!

Jessie. If I'd known you were going to act like this, I wouldn't have told you.

Mama. How am I supposed to act? Tell you to go ahead? O.K. by me, sugar? Might try it myself. What took you so long?

Jessie. There's just no point in fighting me over it, that's all. Want some coffee?

Mama. Your birthday's coming up, Jessie. Don't you want to know what we got you?

Jessie. You got me dusting powder, Loretta got me a new housecoat, pink probably, and Dawson got me new slippers, too small, but they go with the robe, he'll say. (*Mama cannot speak.*) Right? (*Apparently Jessie is right.*) Be back in a minute.

> *Jessie takes the gun box, puts it on top of the stack of towels and garbage bags, and takes them into her bedroom. Mama, alone for a moment, goes to the phone, picks up the receiver, looks toward the bedroom, starts to dial, and then replaces the receiver in its cradle as Jessie walks back into the room. Jessie wonders, silently. They have lived together for so long there is very rarely any reason for one to ask what the other was about to do.*

Mama. I started to, but I didn't. I didn't call him.

Jessie. Good. Thank you.

Mama (starting over, a new approach). What's this all about, Jessie?

Jessie. About?

Jessie now begins the next task she had "on the schedule," which is refilling all the candy jars, taking the empty papers out of the boxes of chocolates, etc. Mama generally snitches when Jessie does this. Not tonight, though. Nevertheless, Jessie offers.

Mama. What did I do?

Jessie. Nothing. Want a caramel?

Mama (ignoring the candy). You're mad at me.

Jessie. Not a bit. I am worried about you, but I'm going to do what I can before I go. We're not just going to sit around tonight. I made a list of things.

Mama. What things?

Jessie. How the washer works. Things like that.

Mama. I know how the washer works. You put the clothes in. You put the soap in. You turn it on. You wait.

Jessie. You do something else. You don't just wait.

Mama. Whatever else you find to do, you're still mainly waiting. The waiting's the worst part of it. The waiting's what you pay somebody else to do, if you can.

Jessie (nodding). O.K. Where do we keep the soap?

Mama. I could find it.

Jessie. See?

Mama. If you're mad about doing the wash, we can get Loretta to do it.

Jessie. Oh now, that might be worth staying to see.

Mama. She'd never in her life, would she?

Jessie. Nope.

Mama. What's the matter with her?

Jessie. She thinks she's better than we are. She's not.

Mama. Maybe if she didn't wear that yellow all the time.

Jessie. The washer repair number is on a little card taped to the side of the machine.

Mama. Loretta doesn't ever have to come over here again. Dawson can just leave her at home when he comes. And we don't ever have to see Dawson either if he bothers you. Does he bother you?

Jessie. Sure he does. Be sure you clean out the lint tray every time you use the dryer. But don't ever put your house shoes in, it'll melt the soles.

Mama. What does Dawson do, that bothers you?

Jessie. He just calls me Jess like he knows who he's talking to. He's always wondering what I do all day. I mean, I wonder that myself, but it's my day, so it's mine to wonder about, not his.

Mama. Family is just accident, Jessie. It's nothing personal, hon. They don't mean to get on your nerves. They don't even mean to be your family, they just are.

Jessie. They know too much.

Mama. About what?

Jessie. They know things about you, and they learned it before you had a chance to say whether you wanted them to know it or not. They were there when it happened and it don't belong to them, it belongs to you, only they got it. Like my mail-order bra got delivered to their house.

Mama. By accident!

Jessie. All the same . . . they opened it. They saw the little rosebuds on it. (*Offering her another candy.*) Chewy mint?

Mama (shaking her head no). What do they know about you? I'll tell them never to talk about it again. Is it Ricky or Cecil or your fits or your hair is falling out or you drink too much coffee or you never go out of the house or what?

Jessie. I just don't like their talk. The account at the grocery is in Dawson's name when you call. The number's on a whole list of numbers on the back cover of the phone book.

Mama. Well! Now we're getting somewhere. They're none of them ever setting foot in this house again.

Jessie. It's not them, Mother. I wouldn't kill myself just to get away from them.

Mama. You leave the room when they come over, anyway.

Jessie. I stay as long as I can. Besides, it's you they come to see.

Mama. That's because I stay in the room when they come.

Jessie. It's not them.

Mama. Then what is it?

Jessie (checking the list on her note pad). The grocery won't deliver on Saturday anymore. And if you want your order the same day, you have to call before ten. And they won't deliver less than fifteen dollars' worth. What I do is tell them what we need and tell them to add on cigarettes until it gets to fifteen dollars.

Mama. It's Ricky. You're trying to get through to him.

Jessie. If I thought I could do that, I would stay.

Mama. Make him sorry he hurt you, then. That's it, isn't it?

Jessie. He's hurt me, I've hurt him. We're about even.

Mama. You'll be telling him killing is O.K. with you, you know.

Want him to start killing next? Nothing wrong with it. Mom did it.

Jessie. Only a matter of time, anyway, Mama. When the call comes, you let Dawson handle it.

Mama. Honey, nothing says those calls are always going to be some new trouble he's into. You could get one that he's got a job, that he's getting married, or how about he's joined the army, wouldn't that be nice?

Jessie. If you call the Sweet Tooth before you call the grocery, that Susie will take your fudge next door to the grocery and it'll all come out together. Be sure you talk to Susie, though. She won't let them put it in the bottom of a sack like that one time, remember?

Mama. Ricky could come over, you know. What if he calls us?

Jessie. It's not Ricky, Mama.

Mama. Or anybody could call us, Jessie.

Jessie. Not on Saturday night, Mama.

Mama. Then what is it? Are you sick? If your gums are swelling again, we can get you to the dentist in the morning.

Jessie. No. Can you order your medicine or do you want Dawson to? I've got a note to him. I'll add that to it if you want.

Mama. Your eyes don't look right. I thought so yesterday.

Jessie. That was just the ragweed. I'm not sick.

Mama. Epilepsy is sick, Jessie.

Jessie. It won't kill me. (*A pause.*) If it would, I wouldn't have to.

Mama. You don't *have* to.

Jessie. No, I don't. That's what I like about it.

Mama. Well, I won't let you!

Jessie. It's not up to you.

Mama. Jessie!

Jessie. I want to hang a big sign around my neck, like Daddy's on the barn. GONE FISHING.

Mama. You don't like it here.

Jessie (smiling). Exactly.

Mama. I meant here in my house.

Jessie. I know you did.

Mama. You never should have moved back in here with me. If you'd kept your little house or found another place when Cecil left you, you'd have made some new friends at least. Had a life to lead. Had your own things around you. Give Ricky a place to come see you. You never should've come here.

Jessie. Maybe.

Mama. But I didn't force you, did I?

Jessie. If it was a mistake, we made it together. You took me in. I appreciate that.

Mama. You didn't have any business being by yourself right then, but I can see how you might want a place of your own. A grown woman should . . .

Jessie. Mama . . . I'm just not having a very good time and I don't have any reason to think it'll get anything but worse. I'm tired. I'm hurt. I'm sad. I feel used.

Mama. Tired of what?

Jessie. It all.

Mama. What does that mean?

Jessie. I can't say it any better.

Mama. Well, you'll have to say it better because I'm not letting you alone till you do. What were those other things? Hurt . . . (*Before Jessie can answer.*) You had this all ready to say to me, didn't you? Did you write this down? How long have you been thinking about this?

Jessie. Off and on, ten years. On all the time, since Christmas.

Mama. What happened at Christmas?

Jessie. Nothing.

Mama. So why Christmas?

Jessie. That's it. On the nose.

A pause. Mama knows exactly what Jessie means. She was there, too, after all.

Jessie (*putting the candy sacks away*). See where all this is? Red hots up front, sour balls and horehound mixed together in this one sack. New packages of toffee and licorice right in back there.

Mama. Go back to your list. You're hurt by what?

Jessie (*Mama knows perfectly well*). Mama . . .

Mama. O.K. Sad about what? There's nothing real sad going on right now. If it was after your divorce or something, that would make sense.

Jessie (*looking at her list, then opening the drawer*). Now, this drawer has everything in it that there's no better place for. Extension cords, batteries for the radio, extra lighters, sandpaper, masking tape, Elmer's glue, thumbtacks, that kind of stuff. The mousetraps are under the sink, but you call Dawson if you've got one and let him do it.

Mama. Sad about what?

Jessie. The way things are.

Mama. Not good enough. What things?

Jessie. Oh, everything from you and me to Red China.

Mama. I think we can leave the Chinese out of this.

Jessie (crosses back into the living room). There's extra light bulbs in a box in the hall closet. And we've got a couple of packages of fuses in the fuse box. There's candles and matches in the top of the broom closet, but if the lights go out, just call Dawson and sit tight. But don't open the refrigerator door. Things will stay cool in there as long as you keep the door shut.

Mama. I asked you a question.

Jessie. I read the paper. I don't like how things are. And they're not any better out there than they are in here.

Mama. If you're doing this because of the newspapers, I can sure fix that!

Jessie. There's just more of it on TV.

Mama (kicking the television set). Take it out, then!

Jessie. You wouldn't do that.

Mama. Watch me.

Jessie. What would you do all day?

Mama (desperately). Sing. *(Jessie laughs.)* I would, too. You want to watch? I'll sing till morning to keep you alive, Jessie, please!

Jessie. No. *(Then affectionately.)* It's a funny idea, though. What do you sing?

Mama (has no idea how to answer this). We've got a good life here!

Jessie (going back into the kitchen). I called this morning and canceled the papers, except for Sunday, for your puzzles; you'll still get that one.

Mama. Let's get another dog, Jessie! You liked a big dog, now, didn't you? That King dog, didn't you?

Jessie (washing her hands). I did like that King dog, yes.

Mama. I'm so dumb. He's the one run under the tractor.

Jessie. That makes him dumb, not you.

Mama. For bringing it up.

Jessie. It's O.K. Handi-Wipes and sponges under the sink.

Mama. We could get a new dog and keep him in the house. Dogs are cheap!

Jessie (getting big pill jars out of the cabinet). No.

Mama. Something for you to take care of.

Jessie. I've had you, Mama.

Mama (frantically starting to fill pill bottles). You do too much for me. I can fill pill bottles all day, Jessie, and change the shelf paper and wash the floor when I get through. You just watch me. You don't have to do another thing in this house if you don't want to. You don't have to take care of me, Jessie.

Jessie. I know that. You've just been letting me do it so I'll have something to do, haven't you?

Mama (realizing this was a mistake). I don't do it as well as you. I just meant if it tires you out or makes you feel used . . .

Jessie. Mama, I know you used to ride the bus. Riding the bus and it's hot and bumpy and crowded and too noisy and more than anything in the world you want to get off and the only reason in the world you don't get off is it's still fifty blocks from where you're going? Well, I can get off right now if I want to, because even if I ride fifty more years and get off then, it's the same place when I step down to it. Whenever I feel like it, I can get off. As soon as I've had enough, it's my stop. I've had enough.

Mama. You're feeling sorry for yourself!

Jessie. The plumber's helper is under the sink, too.

Mama. You're not having a good time! Whoever promised you a good time? Do you think I've had a good time?

Jessie. I think you're pretty happy, yeah. You have things you like to do.

Mama. Like what?

Jessie. Like crochet.

Mama. I'll teach you to crochet.

Jessie. I can't do any of that nice work, Mama.

Mama. Good time don't come looking for you, Jessie. You could work some puzzles or put in a garden or go to the store. Let's call a taxi and go to the A&P!

Jessie. I shopped you up for about two weeks already. You're not going to need toilet paper till Thanksgiving.

Mama (interrupting). You're acting like some little brat, Jessie. You're mad and everybody's boring and you don't have anything to do and you don't like me and you don't like going out and you don't like staying in and you never talk on the phone and you don't watch TV and you're miserable and it's your own sweet fault.

Jessie. And it's time I did something about it.

Mama. Not something like killing yourself. Something like . . . buying us all new dishes! I'd like that. Or maybe the doctor would let you get a driver's license now, or I know what let's do right this minute, let's rearrange the furniture.

Jessie. I'll do that. If you want. I always thought if the TV was somewhere else, you wouldn't get such a glare on it during the day. I'll do whatever you want before I go.

Mama (badly frightened by those words). You could get a job!

Jessie. I took that telephone sales job and I didn't even make enough money to pay the phone bill, and I tried to work at the gift shop at the hospital and they said I made people real un-comfortable smiling at them the way I did.

Mama. You could keep books. You kept your dad's books.

Jessie. But nobody ever checked them.

Mama. When he died, they checked them.

Jessie. And that's when they took the books away from me.

Mama. That's because without him there wasn't any business, Jessie!

Jessie (putting the pill bottles away). You know I couldn't work. I can't do anything. I've never been around people my whole life except when I went to the hospital. I could have a seizure any time. What good would a job do? The kind of job I could get would make me feel worse.

Mama. Jessie!

Jessie. It's true!

Mama. It's what you think is true!

Jessie (struck by the clarity of that). That's right. It's what I think is true.

Mama (hysterically). But I can't do anything about that!

Jessie (quietly). No. You can't. (*Mama slumps, if not physically, at least emotionally.*) And I can't do anything either, about my life, to change it, make it better, make me feel better about it. Like it better, make it work. But I can stop it. Shut it down, turn it off like the radio when there's nothing on I want to listen to. It's all I really have that belongs to me and I'm going to say what happens to it. And it's going to stop. And I'm going to stop it. So. Let's just have a good time.

Mama. Have a good time.

Jessie. We can't go on fussing all night. I mean, I could ask you things I always wanted to know and you could make me some hot chocolate. The old way.

Mama (in despair). It takes cocoa, Jessie.

Jessie (gets it out of the cabinet). I bought cocoa, Mama. And I'd like to have a caramel apple and do your nails.

Mama. You didn't eat a bite of supper.

Jessie. Does that mean I can't have a caramel apple?

Mama. Of course not. I mean . . . (*Smiling a little.*) Of course you can have a caramel apple.

Jessie. I thought I could.

Mama. I make the best caramel apples in the world.

Jessie. I know you do.

Mama. Or used to. And you don't get cocoa like mine anywhere anymore.

Jessie. It takes time, I know, but . . .

Mama. The salt is the trick.

Jessie. Trouble and everything.

Mama (*backing away toward the stove*). It's no trouble. What trouble?
You put it in the pan and stir it up. All right. Fine. Caramel
apples. Cocoa. O.K.

*Jessie walks to the counter to retrieve her cigarettes as Mama looks
for the right pan. There are brief near-smiles, and maybe Mama
clears her throat. We have a truce, for the moment. A genuine but
nevertheless uneasy one. Jessie, who has been in constant motion
since the beginning, now seems content to sit.*

*Mama starts looking for a pan to make the cocoa, getting out all
the pans in the cabinets in the process. It looks like she's making
a mess on purpose so Jessie will have to put them all away again.
Mama is buying time, or trying to, and entertaining.*

Jessie. You talk to Agnes today?

Mama. She's calling me from a pay phone this week. God only
knows why. She has a perfectly good Trimline at home.

Jessie (*laughing*). Well, how is she?

Mama. How is she every day, Jessie? Nuts.

Jessie. Is she really crazy or just silly?

Mama. No, she's really crazy. She was probably using the pay
phone because she had another little fire problem at home.

Jessie. Mother . . .

Mama. I'm serious! Agnes Fletcher's burned down every house
she ever lived in. Eight fires, and she's due for a new one
any day now.

Jessie (*laughing*). No!

Mama. Wouldn't surprise me a bit.

Jessie (*laughing*). Why didn't you tell me this before? Why isn't
she locked up somewhere?

Mama. 'Cause nobody ever got hurt, I guess. Agnes woke everybody
up to watch the fires as soon as she set 'em. One time she
set out porch chairs and served lemonade.

Jessie (*shaking her head*). Real lemonade?

Mama. The houses they lived in, you knew they were going to
fall down anyway, so why wait for it, is all I could ever
make out about it. Agnes likes a feeling of accomplishment.

Jessie. Good for her.

Mama (*finding the pan she wants*). Why are you asking about Agnes?
One cup or two?

Jessie. One. She's your friend. No marshmallows.

Mama (getting the milk, etc.). You have to have marshmallows. That's the old way, Jess. Two or three? Three is better.

Jessie. Three, then. Her whole house burns up? Her clothes and pillows and everything? I'm not sure I believe this.

Mama. When she was a girl, Jess, not now. Long time ago. But she's still got it in her, I'm sure of it.

Jessie. She wouldn't burn her house down now. Where would she go? She can't get Buster to build her a new one, he's dead. How could she burn it up?

Mama. Be exciting, though, if she did. You never know.

Jessie. You do too know, Mama. She wouldn't do it.

Mama (forced to admit, but reluctant). I guess not.

Jessie. What else? Why does she wear all those whistles around her neck?

Mama. Why does she have a house full of birds?

Jessie. I didn't know she had a house full of birds!

Mama. Well, she does. And she says they just follow her home. Well, I know for a fact she's still paying on the last parrot she bought. You gotta keep your life filled up, she says. She says a lot of stupid things. (*Jessie laughs, Mama continues, convinced she's getting somewhere.*) It's all that okra she eats. You can't just willy-nilly eat okra two meals a day and expect to get away with it. Made her crazy.

Jessie. She really eats okra twice a day? Where does she get it in the winter?

Mama. Well, she eats it a lot. Maybe not two meals, but . . .

Jessie. More than the average person.

Mama (beginning to get irritated). I don't know how much okra the average person eats.

Jessie. Do you know how much okra Agnes eats?

Mama. No.

Jessie. How many birds does she have?

Mama. Two.

Jessie. Then what are the whistles for?

Mama. They're not real whistles. Just little plastic ones on a necklace she won playing Bingo, and I only told you about it because I thought I might get a laugh out of you for once even if it wasn't the truth, Jessie. Things don't have to be true to talk about 'em, you know.

Jessie. Why won't she come over here?

Mama is suddenly quiet, but the cocoa and milk are in the pan now, so she lights the stove and starts stirring.

Mama. Well now, what a good idea. We should've had more cocoa. Cocoa is perfect.

Jessie. Except you don't like milk.

Mama (another attempt, but not as energetic). I hate milk. Coats your throat as bad as okra. Something just downright disgusting about it.

Jessie. It's because of me, isn't it?

Mama. No, Jess.

Jessie. Yes, Mama.

Mama. O.K. Yes, then, but she's crazy. She's as crazy as they come. She's a lunatic.

Jessie. What is it exactly? Did I say something, sometime? Or did she see me have a fit and's afraid I might have another one if she came over, or what?

Mama. I guess.

Jessie. You guess what? What's she ever said? She must've given you some reason.

Mama. Your hands are cold.

Jessie. What difference does that make?

Mama. "Like a corpse," she says, "and I'm gonna be one soon enough as it is."

Jessie. That's crazy.

Mama. That's Agnes. "Jessie's shook the hand of death and I can't take the chance it's catching, Thelma, so I ain't comin 'over, and you can understand or not, but I ain't comin'. I'll come up the driveway, but that's as far as I go."

Jessie (laughing, relieved). I thought she didn't like me! She's scared of me! How about that! Scared of me.

Mama. I could make her come over here, Jessie. I could call her up right now and she could bring the birds and come visit. I didn't know you ever thought about her at all. I'll tell her she just has to come and she'll come, all right. She owes me one.

Jessie. No, that's all right. I just wondered about it. When I'm in the hospital, does she come over here?

Mama. Her kitchen is just a tiny thing. When she comes over here, she feels like . . . (*Toning it down a little.*) Well, we all like a change of scene, don't we?

Jessie (playing along). Sure we do. Plus there's no birds diving around.

Mama. I hate those birds. She says I don't understand them. What's there to understand about birds?

Jessie. Why Agnes likes them, for one thing. Why they stay with her when they could be outside with the other birds. What their singing means. How they fly. What they think Agnes is.

Mama. Why do you have to know so much about things, Jessie? There's just not that much *to* things that I could ever see.

Jessie. That you could ever *tell,* you mean. You didn't have to lie to me about Agnes.

Mama. I didn't lie. You never asked before!

Jessie. You lied about setting fire to all those houses and about how many birds she has and how much okra she eats and why she won't come over here. If I have to keep dragging the truth out of you, this is going to take all night.

Mama. That's fine with me. I'm not a bit sleepy.

Jessie. Mama . . .

Mama. All right. Ask me whatever you want. Here.

They come to an awkward stop, as the cocoa is ready and Mama pours it into the cups Jessie has set on the table.

Jessie (as Mama takes her first sip). Did you love Daddy?

Mama. No.

Jessie (pleased that Mama understands the rules better now). I didn't think so. Were you really fifteen when you married him?

Mama. The way he told it? I'm sitting in the mud, he comes along, drags me in the kitchen, "She's been there ever since"?

Jessie. Yes.

Mama. No. It was a big fat lie, the whole thing. He just thought it was funnier that way. God, this milk in here.

Jessie. The cocoa helps.

Mama (pleased that they agree on this, at least). Not enough, though, does it? You can still taste it, can't you?

Jessie. Yeah, it's pretty bad. I thought it was my memory that was bad, but it's not. It's the milk, all right.

Mama. It's a real waste of chocolate. You don't have to finish it.

Jessie (putting her cup down). Thanks, though.

Mama. I should've known not to make it. I knew you wouldn't like it. You never did like it.

Jessie. You didn't ever love him, or he did something and you stopped loving him, or what?

Mama. He felt sorry for me. He wanted a plain country woman and that's what he married, and then he held it against me the rest of my life like I was supposed to change and surprise him somehow. Like I remember this one day he was standing on the porch and I told him to get a shirt on and he went in and got one and then he said, real peaceful, but to the point, "You're right, Thelma. If God had meant for people to go around without any clothes on, they'd have been born that way."

Jessie (sees Mama's hurt). He didn't mean anything by that, Mama.

Mama. He never said a word he didn't have to, Jessie. That was probably all he'd said to me all day, Jessie. So if he said it, there was something to it, but I never did figure that one out. What did that mean?

Jessie. I don't know. I liked him better than you did, but I didn't know him any better.

Mama. How could I love him, Jessie. I didn't have a thing he wanted. (*Jessie doesn't answer.*) He got his share, though. You loved him enough for both of us. You followed him around like some . . . Jessie, all the man ever did was farm and sit . . . and try to think of somebody to sell the farm to.

Jessie. Or make me a boyfriend out of pipe cleaners and sit back and smile like the stick man was about to dance and wasn't I going to get a kick out of that. Or sit up with a sick cow all night and leave me a chain of sleepy stick elephants on my bed in the morning.

Mama. Or just sit.

Jessie. I liked him sitting. Big old faded blue man in the chair. Quiet.

Mama. Agnes gets more talk out of her birds than I got from the two of you. He could've had that GONE FISHING sign around his neck in that chair. I saw him stare off at the water. I saw him look at the weather rolling in. I got where I could practically see that boat myself. But you, you knew what he was thinking about and you're going to tell me.

Jessie. I don't know, Mama! His life, I guess. His corn. His boots. Us. Things. You know.

Mama. No, I don't know, Jessie! You had those quiet little conversations after supper every night. What were you whispering about?

Jessie. We weren't whispering, you were just across the room.

Mama. What did you talk about?

Jessie. We talked about why black socks are warmer than blue socks. Is that something to go tell Mother? You were just jealous because I'd rather talk to him than wash the dishes with you.

Mama. I was jealous because you'd rather talk to him than anything! (*Jessie reaches across the table for the small clock and starts to wind it.*) If I had died instead of him, he wouldn't have taken you in like I did.

Jessie. I wouldn't have expected him to.

Mama. Then what would you have done?

Jessie. Come visit.

Mama. Oh, I see. He died and left you stuck with me and you're mad about it.

Jessie (getting up from the table). Not anymore. He didn't mean to. I didn't have to come here. We've been through this.

Mama. He felt sorry for you, too, Jessie, don't kid yourself about that. He said you were a runt and he said it from the day you were born and he said you didn't have a chance.

Jessie (getting the canister of sugar and starting to refill the sugar bowl). I know he loved me.

Mama. What if he did? It didn't change anything.

Jessie. It didn't have to. I miss him.

Mama. He never really went fishing, you know. Never once. His tackle box was full of chewing tobacco and all he ever did was drive out to the lake and sit in his car. Dawson told me. And Bennie at the bait shop, he told Dawson. They all laughed about it. And he'd come back from fishing and all he'd have to show for it was a . . . a whole pipe cleaner *family* — chickens, pigs, a dog with a bad leg — it was creepy strange. It made me sick to look at them and I hid his pipe cleaners a couple of times but he always had more somewhere.

Jessie. I thought it might be better for you after he died. You'd get interested in things. Breathe better. Change somehow.

Mama. Into what? The Queen? A clerk in a shoe store? Why should I? Because he said to? Because you said to? (*Jessie shakes her head.*) Well I wasn't here for his entertainment and I'm not here for yours either, Jessie. I don't know what I'm here for, but then I don't think about it. (*Realizing what all this means.*) But I bet you wouldn't be killing yourself if he were still alive. That's a fine thing to figure out, isn't it?

Jessie (filling the honey jar now). That's not true.

Mama. Oh no? Then what were you asking about him for? Why did you want to know if I loved him?

Jessie. I didn't think you did, that's all.

Mama. Fine then. You were right. Do you feel better now?

Jessie (cleaning the honey jar carefully). It feels good to be right about it.

Mama. It didn't matter whether I loved him. It didn't matter to me and it didn't matter to him. And it didn't mean we didn't get along. It wasn't important. We didn't talk about it. (*Sweeping the pots off the cabinet.*) Take all these pots out to the porch!

Jessie. What for?

Mama. Just leave me this one pan. (*She jerks the silverware drawer open.*) Get me one knife, one fork, one big spoon, and the can opener, and put them out where I can get them. (*Starts throwing knives and forks in one of the pans.*)

Jessie. Don't do that! I just straightened that drawer!

Mama (*throwing the pan in the sink*). And throw out all the plates and cups. I'll use paper. Loretta can have what she wants and Dawson can sell the rest.

Jessie (*calmly*). What are you doing?

Mama. I'm not going to cook. I never liked it, anyway. I like candy. Wrapped in plastic or coming in sacks. And tuna. I'll eat tuna, thank you.

Jessie (*taking the pan out of the sink*). What if you want to make apple butter? You can't make apple butter in that little pan. What if you leave carrots on cooking and burn up that pan?

Mama. I don't like carrots.

Jessie. What if the strawberries are good this year and you want to go picking with Agnes.

Mama. I'll tell her to bring a pan. You said you would do whatever I wanted! I don't want a bunch of pans cluttering up my cabinets I can't get down to, anyway. Throw them out. Every last one.

Jessie (*gathering up the pots*). I'm putting them all back in. I'm not taking them to the porch. If you want them, they'll be here. You'll bend down and get them, like you got the one for the cocoa. And if somebody else comes over here to cook, they'll have something to cook in, and that's the end of it!

Mama. Who's going to come cook here?

Jessie. Agnes.

Mama. In my pots. Not on your life.

Jessie. There's no reason why the two of you couldn't just live here together. Be cheaper for both of you and somebody to talk to. And if the birds bothered you, well, one day when Agnes is out getting her hair done, you could take them all for a walk!

Mama (*as Jessie straightens the silverware*). So that's why you're pestering me about Agnes. You think you can rest easy if you get me a new babysitter? Well, I don't want to live with Agnes. I barely want to talk with Agnes. She's just around. We go back, that's all. I'm not letting Agnes near this place. You don't get off as easy as that, child.

Jessie. O.K., then. It's just something to think about.

Mama. I don't like things to think about. I like things to go on.

Jessie (*closing the silverware drawer*). I want to know what Daddy said to you the night he died. You came storming out of his room and said I could wait it out with him if I wanted to, but you were going to watch *Gunsmoke*. What did he say to you?

Mama. He didn't have *anything* to say to me, Jessie. That's why I left. He didn't say a thing. It was his last chance not to talk to me and he took full advantage of it.

Jessie (after a moment). I'm sorry you didn't love him. Sorry for you, I mean. He seemed like a nice man.

Mama (as Jessie walks to the refrigerator). Ready for your apple now?

Jessie. Soon as I'm through here, Mama.

Mama. You won't like the apple, either. It'll be just like the cocoa. You never liked eating at all, did you? Any of it! What have you been living on all these years, toothpaste?

Jessie (as she starts to clean out the refrigerator). Now, you know the milkman comes on Wednesdays and Saturdays, and he leaves the order blank in an egg box, and you give the bills to Dawson once a month.

Mama. Do they still make that orangeade?

Jessie. It's not orangeade, it's just orange.

Mama. I'm going to get some. I thought they stopped making it. You just stopped ordering it.

Jessie. You should drink milk.

Mama. Not anymore, I'm not. That hot chocolate was the last. Hooray.

Jessie (getting the garbage can from under the sink). I told them to keep delivering a quart a week no matter what you said. I told them you'd run out of Cokes and you'd have to drink it. I told them I knew you wouldn't pour it on the ground . . .

Mama (finishing her sentence). And you told them you weren't going to be ordering anymore?

Jessie. I told them I was taking a little holiday and to look after you.

Mama. And they didn't think something was funny about that? You who doesn't go to the front steps? You, who only sees the driveway looking down from a stretcher passed out cold?

Jessie (enjoying this, but not laughing). They said it was about time, but why didn't I take you with me? And I said I didn't think you'd want to go, and they said, "Yeah, everybody's got their own idea of vacation."

Mama. I guess you think that's funny.

Jessie (pulling jars out of the refrigerator). You know there never was any reason to call the ambulance for me. All they ever did for me in the emergency room was let me wake up. I could've

done that here. Now, I'll just call them out and you say yes
or no. I know you like pickles. Ketchup?

Mama. Keep it.

Jessie. We've had this since last Fourth of July.

Mama. Keep the ketchup. Keep it all.

Jessie. Are you going to drink ketchup from the bottle or what?
How can you want your food and not want your pots to
cook it in? This stuff will all spoil in here, Mother.

Mama. Nothing I ever did was good enough for you and I want
to know why.

Jessie. That's not true.

Mama. And I want to know why you've lived here this long feeling
the way you do.

Jessie. You have no earthly idea how I feel.

Mama. Well, how could I? You're real far back there, Jessie.

Jessie. Back where?

Mama. What's it like over there, where you are? Do people always
say the right thing or get whatever they want, or what?

Jessie. What are you talking about?

Mama. Why do you read the newspaper? Why don't you wear
that sweater I made for you? Do you remember how I used
to look, or am I just any old woman now? When you have
a fit, do you see stars or what? How did you fall off the
horse, really? Why did Cecil leave you? Where did you put
my old glasses?

Jessie (stunned by Mama's intensity). They're in the bottom drawer
of your dresser in an old Milk of Magnesia box. Cecil left
me because he made me choose between him and smoking.

Mama. Jessie, I know he wasn't that dumb.

Jessie. I never understood why he hated it so much when it's so
good. Smoking is the only thing I know that's always just
what you think it's going to be. Just like it was the last time,
right there when you want it and real quiet.

Mama. Your fits made him sick and you know it.

Jessie. Say seizures, not fits. Seizures.

Mama. It's the same thing. A seizure in the hospital is a fit at
home.

Jessie. They didn't bother him at all. Except he did feel responsible
for it. It *was* his idea to go horseback riding that day. It was
his idea I could do *anything* if I just made up my mind to.
I fell off the horse because I didn't know how to hold on.
Cecil left for pretty much the same reason.

Mama. He had a girl, Jessie. I walked right in on them in the
toolshed.

Jessie (after a moment). O.K. That's fair. (*Lighting another cigarette.*) Was she very pretty?

Mama. She was Agnes's girl, Carlene. Judge for yourself.

Jessie (as she walks to the living room). I guess you and Agnes had a good talk about that, huh?

Mama. I never thought he was good enough for you. They moved here from Tennessee, you know.

Jessie. What are you talking about? You liked him better than I did. You flirted him out here to build your porch or I'd never even met him at all. You thought maybe he'd help you out around the place, come in and get some coffee and talk to you. God knows what you thought. All that curly hair.

Mama. He's the best carpenter I ever saw. That little house of yours will still be standing at the end of the world, Jessie.

Jessie. You didn't need a porch, Mama.

Mama. All right! I wanted you to have a husband.

Jessie. And I couldn't get one on my own, of course.

Mama. How were you going to get a husband never opening your mouth to a living soul?

Jessie. So I was quiet about it, so what?

Mama. So I should have let you just sit here? Sit like your daddy? Sit here?

Jessie. Maybe.

Mama. Well, I didn't think so.

Jessie. Well, what did you know?

Mama. I never said I knew much. How was I supposed to learn anything living out here? I didn't know enough to do half the things I did in my life. Things happen. You do what you can about them and you see what happens next. I married you off to the wrong man, I admit that. So I took you in when he left, I'm sorry.

Jessie. He wasn't the wrong man.

Mama. He didn't love you, Jessie, or he wouldn't have left.

Jessie. He wasn't the wrong man, Mama. I loved Cecil so much. And I tried to get more exercise and I tried to stay awake. I tried to learn to ride a horse. And I tried to stay outside with him, but he always knew I was trying, so it didn't work.

Mama. He was a selfish man. He told me once he hated to see people move into his houses after he built them. He knew they'd mess them up.

Jessie. I loved that bridge he built over the creek in back of the house. It didn't have to be anything special, a couple of boards would have been just fine, but he used that yellow pine and rubbed it so smooth . . .

Mama. He had responsibilities here. He had a wife and son here and he failed you.

Jessie. Or that baby bed he built for Ricky. I told him he didn't have to spend so much time on it, but he said it had to last, and the thing ended up weighing two hundred pounds and I couldn't move it. I said, "How long does a baby bed have to last, anyway?" But maybe he thought if it was strong enough, it might keep Ricky a baby.

Mama. Ricky is too much like Cecil.

Jessie. He is not. Ricky is as much like me as it's possible for any human to be. We even wear the same size pants. These are his, I think.

Mama. That's just the same size. That's not you're the same person.

Jessie. I see it on his face. I hear it when he talks. We look out at the world and we see the same thing: Not Fair. And the only difference between us is Ricky's out there trying to get even. And he knows not to trust anybody and he got it straight from me. And he knows not to try to get work, and guess where he got that. He walks around like there's loose boards in the floor, and you know who laid that floor, I did.

Mama. Ricky isn't through yet. You don't know how he'll turn out!

Jessie (*going back to the kitchen*). Yes I do and so did Cecil. Ricky is the two of us together for all time in too small a space. And we're tearing each other apart, like always, inside that boy, and if you don't see it, then you're just blind.

Mama. Give him time, Jess.

Jessie. Oh, he'll have plenty of that. Five years for forgery, ten years for armed assault . . .

Mama (*furious*). Stop that! (*Then pleading.*) Jessie, Cecil might be ready to try it again, honey, that happens sometimes. Go downtown. Find him. Talk to him. He didn't know what he had in you. Maybe he sees things different now, but you're not going to know that till you see him. Or call him up! Right now! He might be home.

Jessie. And say what? Nothing's changed, Cecil, I'd just like to look at you, if you don't mind? No. He loved me, Mama. He just didn't know how things fall down around me like they do. I think he did the right thing. He gave himself another chance, that's all. But I did beg him to take me with him. I did tell him I would leave Ricky and you and everything

I loved out here if only he would take me with him, but he couldn't and I understood that. (*Pause.*) I wrote that note I showed you. I wrote it. Not Cecil. I said "I'm sorry, Jessie, I can't fix it all for you." I said I'd always love me, not Cecil. But that's how he felt.

Mama. Then he should've taken you with him!

Jessie (*picking up the garbage bag she has filled*). Mama, you don't pack your garbage when you move.

Mama. You will not call yourself garbage, Jessie.

Jessie (*taking the bag to the big garbage can near the back door*). Just a way of saying it, Mama. Thinking about my list, that's all. (*Opening the can, putting the garbage in, then securing the lid.*) Well, a little more than that. I was trying to say it's all right that Cecil left. It was . . . a relief in a way. I never was what he wanted to see, so it was better when he wasn't looking at me all the time.

Mama. I'll make your apple now.

Jessie. No thanks. You get the manicure stuff and I'll be right there.

Jessie ties up the big garbage bag in the can and replaces the small garbage bag under the sink, all the time trying desperately to regain her calm. Mama watches, from a distance, her hand reaching unconsciously for the phone. Then she has a better idea. Or rather she thinks of the only other thing left and is willing to try it. Maybe she is even convinced it will work.

Mama. Jessie, I think your daddy had little . . .

Jessie. (*interrupting her*). Garbage night is Tuesday. Put it out as late as you can. The Davis's dogs get in it if you don't. (*Replacing the garbage bag in the can under the sink.*) And keep ordering the heavy black bags. It doesn't pay to buy the cheap ones. And I've got all the ties here with the hammers and all. Take them out of the box as soon as you open a new one and put them in this drawer. They'll get lost if you don't, and rubber bands or something else won't work.

Mama. I think your daddy had fits, too. I think he sat in his chair and had little fits. I read this a long time ago in a magazine, how little fits go, just little blackouts where maybe their eyes don't even close and people just call them "thinking spells."

Jessie (*getting the slipcover out of the laundry basket*). I don't think you want this manicure we've been looking forward to. I washed this cover for the sofa, but it'll take both of us to get it back on.

Mama. I watched his eyes. I know that's what it was. The magazine
    said some people don't even know they've had one.

Jessie. Daddy would've known if he'd had fits, Mama.

Mama. The lady in this story had kept track of hers and she'd had
    eighty thousand of them in the last eleven years.

Jessie. Next time you wash this cover, it'll dry better if you put
    it on wet.

Mama. Jessie, listen to what I'm telling you. This lady had anywhere
    between five and five hundred fits a day and they lasted
    maybe fifteen seconds apiece, so that out of her life, she'd
    only lost about two weeks altogether, and she had a full-
    time secretary job and an IQ of 120.

Jessie (amused by Mama's approach). You want to talk about the fits,
    is that it?

Mama. Yes. I do. I want to say . . .

Jessie (interrupting). Most of the time I wouldn't even know I'd
    had one, except I wake up with different clothes on, feeling
    like I've been run over. Sometimes I feel my head start to
    turn around or hear myself scream. And sometimes there *is*
    this dizzy stupid feeling a little before it, but if the TV's on,
    well, it's easy to miss.

*As Jessie and Mama replace the slipcover on the sofa and the afghan
on the chair, the physical struggle somehow mirrors the emotional
one in the conversation.*

Mama. I can tell when you're about to have one. Your eyes get
    this big! But, Jessie, you haven't . . .

Jessie (taking charge of this). What do they look like? The seizures.

Mama (reluctant). Different each time, Jess.

Jessie. O.K. Pick one, then. A good one. I think I want to know
    now.

Mama. There's not much to tell. You just . . . crumple, in a heap,
    like a puppet and somebody cut the strings all at once, or
    like the firing squad in some Mexican movie, you just slide
    down the wall, you know. You don't know what happens?
    How can you not know what happens?

Jessie. I'm busy.

Mama. That's not funny.

Jessie. I'm not laughing. My head turns around and I fall down
    and then what?

Mama. Well, your chest squeezes in and out, and you sound like
    you're gagging, sucking air in and out like you can't breathe.

Jessie. Do it for me. Make the sound for me.

Mama. I will not. It's awful-sounding.

Jessie. Yeah. It felt like it might be. What's next?

Mama. Your mouth bites down and I have to get your tongue out of the way fast, so you don't bite yourself.

Jessie. Or you. I bite you, too, don't I?

Mama. You got me once real good. I had to get a tetanus! But I know what to watch for now. And then you turn blue and the jerks start up. Like I'm standing there poking you with a cattle prod or you're sticking your finger in a light socket as fast as you can . . .

Jessie. Foaming like a mad dog the whole time.

Mama. It's bubbling, Jess, not foam like the washer overflowed, for God's sake; it's bubbling like a baby spitting up. I go get a wet washcloth, that's all. And then the jerks slow down and you wet yourself and it's over. Two minutes tops.

Jessie. How do I get to bed?

Mama. How do you think?

Jessie. I'm too heavy for you now. How do you do it?

Mama. I call Dawson. But I get you cleaned up before he gets here and I make him leave before you wake up.

Jessie. You could just leave me on the floor.

Mama. I want you to wake up someplace nice, O.K.? (*Then making a real effort.*) But, Jessie, and this is the reason I even brought this up! You haven't had a seizure for a solid year. A whole year, do you realize that?

Jessie. Yeah, the phenobarb's about right now, I guess.

Mama. You bet it is. You might never have another one, ever! You might be through with it for all time!

Jessie. Could be.

Mama. You are. I know you are!

Jessie. I sure am feeling good. I really am. The double vision's gone and my gums aren't swelling. No rashes or anything. I'm feeling as good as I ever felt in my life. I'm even feeling like worrying or getting mad and I'm not afraid it will start a fit if I do, I just go ahead.

Mama. Of course you do! You can even scream at me, if you want to. I can take it. You don't have to act like you're just visiting here, Jessie. This is your house, too.

Jessie. The best part is, my memory's back.

Mama. Your memory's always been good. When couldn't you remember things? You're always reminding me what . . .

Jessie. Because I've made lists for everything. But now I remember what things mean on my lists. I see "dish towels," and I used to wonder whether I was supposed to wash them, buy them, or look for them because I wouldn't remember where

I put them after I washed them, but now I know it means wrap them up, they're a present for Loretta's birthday.

Mama (*finished with the sofa now*). You used to go looking for your lists, too, I've noticed that. You always know where they are now! (*Then suddenly worried.*) Loretta's birthday isn't coming up, is it?

Jessie. I made a list of all the birthdays for you. I even put yours on it. (*A small smile.*) So you can call Loretta and remind her.

Mama. Let's take Loretta to Howard Johnson's and have those fried clams. I *know* you love that clam roll.

Jessie (*slight pause*). I won't be here, Mama.

Mama. What have we just been talking about? You'll be here. You're well, Jessie. You're starting all over. You said it yourself. You're remembering things and . . .

Jessie. I won't be here. If I'd ever had a year like this, to think straight and all, before now, I'd be gone already.

Mama (*not pleading, commanding*). No, Jessie.

Jessie (*folding the rest of the laundry*). Yes, Mama. Once I started remembering, I could see what it all added up to.

Mama. The fits are over!

Jessie. It's not the fits, Mama.

Mama. Then it's me for giving them to you, but I didn't do it!

Jessie. It's not the fits! You said it yourself, the medicine takes care of the fits.

Mama (*interrupting*). Your daddy gave you those fits, Jessie. He passed it down to you like your green eyes, and your straight hair. It's not my fault!

Jessie. So what if he had little fits? It's not inherited. I fell off the horse. It was an accident.

Mama. The horse wasn't the first time, Jessie. You had a fit when you were five years old.

Jessie. I did not.

Mama. You did! You were eating a popsicle and down you went. He gave it to you. It's *his* fault, not mine.

Jessie. Well, you took your time telling me.

Mama. How do you tell that to a five-year-old?

Jessie. What did the doctor say?

Mama. He said kids have them all the time. He said there wasn't anything to do but wait for another one.

Jessie. But I didn't have another one.

Now there is a real silence.

Jessie. You mean to tell me I had fits all the time as a kid and you

just told me I fell down or something and it wasn't till I
had the fit when Cecil was looking that anybody bothered
to find out what was the matter with me?

Mama. It wasn't *all the time,* Jessie. And they changed when you
started to school. More like your daddy's. Oh, that was
some swell time, sitting here with the two of you turning
off and on like light bulbs some nights.

Jessie. How many fits did I have?

Mama. You never hurt yourself. I never let you out of my sight.
I caught you every time.

Jessie. But you didn't tell anybody.

Mama. It was none of their business.

Jessie. You were ashamed.

Mama. I didn't want anybody to know. Least of all you.

Jessie. Least of all me. Oh, right. That was mine to know, Mama,
not yours. Did Daddy know?

Mama. He thought you were . . . you fell down a lot. That's what
he thought. You were careless. Or maybe he thought I beat
you. I don't know what he thought. He didn't think about
it.

Jessie. Because you didn't tell him!

Mama. If I told him about you, I'd have to tell him about him!

Jessie. I don't like this. I don't like this one bit.

Mama. I didn't think you'd like it. That's why I didn't tell you.

Jessie. If I'd known I was an epileptic, Mama, I wouldn't have
ridden any horses.

Mama. Make you feel like a freak, is that what I should have done?

Jessie. Just get the manicure tray and sit down!

Mama (throwing it to the floor). I don't want a manicure!

Jessie. Doesn't look like you do, no.

Mama. Maybe I did drop you, you don't know.

Jessie. If you say you didn't, you didn't.

Mama (beginning to break down). Maybe I fed you the wrong thing.
Maybe you had a fever sometime and I didn't know it soon
enough. Maybe it's a punishment.

Jessie. For what?

Mama. I don't know. Because of how I felt about your father.
Because I didn't want any more children. Because I smoked
too much or didn't eat right when I was carrying you. It
has to be something I did.

Jessie. It does not. It's just a sickness, not a curse. Epilepsy doesn't
mean anything. It just is.

Mama. I'm not talking about the fits here, Jessie! I'm talking about
this killing yourself. It has to be me that's the matter here.

You wouldn't be doing this if it wasn't. I didn't tell you things or I married you off to the wrong man or I took you in and let your life get away from you or all of it put together. I don't know what I did, but I did it, I know. This is all my fault, Jessie, but I don't know what to do about it now!

Jessie (exasperated at having to say this again). It doesn't have anything to do with you!

Mama. Everything you do has to do with me, Jessie. You can't do *anything,* wash your face or cut your finger, without doing it to me. That's right! You might as well kill me as you, Jessie, it's the same thing. This has to do with me, Jessie.

Jessie. Then what if it does! What if it has everything to do with you! What if you are all I have and you're not enough? What if I could take all the rest of it if only I didn't have you here? What if the only way I can get away from you for good is to kill myself? What if it is? I can *still* do it!

Mama (in desperate tears). Don't leave me, Jessie! *(Jessie stands for a moment, then turns for the bedroom.)* No! *(She grabs Jessie's arm.)*

Jessie (carefully taking her arm away). I have a box of things I want people to have. I'm just going to go get it for you. You . . . just rest a minute.

Jessie is gone. Mama heads for the telephone, but she can't even pick up the receiver this time and, instead, stoops to clean up the bottles that have spilled out of the manicure tray.

Jessie returns, carrying a box that groceries were delivered in. It probably says Hershey Kisses or Starkist Tuna. Mama is still down on the floor cleaning up, hoping that maybe if she just makes it look nice enough, Jessie will stay.

Mama. Jessie, how can I live here without you? I need you! You're supposed to tell me to stand up straight and say how nice I look in my pink dress, and drink my milk. You're supposed to go around and lock up so I know we're safe for the night, and when I wake up, you're supposed to be out there making the coffee and watching me get older every day, and you're supposed to help me die when the time comes. I can't do that by myself, Jessie. I'm not like you, Jessie. I hate the quiet and I don't want to die and I don't want you to go, Jessie. How can I . . . *(Has to stop a moment.)* How can I get up every day knowing you had to kill yourself to make it stop hurting and I was here all the time and I never even saw it. And then you gave me this chance to make it better, convince you to stay alive, and I couldn't do it. How can I live with myself after this, Jessie?

Jessie. I only told you so I could explain it, so you wouldn't blame yourself, so you wouldn't feel bad. There wasn't anything you could say to change my mind. I didn't want you to save me. I just wanted you to know.

Mama. Stay with me just a little longer. Just a few more years. I don't have that many more to go, Jessie. And as soon as I'm dead, you can do whatever you want. Maybe with me gone, you'll have all the quiet you want, right here in the house. And maybe one day you'll put in some begonias up the walk and get just the right rain for them all summer. And Ricky will be married by then and he'll bring your grandbabies over and you can sneak them a piece of candy when their daddy's not looking and then be real glad when they've gone home and left you to your quiet again.

Jessie. Don't you see, Mama, everything I do winds up like this. How could I think you would understand? How could I think you would want a manicure? We could hold hands for an hour and then I could go shoot myself? I'm sorry about tonight, Mama, but it's exactly why I'm doing it.

Mama. If you've got the guts to kill yourself, Jessie, you've got the guts to stay alive.

Jessie. I know that. So it's really just a matter of where I'd rather be.

Mama. Look, maybe I can't think of what you should do, but that doesn't mean there isn't something that would help. *You* find it. *You* think of it. You can keep trying. You can get brave and try some more. You don't have to give up!

Jessie. I'm *not* giving up! This *is* the other thing I'm trying. And I'm sure there are some other things that might work, but *might* work isn't good enough anymore. I need something that *will* work. *This* will work. That's why I picked it.

Mama. But something might happen. Something that could change everything. Who knows what it might be, but it might be worth waiting for! (*Jessie doesn't respond.*) Try it for two more weeks. We could have more talks like tonight.

Jessie. No, Mama.

Mama. I'll pay more attention to you. Tell the truth when you ask me. Let you have your say.

Jessie. No, Mama! We wouldn't have more talks like tonight, because it's this next part that's made this last part so good, Mama. No, Mama. *This* is how I have my say. This is how

I say what I thought about it *all* and I say no. To Dawson
and Loretta and the Red Chinese and epilepsy and Ricky and
Cecil and you. And me. And hope. I say no! (*Then going to
Mama on the sofa.*) Just let me go easy, Mama.

Mama. How can I let you go?

Jessie. You can because you have to. It's what you've always done.

Mama. You are my child!

Jessie. I am what became of your child. (*Mama cannot answer.*) I
found an old baby picture of me. And it was somebody else,
not me. It was somebody pink and fat who never heard of
sick or lonely, somebody who cried and got fed, and reached
up and got held and kicked but didn't hurt anybody, and
slept whenever she wanted to, just by closing her eyes.
Somebody who mainly just laid there and laughed at the
colors waving around over her head and chewed on a polka-
dot whale and woke up knowing some new trick nearly
every day, and rolled over and drooled on the sheet and felt
your hand pulling my quilt back up over me. That's who
I started out and this is who is left. (*There is no self-pity here.*)
That's what this is about. It's somebody I lost, all right, it's
my own self. Who I never was. Or who I tried to be and
never got there. Somebody I waited for who never came.
And never will. So, see, it doesn't much matter what else
happens in the world or in this house, even. I'm what was
worth waiting for and I didn't make it. Me . . . who might
have made a difference to me . . . I'm not going to show
up, so there's no reason to stay, except to keep you company
. . . not reason enough because I'm not . . . very good company. (*Pause.*) Am I?

Mama (*knowing she must tell the truth*). No. And neither am I.

Jessie. I had this strange little thought, well, maybe it's not so
strange. Anyway, after Christmas, after I decided to do this,
I would wonder, sometimes, what might keep me here, what
might be worth staying for, and you know what it was? It
was maybe if there was something I really liked, like maybe
if I really liked rice pudding or cornflakes for breakfast or
something, that might be enough.

Mama. Rice pudding is good.

Jessie. Not to me.

Mama. And you're not afraid?

Jessie. Afraid of what?

Mama. I'm afraid of it, for me, I mean. When my time comes. I
know it's coming, but . . .

Jessie. You don't know when. Like in a scary movie.

Mama. Yeah, sneaking up on me like some killer on the loose, hiding out in the back yard just waiting for me to have my hands full someday and how am I supposed to protect myself anyhow when I don't know what he looks like and I don't know how he sounds coming up behind me like that or if it will hurt or take very long or what I don't get done before it happens.

Jessie. You've got plenty of time left.

Mama. I forget what for, right now.

Jessie. For whatever happens, I don't know. For the rest of your life. For Agnes burning down one more house or Dawson losing his hair or . . .

Mama (quickly). Jessie. I can't just sit here and say O.K., kill yourself if you want to.

Jessie. Sure you can. You just did. Say it again.

Mama (really startled). Jessie! (*Quiet horror.*) How dare you! (*Furious.*) How dare you! You think you can just leave whenever you want, like you're watching television here? No, you can't, Jessie. You make me feel like a fool for being alive, child, and you are so wrong! I like it here, and I will stay here until they make me go, until they drag me screaming and I mean screeching into my grave, and you're real smart to get away before then because, I mean, honey, you've never heard noise like that in your life. (*Jessie turns away.*) Who am I talking to? You're gone already, aren't you? I'm looking right through you! I can't stop you because you're already gone! I guess you think they'll all have to talk about you now! I guess you think this will really confuse them. Oh yes, ever since Christmas you've been laughing to yourself and thinking, "Boy, are they all in for a surprise." Well, nobody's going to be a bit surprised, sweetheart. This is just like you. Do it the hard way, that's my girl, all right. (*Jessie gets up and goes into the kitchen, but Mama follows her.*) You know who they're going to feel sorry for? Me! How about that! Not you, me! They're going to be *ashamed* of you. Yes. *Ashamed!* If somebody asks Dawson about it, he'll change the subject as fast as he can. He'll talk about how much he has to pay to park his car these days.

Jessie. Leave me alone.

Mama. It's the truth!

Jessie. I should've just left you a note!

Mama (screaming). Yes! (*Then suddenly understanding what she has said, nearly paralyzed by the thought of it, she turns slowly to face Jessie, nearly whispering.*) No. No. I . . . might not have thought of all the things you've said.

Jessie. It's O.K., Mama.

Mama is nearly unconscious from the emotional devastation of these last few moments. She sits down at the kitchen table, hurt and angry and desperately afraid. But she looks almost numb. She is so far beyond what is known as pain that she is virtually unreachable and Jessie knows this, and talks quietly, watching for signs of recovery.

Jessie (washes her hands in the sink). I remember you liked that preacher who did Daddy's, so if you want to ask him to do the service, that's O.K. with me.

Mama (not an answer, just a word). What.

Jessie (putting on hand lotion as she talks). And pick some songs you like or let Agnes pick, she'll know exactly which ones. Oh, and I had your dress cleaned that you wore to Daddy's. You looked real good in that.

Mama. I don't remember, hon.

Jessie. And it won't be so bad once your friends start coming to the funeral home. You'll probably see people you haven't seen for years, but I thought about what you should say to get you over that nervous part when they first come in.

Mama (simply repeating). Come in.

Jessie. Take them up to see their flowers, they'd like that. And when they say, "I'm so sorry, Thelma," you just say, "I appreciate your coming, Connie." And then ask how their garden was this summer or what they're doing for Thanksgiving or how their children . . .

Mama. I don't think I should ask about their children. I'll talk about what they have on, that's always good. And I'll have some crochet work with me.

Jessie. And Agnes will be there, so you might not have to talk at all.

Mama. Maybe if Connie Richards does come, I can get her to tell me where she gets that Irish yarn, she calls it. I know it doesn't come from Ireland. I think it just comes with a green wrapper.

Jessie. And be sure to invite enough people home afterward so you get enough food to feed them all and have some left for you. But don't let anybody take anything home, especially Loretta.

Mama. Loretta will get all the food set up, honey. It's only fair to let her have some macaroni or something.

Jessie. No, Mama. You have to be more selfish from now on. (*Sitting at the table with Mama.*) Now, somebody's bound to ask you why I did it and you just say you don't know. That you loved me and you know I loved you and we just sat around tonight like every other night of our lives, and then I came over and kissed you and said, " 'Night, Mother," and you heard me close my bedroom door and the next thing you heard was the shot. And whatever reasons I had, well, you guess I just took them with me.

Mama (quietly). It was something personal.

Jessie. Good. That's good, Mama.

Mama. That's what I'll say, then.

Jessie. Personal. Yeah.

Mama. Is that what I tell Dawson and Loretta, too? We sat around, you kissed me, " 'Night, Mother"? They'll want to know more, Jessie. They won't believe it.

Jessie. Well, then, tell them what we did. I filled up the candy jars. I cleaned out the refrigerator. We made some hot chocolate and put the cover back on the sofa. You had no idea. All right? I really think it's better that way. If they know we talked about it, they really won't understand how you let me go.

Mama. I guess not.

Jessie. It's private. Tonight is private, yours and mine, and I don't want anybody else to have any of it.

Mama. O.K., then.

Jessie (standing behind Mama now, holding her shoulders). Now, when you hear the shot, I don't want you to come in. First of all, you won't be able to get in by yourself, but I don't want you trying. Call Dawson, then call the police, and then call Agnes. And then you'll need something to do till somebody gets here, so wash the hot-chocolate pan. You wash that pan till you hear the doorbell ring and I don't care if it's an hour, you keep washing that pan.

Mama. I'll make my calls and then I'll just sit. I won't need something to do. What will the police say?

Jessie. They'll do that gunpowder test, I guess, and ask you what happened, and by that time, the ambulance will be here and they'll come in and get me and you know how that goes. You stay out here with Dawson and Loretta. You keep Dawson out here. I want the police in the room first, not Dawson, O.K.?

Mama. What if Dawson and Loretta want me to go home with them?

Jessie (returning to the living room). That's up to you.

Mama. I think I'll stay here. All they've got is Sanka.

Jessie. Maybe Agnes could come stay with you for a few days.

Mama (*standing up, looking into the living room*). I'd rather be by myself, I think. (*Walking toward the box Jessie brought in earlier.*) You want me to give people those things?

Jessie (*they sit down on the sofa, Jessie holding the box on her lap*). I want Loretta to have my little calculator. Dawson bought it for himself, you know, but then he saw one he liked better and he couldn't bring both of them home with Loretta counting every penny the way she does, so he gave the first one to me. Be funny for her to have it now, don't you think? And all my house slippers are in a sack for her in my closet. Tell her I know they'll fit and I've never worn any of them, and make sure Dawson hears you tell her that. I'm glad he loves Loretta so much, but I wish he knew not everybody has her size feet.

Mama (*taking the calculator*). O.K.

Jessie (*reaching into the box again*). This letter is for Dawson, but it's mostly about you, so read it if you want. There's a list of presents for you for at least twenty more Christmases and birthdays, so if you want anything special you better add it to this list before you give it to him. Or if you want to be surprised, just don't read that page. This Christmas, you're getting mostly stuff for the house, like a new rug in your bathroom and needlework, but next Christmas, you're really going to cost him next Christmas. I think you'll like it a lot and you'd never think of it.

Mama. And you think he'll go for it?

Jessie. I think he'll feel like a real jerk if he doesn't. Me telling him to, like this and all. Now, this number's where you call Cecil. I called it last week and he answered, so I know he still lives there.

Mama. What do you want me to tell him?

Jessie. Tell him we talked about him and I only had good things to say about him, but mainly tell him to find Ricky and tell him what I did, and tell Ricky you have something for him, out here, from me, and to come get it. (*Pulls a sack out of the box.*)

Mama (*the sack feels empty*). What is it?

Jessie (*taking it off*). My watch. (*Putting it in the sack and taking a ribbon out of the sack to tie around the top of it.*)

Mama. He'll sell it!

Jessie. That's the idea. I appreciate him not stealing it already. I'd like to buy him a good meal.

Mama. He'll buy dope with it!

Jessie. Well, then, I hope he gets some good dope with it, Mama.

And the rest of this is for you. (*Handing Mama the box now. Mama picks up the things and looks at them.*)

Mama (*surprised and pleased*). When did you do all this? During my naps, I guess.

Jessie. I guess. I tried to be quiet about it. (*As Mama is puzzled by the presents.*) Those are just little presents. For whenever you need one. They're not bought presents, just things I thought you might like to look at, pictures or things you think you've lost. Things you didn't know you had, even. You'll see.

Mama. I'm not sure I want them. They'll make me think of you.

Jessie. No they won't. They're just things, like a free tube of toothpaste I found hanging on the door one day.

Mama. Oh. All right, then.

Jessie. Well, maybe there's one nice present in there somewhere. It's Granny's ring she gave me and I thought you might like to have it, but I didn't think you'd wear it if I gave it to you right now.

Mama (*taking the box to a table nearby*). No. Probably not. (*Turning back to face her.*) I'm ready for my manicure, I guess. Want me to wash my hands again?

Jessie (*standing up*). It's time for me to go, Mama.

Mama (*starting for her*). No, Jessie, you've got all night!

Jessie (*as Mama grabs her*). No, Mama.

Mama. It's not even ten o'clock.

Jessie (*very calm*). Let me go, Mama.

Mama. I can't. You can't go. You can't do this. You didn't say it would be so soon, Jessie. I'm scared. I love you.

Jessie (*takes her hands away*). Let go of me, Mama. I've said everything I had to say.

Mama (*standing still a minute*). You said you wanted to do my nails.

Jessie (*taking a small step backward*). I can't. It's too late.

Mama. It's not too late!

Jessie. I don't want you to wake Dawson and Loretta when you call. I want them to still be up and dressed so they can get right over.

Mama (*As Jessie backs up, Mama moves in on her, but carefully*). They wake up fast, Jessie, if they have to. They don't matter here, Jessie. You do. I do. We're not through yet. We've got a lot of things to take care of here. I don't know where my prescriptions are and you didn't tell me what to tell Dr. Davis when he calls or how much you want me to tell Ricky or who I call to rake the leaves or . . .

Jessie. Don't try and stop me, Mama, you can't do it.

Mama (*grabbing her again, this time hard*). I can too! I'll stand in front of this hall and you can't get past me. (*They struggle.*)

You'll have to knock me down to get away from me, Jessie. I'm not about to let you . . .

Mama struggles with Jessie at the door and in the struggle Jessie gets away from her and ——

Jessie (*almost a whisper*). 'Night, Mother. (*She vanishes into her bedroom and we hear the door lock just as Mama gets to it.*)

Mama (*screams*). Jessie! (*Pounding on the door.*) Jessie, you let me in there. Don't you do this, Jessie. I'm not going to stop screaming until you open this door, Jessie. Jessie! Jessie! What if I don't do any of the things you told me to do! I'll tell Cecil what a miserable man he was to make you feel the way he did and I'll give Ricky's watch to Dawson if I feel like it and the only way you can make sure I do what you want is you come out here and make me, Jessie! (*Pounding again.*) Jessie! Stop this! I didn't know! I was here with you all the time. How could I know you were so alone?

And Mama stops for a moment, breathless and frantic, putting her ear to the door, and when she doesn't hear anything, she stands up straight again and screams once more.

Jessie! Please!

And we hear the shot, and it sounds like an answer, it sounds like No.

Mama collapses against the door, tears streaming down her face, but not screaming anymore. In shock now.

Jessie, Jessie, child . . . Forgive me. (*Pause.*) I thought you were mine.

And she leaves the door and makes her way through the living room, around the furniture, as though she didn't know where it was, not knowing what to do. Finally, she goes to the stove in the kitchen and picks up the hot-chocolate pan and carries it with her to the telephone, and holds on to it while she dials the number. She looks down at the pan, holding it tight like her life depended on it. She hears Loretta answer.

Mama. Loretta, let me talk to Dawson, honey.

QUESTIONS

1. Early in the play, on page 1139, Jessie says she wants the gun for "protection." In the context of the entire play, what do you take this to mean?

2. Why do you think Jessie says, on page 1142, that she would rather use her father's gun than her husband's?
3. The playwright specifies that "The time is the present, with the action beginning about 8:15. Clocks on stage in the kitchen and on a table in the living room should run throughout the performance and be visible to the audience." Why?
4. Jessie insists (page 1162) that Ricky is like her, and not like his father Cecil. What do you think she is getting at?
5. On page 1143 Mama says, "People don't really kill themselves, Jessie. No, mam, doesn't make sense, unless you're retarded or deranged." Specify the various reasons that Mama assumes are the motives for Jessie's suicide. Most theories of suicide can be classified into one of two groups, psychoanalytical and sociological. Psychoanalytical theories (usually rooted in Freud) assume that human beings have dual impulses, *eros* (life instinct) and *thanatos* (death instinct). When the death instinct, expressed as hostility and aggression, is turned against others it takes the form of homicide, but when it is turned against the self it takes the form of suicide. Most sociological theories assume that suicide occurs among three types of people: egoistic suicides, people who are excessively individualistic (i.e., who are not integrated into society); altruistic suicides, people who have an excessive sense of duty to society and who die willingly to serve society; and, third, anomic suicides, people who find their usual lifestyles disrupted by sudden social changes such as the loss of a job during an economic depression. Do any of these theories seem helpful in explaining Jessie's suicide? In your opinion why *does* Jessie kill herself? (You may want to do some research on suicide, for instance, by consulting Freud's *Civilization and Its Discontents,* or Andrew F. Henry and James F. Short, *Homicide and Suicide,* or Edwin S. Scheidman, ed., *Essays in Self-Destruction,* or A. Alvarez, *The Savage God.*)
6. The greatest tragedies somehow suggest that the tragic figures are not only particular individuals — Oedipus, Lear, and so forth — but also are universal figures who somehow embody our own hopes and fears. Another way of putting it is to say that the greatest plays are not case histories but are visions of a central aspect of life. To what extent, in your opinion, does *'night, Mother* meet this criterion?

Appendix: Writing Essays about Literature

WHY WRITE?

People write about literature to clarify and account for their responses to works that interest or excite or frustrate them. In putting words on paper you will have to take a second and third look at what is in front of you and what is within you. And so writing is a way of learning. The last word about complex thoughts and feelings is never said, but when we write we hope to make at least a little progress in the difficult but rewarding job of talking about our responses. We learn, and then we hope to interest our readers because we are communicating to them our responses to something that for one reason or another is worth talking about.

This communication is, in effect, teaching. You may think that you are writing for the teacher, but that is a misconception; when you write, *you* are the teacher. An essay on literature is an attempt to help someone see the work as you see it. If this chapter had to be boiled down to a single sentence, that sentence would be: Because you are teaching, your essay should embody those qualities that you value in teachers — probably intelligence, open-mindedness, and effort; and certainly a desire to offer what help one can.

TWO COMMON APPROACHES: EXPLICATION AND ANALYSIS

Explication

An **explication** (literally, "unfolding" or "spreading out") is a line-by-line commentary on what is going on in a text — usually a short poem or short passage of prose.

Consider, for example, the following prose lines from *Hamlet* III.i.127–129, part of a speech in which Hamlet bitterly addresses Ophelia:

> What should such fellows as I do crawling between earth and heaven? We are arrant knaves all; believe none of us.

Now for a student's explication (taken from an explication of the entire speech) of these lines:

```
By speaking of himself and others as "fellows"
(rather than as, say, "men" or "human beings"),
Hamlet somewhat lowers or debases himself. The de-
basement in "fellows" is continued and made
stronger in the rest of the sentence ("What should
such fellows as I do crawling between heaven and
earth?"), because "crawling" suggests the action of
a bug or a reptile. Of course human beings some-
times do crawl, and babies crawl a lot, but since
Hamlet a moment earlier says he is guilty of many
sins, it seems reasonable here to say that "crawl-
ing" suggests that he now regards himself not as a
dignified human being but as a beast. And not only
himself; the shift from "such fellows as I" to "We
are arrant knaves all" shows that Hamlet sees all
humans as deeply corrupted.
```

As this brief example indicates, an explication is not concerned with the writer's life or times, and it is not a paraphrase (a rewording)

— though it may include paraphrase. It is a study — almost word by word — that reveals the meaning of a work. Because the language of a literary work is denser (richer in associations or connotations — as we just saw in the comment on "crawling") than the language of such prose as this paragraph, explication is much concerned with bringing to the surface the meanings in the words that may not be immediately apparent. In the brief comment on *Hamlet,* the student called attention to:

1. The implication of "fellows" (relatively low)
2. The metaphoric implication in "crawling"
3. The implication in Hamlet's shift from "I" to "we"

Explication, in short, seeks to make explicit what is *implicit* (literally, "folded" or "entangled") in the text. It may seem to "read into" the work, but if it is done well, it really "reads out" what is within the work. To this end it calls attention, as it proceeds, to such things as

1. The connotations or implications of words
2. The function of rhymes
3. The shifts in tone or point of view
4. The development of contrasts
5. The significance of variations in the meter
6. Any other contributions to meaning

Organizing an Explication

The organization of an explication rarely causes any difficulty; an explication customarily moves through the work (or the chosen passage) from beginning to end, though, of course, it may begin with a statement of the thesis, such as

Hamlet's disgust with himself is revealed most

strongly in his use of "crawling," which suggests

that he thinks of himself as a bug or reptile.

or

Frost's "Mending Wall" uses few or no difficult

words and contains no obscure references, but the

poem nevertheless uses language in extremely subtle

ways.

Although your explication will for the most part move steadily from the beginning to the end of the selection, try to avoid writing along these lines (or, one might say, along this one line): "In line one . . . In the second line . . . In the third line . . ." That is, don't hesitate to write such things as

```
The poem begins . . . In the next line . . . The

speaker immediately adds . . . He then intro-

duces . . . The next stanza begins by

saying . . .
```

And of course you can discuss the second line before the first if that seems the best way of handling the passage.

A Sample Explication

Below we print a student's first-rate explication of Yeats's "The Balloon of the Mind." If, when you read the explication, you are tempted to throw up your hands and say that you could never write a piece as keen as this one, remember several things: The writer of this explication had already achieved some skill by reading poems and by writing several explications earlier in the term; this explication is a finished piece of work, the outcome of several drafts; each draft was the outcome of sustained thinking; and the writer arrived at many of his insights or perceptions by asking himself questions. (For some questions that will help stimulate responses to poetry, see pages 504–505.)

William Butler Yeats (*Irish. 1865–1939*)

The Balloon of the Mind

> Hands, do what you're bid:
> Bring the balloon of the mind
> That bellies and drags in the wind
> Into its narrow shed.

Now, it happens that in a prose work, *Reveries over Childhood and Youth,* Yeats already had used the figure of a balloon (dirigible) to represent mental activity: "My thoughts were a great excitement, but when I tried to do anything with them, it was like trying to pack a balloon into a shed in a high wind." But because explication usually confronts the work itself, without relating it to biography, the writer of this explication passed over this interesting anticipation and confined himself to the poem's four lines, thus:

Yeats's "Balloon of the Mind" is about poetry, specifically about the difficulty of getting one's floating thoughts down in lines on the page. The first line, a short, stern, heavily stressed command to the speaker's hands, perhaps implies by its severe or impatient tone that these hands will be disobedient or inept or careless if not watched closely: the poor bumbling body so often fails to achieve the goals of the mind. The bluntness of the command in the first line is emphasized by the fact that all the subsequent lines have more syllables. Furthermore, the first line is a gramatically complete sentence, whereas the thought of line 2 spills over into the subsequent lines, implying the difficulty of fitting ideas into confining spaces, that is, of getting one's thoughts into order, especially into a coherent poem. Lines 2 and 3 amplify the metaphor already stated in the title (the product of the mind is an airy but unwieldy balloon), and they also contain a second command, "Bring." Alliteration ties this command, "Bring," to the earlier "bid"; it also ties both of these verbs to their object, "balloon," and to the verb that most effectively describes the balloon, "bellies." In comparison with the peremptory first line of the poem, lines 2 and 3 themselves seem almost

swollen, bellying and dragging, an effect aided by
using adjacent unstressed syllables ("of the,"
"[bell]ies and," "in the") and by using an eye
rhyme ("mind" and "wind") rather than an exact
rhyme. And then comes the short last line: almost
before we could expect it, the cumbersome balloon--
here, the idea that is to be packed into the
stanza--is successfully lodged in its "narrow
shed." Aside from the relatively colorless "into,"
the only words of more than one syllable in the
poem are "balloon," "bellies," and "narrow," and
all three emphasize the difficulty of the task. But
after "narrow"--the word itself almost looks long
and narrow, in this context like a hangar--we get
the simplicity of the monosyllable "shed"; and the
difficult job is done, the thought is safely packed
away, the poem is completed--but again with an off
rhyme ("bid" and "shed"), for neatness can go only
so far when hands and mind and a balloon are
involved.

Writing an explication, like almost all other writing, begins
not with putting a sheet of paper into a typewriter but with jotting
down notes, and the best place for one's preliminary notes is the
page in the book with the poem — assuming, of course, that you
own the book. (If you don't own the book — or even if you do
— it's a good idea to copy out the poem double-spaced, and to
jot notes in the margins and between the lines.) As you read, you
notice things, and you begin to mark up the text thus:

sounds
abrupt

Hands, do what you're bid:

Bring the Balloon of the mind   *no real rhymes?*

That Bellies and drags in the wind

Into its narrow shed.

A pen or pencil will help you to think, and your preliminary jottings — including questions to yourself such as "meaning?" or "Do these words rhyme?" — will lead you to greater understanding.

Note: The reader of an explication needs to see the text, and because the explicated text is usually short, it is advisable to quote it all. (Remember, your imagined audience consists of your classmates; even if they have already read the work you are explicating, they have not memorized it, and so you helpfully remind them of the work by quoting it.) You can quote the entire text at the outset, or you can quote the first unit (for example, a stanza), then explicate that unit, and then quote the next unit, and so on. And if the poem or passage of prose is longer than, say, six lines, it is advisable to number each line at the right for easy reference.

Analysis

If one has world enough and time, one can set out to explicate all of *Moby Dick* or *Hamlet*. More likely, one will explicate a page in *Moby Dick* or a speech in *Hamlet*; in writing about works longer than a page or two, a more common approach than explicating is **analyzing** (literally, "separating into parts in order to understand"). An analysis commonly considers one part and the relation of this part to the whole. For example, it may consider only the functions of the setting in *The Adventures of Huckleberry Finn* or the comedy in *Hamlet* or the allusions in T. S. Eliot's "The Love Song of J. Alfred Prufrock."

Analysis, of course, is not a process used only in talking about literature. It is commonly applied in thinking about almost any complex matter. Martina Navratilova plays a deadly game of tennis: What makes it so good? How does her backhand contribute? What does her serve do to the opponent? In short, given the whole, how do the parts fit together?

If a work is faily long, and you are writing only a few pages and you are not explicating a short passage from the work, almost surely you will write an analysis of some part. Unless you have an enormous amount of time for reflection and revision, you cannot write a meaningful essay of five hundred words or even a thousand words on "Shakespeare's *Hamlet*" or "Melville's *Moby-Dick*." You cannot even write on "Character in *Hamlet*" or "Symbolism in *Moby-Dick*." And probably you won't really want to write on such topics anyway. Probably *one* character or *one* symbol has caught your interest. Trust your feelings; you are likely onto something interesting, and it will be best to think about this smaller topic for the relatively few hours that you have. A "smaller" topic need not be a dull or trivial topic; treated properly, it may illuminate the entire work or, to change the metaphor, it may serve as a mine shaft that gives entry to the work. "Hamlet's Relationship to Horatio," carefully thought about, will in five hundred or a thousand words tell a reader more (and will have taught its author more) than will "*Hamlet* as a Tragedy."

From Topic to Thesis

How do you find a topic and how do you turn it into a **thesis** (an argument or proposition)? An idea may hit you suddenly; as you are reading you find yourself jotting in the margin, "contrast with Joyce's treatment of disillusionment," "too heavy irony," or "ugh." Or an idea may come slowly upon rereading. Perhaps you gradually become aware of the frequency of the word "really" in *The Catcher in the Rye,* and you notice that Holden Caulfield, who is regularly given to saying things such as "if you really want to know" and "I really mean it," at one point explicitly comments on the nature of reality. You work on this and begin to relate it to his abundant discussions of phoneys, and you emerge, perhaps, with the thesis, or argument, that in Holden's mouth "really" is not merely the filler it seems to be but is a clue to his quest for the real in a world of appearances and phoneys.

If you have thought about the topic, converted it into a thesis, and stripped it of irrelevancies, you should be able to formulate it in a few words. (This formula, or something like it, can be your title. There is nothing wrong with a title as direct as "Holden Caulfield's Use of the Word 'Really' "; although it is scarcely exciting, it is informative. Beware of cute titles, especially those which do not give the reader a good idea of what will follow, such as "Really!" or "A Boy's Word." "The Real Holden and Reality" is about as far as one should go.)

Let's dwell a moment longer on the distinction between a topic and a thesis. It may be useful to think of it this way: a topic is a subject (for example, Hamlet's relation to Horatio); to arrive at a thesis you have to add a predicate (for example, "Hamlet's relation to Horatio helps to define Hamlet"). Of course, some theses are more promising than others. Consider these three statements:

1. "Hamlet's relationship to Horatio is interesting."

2. "Hamlet's relations with Horatio are friendly."
3. "Hamlet's relation to Horatio helps to reveal Hamlet's special, heroic qualities."

Now, "Hamlet's relationship to Horatio is interesting" is a thesis, but it is vague and provides little direction, little help in generating ideas and in shaping an essay. "Hamlet's relations with Horatio are friendly" is better, but not much. It provides a focus, but it is not likely to help the writer to see anything beyond the obvious. Only the third version is likely to help a writer to develop an essay: "Hamlet's relation to Horatio helps to reveal Hamlet's special, heroic qualities."

Questions that May Generate a Thesis

Every literary work affords its own topics for analysis, and every essayist must set forth his or her own thesis, but a few useful generalizations may be made. You can often find a thesis by asking one of two questions:

1. *What purpose does this serve?* That is, why is this scene in the novel or play? Why is there a clown in *Hamlet?* Why are these lines unrhymed? Why is this stanza form employed? What is the significance of the parts of the work? (Titles are often highly significant parts of the work: Ibsen's *A Doll's House,* Kesey's *One Flew Over the Cuckoo's Nest,* and Roth's *The Great American Novel* would be slightly different if they had other titles.)

2. *Why do I have this response?* Why do I find this poem clever or moving or puzzling? How did the author make this character funny or dignified or pathetic? How does she communicate the idea that this character is a bore without boring me?

The first of these questions, "What purpose does this serve?" requires that you identify yourself with the author, wondering, for example, whether this opening scene is the best possible for this story. The second question, "Why do I have this response?" requires that you trust your feelings. If you are amused or bored or puzzled or annoyed, assume that these responses are appropriate and follow them up, at least until a rereading of the work provides other responses.

Note: For suggested questions—in order to help stimulate responses—see pages 99–101 (on fiction), pages 504–505 (on poetry), and pages 658–659 (on drama).

Two Examples of Analysis

Let's look first at an analysis of one aspect of a short story, irony in Kate Chopin's "The Story of an Hour." (This extremely brief work is printed on page 41.) After thinking about the topic and consulting the jottings (including underlinings and marginal notes) made while reading and rereading, a student found that her underlying thesis—that there are several ironies in the story— broke down into two parts: The chief irony is that Mrs. Mallard dies just as she is beginning to enjoy life, but there are also smaller ironies, such as that the "sad message" turns out (for a while) not to be sad, and that although Richards is "too late" when he tries to save her at the end, if he had been "late" at the beginning the whole mess would not have occurred. The topic ideas of the paragraphs of the essay turned out to be these:

1. The story has an ironic ending, but there are smaller ironies within it.
2. One of these smaller ironies is that the "sad message" turns out, at least for a while, to bring joy.
3. Two other bits of irony are (a) Richards's well-meaning haste at the beginning is not matched by adequate haste at the end, and (b) the doctors' comments on joy are true in a way that the speakers do not mean.
4. The central irony, however, is that Mrs. Mallard begins to live only after years of marriage, and this new life, which occurs appropriately at springtime, is cut off even as she looks forward not only to summer but to "a long progression of years."

Some such thoughts must have preceded the following essay, but of course they were arrived at only after reading and rereading and writing and rewriting. By the way, don't let the excellence of the following essay discourage you from thinking that you can't do as well. Remember, this essay is the product of much work. As the writer wrote, her ideas got better and better, for in her drafts she put down a point and then realized that it needed strengthening (for instance, with a brief quotation) or that—come to think of it—the point couldn't be substantiated and ought to be deleted.

```
      Ironies of Life in Kate Chopin's "Story of an Hour"

      Kate Chopin's "Story of an Hour"--which takes only a
```

few minutes to read--turns out to have an ironic ending,
but on rereading it one sees that the irony is not concentrated only in the outcome of the plot--Mrs. Mallard
dies just when she is beginning to live--but is also
present in many details.

After we know how the story turns out, if we reread it
we find irony at the very start: Mrs. Mallard's friends
and relatives all assume, mistakenly, that she was deeply
in love with her husband, Brently Mallard, and so they
take great care to tell her gently of his death. They mean
well, and in fact they do well, for they bring her an hour
of life, an hour of joyous freedom, but it is ironic that
they think their news is sad. True, Mrs. Mallard at first
expresses grief when she hears the news, but soon (unknown
to her friends) she finds joy in it. So, Richards's "sad
message," though sad in Richards's eyes, is in fact a
happy message.

Among the small but significant ironic details is the
statement near the end of the story that when Mallard entered the house, Richards tried to conceal him from Mrs.
Mallard, but "Richards was too late.'' This is ironic because almost at the start of the story, in the second paragraph, Richards with the best of motives "hastened" to
bring his sad message; if he had at the start been "too
late," Mallard would have arrived at home first, and Mrs.
Mallard's life would not have ended an hour later but
would have gone on simply as it had been. Yet another
irony at the end of the story is the diagnosis of the doctors. They say she had died of "heart disease--of joy
that kills." In one sense they are right: Mrs. Mallard has

for the last hour experienced a great joy. But of course the doctors totally misunderstand the joy that kills her: it is not joy at seeing her husband alive, but her realization that the great joy she experienced during the last hour is over.

All of these ironic details add richness to the story, but the central irony resides not in the well-intentioned but ironic actions of Richards, or in the unconsciously ironic words of the doctors, but in Mrs. Mallard's own life. She has for years been alive, and yet in a way she had been dead, a body subjected to her husband's will. Now, his apparent death brings her new life. Appropriately, this new life comes to her at the season of the year when "the tops of trees were all aquiver with the new spring life." But, ironically, her new life will last only an hour. She is "Free, free, free"--but only until her husband walks through the doorway. She looks forward to "summer days" but she will not see even the end of this spring day. If her years of marriage were ironic, bringing her a sort of living death instead of joy, her new life is ironic too, not only because it grows out of her moment of grief for her supposedly dead husband, but because its vision of "a long progression of years" is cut short within an hour on a spring day.

Let's look at several principles illustrated by this essay.

1. The title of the essay is not merely the title of the work discussed; rather, it gives the reader a clue, a small idea of the essayist's topic.
2. The opening or introductory paragraph does not begin by saying "In this story . . ." Rather, by naming the author and the title, it lets the reader know exactly what story is

being discussed. It also develops the writer's thesis a bit, so readers know where they will be going.

3. The smaller ironies are discussed in the second and third paragraphs, the central (chief) irony in the last paragraph. That is, the essay does not dwindle or become anticlimactic; rather, it builds up.

4. Some brief quotations are used, both to provide evidence and to let the reader hear—even if only fleetingly—Kate Chopin's writing.

5. The essayist, assuming that the reader has read the work, does not tell the plot in great detail. But, aware that the reader has not memorized the story, the essayist gives helpful reminders.

6. The essayist has opinions, but does not keep saying, "In my opinion" and "I feel that."

7. The present tense is used in narrating the action: "Mrs. Mallard dies"; "Mrs. Mallard's friends and relatives all assume."

8. Although a concluding paragraph is often useful—if it does more than merely summarize what has already been clearly said—it is not essential in a short analysis. In this essay, the last sentence explains the chief irony and therefore makes an acceptable ending.

Next, let's look at a longer analysis of a play. To this student's essay we have added marginal notes calling attention to some of the essay's strengths.

Title is focused; it announces topic and thesis.

Opening paragraph closes in on thesis.

The Solid Structure of The Glass Menagerie

In the "Production Notes" Tennessee Williams calls The Glass Menagerie a "memory play," a term that the narrator in the play also uses. Memories often consist of fragments of episodes which are so loosely connected that they seem chaotic, and therefore we might think that The Glass Menagerie will consist of very loosely related episodes. However, the play covers only one episode and though it gives the illusion of random talk, it really has a firm structure and moves steadily toward a foregone conclusion.

Tennessee Williams divides the play into seven scenes. The first scene begins with a sort of prologue and the last scene concludes with a sort of epilogue that is related to the prologue. In the prologue Tom addresses the audience and comments on the 1930s as a time when America was

"blind" and was a place of "shouting and confusion." Tom also mentions that our lives consist of expectations, and though he does not say that our expectations are unfulfilled, near the end of the prologue he quotes a postcard that his father wrote to the family he deserted: "Hello——Good-bye." In the epilogue Tom tells us that he followed his "father's footsteps," deserting the family. And just before the epilogue, near the end of Scene VII, we see what can be considered another desertion: Jim explains to Tom's sister Laura that he

is engaged and therefore cannot visit Laura again. Thus the end is closely related to the beginning, and the play is the steady development of the initial implications.

The first three scenes show things going from bad to worse. Amanda is a nagging mother who finds her only relief in talking about the past to her crippled

daughter Laura and her frustrated son Tom.
When she was young she was beautiful and
was eagerly courted by rich young men, but
now the family is poor and this harping on
the past can only bore or infuriate Tom
and embarrass or depress Laura, who have
no happy past to look back to, who see no
happy future, and who can only be upset by
Amanda's insistence that they should behave as she behaved long ago. The second
scene deepens the despair: Amanda learns
that the timorous Laura has not been attending a business school but has retreated in terror from this confrontation
with the contemporary world. Laura's helplessness is made clear to the audience,
and so is Amanda's lack of understanding.
Near the end of the second scene, however,
Jim's name is introduced; he is a boy
Laura had a crush on in high school, and
so the audience gets a glimpse of a happier Laura and a sense that possibly Laura's world is wider than the stifling tenement in which she and her mother and
brother live. But in the third scene
things get worse, when Tom and Amanda have
so violent an argument that they are no
longer on speaking terms. Tom is so angry
with his mother that he almost by accident
destroys his sister's treasured collection
of glass animals, the fragile lifeless

Brief plot summary supports thesis.

world which is her refuge. The apartment
is literally full of the "shouting and
confusion" that Tom spoke of in his
prologue.

*Useful summary
and transition.*

The first three scenes have revealed a
progressive worsening of relations; the
next three scenes reveal a progressive improvement in relations. In Scene IV, Tom
and his mother are reconciled, and Tom reluctantly—apparently in an effort to
make up with his mother—agrees to try
to get a friend to come to dinner so that
Laura will have "a gentleman caller." In
Scene V, Tom tells his mother that Jim
will come to dinner on the next night, and
Amanda brightens, because she sees a possibility of security for Laura at last. In
Scene VI, Jim arrives, and despite Laura's
initial terror, there seems, at least in
Amanda's mind, to be the possibility that
things will go well.

The seventh scene, by far the longest,
at first seems to be fulfilling Amanda's
hopes. Despite the ominous fact that the
lights go out because Tom has not paid the
electric bill, Jim is at ease. He is an
insensitive oaf, but that doesn't seem to
bother Amanda, and almost miraculously he
manages to draw Laura somewhat out of her
sheltered world. Even when Jim in his

clumsiness breaks the horn off Laura's
treasured glass unicorn, she is not upset.
In fact, she is almost relieved because
the loss of the horn makes the animal less
"freakish" and he "will feel more at home
with the other horses." In a way, of
course, the unicorn symbolizes the crip—
pled Laura, who at least for the moment
feels less freakish and isolated now that
she is somewhat reunited with society
through Jim. But this is a play about life
in a blind and confused world, and though
in a previous age the father escaped,
there can be no escape now. Jim reveals
that he is engaged, Laura relapses into
"desolation," Amanda relapes into rage and
bitterness, and Tom relapses into dreams
of escape. In a limited sense Tom does es—
cape. He leaves the family and joins the
merchant marine, but his last speech or
epilogue tells us that he cannot escape
the memory of his sister: "Oh, Laura,
Laura, I tried to leave you behind me, but
I am more faithful than I intended to be!"

*The essayist is
thinking and com-
menting, not merely
summarizing the
plot.*

And so the end of the last scene brings us
back again to the beginning of the first
scene: we are still in a world of "the
blind" and of "confusion." But now at the
end the darkness is deeper, the characters
are lost forever in their unhappiness as

Laura "blows the candles out," the darkness being literal but also symbolic of
their extinguished hopes.

Numerous devices, such as repeated references to the absent father, to Amanda's
youth, to Laura's Victrola and of course
to Laura's glass menagerie help to tie the
scenes together into a unified play. But
beneath these threads of imagery, and re-

Useful, thoughtful
summary of thesis.

curring motifs, is a fundamental pattern
which involves the movement from nagging
(Scenes I and II) to open hostilities
(Scene III) to temporary reconciliation
(Scene IV) to false hopes (Scenes V and
VI) to an impossible heightening of false
hopes and then, in a swift descent, to an
inevitable collapse (Scene VII). Tennessee
Williams has constructed his play carefully. G. B. Tennyson says that a "playwright must 'build' his speeches, as the
theatrical expression has it."[1] But a playwright must do more; he must also build
his play out of scenes. Like Ibsen, if
Williams were introduced to an architect
he might say, "Architecture is my business
too."

_____

Documentation.   [1]An Introduction to Drama (New York:
                          Holt, Rinehart and Winston, 1967), p. 13.

The danger in writing about structure, especially if one proceeds
by beginning at the beginning and moving steadily to the end, is

that one will simply tell the plot. This essay on *The Glass Menagerie* manages to say things about the organization of the plot even as it tells the plot. It has a point, hinted at in the pleasantly paradoxical title, developed in the body of the essay, and wrapped up in the last line.

COMPARISON AND CONTRAST

Something should be said about an essay organized around a **comparison** or a **contrast,** say, of the settings in two short stories, of two characters in a novel, or of the symbolism in two poems. (A comparison emphasizes resemblances and a contrast emphasizes differences, but we can use the word "comparison" to cover both kinds of writing.) Probably the student's first thought, after making some jottings, is to discuss one-half of the comparison and then go on to the second half. Instructors and textbooks (though not this one) usually condemn such an organization, arguing that the essay breaks into two parts and that the second part involves a good deal of repetition of categories set up in the first part. Usually they recommend that the student organize his thoughts differently, somewhat along these lines:

1. First similarity
   a. first work (or character, or characteristic)
   b. second work
2. Second similarity
   a. first work
   b. second work
3. First difference
   a. first work
   b. second work
4. Second difference
   a. first work
   b. second work

and so on, for as many additional differences as seem relevant. For example, if one wishes to compare *Huckleberry Finn* with *The Catcher in the Rye,* one may organize the material thus:

1. First similarity: the narrator and his quest
   a. Huck
   b. Holden

2. Second similarity: the corrupt world surrounding the narrator
   a. society in *Huckleberry Finn*
   b. society in *Catcher*
3. First difference: degree to which the narrator fulfills his quest and escapes from society
   a. Huck's plan to "light out" to the frontier
   b. Holden's breakdown

Here is another way of organizing a comparison and contrast:

1. First point: the narrator and his quest
   a. similarities between Huck and Holden
   b. differences between Huck and Holden
2. Second point: the corrupt world
   a. similarities between the worlds in *Huck* and *Catcher*
   b. differences between the worlds in *Huck* and *Catcher*
3. Third point: degree of success
   a. similarities between Huck and Holden
   b. differences between Huck and Holden

But a comparison need not employ either of these structures. There is even the danger that an essay employing either of them may not come into focus until the essayist stands back from the seven-layer cake and announces, in the concluding paragraph, that the odd layers taste better. In one's preparatory thinking, one may want to make comparisons in pairs (good-natured humor: the clown in *Othello,* the clownish gravedigger in *Hamlet;* social satire: the clown in *Othello,* the gravedigger in *Hamlet;* relevance to main theme: . . . ; length of role: . . . ; comments by other characters: . . .), but one must come to some conclusions about what these add up to before writing the final version. This final version should not duplicate the thought processes; rather, it should be organized to make the point clearly and effectively. After reflection, one may believe that although there are superficial similarities between the clown in *Othello* and the clownish gravedigger in *Hamlet,* there are essential differences; then in the finished essay one probably will not wish to obscure the main point by jumping back and forth from play to play, working through a series of similarities and differences. It may be better to discuss the clown in *Othello* and then to point out that, although the gravedigger in *Hamlet* resembles him in A, B, and C, the gravedigger also has other functions (D, E, and F) and is of greater consequence to *Hamlet* than the clown is to *Othello.* Some repetition in the second half of the essay (for example, "The gravedigger's puns come even faster than the clown's. . . .") will serve to bind the two halves into a meaningful whole, making clear the degree of similarity or difference.

The point of the essay presumably is not to list pairs of similarities or differences, but to illuminate a work or works by making thoughtful comparisons. Although in a long essay one cannot postpone until page 30 a discussion of the second half of the comparison, in an essay of, say, fewer than ten pages nothing is wrong with setting forth one-half of the comparison and then, in light of it, the second half. The essay will break into two unrelated parts if the second half makes no use of the first or if it fails to modify the first half, but not if the second half looks back to the first half and calls attention to differences that the new material reveals. One ought to learn how to write an essay with interwoven comparisons, but one ought also to know that there is another, simpler and clearer way to write a comparison.

REMARKS ABOUT MANUSCRIPT FORM

Basic Manuscript Form

Much of what follows is nothing more than common sense.

1. Use 8½ × 11 inch paper of good weight. Keep as lightweight a carbon copy as you wish or make a photocopy, but hand in a sturdy original.
2. If you typewrite, use a reasonably fresh ribbon, double-space, and type on one side of the page only. If you submit a handwritten copy, use lined paper and write on one side of the page only, in ink, on every other line. Most instructors do *not* want papers to be enclosed in any sort of binder. And most instructors want papers to be clipped together in the upper left corner; do not crimp or crease corners and expect them to hold together.
3. Leave an adequate margin — an inch or an inch and a half — at top, bottom, and sides.
4. Number the pages consecutively, using arabic numerals in the upper right-hand corner.
5. Put your name and class or course number in the upper right-hand corner of the first page. It is a good idea to put

your name in the upper right corner of each page so that if a page gets separated it can easily be restored to the proper essay.

6. Create your own title — one that reflects your topic or thesis. For example, a paper on Shirley Jackson's "The Lottery" should *not* be called "The Lottery," but might be called "Suspense in 'The Lottery,' " (On titles, see also page 1186.)

7. Center the title of your essay below the top margin of the first page. Begin the first word of the title with a capital, and capitalize each subsequent word except articles, conjuctions, and prepositions, thus:

```
The Diabolic and Celestial Images

in The Scarlet Letter
```

Notice that you do *not* enclose your title within quotation marks, nor do you underline it — though if it includes the title of a story or poem, *that* is in quotation marks. If it includes the title of a book, *that* is underlined, as in the example just given.

8. Begin the essay an inch or two below the title.

9. Your extensive revisions should have been made in your drafts, but minor last-minute revisions may be made — neatly — on the finished copy. Proofreading may catch some typographical errors, and you may notice some small weaknesses. You can make corrections with the following proofreader's symbols:

Changes in wording may be made by crossing through words and rewriting them:

```
                                    has
The influence of Yeats and Eliot have greatly

diminished.
```

Additions should be made above the line, with a caret below the line at the appropriate place:

```
                                    greatly
The influence of Yeats and Eliot has‸diminished.
```

Transpositions of letters may be made thus:

```
The inlfuence of Yeats and Eliot has greatly
diminished.
```

Deletions are indicated by a horizontal line through the word or words to be deleted. Delete a single letter by drawing a vertical or diagonal line through it, and indicate whether the letters on either side are to be closed up by drawing a connecting arc:

```
The influence of Yeats and and Eliot has greatly
diminished.
```

Separation of words accidentally run together is indicated by a vertical line, *closure* by a curved line connecting the letters to be closed up:

```
The influence of Yeats and Eliot has g reatly
diminished.
```

Paragraphing may be indicated by the symbol ¶ before the word that is to begin the new paragraph:

```
The influence of Yeats and Eliot has greatly dimin-
ished. The influence of William Carlos Williams has
greatly increased.
```

Quotations and Quotation Marks

Excerpts from the literature you are writing about are indispensable. Such quotations not only let the readers know what you are talking about but also present them the material you are responding to, thus letting the readers share your responses.

Here are some mechanical matters:

1. Identify the speaker or writer of the quotation, so that the reader is not left with a sense of uncertainty. Usually this identification precedes the quoted material ("Hamlet says . . .") in accordance with the principle of letting the readers know where they are going, but occasionally it may follow

the quotation, especially if it will provide something of a pleasant surprise. For instance, in a discussion of T. S. Eliot's poetry you might quote a hostile comment on one of the poems and then reveal that Eliot himself was the speaker.

2. The quotation must fit grammatically into your sentence. Suppose you want to use Macbeth's line, "I know I am Thane of Glamis." It would be ungrammatical to write:

```
Near the beginning of the play Macbeth says that he

''know I am Thane of Glamis.''
```

Say instead:

```
Near the beginning of the play Macbeth says that he

knows he is ''Thane of Glamis.''
```

Or, of course, you can say:

```
Near the beginning of the play Macbeth says, ''I

know I am Thane of Glamis.''
```

3. The quotation must be exact. Any material that you add — even one or two words — must be in square brackets, thus:

```
When Pope says that Belinda is "the rival of his

[that is, the sun's] beams," he uses comic

hyperbole.
```

```
Stephen Dedalus sees the ball as a "greasy leather

orb [that] flew like a heavy bird through the grey

light."
```

If you wish to omit material from within a quotation, indicate the ellipsis by three spaced periods. If your sentence ends in an omission, add a closed-up period and then three spaced periods to indicate the omission. The following example is based on a quotation from the sentences immediately above this one:

```
The instructions say that "if you . . . omit mate-
rial from within a quotation, [you must] indicate
the ellipsis. . . . If your sentence ends in an
omission, add a closed-up period and then three
spaced periods. . . ."
```

Notice that although material preceded "If you," periods are not needed to indicate the omission because "If you" began a sentence in the original. Customarily, initial and terminal omissions are indicated only when they are part of the sentence you are quoting. Even such omissions need not be indicated when the quoted material is obviously incomplete — when, for instance, it is a word of phrase. (See the first example in this section, which quotes Pope's phrase "the rival of his beams.") Notice, too, that although quotations must be given word for word, the initial capitalization can be adapted, as here where "If" is reduced to "if."

When a line or more of verse is omitted from a passage that is set off, the three spaced periods are printed on a separate line:

```
Two roads diverged in a yellow wood,

        .   .   .

And both that morning equally lay

In leaves no step had trodden black.
```

4. Distinguish between short and long quotations, and treat each appropriately. *Short quotations* (usually defined as fewer than three lines of poetry or five lines of prose) are enclosed within quotation marks and run into the text (rather than set off, without quotation marks). For example:

```
Leroi Jones's poem ends with a glimpse of the
speaker's daughter peeking into her "clasped
hands," either playfully or madly.
```

```
Pope's Essay on Criticism begins informally with a
contraction, but the couplets nevertheless have an
```

```
authoritative ring: " 'Tis hard to say, if greater
want of skill/Appear in writing or in judging ill."
```

Notice in the first passage that although only two words are being quoted, quotation marks are used, indicating that these are LeRoi Jones's words, not the essayist's. Notice also that in the second example a slash (diagonal line, virgule) is used to indicate the end of a line of verse other than the last line quoted.

The slash is, of course, not used in a *long quotation* when the poetry is set off, indented, and printed as verse, thus:

```
Pope's Essay on Criticism begins informally with a

contraction, but the couplets nevertheless have an

authoritative ring:

     'Tis hard to say, if greater want of skill

     Appear in writing or in judging ill;

     But of the two less dangerous is the offense

     To tire our patience than mislead our sense.
```

To set off a long quotation (three or more lines of poetry, five or more lines of prose), triple-space before and after the quotation and single-space the quotation. Poetry should be centred; prose quotations should not be indented. Some style manuals, however, do call for indenting prose quotations (ten spaces on both right and left margins) and for double-spacing; whichever procedure you adopt, be consistent. Be sparing in your use of long quotations. Use quotations as evidence, not as padding. Do not bore the reader with material that can be effectively reduced by cutting. If you cut, indicate ellipses as explained above under 3.

5. Commas and periods go inside the quotations marks. (Exception: If the quotation is immediately followed by material in parentheses or in square brackets, close the quotation, then give the parenthetic or bracketed material, and then — after the closing parenthesis or bracket — put the comma or period.) Marks of punctuation other than periods and commas (semicolons, colons, and dashes) go outside. Question marks and exclamation points go inside if they are part of the quotation, outside if they are your own:

```
Amanda ironically says to her daughter, "How old
are you, Laura?" Is it possible to fail to hear
Laura's weariness in her reply, "Mother, you know
my age"?
```

6. Use *single* quotation marks for material contained within a quotation that itself is within quotation marks, thus:

```
T. S. Eliot says, "Mr. Richards observes that 'po-
etry is capable of saving us.'"
```

Quotation Marks or Underlining?

Use quotation marks around titles of short works — that is, for titles of chapters in books and for stories, essays, and poems that might not be published by themselves. Underline (to indicate italics) titles of books, periodicals, collections of essays, plays, and long poems such as *The Rime of the Ancient Mariner* and *Paradise Lost*.

A Note on Footnotes

You may wish to use a footnote, telling the reader of your paper that the literary work you are discussing is found in this book on such-and-such a page. Let us assume that you have already mentioned the author and the title of the story, poem, or play, and have just quoted a passage. After the period at the end of the sentence that includes the quotation, or at the end of the quotation if you are offering it as an independent sentence, type or write the number 1, elevating it slightly above the line. Do not put a period after the digit. Near the bottom of the paper, indent five spaces and type or write the number 1, elevated and without a period. Then write your footnote in this form (giving the appropriate page number):

```
1 Reprinted in Sylvan Barnet, Morton Berman, and
  William Burto, An Introduction to Literature, 9th
  ed. (Boston: Scott, Foresman/Little, Brown,
  1989), p. 236.
```

Notice that the abbreviation for "page" is *p.*, not *pg.;* the abbreviation for "pages" is *pp.*, thus: pp. 236–237.

If you have not mentioned the author and title of the work quoted, you must give that information in the note, thus:

[1] William Faulkner, "The Bear," reprinted in [and so on].

In short, you need not give information in the note that is already given in the main body of the essay.

In order to eliminate writing many footnotes, each one merely citing the page of a quotation, you can explain in the first footnote, after the bibliographical information, that further references will be given in the main body of the essay:

[1] Reprinted in Sylvan Barnet, Morton Berman, and William Burto, An Introduction to Literature, 9th ed. (Boston: Scott, Foresman/Little, Brown, 1989), p. 236. All further references to this work will be cited parenthetically, within the text of the essay.

Thus, when you quote the next passage from the story, you do not need another footnote; you need only insert parentheses enclosing the page number immediately after closing the quotation. Here is an example:

At this point Faulkner tells us that the boy "could find the crooked print now almost whenever he liked" (p. 76).

Notice that the closing quotation mark *precedes* the parenthesis and that the period *follows* the parenthesis.

If you are writing about a poem, it will probably be useful in the first footnote to cite the page, but subsequent references probably ought to be not to page numbers but to line numbers, again indicated in parentheses in the main body of your essay. If your quotation from the poem is brief and is worked into your sentence, give this reference immediately after the quotation, thus:

The Duke calls attention to "Neptune . . . / Taming

```
a sea-horse" (lines 54-55) as he descends the
stairs.
```

But if the quotation is long enough to set off, put a period at the end of the quotation (assuming that it is gramatically appropriate to put a period there) and give the citation for lines in parentheses immediately below the quotation, at the right.

```
                                         I repeat,
The Count your master's known munificence
Is ample warrant that no just pretense
Of mine for dowry will be disallowed;
Though his fair daughter's self, as I avowed
At starting, is my object.
                              (lines 48-53)
```

Write "line" or "lines" only in your first citation; in later citations, omit it, and simply give the numbers.

If you are writing about a play, especially one whose lines as well as acts and scenes are numbered, it may be better to refer to act, scene, and line than to page. You can give the act, scene, and line in arabic numerals (5.2.340), or you can give the act in capital roman numerals, the scene in small roman numerals, and the line in arabic numerals; thus

```
Othello says that he is "one that loved not wisely,
but too well" (V.ii.340).
```

A Note on Internal Citations

If you use secondary sources, your instructor may want you to cite your source — usually an authority you are quoting or summarizing — parenthetically, within the body of your paper, rather than in a footnote. Here is an example, citing page 29 of a book.

```
In Comic Women, Tragic Men, Linda Bamber says that
in Shakespeare's plays, "The natural order, the
status quo, is for men to rule women" (29).
```

Or:

> In Shakespeare's plays "the natural order," Bamber
> says, "is for men to rule women" (29), but she goes
> on to modify this statement.

At the end of your paper, on a separate page, give a list headed "Works Cited," listing all of your sources, alphabetically by author, last name first, then the title (underlined, to indicate italics), then, in parentheses, the place of publication, the publisher, and the date. After closing the parenthesis, type a period. For details on how to cite journals, books published in more than one volume, translations, and dozens of other troublesome works, see Joseph Gibaldi and Walter S. Achtert, *MLA Handbook for Writers of Research Papers,* 2d ed. (New York: MLA, 1984). (By the way, MLA stands for Modern Language Association.)

REVIEW: HOW TO WRITE
AN EFFECTIVE ESSAY

Everyone must work out his or her own procedures and rituals (John C. Calhoun liked to plough his farm before writing), but the following suggestions may provide some help.

1. Read the work carefully.
2. Choose a worthwhile and compassable subject, something that interests you and is not so big that your handling of it must be superficial. As you work, shape and narrow your topic — for example, from "The Character of Hester Prynne" to "The Effects of Alienation on Hester Prynne."
3. Reread the work, jotting down notes of all relevant matters. As you read, reflect on your reading and record your reflections. If you have a feeling or an idea, jot it down; don't assume that you will remember it when you get around to writing your essay. The margins of the book are a good place for initial jottings, but many people find that in the long run it is easiest to transfer these notes to 3 × 5 cards, writing on one side only.
4. Sort out your cards into some kind of reasonable divisions, and reject cards irrelevant to your topic. As you work you

may discover a better way to group your notes. If so, start reorganizing. If you are writing an explication, the order probably is essentially the order of the lines or of the episodes, but if you are writing an analysis you may wish to organize your essay from the lesser material to the greater (to avoid anticlimax) or from the simple to the complex (to insure intelligibility). If, for example, you are discussing the roles of three characters in a story, it may be best to build up to the one of the three that you think the most important. If you are comparing two characters it may be best to move from the most obvious contrasts to the least obvious. When you have arranged your notes into a meaningful sequence of packets, you have approximately divided your material into paragraphs.

5. Get it down on paper. Most essayists find it useful to jot down some sort of outline, indicating the main idea of each paragraph and, under each main idea, supporting details that give it substance. An outline — not necessarily anything highly formal with capital and lowercase letters and roman and arabic numerals but merely key phrases in some sort of order — will help you to overcome the paralysis called "writer's block" that commonly afflicts professionals as well as students. A page of paper with ideas in some sort of sequence, however rough, ought to encourage you to realize that you do have something to say. And so, despite the temptation to sharpen another pencil or put a new ribbon into the typewriter, the best thing to do at this point is to sit down and start writing.

   If you don't feel that you can work from note cards and a rough outline, try another method: get something down on paper, writing freely, sloppily, automatically, or whatever, but allowing your ideas about what the work means to you and how it conveys its meaning — rough as your ideas may be — to begin to take visible form. If you are like most people, you can't do much precise thinking until you have committed to paper at least a rough sketch of your initial ideas. Later you can push and polish your ideas into shape, perhaps even deleting all of them and starting over, but it's a lot easier to improve your ideas once you see them in front of you than it is to do the job in your head. On paper one word leads to another; in your head one word often blocks another.

   Just keep going; you may realize, as you near the end of a sentence, that you no longer believe it. O.K., be glad that your first idea led you to a better one, and pick up your better one and keep going with it. What you are doing is, in a sense, by trial and error pushing your way not only toward clear expression but also toward sharper ideas and richer responses.

6. If there is time, reread the work, looking for additional material that strengthens or weakens your main point; take account of it in your outline or draft.

7. By now your thesis should be clear to you, and you ought to be able to give your essay an informative title — *not* simply the title of the story, poem, or play, but something that lets your reader know where you will be going.

With a thesis and title clearly in mind, improve your draft, checking your notes for fuller details, such as supporting quotations. If, as you work, you find that some of the points in your earlier jottings are no longer relevant, eliminate them, but make sure that the argument flows from one point to the next. As you write, your ideas will doubtless become clearer; some may prove to be poor ideas. (We rarely know exactly what our ideas are until we have them set down on paper. As the little girl said, replying to the suggestion that she should think before she spoke, "How do I know what I think until I say it?") Not until you have written a draft do you really have a strong sense of how good your essay may be.

8. After a suitable interval, preferably a few days, read the draft with a view toward revising it, not with a view toward congratulating yourself. A revision, after all, is a re-vision, a second (and presumably sharper) view. When you revise, you will be in the company of Picasso, who said that in painting he advanced by a series of destructions. A revision — say, the substitution of a precise word for an imprecise one — is not a matter of prettifying but of thinking. As you read, correct things that disturb you (for example, awkward repetitions that bore, inflated utterances that grate), add supporting detail where the argument is undeveloped (a paragraph of only one or two sentences is usually an undeveloped paragraph), and ruthlessly delete irrelevancies however well written they may be. But remember that a deletion probably requires some adjustment in the preceding and subsequent material.

Make sure that the argument, aided by transitions, runs smoothly. The details should be relevant, the organization reasonable, the argument clear. Check all quotations for accuracy. Quotations are evidence, usually intended to support your assertions, and it is not nice to alter the evidence, even unintentionally. If there is time (there almost never is), put the revision aside, reread it in a day or two, and revise it again, especially with a view toward deleting wordiness and, on the other hand, supporting generalizations with evidence.

9. Type or write a clean copy, following the principles concerning margins, pagination, footnotes, and so on set forth on pages 1199–1208. If you have borrowed any ideas, be sure to give credit, usually in footnotes, to your sources. Remember that plagiarism is not limited to the unacknowledged borrowing of words; a borrowed idea, even when put into your own words, requires acknowledgment.

10. Proofread and make corrections as explained on pages 1200–1201.

Glossary of Literary Terms

The terms briefly defined here are for the most part more fully defined earlier in the text. Hence many of the entries below are followed by page references to the earlier discussions.

Absurd, Theater of the   plays, especially written in the 1950s and 1960s, which call attention to the incoherence of character and of action, the inability of people to communicate, and the apparent purposelessness of existence (1120)

accent   stress given to a syllable (495–496)

act   a major division of a play

action   (1) the happenings in a narrative or drama, usually physical events (B marries C, D kills E), but also mental changes (F moves from innocence to experience); in short, the answer to the question, "What happens?" (2) less commonly, the theme or underlying idea of a work (591–592)

allegory   a work in which concrete elements (for instance, a pilgrim, a road, a splendid city) stand for abstractions (humanity, life, salvation), usually in an unambiguous, one-to-one relationship. The literal items (the pilgrim, and so on) thus convey a meaning, which is usually moral, religious, or political. To take a nonliterary example: The Statue of Liberty holds a torch (enlightenment, showing the rest of the world the way to freedom), and at her feet are broken chains (tyranny overcome). A caution: Not all of the details in an allegorical work are meant to be interpreted. For example, the hollowness of the Statue of Liberty does not stand for the insubstantiality or emptiness of liberty. (63–66)

alliteration   repetition of consonant sounds, especially at the beginnings of words (*f*ree, *f*orm, *ph*antom) (499)

allusion   an indirect reference; thus when Lincon spoke of "a
nation dedicated to the proposition that all men are created equal,"
he was making an allusion to the Declaration of Independence.

ambiguity   multiplicity of meaning, often deliberate, which leaves
the reader uncertain about the intended significance

anagnorisis   a recognition or discovery, especially in tragedy —
for example, when the hero understands the reason for his or her
fall (598)

analysis   an examination which usually proceeds by separating
the object of study into parts (1185–1186)

anapest   a metrical foot consisting of two unaccented syllables
followed by an accented one. Example, showing three anapests:
"As I came / to the edge / of the wood" (496)

anecdote   a short narrative, usually reporting an amusing event
in the life of an important person (102–103)

antagonist   a character or force which opposes (literally, "wrestles")
the main character

apostrophe   address to an absent figure, or to a thing as if it
were present and could listen. Example: "Oh rose, thou art sick!"
(449–450)

archetype   a theme, image, motive, or pattern that occurs so
often in literary works it seems to be universal. Examples: a dark
forest (for mental confusion), the sun (for illumination)

aside   a remark spoken in the presence of others but (by convention)
assumed not to be heard by them (593)

assonance   repetition of similar vowel sounds in stressed syllables.
Example: light/bride (499)

atmosphere   the emotional tone (for instance, joy, or horror) in
a work, most often established by the setting

ballad   a short narrative poem, especially one that is sung or
recited, often in a stanza of four lines, with 8, 6, 8, 6 syllables,
with the second and fourth lines rhyming. A **popular ballad** is
a narrative song that has been transmitted orally by what used to
be called "the folk"; a **literary ballad** is a conscious imitation
(without music) of such a work, often with complex symbolism.
(506–516)

blank (or **gap**)   an ambiguity or uncertainty that readers in their own ways resolve (12)

blank verse   unrhymed iambic pentameter, that is, unrhymed lines of ten syllables, with every second syllable stressed (502)

cacaphony   an unpleasant combination of sounds

caesura   a strong pause within a line of verse (497)

catastrophe   the concluding action, especially in a tragedy

catharsis   Aristotle's term for the purgation or purification of the pity and terror supposedly experienced while witnessing a tragedy

character   (1) a person in a literary work (Romeo); (2) the personality of such a figure (sentimental lover, or whatever). Characters (in the first sense) are sometimes classified as either "flat" (one-dimensional) or "round" (fully realized, complex). Flat characters who appear in many works, such as the drunken butler or the gossipy neighbor, are "stock characters."

characterization   the presentation of a character, whether by direct description, by showing the character in action, or by the presentation of other characters who help to define each other (30, 36–38, 99–100, 640*n*, 658–659)

cliché   an expression that, through overuse, has ceased to be effective. Examples: acid test, sigh of relief, the proud possessor

climax   the culmination of a conflict; a turning point, often the point of greatest tension in a plot (591–592)

comedy   a literary work, especially a play, characterized by humor and by a happy ending (639–642)

comparison and contrast   to compare is, strictly, to note similarities, whereas to contrast is to note differences. But "compare" is now often used for both activities. (1197–1199)

complication   an entanglement in a narrative or dramatic work which causes a conflict (30)

conceit   in poetry, a complicated or extended metaphor

conflict   a struggle between a character and some obstacle, for example, another character, fate, or between internal forces such as divided loyalties (30, 36, 592)

connotation   the associations (suggestions, overtones) of a word or expression. Thus "seventy" and "three score and ten" both mean "one more than sixty-nine," but because "three score and ten" is a biblical expression it has an association of holiness; see *denotation*. (450)

consonance repetition of consonant sounds, especially in stressed syllables. Also called "half rhyme" or "slant rhyme." Example: arouse/doze (499)

consistency building a reader's attempt at various times while reading to combine into a coherent whole the details encountered thus far; a sort of tentative stock-taking

convention a pattern (for instance the fourteen-line poem, or sonnet) or motif (for instance, the bumbling police officer in detective fiction) or other device occurring so often that it is taken for granted. Thus it is a convention that actors in a performance of *Julius Caesar* are understood to be speaking Latin, though in fact they are speaking English. Similarly, the soliloquy (a character alone on the stage speaks his or her thoughts aloud) is a convention, for in real life sane people do not talk aloud to themselves.

couplet a pair of lines of verse, usually rhyming (500–501)

crisis a high point in the conflict, which leads to the turning point (592)

criticism the analysis or evaluation of a literary work

dactyl a metrical foot consisting of a stressed syllable followed by two unstressed syllables. Example: underwear (496)

denotation the dictionary meaning of a word. Thus "soap opera" and "daytime serial" have the same denotation, but the connotations (associations, emotional overtones) of "soap opera" are less favorable. (450)

dénouement the resolution or the outcome (literally, the "un-knotting") of a plot (31, 36, 592)

deus ex machina literally, "a god out of a machine"; any unexpected and artificial way of resolving the plot — for example, by introducing a rich uncle, thought to be dead, who arrives on the scene and pays the debts that otherwise would overwhelm the young hero

dialogue exchange of words between characters; speech

diction the choice of vocabulary and of sentence structure. There is a difference in diction between "One never knows" and "You never can tell." (425–426, 505)

didactic pertaining to teaching; having a moral purpose

dimeter   a line of poetry containing two feet (497)

discovery   see *anagnorisis* (598)

drama   (1) a play; (2) conflict or tension, as in "The story lacks drama" (589–594)

dramatic monologue   a poem spoken entirely by one character, but addressed to one or more other characters, whose presence is strongly felt (423)

elegy   a lyric poem, usually a meditation on a death

elision   omission (usually of a vowel or unstressed syllable), as in "o'er" (for "over") and in "Th' inevitable hour"

end rhyme   identical sounds at the ends of lines of poetry (499)

end-stopped line   a line of poetry that ends with a pause because the grammatical structure and the sense reach (at least to some degree) completion (497)

English (or **Shakespearean**) **sonnet**   a poem of fourteen lines (three quatrains and a couplet), rhyming *ababcdcdefefgg* (501)

enjambment   a line of poetry in which the grammatical and logical sense run on, without pause, into the next line or lines (497)

epic   a long narrative, especially in verse, which usually records heroic material in an elevated style

epigram   a brief, witty poem or saying

epigraph   an inscription at the beginning of a work. Eliot's "The Love Song of J. Alfred Prufrock" (p. 551) begins with an epigraph from Dante

epiphany   a "showing forth," as when an action reveals a character with particular clarity

episode   an incident or scene which has unity in itself but is also a part of a larger action

epistle   a letter, in prose or verse

essay   a work, usually in prose and usually fairly short, that purports to be true and that treats its subject tentatively. In most literary essays the reader's interest is as much in the speaker's personality as in any argument that is offered.

euphony   literally, "good sound," a pleasant combination of sounds

explication   a line-by-line unfolding of the meaning of a text (1180–1185)

exposition   a setting-forth of information. In fiction and drama, introductory material introducing characters and the situation; in an essay, the presentation of information, as opposed to the telling of a story or the setting forth of an argument (36, 593)

eye rhyme   words that look as though they rhyme, but do not rhyme when pronounced. Example: come/home (498)

fable   a short story (often involving speaking animals) with an easily grasped moral (29)

feminine rhyme   a rhyme of two or more syllables, with the stress falling on a syllable other than the last. Examples: fatter/batter; tenderly/slenderly (499)

fiction   an imaginative work, usually a prose narrative (novel, short story), that reports incidents that did not in fact occur. The word can include all works that invent a world, such as a lyric poem or a play.

figurative language   words intended to be understood in a way that is other than literal. Thus "lemon" used literally refers to a citrus fruit, but "lemon" used figuratively refers to a defective machine, especially a defective automobile. Other examples: "He's a beast," "She's a witch," "A sea of troubles." Literally such expressions are nonsense, but writers use them to express meanings inexpressible in literal speech. Among the commonest kinds of figures of speech are *apostrophe, metaphor,* and *simile* (see the discussions of these words in this glossary). (441–471)

flashback   an interruption in a narrative, which presents an earlier episode

flat character   a one-dimensional character (for instance, the figure who is only and always the jealous husband, or the flirtatious wife) as opposed to a round or many-sided character (37–38)

foil   a character who makes a contrast with another, especially a minor character who helps to set off a major character

foot   a metrical unit, consisting of two or three syllables, with a specified arrangement of the stressed syllable or syllables. Thus the iambic foot consists of an unstressed syllable followed by a stressed syllable. (495–497)

foreshadowing   suggestions of what is to come (39)

free verse   poetry in lines of irregular length, which is usually unrhymed (502–503)

genre   kind or type, roughly analogous to the biological term "species." The four chief literary genres are nonfiction, fiction, poetry, and drama, but these can be subdivided into further genres. Thus "fiction" obviously can be divided into the short story and the novel, and "drama" obviously can be divided into tragedy and comedy. But these can be still further divided — for instance, tragedy into heroic tragedy and bourgeois tragedy, comedy into romantic comedy and satirical comedy.

gesture   physical movement, especially in a play (591, 659)

half rhyme   repetition in accented syllables of the final consonant sound but without identity in the preceding vowel sound; words of similar but not identical sound. Also called near rhyme, slant rhyme, approximate rhyme, and off-rhyme. Examples: light/bet; affirm/perform (498)

hamartia   a flaw in the tragic hero, or an error made by the tragic hero (596)

heptameter   a metrical line of seven feet (497)

hero, heroine   the main character (not necessarily heroic or even admirable) in a work; cf. *protagonist*

heroic couplet   an end-stopped pair of rhyming lines of iambic pentameter (500–501)

hexameter   a metrical line of six feet (497)

hubris, hybris   a Greek word, usually translated as "overweening pride," "arrogance," "excessive ambition," and often said to be characteristic of tragic figures (596)

hyperbole   figurative language using overstatement, as in "He died a thousand deaths" (473)

iamb, iambic   a poetic foot consisting of an unaccented syllable followed by an accented one. Example: alone (496)

image, imagery   imagery is established by language that appeals to the senses, especially sight ("deep blue sea") but also other senses ("tinkling bells," "perfumes of Arabia") (458–471)

in medias res   Latin for "in the middle of things," used to describe the narrative device of beginning in the middle of an unexplained action

innocent eye   a naive and therefore unreliable narrator who does not fully understand what he or she reports (51)

internal rhyme   rhyme within a line (499)

interpretation   the exposition of meaning, chiefly by means of analysis

irony   a contrast of some sort. For instance, in **verbal irony** or **Socratic irony** the contrast is between what is saìd and what is meant ("You're a great guy," meant bitterly). In **dramatic irony** or **Sophoclean irony** the contrast is betwen what is intended and what is accomplished (Macbeth usurps the throne, thinking he will then be happy, but the action leads him to misery), or between what the audience knows (a murderer waits in the bedroom) and what a character says (the victim enters the bedroom, innocently saying "I think I'll have a long sleep") (472–485, 597–598)

Italian (or **Petrarchan**) **sonnet**   a poem of fourteen lines, consisting of an octave (rhyming *abbaabba*) and a sestet (usually *cdecde* or *cdccdc*) (501)

litotes   a form of understatement in which an affirmation is made by means of a negation; thus "He was not underweight," meaning "He was grossly overweight"

lyric poem   a short poem, often songlike, with the emphasis not on narrative but on the speaker's emotion or reverie (409–411)

masculine rhyme   rhyme of one-syllable words (lies/cries) or, if more than one syllable, words ending with accented syllables (behold/foretold) (498–499)

melodrama   a narrative, usually in dramatic form, involving threatening situations but ending happily. The characters are usually stock figures (virtuous heroine, villainous landlord).

metaphor   a kind of figurative language equating one thing with another: "This novel is garbage" (a book is equated with discarded and probably inedible food), "a piercing cry" (a cry is equated with a spear or other sharp instrument) (445–448)

meter   a pattern of stressed and unstressed syllables (495–497)

metonymy   a kind of figurative language in which a word or phrase stands not for itself but for something closely related to it: "saber-rattling" means "militaristic talk or action" (448)

monologue   a relatively long, uninterrupted speech by a character

monometer a metrical line consisting of only one foot (497)

mood the atmosphere, usually created by descriptions of the settings and characters

motif a recurrent theme within a work, or a theme common to many works

motivation grounds for a character's action (38)

myth (1) a traditional story reflecting primitive beliefs, especially explaining the mysteries of the natural world (why it rains, or the origin of mountains); (2) a body of belief, not necessarily false, especially as set forth by a writer. Thus one can speak of Yeats or Hardy as myth-makers, referring to the visions of reality that they set forth in their works.

narrative, narrator a narrative is a story (an anecdote, a novel); a narrator is one who tells a story (not the author, but the invented speaker of the story). On kinds of narrators, see *point of view*. (29–31, 49, 54, 102–105)

novel a long work of prose fiction, especially one that is relatively realistic (103, 400–405)

novella a work of prose fiction longer than a short story but shorter than a novel, say about forty to eighty pages

octave, octet an eight-line stanza, or the first eight lines of a sonnet, especially of an Italian sonnet (501)

octosyllabic couplet a pair of rhyming lines, each line with four iambic feet (500)

ode a lyric exalting someone (for instance, a hero) or something (for instance, a season) (410)

omniscient narrator a speaker who knows the thoughts of all of the characters in the narrative (52)

onomatopoeia words (or the use of words) that sound like what they mean. Examples: buzz, whirr (500)

oxymoron a compact paradox, as in "a mute cry," "a pleasing pain," "proud humility"

parable a short narrative that is at least in part allegorical, and which illustrates a moral or spiritual lesson (13–14, 29, 102)

paradox an apparent contradiction, as in Christ's words: "Whosoever will save his life shall lose it; but whosoever will lose his life for my sake, the same shall save it" (472–485)

paraphrase a restatement, which sets forth an idea in diction other than that of the original

parody a humorous imitation of a literary work, especially of its style

pathos pity, sadness

pentameter a line of verse containing five feet (497)

peripeteia a reversal in the action (598)

persona literally, a mask; the "I" or speaker of a work, sometimes identified with the author but usually better regarded as the voice or mouthpiece created by the author (421–422)

personification a kind of figurative language in which an inanimate object, animal, or other nonhuman is given human traits. Examples: "the creeping tide" (the tide is imagined as having feet), "the cruel sea" (the sea is imagined as having moral qualities) (448–449)

plot the episodes in a narrative or dramatic work — that is, what happens — or the particular arrangement (sequence) of these episodes (36, 99, 591–593, 658)

poem an imaginative work in meter or in free verse, usually employing figurative language

point of view the perspective from which a story is told — for example by a major character, or a minor character, or a fly on the wall; see also *narrative, narrator* (49–54)

prosody the principles of versification (495)

protagonist the chief actor in any literary work. The term is usually preferable to "hero" and "heroine" because it can include characters — for example, villainous or weak ones — who are not aptly called heroes or heroines. (592)

quatrain a stanza of four lines (501)

realism presentation of plausible characters (usually middle-class) in plausible (usually everyday) circumstances, as opposed, for example, to heroic characters engaged in improbable adventures. Realism in literature seeks to give the illusion of reality.

recognition see *anagnorisis* (598)

refrain a repeated phrase, line, or group of lines in a poem, especially in a ballad (501)

repertoire the body of assumptions and values held by a reader or by a writer (11–12)

resolution the dénouement or untying of the complication of the plot (31, 36, 592)

reversal a change in fortune, often an ironic twist (598)

rhetorical question a question to which no answer is expected, or to which only one answer is plausible. Example: Do you think I am unaware of your goings-on?"

rhyme similarity or identity of accented sounds in corresponding positions, as, for example, at the ends of lines: love/dove; tender/slender (498–499)

rhythm in poetry, a pattern of stressed and unstressed sounds; in prose, some sort of recurrence (for example, of a motif) at approximately identical intervals (486–493, 498)

rising action in a story or play, the events that lead up to the climax

rising meter a foot (for example, iambic or anapestic) ending with a stressed syllable (496)

romance narrative fiction, usually characterized by improbable adventures and love (400–401, 403–404)

round character a many-sided character, one who does not always act predictably, as opposed to a "flat" or one-dimensional, unchanging character (37–38)

run-on line a line of verse whose syntax and meaning require the reader to go on, without a pause, to the next line; an enjambed line (497)

sarcasm crudely mocking or contemptuous language; heavy verbal irony (473)

satire literature that entertainingly attacks folly or vice; amusingly abusive writing (435–436, 641–642)

scansion description of rhythm in poetry; metrical analysis (497)

scene (1) a unit of a play, in which the setting is unchanged and the time continuous; (2) the setting (locale, and time of the action); (3) in fiction, a dramatic passage, as opposed to a passage of description or of summary

sentimentality excessive emotion, especially excessive pity, treated as appropriate rather than as disproportionate

sestet a six-line stanza, or the last six lines of an Italian sonnet (501)

sestina   a poem with six stanzas of six lines each, and a concluding stanza of three lines. The last word of each line in the first stanza appears as the last word of a line in each of the next five stanzas, but in a different order. In the final (three-line) stanza, each line ends with one of these six words, and each line includes in the middle of the line one of the other three words.

setting   the time and place of a story, play, or poem (for instance, a Texas town in winter, about 1900) (30, 36, 66–67, 100, 659)

short story   a fictional narrative, usually in prose, rarely longer than thirty pages and often much briefer (103–104, 404)

simile   a kind of figurative language explicitly making a comparison, for example by using *as, like,* or a verb such as *seems* (444–445)

soliloquy   a speech in a play, in which a character, alone on the stage, speaks his or her thoughts aloud (593)

sonnet   a lyric poem of fourteen lines; see *English sonnet, Italian sonnet* (501, 1217, 1220)

speaker   see *persona* (421–434, 504)

spondee   a metrical foot consisting of two stressed syllables (496)

stage direction   a playwright's indication to the actors or readers — for example, offering information about how an actor is to speak a line

stanza   a group of lines forming a unit that is repeated in a poem (500)

stereotype   a simplifed conception, especially an oversimplification — for example, a stock character such as the heartless landlord, the kindly old teacher, the prostitute with a heart of gold. Such a character usually has only one personality trait, and this is boldly exaggerated.

stock character   see *character* (1215)

stream of consciousness   the presentation of a character's unrestricted flow of thought, often with free associations, and often without punctuation (52–53)

stress   relative emphasis on one syllable as compared to another (488–489, 495–496)

structure   the organization of a work, the relationship between the chief parts, the large-scale pattern — for instance, a rising action or complication followed by a crisis and then a resolution

style the manner of expression, evident not only in the choice of certain words (for instance, colloquial language) but in the choice of certain kinds of sentence structure, characters, settings, and themes (83–85, 100–101)

subplot a sequence of events often paralleling or in some way resembling the main story

summary a synopsis or condensation

symbol a person, object, action, or situation that, charged with meaning, suggests another thing (for example, a dark forest may suggest confusion, or perhaps evil), though usually with less specificity and more ambiguity than an allegory. A symbol usually differs from a metaphor in that a symbol is expanded, or repeated, and works by accumulating associations. (63–66, 458–471)

synecdoche a kind of figurative language in which the whole stands for a part ("the law," for a police officer), or a part ("all hands on deck," for all persons) stands for the whole (448)

tale a short narrative, usually less realistic and more romantic than a short story; a yarn (104, 400–401)

tercet a unit of three lines of verse (501)

tetrameter a verse line of four feet (497)

theme what the work is about; an underlying idea of a work; a conception of human experience suggested by the concrete details. Thus the theme of *Macbeth* is often said to be that "Vaulting ambition o'erleaps itself." (36, 39, 101)

thesis the point or argument that a writer announces and develops. A thesis differs from a *topic* by making an assertion. "The fall of Oedipus" is a topic, but "Oedipus falls because he is impetuous" is a thesis, as is "Oedipus is impetuous, but his impetuosity has nothing to do with his fall." (1186–1187)

third-person narrator the teller of a story who does not participate in the happenings (52–53)

tone the prevailing attitude (for instance, ironic, genial, objective) as perceived by the reader. Notice that a reader may feel the tone of the persona of the work is genial while the tone of the author of the same work is ironic. (85, 421–434)

topic a subject, such as "Hamlet's relation to Horatio." A topic becomes a *thesis* when a predicate is added to this subject, thus: "Hamlet's relation to Horatio helps to define Hamlet." (1186–1187)

tragedy   a serious play showing the protagonist moving from good fortune to bad, and ending in death or a deathlike state (595–600)

tragic flaw   a supposed weakness (for example, arrogance) in the tragic protagonist (596, 1219)

tragicomedy   a mixture of tragedy and comedy, usually a play with serious happenings which expose the characters to the threat of death, but which ends happily

transition   a connection between one passage and the next

trimeter   a verse line with three feet (497)

triplet   a group of three lines of verse, usually rhyming (501)

trochee   a metrical foot consisting of a stressed syllable followed by an unstressed syllable. Example: garden (496)

understatement   a figure of speech in which the speaker says less than what he or she means; an ironic minimizing, as in "You've done fairly well for yourself" said to the winner of a multimillion-dollar lottery (472–473)

unity   harmony and coherence of parts, absence of irrelevance

verse   (1) a line of poetry; (2) a stanza of a poem

vers libre   free verse, unrhymed poetry (502)

villanelle   a poem with five stanzas of three lines rhyming *aba*, and a concluding stanza of four lines, rhyming *abaa*. The first and third lines of the first stanza rhyme. The entire first line is repeated as the third line of the second and fourth stanzas; the entire third line is repeated as the third line of the third and fifth stanzas. These two lines form the final two lines of the last (four-line) stanza. (492–493)

voice   see *persona, style,* and *tone* (421–434)

(Continued from p. iv)

Anton Chekhov. "Misery." Reprinted with permission of Macmillan Publishing Company, the estate of the translator, and Chatto & Windus from *The Schoolmistress and Other Stories* by Anton Chekhov, translated from the Russian by Constance Garnett. Copyright 1921 by Macmillan Publishing Company, renewed 1949 by David Garnett. "The Lady with the Pet Dog" from *The Portable Chekhov,* edited and translated by Avrahm Yarmolinsky. Copyright 1947, renewed © 1968 by The Viking Press, Inc. Copyright renewed © 1975 by Avrahm Yarmolinsky. All rights reserved. Reprinted by permission of Viking Penguin Inc. *The Brute,* translated by Eric Bentley. Copyright © 1958, 1986, by Eric Bentley. Reprinted by permission of Applause Theatre Book Publishers, 211 West 71st Street, New York, NY 10023.

Amy Clampitt. "The Cormorant in His Element" from *The Kingfisher: Poems by Amy Clampitt.* Copyright © 1983 by Amy Clampitt. Reprinted by permission of Alfred A. Knopf, Inc.

Lucille Clifton. "In the Inner City" from *Good Times* by Lucille Clifton. Copyright © 1969 by Lucille Clifton. Reprinted by permission of Random House, Inc.

E. E. Cummings. "next to of course god america i" is reprinted from *Is 5* poems by E. E. Cummings, by permission of Liveright Publishing Corporation. Copyright © 1985 by E. E. Cummings Trust. Copyright 1926 by Horace Liveright. Copyright 1954 by E. E. Cummings. Copyright © 1985 by George James Firmage. "in Just-" is reprinted from *Tulips & Chimneys* by E. E. Cummings, edited by George James Firmage, by permission of Liveright Publishing Corporation. Copyright 1923, 1925, and renewed 1951, 1953 by E. E. Cummings. Copyright © 1973, 1976 by the Trustees for the E. E. Cummings Trust. Copyright © 1973, 1976 by George James Firmage.

Walter de la Mare. "The Listeners" from *The Complete Poems.* Copyright © 1969 by The Literary Trustees of Walter de la Mare. Reprinted by permission of The Literary Trustees of Walter de la Mare and The Society of Authors as their representative.

Emily Dickinson. "Wild nights, wild nights," "Because I could not stop for Death," "A narrow Fellow in the Grass," "I heard a Fly buzz — when I died," and "The Soul selects her own Society." Reprinted by permission of the publishers and the Trustees of Amherst College from *The Poems of Emily Dickinson,* edited by Thomas H. Johnson, Cambridge, Mass.: The Belknap Press of Harvard University Press, Copyright 1951, © 1955, 1979, 1983 by The President and Fellows of Harvard College. "Apparently with No Surprise" from *The Complete Poems of Emily Dickinson,* edited by Thomas H. Johnson (Boston: Little, Brown and Company, 1960).

Rita Dove. "Geometry" from *The Yellow House on the Corner.* Copyright © 1980 by Rita Dove. Reprinted by permission of Carnegie-Mellon University Press. "The Fish in the Stone" from *Museum.* Copyright © 1963 by Rita Dove. Reprinted by permission of Carnegie-Mellon University Press.

T. S. Eliot. "The Love Song of J. Alfred Prufrock" from *Collected Poems 1909–1962* by T. S. Eliot, copyright 1936 by Harcourt Brace Jovanovich, Inc., copyright © 1963, 1964 by T. S. Eliot. Reprinted by permission of the publishers, Harcourt Brace Jovanovich, Inc. and Faber and Faber Ltd.

Louise Erdrich. "Fleur," *Esquire,* August 1986. Copyright © 1986 by Louise Erdrich. Reprinted by permission.

William Faulkner. "The Bear." Copyright 1942 and renewed 1970 by Estelle Faulkner and Jill Faulkner Summers. An expanded version of this story appears in *Go Down, Moses* by William Faulkner. "A Rose for Emily." Copyright

1930 and renewed 1958 by William Faulkner. Reprinted from *Collected Stories of William Faulkner*. Reprinted by permission of Random House, Inc. William Faulkner letter from *The New York Times*, December 26, 1954. Copyright 1954 by The New York Times Company. Reprinted by permission.

Lawrence Ferlinghetti. "Constantly Risking Absurdity" from Lawrence Ferlinghetti, *A Coney Island of the Mind*. Copyright © 1958 by Lawrence Ferlinghetti. Reprinted by permission of New Directions Publishing Corporation.

Robert Francis. "The Pitcher." Copyright © 1960 by Robert Francis. Reprinted from *The Orb Weaver* by permission of Wesleyan University Press.

Robert Frost. "Stopping by Woods on a Snowy Evening," "Mending Wall," "The Pasture," "Design," "The Road Not Taken," and "The Oven Bird" from *The Poetry of Robert Frost* edited by Edward Connery Lathem. Copyright © 1969 by Holt, Rinehart and Winston, Inc. Copyright © 1962 by Robert Frost. Copyright © 1975 by Lesley Frost Ballantine. Reprinted by permission of Henry Holt and Company, Inc.

Allen Ginsberg. "A Supermarket in California." From *Collected Poems, 1947–1980* by Allen Ginsberg. Copyright © 1955 by Allen Ginsberg. Reprinted by permission of Harper & Row, Publishers, Inc.

Nikki Giovanni. "MasterCharge Blues" from *Re:Creation* by Nikki Giovanni. Copyright © 1970 by Nikki Giovanni. Reprinted by permission of the author.

Donald Hall. "The Fifty-Dollar Bill." Excerpted from *The Ideal Bakery*. Copyright © 1987 by Donald Hall. Published by North Point Press and reprinted by permission.

Robert Hayden. "Those Winter Sundays" is reprinted from *Angle of Ascent: New and Selected Poems,* by Robert Hayden, by permission of Liveright Publishing Corporation. Copyright © 1975, 1972, 1970, 1966 by Robert Hayden.

Seamus Heaney. "Digging" from *Poems 1965–1975* by Seamus Heaney. Copyright © 1966, 1980 by Seamus Heaney. Reprinted by permission of Farrar, Straus and Giroux, Inc., and Faber and Faber Ltd. "The Haw Lantern" from *The Haw Lantern* by Seamus Heaney. Copyright © 1987 by Seamus Heaney. Reprinted by permission of Farrar, Straus and Giroux, Inc., and Faber and Faber Ltd.

Anthony Hecht. "The Dover Bitch" from *The Hard Hours*. Copyright © 1967 Anthony E. Hecht. Reprinted with permission of Atheneum Publishers, an imprint of Macmillan Publishing Company.

Ernest Hemingway. "Hills Like White Elephants" from *The Short Stories of Ernest Hemingway*. Copyright 1927 Charles Scribner's Sons; copyright renewed 1955 Ernest Hemingway. Reprinted with the permission of Charles Scribner's Sons, an imprint of Macmillan Publishing Company.

Gerard Manley Hopkins. "Spring and Fall," "God's Grandeur" and "The Windover" from *The Poems of Gerard Manley Hopkins,* published by Oxford University Press.

A. E. Housman. "To an Athlete Dying Young," "Eight O'Clock," and "Is my team plowing?" from *The Collected Poems of A. E. Housman*. Copyright © 1965 by Holt, Rinehart and Winston, Inc. Reprinted by permission of Henry Holt and Company, Inc.

Langston Hughes. "Evenin' Air Blues" from *Shakespeare in Harlem*. Copyright 1942 by Alfred A. Knopf, Inc.; copyright renewed. Reprinted by permission of Harold Ober Associates Incoprporated. "Dream Boogie" and "Theme for English B" from *Montage of a Dream Deferred*. Reprinted by permission of Harold Ober Associates Incorporated. Copyright 1951 by Langston Hughes. Copyright renewed 1979 by George Houston Bass. "Dream Deferred." Copyright 1951 by Langston Hughes. Reprinted from *The Panther and the Lash: Poems of Our Times* by Langston Hughes, by permission of Alfred A. Knopf, Inc.

Ted Hughes. "Hawk Roosting" from *New Selected Poems* by Ted Hughes. Copyright © 1959 by Ted Hughes. Reprinted by permission of Harper & Row, Publishers, Inc. and Faber and Faber Ltd.

Henrik Ibsen. *A Doll's House* by Henrik Ibsen, translated by Otto Reinert. Copyright © 1977 by Otto Reinert. From Otto Reinert and Peter Arnott, eds., *Twenty-Three Plays.* Reprinted by permission of Scott, Foresman and Company.

Shirley Jackson. "The Lottery" from *The Lottery* by Shirley Jackson. Copyright 1948 by Shirley Jackson. Copyright renewed © 1976 by Laurence Hyman, Barry Hyman, Mrs. Sarah Webster, and Mrs. Joanne Schnurer. Reprinted by permission of Farrar, Straus and Giroux, Inc.

Randall Jarrell. "The Death of the Ball Turret Gunner" from *The Complete Poems* by Randall Jarrell. Copyright 1945 by Mrs. Randall Jarrell. Copyright renewed © 1972 by Mrs. Randall Jarrell. Reprinted by permission of Farrar, Straus and Giroux, Inc. "The Woman at the Washington Zoo" from the book of the same title. Copyright © 1960 Randall Jarrell. Reprinted with the permission of Atheneum Publishers, an imprint of Macmillan Publishing Company.

James Joyce. "Araby" from *Dubliners* by James Joyce. Copyright 1916 by B. W. Huebsch, Inc. Definitive text copyright © 1967 by the Estate of James Joyce. Reprinted by permission of Viking Penguin Inc.

Franz Kafka. "The Metamorphosis" and "The Hunger Artist" from *The Penal Colony* by Franz Kafka, translated by Willa and Edwin Muir. Copyright 1948 and renewed 1976 by Schocken Books, Inc. Reprinted by permission of Schocken Books, published by Pantheon Books, a Division of Random House.

D. H. Lawrence. "The Horse Dealer's Daughter" from *The Complete Short Stories of D. H. Lawrence,* Volume I. Copyright 1922 by Thomas Seltzer, Inc. Copyright renewed 1950 by Frieda Lawrence. Reprinted by permission of Viking Penguin Inc. "Snake" from *The Complete Poems of D. H. Lawrence,* Collected and Edited by Vivian de Sola Pinto and F. Warren Roberts. Copyright © 1964, 1971 by Angelo Ravagli and C. M. Weekley, Executors of the Estate of Frieda Lawrence Ravagli. Reprinted by permission of Viking Penguin Inc.

Don L. Lee. "But He Was Cool" from *Don't Cry Scream.* Copyright © 1969, by Don L. Lee. Reprinted by permission of Broadside Press.

John Lennon and Paul McCartney. "Eleanor Rigby" by John Lennon and Paul McCartney. © 1966 Northern Songs Limited. All Rights for the U.S., Canada and Mexico Controlled and Administered by SBK Blackwood Music Inc. Under License from ATV Music (Maclen). All Rights Reserved. International Copyright Secured. Used by permission.

Robert Lowell. "Skunk Hour" from *Life Studies* by Robert Lowell. Copyright © 1956, 1959 by Robert Lowell. Reprinted by permission of Farrar, Straus and Giroux, Inc.

Clare Boothe Luce. *Slam the Door Softly.* Reprinted by permission of International Creative Management, Inc. Copyright © 1971 by Clare Boothe Luce/Copyright © 1970 by Clare Boothe Luce (under the title *A Doll's House 1970*).

Phyllis McGinley. "A Garland of Precepts" from *Times Three* by Phyllis McGinley. Copyright 1954 by Phyllis McGinley. Copyright renewed © 1982 by Phyllis Hayden Blake. Originally published in *The New Yorker.* All rights reserved. Reprinted by permission of Viking Penguin Inc.

Archibald MacLeish. "Ars Poetica" from *New and Collected Poems 1917–1982* by Archibald MacLeish. Copyright © 1985 by The Estate of Archibald MacLeish. Reprinted by permission of Houghton Mifflin Company.

Gabriel García Márquez. "A Very Old Man With Enormous Wings: A Tale for Children" from *Leaf Storm and Other Stories* by Gabriel García Márquez.

Piercy). Reprinted from *Circles on the Water* by Marge Piercy, by permission of Alfred A. Knopf, Inc.

Sylvia Plath. "Metaphors," copyright 1963 by Ted Hughes, and "Daddy," copyright 1960 by Ted Hughes, from *The Collected Poems of Sylvia Plath,* edited by Ted Hughes. Reprinted by permission of Harper & Row, Publishers, Inc. and Olwyn Hughes. "Mushrooms." Copyright © 1960 by Sylvia Plath. Reprinted from *The Colossus and Other Poems* by Sylvia Plath, by permission of Alfred A. Knopf, Inc. and Olwyn Hughes.

Katherine Anne Porter. "The Jilting of Granny Weatherall" from *Flowering Judas and Other Stories,* copyright 1930, 1958 by Katherine Anne Porter, reprinted by permission of Harcourt Brace Jovanovich, Inc.

Ezra Pound. "An Immortality" from Ezra Pound, *Collected Early Poems of Ezra Pound.* Copyright © 1976 by the Trustees of the Ezra Pound Literary Property Trust. Reprinted by permission of New Directions Publishing Corporation.

Craig Raine. "A Martian Sends a Postcard Home." © Craig Raine 1979. Reprinted from *A Martian Sends a Postcard Home* by Craig Raine (1979) by permission of Oxford University Press.

John Crowe Ransom. "Piazza Piece" and "Bells for John Whiteside's Daughter." Copyright 1924, 1927 by Alfred A. Knopf, Inc. and renewed 1952, 1955 by John Crowe Ransom. Reprinted from *Selected Poems, Third Edition, Revised and Enlarged* by John Crowe Ransom, by permission of Alfred A. Knopf, Inc.

Henry Reed. "Naming of Parts" from *A Map of Verona* by Henry Reed (1946). Reprinted by permission of Jonathan Cape Ltd.

Adrienne Rich. "Diving into the Wreck" and "Living in Sin." Reprinted from *Poems, Selected and New, 1950–1974,* by Adrienne Rich, by permission of W. W. Norton & Company, Inc. Copyright © 1975, 1973, 1971, 1969, 1966 by W. W. Norton & Company, Inc. Copyright © 1967, 1963, 1962, 1961, 1960, 1959, 1958, 1957, 1956, 1955, 1954, 1953, 1952, 1951 by Adrienne Rich.

Edward Arlington Robinson. "Richard Cory" from *The Children of the Night,* published by Charles Scribner's Sons. "Mr. Flood's Party" from *Collected Poems* by Edward Arlington Robinson, published by Macmillan Publishing Company.

Theodore Roethke. "My Papa's Waltz." Copyright 1942 by Hearst Magazines, Inc. From *The Collected Poems of Theodore Roethke.* Reprinted by permission of Doubleday, a division of Bantam, Doubleday, Dell Publishing Group, Inc.

William Shakespeare. Play and footnotes from *The Tragedy of Hamlet* by William Shakespeare, edited by Edward Hubler. Copyright © 1963 by Edward Hubler. Copyright © 1963, 1987 by Sylvan Barnet. Reprinted by arrangement with NAL Penguin Inc., New York, New York. Play and footnotes from *The Tragedy of Macbeth* by William Shakespeare, edited by Sylvan Barnet. Copyright © 1963 by Sylvan Barnet. Reprinted by permission with NAL Penguin Inc., New York, New York.

Stevie Smith. "Not Waving but Drowning." From Stevie Smith, *Collected Poems.* Copyright © 1972 by Stevie Smith. Reprinted by permission of New Directions Publishing Corporation.

Sophocles. *Antigone* and *Oedipus the King.* © Oxford University Press, 1962. Reprinted from *Sophocles: Three Tragedies* translated by H. D. F. Kitto (1962) by permission of Oxford University Press.

George Starbuck. "Fable for Blackboard from *Bone Thoughts.* Copyright © 1960 by George Starbuck. Reprinted by permission of Yale University Press.

Wallace Stevens. "Anecdote of the Jar," "Emperor of Ice Cream," and "The Snow Man." Copyright 1923 and renewed 1951 by Wallace Stevens. Reprinted from *The Collected Poems of Wallace Stevens* by permission of Alfred A. Knopf, Inc.

Index: Critical Terms

Index: Authors, Titles, First Lines of Poems

The number in *italic* indicates the page on which the selection appears.

To the Student

Please help us make *An Introduction to Literature* an even better book. When we revise our textbooks, we take into account the experiences of both instructors and students with the previous edition. At some time, your instructor will be asked to comment extensively on *An Introduction to Literature,* Ninth Edition. Now we would like to hear from you.

Please complete this questionnaire and return it to **College English Developmental Group, Scott, Foresman/Little, Brown College Division, 1900 East Lake Avenue, Glenview, Illinois, 60025.**

School _____

Course title _____

Other texts required _____

Instructor's full name _____

1. Did you like the book overall? Why or why not?

2. **Fiction**
   Approximately how many stories were assigned? _____
   Which stories did you like most?

   Which stories did you like least?

Which stories had you read previously?

Are there any authors or stories not included you would like to see added?

Did you read "Observations on the Novel" and did you find it useful?

3. **Poetry**
Approximately how many poems were assigned? _____
Which poems did you like most?

Which poems did you like least?

Which poems had you read previously?

Are there any poets or poems not included you would like to see added?

4. **Drama**
Approximately how many plays were assigned? _____
Which plays did you like most?

Which plays did you like least?

Which plays had you read previously?

Are there any plays or playwrights not included you would like to see added?

5. Did you read "Writing Essays about Literature" and did you find it useful?

How might that section be improved?

6. Did you like the looks of the book?

7. Was the type easy to read?

8. Do you feel your instructor should assign this book again next year?

9. Will you keep your copy for your library?

10. Please add any other comments and suggestions.

May we quote you in our promotion efforts for this book?

____Yes   ____ No

Date _____

Name _____

Home Address _____

City, State, Zip _____